OFFICIAL

RUGBY UNION

CLUB

DIRECTORY

1997-98

Published in Great Britain by
Tony Williams Publications Ltd.,
Helland, North Curry,
Taunton, Somerset. TA3 6DU

The publishers wish to confirm that
the views expressed in articles and reviews in this
directory are not necessarily those of the Rugby Football
Union, any sponsors or indeed agencies employed by
the R.F.U. or sponsors.

Printed in Great Britain by
WBC Book Manufacturers Limited
Waterton Industrial Estate
Bridgend. CF31 3XP.
Telephone 01656 668836

Typeset by
Typecast (Jean Bastin)
Telephone 01935 27191

Trade Sales & Distribution:
Tony Williams Publications
Telephone 01823 490080

OFFICIAL RUGBY UNION CLUB DIRECTORY 1997-98

EDITOR: STEPHEN McCORMACK

ISBN 1 869833 97X

House Editor: George Brown

Tony Williams Publications Ltd.

Acknowledgments

This is the fifth year I have been involved with the book and the eighth year spent collecting all the facts and figures relating to the Leagues. In that time I have made lots of friends and acquaintances - all people like me who love rugby and enjoy collecting statistics. For me it started as a hobby and has grown into a mammoth task which has taken over a large portion of my life. Now is the time to say thank you to the people who have made the book successful with the time they have given me in compiling all the records. The people mentioned below are in no particular order. Most of you react in a positive way when I ring and ask for some information and for that I thank you. It is annoying that there are still a few clubs who have an 'attitude' problem and being helpful and friendly is obviously against their nature.

Last season took me all over the place going to different clubs each week to try and visit as many of you as possible but unfortunately there are not enough Saturdays in the season, although the way things are going there might well be one day. Most clubs were very hospitable but two deserve a special mention.

Top of the table was Wharfedale - not only are they blessed with a most beautiful setting but the buffet they lay on is second to none as was the company.

Not far behind was Liverpool St. Helens, whose president Ian Clark has a President's lunch before the game and that day I was lucky enough to sit next to their secretary John Robertson with whom I had an enlightening conversation.

Special thanks go to the following: Bristol - John Harding and Neil Williams. Harlequins - Nick Cross and Alex Saward. Orrell - Fred Holcroft and Geoff Lightfoot. Northampton - Roy Gordon and Terry Morris. Sale - Keith Brooks and Christine Kenrick. Saracens - Bill Edwards. Wasps - John Gasson. West Hartlepool - Dave Crisp and Steve Smith. Bedford - Jack Pope. Blackheath - Ron Bailey. Coventry - John Butler and John Wilkinson. Moseley - Ken Birrell. Newcastle - Kingsley Highland. Nottingham - John Drapkin. Richmond - Mickey Harris and Nigel Griffiths. Rotherham - Allan Williams. Rugby - Roy Batchelor and Dennis Keen. Wakefield - Andy Pritchard and Jim Coulson. Waterloo - Ged Pointon and Keith Alderson. Clifton - Brian Jordan. Exeter - Adrian James and Roy Henderson. Fylde - Stuart Brown. Harrogate - Rodney Spragg and John Ashman. Havant - Roger Boydell. Leeds - Mike Bidgood. Liverpool St. H. - Chris Brown. London Welsh - Paul Bekan. Lydney - Roger and Mike Hook. Morley - Fred Pickstone. Otley - John Finch and Peter Thompson. Reading - Nigel Sutcliffe. Redruth - Nigel Jewell and James Glasson. Rosslyn Park - Bernard Wiggins and Charlie Adiman. Walsall - Howard Clews. Wharfedale - Keith Lewis. Aspatria - Melvin Hanley and Tom Borthwick. Birmingham Solihull - Alan Morden. Hereford - Mandy Miles. Kendal - John Hutton. Lichfield - Barry Broad and Dave Lewis. Manchester - Alan Hanson. Nuneaton - Dave Warden. Preston Grasshoppers - John Hetherington and Leslie Anson. Sandal - Phillip Harrison. Sheffield - Martin Fay and Andy Reichwald. Stourbridge - Cerl and Vernon Davies. Stoke on Trent - Tom Maskery and Simon Robson. Winnington Park - Bob Dean. Worcester - Dick Cummings. Askean - Alan Eastick. Barking - Jeff Coney. Berry Hill - John Cole. Camberley - Sarah Shaw and John Lightly. Charlton Park - John Field and Dave Collen. Cheltenham - Tom Parker. Henley - Peter Cawthra. High Wycombe - Dave Carrod. Met. Police - David Barham. Newbury - Terry Burwell and Malcolm Howe. North Walsham - Tony Marcontoni. Plymouth - Paddy Marsh. Tabard - Peter Cook and Geoff Bird. Weston-super-Mare - Clayton Hope. Vale of Lune - Stuart Vernon. Camborne - Ewart White. Broughton Park - Archie McCallum and Barry Allen. Sudbury - Mike Harris.

Producing this book in such a short space of time is a major task and mistakes are inevitable no matter how careful we are. If you happen to come across any I would be extremely grateful if you would let me know through Tony Williams Publications.

It has proved difficult and time consuming researching the early years of League rugby when it did not receive the same coverage it does today. So if you could fill in any of our gaps or correct us we would appreciate it.

This year's book has seen the introduction of a players' page for all National League One clubs (last season's Division Three). Tracing some of the previous club appearances has proved a nightmare and again your help with this task would be much appreciated. The qualification for the players page is those who made most appearances for that club last season. As we build up our data base of players we would like to change it round so the page reflects the squad likely to start the season and we aim to introduce this in the next edition of the Directory.

It has proved impossible to trace back all League appearances for Newbury and Worcester outside the National Leagues so their players page only reflects National League rugby.

Stephen McCormack

EDITORIAL

An £87.5 million deal with Sky television.

20 players on the victorious British Lions tour to South Africa.

Virtually a Second England XV draws the series in Argentina.

Allied Dunbar pump £12.5 million into the Premiership.

Jewson sponsor the new National Divisions One and Two North and Two South.

Tetley's Bitter sponsor the National Knock Out Cup

and Junior Cup plus the County & u21 Championships

The Northern Division is sponsored by Thwaites.

Has the game ever been in a better position?

From the outside you would think not and it is to be hoped that those inside see it that way.

It is now up to the administrators at the RFU to get their act together and follow the rest of the game into the professional age.

We must hope that the management committee and its chairman can bring harmony to the game. The last thing we want to happen is that the various factions start warring again as a result of some hidden agendas.

The game has never been in a better position to prosper and to progress, and we have the attraction of a cracking season on the horizon, especially with the exciting prospect of playing the top three southern hemisphere sides so that we can judge how far we have really advanced following the Lions' victory in South Africa.

Let us trust that the coming season is remembered for the game on the field and that by the end of it we will all have moved forward.

We welcome our new sponsors, and look forward to a successful four year partnership.

Good luck to you all and hopefully we will have a season to remember - with rugby as the winner.

Stephen McCormack

FOREWORD

by Peter Brook, President, The Rugby Football Union

This admirable directory of all senior clubs, now in its tenth season, is of tremendous use to all those associated with club rugby and I am delighted to pen a foreword recommending it.
A primary source of information, it provides the kind of detail which will introduce readers to new clubs, more games and new friendships within the sport.

Throughout the many changes occurring in rugby union over recent years, the publisher has continued to provide an excellent handbook, which, like the game, has gone from strength to strength. The publication is greatly valued by the Rugby Football Union. It continues to foster a deeper interest in the game and it is wholly appropriate that it should now be sponsored by Carlsberg-Tetley, who are sponsoring the Tetley's Bitter Cup, the senior knockout competition.

I would also like to take this opportunity to thank Jewson for their help in sponsoring National Leagues One and Two and Thwaites for their backing in taking over sponsorship of the Northern Division Leagues.

I hope that everyone involved with rugby has a tremendous 1997/98 season and that they get the most out of reading the official RFU Club Directory.

A WELCOME FROM
CARLSBERG-TETLEY

by Vincent Kelly, Director, Carlsberg-Tetley Brewing Ltd.

Carlsberg-Tetley is immensely proud to be a major sponsor of English rugby. We have recently embarked on a four year deal in which Tetley's Bitter becomes the Official Beer of the England Rugby team with an involvement at all levels of the sport, from the national team right the way through to the local clubs.

Tetley's extensive sponsorship package covers four national competitions – the Tetley's Bitter Cup, the Tetley's Bitter County Championship, the Tetley's Bitter Under-21 Championship and the Tetley's Bitter Vase – which reinforces our commitment to all levels of the sport, from the premier knockout competition in the country right the way through to the Vase, the competition for the 512 lower league teams.

The RFU club directory will continue to provide invaluable information to all those involved in the game of rugby in England.

Carlsberg-Tetley is looking forward to the first year of what is a major rugby sponsorship, and aims to promote and develop the game throughout the country.

Best wishes for the 1997/98 season.

V. Kelly

TETLEY'S BITTER CUP

TETLEY'S
BITTER
VASE

TETLEY'S
BITTER
COUNTY
CHAMPIONSHIP

TETLEY'S
BITTER
UNDER 21
CHAMPIONSHIP

OFFICIAL
BEER
ENGLAND
RUGBY

Welcome to the other NEW SPONSORS

The good news for rugby clubs throughout England is the keenness shown by many of the country's most positive and well-known commercial institutions to become involved with their competitions.

We have experienced the problem caused by long and protracted negotiations which had to be undertaken before Pilkington's successors as sponsor of the National Knock-Out Cup and our Directory could be announced but as this book was being compiled we were thrilled to hear the news of three other sponsorships.

The massive Allied Dunbar involvement with the Premiership (the old National Leagues One and Two) will give tremendous prestige to the top clubs and will of course give every other club huge incentives to reach the top.

The Allied Dunbar Premiership represents Allied Dunbar's first major sponsorship activity and is part of a new initiative planned to take top level English club rugby into the new millenium. Fundamental to the Allied Dunbar Premiership has been the formation of English Rugby Partnership (ERP), an organisation established in February 1997 and based on the partnership between the top 24 clubs and the Rugby Football Union. The ERP will act as the official organising committee of the Allied Dunbar Premiership with responsibility for all operational matters.

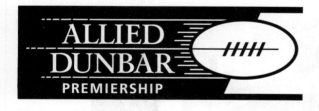

Within the Allied Dunbar Premiership, the top 24 professional clubs will play in Allied Dunbar One and Two. Each of the 12 clubs in Allied Dunbar One and Two will play each other on a home and away basis; totaling 264 Allied Dunbar Premiership matches. At the end of the season, there are two guaranteed relegation and promotion positions between Allied Dunbar One and Two with play-offs deciding the outcome of the two remaining places.

Central to the Allied Dunbar Premiership, is Allied Dunbar's work with the clubs to develop a group disability insurance scheme. This will cover all players in each of the Premiership's 24 clubs.

Allied Dunbar's sponsorship activities also include support for referee development and sponsorship of the Allied Dunbar Premiership match officials. Additionally, an Allied Dunbar squad of players from England, Scotland, Wales and Ireland has also been developed to support local sponsorship initiatives undertaken by the Company's 3,500 strong direct salesforce.

One of the most successful sponsorships of regional association football leagues in England have been enjoyed by JEWSONS, the builders' merchants. They have gained great local publicity from their involvement with the Eastern Counties, Wessex and South Western leagues and have brought much appreciated help to the competitions themselves.

They now take over the Rugby Union's National Leagues One and Two North & South (which used to be National Three and National Four North & South) and we are sure they will be just as successful in this exciting national venture.

BUILDING A RELATIONSHIP WITH JEWSON NATIONAL LEAGUES

"Jewson, Britain's best known builders' merchant, has a long association with rugby union with a commitment to the game at all levels.

We are delighted to announce that from the start of the 1997/98 season Jewson will be the sponsor of the new Division One and Division Two National Leagues.

The Jewson National Leagues include clubs with both current internationals and promising young talent - the future of the game. Yhis partnership with the RFU has a powerful synergy; the RFU has successfully embraced a new era of professionalism and similarly, at Jewson, we recognise that our customers are skilled professionals who deserve a level of service to match. We know that many of these customers are keen rugby fans and we're sure they'll share our excitement in this sponsorship. With nearly 200 branches around the country, Jewson is equipped to supply an unrivalled range of Timber and Building Materials from Kitchen & Bathrooms to Doors & Joinery, Tool & Equipment Hire and Decorating Products. We look forward to actively supporting and working with the RFU and Jewson National League clubs in the coming season."

Richard Fawcett, Chief Executive, Jewson Ltd.

One of the most exciting sponsorships is the Thwaites Brewery link with the Northern Division. Their help will inspire many of the developing clubs in the north of England to strive even harder to achieve their ambitions and fulfill their potential.

EST. **1807**

THWAITES
⊙ B R E W E R Y ⊙
P R O G R E S S   W I T H
T R A D I T I O N

In today's environment competition is at every level. We are continually undergoing change and confronted with challenges and opportunities. Thwaites Brewery is no different and over two centuries it too has faced change but has prospered to become one of the leading regional brewers in the UK.

The only constant throughout this process has been the single-minded determination to brewing which has earned Thwaites a reputation for quality beers.

Thwaites commitment to sport and, in particular, rugby union has never been more evident than over the last 12 months.

As the person who initiated Associations Football's first ever sponsored leagues when working with, dare I use the word, Rothmans in the seventies, and having seen just about every soccer competition benefit from sponsorship since, it is particularly pleasing to see clubs of all sizes within the jurisdiction of the Rugby Union, benefit from the initiatives of these companies who are proud to link their names with their respective leagues.

Tony Williams, Publisher

INDEX

PUBLISHERS MESSAGE

It is with a strong feeling of frustration that I apologise to all readers for the delay in publishing The Directory this year.

Following Courage's late withdrawal from sponsorship of the book last year and Pilkington's kind and enthusiastic support we were determined to make sure this year's publication would arrive in time for the start of the season for all club officials and their supporters.

Sadly, Pilkington pulled out of their involvement with the national knock out cup but once again they stood by us and offered to sponsor the 1997-98 edition of The Official Rugby Union Club Directory.

However, The Rugby Union had linked sponsorship of their official directory with the package offered to the new sponsor taking over from Pilkington and we were obviously pleased with the prospect of a four year agreement with new keen sponsors linked with the R.F.U.

Unfortunately this original plan was decided upon in July and for one reason and another the final sponsorship agreement wasn't signed, sealed and delivered until October.

Only then could we complete the book's cover and the sponsor's pages and finalise the copy for the long suffering printer who was working with us for the first time!

Hopefully you will now enjoy Steve McCormack's brilliant statistics and our new layouts and once again we will promise you that now we are all involved in a new contract with new sponsors and the backing of The Rugby Union the Directory will be out on time next season!

Thank you for bearing with us and I do hope the Directory will contribute towards a happy season.

TONY WILLIAMS

THANK YOU

PILKINGTON

Stories about big business ethics can often be quite shocking and probably the media do make the most of the more sordid stories. But here's a lovely story and we are pleased to report that Pilkington the well known sponsors of the Rugby Union National Cup and makers of quality glass, not only saved the book last year by stepping in when Courage pulled their sponsorship interest away from the book at the last moment, but they also pledged their support for the book this year although they were pulling out of their National Cup involvement.

We would like to thank them very much indeed for their support which was over and above anything they needed to do, especially considering their wonderful service to the game.

We have included here some records which bring their competition's statistics up to date and dedicate the following section of the book to Pilkington plc.

Wishing them good fortune in the future.

TONY WILLIAMS

PILKINGTON CUP 1996-97

FIRST ROUND
Saturday, 14th September 1996

North & Midlands

Birmingham-Solihull 37 Old Halesonians 8
Bradford & Bingley 13 Aspatria 26
Bridlington 23 Nuneaton 16
Camp Hill 17 Wigton 35
Derby 12 Blaydon 13
Lichfield 19 Winnington Park 21
Longton 16 Sheffield 26
Manchester 37 Scunthorpe 10
New Brighton 29 Hereford 13
Preston Grasshoppers 28 Stoke-on-Trent 10
Stourbridge 17 Kendal 28
Sutton Coldfield 15 Sandal 22
Westleigh 19 Tynedale 20
Widnes 30 Ampthill 17
Worcester 59 Vale of Lune 8

South & South-West

Barking 18 Barnstaple 31
Bishop's Stortford 30 Bicester 9
Bridgwater & Albion 22 Newbury 46
Camberley 24 Plymouth Albion 24
Charlton Park 11 Askeans 28
Esher 20 Ruislip 3
Gosport & Fareham 12 Weston-super-Mare 19
Haywards Heath 31 Beckenham 10
Henley 84 Westcombe Park 10
Launceston 25 Cheltenham 37
Marlow 0v Norwich 6
Metropolitan Police 47 Sutton & Epsom 18
North Walsham 17 Gloucester Old Boys 18
Southend 24 High Wycombe 41
Staines 27 Gloucester Spartans 20
Swanage & Wareham 41 Berry Hill 8
Tabard 19 Bracknell 30

SECOND ROUND
Saturday, 12th October 1996

North & Midlands

Bridlington 15 Blaydon 7
Cheltenham 30 Worcester 22
Manchester 19 Wigton 31
New Brighton 12 Preston Grasshoppers 24
Sandal 16 Tynedale 9
Sheffield 29 Kendal 31
Widnes 19 Birmingham-Solihull 9
Winnington Park 19 Aspatria 46

South & South-West

Askeans 18 Swanage & Wareham 21
Barnstaple 27 Plymouth Albion 14
Bishop's Stortford 22 Metropolitan Police 22
(Bishop's Stortford win scoring 3 tries to 2)
Gloucester Old Boys 13 Newbury 26
Haywards Heath 24 Bracknell 58
Norwich 12 Esher 38
Staines 20 Henley 31
Weston-super-Mare 23 High Wycombe 6

THIRD ROUND
Saturday 2nd November 1996

North

Bridlington 22 Wigton 30
Leeds 96 Redruth 6
Liverpool St Helens 30 Walsall 20
Morley 30 Aspatria 26
Otley 34 Wharfedale 27
Preston Grasshoppers 24 Fylde 12
Sandal 20 Kendal 32
Widnes 12 Harrogate 7

South

Cheltenham 23 Henley 19
Esher 26 Bracknell 15
Exeter 32 Barnstaple 3
London Welsh 11 Reading 16
Newbury 58 Clifton 12
Rosslyn Park 27 Havant 15
Swanage & Wareham 9 Lydney 26
Weston-super-Mare 23 Bishop's Stortford 11

FOURTH ROUND
Saturday, 23rd November 1996

Cheltenham 29 Weston-super-Mare 10
Leeds 39 Morley 11
Liverpool St Helens 18 Preston Grasshoppers 28
Wigton 16 Otley 11

Saturday, 30th November 1996
Exeter 12 Kendal 18

Saturday, 7th December 1996
Reading 50 Widnes 3

Saturday, 14th December 1996
Rosslyn Park 30 Exeter 3

Tuesday, 17th Ddecember 1996
Lydney 15 Newbury 28

FIFTH ROUND
Saturday, 21st December 1996

Bath 33 London Irish 0
Bristol v Blackheath
Coventry 79 Kendal 17
Gloucester 55 Leeds 20
Harlequins 47 Cheltenham 11
Leicester 26 Newbury 21
Moseley 49 Wigton 6
Newcastle v West Hartlepool
Nottingham 11 London Scottish 25
Orrell 34 Bedford 31
Preston Grasshoppers 11 Northampton 40
Reading 3 Saracens 41
Rotherham 41 Rosslyn Park 26
Sale 34 Richmond 30
Wakefield 22 Waterloo 17
Wasps 84 Rugby Lions 8

Sunday, 22nd December 1996)
Bristol 60 Blackheath 17
Newcastle 51 West Hartlepool 10

SIXTH ROUND
Saturday, 25th January 1997

Gloucester 18 Bristol 12
London Scottish 15 Newcastle 39
Northampton 26 Coventry 17
Orrell 0 Sale 57
Rotherham 23 Harlequins 42
Wakefield 24 Moseley 14

Sunday, 26th January 1997
Saracens 21 Wasps 17

Saturday, 8th February 1997
Bath 28 Leicester 39

QUARTER FINALS
Saturday, 22nd February 1997

Newcastle   8 v 18   Leicester
Northampton   9 v 22   Sale
Wakefield   21 v 25   Gloucester

Sunday, 23rd February 1997)
Harlequins   28 v 21   Saracens

SEMI-FINALS
Saturday, 29th March 1997

SALE   26 v 16   HARLEQUINS
H.T. 18-6

SALE: J Mallinder (captain); D Rees, J Baxendell, A Hadley, T Beim; S Mannix, D Morris; P Winstanley, S Diamond, A Smith, D Erskine, D Baldwin, J Fowler, D O'Grady, J Mitchell.
Scorers: Tries: Beim (1), Mallinder (1), O'Grady (1). Pens: Mannix (3). Con: Mannix.

HARLEQUINS: P Challinor; D O'Leary, W Carling, P Mensah, S Bromley; T Lacroix, H Harries; J Leonard (captain), T Billups, L Benezech, R Jenkins, A Snow, Gareth Llewellyn, L Cabannes, B Davison. Replacements: J Williams for Challinor 58 minutes, G Allison for Snow 61 minutes, N Walshe for Harries 67 minutes, J Keyter for Carling 68 minutes.
Scorers: Try: Llewellyn. Pens: Lacroix (3). Con: Lacroix.
Referee: S Lander, Liverpool.

GLOUCESTER   13 v 26   LEICESTER
H.T. 3-12

GLOUCESTER: C Catling; M Peters, C Emmerson, M Roberts, M Lloyd; M Maplefoft, S Benton; A Windo, P Greening, A Deacon, P Glanville, R Fidler, D Sims (captain), N Carter, S Devereux.
Scorers: Try: Catling. Pens: Mapletoft (2). Con: Mapletoft.

LEICESTER: J Liley, S Hackney, W Greenwood, S Potter, C Joiner; J Stransky, A Healey; G Rowntree, R Cockerill, D Garforth, J Wells, M Johnson (captain), N Fletcher, N Back, E Miller. Replacements: D Richards for Wells 63 minutes, L Lloyd for Hackney 77 minutes.
Scorers: Try: Hackney. DGs: Stransky (2). Pens: Stransky (5).
Referee: A Spreadbury, Somerset.

PILKINGTON CUP FINAL

Saturday, 10th May 1997. At Twickenham.
Attendance: 75,000

LEICESTER 9   3 SALE

Half Time: 6-3

Penalties	Stransky (3)	Mannix

15	Nial Malone		
14	Craig Joiner	Jim Mallinder (captain)	15
13	Will Greenwood	David Rees	14
12	Stuart Potter	Jos Baxendell	13
11	Leon Lloyd	A Hadley	12
10	Joel Stransky	Tom Beim	11
9	Austin Healey	Simon Mannix	10
		Dewi Morris	9
1	Graham Rowntree		
2	Richard Cockerill	Phil Winstanley	1
3	Darren Garforth	Steve Diamond	2
4	John Wells	Andrew Smith	3
5	(captain) Martin Johnson	Neil Ashurst	4
6	Martin Poole	Dave Erskine	5
7	Neil Back	Dave Baldwin	6
8	Eric Miller	Dylan O'Grady	7
		John Mitchell	8

Replacement:
Dean Richards for Wells 68 minutes.
Temporary replacement:
Aadel Kardooni for Healey 72-76 minutes.

Referee:
B Campsall, Yorkshire.

PREVIOUS FINALS

1972	Gloucester 17	Moseley 6		1984	Bath 10	Bristol 9	
1973	Coventry 27	Bristol 15		1985	Bath 24	London Welsh 15	
1974	Coventry 26	London Scottish 6		1986	Bath 25	Wasps 17	
1975	Bedford 28	Rosslyn Park 12		1987	Bath 19	Wasps 12	
1976	Gosforth 23	Rosslyn Park 14		1988	Harlequins 28	Bristol 22	
1977	Gosforth 27	Waterloo 11		1989	Bath 10	Leicester 6	
1978	Gloucester 6	Leicester 3		1990	Bath 48	Gloucester 6	
1979	Leicester 15	Moseley 12		1991	Harlequins 25	Northampton 13	
1980	Leicester 21	London Irish 9		1992	Bath 15	Harlequins 12	
1981	Leicester 22	Gosforth 15		1993	Leicester 23	Harlequins 16	
1982	Gloucester 12	Moseley 12		1994	Bath 21	Leicester 9	
1983	Bristol 28	Leicester 22		1995	Bath 36	Wasps 16	
				1996	Bath 16	Leicester 15	

INTERMEDIATE CUP
(for the NPI Trophy)
1996-97

SIXTH ROUND
(Saturday, 25th January 1997)

North & Midlands Divisions
Belgrave 16 Northern 27
Market Bosworth 5 Broad Street 26
Middlesbrough 23 Whitchurch 10
Doncaster 27 Huddersfield 16

London & South West Divisions
Colchester 26 Cinderford 16
Sudbury 33 Old Verulamian 26
Thanet Wanderers 34 Guildford & Godalming 18
Torquay Athletic 6 Cambridge 13

QUARTER FINALS
(Saturday, 22nd February 1997)

Doncaster 38 Cambridge 19
Middlesbrough 39 Northern 29
Sudbury 20 Broad Street 13
Thanet Wanderers 30 Colchester 26 (AET)

SEMI-FINALS
(Saturday, 22nd March 1997)

Doncaster 8 Middlesbrough 8 (AET)
(at Otley)
(Doncaster win - greatest quarter-final margin)
Sudbury 13 Thanet Wanderers 18 (AET)
(at Henley)

FINAL
Saturday, 3rd May 1997.
Twickenham.

DONCASTER 13 v 21 THANET WANDERERS

DONCASTER: J Ellis; D E Fairclough, D S Fairclough (captain), S Manson, R Harrison; P Matthews, A Pascoe; D Bosworth, N Waddington, C Yemm, R Senior, M Bailey, K Westgarth, D Senior, M Longworth. Replacement: D Clarke for Westgarth 47 minutes. Scorers: Try: Ellis. Pens: DS Fairclough (2). Con: DS Fairclough.

THANET WANDERERS: G Redmond; E Stokes, P Macaulay, M Coyne, M Meyer; G Harper, J Ward; B Guild, C Smith, T Carlier (captain), T Michael, P Hughes, G Hingley, C Marson, D Langley. Replacements: M Pond for Stokes 40 minutes, S Harris for Michael 61 minutes.
Scorers: Tries: Macaulay, Michael. Pens: Redmond (3). Con: Redmond.

Referee: J Pearson, Durham.

JUNIOR KNOCKOUT CUP
(for the NPI Trophy)
1996-97

SIXTH ROUND
(Saturday, 25th January 1997)

North & Midlands Divisions
Billingham 27 v 11 Market Rasen
Crewe & Nantwich 25 v 3 Loughborough Students
Huddersfield YMCA 37 v 8 Old Abbotstonians
Southport 24 v 10 Alcester

London & South West Divisions
Painswick 19 v 12 Wells
Tadley 19 v 26 Folkestone
Tonbridge 14 v 29 Harpendedn
Topsham 11 v 22 Hadleigh

QUARTER FINALS
(Saturday, 22nd February 1997)

North & Midlands Divisions
Crewe & Nantwich 22 v 13 Billingham
Huddersfield YMCA 47 v 17 Southport
London & South West Divisions
Harpenden 30 v 6 Folkestone
Painswick 10 v 8 Hadleigh

SEMI-FINALS
(Saturday, 22nd March 1997)

Crewe & Nantwich 17 v 12 Painswick
(at Lichfield)
Harpenden 18 v 14 Huddersfield YMCA
(at Burton-on-Trent)

FINAL
Saturday, 3rd May 1997
At Twickenham.

CREWE & NANTWICH 31 v 34 HARPENDEN
(AET Score at 80 mins: 24-24)

HARPENDEN: T Baxter; A Phillips, S Smith, D Talbot, N Sinfield; D Ford, R Humphrey; D Craddock, D Collier, D Alpert, T Stanford, D Foster, D Horsley, A McPherson, D Phillips (captain). Replacements: A Kiff for Alpert 32 minutes, I Hamilton for A Phillips 80 minutes, J Cartmell for Ford 90 minutes, P Butler for Sinfield 98 minutes.
Scorers: Tries: Baxter (2), Talbot, Smith. Pens: Ford (2). Cons: Ford (4).

CREWE & NANTWICH: S Wall; P Harrison, J Nicholls, A Manicom, M Pemberton; C Widdowson, S MacKeen; A Pemberton, N Tilley, S Taylor, J Charlesworth, G Davies, R Harper (captain), S Hayter, A McGarrigle. Replacements: M Morgan for McGarrigle 40 minutes, R Thomas for Manicom 54 minutes, L Gray for Harrison 68 minutes, J Forster for MacKeen 79 minutes.
SCORERS: Tries: McGarrigle, Morgan, Nicholls. DG: Nicholls. Pens: Wall (3). Cons: Wall (2).

Referee: S Savage, North Midlands.

PILKINGTON CUP TRIVIA

During its 26 year run (1972-97), only 23 clubs have managed to reach the Semi-Final stage of the Pilkington Cup. The table below shows how they fared from that point on.

	Winners	Runners-Up	Losing Semi-Finalist
BATH	10	0	0
LEICESTER	5	5	5
GLOUCESTER	3	1	5 (always to the winner)
HARLEQUINS	2	2	7
GOSFORTH	2	1	1
COVENTRY	2	0	6
BRISTOL	1	3	0
BEDFORD	1	0	0
MOSELEY	0	3	3
WASPS	0	3	3
ROSSLYN PARK	0	2	2
LONDON SCOTTISH	0	1	3
LONDON WELSH	0	1	2
NORTHAMPTON	0	1	2
SALE	0	1	2
LONDON IRISH	0	1	1
WATERLOO	0	1	0
ORRELL	0	0	4
NOTTINGHAM	0	0	2
MORPETH	0	0	1
SARACENS	0	0	1
WAKEFIELD	0	0	1
WILMSLOW	0	0	1

MOST WINNERS MEDALS

9   Nigel Redman (Bath)
8   Richard Hill (Bath)
    Graham Dawe (Bath)
7   Stuart Barnes (Bristol 1, Bath 6)
    Andy Robinson (bath)
    Tony Swift (Bath)
    Gareth Chilcott (Bath)

MOST RUNNERS-UP MEDALS

4   Dean Richards (Leicester)
3   Steve Bates (Wasps)
    Paul Dodge (Leicester)
    Adel Kardooni (Leicester)
    Steve Redfern (Leicester)
    Rory Underwood (Leicester)
    John Wells (Leicester)

PLAYERS WITH WINNERS MEDALS FOR TWO CLUBS
    Stuart Barnes (Bristol & Bath)
    Roger barnwell (Coventry & Leicester)
    Roger Cowling (Gloucester & Leicester)

PLAYER WITH RUNNERS-UP MEDALS FOR TWO CLUBS
    Kevin Dunn (Gloucester & Wasps)

PLAYERS APPEARING FOR TWO CLUBS
    Stuart Barnes (Bristol & Bath)
    Roger Barnwell (Coventry & Leicester)
    Barrie Corless (Coventry & Moseley)
    Roger Cowling (Gloucester & Leicester)
    Rob Cunningham (Gosforth & Bath)
    Kevin Dunn (Gloucester & Wasps)
    Simon Halliday (Bath & Harlequins)
    John Olver (Harlequins & Northampton)
    Jonathon Webb (Bristol & Bath)

PILKINGTON CUP

INDIVIDUAL MEDALLISTS

(Dates shown in italics signify an appearance as a substitute)

ACKERMAN, RA	Lon. Welsh	L - 85
ACKFORD, PJ	Harlequins	W - 88, 91 L - 92
ADCASTER, SD	Moseley	W - 82
ADEBAYO, AA	Bath	W - 90, 94, 95, 96
ADEY, GJ	Leicester	W - 79, 80, 81 L - 78
AKENHEAD, R	Moseley	L - 79
ALEXANDER, JR	Harlequins	L - 93
ALSTON, P	Northampton	L - 91
ANDERSON, TR	Gosforth	L - 81
ANDERSON, PG	Rosslyn Park	L - 75
ANDREW, CR	Wasps	L - 87, 95
ARCHER, JS	Gosforth	W - 77 L - 81
ASHURST, N	Sale	L - 97
ASTLEY, KJ	Moseley	L - 79
AYRE, B	Moseley	L - 79
BACK, NA	Leicester	W - 93, 97 L - 94, 96
BAILEY, MD	Wasps	L - 86, 87
BAILWARD, CJ	Bedford	W - 75
BAINBRIDGE, S	Gosforth	L - 81
BAKER, SJW	Gloucester	W - 82
BALCOMBE, P	Wasps	L - *86*
BALDWIN, D	Sale	L - 97
BALDWIN, G	Northampton	L - 91
BALL, I	Waterloo	L - 77
BARKER, RG	Leicester	L - 78
BARKER, N	Bedford	W - 75
BARLOW, RL	Rosslyn Park	L - 75
BARNES, S	Bath	W - 86, 87, 89, 90, 92, 94
	Bristol	W - 83 L - 84
BARNWELL, RC	Coventry	W - 74
	Leicester	W - 79, 80, 81 L - 83
BARTON, J	Coventry	W - 73
BATES, SM	Wasps	L - 86, 87, 95
BATES, I	Leicester	W - 93 L - *83*, 89
BAXENDALE, J	Sale	L - 97
BAYLISS, JA	Gloucester	W - 72
BAZALGETTE, MB	Rosslyn Park	L - 75
BEALE, JD	Moseley	L - 79
BEIM, T	Sale	L - 97
BELL, JAH	Gosforth	L - 81
BELL, TP	Harlequins	W - 88
BELL, DE	Lon. Scot	L - 74
BENNETT, WN	Bedford	W - 75
BERINGER, GG	Lon. Irish	L - 80
BESS, G	Bath	W - 85, 87
BIGGAR, AG	Lon. Scot	L - 74
BIGGAR, MA	Lon. Scot	L - 74
BILLINGHAM, MF	Waterloo	L - 77
BLACKHURST, F	Waterloo	L - 77
BLACKMORE, AG	Bristol	L - 88
BLAKEWAY, PJ	Gloucester	W - 82
BOGIRA, MK	Bristol	W - 83
BONNER, G	Wasps	L - 86, 87
BOOTH, MH	Gloucester	W - 72
BOWRING, K	Lon. Welsh	L - 85
BOYLE, LS	Leicester	L - 94
BOYLE, SB	Gloucester	W - 78 82
BRADLEY, B	Lon. Welsh	L - 85
BRAIN, J	Gloucester	L - 90
BRAY, KA	Harlequins	L - 93
BREAKEY, RW	Gosforth	W - 76, 77 L - 81
BREEZE, J	Gloucester	L - 90
BRINN, A	Gloucester	W - 72
BRITTEN, JK	Gosforth	W - 76, 77
BRODERICK, JM	Coventry	W - 73, 74
BULPITT, MA	Rosslyn Park	L - 76
BURTON, MA	Gloucester	W - 72, 78
BURWELL, T	Leicester	W - 79, 80
BUTLAND, R	Bath	W - 95
BUTLER, JL	Gosforth	L - 81
BUTLER, PE	Gloucester	W - 78
BYRNE, L	Rosslyn Park	L - *76*
CALLARD, JEB	Bath	W - 90, 94, 95, 96
CARDUS, RM	Wasps	L - 86
CARDWELL, R	Coventry	W - 74
CARFOOT, DJ	Waterloo	L - 77
CARLING, WDC	Harlequins	W - 88, 91 L - 92, 93
CARR, JF	Bristol	W - 83 L - 84, 88
CASKIE, D	Gloucester	L - 90
CATT, MJ	Bath	W - 94, 96
CHADWICK, R	Bedford	W - 75
CHALLINOR, AP	Harlequins	L - 92, 93
CHIDGEY, DL	Bristol	L - 84
CHILCOTT, GJ	Bath	W - 84, 85, 86, 87, 89, 90, 92
CHILDS, G	Wasps	L - 95
CHRISTOPHERSON, SF	Waterloo	L - 77
CLARKE, BB	Bath	W - 92, 94, 95
CLEWS, RJ	Gloucester	W - 72, 78
COCKERILL, R	Leicester	W - 93, 97 L - 94, 96
CODD, RA	Rosslyn Park	L - 75
COKER, T	Harlequins	W - 91
COLLINGS, P	Bristol	L - 88
COLLINS, J	Lon. Welsh	L - 85
CONDON, HC	Lon. Irish	L - 80
CONNOR, L	Waterloo	L - 77
COOPER, MJ	Moseley	W - 82 L - 79
CORLESS, TF	Moseley	W - 82
CORLESS BJ	Coventry	W - 74
	Moseley	L - 79
CORSTORPHINE, AE	Lon. Scot	L - 74
COWLING, RJ	Leicester	W - 79, 80, 81
	Gloucester	W - 72
COWMAN, AR	Coventry	W - 73, 74
COX, GNJ	Moseley	W - 82 L - 79
CREED, RN	Coventry	W - 73
CRERAR, RD	Lon. Scot	L - 74
CRONIN, DF	Bath	W - 89, 90
CUE, PC	Bristol	L - 84
CUNNINGHAM, R	Gosforth	L - 81
	Bath	W - 84

Name	Club	Record
CURTIS, PS	Harlequins	W - 88
CUSWORTH, L	Leicester	W - 79, 80, 81 L - 83, 89
CUTTER, AJ	Gosforth	W - 76, 77
DALLAGLIO, LBN	Wasps	L - 95
DANDY, MJW	Bristol	L - 73
DARNELL, IR	Coventry	W - 73, 74
DAVIDSON, JS	Moseley	W - 82
DAVIES, GH	Wasps	L - 87
DAVIS, EG	Harlequins	W - 88, 91 L - 92
DAWE, RGR	Bath	W - 86, 87, 89, 90, 92, 94, 95, 96
DEMMING, R	Bedford	W - 75
DESBOROUGH, JE	Moseley	W - 82
DIAMOND, S	Sale	L - 97
DIX, J	Gloucester	W - 72
DIXON, PJ	Gosforth	W - 76, 77
DOBLE, SA	Moseley	L - 72
DOBSON, I	Leicester	L - 83
DODGE, PW	Leicester	W - 79, 80, 81 L - 78, 83, 89
DOUBLEDAY, RJ	Bristol	W - 83 L - 84, 88
DOUGLAS, MHJ	Lon. Welsh	L - 85
DUCKHAM, DJ	Coventry	W - 73, 74
DUGGAN, MJ	Leicester	L - 78
DUGGAN, IH	Bristol	W - 83 L - 88
DUN, AF	Bristol	L - 88
DUNN, KA	Wasps	L - 95
	Gloucester	L - 90
DUNSTON, I	Wasps	L - 95
EBSWORTH, M	Lon. Welsh	L - 85
EDWARDS, NGB	Harlequins	W - 88 L - 92
EDWARDS, EF	Bedford	W - 75
EGERTON, DW	Bath	W - 87, 89, 90
ELKINGTON, D	Northampton	L - 91
ERSKINE, D	Sale	L - 97
ETHERIDGE, J	Northampton	L - 91
EVANS, BJ	Leicester	L - 83, 89
EVANS, GW	Coventry	W - 73
FAIRBROTHER, KE	Coventry	W - 73, 74
FALLON, JA	Bath	W - 92
FIDLER, JH	Gloucester	W - 78
FIELD, R	Moseley	L - 79
FINLAN, JF	Moseley	L - 72
FISHER, RG	Rosslyn Park	L - 75
FISHER, CD	Waterloo	L - 77
FLETT, MA	Waterloo	L - 77
FLUSKEY, S	Rosslyn Park	L - 76
FORD, P	Gloucester	W - 82
FORFAR, DJ	Leicester	L - 78
FOUHY, D	Lon. Welsh	L - 85
Foulkes-ARNOLD, M	Leicester	L - 83, 89
FOULKS, D	Coventry	W - 74
FOWLIE, DG	Lon. Scot	L - 74
FRASER, G	Lon. Scot	L - 74
FRIELL, AAS	Lon. Scot	L - 74
FRY, MJ	Bristol	L - 73
GADD, J	Gloucester	W - 82 L - 90
GALLAGHER, J	Coventry	W - 74
GARFORTH, DJ	Leicester	W - 93, 97 L - 94, 96
GAYMOND, N	Bath	W - 84, 85
GIFFORD, CJ	Moseley	L - 79
GILLINGHAM, NK	Leicester	W - 80 L - 83
GITTINGS, WJ	Coventry	W - 73, 74
DE GLANVILLE, PR	Bath	W - 92, 94, 95, 96
GLENISTER, RJ	Harlequins	W - 91 L - 93
GOODWIN, JM	Moseley	W - 82
GRAY, JD	Coventry	W - 73
GREAVES, WH	Moseley	L - 79
GREENSTOCK, N	Wasps	L - 95
GREENWOOD, M	Wasps	L - 95
GREENWOOD, W	Leicester	W - 97
GRIFFIN, SM	Gosforth	W - 76
GRIFFITHS, J	Moseley	L - 72
GUSCOTT, JC	Bath	W - 85, 87, 89, 90, 92, 95
GUSTARD, JS	Gosforth	W - 76, 77
HAAG, M	Bath	W - 92, 95, 96
HACKNEY, S	Leicester	L - 96
HADLEY, A	Sale	L - 97
HADLEY, N	Wasps	L - 95
HALL, C	Northampton	L - 91
HALL, BP	Leicester	L - 78
HALL, JP	Bath	W - 84, 85, 86, 87, 89, 94
HALLIDAY, SJ	Harlequins	W - 91 L - 92
	Bath	W - 85, 86, 87, 89, 90
HAMLIN, M	Gloucester	L - 90
HANCOCK, K	Waterloo	L - 77
HANNAFORD, M	Gloucester	L - 90
HANNAFORD, RC	Bristol	L - 73
HARDING, RM	Bristol	W - 83 L - 84, 88
HARE, WH	Leicester	W - 79, 80, 81 L - 78, 89
HARRIMAN, AT	Harlequins	W - 88, 91
HARRIS, JC	Leicester	W - 93 L - 94
HATTER, K	Moseley	L - 72
HAZLERIGG, AG	Leicester	W - 79 L - 78
HEALEY, A	Leicester	W - 97
HEDLEY, J	Gosforth	W - 77
HESFORD, R	Bristol	W - 83
HILL, RJ	Bath	W - 84, 85, 86, 87, 89, 90, 92, 94
HILTON, DIW	Bath	W - 94, 96
HINTON, NP	Rosslyn Park	L - 75, 76
HOBLEY, MJ	Harlequins	L - 92
HOGG, ST	Bristol	W - 83 L - 84, 88
HOLLINS, AJ	Bedford	W - 75
HOLMES, G	Wasps	L - 86
HOLT, BC	Coventry	W - 73
HONE, W	Bristol	L - 88
HOOKER, C	Bedford	W - 75
HOPLEY, P	Wasps	L - 95
HOPLEY, DP	Wasps	L - 95
HORTON, JP	Bath	W - 84, 85
HORTON, NE	Moseley	L - 72
HOWARD, JM	Bedford	W - 75
HOWELL, PR	Gloucester	W - 78
HUGHES, J	Lon. Welsh	L - 85
HUNTER, I	Northampton	L - 91
JACKSON, N	Leicester	W - 81
JACKSON, GT	Waterloo	L - 77
JARDINE, R	Gloucester	W - 78
JARRETT, JS	Gloucester	W - 72
JEAVONS, NC	Moseley	W - 82 L - 79
JOHNSON, D	Gosforth	L - 81
JOHNSON, SR	Leicester	W - 79, 80, 81 L - 78, 83
JOHNSON, MO	Leicester	W - 93, 97 L - 94, 96
JOINER, C	Leicester	W - 97
JONES, W	Lon. Irish	L - 80
JONES, TW	Lon. Welsh	L - 85
JONES, B	Leicester	L - 78
JONES, L	Gloucester	W - 82

JORDEN, AM	Bedford	W - 75
JOYCE, NJ	Leicester	W - 79, 80, 81 L - 78
KARDOONI, A	Leicester	W - 93, *97* L - 89, 94, 96
KEDDIE, RR	Lon. Scot	L - 74
KEEN, B	Bedford	W - 75
d'A KEITH-ROACH, P	Rosslyn Park	L - 75, 76
KENNEY, S	Leicester	W - 79, 80, 81 L - 78
KENT, CP	Rosslyn Park	L - 76
KERR, R	Moseley	L - 72
KILFORD, WA	Leicester	L - 94
KILLICK, N	Harlequins	L - 93
KING, S	Moseley	L - *79*
KNIBBS, RA	Bristol	W - 83 L - 84, 88
KNIGHT, S	Bath	W - *90*
KNIGHT, PM	Bristol	L - 73
LAIRD, R	Moseley	L - 79
LANE, DE	Moseley	L - 72
LANGHORN, RS	Harlequins	W - 88, 91 L - 93
LAWSON, RD	Moseley	W - 82
LEE, MR	Bath	W - 84, 85, 86, 89
LEONARD, J	Harlequins	W - 91 L - 93
LEOPOLD, DA	Lon. Irish	L - 80
LEWIS, E	Lon. Welsh	L - 85
LEWIS, A	Bedford	W - 75
LIGHT, B	Lon. Welsh	L - 85
LILEY, J	Leicester	W - 93 L - 96
LINK, G	Rosslyn Park	L - 75
LLOYD, L	Leicester	W - 97
LLOYD-ROBERTS, G	Rosslyn Park	L - 76
LONGSTAFF, M	Gloucester	W - 82
LOVETT, MS	Lon. Scot	L - 74
LOZOWSKI, RAP	Wasps	L - 87
LUMSDEN, A	Bath	W - 96
LUNT, K	Waterloo	L - 77
LUXTON, TC	Harlequins	L - 92
MacMILLAN, AJ	Gosforth	L - 81
MADDERSON, CS	Harlequins	L - 93
MADSEN, DF	Gosforth	W - 76, 77
MALLETT, J	Bath	W - *95*, 96
MALLINDER, J	Sale	L - 97
MALONE, NG	Leicester	W - 97 L - 96
MANNIX, S	Sale	L - 97
MANTELL, ND	Rosslyn Park	L - 75, 76
MARTIN, CR	Bath	W - 84, 85, 86, 87
McDOWELL, NH	Gosforth	L - 81
McFADYAN, CW	Moseley	L - 72
McHARG, AF	Lon. Scot	L - 74
McKAY, Coventry	Rosslyn Park	L - 75
McKENZIE, RA	Lon. Scot	L - 74
McKIBBIN, R	Lon. Irish	L - 80
McKIBBIN, AR	Lon. Irish	L - 80
MEANWELL, CA	Lon. Irish	L - 80
MILLER, E	Leicester	W - 97
MILLS, SGF	Gloucester	2W - 78, 82
MITCHELL, J	Sale	L - 97
MOGG, RR	Gloucester	W - 78, 82 L - 90
MOLLOY, D	Wasps	L - 95
MOON, RHQB	Harlequins	W - 88
MOORE, BC	Harlequins	W - 91 L - 92
MORDELL, R	Rosslyn Park	L - 76
MORGAN, D	Gloucester	L - 90
MORLEY, AJ	Bristol	W - 83 L - 73, 84
MORRELL, CC	Moseley	L - 72
MORRIS, D	Sale	L - 97
MORRIS, R	Gloucester	W - 72
MORRIS, R	Moseley	L - 72
MORRISON, JSC	Bath	W - 86, 87, 89
MOSS, P	Northampton	L - 91
MOYLES, JL	Rosslyn Park	L - 76
MULLINS, AR	Harlequins	W - 88, 91 L - 92, 93
MUNDEN, AC	Bristol	L - 73
MURPHY, BW	Lon. Irish	L - 80
NANCEKIVELL, R	Northampton	L - 91
NEEDHAM, RJ	Leicester	L - 78
NEWBERRY, JA	Lon. Irish	L - 80
NEWTON, M	Leicester	W - 79
NICHOLLS, MJ	Gloucester	W - 72
NICHOLLS, AH	Bristol	L - 73
NICOL, AD	Bath	W - 96
NINNES, BF	Coventry	W - 73, 74
NUTT, DR	Moseley	W - 82 L - 79
O'DONNELL, P	Lon. Irish	L - 80
O'DRISCOLL, JB	Lon. Irish	L - 80
O'GRADY, D	Sale	L - 97
OJOMOH, SO	Bath	W - 92, *94*, 95, 96
OLVER, JC	Northampton	L - 91
	Harlequins	W - 88
ORLEDGE, RJ	Bristol	L - 73
ORWIN, J	Gloucester	W - 82
PACKMAN, F	Northampton	L - 91
PALMER, JA	Bath	W - 84, 85, 86, 87, 89
PALMER, T	Gloucester	W - 72
PALMER, DJ	Bristol	W - *83 L* - 84, 88
PARSLOE, SG	Gloucester	W - 82
PASCALL, R	Gloucester	L - 90
PASK, P	Northampton	L - 91
PATRICK, B	Gosforth	W - 76, 77 L - 81
PATRICK, HE	Gosforth	W - 76, 77
PEARCE, GS	Northampton	L - 91
PEARN, AFA	Bristol	L - 73
PEARS, D	Harlequins	W - 91 L - 92
PEGLAR, DJ	Wasps	L - 86, 87
PELLOW, R	Wasps	L - 86
PERRY, MH	Moseley	W - 82
PETERS, EW	Bath	W - 96
PHILLIPS, CA	Bristol	L - 88
PICKERING, DA	Lon. Scot	L - 74
PINNEGAR, MCF	Wasps	L - 86, 87
POLLEDRI, P	Bristol	W - 83 L - 84
POMPHREY, NJC	Bristol	W - 83 L - 84, 88
POOLE, MD	Leicester	W - 93, 97 L - 94, 96
POTTER, S	Leicester	W - 93, 97 L - 94, 96
POTTER, MJ	Gloucester	W - 72
PREECE, PS		W - 73
PREEDY, M	Gloucester	W - 82 L - 90
PRESTON, AJ	Gosforth	W - 76
PRICE, C	Lon. Welsh	L - 85
PRINGLE, IN	Moseley	L - 72
PRITCHARD, P	Gloucester	W - 82
PROBYN, JA	Wasps	L - 86, 87
PULLIN, JV	Bristol	L - 73
RAFTER, M	Bristol	W - 83 L - 84
RALSTON, CS	Rosslyn Park	L - 76
RECARDO, A	Moseley	W - 82
REDFERN, SP	Leicester	W - 79, 80, 81 L - 78, 83, 89
REDFERN, SB	Leicester	L - 83
REDMAN, NC	Bath	W - 84, 85, 86, 87, 90, 92, 94, 95, 96
REED, AI	Bath	W - 94
REED, D	Waterloo	L - 77

Name	Club	Result
REES, CWF	Lon. Welsh	L - 85
REES, D	Sale	L - 97
REES, GL	Wasps	L - 86
REES, A	Bath	W - 84
RENDALL, PAG	Wasps	L - 87
RICHARDS, D	Leicester	W - 93, 97 L - 83, 89, 94, 96
RICHARDSON, WP	Leicester	L - 89
RIGBY, MA	Wasps	L - 86, 87
RIPLEY, AG	Rosslyn Park	L - 75, 76
ROBERTS, TC	Gosforth	W - 76, 77 L - 81
ROBINSON, D	Gosforth	W - 76, 77
ROBINSON, RP	Leicester	L - 96
ROBINSON, RA	Bath	W - 87, 89, 90, 92, 94, 95, 96
RODBER, T	Northampton	L - 91
RODGERS, AJ	Bristol	L - 73
RODGERS, AK	Rosslyn Park	L - 75, 76
ROGERS, DP	Bedford	W - 75
ROLINSON, LJ	Coventry	W - 74
ROLLITT, DM	Bristol	L - 73
ROSE, MA	Wasps	L - 86, 87
ROSSBOROUGH, PA	Coventry	W - 73, 74
ROWNTREE, GC	Leicester	W - 93, 97 L - 94, 96
RUSSELL, S	Lon. Welsh	L - 85
RUSSELL, MP	Harlequins	L - 92, 93
RYAN, D	Wasps	L - 95
SAGOE, FK	Bath	W - 89
SALMON, JLB	Harlequins	W - 88
SANDERS, I	Bath	W - 95
SARGENT, GAF	Gloucester	W - 78, 82
SAVILLE, CD	Rosslyn Park	L - 75
SCRIVENS, N	Gloucester	L - 90
SHEASBY, CMA	Harlequins	L - 92, 93
SHEEHAN, JM	Lon. Irish	L - 80
SHEPARD, A	Bristol	W - 83 L - 84
SHORROCK,, DW	Moseley	W - 82
SHORT, JJO	Gosforth	W - 76
SHORT, KS	Lon. Irish	L - 80
SHORT, KF	Waterloo	L - 77
SIMMONS, A	Wasps	L - 86, 87
SIMMS, KG	Wasps	L - 87
SIMONETT, JF	Gloucester	W - 78
SIMPSON, PD	Bath	W - 84, 85, 86, 89
SKINNER, MG	Harlequins	W - 88, 91
SLEIGHTHOLME, JM	Bath	W - 96
SMITH, A	Sale	L - 97
SMITH, SM	Gosforth	L - 81
SMITH, ST	Wasps	L - 86, 87
SMITH, IR	Leicester	W - 79, 80, 81 L - 83, 89
SMITH, T	Leicester	L - 89
SMITH, R	Gloucester	W - 72
SMITH, T	Gloucester	L - 90
SMITH, I	Gloucester	L - 90
SMITH, TJ	Moseley	L - 72
SMYTHE, MJ	Lon. Irish	L - 80
SNOW, ACW	Harlequins	L - 93
SOLE, DMB	Bath	W - 87
SPAVEN, JN	Waterloo	L - 77
SPURRELL, RA	Bath	W - 84, 85, 86
STARLING, D	Rosslyn Park	L - 76
STEELE, J	Northampton	L - 91
STEPHENS, EJF	Gloucester	W - 72
STEVENSON, GB	Lon. Scot	L - 74
STIFF, PJ	Bristol	L - 84
STRANSKY, J	Leicester	W - 97
STRINGER, NC	Wasps	L - 86
SUTHERLAND, IS	Moseley	W - 82
SWAIN, MK	Moseley	L - 72, 79
SWATFIELD, RJ	Bristol	L - 73
SWIFT, AH	Bath	W - 86, 87, 89, 90, 92, 94, 95
TAYLOR, PA	Gloucester	W - 82
TEAGUE, MC	Gloucester	W - 82 L - 90
THACKER, T	Leicester	L - 89
THAME, J	Northampton	L - 91
THOMAS, DG	Bristol	L - 88
THOMAS, A	Moseley	L - 79
THOMPSON, AL	Harlequins	W - 88
THOMPSON, GJ	Harlequins	L - 93
THORBURN, CW	Lon. Scot	L - 74
THORNEYCROFT, H	Northampton	L - 91
THRESHER, SE	Harlequins	W - 88, 91
TICKLE, SG	Waterloo	L - 77
TRESEDER, PA	Rosslyn Park	L - 75, 76
TREVASKIS, B	Bath	W - 84, 85, 87
TRICK, DM	Bath	W - 84, 85, 86
TROUGHTON, AH	Bristol	W - 83
UBOGU, VE	Bath	W - 90, 92, 94, 95
UFTON, J	Wasps	L - 95
UNDERWOOD, R	Leicester	W - 93 L - 89, 94, 96
UNDERWOOD, T	Leicester	W - 93 L - 94
UTTLEY, RM	Gosforth	W - 77
VINE, BJ	Gloucester	W - 78
WALKER, R	Coventry	W - 74
WARD, B	Northampton	L - 91
WARDLOW, CS	Coventry	W - 73
WARREN, DG	Moseley	W - 82
WATKINS, M	Lon. Welsh	L - 85
WATKINS, JA	Gloucester	W - 72, 78
WATSON-JONES, A	Moseley	L - 79
WATT, DEJ	Bristol	L - 73
WEBB, JM	Bath	W - 92
	Bristol	L - 88
WEBSTER, JG	Moseley	L - 72
WEDDERBURN, MA	Harlequins	L - 92
WELLS, JM	Leicester	W - 93, 97 L - 89, 94, 96
WESTON, LE	Rosslyn Park	L - 75, 76
WHEELER, PJ	Leicester	W - 79, 80, 81 L - 78, 83
WHITE, C	Gosforth	W - 76, 77 L - 81
WHITE, L	Lon. Irish	L - 80
WHITE, M	Wasps	L - 95
WHITE, JC	Moseley	L - 72
WILKINSON, RM	Bedford	W - 75
WILLIAMS, K	Leicester	W - 81
WILLIAMS, CG	Gloucester	W - 78
WILLIAMS, CJ	Bristol	L - 73
WINSTANLEY, P	Sale	L - 97
WINTERBOTTOM, PJ	Harlequins	W - 91 L - 92, 93
WITHEY, K	Bath	W - 90
WOOD, P	Gloucester	W - 82
WOODWARD, C	Leicester	W - 80, 81 L - 83
WOOLEY, VJ	Gloucester	W - 78
WYATT, D	Bedford	W - 75
YATES, K	Bath	W - 95
YOUNG, M	Gosforth	W - 76, 77 L - 81
YOUNGS, NC	Leicester	L - 83

* * *

Rugby Memorabilia Society
Programme Survey 1997

Nearly one hundred clubs entered programmes for this year's survey and on the whole the standard was up on previous years. We have been very pleased with the positive response from clubs and the high regard in which our survey is now being held.

Unfortunately, the standard of match programme for several leading clubs was reduced following the arrival of the Promag - an expensive and largely uninformative publication which many rugby supporters dislike.

Leicester was one of the few English Division 1 clubs to resist the temptations of Promag and not surprisingly retained the **Club Programme of theYear** award. They produced an informative programme with excellent statistics and superb analysis of the day's opponents. The programme also contained detailed news of the club at First and Junior XV level and there were well chosen action photographs.

Of the other leading programmes Otley's impressed again. They proved that with limited resouces a real club programme can still be prouced. The statistics were first rate and the historial articles full of interest.

Unlike many £2 programmes, **Newcastle**'s was actually worth the money and was certainly a great improvement on last year's issue. There were many strengths notably the photos and the supporters' section. Newcastle have therefore won the **Most Improved Programme** award.

There was much to admire elsewhere. Gateshead Fell offered good statistics and a genuine sense of humour. Harrogate and Worcester both showed a huge advance on anything previously seen. Old Whitgiftians again showed that given a devoted editor lower division clubs can produce worthwhile programmes. Thurrock's entertaining programme was virtually ad-free and Civil Service sent in a lovely example of 'club flavour' whilst Sedgeley Park and Kenilworth produced enjoyable efforts. Newbury provided a smart-looking and promising issue and Stourbridge again impressed with their 'club' feel with plenty of space devoted to lower XV's and Juniors.

An example of the statistics and analysis provided in the Leicester programme
- their opponents on this occasion were Harlequins.

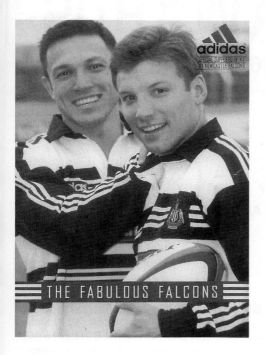

An example of the photography in the Newcastle programme.

There were, however, some disappointments. Priorities are to be questioned elsewhere. For example the £2 Harlequins programme was a major frustration. A club with more history than most, the emphasis on advertisements (about 75 percent) and the ignorance of anything of a historical nature is regrettable. The 'Quins were not alone.

However Harlequins, Orrell and Saracens must be commended for continuing to produce their own programme. The only League 1 Promag-user formally to submit entries was West Hartlepool. We did see all other Promags and thought the editorial element of Bristol's was probably the best.

Why was West Hartlepool the only one to submit an entry? The answer may lie in responses from three other League 1 clubs who advised us that they would not enter because their Promags were 'not good enough', 'worse than Leicester' and 'crap', to quote literally. The solution to their embarrassment is surely in their own hands.

Promags actually look attractive until the reader begins inwardly to digest. The major problems with the Promags are:

1. A programme is part of a club's identity. Local flavour is an important element of the club programme. Promags don't really provide this.

2. In some cases, there is virtually nothing relevant to the day's match to read in the Promag.

3. In trying to be a magazine and a programme it does neither well. Most of the 'magazine' articles have nothing at all to do with the day's game.

There has also been criticism expressed amongst club supporters at Clipson's Corner - a silly 'Mystic Meg' type of production page which is quite likely to tell the home supporters that their team is going to lose today. Just what they want to read!

In short, Promags are a serious setback to the evolution of the club programme and any clubs considering embracing this concept should think of their supporters and get guarantees over content before committing themselves. We have nothing against Sports Programme Promotions and certainly don't want to be negative but the feedback from clubs and so many supporters is that they are currently not good enough.

In conclusion, we hope that the trend upwards with most clubs continues and that clubs and their programme editors realise that the programme is a means of providing supporters and club members with information about the match and the club. They are not magazines - there are plenty of them on newsagents' shelves. It should also be remembered that rugby is a different sport to soccer and that reproducing a soccer programme in the guise of a rugby publication is not necessarily the best for that club or its supporters.

It is our sincere hope if Promags are going to be with us for future seasons that the clubs using them use their influence to improve the product they are provided with and that Sports Programme Promotions recognise the limitations of their publications and raise the standard of the content themselves.

DAVID FOX

R.F.U. AWARDS

1996-97

Player of the Season **Martin Johnson** (Leicester)

Young Player of the Season **Phil Greening** (Gloucester)

Try of the Season **Austin Healey** (Leicester v Llanelli, Heineken Cup)

Unsung Hero **Alan Bell** (retiring RFU Colts physio)

Cellnet Debut of the Season **Richard Hill** (England v Scotland)

Unisys Top Try Scorer **Brian Johnson** (Newbury)

Unisys Top Scorer **Mark Mapletoft** (Gloucester)

Unisys Top Drop Goal Kicker **Steve Kerry** (Preston Grasshoppers)

Best Performance against England **Christophe Lamaison** (France)

*   *   *

Courage Clubs Championship Trophy **Wasps**

The Pilkington Cup **Leicester**

CIS County Championship **Cumbria**

RFU Intermediate Knockout Cup **Thanet Wanderers RUFC**

RFU Junior Knockout Cup **Harpenden RUFC**

Daily Mail Schools Under 18 Cup **Colston Collegiates**

Daily Mail Schools Under 15 Cup **RGS, High Wycombe**

Royal & Sun Alliance Colts Divisional Cup **Midlands**

Royal & Sun Alliance Colts County Cup **East Midlands**

Three of the Winners

BRIAN JOHNSON - proving he can tackle, as well as score tries.

Above: PHIL GREENING
- the Young Player of the Year

TWO FROM GLOUCESTER

Left: MARK MAPLETOFT
- the Top Points Scorer

R.F.U. Contacts

THE RUGBY FOOTBALL UNION

Address: Rugby Road, Twickenham, Middlesex TW1 1DZ.
Main Switchboard: 0181 892 8161
Fax: 0181 892 9826
Ticket Information (Recorded Message):   0181 744 3111
TW1 The Twickenham Shop: 0181 831 6599
The Museum of Rugby and the Twickenham Experience: 0181 892 2000
Terry Burwell, Director, Twickenham Services: 0181 831 6669
Alwynne Evans, Co-ordinator, Twickenham Services: 0181 831 6636
Website: www.rfu.com

NATIONAL CENTRE FOR SCHOOLS AND YOUTH

Address: Castlecroft Stadium, Castlecroft Road, Wolverhampton, WV3 8NA.
Telephone: 01902 380302
Fax: 01902 380311

NATIONAL COACHING AND YOUTH DEVELOPMENT OFFICE

Address: Northonthorpe Mills, Scissett, Huddersfield. HD8 9LA
Telephone: 01484 866363
Fax: 01484 866406

REFEREE CENTRE OF EXCELLENCE

Address: Castlecroft Stadium, Castlecroft Road, Wolverhampton. WV3 8NA.
Telephone: 01902 380280
Fax: 01902 765748

RUGBY FOOTBALL UNION COMPETITION SUB-COMMITTEE

Chairman: Mike Wilson, 6 New Road, Easton on the Hill, Stamford, Lincs. PE9 3NN.
        Telephone: 01780 64019
        Fax: 01780 64676

NATIONAL CLUBS ASSOCIATION EXECUTIVE

Chairman: Trevor Richmond, Inglenook, Carlinghow Hill, Batley, West Yorks. WF17 0AG.
        Telephone: (Home) 01924 472705
                         (Bus.) 01274 480741
        Fax: 01274 497437

Secretary: Colin Sewell, 14 Edmund Road, Southsea, Hants. PO4 0LL.
        Telephone: 01705 342744
        Fax: 01705 421055

Treasurer: Ivor Horscroft, Silver Fields, Chapel Street, Redruth. TR15 2DI.
        Telephone: 01209 215941

National Media

DAILY EXPRESS
Ludgate House, 245 Blackfriars Road, London SE1 9UX

📞 0171 928 8999

DAILY MAIL
Northcliffe House, 2 Derry Street, London. W8 5TT

📞 0171 938 6000

DAILY MIRROR
1 Canada Square, Canary Wharf, London. E14 5AB

📞 0171 293 3000

DAILY TELEGRAPH
1 Canada Square, Canary Wharf, London. E14 5AB

📞 0171 538 5000

THE EUROPEAN
Orbit House, 5 New Fetters Lane, London. EC4A 1AR

📞 0171 377 4903

EVENING STANDARD
Northcliffe House, 2 Derry Street, London. W8 5TT

📞 0171 938 6000

THE GUARDIAN
110 Farringdon Road, London. EC1R 3ER

📞 0171 278 2332

THE INDEPENDENT
1 Canada Square, Canary Wharf, London. E14 5AB

📞 0171 293 2000

DAILY STAR
Ludgate House, 245 Blackfriars Road, London. SE1 9UX

📞 0171 928 8000

THE SUN
P.O. Box 481, Virginia Street, London. E1 9BD

📞 0171 782 4000

THE TIMES
1 Pennington Street, London. E1 9XN

📞 0171 782 5000

MAIL ON SUNDAY
Northcliffe House, 2 Derry Street, London. W8 5TT

📞 0171 938 6000

NEWS OF THE WORLD
1 Virginia Street, London. E1 9XR

📞 0171 782 4000

PRESS ASSOCIATION
Press Association Sport, London House,
Central Park, New Lane, Leeds. LS11 5DZ

📞 0113 234 4411

THE OBSERVER
119 Farringdon Road, London. EC1R 3ER

☎ **0171 278 2332**

SUNDAY EXPRESS
Ludgate House, 245 Blackfriars Road, London. SE1 9UX

☎ **0171 928 8000**

SUNDAY MIRROR
1 Canada Square, Canary Wharf, London. E14 5AB

☎ **0171 510 3000**

SUNDAY TELEGRAPH
1 Canada Square, Canary Wharf, London. E14 5AB

☎ **0171 538 5000**

SUNDAY TIMES
1 Pennington Street, London. E1 9XW

☎ **0171 782 5000**

THE PEOPLE
1 Canada Square, Canary Wharf, London E14 5AP

☎ **0171 510 3000**

INDEPENDENT ON SUNDAY
1 Canada Square, Canary Wharf, London. E14 5AB

☎ **0171 293 3000**

ITN NEWS
200 Grays Inn Road, London. WC1X 8XZ

☎ **0171 833 3000**

BBC TV NEWS
Television Centre, Wood Lane, London. W12 7RJ

☎ **0181 576 1914**

BBC BREAKFAST NEWS
Room 7039, Television Centre, London. W12 7RJ

☎ **0181 576 7501**

SKY NEWS & SKY SPORT
6 Centaurs Business Park, Grant Way,
Isleworth, Middlesex. TW7 5QD

☎ **0171 705 3000**

GMTV
The London Television Centre,
Upper Ground, London. SE1 9TT

☎ **0171 827 7000**

CHANNEL FOUR NEWS
200 Grays Inn Road, London. WC1X 8XZ

☎ **0171 833 3000**

I.R.N.
200 Grays Inn Road, London. WC1X 8XZ

☎ **0171 833 3000**

RADIO FIVE LIVE
Broadcasting House, London. W1 1AA

☎ **0171 580 4468**

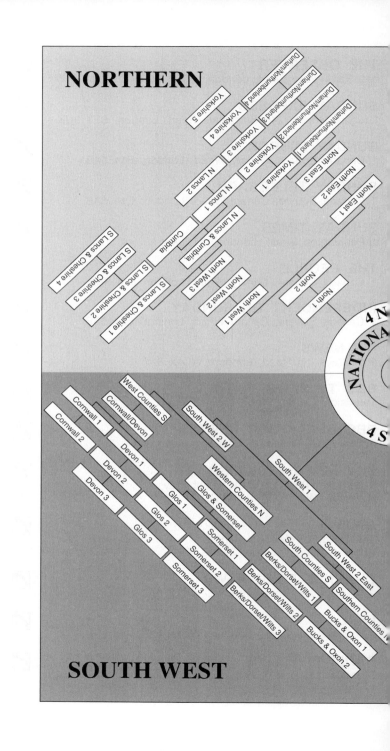

NORTHERN

Durham/Northumberland 4
Durham/Northumberland 3
Durham/Northumberland 2
Durham/Northumberland 1

Yorkshire 5
Yorkshire 4
Yorkshire 3
Yorkshire 2
Yorkshire 1

North East 3
North East 2
North East 1

S Lancs & Cheshire 4
S Lancs & Cheshire 3
S Lancs & Cheshire 2
S Lancs & Cheshire 1

N Lancs 2
N Lancs 1
N Lancs & Cumbria
Cumbria

North West 3
North West 2
North West 1

North 2
North 1

4 N

NATIONAL

4 S

SOUTH WEST

West Counties S

Cornwall 1
Cornwall 2
Cornwall/Devon

Devon 1
Devon 2
Devon 3

South West 2 W

Western Counties N

Glos 1
Glos 2
Glos 3

Glos & Somerset

Somerset 1
Somerset 2
Somerset 3

South West 1

Berks/Dorset/Wilts 1
Berks/Dorset/Wilts 2
Berks/Dorset/Wilts 3

South Counties S

South West 2 East

Southern Counties

Bucks & Oxon 1
Bucks & Oxon 2

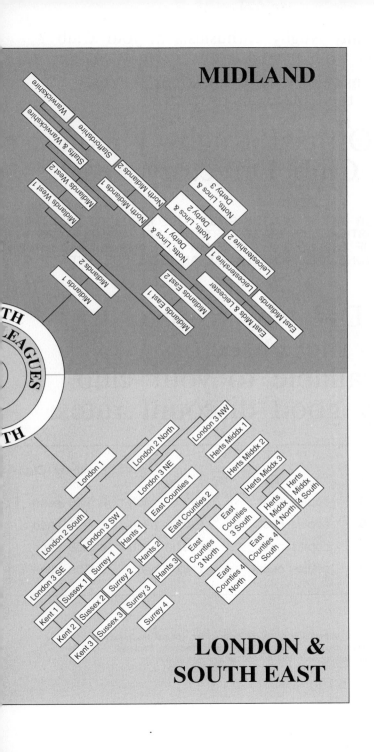

MIDLAND

Warwickshire

Staffs & Warwickshire

Staffordshire

Midlands West 2

Midlands West 1

North Midlands 2

North Midlands 1

Notts, Lincs & Derby 3

Notts, Lincs & Derby 2

Notts, Lincs & Derby 1

Leicestershire 2

Leicestershire 1

East Mids & Leicester

East Midlands

Midlands 2

Midlands 1

Midlands East 2

Midlands East 1

TH
LEAGUES
TH

London 1

London 2 North

London 3 NW

Herts Middx 1

London 3 NE

Herts Middx 2

East Counties 1

Herts Middx 3

East Counties 2

East Counties 3 South

Herts Middx 4 North

Herts Middx 4 South

London 2 South

London 3 SW

Hants 1

East Counties 3 North

East Counties 4 South

London 3 SE

Surrey 1

Hants 2

East Counties 4 North

Kent 1

Sussex 1

Surrey 2

Hants 3

Kent 2

Sussex 2

Surrey 3

Kent 3

Sussex 3

Surrey 4

LONDON &
SOUTH EAST

The English Clubs Championship Regulations 1997/98

1.   Description and Form

1.1   The Competition overall shall be called "The English Clubs Rugby Union Championship" and shall be open to Clubs in membership with the Rugby Football Union and such other Clubs as satisfy the criteria for membership for the RFU in the season 1997/98 but have not done so for the preceding two years.

1.2   With the consent of the Rugby Football Union certain levels or Leagues in the Competition overall may carry separate names or titles which may include the names of sponsors

1.3   All matches in the Competition shall be played under the Laws of the Rugby Football Union and shall comply with the Rules and Regulations of the RFU.

2.   Definitions

For the purposes of these Regulations only:-

"Committee" means the Competitions Committee of the RFU;

"Competition" means the English Clubs Rugby Union Championship to which these regulations or such other regulations as shall be approved by the Committee apply;

"Contract" means any agreement, arrangement or understanding (whether formal or informal) made between any Club (whether or not participating in the Competition) or any other person, firm or company and a player for the provision of material benefit wholly or partially in consideration for the player's participation in the game of rugby football or which entitles the party with whom a player has entered such agreement, arrangement or understanding to require the player to participate in the game of rugby football.

"Division" means a combination of constituent bodies authorised under rule 12.6 of the rules of the RFU;

"Effective Registration" means that a player is registered with a Club in accordance with and pursuant to Regulation No. 3 of the Registration of Players Regulations.

"ERP" means English Rugby Partnership Limited, a company jointly owned by the Clubs playing in Leagues at Levels 1 and 2 known as the Allied Dunbar Premiership and the RFU.

"ERP Play Off Regulations" means the Regulations contained in the Handbook governing the Play Offs between the ninth and tenth placed Clubs in League 1 of the Allied Dunbar Premiership and third and fourth Clubs in League 2 of the Allied Dunbar Premiership.

"Foreign Player" shall mean a person who is not entitled to the rights granted under Part II of the EC Treaty or under Part III of the EEA Treaty (ie a person who does not have European Workers rights).
Note: A passport of a member state of the European Community will normally be accepted as evidence that a player is not a Foreign Player.

"Handbook" means the annual publication of the RFU relating to season 1997/98;

"Loan Player" means a Player who has entered into a contract with a Club and who under an agreement arrangement or understanding between that Club and another Club has Effective Registration with that other Club

"Media Rights" means all television and/or other broadcasting, taping, video record media advertising, publicity and promotion rights of any and every description in and relating to the Competition;

"NCA" means National Clubs Association, an association of clubs at Levels 3 and 4 of Leagues known as National Leagues 1 and 2

"Organising Committee" means ERP or NCA Committee or a Divisional Committee as is appropriate to the League concerned, whose powers are delegated by the Committee;

"Premiership" means the two Leagues at the top two levels.

"Registration of Players Regulations" means those regulations governing the Registration of Players appearing in the Handbook;

"RFU" means Rugby Football Union"

"Season 1997/98" means 16 August 1997 to 23 May 1998 (inclusive).

3.   Committee Responsible for the Competition

The Competition shall be organised by the Committee which may delegate such powers as it deems appropriate (save for the powers contained in Regulations 7.6, 19.1, 19.2 20.1, 21 and 26 herein) and whose decision shall be binding and final on any matter not provided for in and on the interpretation of these Regulations.

4.   Delegation of Administration.

4.1   The Committee appoints the ERP as the Organising Committee of the Premiership.

4.2   The Committee appoints the NCA Committee as the Organising Committee of National Leagues 1 and 2 (North and South)

4.3 The Committee appoints the Division as the organising Committee of all Leagues within their Divisions.

4.4 The Organising Committees shall have power to make administration instructions for the management of the Leagues for which they are responsible in accordance with these Regulations.

4.5 ERP and NCA shall have the power to make further regulations to apply to the Premiership and National Leagues 1 and 2 (North and South) respectively provided that such regulations do not derogate from these Regulations and are approved by the RFU.

4.6 Subject to the right of appeal in Regulation 21, ERP in respect of the Premiership, the NCA in respect of National Leagues 1 and 2 (North and South) and the Divisions in respect of all Leagues within those Divisions shall, subject to Regulation 19.1 of these Regulations, deal with all disputes, transgressions and complaints as laid down by Regulation 20.

5. Structure

5.1 National

There shall be in Season 1997/98 two Premier Leagues each comprising 12 Clubs and National League 1 comprising 14 Clubs.

5.2 Areas

5.2.1 The Northern and Midland RFU Divisions shall combine to provide one National League 2 North and the London and South East and South West Divisions shall combine to provide one National League 2 South each comprising of 14 Clubs.

5.2.2 Promotion from the National Leagues 2 North and South shall be to National League 1.

5.3 Divisions

5.3.1 Each of the Divisions shall have a first League.

5.3.2 Promotion from the North Division League 1 and the Midland Division League 1 shall be to the National League 2 North and from the London and South East Division League 1 and the South West Division League 1 shall be to the National League 2 South.

5.3.3 The Divisional League structure below Division League 1 in each Division shall be such as shall, with the approval of the Committee, be determined by that Division.

5.3.4 Leagues shall comprise such numbers of Clubs as has been approved by the Committee.

5.4 General

5.4.1. Not more than two lower Leagues may support a higher League.

5.4.2 Only Club first XVs may enter the Competition.

5.4.3 A Club may only play in any National League 2 (North and South) or Divisional League according to its RFU Constituent Body allocation unless otherwise specifically agreed by the Committee.

6. Club Positions

The position of a Club in a League shall be established by awarding two competition points for a win and one point for a draw. In the case of equality, positions shall be determined on the basis of match points scored. A Club with a larger difference between match points for and match points against shall be placed higher in a League than a Club with a smaller difference between match points for and match points against. Should two Clubs have the same number of competition points and the same match points difference, the Club having scored more match points shall be placed higher in the League than the Club having the lesser number of match points for. In the event of the match points for still being unable to establish the position of two Clubs, and if the winning of the Competition or promotion or relegation is involved, the Club who has won the highest number of League matches shall be placed higher. If this does not establish the position then the Club who has won the most matches, excluding its first League match of the season, then its second League match, until it can be established which is the higher placed Club.

7. Principles of Promotion and Relegation

7.1 Where one League supports one League, the top two Clubs from the lower League at the end of the Season 1997/98 shall be promoted to the higher League.

7.2 In relation to promotion and relegation between the First Premier League and the Second Premier League there shall, in addition to promotion and relegation provided for in Regulation 7.1 above, be additional promotion and relegation in accordance with the ERP Play-off Regulations.

7.3 Where two Leagues support one League, the top Club in each of the supporting Leagues at the end of the Season 1997/98 shall be promoted to the higher League.

7.4 After promotion has taken place in accordance with Clauses 7.1 7.2, and 7.3 above, the requisite number of Clubs shall be relegated (upon the basis prescribed in Clause 7.5 below) from each League at the end of the Season 1997/98 so that the following Season 1998/99 there are in the Allied Dunbar Premier Leagues 1 and 2, and in all other Leagues the number of Clubs as have been specified by the Committee.

7.5 Except in the cases of relegation from Premier League 1 to Premier League 2 and from Premier League 2 to National League 1 and where specific exceptions are agreed by the Committee, Clubs shall be relegated on a geographical/Divisional/Constituent Body basis as appropriate.

Note: Except in the cases of relegation from Premier League 1 (where up to four clubs will be relegated), Premier League 2, National League 1 and National League 2 [North and South] (where two clubs will be relegated from each League) it is impossible to determine how many Clubs are to be relegated from any particular Leagueuntil it is known into which Leagues Clubs relegated will fall (on a geographical basis). Once the destination of relegated Clubs is known the knock-on effect can be ascertained.

7.6 Notwithstanding the foregoing provisions of this Regulation and the provisions of Regulation 5 above, the Committee may, as it shall in its absolute discretion think fit, at any time:-

7.6.1 diapply, suspend, amend and/or vary the foregoing provisions of this Regulation and/or of Regulation 5 as to promotion and relegation and/or as to the number of Clubs comprising any League or Leagues; and or

7.6.2 transfer any Club from the League in which it would have been placed by virtue of the application of Clauses 7.1 to 7.5 of this Regulation to such other League (whether higher or lower) as the Committee shall think fit.

Any action taken or decision made by the Committee under the powers conferred on it by the foregoing provisions of this Clause 7.6 shall be final and binding.

8. Fixtures

8.1 Save where a specific day is specified by ERP in the case of Premier Leagues 1 and 2, or by the NCA in respect of Leagues 1 and 2 (North and South) or by the Committee in respect of all other Leagues, all League matches shall be played on the Saturdays (unless the Sunday of that weekend is agreed by the Clubs or such a Sunday is specified by the Committee) of weekends specified by the Committee

8.2 All League matches in the Premier Leagues 1 and 2 and National League 1, and National Leagues 2 North and South and such other Leagues specified by the Committee shall be played on a home and away basis.

8.3 All League fixture lists shall be prepared by the Organising Committee of the League concerned and submitted to the Clubs comprising the League by the 15th June in each year. A copy shall be sent to the Secretary (or Chief Executive) of the RFU by the same date.

8.4 Every Club in all League fixtures must play its strongest possible bona fide first XV.

Note: A Club lays itself open to a penalty (which may include deduction of championship points or a fine or compensatory payment) if it does not comply with this Regulation.

9. Eligibility

9.1 Clubs

9.1.1 Any Club in membership with the RFU or any Club satisfying in that year the criteria for membership of the RFU but not being able to satisfy such criteria for the previous two years may enter the Competition subject to the approval of the Committee and of the appropriate Division according to its RFU Constituent Body allocation.

9.1.2 Any Club applying to join the Competition shall only be permitted to do so by being placed in the bottom League in its Division.

9.1.3 ERP has with the agreement of the RFU made additional regulations with which clubs must comply to participate or continue to participate in Premier Leagues 1 and 2.

9.1.4 The Committee shall have the power to impose conditions upon the membership or continued participation of any Club or Clubs in the Competition. Any Club or Clubs failing to comply with such conditions shall not be entitled to enter the Competition or to continue to participate in it.

9.2 Players

9.2.1 A Club in a Competition match may only play or select as a replacement, players who hold Effective Registration for that Club, in accordance with the Registration of Players Regulations.

9.2.2 A Club may not in any one match in the Competition play or select as a replacement more than two Foreign Players.

9.2.3 A Club may not in any one match in the Competition play or select as a replacement more than three Loan Players.

Penalty: A Club shall be deducted not less than two championship points (or such greater number as may be decided by the Organising Committee of the league concerned) on each occasion that it has been represented by an ineligible player or replacement. In addition where the Organising Committee or the Committee is satisfied there has been a breach of Regulation 12.1 or 12.2 of the RFU Registration of Players Regulations then the Club renders itself liable to the deduction of such number of additional Championship points (which shall not be less than 8) as the Committee may decide, relegation of/by one or more Leagues, or permanent or temporary expulsion from the Leagues.

(Warning: The Computerised Listing is the only evidence which will be accepted to substantiate a player's Effective Registration - see Registration of Players Regulation 5).

10. Players in Representative Matches

10.1 Where a representative match involving England's national XV or 'A'XV or Under 21 XV the County Championship Quarter-Finals, Semi Finals or Final is played on a date fixed for a League match, any Club which is affected by three or more players or replacements taking part in such representative match may require the League match to be rearranged for a later date. Such rearranged matches will be fixed by the Organising Committee of the League concerned.

10.2 Where a representative match involving any Senior National Representative Team(s) or Second Senior Representative Team(s) of any of the Home Unions is played on a date fixed for a League match any Club which is affected by 5 or more players or replacements taking part in such representative match(es) may require the League Match to be rearranged for a later date. Such rearranged match will be fixed by the Organising Committee for the League concerned.

11. Replacements and Substitutes

11.1 In all matches in the Competition replacements and substitutes are permitted in accordance with Law 3 and the International Board Resolutions relating thereto.

11.2 In the interests of safety each team playing in the Premiership Leagues 1 and 2 and National Leagues 1 and 2 (North and South) in the Competition shall have available 2 replacements or other players on the field capable of playing in the front row of the scrum should replacements be required whether due to an injury or consequent upon players being ordered off. If on the first or second occasion a front row player requires to be replaced his team cannot provide a replacement or other player capable of playing in the front row of the scrums so that uncontested scrums result, his team shall be deemed to have lost the match. Any match points scored by either side shall be disregarded in computing the differences between match points for and against.

11.3 In the interest of safety every team in the Competition below level 4 shall have available a replacement or other player on the field capable of playing in the front row of the scrum should a replacement be required whether due to an injury or consequent upon a player being ordered off. If on the first occasion a front row player requires to be replaced his team cannot provide a replacement or other player capable of playing in the front row of the scrums so that uncontested scrums result, his team shall be deemed to have lost the match. Any match points scored by either side shall be disregarded in computing the differences between match points for and against.

12. Unplayed, Postponed and Abandoned Matches

12.1 If weather conditions prevent a match being played or a match is abandoned because of such conditions with less than sixty minutes having been played, the match shall be played or replayed on a date directed by the Organising Committee of the League concerned it being the responsibility of the home club to advise the Organising Committee of the reason for non playing or non completion of the match as soon as possible after the event and requesting that the date of the match be fixed by the Organising Committee where a date for the replay has not been agreed between the Clubs involved within 7 days of non completion of a match or its cancellation.

12.2 If a match is abandoned because of weather conditions when sixty or more minutes have been played, then the score at the moment of abandonment shall stand and be deemed the final score in the match. The Referee's decision as to the necessity for abandonment and the number of minutes played at the moment of abandonment shall be final.

12.3 If the Referee finds it necessary to abandon a match for any reason other than weather conditions, then, irrespective of the number of minutes played, the result of that match may be determined by the Organising Committee of the League concerned or that Committee may order the match to be replayed.

12.4 If a match is abandoned under Regulations 12.1, 12.2 or 12.3 above, the home Club shall supply the Chief Executive or ERP or the secretary of the Organising Committee of the League concerned as appropriate with the match card duly signed by the Referee and stating the exact time of the match abandonment, the existing match score at the time and reason for the abandonment.

12.5 In the event of a League match not being played the Organising Committee of the League concerned may at its absolute discretion award the Competition points to either side, divide the Competition points equally between the sides decide that no Competition points shall be awarded or if it is of the view that a club has unjustifiably failed to fulfil its obligations deduct competition points from that Club. In addition or instead it may order the match to be replayed on a date specified by it having had regard to the promotion and relegation issues in the League concerned (including the effect on other Clubs in the League not involved in the league match) the commitments of the Clubs concerned and giving priority to arguments of the Club who was not at fault in the event of a dispute on any re-arranged match date. The Organising Committee of the League concerned shall not have the power to award match points.

12.6 Any Club which is properly suspended from playing Rugby Union Football for disciplinary reasons will not be permitted to re-arrange any League fixtures failing to be played within the period of the suspension. The effects thereof on the non-offending Clubs in the League concerned shall be dealt with by the Organising Committee of the League concerned under Clause 12.7 below.

12.7 In the event of a League match not being played for whatever reason, whether or not competition points are awarded to a Club under this Regulation, if that Club be a contender for promotion or relegation at the end of the season, the difference between the match points for and against of all Clubs (other than that Club) in the League shall be adjusted to exclude all match points scored in matches played against that Club before establishing the final position of that Club in the League in accordance with Regulation 5.

12.8 In the event of a Club failing to fulfil its League fixtures for reasons unacceptable to the Organising Committee of the League concerned, or if a Club voluntarily withdraws from a League, or if a Club is expelled or suspended from a League or from membership of the Competition, the results of all matches played by it shall be deleted. The final League table positions shall be established under Regulation 5 from all matches played between the remaining Clubs in such League.

13. Completion of Match Result Card

Each Club shall be responsible for correctly completing a match result card in accordance with the Regulations or instructions set out in the Administrative Instructions applicable to such Club's League. The Organising Committees are empowered to impose monetary fines for failure to comply with such Instructions and non-payment of fines by the due dates may lead to a deduction of two competition points for each such offence. Providing false information on players or replacements taking part in a match shall be a serious offence.
Penalty: A club shall be deducted not less than eight championship points on each occasion false information has been provided. This will be in addition to any points which may have been deducted if the players or replacements were ineligible.

14. Referees and Touch Judges

14.1 The Referee for each match shall be appointed or provided by the RFU in respect of Premiership Leagues 1, 2 and National Leagues 1 and 2 (North and South) and in respect of the Divisional Leagues by the Referees' Society to which the home Club pay a Referees' Society subscription, subject to any appointments made by the RFU.

14.2 In all matches in Premiership Leagues 1, 2 and National Leagues 1 and 2 North and 2 South two qualified touch judges shall be appointed by the RFU and the RFU Regulation relating to Law 6 shall apply.

14.3 In all other matches each Club shall provide a competent touch judge who should not be a replacement. In an emergency a replacement may act as a touch judge.

14.4 If the Referee appointed or provided under Regulation 14.1 has not arrived at the agreed kick-off time or if the Referee is unable to officiate for the whole of the match for any reason and a replacement Referee is available, the captains of the two Clubs concerned may agree that the Replacement referee can officiate and the result shall count in the Competition. Such agreement shall thereafter be binding upon the Clubs. If there is no agreement then that match shall not count in the Competition and it must be replayed in accordance with the provisions of Regulation 11(a).

15. Kick-Offs and Delayed Arrivals

Kick-off times for all League matches shall in the absence of a requirement from the organising Committee appropriate to the league concerned start at the home Club's usual kick-off time but shall be between 2.15 pm and 3.00 pm. In the absence of a kick-off time being specified by the Committee an early or late kick-off time may be arranged by mutual agreement between the two Clubs concerned. Any delay from the specified or agreed kick-off time may be reported by the non-offending Club to the Organising Committee of the League concerned and may lead to the match being awarded to the non-offending Club.

16. Clash of Colours/Identification of Players

16.1 In the event of Clubs having similar or clashing colours the home Club will be responsible for changing its colours, subject to the satisfaction of the appointed Referee.

16.2 The jerseys of teams competing in the Competition should all be numbered or lettered to ensure the correct identification of all players and replacements during a match.

17. Grounds

17.1 A home Club is responsible for correctly and clearly marking its pitch and it must make proper provision to ensure that (with the exception of the touch judges) all spectators, replacements and officials are kept at a reasonable distance from the field of play.

17.2 When a late decision as to the fitness of the ground for the playing of a league match is necessary, it shall be made by the respective captains of the Clubs involved but if the captains are not able to agree, the decision shall be made by the appointed Referee.

17.3 A late decision is defined as one made within 3 hours of the scheduled kick-off time.

18. Finance

18.1 Monies provided for the 1997/98 Competition and all Competitions thereafter (until otherwise agreed by the Committee) shall belong to the Clubs in the Leagues for whom the monies have been provided and shall be distributed in the case of the Premier Leagues 1 and 2 as ERP shall decide and in respect of all other leagues as the Committee shall decide provided always that the Committee shall decide always that the Committee may as it shall see fit appropriate for the benefit of the Clubs in the competition.

18.2 Any proposal involving an offer of sponsorship, financial assistance or gift for a League or combination of Leagues must be submitted to the RFU for approval.

18.3 Gate receipts at a match shall belong to the home Club.

18.4 The home Club shall be responsible for all match expenses.

18.5 The away Club shall be responsible for its own travelling and accommodation expenses.

18.6 A membership, registration or administration fee may be charged to each participating Club as may from time to time be determined by the Organising Committee of the League concerned with the approval of the Committee.

18.7 Clubs failing to register claims for monies allocated to them by the date notified to them will not be eligible for payment of sponsorship or other monies.

19. Disciplinary Powers

19.1 Without prejudice to the powers of the RFU or the delegation of powers to Constituent Bodies under Rule 12.4 of the Rules of the RFU, the Committee shall have the power to expel or suspend any Club from membership of the Competition or impose such other penalty (including withour prejudice to the generality of the foregoing the imposition of a fine or award of compensation) as is considered appropriate on any Club for a breach of any of these Regulations.

19.2 The Committee shall have the right of its own volition to review any decision made in relation to these Regulations (whether disciplinary organisational, administrative or executive) of any Organising Committee and vary the same.

19.3 The Committee shall have the right to delegate disciplinary powers (other than the power to expel or suspend from membership of the Competition) for any breach of these Regulations to an Organising Committee or a League or National League subject to the rights of appeal as hereinafter provided.

19.4 Specifically an Organising Committee of a League shall have power to discipline any Club participating in such League for breach of any of the Regulations of the Competition by way of loss of match or Competition points, transference of points, review of result, monetary fine or compensation award, and any such Club may be liable to be placed at the bottom of the League concerned and such Club's results deleted from such League table.

20. Complaints

20.1 Any complaint under these Regulations shall be referred in the case of ERP to its Chief Executive, in the case of the NCA to its Secretary but otherwise to the Secretary of the League concerned by telephone within 48 hours of knowledge of the occurrence giving rise to the complaint and thereafter submitted in writing within a further 48 hours. The complaining Club shall also send a copy of such complaint if applicable. The ERP Chief Executive or Secretary on receipt of the written complaint shall require the other party to the complaint if applicable to answer the complaint within seven (7) days of the receipt of the written complaint and the ERP Chief Executive or the Secretary shall give a ruling within a further seven (7) days. If either party to the complaint is dissatisfied with such ruling there shall be a right of appeal to the Board of ERP in the case of the Premier Leagues or otherwise the Organising Committee of the League concerned as set out in Regulation 4, provided notice in writing is given within 7 days of receipt of the League Secretary's or Chief Executive of ERp's decision.

20.2 If either the complaining Club, or the other party to the complaint, or the Club against whom the complaint is made, requires an oral hearing, whether or not a ruling has been given by the League Secretary or the Chief Executive of ERP, it shall be requested in writing and the ERP Board or the Organising Committee responsible for the League concerned shall, within 72 hours of receiving notice of such request, appoint a time, date and place for the hearing of such complaint. The Chief Executive of ERP or League Secretary who has given a ruling shall not be entitled to take any part in the review of a ruling he has given other than to explain the reasons for his ruling.

20.3 Where a complaint is heard before the Organising Committee of a League it shall be the obligation of the complaining Club (or other person making the complaint) to establish that upon the balance of probabilities the complaint is justified. If the Organising Committee considers that the complaint is not justified it may dismiss it without hearing the representations of the Club or person against whom the complaint is made. The Organising Committee cannot find a complaint proved without giving the person or Club against whom the complaint is made an opportunity to make representations or call relevant evidence.

21. Appeals

21.1 Any party aggrieved at the decision of the ERP Board or the Organising Committee may, within seven days of receipt of the decision, appeal in writing to the Secretary (or as appropriate the Chief Executive) of the RFU restating the grounds on which the original appeal was made. The Club shall not be entitled to introduce any further grounds of objection not previously stated to the Organising Committee or the Board of ERP, nor to lodge a second objection arising from the circumstances on which the objection is based.

The Secretary (or as appropriate the Chief Executive) of the RFU shall refer the objection to the Committee to act as an Appeal Committee whose decision shall be final and binding. It shall be at the sole discretion of the Committee whether or not to grant a personal hearing.

21.2 Any party to an appeal (whether made under Regulation 20.2 or this Regulation 21) shall provide such information or evidence and within such time as the Organising Committee or the Appeal Committee (as the case may be) shall require.

21.3 Upon a party to an appeal failing to provide such information within the time required, the Organising Committee or the Appeal Committee (as the case may be) shall be entitled to refuse to hear that party when considering the appeal.

21.4 The Club and/or appellant may be required to pay the cost of the appeal when a personal hearing is requested and granted.

22. Medical Safety

Wherever possible, the home team should ensure a doctor or other medically qualified person is in attendance throughout the match.

23. Media Rights

23.1 Media Rights together with their sole right of exploitation save insofar as has otherwise been expressly agreed belong to the RFU.

23.2 No Club participating in the Competition shall purport to have the right to exploit, license, sell, lease, franchise, grant or in any way dispose of all or any part of the Media Rights save that of each participant in the Competition using the Competition's or Competition sponsor's name.

23.3 Each Club participating in the Competition shall permit access to its ground without demanding any fee or payment therefor to any person firm or company wishing to film, televise or broadcast any Competition match provided such filming, broadcasting or televising is undertaken by the company to whom the RFU sold such rights or has been previously agreed by the RFU but not further or otherwise.

24. Terms and Conditions of Participation

24.1 Each club by commencing its programme of league matches in the competition agrees it has entered into a legally binding obligation with the RFU and as a separate covenant with any sponsor of the league in which the Club plays

24.1.1 to comply in every particular with these Regulations 1 - 26 (inclusive).

24.1.2 to comply at all times with each and every obligation and requirement entered into by the RFU (or organising Committee as the case may be) with those parties including but not limited to the terms and conditions of any sponsorship agreement provided that the details of any such obligations and requirements have been notified to the participating club.

24.2 Each Club in League Levels 1 - 6 (inclusive) by commencing its matches in the competition agrees it has entered into a legally binding obligation with each other club in its league

24.2.1 to play all its fixtures on the dates agreed or on the dates fixed pursuant to these Regulations

24.2.2 to comply at all times with every particular regulation

25. Copyright

The copyright in the fixtures lists of the Competitions shall vest in the RFU and must not be reproduced in whole or in part except with the written consent of the RFU such consent having been given for Season 1997/98, 1998/99 and 1999/2000 to ERP.

26. Omissions and Interpretations and Further Regulations

26.1. The Committee shall have the absolute and unfettered discretion to decide on any matters not provided for in and on the interpretation of these Regulations and/or make any further or alternative regulations for the Competition where there is a requirement therefor. The Committee's decision shall be final and binding.

26.2 Where any provision of these Regulations is held by any Court or competent authority illegal void or unenforceable these Regulations shall continue to be valid as to the other provisions thereof and the remainder of any affected Regulation.

RFU Registration of Players Regulations and Operating Procedures - Season 1997/98

These Regulations together with the Operating Procedures will apply to all Clubs and to all Players seeking to be registered with a Club on or after 1st June 1997.

1. Definitions

For the purpose of these Regulations and the Operating Procedures only:

1.1 **"Club"** means a Club participating in the League;

1.2 **"Committee"** means the Competitions Committee of the RFU or where the context so admits and the power of delegation to the extent permitted by and contained in Regulation 13 hereof has been exercised the Division (or committee or sub-committee thereof appointed by the Division) or other company, person, association, group, body or committee to whom authority is delegated by the Committee;

1.3 **"Computerised Listing"** means the computerised record of a Club and Players' registration details held by the Registrar in the form prescribed by the Committee;

1.4 **"Contract"** means any agreement, arrangement or understanding (whether formal or informal) made between a Union or Division or Province (or other association of clubs) or Club (associated with a Member of a Union) or any other person, firm or company and a Player for the provision of a Material Benefit wholly or partially in consideration for the Player's participation in the Game or which entitles the party with whom the Player has entered any such agreement, arrangement or understanding to require the Player to participate in the Game.

1.5 **"Contracted Overseas Player"** means an Overseas Player who at any time in the six months prior to his application for registration under these Regulations has entered into or been a party to a Contract;

1.6 **"Current Union"** means any rugby football union which is a member of the IRFB other than the RFU;

1.7 **"Division"** means a combination of constituent bodies authorised under Rule 12.6 or rules of the RFU;

1.8 **"Effective Date"** is the date when a Player's application for registration becomes effective in accordance with these Regulations and such Player is accordingly Effectively Registered or has Effective Registration;

1.9 **"Established Club Player"** means a Player for whom application for registration is made who has been a member played for and only played for the Club making such application since the first day of the Season and who has not been Effectively Registered for any other Club during the Season.

1.10 **'Foreign Player'** means a person who is not entitled to the rights granted under Part II of the EC Treaty or under Part III of the EEA Treaty (i.e. a person who does not have European workers rights) (Note: A passport of a Member State of the European Community will normally be accepted as evidence that a Player is not a Foreign Player).

1.11 **"Game"** means rugby football played in accordance with the bye-laws, resolutions and laws of the IRFB;

1.12 **"Handbook"** means the annual publication of the RFU relating to the Season 1997/98;

1.13 **"IRFB"** is the world governing body of the game which is the International Rugby Football Board of which the RFU is a Member;

1.14 **"League"** means the English Clubs Rugby Union Championship (including the Allied Dunbar Premiership).

1.15 **"Loan Player"** means a Player who has entered into a Contract with a Club and who under an agreement, arrangement or understanding between that Club and another Club has Effective Registration with that other Club.

1.16 **"Material Benefit"** means money, consideration, gifts or any other benefits whatsoever contracted, promised or given to a person or at his direction, but does not include reimbursement of expenses incurred for reasonable travel, accommodation, subsistence or other expenses incurred in relation to the Game;

1.17 **"Operating Procedures"** means the RFU Registration of Players Operating Procedures for the Season and appearing in the Handbook;

1.18 **"Overseas Player"** means any Player playing the Game for any team in any Union other than the RFU;

1.19 **"Player"** means any person who is over the age of 18 on that Player's Registration Date;

1.20 **"Registrar"** means the person(s) appointed annually by the Committee for the purposes of dealing with registration for the Premiership, National and Divisional Leagues in accordance with the Operating Procedures and these Regulations such appointees for the Season being set out in the Appendix hereto;

1.21 **"Registration Date"** is the date on which a properly completed and duly signed Registration Form for a Player together with such other documentation as is properly required by the Operating Procedures (and these Regulations) is received and accepted by the Registrar;

1.22 **"Registration Form"** means the form attached as an Appendix to the Operating Procedures;

1.23 **"RFU"** means the Rugby Football Union;

1.24 **"RFU Competition"** means the League, any knock-out competition organised by the RFU and any other competition designated by the RFU as an RFU Competition for the purposes of these Regulations;

1.25 **"Season"** means 16th August 1997 to 17th May 1998 (inclusive)

1.26 **"Transfer Deadline"** means 1st March 1998

1.27 **"Union"** means any Union as defined by bye-law 1 of the rules of the IRFB;

1.28 **"Waiting Period"** means that period of time between the Registration Date and when the player is Effectively Registered pursuant to these Regulations;

2. Eligibility to Play in an RFU Competition

2.1 No Player may play for a Club in an RFU Competition unless he holds Effective Registration with that Club and where a match in a RFU Competition is held after the Transfer Deadline the Player held such Effective Registration with that Club PRIOR to the Transfer Deadline (unless such Player is either an Established Club Player or he achieved his eighteenth birthday after the Transfer Deadline and is thereby entitled to Effective Registration for the first time);

2.2 No Club may lawfully play a match in an RFU Competition unless that Club is only represented in that match by Players with Effective Registration for that Club.

3. Effective Registration

A player will have Effective Registration with a Club:

3.1 if he was Effectively Registered with that Club on 30th May 1997 or

3.2 if application for registration had been properly made to the Registrar appropriate to the Club for registration of that player with that Club prior to 30th May 1997 under the Regulations then in effect and which but for the introduction of these Regulations such registration would have been effective after 30th May 1997 or

3.3 where an application to the Registrar appropriate to the Club is made for registration on the Registration Form together with all such documents and evidence as may be required by the Operating Procedures, the Registrar has accepted such application, the Waiting Period for that Player has elapsed, there has been compliance with paragraph 4 of these Regulations and such application has not been withdrawn by that Player prior to the Effective Date pursuant to paragraph 8.1 of these Regulations.

PROVIDED ALWAYS that Effective Registration has not ceased under any of the provisions of paragraphs 10.2 - 10.9 (inclusive) of these Regulations PROVIDED FURTHER registration will not be deemed to be Effective under the provisions of paragraph 3.1 and 3.2 above where there had been any breach by the Player or the Club of the Regulations relating to the Game published and adopted by IRFB pursuant to bye-law 3(b) of the IRFB.

4. Restrictions upon an application for registration

4.1 The Registrar will not accept an application for registration of a Player who has in the past six months entered into a Contract or who is proposing to enter into a Contract with the Club for which application for registration is made unless and until the Registrar is advised by the RFU that the application for registration may be accepted.

4.2 No application for registration under these Regulations of an Overseas Player who is leaving or proposing to leave his Current Union will be accepted unless and until a clearance from his Current Union has been received to participate in the Game under the jurisdiction of the RFU.

4.3 No application for registration of a Contracted Overseas Player can be accepted by the Registrar until the Registrar is satisfied either that the Player has previously been resident in England, the Isle of Man or the Channel Islands for 180 days (or such other period as may be agreed by the RFU and the Player's Current Union) prior to the commencement of the Season or that upon the expiry of the Waiting Period such Player would have been so resident for the required period.

4.4 No application for registration of an Overseas Player will be accepted unless that Player is resident at the time of such application in England the Channel Islands or the Isle of Man.

4.5 No application for registration of a Foreign Player will be accepted by the Registrar in circumstances where a work permit or other permit or consent to play the Game is or might be required without evidence satisfactory to the Registrar is adduced that the requisite work permit or other permit or consent has been obtained or that no work permit is required.

5. **Evidence of Effective Registration**

The only evidence permissible of a Player's Effective Registration with a Club on any particular date is the Computerised Listing of the Players holding Effective Registration on that particular date such Computerised Listing being held by the Registrar (a copy of which will be provided to any Club upon application (with a stamped addressed envelope) to the appropriate Registrar by the Club).

6. **Limitation on number of Players that may be Effectively Registered with a Club.**

No Club (other than a Club playing below level 6 in the League) will be able to register more than 70 players.

7. **Length of Waiting Period**

Subject to the exception referred to in the proviso to this Regulation 7, the Waiting Periods are as follows:
7.1   7 clear days from the Registration Date for a Player who does not have Effective Registration with any other Club or
7.2   7 clear days from the Registration Date for any seeking to be registered with a Club where such Player had Effective Registration with another Club at the Registration Date or
7.3   2 clear days from the Registration Date for a Player who is a Loan Player re-Registering with the Club with which he has a Contract.
SAVE and PROVIDED that in respect of any application for registration (other than an Established Club Player or for a Player whose eighteenth birthday falls between the Transfer Deadline and the last day of the Season) where the expiry of the Waiting Period would but for this proviso have occurred between the Transfer Deadline and the last day of the Season (inclusive) the Waiting Period will be extended until 1st June 1998 upon which date the Player will become Effectively Registered.

8. **Withdrawal of an application for registration and de-registration**

8.1   A Player (but not a Club) may apply to have any applications for registration with a Club withdrawn provided that any such application is made in writing, is signed by the Player is received by the Registrar by the Effective Date and the Player does not have a binding contract with that Club.
8.2   Any Player (who has not entered into a binding contract with that Club) holding Effective Registration with a Club may upon written application to the relevant Registrar de-register from that Club; the Player will cease to hold Effective Registration 30 days from the receipt of the Player's application to the Registrar
8.3   Any Club may apply to de-register any of its Players and such Player in respect of whom application is made will cease to have Effective Registration with that Club 30 days from the receipt of the application for de-registration by the appropriate Club's Registrar PROVIDED THAT in any application by a Club to de-register a Player the Club has notified and certified to the Registrar that it has notified the Player of its application for that Player's de-registration
8.4   No application for de-registration may be withdrawn during the 30 days' de-registration period.
[Note: A Registrar will only be on notice of a contract with a Player where such a Contract has been registered with the RFU in accordance with IRFB and RFU Regulations)

9. **Limitation on registration**

9.1   No person may hold Effective Registration before his eighteenth birthday
9.2   No Player may hold Effective Registration with more than three (3) Clubs in the Season
9.3   No Player may hold Effective Registration more than three (3) times with any one Club in the Season.
9.4   No Player may hold Effective Registration with more than one Club at any one time.

10. **Loss of Effective Registration**

A Player will cease to have Effective Registration with a Club
10.1   upon being Effectively Registered with another Club.
10.2   upon expiry of 30 days following a valid application for de-registration.
10.3   upon having Effective Registration cancelled or suspended by the Committee.
10.4   upon the expiry of any work permit or other permit or consent required by Law if the Player is to play in an RFU Competition.
10.5   where a Registered Player enters into a Contract or receives Material Benefit and the Contract is not

registered with RFU within three months of being entered into or the date of receipt of Material Benefit.

10.6 where a Registered Player who is a Foreign Player enters into a Contract or receives Material Benefit and such a Player does not have a valid work permit or other permit or consent required by law.

10.7 where Effective Registration is invalidated pursuant to Regulation 12.1 below.

10.8 where that Player plays the Game for any team in or under the control of or a member of a Union other than the RFU more than 6 times in any twelve month period (save for a team selected by the National Selectors of that other Union).

10.9 where that Player plays the Game for Material Benefit for any team in or under the control of or a member of any Union other than the RFU outside the European Community and other than a team selected by the National Selectors of that other Union.

11. Operating Procedures

Any Club seeking to register a Player must comply with the Operating Procedures (together with any amendment(s) or variation(s) thereof as may be notified to Clubs from time to time) and in particular submit with any application to register a Player ALL the requisite documentation and a stamped addressed envelope failing which such application will NOT be accepted by the Registrar.

12. False or Misleading Information

12.1 Where a Club supplies incorrect or misleading information to the Registrar or the RFU in any application to register a Player or any signature on the Registration Form or other document is not the original signature of the person purported to have signed it the application for registration will be void and any Effective Registration will be invalidated.

12.2 Where the Committee is satisfied that any misleading or incorrect information was supplied deliberately or by a Club knowing that such misleading or incorrect information might mislead or with the intention of misleading or where any signature is not that of the person of whom it purports to be may render the Club or Player and/or one or more of the Club's officials liable to disciplinary action under RFU rule 5.12 and in addition penalties that may be imposed under the rules of any RFU Competition

13. Power of Delegation

The Committee shall have the power to delegate any of its powers, duties or obligations under these Regulations other than its powers under Regulations 14 and 15 to any Division, constituent body or other company, person, association, group, body or committee.

14. Power to make new regulations and amend Operating Procedures

Where there has been any omission or error in these Regulations or Operating Procedures the Committee will have power to rectify such error or omission in the manner it sees fit including the power to make new and/or amend these Regulations.

15. Disputes

15.1 Any dispute on the application of these Regulations or Operating Procedures must be referred to the Registrar appropriate to the Club in writing stating the grounds under which any objection or dispute is made.

15.2 If a dispute is not resolved within 7 days of receipt of complaint by the Registrar the Club or Player may submit the complaint in writing to the Secretary (or Chief Executive) of the RFU re-stating the grounds upon which the objection was made. A Club shall not be entitled to introduce any further grounds of objection not previously stated to the Registrar or to lodge a second objection arising from the circumstances on which the objection is based.

15.3 The Chief Executive of the RFU may refer the objection to the Committee whose decision shall be final and binding. It will be at the sole discretion of the Committee whether or not to grant a personal hearing if it has been requested by the Club.

15.4 A Club and/or Player may be required by the RFU to pay the cost of resolving any dispute or any personal hearing that takes place at Club's or Player's request.

16. Omissions and Interpretation

16.1 Where there is any dispute in interpretation of or inconsistency between these Regulations and the

Operating Procedures these Regulations will prevail.

16.2 The Committee shall have the absolute and unfettered discretion to decide on any matter not provided for in and on the interpretation of these Regulations and the Operating Procedures or to rectify any administrative error. The Committee's decision shall be final and binding.

16.3 Where any provision of these Regulations is held by any Court or competent authority illegal, void or unenforceable in whole or in part these Regulations shall continue to be valid as to the other provisions thereof and the remainder of any affected Regulation.

PLAYER REGISTRATION
1997/98
Registrars for season 1997/98 are as follows:

National Leagues
Alwynne Evans
Twickenham Services
Rugby Football Union
Twickenham
Middlesex TW1 1DZ
Tel: 0181 892 8161
Fax 0181 892 4446

London & South East Division
Chris Pool
PO Box 178
Tewin Wood
Herts AL6 OXX
Tel: 01438 798 469
Fax: 01438 798 023

Midland Division
D I Robins
c/o Russells News Agency
PO Box 183
Leicester
LE3 8BZ
Tel: 0116 233 2200
Fax: 0116 233 2204

Northern Division
Bob Archer
Brookfield House
Scotland Head
Winlaton
Tyne & Wear NE21 6PL
Tel: 0191 414 3532
Fax: 0191 414 3532

South West Division
M Gee
The First Eleven Sports Agency
PO Box 11
Reading
Berks. TG6 3DT
Tel: 07071 611 611
Fax: 01189 757 764

Operating Procedures - Season 1997/98

1. Definitions

The words used in these Operating Procedures shall have the meanings set out in Regulation 1 of the Regulations and in addition:

1.1 **"Application Documents"** means those documents required by Paragraph 3 of these Operating Procedures to be submitted to the Registrar and the RFU to obtain Effective Registration of a Player.

1.2 **"Regulations"** means the RFU Registration of Player Regulations for the Season appearing in the Handbook.

1.3 **"Contracted Player"** means a Player who at any time in the six months prior to his application for registration has entered into or been a party to a Contract.

2. General Procedure for obtaining Effective Registration

2.1 The Application Documents MUST be fully and correctly completed and properly signed.

2.2 The Application Documents must be submitted to the Registrar appropriate to the Club making the application by post.

2.3 Clubs in League levels 1 - 4 (inclusive) may submit copy Application Documents to the Registrar appropriate to the Club by facsimile PROVIDED that the original Application Documents are received by that Registrar within 4 working days of the date of the facsimile.

2.4 Any documentation in relation to Contracts or Contracted Overseas Players must be sent by post to the RFU at Twickenham.

3. Documentation to be submitted for Registration

If a Club wishes to register a Player it must submit:

3.1 In relation to a Player who is not a Contracted Player, not an Overseas Player and where the Club does not propose to enter into a Contract with that Player to the Registrar appropriate to that Club.

3.1.1 a fully complete white copy of the Registration Form duly and properly signed by the Player and on behalf of the Club by its Secretary or other delegate officer:

3.1.2 a stamped envelope addressed to the Club making the application.

3.1.3 where a Club wishes Effective Registration to occur after the Transfer Deadline and prior to the end of the Season evidence satisfactory to the Registrar that the Player is an Established Club Player or that the Players' eighteenth birthday falls between the Transfer deadline and the end of the Season

3.1.4 where a Player holds Effective Registration with another Club a copy of a letter to that Player's current Club informing that Club that the Player intends to seek Effective Registration with the applicant Club.

3.2 In relation to a Player to whom a Contract is to be offered contemporaneously to or prior to the Effective Date.

3.2.1 to the Registrar appropriate to that Club the documents referred to in paragraph 3.1 above and

3.2.2 to the RFU (Twickenham Services) the blue copy of the Registration Form, the form of Contract for the RFU's approval and a stamped envelope addressed to the Club.

3.3 in relation to a Contracted Player

3.3.1 to the Registrar appropriate to that Club the documents referred to in paragraph 3.1 above.

3.3.2 to the RFU (Twickenham Services) evidence that the Player's previous Contract has expired or that the other party to it consents to the application for registration with the applicant Club or other evidence satisfactory to the RFU that the Player may be registered with the applicant Club.

3.3.3 where Paragraph 3.2 above applies to the RFU (Twickenham Services) the documents referred to in Paragraph 3.2.2 above.

3.4 in relation to an Overseas Player

3.4.1 to the Registrar appropriate to that Club the documents referred to in paragraph 3.1 above AND a clearance from the Player's Current Union pursuant to Regulation 9.1 of the Regulations of the IRFB.

3.4.2 to the Registrar a certificate from the applicant Club that the Overseas Player is not a Contracted Overseas Player and is resident in England, the Isle of Man or the Channel Islands and

3.4.3 where Paragraph 3.2 above applies to the RFU (Twickenham Services) the documents referred to in Paragraph 3.2.2 above.

3.4.4 Where Paragraph 3.2 above applies and the Overseas Player is a Foreign Player to the Registrar a valid work permit or other permit, or consent required by Law or such evidence as is satisfactory to the Registrar that such a work permit, other permit or consent is not required.

3.5 in relation to a Contracted Overseas Player

3.5.1 to the Registrar appropriate to that Club the documents referred to in Paragraph 3.1 above AND a clearance from the Player's Current Union pursuant to Regulation 9.1 of the Regulations of the IRFB:

3.5.2 to the Registrar evidence satisfactory to the Registrar that the Player has been (or at the expiry of the Waiting Period will have been) resident in England, the Channel Islands or the Isle of Man for 180 days (or such other period as may be agreed by the RFU and the Player's Current Union) prior to commencement of the Season and is so resident at the date of the application and

3.5.3 where Paragraph 3.2 above applies to the RFU (Twickenham Services) the documents referred to in Paragraph 3.2.2 above.

3.6 in relation to a Loan Player where a Club seeks Effective Registration within two working days to the Registrar such documentation as is required under the relevant paragraphs above and evidence satisfactory to the Registrar that the Player is a Loan Player seeking Effective Registration with the Club with whom he has a Contract.

4. Action of Registrar

4.1 Upon receipt of the Application Documents the Registrar will

4.1.1 check the documentation to see it is complete and properly signed.

4.1.2 check that there is no other application for registration pending and that there is no reason why the Player should not be registered

4.1.3 where there is a Contract, a Contracted Player or a Contracted Overseas Player noted on the Registration Form liaise with the RFU to obtain the requisite clearance.

4.2 Where the Registrar is satisfied in relation to 4.1.1 and 4.1.2 above and the requisite clearance from the RFU has been obtained pursuant to 4.1.3 above the Registrar.

4.2.1 will accept the application for Registration [the Registration Date].

4.2.2 calculate the Effective Date and enter the pending registration on the Computerised Listing.

4.2.3 send to the Club making the application a copy of the Computerised Listing (updated to include the application and the Effective Date of the Player's registration) in the stamped addressed envelope.

4.3 Where the Registrar is unable to accept the Application Documents submitted or where clearance from the RFU (Twickenham Services) is not given the Club applying for registration will be notified in the stamped addressed envelope and where appropriate the documentation returned so that the Club may take such action as is required.

4.4 Where no stamped addressed envelope is included with the documentation the Registrar may take NO ACTION until the documentation is completed by a stamped addressed envelope being supplied. The Player will NOT obtain Effective Registration.

5 Action by the RFU

Upon receipt by the RFU (Twickenham Services) of documentation under Paragraph 3 above the RFU will:

5.1 check the documentation received and

5.2 utilising the stamped addressed envelope provided to the RFU either notify the Registrar and the Club of its clearance of the proposed registration OR notify the Registrar and the Club of its reason(s) for refusing clearance of the proposed Registration and invite the Club to take action to remedy the cause of the RFU's refusal of clearance.

6. General - for Information

6.1 No Club may assume that any application for registration of a Player will result in Effective Registration unless and until it has received a Computerised Listing showing the date of Effective Registration for that Player.

6.2 Should the Player's current Club have objection to the Player being Effectively Registered with another Club by reason of existence of a Contract or under RFU rule 5.12 or under RFU Regulations concerning monies owing to that Club or under any IRFB Regulations the objection must be submitted in writing to the Chief Executive of the RFU stating all the grounds upon which the objection is made. The Club shall not be entitled to introduce any further grounds of objection not so stated nor to lodge a second objection arising from the circumstances upon which an objection is based.

6.3 A copy of an updated Computerised Listing will be forwarded at any time to a Club upon request where a stamped addressed envelope is enclosed

6.4 On or before 8th August 1997 the Registrar will post to each Club a complete list of its Players showing those with Effective Registration and those pending movements to and from the Club.

6.5 Where Clubs (Leagues Levels 1 - 6) are required to have limited squad sizes under Regulation 6 and have to reduce their squads such reduction MUST be effected by de-registration by 15th July 1997.

6.6 A Player may only have one application for Effective Registration operative at any one time and if any subsequent application is made whether during or before the Waiting Period it will be returned to the Club making the subsequent application.

6.7 For the avoidance of doubt a Player may play for the Club for which he has Effective Registration in an RFU Competition match until he has Effective Registration with a new Club.

6.8 Where a Club wishes to enter into a Contract with a Player it must submit the blue copy of a Registration Form fully completed with the Contract to the RFU (Twickenham Services) for approval.
Note:
1. If a club does not notify the Rugby Football Union of any Contracts with a PLayer within three months of that Contract being entered into the Player will be de-registered.
2. If the Rugby Football Union is not on notice of a Contract with a Player that Player may be Effectively Regiostered with another club.

6.9 Where a Club wishes to enter a Contract with a Foreign Player it must in addition to the Procedure set out in 6.8 above submit to the Registrar the work permit or other permit required by law or such evidence satisfactory to the Registrar that such work permit or other consent is not required.

6.10 Where a Club has any enquiry in relation into the Regulations and/or these Operating Procedures the Club should contact its appropriate Registrar or the RFU (Twickenham Services) immediately for advice or assistance. Misunderstanding or lack of knowledge WILL NOT be accepted as grounds for an objection under Regulation 15.

The National Knockout Cup 1997/98

1. Description and Form

1.1 The Competition shall be called "The Rugby Football Union Club Knockout Competition" (or such other name as the RFU may decide) and shall be between the 122 Clubs who shall qualify to play in the first and subsequent rounds.

1.2 All matches in the Competition shall be played under the Laws of Rugby Union Football and comply with the Rules and Regulations of the Rugby Football Union (hereinafter called "the RFU").

2 Definitions

In these Regulations

Club means a Club participating in the League in the previous season being a member of the RFU.

Committee means the Competitions Committee of the RFU or where the context so admits the power of delegation contained in Regulation 3.2 having been exercised the Division, Constituent Body or other person, firm or Company, Media Agency or Competition Administrator to whom power has been delegated.

Competition means "The Rugby Football Union Club Knockout Competition" to which these Regulations apply.

Constituent Body means an association or combination of Clubs designated in accordance with Rule 16 of the RFU other than the Army, Cambridge University, The England Schools Union, Oxford University, Royal Air Force, Royal Navy and the Students Union.

Contract means any agreement, arrangement or understanding (whether formal or informal) made between any Club (whether or not participating in the competition) or any other person, firm or company and a player for the provision of material benefit wholly or partially in consideration for the Player's participation in the game of rugby football or which entitles the party with whom a player has entered any such agreement, arrangement or understanding to require the player to participate in the game of rugby football.

Division means a combination of Constituent Bodies authorised under Rule 12.6 of the Rules of the RFU.

Effective Registration means that a player is registered with a Club in accordance with and pursuant to Regulation No. 3 of the Registration of Players Regulations.

ERP means English Rugby Partnership Limited, a company responsible for the organisation and management of the first and second leagues of the Allied Dunbar Premiership.

Foreign Player means any player being a person who is not entitled at the relevant time to the rights granted under Part II of the EC Treaty and/or Part III of the EEA Treaty.

Note: a passport of a Member State of the European Community will normally be accepted as evidence that a player is not a Foreign Player.

Handbook means the annual publication of the RFU relating to the season in which the Competition is played.

League means the English Clubs Rugby Union Championship.

Loan Player means a player who has entered into a contract with any club (whether or not competing in the Competition) and who under an agreement, arrangement or understanding between that Club and another Club has Effective Registration with that other Club.

Media Rights means all Television and/or other broadcasting media advertising, publicity and promotion rights of any and every description in and relating to the Competition.

RFU means Rugby Football Union.

3. Organising Committee

3.1 The Competition will be organised by the Committee.

3.2 The Committee shall have the power to delegate any of its powers, duties or obligations under these Regulations (other than its powers under Regulation 17) to any Division, Constituent Body or other person, firm or Company, Media Agency or Competition Administrator.

3.3 Subject to Regulation 17 the decision of the Committee shall be binding and final on any matter not provided for in and on the interpretation of these Regulations.

4. Eligibility of Clubs

4.1 The Competition shall be open to any Club situated in England, the Channel Islands and the Isle of Man being a member of the R.F.U.

4.2 The Competition shall comprise the 122 Clubs who shall qualify as follows:

4.2.1 in the first round 56 Clubs nominated by the County Constituent Bodies, being two Clubs from each County Constituent Body plus a third Club from Eastern Counties and Yorkshire and the 28 Clubs comprising RFU National Leagues 2 North and 2 South in the season of the Competition:

4.2.2 in the second round the 42 winners from the first round and the 14 Clubs comprising RFU National League 1

4.2.3 in the third round the 28 winners from the second round and the 12 Clubs comprising League 2 of the League competition organised by ERP.

4.2.4 in the fourth round the 20 winners from the third round and the 12 Clubs comprising League 1 of the League Competition organised by ERP

4.2.5 in the fifth round the 16 winners from the fourth round.

5. Eligibility of Players

5.1 A Club in a Competition match may only play or select as a replacement players who hold on the date of the match Effective Registration for that Club.

5.2 A Club may not be represented in the Competition by any person who has played for another Club in the Competition in the current season whether as a Loan Player or not.

5.3 A Club may not in any one match in the competition be represented by and may not select as a replacement more than two Foreign Players.

5.4 A Club may not in any one match in the competition play or select as a replacement more than three Loan Players.

(Warning: The computerised registration list is the only evidence which will be accepted to substantiate a player's Effective Registration - see Registration of Players Regulation)].

[Penalty: Any infringement of these Regulations 5.1 to 5.4 will automatically result in the disqualification from the Competition for that season of the player and Club involved and may expose the Club to disqualification from the Competition in subsequent seasons].

5.5 The Committee shall have the power to reinstate a Club in the Competition when it has been eliminated by a Club which has been in breach of this Regulation 5. This power shall cease to apply at 2.00 p.m. three days before the date when a further round of the Competition immediately following that in which the breach was committed is scheduled to be played.

6. The Competition Format and Draws

6.1 The format of the Competition shall be as follows:

6.1.1 The Competition shall comprise five rounds, Quarter-finals, Semi-finals and a Final.

6.1.2 Rounds 1 and 2 will be played on an Area basis, namely the Northern Division with Midland Division: London and South-East Division with South-West Division. Draws will be made accordingly

6.1.3 Rounds 3, 4, and 5 and the Quarter and Semi-finals will be played on a national basis.

6.2 The draws in the Competition shall be made as follows:

6.2.1 The draw for the first round of the Competition will be made in accordance with arrangements made by the Committee.

6.2.2 The draws for the first and second rounds being made on an area basis, in the event of inequality of Clubs from each area, in respect of either or any of these rounds, there shall be preliminary draws held before the draws for either or any of the first and second rounds, in order to provide an even number of Clubs to participate in the first and second round draws in each area.

6.2.3 The third and subsequent rounds will be drawn on a national basis.

6.2.4 The draw for each round after the first shall be made during the seven days following the weekend specified for the completion of the preceding round, unless agreed otherwise by the Committee.

6.2.5 The first named Club to be drawn in a match shall be considered the home team and, unless otherwise mutually agreed, (or in the case of the semi finals unless directed by the Committee which may require the semi final matches to be played on neutral grounds), the venue of that match shall be the ground of such home team.

7. Dates of Rounds

7.1 Unless specifically directed by the Committee who may upon not less than two weeks notice to the particular Clubs involved change a date for a match, rounds shall be played on the Saturdays of the following weeks:-

Round 1 on week 2   Round 2 on week 5

Round 3 on week 9   Round 4 on week 17

Unless the participating Clubs agree to play on the Sunday of that particular week.

Round 5 will be played on Saturday 24th January 1998.

The Quarter Finals will be played on Saturday 28th February 1998;

The Semi Finals will be played on Saturday 28th March 1998;

and the Final on Saturday 9th May 1998.

8. Drawn Matches

8.1 In all rounds, except the Final, if after 40 minutes of play each way the scores are level, there shall be an immediate period of replay between the same teams of 10 minutes each way, with a one minute interval. If the scores are then still equal, the team that has scored most tries shall go forward into the next round. If this does not produce a result, the team that has scored the most goals from tries goes forward into the next round. If the scores still be equal, the visiting team shall go forward into the next round.

8.2   In the Final, if after 40 minutes play each way the scores are level, there shall be an immediate period of replay between the same teams of 10 minutes each way, with a one minute interval. If the scores are then still equal the team that has scored the most tries shall be the winner. If this does not produce a result, the team that has scored the most goals from tries shall be the winner. If no result is then achieved the match shall be adjudged a draw and the cup shall be held jointly.

9. Referees and Touch Judges

9.1   Referees and touch judges for all matches in the Competition shall be appointed by the RFU and the RFU Regulation relating to Law 6 shall apply.

10. Replacements

10.1   Replacements and substitutions are permitted in all matches in the competition in accordance with Law 3 and the International Board Resolutions relating thereto as printed in the Handbook.

10.2   In the interest of safety every team in the Competition shall have available two replacements or other player(s) on the field capable of playing in the front row of the scrum should a replacement be required whether due to injury or consequent upon a player being ordered off. If on the first or second occasion a front row player requires to be replaced and his team cannot provide a replacement, or other player capable of playing in the front row of the scrum, so that uncontested scrums result, his team shall be deemed to have lost the match.

11. Clash of Colours/Identification of Players

11.1   In the event of Clubs having similar or clashing colours, the home team shall be responsible for changing its colours subject to the satisfaction of the appointed Referee. For the Final the home team will be decided by the toss of a coin at least two days before the match concerned.

11.2   The jerseys of teams competing in the Competition should all be numbered or lettered to ensure the correct identification of all players and replacements during a match.

12. Postponed and Abandoned Matches

If conditions prevent a match being played or a match is abandoned because of such conditions before full time, it shall be played or replayed before the date of the next round on a day to be agreed between the two Clubs concerned or, failing agreement within seven days of the non played or uncompleted match, as directed by the Committee.

13. Notification of Results

The Secretary of the Club qualifying for the next round shall be responsible for informing the person, firm or company appointed by the Committee of the result by 10.00 am on the Monday following the match.

14. Kick-Offs and Delayed Arrivals

All scheduled matches shall start at the time notified by the home Club, but it shall not be earlier than 2.15 pm or later than 3.00 pm in any event. A kick-off time earlier than 2.15 pm or later than 3.00 pm may be ordered by the Committee or arranged by mutual agreement between the two Clubs concerned provided the Committee is advised in writing within 36 hours of any such mutual agreement and does not object thereto within a further 36 hours. Any delay may be reported by the non-offending Club to the Committee who may impose such penalty as it thinks fit.

15. Grounds

15.1   A home Club is responsible for correctly and clearly marking its pitch, and it must make proper provision to ensure that (with the exception of the touch judges) all spectators, replacements and officials are kept at a reasonable distance from the field of play.

15.2   When a late decision (i.e. a decision made or to be made within three hours of the scheduled kick-off time) as to the fitness of a ground for the playing of a match is necessary, it shall be made by the respective captains of the Clubs involved, but if the captains are not able to agree, the decision shall be made by the appointed Referee.

16. Finance

16.1   A reserve fund shall be established to assist in meeting the expenses of Clubs as provided for under Regulation 16.3.

16.2   At all matches in the third and subsequent rounds of the Competition, all spectators (including members, Debenture Holders, sponsors and their guests and season ticket holders) must be charged the advertised entrance, stand and car park prices.

16.2.1 The Committee will allocate from the reserve fund to Clubs playing away from home in the first and second rounds such sums as the Committee in its sole discretion shall decide, in order to assist such

Clubs in paying their travelling and other related expenses. Such allocation shall be made at least seven days before the date of such match and shall be paid as soon as practicable thereafter.

16.2.2 Clubs participating in the third, fourth and fifth rounds and the Quarter Finals shall share the gross gates (excluding VAT) which shall include car park and programme receipts (less cost of printing); the home team bearing all match expenses (which shall include the cost of providing temporary or additional stand accommodation unless, prior to the match, the provision of and the cost thereof has been mutually agreed in writing between the participating Clubs, when such cost shall be charged to the gross gate prior to the gross gate being shared between the participating Clubs) and the visiting team paying its own travelling expenses, each from their half-share of the gross gate.

16.2.3 In each Semi Final the gross gate, (excluding VAT), as defined in Regulations 16.2.2 above, after matchexpenses have been deducted and after the admitted claims of each of the Clubs involved for a party not exceeding 25 have been paid, shall be distributed as to 25% or such greater part as the Committee may decide thereof in equal shares between the two Clubs participating therein. The remaining proceeds from each Semi-Final, together with the gross gate from the Final, excluding VAT, as defined above, after match expenses for the Final have been deducted and after such sums as the Committee in its sole discretion shall decide have been paid to the Clubs in the Final, in order to assist such Clubs in paying their travelling and other expenses in relation to the Final, shall be distributed amongst the Clubs competing in the Competition in such shares as the RFU shall decide.

16.3 Monies provided for the 1997/98 Competition and all Competitions thereafter shall until otherwise decided by the Committee belong to the Clubs who play in the Competition and shall be distributed in such shares as the Committee shall decide.

16.4 A home Club is responsible for the proper promotion of a fixture. It is recommended that in the third and subsequent rounds the minimum charges be £3.00 for admission to the ground with a further £1.00 for a stand seat. A visiting Club shall be entitled to take up to one-third of each ticket category of a home Club if it so desires.

16.5 All match accounts are subject to the scrutiny of the Committee and all match accounts in respect of matches played in the fourth and subsequent rounds must be forwarded by the home Club, together with written confirmation that the half-share of the gross gate has been paid by the home Club to the visiting Club under sub-paragraphs 16.2.2 and 16.2.3 of this Regulation, to reach the Chief Executive of the RFU at Twickenham within four weeks of the game or sponsorship monies may not be paid.

17. Protests, Disputes and Transgressions

Any matters in dispute or any transgressions of these Regulations other than those relating to eligibility of the players where the provisions of the RFU Registration of Players Regulations apply, shall be referred immediately to the Chief Executive of the RFU by telephone if necessary, provided written confirmation follows within 48 hours setting out the grounds of the complaint in full. The Committee shall have absolute discretion to resolve any such protests or disputes as it shall think fit including the right of expulsion from the competition for one or more years and to impose financial penalties or fines and without prejudice to the generality of the foregoing may decline to accept a protest validly made if it considers doing so to be in the interests of the Competition generally. The decision of the Committee shall be final and binding on all parties.

18. Media Rights

18.1 Media Rights together with the sole right of their exploitation belong to the RFU.

18.2 No Club participating in the Competition shall purport to have the right to exploit, licence, sell, lease, franchise, grant or in anyway dispose of all or any part of the Media Rights save that each participating Club may advertise its participation in the Competition using the Competition's or any Sponsor's name.

18.3 Each Club participating in the Competition will permit access to its ground without demanding any fee or payment therefor to any person, firm or Company wishing to film, televise or broadcast all or any part of any game in the Competition provided such filming, broadcasting or televising is undertaken by the company to whom the RFU has sold such rights or has been previously agreed by the RFU but not further or otherwise.

19. Terms and Conditions of Participation

Each Club by commencing its first match in the competition agrees it has entered into a legally binding obligation with the RFU and as separate obligations with other Clubs in the competition and with any Sponsor of the Competition that it will:

19.1 comply in every particular with these Regulations 1 to 19 (inclusive)

19.2 at all times comply with each and every of the obligations and requirements entered into by the RFU with third parties, including, but not limited to, any sponsors of the Competition under the terms and conditions of any sponsorship agreement provided that details of any such obligations and requirements have been notified by the RFU to the participating Clubs.

MAIN FIXTURES 1997-98

AUGUST 1997

Sat, 16th

Welsh Nat Lgs Premier & 1st Divs (1)	Wales
Irish Inter Provincial Championship	
Connacht v Munster	Galway
Leinster v Ulster	Dublin

Sat, 23rd

English Premier League 1 (1)	England
Welsh Nat Lgs Premier & 1st Divs (2)	Wales
Irish Inter Provincial Championship	
Connacht v Ulster	Galway
Munster v Leinster	TBA

Wed, 27th

Wales 'A' v Romania	Wales

Sat, 30th

WALES v ROMANIA	Wrexham
English Premier League 1 (2)	England
English Premier League 2 (1)	England
English National Leagues 1/2 (1)	England
English Divisional Leagues 12s (1)	England
Scottish "League Trophy" Gps A & B (1)	Scotland
Irish Inter Provincial Championship	
Leinster v Connacht	Dublin
Ulster v Munster	Belfast

SEPTEMBER 1997

Sat, 6th

Heineken Cup & Conference (1)	Europe
English Premier League 2 (2)	England
English National Leagues 1/2 (2)	England
English Divisional League 12s (2)	England
English Divisional Leagues 10s/17s (1)	England
Scottish "League Trophy" Gps A & B (2)	Scotland
Welsh Swalec Cup Preliminary Round	Wales
Welsh Nat League Div 1 (3)	Wales
Welsh Nat League Divs 2,3,4 (1)	Wales

Sat, 13th

Heineken Cup & Conference (2)	Europe
English Premier League 2 (3)	England
English National League 1 (3)	England
Scottish "League Trophy" Gps A & B (3)	Scotland
SRU Tennents Cup Round Three	Scotland
Welsh Nat League Div 1 (4)	Wales
Welsh Nat League Divs 2,3,4 (2)	Wales

Sat, 20th

Heineken Cup & Conference (3)	Europe
English Premier League 2 (4)	England
English National League 1 (4)	England
English National League 2 (3)	England
English Divisional League 12s (3)	England
English Divisional Leagues 10s/17s (2)	England
English Divisional League 15s (1)	England
Scottish "League Trophy" Gps A & B (4)	Scotland
SRU Tennents National Lgs Divs 1-7 (1)	Scotland
Welsh Nat League Div 1 (5)	Wales
Welsh Nat League Divs 2,3,4 (3)	Wales

Sat, 27th

Heineken Cup & Conference (4)	Europe
English Premier League 2 (5)	England
English National League 1 (5)	England

English National League 2 (4)	England
English Divisional League 12s (4)	England
English Divisional Leagues 10s/17s (3)	England
English Divisional League 15s (2)	England
Scottish "League Trophy" Gps A & B (5)	Scotland
SRU Tennents National Lgs Divs 1-7 (2)	Scotland
Welsh Swalec Cup First Round	Wales
Welsh Nat League Div 1 (6)	Wales
Welsh Nat League Divs 2,3,4 (4)	Wales

OCTOBER 1997

Sat, 4th

English Knock-Out Cups - S,I,J (2)	England
Heineken Cup & Conference (5)	Europe
English Premier League 2 (6)	England
Scottish "League Trophy" Gps A & B (6)	Scotland
SRU Tennents National Lgs Divs 1-7 (3)	Scotland
Welsh Nat League Div 1 (7)	Wales
Welsh Nat League Divs 2,3,4 (5)	Wales

Tue, 7th

Newport v Barbarians	Newport

Sat, 11th

Heineken Cup & Conference (6)	Europe
English Premier League 2 (7)	England
English National League 1 (6)	England
English National League 2 (5)	England
English Divisional League 12s (5)	England
English Divisional Leagues 10s/17s (4)	England
English Divisional League 15s (3)	England
Scottish "League Trophy" Gps A & B (7)	Scotland
SRU Tennents Cup Round Three	Scotland
Welsh Nat League Div 1 (8)	Wales
Welsh Nat League Divs 2,3,4 (6)	Wales

Sat, 18th

English Premier League 1 (3)	England
English Premier League 2 (8)	England
English National League 1 (7)	England
English National League 2 (6)	England
English Divisional League 12s (6)	England
English Divisional Leagues 10s (5)	England
Scottish "League Trophy" Gps A & B (8)	Scotland
SRU Tennents National Lgs Divs 1-7 (4)	Scotland
Welsh Swalec Cup Second Round	Wales
Welsh Nat League Div 1 (9)	Wales
Welsh Nat League Divs 2,3 (7)	Wales

Sat, 25th

English Premier League 1 (4)	England
English Premier League 2 (9)	England
English National League 1 (8)	England
English National League 2 (7)	England
English Divisional League 12s (7)	England
English Divisional League 17s (5)	England
English Divisional League 15s (4)	England
Scottish "League Trophy" Gps A & B (9)	Scotland
SRU Tennents National Lgs Divs 1-7 (5)	Scotland
Welsh Nat League Premier Div (3)	Wales
Welsh Nat League Div 1 (10)	Wales
Welsh Nat League Divs 2,3 (8)	Wales
Welsh Nat League Div 4 (7)	Wales

NOVEMBER 1997

Sat, 1st

Heineken Cup & Conference Q/Finals	Europe
English Knock-Out Cups - S,I,J (3)	England
SRU Tennents National Lgs Divs 1-7 (6)	Scotland
Welsh Nat League Premier Div (4)	Wales

Sat, 1st Nov. cont.

Welsh Nat League Div 1 (11) — Wales
Welsh Nat League Div 2,3 (9) — Wales
Welsh Nat League Div 4 (8) — Wales

Sat, 8th

Heineken Cup & Conference Q/Finals — Europe
English Premier League 1 (5) — England
English Premier League 2 (10) — England
English National League 1 (9) — England
English National League 2 (8) — England
English Divisional League 12s (8) — England
English Divisional League 10s (7) — England
English Divisional League 17s (6) — England
English Divisional League 15s (5) — England
Welsh Nat League Div 1 (12) — Wales
Welsh Nat League Divs 2,3 (10) — Wales
Welsh Nat League Div 4 (9) — Wales

Sun, 9th

SRU Tennents Cup Round Three — Scotland
SRU Tennents Bowl Preliminary Round — Scotland

Wed, 12th

Wales 'A' v New Zealand — Wales

Sat, 15th

ENGLAND v AUSTRALIA — Twickenham
IRELAND v CANADA — Dublin
WALES v NEW ZEALAND — Wembley
English Premier Leagues 1 & 2 L/Cup — England
English National League 1 (10) — England
English National League 2 (9) — England
English Divisional League 12s (9) — England
English Divisional League 10s (8) — England
English Divisional League 17s (7) — England
English Divisional League 15s (6) — England
SRU Tennents Premiership Divs 1,2,3(1) — Scotland
SRU Tennents National Lgs Divs 1-7 (7) — Scotland

Tue, 18th

Emerging England v New Zealand — TBA

Sat, 22nd

ENGLAND v NEW ZEALAND — Old Trafford
SCOTLAND v AUSTRALIA — Murrayfield
English Knock-Out Cups - I,J (4) — England
English Premier Leagues 1 & 2 L/Cup — England
English National League 1 (11) — England
English National League 2 (10) — England
SRU Tennents National Lgs Divs 1-7(8) — Scotland
Welsh Swalec Cup Third Round — Wales
Welsh Nat League Div 1 (13) — Wales
AIL Championship (1) — Ireland

Tue, 25th

WALES v TONGA — Llanelli
England 'A' v New Zealand — TBA

Mon & Tue, 27th & 28th

Dubai Sevens — Dubai

Sat, 29th

ENGLAND v SOUTH AFRICA — Twickenham
IRELAND v NEW ZEALAND — Dublin
English Premier Leagues 1 & 2 L/Cup — England
English County Championships (1) — England
SRU Tennents Premiership Divs 1,2,3(2) — Scotland
SRU Tennents National Lgs Divs 1-7 (9) — Scotland
Welsh Nat League Div 1 (14) — Wales
Welsh Nat League Divs 2,3 (11) — Wales
Welsh Nat League Div 4 (10) — Wales

DECEMBER 1997

Tue, 2nd

England 'A' v New Zealand — TBA

Sat, 6th

ENGLAND v NEW ZEALAND — Twickenham
SCOTLAND v SOUTH AFRICA — Murrayfield
English Premier Leagues 1 & 2 L/Cup — England
English County Championships (2) — England
Welsh Nat League Divs 2,3 (12) — Wales
Welsh Nat League Div 4 (11) — Wales
AIL Championship (2) — Ireland

Sun, 7th

SRU Tennents Cup Round Four — Scotland
SRU Tennents Shield & Bowl Round One — Scotland

Tue, 9th

Oxford v Cambridge (Bowring Bowl) — Twickenham
Oxford v Cambridge U21s — Stoop Memorial Ground

Sat, 13th

English Premier League 1 (6) — England
English Premier League 2 (11) — England
English County Championships (3) — England
SRU Tennents Premiership Divs 1,2,3(3) — Scotland
SRU Tennents National Lgs Divs 1-7(10) — Scotland
Welsh Nat League Premier Div (5) — Wales
Welsh Nat League Div 1 (15) — Wales
Welsh Nat League Divs 2,3 (13) — Wales
Welsh Nat League Div 4 (12) — Wales
AIL Championship (3) — Ireland

Sat, 20th

ITALY v IRELAND — Italy
Heineken Cup & Conference Semi-finals — Europe
English Premier League 1 (7) — England
English Premier League 2 (12) — England
English National League 1 (12) — England
English National League 2 (11) — England
English Divisional League 12s (11) — England
English Divisional League 10s (9) — England
English Divisional Leagues 17s (8) — England
English Divisional Leagues 15s (7) — England
SRU Tennents Premiership Divs 1,2,3(4) — Scotland
Welsh Nat League Premier Div (6) — Wales
Welsh Nat League Div 1 (16) — Wales
Welsh Swalec Cup Fourth Round — Wales

Sat, 27th

English Premier League 1 (8) — England
English National League 1 (13) — England
English National League 2 (12) — England
SRU Tennents Premiership Divs 1,2,3(5) — Scotland
Welsh Nat League Premier Div (7) — Wales
Welsh Nat League Div 1 (17) — Wales
Welsh Nat League Divs 2,3 (14) — Wales
Welsh Nat League Div 4 (13) — Wales
AIL Championship (4) — Ireland

Tue, 30th

English Premier League 1 (9) — England

JANUARY 1998

Sat, 3rd

English Knock-Out Cup - Senior (4) — England
English Knock-Out Cup - I,J (5) — England
English National League 1 (14) — England
English National League 2 (13) — England
Welsh Nat League Premier Div (8) — Wales

Welsh Nat League Div 1 (18)	Wales
Welsh Nat League Divs 2,3 (15)	Wales
Welsh Nat League Div 4 (14)	Wales
AIL Championship (5)	Ireland

Sat, 10th

Allied Dunbar Premiership 1 (10)	England
Allied Dunbar Premiership 2 (13)	England
English National League 1 (15)	England
English National League 2 (14)	England
English Divisional League 12s (11)	England
English Divisional League 10s (10)	England
English Divisional League 17s (9)	England
English Divisional League 15s (8)	England
SRU Tennents Premiership Divs 1,2,3(6)	Scotland
SRU Tennents National Lgs Divs 1-7(11)	Scotland
Welsh Nat League Div 1 (19)	Wales
Welsh Nat League Divs 2,3 (16)	Wales
Welsh Nat League Div 4 (15)	Wales
AIL Championship (6)	Ireland

Sun & Mon, 11th & 12th

Uruguay Sevens	Uruguay

Sat, 17th

Allied Dunbar Premiership 1 (11)	England
Allied Dunbar Premiership 2 (14)	England
English National League 1 (16)	England
English National League 2 (15)	England
English Divisional League 12s (12)	England
English Divisional League 10s (11)	England
English Divisional League 17s (10)	England
English Divisional League 15s (9)	England
SRU Tennents Premiership Divs 1,2,3(7)	Scotland
SRU Tennents National Lgs Divs 1-7(12)	Scotland
Welsh Nat League Div 1 (20)	Wales
Welsh Nat League Divs 2,3 (17)	Wales
Welsh Nat League Div 4 (16)	Wales
AIL Championship (7)	Ireland

Sat, 24th

English Knock-Out Cup - Senior (5)	England
English Knock-Out Cup - I,J (6)	England
English National League 1 (17)	England
English National League 2 (16)	England
English Divisional League 12s (13)	England
English Divisional League 10s (12)	England
English Divisional League 17s (11)	England
English Divisional League 15s (10)	England
Welsh Swalec Cup Fifth Round	Wales
AIL Championship (8)	Ireland

Sun, 25th

SRU Tennents National Lgs Divs 1-7(13)	Scotland

Sat, 31st

Heineken Cup & Conference Finals	Europe
Allied Dunbar Premiership 1 (12)	England
Allied Dunbar Premiership 2 (15)	England
English National League 1 (18)	England
English National League 2 (17)	England
English Divisional League 12s (14)	England
English Divisional League 10s (13)	England
English Divisional League 17s (12)	England
English Divisional League 15s (11)	England
SRU Tennents Premiership Divs 1,2,3(8)	Scotland
SRU Tennents National Lgs Divs 1-7(14)	Scotland
Welsh Nat League Premier Div (9)	Wales
Welsh Nat League Div 1 (21)	Wales
Welsh Nat League Div 4 (17)	Wales
AIL Championship (9)	Ireland

FEBRUARY 1998

Fri, 6th

Ireland 'A' v Scotland 'A'	Ireland
Ireland U21 v Scotland U21	Ireland
France 'A' v England 'A'	France
England Students v France Students	TBA

Sat, 7th

FRANCE v ENGLAND	Paris
IRELAND v SCOTLAND	Dublin
WALES v ITALY	TBA
Allied Dunbar Premiership 1 & 2 L/Cup	England
English National League 1 (19)	England
English National League 2 (18)	England
English Divisional League 12s (15)	England

Sat, 14th

Allied Dunbar Premiership 1 (13)	England
Allied Dunbar Premiership 2 (16)	England
English National League 1 (20)	England
English National League 2 (19)	England
English Divisional League 12s (16)	England
English Divisional League 10s (14)	England
English Divisional League 17s (13)	England
English Divisional League 15s (12)	England
SRU Tennents Premiership Divs 1,2,3(9)	Scotland
SRU Tennents National Lgs Divs 1-7(15)	Scotland
Welsh Nat League Premier Div (10)	Wales
Welsh Nat League Div 1 (22)	Wales
Welsh Nat League Divs 2,3,4 (18)	Wales
AIL Championship (10)	Ireland

Fri, 20th

Scotland 'A' v France 'A'	Scotland
Scotland U21 v France U21	Scotland
England Students v Wales Students	TBA

Sat, 21st

ENGLAND v WALES	Twickenham
SCOTLAND v FRANCE	Murrayfield
Allied Dunbar Premiership 1 & 2 L/Cup	England
English National League 1 (21)	England
English National League 2 (20)	England
AIL Championship (11)	Ireland

Sat, 28th

English Knock-Out Cup - S, I, J (Q/Fnl)	England
English County Championships Q/Finals	England
SRU Tennents National Lgs Divs 1-7(16)	Scotland
SRU Tennents Cup Round Five	Scotland
SRU Tennents Shield & Bowl Round Two	Scotland
Welsh Swalec Cup Sixth Round	Wales
AIL Championship (12)	Ireland

MARCH 1998

Fri, 6th

Wales 'A' v Scotland 'A'	Wales
Wales U21 v Scotland U21	Wales
France 'A' v Ireland 'A'	France
France U21 v Ireland U21	France

Sat, 7th

FRANCE v IRELAND	Paris
WALES v SCOTLAND	Wembley
Allied Dunbar Premiership 1 (14)	England
Allied Dunbar Premiership 2 (17)	England
English National League 1 (22)	England
English National League 2 (21)	England
English Divisional League 12s (17)	England
English Divisional League 10s (15)	England

Sat, 7th March cont.

English Divisional League 17s (14)   England
English Divisional League 15s (13)   England
Wales Youth v England Colts   Wales

Wed, 11th

East Midlands v Barbarians   Northampton

Sat, 14th

Allied Dunbar Premiership 1 (15)	England
Allied Dunbar Premiership 2 (18)	England
English National League 1 (23)	England
English National League 2 (22)	England
English Divisional League 12s (18)	England
English Divisional League 10s (16)	England
English Divisional League 17s (15)	England
English Divisional League 15s (14)	England
SRU Tennents National Lgs Divs 1-7(17)	Scotland
Welsh Nat League Div 1 (23)	Wales
Welsh Nat League Divs 2,3,4 (19)	Wales
AIL Championship (13)	Ireland

Fri, 20th

Ireland 'A' v Wales 'A'	Ireland
Ireland U21 v Wales U21	Ireland
Scotland 'A' v England 'A'	Scotland
Scotland U21 v England U21	Scotland

Sat, 21st

IRELAND v WALES	Dublin
Allied Dunbar Premiership 1 & 2 L/C	England
English National League 1 (24)	England
English National League 2 (23)	England
English Divisional League 12s (19)	England

Sun, 22nd

SCOTLAND v ENGLAND (Calcutta Cup) Murrayfield
England Colts v Scotland Under 18   Penrith

Wed, 25th

BUSA Finals - Men and Women   Twickenham

Fri, 27th

Hong Kong Sevens start (3 days)   Hong Kong

Sat, 28th

English Knock-Out Cups - S,I,J - S/Fnl	England
English County Championships - S/Finals	England
SRU Tennents National Lgs Divs 1-7(18)	Scotland
Welsh Nat League Div 1 (24)	Wales
Welsh Nat League Divs 2,3,4 (20)	Wales
AIL Championship (14)	Ireland

APRIL 1998

Thu, 2nd

England 'A' v Wales 'A' (18 Group)   TBA

Fri, 3rd

England 'A' v Ireland 'A'	England
England U21 v Ireland U21	England
Wales 'A' v France 'A'	Wales
Wales U21 v France U21	Wales
England v Wales (18 Group) U.S.	Portsmouth

Sat, 4th

ENGLAND v IRELAND	Twickenham
Allied Dunbar Premiership 1 & 2 L/Cup	England
English National Leagues 2 (24)	England
English Divisional League 12s (20)	England
SRU Tennents Cup, Shield & Bowl Q/Fnls	Scotland

Sun, 5th

WALES v FRANCE   Wembley

Sat, 11th

Allied Dunbar Premiership 1 (17)	England
Allied Dunbar Premiership 2 (21)	England
English National League 1 & 2 (25)	England
English Divisional League 12s (21)	England
English Divisional League 10s (17)	England
English Divisional League 17s (16)	England
English Divisional League 15s (15)	England
Welsh Swalec Cup Quarter-finals	Wales
Welsh Nat League Div 1 (25)	Wales
AIL Championship (15)	Ireland

Sat, 18th

English County Championships Final	Twickenham
Allied Dunbar Premiership 1 (18)	England
Allied Dunbar Premiership 2 (21)	England
Welsh Nat League Premier Div (11)	Wales
Welsh Nat League Div 1 (26)	Wales
Welsh Nat League Divs 2,3,4 (21)	Wales
England v Ireland (18 Group)	Stourbridge

Sun, 19th

SRU Tennents Cup, Shield & Bowl S/Fnls Scotland

Sat, 25th

Royal Navy v The Army	Twickenham
Allied Dunbar Premiership 1 (19)	England
Allied Dunbar Premiership 2 (22)	England
English National League 1 (26)	England
English National League 2 (26)	England
English Divisional League 12s (22)	England
English Divisional League 10s (18)	England
English Divisional League 17s (17)	England
Welsh Swalec Cup Semi-finals	Wales
Welsh Nat League Div 1 (27)	Wales
Welsh Nat League Divs 2,3,4 (22)	Wales
England Colts v France Youth	East Midlands

MAY 1998

Sat, 2nd

English Knock-Out Cups - I,J Finals	Twickenham
Allied Dunbar Premiership 1 (20)	England
Welsh Nat League Premier Div (12)	Wales
Welsh Nat League Div 1 (28)	Wales

Wed, 6th

Royal Navy v Royal Air Force   Twickenham

Sat, 9th

English Senior Knock-Out Final	Twickenham
SRU Tennents Cup, Shield & Bowl Finals	Murrayfield
Welsh Nat Leaue Premier Div (13)	Wales
Welsh Nat League Div 1 (29)	Wales
Sun, 10th Allied Dunbar Premiership 1 (21)	England

Wed, 13th

The Army v Royal Air Force   Twickenham

Sat, 16th

Middlesex Sevens Finals	Twickenham
Allied Dunbar Premiership 1 (22)	England
Welsh Nat League Premier Div (14)	Wales
Welsh Nat League Div 1 (30)	Wales

Sat, 23rd

Welsh Swalec Cup Final   Wembley

ALLIED DUNBAR ONE FIXTURES - 1997-98

INCLUDING HEINEKEN CUP AND EUROPEAN CONFERENCE FIXTURES FOR ALLIED DUNBAR ONE CLUBS 1997-98

August 23rd
Bath v Newcastle
Gloucester v Bristol
Northampton v Harlequins
Richmond v London Irish

August 24th
Sale v Saracens

August 30th
Bristol v Wasps
Harlequins v Bath
Leicester v Gloucester
London Irish v Sale

August 31st
Newcastle v Northampton
Saracens v Richmond

HEINEKEN CUP & EUROPEAN CONFERENCE FIXTURES 1997-98

September 6/7th
Leicester v Milan
Swansea v Wasps
Pontypridd v Bath
Harlequins v Munster

Bristol v La Rochelle
Gloucester v Padova
London Irish v Stade Francais
Newcastle v Biarritz
Connacht v Northampton
Colomiers v Richmond
Montferrand v Sale
Narbonne v Saracens

September 27/28th
Leicester v Leinster
Wasps v Glasgow
Borders v Bath
Bourgoin v Harlequins

Bristol v Wales 3
Toulon v Gloucester
London Irish v Dax
Perpignan v Newcastle
Begles-Bordeaux v Northampton
Richmond v Wales 1
Sale v Montpelier
Castres v Saracens

September 13/14th
Leinster v Leicester
Glasgow v Wasps
Bath v Borders
Harlequins v Bourgoin

Wales 3 v Bristol
Gloucester v Toulon
Dax v London Irish
Newcastle v Perpignan
Northampton v Begles-Bordeaux
Wales 1 v Richmond
Montpelier v Sale
Saracens v Castres

October 4/5th
Leicester v Toulouse
Ulster v Wasps
Brive v Bath
Harlequins v Wales 4

Bristol v Agen
Gloucester v Beziers
London Irish v Romanian XV
Newcastle v Edinburgh
Nice v Northampton
Grenoble v Richmond
Wales 2 v Sale
Wales 4 v Saracens

September 20/21st
Toulouse v Leicester
Wasps v Ulster
Bath v Brive
Wales 4 v Harlequins

Agen v Bristol
Beziers v Gloucester
Romanian XV v London Irish
Edinburgh v Newcastle
Northampton v Nice
Richmond v Grenoble
Sale v Wales 2
Saracens v Wales 4

October 11/12th
Milan v Leicester
Wasps v Swansea
Bath v Pontypridd
Munster v Harlequins

La Rochelle v Bristol
Padova v Gloucester
Stade Francais v London Irish
Biarritz v Newcastle
Northampton v Connacht
Richmond v Colomiers
Sale v Montferrand
Saracens v Narbonne

October 18th
Bath v Bristol
Northampton v Leicester
Sale v Newcastle
Richmond v Harlequins

October 19th
Gloucester v London Irish
Wasps v Saracens

October 25th
Harlequins v Sale
Leicester v Bath
Northampton v Bristol

ALLIED DUNBAR ONE FIXTURES - 1996-97

October 26th
London Irish v Wasps
Newcastle v Richmond
Saracens v Gloucester

November 1st
London Irish v Newcastle

November 2nd
Saracens v Bristol
Wasps v Leicester

November 8th
Bath v London Irish
Richmond v Leicester

November 9th
Gloucester v Harlequins
Sale v Bristol
Northampton v Saracens
Wasps v Newcastle

November 15th
England v Australia

November 22nd
England v New Zealand

November 29th
England v South Africa

December 12th
England v New Zealand

December 13th
Bristol v Richmond
Harlequins v Wasps
Leicester v Sale
London Irish v Northampton

December 14th
Newcastle v Gloucester
Saracens v Bath

December 20th
Bath v Gloucester
Leicester v Harlequins
London Irish v Bristol

December 21st
Newcastle v Saracens
Wasps v Sale
Richmond v Northampton

December 27th
Bristol v Newcastle
Gloucester v Richmond
Harlequins v London Irish
Sale v Bath
Northampton v Wasps
Saracens v Leicester

December 30th
Bath v Northampton
London Irish v Saracens
Leicester v Newcastle
Sale v Gloucester
Wasps v Richmond

December 31st
Harlequins v Bristol

January 10th
Bristol v Leicester
Northampton v Sale
Richmond v Bath

January 11th
Wasps v Gloucester
Newcastle v London Irish
Saracens v Harlequins

January 17th
Leicester v Wasps
London Irish v Richmond
Saracens v Sale

January 18th
Harlequins v Northampton
Newcastle v Bath
Bristol v Gloucester

January 31st
Bath v Harlequins
Northampton v Newcastle

February 1st
Gloucester v Leicester
Sale v London Irish
Richmond v Saracens
Wasps v Bristol

February 7th
France v England

February 14th
Bristol v Saracens
Gloucester v Northampton
Leicester v London Irish

February 15th
Bath v Wasps
Richmond v Sale
Newcastle v Harlequins

February 21st
England v Wales

March 7th
Harlequins v Richmond
Leicester v Northampton
London Irish v Gloucester

March 8th
Bristol v Bath
Newcastle v Sale
Saracens v Wasps

March 11th
Gloucester v Wasps

March 14th
Bath v Leicester
Bristol v Northampton
Sale v Harlequins
Richmond v Newcastle

March 15th
Gloucester v Saracens
Wasps v London Irish

March 21st
Scotland v England

March 28th
Bristol v Sale
London Irish v Bath
Leicester v Richmond

March 29th
Harlequins v Gloucester
Newcastle v Wasps
Saracens v Northampton

April 4th
England v Ireland

April 11th
Bath v Saracens
Gloucester v Newcastle
Sale v Leicester
Northampton v London Irish
Richmond v Bristol

April 12th
Wasps v Harlequins

April 18th
Gloucester v Bath
Harlequins v Leicester
Sale v Wasps
Northampton v Richmond

April 19th
Bristol v London Irish
Saracens v Newcastle

April 25th
Bath v Sale
Leicester v Saracens
London Irish v Harlequins
Richmond v Gloucester

April 26th
Newcastle v Bristol
Wasps v Northampton

May 2nd
Gloucester v Sale
Northampton v Bath
Richmond v Wasps

May 3rd
Bristol v Harlequins
Newcastle v Leicester
Saracens v London Irish

May 10th
Bath v Richmond
Harlequins v Saracens
Leicester v Bristol
Sale v Northampton

May 17th
Wasps v Bath
Harlequins v Newcastle
London Irish v Leicester
Sale v Richmond
Northampton v Gloucester

ALLIED DUNBAR TWO FIXTURES - 1996-97

August 30th
Bedford	v	Rotherham
Coventry	v	Moseley
London Scottish	v	Fylde
Orrell	v	Blackheath
West Hartlepool	v	Waterloo
Wakefield	v	Exeter

September 6th
Coventry	v	Exeter
Fylde	v	Bedford
London Scottish	v	Blackheath
Moseley	v	Rotherham
Waterloo	v	Wakefield
West Hartlepool	v	Orrell

September 13th
Blackheath	v	Wakefield
Exeter	v	Bedford
Fylde	v	Coventry
Moseley	v	West Hartlepool
Rotherham	v	Orrell
Waterloo	v	London Scottish

September 20th
Bedford	v	London Scottish
Blackheath	v	Fylde
Exeter	v	Waterloo
Orrell	v	Moseley
Rotherham	v	West Hartlepool
Wakefield	v	Coventry

September 27th
Coventry	v	Bedford
Fylde	v	Rotherham
London Scottish	v	Orrell
Moseley	v	Exeter
Waterloo	v	Blackheath
West Hartlepool	v	Wakefield

October 4th
Bedford	v	Waterloo
Blackheath	v	Coventry
Exeter	v	West Hartlepool
Orrell	v	Fylde
Rotherham	v	London Scottish
Wakefield	v	Moseley

October 11th
Coventry	v	Rotherham
Fylde	v	Exeter
London Scottish	v	Wakefield
Moseley	v	Bedford
Waterloo	v	Orrell
West Hartlepool	v	Blackheath

October 18th
Bedford	v	West Hartlepool
Blackheath	v	Moseley
Exeter	v	London Scottish
Orrell	v	Coventry
Rotherham	v	Waterloo
Wakefield	v	Fylde

October 25th
Coventry	v	Wakefield
Fylde	v	Blackheath
London Scottish	v	Bedford
Moseley	v	Orrell
Waterloo	v	Exeter
West Hartlepool	v	Rotherham

November 8th
Bedford	v	Coventry
Blackheath	v	Waterloo
Exeter	v	Moseley
Orrell	v	London Scottish
Rotherham	v	Fylde
Wakefield	v	West Hartlepool

December 13th
Coventry	v	Blackheath
Fylde	v	Orrell
London Scottish	v	Rotherham
Moseley	v	Wakefield
Waterloo	v	Bedford
West Hartlepool	v	Exeter

December 20th
Blackheath	v	West Hartlepool
Bedford	v	Moseley
Exeter	v	Fylde
Orrell	v	Waterloo
Rotherham	v	Coventry
Wakefield	v	London Scottish

ALLIED DUNBAR TWO FIXTURES - 1997-98

January 10th
Coventry	v	Orrell
Fylde	v	Wakefield
Moseley	v	Blackheath
Waterloo	v	Rotherham
West Hartlepool	v	Bedford

January 11th
London Scottish	v	Exeter

January 17th
Bedford	v	Fylde
Blackheath	v	London Scottish
Exeter	v	Coventry
Orrell	v	West Hartlepool
Rotherham	v	Moseley
Wakefield	v	Waterloo

January 31st
Bedford	v	Orrell
Coventry	v	West Hartlepool
Exeter	v	Blackheath
Fylde	v	Waterloo
Moseley	v	London Scottish
Rotherham	v	Wakefield

February 14th
Blackheath	v	Rotherham
London Scottish	v	Coventry
Orrell	v	Exeter
Wakefield	v	Bedford
Waterloo	v	Moseley
West Hartlepool	v	Fylde

March 7th
Bedford	v	Blackheath
Coventry	v	Waterloo
Exeter	v	Rotherham
Fylde	v	Moseley
London Scottish	v	West Hartlepool
Wakefield	v	Orrell

March 14th
Bedford	v	Wakefield
Coventry	v	London Scottish
Exeter	v	Orrell
Fylde	v	West Hartlepool
Moseley	v	Waterloo
Rotherham	v	Blackheath

March 28th
Blackheath	v	Exeter
London Scottish	v	Moseley
Orrell	v	Bedford
Wakefield	v	Rotherham
Waterloo	v	Fylde
West Hartlepool	v	Coventry

April 11th
Blackheath	v	Orrell
Exeter	v	Wakefield
Fylde	v	London Scottish
Moseley	v	Coventry
Rotherham	v	Bedford
Waterloo	v	West Hartlepool

April 18th
Bedford	v	Exeter
Coventry	v	Fylde
London Scottish	v	Waterloo
Orrell	v	Rotherham
Wakefield	v	Blackheath
West Hartlepool	v	Moseley

April 25th
Blackheath	v	Bedford
Moseley	v	Fylde
Orrell	v	Wakefield
Rotherham	v	Exeter
Waterloo	v	Coventry

ALLIED DUNBAR

PREMIERSHIP ONE

1996-97 DIVISION ONE

PLAYING RECORD & breakdown

	Pd	W	D	L	Pts	HOME W	D	L	Pts	AWAY W	D	L	Pts
Wasps	22	18	1	3	37	9	1	1	19	9	0	2	18
Bath	22	15	1	6	31	10	0	1	20	5	1	5	11
Harlequins	22	15	0	7	30	8	0	3	16	7	0	4	14
Leicester	22	14	1	7	29	10	0	1	20	4	1	6	9
Sale	22	13	2	7	28	8	1	2	17	5	1	5	11
Saracens	22	12	1	9	25	9	1	1	19	3	0	8	6
Gloucester	22	11	1	10	23	7	1	3	15	4	0	7	8
Northampton	22	10	0	12	20	8	0	3	16	2	0	9	4
Bristol	22	8	1	13	17	5	0	6	10	3	1	7	7
London Irish	22	6	0	16	12	4	0	7	8	2	0	9	4
West Hartlepool	22	3	0	19	6	3	0	8	6	0	0	11	0
Orrell	22	3	0	19	6	2	0	9	4	1	0	10	2

POINTS FOR & breakdown

	Lge Pos	Pts	T	C	P	D	HOME Pts	T	C	P	D	AWAY Pts	T	C	P	D
1 Bath	2	863	116	77	41	2	568	78	56	21	1	295	38	21	19	1
2 Harlequins	3	745	96	62	44	3	462	62	37	24	2	283	34	25	20	1
3 Wasps	1	685	75	50	64	6	326	33	19	36	5	359	42	31	28	1
4 Sale	5	603	78	36	46	1	369	48	24	27	0	234	30	12	19	1
5 Leicester	4	600	60	39	74	0	343	33	23	44	0	257	27	16	30	0
6 Saracens	6	568	69	35	48	3	339	40	23	29	2	229	29	12	19	1
7 Northampton	8	515	52	30	59	6	280	27	14	35	4	235	25	10	24	2
8 London Irish	10	502	58	28	49	3	298	31	19	32	3	204	27	9	17	0
9 Gloucester	7	476	46	27	58	6	256	22	13	36	4	220	24	14	22	2
10 Bristol	9	432	48	30	44	0	234	27	18	21	0	198	21	12	23	0
11 West Hartlepool	11	382	44	21	39	1	218	25	12	23	0	164	19	9	16	1
12 Orrell	12	352	41	26	27	4	200	22	12	18	4	150	19	14	9	0

POINTS AGAINST & breakdown

	Lge Pos	Pts	T	C	P	D	HOME Pts	T	C	P	D	AWAY Pts	T	C	P	D
1 Leicester	4	395	38	23	51	2	149	12	7	24	1	246	26	16	27	1
2 Wasps	1	406	42	20	51	1	153	17	10	16	0	253	25	10	35	1
3 Bath	2	411	39	24	52	4	178	19	13	18	1	233	20	11	34	3
4 Harlequins	3	416	47	23	41	4	189	23	10	16	2	227	24	13	25	2
5 Saracens	6	449	45	28	53	3	189	20	13	21	0	260	25	15	32	3
6 Northampton	8	477	47	28	60	2	189	20	10	23	0	288	27	18	37	2
7 Sale	5	525	53	34	60	4	208	23	12	23	0	317	30	22	37	4
8 Gloucester	7	589	67	46	54	0	202	22	13	22	0	387	45	33	32	0
9 Bristol	9	625	76	37	52	5	266	32	17	22	2	359	44	20	30	3
10 London Irish	10	749	95	61	45	5	336	41	28	22	3	411	54	33	23	2
11 West Hartlepool	11	795	109	68	34	4	331	46	28	15	0	464	63	40	19	4
12 Orrell	12	886	125	69	40	1	438	60	30	25	1	448	65	39	15	0

1996-97 DIVISION ONE REVIEW

At the start of April we looked set for a battle royal for the Courage Division One Championship but Wasps fooled everyone to run out comfortably six points clear.

Their rocky spell was a loss at Leicester and a home draw against Bath, but after this they proceeded to win their last four games. Included in those wins were away triumphs at Scaracens, Northampton and Harlequins who all had impressive home records. For Wasps it was a collective will to win and superb defence which were the major reasons for their success. They had a number of key players playing exceptional rugby which was highlighted by the tackle count of their back row which was exceptional.

Bath after an indifferent season came through to finish second and this coming season will be looking for the consistancy which was the hallmark of their game.

Harlequins started the campaign like a house on fire before going into a mid season malaise losing three straight games. The arrival of Thierry Lacroix gave them a consistant goal kicker and saw them start winning again.

Leicester had a good season in real terms, but will be disappointed with just one piece of silverware. Their title hopes disappeared with four successive away defeats and they only just squeezed into Europe for the coming season. With Underwood, Liley, Hackney and Kardooni going in the summer Leicester is becoming a much changed club under the watchful eye of Bob Dwyer.

Sale with two games of their season to go were on the verge of achieving succees beyond their wildest dreams. But a home draw with Leicester in the League saw their European Cup qualifying aspirations disappear. The following week they lost to Leicester in the Pilkington Cup final in a dour affair. It was a strange season for Sale because if you had told them before the season started that they would finish fifth in the League and be runners-up in the Pilkington Cup final they might well have been pleased.

Saracens who were disappointing overall had an excellent home record 89-1-1 but were poor travellers winning only three away matches out of eight. They had a lot of new players and will be looking for consistency in the coming season.

Gloucester were more than pleased with seventh place after a dreadful start to the season. They had a superb mid season winning seven straight games to climb up the table, dashing Leicester's title hopes with a last minute 32-30 win before Gloucesters biggest crowd of the season.

Northampton will be sick of hearing about what Ian McGeechan has done for the British Lions after a terribly disappointing season at Franklin's Gardens. They had a reasonable home record but away from home only the two relegated clubs faired worse.

Bristol's season never really got going. Paul Burke seemed to settle in well and David Tiueti, in his first full season, scored a club record of ten tries. They comfortably won their play-off games but will need to improve to avoid an automatic relegation spot in the coming season. Their cause has not been helped with the departure of their two British Lions, Simon Shaw and Mark Regan.

London Irish will need to improve dramatically to keep their Allied Dunbar Premiership One status next season. They could be said to have been a bit unlucky on losing four of their home games by less than seven points but they lacked real finishing power. Highlight of the season was the 20-19 win against Harlequins.

West Hartlepool used too many players and were unable to get a settled side and find any consistency. They had two good finds in the Johns, Chris and Steven, who were top points and try scorers respectively. Also they had good contributons from Jamie Connolly, Ivan Morgan and Jon Irons.

Orrell were always favourites for relegation after losing over a dozen players during the close season. They had a number of promising youngsters who were out of their depth, but they did not give in and kept trying to play rugby right to the end.

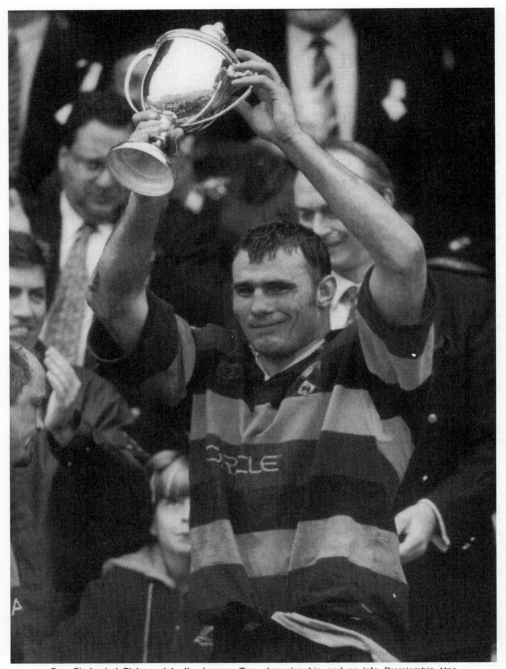

Ben Clarke led Richmond to the League Two championship and so into Premiership One.

Richmond also topped the national Fair Play League, with no yellow or red cards throughout their league campaign.

1996-97 DIVISION ONE

RECORD REVIEW

INDIVIDUAL RECORDS

MOST POINTS IN A MATCH

John Liley's record of 31 remained unchallenged, as the best for this season was 26 by four players. West Hartlepool's John Stabler, in scoring 26 points, has the highest points total for somebody finishing on the losing side. Below is a list of the players scoring 26 points in a match last season.

26	Rob Liley	Leicester v Lon I	31.10.96
26	John Stabler	W Hart v Lon I	28.12.96
26	Simon Mannix	Sale v North	09.03.97
26	Mike Catt	Bath v Sale	26.04.97

Evolution of record

21	Ian Aitchison	Waterloo v Sale	02.01.88
23	Jamie Salmon	Harlequins v Water	27.02.88
24	Dusty Hare	Leicester v Ross P	19.11.88
26	John Liley	Leicester v Bedford	23.09.89
27	David Pears	Harlequins v Bedford	14.10.89
28	Martin Strett	Orrell v Ross Park	28.04.90
31	John Liley	Leicester v Ross P	21.03.92

MOST TRIES IN A MATCH

The record of four was equalled on the opening day of the season by Harlequin flying winger Daren O'Leary. He scored his four tries against a weakened Gloucester side in a 75-19 win
Later in the season Wasps' mid-season signing, Scottish international winger Kenny Logan, set a new record. Logan scored five tries in his side's 62-5 win over bottom of the table Orrell at Sudbury.

Evolution of record (first to)

3	Peter Shillingford	Moseley v Wasps	05.02.88
4	Gary Hartley	Nottingham v Bedford	18.11.89
5	Kenny Logan	Wasps v Orrell	22.03.97

Moseley's Peter Shillingford is the only player to score a hat trick of tries and finish on the losing side.

Gloucester winger Mike Lloyd became the first player to score a hat trick of tries for two different first division sides when he scored three against W Hartlepool. His previous hat trick was for Bristol against Rugby back in March 92.

Harlequins set a record for having the highest number of players to score hat tricks in a season with five. The five were Daren O'Leary, Michael Corcoran, Huw Harries, Dominic Chapman and Nick Walshe.

MOST CONVERSIONS IN A MATCH

Another record to stay in tact but could have been under threat in Bath's 84-7 win late in the season over Sale's virtual second team. Bath scored 12 tries and converted them all but split the kickers with Mike Catt converting eight and Jonathan Callard converting the other four otherwise Stuart Barnes's division one record of 10 could have fallen.

Evolution of record

| 10 | Stuart Barnes | Bath v Bedford | 13.01.90 |

Most in a match

10	Stuart Barnes	Bath v Bedford	13.01.90
9	Paul Challinor	Quins v W Hartlepool	23.03.96
8	Martin Strett	Orrell v Rosslyn P	28.04.90
8	Will Carling	Harlequins v Orrell	05.10.96
8	Mike Catt	Bath v Sale	26.04.97

MOST PENALTIES IN A MATCH

The record of eight remained with penalties not in fashion and a lot of teams running plenty of kickable opportunities. Two players kicked seven falling one short of the record Leicester's John Liley set in the home win over Bath last September. The other was Sale's Simon Mannix who kicked seven in Sale's comfortable 31-15 win over Northampton.

Evolution of record (first to)

6	Dusty Hare	Leicester v Ross P	19.11.88
7	David Pears	Harlequins v Ross P	07.12.91
8	John Liley	Leicester v Bristol	28.10.95

Most in a match

8	John Liley	Leicester v Bristol	28.10.95
7	David Pears	Harlequins v Ross P	07.12.91
7	Jez Harris	Leicester v Bristol	11.12.93
7	Rob Andrew	Wasps v Orrell	11.12.93
7	Jez Harris	Leicester v Gloucs	29.01.94
7	Mark Tainton	Bristol v Leicester	05.11.94
7	John Liley	Leicester v Bath	07.09.96
7	Simon Mannix	Sale v Northampton	08.03.97

MOST DROP GOALS IN A MATCH

Orrell's new Welsh stand-off Matthew McCarthy equalled the Division One record of three drop goals in a match on his league debut against fellow strugglers West Hartlepool. This equalled the record already shared between John Steele, Jez Harris and David Pears.

MOST POINTS IN A SEASON

Wasps' Canadian international Gareth Rees had an inspirational season culminating in him breaking Johm Liley's 1995-96 record of 272 in a season with a new total of 291.

Rees made an impressive start to his league career and reached 100 league points in just seven games - a Division One record in itself. This was later equalled by Quins's French international Thierry Lacroix.

Rees broke Liley's record in the 26-15 away win at Northampton which clinched the title for Wasps. Rees converted both tries, in which he had played a major part, and kicked four penalties.

Evolution of record

126	Dusty Hare	Leicester	1987-88
126	John Liley	Leicester	1989-90
126	Rob Andrew	Wasps	1990-91
202	Jez Harris	Leicester	1993-94
272	John Liley	Leicester	1996-97
291	Gareth Rees	Wasps	1996-97

Most in a season

51	Jonathan Callard	Bath	1996-97
45	Gareth Rees	Wasps	1996-97
43	Jonathan Callard	Bath	1995-96
29	Stuart Barnes	Bath	1989-90
29	Thierry Lacroix	Harlequins	1996-97
27	Will Carling	Harlequins	1996-97
27	Paul Burke	Bristol	1996-97

MOST PENALTIES IN A SEASON

Although the record was not broken Gareth Rees, 62, and Mark Mapletoft, 58, moved into 2nd and 3rd on the all-time list behind Leicester's John Liley.

Most in a season

64	John Liley	Leicester	1995-96
62	Gareth Rees	Wasps	1996-97
58	Mark Mapletoft	Gloucester	1996-97
56	Mark Tainton	Bristol	1994-95
52	Paul Grayson	Northampton	1994-95

MOST TRIES IN A SEASON

This record was broken for the second successive season. This time round it was England and Bath winger Adedayo Adebayo who broke Daren O'Leary's record of 14 from last season with 16. Adebayo finished the season in style, coming up on the rails to pass O'Leary, scoring tries in each of the last 6 games. O'Leary finished second and also passed the old record of 14, finishing the season on 15.

Evolution of record

11	Andrew Harriman	Harlequins	1987-88
11	Daren O'Leary	Harlequins	1993-94
14	Daren O'Leary	Harlequins	1995-96
16	Adedayo Adebayo	Bath	1996-97

Most in a season

16	Adedayo Adebayo	Bath	1996-97
15	Daren 'Leary	Harlequins	1996-97
14	Daren O'Leary	Harlequins	1995-96
13	Steven John	W Hartlepool	1996-97
13	Tom Beim	Sale	1996-97
12	Jeremy Guscott	Bath	1996-97
12	Jon Sleightholme	Bath	1996-97

MOST CONVERSIONS IN A SEASON

Bath's Jonathan Callard broke the record for the second successive season. The previous season he kicked a new record of 43 and last season took the record to 51. Wasps' Gareth Rees also broke the old record with 45. Callard would have had more but Mike Catt finished the season as Bath's front line kicker.

Evolution of record

15	Dusty Hare	Leicester	1987-88
29	Stuart Barnes	Bath	1989-90
43	Jonathan Callard	Bath	1995-96
51	Jonathan Callard	Bath	1996-97

DIVISION ONE

ALL-TIME RECORDS

MOST POINTS

Player	Pts	T	C	P	DG	Apps	PPM
John Liley	1070	25	129	232	1	100	10.70
Jon Callard	844	23	135	155	-	81(2)	10.40
Rob Andrew	748	16	82	161	11	77	10.70
Mark Tainton	637	-	62	165	6		
Tim Smith	593	10	57	142	2	94	6.31

Leicester's John Liley became the first player to score 1000 Division One points and is over 200 points clear of his nearest rival Bath's Jonathan Callard. During the season he became the first player to kick 200 penalties in the top flight. One record he lost was the record of Division One conversions as Bath's Jonathan Callard passed him and set a new record of 135.

MOST TRIES

Player	Tries	Apps	Tries per
Jeremy Guscott	48	98	2.04 games
Daren O'Leary	44	72	1.64 games
Rory Underwood	44	97	2.20 games
Tony Swift	43	90	2.09 games

O'Leary's total includes three tries in 10 games for Saracens 92-93

Bath's Jeremy Guscott broke ex team mate Tony Swift's record of 43 tries in Division One rugby. By the end of the season Daren O'Leary and Rory Underwood had also passed Swift's old record. O'Leary has easily the best strike rate - a try every 1.64 games, well ahead of the next best.

AN ANALYSIS OF PLAYERS USED

Consistency breeds success
- as can be seen from the table below.
The champions Wasps used less players than anyone else, had more ever-presents than anyone else with four and their players averaged 11.4 games each the highest figure in the division.

The number of ever-presents in the division dropped from 15 in 1995-96 to just 8 last season.
The eight for last season were:

Laurant Cabannes (Quins),
Steven John (W Hart),
Lua Tuigamala (Orrell),
Tony Diprose (Saracens)

and the Wasps Quartet of

Nick Greenstock,
Shane Roiser,
Mike White

and captain Lawrence Dallaglio.

Saracen's Captain Tony Diprose was an ever-present for a second successive season and extended his run of consecutive matches to 41 the longest in the division.

The two relegated clubs were also the only two clubs who had half their players making their league debuts. West Hartlepool had 65% of their players making their debuts - this cannot be good for continuity and consistency.

	Players used	League debuts	Ever present	1	2
Bath	33(3)	12	-	36	10.0
Bristol	37(6)	15	-	41	8.9
Gloucester	35(2)	12	-	34	9.4
Harlequins	37(3)	17	1	45	8.9
Leicester	36(2)	17	-	47	9.2
London Irish	43(4)	17	-	40	7.7
Northampton	38(3)	10	-	26	8.7
Orrell	38(2)	19	1	50	8.7
Sale	36(5)	14	-	39	9.2
Saracens	35(5)	16	1	46	9.4
Wasps	29(3)	12	4	41	11.4
W Hartlepool	43(3)	28	1	65	7.7

1 = % of players making league debut
2 = Average appearances per player

ATTENDANCES

This is another new feature in this year's book, and here we have broken them down into Home and Away to see which teams attract the fans on the road.

HOME ATTENDANCES

Team	Average	Highest attendance
Leicester	11454	17000 v Wasps
Bath	6790	8500 v Leicester
		v Harlequins
Northampton	6084	7907 v Leicester
Wasps	5879	10686 v Leicester
Gloucester	4985	6310 v Leicester
Harlequins	4144	6789 v Wasps
Bristol	3871	5320 v Bath
Saracens	3460	6231 v Leicester
London Irish	2856	3960 v Harlequins
Sale	2819	4777 v Bath
West Hartlepool	1936	3000 v Bath
Orrell	1887	3000 v Bath

"ON THE ROAD ATTENDANCES"

Team	Average	Highest Attendance
Harlequins	6157	12504 v Leicester
Bath	5869	10368 v Leicester
Wasps	5625	17000 v Leicester
Leicester	5478	10686 v Wasps
Saracens	5057	10791 v Leicester
Northampton	4572	11839 v Leicester
Gloucester	4279	9597 v Leicester
Sale	4038	7320 v Leicester
London Irish	3805	8263 v Leicester
Orrell	3546	9022 v Leicester
Bristol	3537	9122 v Leicester
West Hartlepool	3162	8709 v Leicester

Leicester averaged 11,454 - an amazing 4800 more than the next best supported club Bath.
Their top attendance was 17,000 for the midweek table topper against Wasps, at the beginning of April.
Six of their attendances topped the 10,000, while only Wasps, against Bath & Leicester, could manage over 10,000.
As a consequence, it is not surprising to find that every team's best attendance 'on the road' was against Leicester. What was more suprising was that Harlequins had the best 'on the road' average - some 300 more than second placed Bath.

FAIR PLAY LEAGUE

This is another new feature which we will publish each season and hopefully get the RFU to make part of their awards evening.

Team	Yellow card	Red card	Total
Harlequins	1	0	5
London Irish	2	0	10
Saracens	2	0	10
Bath	4	0	20
Leicester	4	0	20
Northampton	4	0	20
Wasps	2	1	20
Bristol	4	1	30
Gloucester	8	0	40
Orrell	8	0	40
Sale	9	1	55
West Hartlepool	10	2	70

1996-97 DIVISION ONE

MOST TRIES

16	Adedayo Adabayo	Bath
15	Daren O'Leary	Harlequins
14	Steven John	West Hartlepool
13	Tom Beim	Sale
12	Jon Sleightholme	Bath
12	Jeremy Guscott	Bath
11	Kenny Logan	Wasps
10	David Tiueti	Bristol
9	Mike Catt	Bath
9	Huw Harries	Harlequins
9	Penalty Tries	Leicester
9	Richard Wallace	Saracens
9	Shane Roiser	Wasps
8	Conor O'Shea	London Irish
7	Frederico Mendez	Bath
7	Andy Nicol	Bath
7	Mike Lloyd	Gloucester
7	Jim Staples	Harlequins
7	Jonathan Bell	Northampton
7	Simon Mannix	Sale
7	Dewi Morris	Sale

MOST CONVERSIONS

51	Jon Callard	Bath
45	Gareth Rees	Wasps
29	Thierry Lacroix	Harlequins
27	Paul Burke	Bristol
27	Will Carling	Harlequins
25	Mark Mapletoft	Gloucester
24	Mike Catt	Bath
24	John Liley	Leicester
20	David Humphreys	London Irish
18	Matthew McCarthy	Orrell
17	Simon Mannix	Sale
16	Andy Lee	Saracens
16	Michael Lynagh	Saracens
14	Paul Grayson	Northampton
12	Chris John	West Hartlepool
10	Alastair Hepher	Northampton
8	Joel Stransky	Leicester
7	Rob Liley	Leicester
7	Simon Verbickas	Sale
7	John Stabler	West Hartlepool
6	Adrian Hadley	Sale
4	Conor O'Shea	London Irish
4	Gareth Stocks	Sale
3	Michael Corcoran	Harlequins
3	Paul Challinor	Harlequins
3	Paul Dods	Northampton
3	Gregor Townsend	Northampton
3	Martin Strett	Orrell
3	Andy Tunningley	Saracens
3	Jon Ufton	Wasps
3	Mark Tainton	Bristol
2	Charlie Harrison	Bath
2	Lee Osborne	Gloucester
2	Niall Woods	London Irish
2	Phil Ure	London Irish
2	Frano Botica	Orrell
2	Rob Hitchmough	Orrell
2	Adam Griffin	Sale
2	Alex King	Wasps
2	Matthew Silva	West Hartlepool
1	Lea Tuigamala	Orrell

MOST PENALTIES

62	Gareth Rees	Wasps
58	Mark Mapletoft	Gloucester
44	John Liley	Leicester
40	David Humphreys	London Irish
38	Paul Burke	Bristol
34	Jonathan Callard	Bath
33	Thierry Lacroix	Harlequins
30	Michael Lynagh	Saracens
28	Paul Grayson	Northampton
28	Chris John	West Hartlepool
27	Simon Mannix	Sale
25	Joel Stransky	Leicester
19	Matthew McCarthy	Orrell
17	Alastair Hepher	Northampton
13	Andy Lee	Saracens
10	Gregor Townsend	Northampton
9	John Stabler	West Hartlepool
7	Mike Catt	Bath
7	Gareth Stocks	Sale
6	Simon Verbickas	Sale
5	Mark Tainton	Bristol
5	Will Carling	Harlequins
5	Rob Liley	Leicester
5	Andy Tunningley	Saracens
4	Niall Woods	London Irish
4	Conor O'Shea	London Irish
3	Paul Challinor	Harlequins
3	Martin Strett	Orrell
3	Rob Hitchmough	Orrell
3	Adam Griffin	Sale
3	Adrian Hadley	Sale
2	Michael Corcoran	Harlequins
2	Nick Beal	Northampton
2	Paul Dods	Northampton
2	Frano Botica	Orrell
2	Matthew Silva	West Hartlepool
1	Paul Hull	Bristol
1	Steve Pilgrim	Harlequins
1	Phil Ure	London Irish
1	Alex King	Wasps
1	Jon Ufton	Wasps

MOST DROP GOALS

6	Alex King	Wasps
5	Mark Mapletoft	Gloucester
4	Matthew McCarthy	Orrell
4	Paul Grayson	Northampton
3	David Humphreys	London Irish
3	Thierry Lacroix	Harlequins
2	Mike Catt	Bath
1	Chris Catling	Gloucester
1	Gregor Townsend	Northampton
1	Alastair Hepher	Northampton
1	Chris Yates	Sale
1	Michael Lynagh	Saracens
1	Andy Lee	Saracens
1	Andy Tunningley	Saracens
1	Chris John	West Hartlepool

1996-97 DIVISION ONE

MOST POINTS IN THE SEASON

POINTS	PLAYER	CLUB	Tries	Cons.	Pens.	D.G.
291	Gareth Rees	Wasps	3	45	62	-
269	Mark Mapletoft	Gloucester	6	25	58	5
224	Jonathan Callard	Bath	4	51	34	-
195	John Liley	Leicester	3	24	44	-
189	David Humphreys	London Irish	4	20	40	3
178	Paul Burke	Bristol	2	27	38	-
176	Thierry Lacroix	Harlequins	2	29	33	3
150	Simon Mannix	Sale	7	17	27	-
129	Paul Grayson	Northampton	1	14	28	4
126	Chris John	West Hartlepool	3	12	28	1
125	Michael Lynagh	Saracens	-	16	30	1
120	Mike Catt	Bath	9	24	7	2
116	Matthew McCarthy	Orrell	2	18	19	4
101	Joel Stransky	Leicester	2	8	25	-
84	Andy Lee	Saracens	2	16	13	1
84	Alastair Hepher	Northampton	2	10	17	1
80	Adedayo Adebayo	Bath	16	-	-	-
79	Will Carling	Harlequins	2	27	5	-
75	Daren O'Leary	Harlequins	15	-	-	-
65	Steven John	West Hartlepool	13	-	-	-
65	Tom Beim	Sale	13	-	-	-
64	Gregor Townsend	Northampton	5	3	10	1
60	Conor O'Shea	London Irish	8	4	4	-
60	Jeremy Guscott	Bath	12	-	-	-
60	Jonathan Sleightholme	Bath	12	-	-	-
55	Kenny Logan	Wasps	11	-	-	-
51	John Stabler	West Hartlepool	2	7	9	-
50	David Tiueti	Bristol	10	-	-	-
46	Niall Woods	London Irish	6	2	4	-
45	Alex King	Wasps	4	2	1	6
45	Shane Roiser	Wasps	9	-	-	-
45	Huw Harries	Harlequins	9	-	-	-
45	Richard Wallace	Saracens	9	-	-	-
45	Penalty Try	Leicester	9	-	-	-
44	Rob Liley	Leicester	3	7	5	-
44	Andy Tunningley	Saracens	4	3	5	1

Lawrence Dallaglio (Captain) and Nigel Melville (Director of Rugby) of Wasps with the Courage Division One Trophy.

BATH F.C.

FOUNDED: 1865

Chairman Andrew Brownsword, c/o Bath Rugby, 26 Queen Square, Bath BA1 2HX
01225 325200 (Office), 01225 325201 (Fax)
Chief Executive Tony Swift, c/o Bath Rugby, as above
Coaches Andrew Robinson, Clive Woodward, c/o Bath Rugby, as above
Operations Director David Jenkins, c/o Bath Rugby, as above
Marketing Director Stephen Hands, c/o Bath Rugby, as above
Commercial Manager Andrew Brown, c/o Bath Rugby, as above
Media & Communications Manager Liz Pritchard, c/o Bath Rugby, as above
Youth Developement Manager Gareth Adams, c/o Bath Rugby, as above
Ticket Office Manager Alan Humphreys, c/o Bath Rugby, as above

Bath went through many changes in their management last season which undoubtedly resulted in an empty trophy cabinet for the first time in fifteen years. The phenominally high scores in matches at the end of the season demonstrated the kind of rugby of which Bath is easily capable. A 71-21 win over Gloucester; an 84-7 slaughter of Sale; a 40-14 hammering of Orrell; and a 47-9 thrashing against Leicester, all at home, clearly show Bath's dominance at the end of a mixed season.

The appointment of new coaches, Andy Robinson and Clive Woodward, half way through the season, following the exit of John Hall and Brian Ashton, created the necessary motivation for the team's improvement. Playing a 'fifteen man running game', Bath's focus was to play a southern hemisphere style of rugby similar to the Super12s. The introduction of professionalism meant four days of team training instead of evening training sessions which obviously helped and a reduced squad with two teams plus a development side meant greater focus.

Towards the end of the season, Bath further strengthened their management with the appointment of ex-All Black fitness coach, Jim Blair, and full-time physio, Ian Jones.

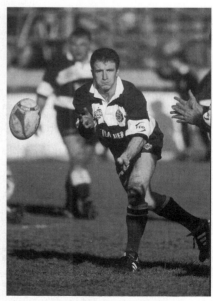

Jon Sleightholme, Bath & England   Mike Catt, Bath & England

Photos - CW Sports Agency

Colours: Blue, white and black.   **Change colours:** Amber/black

BATH

No	Ven.	Date	Opponents	Att.	Res.	Score	Scorers
1	(A)	31.08	v Orrell	3000	W	56-13	Nicol(t)Webster(t)Geoghegan(t)Horne(t)Haag(t)Catt(tdg)Callaed(4c5p)
2	(A)	07.09	v Leicester	10368	L	25-28	Nicol(t)Catt(t)Guscott(t)Callard(2c2p)
3	(H)	14.09	v Wasps	7000	L	36-40	J Robinson(t)Catt(t)Nicol(t)PTry(t)Callard(2c4p)
4	(A)	21.09	v Gloucester	5950	W	45-29	Adebayo(2t)Nicol(t)Catt(t)Ojomoh(t)J Robinson(t)Callard(t2c2p)
5	(H)	28.09	v W Hartlepool	5500	W	46-10	Sleightholme(2t)A Robinson(t)de Glanville(t)Adams(t)Adabayo(t)Callard(5c2p)
6	(A)	05.10	v London Irish	3850	W	56-31	Adebayo(3t)J Robinson(2t)Webster(t)Guscott(t)Redman(t)Callard(t4cp)
7	(H)	29.10	v Bristol	6500	W	76- 7	Guscott(2t)Harrison(tc)Hilton(t)Cusack(t)Adebayo(t)Sleightolme(t)Paul(2t) A Robinson(t)Catt(t4c2pdg)
8	(A)	09.11	v Northampton	7566	L	6- 9	Callard(2p)
9	(H)	07.12	v Harlequins	8500	W	35-20	Guscott(2t)Adebayo(t)Thomas(t)Callard(3c3p)
10	(H)	04.01	v Saracens	5500	W	35-33	Mendez(t)Webster(t)Guscott(t)PenTry(t)Callard(3c3p)
11	(A)	11.01	v Harlequins	5566	L	6-22	Callard(2p)
12	(H)	19.01	v Northampton	7000	W	52-14	Sleightholme(3t)Catt(t)Lyle(t)Mendez(t)Callard(5c4p)
13	(A)	22.02	v Bristol	5320	W	18-13	Redman(t)Guscott(t)Callard(c2p)
14	(H)	08.03	v London Irish	6100	W	46- 3	Sleightholme(3t)Lyle(2t)Mallett(t)Yates(t)A Robinson(t)Callard(3c)
15	(A)	27.03	v W Hartlepool	3000	W	24-16	Haag(t)Adebayo(t)Catt(t)Callard(3cp)
16	(A)	02.04	v Sale	4777	L	5-11	Webster(t)
17	(A)	06.04	v Wasps	10657	D	25-25	Guscott(2t)Adebayo(t)Callard(c)Catt(c2p)
18	(H)	12.04	v Leicester	8500	W	47- 9	Adebayo(2t)Perry(2t)Mendez(t)Lyle(t)Callard(2c)Catt(2c3p)
19	(H)	19.04	v Orrell	6100	W	40-14	Peters(2t)Mendez(t)Ojomoh(t)Adebayo(t)Callard(tc)Catt(4c)
20	(H)	26.04	v Sale	6900	W	84- 7	Guscott(2t)Mendez(2t)Lyle(t)Llanes(t)Adebayo(t)Perry(t)Webster(t) Sleightholme(t)Catt(2t8c)Callard(4c)
21	(H)	30.04	v Gloucester	7100	W	71-21	Nicol(3t)Perry(2t)Sleightholme(2t)Thomas(t)Adebayo(t)Lyle(t)Catt(5c)Callard(t3c)
22	(A)	03.05	v Saracens	4510	L	29-36	Adebayo(t)Mendez(t)Peters(t)Yates(t)Callard(3cp)

1996-97 HIGHLIGHTS

LEAGUE DEBUTS: Matthew Perry, Richard Webster, Henry Paul, Jason Robinson, Brian Cusack, Nathan Thomas, Charlie Harrison, Dan Lyle, Frederico Mendez, Chris Horsman, German Llanes, Joe Ewens.

TRY ON DEBUT:
Richard Webster, Jason Robinson, Charlie Harrison. Mike Horne scored a try on his debut as replacement.

PLAYERS USED: 33 plus 3 as replacement

EVER PRESENT: None - most appearances 20 Mike Catt, Jonathan Callard and Martin Haag

☐ Set a new record for points in a Division One season 863.

☐ Broke the Division One record for most tries in a season, 58 shared by Bath and Harlequins, with an an amazing 116.

☐ England winger Adedayo Adebayo breaks the Division One record for tries in a season scoring 16 in 18 matches. The previous record of 14 was set last season by Harlequins Daren O'Leary. In the process he also broke the Bath record for tries in a season which was 10 shared by Jeremy Guscott and Tony Swift.

☐ Jeremy Guscott broke Tony Swift's all time league record of 43 tries.

	Tries	Apps	Try Every
Jeremy Guscott	48	98	2.04 games
Tony Swift	43	90	2.09 games
Adedayo Adebayo	38	70	1.84 games
Jon Sleightholme	21	36	1.71 games

☐ Scrum Half Andy Nicol and winger Adedayo Adebayo set a new club record of scoring tries in six consecutive matches.

☐ Mike Catt equals Stuart Barnes's record of 26 points in a match in the the clubs record 84- 7 win over Sale. Catt scored two tries and kicked eight conversions out of eight with Jonathan Callard converting the other four.

☐ Jonathan Callard became the first man to score 200 points in a League One season twice and continues to extend the clubs all time records. Callard kicked 51 conversions - a Divisional record as well as a new club record - beating the previous record of 43 (also set by Callard). He now has 135 conversions in League One games passing John Liley's record of 129.

	Pts	T	C	P	D	Apps	Ave.
Jonathan Callard	844	23	135	155	-	81(2)	10.4

BATH'S COURAGE LEAGUE MATCH DETAILS 1996-97

#	15	14	13	12	11	10	9	1	2	3	4	5	6	7	8	Replacements	#
1	Callard	Geoghegan	Guscott	Perry	Adabayo	Catt	Nicol	Hilton	Adams	Ubogu	Haag	Redman	Robinson	Webster	Peters	Horne(15)	1
2	Callard	Sleightholme	de Glanville	Guscott	Ababayo	Catt	Nicol	Hilton	Adams	Ubogu	Haag	Redman	Robinson	Webster	Peters		2
3	Callard	Sleightholme	Guscott	Paul	Robinson	Catt	Nicol	Hilton	Dawe	Mallett	Redman	Cusack	Thomas	Ojomah	Peters	Adabayo(12)	3
4	Callard	Robinson	de Glanville	Guscott	Adabayo	Catt	Nicol	Hilton	Dawe	Ubogu	Haag	Redman	Robinson	Thomas	Ojomoh	Mallett(3)	4
5	Callard	Sleightholme	de Glanville	Paul	Adabayo	Catt	Nicol	Hilton	Adams	Mallett	Haag	Cusack	Robinson	Peters			5
6	Callard	Robinson	de Glanville	Guscott	Adabayo	Catt	Nicol	Yates	Adams	Ubogu	Haag	Redman	Thomas	Webster	Ojomah	Harrison(9),Perry(14)	6
7	Robinson	Sleightholme	Paul	Guscott	Adabayo	Catt	Harrison	Hilton	Dawe	Ubogu	Haag	Cusack	Robinson	Ojomah	Peters	Perry(14),Lyle(7),Sanders(10),McCarthy(1)	7
8	Callard	Sleightholme	de Glanville	Guscott	Adabayo	Catt	Harrison	Yates	Dawe	Mallett	Haag	Cusack	Robinson	Webster	Ojomoh		8
9	Robinson		de Glanville	Guscott	Adabayo	Catt	Sanders	Hilton	Mendez	Mallett	Haag	Lyle	Thomas	Ojomoh		Ubogo(3),Harrison(11)	9
10	Callard	Sleightholme	de Glanville	Guscott	Robinson	Butland	Sanders	Hilton	Mendez	Ubogu	Haag	Redman	Thomas	Ojomoh		Yates(1)	10
11	Callard	Sleightholme	de Glanville	Guscott	Robinson	Catt	Nicol	Hilton	Mendez	Ubogu	Haag	Redman	Thomas	Ojomoh		Butland(tr14)	11
12	Callard	Sleightholme	de Glanville	Guscott	Adabayo	Catt	Sanders	Mendez	Dawe	Ubogu	Haag	Redman	Robinson	Lyle	Ojomoh	Mallett(3)	12
13	Callard	Sleightholme	de Glanville	Guscott	Perry	Catt	Harrison	Yates	Mendez	Mallett	Haag	Redman	Robinson	Lyle		Butland(10)	13
14	Callard	Sleightholme	de Glanville	Guscott	Adabayo	Catt	Harrison	Yates	Mendez	Mallett	Haag	Redman	Robinson	Webster	Lyle	Thomas(6),Mendez(2)	14
15	Callard	Sleightholme	de Glanville	Guscott	Adabayo	Catt	Harrison	Dawe	Horsman	Haag	Redman	Robinson	Webster	Lyle		Geoghegan(15),Hilton(3),Thomas(7)	15
16	Callard	Sleightholme	de Glanville	Guscott	Adabayo	Catt	Nicol	Yates	Dawe	Mallett	Haag	Redman	Robinson	Webster	Lyle	Mendez(2),Hilton(3),Thomas(6)	16
17	Perry	Sleightholme	de Glanville	Guscott	Adabayo	Catt	Nicol	Yates	Mendez	Mallett	Haag	Redman	Robinson	Lyle		Hilton(3),Ojomoh(4),Callard(15)	17
18	Perry	Sleightholme	de Glanville	Guscott	Adabayo	Catt	Nicol	Yates	Mendez	Mallett	Haag	Redman	Thomas	Lyle		Callard(14)Cusack(8)Ojomoh(6)	18
19	Callard	Sleightholme	Guscott	Perry		Catt	Nicol	Yates	Mendez	Mallett	Haag	Ojimoh	Thomas	Peters		Cusack(5)Harrison(9)Butland(14)Horsman(3)	19
20	Callard	Sleightholme	Guscott	Perry		Catt	Harrison	Yates	Mendez	Mallett	Haag	Ojomoh	Thomas	Webster	Lyle	Hilton(1)Horne(15)Peters(6)	20
21	Callard	Sleightholme	Guscott	Perry		Catt	Nicol	Yates	Mendez	Mallett	Haag	Llanes	Thomas	Webster	Lyle	Butland(10)Hilton(3)Peters(tr7)	21
22	Callard	Sleightholme	de Glanville	Ewens	Adabayo	Butland	Nicol	Hilton	Mendez	Mallett	Horsman	Haag	Cusack	Llanes	Peters	Perry(15)French(12)Harrison(9)Yates(1)Thomas(7)Horne(11)	22

BATH LEAGUE STATISTICS
(COMPILED BY STEPHEN McCORMACK)

Season	Div.	P	W	D	L	F	(Tries	Con	Pen	DG)	A	(Tries	Con	Pen	DG)	Most Points	Most Tries
87-88	1	11	6	1	4	197	(28	14	15	4)	156	(17	8	20	4)	40 - Phil Cue	4 - Tony Swift
88-89	1	11	10	0	1	263	(43	17	17	2)	98	(6	4	22	0)	83 - Stuart Barnes	10 - Jeremy Guscott
89-90	1	11	8	0	3	258	(44	29	8	0)	104	(8	6	20	0)	103 - Stuart Barnes	10 - Tony Swift
90-91	1	12	11	0	1	280	(39	23	24	2)	104	(8	6	20	0)	98 - Stuart Barnes	6 - Tony Swift
91-92	1	12	10	1	1	277	(34	18	33	2)	126	(10	7	20	4)	95 - Stuart Barnes	8 - Tony Swift
92-93	1	12	11	0	1	355	(42	23	32	1)	97	(7	4	14	4)	122 - Jon Webb	7 - Stuart Barnes
93-94	1	18	17	0	1	431	(46	27	47	2)	181	(13	7	32	2)	178 - Jon Callard	5 - Mike Catt, Ben Clarke
94-95	1	18	12	3	3	373	(36	26	46	1)	245	(19	6	40	6)	150 - Jon Callard	5 - Adebayo Adebayo
95-96	1	18	15	1	2	575	(68	44	46	3)	276	(26	13	36	4)	236 - Jon Callard	9 - Jeremy Guscott
96-97	1	22	15	1	6	863	(116	77	41	2)	411	(39	24	52	4)	224 - Jon Callard	16 - Adedayo Adebayo
Totals		145	115	7	23	3872	(496	298	309	19)	1798	(143	85	276	28)		

	HOME	AWAY
BIGGEST WIN	(77pts) 84-7 v Sale 26.4.97 49-6 v Saracens 27.4.91	(43pts) 56-13 v Orrell 31.8.96
BIGGEST DEFEAT	(5pts) 13-18 v Sale 29.4.95	(16pts) 6-22 v Harlequins 28.12.96
MOST POINTS SCORED	84-7 v Sale 26.4.97	56-13 v Orrell 31.8.96 56-31 v Lon. Irish 5.10.96
AGAINST	36-40 v Wasps 14.9.96	29-36 v Saracens 3.5.97

MOST CONSECUTIVE VICTORIES - 15

MOST CONSECUTIVE DEFEATS - 2

MOST TRIES IN A MATCH
(FOR) 14 v Bedford 13.1.90, v Sale 26.4.97
(AGAINST) 5 v Sale 27.4.96

MOST APPEARANCES
FORWARD: 118 Grahame Dawe
BACK: 98 Jeremy Guscott

CONSECUTIVE APPEARANCES
50 Tony Swift 9.9.89 - 25.9.93

CONSECUTIVE SCORING MATCHES
Scoring Tries - 6 - Andy Nicol, Adedayo Adebayo
Scoring Points - 15 - Jon Callard

MOST	in a SEASON	in a CAREER	in a MATCH
Points	236 Jon Callard 95-96	844 Jon Callard 89-97	26 Stuart Barnes v W Hartlepool 27.3.93 (A) Mike Catt v Sale 26.4.97 (H)
Tries	16 Adedeyo Adebayo 96-97	48 Tony Swift 87-97	4 Jeremy Guscott v Bedford 13.1.90 (H) Tony Swift v Bedford 13.1.90 (H)
Conversions	51 Jon Callard 96-97	135 Jon Callard 89-97	10 Stuart Barnes v Bedford 13.1.90 (H)
Penalties	45 Jon Callard 95-96	155 Jon Callard 89-97	6 Jon Callard v Harlequins 6.4.96 (H)
Drop Goals	2 Stuart Barnes 87-88 Mike Catt 96-97	9 Stuart Barnes 87-94	1 by 7 players Most - Stuart Barnes 7 times

BATH PLAYING SQUAD

NAME	Ht	Wt	Birthdate	Birthplace	Club	Apps	Pts	T	C	P	DG

BACKS

NAME	Ht	Wt	Birthdate	Birthplace	Club	Apps	Pts	T	C	P	DG
Jonathan Callard	5.10	12.7	01.06.66	Leicester	Newport						
England: 5, A, B. Wales: u21.					Bath	81+2	844	23	135	155	-
Matthew Perry	5.10	13.5	27.01.77	-							
England: A, Colts, u18.					Bath	7+4	25	5	-	-	-
Jon Sleightholme	5.10	14.0	05.08.72	Malton	Hull Ionians						
England: 12, A, Emerging, u21, Colts.					Wakefield	38	127	27	-	-	-
					Bath	36	105	21	-	-	-
Adedayo Adebayo	5.9	13.4	30.11.70	Ibadan (Nig.)							
England: 3, A, Students, u21, u18.					Bath	70+1	184	38	-	-	-
Jeremy Guscott	6.1	13.10	07.07.65	Bath							
England: 48					Bath	98	238	48	8	-	-
Phil de Glanville	5.11	13.6	01.10.68	Loughborough							
England: 24, A, Students, u21.					Bath	93	96	20	-	-	-
Charlie Harrison	5.10	12.0	06.09.72	Chippenham							
					Bath	6+5	9	1	2	-	-
Andy Nicol	5.11	13.4	12.03.71	Dundee	Dundee H.S.F.P.						
Scotland: , A, u19, Schools.					Bath	25	58	11	-	-	1
Mike Catt	5.10	13.0	17.09.71	Port Elizabeth							
England: 22, A, u21.					Bath	65	199	19	28	11	5
Mike Horne			11.11.78								
					Bath	0+3	5	1	-	-	-
Joe Ewens	5.11	13.4	16.01.77	Bristol							
England: u21, u18, u16.					Bath	1	-	-	-	-	-
Rich Butland	5.11	12.7	05.11.71	Cape Town							
England: A, Students, u21.					Bath	14+4	38	1	9	5	-
Ian Sanders	5.9	12.0	22.01.71	Penzance							
England: u21.					Bath	30+4	15	3	-	-	-

FORWARDS

NAME	Ht	Wt	Birthdate	Birthplace	Club	Apps	Pts	T	C	P	DG
Dave Hilton	5.10	15.4	03.04.70	Bristol	Bristol	16	-	-	-	-	-
Scotland: 19, A. England: Colts.					Bath	32+5	15	3	-	-	-
Kevin Yates	5.11	16.2	06.11.72	Medicine Hat (Can)	Chippenham						
England: 2, A, u21.					Bath	27+2	20	4	-	-	-
Frederic Mendez			02.08.72	Argentina							
Argentina: 29					Bath	11+2	35	7	-	-	-
John Mallett	6.1	17.10	28.05.70	Lincoln							
England: 1, A, Emerging, Students, Colts, Schools.					Bath	36+3	9	2	-	-	-
Martin Haag	6.5	16.7	28.07.68	Chelmsford							
England: 2, A, B.					Bath	91+2	38	8	-	-	-
Nigel Redman	6.4	17.2	16.08.64	Cardiff							
England: 20.					Bath	109	41	9	-	-	-
German Llanes											
Argentina:					Bath	6	5	1	-	-	-
Brian Cusack	6.7	17.8	11.07.72	Waterford							
Ireland: A.					Bath	5+2	5	1	-	-	-
Steve Ojomoh	6.2	15.10	25.05.70	Benin City (Nig.)							
England: 11, A, u21, Colts, Schools.					Bath	58+2	20	4	-	-	-
Richard Webster	6.2	14.7	09.07.68	Morriston	Previous Clubs: Swansea, Salford (RL).						
Wales: 13.					Bath	15	25	5	-	-	-
Eric Peters	6.5	16.4	28.01.69	Glasgow	Saracens						
Scotland: 17, A. England: Students.					Bath	21+2	15	3	-	-	-
Nathan Thomas			22.01.76								
Wales:					Bath	11+4	5	1	-	-	-
Dan Lyle	6.5	17.12	28.07.90	San Diego	US Eagles						
					Bath	10+1	30	6	-	-	-
Gary French	5.11	15.0	02.12.68	St Helens	Previous Clubs: Liverpool St. Helens, Orrell.						
England: Emerging.					Bath	1+1	-	-	-	-	-

The Recreation Ground, Bath. BA2 6PW.

Tel: 01255 325200   **Fax:** 01225 325201

CAPACITY: 8,317   **SEATED:** Covered 1,359, Uncovered 4,568   **STANDING:** 2,390

SIMPLE DIRECTIONS:
By Road: Follow signs to Bath City Centre and then signs to the Recreation Ground.
Nearest Railway Station: Bath Spa (B.R.)

CAR PARKING: Minimal on ground, unlimited Park & Ride

ADMISSION:
Seasons: Standing - Adults £135; Children/OAPs £70 - £105;
Seated Adults £160-£295, Children/OAPs £145-£265.
Matchday: Standing - Adults £12, Children/Oaps £6-£8; Seated £16-£18

CLUB SHOP: Yes - manager Carol Walker 01225 311950.

CLUBHOUSE: Matchdays 11.00-11.00, snacks & barmeals available.
Function room: Yes with a capacity between 250-300, contact Rob Rowland 01225 469230

TRAINING NIGHTS: Day time training twice a week plus one evening session.

Bath's Adedayo Adebayo, top League try scorer
Photo - CW Sports Agency

MATCHDAY PROGRAMME

Size	A5
Number of pages	40 plus cover
Price	£2
Programme Editor	
	Liz Pritchard, 01225 325200
Advertising Rates	
	Colour - Full Page £1800,
	Half page £970,
	Qtr page £520

BRISTOL R.F.C.

NICKNAME:

FOUNDED: 1888

Chairman Arthur Holmes, c/o Bristol RFC Ltd, The Memorial Ground, Filton Avenue, Horfield, Bristol BS7 0AQ. 0117 908 5500, 0117 908 5530 (Fax)

Non Executive Directors Derek Brown, Chez Wardazla, Gary White, c/o Bristol RFC Ltd, as above

Company Secretary Andrew Reid, c/o Bristol RFC Ltd, as above

Chief Executive Jeff Lewis, c/o Bristol RFC Ltd, as above. 0117 908 5507 (B)

Director of Marketing Andy Brassington, c/o Bristol RFC Ltd, as above. 0117 908 5502 (B), 0117 908 5530 (Fax), 0831 532 670 (Mobile)

Club Coach Alan Davies, c/o Bristol RFC Ltd, as above

Rugby Development Officer Mark Tainton, c/o Bristol RFC Ltd, as above. 0117 908 5504

Referee Liason Keith Gerrish, 52 West Town Lane, Brislington, Bristol BS4 5DB 0117 977 7009 (H)

Media Liaison John Harding, 10 Fairlyn Drive, Kingswood, Bristol BS15 4PU 0117 956 3558 (H), 0117 983 7537 (Fax), 0860 885 602 (Mobile), 01426 319 289 (Pager)

A season best forgotten as far as Bristol supporters are concerned. One that started with so much promise and commitment but ended having to play Bedford over two-legs to retain a place in top flight rugby.

New club coach Alan Davies had targeted the new European Conference as the competition to bring some silverware to the Memorial Ground's new £2 million West Stand. Bristol started with a convincing victory over Treorchy but defeats by Bridgend, Castres, Narbonne and Bucharest ended that campaign abruptly.

The Anglo-Welsh competition never really got out of the starting blocks as far as Bristol were concerned. After a double over Neath the ties against Pontypridd and Bridgend fell by the wayside.

After crushing Blackheath 60-17 in the fifth round of the Pilkington Cup, the draw for the next round paired Bristol with neighbours Gloucester at Kingsholm and the exit door from another competition.

In the League Bristol started with a narrow victory at London Irish and a good win over Orrell but defeats against Northampton and Harlequins followed. Sale provided a closely fought clash before a run of seven League defeats followed including a 76-7 midweek battering at Bath.

Some local pride remained with success at home to Gloucester but it couldn't be repeated when Bath visited the Memorial Ground five days later. Wins over Sale, Northampton and Orrell brought some ray of hope only for Harlequins and London Irish to return the gloom.

Gloucester snatched a last minute draw at Kingsholm before Bristol completed their official League programme with victory over relegated West Hartlepool. But there was still the play-offs. Bristol secured a nine point cushion from the first leg at Goldington Road and the crowds wept with joy at the final whistle of the return leg as Bristol lived to fight another day.

Hooker Mark Regan and lock Simon Shaw continued to gain England caps though Shaw has now left to join league champions Wasps and Regan's future may lie at Bath. Flyhalf Paul Burke and flanker David Corkery turned out for Ireland in the Five Nations.

In the 1997 summer Regan and Shaw toured South Africa with the British Lions, club captain Martin Corry was with England in Argentina, centre Kevin Maggs and hooker Barry McConell with the Irish Development squad in New Zealand, wing Dave Tiueti with Tonga in South Africa plus centre Frazer Waters and full back Josh Lewsey with England Under 21's in Australia.

Flyhalf Mark Tainton, who joined England as kicking coach in Argentina, became the club's leading points scorer, in all competitions, overtaking Alan Pearn's 2047 points.

Bristol FC: Back Row (L-R); Keith James (Physio), Dean Dewdney, Iain Dixon, Simon Shaw, Eben Rollitt, Fraser Waters, Nathan Millett, Dave Tiueti, Paul Hull, Alan Davies (Coach). Front Row; Mark Denney, Ben Breeze, Ralph Knibbs, Kevin Maggs, Alan Sharp, Martin Corry (Capt), Phil Adams, Mark Regan, Simon Martin, Kris Fulman, Robert Jones.

Photo - Paul Box

Colours: Blue and white hoops

Change colours: Blue and yellow quarters

COURAGE LEAGUE MATCH DETAILS 1996-97

No	Ven.	Date	Opponents	Att.	Res.	Score	Scorers
1	(A)	31.08	v London Irish	1467	W	28-27	Jones(t)Tiueti(t)Waters(t)Burke(2c3p)
2	(H)	07.09	v Orrell	2996	W	38-10	Hull(2t)Breeze(t)PTry(t)Burke(3c4p)
3	(A)	14.09	v Northampton	4593	L	21-29	Corry(t)Corkery(t)Burke(c3p)
4	(H)	21.09	v Harlequins	4823	L	24-35	Corkery(t)Breeze(t)Corry(t)Shaw(t)Tainton(2c)
5	(A)	28.09	v Sale	2041	W	33-31	Tiueti(2t)Regan(t)Burke(t2c3p)
6	(H)	05.10	v Saracens	4795	L	11-21	Tiueti(t)Burke(2p)
7	(A)	29.10	v Bath	6500	L	7-76	Hull(t)Burke(c)
8	(A)	07.12	v Wasps	3832	L	13-15	Hull(t)Corkery(t)Burke(p)
9	(H)	00.00	v Leicester	2553	L	12-38	Tiueti(t)Smith(t)Burke(c)
10	(A)	04.01	v W Hartlepool	1078	L	8-19	Jones(t)Tainton(p)
11	(H)	11.01	v Wasps	3650	L	18-41	Denney(t)Burke(tc2p)
12	(A)	18.01	v Leicester	9122	L	19-53	Filali(t)Tainton(c3p)Hull(p)
13	(H)	18.02	v Gloucester	5406	W	18-13	Burke(6p)
14	(H)	22.02	v Bath	5320	L	13-18	Short(t)Burke(c2p)
15	(A)	09.03	v Saracens	1793	L	15-33	Rollitt(t)Maggs(t)Burke(cp)
16	(H)	22.03	v Sale	3526	W	34-24	Tiueti(2t)Eagle(t)Lewsey(t)Burke(4c2p)
17	(H)	05.04	v Northampton	4254	W	20-11	Rollitt(t)Waters(t)Burke(2c2p)
18	(A)	12.04	v Orrell	1500	W	28-27	Tiueti(2t)Corry(t)Burke(2c3p)
19	(A)	15.04	v Harlequins	2058	L	6-29	Burke(2p)
20	(H)	19.04	v London Irish	3300	L	26-38	Breeze(t)Corkery(t)Hull(t)Jones(t)Burke(3c)
21	(A)	26.04	v Gloucester	4931	D	20-20	Lewsey(t)Maggs(t)Burke(2c2p)
22	(H)	04.05	v W Hartlepool	1965	W	20-17	Martin(t)Temperley(t)Tiueti(t)Burke(c)Tainton(p)

1996-97 HIGHLIGHTS

LEAGUE DEBUTS:
Fraser Waters, Paul Burke, Robert Jones, David Corkery, Andy Collins, Andy Down, Andrew Wadley, Chad Eagle, Richard Smith, Said Filali, Josh Lewsey, Craig Short, Richie Collins, John Brownrigg, David Yapp.

TRY ON DEBUT: FraserWaters, Robert Jones.

PLAYERS USED: 37

EVER PRESENT: None
- most appearances 20 Ben Breeze

❏ Paul Hull breaks the club record for tries in a League career held by Derek Eves. Hull started the season one behind Eves's total of 17 set between 87-95.

	Tries	Apps	Try Every
Paul Hull	23	109	2.04 games
Derek Eves	17	86	2.09 games

❏ David Tiueti, who scored 10 tries, broke Alastair Saveriamutto's record of eight tries in a season set back in the 93-94 season.

❏ Equalled the club record of seven successive defeats.

❏ Mark Tainton extended his club points scoring record to 637 as well as his record for conversions and penalties to 62 and 165 respectively.
Paul Burke in his first season at the club moves into second place on the all time list behind Tainton.

	Pts	T	C	P	D	Apps	Ave.
Mark Tainton	637	-	62	165	6	72(1)	8.85
Paul Burke	178	2	27	38	-	19(1)	9.36
Paul Hull	158	23	4	13	1	109(3)	1.45
Jonathan Webb	155	3	16	37	-	22	7.04

❏ Paul Hull broke Derek Eves's club record of 86 appearances. Hull went on to become the first Bristol player to reach 100 and ended the season on 109 (3). Prop David Hinkins relieved Eves of the record for most appearances by a forward, 86, and ended the season on his century.

❏ Paul Burke, who became only the second Bristol player to score 100 points in a season, broke Mark Tainton's record of 19 conversions in a season with 27.

❏ Suffered their worst ever away defeat losing 7-76 at the hands of their West Country rivals Bath. In the process they conceded a record 11 tries three more than their previous worst against Wasps back in April 91.

BRISTOL'S COURAGE LEAGUE MATCH DETAILS 1996-97

#	15	14	13	12	11	10	9	1	2	3	4	5	6	7	8	Replacements
1	Hull	Tiueti	Waters	Denney	Breeze	Burke	Jones	Sharp	Regan	Fulman	Adams	Shaw	Corry	Corkery	Rollitt	
2	Hull	Tiueti	Denney	Denney	Breeze	Burke	Jones	Sharp	Regan	Fulman	Adams	Shaw	Corry	Corkery	Rollitt	
3	Hull	Maggs	Denney	Denney	Breeze	Burke	Jones	Sharp	Regan	Fulman	Adams	Shaw	Corry	Corkery	Rollitt	
4	Bennett	Tiueti	Waters	Denney	Breeze	Burke	Jones	Collins	Regan	Fulman	Adams	Shaw	Corry	Corkery	Rollitt	Tainton(10)
5	Hull	Tiueti	Waters	Maggs	Breeze	Burke	Jones	Sharp	Regan	Fulman	Adams	Shaw	Dixon	Corkery	Rollitt	Down(9)
6	Hull	Tiueti	Waters	Denney	Breeze	Burke	Jones	Sharp	Regan	Fulman	Adams	Shaw	Dixon	Corkery	Rollitt	
7	Hull	Tiueti	Waters	Maggs	Wring	Burke	Down	Hinkins	Wadley	Fulman	Shaw	Eagle	Dixon	Corkery	Rollitt	Dewdney(9)
8	Hull	Tiueti	Martin	Denney	Breeze	Burke	Smith	Sharp	Regan	Hinkins	Shaw	Eagle	Corkery	Filali	Corry	Barrow(8)
9	Hull	Tiueti	Martin	Denney	Breeze	Burke	Smith	Sharp	Regan	Hinkins	Shaw	Eagle	Corkery	Filali	Barrow	
10	Hull	Tiueti	Maggs	Denney	Breeze	Tainton	Jones	Sharp	Regan	Hinkins	Adams	Eagle	Barrow	Corry	Corry	Temperley(7)
11	Hull	Tiueti	Martin	Denney	Breeze	Burke	Jones	Sharp	Regan	Hinkins	Adams	Eagle	Corkery	Corkery	Rollitt	Maggs(12)
12	Bennett	Tiueti	Hull	Denney	Lewsey	Tainton	Jones	Sharp	Regan	Hinkins	Shaw	Eagle	Filali	Filali	Rollitt	Dewdney(12)Martin(15)
13	Hull	Tiueti	Waters	Maggs	Breeze	Burke	Jones	Hinkins	Regan	Fulman	Shaw	Eagle	Corkery	Rollitt	Short	
14	Hull	Maggs	Waters	Denney	Breeze	Burke	Jones	Hinkins	Regan	Fulman	Shaw	Eagle	Corry	Short	Rollitt	
15	Hull	Tiueti	Waters	Maggs	Breeze	Burke	Jones	Hinkins	Regan	Fulman	Shaw	Eagle	Corry	Corkery	Rollitt	Lewsey(15)
16	Lewsey	Tiueti	Waters	Maggs	Breeze	Burke	Jones	Hinkins	McConnell	Fulman	Adams	Eagle	Corry	Collins	Rollitt	Hull(10)
17	Lewsey	Tiueti	Waters	Maggs	Breeze	Burke	Jones	Hinkins	McConnell	Fulman	Adams	Eagle	Corry	Collins	Rollitt	Corkery(8)Smith(9)
18	Lewsey	Tiueti	Waters	Maggs	Breeze	Burke	Jones	Hinkins	McConnell	Fulman	Adams	Eagle	Corry	Collins	Rollitt	Hull(15)Denney(13)Corkery(4)Short(7)
19	Lewsey	Tiueti	Waters	Maggs	Breeze	Burke	Jones	Hinkins	McConnell	Fulman	Shaw	Eagle	Corkery	Collins	Rollitt	Hull(14)Adams(4)Short(8)
20	Lewsey	Hull	Waters	Maggs	Breeze	Burke	Jones	Hinkins	McConnell	Fulman	Shaw	Eagle	Corkery	Collins	Rollitt	Adams(5)
21	Lewsey	Hull	Waters	Maggs	Breeze	Burke	Dewdney	Hinkins	McConnell	Fulman	Adams	Browning	Corkery	Collins	Rollitt	Barrow(7)
22	Hull	Tiueti	Martin	Denney	Yapp	Tainton	Dewdney	Hinkins	Regan	Fulman	Shaw	Adams	Corkery	Short	Temperley	Browning(14)Burke(10)Jones(9)McConnell(2)Maggs(15)

BRISTOL LEAGUE STATISTICS
(COMPILED BY STEPHEN McCORMACK)

Season	Div.	P	W	D	L	F	(Tries	Con	Pen	DG)	A	(Tries	Con	Pen	DG)	Most Points	Most Tries
87-88	1	10	4	1	5	171	(22	16	16	1)	145	(17	13	16	1)	58 - Jon Webb	3 - Andy Dunn
88-89	1	11	6	0	5	188	(24	10	21	3)	117	(13	4	16	3)	50 - Jon Webb	2 - by 8 players
89-90	1	11	4	0	7	136	(14	4	24	0)	144	(19	7	18	0)	47 - Jon Webb	2 - Paul Hull / John Davis
90-91	1	12	4	1	7	135	(16	7	17	2)	219	(32	20	16	1)	35 - Simon Hogg	4 - Julian Horrobin
91-92	1	12	4	0	8	192	(29	14	13	3)	174	(23	8	19	3)	29 - Mark Tainton	5 - Pete Stiff
92-93	1	12	6	0	6	148	(13	7	23	0)	169	(18	11	15	4)	68 - Mark Tainton	3 - Derek Eves
93-94	1	18	10	0	8	331	(33	20	40	2)	276	(23	13	44	1)	161 - Mark Tainton	8 - A. Saveriamutto
94-95	1	18	7	0	11	301	(21	11	56	2)	353	(32	17	49	4)	196 - Mark Tainton	6 - Derek Eves
95-96	1	18	8	0	10	329	(27	19	47	5)	421	(48	23	43	2)	120 - Mark Tainton	4 - Martin Corry
96-97	1	22	8	1	13	432	(48	30	44	0)	625	(76	37	52	5)	178 - Paul Burke	10 - David Tiueti
Totals		144	61	3	80	2363	(247	138	301	18)	2643	(301	153	288	24)		

	HOME	AWAY
BIGGEST WIN	(36pts) 50-14 v Liverpool St H 22.4.89	(32pts) 32-0 v Nottingham 16.11.91
BIGGEST DEFEAT	(38pts) 5-43 v Bath 30.3.96	(69pts) 7-76 v Bath 30.10.96
MOST POINTS SCORED	50-14 v Liverpool St H 22.4.89	33-31 v Sale 28.9.96
AGAINST	5-43 v Bath 30.3.96	7-76 v Bath 30.10.96

MOST CONSECUTIVE VICTORIES - 4   **MOST CONSECUTIVE DEFEATS - 7**

MOST TRIES IN A MATCH
(FOR) 10 v Rugby 28.3.92
(AGAINST) 11 v Bath 30.10.96 (A)

MOST APPEARANCES
FORWARD: 100 Dave Hinkins
BACK: 109(3) Paul Hull

CONSECUTIVE SCORING MATCHES
Scoring Tries - 3 - Alastair Saveriamutto
Scoring Points - 31 - Mark Tainton

CONSECUTIVE APPEARANCES
81 Derek Eves 11.3.88 - 4.3.95

MOST	in a SEASON	in a CAREER	in a MATCH
Points	196 Mark Tainton 94-95	637 Mark Tainton 87-97	26 Mark Tainton v Leicester 5.11.94 (H)
Tries	10 David Tiueti 96-97	23 Paul Hull 87-97	3 Mike Lloyd v Rugby 28.3.92 (H) / Derek Eves v Rugby 27.3.93 (H)
Conversions	27 Paul Burke 96-97	62 Mark Tainton 87-97	5 Jon Webb v Sale 24.10.87 (H)
Penalties	56 Mark Tainton 94-95	165 Mark Tainton 87-97	7 Mark Tainton v Leicester 5.11.94 (H)
Drop Goals	3 Simon Hogg 88-89 / Arwel Thomas 95-96	6 Mark Tainton 87-97	2 Simon Hogg v Leicester 9.3.91 (H)

BRISTOL PLAYING SQUAD

NAME	Ht	Wt	Birthdate	Birthplace	Club	Apps	Pts	T	C	P	DG

BACKS

NAME	Ht	Wt	Birthdate	Birthplace	Club	Apps	Pts	T	C	P	DG
Paul Hull	5.9	12.10	17.05.68	Lambeth							
England: 4, B, Emerging, u21, Colts.					Bristol	109+3	158	23	4	13	1
John Lewsey											
					Bristol	7+1	10	2	-	-	-
David Tiueti	6.0	14.2	06.06.73	Tonga	North Harbour (NZ)						
					Bristol	22	60	12	-	-	-
Fraser Waters	6.0	13.9	31.03.76	Cape Town (SA)	Bath	0+1	5	1	-	-	-
England: u21, Colts, Schools.					Bristol	14	10	2	-	-	-
Mark Denney	5.8	14.7	25.07.75	Epping Forest	Bedford	2	-	-	-	-	-
England: Students, u21, Colts, u18.					Bristol	38+1	20	4	-	-	-
Ben Breeze	5.10	13.0	08.04.74	Exeter							
					Bristol	27	15	3	-	-	-
Kevin Maggs	5.11	14.0	03.06.74								
England: Colts.					Bristol	31+2	15	3	-	-	-
Paul Burke	5.8	12.0	01.05.73	London	Cork Constitution						
Ireland: 10, A, u21. England: u21, Schools.					London Irish	21	57	-	3	12	5
					Bristol	19+1	17	-	-	-	-
Mark Tainton	5.7	12.0	10.03.69								
England: Colts.					Bristol	72+1	637	-	62	165	6
Robert Jones	5.8	11.8	10.11.65	Trebanos	Swansea						
Wales: 54. British Lions: 3					Bristol	17+1	15	3	-	-	-
Richard Smith											
					Bristol	2+1	5	1	-	-	-
Simon Martin	5.10	13.7	24.01.75	Thornbury							
					Bristol	10+1	5	1	-	-	-
Dean Dewdney					Clifton	6+1	-	-	-	-	-
					Bristol	2+3	-	-	-	-	-
Andy Down											
					Bristol	1+1	-	-	-	-	-

FORWARDS

NAME	Ht	Wt	Birthdate	Birthplace	Club	Apps	Pts	T	C	P	DG
Brian McConnell											
					Bristol	7+1	-	-	-	-	-
Dave Hinkins	6.0	17.0	20.10.66	Exeter	Moseley						
England: Emerging, Students, u18.					Bristol	100	-	-	-	-	-
Kris Fulman											
					Bristol	18	-	-	-	-	-
Mark Regan	5.11	16.2	28.01.72	Bristol							
England: 13, Emerging, u21, Colts, u18.					Bristol	66	20	4	-	-	-
Paul Adams	6.6	17.0	02.02.63								
					Bristol	48+2	-	-	-	-	-
Simon Shaw	6.9	19.0	01.09.73	Kenya							
England: 6, Students, Colts, u21, u18.					Bristol	56	15	3	-	-	-
Chad Eagle											
					Bristol	14	5	1	-	-	-
Martin Corry	6.5	17.0	12.10.73	Birmingham	Newcastle	24+1	40	8	-	-	-
England: 2, A, Emerging, u18.					Bristol	29	30	6	-	-	-
David Corkery	6.4	16.2	06.11.72	Cork							
Ireland: 21, A, u21, Schools.					Bristol	15+2	20	4	-	-	-
Eben Rollitt	6.3	16.5	23.11.72	Bristol	Richmond	2	-	-	-	-	-
England: Students, u21, u18.					Bristol	29	15	3	-	-	-
Richie Collins											
					Bristol	6	-	-	-	-	-
Craig Short											
					Bristol	3+2	5	1	-	-	-
Craig Barrow	6.6	17.0	26.02.69								
England: Students					Bristol	56+4	14	3	-	-	-

Memorial Ground, Filton Avenue, Horfield, Bristol. BS7 0AQ

Tel: 0117 908 5500   **Club Newsline:** 0839 44 66 33   **Fax:** 0117 908 5530
CAPACITY: 10,000   **SEATED:** 1,780   **STANDING:** Enclosure 1,200, Ground 7,020

SIMPLE DIRECTIONS:
  By Road: M4 to junction 19, M32 to junction 2, then join B4469 towards Horfield. At the 2nd set of traffic lights after 'Brunel Ford' and bus garage, ground on left
  Nearest Railway Station: Bristol Parkway or Bristol Temple Meads.

CAR PARKING: Limited spaces available at the ground. Street parking nearby

ADMISSION:
Season Tickets: Adults - Stand £140, Enclosure £90, Ground £75.
Students/OAPs - Stand £100, Enclosure £60, Ground £45.
Matchday: Adults - Stand £12, Enclosure £10, Ground £8.
Students/OAPs - £12, Enclosure £8, Ground £6.

CLUB SHOP: Monday - Friday 9.30-5.00, & matchdays from noon
CLUBHOUSE: Monday-Saturday 12.00-3.00, 6.00-11.00, Matchdays 12.00-11.00. Two bars with food available. Available for functions, contact Catering Manager Robert Laurence 0117 908 5506, 0117 908 5530 (Fax).

TRAINING NIGHTS: Tuesday and Thursday + daytime sessions.

Bristol's Player's Player of the Season: Chad Eagle

MATCHDAY PROGRAMME

Size	B5
Number of pages	48 plus cover
Price	£1
Programme Editor	John Harding (Media Liason)

Advertising Rates
Contact - Sports Programme Promotions 0117 977 0188

GLOUCESTER R.F.C.

NICKNAME: Cherry & whites   **FOUNDED:** 1873

President Reg Collins, 11 Gilpin Avenue, Hucclecote, Gloucester GL1 3AX
01452 614335 (H)

Chairman Alan Brinn, 108 Estcourt Road, Gloucester
01452 303722 (B)

Club Secretary Andy Mitchell, c/o Gloucester RFC, Kingsholm, Gloucester, GL1 3AX
01452 381087 (B), 01452 383321 (Fax)

Fixtures Secretary Eric Stephens, 1 Court Gardens, Hempstead, Gloucester.
01452 529000 (H), 01684 291777 (B), 01684 298777 (Fax)

Press Officer Jonathan Davis, c/o Gloucester R.F.C., as above
01452 381087 (B)   01452 383321 (Fax)

Director of Coaching Richard Hill, 01452 381087/301037

At the start of the season, rugby director Richard Hill declared a mid table league position as a realistic target for Gloucester. He delivered it too, but there were some fairly coronary inducing periods along the way. Indeed by October some good judges were already regarding the Cherry-and-Whites as bankers for League Two for 1997/98. Not unreasonably considering that the first five league games had been lost, most of them by the sort of margin called healthy, if you happen to be on the winning side.

Then on a chilly Sunday afternoon at Kingsholm, reports of Gloucester's demise turned out to be exaggerated. Eventual champions Wasps, were beaten in some style and the season was back on track. After that most things went right with a place in the Pilkington Cup Semi-Finals, where the home side were, they considered, a shade unlucky to lose to Leicester, an opinion which was reinforced by a floodlit win over the same opposition just a few evenings later.

Gloucester were then freed from relegation worries for the first time in three seasons. A side which had looked mere points fodder earlier on had become a team to be reckoned with and Kingsholm had regained much of it's mythology of invincibility.

The architects of the revival were undoubtedly the pack, inspirationally led by Dave Sims and entirely composed of locally bred players. Even Leicester's famous ABC club had problems with the front row trio of Deacon, Greening and Windo while Sims lock partner Rob Fidler developed well enough to be considered for England's Argentina tour. As for the back row, Glanville, Devereaux and Carter just never stopped running.

But it was by no means all forward play. Macletoft in his first season at fly half was a revelation and topped the national points table. Chris Catling ended his season recognised as one of the best young full backs in the country, and scrum half Scott Benton is attracting considerable attention too. Greening's arrival on the international scene is no more than the Kingsholm faithful have been expecting for a couple of years.

Imaginative signings in the post season period should provide Gloucester with a very formidable three quarter line indeed. Add that to a battle hardened pack and the future looks bright.

Gloucester RFC: Back Row (L-R); Laurie Beck, Nathan Carter, Pete Glanville, Simon Devereux, Martin Roberts, Craig Emmerson, Audley Lumsden, Eral Anderson. Middle Row; John Fidler (Team Manager), Mike Peters, Trevor Woodham, Tony Windo, Phil Vickery, Rob Fidler, Ed Pearce, Andy Metcalfe, Alastair Saverimutto, John Brain (Asst Coach), Richard Hill (Director of Coaching). Front Row; Andy Stanley, Andy Deacon, Phil Greening, Dave Sims (Capt), Scott Benton, Mark Mapletoft, Chris Catling.

Colours: Cherry, white, black.   **Change colours:** Black, red

87

No	Ven.	Date	Opponents	Att.	Res.	Score	Scorers
1	(A)	31.08	v Harlequins	3654	L	19-75	Lloyd(t)Mulraine(t)Osborne(t2c)
2	(H)	07.09	v Sale	4014	L	12-16	Mapletoft(4p)
3	(A)	14.09	v Saracens	4111	L	11-41	Lloyd(t)Mapletoft(2p)
4	(H)	21.09	v Bath	5950	L	29-45	Deacon(t)Sims(t)Greening(t)Mapletoft(c4p)
5	(A)	28.09	v Leicester	9597	L	14-32	Anderson(t)Mapletoft(3p)
6	(H)	06.10	v Wasps	5886	W	28-23	Saveriamutto(t)Catling(t)Mapletoft(6p)
7	(A)	09.11	v W Hartlepool	1800	W	23-14	Lumsden(t)Mapletoft(t2c3p)
8	(A)	16.11	v Orrell	1800	W	49- 3	Saveriamutto(2t)Benton(t)Windo(T)Lumsden(t)Peters(t)Mapletoft(5c3p)
9	(H)	07.12	v London Irish	3635	W	29-19	Benton(t)Roberts(t)Mapletoft(2c4pdg)
10	(A)	11.01	v London Irish	2362	W	21-20	Glanville(t)Fidler(t)Mapletoft(c2pdg)
11	(H)	18.01	v W Hartlepool	4072	W	37-10	Lloyd(3t)Windo(t)Mapletoft(t3cpdg)
12	(H)	08.02	v Orrell	4464	W	30- 0	Peters(t)Lloyd(t)Mapletoft(2t2c2p)
13	(A)	18.02	v Bristol	5406	L	13-18	Glanville(t)Catling(dg)Mapletoft(cp)
14	(H)	04.03	v Northampton	4748	W	19- 6	Benton(t)Mapletoft(c4p)
15	(A)	09.03	v Wasps	4007	L	10-36	Catling(t)Mapletoft(cp)
16	(H)	05.04	v Saracens	4523	W	9- 6	Mapletoft(p2dg)
17	(H)	08.04	v Leicester	6310	W	32-30	Lumsden(t)Greening(t)Mapletoft(2c6p)
18	(A)	12.04	v Sale	2614	L	12-52	Lumsden(t)Mapletoft(tc)
19	(H)	19.04	v Harlequins	6106	L	11-27	Benton(t)Mapletoft(2p)
20	(H)	26.04	v Bristol	4931	D	20-20	Carter(t)Lloyd(t)Mapletoft(2c2p)
21	(A)	30.04	v Bath	7100	L	21-71	Deacon(t)Saveriamutto(t)Mapletoft(t2p)
22	(A)	03.05	v Northampton	4620	W	27-25	Catling(t)Lumsden(t)Mapletoft(c5p)

1996-97 HIGHLIGHTS

LEAGUE DEBUTS:
Dave Timmington, Charlie Mulraine, Paul Vickery, Richard Ward, Rob York, Chris Catling, Ed Pearce, Craig Emmerson, Eral Anderson, Audley Lumsden, Nathan Carter, Chris Fortey.

TRY ON DEBUT:
Charlie Mulraine.

PLAYERS USED: 35 plus 2 as replacement.

EVER PRESENT: None - most appearances 21 David Sims, Mark Mapletoft and Rob Fidler

❏ Only West Hartlepool and Orrell scored fewer tries.

❏ Stopped the opposition scoring tries in five games the best record in the division.

❏ Suffered worst ever away defeat on the opening day of the season. They fielded their infamous second team and were heavily beaten 19-75.

❏ In the above game they conceded a record 11 tries. They equalled this feat in their late season hammering at Bath.

❏ Scored more tries away from home.

❏ Captain Dave Sims became the second player after Ian Smith to reach 100 league appearances.

❏ Mark Mapletoft re-wrote Gloucester's record books in a tremendous season which ended with his selection for England's summer tour to Argentina. He ended the season with 269 points, third on the division one all time list, to destroy the club record of 85 which Mapletoft shared with Tim Smith.
His 25 conversions and 58 penalties easily beat the previous records of 12 and 24 respectively held by Tim Smith.
Mapletoft became only the second Gloucester player to pass career totals of 200 and 300 after Tim Smith.

	Pts	T	C	P	D	Apps	Ave.
Tim Smith	593	10	57	142	2	94	6.31
Mark Mapletoft	375	8	34	84	5	34	11.03

He also equalled and then broke the club record for points in a match. First he equalled Tim Smith's record of 20 and in the famous win against Leicester he converted both tries and kicked six penalties for a 22 point haul. The six penalties equalled the club record he already shared with Tim Smith

❏ Mid-season they set a club record of seven successive wins.

GLOUCESTER'S COURAGE LEAGUE MATCH DETAILS 1996-97

No.	15	14	13	12	11	10	9	1	2	3	4	5	6	7	8	Replacements
1	Hart	Lloyd	Caskie	Osborne	Timmington	Kimber	Powles		Hawker	Vickery	Ward	Sims	York	Smith	Devereux	
2	Catling	Anderson	Saveriamutto	Roberts	Lloyd	Mapletoft	Benton	Windo	Greening	Deacon	Fidler	Sims	Glanville	Carter	Devereux	Edwards(7)
3	Catling	Timmington	Emmerson	Roberts	Lloyd	Mulraine	Benton	Windo	Greening	Deacon	Fidler	Sims	Glanville	Carter	Devereux	Caskie(10)
4	Catling	Holford	Emmerson	Roberts	Lloyd	Mulraine	Benton	Windo	Greening	Deacon	Fidler	Sims	Glanville	Carter	Devereux	Beck(9)
5	Catling	Anderson	Emmerson	Roberts	Lloyd	Mapletoft	Benton	Windo	Greening	Deacon	Fidler	Sims	Smith	Pearce	Devereux	
6	Catling	Lumsden	Saveriamutto	Roberts	Lloyd	Mapletoft	Benton	Windo	Greening	Deacon	Fidler	Sims	Glanville	Carter	Devereux	Vickery(3),Pearce(6)
7	Catling	Saveriamutto	Saveriamutto	Roberts	Lumsden	Mapletoft	Benton	Windo	Greening	Deacon	Fidler	Sims	Glanville	Pearce	Devereux	
8	Catling	Peters	Saveriamutto	Roberts	Lumsden	Mapletoft	Benton	Windo	Greening	Deacon	Fidler	Sims	Glanville	Pearce	Devereux	Stanley(5),Beck(9),Fortey(2)
9	Catling	Peters	Saveriamutto	Roberts	Lumsden	Mapletoft	Benton	Windo	Greening	Deacon	Fidler	Sims	Glanville	Carter	Devereux	Caskie(13)
10	Catling	Peters	Caskie	Roberts	Lumsden	Mapletoft	Benton	Windo	Greening	Deacon	Fidler	Sims	Glanville	Carter	Devereux	Hart(10)
11	Catling	Peters	Caskie	Roberts	Lumsden	Mapletoft	Benton	Windo	Greening	Deacon	Fidler	Sims	Pearce	Carter	Devereux	Mulraine(9)
12	Catling	Peters	Caskie	Roberts	Lloyd	Mapletoft	Benton	Windo	Greening	Deacon	Fidler	Sims	Pearce	Carter	Devereux	Fortey(2)
13	Catling	Peters	Caskie	Roberts	Lloyd	Mapletoft	Benton	Windo	Greening	Deacon	Fidler	Sims	Pearce	Carter	Devereux	
14	Catling	Peters	Caskie	Roberts	Lloyd	Mapletoft	Benton	Windo	Greening	Deacon	Fidler	Sims	Glanville	Carter	Devereux	Vickery(3)
15	Catling	Peters	Caskie	Roberts	Lloyd	Mapletoft	Benton	Windo	Greening	Deacon	Fidler	Sims	Glanville	Carter	Devereux	Stanley(7),Kimber(10),Beck(9)
16	Catling	Peters	Emmerson	Roberts	Lloyd	Mapletoft	Benton	Windo	Greening	Deacon	Fidler	Sims	Glanville	Carter	Devereux	Lumsden(15)Stanley(6)Woodman(1)
17	Lumsden	Peters	Emmerson	Roberts	Lloyd	Mapletoft	Benton	Windo	Greening	Deacon	Fidler	Sims	Stanley	Carter	Devereux	
18	Lumsden	Peters	Emmerson	Roberts	Lloyd	Mapletoft	Benton	Windo	Greening	Deacon	Fidler	Sims	Stanley	Carter	Devereux	Woodman(1)Caskie(12)
19	Lumsden	Emmerson	Emmerson	Roberts	Lloyd	Benton	Benton	Windo	Greening	Deacon	Fidler	Sims	Stanley	Carter	Devereux	Hawker(2)
20	Catling	Peters	Emmerson	Lloyd	Lloyd	Benton	Benton	Windo	Greening	Deacon	Fidler	Sims	Stanley	Carter	Devereux	Beck(9)
21	Catling	Lumsden	Emmerson	Caskie	Lloyd		Beck	Windo	Hawker	Deacon	Fidler	Sims	Stanley	Stanley	Devereux	Saveriamutto(12)Woodman(tr3)
22	Catling	Lumsden	Emmerson	Saveriamutto	Lloyd	Mapletoft	Beck	Windo	Hawker	Deacon	Fidler	Sims	Glanville	Carter	Devereux	Stanley(7)Woodman(2)

GLOUCESTER LEAGUE STATISTICS
(COMPILED BY STEPHEN McCORMACK)

Season	Div.	P	W	D	L	F (Tries Con Pen DG)	A (Tries Con Pen DG)	Most Points	Most Tries
87-88	1	10	6	1	3	206 (32 18 14 0)	121 (9 2 23 4)	42 - Nick Marment	6 - Jim Breeze
88-89	1	11	7	1	3	215 (31 14 21 0)	112 (14 7 13 1)	85 - Tim Smith	6 - Mike Hamlin
89-90	1	11	8	1	2	214 (32 10 21 1)	139 (16 9 19 0)	75 - Tim Smith	6 - Derek Morgan
90-91	1	12	6	0	6	207 (29 17 19 0)	163 (19 9 22 1)	75 - Tim Smith	3 - by 4 players Ian Smith, Chris Dee, Derek Morgan & Paul Ashmead.
91-92	1	12	7	1	4	193 (19 12 29 2)	168 (16 10 26 2)	81 - Tim Smith	5 - Simon Morris
92-93	1	12	6	0	6	173 (17 8 24 0)	151 (12 5 25 2)	71- Tim Smith	3 - Tim Smith Derek Morgan
93-94	1	18	6	2	10	247 (21 11 36 4)	356 (29 23 53 2)	82 - Tim Smith	3 - Paul Holford & Bruce Fenley
94-95	1	18	6	1	11	269 (25 15 32 6)	336 (37 17 37 2)	85 - Mark Mapletoft	8 Paul Holford
95-96	1	18	6	0	12	275 (20 8 46 7)	370 (38 21 40 6)	79 - Tim Smith	5 - Paul Holford
96-97	1	22	11	1	10	476 (46 27 58 6)	589 (62 46 54 0)	269 - Mark Mapletoff	7 - Mike Lloyd
Totals		144	69	8	67	2475 (272 140 300 26)	2505 (252 149 312 20)		

HOME

BIGGEST WIN	(54pts) 61-7 v Sale 16.4.88
BIGGEST DEFEAT	(16pts) 29-45 v Bath 21.9.96
MOST POINTS SCORED	61-7 v Sale 16.4.88
AGAINST	29-45 v Bath 21.9.96

AWAY

(46pts) 49-3 v Orrell 16.11.96
(56pts) 19-75 v Harlequins 31.8.96
49-3 v Orrell 16.11.96
19-75 v Harlequins 31.8.96

MOST CONSECUTIVE VICTORIES - 7

MOST CONSECUTIVE DEFEATS - 7

MOST TRIES IN A MATCH
(FOR) 11 v Sale 16.4.88
(AGAINST) 11 v Harlequins 31.8.96
v Bath 30.4.97

MOST APPEARANCES
FORWARD: 108 Ian Smith
BACK: 94 Tim Smith

CONSECUTIVE SCORING MATCHES
Scoring Tries - 3 - Jim Breeze, Tim Smith,
Mike Hamlin & Paul Holford.
Scoring Points - 21 - Mark Mapletoft

CONSECUTIVE APPEARANCES
47 Dave Sims 11.4.92 - 25.3.95

MOST	in a SEASON	in a CAREER	in a MATCH
Points	269 Mark Mapletoft 96-97	593 Tim Smith 87-96	22 Mark Mapletoft v Leicester 8.4.97 (H)
Tries	8 Paul Holford 94-95	17 Paul Holford -96	3 Derek Morgan v Rosslyn P 11.11.89 (H) Mike Lloyd v W. Hartlepool 18.1.97 (H)
Conversions	23 Mark Mapletoft 96-97	57 Tim Smith 87-96	6 Paul Mansell v Sale 16.4.88 (H)
Penalties	58 Mark Mapletoft 96-97	142 Tim Smith 87-96	6 Tim Smith v Harlequins 12.3.90 (H) Mark Mapletoft v Wasps 6.10.96 (H) v Leicester 8.4.97 (H)
Drop Goals	6 Martyn Kimber 94-95/ 95-96	12 Martyn Kimber 94-95	2 Martyn Kimber v Bath 4.3.95 (A) Mark Mapletoft v Saracens 5.4.97 (H)

GLOUCESTER PLAYING SQUAD

NAME	Ht	Wt	Birthdate	Birthplace	Club	Apps	Pts	T	C	P	DG
BACKS											
Audley Lumsden	6.0	13.7	06.06.67	London	Bath	44+1	86	18	-	-	-
England: A, B, Students, Colts.					Gloucester	9+1	25	5	-	-	-
Chris Catling	6.2	13.7	17.06.76		Exeter	6	5	1	-	-	-
England: u21, Students, Schools.					Gloucester	19	18	3	-	-	1
Mike Lloyd	6.2	16.0	21.07.70		Keynsham						
England: u21.					Bristol	22	5	1	-	-	-
					Bath	5	5	1	-	-	-
					Gloucester	23	35	7	-	-	-
Mike Peters	6.0	14.0	21.10.68	Trinidad							
					Gloucester	15	10	2	-	-	-
Craig Emmerson	5.11	13.0	14.09.71	Halifax	West Hartlepool						
England: Colts					Harlequins		-	-	-	-	-
					Morley		-	-	-	-	-
					Gloucester	10	-	-	-	-	-
Martin Roberts	6.3	15.2		Gloucester	Cheltenham						
					Gloucester	47+1	66	3	6	13	-
Alastair Saveriamutto	5.9	12.8	04.03.70		Bristol	16	40	8	-	-	-
					Coventry	8	8	1	-	-	1
					Gloucester	6+1	20	4	-	-	-
Mark Mapletoft	5.7	13.0	25.12.71	Mansfield	Rugby	41	201	6	14	45	3
England: 1, A, u21, u18, 7s.					Gloucester	34+1	375	8	34	84	5
Scott Benton	5.11	13.0	08.09.74	Bradford	Morley						
England: Colts					Gloucester	23	20	4	-	-	-
Laurie Beck	5.10	12.7	02.01.70	Cheltenham	Cheltenham						
South West: u21.					Gloucester	2+4	-	-	-	-	-
Dan Caskie	5.8	13.4	12.12.67	Almondsbury							
Scotland: B, u21, Students.					Gloucester	91+3	17	4	-	-	-
Martyn Kimber	6.0	13.10	20.09.68	Auckland	Stroud						
					Gloucester	34	60	1	2	5	12
Charlie Mulraine	5.8	12.10	24.12.73	Leamington							
					Gloucester	3+1	5	1	-	-	-
FORWARDS											
Tony Windo	6.0	16.0	30.04.69	Gloucester							
England: u21.					Gloucester	55	30	6	-	-	-
Andy Deacon	6.2	17.0	21.02.65	Gloucester	Longlevens						
					Gloucester	66+1	25	5	-	-	-
John Hawker	5.11	13.9	17.05.63	Gloucester	Matson						
					Gloucester	56+1	8	2	-	-	-
Phil Greening	5.11	17.0	03.10.75	Gloucester	Spartans						
England: 3, A, u21, u16.					Gloucester	28+1	10	2	-	-	-
Dave Sims	6.7	18.0	22.11.69	Gloucester	Longlevens						
England: A, B, u21.					Gloucester	104	38	8	-	-	-
Rob Fidler	6.5	17.8	21.09.74	Gloucester	Cheltenham						
England: u21, Colts.					Gloucester	32	5	1	-	-	-
Nathan Carter	6.0	15.0	22.06.72	Gloucester	Gordon League						
					Gloucester	16	5	1	-	-	-
Simon Deveraux	6.3	16.10	20.10.68	Gloucester	Spartans						
					Gloucester	36+2	-	-	-	-	-
Pete Glanville	6.3	16.3	10.06.71	Gloucester	Longlevens						
					Gloucester	49	10	2	-	-	-
Andy Stanley	6.0	14.7	15.09.65	Gloucester	Gordon League						
					Gloucester	19+4	-	-	-	-	-
Ed Pearce	6.6	17.0	02.09.75	Bristol	Bath	2+1	-	-	-	-	-
England: u21, u18.					Gloucester	7+1	-	-	-	-	-
Paul Vickery											
					Gloucester	2+3	-	-	-	-	-
Trevor Woodman											
					Gloucester	0+4	-	-	-	-	-
Chris Fortey	6.0	16.7	25.08.75	Gloucester							
					Gloucester	2+1	-	-	-	-	-

Kingsholm, Gloucester. GL1 3AX.

Tel: 01452 381087   **Fax:** 01452 383321

CAPACITY: 11,000   **SEATED:** 1,250   **STANDING:** 9,750

SIMPLE DIRECTIONS:
    By Road: From M5 junction 11 towards Gloucester, first roundabout turn right towards Gloucester/Wales, next roundabout turn left, next roundabout go straight over and the ground is 300 yards on the right.
    Nearest Railway Station: Gloucester (B.R.). The station is about a 10 minute walk from the ground.

CAR PARKING: 250 spaces available at the ground, £5

ADMISSION: Season tickets
               Seated - Adults £150; OAPs £110; Juniors (u16) £75.
               Standing - Adults £80; OAPs £60; Juniors (u16) £40.
               Matchday tickets
               Seated - Adults £14; OAPs & Juniors no concessions
               Standing - Adults £10; OAPs £8; Juniors (u16) £6.

CLUB SHOP: Yes - manager Jonathan Davis. 01452 381087.

CLUBHOUSE: Normal Licensing Hours, snacks available
    Function room: Available for hire, capacity 150; contact Mrs D Long 01452 422070.

TRAINING NIGHTS: Monday, Tuesday and Thursday.

Gloucester Captain Peter Glanville

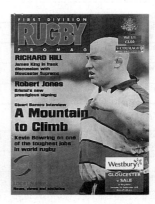

MATCHDAY PROGRAMME

Size	B5
Number of pages	46
Price	£2
Programme Editor	Promag
	01179 779188
Advertising Rates	Contact Promag

HARLEQUIN F.C.

NICKNAME: Quins   FOUNDED: 1866

President David Brooks, c/o NEC Harlequins FC, Stoop Memorial Ground,
Craneford Way, Twickenham TW2 7SQ. 0181 892 0822, 0181 744 2764 (Fax).
Chief Executive Donald Kerr, c/o NEC Harlequins FC, as above
Company Secretary Guy Williams, c/o NEC Harlequins FC, as above
Marketing Director Jamie Salmon, c/o NEC Harlequins FC, as above
Director of Coaching Andy Keast, c/o NEC Harlequins FC, as above
Media Liason Alex Saward, 152 Woodseer Street, London, E1 5HQ,
0171 377 1151 (Tel & Fax), 0850 595768 (Mobile)

The club made a positive response to the demands of professional rugby in 1996/97. Planning consent was obtained for the first phase of the redevelopment of the Stoop Memorial Ground and the playing side was strengthened with players from France, Wales and the United States, as well as by two recruits from the world of Rugby League. The 4,500 seats and 22 hospitality boxes in the new East Stand were in use by February and by the end of the season the superb bar and catering facilities had been completed, while on the field the players had taken the club to the Quarter Finals of the Heineken Cup, the Semi Finals of the Pilkington Cup and a third place in the Courage League.

The timing of the fixtures in the league meant that Quins' did not meet any of the more fancied sides in the competition until the season was a couple of months old. It also gave them a tough run in at the end of the competition. Quins' early lead in the championship was dented by the defeat at Sale at the end of October. This was followed swiftly by losses to Bath and Leicester which ended the club's sojourn at the top of the table. After Christmas wins against Wasps at Loftus Road and against Bath the following week gave them a pause for thought but defeat at London Irish finally ended Quins' remaining hopes for the title. In previous years this might have been the excuse for the players to ease up but with the battle for European places still being hotly disputed by half a dozen clubs there was to be no respite. By winning their next five league matches, which included away wins at Gloucester and Leicester, Quins made certain of their place in Europe for the second year running.

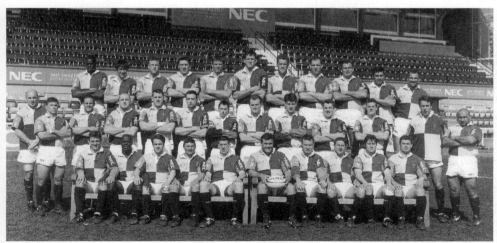

NEC Harlequins   Photo - Joe McCabe

Colours: Light blue, magenta, chocolate, french grey, light green & black.   **Change colours:** None.

HARLEQUINS

No	Ven.	Date	Opponents	Att.	Res.	Score	Scorers
1	(H)	31.08	v Gloucester	3654	W	75-19	O'Leary(4t)Mensah(t)Snow(t)Staples(t)Benezech(t)Cabannes(t)Bromley(t)PTry(t)Carling(7c2p)
2	(A)	07.09	v W Hartlepool	2200	W	41-21	Challinor(2t)Luger(2t)Mensah(t)Walshe(t)Carling(4cp)
3	(H)	14.09	v London Irish	4599	W	66- 7	Corcoran(3tcp)Wood(2t)Jenkins(2t)Staples(2t)Connolly(t)O'Leary(t)Carling(3c)
4	(A)	21.09	v Bristol	4825	W	35-24	Staples(t)Wood(t)O'Leary(t)Connolly(t)PTry(t)Carling(4c)Corcoran(c)
5	(A)	28.09	v Northampton	7602	W	20-15	Staples(t)Harries(t)Carling(tcp)
6	(H)	05.10	v Orrell	3335	W	89-18	Harries(3t)Paul(2t)Connolly(2t)Bromley(2t)Benezech(t)Davison(t)Watson(t)PTry(t)Carling(t8cp)
7	(A)	30.10	v Sale	3929	L	13-24	Walshe(t)Connolly(t)Corcoran(p)
8	(A)	07.12	v Bath	8500	L	20-35	Harries(t)Challinor(t2c2p)
9	(H)	28.12	v Leicester	5772	L	18-34	Harries(2t)Challinor(cp)Pilgrim(p)
10	(A)	05.01	v Wasps	9766	W	19-17	Connolly(t)Lacroix(c4p)
11	(H)	11.01	v Bath	5566	W	22- 6	Staples(t)Lacroix(c4pdg)
12	(A)	19.01	v Saracens	5975	L	20-28	Harries(t)O'Leary(t)Lacroix(2c2p)
13	(H)	08.02	v Sale	2889	L	30-31	Gareth Llewellyn(t)Harries(t)Lacroix(c6p)
14	(A)	08.03	v Orrell	2360	W	56-20	Chapman(3t)O'Leary(2t)Mensah(t)Davison(t)Lacroix(t5c2p)
15	(H)	22.03	v W Hartlepool	1903	W	48-10	Walshe(3t)Corcoran(2t)O'Leary(t)Keyter(t)Lacroix(5cp)
16	(A)	05.04	v London Irish	3960	L	19-20	Chapman(t)Lacroix(c3pdg)
17	(H)	09.04	v Saracens	4614	W	27- 0	Mensah(t)O'Leary(t)Staples(t)Lacroix(3c2p)
18	(H)	15.04	v Bristol	2058	W	29- 6	Wood(2t)O'Leary(t)Lacroix(c3pdg)
19	(A)	19.04	v Gloucester	6106	W	27-11	Williams(t)O'Leary(t)Lacroix(t3c2p)
20	(A)	26.04	v Leicester	12504	W	13-12	O'Leary(t)Lacroix(c2p)
21	(H)	30.04	v Gloucester	3654	W	36-16	Mensah(2t)Mullins(t)O'Leary(t)Wood(t)Lacroix(4cp)
22	(H)	03.05	v Wasps	6789	L	22-42	Allison(t)Cabannes(t)Keyter(t)Lacroix(cp)Corcoran(c)

1996-97 HIGHLIGHTS

LEAGUE DEBUTS:
Keith Wood, Laurant Benezech, Gareth Llewellyn, Laurant Cabannes, Dan Luger, Gary Connolly, Michael Corcoran, Glyn Llewellyn, Huw Harries, Robbie Paul, Thierry Lacroix, Dominic Chapman, Tom Billups, Luke Gross, Altan Ozdemir, Simon Owen, Richard Sharples

PLAYERS USED: 37 plus 3 as replacement.

EVER PRESENT: Laurant Cabannes

❏ Quins were the only club in the division to score a try in every game.

❏ Both Michael Corcoran and Domonic Chapman scored hat-tricks of tries on their league debuts.

❏ At the start of the season Paul Challinor held the seasonal record for conversions with 18. This was broken twice during the season. First Will Carling took on the kicking duties and took Challinor's record on to 27. On his arrival former French international Thierry Lacroix took over the kicking responsibilities and proceeded to rattle up 29 conversions and relieve Carling of his record.

❏ Second highest try scorers in the division after Bath - 96 to 116.

❏ Star of the show was Thierry Lacroix who helped himself to a number of club records. He equalled the first division record for reaching a 100 points in just seven games. Next to go was Kent Bray's record of 143 points in a season as Lacroix pushed the record out to 176 and an impressive record of 13.5 points per game.

	Pts	T	C	P	D	Apps	Ave.
Thierry Lacroix 96-97	176	2	29	33	3	13	13.53
Kent Bray 93-94	143	1	12	38		16	8.94

❏ Not to be out done winger Daren O'Leary broke the club record for tries in a season for the second successive season. This time round he notched up 15 one more than last season when he set a new club and division record. O'Leary now lies second on the division one all-time list with the best strike rate for anyone with 40 tries or more.

	Tries	Apps	Try Every
Jeremy Guscott	48	98	2.04 games
Daren O'Leary	44	72	1.64 games
Rory Underwood	43	97	2.25 games
Tony Swift	43	90	2.09 games

Included in O'Leary's total are three tries in 10 appearances for Saracens in 1992-93.

HARLEQUIN'S COURAGE LEAGUE MATCH DETAILS 1996-97

#	15	14	13	12	11	10	9	1	2	3	4	5	6	7	8	Replacements
1	Staples	O'Leary	Carling	Mensah	Bromley	Challinor	Kitchen	Leonard	Wood	Benezech	Snow	Ga Llewellyn	Davison	Cabannes	Allison	Pilgrim(14),Pickup(6)
2	Staples	O'Leary	Carling	Mensah	Luger	Challinor	Walshe	Leonard	Wood	Mullins	Snow	Ga Llewellyn	Jenkins	Cabannes	Davison	Davison(8)
3	Staples	O'Leary	Carling	Connolly	Corcoran	Challinor	Harries	Leonard	Wood	Benezech	Gl Llewellyn		Jenkins	Cabannes	Davison	Mensah(10),Brown(2)
4	Staples	O'Leary	Carling	Connolly	Corcoran	Challinor	Harries	Leonard	Wood	Benezech	Gl Llewellyn		Jenkins	Cabannes	Davison	Pickup(7)
5	Staples	O'Leary	Connolly	Mensah	Paul	Carling	Harries	Leonard	Wood	Benezech	Gl Llewellyn		Jenkins	Cabannes	Davison	Pickup(6)
6	Staples	O'Leary	Connolly	Paul	Bromley	Carling	Harries	Leonard	Wood	Benezech	Gl Llewellyn	Snow	Watson	Cabannes	Davison	Wright(9)
7	Williams	O'Leary	Connolly	Paul	Corcoran	Carling	Walshe	Leonard	Wood	Benezech	Gl Llewellyn		Jenkins	Cabannes	Davison	Wright(9)
8	Bromley	Bromley	Carling	Mensah	Luger	Mensah	Harries	Mullins	Wood	Benezech	Gl Llewellyn		Jenkins	Cabannes	Davison	Brown(15),Allison(8),Paul(14)
9	Pilgrim	O'Leary	Carling	Connolly	Bromley	Challinor	Harries	Leonard	Wood	Benezech	Snow		Allison	Cabannes	Davison	Pickup(5)
10	Paul	Luger	Carling	Connolly	Mensah	Lacroix	Harries	Leonard	Delaney	Benezech	Gl Llewellyn		Jenkins	Cabannes	Davison	Watson(6),Wright(11)
11	Staples	O'Leary	Paul	Mensah	Luger	Lacroix	Harries	Leonard	Woods	Benezech	Gl Llewellyn		Jenkins	Cabannes	Davison	Mullins(1),Williams(11),Harries(15)
12	Staples	O'Leary	Carling	Mensah	Luger	Lacroix	Harries	Leonard	Delaney	Benezech	Gl Llewellyn		Watson	Cabannes	Davison	
13	Staples	O'Leary	Mensah	Carling	Luger	Lacroix	Harries	Leonard	Delaney	Benezech	Gl Llewellyn		Watson	Cabannes	Davison	Watson(4)
14	Pilgrim	O'Leary	Mensah	Keyter	Chapman	Lacroix	Harries	Leonard	Billups	Benezech	Gl Llewellyn	Ga Llewellyn	Jenkins	Cabannes	Davison	Allison(6)
15	Challinor	O'Leary	Keyter	Keyter	Corcoran	Lacroix	Harries	Leonard	Billups	Benezech	Ga Llewellyn	Gross	Jenkins	Watson	Davison	Mullins(1),Williams(15)
16	Chapman	O'Leary	Carling	Mensah	Williams	Williams	Walshe	Leonard	Billups	Mullins	Ga Llewellyn	Gross	Jenkins	Cabannes	Davison	Harries(9),Pickup(6)
17	Staples	O'Leary	Carling	Mensah	Williams	Lacroix	Walshe	Leonard	Wood	Benezech	Ga Llewellyn	Gross	Jenkins	Cabannes	Davison	Harries(9),Pickup(6)
18	Staples	O'Leary	Carling	Mensah	Williams	Lacroix	Harries	Leonard	Wood	Ozdemir	Ga Llewellyn	Gross	Jenkins	Cabannes	Davison	Keyter(15),Delaney(2),Allison(tr8)
19	Staples	O'Leary	Carling	Mensah	Williams	Lacroix	Wright	Leonard	Wood	Ozdemir	Ga Llewellyn	Gross	Jenkins	Cabannes	Davison	Benezech(3),Allison(8),Keyter(12)
20	Staples	O'Leary	Carling	Mensah	Bromley	Lacroix	Wright	Leonard	Wood	Benezech	Ga Llewellyn	Gross	Allison	Cabannes	Davison	Corcoran(11),Keyter(15),Owen(6)
21	Staples	O'Leary	Carling	Mensah	Williams	Lacroix	Walshe	Leonard	Wood	Ozdemir	Snow	Gross	Owen	Cabannes	Davison	Keyter(13),Sharples(9),Delaney(2),Leonard(3),Pickup(8)
22	Staples	O'Leary	Keyter	Lacroix	Corcoran	Challinor	Sharples	Leonard	Billups	Benezech	Ga Llewellyn	Gross	Allison	Cabannes	Davison	Mullins(3),Delaney(6),Owen(8),Davies(12)

HARLEQUINS LEAGUE STATISTICS
(COMPILED BY STEPHEN McCORMACK)

Season	Div.	P	W	D	L	F	(Tries	Con	Pen	DG)	A	(Tries	Con	Pen	DG)	Most Points	Most Tries
87-88 Harriman	1	11	6	1	4	261	(38	26	18	1)	128	(19	5	11	3)	58 - Stuart Thresher 11	- Andrew
88-89	1	11	5	0	6	194	(25	17	18	2)	184	(23	16	20	0)	71 - Stuart Thresher 4	- Jon Eagle, Mickey Skinner
89-90	1	11	6	0	5	218	(26	15	26	2)	180	(22	10	21	3)	114 - David Pears	5 - Craig Luxton
90-91	1	12	8	0	4	267	(32	20	28	5)	162	(17	8	24	2)	120 - David Pears	9 - Andrew Harriman
91-92	1	12	5	1	6	213	(27	15	23	2)	207	(28	16	18	3)	109 - David Pears	4 - David Pears
92-93	1	12	5	1	6	197	(23	11	19	1)	187	(17	9	26	2)	57 - Stuart Thresher	3 - by 4 players Will Carling, Stuart Thresher, Paul Challinor & Rob Glenister.
93-94	1	18	8	0	10	333	(30	15	50	1)	287	(34	18	27	0)	143 - Kent Bray	11 - Daren O'Leary
94-95	1	18	6	1	11	275	(27	10	37	3)	348	(38	25	32	4)	103 - Paul Challinor	4 - Peter Mensah
95-96	1	18	13	0	5	524	(68	32	27	13)	314	(26	11	51	3)	112 - Paul Challinor	14 - Daren O'Leary
96-97	1	22	15	0	7	745	(96	62	44	3)	416	(47	23	41	4)	176 - Thierry Lacroix	15 - Daren O'Leary
Totals		145	78	4	63	3227	(392	223	290	33)	2413	(271	141	271	24)		

HOME		AWAY

BIGGEST WIN (71pts) 89-18 v Orrell 5.10.96
(70pts) 91-21 v West Hartlepool 23.3.96

BIGGEST DEFEAT (31pts) 26-57 v Wasps 17.9.94
(26pts) 15-41 v Bath 6.4.96

MOST POINTS SCORED 89-18 v Orrell 5.10.96
91-21 v West Hartlepool 23.3.96

AGAINST 26-57 v Wasps 17.9.94
15-41 v Bath 6.4.96

MOST CONSECUTIVE VICTORIES - 6
MOST CONSECUTIVE DEFEATS - 4

MOST TRIES IN A MATCH
(FOR) 14 v West Hartlepool 23.3.96, v Orrell 5.10.96
(AGAINST) 9 v Wasps 17.9.94

MOST APPEARANCES
FORWARD: 117(2) Andy Mullins
BACK: 93 Will Carling

CONSECUTIVE APPEARANCES
42 Andy Mullins 16.11.91 - 30.4.94

CONSECUTIVE SCORING MATCHES
Scoring Tries - 5 - Daren O'Leary
Scoring Points - 13 - Thierry Lacroix

MOST	in a SEASON	in a CAREER	in a MATCH
Points	176 Thierry Lacroix 96-97	431 David Pears 89-96	27 David Pears v Bedford 14.10.89 (A)
Tries	15 Daren O'Leary 96-97	44 Daren O'Leary 93-96	4 Daren O'Leary v Gloucester 31.8.96 (H)
Conversions	29 Thierry Lacroix 96-97	57 David Pears 89-96	9 Paul Challinor v W Hartlepool 23.3.96 (A)
Penalties	38 Kent Bray 93-94	83 David Pears 89-96	7 David Pears v Rosslyn Park 7.12.91 (A)
Drop Goals	7 David Pears 95-96	14 David Pears 89-96	3 David Pears v Wasps 16.9.95 (H)

HARLEQUINS PLAYING SQUAD

NAME	Ht	Wt	Birthdate	Birthplace	Club	Apps	Pts	T	C	P	DG
Jim Staples	6.2	13.10	20.10.65	London	London Irish	58	55	13	-	-	-
Ireland: 26, A, B, u25, Exiles. (Prev. clubs: Bromley, Sidcup)					Harlequins	38	102	16	5	3	1
Jaime Williams	6.1	13.9	16.03.76	Martin (N.Z.)	Wimbledon						
					Harlequins	6+1	5	1	-	-	-
Daren O'Leary	6.0	13.0	27.06.73	Harrow Wood	Saracens	10	15	3	-	-	-
England: A, Emerging, u21, Students.					Harlequins	62	205	41	-	-	-
Peter Mensah	6.0	13.8	10.11.66	Ghana	Old Millhillians						
England: A, Emerging.					Harlequins	37+1	70	14	-	-	-
Will Carling	5.11	14.2	12.12.65	Bradford-on-Avon							
England: 72, B, Schools. British Lions.					Harlequins	93	157	19	27	5	-
Spencer Bromley	6.1	14.10	12.12.69	Manchester	Rugby	21+1	10	2	-	-	-
					Liverpool St. H.	?	8	2	-	-	-
England: u21, Students.					Harlequins	30	70	14	-	-	-
Paul Challinor	6.0	13.2	05.12.69	Wolverhampton							
England: A, u18.					Harlequins	65	363	10	30	65	10
Thiery Lacroix	6.0	13.5	02.03.67	France	Previous Clubs: Dax, Natal.						
France: 38					Harlequins	13	-	-	-	-	-
Huw Harries	5.11	13.7	21.02.73	Cardiff	Previous Clubs: Cardiff, Llanelli.						
Wales: Students, u21, u19, u18, u15.					Harlequins	13+2	45	9	-	-	-
Nick Walshe	5.10	13.0	01.11.73	Chiswick	Rosslyn Park	23+2	10	2	-	-	-
England: Students.					Harlequins	11	27	5	1	-	-
Michael Corcoran	6.3	14.7	29.11.69	London	London Irish	70	730	22	64	465	1
Ireland: Development XV, Exiles.					Harlequins	5+1	37	5	3	2	-
Jason Keyter	5.11	13.2	20.12.73	Port Elizabeth	Bristol	9	-	-	-	-	-
England: A, u21, Colts.					Harlequins	15+3	35	7	-	-	-
Chris Wright	5.6	11.7	08.02.68	Heswell	Orrell	24	24	6	-	-	-
England: B.				(Prev. club: New Brighton)	Wasps	5+7	-	-	-	-	-
					Harlequins	8+13	10	2	-	-	-
Domonic Chapman	5.8	11.12	07.03.76	Kingston	Esher						
England: Colts.					Harlequins	2	20	4	-	-	-

FORWARDS

NAME	Ht	Wt	Birthdate	Birthplace	Club	Apps	Pts	T	C	P	DG
Jason Leonard	5.10	17.2	14.08.68	Barking	Barking						
England: 55, B, Colts. British Lions: 2.					Saracens	19	4	1	-	-	-
					Harlequins	-	-	-	-	-	-
Laurant Benezech	6.1	16.3	19.12.66	Parmiers	Previous Clubs: Toulouse, Racing Club.						
France: 15, Universities, Schools.					Harlequins	17+1	10	2	-	-	-
Andy Mullins	5.11	16.0	12.12.64	Blackheath	Old Alleylenians						
England: 1, A, B.					Harlequins	117+2	14	3	-	-	-
Keith Wood	6.0	16.10	27.01.72	Limerick	Garryowen						
Ireland: 9, A, u21, Schools.					Harlequins	15	25	5	-	-	-
Altan Ozdemir	5.7	16.0	03.09.74	Sutton Coldfield	Bristol	7	-	-	-	-	-
England: u21, u18, u16.					Harlequins	3	-	-	-	-	-
Luke Cross	6.9	17.2	21.11.69	Indiana (USA)	Cincinatti						
US Eagles.					Harlequins	8	-	-	-	-	-
Gareth Llewellyn	6.6	18.0	27.02.69	Cardiff	Previous Clubs: Llanharan, Neath.						
Wales: 57, A, Schools.					Harlequins	17	5	1	-	-	-
Ian Pickup	6.4	16.0	27.06.69	York	Rosslyn Park	23+1	20	4	-	-	-
England: Universities.				(Prev. club: Coventry)	Harlequins	0+7	-	-	-	-	-
Bill Davison	6.6	16.6	08.04.69	Kitwe (Zam.)	Richmond	0+1	-	-	-	-	-
			(Prev. club: Sheffield)		Rosslyn Park	24	10	2	-	-	-
					Harlequins	-	-	-	-	-	-
Laurant Cabannes	6.2	14.7	06.02.64	Reims	Previous Clubs: Dax, Racing Club.						
France: , A, B, Army.					Harlequins	22	10	2	-	-	-
Rory Jenkins	6.2	15.12	29.06.70	Leicester	Previous Clubs: Brixham, Wasps.						
England: A, Emerging, Students, u21, Colts.					London Irish	15	5	1	-	-	-
					Harlequins	46	10	2	-	-	-
Alex Snow	6.7	17.0	29.04.69	Chelsea	Heriots F.P.						
England: Emerging, Students. Scotland: Students.					Harlequins	60	15	3	-	-	-
Mick Watson	6.6	18.7	02.08.69	Sunderland	Alton						
Army, Combined Services.					West Hartlepool	27	25	5	-	-	-
					Harlequins	24+4	30	6	-	-	-
Simon Owen	6.5	16.8	22.03.71	Birmingham	Moseley	19	15	3	-	-	-
England: u21				(Prev. club: Newcastle)	Harlequins	1+2	-	-	-	-	-

Tel: 0181 410 6000   **Advance Ticket Line:** 0181 410 6010   **Fax:** 0181 410 6001

CAPACITY: 8,250   **SEATED Covered:** 4,500   **SEATED Uncovered:** 3,750

SIMPLE DIRECTIONS:
    By Road: On the A316 going towards the M3. Ground is situated on the left hand side, close to the R.F.U. ground. The car parks are off the A316 Westbound only. No entry for vehicles from Craneford Way
    Nearest Railway Station: Twickenham (BR). 15 minutes walk from the ground.

CAR PARKING: Sponsors only in the ground. 500 nearby @ £5

ADMISSION:
Season ticket all seated - Adult £150.
Matchday - All seated Adults East & West £15, Children/OAPs £10.
            All seated Adults North & South £12, Children/OAPs £6.
Family Ticket (2 Adults & 2 Children) £30.

CLUB SHOP: Yes, Tel: 0181 410 6005

CLUBHOUSE: Matchdays & Training nights only, With two bars and food is available.
    Function room: Yes; 500-600 seated, 1000 buffet, 2000 bar, contact Brian Terry 0181 410 6054

TRAINING NIGHTS: Tuesday and Thursday.

NEC Harlequins Player of the Year; Kieth Wood
Photo - Joe McCabe

MATCHDAY PROGRAMME

Size	A5
Number of pages	62
Price	£2
Programme Editor	

Advertising Rates
                Contact - Geoff Hill 01703 868595,
                            01703 868380 (Fax),
                            0831 683843 (Mobile)

LEICESTER F.C.

NICKNAME: Tigers   **FOUNDED:** 1880

President Garry Adey, c/o Leicester FC, Welford Road Ground, Aylestone Road, Leicester LE2 7LF.
0116 254 1607 (B), 0116 285 4766 (Fax)

Chief Executive Peter Wheeler, c/o Leicester FC, as above

Commercial Manager Keith Grainger, c/o Leicester FC, as above

Club Secretary Tudor Thomas, 52 Main Street, Cosby, Leics. LE9 5UU
0116 286 3142 (H)

Press Officer Stuart Farmer, 2 Lundy Close, Hinckley, Leics. LE10 0SS.
01455 631934 (B), 01455 636367 (Fax), 0802 961057 (Mobile).

Chairman Peter Tom, c/o Leicester FC, as above

This first professional season must surely go down as one of Leicester's most successful, with the pinnacle coming when six players were included in the successful British Lions touring party to South Africa, including the captain, Martin Johnson.

In addition there were first international caps for Irish back row Eric Miller, scrum half Austin Healey, and the remaining two members of the 'ABC' club, Darren Garforth and Richard Cockerill.

The club was involved in the latter stages of all three major competitions, overcoming Sale in the Pilkington Cup finally to put some silverware on display at Welford Road. In the showpiece Heineken European Cup Final in January, when Cardiff was 'invaded' by 25,000 fanatical Tigers supporters, Leicester were eclipsed by Brive in one of the best club performances of all time. It was a great achievement for Leicester to get to the final at their first attempt, beating Harlequins, Toulouse and Pau on the way, the latter being the only English victory in France.

The Courage League proved a bridge too far when postponements due to cup success forced Leicester to play almost a third of their entire league campaign in the space of eighteen punishing days in April. Crucially for the first time they suffered three successive league defeats, only gaining the coveted fourth place qualification for next season's Heineken Cup by clawing back a seventeen point deficit to draw 20-20 at Sale on the last league weekend of the season.

In the summer of 1996 Leicester signalled their intent to remain a leading force in the game with the acquisition of Wallaby World Cup winning coach Bob Dwyer, whilst strengthening their playing ranks with the likes of Will Greenwood, Austin Healey, Craig Joiner and Rob Liley. Springbok World Cup winning fly half Joel Stransky joined in December and was instrumental in the successful cup campaign. Not wishing to stand still Tigers have recruited Fijian backs Waisale Serevi and Marika Vunibaka and Springbok lock Fritz van Heerden to take them forward into 1997/98.
STUART FARMER

Leicester Tigers: Back Row (L-R); Bob Dwyer (Director of Coaching), Ruth Cross (Physio), Mark Geeson (Physio), Darren Garforth, Duncan Hall (Dir Coaching Developement), Richard Cockerill, Graham Rowntree, Perry Freshwater, Will Greenwood, John Wells, Neil Fletcher, Matt Poole, Martin Johnson, Leon Lloyd, Eric Miller, Niall Malone, Dave Redding (Fitness Coach), Cliff Shephard (Team Secretary), Ian Smith (Asst Coach), John Duggan (Fitness Coach). Front Row: Dorian West, Rob Liley, Stuart Potter, Steve Hackney, Dean Richards (Capt), Rory Underwood, Neil Back, John Liley, Aadel Kardooni.
Photo - Allsport

Colours: Scarlet, green & white hoops.   **Change colours:** Blue with scarlet, green & white band.

LEICESTER

No	Ven.	Date	Opponents	Att.	Res.	Score	Scorers
1	(A)	31.08	v Saracens	6231	L	23-25	Underwood(t)J Liley(t2c3p)
2	(H)	07.09	v Bath	10368	W	28-25	PTry(t)J Liley(c7p)
3	(A)	14.09	v Orrell	2300	W	29-12	Greenwood(t)Potter(t)Hackney(t)J Liley(c4p)
4	(A)	22.09	v Wasps	10686	L	7-14	PTry(t)J Liley (c)
5	(H)	28.09	v Gloucester	9597	W	32-14	Hackney(t)Cockerill(t)Underwood(t)PTry(t)J Liley(3c2p)
6	(A)	05.10	v W Hartlepool	2300	W	30-19	Drake-lee(t)Greebwood(t)PTry(t)J Liley(3c3p)
7	(H)	31.10	v London Irish	8263	W	46-13	W Johnson(t)Austin(t)PTry(t)Kardooni(t)R Liley(2t5c2p)
8	(H)	08.12	v Northampton	11839	W	23- 9	Back(t)Potter(t)J Liley(c2p)R Liley(cp)
9	(A)	00.00	v Bristol	2553	W	38-12	Potter(2t)Hackney(t)R Liley(t)J Liley(3c4p)
10	(A)	28.12	v Harlequins	5772	W	34-18	Underwood(2t)Greenwood(t)J Liley(tc4p)
11	(A)	11.01	v Northampton	7907	L	19-22	Back(2t)J Liley(3p)
12	(H)	18.01	v Bristol	9122	W	53-19	Greenwood(t)Underwood(t)Stransky(t)Healey(t)Lloyd(t)PenTry(t)Liley(4c5p)
13	(H)	04.03	v Sale	7320	W	25- 9	PenTry(t)Stransky(c6p)
14	(H)	08.03	v W Hartlepool	8709	W	48- 3	Garforth(t)Healey(t)Greenwood(t)Jioner(t)Austin(t)Stransky(t3c4p)
15	(H)	02.04	v Wasps	17000	W	18-12	Stransky(6p)
16	(H)	05.04	v Orrell	9022	W	36-14	Malone(2t)Hackney(t)Underwood(t)Poole(t)Joiner(t)J Liley(3c)
17	(A)	08.04	v Gloucester	6310	L	30-32	Joiner(t)Kardooni(t)Underwood(t)Hackney(t)Stransky(2c2p)
18	(A)	12.04	v Bath	8500	L	9-47	Stransky(3p)
19	(A)	16.04	v London Irish	3456	L	18-25	Poole(t)Fletcher(t)R Liley(c2p)
20	(H)	19.04	v Saracens	10791	W	22-18	PenTry(t)J Liley(c5p)
21	(H)	26.04	v Harlequins	12504	L	12-13	Stransky(2p)J Liley(2p)
22	(A)	03.05	v Sale	4777	D	20-20	PenTry(t)Potter(t)Stransky(2c2p)

1996-97 HIGHLIGHTS

LEAGUE DEBUTS:
Matthew Jones, Austin Healey, Eric Miller, Will Greenwood, Gary Becconsall, Rob Liley, Lewis Moody, Neil Fletcher, Leon Lloyd, Greg Austin, Joel Stransky, Perry Freshwater, Craig Joiner, M Jasnikowski, D Addison, N Ezulike.

TRY ON DEBUT: Greg Austin, Joel Stransky.

PLAYERS USED: 36 plus 2 as replacement.

EVER PRESENT: None
        - most appearances 20 Darren Garforth.

❏ Lost three consecutive league games for the first time.

❏ Penalty tries headed Leicester's try scoring list.

❏ South African international Joel Stransky becomes the fourth Leicester player to score 100 points in a season. The other three being Dusty Hare, John Liley and Jez Harris. The only other club to have achieved this is Bath also this saeson when Mike Catt joined the club.

❏ On a similar theme they had three players score 20 points in a match. The three were John Liley, Rob Liley

and Joel Stransky. The only team to better this is Quins who had four players achieve this feat this season.

❏ Full back John Liley becomes the first player to reach 1000 National league points and then goes on to become the first player to reach 1000 division one points. Liley topped Leicester scoring list for a record sixth time and in all six of these seasons he has passed 100 league points which is a division record in itself.

	Pts	T	C	P	D	Apps	Ave.
Wakefield	22	1	2	5		5	4.40
Leicester	1070	25	129	232	1	100	10.70
Total	1092	26	131	237	1	105	10.70

Liley becomes the first Leicester back to reach 100 league appearances and the second player in the club after flanker John Wells.

❏ They suffered their worst ever league defeat when they lost 9-47 at Bath's Recreation Ground. Their previous worst defeat was also there in January 1992 when they lost 6-37.

❏ England international winger Rory Underwood was the player who scored most tries, 7, after penalty tries. That took him into joint second place on the division one all-time list behind fellow international Jeremy Guscott and level with Harlequins Daren O'Leary.

LEICESTER'S COURAGE LEAGUE MATCH DETAILS 1996-97

#	15	14	13	12	11	10	9	1	2	3	4	5	6	7	8	Replacements
1	J Liley	Hackney	Potter	Malone	Underwood	Jones	Healey	Rowntree	Cockerill	Garforth	Johnson	Poole	Miller	Drake-Lee	Richards	
2	J Liley	Hackney	Potter	Greenwood	Underwood	Malone	Healey	Rowntree	Cockerill	Garforth	Johnson	Poole	Wells	Miller	W Johnson	
3	J Liley	Hackney	Potter	Greenwood	Underwood	R Liley	Healey	Becconsall/Rowntree	Cockerill	Garforth	Johnson	Field	Moody		Richards	
4	J Liley	Hackney	Potter	Greenwood	Underwood	R Liley	Healey	Rowntree	Cockerill	Garforth	Johnson	Poole	Wells	Miller	Richards	Jones(14),Drake-Lee(8)
5	J Liley	Hackney	Potter	Greenwood	Underwood	R Liley	Healey	Rowntree	Cockerill	Garforth	Johnson	Poole	Wells	Drake-Lee	Miller	O Wingham(8)
6	J Liley	Hackney	Potter	Greenwood	Underwood	R Liley	Healey	Rowntree	Cockerill	Garforth	Johnson	Fletcher	Wells	Drake-Lee	Miller	
7	J Liley	Lloyd	Austin	Malone	Underwood	R Liley	Kardooni	Jelley	West	Rowntree	Johnson	Fletcher	W Johnson	Drake-Lee	Richards	
8	J Liley	Hackney	Potter	Greenwood	Lloyd	R Liley	Healey	Rowntree	Cockerill	Garforth	Johnson	Field	Wells	Back	Richards	Miller(8)
9	J Liley	Hackney	Potter	Greenwood	Lloyd	R Liley	Healey	Rowntree	West	Garforth	Johnson	Fletcher	Wells	Back	Richards	
10	J Liley	Hackney	Lloyd	Greenwood	Underwood	Malone	Healey	Rowntree	Cockerill	Garforth	Johnson	Poole	Wells	Miller	Richards	W Johnson(6)
11	J Liley	Hackney	Potter	Greenwood	Underwood	R Liley	Healey	Rowntree	West	Garforth	Johnson	Poole	W Johnson	Back	Richards	Stransky(14)
12	J Liley	Underwood	Potter	Greenwood	Lloyd	Stransky	Healey	Freshwater	Cockerill	Garforth	Johnson	Fletcher	Wells	Back	Richards	W Johnson(7),Kardooni(9),Rowntree(tr)
13	J Liley	Hackney	Joiner	Greenwood	Lloyd	Stransky	Healey	Rowntree	Cockerill	Garforth	Johnson	Fletcher	Wells	Back	Richards	W Johnson,Austin(15),Drake-Lee(tr 6),Freshwater(tr 1&2)
14	J Liley	Hackney	Potter	Greenwood	Joiner	Stransky	Healey	Rowntree	West	Garforth	Johnson	Field	Drake-Lee	Back	Miller	Austin(12),Kardooni(9),R Liley(tr 10),Richards(tr 7)
15	Malone	Hackney	Joiner	Greenwood	Lloyd	Stransky	Healey	Rowntree	Cockerill	Garforth	Johnson	Poole	Miller	Back	Richards	Fletcher(5),Underwood(11),Kardooni(9)
16	J Liley	Hackney	Malone	Underwood	Lloyd	R Liley	Kardooni	West	Cockerill	Garforth	Fletcher	Poole	Drake-Lee	Back	Miller	Debney(14),Healey(11),Rowntree(3),Johnson(4),Richards(8)
17	J Liley	Hackney	Malone	Lloyd	Joiner	Stransky	Kardooni	Rowntree	Cockerill	Garforth	Johnson	Poole	Miller	Back	Richards	Underwood(11),Fletcher(5),Drake-Lee(8)
18	J Liley	Hackney	Potter	Greenwood	Joiner	Stransky	Healey	Rowntree	Cockerill	Garforth	Johnson	Poole	Miller	Back	Richards	Malone(12),Underwood(14),Edwards(15),Fletcher(5),Drake-Lee(8)
19	Malone	Joiner	Jasnikowski	Ezulike	Potter	Healey	Jelley	West	Rowntree	Garforth	Johnson	Fletcher	Wingham	Drake-Lee	Addison	Austin(12),Moody(8),Garforth(1),Cockerill(2)
20	J Liley	Hackney	Malone	Underwood	Joiner	R Liley	Kardooni	Rowntree	Cockerill	Garforth	Johnson	Poole	Wells	Back	Miller	Drake-Lee(8)
21	J Liley	Hackney	Potter	Potter	Underwood	Stransky	Kardooni	Rowntree	Cockerill	Garforth	Johnson	Poole	Moody	Back	Miller	Healey(14),Wells(8),R Liley(10),Fletcher(5),West(2)
22	Malone	Underwood	Potter	Joiner	Lloyd	Stransky	Healey	Rowntree	Cockerill	Garforth	Johnson	Poole	Wells	Back	Miller	Richards(5),Drake-Lee(8)

LEICESTER LEAGUE STATISTICS
(COMPILED BY STEPHEN McCORMACK)

Season	Div.	P	W	D	L	F	(Tries	Con	Pen	DG)	A	(Tries	Con	Pen	DG)	Most Points	Most Tries
87-88	1	10	9	0	1	225	(21	15	31	6)	133	(14	10	17	2)	126 - Dusty Hare	5 - Barry Evans
88-89	1	11	6	1	4	189	(19	10	29	2)	199	(25	12	21	4)	97 - Dusty Hare	3 - Barry Evans & Dean Richards.
89-90	1	11	6	0	5	248	(36	16	22	2)	184	(24	14	17	3)	126 - John Liley	7 - John Liley
90-91	1	12	8	0	4	244	(29	19	25	5)	140	(12	7	21	5)	110 - John Liley	8 - Rory Underwood
91-92	1	12	6	1	5	262	(33	20	26	4)	216	(26	11	28	2)	125 - John Liley	9 - Rory Underwood
92-93	1	12	9	0	3	220	(21	17	23	4)	116	(13	3	14	1)	106 - John Liley	3 - Tony Underwood Nigel Richardson
93-94	1	18	14	0	4	425	(41	23	47	11)	210	(18	9	32	2)	202 - Jez Harris	8 - Tony Underwood
94-95	1	18	15	1	2	400	(27	17	64	13)	239	(15	10	44	4)	181 - Jez Harris	5 - Steve Hackney
95-96	1	18	15	0	3	476	(42	28	66	4)	242	(16	9	41	7)	272 - John Liley	8 - Rory Underwood
96-97	1	22	14	1	7	600	(60	39	74	0)	395	(38	23	51	2)	195 - John Liley	9 - Penalty Tries
Totals		144	102	4	38	3289	(329	204	407	51)	2074	(201	108	286	32)		

	HOME	AWAY
BIGGEST WIN	(61pts) 66-5 v Newcastle Gos. 12.3.94	(26pts) 38-12 v Bristol 18.12.96
BIGGEST DEFEAT	(10pts) 21-31 v Harlequins 26.11.89	(38pts) 9-47 v Bath 12.4.97

MOST POINTS SCORED — 66-5 v Newcastle Gos. 12.3.94 — 43-19 v Moseley 27.4.91

AGAINST — 21-31 v Harlequins 26.11.89 — 9-47 v Bath 12.4.97

MOST CONSECUTIVE VICTORIES - 9   MOST CONSECUTIVE DEFEATS - 3

MOST TRIES IN A MATCH
(FOR) 11 v Bedford 23.9.89
(AGAINST) 7 v Bath 11.1.92

MOST APPEARANCES
FORWARD: 114 John Wells
BACK: 100(2) John Liley

CONSECUTIVE APPEARANCES
32 Darren Garforth 28.3.92-3.4.94

CONSECUTIVE SCORING MATCHES
Scoring Tries - 3 - Rory Underwood
Scoring Points - 24 - John Liley

MOST	in a SEASON	in a CAREER	in a MATCH
Points	272 John Liley 95-96	1070 John Liley 88-97	31 John Liley v Rosslyn Park 21.3.92 (H)
Tries	9 Rory Underwood 91-92 Penalty Tries 96-97	43 Rory Underwood 87-97	4 Tony Underwood v Newcastle G. 12.3.94 (H)
Conversions	26 John Liley 95-96	129 John Liley 88-97	7 John Liley v Rosslyn Park 21.3.92 (H)
Penalties	64 John Liley 95-96	232 John Liley 88-97	8 John Liley v Bristol 28.10.95 (H)
Drop Goals	13 Jez Harris 94-95	37 Jez Harris 87-96	3 Jez Harris v Wasps 23.11.91 (H) v Bath 15.4.95 (H)

LEICESTER PLAYING SQUAD

NAME	Ht	Wt	Birthdate	Birthplace	Club	Apps	Pts	T	C	P	DG
BACKS											
John Liley	6.0	13.10	21.08.67	Wakefield	Sandal						
England: A.					Wakefield	5	22	2	4	2	-
					Leicester	100+2	1070	25	129	232	1
Nial Malone	5.11	14.0	30.04.71	Leeds	London Irish	1	-	-	-	-	-
Ireland: 3, A, Students, u21, Schools.					Leicester	25+3	16	2	-	1	1
Steve Hackney	5.11	13.10	13.06.68	Stockton-on-Tees	West Hartlepool						
England: A, Colts, u18.					Nottingham	25	8	2	-	-	-
					Leicester	77	121	25	-	-	-
Leon Lloyd	6.4	14.0	22.09.77	Coventry	Barker's Butt						
England: Colts.					Leicester	9	5	1	-	-	-
Rory Underwood	5.9	13.8	19.06.63	Middlesbrough							
England: 85, A, Colts, u23. British Lions: 6					Leicester	97+3	192	43	-	-	-
Craig Joiner	5.10	14.0	21.04.74	Glasgow	Melrose						
Scotland: 17, A, u21, Schools.					Leicester	10	15	3	-	-	-
Stuart Potter	5.11	14.7	11.11.67	Lichfield	Lichfield						
England: A, B.					Nottingham	30	20	5	-	-	-
					Leicester	72	65	13	-	-	-
Will Greenwood	6.4	15.0	20.10.72	Blackburn	Preston Grasshoppers						
England: A, Students, u21.					Waterloo	4	5	1	-	-	-
					Harlequins	24	47	6	1	5	-
					Leicester	13	25	5	-	-	-
Austin Healey	5.10	13.7	26.10.73	Wallasey	Waterloo	20	18	3	-	-	-
England: 3, A, Students, u21.					Orrell	32+1	27	4	2	1	-
					Leicester	16+2	10	2	-	-	-
Aadel Kardouni	5.8	12.12	17.05.68	Teheran	Wasps	1	-	-	-	-	-
England: A, B.					Leicester	94+3	84	18	-	-	-
Rob Liley	6.1	13.0	03.03.70	Wakefield	Wakefield	23	214	2	23	51	2
England: A, u21, Students.					Sale	25	209	3	28	44	2
					Leicester	11+2	44	3	7	5	-
Joel Stransky	5.11	13.5	16.07.67	Johannesburg	Previous Clubs: Western Province, N. Transvaal, Natal.						
South Africa:					Leicester	8+1	101	2	8	25	-
Paul Delaney	6.0	13.7	17.10.74	Wellsbourne							
					Leicester	2+1	-	-	-	-	-
FORWARDS											
Graham Rowntree	6.0	17.5	18.04.71	Stockton-on-Tees	Nuneaton						
England: 15, A, u21, Colts, u18.					Leicester	82+1	5	-	-	-	-
Darren Garforth	5.10	18.0	09.04.66	Coventry	Nuneaton		8	2			
England: 4.					Leicester	96+1	19	4	-	-	-
Richard Cockerill	5.10	15.10	16.12.70	Rugby	Coventry	12	-	-	-	-	-
England: 2					Leicester	75+1	20	4	-	-	-
Dorian West	5.11	16.0	03.10.67	Wrexham	Nottingham	41	30	6	-	-	-
England: A.					Leicester	6+2	-	-	-	-	-
Derek Jelley	6.0	16.10	04.03.72	Nuneaton							
					Leicester	10+1	-	-	-	-	-
Martin Johnson	6.7	18.4	09.03.70	Solihull							
England: 30, A, u21, Colts, u18. British Lions: 2					Leicester	85+1	10	2	-	-	-
Matt Poole	6.7	18.11	06.02.69	Leicester							
England: Emerging, u21, Colts, u18.					Leicester	90+1	25	5	-	-	-
Dean Richards	6.4	18.0	11.07.63	Nuneaton							
England: 48, A, u23, u18. British Lions: 5					Leicester	91+3	51	12	-	-	-
Neil Back	5.10	14.4	16.01.69	Coventry	Nottingham						
England: 5, A, B, u21, Colts, u18.					Leicester	82	79	16	-	-	-
Eric Miller	6.3	15.7	23.09.75	Dublin	Old Wesley						
Ireland: 4, A, u21, Students, Schools.					Leicester	13	-	-	-	-	-
John Wells	6.2	15.7	12.05.63	Driffield							
England: A, Students, u23, u18.					Leicester	113+1	34	8	-	-	-
Bill Drake-Lee	6.0	15.0	09.08.70	Kettering	Kettering						
					Leicester	20+6	5	-	-	-	-
Neil Fletcher	6.7	17.0	04.06.76		Moseley						
					Leicester	7+4	5	1	-	-	-

Welford Road Ground, Aylestone Road., Leicester. LE2 7LF.

Tel: 0116 254 1607

Fax: 0116 285 4766

CAPACITY: 16,000   **SEATED:** 12,000   **STANDING:** 4,000

SIMPLE DIRECTIONS:

By Road: From the M1, junction 21. Along the A46 into Leicester. At the Post House Hotel traffic lights turn right onto B5418 (Braunstone Lane East). After 1 mile turn left at 'T' junction traffic lights onto A426 (Aylestone Road). Ground 2 miles on right.

Nearest Railway Station: Leicester (London Road). The ground is about 3/4 mile walk along Waterloo Way. (Station Tel. No. 0116 248 1000)

CAR PARKING: None available at the ground.

ADMISSION:

Membership - Adults from £95 standing to £220 Reserved centre; OAPs/students £65 to £175; Juniors £45 to £160. Matchday - Varied according to match.

CLUB SHOP: Yes, manager Sarah Watson, 0116 254 1607

CLUBHOUSE: Has three bars with snacks, barmeals & restaurant food available.

Function room: Various rooms are available. For further details contact Tracey Branson, 0116 255 1894.

TRAINING NIGHTS: Tuesday and Thursday.

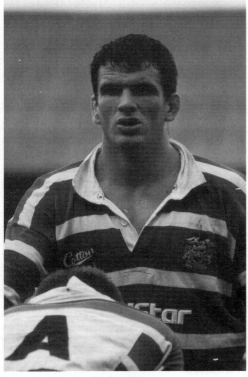

Martin Johnson,
Leicester Tigers' victorious Lions captain
Photo - Darren Griffiths

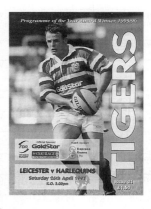

MATCHDAY PROGRAMME

Size	170mm x 240mm
Number of pages	36
Price	£1.50
Programme Editor	Stuart Farmer, Press Officer

Advertising Rates
On application to Commercial Manager
Keith Grainger, c/o Leicester FC

LONDON IRISH R.F.C.

NICKNAME: The Irish   **FOUNDED:** 1898

Chief Executive Duncan Leopold, c/o London Irish RFC, The Avenue, Sunbury on Thames, Middx TW16 5EQ
01932 783034 (Club), 01932 784462 (Fax)

Director of Rugby Willie Anderson, c/o London Irish RFC, as above

Commercial Manager David Banks, c/o London Irish RFC, as above.

Facilities Manager Tony Jack, c/o London Irish RFC, as above

Rugby Administrator Kieran McCarthy, c/o LOndon Irish RFC, as above

President Ronnie Johnston, c/o London Irish RFC, as above. 01276 22684 (H).

The 1996/97 season can best be described as both tiring and trying. The first season of professionalism opened with the whole of rugby in a state of flux and it ended in a similar vein, though with much happening along the way, with the game gaining a higher profile than ever before.

London Irish found itself at the Wasps league match on 9th November, having played seven league matches and having secured just two league points. That particular Wasps game brought about a change of fortune for apart from being unlucky to lose the match by two points it heralded the arrival of Willie   Anderson as director of rugby. A lot of ground had to be made up and the target of at least quality for the play-offs was achieved, culminating in facing Coventry on a two-leg basis to decide on who would maintain 1st Division status at the end of 160 minutes of rugby. London Irish lost the first leg, which was played away, 14-16, in front of a huge vociferous partisan crowd. However, the second-leg at Sunbury proved to be a different story in front of a green coloured capacity attendance where a comprehensive and clinical display saw The Irish win by 28-7 and affirm a premier league position.

An unfortunate away draw against Bath in the Pilkington Cup produced an early exit from the competition at the fifth round stage. In addition, participation in the inaugural European Conference tournament proved to be a formidable, though valuable, experience for the younger players in the squad due to the unavailability of the senior players who had opted to play for the Irish Provinces in the European Cup.

The success of the under age groups continued with the development U19, youth and mini, it was also pleasing to note the endurance of the other eight amateur adult sides that take the field each Saturday. Representative honours were enjoyed by many senior squad players with ten being selected for the Irish Squad tour to New Zealand in May and Jeremy Davidson's inclusion in the British Lions squad to tour South Africa.

London Irish in complete control!.

Colours: Green/white/green   **Change colours:** Black with cream stripe/black/black

LONDON IRISH

No	Ven.	Date	Opponents	Att.	Res.	Score	Scorers
1	(H)	31.08	v Bristol	1467	L	27-28	Woods(2tp)Henderson(t)Humphreys(3p)
2	(H)	07.09	v Northampton	3170	W	34-21	Davidson(t)Costello(t)Woods(t)Humphreys(2c4pdg)
3	(A)	14.09	v Harlequins	4599	L	7-66	Flood(t)Humphreys(c)
4	(H)	21.09	v Sale	2650	L	19-25	Halpin(t)Humphreys(c3pdg)
5	(H)	28.09	v Saracens	2670	L	23-37	Woods(t)PTry(t)Humphreys(2c3p)
6	(H)	05.10	v Bath	3850	L	31-56	O'Shea(2t)Briers(t)Walsh(t)Humphreys(4cp)
7	(A)	31.10	v Leicester	8263	L	13-46	Henderson(t)Humphreys(c2p)
8	(H)	16.11	v Wasps	3720	L	20-22	Richards(t)Humphreys(4pdg)
9	(A)	07.12	v Gloucester	3835	L	19-29	Henderson(2t)Humphreys(3p)
10	(H)	28.12	v W Hartlepool	1620	W	52-41	Walsh(2t)Bishop(t)Davidson(t)O'Shea(t)Henderson(t)Humphreys(5c4p)
11	(H)	11.01	v Gloucester	2362	L	20-21	O'Shea(t)Humphreys(5p)
12	(A)	22.02	v Orrell	1200	L	27-32	O'Shea(2t)O'Connell(t)Humphreys(t2cp)
13	(A)	08.03	v Bath	6100	L	3-46	Humphreys(p)
14	(A)	26.03	v Wasps	3010	L	18-31	Flood(t)Fulcher(t)O'Shea(c2p)
15	(H)	05.04	v Harlequins	3960	W	20-19	Walsh(t)O'Shea(t)Humphreys(2c2p)
16	(A)	12.04	v Northampton	5470	L	21-31	Dawson(t)Hennessy(t)O'Shea(cp)Humphreys(2p)
17	(H)	16.04	v Leicester	3456	W	25-18	Fulcher(t)Burrows(t)Bishop(t)O'Connell(t)O'Shea(cp)
18	(A)	19.04	v Bristol	3300	W	38-26	Fulcher(t)Hennessy(t)Spicer(t)Woods(t)O'Shea(c)Humphreys(2t2p)
19	(A)	23.04	v Sale	2320	L	25-41	Yeabsley(2t)Hennessy(t)O'Shea(t)Woods(cp)
20	(A)	26.04	v W Hartlepool	1900	W	33-18	Humphreys(t)O'Connell(t)Redmond(t)Richards(t)Woods(tc2p)
21	(A)	30.04	v Saracens	1865	L	0-45	
22	(H)	03.05	v Orrell	2500	L	27-48	Allen(t)Dougan(t)Ewington(t)Walsh(t)Ure(2cp)

1996-97 HIGHLIGHTS

LEAGUE DEBUTS:
Niall Woods, Malcolm O'Kelly, Jeremy Davidson, Nigel Richardson, Victor Costello, Phil Drury, Ivan McKenzie, Kieran Dawson, Alastair Allen, Peter Richards, Kevin O'Kane, Ken O'Connell, David Charles, Tyrone Howe, Noel Burrows, Niall Hogan, Peter Faiers.

TRY ON DEBUT: Niall Woods.

PLAYERS USED: 43 plus 4 as replacement.

EVER PRESENT: None
— most appearances 20 Conor O'Shea.

❏ Irish international stand-off David Humphreys broke the record for conversions in a match when he converted five of the six tries in the 52-41 home victory over Wet Hartlepool. The previous record of four was shared by Brian Mullen and Michael Corcoran.

❏ Before his departure to Wasps, Rob Henderson had extended his club record for consecutive league appearances to 29.

❏ Their 7-66 loss at Harlequins was their worst ever defeat in terms of both highest score against and

worst points difference. They also condeced a record 11 tries. To rub salt into the wound ex Irish player Michael Corcoran scored 20 points for Quins on his debut.

❏ Irish international Conor O'Shea topped the try scoring list for the second successive season. That puts him on 18 tries and moves him ahead of Simon Geoghegan into third place on the clubs all-time try scorers list.

	Tries	Apps	Try Every
Michael Corcoran	22	70	3.18 games
Rob Henderson	20	56	2.80 games
Conor O'Shea	18	36	2.00 games

O'Shea easily has the best strike rate and next season should pass both Henderson and Corcoran.

❏ Irish international stand-off David Humphreys becomes the fourth Irish player to score 100 points in a season and also moves into third place on the all-time points scorers list. The three other players to score 100 points in a season were Brian Mullen, twice, Ian Aitchison and Michael Corcoran, four times. The two players above him on the all-time list are Corcoran, 730, and Mullen, 265, followed by Humphreys on 202.

❏ When beating West Hartlepool 52-41 they achieved their highest ever score in a league match.

LONDON IRISH'S COURAGE LEAGUE MATCH DETAILS 1996-97

	15	14	13	12	11	10	9	1	2	3	4	5	6	7	8	Replacements
1	O'Shea	Bishop	Henderson	Flood	Woods	Humphreys	Ewington	Mooney	Kellam	Halpin	O'Kelly	Davidson	Bird	Richardson	Costello	Burns(15)
2	O'Shea	Bishop	Henderson	Flood	Woods	Humphreys	Ewington	Mooney	Kellam	Halpin	Fulcher	O'Kelly	Davidson	Richardson	Costello	
3	O'Shea	Bishop	Henderson	Flood	Woods	Humphreys	Ewington	Mooney	Kellam	Halpin	Fulcher	O'Kelly	Davidson	Richardson	Costello	Burns(10),Walsh(8)
4	O'Shea	Bishop	Henderson	Drury	Woods	Humphreys	Ewington	Mackenzie	Halpin	Fulcher	Davidson	Walsh	Dougan	Costello		Richardson(8)
5	O'Shea	Bishop	Henderson	Flood	Woods	Humphreys	Briers	Mooney	Kellam	Halpin	Fulcher	Davidson	Dougan	Dawson	Walsh	
6	O'Shea	Bishop	Henderson	Flood	Woods	Humphreys	Briers	Fitzpatrick	Kellam	Mooney	Fulcher	Davidson	Dougan	Dawson	Walsh	Yeabsley(7)
7	Allen	Henderson	Henderson	Bishop	Woods	Humphreys	Mooney	O'Kane	Fitzpatrick	Fulcher	O'Kelly	Davidson	O'Connell	Dawson	Costello	
8	O'Shea	Charles	Henderson	Bishop	Woods	Humphreys	Mooney	Mooney	Kellam	Halpin	Fulcher	Davidson	O'Connell	Dawson	Costello	
9	O'Shea	Woods	Henderson	Burns	Bishop	Humphreys	Richards	Mooney	Kellam	Halpin	Davidson	O'Kelly	O'Connell	Dawson	Costello	Fraser(10)
10	O'Shea	Bishop	Henderson	Burns	Woods	Humphreys	Richards	Mooney	Kellam	Halpin	Fulcher	Davidson	O'Connell	Dawson	Walsh	Costello(7),Fitzpatrick(1),Hennessy(14)
11	Bishop	Henderson	Henderson	Burns	Woods	Humphreys	Richards	Fitzpatrick	Kellam	Halpin	Fulcher	Davidson	O'Connell	Dawson	Walsh	Mooney(3)
12	O'Shea	Woods	Burns	Burns	Howe	Humphreys	Ewington	Fitzpatrick	Kellam	Mooney	Fulcher	Meadows	O'Connell	Dawson	Walsh	Walsh(7)
13	O'Shea	Woods	Bishop	Burrows	Howe	Humphreys	Ewington	Fitzpatrick	Kellam	Halpin	Fulcher	Davidson	O'Connell	Dawson	Costello	Walsh(8),Redmond(2),McLoughlin(3)
14	O'Shea	Bishop	Flood	Burrows	Hennessy	Humphreys	Ewington	Fitzpatrick	Redmond	Halpin	Fulcher	Davidson	O'Connell	Bird	Allen	Allen(13)
15	O'Shea	Bishop	Bishop	Burrows	Hennessy	Humphreys	Hogan	Fitzpatrick	Redmond	Halpin	Fulcher	Davidson	O'Connell	Dawson	Yeabsley	Burns(12)Walsh(5)Bird(8)
16	O'Shea	Bishop	Bishop	Burns	Hennessy	Humphreys	Hogan	Fitzpatrick	Redmond	Halpin	Fulcher	Meadows	O'Connell	Dawson	Yeabsley	Mooney(1)Kellam(2)Spicer(5)Burrows(10)Bird(7)
17	O'Shea	Bishop	Bishop	Burrows	Hennessy	Burns	Hogan	Mooney	Kellam	Halpin	Fulcher	Walsh	Bird	Spicer	Dawson	Dawson(6)Redmond(2)
18	O'Shea	Bishop	Bishop	Burrows	Hennessy	Humphreys	Hogan	Fitzpatrick	Redmond	Halpin	Fulcher	Davidson	O'Connell	Dawson	Spicer	Burns(14)Redmond( )
19	O'Shea	Woods	Burns	Burrows	Hennessy	Hogan	Hogan	Mooney	Kellam		Fulcher	Davidson	Spicer	Dawson	Yeabsley	Bishop(12)O'Kelly(5)Walsh(7)McLoughlin(3)
20	O'Shea	Woods	Bishop	Burns	Hennessy	Humphreys	Richards	Fitzpatrick	Redmond	Halpin	Fulcher	Davidson	O'Connell	Spicer	Spicer	Burrows(15)O'Kelly(5)
21	Joy	Allen	Drury	Flood	Jensen	Ure	Richards	Mooney	Kellam	Faiers	Meadows	O'Kelly	Bird	Yeabsley	Walsh	
22	Joy	Jensen	Drury	Haly	Ure	Ure	Ewington	Mooney	Kellam	McLoughlin	Meadows	O'Kelly	Dougan	Richardson	Walsh	Yeabsley(6)Condon(15)Cockle(7)McCormack(1)

LONDON IRISH LEAGUE STATISTICS

(COMPILED BY STEPHEN McCORMACK)

Season	Div.	P	W	D	L	F	(Tries	Con	Pen	DG)	A	(Tries	Con	Pen	DG)	Most Points	Most Tries
87-88	2	11	4	1	6	120	(15	6	14	2)	177	(22	10	20	3)	27 - Paul Bell	4 - Harry Harbison
88-89	2	11	5	2	4	194	(20	9	26	6)	222	(25	13	29	3)	100 - Brian Mullen	5 - S. Geoghegan
89-90	2	11	6	0	5	228	(25	19	27	3)	247	(33	20	21		111 - Ian Aitcheson	6 - Shaun Brown
90-91	2	12	9	1	2	239	(30	16	22	7)	192	(21	12	26	2)	117 - Brian Mullen	6 - Rob Saunders
91-92	1	12	3	3	6	147	(11	8	25	4)	237	(31	13	26	3)	71 - M. Corcoran	4 - M. Corcoran
92-93	1	12	6	0	6	175	(9	5	33	7)	223	(25	16	20	2)	111 - M. Corcoran	3 - S. Geoghegan
93-94	1	18	4	0	14	217	(19	7	34	2)	391	(40	22	43	6)	75 - M. Corcoran	5 - M. Geoghegan
94-95	2	18	9	0	9	363	(36	18	46	3)	381	(31	17	52	12)	164 - M. Corcoran	6 - R. Henderson
95-96	2	18	15	0	3	583	(62	36	63	4)	405	(45	30	37	3)	301 - M. Corcoran	10 - Conor O'Shea
96-97	1	22	6	0	16	502	(58	28	49	3)	749	(95	61	45	5)	189 - David Humphreys	8 - Conor O'Shea
Totals		145	67	7	71	2768	(285	152	339	41)	3154	(368	214	319	43)		

	HOME	AWAY
BIGGEST WIN	(41pts) 49-8 v Moseley 30.9.95	(34pts) 50-16 v Waterloo 23.9.95
BIGGEST DEFEAT	(33pts) 32-65 v Northampton 9.9.95	(59pts) 7-66 v Harlequins 14.9.96
MOST POINTS SCORED	52-41 v W. Hartlepool 28.12.96	50-16 v Waterloo 23.9.95
AGAINST	32-65 v Northampton 9.9.95	7-66 v Harlequins 14.9.96

MOST CONSECUTIVE VICTORIES - 8

MOST TRIES IN A MATCH
(FOR) 8 v Moseley 30.9.95 (H)
(AGAINST) 11 v Harlequins 14.9.96 (A)

CONSECUTIVE APPEARANCES
29 Rob Henderson

MOST CONSECUTIVE DEFEATS - 7

MOST APPEARANCES
FORWARD: 80 Gary Halpin
BACK: 70 Michael Corcoran

CONSECUTIVE SCORING MATCHES
Scoring Tries - 4 - Rob Saunders
Scoring Points - 24 - Michael Corcoran

MOST	in a SEASON	in a CAREER	in a MATCH
Points	301 M. Corcoran 95-96	730 M. Corcoran 89-96	30 M. Corcoran v Waterloo 23.9.95 (A)
Tries	10 Conor O'Shea 95-96	22 M. Corcoran 89-96	3 Rob Saunders v Rugby 13.10.90 (H) Conor O'Shea v Moseley 30.9.95 (H)
Conversions	36 M. Corcoran 95-96	64 M. Corcoran 89-96	5 David Humphreys v W Hartlepool 28.12.96 (H)
Penalties	63 M. Corcoran 95-96	165 M. Corcoran 89-96	7 M. Corcoran v Lon. Scottish 13.1.96 (H)
Drop Goals	6 Paul Burke 92-93	10 Brian Mullen 88-92	2 Ralph Kuhn v Lon. Scottish 14.1.89 (A) Brian Mullen v Richmond 8.4.89 (A) Ian Aitchison v Plymouth 13.1.90 (H) Paul Burke v Bristol 24.1.92 (H)

LONDON IRISH PLAYING SQUAD

NAME	Ht	Wt	Birthdate	Birthplace	Club	Apps	Pts	T	C	P	DG

BACKS

NAME	Ht	Wt	Birthdate	Birthplace	Club	Apps	Pts	T	C	P	DG
Conor O'Shea	6.2	15.0	21.10.70	Limerick	Lansdowne						
Ireland: 15, A, Leinster.					London Irish	36	110	18	4	4	-
Niall Woods	6.0	13.0	21.05.71		Blackrock						
Ireland: 7, A, Leinster.					London Irish	19	46	6	2	4	-
Nick Burrows	6.1	13.12	19.05.73		Prev. Clubs: Eastern Province, Transvaal.						
					London Irish	6+2	5	-	-	-	-
Sean Burns	5.10	13.11	10.08.71	Nuneaton	Nuneaton						
Ireland: u21, Exiles. England: Students.					London Irish	34+7	10	2	-	-	-
Justin Bishop	6.0	13.0	08.11.74	Crawley	East Grinstead						
Ireland: u21. England: u21.					London Irish	44+2	35	7	-	-	-
David Humphreys	5.10	12.3	10.09.71	Belfast	Previous Clubs: Queens University, Ballymena.						
Ireland: 7, A.					London Irish	23	202	6	20	40	4
Niall Hogan	5.8	12.0	20.04.71								
Ireland: 12, A, Students.					London Irish	6	-	-	-	-	-
Peter Richards	5.10	12.0	10.03.78								
England: Schools.					London Irish	6	10	2	-	-	-
Ray Hennessy	6.2	14.6	18.02.70								
Ireland: u21, Students.					London Irish	49+2	31	6	-	-	1
Paul Flood	6.0	13.10	25.11.70	Birmingham	Bridgend						
England: u21, Students, Schools.					London Irish	21	23	4	-	-	-
Tim Ewington	6.0	12.7	10.02.68	Sydney							
					London Irish	26	10	2	-	-	-
Tyrone Howe	6.0	13.4	02.04.71	Newtownards							
Ireland: A, Students.					London Irish	2	-	-	-	-	-

FORWARDS

NAME	Ht	Wt	Birthdate	Birthplace	Club	Apps	Pts	T	C	P	DG
Justin Fitzpatrick	6.3	17.2	21.11.73								
England: Students.					London Irish	27+1	-	-	-	-	-
Tony Redmond	5.10	15.8	14.01.71	Wigan	Orrell	10	-	-	-	-	-
English: Universities. Irish: Exiles.					London Irish	7+2	5	1	-	-	-
Gary Halpin	6.0	17.6	13.02.66	Dublin							
Ireland: 13.					London Irish	80	45	9	-	-	-
Liam Mooney	6.0	17.10	18.05.73	Dublin	Plymouth						
Ireland: u21, Students. England: Students, Schools.					London Irish	21+3	-	-	-	-	-
Rob Kellan	5.10	15.10	04.02.71	Newbury	Newbury						
England: u21, Students.					London Irish	61+1	5	1	-	-	-
Gabriel Fulcher	6.5	17.0	27.11.69	Surrey	Cork Constitution						
Ireland: 19, A, u21, Students.					London Irish	18	15	3	-	-	-
Jeremy Davidson	6.6	18.0	28.04.74	Belfast							
Ireland: 12, A, u21.					London Irish	16	5	1	-	-	-
Ken O'Connell	6.1	15.2	25.07.68								
Ireland: 2, A.					London Irish	13	15	3	-	-	-
Ciaran Bird	6.2	16.0	29.11.71	Chingford							
England: u21.					London Irish	33+3	25	5	-	-	-
Kevin Spicer	6.4	16.7	28.07.73								
Ireland: u21, Students.					London Irish	4+1	5	1	-	-	-
Barry Walsh	6.6	15.4	27.05.68	Limerick							
Ireland: A.					London Irish	30+6	50	10	-	-	-
Malcolm O'Kelly	6.7	16.7	19.07.74								
Ireland: A, u21, Students.					London Irish	8+2	5	1	-	-	-
Ian McLoughlan	6.2	16.10	04.01.77								
					London Irish	1+2	-	-	-	-	-
Alastair Meadows	6.5	17.0	20.04.71	Kendal	Newcastle	19	9	2	-	-	-
England: u21, Students.					London Irish	10+1	5	1	-	-	-

The Avenue, Sunbury-on-Thames, Middlesex. TW16 5EQ

Tel: 01932 783034   **Fax:** 01932 784462

CAPACITY: 7,200   **SEATED:** Covered 500, Uncovered 1,500   **STANDING:** 5,200

SIMPLE DIRECTIONS:
  By Road: From junction 1 on M3, take the A308 to Kingston. The Avenue is the 2nd turn on the right.
  Nearest Railway Station: Sunbury (Network South East). Turn left at exit, after 400 yds take 2nd right, ground 500yds on right.
CAR PARKING: 200 spaces available in ground. A further 400 spaces nearby

ADMISSION: Season Adults Standing £100, Seated £150.
Matchdays - Adults Standing £10; Seated £15. Children/OAPs £5.

CLUB SHOP: Yes. Shop manager - P. McDonough 01932 783034
CLUBHOUSE: Open 12am -11pm Matchdays. Snacks available.
  Function room: Can hold 150 seated or 250 for buffet. Contact David Banks 01932 783034
TRAINING NIGHTS: Monday, Wednesday & Thursday.

London Irish ground.

MATCHDAY PROGRAMME

Size	B5
Number of pages	72 plus cover
Price	£2
Programme Editor	David Banks 01934 783034

Advertising Rates
        Colour - Full page £1700, half page £1000
        Mono - Full page £850, half page £700

NEWCASTLE R.F.C.

NICKNAME: The Falcons   **FOUNDED:** 1877

President Trevor Bennett, c/o Newcastle R.U.F.C. Kingston Park, Brunton Rd., Kenton Bank Foot,
Newcastle upon Tyne. NE13 8AF. 0191 214 0422 (B)   0191 214 0488 (Fax)

Director of Rugby Rob Andrew, c/o Newcastle R.U.F.C. as above

Chairman Sir John Hall, c/o Newcastle R.U.F.C. as above

General Manager Ken Nottage, c/o Newcastle R.U.F.C. as above

Season 96/97 must surely have been the most exciting year since the club was formed in 1877.

The Falcons sent records tumbling with some of the best rugby ever seen in the North East at our Kingston Park Stadium with five current British Lions playing in a team of multi talented players, many of them internationals, from five different nations. The team work and understanding that the squad developed augur well for our future results in the Allied Dunbar Premiership One in 1997/98.

Our second team and development squad provided classic entertainment for the spectators who turned up to watch them in ever increasing numbers, our crowd base has moved on from around 800 at the start of the season to approximately 4,000 with two sell out attendances of 5,700. A new innovation at the club was the setting up of a supporter club that has already recruited 180 members from scratch during the season, providing away support that had never been a feature in the past.

Rugby in Newcastle is now big business and the support and expertise we received from the input of Sir John Hall and the Sporting Club is providing a solid and magnificent base for Rob Andrew to build a fascinating and bright future for the Falcons in the professional game, competing in World Club Rugby. The Black and White army is on the mark supporting the Falcons stretching our ground facilities to the limit.

The youth and mini policy that is very much part and parcel of our future is showing the benefits of the investment the club has made over the years. Our Under-15s tournament, which Telewest Communications sponsored, is now recognised as a premier competition in which to take part.

The magnificent corporate support we have had from the local business community has undoubtedly been a major factor in our development, and the board of the club are totally appreciated for their interest and participation. So we can all look forward to the new season with great expectations.

Newcastle Rugby Club: Back Row (L-R); Tony Underwood, Ross Wilkinson, Alan Tait, Pat Lam, Va'aiga' Tuigamala, Andy Hetherington, Steve Douglas, Steve Black. Middle Row; Steve Bates, Ross Nesdale, Richard Arnold, Tim Stimpson, Garath Archer, Doddie Weir, Richard Metcalfe, John Dixon, Peter Walton, Nick Popplewell, Matt Long, Neil Metcalfe. Front Row; Paul Van Zandvleit, Gary Armstrong, Andy Blyth, Matt Tetlow, Martin Shaw, Graham Childs, John Bentley, Dean Ryan, Rob Andrew, David Quinn, George Graham, Peter Lewington, Steve O'Neill.

Colours: Black and white hoops   **Change colours:** Black, white and green.

NEWCASTLE FALCONS

COURAGE LEAGUE MATCH DETAILS 1996-97

No	Ven.	Date		Opponents	Att.	Res.	Score	Scorers
1	(H)	07.09	v	Waterloo	1479	W	30-13	Wilkinson(t)Armstrong(t)Popplewell(t)Andrew(t2c2p)
2	(A)	14.09	v	Nottingham	733	W	74-29	Armstrong(4t)Archer(t)Blyth(t)Childs(t)Wilkinson(t)Underwood(t)Andrew(t7c)
3	(H)	21.09	v	Blackheath	1457	W	61- 0	Armstrong(2t)Bentley(t)Weir(t)Arnold(t)Graham(2t)Frankland(t) Underwood(t)Stimpson(t)Andrew(4cp)
4	(A)	28.09	v	Richmond	6567	D	20-20	Underwood(t)Armstrong(t)Andrew(2c2p)
5	(H)	05.10	v	Rugby	2328	W	156-5	3t - Armstrong,Nesdale,Graham,Ryan. 2t - Popplewell,Underwood, Bentley,Tetlow. 1t - Bates,Blyth,Stimpson,Weir. Andrew(18c)
6	(A)	12.10	v	Wakefield	1900	W	47-17	Archer(t)O'Neill(t)Bentley(t)Ryan(t)Stimpson(t)Armstrong(t)Popplewell(t) Andrew(6c)
7	(A)	19.10	v	Moseley	2003	W	75- 9	Bentley(3t)Tetlow(2t)O'Neill(t)Ryan(t)Nesdale(t) Popplewell(t)Armstrong(t)Underwood(t)Andrew(3c)Stimpson(7c)
8	(H)	26.10	v	Bedford	2261	W	49-12	Tetlow(t)Bentley(t)Archer(t)Armstrong(t)Blyth(t)PenTry(t)Stimpson(tc) Andrew(3c2p)
9	(A)	02.11	v	Coventry	7800	L	18-19	Andrew(5pdg)
10	(A)	16.11	v	Lon. Scottish	2566	W	28-12	Stimpson(3t)Andrew(2c3p) Weir(t)Lam(t)Hetherington(t)Andrew(6cp)
11	(A)	08.02	v	Rugby	1190	W	70- 8	Bentley(3t)Nesdale(2t)Underwood(t)Armstrong(t)Van Zandvliet(t)
12	(H)	08.03	v	Wakefield	2092	W	57-10	Bentley(4t)Underwood(2t)Tait(t)Vanzandvliet(t)Andrew(t6c)
13	(H)	16.03	v	Nottingham	1739	W	53-17	Bates(3t)Archer(2t)Shaw(t)Lam(t)Ryan(t)Armstrong(t)Andrew(3c)Stimpson(c)
14	(H)	22.03	v	Moseley	1690	W	88-19	Bentley(3t)Tuigamala(3t)Lam(2t)Stimpson(2t5c)Armstrong(t)Nesdale(t)Wilson(t) PenTry(t)Andrew(4c)
15	(H)	29.03	v	Richmond	5645	W	37-17	Ryan(t)Popplewell(t)Archer(t)Weir(t)Andrew(4c3p)
16	(A)	05.04	v	Bedford	5200	L	28-34	Tait(t)Lam(t)Graham(t)Andrew(2c3p)
17	(H)	12.04	v	Coventry	3200	W	49-17	Nesdale(2t)Bentley(t)Childs(t)Tait(t)Tuigamala(t)Stimpson(t)Andrew(t3cp)
18	(A)	16.04	v	Blackheath	4650	W	72-10	Tuigamala(2t)Lam(2t)Walton(2t)Nesdale(t)Ryan(t)Shaw(t)Bentley(t) Stimpson(t4c)Andrew(t2c)
19	(A)	19.04	v	Rotherham	3025	W	45-21	Bentley(t)Lam(t)Archer(t)Tuigamala(t)Bates(t)PenTry(t)Andrew(t5c)
20	(H)	26.04	v	Lon. Scottish	2507	W	71-20	Armstrong(2t)Tuigamala(2t)Graham(t)Childs(t)Bentley(t) O'Neill(t)Walton(t)Stimpson(t3c)Andrew(t5c) Andrew(7c)
21	(A)	30.04	v	Waterloo	2500	W	66-24	Lam(2t)Walton(2t)Tuigamala(2t)Blyth(t)O'Neill(t)V-Zandvliet(t)Stimpson(tc)
22	(H)	04.05	v	Rotherham	3406	W	61-13	Lam(5t)Armstrong(2t)Bentley(t)Childs(t)Tait(t)Andrew(c)Stimpson(c)Tuigamala(c)

1996-97 HIGHLIGHTS

LEAGUE DEBUTS: Tim Stimpson, Andrew Blyth, Graham Childs, Ross Nesdale, George Graham, Gareth Archer, Steve O'Neill, John Bentley, Steve Bates, Alan Tait, Pat Lam, Va'aiga Tuigamala.

TRY ON DEBUT:
Gareth Archer, Steve Bates, John Bentley, Pat Lam.

PLAYERS USED: 28 plus 4 as replacement.

EVER PRESENT: Rob Andrew

❏ Rob Andrew scores in all 22 games to break Simon Mason's record. Mason, who set his record in 1994-95, held the record scoring in 18 consecutive games.

❏ Gary Armstrong set a new club record of scoring tries in eight consecutive games. This easily beat the club record of three shared by a number of players. His eight also equalled the National league record held by Sale's Winger Simon Verbickas. Verbickas achieved his feat in the 1993-94 season helping Sale to the second division Championship.

❏ Newcastle set new National and Division two records for points scored, 1255, tries scored, 189, and conversions kicked, 119.

❏ Gary Armstrong and John Bentley both scored a club record four tries in a match but on the final day of the season this was beaten. In the home fixture against Rotherham the Western Samoan flanker Pat Lam scored five. This also equalled the division two and National league record. The divion two record he now shares with Sale's Simon Verbickas. The other players to score five National league tries are Kenny Logan of Wasps and Otley's Mark Kirkby.

❏ Rob Andrew broke Simon Mason's record of 193 points in a season set in 1994-95. Andrew finished the season on 297 his total included a National league record for conversions in a season 95. In Newcastle's national league record breaking 156-5 win over Rugby Andrew set a club record for points in a match, 36, and a national League record of 18 conversions.

	Pts	T	C	P	D	Apps	Ave.
R Andrew 96-97	297	7	95	23	1	22	13.50
S Mason 94-95	193	1	22	45	2	18	10.72
D Johnson 91-92	147	1	31	26	1	12	12.25

NEWCASTLE FALCON'S COURAGE LEAGUE MATCH DETAILS 1996-97

	15	14	13	12	11	10	9	1	2	3	4	5	6	7	8	Replacements	
1	Stimpson	Wilkinson	Blyth	Childs	Underwood	Andrew	Armstrong	Popplewell	Nesdale	Graham	Metcalfe	Weir	Walton	Arnold	Ryan		1
2	Belgian	Wilkinson	Blyth	Childs	Underwood	Andrew	Armstrong	Long	Nesdale	Graham	Archer	Weir	O'Neill	Arnold	Ryan		2
3	Stimpson	Bentley	Blyth	Childs	Underwood	Andrew	Armstrong	Popplewell	Frankland	Graham	Archer	Weir	O'Neill	Arnold	Ryan		3
4	Stimpson	Bentley	Blyth	Childs	Underwood	Andrew	Armstrong	Popplewell	Nesdale	Graham	Archer	Weir	O'Neill	Arnold	Ryan		4
5	Stimpson	Bentley	Blyth	Tetlow	Underwood	Andrew	Armstrong	Popplewell	Nesdale	Graham	Archer	Weir	O'Neill	Arnold	Ryan	Bates(11)	5
6	Stimpson	Bentley	Blyth	Tetlow	Underwood	Andrew	Armstrong	Popplewell	Frankland	Graham	Archer	Weir	O'Neill	Arnold	Ryan		6
7	Stimpson	Bentley	Blyth	Tetlow	Underwood	Andrew	Armstrong	Popplewell	Nesdale	Graham	Metcalfe	Weir	Walton	O'Neill	Ryan	Shaw(11)	7
8	Stimpson	Bentley	Tetlow		Shaw	Andrew	Armstrong	Popplewell	Nesdale	Graham	Archer	Weir	Walton	O'Neill	Ryan	v Zandvliet(3)	8
9	Stimpson	Bentley	Tetlow		Underwood	Andrew	Armstrong	Popplewell	Nesdale	Graham	Archer	Weir	Walton	O'Neill	Ryan		9
10	Stimpson	Shaw	Tetlow	Childs	Underwood	Andrew	Bates	v Zandvliet	Nesdale	Graham	Archer	Weir	Walton	O'Neill	Ryan		10
11	Stimpson	Tait	Childs		Underwood	Andrew	Armstrong	Popplewell	Nesdale	Graham	Archer	Weir	Lam	Arnold	Ryan	Tetlow(15),Hetherington(7)	11
12	Stimpson	Bentley	Tait	Tuigamala	Underwood	Andrew		Long	Nesdale	Graham	Archer	Weir	Lam	Arnold	Ryan	Shaw(14),Smith(1)	12
13	Shaw	Childs		Tuigamala	Underwood	Andrew	Armstrong	Long	Nesdale	v Zandvliet	Archer	Weir	Lam	Arnold	Ryan	Blyth(14),Bates(11)	13
14	Stimpson	Bentley		Tuigamala	Underwood	Andrew	Armstrong	Popplewell	Nesdale	Graham	Archer	Weir	Lam	Arnold	Ryan	Wilson(13),Bates(9),Vyvyan(5),Zandvliet(3)	14
15	Stimpson	Bentley	Tait	Tuigamala	Underwood	Andrew	Armstrong	Popplewell	Nesdale	Graham	Archer	Weir	Lam	Arnold	Ryan	O'Neill(8)	15
16	Stimpson	Bentley	Tait	Tuigamala	Underwood	Andrew	Armstrong	Popplewell	Nesdale	Graham	Archer	Weir	O'Neill	Arnold	Lam	Childs(11),Vyvyan(r6)	16
17	Stimpson	Bentley	Tait	Tuigamala	Underwood	Andrew	Armstrong	Popplewell	Nesdale	Graham	Archer	Weir	Lam	Arnold	Ryan	Shaw(13),Walton(7),Frankland(6),v Zandvliet(1)	17
18	Stimpson	Bentley	Shaw	Tuigamala	Underwood	Andrew	Armstrong	Popplewell	Nesdale	Graham	Archer	Weir	Lam	Arnold	Ryan	Bates(9),Frankland(2),O'Neill(3)	18
19	Stimpson	Bentley	Shaw	Tuigamala	Underwood	Andrew	Armstrong	Popplewell	Nesdale	Graham	Archer	Weir	Walton	Lam	Arnold	Blyth(13),Frankland(2),Bates(9),O'Neill(6)	19
20	Stimpson	Bentley	Shaw	Tuigamala	Childs	Andrew	Armstrong	Popplewell	Nesdale	Graham	Metcalfe	Weir	O'Neill	Arnold	Watton	Blyth(13),Vyvyan(6)	20
21	Blyth	Tetlow		Tuigamala	Childs	Andrew	Armstrong	Popplewell	Nesdale	Graham	Archer	Weir	Walton	Arnold	Ryan	O'Neill(7),Bentley(11),Frankland(2),Bates(15),Lam(8)	21
22	Bentley	Tait		Tuigamala	Childs	Andrew	Armstrong	Graham	Nesdale	v Zandvliet	Metcalfe	Weir	Lam	Arnold	Watton	O'Neill(5),Tetlow(14)	22

NEWCASTLE LEAGUE STATISTICS
(COMPILED BY STEPHEN McCORMACK)

Season	Div.	P	W	D	L	F (Tries Con Pen DG)					A (Tries Con Pen DG)					Most Points	Most Tries
87-88	2	10	2	1	7	124	(14	4	16	4)	145	(21	5	16	1)	56 - David Johnson	4 - David Walker
88-89	2	11	4	0	7	176	(21	13	21	1)	248	(41	14	12	6)	57 - Peter Clark	3 - David Walker
89-90	2	11	1	1	9	108	(11	5	17	1)	266	(39	25	20	0)	62 - Graham Spearman	1 - by 11 players
90-91	2	12	6	0	6	169	(20	10	21	2)	140	(16	8	15	5)	66 - David Johnson	5 - Steve Douglas
91-92	2	12	7	0	5	371	(57	31	26	1)	140	(16	8	15	5)	147 - David Johnson	10 - Peter Walton
92-93	2	12	10	0	2	241	(22	16	30	3)	106	(7	4	20	1)	136 - David Johnson	6 - Ross Wilkinson
93-94	1	18	2	1	15	190	(17	6	27	4)	483	(54	27	51	2)	79 - David Johnson	4 - Ross Wilkinson
94-95	2	18	8	2	8	373	(37	22	46	2)	281	(20	8	52	4)	193 - Simon Mason	8 - Tony Penn
95-96	2	18	5	1	12	348	(38	22	24	1)	405	(40	26	44	7)	73 - Richard Cramb	4 - Mike Brummitt & Gary Armstrong
96-97	2	22	19	1	2	1255	(189	119	23	1)	346	(46	25	20	2)	297 - Rob Andrew	23 - John Bentley
Totals		144	64	7	73	3355	(426	246	251	20)	2560	(300	247	269	33)		

	HOME	AWAY
BIGGEST WIN	(151pts) 156-5 v Rugby 5.10.96	(66pts) 75-9 v Moseley 19.10.96
DEFEAT	(43pts) 9-52 v Northampton 21.10.95	(61pts) 5-66 v Leicester 12.3.94
MOST POINTS SCORED	156-5 v Rugby 5.10.96	75-9 v Moseley 19.10.96
AGAINST	9-52 v Northampton 21.10.95	5-66 v Leicester 12.3.94

MOST CONSECUTIVE VICTORIES - 6

MOST TRIES IN A MATCH
(FOR) 24 v Rugby 5.10.96 (H)
(AGAINST) 10 v Leicester 12.3.94

CONSECUTIVE APPEARANCES
44 Neil Frankland 13.1.90 - 2.10.93

MOST CONSECUTIVE DEFEATS - 12

MOST APPEARANCES
FORWARD: 96(5) Neil Frankland
BACK: 105 Ross Wilkinson

CONSECUTIVE SCORING MATCHES
Scoring Tries - 8 - Gary Armstrong
Scoring Points - 22 - Rob Andrew

MOST	in a SEASON	in a CAREER	in a MATCH
Points	297 Rob Andrew 96-97	484 David Johnson 87-94	36 Rob Andrew v Rugby 5.10.96 (H)
Tries	23 John Bentley 96-97	25 Gary Armstrong 95-97	5 Pat Lam v Rotherham 4.5.97 (H)
Conversions	95 Rob Andrew 96-97	102 Rob Andrew 95-97	18 Rob Andrew v Rugby 5.10.96 (H)
Penalties	45 Simon Mason 94-95	105 David Johnson 87-94	6 David Johnson v Morley 11.1.92 (H)
Drop Goals	4 David Johnson 87-88	10 David Johnson 87-94	2 David Johnson v Bedford 5.12.87 (A)

NEWCASTLE PLAYING SQUAD

NAME	Ht	Wt	Birthdate	Birthplace	Club	Apps	Pts	T	C	P	DG

BACKS

NAME	Ht	Wt	Birthdate	Birthplace	Club	Apps	Pts	T	C	P	DG
Tim Stimpson	6.3	15.7	10.09.73	Liverpool	Wakefield						
England: 6, A, Emerging, u21, Students, u18, u16.					West Hartlepool	23	203	7	21	42	2
					Newcastle	21	116	14	23	-	-
Tony Underwood	5.9	12.10	17.02.69	Ipoh (Mal.)	Leicester	42	111	24			
England: 25, B, Students, Schools.					Newcastle	20	60	12	-	-	-
John Bentley	6.0	15.7	05.09.66		Sale	8	11	2	-	1	-
England: 3.		(via Leeds (RL) & Halifax (RL) to)			Newcastle	17+1	115	23	-	-	-
Alan Tait	6.0	14.0	02.07.64		Previous Clubs: Kelso, Widnes (RL), Leeds (RL).						
Scotland: 10		G.B. (RL).			Newcastle	20	4	-	-	-	-
Va'aiga Tuigamala					Wasps	15	3	-	-	-	-
Western Samoa: 1			New Zealand:		Newcastle	11	57	11	2	-	-
Rob Andrew	5.9	12.8	18.02.63	Richmond (Yorks)	Previous Clubs: Nottingham, Toulouse.						
England: 71		British Lions: 5			Wasps	77	748	16	82	161	11
					Newcastle	25	323	7	102	27	1
Gary Armstrong	5.8	13.8	30.09.66	Edinburgh	Jed-Forest						
Scotland: 34					Newcastle	24	25	125	-	-	-
Steve Bates	5.10	13.0	04.03.63	Merthyr Tydfil	Wasps	91+1	28	6	-	-	-
England: 1, A, B.					Newcastle	1+6	28	5	-	-	-
Matt Tetlow											
					Newcastle	18+3	30	6	-	-	-
Graham Childs	6.0	13.7	03.04.68	Fareham	Northern						
England: A, u21.					Wasps	61	55	12	-	-	-
					Newcastle	17+1	20	4	-	-	-
Andrew Blyth	6.0	13.9	02.10.75	Hexham	West Hartlepool	10	10	2			
England: A, u21, Colts, u18.					Newcastle	10+3	20	4	-	-	-

FORWARDS

NAME	Ht	Wt	Birthdate	Birthplace	Club	Apps	Pts	T	C	P	DG
George Graham	5.7	17.0	19.01.66	Stirling	Previous Clubs: Lon. Scottish, Stirling Co., Carlisle (RL).						
Scotland: A, B.					Newcastle	19	35	7	-	-	-
Ross Nesdale	5.10	16.2	30.07.69	Auckland	Auckland						
Ireland: 3.					Newcastle	21	55	11	-	-	-
Nick Popplewell	5.10	17.3	06.04.64	Dublin	Greystones						
Ireland: 44		British Lions: 3			Wasps	13	-	-	-	-	-
					Newcastle	20	45	9	-	-	-
Paul Van Zandvliet	6.0	17.0	14.10.66	Newcastle	Whitley Bay Rockliff						
					Newcastle	54+4	40	8	-	-	-
Neil Frankland	5.11	14.0	16.02.63	Leeds	Ilkley						
					Newcastle	96+5	34	7	-	-	-
Dodie Weir	6.6	17.7	04.07.70	Edinburgh	London Scottish	3	4	1	-	-	-
Scotland: 45, A, Students, u21, u18. (via Melrose to)					Newcastle	24	25	5	-	-	-
Gareth Archer	6.6	18.0	15.12.74	South Shields	Bristol	16	5	1			
England: 2, A, u21, Colts, u18.					Newcastle	36+1	45	9	-	-	-
Richard Metcalfe	7.1	19.0	21.11.73	Leeds	Sandal						
England: A, u21.					Newcastle	35+2	10	2	-	-	-
Peter Walton	6.3	18.0	03.06.69	Alnwick	Alnwick						
Scotland: 10, A, Schools. England: Colts.					Northampton	27	10	2	-	-	-
					Newcastle	26+1	70	16	-	-	-
Pat Lam	6.1	15.10	29.09.68		Prev. Clubs: Auckland, N. Harbour, Canterbury (NZ)						
Western Samoa		New Zealand:			Newcastle	10+1	75	15	-	-	-
Steve O'Neill	6.1	16.7	10.10.72	Blaydon	Blaydon						
Durham					Newcastle	11+5	20	4	-	-	-
Dean Ryan	6.6	17.0	22.06.66	Tuxford	Saracens	13	-	-	-	-	-
England: 3, A, B.					Wasps	69	56	12	-	-	-
					Newcastle	23	50	10	-	-	-
Richard Arnold	6.4	15.12	16.08.65	Taranaki (NZ)							
					Newcastle	76	54	12	-	-	-
Andrew Hetherington	5.11	15.0	03.09.68	Usk							
England: University, Schools.					Newcastle	36+4	5	-	-	-	-

Kingston Park, Brunton Rd., Kenton Bank Foot, Newcastle NE13 8AF

Tel: 0191 214 0422

Fax: 0191 214 0422

CAPACITY: 8,000   **SEATED:** 2,200   **STANDING:** 5,800

SIMPLE DIRECTIONS:
By Road: Travelling from North or South on the City bypass take the Newcastle Airport sign & follow signs for Kingston Park (Rugby Ground), approx 1 mile
Nearest Railway Station: Newcastle Central then Metro to Kingston Park or Bank Foot

CAR PARKING: 600 at ground, 800-1000 nearby

ADMISSION:
Season; Standing, Adults £99, Children/OAPs £65. Seated, Adults £165, Children/OAPs no concession
Matchday; Standing, Adults £12, Children/OAPs £7. Seated, Adults £15, Children/OAPs no concession

CLUB SHOP: Yes; Manager TBA

CLUBHOUSE: Normal Licensing Hours, three bars with food available
Function room: Yes available for hire, capacity 200 - contact Stephen Wafer 0191 286 6200

TRAINING NIGHTS: Tuesday & Thursday

Captain: Dean Ryan.

Player of the Year: Garry Armstrong

MATCHDAY PROGRAMME

Size	A5
Number of pages	44 plus cover
Price	£2
Programme Editor	T B A, contact Club Line
Advertising Rates	Negotiable Contact - Gen Manager

NORTHAMPTON R.F.C.

NICKNAME: Saints

FOUNDED: 1880

Director of Rugby Ian McGeechan O.B.E. Trinity Pavilion, Abbey Street, St. James', Northampton. NN5 5LN.
Tel: 01604 751543   Fax: 01604 599100

Rugby Administrator Ros Hargreaves, Trinity Pavilion, as above

Chief Executive Geoff Allen, Sturtridge Pavilion, Weedon Road, St. James', Northampton. NN5 5BG.
Tel: 01604 751543   Fax: 01604 599110

So near, yet so far.

There are any number of cliches you could use to describe the 1996/97 Saints' season, but overall the impression is one of flattering to deceive.

At various stages in the campaign the Saints were in the top four of the league only to fall away to eighth. They were in the quarter finals of the European Conference, the only English side left to stand out against a French monopoly, and they were also two games from Twickenham in the Pilkington Cup.

In the league it was wretched away results that prevented a serious tilt at a top four spot (and with it entry into the European Cup), but in the cup competitions the side faltered at Franklin's Gardens in front of their own passionate supporters - those who had earned the club the nickname of Fortress Franklin's.

The big question those same fans will be asking throughout the summer is whether the Saints can build on the successful parts of the season just gone in what will be an infinitely stronger division next season: the Allied Dunbar Premiership.

Coming up are Richmond and Newcastle, both seemingly with unlimited reserves of cash; London Irish and Bristol survived by the skin of their teeth in play-off games, while Gloucester have an initial £2 million to play with.

Other teams engaged in a mindless exercise of bringing in Rugby League stars on short-term contracts. Amid all this, the Saints tried to retain the old rugby traditions allied to a more professional approach.

The administration of the game still has to catch up and Saints Director of Rugby Ian McGeechan was constantly bemoaning the lack of structure to the season. Club versus country is now a clearly defined problem, which simply did not exist before.

The politics of the game threaten to rumble on for many years, but for Saints fans, and indeed for all clubs, they want to see their team up there challenging for honours.

Skipper Tim Rodber with the Carlsberg-Tetley trophy.

Extract from the review by Brian Barron (editor of Saints matchday magazine) in the Saints yearbook.

Colours: Black, green, gold

Change colours: White with black, green & gold hoops.

NORTHAMPTON

No	Ven.	Date	Opponents	Att.	Res.	Score	Scorers
1	(H)	31.08	v W Hartlepool	4775	W	46-20	Bell(2t)Beal(t)Moir(t)Dawson(t)PTry(t)Grayson(5c2p)
2	(A)	07.09	v London Irish	3170	L	21-34	Rodber(t)PTry(t)Dods(t3c)
3	(H)	14.09	v Bristol	4593	W	29-21	Bell(t)Beal(t)Rodber(t)Grayson(t2pdg)
4	(H)	21.09	v Orrell	4474	W	41- 7	Bell(2t)Hunter(t)Thorneycroft(t)Dawson(t)Rodber(t)MacKinnon(t)Grayson(3c)
5	(H)	28.09	v Harlequins	7602	L	15-20	Bell(t)Beal(t)Grayson(cp)
6	(H)	05.10	v Sale	5127	W	30-12	Beal(t)Clarke(t)Grayson(c4p2dg)
7	(A)	29.10	v Saracens	4254	L	23-24	Allen(t)Beal(t)Grayson(2c3p)
8	(H)	09.11	v Bath	7566	W	9- 6	Grayson(2pdg)
9	(A)	08.12	v Leicester	11839	L	9-23	Grayson(2p)Townsend(dg)
10	(A)	28.12	v Wasps	4838	L	13-18	Chandler(t)Grayson(c2p)
11	(H)	11.01	v Leicester	7907	W	22-19	Townsend(t)Grayson(c5p)
12	(A)	19.01	v Bath	7000	L	14-52	McNaughton(t)Grayson(p)Beal(2p)
13	(H)	08.02	v Saracens	7525	W	17-10	Hunter(t)Grayson(4p)
14	(A)	04.03	v Gloucester	4748	L	6-19	Dods(2p)
15	(A)	09.03	v Sale	2486	L	15-31	Townsend(5p)
16	(A)	29.03	v Orrell	1100	W	50-14	Seely(2t)Wright(t)Bell(t)Cohen(t)Thorneycroft(t)Townsend(t3c3p)
17	(A)	05.04	v Bristol	4254	L	11-20	Hunter(t)Townsend(2p)
18	(H)	12.04	v London Irish	5470	W	31-21	Townsend(t)Hunter(t)Hepher(t2c4p)
19	(A)	19.04	v W Hartlepool	2200	W	57-17	Townsend(2t)Allen(2t)Cassell(2t)Merlin(t)Thorneycroft(t)Beal(t)Hepher(6c)
20	(H)	26.04	v Wasps	7274	L	15-26	Hepher(5p)
21	(A)	30.04	v Harlequins	4405	L	16-36	Hepher(tc2pdg)
22	(H)	03.05	v Gloucester	4602	L	25-27	PenTry(t)Hepher(c6p)

1996-97 HIGHLIGHTS

LEAGUE DEBUTS:
Chris Johnson, Matt Stewart, Don MacKinnon, Shem Tatupu, John Hearn, Jason Chandler, Dominic Malone, Gavin Walsh, Ben Cohen, S Barnes.

PLAYERS USED: 38 plus 3 as replacement.

EVER PRESENT: None
- most appearances 20 (1) Harvey Thornecroft.

❑ Winger Harvey Thorneycoft becomes the first Northampton player to reach 100 appearances and ends the season on 111(2). He is also heads the clubs all-time try scoring list just one ahead of England A centre Matt Allen.

	Tries	Apps	Try Every
Harvey Thorneycroft	26	111(2)	4.27 games
Matt Allen	25	47	1.88 games

Allen has made a prodigious start to his career and has one of the best strike rates around in league rugby.

❑ Captain Tim Rodber passes Gary Pearce's record for appearances by a forward 76. Rodber ends the season with a ner record of 88(1) and next season should become the club's second player to 100 appearances after winger Harvey Thorneycroft.

❑ Had an excellent home record with nine wins and two losses but a disastrous away record - exactly the opposite - two wins and nine losses. The two away wins were at Orrell and West Hartlepool.

❑ England Stand-off Paul Grayson broke the record for drop goals in a season with four. The previous record of three was held by John Steele and Grayson himself. Grayson passed 1000 league points in his career which started in 1988 with Preston Grasshoppers.

	Pts	T	C	P	D	Apps	Ave.
Preston G	265	5	19	62	7	27	9.81
Waterloo	126	1	8	29	6	10	12.60
Northampton	665	7	111	127	10	61	10.90
TOTAL	1056	13	138	218	23	98	10.76

Grayson also extended his club record for conversions and penalties past the 100 mark to end on 111 and 127 respectively. He is also just one drop goal behind John Steele's club record of 11.

❑ Grayson topped the Northampton points scoring list for the fourth consecutive season and is just one behind John Steele's record of five. In total it was the seventh successive season that Grayson had topped 100 league points - every season since 1990-91.

Preston G	1990-91, 1991-92.
Waterloo	1992-93
Northampton	1993-93 through 1996-97

NORTHAMPTON'S COURAGE LEAGUE MATCH DETAILS 1996-97

#	15	14	13	12	11	10	9	1	2	3	4	5	6	7	8	Replacements
1	Beal	Moir	Bell	Townsend	Thorneycroft	Grayson	Dawson	Volland	Johnson	Stewart	Foale	Merlin	MacKinnon	Pountney	Rodber	Seely(8)
2	Beal	Hunter	Bell	Allen	Dods	Townsend	Dawson	Volland	Clarke	Lewis	Foale	Merlin	MacKinnon	Pountney	Rodber	Wright(4)
3	Beal	Allen	Bell	Allen	Thorneycroft	Grayson	Dawson	Volland	Clarke	Lewis	Phillips	Foale	MacKinnon	Pountney	Rodber	
4	Hunter	Beal	Townsend	Bell	Thorneycroft	Townsend	Dawson	Volland	Clarke	Stewart	Phillips	Foale	MacKinnon	Pountney	Rodber	Allen(12)
5	Hunter	Beal	Townsend	Bell	Thorneycroft	Grayson	Dawson	Volland	Clarke	Lewis	Phillips	Foale	MacKinnon	Pountney	Rodber	Allen(12)
6	Beal	Moir	Townsend	Allen	Thorneycroft	Grayson	Dawson	Volland	Johnson	Hynes	Phillips	Foale	MacKinnon	Pountney	Rodber	Clarke(2),Tatupu(6)
7	Beal	Moir	Townsend	Bell	Thorneycroft	Grayson	Dawson	Volland	Clarke	Hynes	Phillips	Hearn	Tatupu	Pountney	Rodber	Allen(12),Fountaine(5)
8	Beal	Hunter	Townsend	Allen	Thorneycroft	Grayson	Dawson	Johnson	Clarke	Hynes	Phillips	Foale	Tatupu	Pountney	Hunter	Cassell(8)
9	Grayson	Beal	Bell	Allen	Thorneycroft	Townsend	Dawson	Volland	Johnson	Hynes	Phillips	Chandler	Cassell	Pountney	Rodber	Hunter(12)
10	Beal	Hunter	McNaughton	Allen	Thorneycroft	Grayson	Malone	Volland	Clarke	Walsh	Phillips	Chandler	Tatupu	Pountney	Cassell	Cassell(8)
11	Beal	Bell	Townsend	Allen	Thorneycroft	Grayson	Taylor	Volland	Clarke	Walsh	Phillips	Chandler	Tatupu	Pountney	Cassell	Cassell(6)
12	Hunter	Beal	McNaughton	Allen	Thorneycroft	Grayson	Taylor	Volland	Clarke	Hynes	Phillips	Chandler	Tatupu	Cassell	Seely	Malone(10)
13	Beal	Bell	Townsend	Allen	Thorneycroft	Grayson	Taylor	Volland	Beddow	Hynes	Phillips	Chandler	Tatupu	Pountney	Rodber	
14	Dods	Moir	Townsend	Allen	Thorneycroft	Grayson	Taylor	Beddow	Beddow	Stewart	Phillips	Chandler	Seely	Cassell	Rodber	Barnes(5)Beales(10)Taylor(tr14)
15	Hunter	Moir	Bell	Bell	Thorneycroft	Townsend	Dawson	Hynes	Beddow	Stewart	Phillips	Chandler	Tatupu	Cassell	Rodber	Volland(1)Walsh(3)Hepher(15)Seely(5)
16	Hepher	Cohen	Bell	Allen	Thorneycroft	Townsend	Dawson	Hynes	Clarke	Stewart	Chandler	Phillips	Tatupu	Wright	Seely	Rodber(6),Beddow(2),Foale(4)
17	Hunter	Beal	Bell	Bell	Thorneycroft	Townsend	Dawson	Volland	Clarke	Stewart	Phillips	Chandler	Rodber	Wright	Seely	Cohen(12)Foale(5)Johnson(6)
18	Hunter	Beal	Townsend	Allen	Thorneycroft	Hepher	Dawson	Volland	Clarke	Hynes	Phillips	Foale	Merlin	Cassell	Seely	Barnes(6)Moir(tr11)
19	Hunter	Beal	Townsend	Allen	Thorneycroft	Hepher	Dawson	Volland	Clarke	Hynes	Phillips	Merlin	Merlin	Cassell	Seely	Moir(13)Hearn(5)Johnson(2)Stewart(3)Barnes(6)Taylor(12)
20	Hunter	Beal	Townsend	Allen	Thorneycroft	Hepher	Dawson	Volland	Clarke	Stewart	Phillips	Bayfield	Foale	Cassell	Seely	Moir(13)
21	Moir	Cohen	McNaughton	Allen	Thorneycroft	Hepher	Taylor	C Allen	Johnson	Lewis	Phillips	Hearn	Barnes	Cassell	Merlin	Hunter(11)Foale(5)Seely(8)
22	Hunter	Moir	Bell	Cohen	Allen	Taylor	Taylor	Volland	Beddow	Stewart	Phillips	Bayfield	Foale	Cassell	Seely	Bramhall(9)Barnes(5)Clarke(2)Tcroft(14)McNaughton(15)

NORTHAMPTON LEAGUE STATISTICS
(COMPILED BY STEPHEN McCORMACK)

Season	Div.	P	W	D	L	F	(Tries	Con	Pen	DG)	A	(Tries	Con	Pen	DG)	Most Points	Most Tries
87-88	2	10	1	0	9	81	(10	7	9	0)	226	(33	20	16	2)	27 - Phil Larkin	4 - Paul Alston
88-89	2	11	5	2	4	165	(28	10	10	1)	131	(12	7	17	6)	43 - John Steele	6 - Frank Packman
89-90	2	11	9	1	1	192	(23	11	22	4)	135	(12	6	22	3)	105 - John Steele	4 - Frank Packman & John Thame
90-91	1	12	5	1	6	149	(15	10	20	3)	254	(38	18	19	3)	83 - John Steele	3 - Wayne Shelford
91-92	1	12	9	1	2	209	(22	11	30	3)	136	(11	7	23	3)	110 - John Steele	5 - Harvey Thorneycroft
92-93	1	12	8	0	4	215	(24	16	20	1)	150	(11	4	27	2)	52 - John Steele	6 - Harvey Thorneycroft
93-94	1	18	9	0	9	305	(23	14	50	4)	342	(34	17	40	6)	132 - Paul Grayson	2 - by 7 players
94-95	1	18	6	0	12	267	(16	11	52	3)	335	(35	20	36	4)	189 - Paul Grayson	3 - Grant Seely & Matt Dawson
95-96	2	18	18	0	0	867	(128	88	14	3)	203	(23	14	16	4)	215 - Paul Grayson	20 - Matt Allen
96-97	1	22	10	0	12	515	(52	30	59	6)	477	(47	28	60	2)	129 - Paul Grayson	7 - Jonathon Bell
Totals		144	80	5	59	2965	(341	208	286	28)	2389	(256	141	276	35)		

	HOME	AWAY
BIGGEST WIN	(64pts) 69-5 v Waterloo 13.4.96	(66pts) 69-3 v Waterloo 28.10.95
BIGGEST DEFEAT	(47pts) 3-50 v London Scottish 3.10.87	(60pts) 0-60 v Orrell 27.10.90
MOST POINTS SCORED	69-5 v Waterloo 13.4.96	69-3 v Waterloo 28.10.95
AGAINST	3-50 v London Scottish 3.10.87	0-60 v Orrell 27.10.90

MOST CONSECUTIVE VICTORIES - 20

MOST CONSECUTIVE DEFEATS - 6

MOST TRIES IN A MATCH
(FOR) 11 v Blackheath 14.10.95,
v Waterloo 28.10.95 & 13.4.96
(AGAINST) 11 v Orrell 27.10.90

MOST APPEARANCES
FORWARD: 88(1) Tim Rodber
BACK: 111(2) Harvey Thorneycroft

CONSECUTIVE APPEARANCES
31 Frank Packman

CONSECUTIVE SCORING MATCHES
Scoring Tries - 4 - Ian Hunter
Scoring Points - 18 - Paul Grayson

MOST	in a SEASON	in a CAREER	in a MATCH
Points	215 Paul Grayson 95-96	665 Paul Grayson 93-97	26 Paul Grayson v Bristol 2.10.93 (A)
Tries	20 Matt Allen 95-96	23 Matt Allen 94-96	4 Craig Moir v Waterloo 13.4.96 (H)
Conversions	76 Paul Grayson 95-96	111 Paul Grayson 93-97	7 Paul Grayson v Lon Irish 9.9.95 (H) v Lon Scottish 4.11.95 (H) v Lon Scottish 27.4.96 (A) Michael Dods v Blackheath 14.10.95 (H)
Penalties	52 Paul Grayson 94-95	127 Paul Grayson 93-96	6 Paul Grayson v W Hartlepool 5.11.94 (H) Alastair Hepher v Gloucester 3.5.97 (H)
Drop Goals	4 Paul Grayson 96-97	11 John Steele 88-94	3 John Steele v Wasps 23.3.91 (A)

NORTHAMPTON PLAYING SQUAD

NAME	Ht	Wt	Birthdate	Birthplace	Club	Apps	Pts	T	C	P	DG
BACKS											
Ian Hunter	6.2	14.10	15.02.68	Harrow	Nottingham	2	-	-	-	-	-
England: 7, A, Students					Northampton	69+2	84	16	-	3	1
Nick Beal	6.2	13.8	02.12.70	York	High Wycombe						
England: 2, A.					Northampton	68	14	16	11	12	1
Craig Moir			28.10.73								
Wales: u21, Schools.					Northampton	27+4	50	10	-	-	-
Harvey Thorneycroft	6.0	15.11	22.02.69	Northampton	Nottingham	12	3	-	-	-	-
England: A, Students, u21, Colts.					Northampton	111+2	26	123	-	-	-
Jonathan Bell	5.11	15.0	07.02.74	Belfast							
Ireland: 21, A, Students, u21, Schools.					Northampton	19	60	12	-	-	-
Gregor Townsend	6.1	13.7	16.04.73	Edinburgh	Gala						
Scotland: 25, A, Students, u21, u18.					Northampton	23	129	18	3	10	1
Matt Allen	6.2	15.2	28.02.74	Farnborough							
England: A, Students, u21.					Northampton	47+2	125	25	-	-	-
Paul Grayson	6.0	12.7	30.05.71	Chorley	Preston G/hoppers	?	265	5	19	62	6
England: 8, A, Emerging, u21.					Waterloo	10	126	1	8	29	6
					Northampton	61	665	7	111	127	10
Matt Dawson	5.11	12.10	31.10.72	Birkenhead							
England: 6, A, u21, u18.					Northampton	72+1	100	18	1	2	1
Brett Taylor			31.07.68								
					Northampton	20+6	-	-	-	-	-
Alastair Hepher			03.10.74								
					Northampton	8+1	87	2	10	17	2
Michael Dods	5.10	11.9	30.12.68	Galashiels	Gala						
Scotland: , A, u21, u18.					Northampton	11	76	8	15	1	-
Ben Cohen											
					Northampton	2+1	5	1	-	-	-
Rob McNaughton											
					Northampton	44+2	18	4	-	-	-
FORWARDS											
Matt Volland	6.0	16.7	30.06.74	Peterborough							
England: u21.					Northampton	39+2	-	-	-	-	-
Chris Johnson					Leicester	7+1	5	1	-	-	-
England: Students					Northampton	3+2	-	-	-	-	-
Matt Stewart											
Scotland: 5					Northampton	9+1	-	-	-	-	-
Martin Hynes	5.9	16.0	23.08.68	Wigan	Orrell	65	4	1	-	-	-
England: A					Northampton	36	-	-	-	-	-
Allan Clarke	5.9	14.0	29.07.67	Dungannon							
Ireland: 5, A, u21.					Northampton	39+2	35	7	-	-	-
Martin Bayfield	6.10	19.0	21.12.66	Bedford							
England: 31, A, Schools. British Lions: 7.					Northampton	60	24	5	-	-	-
Jon Phillips	6.6	17.0	16.08.72	Peterborough							
England: u21, Colt.					Northampton	66	15	3	-	-	-
Jason Chandler											
					Northampton	10	5	1	-	-	-
Justyn Cassell					Saracens	33	13	3	-	-	-
					Harlequins	11+1	10	2	-	-	-
					Northampton	16+4	15	3	-	-	-
Tim Rodber	6.6	16.7	02.07.65	Richmond (Yorks)							
England: 32, A, B, u21.					Northampton	88+1	77	16	-	-	-
Grant Seely	6.4	16.2	07.01.74	Aylesbury	Aylesbury						
England: u21.					Northampton	32+3	95	19	-	-	-
Budge Pountney	6.2	15.0	13.11.73	Southampton							
England: Students, u21.					Northampton	41+2	50	10	-	-	-
Simon Foale	6.4	16.9		Northampton							
					Northampton	24+8	5	1	-	-	-
Shem Tatupu					Wigan (RL)						
					Northampton	8+1	-	-	-	-	-
Dave Merlin	6.4	16.5	22.05.72		Worcester						
					Northampton	12+3	25	5	-	-	-

Tel: 01604 751543   **Fax:** 01604 599110

CAPACITY: 9,000   **SEATED Covered:** 4,450   **STANDING Covered:** 3,300
                                            Uncovered: 650   **Uncovered:** 600

SIMPLE DIRECTIONS:
   By Road: From the M1 junction 16, follow the signs for Northampton and then follow town centre signs, turn right into Abbey Street.
   Nearest Railway Station: Northampton

CAR PARKING: 1000, £2/3.

ADMISSION:
Season; Standing Adults £119, Children/OAPs £62. Seated Adults £155-£197, Children/OAPs £80-£87
Matchday; Standing Adults £10, Children/OAPs £5. Seated Adults £12-£14, Children/OAPs £6-7

CLUB SHOP: Yes, Manager Joanne Bage 01604 599111

CLUBHOUSE: Matchday & Training nights only, bar meals available
   Function room: Yes available for hire, capacity 200,
   contact Paula Towers 01604 599114, or Ken Ball 01604 599119

TRAINING NIGHTS: Tuesday & Thursday

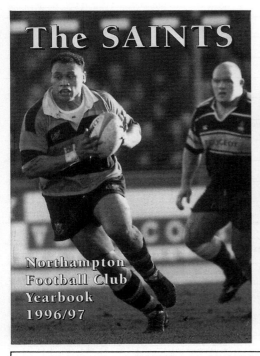

Shem Tatupu - Player of the Year

MATCHDAY PROGRAMME

Size	A5	**Editor**	Brian Barron 01604 29483
Number of pages	36	**Advertising Rates**	Full page £1500 + Vat
Price	£2	Colour	Half page £875 + Vat
			Qtr page £ 500 + Vat

RICHMOND F.C.

FOUNDED: 1861

President David Buchanan, 12 Rosehill Road, London SW18 2NX
0181 870 2714 (H), 0181 871 4907 (B).

Chief Executive Symon Elliott, c/o Richmond FC, The Athletic Ground,
Kew Foot Road, Richmond, Surrey TW9 2SS.
0181 332 7112 (B), 0181 332 7113 (Fax)

General Manager Peter Moore, c/o Richmond FC, as above

Director of Rugby John Kingston, c/o Richmond FC, as above

Press Officer Michelle Lawrence, 0181 332 7112

Richmond, with some style, achieved their second successive promotion to move into the top League for the first time in their history. In finishing as champions of the league, they won all but one match, scoring 986 league points in the process.

This side had changed substantially from the previous season with the influx of several top names to the club, but it was most pleasing to see that many of the individuals involved in the winning of the League Three championship the year before had a role to play in securing promotion for the side. A total of 38 squad members actually played in the promotion campaign and it is testimony to the quality of the players already at the club together with the speed at which the newcomers settled that we were able to win the League with such injury problems.

Many of the international names shone at League Two level, but Andy Moore at scrum half proved to be the most consistent performer and deservedly won his award as Player of the Year. The development of Spencer Brown on the left wing in the second half of the season led to him winning the Young Player of the Year award and he is clearly a player to look out for in the future.

The Premier Division will provide a stern test but already recruitment has been active over the summer period, and, given the quality of players which lie within the club and the continuing development of the always active youth section, Richmond move into the top sector of the game with confidence.

The side will once again be captained by Ben Clarke from the back row, with Adrian Davies (who suffered injury over the last season) being made vice-captain for this season.

The club was pleased to gave several Internatioional representatives over the season, with Simon Mason (Ireland), Ben Clarke (England), Craig Quinnell, Scott Quinnell, Allan Bateman (all Wales) all representing their country. The selection of Allan Bateman and Scott Quinnell for the British Lions also brought much pleasure to the club. Barry Williams another current British Lion is joining us next season and he will be looking to fill the not inconsiderable boots of Brian Moore.

Richmond FC celebrating after winning The Divison Two Championship

Colours: Old gold, red & black.   Change colours: Black with wide red and thin gold bands.

RICHMOND

No	Ven.	Date	Opponents	Att.	Res.	Score	Scorers
1	(A)	07.09	v Coventry	3850	D	16-16	Whitford(t)Boyd(t)Mason(2p)
2	(H)	14.09	v Rotherham	1032	W	64-38	S Quinnell(3t)Fallon(t)A Moore(t)Davies(t)B Moore(t)Mason(2t8cp)
3	(A)	21.09	v Bedford	3510	W	44-17	Cottrell(2t)Hutton(t)A Moore(t)Whitford(t)Davies(t)Mason(4c2p)
4	(H)	28.09	v Newcastle	6567	D	20-20	S Quinnell(t)PenTry(t)Mason(2cp)Davies(dg)
5	(A)	05.10	v Moseley	1612	W	87-15	S Quinnell(3t)Fallon(3t)C Quinnell(2t)Hutton(t)Bateman(t)Davies(t)Cottrell(t)B Clarke(t)Mason(7cp)
6	(H)	12.10	v London Scot	4500	W	54-13	Bateman(2t)Fallon(t)S Quinnell(t)Davies(t)Mason(t5c3p)
7	(H)	19.10	v Rugby	1600	W	64- 8	Fallon(2t)Bateman(2t)Leach(2t)Davies(2t(Masont7c)
8	(A)	26.10	v Blackheath	3405	W	40-21	Harvey(t)B Clarke(t)PenTry(t)Mason(2c6p)Davies(dg)
9	(H)	02.11	v Waterloo	1500	W	64-13	S Quinnell(4t)C Quinnell(3t)Brown(2t)Bateman(t)Mason(7c)
10	(A)	09.11	v Wakefield	1200	W	23- 7	B Clarke(t)S Quinnell(t)Fallon(t)Gregory(c2p)
11	(A)	16.11	v Nottingham	611	W	70- 5	Brown(2t)Bateman(2t)Fallon(t)S Quinnell(t)C Quinnell(t)Whitford(t)Boyd(t)Mason(t7c2p)
12	(H)	28.12	v Coventry	3200	W	39-12	S Quinnell(2t)Brown(t)B Clarke(t)Boyd(t)Mason(4c2p)
13	(H)	25.01	v Bedford	2875	W	34-33	Brown(t)Rodgers(t)Vander(t)B Clarke(t)Cottrell(t)Mason(3cp)
14	(H)	08.02	v Moseley	1452	W	37-27	C Quinnell(2t)Brown(t)Vander(t)B Clarke(t)Mason(t2cp)
15	(A)	22.02	v Rotherham	2025	W	28- 6	Bateman(t)Fallon(t)Brown(t)Mason(2c3p)
16	(A)	08.03	v London Scot	1348	W	37-18	Cuthbert(t)Fallon(t)C Quinnell(t)Va'a(t)Mason(t3c2p) Mason(t8cp)
17	(A)	22.03	v Rugby	575	W	72-31	S Quinnell(3t)Jones(t)Deane(t)Fallon(t)A Moore(tdg)B Clarke(t)Cottrell(t)
18	(A)	29.03	v Newcastle	5645	L	17-37	Fallon(2t)Clarke(t)Mason(c)
19	(H)	05.04	v Blackheath	1706	W	29-24	Cooke(t)Crompton(t)L Jones(t)B Clarke(t)Mason(3p)
20	(A)	12.04	v Waterloo	1500	W	58-29	C Quinnell(2t)S Quinnell(t)Bateman(t)A Moore(t)Cottrell(t)Davies(t)Fallon(t)Mason(6c2p)
21	(H)	19.04	v Wakefield	1359	W	55-22	Fallon(3t)Brown(2t)S Quinnell(t)B Clarke(t)Codling(t)Mason(t5c)
22	(H)	26.04	v Nottingham	1658	W	34- 0	A Moore(2t)Brown(t)Davies(t)B Clarke(t)Mason(3p)

1996-97 HIGHLIGHTS

LEAGUE DEBUTS: Simon Mason, Tom Whitford, Steve Cottrell, Adrian Davies, Andy Moore, Dan McFarland, Brian Moore, Darren Crompton, Craig Quinnell, Richard West, Ben Clarke, Scott Quinnell, Allan Bateman, Adam Vander, Rick Leach, Chris Clark, Steve Atherton, Earl Va'a, Mel Deane, Jeremy Cooke, Adam Jones.

TRY ON DEBUT:
Tom Whitford, Earl Va'a and Jeremy Cooke.

PLAYERS USED: 33 plus 4 as replacement.

EVER PRESENT: Andy Moore.

❏ Set a new record for consecutive victories with 12 easily beating the previous record of seven.

❏ Winger Spencer Brown set a new record scoring tries in five consecutive matches. The previous record (3) was shared by Jim Fallon, Rick Forde and Mike Hutton.

❏ Jim Fallon, in his second spell, passed Mike Hutton to go top of the club's all-time try scoring list with 28.

❏ Welsh international No 8 Scott Quinnell nearly doubled the previous record of 11 tries in a season

set by Adrian Boyd last season. Quinnell scores 21 tries in 20 games.

❏ Irish international full back Simon Mason re-wrote the record book in an amazing season. He broke the Division Two record of Michael Corcoran (301) and the club record of John Gregory (196) for points in a season with 324 from 21 games. His 324 included 83 conversions, smashing Martin Livesey's 1989-90 record of 24 and wiping out Livesey's career record of 74 set between 88-94. The 36 penalties Mason kicked last season was just four short of the 40 set by Gregory in 95-96.
Below is a comparison of the club and Division Two season records.

	Pts	T	C	P	D	Apps	Ave.
S Mason 96-97	324	10	83	36	-	21	15.43
J Gregory 95-96	196	4	28	40	-	17	11.57
M Corcoran 95-96	301	8	36	63	-	18	16.72

❏ Mason broke John Gregory's record of 23 points in a match three times during the season. His highest was the 29 he scored against Rotherham in September. In that game he set a new record for conversions with eight which he later equalled in the away game at Rugby. He also equalled the club record of six penalties in a match, held by three other players, in the away fixture at Blackheath

RICHMOND'S COURAGE LEAGUE MATCH DETAILS 1996-97

#	15	14	13	12	11	10	9	1	2	3	4	5	6	7	8	Replacements
1	Mason	Boyd	Whitford	Cottrell	Hutton	Davies	A.Moore	McFarland	B.Moore	Crompton	C.Quinnell	West	Jones	B.Clarke	S.Quinnell	
2	Mason	Fallon	Whitford	Cottrell	Hutton	Davies	A.Moore	McFarland	B.Moore	Crompton	C.Quinnell	West	Jones	Clarke	S.Quinnell	
3	Mason	Fallon	Whitford	Cottrell	Hutton	Davies	A.Moore	McFarland	B.Moore	Crompton	C.Quinnell	West	Jones	B.Clarke	S.Quinnell	
4	Mason	Fallon	Bateman	Cottrell	Hutton	Davies	A.Moore	McFarland	B.Moore	Crompton	C.Quinnell	West	Vander	B.Clarke	S.Quinnell	
5	Mason	Fallon	Bateman	Cottrell	Hutton	Davies	A.Moore	McFarland	Rodgers	Crompton	C.Quinnell	West	Leach	B.Clarke	S.Quinnell	
6	Mason	Fallon	Bateman	Cottrell	Hutton	Davies	A.Moore	McFarland	B.Moore	Crompton	C.Quinnell	West	Leach	B.Clarke	S.Quinnell	
7	Mason	Fallon	Bateman	Cottrell	Hutton	Davies	A.Moore	Foster	Rodgers	Codling	C.Quinnell	West	Leach	B.Clarke	S.Quinnell	Palmer(8)
8	Mason	Fallon	Bateman	Cottrell	Hutton	Davies	A.Moore	McFarland	B.Moore	Crompton	C.Quinnell	West	Jones	B.Clarke	S.Quinnell	Harvey(14)
9	Mason	Fallon	Bateman	Cottrell	Hutton	Boyd	A.Moore	Foster	B.Moore	Yeldham	C.Quinnell	West	Jones	B.Clarke	S.Quinnell	
10	Gregory	Fallon	Cottrell	A.Clarke		Davies	A.Moore	McFarland	B.Moore	Crompton	C.Quinnell	West	Jones	B.Clarke	S.Quinnell	Harvey(10)
11	Mason	Fallon	Bateman	Whitford	Brown	Boyd	A.Moore	Foster	B.Moore	Crompton	C.Quinnell	West	Jones	B.Clarke	S.Quinnell	Rodgers(8)Yeldham(3)Codling(4)
12	Mason	Fallon	Bateman	Hutton	Brown	Boyd	A.Moore	C.Clark	B.Moore	Crompton	C.Quinnell	West	Vander	B.Clarke	S.Quinnell	Short(11)
13	Mason	Fallon	Bateman	Cottrell	Brown	Boyd	C.Clark	Rodgers		Crompton	C.Quinnell	West	Vander	B.Clarke	S.Quinnell	Atherton(8)Short(13)
14	Mason	Fallon	Whitford	Cottrell	Brown	Boyd	C.Clark	Rodgers		Crompton	C.Quinnell	West	Vander	B.Clarke	S.Quinnell	
15	Mason	Fallon	Bateman	Cottrell	Brown	Boyd	C.Clark	Cuthbert	Rodgers	Crompton	C.Quinnell	West	Vander	B.Clarke	S.Quinnell	
16	Mason	Fallon	Bateman	Cottrell	Brown	Proctor	C.Clark	Cuthbert		Crompton	C.Quinnell	Atherton	Jones	B.Clarke	S.Quinnell	Davies(14)Leach(8)
17	Mason	Fallon	Deane	Cottrell	Brown	Va'A	A.Moore	Foster	B.Moore	Crompton	C.Quinnell	Atherton	Jones	B.Clarke	S.Quinnell	Davies(10)Darragh(8)Codling(4)
18	Mason	Fallon	Cottrell	Bateman	Brown	Davies	A.Moore	Foster	B.Moore	Crompton	C.Quinnell	Atherton	Vander	B.Clarke	S.Quinnell	Cuthbert(2)L.Jones(8)
19	Cooke	Fallon	Cottrell	Cottrell	A.Jones	Davies	A.Moore	Foster	Cuthbert	Crompton	C.Quinnell	Atherton	Vander	B.Clarke	S.Quinnell	Yeldham(3)
20	Mason	Fallon	Bateman	Cottrell	A.Jones	Davies	A.Moore	Foster	Cuthbert	Crompton	C.Quinnell	Atherton	Vander	B.Clarke	S.Quinnell	L.Jones(7)Yeldham(3)Codling(4)
21	Mason	Fallon	Bateman	Cottrell	Brown	Davies	A.Moore	Foster	B.Moore	Crompton	C.Quinnell	Codling	B.Clarke	Vander	S.Quinnell	L.Jones(8)Va'a(12)
22	Mason	Fallon	Bateman	Va'a	Brown	Davies	A.Moore	Foster	B.Moore	Crompton	C.Quinnell	Atherton	L.Jones	Vander	B.Clarke	Hutton(10)Codling(5)Cuthbert(2)

RICHMOND LEAGUE STATISTICS

(COMPILED BY STEPHEN McCORMACK)

Season	Div.	P	W	D	L	F (Tries Con Pen DG)	A (Tries Con Pen DG)	Most Points	Most Tries
87-88	2	11	6	0	5	140 (14 6 20 4)	156 (22 7 16 2)	60 - Simon Smith	5 - Simon Pennock
88-89	2	11	4	1	6	112 (8 4 21 3)	216 (24 18 25 3)	74 - Martin Livesey	3 - Paul Seccombe
89-90	2	11	7	1	3	282 (41 29 20 0)	135 (16 4 19 2)	120 - Martin Livesey	7 - Jim Fallon
90-91	2	12	3	1	8	134 (17 9 14 2)	245 (25 14 31 8)	38 - Martin Livesey	6 - Mike Hutton
91-92	3	12	10	1	1	296 (39 22 26 6)	124 (13 9 17 1)	95 - Martin Livesey	6 - Phil Della-Savina
92-93	2	12	5	0	7	204 (19 4 25 2)	196 (15 8 33 2)	95 - Martin Livesey	3 - David Sole
93-94	3	18	9	0	9	337 (30 26 40 5)	300 (30 18 37 1)	90 - Martin Livesey	6 - Paul Greenwood
94-95	3	18	6	1	11	319 (31 19 41 1)	290 (27 16 39 2)	136 - John Gregory	4 - Andy Cuthbert & Adrian Boyd
95-96	3	18	13	1	4	476 (57 31 43 0)	266 (27 19 27 4)	196 - John Gregory	11 - Adrian Boyd
96-97	2	22	19	1	2	986 (139 84 38 3)	410 (48 31 34 2)	324 - Simon Mason	21 - Scott Quinnell
Totals		145	82	7	56	3286 (395 234 288 26)	2338 (247 144 278 27)		

	HOME	AWAY
BIGGEST WIN	(78pts) 86-8 v Headingley 28.4.90	(72pts) 87-15 v Moseley 5.10.96
DEFEAT	(25pts) 15-40 v London Scottish 17.11.90	(41pts) 9-50 v Sale 10.9.88
MOST POINTS SCORED	86-8 v Headingley 28.4.90	87-15 v Moseley 5.10.96
AGAINST	15-40 v London Scottish 17.11.90	9-50 v Sale 10.9.88

MOST CONSECUTIVE VICTORIES - 13   **MOST CONSECUTIVE DEFEATS - 9**

MOST TRIES IN A MATCH   **MOST APPEARANCES**
(FOR) 16 v Headingley 28.4.90   FORWARD:
(AGAINST) 8 v Sale 10.9.88   BACK:

CONSECUTIVE APPEARANCES

CONSECUTIVE SCORING MATCHES
Scoring Tries - 5 - Spencer Brown
Scoring Points - 19 - Martin Livesey

MOST	in a SEASON	in a CAREER	in a MATCH
Points	324 Simon Mason 96-97	512 Martin Livesey 88-94	29 Simon Mason v Rotherham 14.9.96 (H)
Tries	21 Scott Quinnell 96-97	27 Jim Fallon 89-90 & 96-97	4 Scott Quinnell v Waterloo 2.1.96 (H)
Conversions	83 Simon Mason 96-97	83 Simon Mason 96-97	8 Simon Mason v Rotherham 14.9.96 (H) v Rugby 22.3.97 (A)
Penalties	36 Simon Mason 96-97	100 Martin Livesey 88-94	6 Nick Preston v Bedford 27.3.88 (H) Martin Livesey v Lon Irish 8.4.89 (H) Jon Clark v Lydney 14.3.92 (H) Simon Mason v Blackheath 26.10.96 (A)
Drop Goals	6 Martin Livesey 91-92	14 Martin Livesey 88-94	3 Martin Livesey v Northampton 19.11.88 (H)

NAME	Ht	Wt	Birthdate	Birthplace	Club	Apps	Pts	T	C	P	DG
BACKS											
Simon Mason			22.10.73	Birkenhead	Liverpool St. Helens	15	140	3	16	30	1
Ireland: 3, A, Students, u21.					Newcastle	18	193	1	21	45	2
					Orrell	16	166	4	16	38	-
					Richmond	21	324	10	83	36	-
Spencer Brown	5.11	12.9	11.07.73	Eton	Deal						
Navy					Richmond	15	60	12	-	-	-
Jim Fallon	6.1	14.4	27.03.66	Devon							
England: A, B.					Richmond		-	-	-	-	-
Allan Bateman	5.9	13.3	06.03.65		Cronulla (RL)						
Wales: 9.					Richmond	17	50	10	-	-	-
Steve Cottrell	6.1	14.7	22.10.67	Christchurch	Rotherham	3	-	-	-	-	-
N.Z. Development XV, Universities.					Richmond	19	35	7	-	-	-
Earl Va'a	5.6	13.0	01.05.72								
					Richmond	3+1	5	1	-	-	-
Adrian Davies	5.9	12.8	09.02.69	Bridgend	Cardiff						
Wales: 9, A, B, u21, Schools.					Richmond	13+2	54	9	-	-	-
Andy Moore	5.11	13.2	06.09.68	Cardiff	Cardiff						
Wales: 4, Students, u20, u19.					Richmond	21	25	5	-	-	-
Agustin Pichot			22.08.74	Buenos Aires							
Argentina: 10, u21, u19.					Richmond		-	-	-	-	-
Adrian Boyd	5.10	11.9	09.08.72	Enfield	Previous Clubs: Orpington, Westcombe Park.						
England: Students, u21.					Richmond	32	90	18	-	-	-
Jonathan Gregory	6.1	13.8	02.06.73	Chertsey							
					Richmond	38	346	5	48	75	-
Andy Clark	5.7	12.13	14.08.74								
England: u21, Students					Richmond	6	25	5	-	-	-
Mike Hutton	6.0	15.7	09.04.70								
England: u21.					Richmond	93+1	100	22	-	-	-
FORWARDS											
Chris Clark	6.0	16.0	01.09.71	Poole	Swansea						
England: A, u21, u18.					Bath	7+2	-	-	-	-	-
					Richmond	4	-	-	-	-	-
Darren Crompton	6.1	17.0	12.09.72	Exeter	Bath	5+1	-	-	-	-	-
England: A, Emerging, u21, u18.					Richmond	20	5	1	-	-	-
Andy Cuthbert	5.10	14.7	11.02.68								
England: u21.					Richmond	50+2	65	13	-	-	-
Richard West	6.9	19.10	28.03.71	Hereford	Gloucester	49+2	10	2	-	-	-
England: 1, A, Emerging, u21, Students.					Richmond	14	-	-	-	-	-
Craig Quinnell			09.07.75	Swansea							
Wales: 6, u21, u19, Schools.					Richmond	19	55	11	-	-	-
Scott Quinnell	6.4	18.5	02.08.72	Swansea	Previous Clubs: Llanelli, Wigan (RL).						
Wales: 14, A, B, Youth, u18.					Richmond	20	105	21	-	-	-
Steve Atherton	6.6	17.12	17.03.65		Natal						
South Africa: 10					Richmond	7+1	-	-	-	-	-
Alex Codling	6.4	17.10	25.09.63		Blackheath	23	5	1	-	-	-
					Richmond	4+4	5	1	-	-	-
Ben Clarke	6.5	18.0	15.04.68	Bishops Stortford	Saracens	22	35	8	-	-	-
England: 33, A, Students.					Bath	61	68	14	-	-	-
					Richmond	21	50	10	-	-	-
Adam Vander	6.2	15.7	27.01.74		Prev. Clubs: Rosslyn Park, Bath.						
England: u19, u18.					Richmond	11	10	2	-	-	-
Luke Jones	6.3	14.7	06.11.70	Suffolk							
					Richmond	35+3	-	-	-	-	-
Barrie Williams											
Wales: 1					Richmond		-	-	-	-	-
Jim Foster	6.1	16.10	24.03.67		Chinnor						
					Richmond	76	13	3	-	-	-
Matt Yeldham	5.11	17.0	29.01.69								
England: Students.					Richmond	45+6	8	2	-	-	-
Rolando Martin											
Argentina: 28, Students.					Richmond		-	-	-	-	-
Dan McFarland					Morley						
					Richmond	8	-	-	-	-	-

The Athletic Ground, Kew Foot Road, Richmond, Surrey. TW9 2SS.

Tel: 0181 332 7112
CAPACITY: 8,000   **SEATED:** 3,340
Fax: 0181 332 7113
STANDING: 4,660

SIMPLE DIRECTIONS:
  By Road: On main A316 past Richmond Circus roundabout heading towards Twickenham.
  Nearest Railway Station: Richmond (BR & Underground)

CAR PARKING: 400 on ground £3.

ADMISSION:
  Season; Standing Adult £145, OAPs £ 79. Seated Adult £ 195, OAPs £ 99
  Matchday; Standing Adults £11, OAPs £5, Children £1. Seated Adults £15, OAPs £13, CHildren £5

CLUB SHOP: Yes; Manager Jen Gadsby Peet 0181 933 8321

CLUBHOUSE: Normal licensing hours (except Sunday Evening). Two Bars with snacks, barmeals & restaurant.
  Function room: Yes available for hire, capacity 180 - contact Miss Louise Veale c/o Club

TRAINING NIGHTS: Tuesdays & Thursdays

Player of the Year; Andy Moore

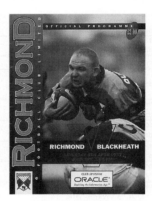

MATCHDAY PROGRAMME

Size	A5
Number of pages	44 plus cover
Price	£2

Programme Editor
Michelle Lawrence 0181 332 7112

Advertising Rates	Colour Full page £1500
	1/2 page £800

SALE F.C.

FOUNDED: 1861

President Richard Trickey, c/o Sale FC, Heywood Road, Sale M33 3WB
0161 973 6348 (Club), 0161 969 4124 (Fax)

Chairman Nick Lunt, c/o Sale Fc. as above

Chief Executive Howard Thomas, c/o Sale FC, as above

Club Secretary Mike Atherton, c/o Sale FC, as above
0161 973 6013 (H), 0161 973 6348 (Club), 0161 969 4124 (Fax)

At the start of the 1996/97 season the usual predictions about relegation were present. Sale, during the close season, had internal turmoil with the departure of Paul Turner. No big name signings apart from Dewi Morris were coming to Heywood Road and there was no financial backer on the horizon.

However, the team, under new coach John Mitchell worked hard all summer and it transpired that the season was relatively succcessful with a league position of fifth and a Pilkington Cup Final appearance for the first time ever.

In truth the main ambition for the club was a place in the European Cup. This was not to be, and Sale were pipped by Leicester after a bruising and controversial 20-20 draw in the last match of the season. The club can look to early season form for missing out on Europe. Bristol won at Sale as did Wasps by 33-31 and the lack of a goal kicker and a fly half were apparent. Simon Mannix arrived from New Zealand and results improved. On a memorable night in October Sale ended Harlequins' unbeaten record in the League, winning under the lights of Heywood Road by 24-13. This signalled a run of good form with notable victories over Harlequins away, by a last minute drop goal, and Bath at home with arguably the finest display of defensive rugby ever seen by a Sale team. Despite all this a European Cup place was not to be.

In the Pilkington Cup, victories over Richmond, Orrell and Northampton took the club to only their third semi-final. Yet another brilliant performance against Harlequins gave Sale a place in the final for the first time. A narrow defeat by Leicester in a poor game at Twickenham followed.

Yes it was a good season, but hardened Sale supporters still think of what might have been.

Sale FC: Back Row (L-R); Luke Hewson, Phil Winstanley, Andy Morris, Simon Mannix, Murray Driver, Simon Verbikas, Chris Yates, Tom Beim. Standing; John Mitchell (Player/Coach), Dylan O'Grady, Sean Fletcher, Dave Erskine, Richard McCartney, John Fowler, Charles Vyvyan, Dave Baldwin, Andrew Smith, Mark Nelson (Asst Coach). Seated; Mark Warr, Steve Diamond, Dewi Morris, Jim Mallinder (Capt), Adrian Hadley (Player/Manager), John O'Reilly, Joss Baxendell,David Rees. Front Row; Robbie Dickson (Equipment Officer), Alan Blease (Asst Manager).

Colours: Royal blue & white hoops/blue shorts.   **Change colours:** Red & black hoops/red shorts.

COURAGE LEAGUE MATCH DETAILS 1996-97

No	Ven.	Date	Opponents	Att.	Res.	Score	Scorers
1	(H)	31.08	v Wasps	2394	L	31-33	Beim(2t)O'Grady(t)Rees(t)Stocks(c3p)
2	(A)	07.09	v Gloucester	4014	W	16-12	Diamond(t)Griffin(c3p)
3	(H)	14.09	v W Hartlepool	1296	W	58-18	Morris(2t)Baxendell(2t)Warr(2t)Rees(t)Vyvyan(t)Verbickas(t5cp)
4	(A)	21.09	v London Irish	2650	W	25-19	Warr(t)Ryan(t)Stocks(t2cp)Verbickas(p)
5	(H)	28.09	v Bristol	2041	L	31-33	Ryan(t)A Morris(t)Mallinder(t)PTry(t)Stocks(c3p)
6	(A)	05.10	v Northampton	5127	L	12-30	Mallinder(t)Ryan(t)Verbickas(c)
7	(H)	30.10	v Harlequins	3929	W	24-13	Morris(2t)Vyvyan(t)Mannix(3p)
8	(H)	09.11	v Orrell	2204	W	37-11	O'Grady(2t)Erskine(t)Baldwin(t)Beim(t)Mannix(3c2p)
9	(A)	08.12	v Saracens	1424	D	17-17	McCartney(t)Mannix(4p)
10	(A)	18.01	v Orrell	2500	W	40- 8	Mannix(2t)Morris(2t)Mallinder(t)Beim(t)O'Grady(t)A Smith(t)
11	(A)	08.02	v Harlequins	2889	W	31-30	Baldwin(2t)Fowler(t)Vyvyan(t)Hadley(c2p)C Yates(dg)
12	(A)	04.03	v Leicester	7320	L	9-25	Mannix(3p)
13	(H)	09.03	v Northampton	2486	W	31-15	C Yates(t)Mannix(t7p)
14	(A)	22.03	v Bristol	3524	L	24-34	Mallinder(t)C Yates(t)Verbickas(c4p)
15	(H)	02.04	v Bath	4777	W	11- 5	Beim(t)Mannix(2p)
16	(A)	05.04	v W Hartlepool	1800	W	43-22	Beim(3t)Mitchell(t)D Morris(t)Rees(t)Mannix(t4c)
17	(H)	12.04	v Gloucester	2614	W	52-12	Beim(2t)Hadley(t)Erskine(t)Fowler(t)PenTry(t)Mannix(2t6c)
18	(H)	15.04	v Saracens	2702	W	33-23	Driver(2t)Hadley(t)C Yates(t)Mannix(2c3p)
19	(A)	20.04	v Wasps	6270	L	10-36	Beim(t)Hadley(c)Mannix(p)
20	(H)	23.04	v London Irish	2320	W	41-25	Beim(2t)Rees(2t)Erskine(t)Mallinder(t)Hadley(4cp)
21	(A)	26.04	v Bath	6900	L	7-84	Hewson(t)Griffin(c)
22	(H)	03.05	v Leicester	4250	D	20-20	Winstanley(t)Mannix(t2c2p)

1996-97 HIGHLIGHTS

LEAGUE DEBUTS:
Tom Beim, John Devereux, Phil Winstanley, John Mitchell, Simon Mannix, Dewi Mooris, John O'Reilly, Adrian Hadley, Murray Driver, Darren Wright, J Fletcher, M Moore, Adam Griffin, M Karraitian.

TRY ON DEBUT: Tom Beim.

PLAYERS USED: 36 plus 5 as replacement.

EVER PRESENT: None - most appearances 21
— Jim Mallinder and Jos Baxendell.

☐ Dave Baldwin and Jim Mallinder both reach 100 league appearances in the last minute win at Harlequins.

☐ Only Bath, 116, and Harlequins, 96, scored more than Sale's 76 tries.

☐ Suffered their worst ever defeat losing 7-84 at Bath. This was the week before they played Leicester in the final league game of the season to decide who went into Europe and they fielded a virtual second XV.

☐ Full back and now England International Jim Mallinder extended his club record for tries to 33. This is 13 more than number two on the list Simon Verbickas.

☐ New Zealand international stand-off Simon Mannix makes an immediate impact as he helped Sale defeat an unbeaten Harlequins on his debut. Mannix went from strength to strength and ended the season with 150 points and an impressive reputation.
He broke the Sale record for points in a match when he scored 26 points in his sides 31-15 win at home to Northampton. Included in his 26 points were seven penalties which broke the previous record of five held by David Pears and Rob Liley.
His 150 points was the second highest in a season for Sale and he became the fourth Sale player to score 100 points in a season.

	Pts	T	C	P	D	Apps	Ave.
Rob Liley 95-96	167	3	22	34	2	18	9.28
Simon Mannix 96-97	150	7	17	27	-	12	12.50

Mannix had an average over three points per match higher than Liley

SALE'S COURAGE LEAGUE MATCH DETAILS 1996-97

No.	15	14	13	12	11	10	9	1	2	3	4	5	6	7	8	Replacements
1	Mallinder	Rees	Stocks	Birt	Beim	Baxendell	D Morris	P Smith	Diamond	A Smith	Fowler	Baldwin	O'Grady	A Morris	Vyvyan	Warr(12),P Smith(3),Hewson(7),Verbickas(11)
2	Mallinder	Rees	Devereux	Birt	Beim	Baxendell	D Morris	P Smith	Diamond	A Smith	Fowler	Baldwin	O'Grady	A Morris	Vyvyan	Griffin(12)
3	Mallinder	Rees	Baxendell	Devereux	Beim	Ryan	D Morris	Winstanley	Diamond	A Smith	Fowler	Baldwin	O'Grady	A Morris	Vyvyan	Warr(12),P Smith(3),Hewson(7),Verbickas(11)
4	Mallinder	Rees	Baxendell	Stocks	Yates	Ryan	D Morris	P Smith	Diamond	A Smith	Fowler	Baldwin	O'Grady	A Morris	Vyvyan	Mitchell(8),Verbickas(15)
5	Mallinder	Rees	Baxendell	Stocks	C Yates	Ryan	Warr	Winstanley	Diamond	A Smith	Fowler	Baldwin	O'Grady	A Morris	Vyvyan	Verbickas(11)
6	Mallinder	Rees	Baxendell	Stocks	Verbickas	Ryan	Warr	P Smith	Diamond	A Smith	Fowler	Baldwin	O'Grady	A Morris	Vyvyan	Winstanley(1)
7	Mallinder	Rees	Baxendell	Stocks	Beim	Mannix	D Morris	P Smith	Diamond	A Smith	Fowler	Baldwin	Erskine	A Morris	Vyvyan	O'Reilly(9),A Morris(8)
8	Mallinder	Rees	Baxendell	Stocks	Beim	Mannix	O'Reilly	Winstanley	Diamond	A Yates	Fowler	Baldwin	Erskine	A Morris	Vyvyan	Devereux(12),A Morris(7)
9	Devereux	Rees	Baxendell	Stocks	Beim	Mannix	D Morris	Winstanley	Diamond	A Yates	McCartney	Baldwin	O'Grady	A Morris	Erskine	Wall(1)
10	Mallinder	Rees	Baxendell	Devereux	Beim	Mannix	D Morris	P Smith	Diamond	A Smith	Fowler	Baldwin	O'Grady	A Morris	Vyvyan	Hadley(10)Ashurst(8)
11	Mallinder	Rees	Yates	Hadley	Beim	Baxendell	D Morris	Winstanley	Diamond	P Smith	Fowler	Baldwin	Mitchell	A Morris	Vyvyan	
12	Mallinder	Rees	Baxendell	Hadley	Beim	Mannix	D Morris	Winstanley	Diamond	A Smith	Fowler	Baldwin	Mitchell	A Morris	Vyvyan	A Morris(5)Driver(1)Dryden(tr1)
13	Mallinder	Rees	Baxendell	C Yates	Beim	Mannix	D Morris	Winstanley	Diamond	A Smith	Fowler	Baldwin	Erskine	O'Grady	Mitchell	A Morris(7)Driver(1)Wright(tr10)
14	Mallinder	Rees	Wright	C Yates	Verbickas	Baxendell	D Morris	Winstanley	Diamond	A Smith	Fowler	Baldwin	Erskine	O'Grady	Mitchell	Ashurst(6)
15	Mallinder	Rees	Baxendell	C Yates	Beim	Mannix	O'Reilly	Winstanley	Diamond	A Smith	Fowler	Baldwin	Ashurst	Erskine	Mitchell	Mitchell(6)
16	Mallinder	Rees	Hadley	Baxendell	Beim	Mannix	O'Reilly	Driver	Hewson	A Smith	Fowler	Baldwin	Erskine	O'Grady	Mitchell	Wright(13)A Yates(1)A Morris(7)Sanderson(8)
17	Mallinder	Rees	Baxendell	Hadley	Beim	Mannix	D Morris	Winstanley	Diamond	A Smith	Fowler	Baldwin	Erskine	O'Grady	Mitchell	A Morris(7)Hewson(2)C Yates(13)A Yates(3)O'Reilly(9)
18	Mallinder	Rees	Baxendell	Hadley	Beim	Mannix	D Morris	Winstanley	Diamond	A Smith	Fowler	Baldwin	Mitchell	A Morris	Vyvyan	Erskine(4)
19	Mallinder	Rees	Baxendell	Hadley	Beim	Mannix	D Morris	Winstanley	Diamond	A Smith	Erskine	Baldwin	Mitchell	O'Grady	Vyvyan	Yates(10)
20	Mallinder	Rees	C Yates	Hadley	Beim	Baxendell	D Morris	A Yates	Driver	Hewson	Fowler	Baldwin	Mitchell	A Morris	Vyvyan	O'Grady(4)Ryan(15)O'Reilly(9)Fletcher(5)
21	Griffin	Moore	C Yates	Wright	Verbickas	Ryan	O'Reilly	A Yates	Hewson	Driver	McCartney	Fletcher	Ashurst	A Morris	Karratian	Warr(9)Aby(15)Batt(3)Dobson(7)
22	Mallinder	Rees	Baxendell	Hadley	Beim	Mannix	D Morris	Winstanley	Diamond	A Smith	Erskine	Baldwin	Mitchell	O'Grady	Vyvyan	A Morris(8)Fletcher(tr4)

SALE LEAGUE STATISTICS
(COMPILED BY STEPHEN McCORMACK)

Season	Div.	P	W	D	L	F (Tries Con Pen DG)	A (Tries Con Pen DG)	Most Points	Most Tries
87-88	1	11	0	0	11	95 (9 4 16 1)	375 (60 40 15 3)	49 - Graham Jenion	3 - Howard Fitton
88-89	2	11	6	0	5	195 (18 9 32 3)	152 (16 8 23 1)	102 - David Pears	3 - David Pears
89-90	2	11	4	0	7	153 (16 7 25 0)	182 (23 12 22 0)	29 - Graham Jenion	4 - Phil Stansfield
90-91	2	12	5	1	6	224 (32 15 18 4)	156 (23 11 8 6)	82 - Richard Booth	5 - Jeff Powell
91-92	2	12	6	0	6	204 (23 11 28 2)	209 (25 11 27 2)	79 - Matthew Alexander	5 - Jim Mallinder
92-93	2	12	7	1	4	237 (26 13 22 5)	102 (5 4 20 3)	63 - Phil Jee	7 - Mark Warr
93-94	2	18	13	2	3	438 (57 30 28 3)	160 (9 5 32 3)	144 - Paul Turner	16 - Simon Verbickas
94-95	1	18	7	2	9	327 (39 24 24 4)	343 (32 15 46 5)	92 - Paul Turner	5 - Gareth Stocks & Jim Mallinder
95-96	1	18	9	1	8	365 (39 22 35 7)	371 (39 16 41 7)	167 - Rob Liley	6 - Jos Baxendell
96-97	1	22	13	2	7	603 (39 22 35 7)	525 (39 16 41 7)	150 - Simon Mannix	13 - Tim Beim
Totals		145	70	9	66	2841 (337 171 274 30)	2575 (285 156 294 34)		

	HOME	AWAY
BIGGEST WIN	(79pts) 88-9 v Otley 12.2.94	(32pts) 40-8 v Orrell 18.1.97
BIGGEST DEFEAT	(29pts) 17-46 v Bath 28.4.88	(77pts) 7-84 v Bath 26.4.97
MOST POINTS SCORED	88-9 v Otley 12.2.94	43-22 v W. Hartlepool 5.4.97
AGAINST	17-46 v Bath 28.4.88	7-84 v Bath 26.4.97

MOST CONSECUTIVE VICTORIES - 7

MOST TRIES IN A MATCH
(FOR) 14 v Otley 12.2.94 (H)
(AGAINST) 12 v Harlequins 23.4.88 (A)
v Bath 24.4.97 (A)

CONSECUTIVE APPEARANCES
39 Philip Stansfield 22.10.88-14.3.92

MOST CONSECUTIVE DEFEATS - 11

MOST APPEARANCES
FORWARD: 109 Dave Baldwin
BACK: 110 Jim Mallinder

CONSECUTIVE SCORING MATCHES
Scoring Tries - 8 - Simon Verbickas
Scoring Points - 17 - Rob Liley

MOST	in a SEASON	in a CAREER	in a MATCH
Points	167 Rob Liley 95-96	305 Paul Turner 92-96	27 Simon Mannix v Northampton 9.3.97 (H)
Tries	16 Simon Verbickas 93-94	33 Jim Mallinder 88-97	5 Simon Verbickas v Otley 12.2.94 (H)
Conversions	29 Paul Turner 93-94	55 Paul Turner 92-96	9 Paul Turner v Otley 12.2.94 (H)
Penalties	34 Rob Liley 95-96	47 Paul Turner 92-96	7 Simon Mannix v Northampton 9.3.97 (H)
Drop Goals	4 Paul Turner 95-96	13 Paul Turner 92-96	2 David Pears v Bedford 22.2.89 (H) Paul Turner v Morley 3.10.92 (H) v Wakefield 9.4.94 (A) v Orrell 6.1.96 (H)

SALE PLAYING SQUAD

NAME	Ht	Wt	Birthdate	Birthplace	Club	Apps	Pts	T	C	P	DG
BACKS											
Jim Mallender	6.3	16.0	16.03.66	Halifax	Rounday						
England: 2, A.					Sale	110	159	33	-	-	2
David Rees	5.9	13.7	15.10.74	London	Northern						
England: A, u21, Students, u16.					Sale	25+1	30	6	-	-	-
Tom Beim	6.0	14.0	11.12.75	Frimley	Gloucester	2	5	1	-	-	-
England: u21, u18, u16.					Sale	16	65	13	-	-	-
Adrian Hadley	6.1	15.4	01.03.63	Cardiff	Previous Clubs: Salford (RL), Widnes (RL), Cardiff.						
Wales: 27, B, Youth.					Sale	8+1	31	2	6	3	-
Jos Baxendell	6.0	14.4	03.12.72	Manchester	Sheffield	14	10	2	-	-	-
England: A.					Sale	61	55	11	-	-	-
Chris Yates	6.1	16.10	13.05.71	Otahute (NZ)	Old Aldwinians						
					Sale	32+2	58	+11	-	-	1
John O'Reilly	5.10	13.9	07.01.76		Bristol						
					Sale	4+3	-	-	-	-	-
Simon Mannix	5.8	13.9	10.08.71	Wellington (NZ)	Wellington						
New Zealand: 1					Sale		150	7	17	27	-
Dewi Morris	6.0	14.0	09.02.64	Crickhowell	Winnington Park						
England: 26.		British Lions: 3			Waterloo	20	8	2	-	-	-
					Orrell	62	106	24	-	-	-
					Sale	15	35	7	-	-	-
Simon Verbickas	6.1	13.7	22.04.75	Manchester	Broughton Park	1	2	-	1	-	-
England: u21.					Sale	23+3	32	20	7	6	-
Neil Ryan	5.9	13.4	29.11.77	Wigan	Waterloo						
England: u21, u18.					Sale	5+3	20	4	-	-	-
John Deveraux	6.1	15.0	30.03.66	Pontycymmer	Previous Clubs: Bridgend, Widnes (RL)						
Wales: u21.					Sale	4+1	-	-	-	-	-
Darren Wright					Sale	2+2	-	-	-	-	-
FORWARDS											
Paul Smith	6.0	17.0	28.03.69	Nantwich							
England: 16					Sale	46+1	-	-	-	-	-
Andrew Smith	6.1	17.5	28.03.69	Nantwich	Chester						
England: Emerging.					Sale	72	5	1	-	-	-
Steve Diamond	5.9	14.7	03.02.68	Manchester	Metrovick						
England: A.					Sale	95	20	4	-	-	-
Murray Driver	6.0	17.7	05.04.72	Hamilton (NZ)	Waikato						
New Zealand: Colts, u19, u17.					Sale	6+2	10	2	-	-	-
Luke Hewson	6.0	16.0	06.12.72	Stafford	Sale	10+5	5	1	-	-	-
Alan Yates	6.0	18.0	05.02.63								
					Sale	14+2	-	-	-	-	-
Phil Winstanley	6.0	16.10	19.06.68	Orrell	Orrell	36+2	17	3	-	1	-
					Sale	13+1	5	1	-	-	-
John Fowler	6.8	17.8	06.02.68	Bexley	Richmond	9	4	1	-	-	-
England: A.					Rosslyn Park	17	-	-	-	-	-
					Newcastle	15	-	-	-	-	-
					Sale	43	25	5	-	-	-
Dave Baldwin	6.6	19.0	03.09.65	Ilkley	Bramley						
England: A, B.					Wakefield	11	-	-	-	-	-
					Sale	109	63	13	-	-	-
John Mitchell	6.4	17.3	23.03.64	Hawera (NZ)	Waikato						
					Sale	10+2	5	1	-	-	-
Charlie Vyvyan	6.6	17.4	01.09.65	Wimbledon	Richmond	?	16	4	-	-	-
England: Students					Wharfedale	33	33	7	-	-	-
					Sale	40	55	11	-	-	-
Dylan O'Grady	6.3	16.7	19.01.71	Manchester	Metrovick						
Irish Exiles					Sale	43+3	50	10	-	-	-
Dave Erskine	6.5	17.0	14.10.69	London	Previous Clubs: Boroughmuir, Ciyms (Ire)						
Ireland: A.					Sale	67+4	50	10	-	-	-
Andy Morris	6.0	15.0	01.09.71	Blackburn	Sheffield.	22	10	2	-	-	-
England: u21, Students.					Nottingham	5	-	-	-	-	-
					Sale	15+9	5	1	-	-	-
Neil Ashurst	6.2	16.7	12.05.69	St. Helens	West Park						
England: u21, Colts.					Orrell	39+2	31	7	-	-	-
					Sale	37+3	35	7	-	-	-

Tel: 0161 973 6348

Fax: 0161 969 4124

CAPACITY: 7,500   **SEATED:** 7,000   **STANDING:** 500

SIMPLE DIRECTIONS:
By Road: From M6 junction 19 follow the A556/A56 for approx 8 miles. Turn right into Marsland Road and Heywood Road is on the right after half a mile.
Nearest Railway Station: Brooklands - Metro

CAR PARKING: None on ground, 100 nearby

ADMISSION: Season - Standing; Adults £90, Children/OAPs £45. Seated; Adults £135, Children/OAPs £80.
Matchday - Standing; Adults £10, Children/OAPs £5. Seated; Adults £15, Children OAPs £10.

CLUB SHOP: Yes.

CLUBHOUSE: Monday-Friday 7.00-11.00. Saturday 11.00-11.00. Sunday 12.00-3.00. Snacks available matchdays.
Function room: Yes, capacity 150, contact Liz Burne 0161 973 6348

TRAINING NIGHTS: Tuesday and Thursday

Dewi Morris on another attack during a very successful year with Sale FC

MATCHDAY PROGRAMME

Size   A5

Number of pages   36 plus cover

Price   £1.50

Programme Editor   Jon Elwood, c/o Sale FC

Advertising Rates
Colour Full page £1500, Half page £800.
Mono Full page £1000, Half page £600.

Have you many Rugby enthusiasts at your Club ?
Does you Club need to raise extra funds ?

If the answer to these questions is Yes -
then place an order for

The Official Rugby Union Club Directory

WITH EVERY CLUB IN THE LEAGUE STRUCTURE INCLUDED AND ITS
UNRIVALLED STATISTICAL COVERAGE OF THE CLUBS AND PLAYERS IN
THE TOP LEVELS OF THE LEAGUE SYSTEM IT CAN ANSWER ALL SORTS
OF QUESTIONS AND WOULD MAKE AN IDEAL PRESENT.

Did you realise the Directory is available to your club at very good discount rates.

If you order				Profit for Club
1	copy cost	£14.99		
2 or 3	copies cost	£13.50 each	£ 1.49 each	
between 4 & 9	copies cost	£10.00 each	£ 4.99 each	
between 10 & 19	copies cost	£ 9.00 each	£ 5.99 each	
20 or more	copies cost	£ 8.00 each	£ 6.99 each	

To find out more information or to place an order, contact the publishers:
Tony Williams Publications Ltd., Helland, North Curry, Taunton, Somerset. TA3 6DU.
or Telephone 01823 490080 or Fax 01823 490281

SARACENS

No	Ven.	Date	Opponents	Att.	Res.	Score	Scorers
1	(H)	31.08	v Leicester	6231	W	25-23	Bracken(t)Lynagh(c5p)Tunningley(dg)
2	(A)	08.09	v Wasps	9609	L	21-36	Hill(t)PTry(t)Lynagh(2p)Tunningley(cp)
3	(H)	14.09	v Gloucester	4111	W	41-11	Copsey(2t)Chesney(t)P Wallace(t)R Wallace(t)Lee(5c2p)
4	(A)	21.09	v W Hartlepool	1700	L	16-25	R Wallace(t)Ebongalame(t)Lee(p)Tunningley(p)
5	(A)	28.09	v London Irish	2670	W	37-23	Johns(t)Hill(t)Ravenscroft(t)Ebongalame(t)R Wallace(t)Lee(cdg)Tunningley(2cp)
6	(A)	05.10	v Bristol	4795	W	21-11	Chesney(2t)Lee(tp)Tunningley(p)
7	(H)	29.10	v Northampton	4254	W	24-23	Ebongalame(t)Ravenscroft(t)Sella(t)Lynagh(3p)
8	(H)	08.12	v Sale	1424	D	17-17	Olver(t)Lynagh(4p)
9	(A)	04.01	v Bath	5500	L	33-35	Smith(t)Diprose(t)R Wallace(t)Clark(t)Lynagh(2c3p)
10	(H)	19.01	v Harlequins	5975	W	28-20	Copsey(t)Diprose(t)Sella(t)Lynagh(2c2pdg)
11	(A)	08.02	v Northampton	7525	L	10-17	Sella(t)Lynagh(cp)
12	(H)	04.03	v Orrell	1796	W	24-15	Diprose(t)Copsey(t)Lynagh(c4p)
13	(H)	09.03	v Bristol	1793	W	33-15	Singer(t)Sella(t)Clark(t)P Wallace(t)Lee(2c3p)
14	(H)	30.03	v W Hartlepool	2144	W	51- 8	Diprose(t)Tunningley(t)Ravenscroft(t)P Wallace(t)Friel(t)Sella(t)Bracken(t)Lynagh(2cp)Lee(t2c)
15	(A)	05.04	v Gloucester	4523	L	6- 9	Lee(p)Tunningley(p)
16	(A)	09.04	v Harlequins	4614	L	0-27	
17	(H)	12.04	v Wasps	3962	L	15-28	Botterman(t)Diprose(t)Lee(cp)
18	(A)	15.04	v Sale	2702	L	23-33	Botterman(t)R Wallace(t)Lee(2c3p)
19	(A)	19.04	v Leicester	10791	L	18-22	P Wallace(t)Pienaar(t)Ebongalame(t)Lynagh(p)
20	(A)	26.04	v Orrell	1200	W	44-22	Hill(t)Johns(t)Pienaar(t)P Wallace(t)Singer(t)Sorrell(t)PenTry(t)Lee(3cp)
21	(H)	30.04	v London Irish	1865	W	45- 0	R Wallace(3t)Tunningley(2t)Olsen(t)Pienaar(t)Lynagh(5c)
22	(H)	03.05	v Bath	4510	W	36-29	Pienaar(t)R Wallace(t)Singer(t)Tunningley(t)Lynagh(2c4p)

1996-97 HIGHLIGHTS

LEAGUE DEBUTS: Phillipe Sella, Richard Wallace, Michael Lynagh, Kyran Bracken, Paul Wallace, Paddy Johns, Adrian Olver, Muna Ebongalame, Tony Daly, Matthew Evans, Courtney Smith, Francois Pienaar, Brimah Kebbie, Kevin Sorrell, Brendan Reidy, Marcus Olsen.

TRY ON DEBUT: Kyran Bracken, Muna Ebongalame, Courtney Smith, Marcus Olsen.

PLAYERS USED: 35 plus 5 as replacement

EVER PRESENT: Tony Diprose.

In his debut season former Australian World Cup winner Michael Lynagh scored 126 points in just 12 games. This put him in joint fourth place with Andy Lee for points in a season - but second in points per match.

	Pts	T	C	P	D	Apps	Ave.
Andy Tunningley 94-95	162	3	21	35	-	18	9.00
Andy Tunningley 93-94	149	5	14	31	1	17	8.76
Andy Kennedy 88-89	138	5	14	30	-	10	13.80
Michael Lynagh 96-97	126	-	16	30	1	12	10.50
Andy Lee 95-96	126	2	7	29	5	14	9.00

South African World cup winning captain Francois Pienaar scored tries in each of the last four matches. This in the second best run for the club after Dave McLagen's six back in the 87-88 season.

Both Michael Lynagh and Andy Lee equalled the club record of five conversions in a match. They now share the record with Nick Holmes and Andy Kennedy.

Irish international winger Richard Wallace became only the second Sarries player to score a hat-trick of tries in a league match. He achieved the feat late in the season against London Irish. The only other Saracen's player to do this was Laurie Smith back in April 89.

Former England international John Buckton extended his club record for appearances to 105. Buckton was the only Saracens player playing last season who played in the inagural league campaign back in 87-88.

In terms of tries only Leicester, Bath and Wasps conceded less.

Canadian international winger scored a try on his league debut then left the club to join London Scottish.

Had an excellent home record with just one loss to Champions Wasps.

SARACENS' COURAGE LEAGUE MATCH DETAILS 1996-97

	15	14	13	12	11	10	9	1	2	3	4	5	6	7	8	Replacements	
1	Tunningley	Chesney	Sella	Ravenscroft	R Wallace	Lynagh	Bracken	Holmes	Botterman	P Wallace	Johns	Copsey	Green	Hill	Diprose	Diprose	1
2	Tunningley	Chesney	Sella	Ravenscroft	R Wallace	Lynagh	Bracken	Andrews	Botterman	P Wallace	Johns	Copsey	Green	Hill	Diprose	Edwards(10),Zaltman(6)	2
3	Tunningley	Chesney	Sella	Ravenscroft	R Wallace	Lee	Bracken	Olver	Olney	P Wallace	Johns	Copsey	Clark	Hill	Diprose		3
4	Tunningley	R Wallace	Sella	Dooley	Boogaardene	Lee	Bracken	Olver	Olney	P Wallace	Johns	Copsey	Metcalfe	Hill	Diprose		4
5	Tunningley	R Wallace	Sella	Ravenscroft	Boogaardene	Lee	Bracken	Olver	Olney	P Wallace	Johns	Copsey	Clark	Hill	Diprose	Zaltman(5)	5
6	Tunningley	R Wallace	Sella	Ravenscroft	Chesney	Lee	Bracken	Daly	Botterman	P Wallace	Johns	Copsey	Clark	Hill	Diprose	Olney(15)	6
7	Tunningley	Boogaardene	Sella	Ravenscroft	R Wallace	Lynagh	Bracken	Daly	Botterman	P Wallace	Johns	Copsey	Clark	Hill	Diprose		7
8	Evans	Chesney	Buckton	Ravenscroft	R Wallace	Lynagh	Bracken	Olver	Botterman	P Wallace	Johns	Copsey	Clark	Hill	Diprose		8
9	Evans	R Wallace	Sella	Ravenscroft	C Smith	Lynagh	Bracken	Daly	Botterman	Olver	Yandell	Copsey	Clark	Pienaar	Diprose		9
10	Evans	R Wallace	Sella	Ravenscroft	Chesney	Lynagh	Bracken	Daly	Botterman	Olver	Yandell	Copsey	Pienaar	Hill	Diprose	Johns(4),Clark(6)	10
11	Tunningley	R Wallace	Sella	Ravenscroft	Boogaardene	Lynagh	Bracken	Daly	Botterman	P Wallace	Yandell	Copsey	Pienaar	Hill	Diprose	Friel(9)	11
12	Tunningley	Chesney	Sella	Ravenscroft	Kebble	Lynagh	Bracken	Daly	Olver	Olver	Yandell	Copsey	Clark	Hill	Diprose	Johns(5),Ogilvie(7)	12
13	Singer	R Wallace	Sella	Ravenscroft	Chesney	Lee	Bracken	Olver	Botterman	P Wallace	Yandell	Copsey	Green	Clark	Clark	Langley(4),Tunningley(15)	13
14	Tunningley	Kebble	Sella	Ravenscroft	Chesney	Lynagh	Bracken	Daly	Botterman	P Wallace	Yandell	Copsey	Green	Hill	Diprose	Lee(10)Friel(14)Olver(1)Burrow(4)Johns(5)	14
15	Tunningley	Chesney	Sella	Ravenscroft	R Wallace	Lee	Bracken	Daly	Botterman	P Wallace	Johns	Copsey	Green	Hill	Diprose	Pienaar(6)	15
16	Tunningley	Chesney	Sorrell	Ravenscroft	Chesney	Lee	Bracken	Olver	Botterman	P Wallace	Johns	Copsey	Pienaar	Hill	Diprose		16
17	Singer	R Wallace	Sella	Ravenscroft	Boogaardene	Lee	Bracken	Daly	Botterman	Olver	Johns	Copsey	Pienaar	Hill	Diprose	Yandell(4)	17
18	Singer	R Wallace	Sella	Ravenscroft	Boogaardene	Lee	Bracken	Reidy	Olney	P Wallace	Johns	Yandell	Pienaar	Hill	Diprose	Botterman(2)Copsey(4)	18
19	Singer	R Wallace	Sella	Ravenscroft	Boogaardene	Lynagh	Bracken	Daly	Botterman	P Wallace	Copsey	Johns	Pienaar	Hill	Diprose	Lee(10)Olver(1)Yandell(4)	19
20	Tunningley	R Wallace	Sella	Sorrell	Singer	Lee	Olver	Freil	Botterman	P Wallace	Johns	Copsey	Pienaar	Hill	Diprose	Reidy(2)	20
21	Tunningley	R Wallace	Sella	Sorrell	Singer	Lynagh	Olsen	Daly	Reidy	P Wallace	Johns	Copsey	Pienaar	Hill	Diprose	Olver(1)Olney(2)Yandell(7)Burrow(4)	21
22	Tunningley	R Wallace	Sella	Ravenscroft	Singer	Lynagh	Olsen	Daly	Botterman	P Wallace	Johns	Copsey	Pienaar	Hill	Diprose	Evans(tr12)	22

SARACENS LEAGUE STATISTICS
(COMPILED BY STEPHEN McCORMACK)

Season	Div.	P	W	D	L	F	(Tries	Con	Pen	DG)	A	(Tries	Con	Pen	DG)	Most Points	Most Tries
87-88	2	11	7	2	2	228	(38	17	13	1)	86	(11	6	8	2)	46 - Nick Holmes	10 - Dave McLagen
88-89	2	11	11	0	0	288	(37	19	23	1)	80	(9	4	11	1)	138 - Andy Kennedy	7 - Dave McLagen
89-90	1	11	7	1	3	168	(25	16	11	1)	167	(26	9	14	1)	50 - Andy Kennedy	4 - Ben Clarke
90-91	1	12	5	0	7	151	(20	10	14	3)	228	(32	20	18	2)	36 - Ben Rudling	4 - Ben Clarke
91-92	1	12	7	1	4	176	(18	10	22	6)	165	(17	8	27	0)	91 - Ben Rudling	4 - Martin Gregory
92-93	1	12	3	0	9	137	(13	6	16	4)	180	(15	9	28	1)	43 - Ben Rudling	3 - Darren O'Leary & Barry Crawley
93-94	2	18	11	1	6	299	(30	16	34	5)	238	(16	10	41	5)	149 - Andy Tunningley	5 - Richard Hill & Andy Tunningley
94-95	2	18	15	1	2	389	(43	21	38	6)	213	(20	13	28	1)	162 - Andy Tunningley	7 - John Green
95-96	1	18	5	0	13	284	(22	12	44	6)	451	(48	32	43	6)	126 - Andy Lee	4 - Peter Harries
96-97	1	22	12	1	9	568	(69	35	48	3)	449	(45	28	53	3)	126 - Michael Lynagh	9 - Richard Wallace
Totals		145	83	7	55	2688	(315	162	273	36)	2257	(239	139	271	22)		

	HOME	AWAY
BIGGEST WIN	(45pts) 45-0 v Lon. Irish 30.4.97	(36pts) 48-12 v Blackheath 23.3.88
BIGGEST DEFEAT	(43pts) 6-49 v Bath 27.4.91	(49pts) 3-52 v Sale 18.9.93
MOST POINTS SCORED	50-10 v Bedford 19.11.88	48-12 v Blackheath 23.3.88
AGAINST	6-49 v Bath 27.4.91	3-52 v Sale 18.9.93

MOST CONSECUTIVE VICTORIES - 17   **MOST CONSECUTIVE DEFEATS - 7**

MOST TRIES IN A MATCH
(FOR) 9 v Gosforth 22.4.89
(AGAINST) 9 v Sale 18.9.93

MOST APPEARANCES
FORWARD: 95 Richard Andrews
BACK: 106 John Buckton

CONSECUTIVE APPEARANCES
68 Brian Davies

CONSECUTIVE SCORING MATCHES
Scoring Tries - 6 - Dave McLagen
Scoring Points - 19 - Andy Tunningley (twice)

MOST	in a SEASON	in a CAREER	in a MATCH
Points	162 Andy Tunningley 94-95	462 Andy Tunningley 90-97	26 Andy Lee v W. Hartlepool 14.10.95 (H)
Tries	10 Dave McLagen 87-88	17 Dave McLagen 87-90 John Buckton 87-95	3 Laurie Smith v Gosforth 22.4.89 (A) Richard Wallace v L. Irish 30.4.97 (H)
Conversions	21 Andy Tunningley 94-95	49 Andy Tunningley 90-97	5 Nick Holmes v Blackheath 23.3.88 (A) v Lon Scottish 23.4.88 (H) Andy Kennedy v Bedford 19.11.88 (H) v Moseley 28.10.89 (H)
Penalties	35 Andy Tunningley 94-95	92 Andy Tunningley 90-97	6 Andy Tunningley v Fylde 15.10.94 (H) Andy Lee v W. Hartlepool 14.10.95 (H)
Drop Goals	6 Andy Lee 94-95	16 Andy Lee 89-95	2 Andy Lee v Wasps 22.2.92 (A) v Lon Scottish 5.11.94 (H) v W Hartlepool 14.10.95 (H) Ben Rudling v Lon Irish 11.4.92 (H) Gareth Hughes v Bath 24.4.93 (H)

SARACENS PLAYING SQUAD

NAME	Ht	Wt	Birthdate	Birthplace	Club	Apps	Pts	T	C	P	DG

BACKS

NAME	Ht	Wt	Birthdate	Birthplace	Club	Apps	Pts	T	C	P	DG
Andy Tunningley	6.2	14.0	29.03.67	Harrogate	Sandal						
England: A.					Saracens	78+1	462	16	49	62	3
Kevin Sorrell	6.0	12.8	06.03.77								
England: u18					Saracens	3+1	5	1	-	-	-
Phillipe Sella	5.11	13.8	14.02.62	Cairac (Fra)	Agen						
France: 111					Saracens	20	25	5	-	-	-
Stephen Ravenscroft	5.11	14.2	02.11.70	Bradford	Previous Clubs: Bradford & Bingley, Otley.						
England: Students; North.					Saracens	68	25	5	-	-	-
Andy Lee	5.9	13.7	10.11.68	Woodford							
England: Students, u21.					Saracens	54+2	29	8	27	50	16
Richard Wallace	5.11	14.0	16.01.68	Cork	Previous Clubs: Garryowen, Cork Constitution.						
Ireland: , u25, Students, u21.					Saracens	20	45	9	-	-	-
Kyran Bracken	5.11	12.10	22.11.71	Dublin	Bristol	47	35	7	-	-	-
England: 13, A, u21.					Saracens	19	40	2	-	-	-
Michael Lynagh				Queensland	Benetton Treviso						
Australia: 72					Saracens	12	125	-	16	30	-
Phillip Friel	5.8	12.7	14.01.73	Romford							
					Saracens	2+3	5	1	-	-	-
Kris Chesney	6.6	16.12	02.03.74	Ilford	Barking						
England: u21					Saracens	17+2	25	5	-	-	-
Muna Ebongalame	5.8	12.0	09.06.73	Cameroon	Luton						
					Saracens	7+1	20	4	-	-	-
Matt Singer			07.11.72	Bristol							
					Saracens	10	22	3	2	1	-
John Buckton	6.2	12.11	22.12.61	Hull	Hull ER						
England: 3, A, B.					Saracens	105	73	17	-	-	-

FORWARDS

NAME	Ht	Wt	Birthdate	Birthplace	Club	Apps	Pts	T	C	P	DG
Greg Botterman	5.11	15.6	03.03.68	Welwyn G.C.							
England: Emerging England.					Saracens	82+3	20	4	-	-	-
Adrian Olver											
					Saracens	12+4	-	-	-	-	-
Paul Wallace	6.1	16.0	30.12.71	Cork							
Ireland: , A, Students, u21, Schools.					Saracens	18+2	25	5	-	-	-
Paddy Johns	6.6	16.10	19.02.68	Portadown	Dungannon						
Ireland: , B, u25, u21.					Saracens	16+3	10	2	-	-	-
Tony Copsey	6.6	17.8	25.01.65	Romford	Llanelli						
Wales: 16.					Saracens	26+1	20	4	-	-	-
Tony Diprose	6.5	16.10	22.09.72	Orsett							
England: 2, A, Emerging, Students, u21.					Saracens	77+1	55	11	-	-	-
John Green	6.4	18.0	17.03.67	Romford	Bridgend						
England: Students, School. Irish Exiles.					Saracens	50	45	9	-	-	-
Richard Hill	6.2	15.8	23.05.72								
England: 5, A, Students, u21, Colts, Schools.					Saracens	60	65	13	-	-	-
Francois Pienaar											
South Africa:					Saracens	10+1	20	4	-	-	-
Craig Yandell	6.7	17.2	16.08.72	Weston-s-Mare	Previous Clubs: Llandovery, Narbeth.						
England: Students, u21.					Saracens	12+6	-	-	-	-	-
Mark Langley	6.4	17.10	09.06.67	Cardiff	Previous Clubs: Bridgend, Penarth, Swansea.						
Wales: Students, u21.					Saracens	63+1	15	3	-	-	-
Mark Burrow	6.6	17.8	09.07.69	Chelmsford							
					Saracens	40+2	-	-	-	-	-

Have you many Rugby enthusiasts at your Club ?
Does you Club need to raise extra funds ?

If the answer to these questions is Yes -
then place an order for

The Official Rugby Union Club Directory

WITH EVERY CLUB IN THE LEAGUE STRUCTURE INCLUDED AND ITS
UNRIVALLED STATISTICAL COVERAGE OF THE CLUBS AND PLAYERS IN
THE TOP LEVELS OF THE LEAGUE SYSTEM IT CAN ANSWER ALL SORTS
OF QUESTIONS AND WOULD MAKE AN IDEAL PRESENT.

Did you realise the Directory is available to your club at very good discount rates.

If you order				Profit for Club
1	copy cost	£14.99		
2 or 3	copies cost	£13.50 each	£ 1.49 each	
between 4 & 9	copies cost	£10.00 each	£ 4.99 each	
between 10 & 19	copies cost	£ 9.00 each	£ 5.99 each	
20 or more	copies cost	£ 8.00 each	£ 6.99 each	

WASPS FC

NICKNAME: WASPS   FOUNDED: 1867

Chief Executive Geoff Huckstep, c/o Wasps RFC, Loftus Road Stadium, South Africa Road, London W12 7PA.
0181 740 2523 (B), 0181 740 2508 (Fax)
Commercial Manager Katie Rowland, c/o Wasps RFC, as above
0181 740 2547 (B), 0181 740 2512 (Fax)
Director of Rugby Nigel Melville, Repton Avenue, Sudbury, near Wembley, Middx HA0 3DW
0181 902 4220 (B), 0181 900 2659 (Fax)
Press Officer Mr Eddie Laxton, Public Relations Oxford, Aston Park, Aston Rowant, Oxford OX9 5SW
0421 371696 (Mobile), 01844 351363 (B), 01844 354939 (Fax)

Six points clear of all the opposition made Wasps worthy Champions of England last season. The club unanimously recognised as 'the most difficult team in the League to overcome', won the first ever professional title convincingly, the best prepared and fittest of the dozen sides playing. Though we slipped out of the European Cup losing 26-24 to Cardiff in the early stages we overwhelmed previous champions Toulouse 71-17.

Captain Lawrence Dallaglio, added five more England caps and became a British Lion. Four players were capped for England for the first time during this season - Andy Gomarsall (6), Chris Sheasby (5), Nick Greenstock (2) and Alex King (1). Will Green was called up by England in Argentina while Peter Scrivener and Buster White remain on International stand-by at home. Kenny Logan, Damian Cronin and Andy Reed all got more caps for Scotland and Rob Henderson and Darren Molloy toured New Zealand with Ireland, while Gareth Rees, our top scorer with 293 points in the League, was performing for Canada.

Wasps had four players in the England U21 Tour to Australia coached by our own Rob Smith - Paul Sampson, Joe Worsley, Martyn Wood and Joe Beardshaw. Watch out for these names in the near future.

Director of rugby Nigel Melville, spent the summer balancing his squad and the arrival of forty stone worth of second row forwards will ensure a more plentiful supply of good ball this season, Simon Shaw from Bristol and Kiwi Mark Weedon, but they will have to battle for the First Team spots. "We intend to finish the coming season at least where we began, as English Champions and that is by no means the limit of our ambitions", said Nigel.

Wasps Squad 1997-98: Back Row (L-R); Kevin Dunn, Paul Sampson, Ian Dunston, Simon Mitchell, Aaron James, Guy Gregory, Phil Hopley, Richard Kinsey, Andy Reed, Chris Sheasby, Peter Scrivenor, Darren Molloy, Joe Worsley, Adam Black, Jon Ufton, Laurence Scrase, Paul Volley, Alistair Johnson, Murray Fraser. Front Row; Michael Skinner, Shane Roiser, Kenny Logan, Alex King, Buster White, Gareth Rees, Damian Cronin, Lawrence Dallaglio, Martyn Wood, Nick Greenstock, Rob Henderson, Andy Gomarsall, Will Green, Dugald Macer.

Colours: Black with gold wasp on left breast & gold stipes on shoulders.   **Change colours:** Black & gold hoops.

No	Ven.	Date	Opponents	Att.	Res.	Score	Scorers
1	(A)	31.08	v Sale	2394	W	33-31	Gomersall(2t)Sampson(t)Rees(3c4p)
2	(H)	08.09	v Saracens	9609	W	36-21	Gomersall(t)Mitchell(t)Rees(t6p)King(dg)
3	(A)	14.09	v Bath	7000	W	40-36	Sheasby(2t)Sampson(t)Mitchell(t)Rees(4c3p)King(dg)
4	(H)	22.09	v Leicester	10686	W	14- 7	P Hopley(t)Rees(3p)
5	(A)	28.09	v Orrell	2000	W	41-27	Scrase(2t)Roiser(2t)Sheasby(t)Tuigamala(t)Rees(4c2p)
6	(A)	06.10	v Gloucester	5886	L	23-28	Scrase(t)Gomersall(t)Rees(c3p)King(c)
7	(A)	16.11	v London Irish	3720	W	22-20	Dallaglio(t)Roiser(t)Sampson(t)Ufton(2cp)
8	(H)	07.12	v Bristol	3832	W	15-13	White(t)King(tp)Ufton(c)
9	(H)	28.12	v Northampton	4838	W	18-13	Rees(6p)
10	(H)	05.01	v Harlequins	9766	L	17-19	Cronin(t)Rees(3p)King(dg)
11	(A)	11.01	v Bristol	3650	W	41-18	Tuigamala(2t)Reed(t)Greenstock(t)Roiser(t)Sheasby(t)Rees(4cp)
12	(A)	08.02	v W Hartlepool	2200	W	48-23	Gomersall(t)White(t)King(t)PenTry(t)Mitchell(t)Sheasby(t)Henderson(t)Rees(5cp)
13	(H)	23.02	v W Hartlepool	1000	W	36-12	Reed(t)Sheasby(t)Ufton(t)Gregory(t)PenTry(t)Rees(t3c)
14	(H)	09.03	v Gloucester	4007	W	36-10	King(t)Greenstock(t)Roiser(t)Rees(3c5p)
15	(H)	22.03	v Orrell	1000	W	62- 5	Logan(5t)Roiser(2t)Greenstock(t)Scrivener(t)Rees(6cp)King(c)
16	(H)	26.03	v London Irish	3010	W	31-18	PenTry(2t)Greenstock(t)Rees(2c3p)King(dg)
17	(A)	02.04	v Leicester	17000	L	12-18	Rees(4p)
18	(H)	06.04	v Bath	10657	D	25-25	King(tdg)Rees(c5p)
19	(A)	12.04	v Saracens	3962	W	28-15	Logan(2t)Sheasby(t)Rees(2c3p)
20	(H)	20.04	v Sale	6270	W	36-10	Henderson(t)Logan(t)Roiser(t)Greenstock(t)Rees(2c3p)King(dg)
21	(A)	19.04	v Northampton	7274	W	26-15	Roiser(t)Logan(t)Rees(2c4p)
22	(A)	03.05	v Harlequins	6789	W	42-22	Henderson(2t)Logan(2t)Green(t)Rees(t3c2p)

1996-97 HIGHLIGHTS

LEAGUE DEBUTS: Paul Sampson, Gareth Rees, Alex King, Damian Cronin, Chris Sheasby, Va aiga Tuigamala, Mike Griffiths, Andy Reed, Rob Henderson, Kenny Logan, Martin Wood.

TRY ON DEBUT: Paul Sampson and Simon Mitchell.

PLAYERS USED: 29 plus 3 as replacement.

EVER PRESENT: 4 Nick Greenstock, Shane Roiser, Mike White and Laurence Dallaglio.

❏ Wasps had four ever presents the most by any team in National league rugby.

❏ Shane Roiser broke his own record of eight tries in a season with nine but was still to lose his record. That went to Scottish international winger Kenny Logan. He scored 11 tries in just 13 matches including a Division one record of five in a amatch. He scored the five in the 62-5 home win against bottom of the table Orrell.

❏ Logan also scored tries in four consecutive league games also a new club record. The previos record of three was shared by Chris Oti and Simon Smith.

❏ In scoring his five tries against Orrell Logan Notched up 25 points for a new club record for most points in

a match. The previous record was Rob Andrew's 24 against Bristol back in April 91.

❏ Canadian international Gareth Rees re-wrote the Wasps record books during their championship season - also his first in English league rugby.
He started off by reaching 100 Division one points in just seven league games to establish a new division record. He then went on to pass Rob Andrew's club record of 159 points and finished by breaking John Liley's Division one record of 272
Below is a comparison of both records.

	Pts	T	C	P	D	Apps	Ave.
Gareth Rees 96-97	291	3	45	62	-	20	14.55
Rob Andrew 93-94	159	2	16	38	1	13	12.23

	Pts	T	C	P	D	Apps	Ave.
Gareth Rees 96-97	291	3	45	62	-	20	14.55
John Liley 95-96	272	5	26	64	1	17	16.00

❏ In the process of the above he broke Andrew's season records for Conversions and Penalties of 19 and 38 with 45 and 62 respectively.

❏ England A stand-off Alex King broke Rob Andrews record of three drop goals in a season. Andrew had twice scored three drop goals in a season but King easily beat this dropping six.

❏ Only home defeat at the hands of London rivals Harlequins.

WASPS' COURAGE LEAGUE MATCH DETAILS 1996-97

#	15	14	13	12	11	10	9	1	2	3	4	5	6	7	8	Replacements
1	Ufton	Sampson	Greenstock	Scrase	Roiser	Rees	Gomersall	Molloy	Dunn	Dunston	Greenwood	Hadley	White	Dallaglio	Scrivener	Griffiths(3)
2	Rees	Sampson	Greenstock	James	Roiser	King	Gomersall	Molloy	Mitchell	Dunston	Greenwood	Cronin	White	Dallaglio	Sheasby	
3	Rees	Sampson	Greenstock	Tuigamala	Roiser	King	Gomersall	Molloy	Mitchell	Green	Greenwood	Cronin	White	Dallaglio	Sheasby	Griffiths(3)
4	Rees	Sampson	Greenstock	Tuigamala	Roiser	King	Gomersall	Molloy	Mitchell	Griffiths	Cronin	Greenwood	White	Dallaglio	Sheasby	P Hopley(14)
5	Rees	Scrase	Greenstock	Tuigamala	Roiser	King	Gomersall	Molloy	Mitchell	Griffiths	Cronin	Greenwood	White	Dallaglio	Sheasby	Hadley(8)
6	Rees	Scrase	Greenstock	James	Roiser	King	Gomersall	Molloy	Dunn	Green	Cronin	Greenwood	White	Dallaglio	Scrivener	Kinsey(8),Macer(11)
7	Ufton	Sampson	Greenstock	Tuigamala	Roiser	King	Gomersall	Molloy	Mitchell	Green	Cronin	Reid	White	Dallaglio	Sheasby	
8	Ufton	Sampson	Greenstock	Tuigamala	Roiser	King	Gomersall	Molloy	Mitchell	Green	Cronin	Reed	White	Dallaglio	Sheasby	Dunston(3)
9	Rees	Roiser	Greenstock	James	Tuigamala	King	Gomersall	Griffiths	Mitchell	Green	Cronin	Reed	White	Dallaglio	Sheasby	Molloy(1),Kinsey(4)
10	Rees	Ufton	Greenstock	Tuigamala	Roiser	King	Gomersall	Molloy	Mitchell	Green	Cronin	Reed	Dallaglio	White	Sheasby	Dunston(7),Kinsey(4)
11	Rees	Ufton	Greenstock	Tuigamala	Roiser	King	Gomersall	Molloy	Macer	Green	Cronin	Reed	Dallaglio	White	Sheasby	Dunn(2),Dunston(3),Kinsey(4),Wood(9)
12	Rees	Sampson	Greenstock	Henderson	Roiser	King	Gomersall	Molloy	Mitchell	Green	Cronin	Reed	Dallaglio	White	Sheasby	Kinsey(9),Macer(7),Wood(10)
13	Rees	Ufton	Greenstock	Henderson	Roiser	Gregory	Gomersall	Molloy	Mitchell	Green	Cronin	Reed	Dallaglio	White	Sheasby	Dunston(1),Dunn(2)
14	Logan	Greenstock	Greenstock	Henderson	Roiser	King	Gomersall	Molloy	Mitchell	Green	Cronin	Reed	Dallaglio	White	Greenwood	Greenwood(4)
15	Rees	Roiser	Greenstock	Henderson	Logan	King	Gomersall	Molloy	Mitchell	Green	Cronin	Reed	Dallaglio	White	Scrivener	Ufton(15),Wood(9),Dunn(2),Kinsey(5)
16	Rees	Roiser	Greenstock	Henderson	Logan	King	Gomersall	Molloy	Mitchell	Green	Greenwood	Reed	Dallaglio	White	Scrivener	Ufton(14),Volley(7)
17	Rees	Roiser	Greenstock	Henderson	Logan	King	Gomersall	Molloy	Mitchell	Green	Greenwood	Reed	Dallaglio	White	Sheasby	Cronin(4),Dunn(2),Scrivener(7)
18	Rees	Roiser	Greenstock	Henderson	Logan	King	Gomersall	Molloy	Mitchell	Green	Greenwood	Reed	Dallaglio	White	Sheasby	Dunn(2),Scrivener(8),Dunston(3)
19	Rees	Roiser	Greenstock	Henderson	Logan	King	Gomersall	Molloy	Mitchell	Green	Greenwood	Reed	Dallaglio	White	Sheasby	Cronin(4),Dunn(2)
20	Rees	Roiser	Greenstock	Henderson	Logan	King	Wood	Molloy	Mitchell	Green	Greenwood	Reed	Dallaglio	White	Sheasby	Cronin(5),Scrivener(7)
21	Rees	Roiser	Greenstock	Henderson	Logan	King	Wood	Molloy	Mitchell	Green	Greenwood	Reed	Dallaglio	White	Sheasby	Ufton(10),Cronin(5),Scrivener(7)
22	Ufton	Roiser	Greenstock	Henderson	Logan	Rees	Gomersall	Molloy	Mitchell	Green	Greenwood	Reed	Dallaglio	White	Sheasby	Scrivener(8),Dunn(2),Cronin(7)

WASPS LEAGUE STATISTICS
(COMPILED BY STEPHEN McCORMACK)

Season	Div.	P	W	D	L	F	(Tries	Con	Pen	DG)	A	(Tries	Con	Pen	DG)	Most Points	Most Tries
87-88	1	11	8	1	2	218	(29	12	25	1)	136	(14	7	21	1)	57 - Nick Stringer	5 - Mark Bailey, Simon Smith.
88-89	1	11	7	1	3	206	(24	15	24	2)	138	(13	7	20	4)	103 - Rob Andrew	4 - Mark Bailey
89-90	1	11	9	0	2	250	(39	17	20	0)	106	(9	5	19	1)	90 - Rob Andrew	7 - Mark Bailey
90-91	1	12	9	1	2	252	(35	17	26	0)	151	(12	8	25	4)	126 - Rob Andrew	7 - Chris Oti
91-92	1	12	6	0	6	177	(18	6	29	2)	180	(17	8	27	0)	101 - Steve Pilgrim	5 - Chris Oti
92-93	1	12	11	0	1	186	(19	8	24	1)	118	(6	5	25	1)	54 - Alan Buzza	4 - Phil Hopley, Chris Oti
93-94	1	18	10	1	7	362	(33	19	50	3)	340	(28	13	50	8)	159 - Rob Andrew	5 - Damian Hopley
94-95	1	18	13	0	5	470	(58	30	37	3)	313	(24	14	53	2)	135 - Rob Andrew	7 - Phil Hopley
95-96	1	18	11	0	7	439	(53	30	30	8)	322	(28	16	42	8)	91 - Guy Gregory	8 - Shane Roiser
96-97	1	22	18	1	3	685	(75	50	64	6)	406	(42	20	51	1)	291 - Gareth Rees	11 - Kenny Logan
Total		145	102	5	38	3245	(383	124	329	26)	2210	(193	103	333	30)		

HOME

BIGGEST WIN	(57pts) 62-5 v Orrell 22.3.97
BIGGEST DEFEAT	(31pts) 3-34 v Harlequins 9.3.96
MOST POINTS SCORED	62-5 v Orrell 22.3.97
AGAINST	3-34 v Harlequins 9.3.96

AWAY

(31pts) 57-26 v Harlequins 17.9.94
(32pts) 6-38 v Leicester 12.10.93
57-26 v Harlequins 17.9.94
24-42 v Orrell 30.4.94

MOST CONSECUTIVE VICTORIES - 9

MOST CONSECUTIVE DEFEATS - 4

MOST TRIES IN A MATCH

(FOR) 9 v Coventry 13.4.88 (H); v Bedford 12.3.90
(A); v Liverpool St H 20.4.91; v Orrell 22.3.97 (H)
(AGAINST) 6 v Orrell 30.4.94

MOST APPEARANCES
FORWARD: 98 Mike White
BACK: 91 Steve Bates 87-96

CONSECUTIVE APPEARANCES
36 Richard Kinsey 29.2.92 - 30.4.94

CONSECUTIVE SCORING MATCHES
Scoring Tries - 4 - Kenny Logan
Scoring Points - 16 - Rob Andrew

MOST	in a SEASON	in a CAREER	in a MATCH
Points	291 Gareth Rees 96-97	748 Rob Andrew 87-96	25 Kenny Logan v Orrell 22.3.97 (H)
Tries	11 Kenny Logan 96-97	22 Chris Oti 88-94	5 Kenny Logan v Orrell 22.3.97 (H)
Conversions	41 Gareth Rees 96-97	82 Rob Andrew 87-96	6 Rob Andrew v Liverpool St H 20.4.91 (H) v Bristol 27.4.91 (H) Guy Gregory v W Hartlepool 20.4.96 (H) Gareth Rees v Orrell 22.3.97 (H)
Penalties	62 Gareth Rees 96-97	161 Rob Andrew 87-96	7 Rob Andrew v Orrell 11.12.93 (H)
Drop Goals	6 Alex King 96-97	11 Rob Andrew 87-96	2 Jon Ufton v Saracens 23.9.95 (H) Rob Andrew v Sale 30.9.95 (A) Guy Gregory v Leicester 6.4.96 (A)

WASPS PLAYING SQUAD

NAME	Ht	Wt	Birthdate	Birthplace	Club	Apps	Pts	T	C	P	DG

BACKS

NAME	Ht	Wt	Birthdate	Birthplace	Club	Apps	Pts	T	C	P	DG
Gareth Rees	6.0	15.0	30.06.67	Vancouver Is. (Can)							
Canada:					Wasps	20	291	3	45	62	-
Jon Ufton	6.1	13.10	31.01.74	Dulwich	Old Whitgiftians						
England: Students, u21, Colts, u18.					Wasps	41+4	63	6	9	3	2
Kenny Logan					Stirling County						
Scotland: 30					Wasps	9	55	11	-	-	-
Shane Roiser	5.10	13.7	07.06.73	London	Rosslyn Park	26	50	10	-	-	-
England: Studenmts, u21.					Wasps	42	95	19	-	-	-
Rob Henderson	6.1	15.4	27.10.72	Dover	London Irish						
Ireland: A, Exiles, u21.					Wasps	11	15	3	-	-	-
Nick Greenstock	6.2	15.4	03.11.73	Dubai							
England: 3, A, Emerging, u21, u18.					Wasps	40	75	15	-	-	-
Alex King	6.0	13.4	17.01.75	Brighton	Hove						
England: 1, A, u21, Colts.					Rosslyn Park	7	70	2	9	14	-
					Wasps	19	4	4	2	1	6
Guy Gregory	6.0	13.7	13.02.69	Chalfont St Giles	Nottingham	48	331	2	27	70	10
England: Emerging, u21, Students.					Wasps	14	144	4	23	24	2
Andy Gomersall	5.10	14.0	24.07.74	Durham	Bedford						
England: 6, A, Emerging, u21, Colts, u18.					Wasps	36+5	5+11	-	-	-	-
Martin Wood	5.9	13.0	25.04.77								
					Wasps	2+3	-	-	-	-	-
Paul Samspon	5.10	11.10	12.07.77	Wakefield	Otley	2	-	-	-	-	-
England: u21, Colts, u18.					Wasps	7	15	3	-	-	-
Laurence Scrase	6.0	12.7	10.09.72	Dubai							
					Wasps	15	25	5	-	-	-
Aaron James	5.10	13.11	20.09.67	Otautan (NZ)							
					Wasps	19	5	1	-	-	-

FORWARDS

NAME	Ht	Wt	Birthdate	Birthplace	Club	Apps	Pts	T	C	P	DG
Will Green	5.11	17.2	25.10.73	Littlehampton							
					Wasps	22	5	1	-	-	-
Darren Molloy	6.2	17.7	31.08.72	London							
Ireland: A. England: Emerging, u21, Students.					Wasps	44+2	5	1	-	-	-
Ian Dunston	5.10	17.4	11.06.68	London							
England: Colts.					Wasps	48+5	13	3	-	-	-
Simon Mitchell	5.10	16.0	23.11.67	Saltburn	West Hartlepool	82+1	32	7	-	-	-
England: Emerging.					Harlequins	13+1	-	-	-	-	-
					Wasps	19	15	3	-	-	-
Kevin Dunn	5.10	14.5	05.06.65	Gloucester	Gloucester	42+3	16	4	-	-	-
England: A, B.					Wasps	54+7	10	2	-	-	-
Damian Cronin	6.6	17.10	17.04.63	Wegberg (Ger.)	London Scottish	29	24	5	-	-	-
Scotland: 41.					Bath		-	-	-	-	-
				via Bordeaux to	Wasps	13+5	-	-	-	-	-
Andy Reed	6.7	17.10	04.05.69	St. Austell	Camborne	10+1	8	2	-	-	-
Scotland: u15. England: Colts.					Plymouth	10	8	2	-	-	-
					Bath	24	-	-	-	-	-
					Wasps	16	10	2	-	-	-
Matt Greenwood	6.6	17.8	25.09.64	Leeds	Roundhay						
England: A, u21.					Nottingham	27	4	1	-	-	-
					Wasps	77+1	25	5	-	-	-
Mike White	6.1	15.7	30.03.66	Poole							
					Wasps	98	66	14	-	-	-
Lawrence Dallaglio	6.4	6.10	10.08.72	Shepherds Bush							
England: 12, A, Emerging, u21, Colts.					Wasps	71+4	60	12	-	-	-
Chris Sheasby	6.3	16.0	30.11.66	Windsor	Harlequins	58+3	44	9	-	-	-
England: 5, A, Students, Colts.					Wasps	18	35	7	-	-	-
Peter Scrivener	6.6	17.12	27.10.73								
England: Students, u21, u18.					Wasps	22+5	15	3	-	-	-
Richard Kinsey	6.5	18.7	05.02.64	Barnet							
					Wasps	65+9	20	4	-	-	-

Loftus Road Stadium, South Africa Road, London W12 7PA

Tel: 0181 743 0262

Fax:

CAPACITY: 19,000

All SEATED: 19,000

SIMPLE DIRECTIONS:
By Road: A40(M) Westway (London-Oxford). Turn south at White City (BBC) into Wood Lane. Turn right into South Africa Road, ground 200yards on right
London Transport: White City (Central Line). In Wood Lane, turn right, then left into South Africa Road. Shepherds Bush (Hammersmith & City Line).
By Bus: 72, 95, 220 to White City Station.

CAR PARKING: 750 spaces at BBC White City

CLUB SHOP: Yes, Leon Gold 0181 740 2550, shop tel no 0181 749 6862

CLUBHOUSE: Matchdays 1.00-8.00, with snacks & bar meals available
Function room: No.

TRAINING NIGHTS: Tuesday, Wednesday & Thursday.

ADMISSION:
Season: Adults £140-£175, Children/OAPs £70-£90
Matchday: Adults £10-£15 depending on stand, Children/OAPs £5-£8

Wasps' Captain; Lawrence Dallaglio

MATCHDAY PROGRAMME

Size	A5
Number of pages	48 plus cover
Price	£2
Programme Editor	Katie Rowland 0181 740 2547
Advertising Rates	Colour Full page £1200 Half page £750

DIVISION ONE

RECORDS SECTION

DIVISION ONE - THE LAST TEN YEARS

	Champions	Runners-up	Relegated
1987-88	**LEICESTER**	WASPS	Coventry, Sale
1988-89	**BATH**	GLOUCESTER	Waterloo, Liverpool St. Helens
1989-90	**WASPS**	GLOUCESTER	Bedford
1990-91	**BATH**	WASPS	Moseley, Liverpool St. Helens
1991-92	**BATH**	ORRELL	Nottingham, Rosslyn Park
1992-93	**BATH**	WASPS	Saracens, London Scottish, West Hartlepool, Rugby.
1993-94	**BATH**	LEICESTER	London Irish, Newcastle Gosforth
1994-95	**LEICESTER**	BATH	Northampton
1995-96	**BATH**	LEICESTER	
1996-97	**WASPS**	BATH	Orrell, West Hartlepool

Most Points

1987-88	126	Dusty Hare (Leicester)
1988-89	103	Rob Andrew (Wasps)
1989-90	126	John Liley (Leicester)
1990-91	126	Rob Andrew (Wasps)
1991-92	125	John Liley (Leicester)
1992-93	122	Jon Webb (Bath)
1993-94	202	Jez Harris (Leicester)
1994-95	196	Mark Tainton (Bristol)
1995-96	272	John Liley (Leicester)
1996-97	291	Gareth Rees (Wasps)

Most Tries

1987-88	11	Andrew Harriman (Harlequins)
1988-89	10	Jeremy Guscott (Bath)
1989-90	10	Tony Swift (Bath)
1990-91	9	Andrew Harriman (Harlequins)
1991-92	9	Rory Underwood (Leicester)
1992-93	7	Stuart Barnes (Bath)
1993-94	11	Daren O'Leary (Harlequins)
1994-95	8	Paul Holford (Gloucester)
1995-96	14	Daren O'Leary (Harlequins)
1996-97	16	Adedayo Adebayo (Bath)

Most Penalties

1987-88	31	Dusty Hare (Leicester)
1988-89	25	Dusty Hare (Leicester)
1989-90	24	David Pears (Harl)
1990-91	26	Rob Andrew (Wasps)
1991-92	28	John Steele (N'hampton)
1992-93	31	Michael Corcoran (Lon I)
1993-94	41	Jez Harris (Leicester)
1994-95	56	Mark Tainton (Bristol)
1995-96	64	John Liley (Leicester)
1996-97	62	Gareth Rees (Wasps)

Most Conversions

1987-88	15	Dusty Hare (Leicester)
1988-89	13	Rob Andrew (Wasps) Stuart Barnes (Bath)
1989-90	29	Stuart Barnes (Bath)
1990-91	21	Martin Strett (Orrell)
1991-92	19	John Liley (Leicester)
1992-93	19	Jonathan Webb (Bath)
1993-94	25	Jonathan Callard (Bath)
1994-95	19	Rob Andrew (Wasps)
1995-96	43	Jonathon Callard (Bath)
1996-97	51	Jonathon Callard (Bath)

Most Drop Goals

1987-88	2	Stuart Barnes
1988-89	6	Simon Hodgkinson (s)
1989-90	2	David Pears (Harl)
1990-91	5	David Pears (Harls)
1991-92	2	Huw Davies (Wasps)
1992-93	6	Paul Burke (London I)
1993-94	11	Jez Harris (Leicester)
1994-95	13	Jez Harris (Leicester)
1995-96	7	David Pears (Harlequins)
1996-97	6	Alex King (Wasps)

TEAM RECORDS

Highest score:	W Hartlepool 21 Harlequins 91. 23.3.96
Highest aggregate:	112: As above
Highest score by a losing side:	London Irish 52 W Hartlepool 41. 28.12.96
Highest scoring draw:	38-38 Bath v Sale 27.4.96
Most consecutive wins:	17 Bath 1993-94 through 1994-95
Most consecutive defeats:	18 West Hartlepool 1995-96
Most points for in a season:	863 Bath 1996-97
Least points for in a season:	70 Bedford 1989-90
Most points against in a season:	886 Orrell 1996-97
Least points against in a season:	95 1Orrell 1991-92
Most tries for in a season:	116 Bath 1996-97
Most tries against in a season:	125 Orrell 1996-97
Least tries for in a season:	8 Waterloo 1988-89
Least tries against in a season:	6 Bath 1988-89, Wasps 1992-93
Most conversions for in a season:	77 Bath 1996-97
Most conversions against in a season:	69 Orrell 1996-97
Most penalties for in a season:	74 Leicester 1996-97
Most penalties against in a season:	60 Northampton & Sale 1996-97
Least penalties for in a season:	7 Bedford 1989-90
Least penalties against in a season:	11 Harlequins 1987-88
Most drop goals for in a season:	13 Leicester 1994-95 & Harlequins 1995-96
Most drop goals against in a season:	8 Wasps 1993-94 & 1995-96

INDIVIDUAL RECORDS

Most points in a season:	291 Gareth Rees (Wasps) 1996-97
Most tries in a season:	16 Adedayo Adebayo (Bath) 1996-97
Most conversions in a season:	51 Jonathon Callard (Bath) 1996-97
Most penalties in a season:	64 John Liley (Leicester) 1995-96
Most drop goals in a season:	13 Jez Harris (Leicester) 1994-95
Most points in a match:	31 John Liley, **Leicester** v Rosslyn Park 21.2.92
Most tries in a match:	5 Kenny Logan, **Wasps** v Orrell 22.3.97
Most conversions in a match:	10 Stuart Barnes, **Bath** v Bedford 13.1.90
Most penalties in a match:	8 John Liley, **Leicester** v Bristol 28.10.95
Most drop goals in a match:	3 John Steele, **Northampton** v Wasps 23.3.91
	Jez Harris, **Leicester** v Wasps 23.11.91
	David Pears, **Harlequins** v Wasps 16.9.95
	Matthew McCarthy, **Orrell** v W Hartlepool 7.12.96

Andy Gomarsall of Wasps and England.

DIVISION ONE - ALL TIME RECORDS

100+ POINTS IN A SEASON

POINTS	PLAYER	CLUB	SEASON	Tries	Cons.	Pens.	D.G.
291	Gareth Rees	Wasps	1996-97	3	45	62	
272	John Liley	Leicester	1995-96	5	26	64	1
269	Mark Mapletoft	Gloucester	1996-97	6	25	58	5
236	Jonathan Callard	Bath	1995-96	3	43	45	
224	Jonathan Callard	Bath	1996-97	4	51	34	
202	Jez Harris	Leicester	1993-94	2	18	41	11
196	Mark Tainton	Bristol	1994-95		11	56	2
195	John Liley	Leicester	1996-97	3	24	44	
189	Paul Grayson	Northampton	1994-95	1	11	52	2
189	David Humphreys	London Irish	1996-97	4	20	40	3
181	Jez Harris	Leicester	1994-95		11	40	13
178	Jonathan Callard	Bath	1993-94	4	25	36	
178	Paul Burke	Bristol	1996-97	2	27	38	
176	Thierry Lacroix	Harlequins	1996-97	2	29	33	3
167	Rob Liley	Sale	1995-96	3	22	34	2
166	Simon Mason	Orrell	1995-96	4	16	38	
161	Mark Tainton	Bristol	1993-94		19	40	1
159	Rob Andrew	Wasps	1993-94	2	16	38	1
150	Jonathan Callard	Bath	1994-95	1	14	39	
150	Simon Mannix	Sale	1996-97	7	17	27	
143	Kent Bray	Harlequins	1993-94	1	12	38	
135	Rob Andrew	Wasps	1994-95	2	19	26	3
132	Paul Grayson	Northampton	1993-94	2	10	33	1
129	Paul Grayson	Northampton	1996-97	1	14	28	4
126	Dusty Hare	Leicester	1987-88		15	31	1
126	John Liley	Leicester	1989-90	7	16	22	
126	Rob Andrew	Wasps	1990-91	4	16	26	
126	Andy Lee	Saracens	1995-96	2	7	29	5
126	Chris John	West Hartlepool	1996-97	3	12	28	1
125	Michael Lynagh	Saracens	1996-97		16	30	1
124	John Liley	Leicester	1991-92	3	19	25	
122	Jonathan Webb	Bath	1992-93	3	19	23	
120	David Pears	Harlequins	1990-91	1	16	23	5
120	Mark Tainton	Bristol	1995-96		12	30	2
120	Mike Catt	Bath	1996-97	9	24	7	2
116	Matthew McCarthy	Orrell	1996-97	2	18	19	4
114	David Pears	Harlequins	1989-90	2	14	24	2
112	Paul Challinor	Harlequins	1995-96	5	18	12	5
111	Michael Corcoran	London Irish	1992-93	2	4	41	
110	John Liley	Leicester	1990-91	2	18	22	
110	John Steele	Northampton	1991-92		10	28	2
110	Tim Stimpson	West Hartlepool	1995-96	5	8	23	
109	Martin Strett	Orrell	1990-91	1	21	20	1
107	David Pears	Harlequins	1991-92	4	15	21	
106	John Liley	Leicester	1992-93	2	15	22	
104	Martin Strett	Orrell	1989-90	4	14	20	
104	Martin Strett	Orrell	1991-92	1	8	26	2
103	Rob Andrew	Wasps	1988-89	2	13	21	2
103	Stuart Barnes	Bath	1989-90	6	29	7	
101	Steve Pilgrim	Wasps	1991-92	2	6	27	
101	Joel Stransky	Leicester	1996-97	2	8	25	

MOST POINTS IN A MATCH

31	John Liley	Leicester v Rosslyn Park	21.03.92
28	Martin Strett	Orrell v Rosslyn Park	28.04.90
28	John Liley	Leicester v Bristol	28.10.95
27	David Pears	Harlequins v Bedford	14.10.89
26	John Liley	Leicester v Bedford	23.09.89
26	Stuart Barnes	Bath v West Hartlepool	27.03.93
26	Paul Grayson	Northampton v Bristol	02.10.93
26	Mark Tainton	Bristol v Leicester	05.12.94
26	Andy Lee	Saracens v West Hartlepool	14.10.95
26	Paul Challinor	Harlequins v West Hartlepool	23.03.96
26	Rob Liley	Leicester v London Irish	31.10.96
26	John Stabler	West Hartlepool v London Irish	28.12.96
26	Simon Mannix	Sale v Northampton	09.03.97
26	Mike Catt	Bath v Sale	26.04.97
25	John Callard	Bath v Orrell	30.09.95
25	John Liley	Leicester v Leicester v Bristol	13.04.96
24	Dusty Hare	Leicester v Rosslyn Park	19.11.88
24	Stuart Barnes	Bath v Bedford	13.01.90
24	Rob Andrew	Wasps v Bristol	27.04.91
24	Will Carling	Harlequins v Orrell	05.10.96
23	Jaime Salmon	Harlequins v Waterloo	27.02.88
23	Rob Andrew	Wasps v Rosslyn Park	22.10.88
23	David Pears	Harlequins v Saracens	20.10.90
23	Rob Andrew	Wasps v Orrell	11.12.93
23	Jez Harris	Leicester v Gloucester	29.01.94
23	Arwel Thomas	Bristol v Orrell	04.11.95
23	Simon Mason	Orrell v Saracens	13.01.96
23	John Liley	Leicester v Orrell	30.03.96
23	Andy Lee	Saracens v West Hartlepool	30.03.96
23	John Callard	Bath v Orrell	31.08.96
23	John Liley	Leicester v Bath	07.09.96
23	Gareth Rees	Wasps v Saracens	08.09.96
23	John Liley	Leicester v Bristol	18.01.97
23	Joel Stransky	Leicester v West Hartlepool	08.03.97
22	Dusty Hare	Leicester v Sale	26.03.88
22	John Graves	Rosslyn Park v Bedford	31.03.90
22	Stuart Thresher	Harlequins v London Irish	31.10.92
22	Jonathan Callard	Bath v Northampton	18.09.93
22	Michael Corcoran	London Irish v Wasps	26.03.94
22	Rob Andrew	Wasps v Sale	15.10.94
22	Jez Harris	Leicester v Sale	29.10.94
22	Guy Gregory	Wasps v Orrell	13.04.96
22	Mike Catt	Bath v Bristol	29.10.96
22	David Humphreys	London Irish v West Hartlepool	28.12.96
22	Jonathan Callard	Bath v Northampton	19.01.97
22	Matthew McCarthy	Orrell v London Irish	22.02.97
22	Mark Mapletoft	Gloucester v Leicester	08.04.97
22	Simon Mannix	Sale v Gloucester	12.04.97
21	Ian Aithison	Waterloo v Sale	02.01.88
21	David Pears	Harlequins v Rosslyn Park	07.12.91
21	Ben Rudling	Saracens v Harlequins	21.03.92
21	Jonathan Webb	Bath v Rugby	09.01.93
21	Jez Harris	Leicester v Bristol	11.12.93
21	Jez Harris	Leicester v Northampton	08.01.94
21	Guy Gregory	Wasps v West Hartlepool	20.04.96
21	Thierry Lacroix	Harlequins v Orrell	08.03.97
21	Gareth Rees	Wasps v Gloucester	09.03.97
21	Alastair Hepher	Northampton v London Irish	12.04.97

MOST TRIES IN A MATCH

5	Kenny Logan	Wasps v Orrell	22.03.97
4	Gary Hartley	Nottingham v Bedford	18.11.89
4	Tony Swift	Bath v Bedford	13.01.90
4	Jeremy Guscott	Bath v Bedford	13.01.90
4	Paul Hamer	Orrell v Rugby	13.03.93
4	Tony Underwood	Leicester v Newcastle Gosforth	12.03.94
4	Daren O'Leary	Harlequins v Gloucester	31.08.96
3	Peter Shillingford	Moseley v Wasps	05.02.88
3	Mark Charles	Leicester v Sale	26.03.88
3	Andrew Harriman	Harlequins v Nottingham	01.04.88
3	Simon Smith	Wasps v Coventry	13.04.88
3	Andrew Harriman	Harlequins v Sale	23.04.88
3	Jeremy Guscott	Bath v Moseley	12.11.88
3	Mark Bailey	Wasps v Moseley	19.11.88
3	John Liley	Leicester v Bedford	23.09.89
3	Mike Wedderburn	Harlequins v Bedford	14.10.89
3	Mark Bailey	Wasps v Gloucester	14.10.89
3	Derrick Morgan	Gloucester v Rosslyn Park	11.11.89
3	Jonathan Callard	Bath v Bedford	13.01.90
3	Chris Gerard	Leicester v Moseley	13.01.90
3	Paul Manley	Orrell v Rosslyn Park	31.03.90
3	Dewi Morris	Orrell v Liverpool StH	13.10.90
3	Dewi Morris	Orrell v Northampton	27.10.90
3	Rory Underwood	Leicester v Northampton	21.01.91
3	Andrew Harriman	Harlequins v Bristol	30.03.91
3	Will Carling	Harlequins v Bristol	30.03.91
3	Graham Childs	Wasps v Liverpool StH	20.04.91
3	Rob Andrew	Wasps v Bristol	27.04.91
3	Rory Underwood	Leicester v Moseley	27.04.91
3	Steve Hackney	Leicester v London Irish	04.01.92
3	Tony Swift	Bath v Leicester	11.01.92
3	Rory Underwood	Leicester v Rosslyn Park	21.03.92
3	Mike Lloyd	Bristol v Rugby	28.03.92
3	Martin Pepper	Nottingham v Rosslyn Park	04.04.92
3	Chris Oti	Wasps v Bristol	25.04.92
3	Stuart Barnes	Bath v West Hartlepool	27.03.93
3	Derek Eves	Bristol v Rugby	22.03.93
3	Ian Wynn	Orrell v Wasps	30.04.94
3	Simon Morris	Gloucester v West Hartlepool	17.09.94
3	Damian Hopley	Wasps v Sale	15.10.94
3	Jeremy Guscott	Bath v Bristol	14.10.95
3	Graeme Smith	Orrell v Wasps	28.10.95
3	Rob Kitchen	Harlequins v Bristol	06.01.96
3	Graeme Smith	Orrell v Saracens	13.01.96
3	Aadel Kardooni	Leicester v West Hartlepool	17.02.96
3	Spencer Bromley	Harlequins v Sale	30.03.96
3	Aadel Kardooni	Leicester v Sale	17.04.96
3	Michael Corcoran	Harlequins v London Irish	14.09.96
3	Adedayo Adebayo	Bath v London Irish	05.10.96
3	Huw Harries	Harlequins v Orrell	05.10.96
3	Mike Lloyd	Gloucester v West Hartlepool	18.01.97
3	Jonathan Sleightholme	Bath v Northampton	19.01.97
3	Jonathan Sleightholme	Bath v London Irish	08.03.97
3	Domonic Chapman	Harlequins v Orrell	08.03.97
3	Nick Walshe	Harlequins v West Hartlepool	22.03.97
3	Tom Beim	Sale v West Hartlepool	05.04.97
3	Andy Nicol	Bath v Gloucester	30.04.97
3	Richard Wallace	Saracens v London Irish	30.04.97

Designed to perform

DIVISION ONE

MOST APPEARANCES

125	**Jim Mallinder**	Roundhay 15, Sale 110.	Full Back
120	**Dave Baldwin**	Wakefield 11, Sale 109.	Lock
118	**Graham Dawe**	Bath	Hooker
117	**Andy Robinson**	Bath	Flanker
117	**Andy Mullins**	Harlequins	Prop
114	**Matt Greenwood**	Roundhay 10, Nottingham 27, Wasps 77.	Utility Forward
	Simon Mitchell	W Hartlepool 82, Harlequins 13, Wasps 19.	Hooker
113	**John Wells**	Leicester	Flanker
111	**Harvey Thorneycroft**	Northampton	Winger
109	**Paul Hull**	Bristol	Full Back
	Nigel Redman	Bath	Lock
105	**John Liley**	Wakefield 5, Leicester 100.	Full Back
	Dean Ryan	Saracens 13, Wasps 69, Newcastle 23.	No. 8
	John Buckton	Saracens	Centre
	Ross Wilkinson	Newcastle	Centre
104	**Ben Clarke**	Saracens 22, Bath 61, Richmond 21.	Flanker
	Dave Sims	Gloucester	Lock
102	**Rob Andrew**	Wasps 77, Newcastle 25.	Stand Off
	Stuart Potter	Nottingham 30, Leicester 72.	Centre
	Steve Hackney	Nottingham 25, Leicester 77.	Winger
100	**Dave Hinkins**	Bristol	Prop
98	**Mike White**	Wasps	Flanker
98	**Jeremy Guscott**	Bath	Centre
97	**Rory Underwood**	Leicester	Winger
97	**Dewi Morris**	Waterloo 20, Orrell 62, Sale 15.	Scrum Half
96	**Darren Garforth**	Leicester	Prop
96	**Neil Frankland**	Newcastle	Flanker
96	**Jim Staples**	London Irish 58, Harlequins 38.	Full Back

LAURENT CABANNES of Harlequins & France in action against Sale.

Photo: Joe McCabe. 0181 394 0776

DIVISION ONE - TEN YEAR RECORD

	87/88	88/89	89/90	90/91	91/92	92/93	93/94	94/95	95/96	96/97
BATH	4	1	3	1	1	1	1	2	1	2
BEDFORD	-	-	12	-	-	-	-	-	-	-
BRISTOL	9	7	9	11	10	6	4	6	6	9
COVENTRY	11	-	-	-	-	-	-	-	-	-
GLOUCESTER	5	2	2	6	4	5	8	7	8	6
HARLEQUINS	3	8	7	3	8	8	6	8	3	3
LEICESTER	1	6	5	4	6	3	2	1	2	4
LIVERPOOL ST HELENS	-	12	-	13	-	-	-	-	-	-
LONDON IRISH	-	-	-	-	9	7	9	-	-	10
LONDON SCOTTISH	-	-	-	-	-	10	-	-	-	-
MOSELEY	7	10	11	12	-	-	-	-	-	-
NEWCASTLE	-	-	-	-	-	-	10	-	-	-
NORTHAMPTON	-	-	-	9	3	4	5	10	-	8
NOTTINGHAM	8	4	6	8	12	-	-	-	-	-
ORRELL	6	5	8	5	2	9	7	5	7	12
ROSSLYN PARK	-	9	10	7	13	-	-	-	-	-
RUGBY	-	-	-	-	11	13	-	-	-	-
SALE	12	-	-	-	-	-	-	4	5	5
SARACENS	-	-	4	10	5	11	-	-	9	7
WASPS	2	3	1	2	7	2	3	3	4	1
WATERLOO	10	11	-	-	-	-	-	-	-	-
WEST HARTLEPOOL	-	-	-	-	-	12	-	9	10	11

New Zealander, Richard Le Bas was Moseley's leading points scorer during the 1996-97 League campaign.

ALLIED DUNBAR

PREMIERSHIP TWO

1996-97 DIVISION TWO

PLAYING RECORD & breakdown

	Pd	W	D	L	Pts	HOME				AWAY			
						W	D	L	Pts	W	D	L	Pts
Richmond	22	19	2	1	40	10	1	0	21	9	1	1	19
Newcastle	22	19	1	2	39	11	0	0	22	8	1	2	17
Coventry	22	16	1	5	33	9	1	1	19	7	0	4	14
Bedford	22	15	0	7	30	9	0	2	18	6	0	5	12
London Scottish	22	11	0	11	22	6	0	5	12	5	0	6	10
Wakefield	22	11	0	11	22	5	0	6	10	6	0	5	12
Rotherham	22	10	0	12	20	6	0	5	12	4	0	7	8
Moseley	22	9	0	13	18	7	0	4	14	2	0	9	4
Waterloo	22	8	0	14	16	5	0	6	10	3	0	8	6
Blackheath	22	7	0	15	14	4	0	7	8	3	0	8	6
Rugby	22	3	0	19	6	2	0	9	4	1	0	10	2
Nottingham	22	2	0	20	4	1	0	10	2	1	0	10	2

POINTS FOR & breakdown

	Lge Pos	Pts	T	C	P	D	HOME					AWAY				
							Pts	T	C	P	D	Pts	T	C	P	D
1 Newcastle	2	1255	189	119	23	1	712	111	65	9	0	543	78	54	14	1
2 Richmond	1	986	139	84	38	3	494	72	43	15	1	492	67	41	23	2
3 Coventry	3	738	96	57	41	7	437	57	37	22	4	301	39	20	19	3
4 Bedford	4	720	103	68	23	0	436	62	45	12	0	284	41	23	11	0
5 Lon. Scottish	5	549	58	41	53	6	311	33	25	31	1	238	25	16	22	5
6 Rotherham	7	525	62	28	50	3	263	30	13	27	2	262	32	15	23	1
7 Waterloo	9	506	53	41	52	1	243	26	19	24	1	263	27	22	28	0
8 Wakefield	6	504	61	38	40	1	286	36	26	18	0	318	25	12	22	1
9 Moseley	8	492	54	36	49	1	298	33	20	30	1	194	21	16	19	0
10 Blackheath	10	412	43	31	42	3	225	24	18	21	2	187	19	13	21	1
11 Nottingham	12	344	39	22	35	0	178	18	11	22	0	166	21	11	13	0
12 Rugby	11	317	40	20	23	1	185	22	12	17	0	132	19	8	6	1

POINTS AGAINST & breakdown

	Lge Pos	Pts	T	C	P	D	HOME					AWAY				
							Pts	T	C	P	D	Pts	T	C	P	D
1 Newcastle	2	346	46	25	20	2	143	22	9	5	0	203	24	16	15	2
2 Coventry	3	394	45	26	27	2	166	18	8	19	1	228	27	18	18	1
3 Richmond	1	410	48	31	34	2	208	23	15	20	1	202	25	16	14	1
4 Bedford	4	482	54	31	47	3	234	25	14	25	2	248	29	17	22	1
8 Wakefield	6	557	66	40	47	2	269	32	20	23	0	288	34	20	24	2
6 Lon. Scottish	5	568	63	44	54	1	200	21	16	20	1	368	42	28	34	0
7 Blackheath	10	641	83	50	38	4	256	31	19	18	3	385	52	31	20	1
=8 Rotherham	7	661	83	54	45	1	269	33	19	21	1	392	50	35	24	0
=8 Waterloo	9	661	86	57	36	3	304	38	27	18	2	357	48	30	18	1
10 Moseley	8	741	104	58	33	2	358	51	29	14	1	383	53	29	19	1
11 Nottingham	12	827	110	68	43	4	466	56	33	18	2	421	54	35	25	2
12 Rugby	11	1060	150	101	35	1	467	64	42	20	1	593	86	59	15	0

1996-97 DIVISION TWO REVIEW

The top two were never really in much doubt - the order in which they would finish the season was.

In the end **Richmond** won it by just a point. They lost only once, heavily at Newcastle, and were held to draws twice - at Coventry on the opening day of the season, and at home to Newcastle. Led by Ben Clarke they topped the National Fair Play League with no yellow or red cards in League games, although Brian Moore was sent off in the Pilkington Cup game at Sale.

Irish international full back Simon Mason had a superb season contributing 324 points including ten tries, and there were other outstanding contributions from Scott Quinnell, Jim Fallon, Spencer Brown and Alan Tait to name but a few. Not contented with their lot they signed two Argentinians just as the season finished and late in the summer Australian international full back Matthew Pini.

Second placed **Newcastle** set a number of records including most points in a season, 1255, and most tries in a season, 189; both were Division Two and National League records. They suffered just two defeats all season at the hands of Coventry and Bedford whilst going undefeated at home. There were major contributions from just about every position but special mention must go to winger John Bentley who scored 23 tries in seventeen games - an amazing feat - on his return to Union. Director of rugby Rob Andrew did his bit with 297 points and was also the club's only ever present and passed personal milestones in his career in League rugby of 100 appearances and 1000 points.

The best of the rest were easily **Coventry** and **Bedford** whose new squads only came together at the start of the season - in Coventry's case and after the season started for Bedford who welcomed Martin Offiah back into rugby union. He did not disappoint with ten tries in just fourteen matches including tries in his last six games of the season. They now have a number of overseas players on their books including former Springbok Rudolf Straeuli and will start the coming season as one of the favourites for promotion after a summer of more recruitment.

Coventry had a super season with summer signings Jez Harris, rattling up 236 points, and Andy Smallwood, 17 tries, making major contributions. The squad lacks depth and strengthening is vital if they are to mount a serious challenge in the coming season but I am sure director of rugby Derek Eves has this matter in hand.

Of the remainder **London Scottish** were probably the best but they relied too heavily on the boot of ex-Northampton stand-off John Steele who scored nearly half their points and was probably one of the deadliest kickers in the division.

Wakefield won four of their last six matches to finish a creditable sixth. Scrum half Dave Scully topped the try scoring list for a second successive season with nine and is just four short of his half century. Scully also needs just three more appearances to be the first player to 150 league games in the National Leagues.

Rotherham acquitted themselves superbly in Division Two rugby to finish seventh. They achieved this without a settled side suffering numerous injuries in the second half of the season.

Moseley rescued their season late on with six successive home wins to climb the table after a disasterous first half of the campaign. Part of their late success was due to winger Domonic O'Mahoney who scored fifteen tries in thirteen games and stand-off Richard Le Bas who scored 177 points in just fourteen games.

Le Bas has left to join ambitious Worcester but Moseley have signed the Leicester pair of John Liley and Stue Hackney for the new season.

Waterloo were another side to rally late on with four wins out of the last five matches - scoring nearly half their season's total of tries in their closing six games.

Blackheath started the season positively but fell away dramatically to plummet down the table. They managed to stay clear of relegation, although they suffered from injuries losing new recruit Chris Braithwaite through injury from the middle part of the season.

The two relegated sides **Rugby** and **Nottingham** were eight and ten points behind Blackheath respectively. Rugby's veteran winger Eddie Saunders was the club's only ever present and topped their try scoring list for the seventh time in ten seasons with eight. Defensively Rugby were a nightmare conceding 200 points and 40 tries more than the next worst in the Division. Nottingham, who were rooted to the bottom of the table for nearly the whole time, were not helped by having to use five goal kickers during the season and losing the promising Rich Tomlinson to Worcester.

1996-97 DIVISION TWO

RECORD REVIEW

INDIVIDUAL RECORDS

MOST POINTS IN A MATCH

This record was broken twice on the same day - 5th October 1996.

At the start of the day the record stood at 30 to London Irish's Michael Corcoran.

By the end of the day the record was the property of Coventry's Jez Harris who scored 42 points in Coventry's record 102-22 win over Nottingham. His 42 points were made up of two tries, 13 conversions and two penalties. In Newcastle's National League record win 156-5 at home to Rugby on the same day Rob Andrew scored 36 points. Andrew's 36 points came from converting 18 of his sides 24 tries.

Late in the season London Scottish stand off John Steele equalled the old record of 30 against Rugby with two tries, four conversions and four penalties.

Evolution of record

26	Andy Mitchell	London Scot v North	03.10.87
28	David Johnson	New Gos v Morley	11.01.92
30	Michael Corcoran	L. Irish v Waterloo	23.09.95
42	Jez Harris	Coventry v Nott	05.10.96

Most in a match

42	Jez Harris	Coventry v Nott	05.10.96
36	Rob Andrew	Newcastle v Rugby	05.10.96
30	Michael Corcoran	L. Irish v Waterloo	23.09.95
30	John Steele	London S v Rugby	28.03.97
29	Simon Mason	Rich v Roth	14.09.96

MOST TRIES IN A MATCH

This record was equalled on the last day of the Division Two season when Western Samoan flanker Pat Lam scored five tries for Newcastle at home to Rotherham. Lam equalled the record set by Sale winger Simon Verbickas in their home win against Otley in February 1994.

Evolution of record (first to)

3	Jerry Macklin	Lon Scot v North	03.10.87
5	Simon Verbickas	Sale v Otley	12.02.94
5	Pat Lam	Newcastle v Roth	04.05.97

MOST CONVERSIONS IN A MATCH

Newcastle's Rob Andrew doubled the previous record of nine when he converted 18 of his side's 24 tries in their record 156-5 win over Rugby. Andrew's 19 conversions took the record from a three way tie between David Johnson, Guy Gregory and Paul Turner.

Evolution of record

6	Chris Howard	Rugby v Gosforth	11.11.89
9	David Johnson	New Gos v Morley	11.01.92
9	Guy Gregory	Nott v Morley	24.10.92
9	Paul Turner	Sale v Otley	12.02.94
18	Rob Andrew	Newcastle v Rugby	05.10.96

Most in a match

18	Rob Andrew	Newcastle v Rugby	05.10.96
13	Jez Harris	Coventry v Nott	05.10.96
9	David Johnson	New Gos v Morley	11.01.92
9	Guy Gregory	Nott v Morley	24.10.92
9	Paul Turner	Sale v Otley	12.02.94

MOST PENALTIES IN A MATCH

With tries the order of the day nobody kicked more than six penalties in a match and did not threaten Alastair Kerr's record of eight set in 1995-96 for Moseley against Waterloo.

Evolution of record (first to)

7	Michael Corcoran	Lon I v Lon S	13.01.96
8	Alastair Kerr	Moseley v Waterloo	17.02.96

Most in a match

8	Alastair Kerr	Moseley v Water	17.02.96
7	Michael Corcoran	Lon I v Lon S	13.01.96
7	Matt Inman	Roth v Rich	14.09.96

MOST DROP GOALS IN A MATCH

The existing record of three remained in tact with the most in a match last season being two.

MOST POINTS IN A SEASON

Richmond's Irish international full back Simon Mason broke London Irish's Michael Corcoran's record of 301 with 324 in Richmond's Championship season. Although Mason scored more points than Corcoran his points per match average was just below 15.43 to 16.72.
Mason equalled Corcoran's record of 20 points in a match five times in a season.

Evolution of record

75	Andy Finnie	Bedford	1987-88
138	Andy Kennedy	Saracens	1988-89
147	David Johnson	Newcastle Gos	1991-92
172	Guy Gregory	Nottingham	1993-94
213	Mike Jackson	Wakefield	1994-95
310	Michael Corcoran	London Irish	1995-96
324	Simon Mason	Richmond	1996-97

MOST TRIES IN A SEASON

Newcastle's John Bentley broke Northampton Centre Matt Allen's record of 20 tries in a season from 1995-96 with 23 last season. Fellow team mate Gary Armstrong and Richmond's Scott Quinnell also broke Allen's record of last season with 21.
Armstrong scored tries in eight successive matches to equal the National League record set by Sale winger Simon Verbikas during Sale Division Two championship season of 1993-94 Bentley and Quinnell equalled Matt Allen's record of scoring four hat tricks in a season.

Evolution of record

10	Dave McLagan	Saracens	1987-88
11	Nick Grecian	London Scot	1991-92
16	Simon Verbickas	Sale	1993-94
20	Matt Allen	Northampton	1996-97
23	John Bentley	Newcastle	1996-97

Most in a season

23	John Bentley	Newcastle	1996-97
21	Gary Armstrong	Newcastle	1996-97
21	Scott Quinnell	Richmond	1996-97
20	Matt Allen	Northampton	1995-96
20	Jim Fallon	Richmond	1996-97
17	Andy Smallwood	Coventry	1996-97

MOST CONVERSIONS IN A SEASON

Newcastle's Rob Andrew broke the record set last season by Northampton's Paul Grayson. Grayson kicked 76 conversions whilst Andrew

took the record to 95 - its hard to imagine that ever being broken.
Richmond's Simon Mason also passed the old record with 83.

Evolution of record

14	Andy Kennedy	Saracens	1988-89
24	Martin Livesey	Richmond	1989-90
31	David Johnson	Newcastle Gos	1991-92
76	Paul Grayson	Northampton	1995-96
95	Rob Andrew	Newcastle	1996-97

Most in a season

95	Rob Andrew	Newcastle	1996-97
83	Simon Mason	Richmond	1996-97
76	Paul Grayson	Northampton	1995-96
67	Mike Rayer	Bedford	1996-97
48	Jez Harris	Coventry	1996-97

MOST PENALTIES IN A SEASON

It was a season of tries and penalty kicks were not in fashion. The exception to that was John Steele of London Scottish who kicked 48 and moved into 4th place on the all time list.

Most in a season

63	Michael Corcoran	London Irish	1995-96
57	Mike Jackson	Wakefield	1994-95
48	Steve Swindells	Waterloo	1994-95
47	John Steele	London Scot	1996-97
45	Simon Mason	Newcastle Gos	1994-95

ANALYSIS OF PLAYERS USED

	Players used	League debuts	Ever present	1	2
Bedford	46(1)	30	1	65	7.2
Blackheath	31	14	-	45	10.6
Coventry	35(4)	16	-	46	9.4
London Scot	38	15	1	39	8.7
Moseley	46(1)	26	-	56	7.2
Newcastle	28(4)	12	1	43	11.8
Nottingham	41(3)	15	2	36	8.0
Richmond	33(4)	21	-	64	10
Rotherham	36(6)	15	1	42	9.8
Rugby	45(2)	19	1	42	7.3
Wakefield	31(3)	14	2	45	10.6
Waterloo	38(5)	17	2	45	8.7

1 = % of players making league debut
2 = Average appearances per player

Rob Andrew's Newcastle Falcons used just 28 players, the lowest number in the National Leagues along with Division Three Champions Exeter. Andrew was the club's only ever-present.

Bedford gave league debuts to 30 players out of the 46 they used - an incredible 65%. No wonder they found consistency difficult to achieve.

Moseley, who along with Bedford used a Divisional high 46 players, fielded just 2 players in their final game of the season who had started in the opening game of the season - Carl Hall and Nathan Webber.

Overall in the Division there were 11 ever-presents:

Jeff Probyn (Bedford)
Chris Tarbuck (London Scottish)
Rob Andrew (Newcastle)
Alan Rayer (Nottingham)
Richard Bygrave (Nottingham)
John Dudley (Rotherham)
Eddie Saunders (Rugby)
Peter Massey (Wakefield)
Simon Croft (Wakefield)
Marcus Coast (Waterloo)
Tony Handley (Waterloo)

ATTENDANCES

Another new feature in this years book and we have broken it down into Home and Away to see which teams attract the fans on the road.

HOME ATTENDANCES

Team	Average	Highest attendance
Coventry	3486	7800 v Newcastle
Bedford	2832	5200 v Newcastle
Richmond	2656	6567 v Newcastle
Newcastle	2528	5645 v Richmond
Blackheath	2331	4650 v Newcastle
Rotherham	1420	3025 v Newcastle
Moseley	1047	2003 v Newcastle
Lon. Scottish	1045	2566 v Newcastle
Wakefield	909	1900 v Newcastle
Waterloo	904	2500 v Newcastle
Rugby	683	1190 v Newcastle
Nottingham	499	760 v Bedford

FAIR PLAY LEAGUE

This is another new feature which we will publish each season and hopefully get the RFU to make part of their awards evening.

This season's Division Two award goes to Champions Richmond but just behind them are London Scottish who share the same ground - could it be something in the air!!

Team	Yellow card	Red card	Total
Richmond	0	0	0
London Scottish	1	0	5
Moseley	2	0	10
Wakefield	3	0	15
Rotherham	4	0	20
Waterloo	2	1	20
Blackheath	0	2	20
Bedford	5	0	25
Coventry	6	0	30
Nottingham	6	0	30
Newcastle	8	1	50
Rugby	6	2	50

"ON THE ROAD ATTENDANCES"

Team	Average	Highest attendance
Newcastle	3466	7800 v Coventry
Richmond	2298	5645 v Newcastle
Bedford	2166	6200 v Coventry
Coventry	1751	3620 v Bedford
Lon. Scottish	1503	2620 v Bedford
Nottingham	1413	3100 v Bedford
Moseley	1380	3500 v Coventry
Wakefield	1359	3100 v Coventry
Rotherham	1269	3000 v Coventry
Blackheath	1166	2380 v Bedford
Rugby	1134	2328 v Newcastle
Waterloo	1121	2000 v Coventry

Third placed Coventry averaged 3486, some 600+ more than the next best supported club - Bedford. Coventry had just one attendance less than 2000 - that was the game against Rugby, which attracted 1900. They had the top attendance in the division with 7800, for the home game against Newcastle. Bedford who averaged 2832, second behind Coventry, had just two attendances under 2000.

Ron Andrew's Newcastle side gave ten teams their top attendances - the exception being Nottingham whose top attendance was 760 for the match against Bedford, some 27 more than watched the Newcastle fixture.

In the 'on the road' figures Newcastle easily came out on top. They were 1200 clear of rivals Richmond, and had a better away average attendance than home - 3466 compared to 2528.

Most teams had their best 'on the road' attendances against either Bedford or Coventry, both traditionally well supported clubs.

1996-97 DIVISION TWO

MOST TRIES

23	John Bentley	Newcastle
21	Gary Armstrong	Newcastle
21	Scott Quinnell	Richmond
20	Jim Fallon	Richmond
17	Andy Smallwood	Leeds
15	Domonic O 'Mahoney	Moseley
15	Pat Lam	Newcastle
14	Andy McAdam	Coventry
14	Tim Stimpson	Newcastle
13	Guy Easterby	Rotherham
13	Ben Whetstone	Bedford
12	Spencer Brown	Richmond
11	Ross Nesdale	Newcastle
11	Va'aiga Tulugamala	Newcastle
11	Ben Clarke	Clifton
11	Craig Quinnell	Richmond
10	Martin Offiah	Bedford
10	Simon Mason	Richmond
10	Allan Bateman	Richmond
9	Junior Paramore	Bedford
9	Tony Underwood	Newcastle
9	Dave Scully	Wakefield
9	Adrian Davies	Richmond
8	Mike Hanslip	Blackheath
8	Ian Patten	Coventry
8	Dean Ryan	Newcastle
8	Richard Heaslegrave	Rotherham
8	Eddie Saunders	Rugby
7	David Blyth	Waterloo
7	Peter Massey	Wakefield
7	Paul Bale	Rugby
7	George Graham	Newcastle
7	Gareth Archer	Newcastle
7	Chris Tarbuck	London Scottish
7	Mike Rayer	Bedford
7	Rob Andrew	Newcastle

MOST PENALTIES

47	John Steele	London Scottish
36	Simon Mason	Richmond
36	Richard LeBas	Moseley
35	Jez Harris	Coventry
35	Mike Jackson	Wakefield
25	Chris Braithwaite	Blackheath
23	Mike Rayer	Bedford
23	Chris Thompson	Waterloo
23	Rob Andrew	Newcastle
21	Matt Inman	Rotherham
21	Dean Lax	Rotherham
18	Lyndon Griffiths	Waterloo
15	Jim Quantrill	Rugby
10	David Evans	Nottingham
9	Tony Handley	Waterloo
9	John Gallagher	Blackheath
9	Nick Carroll	Nottingham
8	Sam Howard	Blackheath
7	Wayne Barr	Rugby
7	Simon Hodgkinson	Nottingham
6	Chris Dossett	Moseley
5	Ian Stent	London Scottish
5	Craig Quick	Moseley
5	Dave Scully	Wakefield
4	James Brown	Coventry
4	Gary Hartley	Nottingham
4	Stewart Moffitt	Rotherham
3	Rich Tomlinson	Nottingham
2	Matt Gallagher	Coventry
2	Matt Birch	Moseley
2	Steve Wills	Nottingham
2	John Gregory	Richmond
2	Simon Binns	Rotherham
2	Rob Ashforth	Rotherham
2	Martin Emmett	Waterloo

MOST CONVERSIONS

95	Rob Andrew	Newcastle
83	Simon Mason	Richmond
67	Mike Rayer	Bedford
48	Jez Harris	Coventry
39	John Steele	London Scottish
33	Mike Jackson	Wakefield
27	Richard LeBas	Moseley
23	Chris Braithwaite	Blackheath
23	Tim Stimpson	Newcastle
20	Lyndon Griffiths	Waterloo
14	Matt Inman	Rotherham
11	Jim Quantrill	Rugby
10	David Evans	Nottingham
10	Tony Handley	Waterloo
10	Chris Thompson	Waterloo
9	Wayne Barr	Rugby
7	Nick Carroll	Nottingham
7	Dean Lax	Rotherham
6	John Gallagher	Blackheath
6	Matt Gallagher	Coventry

MOST DROP GOALS

5	Jez Harris	Coventry
4	John Steele	London Scottish
3	Adrian Davies	Richmond
2	Chris Braithwaite	Blackheath
2	Matt Gallagher	Coventry
2	Simon Binns	Rotherham
1	Andy Park	Blackheath
1	Ronnie Eriksson	London Scottish
1	Ian Stent	London Scottish
1	Chris Dossett	Moseley
1	Rob Andrew	Newcastle
1	Richard Heaselgrave	Rotherham
1	Alsatair Kennedy	Rugby
1	Mike Jackson	Wakefield
1	Tony Handley	Waterloo

1996-97 DIVISION TWO

MOST POINTS IN THE SEASON

POINTS	PLAYER	CLUB	Tries	Cons.	Pens.	D.G.
324	Simon Mason	Richmond	10	83	36	-
297	Rob Andrew	Newcastle	7	95	23	1
256	John Steele	Northampton	5	39	47	4
238	Mike Rayer	Bedford	7	67	23	-
236	Jez Harris	Coventry	4	48	35	5
199	Mike Jackson	Wakefield	5	33	35	1
177	Richard Le Bas	Moseley	3	27	36	-
137	Chris Braithwaite	Blackheath	2	23	25	2
116	Tim Stimpson	Newcastle	14	23	-	-
115	John Bentley	Newcastle	23	-	-	-
105	Gary Armstrong	Newcastle	21	-	-	-
105	Scott Quinnell	Richmond	21	-	-	-
100	Jim Fallon	Richmond	20	-	-	-
99	Lyndon Griffiths	Waterloo	1	20	18	-
92	Dean Lax	Rotherham	3	7	21	-
91	Matt Inman	Rotherham	-	14	21	-
89	Chris Thompson	Waterloo	-	10	23	-
85	Andy Smallwood	Coventry	17	-	-	-
75	Domonic O'Mahoney	Moseley	15	-	-	-
75	Pat Lam	Newcastle	15	-	-	-
72	Jim Quantrill	Rugby	1	11	15	-
70	Dave Scully	Wakefield	9	5	5	-
70	Andy McAdam	Coventry	14	-	-	-
65	Guy Easterby	Rotherham	13	-	-	-
65	Ben Whetstone	Bedford	13	-	-	-
64	John Gallagher	Blackheath	5	6	9	-
60	Tony Handley	Waterloo	2	10	9	1
60	Spencer Brown	Richmond	12	-	-	-
57	Va'aiga Tuigamala	Newcastle	11	1	-	-
55	Ben Clarke	Richmond	11	-	-	-
55	Craig Quinnell	Richmond	11	-	-	-
55	Ross Nesdale	Newcastle	11	-	-	-
55	David Evans	Nottingham	1	10	10	-
54	Wayne Barr	Rugby	3	9	7	-
54	Adrian Davies	Richmond	9	-	-	3
50	Martin Offiah	Bedford	10	-	-	-
50	Allan Bateman	Richmond	10	-	-	-

BEDFORD R.U.F.C.

NICKNAME: The Blues

FOUNDED: 1886

Chairman - Frank Warren
Sports Network Europe, Centurian Ho.,
Bircherley Green, Hertford. SG14 2RE
Tel: 01992 505550 (B)   01992 505552 (Fax)

Commercial Manager - Peter Hicks
c/o Bedford RFC, as opposite

Chief Executive - Geoff Cooke OBE
Bedford RFC, Goldington Road, Bedford. MK40 3NF
Tel: 01234 347980 (B)   01234 347511 (Fax)

Press Officer - Richard Hart
c/o Bedford RFC, as above. 0410 323962 (Mob)

Director of Rugby - Paul Turner
c/o Bedford RFC, as above

In 1975 'Budge' Rogers and company led Bedford to their famous Cup Final victory over Rosslyn Park. Now, after waiting more than twenty years to reach the same heights, Bedford have a mission under chairman Frank Warren - simply to become the best club in Britain within the next five years.

After relaunching the Blues with a management structure dubbed the 'dream team' in August 1996, it was perhaps unreasonable to expect promotion ten months later. But, after finishing fourth, and narrowly missing out on First League rugby in their play-off match against Bristol, the Blues enter the new season arguably as co-favourites with Coventry to win the Second Division title.

With former England and Lions manager Geoff Cooke appointed as director of rugby, the mercurial Welsh fly-half Paul Turner acquired from Sale as captain and coach and Bob Burrows, former Head of ITV Sport, as chief executive, Bedford comprehensively embraced the new professional era just in time for the season's kick-off. Perhaps the most influential addition to the 'dream team' was boxing promoter Frank Warren, who injected substantial backing in a joint venture deal between his company Sports Network Europe and the club.

On the field Bedford boasted no fewer than eight players of international status this season as Cooke and Turner persuaded the stars to arrive at Goldington Road. Great Britain rugby league internationals Martin Offiah and Steve McCurrie successfully switched codes to union; Springbok No 8 and 1995 World Cup winner Rudolf Straeuli and Western Samoan flanker Junior Paramore happily settled; Canadian 'Stormin' Norm Hadley also boosted the pack; veteran England prop Jeff Probyn, now 41, added invaluable experience, while Turner's Welsh counterpart, full-back Mike Rayer, broke the club record for individual points in a season amassing 361 (9T, 101C, 38P) with his accurate boot and crucial tries. With the likes of young stars Scot Murray, Roy Winters and Ben Whetstone improving all the time, the Blues created a fine balance between experience and youth.

By February, with the club vying for promotion, Warren was appointed chairman, taking over from Ian Bullerwell. He and partner Chris Roberts have whole-heartedly pledged their support in a five year deal and have now acquired a 90 percent shareholding agreed by the old members' club. Cooke will also take a more hands-on role next season as chief executive.

And the abiding memory last term? Bedford's barnstorming 34-28 victory over Newcastle at Goldington Road, described by many reporters as the game of the season and enhancing the Blues' reputation as a growing force. Next season consistency will be the key but, with further big signings on the cards, Messrs. Warren and Cooke are in enviable shape. RICHARD HART

L-R - Back Row: Leigh Mansell, Junior Paramore, Mark Upex, Roy Winters, Martin Pepper, Judd Marshall. Middle: Richard Greed (coach), Graham radford (Team Man.), Jeff Probyn, Simon Brown, Richard White, Scot Murray, Paul Hewtt, Matt Oliver, Paul Simmons, Martin Offiah, Geoff Cooke, Frank Warren. Front: Mike rayer, John Farr, Paul Turner (Capt./Dir. of Rugby), Ian Bullerwell, Ben Whetstone, Ben Hyde.

Colours: Oxford & Cambridge blue hoops

Change colours: Navy blue with light blue and cerise hoop

BEDFORD

No	Ven.	Date	Opponents	Att.	Res.	Score	Scorers
1	(H)	07.09	v Nottingham	3100	W	41-23	Oliver(t)Whetstone(t)Crossland(t)PTry(2t)Rayer(5c2p)
2	(A)	14.09	v Blackheath	2834	L	3-11	Rayer(p)
3	(H)	21.09	v Richmond	3510	L	17-44	Whetstone(t)Farr(t)Rayer(tc)
4	(A)	29.09	v Rugby	1150	W	34- 6	Pechey(2t)Crossland(t)Paramore(t)Hewitt(t)Rayer(3cp)
5	(H)	05.10	v Wakefield	1800	W	25-19	Hyde(t)Mansell(t)Rater(t2c2p)
6	(A)	12.10	v Waterloo	800	W	34-11	McCurrie(2t)Murray(t)Brown(t)Upex(t)Rayer(3cp)
7	(H)	19.10	v Rotherham	2800	W	44-30	Probyn(t)Paramore(t)Offiah(t)White(t)Simmonds(t)Rayer(t4c2p)
8	(A)	26.10	v Newcastle	2261	L	12-49	Whetstone(t)Rayer(tc)
9	(H)	02.11	v Moseley	2226	W	64- 9	Offiah(2t)Hyde(t)Winters(t)Turner(t)Upex(t)Rennell(t)Hewitt(t)Whetstone(t)Pechey(t)Rayer(7c)
10	(A)	09.11	v LondonScot	2317	W	27-26	Hewitt(t)Pechey(t)Whetstone(t)Rayer(3c2p)
11	(H)	16.11	v Coventry	3640	W	30-23	Pechey(t)Paramore(t)Whetstone(t)Rayer(3c3p)
12	(A)	28.12	v Nottingham	760	W	36-13	Probyn(2t)Skingsley(t)Brown(t)Oliver(t)Stone(t)Rayer(3c)
13	(H)	18.01	v Rugby	1696	W	57- 6	Marshall(2t)Brown(2t)Whetstone(t)Murray(t)Hewitt(t)Pflugler(t)Paramore(t)Rayer(6c)
14	(A)	26.01	v Richmond	2875	L	33-34	Pflugler(2t)Oliver(t)Rayer(t2c2p)
15	(H)	08.02	v Wakefield	1500	W	29-17	Paramore(2t)McCurrie(t)Murray(t)Rayer(3cp)
16	(H)	22.02	v Blackheath	2380	W	72-18	Paramore(2t)Offiah(2t)Probyn(t)Platford(t)Turner(t)Murray(t)Whetstone(t)Edwards(t)Oliver(t)Rayer(7cp)
17	(H)	08.03	v Waterloo	1800	W	38- 6	Edwards(t)Offiah(t)Whetstone(t)Allen(t)PenTry(t)Rayer(5cp)
18	(A)	22.03	v Rotherham	1850	W	32-11	McCurrie(2t)Whetstone(t)Offiah(t)Rayer(3c2p)
19	(H)	05.04	v Newcastle	5200	W	34-28	Hewitt(t)Edwards(t)Whetstone(t)Boyd(t)Offiah(t)Rayer(3cp)
20	(A)	12.04	v Moseley	1216	L	34-40	Stone(t)Paramore(t)Offiah(t)Whetstone(t)Turner(c)Rayer(t2cp)
21	(H)	19.04	v London Scot	2620	L	14-28	Whetstone(t)Offiah(t)Rayer(2c)
22	(A)	26.04	v Coventry	6200	L	10-30	Pflugler(t)Platford(t)

1996-97 HIGHLIGHTS

LEAGUE DEBUTS: Mike Rayer, Stuart Crossland, Paul Turner, Simon Brorwn, Martin Pepper, Jeff Probyn, Paul Hewitt, Roy Winters, Rob Scott, Shaun Cassidy, Mark Petchey, Steve McCurrie, Scott Murray, Junior Paramore, Graham HigginBotham, Ben Ryan, Richard White, Martin Offiah, Judd Marshall, Hienz Pflugler, Norm Hadley, Clement Boyd, Neil McCarthy, Shaun Platford, Rudolf Streuli, Darren Edwards, Ryan O'Neil, Chris Bajak, Naude Roussouw, Andy Matchett.

TRY ON DEBUT: Stuart Crossland, Martin Offiah, Darren Edwards.

PLAYERS USED: 46 plus 1 as replacement.

EVER PRESENT: Jeff Probyn.

❑ After ten seasons and 145 matches still nobody has managed a hat-trick of tries in a match. Two tries have been scored on 26 occasions.

❑ Second row forward Mark Upex broke the record for most league appearances. On the last day of the season he passed Andy Finnie's record of 95

❑ 30 players scored tries - most in the division & three more than London Scottish and Newcastle.

❑ Welsh international utility back Mike Rayer broke Andy Finnie's record's for points and conversions in a season with 238 and 67 respectively. Finnie set his records during Bedford's 1994-95 division three championship winning season with 228 and 24 respectively.

	Pts	T	C	P	D	Apps	Ave.
Mike Rayer 96-97	238	7	67	23	-	21	11.33
Andy Finnie 94-95	228	-	24	56	4	18	12.67

❑ Rayer also broke the record of five conversions in a match held by Steve Batty and Andy Finnie. Rayer twice kicked seven conversions against Moseley and Blackheath.

❑ Centre, Ben Whetstone, and Winger, Martin Offiah, both broke Vince Turner's record of scoring tries in consecutive matches. Turner did it in games whilst Whetstone and Offiah went one better with 6.

❑ Whetstone broke Matt Oliver's record of eight tries in a season . He set a new mark of 13 from 18 games. This extended his career record to 30.

❑ One of only two teams to beat Newcastle.

❑ Stopped the opposition scoring a try in four games jointly the best record in the division along with Blackheath and Coventry.

BEDFORD'S COURAGE LEAGUE MATCH DETAILS 1996-97

	15	14	13	12	11	10	9	1	2	3	4	5	6	7	8	Replacements	
1	Rayer	Crossland	Whetstone	Oliver	Cooke	Turner	Farr	Brown	Pepper	Upex	Thompson	Skingsley	Hewitt	Winters			1
2	Rayer	Crossland	Oliver	Whetstone	Cooke	Turner	Stone	Brown	Pepper	Probyn	Scott	Thompson	Rennell	Cassidy	Winters	Hewitt(11)	2
3	Rayer	Crossland	Whetstone	Oliver	Oliver	Turner	Farr	Brown	McCurrie	Probyn	Upex	Murray	Paramore	Hewitt	Winters		3
4	Rayer	Crossland	Higginbotham/Petchey	Ryan	Turner	Hyde	Brown	McCurrie	Probyn	Upex	Murray	Paramore	Hewitt	Winters		Kemble(11)White(12)	4
5	Rayer	Crossland	Oliver	McCurrie	Hewitt	Turner	Hyde	Mansell	Pepper	Probyn	White	Murray	Paramore	Kemble	Winters		5
6	Rayer	Crossland	Oliver	Petchey	Oliver	Turner	Farr	Brown	McCurrie	Probyn	Upex	Murray	Deans	Paramore	Winters	Kemble(8)	6
7	Rayer	Hewitt	Whetstone	Oliver	Offiah	Turner	Farr	Brown	Simmonds	Probyn	Upex	Murray	White	Paramore	Winters		7
8	Rayer	Hewitt	Whetstone	Petchey	Offiah	Turner	Farr	Brown	Simmonds	Orobyn	Upex	White	Paramore	Winters			8
9	Rayer	Hewitt	Whetstone	Oliver	Offiah	Turner	Hyde	Brown	Simmonds	Probyn	Upex	White	Winters	Marshall	Rennell	Stone(10)Petchey(6)	9
10	Rayer	Hewitt	Whetstone	Oliver	Offiah	Tapper	Hyde	Brown	Simmonds	Probyn	Upex	White	Deans	Marshall	Paramore	Pepper(7)Petchey(10)	10
11	Rayer	Hewitt	Whetstone	Petchey	Offiah	Turner	Hyde	Brown	Simmonds	Probyn	Upex	White	Winters	Paramore	Kemble	Pepper(6)	11
12	Cooke	Hewitt	Whetstone	Oliver	Offiah	Rayer	Hyde	Brown	Simmonds	Probyn	Thompson	Murray	Winters	Pepper	Paramore	Stone(9)Petchey(11)Skingsley(tr7)	12
13	Rayer	Hewitt	Whetstone	Oliver	Offiah	Turner	Stone	Brown	Simmonds	Probyn	Murray	Hadley	Winters	Paramore	Marshall	McCurrie(2)Hyde(9)	13
14	Rayer	Whetstone	Oliver	Pfluger	Offiah	Turner	Hyde	Brown	Simmonds	Probyn	Murray	Hadley	Winters	Paramore	Stone(9)		14
15	Rayer	Hewitt	Pfluger	Oliver	Offiah	Turner	McCurrie	Boyd	McCarthy	Probyn	Platford	Hadley	Murray	Paramore	Straeuli	Stone(13)	15
16	Rayer	Hewitt	Pfluger	McCurrie	Turner	Stone	Boyd	McCarthy	Probyn	Platford	Hadley	Murray	Streuli	Paramore		Oliver(13),Edwards(9),Winters(8)	16
17	Rayer	Allen	Whetstone	Oliver	Offiah	Turner	Edwards	Boyd	McCarthy	Probyn	Platford	Hadley	Murray	Paramore	Straeuli	Winters(5)	17
18	Rayer	Cooke	Whetstone	Allen	Oliver	Turner	Stone	Boyd	McCarthy	Probyn	Platford	Hadley	Murray	Paramore	Straeuli	Offiah(14)Pfluger(13)McCurrie(9)Winters(4)Simmonds(2)	18
19	Rayer	Hewitt	Whetstone	McCurrie	Offiah	Turner	Edwards	Simmonds	Murray	Probyn	Murray	Winters	Winters	Parramore	Straeuli	McCarthy(2)Deans(4)	19
20	Rayer	O'Neill	Whetstone	Allen	Offiah	Pfluger	Stone	Boyd	Simmonds	Probyn	Murray	Hadley	Winters	Parramore	Straeuli	McCurrie(12)Deans(11)Turner(10)Matchett(9)20	20
21	Rayer	Hewitt	Whetstone	McCurrie	Offiah	Turner	Matchett	Brown	McCarthy	Probyn	Murray	Hadley	Deans	Paramore	Straeuli	Simmonds(2)Allen(14)Pepper(6)	21
22	Cooke	O'Neill	Oliver	McCurrie	Bajak	Pfluger	Stone	Mansell	McCarthy	Probyn	Upex	Hadley	Deans	Pepper		Roussouw Binny(2)Platford(4)Winters(6)Matchett(9)	22

BEDFORD LEAGUE STATISTICS
(COMPILED BY STEPHEN McCORMACK)

Season	Div.	P	W	D	L	F	(Tries	Con	Pen	DG)	A	(Tries	Con	Pen	DG)	Most Points	Most Tries
87-88	2	11	6	2	3	168	(18	12	22	2)	164	(17	9	23	3)	75 - Andy Finnie	3 - by 3 players Steve Harris, Steve Batty & Brian Gabriel.
88-89	2	11	6	2	3	141	(13	7	21	4)	187	(23	13	20	3)	56 - Andy Finnie	2 - Steve Harris & Gary Colleran
89-90	1	11	0	0	11	70	(9	5	7	1)	467	(83	42	15	2)	13 - Richard Creed	3 - Mark Howe
90-91	2	12	4	2	6	138	(16	7	16	4)	203	(27	10	22	3)	78 - Andy Finnie	3 - Tim Young
91-92	2	12	4	0	8	168	(20	11	19	3)	204	(24	15	25	1)	92 - Andy Finnie	5 - Mark Rennell
92-93	2	12	6	2	4	186	(13	8	32	3)	183	(15	9	24	6)	75 - Andy Finnie	3 - Mark Rennell
93-94	3	18	12	0	6	332	(29	14	50	3)	260	(27	13	32	1)	172 - Andy Finnie	8 - Vince Turner
94-95	3	18	13	1	4	421	(38	24	56	5)	250	(27	14	28	1)	228 - Andy Finnie	6 - Ben Whetsone
95-96	2	18	5	1	12	289	(35	18	23	3)	520	(66	41	33	3)	85 - Andy Finnie	8 - Matt Oliver
96-97	2	22	15	0	7	720	(103	68	23	0)	482	(54	31	47	3)	238 - Mike Rayer	13 - Ben Whetstone
Totals		145	71	10	64	2633	(294	174	269	28)	2920	(363	197	269	26)		

	HOME	AWAY
BIGGEST WIN	(55pts) 64-9 v Moseley 2.11.96	(44pts) 59-15 v Harrogate 15.4.95
DEFEAT	(63pts) 71-8 v Harlequins 14.10.89	(76pts) 0-76 v Bath 13.1.90
MOST POINTS SCORED:	72-18 v Blackheath 22.2.97	59-15 v Harrogate 15.4.95
AGAINST:	8-71 v Harlequins 14.10.89	0-76 v Bath 13.1.90

MOST CONSECUTIVE VICTORIES - 7   **MOST CONSECUTIVE DEFEATS - 14**

MOST TRIES IN A MATCH
(FOR) 11 v Blackheath 22.2.97
(AGAINST) 14 v Bath 13.1.90

MOST APPEARANCES
FORWARD: 97 Mark Upex
BACK: 96 Andy Finnie

CONSECUTIVE APPEARANCES
46 Paul Alston 19.9.92 to 12.4.95

CONSECUTIVE SCORING MATCHES
Scoring Tries - 6 - Ben Whetstone & Martin Offiah
Scoring Points - 36 - Andy Finnie

MOST	in a SEASON	in a CAREER	in a MATCH
Points	238 Mike Rayer 96-97	867 Andy Finnie 87-96	25 Andy Finnie v Coventry 27.3.93 (H)
Tries	13 Ben Whetstone 96-97	30 Ben Whetstone 92-97	2 on 26 occasions incl. Vince Turner on 3 occasions
Conversions	67 Mike Rayer 96-97	87 Andy Finnie 87-96	7 Mike Rayer v Moseley 2.11.96 (H) v Blackheath 22.2.97 (H)
Penalties	56 Andy Finnie 94-95	203 Andy Finnie 87-96	7 Andy Finnie v Coventry 27.4.94 (H)
Drop Goals	4 Andy Finnie 90-91 & 94-95	22 Andy Finnie 87-96	2 Andy Finnie v Coventry 27.3.94 (H) v Clifton 14.1.95 (A)

BEDFORD PLAYING SQUAD

NAME	Ht	Wt	Birthdate	Birthplace	Club	Apps	Pts	T	C	P	DG

BACKS

NAME	Ht	Wt	Birthdate	Birthplace	Club	Apps	Pts	T	C	P	DG
Mike Rayer	5.10	13.3	21.07.65	Cardiff	Cardiff						
Wales: 21, B, Youth.					Bedford	21	238	7	67	23	-
Martin Offiah	6.2	14.4	29.12.66	London	Previous Clubs: Rosslyn Park, Widnes (RL), Wigan (RL), London Broncos (RL)						
RL - England: Great Britain:					Bedford	13+1	50	10	-	-	-
Ben Whetstone	5.11	14.7	29.06.70	Holbeach	Ely						
					Bedford	73	153	30	-	-	-
Matt Oliver	6.1	13.7	30.11.76	Northampton							
					Bedford	32+1	60	12	-	-	-
Marcus Cooke	6.4	14.0	14.07.75	Cuckfield	Burton-on-Trent						
					Bedford	38	28	5	-	-	-
Paul Turner	5.10	11.8	16.02.59	Newport	Newbridge						
Wales: 3.					Sale	52+1	305	3	55	47	3
					Bedford	18+1	12	2	1	-	-
Heinz Pflugler	6.0	13.7	04.11.69	Pretoria (SA)	Previous Clubs: Transvaal, Natal.						
					Bedford	6+1	20	4	-	-	-
Steve McCurrie	5.10	17.8	01.06.73	Whitehaven	Widnes (RL)						
RL - England:, u21. Great Britain:					Bedford	8+4	25	5	-	-	-
Paul Hewitt	6.2	16.5	04.10.71	Pontypool	Pontypool						
Wales: u19, Students.					Sale	10+2	5	1	-	-	-
					Bedford	16	25	5	-	-	-
Paul Allen	5.11	14.0	05.11.71	Poole							
					Bedford	22+1	20	4	-	-	-
Ben Hyde	5.6	11.7	14.03.75	Cheltenham							
England: Colts, u18, u16.					Bedford	9+2	10	2	-	-	-

FORWARDS

NAME	Ht	Wt	Birthdate	Birthplace	Club	Apps	Pts	T	C	P	DG
Simon Brown	5.10	16.0	31.10.72	Oxford	Harlequins	20+1	5	1	-	-	-
England: u21, u18					Bedford	14	20	4	-	-	-
Martin Pepper	5.11	15.7	14.12.67	Beverley	Headingley	34	4	1	-	-	-
					Harlequins	16	-	-	-	-	-
England: A, Students					Nottingham	22	21	5	-	-	-
					Bedford	5+3	-	-	-	-	-
Jeff Probyn	5.10	16.0	27.04.56	London	Previous Clubs: Richmond, Askeans.						
England: 37, B (4).					Wasps	70	9	2	-	-	-
					Bedford	22	20	4	-	-	-
Paul Simmonds	5.11	15.0	26.06.71	Luton	Harlequins	0+1	-	-	-	-	-
					Bedford	10+2	5	1	-	-	-
Clement Boyd	6.1	18.7	08.11.73	Belfast	Previous Clubs: Currie (Scot), Instonians (Ire).						
Ireland: u21, Students, Schools.					Bedford	6	5	1	-	-	-
Matt Deans	6.3	15.0	27.05.71	Zimbabwe	Cambridge						
					Bedford	41+3	25	5	-	-	-
Junior Paramore	6.2	17.0	18.11.68	Western Samoa	Previous Clubs: Hunter Mariners (RL), Castleford (RL).						
Western Samoa:					Bedford	18	45	9	-	-	-
Mark Upex	6.5	16.7	01.04.66	Cambridge							
					Bedford	97	15	3	-	-	-
Scott Murray	6.6	16.7	15.01.76	Edinburgh	Prev. Clubs: Edinburgh Acads., Preston Lodge, Dundee HSFP.						
					Bedford	16	20	4	-	-	-
Shaun Platford	6.6	17.6	05.05.68	Zabia	Natal						
					Bedford	4+1	10	2	-	-	-
Rudolph Straueli	6.3	17.4	20.08.63	South Africa	Prev. Clubs: Penarth, N. Transvaal, Transvaal.						
South Africa:					Bedford	7	-	-	-	-	-
Norman Hadley	6.7	20.7	03.12.64	Winnipeg (Can)	Wasps	15+1	-	-	-	-	-
Canada:					Bedford	10	-	-	-	-	-
Roy Winters	6.4	16.0	13.12.75	Cockfield	Haywards Heath						
England: u21, Students, Colts, Schools.					Bedford	15+4	5	1	-	-	-

Goldington Road, Bedford. MK40 3NF.

CAPACITY: 6,000   **SEATED:** 3,000   **STANDING:** 3,000

SIMPLE DIRECTIONS:
By Road: M1 Jnc 13, to Bedford, follow signs for Cambridge A428 (Not bypass), over River Bridge, left into The Embankment, 3rd right into Bushmead Avenue, continue to junction, ground opposite.
Nearest Railway Station: Bedford Midland Road. The ground is approx a 20 minute walk.

CAR PARKING: Approx 100 at the ground. Charge £2.

ADMISSION: **Standing** - Season £100, OAPs £80 :: Matchdays £7, OAPs £5, Children £2.
                     Seated - Season £150, OAPs £120 :: Matchdays £10, OAPs £8, Children £5.

CLUB SHOP: Yes, Manager John Finch 01992 505550

CLUBHOUSE: Open during normal licensing hours. Two bars, with bar food available
Function facilities: Yes. Contact Chris Wiltshire 01234 347980.

TRAINING NIGHTS: Tuesday & Thursday

Junior Paramore (left) being welcomed to the club in October by Captain & Coach, Paul Turner, the former Welsh fly-half.

Junior, a Western Samoan international, went on to finish the season as the club's Player of the Year.

Photo: Bob Johns
Herald Newspapers, Bedford.

MATCHDAY PROGRAMME

Size	B5
Number of pages	52
Price	£2.00
Programme Editor	Richard Hart
	01234 347980

Advertising Rates   Contact - Peter Hicks
Colour (B & W) - Full page £600 (£500), 1/2 page £300 (£250), 1/4 page £150 (£125).

BLACKHEATH F.C.

NICKNAME: The Club

FOUNDED: 1858

President Pat King, 14 Regents Court, St George's Avenue, Weybridge, Surrey KT13 0DQ. 01932 847013 (H)

Chairman Frank McCarthy, Easter Hill, Romford Road, Pembury, Nr Tunbridge Wells, Kent. 01892 822149 (H)

Club Secretary Barry Shaw, 86 Crown Woods Way, Eltham, London. SE9 2NN.
0181 850 7976 (H), 0171 494 1454 (B), 0181 850 7421 (Fax)

Fixtures Secretary J Collett, 8 Vanbrugh Fields, Blackheath, London. SE3 7TZ.
0181 858 7571 (H), 0181 539 3348 (B)

Rugby Administrator Chris Friday, 0181 289 6152 (B), 0181 249 0607 (Fax)

Chairman of Developement Tony Kennett, 01732 459480 (H), 01732 464112 (Fax)

Press Officer Phil Ubee, 0181 293 0853 (B), 0181 305 1702 (H)

Director of Coaching Hika Reid, 0181 293 0853 (B), 01375 892406 (H)

The season started brightly for 'The Club'. Experienced signings Chris Wilkins, Chris Braithwaite, Mark Russell, Steve Shortland and Garry Holmes blended well into the squad which was captained for the first time by former All Black John Gallagher. Following a short tour to Wales which produced wins at Newbridge and Cross Keys, and a draw at Newport, the League programme got under way with home victories against Rotherham and Bedford. Confidence was rocked by a heavy defeat at Newcastle but the team responded well, to record victories at home against Moseley and away at London Scottish.

With five wins from seven League games, Blackheath were certainly in contention for honours. However, the defeat by Coventry at Rectory Field was perhaps the turning point of the season, for it seriously damaged hopes of a top four finish and was followed by a poor performance at Nottingham and consecutive home losses to Richmond and Rugby. Narrow defeats by Waterloo and Wakefield followed, and the bubble had truly burst.

Head coach Danny Vaughan resigned after sixteen distinguished years at the club as both player and coach, and was replaced by former New Zealand international Hika Reid, who immediately set about refining the Blackheath style of play and reassessing the players at his disposal. The second half of the season was therefore largely seen as preparation for the new campaign, and though there were disappointments, the highlight was undoubtedly the visit to Richmond, where Blackheath led for much of the game and fought back strongly in the last quarter, narrowly losing by 29-24. Important victories against Nottingham and Rugby followed, and a sound base had been laid on which to build for the new season.

What became obvious as the season progressed however, was that semi-professioinal players now have little chance of competing against full-time professioinals. the new season will therefore see a number of full-timers at the Record Field as the oldest independent rugby club in the world takes the final step into the truly professional arena.
PHIL UBEE

Blackheath about to stop a break away in their league game against Richmond   Photo - John Kay Photography.

Colours: Red & black hoops, blue trim/black.   **Change colours:** Blue with red & black hoops/black.

COURAGE LEAGUE MATCH DETAILS 1996-97

No	Ven.	Date	Opponents	Att.	Res.	Score	Scorers
1	(H)	07.09	v Rotherham	1522	W	44- 5	Hoare(3t)Hanslip(t)Friday(t)Braithwaite(5c3p)
2	(H)	14.09	v Bedford	2834	W	11- 3	Braithwaite(t2p)
3	(A)	21.09	v Newcastle	1457	L	0-61	
4	(H)	28.09	v Moseley	1724	W	28- 3	Friday(t)Walton(t)McAllister(t)Braithwaite(2c3p)
5	(A)	05.10	v London Scot	878	W	31-23	Hanslip(2t)Fitzgerald(t)Braithwaite(2c4p)
6	(H)	12.10	v Coventry	2701	L	10-16	Friday(t)Braithwaite(cp)
7	(A)	19.10	v Nottingham	329	W	22-12	Hanslip(t)Park(dg)Gallagher(c3p)
8	(H)	26.10	v Richmond	3405	L	21-40	Park(t)Hanslip(t)Gallagher(c3p)
9	(H)	02.11	v Rugby	1755	L	24-33	Park(t)Gallagher(2t3cp)
10	(A)	09.11	v Waterloo	600	L	10-16	Griffiths(t)Gallagher(cp)
11	(H)	16.11	v Wakefield	1775	L	13-17	Hanslip(t)Howard(c2p)
12	(A)	28.12	v Rotherham	1300	L	11-39	Taylor(t)Howard(2p)
13	(A)	18.01	v Moseley	533	L	18-21	Harris(t)Ekoku(t)Braithwaite(c2p)
14	(H)	08.02	v London Scot	2009	L	13-19	Shortland(t)Howard(2p)Gallagher(c)
15	(A)	22.02	v Bedford	2380	L	18-72	Fitzgerald(t)Hanslip(t)Braithwaite(c2p)
16	(A)	08.03	v Coventry	2000	L	10-74	Gallagher(t)Braithwaite(cp)
17	(H)	22.03	v Nottingham	1287	W	24- 0	Shadbolt(t)Griffiths(t)Braithwaite(c2p2dg)
18	(A)	05.04	v Richmond	1706	L	24-29	McCorduck(t)Gallagher(t)Braithwaite(t3cp)
19	(A)	12.04	v Rugby	510	W	32-24	Gallagher(t)Fitzgerald(t)Wilkins(t)Russell(t)Braithwaite(3c2p)
20	(H)	16.04	v Newcastle	4650	L	10-72	Ridgway(t)Braithwaite(cp)
21	(H)	19.04	v Waterloo	1980	L	27-48	Griffiths(3t)Howard(t)Braithwaite(2cp)
22	(A)	26.04	v Wakefield	600	L	11-14	Fitzgerald(t)Howard(2p)

1996-97 HIGHLIGHTS

LEAGUE DEBUTS: John Gallagher, Chris Braithwaite, Rob McCorduck, Chris Wilkins, Gary Holmes, Abi Ekoku, Mark Russell, Steve Shortland, Dave Fitzgerald, Peter McAllister, Andy Park, Mark Skrypec, Dean Kenny, Matt Tassle.

PLAYERS USED: 31

EVER PRESENT: None - most appearances 20
- John Gallagher and Chris Wilkins.

❑ Winger Mark Hanslip became the first player to top the club's try scoring list twice. He also moves into second place on the club's all-time list with 15.

❑ Suffered their worst ever run of defeats. They lost nine consecutive games to eclipse the previous record of six.

❑ Mike Harris and Richard Smith extended their club records for appearances by a forward and a back to 98(1) and 75 respectively.

❑ Blackheath stop the opposition scoring in four games which was the joint best record in the division. The other clubs on four were Bedford and Coventry.

❑ Scored a club record 43 tries.

❑ Ex Wasps stand-off Chris Braithwaite scored 19 points in his debut on the opening day of the season when they beat Rotherham 44-5. That was the best performance by someone making his Blackheath debut. Braithwaite went on to become only the second Blackheath player to score 100 points in a season after Sam Howard. Howard had achieved this feat in the previous two seasons. But for injury Braithwaite would probably beaten Howards record of 153 points set last season.

	Pts	T	C	P	D	Apps	Ave.
Sam Howard 95-96	153	2	19	30	5	17	9.00
Braithwaite 96-97	137	2	23	25	2	14	9.78

Braithwaite broke Howard's record of 19 conversions in a season with 23.

❑ Achieved their best ever home win beating Rotherham on the opening day of the season 44-5.

❑ Suffered their worst ever defeats both home and away. At home they lost 10-72 to Newcastle in April. Away from home they lost 10-74 at Coventry in March.

❑ Chris Braithwaite equalled Jon King's record of two dropped goals in a match.

BLACKHEATH'S COURAGE LEAGUE MATCH DETAILS 1996-97

#	15	14	13	12	11	10	9	1	2	3	4	5	6	7	8	Replacements
1	Gallagher	Hanslip	Coyne	Smith	Hoare	Braithwaite	Friday	Shadbolt	Ridgway	Holmes	Furneaux	McCorduck	Walton	Wilkins	Harris	
2	Gallagher	Ekoku	Coyne	Smith	Hoare	Braithwaite	Friday	Shadbolt	Ridgway	Holmes	Russell	Shortland	Walton	Wilkins	Harris	
3	Gallagher	Ekoku	Coyne	Smith	Hoare	Braithwaite	Friday	Shadbolt	Ridgway	Holmes	Russell	Shortland	Walton	Wilkins	Harris	Welsh(13)
4	Gallagher	Ekoku	Fitzgerald	McAllister	Hanslip	Braithwaite	Friday	Shadbolt	Ridgway	Holmes	Russell	Shortland	Walton	Wilkins	Harris	
5	Gallagher	Ekoku	Fitzgerald	McAllister	Hanslip	Braithwaite	Friday	Shadbolt	Ridgway	Holmes	Russell	Shortland	Walton	Wilkins	Harris	
6	Gallagher	Ekoku	Fitzgerald	McAllister	Hanslip	Braithwaite	Friday	Shadbolt	Ridgway	Holmes	Russell	Shortland	Walton	Wilkins	Harris	
7	Gallagher	Ekoku	Fitzgerald	McAllister	Hanslip	Park	Friday	Shadbolt	Ridgway	Holmes	Russell	Shortland	Walton	Wilkins	Harris	Taylor(1)
8	Gallagher	Ekoku	Fitzgerald	McAllister	Hanslip	Park	Friday	Shadbolt	Ridgway	Holmes	Russell	McCorduck	Walton	Wilkins	Harris	
9	Gallagher	Ekoku	Fitzgerald		Hanslip	Park	Friday	Holmes	Ridgway	Pope	Shortland	Walton	Watton	Wilkins	Harris	
10	Gallagher	Griffiths	Coyne	Smith	Hanslip	Park	Welsh	Holmes	Ridgway	Taylor	Shortland	McCorduck	Russell	Wilkins	Harris	
11	Gallagher	Griffiths	Coyne	Smith	Hanslip	Howard	Welsh	Holmes	Ridgway	Taylor	Shortland	McCorduck	Russell	Wilkins	Harris	Walton(4)
12	Gallagher	Ekoku	Coyne	Fitzgerald	Hanslip	Howard	Welsh	Holmes	Ridgway	Taylor	Skrypec	Shortland	McCorduck	Wilkins	Harris	Walton(6)
13	Gallagher	Ekoku	Coyne	Fitzgerald	Hanslip	Braithwaite	Kenny	Holmes	Ridgway	Taylor	Skrypec	Shortland	Russell	Harris	Furneaux	Furneaux(4)
14	Gallagher	Griffiths	Coyne	Fitzgerald	Hanslip	Howard	Kenny	Pope	Ridgway	Taylor	Furneaux	Shortland	Booth	Wilkins	Russell	Welsh(9)
15	Gallagher	Griffiths	Fitzgerald	Smith	Hanslip	Braithwaite	Kenny	Pope	Ridgway	Taylor	Skrypec	Shortland	Booth	Willis	Russell	Holmes(3),Harris(4)
16	Gallagher	Griffiths	Fitzgerald	Smith	Hanslip	Braithwaite	Kenny	Pope	Howe	Holmes	Skrypec	Shortland	Booth	Harris	Russell	Shadbolt(14)Park(11)Taylor(3)Tassle(13)
17	Gallagher	Smith	Coyne	Fitzgerald	Griffiths	Hanslip	Kenny	Pope	Ridgway	Taylor	Skrypec	Furneaux	Booth	Wilkins	Russell	McCorduck(4)Shadbolt(3)Hoare(12)
18	Gallagher	Smith	Fitzgerald	Coyne	Griffiths	Braithwaite	Kenny	Pope	Ridgway	Taylor	Skrypec	McCorduck	Booth	Harris	Russell	Tassle(11)Shadbolt(3)
19	Gallagher	Smith	Coyne	Fitzgerald	Griffiths	Braithwaite	Kenny	Pope	Ridgway	Taylor	Skrypec	McCorduck	Booth	Wilkins	Russell	Hoare(12)Tassle(11)Friday(9)
20	Gallagher	Smith	Coyne	Fitzgerald	Griffiths	Braithwaite	Friday	Ridgway	Pope	Taylor	McCorduck	Skrypec	Booth	Wilkins	Russell	Hoare(12)Friday(9)Shortland(7)Shadbolt(8)
21	Howard	Hoare	Smith	Fitzgerald	Griffiths	Braithwaite	Friday	Pope	Howe	Taylor	Skrypec	Shortland	McCorduck	Booth	Harris	Shadbolt(3)
22	Hoare	Smith	Fitzgerald	Tassle	Griffiths	Howard	Kenny	Pope	Howe	Taylor	Skrypec	Shortland	McCorduck	Booth	Harris	Friday(9)Shadbolt(3)

BLACKHEATH LEAGUE STATISTICS
(COMPILED BY STEPHEN McCORMACK)

Season	Div.	P	W	D	L	F	(Tries	Con	Pen	DG)	A	(Tries	Con	Pen	DG)	Most Points	Most Tries
87-88	2	11	2	0	9	102	(14	5	11	1)	187	(27	11	17	2)	30 - Nick Colyer	2 - by 3 players - Pat Jones, Giles Marshall & Martin Holcombe
88-89	2	11	4	1	6	181	(19	12	19	8)	144	(17	5	22	0)	70 - Colin Parker	3 - Mickey Scott & Peter Vaughan
89-90	2	11	3	2	6	141	(15	12	15	4)	205	(25	12	27	0)	57 - Colin Parker	3 - Jon king
90-91	2	12	4	0	8	134	(12	4	22	4)	169	(18	8	25	2)	48 - Colin Parker	3 - Pat Jones
91-92	2	12	4	0	8	140	(12	4	25	3)	266	(37	20	26	0)	61 - Neil Munn	2 - Andy Mercer
92-93	2	12	4	2	6	142	(9	5	27	2)	231	(23	13	26	4)	97 - Grant Eagle	5 - Joe McIntyre
93-94	3	18	11	0	7	305	(36	13	30	3)	222	(18	12	34	2)	78 - Stuart Burns	9 - Mike Friday
94-95	3	18	12	2	4	299	(27	13	44	2)	190	(18	11	25	1)	147 - Sam Howard	5 - Matt Griffiths
95-96	2	18	6	1	11	341	(37	21	33	5)	469	(52	32	44	5)	153 - Sam Howard	5 - Mike Hanslip
96-97	2	22	7	-	15	412	(43	31	42	3)	641	(83	50	38	4)	137 - Chris Braithwaite	8 - Mike Hanslip
Totals		145	57	8	80	2197	(224	120	268	35)	2624	(318	174	284	20)		

	HOME	AWAY
BIGGEST WIN	(39pts) 44-5 v Rotherham 7.9.96	(28pts) 28-0 v Exeter 29.4.95
DEFEAT	(62pts) 10-72 v Newcastle 16.4.97	(64pts) 10-74 v Coventry 8.3.97
MOST POINTS SCORED	44-5 v Rotherham 7.9.96	32-24 v Rugby 12.4.97
AGAINST	1-72 v Newcastle 16.4.97	0-74 v Coventry 8.3.97

MOST CONSECUTIVE VICTORIES - 4　　**MOST CONSECUTIVE DEFEATS - 9**

MOST TRIES IN A MATCH
(FOR) 7 v Newcastle G. 7.10.95, v Moseley 27.4.96
(AGAINST) 12 v Coventry 8.3.97 (A)
v Newcastle 16.4.97 (H)

MOST APPEARANCES
FORWARD: 98(1) Mike Harris
BACK: 75 Richard Smith

CONSECUTIVE APPEARANCES
46 Mike Friday 1993-96

CONSECUTIVE SCORING MATCHES
Scoring Tries - 3 - Peter Mitchell
Scoring Points - 11 - Sam Howard

MOST	in a SEASON	in a CAREER	in a MATCH
Points	153 Sam Howard 95-96	349 Sam Howard 93-97	20 Grant Eagle v Moseley 28.3.92 (H)
Tries	9 Mike Friday 93-94	19 Mike Friday 93-97	3 Mike Friday v Morley 6.11.93 (H) Mitch Hoare v Rotherham 7.9.96 (H) Matt Griffiths v Waterloo 19.4.97 (H)
Conversions	23 Chris Braithwaite 96-97	32 Sam Howard 93-97	5 Sam Howard v Moseley 27.4.96 (A)
Penalties	38 Sam Howard 94-95	76 Sam Howard 93-97	6 Grant Eagle v Moseley 28.3.92 (H) v Rosslyn Park 9.1.93 (H) Sam Howard v Morley 7.1.95 (H)
Drop Goals	8 Jon King 88-89	16 Jon King 87-91	2 Jon King v Coventry 19.11.88 (A) v Lon. Irish 22.4.89 (A) v Lon. Irish 28.4.90 (H) Chris Braithwaite v Nottingham 22.3.97 (H)

BLACKHEATH PLAYING SQUAD

NAME	Ht	Wt	Birthdate	Birthplace	Club	Apps	Pts	T	C	P	DG
BACKS											
John Gallagher	6.1	13.2	29.01.69	Blackheath							
New Zealand 18.		Ireland A			Blackheath	20	64	5	6	9	-
Mark Hanslip	5.10	11.7	04.05.73	London							
					Blackheath	36	75	15	-	-	-
Richard Smith	6.0	14.0	14.06.67								
					Blackheath	75+1	28	6	-	-	-
Mitch Hoare	5.10	13.7	28.12.73	Coventry	Previous Clubs: Coventry, Wasps.						
					Blackheath	14+3	15	3	-	-	-
Mike Friday	5.9	12.1	25.04.72								
					Blackheath	61+3	95	19	-	-	-
Sam Howard	6.0	13.7	31.07.74								
England: u21, Students, u16					Blackheath	56	349	6	32	76	9
Matt Griffiths	5.8	13.4	30.02.72		Wasps	1					
					Blackheath	55	74	15	-	-	-
Chris Braithwaite	5.11	12.10	26.12.71		Wasps	9+1	76	6	8	8	2
					Blackheath	14	137	2	23	25	2
Dean Kenny											
					Blackheath	9	-	-	-	-	-
Dave Fitzgerald											
					Blackheath	17	20	4	-	-	-
Andy Park					Blackheath	4+1	13	2	-	-	1
Owen Coyne	5.10	14.0	24.08.70								
England: u21.					Blackheath	62	10	2	-	-	-
Abi Ekoku	6.5	17.5		London							
					Blackheath	10	5	1	-	-	-
Matt Tassle					Blackheath	1+3	-	-	-	-	-
FORWARDS											
Paul Shadbolt	5.10	17.10	01.10.73		Saracens						
England: u21.					Blackheath	32+6	30	6	-	-	-
Colin Ridgeway	5.11	15.7	22.04.72	Stroud							
					Blackheath	58	30	6	-	-	-
Stephen Pope	5.11	17.2	24.11.73		Wasps						
England: u16					Blackheath	15+2	-	-	-	-	-
John Taylor											
					Blackheath	28+5	10	2	-	-	-
Bobby Howe	5.8	14.0	12.04.63	Beckenham	Askeans						
					Blackheath	27+1	-	-	-	-	-
Mark Russell	6.4	17.6	16.12.65	Nairobi (Ken)	Harlequins	44	9	2	-	-	-
England: A, B.					Blackheath	18	5	1	-	-	-
Steve Shortland	6.7	18.6	26.01.68		Northampton	4	4	1	-	-	-
England: u21, Students.					Harlequins	5	4	1	-	-	-
					Wasps	12	15	3	-	-	-
					Blackheath	16+1	5	1	-	-	-
Gary Furneaux	6.5	18.0	25.03.67								
					Blackheath	28+1	-	-	-	-	-
Rob McCorduck	6.4	16.0	09.01.72		Abertillery						
					Blackheath	9+1	-	-	-	-	-
Chris Wilkins	6.3	16.2	03.07.71		Wasps	17	10	2	-	-	-
England: A, u21, u18, u16.					Blackheath	20	10	2	-	-	-
Micky Harris	6.4	17.1	07.09.67		Wasps						
England: u21, Colts, u18, u16.					Blackheath	98+1	100	9	6	14	-
Mark Skrypec					Nottingham	3	-	-	-	-	-
					Blackheath	10	-	-	-	-	-
Domonic Walton	6.3	17.0	16.11.70	Farnborough							
					Blackheath	70+2	25	5	-	-	-
Gary Holmes	5.11	16.0	07.07.65	Hampstead	Wasps	60	5	1	-	-	-
England: A, B, Colts.					Saracens	12	5	1	-	-	-
					Blackheath	13+1	-	-	-	-	-

Tel: 0181 858 1578
CAPACITY: 6,000   **SEATED:** 572   **Fax:** 0181 293 0854
STANDING: 5,428

SIMPLE DIRECTIONS:
By Road: The entrance to the Rectory Field is approx 800 yards from the start of Charlton Road B210 at its junction with Stratheden Road/Westcombe Hill which is a turning off Shooters Hill Road A2.
Nearest Railway Station: Blackheath (BR) or Westcombe Park (BR)

CAR PARKING: 250

ADMISSION: Season Adults £89, U17 Free: Matches £10 includes Programme

CLUB SHOP: Yes; Manageress Mandy Allen 0181 293 5980

CLUBHOUSE: Normal Licensing hours, snacks available.
Function room: Yes; capacity 100

TRAINING NIGHTS: Tuesday & Thursday

Blackheath's Captain John Gallagher
Photo - Jack Kay Photography

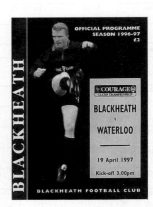

MATCHDAY PROGRAMME

Size	A5
Number of pages	36 plus cover
Price	With admission
Programme Editor	Pro-Mag. 0117 9779188

Advertising Rates

Colour   Full page £995,
Half page £695

COVENTRY F.C.

NICKNAME: Cov

FOUNDED: 1874

President   L R Evans, 3 Croft Close, Wolvey, nr Hinckley, Leics. LE10 3LE.
01455 220448 (H) 01203 302865 (B)
Chairman   G S Sugrue, 14 Elphin Close, Keresley, Coventry. CV6 2NE.
01203 336390 (H)   01203 679922 (B)   01203 672274 (Fax)
Honorary Secretary   P B Jackson, c/o Coventry FC, Barkers Butts Lane, Coundon, Coventry. CV6 1DU
0121 747 2498 (H)
General Manager   S B Ginn, 37 Blackthorne Road, Kenilworth, Warwickshire. CV8 2DS.
01926 511224 (H)   01203 601174 (B)   01203 601194 (Fax)
Fixtures Secretary & Office Admin. Man.   J Butler, 62 Spring Lane, Whittington, Lichfield, Staffs. WS14 9NA.
01543 432654 (H)   01203 601174 (B)   01203 601194 (Fax)

Following promotion from Division Three, Season 1996/7 was always going to be challenging. The fact that the squad were serious promotion candidates for all the season emphasised the work put in by director of rugby, Derek Eves. There was disappointment in the final analysis, for having reached the play-offs and recorded a home win against London Irish, defeat in the second leg meant Second League rugby remained at Coundon Road.

Many achievements were recorded during a season when nine new recruits made league debuts. In compiling 317 points overall to surpass Peter Rossborough's 20 year old club record, Jez Harris set a new club league record of 249 points for the season, whilst in addition setting up a new overall league of 42 points in the club's league record win by 102-22 v Nottingham. The overall points tally of 1268 was also a record, as was the seventeen league tries run in by another of the newcomers, Andy Smallwood.

Club skipper Rob Hardwick was awarded his first full cap following his appearance as a replacement against Italy, whilst lock forward Danny Grewcock received England 'A' honours, both being selected for the Summer tour to Argentina. Hardwick, Grewcock, Eves and centre three quarter Richie Robinson all represented the Barbarians, young reserve fly half James Brown gaining his England Colts cap and a place in the English Under 21 summer tour party.

L-R - Back Row: Bamber Evans (Pres.), Peter Jackson (Hon. Sec.), John King (Match Sec.), Richard Blundell, Ian Patten, Mark Crane, Danny Grewcock, Andy Blackmore, Julian Horrobin, David John, Steve Chapman, Wayne Kilford, Steve Thomas (Team Man.), Gerry Sugrue (Chairman). Middle: Dave Addleton, Derek Eves, Rob Hardwick (Capt.), Gareth Treligas, Jez Harris. Front: Claire Gee (Physio), Jackie Burke (Physio), Andy Smallwood, Mick Curtis, Paul Lydster, Tigger Dawson, Matt Gallagher, Richie Robinson.

Photo: Courtesy of the Coventry Evening Telegraph.

Colours: Navy blue & white hoops

Change colours: Navy blue

COVENTRY

No	Ven.	Date	Opponents	Att.	Res.	Score	Scorers
1	(H)	07.09	v Richmond	3850	D	16-16	Dawson(t)Harris(c3p) Harris(2p)
2	(A)	14.09	v Rugby	1300	W	61- 3	Robinson(2t)Smallwood(2t)Hardwick(2t)Kilford(t)Patten(t)Gallagher(t5c)
3	(H)	21.09	v Wakefield	3100	L	24-25	Horrobin(t)Kilford(t)Gallagher(c2p)Harris(2dg)
4	(A)	28.09	v Waterloo	700	W	36-17	Smallwood(2t)Eves(t)Kilford(t)Harris(2c4p)
5	(H)	05.10	v Nottingham	2500	W	102-22	McAdam(3t)Eves(3t)Curtis(2t)Lydster(2t)Crofts(t)Gallagher(t)Harris(2t13c2p)
6	(A)	12.10	v Blackheath	2701	W	16-10	Crane(t)Harris(c3p)
7	(H)	19.10	v London Scot	2500	W	66- 6	McAdam(3t)Grewcock(t)Dawson(t)Kilford(t)Smallwood(t)PenTry(t)Harris(t6c3p)
8	(A)	26.10	v Rotherham	1250	W	42-11	McAdam(2t)Smallwood(2t)Patten(t)Crane(t)Gallagher(t)Harris(2cp)
9	(H)	02.11	v Newcastle	7800	W	19-18	Kilford(t)Smallwood(t)Harris(2pdg)
10	(A)	09.11	v Moseley	1720	W	35-19	Dawson(t)Smallwood(t)PenTry(t)Crofts(t)Crane(t)Brown(2c2p)
11	(A)	16.11	v Bedford	3620	L	23-30	Patten(t)Dawson(t)Harris(2c3p)
12	(A)	28.12	v Richmond	3200	L	10-39	Smallwood(t)Harris(cdg)
13	(H)	18.01	v Waterloo	2000	W	28-16	McAdam(t)Patten(t)Smallwood(t)Harris(tc2p)
14	(A)	08.02	v Nottingham	422	W	29- 0	Minshull(t)Eves(t)Patten(t)Robinson(t)Smallwood(t)Harris(2c)
15	(H)	23.02	v Rugby	1900	W	24-10	Grewcock(2t)McAdam(t)Hardwick(t)Harris(2c)
16	(H)	08.03	v Blackheath	2000	W	74-10	Horrobin(3t)Patten(2t)Smallwood(2t)Dawson(t)Addleton(t)Hardwick(t) Blackmore(t)Gallagher(t)Harris(7c)
17	(A)	22.03	v London Scot	483	W	14-13	Smallwood(t)Harris(2p)Gallagher(dg)
18	(H)	05.04	v Rotherham	3000	W	21-15	Smallwood(t)Addleton(t)Harris(c3p)
19	(A)	12.04	v Newcastle	3200	L	17-49	Smallwood(t)McAdam(t)Harris(2cp)
20	(H)	19.04	v Moseley	3500	W	33-18	McAdam(t)Patten(t)Eves(t)Gallagher(dg)Harris(3c3p)
21	(H)	26.04	v Bedford	6200	W	30-10	Robinson(2t)McAdam(2t)Harris(2c2p)
22	(A)	03.05	v Wakefield	450	L	18-33	Curtis(t)Irwin(t)Brown(c2p)

1996-97 HIGHLIGHTS

LEAGUE DEBUTS: Wayne Kilford, David John, Matt Gallager, Richie Robinson, Andy Smallwood, Jez Harris, Tigger Dawson, Mark Crane, Andrew McAdam, James Brown, John Farr, Alan Sharp, Adam Irwin, Jason Soden, Richard Lloyd, Dinos Andreou.

TRY ON DEBUT: Tigger Dawson.

PLAYERS USED: 35 plus 5 as replacement.

EVER PRESENT: None - most appearances 21 - Matt Gallagher and Derek Eves.

☐ In their opening game of the season at home to Richmond all seven of Coventry's backs were making their league debuts.

☐ Winger Andy Smallwood breaks the club record of scoring tries in three consecutive games. Smallwood twice scores tries in four consecutive games.

☐ Ex Leicester stand-off Jez Harris re-writes Coventry's points scoring list. Harris broke the National League record for points in a match when he scored 42 points in the club's record 102-22 win over Nottingham. It broke Richard Angell's club record of 25 points in a match. His 13 conversions against Nottingham broke Marc

Thomas's club record of 7 set against Otley in March 96. Harris ended the season with 236 points easily beating Angell's club record of 151 set during the 93-94 division three promotion season.

	Pts	T	C	P	D	Apps	Ave.
Jez Harris 96-97	236	4	48	35	5	20	11.80
Richard Angell 93-94	151	3	23	29	-	16	9.44

Harris broke Angell's record for conversions, 23, and penalties, 29, with 48 and 35 respectively. Harris who is known as a drop goal expert set a new club record for a season with 5.

☐ Another record to fall to Harris was the record of scoring points in consecutive games. Prior to last season Craig Quick held the record with 10 but Harris went one better to 11.

☐ Andy Smallwood destroyed Julian Horrobin's club record of 11 tries in a season. Smallwood scored 17 tries in 20 games and in the process moved into joint second on the club's all-time list behind Kevin Hickey.

☐ Lost only once at home to Wakefield

☐ One of only two teams to score in all 22 games.

☐ Conceded just 22 tries at home - the lowest total in the division.

COVENTRY'S COURAGE LEAGUE MATCH DETAILS 1996-97

#	15	14	13	12	11	10	9	1	2	3	4	5	6	7	8	Replacements
1	Kilford	John	Gallagher	Robinson	Smallwood	Harris	Dawson	Hardwick	Addleton	Crane	Grewcock	Blackmore	Horrobin	Eves	Patten	
2	Kilford	John	Gallagher	Robinson	Smallwood	Harris	Dawson	Hardwick	Addleton	Crane	Grewcock	Blackmore	Horrobin	Eves	Patten	Reayer(15),Lewis(3)
3	Kilford	McAdam	Gallagher	Robinson	Smallwood	Harris	Dawson	Hardwick	Addleton	Crane	Grewcock	Blackmore	Horrobin	Eves	Patten	
4	Kilford	McAdam	Gallagher	Robinson	Smallwood	Harris	Dawson	Hardwick	Addleton	Crane	Grewcock	Blackmore	Horrobin	Eves	Patten	
5	Gallagher	McAdam	Reayer	Curtis	Woodman	Harris	Lydster	Hardwick	Addleton	Tregilgas	Hyde	Blackmore	Crofts	Eves	Patten	Blundell(7)
6	Kilford	McAdam	Gallagher	Robinson	Smallwood	Harris	Dawson	Hardwick	Addleton	Crane	Grewcock	Blackmore	Horrobin	Eves	Patten	Blundell(1)
7	Kilford	McAdam	Gallagher	Robinson	Smallwood	Harris	Dawson	Lewis	Addleton	Crane	Grewcock	Blackmore	Horrobin	Eves	Patten	
8	Gallagher	McAdam	Curtis	Robinson	Smallwood	Harris	Dawson	Lewis	Addleton	Crane	Grewcock	Blackmore	Horrobin	Eves	Patten	
9	Kilford	McAdam	Gallagher	Robinson	Smallwood	Harris	Dawson	Hardwick	Addleton	Crane	Grewcock	Blackmore	Horrobin	Eves	Patten	Crofts(5)
10	Kilford	McAdam	Gallagher	Robinson	Smallwood	Brown	Dawson	Hardwick	Blundell	Crane	Hyde	Grewcock	Crofts	Eves	Horrobin	Chapman(13)
11	Kilford	McAdam	Gallagher	Robinson	Smallwood	Harris	Dawson	Hardwick	Addleton	Crane	Grewcock	Patten	Crofts	Eves	Horrobin	
12	Kilford	John	Gallagher	Robinson	Smallwood	Harris	Dawson	Hardwick	Addleton	Crane	Grewcock	Blackmore	Crofts	Eves	Patten	Horrobin(6)
13	Kilford	McAdam	Gallagher	Robinson	Smallwood	Harris	Farr	Hardwick	Addleton	Crofts	Grewcock	Blackmore	Horrobin	Eves	Patten	
14	Gallagher	Minshull	Gallagher	Robinson	Smallwood	Harris	Dawson	Hardwick	Addleton	Crane	Grewcock	Blackmore	Horrobin	Eves	Patten	Salisbury(7)
15	Kilford	McAdam	Gallagher	Robinson	Smallwood	Harris	Dawson	Hardwick	Addleton	Crane	Grewcock	Blackmore	Horrobin	Eves	Patten	Lydster(9),Morgan(3)
16	Kilford	McAdam	Gallagher	Robinson	Smallwood	Harris	Dawson	Hardwick	Addleton	Crane	Grewcock	Blackmore	Horrobin	Eves	Patten	Crofts(5)
17	Kilford	McAdam	Gallagher	Robinson	Smallwood	Harris	Dawson	Hyde	Addleton	Hardwick	Grewcock	Grewcock	Horrobin	Eves	Patten	Crofts(4)
18	Kilford	McAdam	Gallagher	Robinson	Smallwood	Harris	Dawson	Sharp	Addleton	Hardwick	Grewcock	Blackmore	Horrobin	Eves	Patten	Crane(3)
19	Kilford	McAdam	Gallagher	Robinson	Smallwood	Harris	Dawson	Sharp	Addleton	Hardwick	Grewcock	Blackmore	Horrobin	Eves	Patten	Minshull(13),Curtis(11),Crane(6),Crofts(8)
20	Gallagher	McAdam	Minshull	Robinson	Smallwood	Harris	Dawson	Sharp	Hardwick	Addleton	Grewcock	Blackmore	Horrobin	Eves	Patten	Crane(1)
21	Gallagher	McAdam	Minshull	Robinson	Smallwood	Harris	Dawson	Hardwick	Addleton	Crane	Grewcock	Blackmore	Horrobin	Eves	Patten	
22	Kilford	Sheperd	Reayer	Curtis	Irwin	Brown	Lydster	Tregilgas	Soden	Crane	Hyde	Andreou	Crofts	Lloyd	Salisbury	Williams(3),Southwell(7)

COVENTRY LEAGUE STATISTICS
(COMPILED BY STEPHEN McCORMACK)

Season	Div.	P	W	D	L	F	(Tries	Con	Pen	DG)	A	(Tries	Con	Pen	DG)	Most Points	Most Tries
87-88	1	11	3	1	7	139	(14	10	19	2)	246	(35	17	23	1)	28 - Martin Fairn	3 - Paul Suckling
88-89	2	11	6	0	5	150	(22	7	12	4)	143	(16	11	16	3)	36 - Martin Fairn	4 - Dick Travers
89-90	2	11	6	1	4	206	(25	11	24	4)	185	(23	9	21	4)	79 - Steve Thomas	6 - Steve Thomas
90-91	2	12	8	0	4	172	(23	13	17	1)	129	(19	10	10	1)	37 - Richard Angell	4 - Richard Angell
91-92	2	12	7	0	5	187	(18	11	29	2)	196	(22	15	25	1)	13 - Steve Thomas	4 - Kevin Hickey
92-93	2	12	3	0	9	192	(21	15	16	3)	236	(24	13	26	4)	53 - Richard Angell	4 - Barry Evans
93-94	3	18	14	0	4	406	(47	27	37	2)	259	(29	12	26	4)	151 - Richard Angell	9 - Doug Woodman
94-95	2	18	2	0	16	213	(16	5	35	6)	436	(43	28	50	5)	90 - Richard Angell	5 - Mark Douglas
95-96	3	18	15	0	3	524	(67	36	35	4)	264	(25	20	29	4)	84 - Craig Quick	11 - Julian Horrobin
96-97	2	22	16	1	5	738	(96	57	41	7)	394	(45	26	37	2)	236 - Jez Harris	17 - Andy Smallwood
Totals		145	80	3	62	2927	(349	192	265	35)	2488	(281	161	263	29)		

	HOME	AWAY
BIGGEST WIN	(80pts) 102-22 v Nottingham 5.10.96	(58pts) 61-3 v Rugby 14.9.96
DEFEAT		(43pts) 6-49 v Wasps 13.4.88
MOST POINTS SCORED	102-22 v Nottingham 5.10.96	61-3 v Rugby 14.9.96
AGAINST	16-33 v Saracens 29.10.94	6-49 v Wasps 13.4.88
		17-49 v Newcastle 12.4.97

MOST CONSECUTIVE VICTORIES - 9   **MOST CONSECUTIVE DEFEATS - 13**

MOST TRIES IN A MATCH
(FOR) 14 v Nottingham 5.10.96
(AGAINST) 9 v Wasps 13.4.88

MOST APPEARANCES
FORWARD: 96 Dave Addleton
BACK: 66+1 Richard Angell

CONSECUTIVE APPEARANCES
35 Richard Angell & Warwick Bullock

CONSECUTIVE SCORING MATCHES
Scoring Tries - 4 - Andy Smallwood
Scoring Points - 11 - Jez Harris

MOST	in a SEASON	in a CAREER	in a MATCH
Points	236 Jez Harris 96-97	396 Richard Angell 90-96	42 Jez Harris v Nottingham 5.10.96 (H)
Tries	17 Andy Smallwood 96-97	18 Kevin Hickey 88-95	3 Peter Rowlands v Lon Irish 10.9.89 (A) Graham Robbins v Waterloo 13.1.90 (H) Richard Gee v Morley 19.9.92 (H) Julian Horrobin v Otley 30.3.96 (H) v Blackheath 8.3.97 (H) Derek Eves v Nottingham 5.10.96 (H) Andy McAdam v Nottingham 5.10.96 (H) v Lon. Scottish 19.10.96 (H)
Conversions	48 Jez Harris 96-97	48 Richard Angell 90-96 Jez Harris 96-97	13 Jez Harris v Nottingham 5.10.96 (H)
Penalties	35 Jez Harris 96-97	81 Richard Angell 90-96	6 Steve Thomas v Sale 23.9.89 (A)
Drop Goals	5 Jez Harris 96-97	10 Mark Lakey 87-95	2 Mark Lakey v Moseley 3.4.93 (H) v Lon Irish 8.10.94 (H) Jez Harris v Wakefield 21.9.96 (H)

COVENTRY PLAYING SQUAD

NAME	Ht	Wt	Birthdate	Birthplace	Club	Apps	Pts	T	C	P	DG
BACKS											
Wayne Kilford	5.11	13.0	25.09.68	Malvern	Nottingham	20	23	1	2	5	-
					Leicester	22	23	4	-	1	-
					Coventry	17	25	5	-	-	-
Matt Gallagher	6.1	13.0	21.03.73	Solihull	Nottingham	44	114	4	8	26	-
					Coventry	21	44	4	6	2	2
Andy Smallwood			13.01.72		Nottingham	47	60	12	-	-	-
					Coventry	47	60	12	-	-	-
Andy McAdam	6.1	13.5	23.03.71	Coventry	Barker's Butts						
					Leicester	6	-	-	-	-	-
					Coventry	18	70	14	-	-	-
Ritchie Robinson	6.1	14.0	05.07.67	Kendal	Leicester	24	15	3	-	-	-
					Coventry	20	25	5	-	-	-
Jez Harris	5.6	12.6	22.02.65	Kettering	Leicester	69+1	461	4	37	86	37
					Coventry	20	236	4	48	35	5
James Brown	5.8	10.10	08.12.77	Solihull	Coventry	2	18	-	3	4	-
Tigger Dawson	5.10	11.0	29.01.75	Crewe	Coventry	19	25	5	-	-	-
Jason Minshull					Coventry	33+1	29	7	-	-	-
Gareth Reayer	6.2	14.5	11.03.69	Oxford	Coventry	10+1	25	5	-	-	-
Mick Curtis	5.10	15.7	27.06.72	Coventry	Coventry	34+1	20	4	-	-	-
Paul Lydster	6.1	14.0	28.05.70	Coventry	Broadstreet						
					Coventry	13+1	45	9	-	-	-
Doug Woodman	6.0	14.4	07.03.62	Bristol	Clifton						
					Bristol	17	12	3	-	-	-
					Coventry	31	70	14	-	-	-
FORWARDS											
Mark Crane	6.0	15.0	10.10.71	Bristol	Clifton	11	25	5	-	-	-
					Coventry	16+3	15	3	-	-	-
Rob Hardwick	6.0	19.12	23.03.69	Kenilworth	Coventry	74	39	8	-	-	-
Dave Addleton	5.9	14.2	30.03.63	Coventry	Barkers Butts						
					Coventry	96	10	2	-	-	-
Alan Sharp	5.9	17.0	17.10.69	Bristol	Clifton						
					Bristol	76	-	-	-	-	-
					Coventry	5	-	-	-	-	-
Danny Grewcock	6.6	17.7	07.11.72	Coventry	Barkers Butts						
					Coventry	31	15	3	-	-	-
Andy Blackmore	6.2	16.0	01.11.65	Bristol	Bristol	75	9	2	-	-	-
					Coventry	26	5	1	-	-	-
Derek Eves	5.10	15.0	07.01.66	Bristol	Bristol	86	80	17	-	-	-
					Coventry	31	55	11	-	-	-
Ian Patten	6.5	16.0	31.08.70	Bristol	Bristol	35	15	3	-	-	-
					Coventry	24	45	9	-	-	-
Julian Horrobin	6.3	15.4			Bristol	10	16	4	-	-	-
					Coventry	60+1	85	17	-	-	-
Lee Crofts	6.4	17.7	07.09.68	Coventry	Broad Street						
					Coventry	43+4	35	7	-	-	-
Richard Lloyd	5.10	14.0	01.12.77	Solihull	Coventry	1	-	-	-	-	-
Julian Hyde	6.4	18.0			Coventry	77	13	3	-	-	-
Richard Blundell	5.10	15.0	08.09.77	Coventry	Coventry	1+3	-	-	-	-	-

Barker Butts Lane, Coundon Road, Coventry. CV6 1DU.

CAPACITY: 9,900   **SEATED:** 900   **STANDING - Covered:** 4,000   **Uncovered:** 5,000

SIMPLE DIRECTIONS:
    By Road: From ringroad take the A414 to Birmingham, turn right at traffic lights and follow road across railway lights. Coming into Coventry on the A45 pick up A414 turn left at Hollyhead P.H. right at traffic lights ground on right.
    Nearest Railway Station: Coventry

CAR PARKING: None

ADMISSION: Season (Seated or Standing) - £70.00, Juniors & OAPs £35.00
               Matchday (Seated or Standing) - £7, Juniors & OAPs £4

CLUB SHOP: Open Monday to Friday 9 - 5 & on matchdays from 1 - 5.30pm. Manager Richard Blundell 01203 601174.

CLUBHOUSE: Open matchdays Noon - 11pm (except during match) and training evenings (Mon & Wed.). Bar meals and snacks are available.
    Function facilities: With a capacity of 200, contact Mrs Sharon Daniels 01203 601174.

TRAINING NIGHTS: Monday and Wednesday.

CLUB CAPTAIN, ROB HARDWICK,
pictured following his first cap as replacement v Italy.

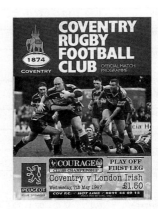

MATCHDAY PROGRAMME

Size	A5
Number of pages	32
Price	£1.50
Programme Editor	J Butler
	01203 601174
Advertising Rates	Full page £1000
	1/2 page £750
	1/4 page £450

EXETER F.C.

NICKNAME: Exe

FOUNDED: 1872

President R J Roach, c/o Exeter RFC, The County Ground, Church Road, Exeter, Devon EX2 9BQ.

Chairman Mr S Byrne, c/o Exeter RFC, as above

Chief Executive Mr B P 'Tug' Wilson, c/o Exeter RFC, as above
01404 813316 (H), 01392 278759 (B), 01392 427582 (Fax)

Match Arrangement Secretary Mr R Huxtable, 21 Somerset Avenue, St Thomas, Exeter, Devon
01392 277385 (H), 01392 277385 (Fax)

Rugby Manager Mr R Henderson, Trehill Cottage, Kenn, Exeter, Devon
01392 833237 (H), 01392 426121 (Fax)

Treasurer Mr S L Williams, 01392 824777 (B)

The second season of National League success here finally provided the club with the opportunity to join the elite of English rugby. Once again the success was based on good team work and the will to play open running rugby at every opportunity.

The Championship was won on the last day of a very long season with a 13-3 win at Reading. This completed a run of fourteen games without defeat, a club and National League Three record. The only defeat at the County Ground was in the Pilkington Cup to Kendal, a black day on an otherwise very bright and successful season.

Eight players from the club represented the South West Division - Andy Maunder, Andy Green, Andy Turner, Rob Baxter, Keith Brooking, Bob Armstrong, Nick Southern and Richard Gibbins. In addition Mark Curry represented Somerset who reached the final of the County Championships. The loss of these players to divisional rugby had much to do with the poor Cup performance.

However, after two away defeats at Rosslyn Park and Harrogate it seemed that the club was going to miss out on promotion. The return from Plymouth of Bob Armstrong and the buying of Iain Dixon from Bristol, plus the return to form of many key players, started the long run of wins which resulted in the Championship Cup coming to the County Ground.

Two years of success with two National titles under our belt has ensured that the club supporters have had real value for money. Next season is seen as a real test of our resolve to keep Premiership Rugby in the far South West. The current squad will be retained and strengthened with Craig Barrow (Bristol) and James Alvis (Newport) joining the club.

The Exeter club are looking forward to the challenge of playing in the new Allied Dunbar Premiership Division and have every intention of retaining their new status for many years to come.

Exeter RFC:

Colours: Black/black/black with white tops.   Change colours: White with black stripe.

COURAGE LEAGUE MATCH DETAILS 1996-97

No	Ven.	Date	Opponents	Att.	Res.	Score	Scorers
1	(H)	31.08	v Rosslyn Park		W	47- 6	Doyle(2t)Woodman(t)Hutchinson(2t)Maunder(t)Gibbins(t)Green(3c2p)
2	(A)	07.09	v Wharfdale		W	29-17	Maunder(t)Green(t2c4pdg)
3	(A)	14.09	v Walsall		W	35-11	Hutchinson(t)Woodman(t)Dovell(t)PenTry(t)Green(3c3p)
4	(H)	21.09	v Harrogate		W	22- 7	Dovell(3t)Maunder(t)Green(c)
5	(A)	28.09	v Leeds		L	24-33	Turner(2t)Thomas(t)Doyle(t)Stewart(2c)
6	(H)	05.10	v London Welsh		W	18-17	Webb(2t)Hutchinson(t)Green(p)
7	(A)	12.10	v Lydney		W	24-12	Turner(t)Webb(t)Southern(t)Green(3cp)
8	(H)	19.10	v Redruth		W	44- 0	Armstrong(3t)Woodman(2t)Doyle(t)Curry(t)Dovell(tc)Stewart(c)
9	(A)	26.10	v Morley		L	9-19	Green(2pdg)
10	(H)	09.11	v Clifton		W	71-10	Southern(t)Turner(t)Curry(t)PenTry(t)Baxter(t)Stewart(t)Woodman(t) Batchelor(t)Doyle(t)Green(t4cp)Fabian(5c)
11	(A)	16.11	v Fylde		L	11-26	Fabian(t2p)
12	(H)	21.12	v Havant		W	46- 5	Dovell(4t)Hutchinson(2t)Rowe(t)Woodman(t)Green(3c)
13	(A)	18.01	v Rosslyn Park		L	10-38	Doyle(t)Green(cp)
14	(H)	25.01	v Wharfdale		W	14- 8	Thomas(tdg)Green(2p)
15	(H)	01.02	v Walsall		W	24-22	Southern(t)Baxter(t)Green(c4p)
16	(A)	08.02	v Harrogate		L	12-15	Woodman(t)Green(tc)
17	(H)	15.02	v Leeds		W	26-25	Woodman(t)Batchelor(t)Green(2c4p)
18	(A)	22.02	v London Welsh		W	36-15	Armstrong(t)Dixon(t)Turner(t)Maunder(t)Curry(t)Green(4cp)
19	(H)	01.03	v Lydney		W	60- 9	Woodman(2t)Hutchinson(2t)Batchelor(t)Turner(t)Armstrong(t)Doyle(t) Thomas(t)Green(6cp)
20	(A)	08.03	v Redruth		W	31-18	Maunder(2t)Doyle(t)Armstrong(t)Green(4cp)
21	(H)	15.03	v Morley		W	26-24	Dixon(t)Thomas(t)Green(2c4p)
22	(A)	22.03	v Clifton		W	60- 3	Dovell(2t)Doyle(t)Woodman(t)Curry(t)Hutchinson(t)Batchelor(t)Thomas(t) Green(t6cp)
23	(A)	29.03	v Liverpool StH		W	25-18	Woolterton(2t)Woodman(t)Green(2c2p)
24	(H)	05.04	v Fylde		W	21-13	Green(7p)
25	(A)	12.04	v Havant		W	36- 8	Thomas(2t)Woodman(t)Brooking(t)Turner(t)Dixon(t)Green(3c)
26	(H)	19.04	v Liverpool StH		W	45-14	Maunder(2t)Dixon(2t)Armstrong(t)Turner(t)Woodman(t)Green(2c2p)
27	(A)	26.04	v Otley		W	26-14	Dixon(3t)Green(c3p)
28	(H)	03.05	v Reading		W	30-16	Doyle(t)Dovell(t)Fabian(p)Green(t3c2p)
29	(H)	10.05	v Otley		W	48-19	Armstrong(2t)Dixon(t)Dovell(t)Maunder(t)Turner(t)Woodman(t)Green(3c)Fabian(2cp)
30	(A)	17.05	v Reading		W	13- 3	Doyle(t)Green(c)Fabian(2p)

1996-97 HIGHLIGHTS

LEAGUE DEBUTS: Del Cross, Bob Armstrong, Mark Curry, John Fabian, Andy Dart, Joff Rowe, Lee Martin.

PLAYERS USED: 27 plus 7 as replacement.

EVER PRESENT: Richard Gibbins, Mark Woodman and Rob Baxter.

❏ Won their last 14 games to take the title by one point from long time leaders Fylde. Those 14 consecutive wins produced a new club record easily beating the previous record of 6.

❏ Mark Woodman with 15 broke Andy Maunder's record of 8 tries in a season set in 95-96.

❏ Set a new club record of 10 tries in a match v Clifton.

❏ Another record breaking season for the Andy & Andy show.

We start with Scrum-half Andy Maunder who has created a new National League record with 139 league appearances. He also scored nine tries taking his Exeter career total to 40 - well clear of his nearest rival.

The other Andy - Green - either broke or extended ten club records. In the in a match section he beat his own record for points in a match scoring 24 at Wharfdale early in the season. This was one more than his previous best against Aspatria in 95-96. He twice equalled his own record of six conversions in a match. The seven penalties he kicked against Fylde broke his previous record of six against Havant in 95-96.

In the "In a season" section he broke his own records for season, conversions and penalties with 300, 58 and 50 respectively, and he took his career total for points past the 1000 point mark.

EXETER'S COURAGE LEAGUE MATCH DETAILS 1996-97

15	14	13	12	11	10	9	1	2	3	4	5	6	7	8	Replacements	
Doyle	Woodman	Turner	Thomas	Dovell	Green	Maunder	Gibbins	Woolterton	Reed	Baxter	Cross	Southern	Hutchinson	Armstrong		1
Doyle	Woodman	Turner	Thomas	Dovell	Green	Maunder	Gibbins	Woolterton	Reed	Baxter	Cross	Southern	Hutchinson	Armstrong		2
Doyle	Woodman	Turner	Thomas	Dovell	Green	Maunder	Gibbins	Woolterton	Reed	Baxter	Cross	Southern	Hutchinson	Armstrong	Crompton(7)	3
Doyle	Woodman	Turner	Thomas	Dovell	Green	Maunder	Gibbins	Woolterton	Reed	Baxter	Cross	Southern	Hutchinson	Armstrong		4
Doyle	Woodman	Turner	Thomas	Dovell	Stewart	Maunder	Gibbins	Woolterton	Reed	Baxter	Cross	Southern	Hutchinson	Armstrong		5
Doyle	Woodman	Turner	Thomas	Dovell	Green	Maunder	Gibbins	Woolterton	Reed	Baxter	Cross	Southern	Hutchinson	Armstrong	Batchelor(8)Stewart(15)	6
Doyle	Woodman	Webb	Turner	Dovell	Green	Maunder	Gibbins	Woolterton	Reed	Baxter	Curry	Batchelor	Southern	Armstrong	Fabian(10)	7
Doyle	Woodman	Webb	Turner	Dovell	Thomas	Maunder	Gibbins	Woolterton	Reed	Baxter	Curry	Southern	Hutchinson	Armstrong	Stewart(10)Dart(12)	8
Doyle	Woodman	Turner	Webb	Dovell	Green	Dart	Gibbins	Brooking	Reed	Baxter	Curry	Rowe	Hutchinson	Armstrong	Adams(7)	9
Fabian	Woodman	Turner	Webb	Doyle	Green	Maunder	Gibbins	Woolterton	Reed	Baxter	Curry	Southern	Hutchinson	Batchelor	Stewart(10)	10
Fabian	Woodman	Turner	Thomas	Doyle	Green	Maunder	Gibbins	Brooking	Gibbins	Baxter	Curry	Martin	Hutchinson	Rowe	Martin(6)	11
Doyle	Woodman	Turner	Thomas	Dovell	Green	Maunder	Sluman	Brooking	Gibbins	Baxter	Curry	Southern	Hutchinson	Rowe	Martin(6)	12
Doyle	Woodman	Turner	Thomas	Dovell	Green	Maunder	Gibbins	Brooking	Sluman	Baxter	Curry	Southern	Hutchinson	Rowe		13
Doyle	Woodman	Turner	Thomas	Dovell	Green	Maunder	Gibbins	Woolterton	Sluman	Baxter	Curry	Batchelor	Hutchinson	Rowe	Hudson(8)	14
Doyle	Woodman	Thomas	Webb	Dovell	Green	Maunder	Gibbins	Woolterton	Sluman	Baxter	Curry	Southern	Dixon	Batchelor		15
Doyle	Woodman	Thomas	Webb	Dovell	Green	John	Gibbins	Woolterton	Sluman	Baxter	Curry	Southern	Dixon	Batchelor	Thorpel(15)Rowe(6)Turner(12)	16
Doyle	Woodman	Turner	Thomas	Dovell	Green	John	Gibbins	Brooking	Sluman	Baxter	Curry	Batchelor	Dixon	Armstrong	Maunder(9)	17
Doyle	Thomas	Turner	Turner	Dovell	Green	John	Gibbins	Brooking	Sluman	Baxter	Curry	Batchelor	Dixon	Armstrong	Maunder(9),Woolterton(2)	18
Doyle	Woodman	Turner	Thomas	Webb	Green	Maunder	Gibbins	Woolterton	Sluman	Baxter	Curry	Batchelor	Hutchinson	Armstrong	Reed(3)	19
Doyle	Woodman	Turner	Webb	Webb	Green	Maunder	Gibbins	Woolterton	Reed	Baxter	Cross	Batchelor	Dixon	Armstrong	Hutchinson(8)Dovell(12)	20
Doyle	Woodman	Turner	Thomas	Dovell	Green	Maunder	Gibbins	Woolterton	Sluman	Baxter	Curry	Batchelor	Dixon	Armstrong	Brooking(3)	21
Doyle	Woodman	Turner	Turner	Dovell	Green	Maunder	Gibbins	Woolterton	Reed	Baxter	Curry	Dixon	Hutchinson	Batchelor	Thomas(13)Maunder(8)Rowe(6)	22
Doyle	Woodman	Webb	Webb	Dovell	Green	John	Gibbins	Woolterton	Sluman	Baxter	Curry	Batchelor	Dixon	Armstrong	May(9)	23
Doyle	Woodman	Turner	Thomas	Dovell	Green	John	Gibbins	Brooking	Sluman	Baxter	Curry	Batchelor	Hutchinson	Armstrong	Woolterton(8)Southern(7)	24
Doyle	Woodman	Turner	Thomas	Dovell	Green	John	Gibbins	Woolterton	Reed	Baxter	Curry	Batchelor	Dixon	Armstrong	Rowe(8)Sluman(7)	25
Doyle	Woodman	Turner	Thomas	Dovell	Green	Maunder	Gibbins	Brooking	Reed	Baxter	Batchelor	Southern	Dixon	Armstrong	Woolterton(1)Fabian(11)May(9)Colburn(8)	26
Doyle	Woodman	Turner	Thomas	Dovell	Green	Maunder	Gibbins	Woolterton	Sluman	Baxter	Curry	Batchelor	Dixon	Armstrong	Southern(6)	27
Doyle	Woodman	Turner	Thomas	Dovell	Green	Maunder	Gibbins	Brooking	Sluman	Baxter	Curry	Southern	Dixon	Armstrong	Fabian(13)Rowe(6)	28
Fabian	Woodman	Turner	Thomas	Dovell	Green	Maunder	Gibbins	Woolterton	Sluman	Baxter	Curry	Southern	Dixon	Armstrong	Doyle(11)Batchelor(6)May(9)	29
Fabian	Woodman	Turner	Thomas	Doyle	Green	Maunder	Gibbins	Woolterton	Sluman	Baxter	Curry	Southern	Dixon	Armstrong		30

EXETER LEAGUE STATISTICS

(COMPILED BY STEPHEN McCORMACK)

Season	Div.	P	W	D	L	F	(Tries	Con	Pen	DG)	A	(Tries	Con	Pen	DG)	Most Points	Most Tries
87-88	3	11	3	2	6	128	(15	4	16	4)	197	(27	16	19	0)	42 - Andy Green	3 - Andy Green & Mike Gathery
88-89	3	11	4	0	7	142	(17	7	14	6)	180	(22	10	20	4)	65 - Malcolm Collins	5 - Andy Maunder
89-90	3	11	5	1	5	149	(15	7	25	0)	153	(17	5	19	6)	99 - Andy Green	2 - Andy Green & Andy Maunder
90-91	3	12	7	2	3	160	(20	7	22	0)	139	(16	6	21	0)	92 - Andy Green	4 - Jeff Tutchings
91-92	3	12	8	2	2	203	(29	12	19	2)	138	(14	5	22	2)	77 - Andy Green	4 - John Davies & Mark Chatterton
92-93	3	11	8	1	2	247	(25	10	31	3)	169	(16	7	24	1)	122 - Andy Green	5 - Andy Maunder
93-94	3	18	9	1	8	308	(32	20	34	2)	271	(23	15	38	4)	125 - Andy Green	5 - Andy Maunder
94-95	3	18	3	1	14	153	(11	4	26	4)	319	(30	17	43	2)	35 - Ian Stewart	3 - Mark Chatterton
95-96	4	18	14	0	4	448	(52	31	35	7)	230	(22	6	30	6)	191 - Andy Green	8 - Andy Maunder
96-97	3	30	25	0	5	923	(62	38	40	4)	443	(46	24	54	1)	300 - Andy Green	15 - Mark Maunder
Totals		152	86	10	56	2861	(278	140	262	32)	2239	(233	111	290	26)		

	HOME	AWAY
BIGGEST WIN	(61pts) 71-10 v Clifton 9.11.96	(57pts) 60-3 v Clifton 22.3.97
DEFEAT		(35pts) 13-48 v Fylde 3.10.87
MOST POINTS SCORED	71-10 v Clifton 9.11.96	60-3 v Clifton 22.3.97
AGAINST	28-33 v Leeds 13.3.93	13-48 v Fylde 3.10.87

MOST CONSECUTIVE VICTORIES - 14   **MOST CONSECUTIVE DEFEATS - 8**

MOST TRIES IN A MATCH   **MOST APPEARANCES**
(FOR) 10 v Clifton 9.11.96 (H)   FORWARD: 105 Harry Langley
(AGAINST) 8 v Fylde 3.10.87 (A)   BACK: 139(3) Andy Maunder

CONSECUTIVE APPEARANCES   **CONSECUTIVE SCORING MATCHES**
88 Andy Maunder 12.9.87 - 17.9.94   Scoring Tries - 3 - Andy Maunder, John Davis, Ian Dixon & Bob Armstrong
Scoring Points - 32 - Andy Green

MOST	in a SEASON	in a CAREER	in a MATCH
Points	300 Andy Green 96-97	1085 Andy Green 87-97	24 Andy Green v Wharfdale 7.9.96 (A)
Tries	15 Andy Maunder 95-96	40 Andy Maunder 87-96	4 Simon Dovell v Havant 21.12.96 (H)
Conversions	58 Andy Green 96-97	140 Andy Green 87-97	6 Andy Green v Aspatria 23.3.96 (H) v Lydney 1.3.97 (H) v Clifton 22.3.97 (A)
Penalties	50 Andy Green 96-97	213 Andy Green 87-97	7 Andy Green v Fylde 5.4.97 (H)
Drop Goals	6 Andy Green 95-96	22 Andy Green 87-96	2 Andy Green v Sheffield 23.4.88 (H)

EXETER PLAYING SQUAD

NAME	Ht	Wt	Birthdate	Birthplace	Club	Apps	Pts	T	C	P	DG

BACKS

Ian Stewart

| | | | | | Exeter | 80+3 | 166 | 16 | 9 | 17 | 8 |

Simon Dovell 5.10 13.11 09.01.69 Barnstaple
Devon, u21, Colts.

| | | | | | Exeter | 88+3 | 123 | 25 | - | - | - |

Sean Doyle 6.0 14.10 21.08.74 Exeter — Tiverton
Devon, South West u21.

| | | | | | Exeter | 58+1 | 90 | 18 | - | - | - |

Mark Woodman 6.0 15.0 18.09.70 Exeter — Prev. Clubs: Crediton, Bath.
Devon.

| | | | | | Exeter | 39 | 85 | 17 | - | - | - |

Andy Turner 6.1 14.0 27.11.70 Saddleworth
South West, u21. Devon, u21.

| | | | | | Exeter | 81+1 | 60 | 12 | - | - | - |

Jason Thomas 5.9 11.7 02.03.75 Aberdare — Paignton
Devon. Welsh Elite 2000

| | | | | | Exeter | 48+2 | 58 | 11 | - | - | - |

Andy Green 5.5 10.7 23.05.64 Barnstaple — Prev. Clubs: South Molton, Bristol.
Devon, u21, Colts. South West, B.

| | | | | | Exeter | 122 | - | - | - | - | - |

Andy Maunder 6.0 14.0 08.04.66 Tiverton — Tiverton
Devon. South West.

| | | | | | Exeter | 139+3 | 184 | 40 | - | - | - |

Jon Fabian 6.3 14.7 18.09.76 Plymouth — Plymouth
England: Students, Universities. South West u21.

| | | | | | Exeter | 4+3 | 37 | 1 | 7 | 6 | - |

Richard John 5.10 13.0 30.05.74 Exeter — Crediton
South West, Colts, u21.

| | | | | | Exeter | 10 | 5 | 1 | - | - | - |

Mel Webb

| | | | | | Exeter | 14 | 20 | 4 | - | - | - |

Andy Dart

| | | | | | Exeter | 1+1 | - | - | - | - | - |

FORWARDS

Richard Gibbins

| | | | | | Exeter | 106 | 15 | 3 | - | - | - |

Phil Sluman 6.0 17.0 15.03.67 Exeter
Devon

| | | | | | Exeter | 68+3 | 9 | 2 | - | - | - |

Wayne Reed 5.10 17.4 27.10.71 Tiverton — Crediton
Devon u21.

| | | | | | Exeter | 20 | 1 | 5 - | 1 | - | - |

Keith Brooking 6.0 16.0 07.05.73 Newton Abbott
South West. Devon. Welsh Exiles u21.

| | | | | | Exeter | 34+2 | 5 | 1 | - | - | - |

Mark Wooltorton 5.10 14.0 03.03.67 Mirfield — Morley
Devon. Combined Services. Yorkshire Colts.

| | | | | | Plymouth | 3+1 | - | - | - | - | - |
| | | | | | Exeter | 24+3 | 10 | 2 | - | - | - |

Rob Baxter 6.5 16.7 10.03.71 Tavistock — Gloucester
England: Colts. Devon, u21. South West, u21.

| | | | | | Exeter | 86 | 20 | 4 | - | - | - |

Mark Curry 6.7 17.0 22.10.73 Taunton — Bristol u21
Somerset, u21, Colts.

| | | | | | Exeter | 23 | 20 | 4 | - | - | - |

Roger Hutchinson 6.0 14.7 21.11.69 Singapore
England Students. South West.

| | | | | | Exeter | 59+4 | 45 | 9 | - | - | - |

Iain Dixon

					London Scottish	27	8	2	-	-	-
					Bristol	6+1	-	-	-	-	-
					Exeter	19	49	10	-	-	-

Bob Armstrong 6.4 18.0 17.08.67 Liverpool — Plymouth
Combined Services. South West.

| | | | | | Bristol | 38+2 | - | - | - | - | - |
| | | | | | Exeter | 22 | 45 | 9 | - | - | - |

Nick Southern 5.11 14.0 30.09.67 Plymouth

| | | | | | Exeter | 46+2 | 25 | 5 | - | - | - |

John Batchelor 6.4 17.7 08.05.70 Essex — Upper Clapton
Essex. Eastern Counties. Somerset.

| | | | | | Exeter | 55+2 | 30 | 6 | - | - | - |

Joff Rowe 6.1 17.0 18.10.68 St. Ives — Prev. Clubs: St. Ives, Plymouth.
Cornwall, u21. British Police.

| | | | | | Exeter | 4+4 | 5 | 1 | - | - | - |

Tel: 01392 78759   **Fax:** 01392 438802

Capacity: 6,000   **Seated:** 900   **Standing:** 5,100

Simple Directions: From M5 junction 30 follow A377 to town centre. At Sainsbury store turn left (Cowick Street), under the railway bridge. Turn left at traffic lights and then first right. The ground is approx 100 metres ahead.

Nearest Railway Station: Exeter (St. Davids) (B.R.)

Car Parking: 200 spaces inside ground.

Admission: Season tickets - Adults Standing £60, Seated £80. Children/OAPs half price.
   Matchdays - Adults Standing £6, Seated £8, Children/OAPs half price

Club Shop: Yes - manager Mrs L Sluman 01392 437907.

Clubhouse: Monday, Tuesday & Thursday evenings 6.00-11.00. Matchdays 12.00-11.00. Snacks and bar meals available
   Functions available capacity 80, contact Mrs K Chalmers.

Training Nights: Tuesday and Thursday.

Exeter Captain Rob Baxter celebrates another trophy.

Photo - Nigel Chanter

MATCHDAY PROGRAMME

Size   A5

Number of pages   28 + cover + centrefold

Price   £1

Programme Editor Mr A S E Lee, 01392 823903

Advertising Rates
   66x23mm £55, 66x46mm £100, 66x92mm £175,
                        132x46mm £175, 132x92mm £310,
                        132x184mm £530, all plus VAT
   Contact - Mike Dalton, Commercial Manager

FYLDE R.U.F.C.

FOUNDED: 1919

President   David Lyon, Atherton, Ribby Road, Wrea Green, Preston, Lancs. PR4 2NA. 01772 682294 (H)
Chairman   Barry Fothergill, 97 Heyhouses Lane, Lytham St. Annes, Lancs. FY8 3RN.   01253 726958 (H)
Club Secretary   Peter Makin, Links Grange, Greenways, St. Annes, Lancs. FY8 3LY.
01253 722713 (H)   01772 259625 (B) 01772 259628 (Fax)
Rugby Manager   Andrew McFarlane, 01253 739137 (B)   01253 739137 (Fax)
Fylde RUFC, The Woodlands Memorial Ground, Ansdell, Lytham St Annes, Lancs. FY8 4EL.
Business Operations Manager   P Walsh, c/o Fylde RUFC, as above
01253 739137 (B)   01253 739137 (Fax)
Fixture Secretary   Graham Benstead 01253 736922 (B)   01253 730898 (H)
Press Officer   S Brown 01253 883100

In the last game of season 1995/96, Fylde, the League's bottom club, defeated Richmond, the Division Three runners-up. Realistically, no one would have considered this to be any more than a token omen for Fylde's fortunes in 1996/97. As it turned out, the club was reinforced by a returning and rejuvinated Craig Burns at prop, 'old boy' Martin Greatorex (back-row), 'new boys' Dave Wright (prop) and Paul Holmes (2nd Row) and the home coming of Mark Preston from rugby league. Later on in the season, further additions came from Andy MacFarlane (No 8), Tony Ireland (back row) after injury, and Gavin Moffat at full back. These players cemented a Fylde side which surprised everyone with their free running rugby in the early matches, and stealing a march on more fancied rivals they rushed to the top of Division Three, a position they did not relinquish until the last Saturday of the season.

The pinnacle of the campaign was undoubtedly a truly gutsy performance in a titanic battle with the all powerful Leeds side at Fylde in December. Fylde won 13-0, the only League game in which Leeds failed to score. But if the early season proved satisfying and enjoyable, the tougher second half of the programme produced a stuttering, nerve racking run in to the end of the season, in which free running rugby fell by the wayside.

Only great determination and team spirit, inspired by captain Garath Russell, who was always in the thick of the action, pulled us through, despite a number of set backs, particularly at Leeds. The last two games had to be won to achieve promotion, and this Fylde did quite comfortably, edging out Leeds, but being pipped for the championship by Exeter.

Full marks to all the players and coaching staff who held their nerve over a strenuous season - 30 League games proved to be a few too many. No one underestimates the magnitude of the challenge in Division Two, and team strengthening will be required. As a first step, Andy MacFarlane has been appointed full time rugby manager.

Fylde RUFC after the match at Lydney which sealed their promotion to Premiership 2 for this season

Colours: Claret, gold and white/white/claret.   **Change colours:** Maroon.

191

FYLDE

No	Ven.	Date	Opponents	Att.	Res.	Score	Scorers
1	(A)	31.08	v Redruth		W	28-16	Bell(t)Lancaster(t)Preston(t)Gough(2c3p)
2	(H)	07.09	v Morley		W	19-17	Anderton(t)Gough(c3pdg)
3	(A)	14.09	v Clifton		W	45-17	Preston(3t)irving(2t)Bell(t)Gough(t5c)
4	(H)	21.09	v Walsall		W	28-10	Preston(t)Anderton(t)Gough(6p)
5	(H)	28.09	v Havant		W	44-17	Anderton(2t)Preston(t)Parker(t)O'Toole(t)Lavin(t)Gough(4c2p)
6	(A)	05.10	v Liverpool StH		W	40-12	Anderton(t)Irving(t)Bell(t)O'Toole(t)Gough(4c4p)
7	(H)	12.10	v Otley		W	28-14	Preston(t)Barclay(t)Anderton(t)Gough(2c3p)
8	(A)	19.10	v Reading		D	19-19	Barclay(t)Parker(t)Tanner(3p)
9	(H)	26.10	v Rosslyn Park		W	40- 8	Parker(t)Preston(t)Anderton(t)Gough(t4c4p)
10	(A)	09.11	v Wharfdale		W	19-13	Russell(t)Gough(c4p)
11	(H)	16.11	v Exeter		W	26-11	Preston(t)Seed(t)Gough(2c4p)
12	(A)	21.12	v Harrogate		L	19-27	Preston(2t)Gough(3p)
13	(H)	28.12	v Leeds		W	13- 0	Barclay(t)Gough(cpdg)
14	(H)	11.01	v Lydney		W	24-16	Preston(2t)Gough(c4p)
15	(H)	18.01	v Redruth		W	55- 6	Parker(2t)Preston(t)Holmes(t)O'Toole(t)Russell(t)Moffatt(t)Gough(t6cp)
16	(A)	25.01	v Morley		W	30-18	Preston(2t)Gough(c6p)
17	(H)	01.02	v Clifton		W	29-20	Anderton(t)O'Toole(t)McFarlane(t)Gough(t3cp)
18	(A)	08.02	v Walsall		W	28-12	Greatorex(t)Bell(t)Gough(t2c3p)
19	(A)	15.02	v Havant		W	60-13	O'Toole(2t)Preston(2t)Russell(t)Parker(t)Tanner(t)Barclay(t)Gough(t6cp)
20	(H)	22.02	v Liverpool St H		W	30-13	Tanner(t)Anderton(t)O'Toole(t)Gough(3c3p)
21	(A)	01.03	v Otley		W	22- 7	Parker(t)Parker(t)Tanner(t)Anderton(t)Gough(c)
22	(H)	08.03	v Reading		L	16-21	Anderton(t)Gough(c3p)
23	(A)	15.03	v Rosslyn Park		L	5-18	O'Toole
24	(H)	22.03	v Wharfdale		W	39-18	Russell(2t)Parker(tc)O'Toole(dg)Gough(2c5p)
25	(A)	29.03	v London Welsh		W	13- 9	O'Toole(t)Gough(c2p)
26	(A)	05.04	v Exeter		L	13-21	Preston(t)Gough(tp)
27	(H)	12.04	v Harrogate		W	22-17	Burns(t)Gough(c5p)
28	(A)	20.04	v Leeds		L	0-34	
29	(H)	26.04	v London Welsh		W	39- 9	Preston(2t)Russell(t)Gough(3c5pdg)
30	(A)	03.05	v Lydney		W	20-6	Burns(t)Gough(5p)

1996-97 HIGHLIGHTS

LEAGUE DEBUTS:
Julian Irving, Paul Holmes, Gavin Moffatt, Jon Webster, Carl Lavin, Dave Tanner, Dave Wright.

TRY ON DEBUT: Carl Lavin.

PLAYERS USED: 29 plus 6 as replacement.

EVER PRESENT: Chris O'Toole, Steve Gough
and Craig McIntyre.

❏ Set a new club record of nine consecutive wins beating the old record of six.

❏ Second rower John Taylor became the first player from the club to reach 100 league appearances and ended the season on 108. Stand-off Steve Gough took the record for most appearances by a Back off Andy Parker and ended the season on 103.

❏ Steve Gough re-wrote the record books by scoring an incredible 404 points to set a National League record. The previous Fylde record was 138 by Gough himself last season. He passes Steve Burnage's career record of 318 and ends the season on 641. Both season records for conversions and penalties are his with 57 and 82 respectively.
Gough also breaks the record for penalties in a match by twice kicking six to beat the previous record of four shared by four players.

❏ Winger Mark Preston on his return to the club after his Rugby League exploits set a new record of 20 tries in a season to top Brendan Hanavan's club record of 12 set in 93-94.

❏ Winger Greg Anderton set a new record by scoring tries in four consecutive matches.

FYLDE'S COURAGE LEAGUE MATCH DETAILS 1996-97

#	15	14	13	12	11	10	9	1	2	3	4	5	6	7	8	Replacements
1	Parker	Irving	Seed	Barclay	Preston	Gough	O'Toole	Burns	McIntyre	Lancaster	Taylor	Holmes	Bell	Bell	Moffatt	Moffatt(9)
2	Parker	Preston	Seed	Barclay	Preston	Gough	O'Toole	Burns	McIntyre	Webster	Taylor	Holmes	Bell	Bell	Eckersley	Eckersley,Irving(13)
3	Parker	Irving	Barclay	Barclay	Anderton	Gough	Lancaster	Burns	McIntyre	Webster	Taylor	Holmes	Bell	Bell	Eckersley	Knight(14)
4	Parker	Preston	Connell	Barclay	Anderton	Gough	O'Toole	Lancaster	McIntyre	Lancaster	Taylor	Holmes	Bell	Eckersley	Eckersley	Evans(12);Dixon(8);Kaye(7)
5	Parker	Preston	Connell	Connell	Anderton	Gough	O'Toole	Burns	McIntyre	Lancaster	Taylor	Bell	Russell	Lavin	Eckersley	Mullen(4)
6	Tanner	Parker	Irving	Barclay	Anderton	Gough	O'Toole	Burns	McIntyre	Lancaster	Taylor	Holmes	Russell	Lavin	Eckersley	Blackburn
7	Parker	Parker	Irving	Anderton	Anderton	Gough	O'Toole	Burns	McIntyre	Lancaster	Taylor	Eckersley	Russell	Bell	Bell	Kaye(6)
8	Parker	Preston	Barclay	Anderton	Anderton	Gough	O'Toole	Burns	McIntyre	Lancaster	Bell	Holmes	Russell	Kaye	Duggan	Duggan(5),Tanner(12),Dixon(8)
9	Parker	Preston	Tanner	Anderton	Anderton	Gough	O'Toole	Burns	McIntyre	Lancaster	Taylor	Holmes	Bell	Greatorex	Greatorex	Greatorex
10	Parker	Preston	Barclay	Seed	Anderton	Gough	O'Toole	Burns	McIntyre	Lancaster	Taylor	Holmes	Greatorex	Greatorex	Duggan	Webster(3)
11	Parker	Preston	Barclay	Seed	Anderton	Gough	O'Toole	Burns	McIntyre	Lancaster	Taylor	Holmes	Russell	Greatorex	Eckersley	Tanner(12)
12	Parker	Preston	Barclay	Seed	Anderton	Gough	O'Toole	Burns	McIntyre	Lancaster	Bell	Holmes	Russell	Greatorex	Connell	Connell(12)
13	Barclay	Preston	Barclay	Seed	Anderton	Gough	O'Toole	Burns	McIntyre	Lancaster	Taylor	Holmes	Greatorex	Greatorex	McFarlane	Bell(7)
14	Barclay	Preston	Connell	Seed	Anderton	Gough	O'Toole	Burns	McIntyre	Lancaster	Taylor	Holmes	Russell	Greatorex	McFarlane	Wright(1)Irving(12)
15	Barclay	Preston	Connell	Parker	Anderton	Gough	O'Toole	Lancaster	McIntyre	Lancaster	Taylor	Holmes	Bell	Greatorex	McFarlane	Moffatt(15)
16	Parker	Preston	Connell	Parker	Anderton	Gough	Lancaster	Burns	McIntyre	Lancaster	Taylor	Holmes	Russell	Greatorex	McFarlane	Ferri(12)
17	Parker	Preston	Connell	Anderton	Anderton	Gough	Lancaster	Burns	McIntyre	Lancaster	Bell	Holmes	Russell	Greatorex	McFarlane	Bell(7)
18	Parker	Preston	Barclay	Anderton	Anderton	Gough	O'Toole	Burns	McIntyre	Lancaster	Bell	Holmes	Russell	Greatorex	McFarlane	Bell(7)
19	Parker	Preston	Barclay	Bell	Anderton	Gough	Lancaster	Burns	McIntyre	Rigby	Taylor	Holmes	Russell	Greatorex	McFarlane	Wright(1)Webster(6)
20	Parker	Preston	Barclay	Anderton	Anderton	Gough	Lancaster	Burns	McIntyre	Lancaster	Bell	Holmes	Bell	Greatorex	McFarlane	Davy(15)Webster(6)
21	Barclay	Parker	Barclay	Anderton	Parker	Gough	O'Toole	Burns	McIntyre	Wright	Bell	Holmes	Russell	Greatorex	McFarlane	Eckersley(7),Moffatt(14).
22	Barclay	Connell	Connell	Anderton	Anderton	Gough	O'Toole	Murns	McIntyre	Wright	Taylor	Holmes	Bell	Greatorex	McFarlane	Connell(14)
23	Barclay	Preston	Connell	Irving	Anderton	Gough	Lancaster	Lancaster	McIntyre	Wright	Taylor	Holmes	Greatorex	Greatorex	McFarlane	Webster(1)Bell(5)
24	Moffatt	Preston	Connell	Tanner	Parker	Gough	O'Toole	Burns	McIntyre	Lancaster	Taylor	Holmes	Russell	Ireland	McFarlane	Greatorex(7)Barclay(10)
25	Moffatt	Preston	Tanner	Tanner	Parker	Gough	O'Toole	Burns	McIntyre	Lancaster	Taylor	Holmes	Russell	Ireland	McFarlane	Barclay(15)
26	Parker	Preston	Connell	Connell	Tanner	Gough	O'Toole	Burns	McIntyre	Lancaster	Taylor	Holmes	Russell	Ireland	McFarlane	Bell(4)Wright(3)
27	Parker	Connell	Connell	Tanner	Anderton	Gough	O'Toole	Lancaster	McIntyre	Taylor	Taylor	Eckersley	Russell	Ireland	McFarlane	Wright(3)Duggan(7)
28	Moffatt	Preston	Connell	Tanner	Anderton	Gough	O'Toole	Burns	McIntyre	Wright	Taylor	Holmes	Bell	Lavin	McFarlane	Barclay(9)
29	Moffatt	Preston	Barclay	Tanner	Anderton	Gough	O'Toole	Burns	McIntyre	Wright	Taylor	Holmes	Russell	Ireland	McFarlane	Lancaster(1)Bell(7)Davy(2)
30	Moffatt	Preston	Barclay	Tanner	Anderton	Gough	O'Toole	Burns	McIntyre	Wright	Taylor	Holmes	Russell	Ireland	McFarlane	

FYLDE LEAGUE STATISTICS
(COMPILED BY STEPHEN McCORMACK)

Season	Div.	P	W	D	L	F	(Tries	Con	Pen	DG)	A	(Tries	Con	Pen	DG)	Most Points	Most Tries
87-88	3	11	6	0	5	269	(41	30	14	1)	164	(26	12	11	1)	121 - Steve Burnage	10 - Brendan Hanavan
88-89	3	11	4	0	7	136	(13	6	24	0)	181	(26	13	14	3)	88 - Steve Burnage	4 - Mark Hesketh
89-90	3	11	5	0	6	169	(19	9	23	2)	222	(30	15	24	0)	91 - Steve Burnage	7 - Brendan Hanavan
90-91	3	12	7	2	3	183	(25	10	19	2)	115	(14	7	13	2)	62 - Mike Jackson	5 - Brendan Hanavan
91-92	3	12	9	1	2	198	(21	12	28	2)	109	(11	4	16	3)	106 - Mike Jackson	4 - Antony Ireland
92-93	2	12	0	3	9	108	(9	3	18	1)	290	(31	18	30	3)	40 - Mike Jackson	2 - Steve Gough & John Nicholson
93-94	3	18	13	0	5	339	(46	20	21	2)	219	(19	11	31	3)	109 - Andy Parker	12 - Brendan Hanavan
94-95	2	18	8	0	10	250	(25	13	28	5)	329	(28	15	53	0)	91 - Andy Parker	5 - 3 players - Brendan Hanavan, Steve Gough & Greg Anderton.
95-96	3	18	3	1	14	283	(28	16	37	0)	448	(45	26	51	6)	138 - Steve Gough	5 - Greg Anderton
96-97	3	30	24	1	5	813	(86	58	85	4)	439	(38	21	65	4)	404 - Steve Gough	20 - Mark Preston
Totals		153	79	8	66	2748	(313	177	250	19)	2516	(268	142	308	25)		

	HOME	AWAY
BIGGEST WIN	(61pts) 68-7 v Birmingham 7.11.87	(47pts) 60-13 v Havant 15.2.97
DEFEAT	(22pts) 15-37 v Saracens 8.4.95	(48pts) 3-51 v Sale 19.9.92
MOST POINTS SCORED	68-7 v Birmingham 7.11.87	60-13 v Havant 15.2.97
AGAINST	15-37 v Saracens 8.4.95	3-51 v Sale 19.9.92

MOST CONSECUTIVE VICTORIES - 9

MOST CONSECUTIVE DEFEATS - 6

MOST TRIES IN A MATCH
(FOR) 10 v Birmingham 7.11.87
v Redruth 9.4.94 (H)
(AGAINST) 7 v Plymouth 19.11.88

MOST APPEARANCES
FORWARD: 108 John Taylor
BACK: 103 Andy Parker, Steve Gough

CONSECUTIVE SCORING MATCHES
Scoring Tries - 4 - Greg Anderton
Scoring Points - 20 - Steve Burnage

CONSECUTIVE APPEARANCES
41 Andy Parker 12.3.94 to date

MOST	in a SEASON	in a CAREER	in a MATCH
Points	404 Steve Gough 96-97	641 Steve Gough 92-97	28 Steve Burnage v Birmingham 7.11.87 (H)
Tries	20 Mark Preston 96-97	41 Brendan Hanavan 87-96	4 Brendan Hanavan v Exeter 3.10.87 (H) v Birmingham 7.11.87 (H) v Redruth 9.4.94 (H)
Conversions	57 Steve Gough 96-97	75 Steve Gough 92-97	9 Steve Burnage v Birmingham 7.11.87 (H)
Penalties	82 Steve Gough 96-97	122 Steve Gough 92-97	6 Steve Gough v Walsall 21.9.96 (H) v Morley 25.1.97 (A)
Drop Goals	5 Ian Barclay 94-95	7 Ian Barclay 87-95	2 Ian Barclay v Waterloo 25.3.95 (A)

FYLDE PLAYING SQUAD

NAME	Ht	Wt	Birthdate	Birthplace	Club	Apps	Pts	T	C	P	DG

BACKS

NAME	Ht	Wt	Birthdate	Birthplace	Club	Apps	Pts	T	C	P	DG
Andy Parker	6.1	13.6	04.04.67	Blackpool							
Lancashire					Fylde	103+2	273	17	31	43	-
Gavin Moffatt	6.1	13.7	09.09.72	Lancaster	Vale of Lune						
					Fylde	5+3	5	1	-	-	-
Mark Preston	5.10	12.7	03.04.67	Lytham St. Annes	Prev. Clubs: Wigan (RL), Halifax (RL).						
England: u21, B.	Lancashire.				Fylde	36	132	28	-	-	-
Greg Anderton	5.10	15.0	26.02.75	Preston							
North Lancashire					Fylde	70	140	28	-	-	-
Dave Tanner	5.10	14.7	29.09.65	Keighley	Wigan (RL)						
Lancashire					Fylde	15+3	24	3	-	3	-
Stuart Connell	5.10	14.7	17.04.67	Bolton	Cockermouth						
Cumbria					Fylde	39+2	8	2	-	-	-
Steve Gough	5.9	12.0	22.04.66	Leigh							
England: Colts.	Lancashire.				Fylde	103	641	23	75	122	5
Chris O'Toole	5.9	14.0	08.02.66	St. Helens	Prev. Clubs: Orrell, Liverpool St. Helens.						
Lancashire.					Fylde	77	73	14	-	-	1
Paddy Seed	6.1	15.0	28.09.67	Blackpool							
Lancashire.					Fylde	67+2	44	9	-	-	-
Ian Barclay	6.0	13.7	28.07.69	Lytham St. Annes							
Lancashire					Fylde	101+4	132	15	3	10	7
Julian Irving	6.0	14.7	13.02.71	Oldham							
					Fylde	8+2	15	3	-	-	-
Mark Evans	5.9	12.7	21.02.75	Leeds							
					Fylde	9+3	5	1	-	-	-

FORWARDS

NAME	Ht	Wt	Birthdate	Birthplace	Club	Apps	Pts	T	C	P	DG
Craig Burns	6.0	15.0	01.08.64	Blackburn	Blackburn						
Lancashire. Anglo-Scots.					Fylde	94	19	4	-	-	-
Craig McIntyre	5.11	14.7	19.04.69	Lytham St. Annes							
					Fylde	48+2	5	1	-	-	-
Richard Lancaster	6.1	17.7	12.03.73	Lancaster	Aspatria						
Cumbria					Fylde	28+1	5	1	-	-	-
Jon Webster	5.10	16.0	04.11.75	Preston	Preston G/hopper						
					Fylde	2+3	-	-	-	-	-
Dave Wright	6.1	17.0	18.10.70	Nottingham	Nottingham						
					Fylde	11+3	-	-	-	-	-
Paul Holmes	6.6	16.7	18.11.75	Lancaster	Vale of Lune						
Scotland: u21.	England: Students.				Fylde	22	5	1	-	-	-
John Taylor	6.5	16.8	05.10.66	S. Point (Aden)							
Lancashire					Fylde	108	30	7	-	-	-
Gareth Russell	5.11	15	30.07.72	Rochdale							
Lancashire.					Fylde	81	50	10	-	-	-
Alastair Bell	6.3	16.7	15.04.74	Carlisle	Carlisle (RL)						
Cumbria					Fylde	36+6	20	4	-	-	-
Andy McFarlane	6.4	16.0	15.04.61	London	Sale	65+1	17	4	-	-	-
Lancashire, North.					Orrell	4+1	-	-	-	-	-
					Fylde	26	9	2	-	-	-
Martin Greatorex	6.1	15.7	31.08.72	Manchester	Saracens						
					Fylde	48+2	20	4	-	-	-
Nick Eckersley	6.3	15.0	02.04.61	Farnworth							
					Fylde	16+2	-	-	-	-	-
Tony Ireland	6.0	15.0	05.03.66	Lancaster	Prev. Clubs: Waterloo, Vale of Lune.						
					Fylde	19	16	4	-	-	-
Steve Rigby	5.10	17.6	05.06.59	Lytham St. Annes							
					Fylde	30+1	-	-	-	-	-
Carl Lavin	6.0	14.0	14.03.77	Blackpool							
					Fylde	3	5	1	-	-	-
John Duggan	6.3	16.7	16.03.74	Leicester							
					Fylde	10+2	5	1	-	-	-

TELEPHONE: 01253 734733

CAPACITY: 5,440   **SEATED:** 440   **STANDING:** 5,000

SIMPLE DIRECTIONS: From the end of the M55 follow signs for Lytham St. Annes - B5230 then B5261 onto Queensway - ground is three miles on the left opposite Blossoms P.H. and R.C. Church.
Nearest Railway Station: Ansdell & Fairhaven. Left outside station, down the hill away from the sea, along Woodlands Road to T junction (R.C. Church & Blossoms PH) - ground is directly opposite to the right.
Car Parking: 150 spaces available F.O.C. at the ground.

ADMISSION: (Standing only)   Matchdays - Non members £8, OAPs £5; members £5, OAPs £3.
                              Season (members only) £50, OAPs £25.

CLUB SHOP: Yes, open matchdays 1-6pm & Sundays 10-Noon. Contact D Walsh 01253 729253.
CLUBHOUSE: Open matchdays Noon-11pm, Sundays Noon-3pm, Tues, Thurs & Fri 7.30-11pm. Has three bars with wide range of food available. Function facilities for approx 400. Contact D Walsh 01253 729253.
TRAINING NIGHTS: Tuesday and Thursday.

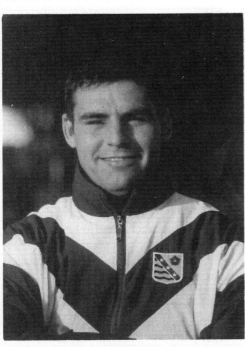

Gareth Russell
Fylde RUFC Captain
1996-97 & 1997-98

MATCHDAY PROGRAMME

Size	A5
Number of pages	32
Price	£2.00
Programme Editor	G Gill
	01253 738080 (B)
Advertising Rates	Full page £400
	1/2 page £250
	1/4 page £150
	Back page £500

LONDON SCOTTISH F.C.

NICKNAME: Scottish   **FOUNDED:** 1878

Director of Rugby John Steele, c/o London Scottish FC, Richmond Athletic Ground, Richmond, Surrey. TW9 2SS. 0410 042447 (H), 0181 332 2473 (B), 0181 948 6183 (Fax)

Chief Executive Richard Yerbury, c/o London Scottish FC, as above

Commercial Director Angus Stewart, c/o London Scottish FC, as above

Club Secretary John J Smith, c/o London Scottish FC, as above
01784 459463 (H), 0181 332 2473 (B), 0181 948 6183 (Fax)

Press Officer Angus Stewart, c/o London Scottish FC, as above

London Scottish's first professional season saw them finish fifth in what was a very competitive league. The club had a good start of four wins against a background of financial uncertainty in the new professional era. A comparatively young squad of players was complimented by new recruits such as Chris Tarbuck from Leicester, Paul Johnston from Zimbabwe, Ed Jones from New Zealand and Courtney Smith from Canada. With these additions the side developed and matured, finishing one place behind the promotion and play-off teams.

Increasing representative honours are an indicator of things to come. These include further caps for centre Ronnie Eriksson and International 'A' honours for captain Simon Holmes and fullback Derek Lee. These add to the club's proud record of having produced more international players for Scotland and more Scotland captains than any other club.

The players and management now have their sights firmly fixed on promotion to Division One.

Scotland International Ronnie Eriksson in action against Gary Armstrong of Newcastle. Ronnie will be 1st XV Captain for 1997/98 season.
Photo - Harry Hern

Colours: Dark blue/white/red.   **Change colours:** Blue and white quarters.

COURAGE LEAGUE MATCH DETAILS 1996-97

No	Ven.	Date	Opponents	Att.	Res.	Score	Scorers
1	(H)	07.09	v Rugby	401	W	43- 7	Furley(t)Griffiths(t)Hunter(t)Holmes(t)Steele(4c5p)
2	(A)	14.09	v Wakefield	750	W	30-27	Tarbuck(2t)Hamilton(t)Steele(3c3p)
3	(H)	21.09	v Waterloo	448	W	42-30	G Smith(t)Erikson(t)Duthie(2t)Steele(t4c3p)
4	(A)	28.09	v Nottingham	458	W	26-12	Duthie(t)Erikson(t)Steele(2c3pdg)
5	(H)	05.10	v Blackheath	878	L	23-31	Watson(t)Tarbuck(t)Steele(2c3p)
6	(A)	12.10	v Richmond	4500	L	13-54	Millard(t)Steele(c2p)
7	(A)	19.10	v Coventry	2500	L	6-66	Stent(2p)
8	(H)	26.10	v Moseley	1110	W	42-10	Wichary(3t)Tarbuck(2t)Duthie(t)Steele(3c2p)
9	(A)	02.11	v Rotherham	1100	L	18-28	Robinson(t)Turner(t)Steele(c2p)
10	(H)	09.11	v Bedford	2317	L	26-27	Rayner(t)Steele(t2c4p)
11	(H)	16.11	v Newcastle	2566	L	12-28	Jankovich(t)Watson(t)Steele(c)
12	(H)	18.01	v Nottingham	1209	W	33-10	Thompson(t)Jankovich(t)Steele(t3c4p)
13	(A)	08.02	v Blackheath	2009	W	19-13	Robinson(t)Holmes(t)Erikson(dg)Stent(pdg)
14	(H)	08.03	v Richmond	1348	L	18-37	Tarbuck(2t)Steele(cpdg)
15	(H)	22.03	v Coventry	483	L	13-14	Hunter(t)Stent(c2p)
16	(A)	28.03	v Rugby	520	W	45-16	Robinson(t)Erikson(t)Sly(t)Steele(2t4c4p)
17	(H)	31.03	v Wakefield	243	W	34- 3	Hunter(t)Holmes(t)C Smith(t)Steele(2c5p)
18	(A)	05.04	v Moseley	802	L	16-44	C Smith(t)Millard(t)Steele(pdg)
19	(H)	12.04	v Rotherham	501	W	25- 3	Millard(t)Milligan(t)Johnstone(t)Steele(2c2p)
20	(A)	19.04	v Bedford	2620	W	28-14	A Jackson(t)Tarbuck(t)Milligan(t)Steele(2c2pdg)
21	(A)	26.04	v Newcastle	2507	L	20-71	Hunter(t)Stent(t)Lee(tcp)
22	(A)	03.05	v Waterloo	448	L	17-23	Burnell(t)McKenzie(t)Steele(2cp)

1996-97 HIGHLIGHTS

LEAGUE DEBUTS: Graeme Smith, Andy Furley, Steve Griffiths, Chris Tarbuck, Jamie Hamilton, Ed Rayner, Adam Jackson, Colin Morley, Ivan McKenzie, Eddie Jones, Courtney Smith, Matt Kirke, Ken Milligan, Derrick Lee, Garth Wakeford.

TRY ON DEBUT: Andy Furley, Steve Griffiths.

PLAYERS USED: 38

EVER PRESENT: Chris Tarbuck

❏ Scottish international prop Paul Burnell becomes the first London Scottish player to reach 100 league appearances. He ends the season on 105. Dave Millard extends his record for most appearances by a Back to 90(6).

❏ Back row forward Chris Tarbuck tops the try scoring list in his first season with the club. Tarbuck scored seven tries in 22 matches as he became the first forward to top the try scoring list.

❏ Conceded a record 11 tries when suffering their highest score against losing 20-71 at Newcastle.

❏ Achieved their biggest ever away win when beating Rugby 45-16 a 29 point victory.

❏ John Steele passes Nick Grecian's career record of 355 on his way to a new season's best of 256 beating the 140 he scored last season.

	Pts	T	C	P	D	Apps	Ave.
John Steele 95-96	140	4	18	26	2	13	10.77
John Steele 96-97	256	5	39	47	4	18	14.22

Steele topped the points scoring list for a third consecutive year to equal Nick Grecian's feat from the early nineties.

Steele's new career total now stands at 474.

	Pts	T	C	P	D	Apps	Ave.
John Steele	474	9	63	91	10	37	12.81
Nick Grecian	355	23	41	52	1	71	5.00

Steele broke Grecian's career records for conversions, 41, and penalties,52, with 63 and 91 respectively. He also broke Murray Walker's record for career drop goals which stood at nine before Steele made it 10.

❏ Andy Mitchell's long standing record for points in a match, 26 v Northampton in Oct 87, was also broken when yes that man Steele again scored 30 points in the away win at rugby.

❏ Had 27 players score tries second only to Bedford.

LONDON SCOTTISH COURAGE LEAGUE MATCH DETAILS 1996-97

	15	14	13	12	11	10	9	1	2	3	4	5	6	7	8	Replacements	
1	Robinson	G.Smith	Furley	Erikson	Watson	Steele	Kelly	McLellan	McKenzie	Burnell	Griffiths	Hunter	Duthie	Holmes	Tarbuck	D.Jackson(6)	1
2	Robinson	G.Smith	Furley	Erikson	Watson	Steele	Hamilton	Signorini	McGavin	Burnell	Griffiths	Hunter	Duthie	Holmes	Tarbuck	Nesbit(4)	2
3	Robinson	G.Smith	Rayner	Erikson	Wichary	Steele	Hamilton	Signorini	McGivin	Burnell	Nesbit	Hunter	Duthie	Holmes	Tarbuck	Millard(12)	3
4	Robinson	Watson	Rayner	Erikson	Wichary	Steele	Hamilton	McLellan	McKenzie	Burnell	Nesbit	Hunter	Duthie	Holmes	Tarbuck	D.Jackson Tarbuck	4
5	Robinson	Watson	Rayner	Erikson	Wichary	Steele	Signorini	McLellan	McLellan	Burnell	Griffiths	Hunter	Duthie	Holmes	Tarbuck	Hamilton(13)D.Jackson(14)	5
6	Robinson	Watson	Rayner	Erikson	Turner	Steele	Millard	Baird	McLellan	Burnell	Griffiths	A.Jackson	Duthie	Holmes	Tarbuck		6
7	Wichary	Watson	Rayner	Furley	Turner	Stent	Hamilton	Baird	McGavin	Burnell	Griffiths	Hunter	Duthie	Holmes	Tarbuck	Nesbit(4)Millard(13)	7
8	Robinson	Turner	Rayner	Erikson	Wichary	Steele	Baird	Baird	McLellan	Burnell	Hunter	A.Jackson	Duthie	Holmes	Tarbuck	Nesbit(5)	8
9	Robinson	Turner	Erikson	Rayner	Wichary	Steele	Baird	Baird	McLellan	Burnell	Hunter	A.Jackson	Duthie	Holmes	Tarbuck	Morley(12)Nesbit(4)	9
10	Robinson	Turner	Rayner	Sly	Wichary	Steele	Baird	McLellan	Baird	Burnell	Hunter	A.Jackson	Duthie	Jankovich	Tarbuck	Watson(11)	10
11	Robinson	Watson	Erikson	Erikson	Wichary	Steele	Baird	McLellan	Burnell	Hunter	A.Jackson	Duthie	Holmes	Tarbuck	Jankovich(4)Millard(9)Johnstone(1)		11
12	Robinson	C.Smith	Rayner	Thompson	Morley	Steele	Hamilton	Johnstone	McKenzie	Burnell	Hunter	A.Jackson	Duthie	Holmes	Tarbuck	Jankovich(5)	12
13	Robinson	C.Smith	Rayner	Erikson	Morley	Stent	Johnstone	McKenzie	Burnell	Kirke	Jones	Jankovich	Holmes	Tarbuck	Duthie(5)		13
14	Lee	Milligan	Rayner	Erikson	C.Smith	Steele	Johnstone	McKenzie	Burnell	Hunter	Jones	Duthie	Holmes	Tarbuck	Griffiths(5)Morley(14)Jankovich(6)		14
15	Robinson	G.Smith	Rayner	Erikson	Stent	Millard	Johnstone	McKenzie	Burnell	Hunter	Jones	D.Jackson	Jankovich	Tarbuck	Griffiths(7)		15
16	Robinson	G.Smith	Rayner	Erikson	C.Smith	Morley	Kelly	McKenzie	Burnell	Griffiths	Jones	Hunter	Holmes	Tarbuck	Millard(9)Milligan(14)Sly(13)Duthie(5)		16
17	Robinson	Milligan	Sly	Erikson	C.Smith	Steele	Johnstone	McKenzie	Burnell	Jones	Hunter	Duthie	Holmes	Tarbuck	Thompson(12)		17
18	Stent	Milligan	Sly	Thompson	C.Smith	Steele	Johnstone	Kelly	McKenzie	Burnell	Jones	Hunter	Duthie	Holmes	Tarbuck	A.Jackson(4)G.Smith(11)	18
19	Robinson	C.Smith	Sly	Erikson	Milligan	Steele	Johnstone	McKenzie	Burnell	Jones	Hunter	Duthie	Holmes	Tarbuck	Tarbuck		19
20	Robinson	Watson	Sly	Eriksson	Milligan	Millard	Johnstone	McKenzie	Burnell	A.Jackson	Wakeford	Holmes	Tarbuck	Hunter(5)		20
21	Lee	Watson	Sly	Eriksson	Robinson	Stent	Johnstone	McKenzie	Burnell	Jones	Duthie	Jankovich	Tarbuck	Wakeford(7)		21
22	Lee	G.Smith	Sly	Eriksson	Milligan	Steele	Johnstone	McKenzie	Burnell	Jones	Hunter	Tarbuck	Holmes	Wakeford A.Jackson(5)Kelly(3)McLellan(2)		22

LONDON SCOTTISH LEAGUE STATISTICS
(COMPILED BY STEPHEN McCORMACK)

Season	Div.	P	W	D	L	F (Tries Con Pen DG)	A (Tries Con Pen DG)	Most Points	Most Tries
87-88	2	11	4	1	6	141 (18 9 16 1)	158 (20 9 18 2)	38 - Andy Mitchell	4 - Lindsay Renwick
88-89	2	11	3	1	7	146 (15 7 23 1)	160 (15 8 26 2)	49 - Gavin Hastings	3 - Nick Grecian
89-90	3	11	11	0	0	258 (40 22 14 4)	92 (7 2 20 0)	64 - Gavin Hastings	4 - Tim Exeter
90-91	2	12	7	0	5	240 (37 19 15 3)	178 (19 12 24 2)	89 - Nick Grecian	9 - Lindsey Renwick
91-92	2	12	11	0	1	304 (45 23 25 1)	130 (14 4 21 1)	124 - Nick Grecian	11 - Nick Grecian
92-93	1	12	3	1	8	192 (23 10 17 2)	248 (31 15 21 0)	40 - Nick Grecian	4 - Lindsay Renwick
93-94	2	18	6	0	12	232 (17 9 36 7)	325 (30 17 40 7)	81 - Murray Walker	3 - Ronnie Eriksson
94-95	2	18	9	0	9	351 (30 18 44 11)	321 (28 17 45 4)	78 - John Steele	4 - Dave Millard & Fraser Harrold
95-96	2	18	10	2	6	361 (38 24 39 2)	389 (43 24 37 5)	140 - John Steele	5 - Dave Millard
96-97	2	22	11	0	11	549 (58 41 53 6)	568 (63 44 54 1)	256 - John Steele	5 - Chris Tarbuck
Totals		145	75	5	65	2774 (321 182 282 38)	2569 (270 152 306 24)		

	HOME	AWAY
BIGGEST WIN	(47pts) 50-3 v Northampton 3.10.87	(29pts) 45-16 v Rugby 29.3.97
DEFEAT	(40pts) 19-59 v Northampton 27.4.96	(60pts) 6-66 v Coventry 19.10.96
MOST POINTS SCORED	50-3 v Northampton 3.10.87	45-20 v Rugby 31.10.91
		45-16 v Rugby 29.3.97
AGAINST	19-59 v Northampton 27.4.96	20-71 v Newcastle 26.4.97

MOST CONSECUTIVE VICTORIES - 12

MOST TRIES IN A MATCH
(FOR) 7 on 3 occasions
(AGAINST) 11 v Newcastle 26.4.97

CONSECUTIVE APPEARANCES
53 Nick Grecian 10.9.88 - 21.11.92

MOST CONSECUTIVE DEFEATS - 6

MOST APPEARANCES
FORWARD: 106 Paul Burnell
BACK: 90(6) Dave Millard

CONSECUTIVE SCORING MATCHES
Scoring Tries - 6 - Nick Grecian
Scoring Points - 12 - Nick Grecian

MOST	in a SEASON	in a CAREER	in a MATCH
Points	256 John Steele 96-97	474 John Steele 94-97	30 John Steele v Rugby 29.3.97 (A)
Tries	11 Nick Grecian 91-92	23 Lindsey Renwick 87-94 Nick Grecian 88-94	3 Jerry Mackin v Northampton 3.10.87 (H)
Conversions	39 John Steele 96-97	63 John Steele 94-97	5 Andy Mitchell v Northampton 3.10.87 (H) Gavin Hastings v Vale of Lune 23.9.89 (H) Mark Appleson v Rugby 31.10.92 (A)
Penalties	47 John Steele 96-97	91 John Steele 94-97	5 John Steele v Wakefield 17.2.96 (H) v Rugby 7.9.96 (H) v Wakefield 31.3.97 (H)
Drop Goals	5 Murray Walker 93-94	10 John Steele 94-97	3 Murray Walker v Hartlepool 23.4.94 (H)

LONDON SCOTTISH PLAYING SQUAD

NAME	Ht	Wt	Birthdate	Birthplace	Club	Apps	Pts	T	C	P	DG

BACKS

NAME	Ht	Wt	Birthdate	Birthplace	Club	Apps	Pts	T	C	P	DG
Nick Robinson			07.12.68								
					London Scottish	33	30	6	-	-	-
Graeme Smith	6.2	13.6	31.12.75	Paisley	Orrell	13	50	10	-	-	-
					London Scottish	6+1	5	1	-	-	-
Courtney Smith					Saracens	1	5	1	-	-	-
					London Scottish	7	10	2	-	-	-
Andy Furley											
					London Scottish	6	5 -	1	-	-	-
Ken Milligan											
					London Scottish	7+1	10	2	-	-	-
Derrick Lee	5.10	12.8			Previous Clubs: Ayr, Watsonians.						
Scotland: 'A, Students, u21, u18, u15.					London Scottish	3	10	1	1	1	-
Dave Millard	6.1		19.09.64								
					London Scottish	91+6	113	24	-	-	-
John Steele			09.08.64	Cambridge	Northampton	58	425	7	40	95	11
					London Scottish	37	474	9	63	91	10
Mark Sly			12.03.67								
					London Scottish	38+2	19	4	-	-	-
Ronnie Eriksson			22.04.72								
Scotland:					London Scottish	58	58	11	-	-	1
Toby Watson			27.07.72								
					London Scottish	29+1	30	6	-	-	-
Ian Stent			22.12.72	Camberley							
					London Scottish	7+1	42	1	2	10	2
Jamie Hamilton	5.9	12.6	01.07.70	Guildford	Leicester	9+6	5	1	-	-	-
					London Scottish	5+1	5	1	-	-	-

FORWARDS

NAME	Ht	Wt	Birthdate	Birthplace	Club	Apps	Pts	T	C	P	DG
James Kelly			16.02.76								
					London Scottish	5+2	-	-	-	-	-
Jamie Mclellan			12.05.69								
					London Scottish	22+2	5	1	-	-	-
Paul Burnell	6.1	17.2	29.05.65	Edinburgh	Leicester						
Scotland:			British Lions:		London Scottish	106	5	1	-	-	-
Paul Johnson											
					London Scottish	10+1	10	2	-	-	-
Ivan McKenzie					London Irish	1	-	-	-	-	-
					London Scottish	11	5	1	-	-	-
Steve Griffiths											
					London Scottish	6+2	5	1	-	-	-
Rob Hunter			23.05.72								
					London Scottish	22+1	25	5	-	-	-
Max Duthie			22.01.70		Rosslyn Park						
					Sale		-	-	-	-	-
					London Scottish	25+2	30	6	-	-	-
Simon Holmes			12.12.66								
					London Scottish	39	30	6	-	-	-
Chris Tarbuck	6.4	15.7	20.08.69	Harlow	Saracens	44	12	3	-	-	-
					Leicester	16+2	20	4	-	-	-
					London Scottish	22	35	7	-	-	-
Eddie Jones											
					London Scottish	11	-	-	-	-	-
Garth Wakeford											
					London Scottish	2+1	-	-	-	-	-
Adam Jackson											
					London Scottish	8+2	5	1	-	-	-

Richmond Athletic Ground, Richmond, Surrey. TW9 2SS

TELEPHONE: 0181 332 2473   Fax: 0181 948 6183

CAPACITY: 5,000   **SEATED:** 850   **STANDING (uncovered):** 4,150

SIMPLE DIRECTIONS:
By Road: The ground is situated on the A316, about 100 yards from Richmond Circus, heading towards Twickenham.
Nearest Railway Station: Richmond (BR & Underground). Turn right out of the station & walk for about 150 yards to traffic lights. Turn right and the ground is facing you.

CAR PARKING: 200 parking spaces available at the ground with a public car park close by.

ADMISSION: Season Ticket: Adult - Seated £85 Standing £70
                        Match Day: Seated - Adult £10, Children/OAPs £6.   Standing - Adult £8, Children/OAPs £4

CLUB SHOP: Yes. Contact Angus Stewart at the club.

CLUBHOUSE: Open match days and evenings. Has two bars and bar meals are available.
Function room: Yes available for hire, capacity 250

TRAINING NIGHTS: Mondays & Wednesdays

London Scottish's Paul Burnell, Scotland & British Lions, continues as Club Captain for 1997/98
Photo - Sporting Pictures (UK) Ltd

MATCHDAY PROGRAMME

Size	A5
Number of pages	28
Price	£2.00
Programme Editor	David McGavin
	0181 332 2473
Advertising Rates	Colour Full page £1000
	1/2 page £650
	Mono Full page £750
	1/2 page £450

MOSELEY F.C.

NICKNAME: Mose   **FOUNDED:** 1873

President Peter Woodroofe, c/o Moseley FC, The Reddings, Reddings Road, Moseley, Birmingham B13 8LW.
0121 449 2149 (B), 0121 442 4147 (Fax)

Chairman Peter Veitch, c/o Moseley FC, as above 0121 449 2149 (B), 0121 442 4147 (Fax)

Club Secretary Mrs. J Thomas, c/o Moseley FC, as above
0121 449 3293 (H), 0121 449 2149 (B), 0121 442 4147 (Fax)

General Manager David Coleman, c/o Moseley FC, as above 0121 449 2149 (B), 0121 442 4147 (Fax)

Director of Rugby Allan Lewis, c/o Moseley FC, as above 0121 449 2149 (B), 0121 442 4147 (Fax)

Press Officer David Coleman, c/o Moseley FC, as above 0121 449 2149 (B), 0121 442 4147 (Fax)

Commercial Manager Mark Sheasby, c/o Moseley FC, as above 0121 449 2149 (B), 0121 442 4147 (Fax)

Colts Co-ordinator Tom Campbell, c/o Moseley FC, as above 0121 449 2149 (B), 0121 442 4147 (Fax)

Moseley's first season of professional rugby was definitely one of two halves. In the first round of league matches played before Christmas, the Reddings Road outfit only managed one win against Nottingham. The almost total transformation of the side after Christmas saw Moseley win eight out of the eleven league fixtures to finish eighth in the table. This remarkable transformation was brought about by the arrival of internationals Darragh O'Mahony, Henry Hurley and Alain Rolland from Ireland, Al Charron and Kevin Whitley from Canada and Scotland's Ian Smith. The former Wales and Llanelli assistant coach Allan Lewis was appointed director of rugby in January and under his tutorage the side began to gel into one of the form sides in the division.

Canadian No 8 Al Charron and Scottish flanker Ian Smith provided an experienced back row whilst the Irishman Darragh O'Mahony proved to be one of the most deadly finishers in the Second Division scoring fifteen league tries and 25 in all. Fly-half Richard Le Bas topped the scoring with 177 league points.

The arrival of experienced international players brought out the best in many of the younger members of the squad. Centre Dan Harris was selected for the England under-21 tour to Australia and flanker James Cockle was named in the training squad. In fact the side that played so well in the second round of the league contained six players who were 22 or under.

If Moseley start the season as they finished, the Birmingham club will be genuine promotion contenders.

Moseley FC: Back Row (L-R); Stuart Nottingham (Physio), Andy Binns, James Cockle, Robin Poll, Al Charron, Kevin Whitley, Neil Mitchell, Mike Ord, Martin Ridge, Rod Martin, Norm Wainwright (Sec), Allan Lewis (Dir of Rugby). Seated; Denley Isaacs (Coach), Darragh O'Mahony, Stu Mackinnon, Nathan Webber, Peter Woodroofe (President), Andy Houston, Peter Veitch (Chairman), Richard Denhardt, Damien Geraghty, Henry Hurley, Paul White (Chairman of Rugby). Front Row; Richard Le Bas, Richard Turner, Carl Hall, Dan Harris

Colours: Red & black hoops.   **Change colours:** Light grey & navy blue hoops.

MOSELEY

No	Ven.	Date	Opponents	Att.	Res.	Score	Scorers
1	(H)	07.09	v Wakefield	657	L	17-30	Houston(t)Dossett(4p)
2	(A)	14.09	v Waterloo	500	L	13-20	Johal(t)Quick(c2p)
3	(H)	21.09	v Nottingham	883	W	34-22	McKinnon(2t)Harris(t)Wilkinson(t)Birch(t)Dossett(3cp)
4	(A)	28.09	v Blackheath	1724	L	3-28	Dossett(p)
5	(H)	05.10	v Richmond	1612	L	15-87	McKinnon(t)Poll(t)Birch(cp)
6	(A)	12.10	v Rugby	530	L	22-29	Batey(t)Faiva(t)McKinnon(t)Birch(2cp)
7	(H)	19.10	v Newcastle	2003	L	9-75	Quick(3p)
8	(A)	26.10	v London Scot	1110	L	10-42	Wilkinson(t)Le Bas(cp)
9	(A)	02.11	v Bedford	2226	L	9-64	Le Bas(3p)
10	(H)	09.11	v Coventry	1720	L	19-35	Harris(t)Dossett(dg)Le Bas(c3p)
11	(A)	16.11	v Rotherham	1050	L	9-18	Le Bas(3p)
12	(H)	18.01	v Blackheath	533	W	21-18	Ridge(t)O'Mahoney(t)Le Bas(c3p)
13	(A)	02.02	v Nottingham	463	W	22-11	O'Mahoney(3t)Le Bas(2cp)
14	(A)	08.02	v Richmond	800	L	27-37	O'Mahoney(2t)Charron(t)Le Bas(3c2p)
15	(H)	22.03	v Waterloo	702	W	17-13	O'Mahoney(t)La Bas(4p)
16	(H)	08.03	v Rugby	477	W	34-11	O'Mahoney(2t)Jones(t)Denhardt(t)Le Bas(c4p)
17	(A)	22.03	v Newcastle	1690	L	19-88	Hall(t)Turner(t)PenTry(t)Stuart(2c)
18	(A)	29.03	v Wakefield	800	W	42-13	O'Mahoney(2t)Martin(t)Ridge(t)Le Bas(t4c3p)
19	(H)	05.04	v London Scot	802	W	44-16	O'Mahoney(2t)Binns(t)Harris(t)Smith(t)Le Bas(t4c2p)
20	(H)	12.04	v Bedford	1216	W	40-34	O'Mahoney(t)Binns(t)Harris(t)Turner(t)Le Bas(t3c3p)
21	(A)	19.04	v Coventry	3500	L	18-33	Binns(t)Cockle(t)Le Bas(c2p)
22	(H)	26.04	v Rotherham	916	W	48-17	Charron(2t)O'Mahoney(t)Mitchell(t)Martin(t)Hall(t)Le Bas(6c2p)

1996-97 HIGHLIGHTS

LEAGUE DEBUTS: Craig Quick, Stuart Langley, Carl Hall, Manu Faiva, Jim Withers, Robin Poll, Jason John, Dan Harris, Michael Brookes, Tim Robinson, Gavin Batey, Martin Ridge, Henry Hurley, Richard Le Bas, Andy Freke, Dominic O'Mahoney, Alain Rolland, John Ellis, Damian Geraghty, Kevin Whitley, Al Charron, Andy Binns, James Cockle, Richard Turner, Ian Smith, Bill Fuller.

TRY ON DEBUT: Dan Harris, Richard Turner
and Gavin Batey.

PLAYERS USED: 46 plus as replacement.

EVER PRESENT: None - most appearances 18
- Nathan Webber and Dan Harris.

❏ Suffered their worst ever home defeat when losing 87-15 to Richmond. Their previous worst defeat was 43-19 v Leicester in April 91.

❏ Suffered their worst ever away defeat losing 88-19 at Newcastle. Their previous worst defeat was 50-7 at Northampton in September 95.

❏ Lost a club record 8 consecutive games one than the previous record of seven.

❏ If ever we had a game of two halfs it was Moseley's season. In the first half they lost 10 out of the 11 games whilst in the second half they won 8 out of 11.

❏ Two players dominated Moseley's season - Irish winger Domonic O'Mahoney and New Zealand stand-off Richard LeBas.
O'Mahoney made a dramatic start to his career in English rugby with 15 tries in just 11 games for a new record for tries in a season. It destroyed the previous record of seven set last season by Alastair Kerr. He scored tries in five consecutive games which was also a record beating the three of Peter Shillingford and Simon Purdy.

❏ The other star of the show LeBas helped himself to a new club record for points in a season beating Alastair Kerr's record from last season 177 to 172.

	Pts	T	C	P	D	Apps	Ave.
Richard LeBas	177	3	27	36	-	14	12.64
Alastair Kerr	172	7	13	36	2	15	11.47

In the process of his record LeBas breaks Kerr's record of 13 conversions more tham doubling it to 27.

❏ LeBas failed by one to equal Carl Arntzen's record of scoring 11 consecutive matches.

❏ Only scored tries in 18 matches only Nottingham with 16 had a worse record.

MOSELEY'S COURAGE LEAGUE MATCH DETAILS 1996-97

#	15	14	13	12	11	10	9	1	2	3	4	5	6	7	8	Replacements
1	Quick	Bonney	Hall	S Langley	Dossett	Houston	Faiva	McKinnon	Doyle	Webber	B Langley	Watson	Johal	Ord	Withers	
2	Quick	Bonney	Hall	S Langley	Dossett	Houston	Faiva	McKinnon	Doyle	Webber	B Langley	Watson	Johal	Ord	Poll	Chudleigh(9)
3	Dossett	John	Bonney	Harris	Wilkinson	Birch	Chudleigh	McKinnon	Ball	Webber	B Langley	Watson	Ord	Poll	Brookes	
4	Dossett	John	Bonney	Harris	Wilkinson	Birch	Chudleigh	McKinnon	Ball	Webber	B Langley	Watson	Johal	Poll	Brookes	
5	Robinson	John	Hall	Harris	Wilkinson	Birch	Faiva	McKinnon	Doyle	Webber	Denhardt	Watson	Poll	Ord	B Langley	
6	Robinson	John	Harris	S Langley	Birch	Faiva	Williams	Ball	McKinnon	Denhardt	Watson		Johal	Ord	B Langley	Dossett(11)
7	Quick	John	Ridge	Bonney	Wilkinson	Houston	Faiva	Hurley	Ball	McKinnon	Denhardt	Watson	Johal	Ord	Poll	Dossett(15)/B Langley(8)
8	Quick	John	Ridge	Bonney	Wilkinson	Houston	Faiva	Hurley	Ball	McKinnon	Denhardt	Watson	Brookes	Ord	B Langley	
9	Dossett	John	Bonney	Harris	Wilkinson	Le Bas	Chudleigh	Doyle	Webber	Denhardt	Watson	Brookes	Ord	Poll	B Langley	Williams(1)
10	Dossett	Wilkinson	Ridge	Harris	O'Mahoney	Le Bas	Chudleigh	Doyle	Webber	Denhardt	Watson	Brookes	Johal	Ord	Denhardt	Ball(2)/Bonney(12)
11	Dossett	John	Ridge	Harris	O'Mahoney	Le Bas	Rolland	Hurley	Ball	Webber	N Mitchell	Watson	Johal	Denhardt	Denhardt	
12	S Langley	Harris	Ridge	Stuart	O'Mahoney	Le Bas	Ellis	Geraghty	McKinnon	Denhardt	Whitley	N Mitchell	Ord	Charron	Wilkinson(12)	
13	S Langley	Harris	Ridge	Hall	O'Mahoney	Le Bas	Hurley	Ball	Webber	Denhardt	Whitley	N Mitchell	Ord	Cockle	Charron	Binns(15)
14	Binns	Wilkinson	Ridge	Harris	O'Mahoney	Le Bas	Hurley	Ball	Webber	Denhardt	Whitley	N Mitchell	Johal	Cockle	Charron	A Mitchell(1)
15	Binns	Martin	Ridge	Harris	O'Mahoney	Le Bas	Rolland	Ball	Webber	Denhardt	Whitley	N Mitchell	Johal	Cockle	Charron	
16	Binns	Martin	Ridge	Harris	O'Mahoney	Le Bas	Rolland	Hurley	Geraghty	Webber	Denhardt	N Mitchell	Johal	Smith	Charron	Turner(10)/Ord(7)/Jones(15)/McKinnon(1)
17	Martin	Stuart	Hall	O'Mahoney	Binns	Turner	Hurley	Fidler	Webber	Denhardt	N Mitchell	Cockle	Ord	Charron		Johal(6)/McKinnon(1)
18	Binns	Martin	Ridge	Harris	O'Mahoney	Le Bas	Turner	Hurley	Geraghty	Webber	Denhardt	N Mitchell	Cockle	Smith	Charron	Whitley(4)
19	Binns	Martin	Ridge	Harris	O'Mahoney	Le Bas	Turner	Hurley	Geraghty	Webber	Denhardt	N Mitchell	Cockle	Smith	Charron	Charron
20	Binns	Martin	Ridge	Harris	O'Mahoney	Le Bas	Turner	Hurley	Geraghty	Webber	Denhardt	N Mitchell	Cockle	Smith	Charron	
21	Binns	Martin	Ridge	Ridge	O'Mahoney	Le Bas	Turner	Hurley	Geraghty	Webber	Denhardt	Mitchell	Cockle	Smith	Charron	
22	Binns	Martin	Hall	Harris	O'Mahoney	Le Bas	Turner	Hurley	Geraghty	Webber	Denhardt	N Mitchell	Cockle	Smith	Charron	Rolland(9)/Ball(2)/Poll(8)/Jones(13)

MOSELEY LEAGUE STATISTICS

(COMPILED BY STEPHEN McCORMACK)

Season	Div.	P	W	D	L	F (Tries Con Pen DG)	A (Tries Con Pen DG)	Most Points	Most Tries
87-88	1	11	5	0	6	167 (25 8 17 0)	170 (22 14 17 1)	48 - John Gordon	8 - Peter Shillingford
88-89	1	11	3	0	8	113 (13 8 14 1)	242 (34 20 20 2)	46 - Carl Arntzen	4 - Peter Shillingford
89-90	1	11	2	0	9	138 (20 8 14 0)	258 (37 28 17 1)	52 - Carl Arntzen	6 - Simon Robson
90-91	1	12	1	1	10	113 (12 7 15 2)	244 (34 18 21 3)	68 - Carl Arntzen	2 - by 3 players Carl Arntzen, Graham Smith & Laurence Boyle
91-92	2	12	6	0	6	215 (31 14 18 3)	196 (25 9 25 1)	62 - Alastair Kerr	6 - Dave Spiller
92-93	2	12	6	2	4	184 (19 7 22 3)	150 (8 23 5 0)	40 - Bob Massey	3 - Nick Parry & Bob Massey
93-94	2	18	9	1	8	266 (23 14 40 1)	220 (21 10 32 1)	83 - Simon Hodgkinson	5 - Mark Linnett
94-95	2	18	8	1	9	299 (20 14 54 3)	303 (33 15 32 4)	156 - Simon Hodgkinson	2 - by 6 players
95-96	2	18	7	0	11	327 (29 16 43 7)	447 (53 31 37 3)	172 - Alastair Kerr	7 - Alastair Kerr
96-97	2	22	9	0	13	492 (54 36 49 1)	741 (104 58 33 2)	177 - Richard Le Bas	Dominic O'Mahoney
Totals		145	56	5	84	2314 (246 132 286 21)	2971 (273 211 257 23)		

HOME

BIGGEST WIN	(32pts) 47-15 v Sale 4.4.92
DEFEAT	(72pts) 15-87 v Richmond 5.10.96
MOST POINTS SCORED	48-17 v Rotherham 26.4.97
AGAINST	15-87 v Richmond 5.10.96

MOST CONSECUTIVE VICTORIES - 5

MOST TRIES IN A MATCH
(FOR) 9 v Sale 4.4.92
(AGAINST) 14 v Richmond 5.10.96 (H)
v Newcastle 22.3.97 (A)

CONSECUTIVE APPEARANCES
32 Mark Linnett 3.11.92 - 1.10.94

AWAY

	(29pts) 42-13 v Wakefield 29.03.97
	(69pts) 19-88 v Newcastle 22.03.97
	42-13 v Wakefield 29.03.97
	19-88 v Newcastle 22.3.97

MOST CONSECUTIVE DEFEATS - 8

MOST APPEARANCES
FORWARD: 84 Mark Linnett
BACK: 63 Alastair Kerr

CONSECUTIVE SCORING MATCHES
Scoring Tries - 5 - Dominic O'Mahoney
Scoring Points - 11 - Carl Arntzen

MOST	in a SEASON	in a CAREER	in a MATCH
Points	177 Richard Le Bas 96-97	364 Alastair Kerr 91-96	27 Simon Hodgkinson v L. Irish 8.4.95 (H)
Tries	15 Dominic O'Mahoney 96-97	20 Peter Shillingford 87-94	3 Peter Shillingford v Wasps 5.2.88 (H) Dave Spiller v Sale 4.4.92 (H) Dominic O'Mahoney v Nottinghamn 2.2.97 (A)
Conversions	27 Richard Le Bas 96-97	38 Alastair Kerr 91-96	6 Richard Le Bas v Rotherham 26.4.97 (H)
Penalties	41 Simon Hodgkinson 94-95	61 Alastair Kerr 91-96	8 Alastair Kerr v Waterloo 17.2.96 (H)
Drop Goals	3 Simon Hodgkinson 94-95	5 Alastair Kerr 91-96	2 Alastair Kerr v Plymouth 21.12.92 (H) A. Houston v Blackheath 14.11.95

MOSELEY PLAYING SQUAD

NAME	Ht	Wt	Birthdate	Birthplace	Club	Apps	Pts	T	C	P	DG

BACKS

NAME	Ht	Wt	Birthdate	Birthplace	Club	Apps	Pts	T	C	P	DG
Andy Binns	5.10	13.0	29.06.76	Yorkshire							
					Moseley	9+1	15	3	-	-	-
Domonic O'Mahoney	5.9	11.0	18.02.72	Cork							
Ireland: 2, A.					Moseley	13	75	15	-	-	-
Carl Hall	5.10	14.7	10.08.69	Auckland (NZ)	Leeds (RL)						
Fiji (RL).					Moseley	5	10	2	-	-	-
Martin Ridge											
					Moseley	13	10	2	-	-	-
Dan Harris	5.10	13.12	17.05.77	High Wycombe							
England: u21, Schools.					Moseley	18	20	4	-	-	-
Richard Le Bas											
					Moseley	14	177	3	27	36	-
Rod Martin	6.0	14.0	25.11.75	Southend							
					Moseley	8	10	2	-	-	-
Richard Turner	5.7	10.0	06.03.71	Hereford	Hereford						
					Moseley	6+1	10	2	-	-	-
Rob Stuart	5.11	13.0	19.09.72	Devizes	Bath						
Scotland: u21, Exiles.					Moseley	5	4	-	2	-	-
Alain Rolland											
					Moseley	6+1	-	-	-	-	-
David Wilkinson											
					Moseley	9+1	10	2	-	-	-
Andrew Dart	5.9	10.8	25.07.76	Taunton	Exeter	1+1	-	-	-	-	-
					Moseley	-	-	-	-	-	-
Steve Hackney	5.11	13.7	13.06.68	Stockton	Nottingham	25	8	2	-	-	-
					Leicester	77	121	25	-	-	-
					Moseley	-	-	-	-	-	-

FORWARDS

NAME	Ht	Wt	Birthdate	Birthplace	Club	Apps	Pts	T	C	P	DG
Henry Hurley					Old Wesley						
					Moseley	12	-	-	-	-	-
Nathan Webber	6.1	16.8	20.06.74	Stratford-on-Avon							
England: A, u21.					Moseley	53	-	-	-	-	-
Damian Geraghty	5.11	14.0	29.03.68	Wellington(NZ)							
Wellington					Moseley	9+1	-	-	-	-	-
Rob Denhardt	6.5	17.0	13.09.67	Birmingham							
England: Colts.					Moseley	40	-	-	-	-	-
Neil Mitchell	6.7	18.5	22.06.66	Newcastle							
England: Colts					Moseley	8	5	1	-	-	-
James Cockle	6.3	16.6									
England: u18.					Moseley	9	5	1	-	-	-
Al Charron	6.6	17.7	27.07.66	Ottawa							
Canada: 34					Moseley	11	15	3	-	-	-
Rubin Poll	6.4	16.0	16.02.74	Shrewsbury							
England: u21.					Moseley	23+2	15	3	-	-	-
Dean Ball	5.7	14.10	24.07.71								
					Moseley	59+2	5	1	-	-	-
Ian Smith	6.0	13.10	16.03.66	Gloucester	Gloucester	108	25	6	-	-	-
Scotland: 23, A.	England: B.				Moseley	7	5	1	-	-	-
Jag Johal	5.10	16.10	19.07.74								
					Moseley	19+3	10	2	-	-	-
Stuart McKinnon	6.0	17.7	06.01.69	Kuala Lumpar							
					Moseley	14+2	20	4	-	-	-
Kevin Whiteley	6.6	17.0	12.08.69	Brunei							
Canada: 1, A, u21.					Moseley	4+1	-	-	-	-	-

The Reddings, Reddings Road, Moseley, Birmingham. B13 8LW.

CAPACITY: 5,041   **SEATED Covered:** 665 **Uncovered:** 376   **STANDING:** 4,000

SIMPLE DIRECTIONS:
   By Road: A 38 South of Birmingham to Edgbaston Road, turn at traffic lights passing Edgbaston County Cricket ground on left, to traffic island, right into Russell Rd, left into Moorcroft Rd, left into Reddings Rd
   Nearest Railway Station: Birmingham New Street, then Bus no 50

CAR PARKING: 150 at ground, 400 nearby

ADMISSION: Season £ 70, Oap's £ 50; Matches £ 10, Oap's £7, Juniors 7-14 Free

CLUB SHOP: Yes; Manager David Ireland 0121 745 6007

CLUBHOUSE: Normal Licensing hours, Three bars with snacks, bar meals & dining room
   Function room: Yes available for hire, capacity 200 Contact Terry Hazlewood 0121 442 2095

TRAINING NIGHTS: Tuesday & Thursday

Captain; Ian Smith

Leading Try Scorer; Darragh O'Mahoney

MATCHDAY PROGRAMME

Size	B5
Number of pages	22
Price	£2 part of entry
Programme Editor	David Coleman

Advertising Rates
          Contact - Mark Sheasby Commercial Mgr

ORRELL R.U.F.C.

FOUNDED: 1927

President Des Seabrook, c/o Orrell RUFC, Edge Hall Road, Orrell, Nr Wigan WN5 8TL.

Chairman Ron Pimblett, c/o Orrell RUFC, as above

Club Secretary John Arrowsmith, 1 Fisher Drive, Orrell, Wigan, Lancs. WN5 8QX
01942 216879 (H), 01695 632116 (Fax)

Fixtures Secretary c/o Orrell RUFC, as above

Press Officer Geoff Lightfoot, 38 Coultshead Avenue, Billinge, Wigan WN5 7HT.
01744 603199/636689 (H & B), 01744 603199 (Fax)

Director of Commercial Affairs Ken Stringer, 01695 632114, 01695 632116 (Fax).

Director of Coaching Ged Glynn, 01695 623193

For an ever present in the First Division, relegation as far as Orrell were concerned was always something that happened to others. Unfortunately, all that has now changed and the Lancashire club is having to prepare for life in the Second Division as from next term. Having made a concious decision at the beginning of the season that they were not going to spend money they had not got and, by steadfastly refusing to chase the big spending monied outfits, the club was faced with the mass exodus of most of their first team squad. However, with the appointment of Peter Williams as director of rugby a number of very talented, albeit young, players were recruited and the former All Black and rugby league international Frano Botica together with Great Britain Rugby League international David Lyon were brought in to cement the side together.

The loss of Botica to Llanelli was a major blow and with the New Zealander in the Valleys the side was without its lynch pin and, despite the obvious quality of some of the youngsters, the lack of experience and their need for leadership was all too often cruelly exposed. Yet, despite these setbacks, the team now under the leadership of David Lyon refused to throw in the towel and continued to battle through to the end.

There is little doubt that many of the younger players have 'come of age' this season and there is the nucleus of a side well capable of bouncing back. With Peter Williams' departure, an early victim of the professional age, the club wasted no time in appointing the Rotherham and Cambridge coach Ged Glynn to take this task forward. There will obviously be a period of regrouping and retrenchment but optimism is high that it will not be too long before Edge Hall Road is once again back on most of the top clubs itineraries.

GEOFF LIGHTFOOT

Orrell's Captain, David Lyon

Colours: Black & amber

Change colours: Red, black, amber

ORRELL

No	Ven.	Date	Opponents	Att.	Res.	Score	Scorers
1	(H)	31.08	v Bath	3000	L	13-56	Tuigamala(t)Heslop(t)Botica(p)
2	(A)	07.09	v Bristol	2996	L	10-38	Anglesea(t)Botica(cp)
3	(H)	14.09	v Leicester	2300	L	12-29	Naylor(t)Saveriamutto(t)Botica(c)
4	(A)	21.09	v Northampton	4474	L	7-41	Tuigamala(tc)
5	(H)	28.09	v Wasps	2000	L	27-41	Lyon(t)Heslop(t)Bennett(t)Naylor(t)Strett(2cp)
6	(A)	05.10	v Harlequins	3335	L	18-89	Cook(t)Anglesea(t)Strett(c2p)
7	(A)	09.11	v Sale	2204	L	11-37	Nelson(t)Hitchmough(2p)
8	(H)	16.11	v Gloucester	1800	L	3-49	Hitchmough(p)
9	(H)	07.12	v W Hartlepool	1800	W	22-15	Cook(t)McCarthy(c2p3dg)
10	(A)	11.01	v W Hartlepool	1123	L	8-24	Hitchmough(t)McCarthy(p)
11	(H)	18.01	v Sale	2500	L	8-40	Worsley(t)McCarthy(p)
12	(A)	08.02	v Gloucester	4464	L	0-30	
13	(H)	22.02	v London Irish	1200	W	32-27	Tuigamala(t)Naylor(t)McCarthy(2c6p)
14	(A)	04.03	v Saracens	1796	L	15-24	Naylor(t)Higgs(t)McCarthy(cp)
15	(H)	08.03	v Harlequins	2360	L	20-56	Taberner(t)McCarthy(t2c2p)
16	(A)	22.03	v Wasps	1000	L	5-62	Heslop(t)
17	(H)	29.03	v Northampton	1100	L	14-50	Bennett(t)McCarthy(2pdg)
18	(A)	05.04	v Leicester	9022	L	14-36	Cook)t)PenTry(t)McCarthy(2c)
19	(H)	12.04	v Bristol	1500	L	27-28	Hitchmough(2t)Anglesea(t)Rees(t)McCarthy(2cp)
20	(A)	19.04	v Bath	6100	L	14-40	Lyon(t)Hope(t)Hitchmough(2c)
21	(H)	26.04	v Saracens	1200	L	22-44	Anglesea(t)Turner(t)McCarthy(t2cp)
22	(A)	03.05	v London Irish	2500	W	48-27	Bennett(2t)Lyon(2t)Hitchmough(t)Naylor(t)McCarthy(6c2p)

1996-97 HIGHLIGHTS

LEAGUE DEBUTS: Rob Hitchmough, David Lyon, Frano Botica, Steve Cook, Michael Worsley, Stuart Turner, Robin Saveriamutto, Paul Ledson, Paul Clayton, John Seabrook, Jason Smith, Neil Gregory, Richard Higgs, Richard Nelson, Matthew McCarthy, Willie Munro, Paul Newton, Guy Hope.

TRY ON DEBUT: Guy Hope, Richard Nelson, Robin Saveriamutto.

PLAYERS USED: 38 plus 2 as replacement.

EVER PRESENT: Lua Tuigamala

❏ Lost a club record 11 consecutive league games - never previosly lost more than four.

❏ Became the first club to concede 100 tries in a division one sesson.

❏ They did the double over London Irish.

❏ Only 17 players scored tries - the lowest total in the division.

❏ Conceded a division one record 886 points.

❏ After making his debut mid-season Matthew McCarthy went on to score 116 points in 14 matches. That put him second behind Simon Mason for points in a season.

	Pts	T	C	P	D	Apps	Ave.
Mason 95-96	166	4	16	38	-	16	10.38
McCarthy 96-97	116	2	18	19	4	14	8.28

McCarthy broke the record for drop goals in a game when he dropped three in Orrell's first win of the season which was also his debut. Three also equalled the first division record.

❏ Martin Strett on his return from Rugby League regained the club all-time points scoring record from Gerry Ainscough.

	Pts	T	C	P	D	Apps	Ave.
Martin Strett	338	6	46	70	4	42	8.05
Gerry Ainscough	337	12	34	71	2	66	5.10

❏ Another player who returned from Rugby League was Nigel Heslop . He passed Phil Halsall and moved into second place on the club's all-time try scorers list behind Dewi Morris

	Tries	Apps	Try Every
Dewi Morris	24	62	2.58 games
Nigel Heslop	21	59	2.81 games
Phil Halsall	19	59	3.10 games

ORRELL'S COURAGE LEAGUE MATCH DETAILS 1996-97

Match	15	14	13	12	11	10	9	1	2	3	4	5	6	7	8	Replacements
1	Hitchmough	Naylor	Lyon	Tuigamala	Heslop	Botica	Cook	Worsley	Moffatt	Turner	Cusani	O'Neill	Bennett	Huxley	McFarlane	Hanson(1)
2	Hitchmough	Naylor	Lyon	Tuigamala	Heslop	Botica	Cook	Cundick	Scott	Turner	Cusani	O'Neill	Anglesea	McFarlane	McFarlane	
3	Hitchmough	Naylor	Lyon	Tuigamala	Heslop	Botica	Cook	Cundick	Scott	Turner	Cusani	Rees	Anglesea	Huxley	McFarlane	Ledson(1)Saveriamutto(10)
4	Taberner	Naylor	Lyon	Tuigamala	Heslop	Hitchmough/Cook	Cook	Ledson	Scott	Turner	Cusani	Rees	Anglesea	Clayton	McFarlane	Huxley(8)
5	Hitchmough	Naylor	Lyon	Tuigamala	Heslop	Strett	Cook	Worsley	Scott	Turner	O'Neill	Rees	Anglesea	Huxley	Bennett	McFarlane(6)
6	Hitchmough	Naylor	Lyon	Tuigamala	Smith	Strett	Cook	Worsley	Scott	Turner	O'Neill	Rees	Anglesea	Gregory	Bennett	
7	Hitchmough	Clayton	Seabrook	Tuigamala	Heslop	Taberner	Cook	Worsley	Moffatt	Turner	Cusani	Rees	Anglesea	Higgs	Nelson	Saveriamutto(10)
8	Hitchmough	Clayton	Lyon	Tuigamala	Heslop	Taberner	Cook	Worsley	Scott	Turner	Cusani	Rees	Wood	Nelson	Horrocks(11)	
9	Taberner	Hamer	Lyon	Tuigamala	Heslop	Taberner	Cook	Worsley	Moffatt	Turner	Brierley	Rees	Anglesea	Higgs	Nelson	Bennett(8)Hitchmough(11)
10	Taberner	Naylor	Lyon	Tuigamala	Heslop	McCarthy	Cook	Worsley	Moffatt	Turner	Cusani	Rees	Bennett	Higgs	Anglesea	Brierley(5)Hitchmough(15)
11	Taberner	Naylor	Lyon	Tuigamala	Heslop	McCarthy	Cook	Worsley	Moffatt	Turner	Cusani	Rees	Bennett	Higgs	Anglesea	Hitchmough(11)
12	Taberner	Naylor	Lyon	Tuigamala	Hitchmough	McCarthy	Cook	Cundick	Scott	Turner	Cusani	Rees	Anglesea	Higgs	Huxley	Rees(tr6)
13	Taberner	Naylor	Lyon	Tuigamala	Hitchmough	McCarthy	Cook	Worsley	Scott	Turner	Cusani	Brierley	Anglesea	Higgs	Huxley	Bennett(5)
14	Munro	Naylor	Lyon	Tuigamala	Hamer	McCarthy	Cook	Worsley	Hitchin	Turner	Cusani	Rees	Anglesea	Higgs	Huxley	Ledson(1)Horrocks(11)Brierley(5)Rawlinson(2)
15	Taberner	Naylor	Lyon	Tuigamala	Hitchmough	McCarthy	Newton	Cundick	Hitchin	Turner	Cusani	Rees	Anglesea	Higgs	Huxley	Bennett(8)Wood(6)Rawlinson(2)
16	Taberner	Naylor	Lyon	Tuigamala	Heslop	McCarthy	Cook	Worsley	Hitchin	Turner	Cusani	Rees	Anglesea	Higgs	Bennett	Moffatt(2)Munro(15)Hamer(12)Brierley(5)
17	Lyon	Naylor	Hamer	Tuigamala	Heslop	McCarthy	Cook	Worsley	Moffatt	Turner	Cusani	Rees	Wood	Higgs	Bennett	Hitchin(15)Anglesea(4)
18	Lyon	Naylor	Hamer	Tuigamala	Heslop	McCarthy	Cook	Worsley	Hitchin	Turner	Brierley	Rees	Bennett	Higgs	Anglesea	Hitchmough(15)Moffatt(2)Huxley(4)Saveriamutto(9)
19	Lyon	Naylor	Hamer	Tuigamala	Hitchmough	McCarthy	Cook	Worsley	Hitchin	Turner	Brierley	Rees	Bennett	Higgs	Anglesea	Moffatt(2)Cusani(4)Taberner(15)
20	Lyon	Naylor	Hope	Tuigamala	Hitchmough	McCarthy	Cook	Saveriamutto	Worsley	Turner	Cusani	Rees	Bennett	Higgs	Anglesea	Cook(9)Horrocks(11)Cundick(3)Brierley(5)
21	Taberner	Naylor	Hope	Tuigamala	Hitchmough	McCarthy	Cook	Saveriamutto	Worsley	Turner	Cusani	Rees	Bennett	Higgs	Anglesea	Moffatt(2)Turner(3)Horrocks(12)
22	Lyon	Naylor	Horrocks	Tuigamala	Hitchmough	McCarthy	Saveriamutto	Worsley	Moffatt	Turner	Cusani	Rees	Anglesea	Higgs	Bennett	Cundick(1)Rawlinson(1)

ORRELL LEAGUE STATISTICS
(COMPILED BY STEPHEN McCORMACK)

Season	Div.	P	W	D	L	F	(Tries	Con	Pen	DG)	A	(Tries	Con	Pen	DG)	Most Points	Most Tries
87-88	1	11	5	1	5	192	(24	12	24	0)	153	(17	5	23	2)	72 - Gerry Ainscough	6 - Gerry Ainscough
88-89	1	11	6	1	4	148	(13	9	24	2)	157	(14	7	27	2)	54 - Gerry Ainscough	3 - Nigel Heslop
89-90	1	11	5	0	6	221	(28	17	25	0)	132	(9	3	28	2)	104 - Martin Strett	5 - Paul Manley & Nigel Heslop
90-91	1	12	7	0	5	247	(34	21	21	2)	105	(12	6	14	1)	109 - Martin Strett	7 - Phil Halsall & Dewi Morris
91-92	1	12	10	0	2	204	(26	8	26	2)	95	(8	2	17	2)	104 Martin Strett	7 - Dewi Morris
92-93	1	12	5	0	7	175	(20	6	21	0)	183	(19	11	22	0)	63 - Gerry Ainscough	6 - Dewi Morris
93-94	1	18	8	0	10	327	(36	24	33	0)	302	(25	16	43	4)	84 - Simon Langford	8 - James Naylor
94-95	1	18	6	3	9	256	(23	9	38	3)	326	(30	19	44	2)	81 - Simon Langford	7 - Ian Wynn
95-96	1	18	7	0	11	323	(33	19	39	1)	477	(56	37	35	6)	166 - Simon Mason	10 - Graeme Smith
96-97	1	22	3	0	19	352	(41	26	27	4)	886	(125	69	40	1)	116 - Michael McCarthy	5 - Jim Naylor
Totals		145	62	5	78	2445	(278	151	278	14)	2816	(315	178	293	22)		

HOME

BIGGEST WIN (66pts) 66-0 v Rugby 13.3.93
BIGGEST DEFEAT (43pts) 13-56 v Bath 31.08.96
MOST POINTS SCORED 66-0 v Rugby 13.3.93
AGAINST 13-56 v Bath 31.08.96
20-56 v Harlequins 8.3.97

AWAY

(33pts) 36-3 v Bristol 17.11.90
(71pts) 18-89 v Harlequins 5.10.96
36-3 v Bristol 17.11.90
18-89 v Harlequins 5.10.96

MOST CONSECUTIVE VICTORIES - 5

MOST TRIES IN A MATCH
(FOR) 11 v Rugby 13.3.93 (H), v Northampton 27.10.90 (H), v Rosslyn Park 28.4.90 (H).
(AGAINST) 14 v Harlequins 5.10.96 (A)

CONSECUTIVE APPEARANCES
39 David Southern 26.9.87 - 17.11.90

MOST CONSECUTIVE DEFEATS - 11

MOST APPEARANCES
FORWARD: 86 Paul Manley
BACK: 90 Simon Langford

CONSECUTIVE SCORING MATCHES
Scoring Tries - 3 - Gerry Ainscough, Martin Strett & Phil Halsall.
Scoring Points - 17 - Martin Strett

MOST	in a SEASON	in a CAREER	in a MATCH
Points	166 Simon Mason 95-96	337 Gerry Ainscough 87-95	28 Martin Strett v Rosslyn Park 28.4.90 (H)
Tries	10 Graeme Smith 95-96	24 Dewi Morris 90-95	4 Paul Hamer v Rugby 13.3.93 (H)
Conversions	21 Martin Strett 90-91	46 Martin Strett 88-93	8 Martin Strett v Rosslyn Park (H)
Penalties	38 Simon Mason 95-96	71 Gerry Ainscough 87-95	6 Martin Strett v Gloucester 28.3.92 (H) Matthew McGrath v Lon. Irish 22.2.97 (H)
Drop Goals	4 Matthew McCarthy 96-97	4 Martin Strett 88-93 Matthew McCarthy 96-97	3 Matthew McCarthy v W. Hartlepool 7.12.98 (H)

ORRELL PLAYING SQUAD

NAME	Ht	Wt	Birthdate	Birthplace	Club	Apps	Pts	T	C	P	DG

BACKS

NAME	Ht	Wt	Birthdate	Birthplace	Club	Apps	Pts	T	C	P	DG
Rob Hitchmough England: u21.					Orrell	15+4	33	4	2	3	-
James Naylor England: A, u21.	5.11	14.0	06.02.74	Halifax	Old Crossleyans						
					Orrell	60	80	16	-	-	-
David Lyon	6.1	14.8	03.09.65		Prev. Clubs: Warrington (RL), St. Helens (RL).						
					Orrell	20	20	4	-	-	-
Lua Tuigamala	6.2	14.8	10.10.75	Western Samoa							
					Orrell	22	27	5	1	-	-
Guy Hope					Orrell	2	5	1	-	-	-
Steve Taberner	5.10	13.0	15.09.62	Orrell							
					Orrell	89+5	70	14	-	-	1
Steve Cook	5.9	13.2	04.08.74	St. Helens	Liverpool St. Helens						
					West Hartlepool	18+4	20	4	-	-	-
					Orrell	18+1	15	3	-	-	-
Paul Newton					Orrell	1	-	-	-	-	-
Matthew McCarthy					Orrell	14	114	2	18	19	4
Paul Hamer	6.0	13.4	12.11.66	St. Helens	St. Helens						
					Sale	14	29	3	1	5	-
					Orrell	51+2	63	11	1	-	2
Robin Saveriamutto					Orrell	3+3	5	1	-	-	-
Phil Horrocks	6.2	15.7	24.09.69	Wigan							
					Orrell	9+4	15	3	-	-	-

FORWARDS

NAME	Ht	Wt	Birthdate	Birthplace	Club	Apps	Pts	T	C	P	DG
Michael Worsley England: u21.	6.1	17.0	01.12.76		Sale						
					Orrell	17	5	1	-	-	-
Stuart Turner					Waterloo	38	-	-	-	-	-
					Orrell	21+1	5	1	-	-	-
Alex Moffatt	5.2	13.0	29.06.68								
					Orrell	14+6	-	-	-	-	-
Neil Hitchin					Orrell	71+1	-	-	-	-	-
Martin Scott	6.0	15.10	05.07.67	Falkirk	Prev. Clubs: Dunfermilne, Edinburgh Acad.						
					Orrell	28	5	1	-	-	-
Jason Cundick	6.0	17.0	09.09.73		Winnington Park						
					Orrell	23+2	-	-	-	-	-
Charles Cusani	6.6	17.0	22.10.65	Wigan							
					Orrell	81+1	12	3	-	-	-
Paul Rees	6.6	17.0	03.05.75		Winnington Park						
					Orrell	18+1	5	1	-	-	-
Chris Brierley	6.4	18.0	31.07.62	Colchester	Sale	2	-	-	-	-	-
					Orrell	48+8	-	-	-	-	-
Jeff Huxley	6.3	16.7	28.06.63								
					Orrell	33+2	5	1	-	-	-
Alex Bennett	6.3	17.0	01.04.75		Otley						
					Orrell	17+4	20	4	-	-	-
Peter Anglesea	6.4	15.8	30.10.71								
					Orrell	25+2	25	5	-	-	-
Richard Higgs					Orrell	15	5	1	-	-	-

Edgehall Road, Orrell, Wigan, Lancs. WN5 8TL.

Tel: 01695 632114   **Fax:** 01695 632116

CAPACITY: 4,950   **SEATED:** 250   **STANDING:** 4,700

SIMPLE DIRECTIONS:
    By Road: The ground is situated about 2 miles from the M6 junction 26. Turn left at the traffic lights at end of the slip road, then turn left at the set of traffic lights at the Stag Inn. After about 400 yds. turn left again at the traffic lights and after another 400 yds. make another left turn at the traffic lights which will take you into Edgehall Road.
    Nearest Railway Station: Orrell

CAR PARKING: 300 spaces are available at the ground.

ADMISSION: Matchday - Standing Adults £6, Children/OAPs £3. Seated £2 extra.

CLUB SHOP: Yes - run by the Commercial Department. 01695 623193.

CLUBHOUSE: With one public bar where food is available.
    Function room: The club can cater for functions.
    Please contact the Commercial Department for details 01695 623193.

TRAINING NIGHTS: Tuesday and Thursday.

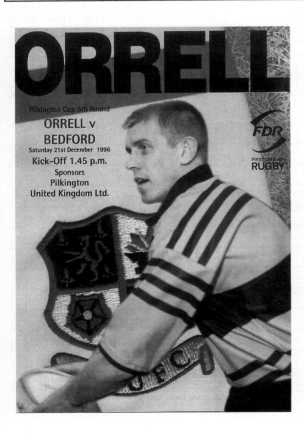

MATCHDAY
PROGRAMME

Size
    A5

Number of pages
    48, Full colour

Price
    £1.50

Programme Editor
    Geoff Lightfoot,
    01744 603199

Advertising Rates
    Contact - Commercial Manager

ROTHERHAM R.U.F.C.

NICKNAME: Roth   FOUNDED: 1923

President A Carruthers c/o Rotherham B.C., Walker Place, Rotherham
01709 382121 (B)
Club Secretary Allan Williams, 116 Grange Road, Rotherham. S60 3LL.
01709 364190 (H)
Chief Executive M Yarlett, High Beeches, Morgate, Rotherham
01709 364306 (H); 01709 540982 (B); 01709 700648 (Fax)
Press Officer/Playing Mgr S Cousins, c/o Yorkshire Window Co, Hellaby Ind Estate, Hellaby, Rotherham
01246 413681 (H); 01709 540982 (B); 01709 700648 (Fax)
Director of Rugby c/o Rotherham RUFC, Clifton Lane, Rotherham
01709 370763 (B)
Fixtures Secretary Andy Fraser, 01142 482051 (H)
Commercial Manager Paul Housley, 01709 370763 (Club); 01142 862351 (H); 0976 843722 (Mob)

After six promotions in nine seasons to the dizzy heights of National League Two and operating on a small budget in the new professional era Rotherham's first aim was survival. To ensure this survival they recruited sensibly from the successful Yorkshire U-21 side and from the student body. A final position of seventh in National League Two was eminently satisfactory but slightly disappointing from the strong run around mid season which put Rotherham fifth in the table. With many of the regulars who had taken Rotherham forward retiring the average age of the side was always under 25 and at times nearer under 23.

A heavy defeat at Blackheath in the first game did not augur well but despite defeat the next week at Richmond the side showed traditional Rotherham qualities of grit and determination in losing 64-38 and hope for the future was high. This hope was fully justified with four straight wins over Rugby, Wakefield, Waterloo and Nottingham. A narrow loss at Bedford and a first home defeat by Coventry stopped the surge but victories at home to London Scottish and Moseley left the newcomers to the league happily placed at Christmas.

A Pilkington Cup victory over Rosslyn Park set up a sixth Round tie with Harlequins at home and a record crowd of 4,000 saw the illustrious visitors made to work very hard for a 42-23 victory. In the league, victories over Blackheath, Nottingham, Waterloo and Rugby comfortably put Rotherham safe and this comfort zone plus an horrific injury list undoubtedly contributed to defeat in the last six games, a new and unpleasant experience for the club.

The omens for next season look fairly bright as a young side will only improve and a few key areas of recruitment could yet see Rotherham once again surprise a lot of people.

Rotherham RUFC Back Row (L-R); Kevin Plant, Steve Burnhill, Mark Pinder, Steve Hough, Ian Kearney, Ian Gresser, Matt Mills, Gavin Webster, Dan Cook, Tim Turner, John Dudley, Craig West, Ged Glynn. Middle Row; Nick Miller, Richard Selkirk, Lee Rick, Alan Buzza, Paul Scott, Simon Binns, Matt Inman. Front Row; Scott Wilson, Richard Wareham, Guy Easterby, Simon Bunting, Neil Spence, Richard Heaselgrave, Jon Harper, Chris Barrett, Sam Coy.

Colours: Maroon, sky, navy & white 1" hoops.   **Change colours:** Maroon.

ROTHERHAM

No	Ven.	Date	Opponents	Att.	Res.	Score	Scorers
1	(A)	07.09	v Blackheath	1522	L	5-44	Heaselgrave(t)
2	(A)	14.09	v Richmond	1032	L	38-64	Easterby(2t)Miller(t)Inman(c7p)
3	(H)	21.09	v Rugby	750	W	49-18	Binns(2t)Miller(t)Buzza(t)Dudley(2t)Easterby(t)Inman(4c2p)
4	(A)	28.09	v Wakefield	1000	W	29-25	Heaselgrave(t)Burnhill(t)Mills(t)Inman(c4p)
5	(H)	05.10	v Waterloo	850	W	38-23	Harper(t)Burnhill(t)Binns(t)Easterby(t)Heaselgrave(tdg)Inman(2c2p)
6	(A)	12.10	v Nottingham	646	W	44-21	PenTry(t)Buzza(t)Harper(t)Burnhill(t)Binns(t)Webster(t)Inman(4c2p)
7	(A)	19.10	v Bedford	2800	L	30-44	Heaselgrave(2t)Buzza(t)Wareham(t)Inman(2c2p)
8	(H)	26.10	v Coventry	1250	L	11-42	Kearney(t)Inman(2p)
9	(H)	02.11	v London Scot	1100	W	28-18	Heaselgrave(t)Easterby(t)Lax(6p)
10	(H)	09.11	v Moseley	1050	W	18-9	Easterby(t)Bayston(t)Lax(c2p)
11	(H)	16.11	v Blackheath	1300	W	39-11	Webster(2t)Miller(t)Easterby(t)Wareham(t)Binns(dg)Lax(4cp)
12	(H)	18.01	v Wakefield	1325	L	12-19	Lax(4p)
13	(A)	08.02	v Waterloo	500	W	27-23	Easterby(t)Lax(tc4p)Binns(dg)
14	(H)	22.02	v Richmond	2025	L	6-28	Lax(2p)
15	(H)	08.03	v Nottingham	1100	W	30-24	Easterby(2t)Miller(t)PenTry(t)Lax(tcp)
16	(A)	15.03	v Rugby	360	W	41-16	Binns(2t)Harper(t)Easterby(t)Bunting(t)Bramley(t)Ashforth(4cp)
17	(H)	22.03	v Bedford	1850	L	11-32	Hill(t)Binns(p)Ashforth(p)
18	(A)	05.04	v Coventry	2800	L	15-21	Buzza(t)Miller(t)Binns(cp)
19	(A)	12.04	v London Scot	501	L	3-25	Moffitt(p)
20	(H)	19.04	v Newcastle	3025	L	21-45	Heaselgrave(2t)Moffitt(c3p)
21	(A)	26.04	v Moseley	916	L	17-48	Hill(t)Easterby(t)Sinclair(t)Ashforth(c)
22	(A)	04.05	v Newcastle	3406	L	13-61	Moffitt(t)Lax(tp)

1996-97 HIGHLIGHTS

LEAGUE DEBUTS:
Nick Miller, Alan Buzza, Simon Binns, Guy Easterby, Gavin Webster, Neil Spence, Matt Inman, Ian Kearney, Dean Lax, Doug Elliott, Dan Cook, Stewart Moffatt, Rob Ashforth, Nick Hill, Richard Bramley, Ian Carroll, Lee Cholewa, Andy Watkins, Ian Worsley.

PLAYERS USED: 36 plus 6 as replacement only.

EVER PRESENT: John Dudley

❏ Only scoring record broken was Paul Scott's 1988-89 record of scoring 12 tries in a season achieved in North East One. The new record holder is scrum-half Guy Easterby in his debut season having joined Rotherham from Harrogate. Easterby's 13 tries came in 21 games.

❏ Winger Matt Inman sets a new record for points on debut when he kicks 23 in the away 38-64 defeat at Richmond

❏ John Dudley passes Richard Selkirk in the most league appearances list and ends the season on a new record of 120. Selkirk is second on 106 adding just three appearances to his previous record of 103.

❏ Dean Lax another points scoring winger equalled the record of six penalties in a match in the 28-18 home win against London Scottish in only his second league appearance. The only other player to achieve this was David Francis back in the 1988-89 season against Keighley.

❏ Their 13-61 loss at Newcastle was a record in terms of both biggest margin and highest score against. The 11 tries against was also e record in a league match.

❏ Newcastle also registered the biggest score in a Rotherham home fixture when they won 45-21. The previous highest score against was 43 set by Richmond at the end of last season.

❏ Finished two points behind Wakefield for the honour of being the top placed Yorkshire team in the Courage League.

❏ One of two teams in the division to score more tries away from home than at home

❏ Rotherham have now played in seven different divisions in ten seasons since starting in North East One back in 1987-88. In that time they have won promotion six times.

ROTHERHAM'S COURAGE LEAGUE MATCH DETAILS 1996-97

#	15	14	13	12	11	10	9	1	2	3	4	5	6	7	8	Replacements
1	Heaselgrave	Miller	Buzza	Harper	Burnhill	Binns	Easterby	Rick	Wareham	Coy	Webster	Mills	Dudley	Spence	Selkirk	McIntyre(13)Scott(10)Bunting(7)
2	Heaselgrave	Miller	Burnhill	Harper	Inman	Binns	Easterby	Rick	Wareham	Coy	Webster	Mills	Kearney	Spence	Dudley	
3	Heaselgrave	Miller	Burnhill	Harper	Inman	Binns	Easterby	Rick	Wareham	Coy	Webster	Mills	Kearney	Spence	Dudley	Wilson(3)
4	Heaselgrave	Burnhill	Buzza	Harper	Inman	Binns	Easterby	Rick	Wareham	Coy	Webster	Mills	Kearney	Spence	Dudley	
5	Heaselgrave	Burnhill	Buzza	Harper	Inman	Binns	Easterby	Rick	Wareham	Bunting	Webster	Mills	Kearney	Spence	Dudley	
6	Heaselgrave	Burnhill	Buzza	Harper	Inman	Binns	Easterby	Rick	Wareham	Wilson	Webster	Mills	Kearney	Spence	Dudley	Barrett(5)
7	Inman	Burnhill	Burnhill	Harper	Lax	Buzza	Easterby	Rick	Wareham	Coy	Webster	Gresser	Kearney	West	Dudley	
8	Heaselgrave	Burnhill	Harper	Buzza	Inman	Binns	Easterby	Rick	Wareham	Coy	Webster	Gresser	Kearney	Spence	Dudley	
9	Buzza	Heaselgrave	Harper	Elliott	Lax	Binns	Easterby	Rick	Wareham	Coy	Webster	Richardson	West	Spence	Dudley	
10	Heaselgrave	Miller	Buzza	Elliott	Lax	Burnhill	Easterby	Rick	Bayston	Coy	Webster	Richardson	Kearney	Spence	Dudley	West(5)
11	Heaselgrave	Miller	Burnhill	Buzza	Lax	Binns	Easterby	Rick	Wareham	Coy	Cook	Carroll	Webster	West	Dudley	Pinder(6)
12	Heaselgrave	Miller	Buzza	Harper	Burnhill	Burnhill	Easterby	Rick	Wareham	Coy	Cook	Carroll	Webster	Spence	Dudley	West(13)
13	Buzza	Miller	Burnhill	Harper	Lax	Binns	Easterby	Rick	Wareham	Coy	Carroll	Mills	West	Spence	Dudley	Worsley(15)Heaselgrave(14)Bunting(3)
14	Moffatt	Lax	Burnhill	Harper	Buzza	Binns	Worsley	Bunting	Wareham	Coy	Webster	Cook	Bramley	West	Dudley	Rick(4)Spence(7)Richardson(5)
15	Heaselgrave	Miller	Burnhill	Turner	Lax	Binns	Easterby	Bunting	Wareham	Coy	Webster	Cook	West	Spence	Dudley	Hughes(12)Pinder(7)
16	Buzza	Miller	Harper	Ashforth	Binns	Binns	Easterby	Bunting	Wareham	Wilson	Webster	Cook	Bramley	West	Dudley	McIntyre(15)Selkirk(14)
17	Moffatt	Miller	Harper	Ashforth	Hill	Binns	Easterby	Bunting	Wareham	Coy	Webster	Cook	Bramley	West	Dudley	Wilson(3)Selkirk(6)
18	Moffatt	Miller	Buzza	Ashforth	Hill	Binns	Easterby	Bunting	Wareham	Coy	Webster	Cook	Bramley	West	Dudley	Harper(11)Kearney(7)Wilson(3)
19	Moffatt	Miller	Buzza	Ashforth	Harper	Binns	Easterby	Bunting	Wareham	Coy	Webster	Cook	Bramley	West	Dudley	Kearney(6)Lax(10)Worsley(11)Wilson(1)Sinclair(R6)
20	Moffatt	Burnhill	Harper	Hill	Binns	Ashforth	Easterby	Bunting	Coy	Mills	Webster	Cook	Dudley	Pinder	Selkirk	Heaselgrave(14)Wilson(3)Richardson(5)
21	Moffatt	Heaselgrave	Harper	Buzza	Ashforth	Ashforth	Easterby	Bunting	Wareham	Wilson	Webster	Cook	Dudley	West	Selkirk	Richardson(7)Sinclair(15)Cholewa(10)
22	Moffatt	Heaselgrave	Buzza	Harper	Lax	Cholewa	Easterby	Bunting	Wareham	Coy	Webster	Cook	Pinder	Watkins	Dudley	Richardson(6)Worsley(3)Walter(12)

ROTHERHAM LEAGUE STATISTICS
(COMPILED BY STEPHEN McCORMACK)

Season	Div.	P	W	D	L	F (Tries Con Pen DG)					A (Tries Con Pen DG)					Most Points	Most Tries
87-88	NE1	10	8	0	2	175	(22	9	21	2)	52	(3	2	9	2)	55 - Kevin Plant	6 - Richard Selkirk
88-89	NE1	10	10	0	0	273	(40	22	21	2)	54	(3	3	11	1)	115 - Kevin Plant	12 - Paul Scott
89-90	N2	10	9	0	1	214	(26	16	24	2)	134	(15	10	18	0)	98 - Kevin Plant	6 - Paul Scott
90-91	N1	10	6	1	3	198	(28	13	17	3)	107	(11	6	16	1)	81 - Kevin Plant	4 - by 3 players
																John Dudley, Danny Walker & Richard Selkirk.	
91-92	N1	10	10	0	0	245	(36	19	21	0)	123	(7	5	10	0)	60 - Steve Worrall	7 - Richard Selkirk
92-93	D4N	12	10	1	1	259	(32	15	21	2)	123	(13	6	16	0)	50 - Steve Worrall	8 - Andy Challinor
93-94	D5N	12	10	1	1	335	(42	25	23	2)	142	(12	8	22	0)	118 - Kevin Plant	8 - John Dudley
94-95	4	18	17	0	1	576	(70	38	48	2)	267	(25	14	34	4)	202 - Kevin Plant	8 - John Dudley & Paul Scott
95-96	3	18	12	0	6	384	(43	20	37	6)	368	(33	19	47	8)	155 - Kevin Plant	
96-97	2	22	11	0	11	525	(62	28	50	3)	661	(83	34	45	1)	92 - Dean Lax	13 - Guy Easterby
Totals		132	103	3	26	3184	(401	205	283	24)	2031	(205	127	228	17)		

	HOME	AWAY
BIGGEST WIN	(73pts) 76-3 v Durham 19.3.94	(40pts) 46-6 v Westoe 8.4.89
DEFEAT	(37pts) 6-43 v Richmond 30.9.95	(48pts) 13-61 v Newcastle 4.5.97
MOST POINTS SCORED	76-3 v Durham 19.3.94	46-6 v Westoe 8.4.89
AGAINST	21-45 v Newcastle 19.4.97	13-61 v Newcastle 4.5.97

MOST CONSECUTIVE VICTORIES - 17   **MOST CONSECUTIVE DEFEATS** - 6

MOST TRIES IN A MATCH
(FOR) 11 v Durham 19.3.94
(AGAINST) 11 v Newcastle 4.5.97 (A)

MOST APPEARANCES
FORWARD: 120 John Dudley
BACK: 99(1) Paul Scott

CONSECUTIVE APPEARANCES
89 Richard Selkirk 12.9.87 - 1.4.94

CONSECUTIVE SCORING MATCHES
Scoring Tries - 4 - Grant Treece
Scoring Points - 14 - Kevin Plant (twice)

MOST	in a SEASON	in a CAREER	in a MATCH
Points	202 Kevin Plant 94-95	922 Kevin Plant 87-96	24 Paul Scott v Westloe 8.4.89 (A)
Tries	13 Guy Easterby 96-97	42 Paul Scott 87-96	6 Paul Scott v Westoe 8.4.89 (A)
Conversions	33 Kevin Plant 94-95	141 Kevin Plant 87-96	9 Kevin Plant v Durham 19.2.94 (H)
Penalties	41 Kevin Plant 90-91	182 Kevin Plant 87-96	6 David Francis v Keighley 8.4.89 (H) Dean Lax v Lon. Scottish 2.11.96 (H)
Drop Goals	5 Kevin Plant 95-96	17 Kevin Plant 87-96	2 Kevin Plant v Coventry 28.10.95

ROTHERHAM PLAYING SQUAD

NAME	Ht	Wt	Birthdate	Birthplace	Club	Apps	Pts	T	C	P	DG
BACKS											
Richard Heaselgrave	5.11	13.0		Birmingham							
					Rotherham	38+1	73	14	-	-	-
Nick Miller											
					Rotherham	12	25	5	-	-	-
Alan Buzza					Wasps						
					Rotherham	19	20	4	-	-	-
Jon Harper	6.0	13.7	09.09.74	London							
					Rotherham	43+1	55	11	-	-	-
Steve Burnhill	5.11	13.0		Cleckheaton	Leicester	4+1	4	1	-	-	-
					Sale	39+1	36	9	-	-	-
					Rotherham	23	20	4	-	-	-
Simon Binns	5.11	13.7	20.09.74								
					Rotherham	16	39	5	1	2	3
Guy Easterby					Harrogate	77	127	17	7	8	2
					Rotherham	21	65	13	-	-	-
Stewart Moffatt											
					Rotherham	7	19	1	1	4	-
Rob Ashforth											
					Rotherham	6	16	-	5	2	-
Nick Hill											
					Rotherham	5	10	2	-	-	-
Lee Cholewa											
					Rotherham	1+1	-	-	-	-	-
Dean Lax											
					Rotherham	9+1	92	3	7	2	-
FORWARDS											
Richard Wareham	5.11	16.7		Wakefield	Leicester						
					Moseley	15	-	-	-	-	-
					Rotherham	34	15	3	-	-	-
Sam Coy	5.11	18.7	19.01.66	Rotherham							
					Rotherham	102+1	15	3	-	-	-
Simon Bunting	6.1	16.7	17.09.70	Rotherham							
					Rotherham	44+2	10	2	-	-	-
Gavin Webster											
					Rotherham	20	15	3	-	-	-
Matt Mills	6.6	16.0	29.12.73	Selby							
					Rotherham	20	5	1	-	-	-
Dan Cook											
					Rotherham	10	-	-	-	-	-
Mark Pinder	6.0	16.7	18.12.70	Rotherham							
					Rotherham	12+2	-	-	-	-	-
Ian Carroll					Otley						
					Rotherham	3	-	-	-	-	-
John Dudley	6.4	18.0	16.07.66	Sheffield							
					Rotherham	120	141	30	-	-	-
Ian Kearney											
					Rotherham	8+2	5	1	-	-	-
Richard Bramley					Wakefield	18+3	5	-	-	-	-
					Rotherham	5	5	1	-	-	-
Craig West	6.2	17.0	08.02.64	Rotherham							
					Rotherham	97+2	98	21	-	-	-
Neil Spence											
					Rotherham	12+1	-	-	-	-	-
Scott Wilson	5.11	16.0	14.01.72	Rotherham							
					Rotherham	14+5	-	-	-	-	-
Brian Richardson	6.7	17.0	08.06.59	Edinburgh	Boroughmuir						
					Rotherham	46+4	-	-	-	-	-
Richard Selkirk	6.1	17.0	19.06.62	Sheffield							
					Rotherham	106+2	196	44	-	-	-
Lee Rick	6.2	17.7	20.03.69	Rotherham							
					Rotherham	73+1	10	2	-	-	-

Clifton Lane Sports Ground, Badsley Moor Lane, Rotherham. S65 2AA.

CAPACITY: 4,000   **SEATED Covered:** 300 Uncovered: 700   **STANDING Covered:** 1500 Uncovered: 1500

SIMPLE DIRECTIONS:
   By Road: M1 Jnc 33. Follow Rotherway for half mile to roundabout. Take 2nd exit signposted Bawtry. Traffic lights straight on up hill to roundabout. Exit 1st left, follow road into town centre. Ground approx 1 mile on right.
   M18 Jnc 1. follow signs Rotherham. After 2 miles at 2nd roundabout (Brecks Hotel) fork right. At next roundabout (Stag Inn) 2nd exit. Follow road into town centre. Ground approx 1 mile on right.
   Nearest Railway Station: Rotherham

CAR PARKING: 20 on ground, 1,000 No Charge nearby.

ADMISSION: Matches £5.00, Oap's £3.00

CLUB SHOP: Yes, Contact Paul Housley, Commercial Mgr

CLUBHOUSE: Normal Licensing Hours
   Function room: Yes available for hire, capacity 200 Contact Paul Housley or Julie Docherty 01709 370763

TRAINING NIGHTS: Monday, Tuesday & Thursday

Rotherham's 1996/97 Captain John Dudley on the ground against Moseley

MATCHDAY PROGRAMME

Size	A5
Number of pages	38
Price	£1
Programme Editor	A Williams 01709 364190

Advertising Rates
   Full page £200, 1/2 page £100, 1/4 page £ 50

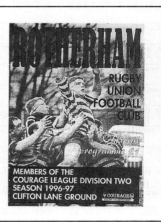

WAKEFIELD R.F.C.

NICKNAME: Field

FOUNDED: 1901

President   Alan Calvert
Chairman   Nigel Foster
Club Secretary   J B Coulson, 39 Melbourne Road, St. Johns, Wakefield. WF1 2RL.
01924 373586 (H) 01924 374801 (B & Fax)
Fixtures Secretary   W Halstead, 84 Whitcliffe Road, Cleckheaton, W. Yorks. BD19 3DR.
01274 872710 (H)

Wakefield entered the first ever professional rugby season with players contracted to the club, both old and new, for the first time. The optimists felt a place in the top three or four was possible - the realists felt fifth would be the best possible placing, behind all those clubs who had had large sums invested in them. Indeed the financial investment in the Second League clubs who finished in the top four overshadowed all but the top two or three clubs in the First League. That we finished fifth, and top Yorkshie club, speaks volumes for the efforts of both players and coaching staff led by Jim Kilfoyle.

Injuries played a key part in our season, so much so that the first choice back row only played one league game together in September before injuries and work duties stopped them playing together again.

Wakefield dipped their toes in the water of rugby league with Dean Hanger and Daryl Shelford joining from Huddersfield. Yet again injuries hampered their progress with Hanger sustaining a knee injury that involved him returning to Huddersfield for an operation, and Shelford breaking an arm on his debut at Rugby in October.

Best results last season were a double over Coventry and also doubles over Blackheath, Nottingham and Rugby, a win over a near full strength Orrell side with a near second fifteen and a narrow 26-21 defeat by Gloucester in the Cup.

The future though is looking bright with at least eight players 21 and under playing in league games at one stage or another. It was hoped that the majority of these will be signed on contracts (some full time) before next season. With the appointments of an experinced full time player\coach and a more professional training regime, morale and optimism are high that next season will see an improvement from fifth place into the top four.

Dave Scully made his long deserved debut with the Barbarians and went on to skipper them in the Middlesex and Air France Sevens in Hong Kong - rich rewards in his benefit season. Dean Hardcastle represented England U21's and Glen Wilson England Students.

Wakefield RFC: Back Row (L-R); A Gomersal, P Hanley, P Hayward, D Shelford, D Falkingham, A Bailey, P Stewart, C Rushworth, R Latham, R Szabo, D Hendry, S Pevy, J Adams, C Harris. Front Row; J Kilfoyle, P Hanley, R Thompson, I Winn, M Jackson, S Croft, D Scully, P Lancaster, P Massey, P White, T Garnett, R Burman
Photo - Gordon Bunney

Colours: Black & gold quarters/black/black.

Change colours: Red

COURAGE LEAGUE MATCH DETAILS 1996-97

No	Ven.	Date	Opponents	Att.	Res.	Score	Scorers
1	(A)	07.09 v	Moseley	657	W	30-17	Hendry(t)White(t)Thompson(t)Scully(tcp)Jackson(cp)
2	(H)	14.09 v	London Scot	750	L	27-30	Massey(t)Scully(t)Jackson(c5p)
3	(A)	21.09 v	Coventry	3100	W	25-24	Petyt(t)Garnett(t)Rushworth(t)Scuylly(2c2p)
4	(H)	28.09 v	Rotherham	1000	L	25-29	Massey(t)Petyt(t)Scully(t2c2p)
5	(A)	05.10 v	Bedford	2200	L	19-25	Scully(t)Lancaster(t)Jackson(2pdg)
6	(H)	12.10 v	Newcastle	1900	L	17-47	Manley(t)Jackson(t2cp)
7	(H)	19.10 v	Waterloo	600	W	45-12	Wynn(2t)PenTry(2t)Manley(t)Garnett(t)Jones(t)Jackson(5c)
8	(A)	26.10 v	Rugby	440	W	22-17	Scully(t)Stewart(t)PenTry(t)Jackson(2cp)
9	(A)	02.11 v	Nottingham	495	W	40-18	Scully(t)Stewart(t)Wilson(t)Jackson(t3c3p)
10	(H)	09.11 v	Richmond	1200	L	7-23	Scully(t)Jackson(c)
11	(A)	16.11 v	Blackheath	1775	W	17-13	McClarron(t)Jackson(4p)
12	(A)	18.01 v	Rotherham	1325	W	19-12	McClarron(t)Jackson(c4p)
13	(H)	08.02 v	Bedford	1500	L	17-29	PenTry(t)Thompson(t)Jackson(2cp)
14	(A)	08.03 v	Newcastle	2092	L	10-57	Stewart(2t)
15	(A)	22.03 v	Waterloo	1000	L	11-16	Jackson(t2p)
16	(A)	24.03 v	London Scot	243	L	3-34	Jackson(p)
17	(H)	29.03 v	Moseley	800	L	13-42	Massey(t)Jackson(c2p)
18	(H)	05.04 v	Rugby	550	W	53-12	Hendry(2t)Massey(2t)Wilson(t)Scully(t)Croft(t)Garnett(t)Jackson(5cp)
19	(H)	12.04 v	Nottingham	650	W	31-16	Garnett(t)Shelford(t)Scully(t)Jackson(2c4p)
20	(A)	19.04 v	Richmond	1359	L	22-55	Massey(t)White(t)Jackson(t2cp)
21	(H)	26.04 v	Blackheath	600	W	14-11	Thompson(t)Wynn(t)Jackson(2c)
22	(H)	03.05 v	Coventry	450	W	37-18	Maynard(t)Manley(t)Hendry(t)PenTry(t)Jackson(t3c2p)

1996-97 HIGHLIGHTS

LEAGUE DEBUTS:
Peter Massey, Jamie Bartle, Ian Wynn, Phil Lancaster, Scott Plevey, Paul Manley, Dixie Hendry, Dean Hanger, Darryl Shelford, Gavin Reynolds, Steve Jones, Alastair McClarron, S Dykes, Dean Hardcastle.

TRY ON DEBUT: Dixie Hendry.

PLAYERS USED: 31 plus 3 as replacement.

EVER PRESENT: Peter Massey, Ian Wynn
and Simon Croft.

❏ Terry Garnett became the first Wakefield forward to pass 100 league appearances as he extended his record for appearances by a forward to 113.

❏ Had a better away record than home record.

❏ Were the only team to do the double over Coventry.

❏ Mike Jackson became the seventh Wakefield player to drop a goal in a league game.

❏ Club stalwart and scrum-half Dave Scully tops the try scoring list for a record fourth time after sharing the record of three with Jonathan Sleightholme.
Scully has started 139 out of Wakefield's 145 league games since league Rugby began in September 1987. He also extended his all time try scoring record to 46.
Winger Richard Thompson moved into joint third place on the list with former England Captain Mike Harrison.

	Tries	Apps	Try Every
Dave Scully	46	139	3.02 games
Jon Sleightholme	27	38	1.14 games
Mike Harrison	22	47	2.14 games
R Thompson	22	76	3.45 games

❏ Stand-off Mike Jackson easily broke the record for conversions in a season with 33. The previous record of 19 was shared by both Ray Adamson and Jackson himself. He also extended his club points scoring record past 500 and 600 to finish up on 679. Second on the all-time scoring list to Jackson now is Dave Scully.

	Pts	T	C	P	D	Apps	Ave.
Mike Jackson	679	9	77	159	1	68	9.99
Dave Scully	236	46	5	7	-	139	1.70

❏ Suffered their worst ever defeats, home and away, in both biggest deficit and most points scored against. Both defeats were at the hands of runners-up Newcastle.

WAKEFIELD'S COURAGE LEAGUE MATCH DETAILS 1996-97

	15	14	13	12	11	10	9	1	2	3	4	5	6	7	8	Replacements	
1	Massey	Bartle	Wynn	Maynard	Thompson	Jackson	Scully	Lancaster	Plevey	Latham	Croft	Stewart	Rushworth	Manley	Hendry	White(14)	1
2	Massey	Hanger	Wynn	Maynard	Thompson	Jackson	Szabo	Lancaster	Garnett	Latham	Croft	Stewart	Rushworth	Manley	Hendry	Shelford(12)Falkingham(5)	2
3	Massey	Hanger	Wynn	Maynard	Thompson	Petyt	Scully	Lancaster	Garnett	Reynolds Croft	Bailey	Rushworth	Griffiths	Manley	Hendry	Burman(3)Adams(7)	3
4	Massey	Hanger	Wynn	Maynard	Thompson	Petyt	Scully	Lancaster	Garnett	Szabo	Croft	Bailey	Wilson	Adams	Rushworth Burman(1)		4
5	Massey	Jones	Wynn	Maynard	Thompson	Jackson	Scully	Lancaster	Garnett	Szabo	Croft	Bailey	Wilson	Manley	Stewart		5
6	Massey	Jones	Wynn	Maynard	White	Jackson	Scully	Lancaster	Garnett	Szabo	Croft	Bailey	Wilson	Manley	Stewart		6
7	Massey	Hanger	Wynn	Maynard	Jones	Jackson	Scully	Lancaster	Garnett	Latham	Croft	Bailey	Wilson	Manley	Stewart	Adams(8)	7
8	Massey	Hanger	Wynn	Shelford	Jones	Jackson	Scully	Lancaster	Garnett	Latham	Croft	Bailey	Wilson	Manley	Stewart	Maynard(12)	8
9	Massey	McClarron	Wynn	Maynard	Jines	Jackson	Scully	Lancaster	Garnett	Latham	Croft	Bailey	Wilson	Bailey	Stewart		9
10	Massey	McClarron	Wynn	Maynard	Jones	Jackson	Scully	Lancaster	Garnett	Latham	Croft	Bailey	Wilson	Manley	Stewart	Adams(8)	10
11	Massey	McClarron	Wynn	Maynard	Thompson	Jackson	Scully	Lancaster	Garnett	Latham	Croft	Bailey	Wilson	Manley	Stewart		11
12	Massey	McClarron	Wynn	Maynard	Thompson	Jackson	Scully	Lancaster	Garnett	Latham	Croft	Bailey	Wilson	Manley	Hendry		12
13	Massey	McClarron	Wynn	Maynard	Thompson	Jackson	Scully	Lancaster	Garnett	Latham	Croft	Bailey	Stewart	Manley	Wilson	White(15)	13
14	Massey	McClarron	Shelford	Maynard	White	Jackson	Scully	Lancaster	Garnett	Croft	Bailey	Stewart	Manley	Hendry	Wynn(13)Birkby(12)Szabo(3)Wilson(4)		14
15	Massey	McClarron	Wynn	Shelford	Thompson	Jackson	Birkby	Lancaster	Garnett	Szabo	Croft	Stewart	Wilson	Manley	Hendry	Bailey(8)	15
16	Massey	McClarron	Wynn	Shelford	Thompson	Jackson	Hardcastle	Lancaster	Garnett	Latham	Croft	Bailey	Stewart	Manley	Wilson	White(10)Hendry(7)Lancaster(1)	16
17	Massey	McClarron	Wynn	Shelford	Thompson	Jackson	Lancaster	Garnett	Szabo	Croft	Bailey	Stewart	Dykes	Wilson	Hardcastle(8)Shuttleworth(10)		17
18	Massey	White	Wynn	Maynard	Thompson	Jackson	Scully	Lancaster	Garnett	Latham	Croft	Bailey	Stewart	Wilson	Hendry	Shelford(12)Shuttleworth(10)Bartle(9)Szabo(3)Dykes(8)	18
19	Massey	White	Wynn	Shelford	Thompson	Jackson	Scully	Lancaster	Garnett	Croft	Bailey	Stewart	Manley	Hendry	Szabo(2)Wilson(4)Birkby(9)		19
20	Massey	White	Wynn	Maynard	Thompson	Jackson	Scully	Lancaster	Garnett	Szabo	Croft	Bailey	Stewart	Manley	Hendry	Bartle(9)Latham(3)Shuttleworth(15)Shelford(12)	20
21	Massey	White	Wynn	Maynard	Thompson	Birkby	Lancaster	Garnett	Latham	Croft	Bailey	Stewart	Manley	Hendry	Scully(9)Hardcastle(1)		21
22	Massey	White	Wynn	Maynard	Thompson	Jackson	Scully	Lancaster	Garnett	Szabo	Croft	Wilson	Stewart	Manley	Hendry	Plevey(2)Latham(3)Hardcastle(1)	22

WAKEFIELD LEAGUE STATISTICS
(COMPILED BY STEPHEN McCORMACK)

Season	Div.	P	W	D	L	F	(Tries	Con	Pen	DG)	A	(Tries	Con	Pen	DG)	Most Points	Most Tries
87-88	3	11	10	0	1	308	(45	25	26	0)	90	(8	5	13	3)	105 - Ray Adamson	8 - Simon Cowling
88-89	3	11	9	0	2	282	(46	25	16	0)	114	(12	6	15	3)	69 - Andy Atkinson	8 - Dave Scully
89-90	3	11	7	1	3	210	(34	16	13	1)	126	(15	6	16	2)	31 - Ray Adamson	7 - Mike Harrison & Mike Murtagh
90-91	2	12	8	0	4	188	(25	11	21	1)	109	(8	4	21	2)	89 - Andy Atkinson	4 - Raz Bowers & Dave Scully
91-92	2	12	7	0	5	187	(30	14	13	0)	194	(27	16	14	4)	32 - Rob Liley - John Sleightholme	8 - Jon Sleightholme
92-93	2	12	8	1	3	186	(17	10	24	3)	123	(10	5	15	6)	101 - Rob Liley	7 - Jon Sleightholme
93-94	2	18	8	3	7	347	(34	18	47	0)	240	(21	9	35	4)	90 - Mike Jackson	12 - Jon Sleightholme
94-95	2	18	12	1	5	354	(29	16	58	1)	261	(18	9	47	4)	213 - Mike Jackson	7 - Richard Thomspon
95-96	2	18	8	0	10	328	(31	19	43	3)	331	(32	18	42	3)	177 - Mike Jackson	7 - Dave Scully
96-97	2	22	11	0	11	504	(61	38	40	1)	557	(66	40	47	2	199 - Mike Jackson	9 - Dave Scully
Totals		145	88	6	51	2894	(352	192	301	10)	2145	(217	118	265	33)		

	HOME	AWAY
BIGGEST WIN	(70pts) 70-0 v Metropolitan Police 24.9.88	(47pts) 50-3 v Birmingham 31.10.87
DEFEAT	(30pts) 17-47 v Newcastle 12.10.96	(47pts) 10-57 v Newcastle 8.3.97
MOST POINTS SCORED	70-0 v Metropolitan Police 24.9.88	50-3 v Birmingham 31.10.87
AGAINST	17-47 v Newcastle 12.10.96	10-57 v Newcastle 8.3.97

MOST CONSECUTIVE VICTORIES - 10   **MOST CONSECUTIVE DEFEATS - 5**

MOST TRIES IN A MATCH
(FOR) 14 v Metropolitan Police 24.9.88
(AGAINST) 9 v Newcastle 8.3.97
v Richmond 19.4.97

MOST APPEARANCES
FORWARD: 113 Terry Garnett
BACK: 139(1) Dave Scully

CONSECUTIVE SCORING MATCHES
Scoring Tries - 3 -
Scoring Points - 21 - Mike Jackson

CONSECUTIVE APPEARANCES
49 Dave Scully

MOST	in a SEASON	in a CAREER	in a MATCH
Points	213 Mike Jackson 94-95	679 Mike Jackson 93-97	23 Rob Liley v Rugby 11.9.93 (H)
Tries	12 Jon Sleightholme 93-94	46 Dave Scully 87-97	3 by 6 players - Simon Cowling (x2), Mike Harrison (x2), Andy Holloway, Andy Atkinson, Mike Murtagh, Jon Sleightholme.
Conversions	33 Mike Jackson 96-97	77 Mike Jackson 93-97	7 Ray Adamson v Birmingham 31.10.87 (A)
Penalties	57 Mike Jackson 94-95	159 Mike Jackson 93-97	6 Ray Adamson v Vale of Lune 27.2.88 (H) Mike Jackson v Nottingham 1.10.94 (A) v Lon. Irish 22.10.94 (H)
Drop Goals	2 Rob Liley 92-93	2 Steve Townend 87-93 Rob Liley 91-93	1 by 7 players - Steve Townend (x2), Rob Liley (x2), Richard Petyt, Brian Barley, Andy Metcalfe, Ian Shuttleworth, Mike Jackson.

WAKEFIELD PLAYING SQUAD

NAME	Ht	Wt	Birthdate	Birthplace	Club	Apps	Pts	T	C	P	DG
BACKS											
Peter Massey	5.11	13.7	03.04.75	Pontefract	Morley						
England: u21, Colts.					Wakefield	22	35	7	-	-	-
Richard Thompson	6.0	13.7	03.12.69	Leeds	West Hartlepool	6	5	1	-	-	-
England: u18, u16. Yorkshire. North.					Wakefield	72	108	22	-	-	-
Alastair McClarron	6.3	14.0	19.06.73	Driffield							
					Wakefield	10	10	2	-	-	-
Paul White	5.10	12.7	15.12.64		Morley						
Irish Exiles					Wakefield	35+6	35	7	-	-	-
Alex Birkby		12.5	21.07.77	Sheffield							
Yorkshire Colts, u21.					Wakefield	3+2	-	-	-	-	-
Jamie Bartle	5.11	12.0	24.09.76	Sheffield							
Yorkshire u21.					Wakefield	1+2	-	-	-	-	-
Mike Jackson	6.1	13.10	21.01.67	Manchester	Fylde	53	222	5	21	53	-
North. Lancashire.					Wakefield	68	679	9	77	159	1
Dave Scully	5.8	12.0	07.08.65	Doncaster							
England: B, Sevens. North.					Wakefield	147+1	236	46	5	7	-
Phil Maynard	5.11	14.5	08.01.70	Wakefield							
England: Colts. Yorkshire. North.					Wakefield	72+6	52	11	-	-	-
Darryl Shelford											
					Wakefield	6+3	5	1	-	-	-
Ian Shuttleworth											
					Wakefield	7+3	8	1	-	-	1
Richard Petyt	6.0	13.7	04.07.67	Keighley	Prev. Clubs: Newcastle, Otley.						
					Wakefield	22	28	5	-	-	1
Ian Wynn	6.2	14.0	19.08.68	St. Helens	Orrell	59+1	80	16	-	-	-
Scottish Exiles.					Wakefield	21+1	15	3	-	-	-
FORWARDS											
Phil Lancaster	6.1	16.7	15.01.64	Hartlepool	West Hartlepool	101	13	3	-	-	-
North. Durham.					Wakefield	20+1	5	1	-	-	-
Scott Plevey	5.10	13.5	28.09.76	Doncaster							
Yorkshire Colts.					Wakefield	1+1	-	-	-	-	-
Rod Latham	6.1	18.4	01.08.69	Ghana							
North. Yorkshire.					Wakefield	76+4	-	-	-	-	-
Dean Hardcastle	5.10	16.2	26.01.76	Doncaster							
England: u21. North u21. Yorkshire u21.					Wakefield	1+3	-	-	-	-	-
Terry Garnett	5.11	16.9	10.05.67	Hull							
England: Colts. Yorkshire. North.					Wakefield	113	20	4	-	-	-
Simon Croft	6.7	17.12	22.03.65	Harrogate	Harrogate						
England: Colts. Yorkshire.					Wakefield	70	10	2	-	-	-
Paul Stewart	6.6	16.9		Halifax							
North. Yorkshire.					Wakefield	93+2	44	9	-	-	-
Paul Manley	6.1	15.7	21.06.68	Stockport	Orrell	86	29	7	-	-	-
					Wakefield	19	15	3	-	-	-
Alastair Bailey	6.7	17.3	27.06.73	Essex							
England: Colts.					Wakefield	29+1	-	-	-	-	-
Glen Wilson	6.2	15.10		Wakefield							
England: Students.					Wakefield	13+2	10	2	-	-	-
Derek Hendry	6.3	15.7	15.05.71	South Africa							
					Wakefield	19	15	3	-	-	-
Richard Szabo	6.0	16.10	13.07.66	Leeds	Morley						
Yorkshire. North.					Wakefield	34+4	-	-	-	-	-
John Adams			02.09.65	Wakefield	Sandal						
					Wakefield	4+4	5	1	-	-	-
Chris Rushworth	6.3	16.3	27.02.67								
					Wakefield	16+1	20	4	-	-	-

Tel: 01924 374801   **Fax:** 01924 374801

CAPACITY: 2,450   **SEATED:** 450   **STANDING:** 2,000

SIMPLE DIRECTIONS:
   By Road: From M1 Jnc 41, A650 into Wakefield City Centre, turn left at Queen Elizabeth Grammar School onto Westfield Road, ground in front 250 yards.
   From M62 Jnc 30, A642 into Wakefield, turn right at traffic lights immediately after Hospital onto Eastmoor Road, ground 300 yards on left.
   Nearest Railway Station: Wakefield Westgate

CAR PARKING: No parking in ground, 200 spaces nearby £1.

ADMISSION: Season Male £75, Oap £45, Ladies £50, Oap £35;

Match £7.00, Seated £8.00, Oap £5.00, Children £3.00

CLUB SHOP: Yes; Manager Cath Brocklebby via club

CLUBHOUSE: Normal Licensing Hours. Three bars with snacks & bar meals available
   Function room: Yes; Capacity 150; Contact Dianne Cole via club

TRAINING NIGHTS: Seniors Monday & Thursday, Colts Wednesday.

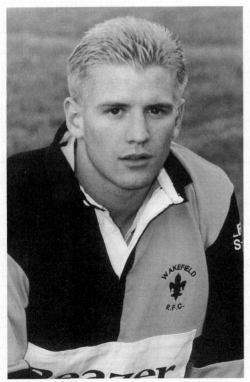

Peter Massey; Players & Supporters Player of The Year.

Photo - Gordon Bunney

MATCHDAY PROGRAMME

Size   B5

Number of pages   30

Price   £1

Programme Editor

Advertising Rates
   Full page Colour £ 350, Mono £ 300
   1/2 page Colour £ 200, Mono £ 175
   1/4 page Mono £ 100.

WATERLOO F.C.

FOUNDED: 1882

President D R Morgan, Mansley House, Larkhill Lane, Formby, Lancs L37 1LX
017048 77072
Chairman R H Wilson, Netherwood, Far Moss Road, Blundellsands, Liverpool L23 8TG
0151 924 1398 (H), 0151 928 9288 (B), 0151 928 4190 (Fax)
Club Secretary Keith Alderson, 66 St Michaels Road, Blundellsands, Liverpool. L23 7UW.
0151 924 1168 (H)   0151 933 8088 (B)   0151 949 0981 (Fax)
Commercial Manager F Spencer, c/o Waterloo FC, St Anthonys Road, Blundellsands, Liverpool, L23 8TW
0151 924 4552 (B), 0151 924 0900 (Fax)
Director of Rugby Tony Russ, c/o Waterloo FC, as above
0151 924 4552 (B), 0151 924 0900 (Fax)
Fixtures Secretary J Rimmer, 01772 614277 (H), 01772 885000 (B)
Chairman of Rugby J Greenwood, 01772 655223 (H & B)

Waterloo got off to a shocking start to the season, losing seven of the first eight games to find themselves deep in the relegation zone with Nottingham and Rugby. The ship steadied somewhat in November with wins against Blackheath and Rugby but the year petered out with defeat in the Pilkington Cup and the start of the freeze. The club reacted to their predicament with the appointment of Tony Russ who left Ulster to take up his job at Blundellsands on December 1st. Shortly afterwards several new players were brought to the club, the most notable being Bridgend half backs Wayne Morris and Lyndon Griffiths, North Harbour centre Mike Mullins and local boy Shaun Woof, who all helped to turn things round to the point where the club won five of the last seven league games to finish in ninth place and well clear of the relegation zone. With the recruitment of further new players during the close season well Waterloo look forward to a more successful season and a place in the play offs come next May

Waterloo FC:

Colours: Myrtle, scarlet & white hoops/green shorts.   **Change colours:** White with myrtle,scarlet & white thin striped 'V'

COURAGE LEAGUE MATCH DETAILS 1996-97

No	Ven.	Date	Opponents	Att.	Res.	Score	Scorers
1	(A)	07.09 v	Newcastle	1479	L	13-30	Blyth(t)Handley(c2p)
12	(H)	14.09 v	Moseley	500	W	20-13	Wright(t)Beckett(t)White(t)Handley(cp)
3	(A)	21.09 v	London Scot	448	L	30-42	D Thompson(t)Wright(t)White(t)C Thompson(3c3p)
4	(H)	28.09 v	Coventry	700	L	17-36	PenTry(2t)C Thompson(2cp)
5	(A)	05.10 v	Rotherham	850	L	23-38	Coast(t)White(t)C Thompson(2c3p)
6	(H)	12.10 v	Bedford	800	L	11-34	Blyth(t)Handley(dg)C Thompson(p)
7	(A)	19.10 v	Wakefield	600	L	12-45	C Thompson(4p)
8	(H)	26.10 v	Nottingham	450	L	19-20	Coast(t)C Thompson(c4p)
9	(A)	02.11 v	Richmond	1500	L	13-64	Blyth(t)Emmett(c2p)
10	(H)	09.11 v	Blackheath	600	W	16-10	Aitchison(t)Handley(c3p)
11	(A)	16.11 v	Rugby	430	W	56-15	Coast(2t)Stevenson(2t)Blyth(t)Buckton(t(Aitchison(t)Handley(t5c2p)
12	(A)	18.01 v	Coventry	2000	L	16-28	Blyth(t)C Thompson(c3p)
13	(H)	08.02 v	Rotherham	500	L	23-27	Coast(t)Holt(t)C Thompson(2c3p)
14	(A)	22.02 v	Moseley	702	L	13-17	Bruce(t)C Thompson(c2p)
15	(A)	08.03 v	Bedford	1800	L	6-38	Griffiths(2p)
16	(H)	22.03 v	Wakefield	1000	W	16-11	Griffiths(tc3p)
17	(A)	05.04 v	Nottingham	262	W	33-13	Handley(t)Pilecki(t)Blyth(t)Woof(t)Griffiths(2c3p)
18	(H)	12.04 v	Richmond	1500	L	29-58	Morris(t)Wolfenden(t)Blyth(t)PenTry(t)Griffiths(3cp)
19	(A)	19.04 v	Blackheath	1980	W	48-27	Woof(2t)Wolfenden(2t)Bruce(t)Mullins(t)Griffiths(6c2p)
20	(H)	26.04 v	Rugby	700	W	45-12	Mullins(2t)Buckton(t)Wright(t)Woof(t)Bruce(t)Allott(t)Griffiths(5c)
21	(H)	30.04 v	Newcastle	2500	L	24-66	Pilecki(t)Morris(t)Buckton(t)Griffiths(3cp)
22	(H)	03.05 v	London Scot	700	W	23-17	Wolfenden(t)Griffiths(6p)

1996-97 HIGHLIGHTS

LEAGUE DEBUTS:
David Thompson, Jason Green, Marcus Coast, Gareth Monaghan, Steve Bibby, Jason Brittin, Karl Temmen, Damian Evans, Nick Regenvanu, Andy Whalley, Steve Rule, Bart Pilecki, Shaun Woof, Lyndon Griffiths, Matt Holt, Mike Mullins, Wayne Morris.

PLAYERS USED: 38 plus 5 as replacement.

EVER PRESENT: Tony Handley and Marcus Coast.

❏ Second rower and club captain Nick Allott becomes the first man at the club to reach 100 league appearances and extends his club record to 102.

❏ One of only two teams in the division to score more tries away from home than at home.

❏ Centre Nigel Hill extends his club record for appearances by a back to 64 after having shared the record with Ian Aitchison.

❏ In beating Rugby 56-15 away they set a new victory for both biggest win and highest score for in any league match.

❏ In the above match they also set a new record by scoring seven tries in a match for the first time. The previous record of six was set against Bedford in January 96.

❏ Veteran Ian Aitchison extended his career record to 336 with the aid of two more tries.

	Pts	T	C	P	D	Apps	Ave.
	336	5	23	80	9	50	6.72

❏ Welsh stand-off Lyndon Griffiths made an impressive start to his league career scoring 99 points in the clubs last 10 games.
Griffiths broke Ian Aitchison's club record of four conversions in a game when he converted all six tries in the impressive 48-27 win at Blackheath.
Those six helped him break Martin Emmett's record of 12 conversions in a season. The record now stands at 20 which is just three behind Ian Aitchison's career total of 23.

❏ Back row forward David Blyth fails by one to equal Steve Bracegirdle's record of eight tries in a season set back in 1990-91. Blyth is the first forward to top the clubs try scoring chart outright. In 93-94 flanker John Ashcroft finished joint leading try scorer.

WATERLOO'S COURAGE LEAGUE MATCH DETAILS 1996-97

15	14	13	12	11	10	9	1	2	3	4	5	6	7	8	Replacements	#
D Thompson	Green	Hill	Hill	Monaghan	Handley	Wright	Fenton	Hackett	Beckett	White	Kay	Blyth	Buckton	Bibby	Brittin(2)Temmen(4)	1
D Thompson	Green	Hill	Hill	Monaghan	Handley	Wright	Fenton	Hackett	Beckett	White	Allott	Blyth	Buckton	Bibby	Brittin	2
D Thompson	Coast	Hill	Hill	Monaghan	Handley	Wright	Fenton	Hackett	Beckett	White	Allott	Blyth	Buckton	Bibby	D Evans(13)Donovan(1)	3
D Thompson	Coast	Hill	Hill	Monaghan	Handley	Wright	Fenton	Hackett	Beckett	White	Allott	Blyth	Buckton	Bibby	Brittin(3)Wolfenden(4)	4
D Thompson	C Thompson	Coast	Hill	Monaghan	Handley	Wright	Peters	Hackett	Beckett	White	Allott	Wolfenden	Buckton	Bibby	Brittin(3)Wolfenden(4)	5
D Thompson	C Thompson	Coast	Hill	Monaghan	Handley	Wright	Fenton	Hackett	Beckett	White	Allott	Wolfenden	Buckton	Bibby	Topping(9)	6
D Thompson	C Thompson	Coast	Hill	Monaghan	Handley	Wright	Bloomfield	Peters	Beckett	Temmen	Allott	Regenvanu	Buckton	Bibby	Brittin(2)	7
D Thompson	C Thompson	Coast	Hill	Monaghan	Handley	Wright	Bloomfield	Peters	Beckett	Temmen	Allott	Regenvanu	Buckton	Blyth	Regenvanu(5)Kennedy(3)	8
Emmett	Coast	Stevenson	Hill	Whalley	Handley	Young	Fenton	Hackett	Beckett	Rule	Wilkinson	Blyth	Regenvanu	Bibby	Hackett(11)	9
Handley	Coast	Stevenson	Hill	Monaghan	Handley	Young	Britton	Beckett	Beckett	White	Rule	Regenvanu	Buckton	Blyth	Temmen(5)	10
Handley	Coast	Stevenson	Hill	Monaghan	Aitchison	Young	Beckett	Hackett	Plecki	White	Kay	Regenvanu	Buckton	Blyth	Temmen(8)Bloomfield(5)Donovan(10)	11
C Thompson	Coast	Handley	Hill	Whalley	Aitchison	Wright	Plecki	Hackett	Beckett	White	Kay	Regenvanu	Buckton	Blyth	Topping(2)Stevenson(6)	12
C Thompson	Coast	Handley	Hill	Bruce	Aitchison	Wright	Plecki	Hackett	Beckett	White	Allott	Blyth	Buckton	Blyth	Bibby(7)	13
C Thompson	Coast	Woof	Hill	Bruce	Aitchison	Beckett	Plecki	Hackett	Beckett	White	Allott	D Evans	Buckton	Blyth	Handley(9),C.Evans(6)	14
Handley	Coast	Mullins	Hill	Bruce	Griffiths	Wright	Plecki	Hackett	Beckett	White	Allott	Kay	Buckton	Blyth		15
Handley	Coast	Mullins	Hill	Bruce	Griffiths	Wright	Plecki	Hackett	Beckett	White	Allott	Kay	Buckton	Blyth		16
Handley	Coast	Mullins	Woof	Bruce	Griffiths	Morris	Plecki	Hackett	Beckett	White	Allott	Kay	Buckton	Blyth	Cooper(6)Rule(4)	17
Handley	Coast	Mullins	Woof	Bruce	Griffiths	Morris	Plecki	Hackett	Beckett	Temmen	Allott	Wolfenden	Buckton	Blyth	Wright(9)C Thompson(15)Cooper(6)	18
Handley	Coast	Mullins	Woof	Bruce	Griffiths	Morris	Plecki	Hackett	Beckett	White	Allott	Wolfenden	Buckton	Blyth		19
Handley	Coast	Mullins	Woof	Bruce	Griffiths	Wright	Plecki	Hackett	Beckett	White	Allott	Wolfenden	Buckton	Blyth	Fenton(3)Hackett(2)Young(9)Emmett(6)	20
Handley	Coast	Mullins	Woof	Bruce	Griffiths	Morris	Plecki	Hackett	Beckett	White	Allott	Wolfenden	Buckton	Blyth	Wright(9)Fenton(1)Holt(2)Temmen(5)C Thompson(10)	21
Handley	Coast	Woof	Mullins	Bruce	Griffiths	Wright	Plecki	Hackett	Beckett	White	Temmen	Wolfenden	Buckton	Blyth	Holt(2)	22

WATERLOO LEAGUE STATISTICS
(COMPILED BY STEPHEN McCORMACK)

Season	Div.	P	W	D	L	F	(Tries	Con	Pen	DG)	A	(Tries	Con	Pen	DG)	Most Points	Most Tries
87-88	1	10	4	0	6	123	(13	4	14	7)	208	(23	13	27	3)	66 - Ian Aitchison	4 - Peter Cooley
88-89	1	11	1	1	9	120	(8	5	25	1)	235	(31	15	23	4)	77 - Ian Aitchison	4 - Peter Cooley
89-90	2	11	3	0	8	147	(16	7	21	2)	193	(29	16	16	0)	43 - Richard Angell	5 - Peter Cooley
90-91	2	12	4	0	8	154	(15	8	24	2)	206	(30	13	16	4)	57 - Ian Aitchison	8 - Steve Bracegirdle
91-92	2	12	8	0	4	206	(21	13	31	1)	184	(27	14	15	1)	92 - Ian Aitchison	4 - Gary Meredith
92-93	2	12	10	0	2	228	(17	10	33	8)	138	(7	2	32	1)	126 Paul Grayson	3 - Austin Healey
93-94	2	18	6	2	10	231	(13	8	47	3)	346	(35	24	40	1)	137 - Steve Swindells	2 - by 3 players - Gary Meredith, Steve Swindells & John Ashcroft.
94-95	2	18	8	0	10	287	(20	8	52	5)	331	(33	14	42	4)	160 - Steve Swindells	4 - Neil Ryan & Steve Wright
95-96	2	18	7	2	9	309	(26	16	45	4)	482	(57	37	40	1)	134 - Martin Emmett	4 - Peter McCaugheran
96-97	2	22	7	0	15	506	(53	41	52	1)	661	(86	57	36	3)	99 - Lyndon Griffiths	7 - David Blyth
Totals		144	58	5	71	2311	(202	120	344	34)	2984	(358	205	286	22)		

	HOME	AWAY
BIGGEST WIN	(33pts) 45-12 v Rugby 26.4.97	(41pts) 56-15 v Rugby 16.11.96
DEFEAT	(66pts) 3-69 v Northampton 28.10.96	(64pts) 5-69 v Northampton 13.4.96
MOST POINTS SCORED	45-12 v Rugby 26.4.97	56-15 v Rugby 16.11.96
AGAINST	3-69 v Northampton 28.10.96	5-69 v Northampton 13.4.96

MOST CONSECUTIVE VICTORIES - 7

MOST CONSECUTIVE DEFEATS - 11

MOST TRIES IN A MATCH
(FOR) 7 v Rugby 26.4.97
(AGAINST) 11 v Northampton 28.10.95

MOST APPEARANCES
FORWARD: 102 Nick Allott
BACK: 64 Nigel Hill

CONSECUTIVE APPEARANCES
39 Shaun Gallagher

CONSECUTIVE SCORING MATCHES
Scoring Tries - 4 - Steve Bracegirdle
Scoring Points - 14 - Steve Swindells

MOST	in a SEASON	in a CAREER	in a MATCH
Points	160 Steve Swindells 94-95	346 Ian Aitchison 87-97	23 Martin Emmett v Bedford 13.1.96 (H)
Tries	8 Steve Bracegirdle 90-91	14 Steve Bracegirdle 90-93	2 by 11 players - Steve Bracegirdle (x2)
Conversions	20 Lyndon Griffiths 96-97	22 Ian Aitchison 87-95	6 Lyndon Griffiths v Blackheath 19.4.97 (A)
Penalties	48 Steve Swindells 94-95	88 Steve Swindells 92-95	6 Ian Aitchison v Blackheath 25.4.92 (A) Steve Swindells v Otley 12.3.94 (A) v Newcastle Gos. 10.9.94 (H) Martin Emmett v Bedford 13.1.96 (H)
Drop Goals	6 Paul Grayson 92-93	9 Ian Aitchison 87-95	2 Ian Aitchison v Gloucester 31.10.87 (H) v Sale 2.1.88 (H) Ian Croper v Sale 9.3.91 (H) Paul Grayson v Sale 13.3.93 (H) Neil Ryan v Lon. Irish 24.9.94 (H) v Newcastle Gos. 14.10.95 (A)

WATERLOO PLAYING SQUAD

NAME	Ht	Wt	Birthdate	Birthplace	Club	Apps	Pts	T	C	P	DG

BACKS

NAME	Ht	Wt	Birthdate	Birthplace	Club	Apps	Pts	T	C	P	DG
Tony Handley	5.11	13.7	12.11.73	Salford							
England: Students, Colts.		North.			Waterloo	65+1	88	3	11	16	1
Marcus Coast	6.1	15.0	14.05.76	Bebington	New Brighton						
North u21					Waterloo	22	25	5	-	-	-
Simon Wright	5.8	12.7	15.02.65		Prev. Clubs: New Brighton, Liverpool St.H.						
Cheshire					Waterloo	53+2	53	10	-	-	1
Wayne Morris	6.0	12.8	06.12.72	Swansea	Prev. Clubs: Pontypool, Bridgend.						
Wales: u21.					Waterloo	4	10	2	-	-	-
Lyndon Griffiths	5.6	11.0	17.02.74	Bridgend							
Wales: u21.					Waterloo	10	99	1	20	18	-
Shaun Woof	6.2	15.0	06.03.77	Liverpool	Caldy						
Cheshire					Waterloo	7	20	4	-	-	-
Mike Mullins	6.0	13.6	29.10.70	Auckland							
North Harbour					Waterloo	8	15	3	-	-	-
Ian Bruce	5.10	14.0		Colombo	Orrell		15	3	-	-	-
Scotland: u21, Exiles.					Waterloo	21	30	6	-	-	-
Chris Thompson	6.0	12.3	13.11.71	Widnes	Sheffield						
England: u21, Students.		North.			Waterloo	22+2	116	-	13	30	-
Nigel Hill			14.12.67	Amersham	Prev. Clubs: Oxford, Moseley.						
South West u21, Colts.					Waterloo	64+2	5	1	-	-	-
Paddy Young	5.10	13.8	14.06.73	Belfast							
					Waterloo	5+4	-	-	-	-	-
David Thompson											
					Waterloo		-	-	-	-	-
Gareth Monaghan	5.10	11.7	22.06.71	Manchester	Leigh						
Lancashire, u21, Colts.					Waterloo	9	-	-	-	-	-
Phil Graham	5.10	13.7	02.12.76	Carlisle	Liverpool St Helens						
North u21.					Waterloo		-	-	-	-	-

FORWARDS

NAME	Ht	Wt	Birthdate	Birthplace	Club	Apps	Pts	T	C	P	DG
Matt Holt	6.0	16.0	30.10.71	Brisbane	W. Brisbane						
Queensland Reds, u21, u19.					Waterloo	8+2	-	-	-	-	-
Bart Pilecki	6.2	19.0		Brisbane							
Queensland					Waterloo	12	10	2	-	-	-
Russell Kirby	6.0	16.10	30.05.71	Solihull	Prev. Clubs: Birkenhead P., Rugby.						
Warwickshire					Waterloo		-	-	-	-	-
Mark Beckett	6.2	19.7	16.10.65	Hartlepool	Prev. Clubs: Askeans, West Hartlepool.						
North, Lancashire.					Waterloo	72	4	1	-	-	-
Paul Hackett	5.11	10.0	28.02.64	Liverpool	Crewe & Nantwich						
North, Cheshire.					Waterloo	92+2	2	5	-	-	-
Paul White	6.4	17.2	08.05.70	Worthing	Worthing						
London u21, Colts.					Waterloo	49+2	25	5	-	-	-
Ben Kay	6.6	17.0	14.12.75	Liverpool							
England: u21.					Waterloo	29	10	2	-	-	-
Nick Allott	6.5	17.0	12.01.64	Cheadle Hulme	Liverpool St. Helens						
North, Lancashire.					Waterloo	101	24	5	-	-	-
David Blyth	6.3	17.0	14.03.71	Glasgow	Newcastle	0+1		-	··		
England: u21, Colts. Scottish Exiles.					West Hartlepool	9	-	-	-	-	-
					Waterloo	55	45	9	-	-	-
Carl Wolfenden	6.2	15.11	05.02.69	Waterloo							
Lancashire u21.					Waterloo	14+5	25	5	-	-	-
Karl Temmen	6.10	19.0	23.09.74	Salisbury	Preston G/hoppers						
North u21. Lancashire, u21, Colts.					Waterloo	5+4	-	-	-	-	-
Peter Buckton	6.2	14.0	24.11.60	Hull							
England: A, u23, Students.					Waterloo	81	70	14	-	-	-
Steve Bibby					Orrell	49+5	14	3	-	-	-
					Waterloo	7+1	-	-	-	-	-
Jason Brittin	5.10	15.5	24.10.73	Hawkes Bay							
					Waterloo	2+3	-	-	-	-	-
Paul Cooper	6.0	15.0	05.09.66	Liverpool							
					Waterloo	32+7	4	1	-	-	-
Mike Regenvanu	6.1	14.0	06.02.74	Brisbane							
Queensland u21.					Waterloo	4+1	-	-	-	-	-

The Pavillion, St Anthony's Rd., Blundellsands, Liverpool. L23 8TW.

Tel: 0151 924 4552

CAPACITY: 8,900 **SEATED:** 900 **STANDING:** 8,000

SIMPLE DIRECTIONS:
  By Road: End of M57, follow signs for Crosby, Waterloo FC sign posted to ground
  Nearest Railway Station: Crosby & Blundellsands, 1/2 mile down St Anthonys Rd.

CAR PARKING: 100 Saturdays only

ADMISSION: Matchdays - Adults Standing £5.50, Seated £6.50; Children & OAPs £3.00

CLUB SHOP: Yes; Manager Frank Phillips Tel c/o Club

CLUBHOUSE: Normal Licensing hours; Three bars, with snacks & bar meals available
  Function room: Yes, available for hire, capacity 150, contact Frank Spencer 0151 924 4552

TRAINING NIGHTS: Tuesday & Thursday

MATCHDAY PROGRAMME

Size	A5
Number of pages	34
Price	£1
Programme Editor	contact - Commercial Manager
Advertising Rates	Full page £500
	Half page £250
	Qtr page £125

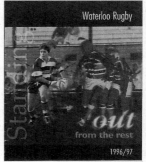

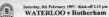

Saturday, 8th February 1997 - Kick-off 2.15 pm
WATERLOO v Rotherham

WEST HARTLEPOOL R.F.C.

NICKNAME: West

FOUNDED: 1881

President R Bateman, c/o West Hartlepool RC, Brierton Lane, Hartlepool, TS25 5DR
01429 233149 (B), 01429 261857 (Fax)

Chairman B A Hindle, c/o West Hartlepool RFC, as above

Club Secretary A Savage, c/o West Hartlepool RFC, as above
Fixtures Secretary D Butcher, 55 Arncliffe Gardens, Hartlepool.
01429 298241 (H), 01429 233149 (B), 01429 862818 (Fax)
Director of Rugby M Brewer, c/o West Hartlepool RFC, as above

West Hartlepool's relegation from the First Division came at the end of a season of inconsistency, when they played some excellent rugby at home, but produced some distinctly moderate efforts away from Brierton Lane where they haven't won a League game for two seasons.

An early win against Saracens was a boost but they let leads slip at Orrell and London Irish where they lost despite scoring 41 points. Successive wins against Bristol and Orrell followed immediately but that was the end of their League success as London Irish's strong finish in April moved them out of the automatic relegation spot and above West, who flattered to deceive at times late in the season.

Stephen John's thirteen League tries bettered the previous League record, and there were tremendously consistent performances from Kiwis Ivan Morgan and Jamie Connolly, who will play a major role in West's plans for the future. Chris John broke John Stabler's points record for a season, albeit in a larger League, though Stabler had the consolation of scoring 26 points in a game (at London Irish).

With few of the squad contracted on a full time basis, it was easy to see the difference between West and the clubs with the luxury of regular daily practice opportunities. The realities of the north east mean it is unlikely that West will ever achieve a full time sqaud, but playing problems recently have not diminished West's ambition to play at the highest level.

Mark Ring's legacy was a strong contingent of talented youngsters (six in the England Under 21 squad, including Chris Murphy who skippered the Under 21s) and this allied to new director of rugby, All Black Michael Brewer whose obvious talents should spell a successful campaign next time round.

West Hartlepool Rugby Club; 1st XV squad 96-97.

Colours: Red, white, green.

Change colours: Blue, white

WEST HARTLEPOOL

COURAGE LEAGUE MATCH DETAILS 1996-97

No	Ven.	Date	Opponents	Att.	Res.	Score	Scorers
1	(A)	31.08	v Northampton	4775	L	20-46	Stabler(t)Ions(t)Silva(tc)C John(p)
2	(H)	07.09	v Harlequins	2200	L	21-41	S John(2t)C John(c3p)
3	(A)	14.09	v Sale	1296	L	18-58	Silva(t)S John(t)C John(c2p)
4	(H)	21.09	v Saracens	1700	W	25-16	Ring(t)Morgan(t)C John(t2c2p)
5	(A)	28.09	v Bath	5500	L	10-46	S John(t)Silva(c)C John(p)
6	(H)	05.10	v Leicester	2300	L	19-30	S John(2t)Wood(t)C John(2c)
7	(H)	09.11	v Gloucester	1800	L	14-23	Wood(t)C John (3p)
8	(A)	07.12	v Orrell	1800	L	15-22	Wood(t)Cordle(t)C John(c)Silva(p)
9	(A)	28.12	v London Irish	1620	L	41-52	Connolly(t)Ions(t)Morgan(t)Stabler(t3c5p)
10	(H)	04.01	v Bristol	1078	W	19- 8	Connolly(t)Stabler(c3p)Silva(p)
11	(H)	11.01	v Orrell	1123	W	24- 8	Earnshaw(2t)Botham(t)Harvey(t)Stabler(2c)
12	(A)	18.01	v Gloucester	4072	L	10-37	C John(t)Stabler(cp)
13	(H)	08.02	v Wasps	2200	L	23-48	Botham(t)Peacock(t)C John(tc2p)
14	(A)	23.02	v Wasps	1000	L	12-36	S John(2t)C John(c)
15	(A)	08.03	v Leicester	8709	L	3-48	C John(p)
16	(A)	22.03	v Harlequins	1903	L	10-48	Earnshaw(t)S John(t)
17	(H)	27.03	v Bath	3000	L	16-24	Barnes(t)S John(t)C John(2p)
18	(A)	30.03	v Saracens	2144	L	8-51	Moseley(t)C John(p)
19	(H)	05.04	v Sale	1800	L	22-43	S John(2t)C John(4p)
20	(H)	19.04	v Northampton	2200	L	17-57	Silva(2t)C John(2cp)
21	(H)	26.04	v London Irish	1900	L	18-33	S John(t)Mitchell(t)C John(c2p)
22	(A)	04.05	v Bristol	1965	L	17-20	Ions(t)C John(3pdg)

1996-97 HIGHLIGHTS

LEAGUE DEBUTS: Chris John, Steven John, Jaime Connolly, Matthew Silva, Wayne de Jonge, Andrew Peacock, Kevin Moseley, Ivan Morgan, Virgil Hartland, Mark Roderick, Gerald Cordle, Stuart Whitehead, George Truelove, Phil Harvey, Craig Hart, Andy Tate, Alastair Remus, Danny Kano, Matthew Kennedy, John Marston, Liam Botham, Mark Challinor, John Painter, Charles Yoeman, David Barnes, Lee Francis, Ben Ryan, Gareth Rowlands, N Hood.

TRY ON DEBUT: Steven John.

PLAYERS USED: 43 plus 3 as replacement.

EVER PRESENT: Steven John.

❏ John Stabler scores 26 points at London Irish to establish a new record for points in a match. The previous record of 23 was also held by Stabler.

❏ In the above game West lost 41-52 to achieve the highest score by a losing side in League rugby. This record was later beaten by Walsall.

❏ West were the only team in the division not to win an away match. They have now lost 20 consecutive away games since they beat Bristol in April 95.

❏ Scored tries in more games than Leicester - 21 to 19.

❏ Stand-off John Stabler made six appearances during the season and in the process passed the record for most appearances by a Back. Those six Appearances took him to 91(3) four more than the previous record holder winger Owen Evans.

❏ The two Johns, Chris and Steven, both broke records during the season.
Centre and wing Steven set a new record of 13 tries in a season. the previous record of nine was set by scrum-half Jonathan Wrigley back in 1990-91.

❏ Chris, who played full back, centre and stand-off, broke John Stabler's record for points and penalties in a season with 126 and 28. The previous records were 118 and 26 respectively.

	Pts	T	C	P	D	Apps	Ave.
Chris John 96-97	126	3	12	28	1	18	7.00
John Stabler 90-91	118	2	16	26	-	12	9.80

❏ Only Orrell with 352 points, scored fewer points than West's 382.

❏ One of three teams to concede tries in all 22 games.

WEST HARTLEPOOL'S COURAGE LEAGUE MATCH DETAILS 1996-97

15	14	13	12	11	10	9	1	2	3	4	5	6	7	8	Replacements	No.
C.John	Wood	S.John	Connolly	Stabler	Stabler	Patterson	de Jonge	Peacock	Whitehead	Murphy	Moseley	Mitchell	Brown	Morgan	Ring(15),Hartland(1)	1
Silva	Wood	Connolly	Ring	S.John	C.John	Roderick	de Jonge	Whitelock	Whitelock	Murphy	Moseley	Mitchell	Ions	Morgan	Stabler(13),Patterson(9)	2
C.John	Wood	S.John	Ring	Silva	Stabler	Roderick	de Jonge	Whitelock	Hartland	Murphy	Mitchell	Mitchell	Ions	Wappett	Wappett(5)	3
Silva	Wood	S.John	C.John	Cordle	Ring	Roderick	de Jonge	Whitehead	Hartland	Murphy	Mitchell	Ions	Brown	Morgan	Whitelock(3);Herbert(2)	4
Silva	Oliphant	S.John	C.John	Truelove	Ring	Roderick	de Jonge	Hartland	Hartland	Mitchell	Hart	Ions	Brown	Morgan	Earnshaw,Wappett(4),Lee(9)	5
Silva	Truelove	S.John	C.John	Wood	Ring	Harvey	de Jonge	Peacock	Hartland	Murphy	Mitchell	Ions	Brown	Tate	Whitelock(3),Oliphant(15),Remus(5)	6
Silva	Truelove	S.John	C.John	S.John	Ring	Karno	de Jonge	Peacock	Hartland	Murphy	Moseley	Ions	Brown	Brown	Whitelock(3)	7
Silva	Wood	Connolly	C.John	S.John	Ring	Roderick	de Jonge	Kennedy	Mitchell	Murphy	Moseley	Ions	Tate	Morgan	Cordle(12);Whitehead(2);Whitelock(3)	8
Silva	Wood	Connolly	S.John	Cordle	Stabler	Roderick	de Jonge	Peacock	Whitelock	Murphy	Moseley	Ions	Remus	Morgan	Oliphant(11),Marston(6)	9
Silva	Wood	Connolly	S.John	S.John	Stabler	Harvey	Whitehead	Peacock	Whitelock	Murphy	Moseley	Challinor	Roderick	Morgan		10
Silva	Wood	Botham	Connolly	Wood	Stabler	Harvey	Whitehead	Peacock	Whitelock	Murphy	Moseley	Ions	Earnshaw	Morgan	Peacock(2),Kennedy(3)	11
Silva	Wood	Botham	Connolly	Stabler	Stabler	Harvey	Whitehead	Peacock	Whitelock	Murphy	Moseley	Roderick	Roderick	Morgan	C.John(14),Peacock(2),Painter(1)Yoeman(6)	12
M.Silva	Wood	Botham	Connolly	C.John	Harvey	Harvey	Painter	Peacock	de Jonge	Murphy	Moseley	Ions	Ions	Morgan	Barnes(1),Kennedy(6)	13
M.Silva	M.Wood	Botham	Connolly	C.John	Harvey	Roderick	Barnes	Kennedy	de Jonge	Murphy	Francis	Roderick	Emerson	Morgan		14
Silva	Wood	Botham	Connolly	C.John	Harvey	Roderick	Barnes	Kennedy	de Jonge	Murphy	Moseley	Ions	Yoeman	Morgan	Stabler(14)Peacock(2)Francis(4)Harvey(4)Emmerson(7)	15
Silva	Truelove	Botham	Connolly	C.John	Roderick	Roderick	Barnes	de Jonge	de Jonge	Murphy	Moseley	Emmerson	Emmerson	Morgan	Armitage(13)Stabler(10)Harvey(9)Whitelock(3)	16
Silva	Truelove	Botham	Connolly	C.John	Ryan	Roderick	Barnes	de Jonge	de Jonge	Murphy	Moseley	Ions	Earnshaw	Whitelock	Whitelock(3)	17
Silva	Truelove	Botham	Connolly	C.John	Ryan	Roderick	Barnes	de Jonge	de Jonge	Murphy	Moseley	Ions	Earnshaw	Morgan	Roderick(11)Kennedy(2)Francis(5)Knowles(15)	18
Oliphant	Truelove	Connolly	Knowles	C.John	Ryan	Roderick	Barnes	Peacock	Hartland	Francis	Francis	Ions	Earnshaw	Morgan	Kennedy(2)Rowlands(5)Mitchell(6)	19
Silva	Truelove	Knowles	Connolly	C.John	Ryan	Roderick	Barnes	Peacock	Murphy	Murphy	Rowlands	Ions	Earnshaw	de Jonge	de Jonge(4)Whitelock(5)Harvey(9)Botham(12)Kennedy(2)	20
Silva	Wood	Botham	Connolly	C.John	Ryan	Ryan	Barnes	Kennedy	Whitelock	Whitelock	Rowlands	Ions	Ions	Morgan	de Jonge(3)Hart(8)	21
Silva	Cordle	Botham	Connolly	C.John	Roderick	Roderick	Painter	Peacock	Mitchell	Mitchell	Rowlands	Hood	Ions	Morgan	Kennedy(2)de Jonge(1)	22

WEST HARTLEPOOL LEAGUE STATISTICS
(COMPILED BY STEPHEN McCORMACK)

Season	Div.	P	W	D	L	F (Tries Con Pen DG)	A (Tries Con Pen DG)	Most Points	Most Tries
87-88	3	11	10	0	1	249 (33 12 27 4)	105 (11 5 16 1)	83 - John Stabler	6 - Owen Evans
88-89	3	11	5	1	5	164 (19 11 18 4)	133 (18 8 14 1)	60 - John Stabler	8 - Dave Cooke
89-90	3	11	5	2	4	175 (20 10 23 2)	120 (8 4 21 1)	65 - Gary Armstrong	5 - Dave Cooke
90-91	3	12	10	1	1	282 (42 24 21 1)	90 (13 4 10 0)	87 - John Stabler	9 - John Wrigley
91-92	2	12	11	0	1	244 (33 17 26 0)	89 (12 4 11 0)	118 - John Stabler	7 - John Wrigley
92-93	1	12	3	0	9	149 (14 8 21 0)	236 (24 12 28 2)	89 - John Stabler	3 - Alan Brown
93-94	2	18	13	2	3	389 (39 25 43 5)	271 (22 13 36 9)	103 - John Stabler	7 - John Wrigley
94-95	1	18	6	1	11	312 (35 19 33 0)	412 (45 29 38 5)	93 - Tim Stimpson	5 - Paul Hodder
95-96	1	18	0	0	18	288 (30 15 34 2)	634 (77 51 42 7)	110 - Tim Stimpson	5 - Tim Stimpson
96-97	1	22	3	0	19	382 (44 21 39 1)	795 (109 68 34 4)	126 - Chris John	13 - Steve John
Totals		145	66	7	72	2634 (309 162 285 19)	2891 (339 199 250 30)		

	HOME	AWAY
BIGGEST WIN	(43pts) 47-4 v Broughton Park 9.3.91	(37pts) 43-6 v Birmingham 6.2.88
BIGGEST DEFEAT	(70pts) 21-91 v Harlequins 23.3.96	(46pts) 9-55 v Northampton 3.4.93
MOST POINTS SCORED	48-20 v Otley 15.1.94	43-6 v Birmingham 6.2.88
AGAINST	21-91 v Harlequins 23.3.96	9-55 v Northampton 3.4.93

MOST CONSECUTIVE VICTORIES - 9   **MOST CONSECUTIVE DEFEATS - 19**

MOST TRIES IN A MATCH   **MOST APPEARANCES**
(FOR) 8 v Birmingham 6.2.88   FORWARD: 101 Phil Lancaster
(AGAINST) 14 v Harlequins 23.3.96   BACK: 91(3) John Stabler

CONSECUTIVE SCORING MATCHES

CONSECUTIVE APPEARANCES   Scoring Tries - 4 - Owen Evans & Steve Cook
64 John Stabler 11.7.89 - 26.3.94   Scoring Points - 36 - John Stabler

MOST	in a SEASON	in a CAREER	in a MATCH
Points	126 Chris John 96-97	630 John Stabler 87-97	26 John Stabler v Lon. Irish 28.12.96 (A)
Tries	13 Steven John 96-97	32 Owen Evans 87-96	3 Owen Evans v Nuneaton 23.4.88 (H) Peter Robinson v V. of Lune 2.3.91 (A) John Wrigley v Moseley 14.12.91 (H)
Conversions	19 John Stabler 90-91	83 John Stabler 87-97	6 John Stabler v Broughton P. 9.3.91 (H)
Penalties	28 Chris John 96-97	127 John Stabler 87-97	6 John Stabler v Met Police 6.1.88 (A)
Drop Goals	3 John Stabler 88-89	8 John Stabler 87-97	2 Kevin Oliphant v V. of Lune 7.11.88 (A) John Stabler v Sheffield 19.11.88 (H)

WEST HARTLEPOOL PLAYING SQUAD

NAME	Ht	Wt	Birthdate	Birthplace	Club	Apps	Pts	T	C	P	DG
BACKS											
Chris John	6.1	14.2	19.02.73	Cardiff	Cardiff						
Wales: Students					**West Hartlepool**	18+1	126	3	12	28	-
Steven John	5.10	13.0	11.10.73	Cardiff	Cardiff						
Wales: Schools					**West Hartlepool**	22	65	13	-	-	-
Jamie Connolly	5.10	14.0	06.02.73	New Zealand	Canterbury						
South Island. Canterbury.					**West Hartlepool**	17	10	2	-	-	-
Liam Botham	6.0	13.10	26.08.77	Doncaster							
England: u21.					**West Hartlepool**	11+1	10	2	-	-	-
Matthew Silva	6.1	14.7	15.03.70	Cardiff	Prev. Clubs: Halifax (RL), Newbridge.						
England: u21. North.					**West Hartlepool**	21	25	3	2	2	-
Mike Wood	5.11	12.2	15.07.76	Stockton							
England: u21. North.					**West Hartlepool**	23	35	7	-	-	-
Mark Roderick	5.10	13.8	17.09.71	Morriston							
					West Hartlepool	14+1	-	-	-	-	-
Ben Ryan	5.11	12.8	11.09.71	Wimbledon	Bedford						
					West Hartlepool	4	-	-	-	-	-
George Truelove	6.4	14.4	22.09.75	Newcastle	Saracens	1	-	-	-	-	-
England: Colts, 18 Group.					**West Hartlepool**	7	-	-	-	-	-
Phil Harvey	5.6	11.0	01.05.76	Bishop Auckland	Prev. Clubs: Bath, Saracens.						
England: u21.					**West Hartlepool**	5+3	5	1	-	-	-
Toby Knowles	5.10	13.4	16.05.74	Durham	Durham City						
England: u21, Colts.					**West Hartlepool**	5+2	-	-	-	-	-
John Stabler	6.2	13.2	05.02.63	Hartlepool							
North.					**West Hartlepool**	91+3	630	13	83	127	8
Kevan Oliphant	5.8	12.4	11.01.67	Hartlepool							
England: Colts.					**West Hartlepool**	85+2	199	5	20	41	5
Mark Ring	6.1	13.3	15.10.62	Cardiff	Cardiff						
Wales					**West Hartlepool**	10+1	5	1	-	-	-
FORWARDS											
Virgil Hartland	5.10	15.2	23.04.77	Gloucester	Prev. Club: Gloucester						
John Painter	5.1	16.4	26.02.64	Hartlepool							
					West Hartlepool	2+1	-	-	-	-	-
David Barnes	6.1	16.2	17.07.76	Leicester	Kendal						
England: u21.					**West Hartlepool**	9+1	5	1	-	-	-
Andrew Peacock	6.0	15.7	03.12.68	Newport	Newport						
Monmouth.					**West Hartlepool**	15+3	5	1	-	-	-
Dave Mitchell	6.4	15.7	19.10.71	Richmond	Harrogate						
England: Schools					**West Hartlepool**	63+6	15	3	-	-	-
Gareth Rowlands	6.5	17.6	12.03.71	Bridgend	Bridgend						
Canada					**West Hartlepool**	3+1	-	-	-	-	-
Nick Hood	6.1	14.0	14.03.75	Sunderland							
					West Hartlepool	2	-	-	-	-	-
Jon Ions	6.1	14.4	12.12.76	Wakefield	Wakefield						
England: u21.					**West Hartlepool**	23	20	4	-	-	-
Ivan Morgan	6.4	15.2	30.01.76	New Zealand	Canterbury						
Canterbury					**West Hartlepool**	20	10	2	-	-	-
Phil Whitelock	5.7	15.3	16.03.63	Hartlepool							
Durham					**West Hartlepool**	83+6	25	6	-	-	-
Wayne DeJonge	5.10	17.7	16.07.68	Sydney (Aust.)							
N.S.W. Country					**West Hartlepool**	19+3	-	-	-	-	-
Russell Earnshaw	6.4	15.3	08.04.75	Billingham	Stockton						
England: u21.					**West Hartlepool**	9	15	3	-	-	-
Matthew Kennedy	5.8	15.7	04.10.79	Sydney (Aust)	**West Hartlepool**	4+6	-	-	-	-	-
Lee Francis	6.5	16.1	15.11.74	Saltburn	York						
					West Hartlepool	2+2	-	-	-	-	-
Kevin Moseley	6.7	17.6	02.07.65	Caerphilly	Prev. Clubs: Newport, Pontypool						
Chris Murphy	6.8	17.10	02.02.76	Hull	West Hartlepool	36+1	-	-	-	-	-
Gerald Cordle	5.11	15.4	29.09.60	Cardiff	Cardiff						
					West Hartlepool	4+1	5	1	-	-	-

Brierton Lane, Hartlepool, Cleveland. TS25 5DR.

Tel: 01429 233149   **Fax:** 01429 261857   **Tel:** Clubhouse 01429 272640
CAPACITY: 6,500   **SEATED:** 450   **STANDING: Covered,** 3,000, **Uncovered,** 3050

SIMPLE DIRECTIONS:
By Road:
From the A1 or A19 take the A689 to Hartlepool. Within a mile of the first houses turn left into Brierton Lane (opposite the Travellers Rest P.H.). The ground is 800 yards on the left.
Nearest Railway Station:
Hartlepool. The station is about 2 miles from the ground.

CAR PARKING:
200 spaces available in the ground, £1

ADMISSION:
Season tickets - Standing Adults £85, Children/OAP £50; Seated Adults £115, Children/OAP £80.
Match day - Standing Adults £8, Children/OAP £4; Seated Adults £10, Children/OAP £5.

CLUB SHOP: Yes - manager Ann Atkinson c/o club office.

CLUBHOUSE: Normal Licensing hours, snacks & bar meals available.
Function room: Limited availability capacity 150, franchised - contact the club office.

TRAINING NIGHTS: Tuesday and Thursday.

West Hartlepool's, West Stand, Brierton Lane.

MATCHDAY PROGRAMME

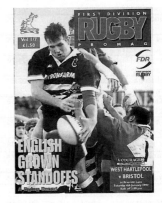

Size	B5
Number of pages	50
Price	£1.50
Programme Editor	Rod Hobbs, (0117 908 6697)
Advertising Rates	Colour Full page £1000
	Half page £500
	Qtr page £300
	Third page £400

DIVISION TWO

RECORDS SECTION

DIVISION TWO - THE LAST TEN YEARS

	Champions	Runners-up	Relegated
1987-88	**ROSSLYN PARK**	LIVERPOOL St. HELENS	
1988-89	**SARACENS**	BEDFORD	London Welsh, London Scottish
1989-90	**NORTHAMPTON**	LIVERPOOL St. HELENS	
1990-91	**RUGBY**	LONDON IRISH	Richmond, Headingley
1991-92	**LONDON SCOTTISH**	WEST HARTLEPOOL	Plymouth Albion, Liverpool St Helens
1992-93	**NEWCASTLE GOSFORTH**	WATERLOO	Bedford, Rosslyn Park, Richmond Blackheath, Coventry, Fylde, Morley
1993-94	**SALE**	WEST HARTLEPOOL	Rugby, Otley
1994-95	**SARACENS**	WAKEFIELD	Fylde, Coventry
1995-96	**NORTHAMPTON**	LONDON IRISH	
1996-97	**RICHMOND**	NEWCASTLE	Rugby, Nottingham

	Most Points		Most Tries
1987-88	75 Andy Finnie (Bedford)	10	Dave McLagan (Saracens)
1988-89	138 Andy Kennedy (Saracens)	7	Dave McLagan (Saracens)
1989-90	107 Ian Aitchison (Lon. Irish)	7	Jim Fallon (Richmond)
1990-91	117 Brian Mullen (Lon. Irish)	9	Lindsay Renwick (Lon. Scottish)
1991-92	147 David Johnson (Newcastle Gos.)	11	Nick Grecian (Lon. Scottish)
1992-93	136 David Johnson (Newcastle Gos.)	7	Jon Sleightholme (Wakefield)
1993-94	172 Guy Gregory (Nottingham)	16	Simon Verbickas (Sale)
1994-95	213 Mike Jackson (Wakefield)	8	Tony Penn (Newcastle Gos.)
1995-96	301 Michael Corcoran (Lon Irish)	20	Matt Allen (Northampton)
1996-97	334 Simon Mason (Richmond)	23	John Bentley (Newcastle)

	Most Penalties		Most Conversions		Most Drop Goals
1987-88	12 Nick Holmes (Saracens)	19 Andy Finnie (Bedford)		4	Simon Smith (Bedford) David Johnson (Gosforth)
1988-89	18 Simon Irving (Headingley)	30 Andy Kennedy (Saracens)		8	Jon King (Blackheath)
1989-90	24 Martin Livesey (Richmond)	22 Ian Aitchison (L. Irish) John Steele (Northampton)		4	Jon King (Blackheath)
1990-91	16 Nick Grecian (L. Scottish)	22 Brian Mullen (L. Irish)		5	Brian Mullen (L. Irish)
1991-92	31 David Johnson (Newcastle)	26 David Johnson (Newcastle) John Stabler (W. Hartlepool)		3	Andy Finnie (Bedford)
1992-93	16 David Johnson (Newcastle)	30 David Johnson (Newcastle)		9	Guy Gregory (Nottingham)
1993-94	29 Paul Turner (Sale)	43 Guy Gregory (Nottingham)		5	Guy Gregory (Nottingham) Murray Walker (L. Scottish)
1994-95	21 Simon Mason (Newcastle) Andy Tunningley (Saracens)	57 Mike Jackson (Wakefield)		6	Andy Lee (Saracens)
1995-96	76 Paul Grayson (Northampton)	63 Michael Corcoran (L. Irish)		5	Sam Howard (Blackheath)
1996-97	47 John Steele (Lon Scot)	95 Rob Andrew (Newcastle)		5	Jez Harris (Coventry)

TEAM RECORDS

Highest score:	Newcastle 156 Rugby 5. 5.10.96
Highest aggregate:	161: As above
Highest score by a losing side:	Mosley 36 Blackheath 51. 27.4.96
Highest scoring draw:	24-24 Lon Scot v Lon Wesh 13.4.88
	Nottingham v Newcastle G 13.1.96
Most consecutive wins:	18 Northampton 1995-96
Most consecutive defeats:	13 Coventry 1993-94
Most points for in a season:	1255 Newcastle 1996-97
Least points for in a season:	81 Northampton 1987-88
Most points against in a season:	1060 Rugby 1996-97
Least points against in a season:	80 Saracens 1989-90
Most tries for in a season:	189 Newcastle 1996-97
Most tries against in a season:	150 Rugby 1996-97
Least tries for in a season:	7 Morley 1992-93
Least tries against in a season:	5 Sale 1992-93
Most conversions for in a season:	119 Newcastle 1996-97
Most conversions against in a season:	101 Rugby 1996-97
Most penalties for in a season:	63 London Irish 1995-96
Most penalties against in a season:	54 London Scottish 1996-97
Least penalties for in a season:	6 Gosforth 1987-88
Least penalties against in a season:	8 Saracens 1987-88, Sale 1990-91
Most drop goals for in a season:	11 London Scottish 1994-95
Most drop goals against in a season:	12 London Irish 1994-95

INDIVIDUAL RECORDS

Most points in a season:	334 Simon Mason (Richmond) 1996-07
Most tries in a season:	23 John Bentley (Newcastle) 1996-97
Most conversions in a season:	95 Rob Andrew (Newcastle) 1996-97
Most penalties in a season:	63 Michael Corcoran (London Irish) 1995-96
Most drop goals in a season:	9 Guy Gregory (Nottingham) 1992-93
Most points in a match:	42 Jez Harris, **Coventry** v Nottingham 5.10.96
Most tries in a match:	5 Simon Verbickas, **Sale** v Otley 12.2.94
	Pat Lam, **Newcastle** v Rotherham 4.5.97
Most conversions in a match:	18 Rob Andrew **Newcastle** v Rugby 5.10.96
Most penalties in a match:	8 Alastair Kerr, **Moseley** v Waterloo 17.2.96
Most drop goals in a match:	3 Martin Livesey, **Richmond** v Northampton 19.11.88
	Murray Walker, **London Scot** v W Hartlepool 23.4.94

Darragh O'Mahony scores in Moseley's impressive defeat of Bedford. This was O'Mahony's 14th try in only his 9th League game for Bedford. He finished the season with 15 from 11 games.

Rotherham's Richard Heaselgrave congratulates try-scorer Simon Binns during the Pilkington Cup match against Harlequins. Photo: Courtesy Rotherham Advertiser.

100+ POINTS IN A SEASON

POINTS	PLAYER	CLUB	SEASON	Tries	Cons.	Pens.	D.G.
324	Simon Mason	Richmond	1996-97	10	83	36	
310	Michael Corcoran	London Irish	1995-96	8	36	63	
297	Rob Andrew	Newcastle	1996-97	7	95	23	1
256	John Steele	Northampton	1996-97	5	39	47	4
238	Mike Rayer	Bedford	1996-97	7	67	23	
236	Jez Harris	Coventry	1996-97	4	48	35	5
218	Paul Grayson	Northampton	1995-96	3	76	14	3
213	Mike Jackson	Wakefield	1994-95	2	16	57	
199	Mike Jackson	Wakefield	1996-97	5	33	35	1
193	Simon Mason	Newcastle	1994-95	1	21	45	2
177	Mike Jackson	Wakefield	1995-96	2	19	43	
177	Richard Le Bas	Moseley	1996-97	3	27	36	
172	Alastair Kerr	Moseley	1995-96	7	13	36	2
171	Guy Gregory	Nottingham	1993-94	1	11	43	5
164	Michael Corcoran	London Irish	1994-95	3	16	38	1
162	Andy Tunningley	Saracens	1994-95	3	21	35	
160	Steve Swindells	Waterloo	1994-95		8	48	
158	Simon Hodgkinson	Nottingham	1995-96	1	18	35	4
156	Simon Hodgkinson	Moseley	1994-95		12	41	3
153	Sam Howard	Blackheath	1995-96	2	19	30	5
149	Andy Tunningley	Saracens	1993-94	5	14	31	1
147	David Johnson	Newcastle Gosforth	1991-92	1	31	26	3
144	Paul Turner	Sale	1993-94	1	29	24	3
140	John Steele	London Scottish	1995-96	4	18	26	2
138	Andy Kennedy	Saracens	1988-89	5	14	30	
137	Steve Swindells	Waterloo	1993-94	2	5	39	
137	Chris Braithwaite	Blackheath	1996-97	2	23	25	2
136	David Johnson	Newcastle Gosforth	1992-93	1	16	30	3
134	Martin Emmett	Waterloo	1995-96	1	12	35	
126	Paul Grayson	Waterloo	1992-93	1	8	29	6
124	Nick Grecian	London Scottish	1991-92	11	13	18	
120	Martin Livesey	Richmond	1989-90	3	24	20	
119	Peter Rutledge	Otley	1993-94	3	10	28	
118	John Stabler	West Hartlepool	1991-92	2	16	26	
117	Brian Mullen	London Irish	1990-91	1	16	22	5
116	Tim Stimpson	Newcastle	1996-97	14	23		
115	Mark Mapletoft	Rugby	1993-94	5	9	22	2
115	John Bentley	Newcastle	1996-97	23			
111	Ian Aitchison	London Irish	1989-90		18	22	3
106	Guy Gregory	Nottingham	1992-93	1	10	18	9
105	John Steele	Northampton	1989-90	2	11	22	3
105	Gary Armstrong	Newcastle	1996-97	21			
105	Scott Quinnell	Richmond	1996-97	21			
103	John Stabler	West Hartlepool	1993-94	1	16	20	2
102	David Pears	Sale	1988-89	3	3	26	2
101	Rob Liley	Wakefield	1992-93	1	9	24	2
100	Chris Howard	Rugby	1989-90	3	17	16	1
100	Brian Mullen	London Irish	1988-89		8	25	3
100	Matt Allen	Northampton	1995-96	20			
100	Jim Fallon	Richmond	1996-97	20			

DIVISION TWO - ALL TIME RECORDS

MOST POINTS IN A MATCH

42	Jez Harris	Coventry v Nottingham	05.10.96
36	Rob Andrew	Newcastle v Rugby	05.10.96
30	Michael Corcoran	London Irish v Waterloo	23.09.95
30	John Steele	London Scottish v Rugby	29.03.97
29	Simon Mason	Richmond v Rotherham	14.09.96
28	David Johnson	Newcastle Gosforth v Morley	11.01.92
28	David Johnson	Newcastle Gosforth v Liverpool StH	29.02.93
27	Simon Hodgkinson	Moseley v London Irish	08.04.95
26	Andy Mitchell	London Scottish v Northampton	03.10.87
26	Michael Corcoran	London Irish v Bedford	21.10.95
26	Michael Corcoran	London Irish v Blackheath	28.10.95
25	Chris Howard	Rugby v Newcastle Gosforth	11.11.89
25	Andy Finnie	Bedford v Coventry	27.03.93
25	Guy Gregory	Nottingham v Otley	11.09.93
25	Simon Verbickas	Sale v Otley	12.02.94
25	John Steele	London Scottish v Bedford	14.10.95
25	Simon Mason	Richmond v Nottingham	16.11.96
25	Pat Lam	Newcastle v Rotherham	04.05.97
24	Simon Irving	Headingley v London Scottish	12.11.88
24	Andy Kennedy	Saracens v Nottingham	12.11.88
24	Nick Grecian	London Scottish v Blackheath	16.11.91
24	Alastair Kerr	Moseley v Waterloo	17.02.96
24	Simon Mason	Richmond v London Scottish	12.10.96
24	Jez Harris	Coventry v London Scottish	19.10.96
24	Simon Mason	Richmond v Rugby	22.03.97
23	Simon Hodgkinson	Nottingham v Blackheath	26.09.92
23	David Johnson	Newcastle Gosforth v Nottingham	10.10.92
23	Guy Gregory	Nottingham v Morley	24.10.92
23	Gary Abraham	Rosslyn Park v Morley	27.03.93
23	Rob Liley	Wakefield v Rugby	11.09.93
23	Paul Turner	Sale v Otley	12.02.94
23	Martin Emmett	Waterloo v Bedford	13.01.96
23	John Steele	London Scottish v Rugby	07.09.96
23	Matt Inman	Rotherham v Richmond	14.09.96
23	John Steele	London Scottish v Nottingham	18.01.97
22	Gary Clark	Gosforth v London Welsh	12.11.88
22	Andy Kennedy	Saracens v Bedford	19.11.88
22	Rob Liley	Wakefield v London Scottish	28.03.92
22	Ian Aitchison	Waterloo v Blackheath	25.04.92
22	John Graves	Rosslyn Park v Coventry	13.02.93
22	Andy Tunningley	Saracens v London Scottish	11.12.93
22	Simon Mason	Newcastle Gosforth v Nottingham	15.10.94
22	Mike Jackson	Wakefield v London Scottish	08.04.95
22	Michael Corcoran	London Irish v Newcastle Gosforth	29.04.95
22	Michael Corcoran	London Irish v Blackheath	28.10.95
22	John Steele	London Scottish v Waterloo	21.09.96
22	Simon Mason	Richmond v Moseley	05.10.96
21	Andy Kennedy	Saracens v London Welsh	22.10.88
21	Mark Thomas	Coventry v Morley	19.09.92
21	Paul Turner	Sale v Fylde	19.09.92
21	Steve Swindells	Waterloo v Nottingham	30.04.94
21	Michael Corcoran	London Irish v Wakefield	14.10.95
21	Michael Corcoran	London Irish v London Scottish	13.01.96
21	Alastair Kerr	Moseley v Blackheath	27.04.96
21	John Steele	London Scottish v Bedford	09.11.96
21	Tony Handley	Waterloo v Rugby	16.11.96

MOST TRIES IN A MATCH

5	Simon Verbickas	Sale v Otley	12.02.94
5	Pat Lam	Newcastle v Rotherham	04.05.97
4	Craig Moir	Northampton v Waterloo	13.04.96
4	Gary Armstrong	Newcastle v Nottingham	14.09.96
4	Scott Quinnell	Richmond v Waterloo	02.11.96
4	John Bentley	Newcastle v Wakefield	08.03.97
3	Jerry Macklin	London Scottish v Northampton	03.10.97
3	Orsen Blewitt	Northampton v Bedford	21.11.87
3	John Roberts	Headingley v Northampton	16.04.88
3	Pete Rowland	Coventry v London Irish	10.09.88
3	Dave Kennell	Headingley v Gosforth	14.01.89
3	Laurie Smith	Saracens v Gosforth	22.04.89
3	Nigel Saunders	Plymouth v Blackheath	14.10.89
3	Graham Robbins	Coventry v Waterloo	13.01.90
3	Rob Saunders	London Irish v Rugby	13.10.90
3	Jonathan Wrigley	W Hartlepool v Moseley	14.12.91
3	Peter Walton	Newcastle Gosforth v Blackheath	14.12.91
3	Jon Sleightholme	Wakefield v Blackheath	04.01.92
3	Gary Clark	Newcastle Gos v Liverpool StH	29.02.92
3	Richard Arnold	Newcastle Gos v Liverpool StH	29.02.92
3	Dave Spiller	Moseley v Sale	04.04.92
3	Richard Gee	Coventry v Moseley	19.09.92
3	Malcolm Walker	Nottingham v Moseley	24.10.92
3	Mark Warr	Sale v Otley	12.02.94
3	Matt Allen	Northampton v London Irish	09.09.95
3	Conor O'Shea	London Irish v Moseley	30.09.95
3	Gregor Townsend	Northampton v Blackheath	14.10.95
3	Grant Seeley	Northampton v Blackheath	14.10.95
3	Matt Allen	Northampton v Newcastle Gos	21.10.95
3	Matt Allen	Northampton v Waterloo	28.10.95
3	Gregor Townsend	Northampton v London Scottish	04.11.95
3	Gregor Townsend	Northampton v London Irish	11.11.95
3	Gary Armstrong	Newcastle Gos v Waterloo	28.04.90
3	Alan Royer	Nottingham v Moseley	30.03.96
3	Matt Allen	Northampton v London Scottish	27.04.96
3	Mitch Hoare	Blackheath v Rotherham	07.09.96
3	Scott Quinnell	Richmond v Rotherham	14.09.96
3	Andy McAdam	Coventry v Nottingham	05.10.96
3	Derek Eves	Coventry v Nottingham	05.10.96
3	Jim Fallon	Richmond v Moseley	05.10.96
3	Scott Quinnell	Richmond v Moseley	05.10.96
3	Gary Armstrong	Newcastle v Rugby	05.10.96
3	Ross Nesdale	Newcastle v Rugby	05.10.96
3	George Graham	Newcastle v Rugby	05.10.96
3	Dean Ryan	Newcastle v Rugby	05.10.96
3	Eddie Saunders	Rugby v Moseley	12.10.96
3	Jim Fallon	Richmond v Rugby	19.10.96
3	John Bentley	Newcastle v Moseley	19.10.96
3	Andy McAdam	Coventry v London Irish	19.10.96
3	Steve Wichary	London Scottish v Moseley	26.10.96
3	Craig Quinnell	Richmond v Waterloo	02.11.96
3	Tim Stimpson	Newcastle v London Scottish	16.11.96
3	Domonic O'Mahoney	Moseley v Nottingham	02.02.97
3	John Bentley	Newcastle v Rugby	08.02.97
3	Julian Horrobin	Coventry v Blackheath	08.03.97
3	Steve Bates	Newcastle v Nottingham	16.03.97
3	John Bentley	Newcastle v Moseley	22.03.97
3	Va'aiga Tuigamala	Newcastle v Moseley	22.03.97
3	Scott Quinnell	Richmond v Rugby	22.03.97
3	Matt Griffiths	Blackheath v Waterloo	19.04.97
3	Jason Hall	Nottingham v Rugby	19.04.97
3	Jim Fallon	Richmond v Wakefield	19.04.97

DIVISION TWO

MOST APPEARANCES

147	Dave Scully	Wakefield	Scrum Half
139	Andy Maunder	Exeter	Scrum Half
122	Andy Green	Exeter	Stand Off
121	Peter Buckton	Liverpool St. Helens 40, Waterloo 81.	Flanker
	Phil Lancaster	W. Hartlepool 101, Wakefield 20.	Prop
	Mike jackson	Fylde 53, Wakefield 68.	Stand Off
120	John Dudley	Rotherham	Back Row
117	Derek Eves	Bristol 86, Coventry 31.	Flanker
115	Ian Smith	Gloucester 108, Moseley 7.	Flanker
113	Terry Garnett	Wakefield	Hooker
108	John Taylor	Fylde	Lock
107	Paul Burnell	Leicester 1, London Scottish 106.	Prop
106	Richard Selkirk	Rotherham	Back Row
105	Micky Harris	Wasps 7, Blackheath 98.	Back Row
	Nick Allott	Liverpool St. Helens 4, Waterloo 101.	Lock
	Paul Manley	Orrell 86, Wakefield 19.	Back Row
103	Andy Parker	Fylde	Full Back
	Steve Gough	Fylde	Stand Off
102	Sam Coy	Rotherham	Prop
101	Andy Blackmore	Bristol 75, Coventry 26.	Lock
	Ian Barclay	Fylde	Centre
98	Guy Easterby	Harrogate 77, Rotherham 21.	Scrum Half
97	Mark Upex	Bedford	Lock
	Craig West	Rotherham	Back Row
96	Dave Addleton	Coventry	Hooker
95	Andy McFarlane	Sale 65, Orrell 4, Fylde 26.	No. 8
	John Steele	Northampton 58, London Scottish 37.	Stand Off

DIVISION TWO - TEN YEAR RECORD

	87/88	88/89	89/90	90/91	91/92	92/93	93/94	94/95	95/96	96/97
BEDFORD	5	2	-	8	10	7	-	-	10	4
BLACKHEATH	11	8	10	10	11	10	-	-	7	10
COVENTRY	-	5	4	4	6	11	-	10	-	3
FYLDE	-	-	-	-	-	12	-	9	-	-
GOSFORTH/NEW	10	10	12	6	4	1	-	3	8	2
HEADINGLEY	4	7	8	13	-	-	-	-	-	-
LIVERPOOL StH	2	-	2	-	13	-	-	-	-	-
LONDON IRISH	8	6	5	2	-	-	-	5	2	-
LONDON SCOTTISH	7	11	-	5	1	-	8	4	3	5
LONDON WELSH	9	12	-	-	-	-	-	-	-	-
MORLEY	-	-	-	-	9	13	-	-	-	-
MOSELEY	-	-	-	-	7	6	5	6	6	8
NORTHAMPTON	12	3	1	-	-	-	-	-	1	-
NOTTINGHAM	-	-	-	-	-	4	6	7	9	12
OTLEY	-	-	-	-	-	-	10	-	-	-
PLYMOUTH	-	-	7	11	12	-	-	-	-	-
RICHMOND	6	9	3	12	-	9	-	-	-	1
ROOSLYN PARK	1	-	-	-	-	8	-	-	-	-
ROTHERHAM	-	-	-	-	-	-	-	-	-	7
RUGBY	-	-	6	1	-	-	9	-	-	11
SALE	-	4	9	7	8	5	1	-	-	-
SARACENS	3	1	-	-	-	-	3	1	-	-
WAKEFIELD	-	-	-	3	5	3	4	2	4	6
WATERLOO	-	-	11	9	3	2	7	8	5	9
WEST HARTLEPOOL	-	-	-	-	2	-	2	-	-	-

Two Leeds RUFC players who will be doing their best to gain that elusive promotion this coming season.

Top: Colin Stephens. Photos: PHOTOGENIC, D J Williams. Bottom: Mark Perego.
Tel: 0113 260 3398

JEWSON

NATIONAL

LEAGUE ONE

1996-97 DIVISION THREE

PLAYING RECORD & breakdown

	Pd	W	D	L	Pts	HOME				AWAY			
						W	D	L	Pts	W	D	L	Pts
Exeter	30	25	0	5	50	15	0	0	30	10	0	5	20
Fylde	30	24	1	5	49	14	0	1	28	10	1	4	21
Leeds	30	24	0	6	48	15	0	0	30	9	0	6	18
Morley	30	22	0	8	44	12	0	3	24	10	0	5	20
Harrogate	30	18	0	12	36	13	0	2	26	5	0	10	10
Raeding	30	17	1	12	35	11	1	3	23	6	0	9	12
Wharfedale	30	17	0	13	34	10	0	5	20	7	0	8	14
Rosslyn Park	30	17	0	13	34	14	0	1	28	3	0	12	6
Otley	30	13	0	17	26	9	0	6	18	4	0	11	8
Lydney	30	13	0	17	26	9	0	6	18	4	0	11	8
London Welsh	30	12	0	18	24	10	0	5	20	2	0	13	4
Liverpool St. Helens	30	9	0	21	18	7	0	8	14	2	0	13	4
Walsall	30	8	0	22	16	6	0	9	12	2	0	13	4
Havant	30	8	0	22	16	6	0	9	12	2	0	13	4
Redruth	30	8	0	22	16	7	0	9	14	1	0	14	2
Clifton	30	4	0	26	8	3	0	12	6	1	0	14	2

POINTS FOR & breakdown

	Lge Pos	Pts	T	C	P	D	HOME					AWAY				
							Pts	T	C	P	D	Pts	T	C	P	D
1 Leeds	3	1209	158	94	71	6	731	102	61	30	3	478	56	33	41	3
2 Morley	4	928	123	65	56	5	506	68	38	29	1	422	55	27	27	4
3 Exeter	1	923	121	69	56	4	542	73	39	32	1	381	48	30	24	3
4 Reading	6	869	109	75	56	2	518	69	49	24	1	351	40	26	32	1
5 Harrogate	5	832	105	68	51	6	527	69	43	27	5	305	36	25	24	1
6 Fylde	2	813	86	58	85	4	452	44	35	50	4	361	42	23	35	0
7 Otley	9	720	90	60	47	3	389	46	33	30	1	331	44	27	17	2
8 Wharfedale	7	710	96	52	40	2	400	55	28	21	2	310	41	24	19	0
9 Lydney	10	668	74	35	76	0	390	43	20	45	0	278	31	15	37	0
10 Liverpool St. H.	12	665	90	49	36	3	404	57	31	16	3	261	33	18	20	0
11 Walsall	13	640	58	43	84	4	356	29	20	55	2	284	294	23	29	2
12 London Welsh	11	634	69	41	61	8	380	39	22	42	5	254	30	19	19	3
13 Rosslyn Park	8	630	80	37	50	2	377	51	25	22	2	253	29	12	28	0
14 Havant	14	590	65	39	52	7	304	33	20	30	3	276	32	19	22	4
15 Redruth	15	565	64	40	55	0	31*9	34	22	35	0	246	30	18	20	0
16 Clifton	16	518	62	38	40	4	292	38	21	18	2	226	24	17	22	4

POINTS AGAINST & breakdown

	Lge Pos	Pts	T	C	P	D	HOME					AWAY				
							Pts	T	C	P	D	Pts	T	C	P	D
1 Leeds	3	432	48	27	42	4	148	18	8	13	1	284	30	19	29	3
2 Fylde	2	439	38	21	65	4	197	16	9	32	1	242	22	12	33	3
3 Exeter	1	443	46	24	54	1	195	18	12	27	0	248	28	12	27	1
4 Morley	4	572	56	32	69	7	268	26	12	35	5	304	30	20	36	2
5 Harrogate	5	599	67	89	57	5	285	35	19	21	3	314	32	20	36	2
6 Rosslyn Park	8	620	70	45	58	2	201	21	14	24	0	419	49	31	34	2
7 Reading	6	631	74	45	54	3	260	30	19	24	0	371	44	26	30	3
8 Wharfedale	7	635	72	34	63	6	305	32	17	34	3	330	40	17	29	3
=9 Otley	9	766	88	46	74	4	326	38	17	33	1	440	50	29	41	3
=9 Lydney	10	766	97	58	53	2	301	39	26	18	0	465	58	32	35	2
11 London Welsh	11	777	100	56	51	4	324	38	25	28	0	453	62	31	23	4
12 Liverpool St H.	12	827	99	61	66	4	357	41	28	29	3	470	58	33	37	1
13 Havant	14	954	126	75	50	8	462	62	37	22	4	492	64	38	28	4
14 Walsall	13	980	126	79	62	2	375	54	34	28	1	605	72	45	34	1
15 Redruth	15	1116	159	96	40	3	362	47	29	20	3	754	112	67	20	0
16 Clifton	16	1347	184	125	58	0	577	85	50	24	0	750	99	75	34	1

1996-97 DIVISION THREE REVIEW

A Hollywood script writer could not have produced a better ending to the season with Exeter snatching the title from long time leaders Fylde on the last day of the season.

Exeter came up on the rails by winning their last fourteen games, which included home wins against Fylde, Leeds and Morley, their nearest rivals, to win the title by a point. Their last day win at Reading, 13-3, saw them leapfrog over both Leeds and Fylde from third to first.

They were well marshalled by the experienced half back pairing of scrum half Andy Maunder and stand-off Andy Green, both of whom played in Exeter's first ever league game back in September 1987. Their back row was impressive and they ran in thirty tries between them.

Fylde led for virtually the whole season and suffered a late season blip losing three of their last five away games. They sealed promotion with a 20-6 win at hostile Lydney in a bad tempered match. Stand-off Steve Gough had an amazing season scoring a new National League record 404 points. Ex-Rugby League star, but originally from Fylde back in 1987-88, Mark Preston made a spectacular return running in 20 tries and earning a reputation as one of the best finishers around.

Leeds' campaign was decided mid season when they suffered five straight away defeats. They mounted a superb late challenge winning their last twelve games but it was not to be. They finished the season as the division's leading points and try scorers scoring over 70 points in a match six times. Along with Newbury they were the only team to have three players score over 100 points in the season.

They were bitterly disappointed and have again recruited during the summer as they look to gain promotion to the Premiership.

Any chance of promotion for Morley fell apart when they lost four consecutive games after the New Year, two of which were at home to Yorkshire rivals Harrogate and Wharfedale, and both games they should have won. Back rowers Ben Wade and Simon Smith made major contributions with seventeen and thirteen tries respectively. The ever reliable Jamie Grayshon scored another 195 points to pass the 1000 point mark in League rugby.

Harrogate had a superb second half of the season, winning their last ten home games, including wins over Fylde and Exeter, to finish a highly creditable fifth. Ralph Zoing again topped the points scoring list and passed 1000 career League points. The down side to the season was finishing bottom of the National Clubs Fair Play League.

Reading were another team who started slowly before finding their form and had an excellent second half of the season to reach their highest ever League position of sixth.

Wharfedale surprised everybody including themselves with a superb seventh place. They were light up front so they ran everything and were rewarded with 96 tries, including 21 from full back Andrew Hodgson who played rugby league in the summer for the Bradford Bulls. Wharfedale relied heavily on team spirit and a local community atmosphere which served them well.

Rosslyn Park was a team nobody could figure out; at home they were superb with a 14-1 record but away a disasterous 3-12 record held them to a mid table finish

Otley will be satisfied with a mid table finish. Their back division, and hopefully they can hold onto the players, were superb and had an average age of just over twenty. Winger Mark Kirkby was the division's leading try scorer with 22, while full back Peter Rutledge again broke the club's points scoring record for a season with 287.

Lydney will also be satisfied with their season after promotion the previous year although they relied heavily on the kicking of Paul Morris who scored a club record 275 points. They were ably led by captain Nick Nelmes who was the clubs only ever present. Another team good at home but poor away.

London Welsh had nearly half their points come from stand-off Craig Raymond which is not ideal. They found a livewire scrum half Tom Lewsey who ended up as leading try scorer with thirteen, but they were another side who travelled badly.

Liverpool St. Helens looked dead and buried at one stage of the season but managed to pull it round and avoid relegation. Two good home wins at Wharfedale and Harrogate helped but the result at Walsall where they won 29-20 proved decisive.

Walsall did not score enough tries; they managed just 58 which was the lowest in the division. Fifty-three per cent of their points came from stand-off Richard Mills which is too high a figure.

Havant won their last two games of the season to add some respectability to a very disappointing campaign. They were another side not to score enough points and were unable to find a settled goal kicker which is so vital.

Redruth won their opening away game of the season, then lost the next fourteen ending up with the worst away record in the division along with Clifton. They have a number of young players coming through who can hopefully lead the club back up again.

Clifton used an incredible 63 players with their training nights looking like a scene out of 'Casualty' most weeks. They never found a settled side and like Havant did not have a reliable goal kicker with at least ten players kicking points at various stages of the season.

1996-97 DIVISION THREE

RECORD REVIEW

INDIVIDUAL RECORDS

MOST POINTS IN A MATCH

This was one of the oldest records in the book dating back to November 1987 when Fylde's Steve Burnage scored 28 points in a 68-7 win over Birmingham. Burnage's total included a then record nine conversions.

Burnage's record, after standing for nine years, was broken four times during the season. First up was Lydney's Paul Morris who scored 29 points in his sides 34-22 home win over Otley. Morris's haul included nine penalties, a record in its own right, and a conversion.

A week later Havant full back Rob Ashworth equalled Morris's record. Ashworth achieved it in his sides 34-19 home win over Clifton and his points also came from nine penalties and a conversion.

Liverpool St Helens' winger Paul Brett playing in his first full season of league rugby then took over and twice improved the record. First he added a point to the previous record set earlier in the season when he scored 30 points v Redruth. He scored a hat trick of tries, six conversions and a penalty in his clubs 72-17 win.

Then on the 15th February he smashed the record scoring 39 points in Liverpool's 89-13 win over the hapless Clifton. Brett again scored a hat trick of tries and converted 12 of his side's 13 tries in an exceptional kicking display.

Evolution of record

28	Steve Burnage	Fylde v Birmingham	07.11.87
29	Paul Morris	Lydney v Otley	14.09.96
29	Rob Ashworth	Havant v Clifton	21.09.96
30	Paul Brett	Liverpool v Redruth	01.02.97
39	Paul Brett	Liverepool v Clifton	15.02.97

MOST TRIES IN A MATCH

The record at the start of the season was four shared by a number of players over the years. The record was equalled three times before being broken in the second half on the season. First to equal the record was Leeds' winger Richard Matthias, who the previous season played Division One rugby for Orrell. His tries came in his clubs 80-0 over Clifton and gave him eight tries in three games.

Exeter's Simon Dovell was next to equal the record scoring half his side's eight tries in a comfortable 46-5 home win over Havant. Those four tries also gave Dovell a new club record. Next up, and only the second forward to score four tries in a Division Three match, was Morley flanker Ben Wade. Wade's four came away from home in his clubs record away win 71-25 at yes you've guessed Clifton. Again Wade's four tries was a new club record.

The record was finally broken by Otley's young winger Mark Kirkby who was playing his first full season of league rugby following a handful of appearances last season.

Kirkby scored five of his side's six tries in a 40-28 away win at Redruth. Kirkby made a startling impression in his first full season finishing as the Division's leading try scorer with 22.

Evolution of record (first to)

3	Kevin Norris	Plymouth v Sheffield	12.09.87
4	Brendan Hanavan	Fylde v Exeter	03.10.87
5	Mark Kirkby	Otley v Redruth	08.02.97

MOST CONVERSIONS IN A MATCH

This was another record in the book from the inaugral season of league rugby and was held by Fylde's Steve Burnage. As part of his record 28 point haul against Birmingham back in November 1987 he had converted nine of his side's 10 tries.

The record was equalled by Leeds centre, another ex Orrell player, Gerry Ainscough in their 80-0 whitewash over Clifton in early December.

On the 15th February Reading's Jason Dance equalled the record in their 71-3 thrashing of Redruth but was unable to claim the record. Why? because Liverpool's Paul Brett set a new record converting 12 of his sides 13 tries in the 89-13 win over Clifton.

Evolution of record

9	Steve Burnage	Fylde v Birmingham	07.11.87
9	Gerry Ainscough	Leeds v Clifton	07.12.96
12	Paul Brett	Liverpool v Clifton	15.02.96

Most in a match

12	Paul Brett	Liverpool v Clifton	15.02.97
10	Jason Dance	Reading v Clifton	01.03.97
9	Steve Burnage	Fylde v Birmingham	07.11.87
9	Gerry Ainscough	Leeds v Clifton	07.12.96
9	Jason Dance	Reading v Redruth	15.02.97
9	Jamie Grayshon	Morley v Walsall	17.05.97

MOST PENALTIES IN A MATCH

The record of seven was broken twice early in the season. First to break the record was Lydney's Paul Morris in their 34-22 win over Otley.

The following weekend Havant full back Rob Ashworth equalled the record in his sides 34-19 win over Clifton.

Evolution of record (first to)

6	John Stabler	W Hart v Met Police	06.01.88
7	Andy Finnie	Bedford v Coventry	23.04.94
9	Paul Morris	Lydney v Otley	14.09.96

Most in a match

9	Paul Morris	Lydney v Otley	14.09.96
9	Rob Ashworth	Havant v Clifton	21.09.96
8	Richard Mills	Walsall v Leeds	12.10.96
7	Andy Finnie	Bedford v Coventry	23.04.94
7	Denzil Evans	Rugby v Richmond	15.10.94
7	Phil Belshaw	Reading v Morley	14.10.95
7	Jamie Grayshon	Morley v Rugby	21.10.95
7	Andy Green	Exeter v Fylde	05.04.97
7	Richard Mills	Walsall v Redruth	19.04.97
7	Nat Saumi	Redruth v Clifton	03.05.97

MOST POINTS IN A SEASON

With the advent of the 30 game league programme it was inevitable that the records it this field would be under threat and so it proved. Fylde's stand-off Steve Gough added 174 points to the previous record of 228 set by Bedford's Andy Finnie in the 1994-95 season. Gough also had the highest points per game average of any of the players to top the leading points scorers list.

Evolution of record

121	Steve Burnage	Fylde	1987-88
123	Chris Howard	Rugby	1988-89
172	Andy Finnie	Bedford	1993-94
228	Andy Finnie	Bedford	1994-95
404	Steve Gough	Fylde	1996-97

MOST TRIES IN A SEASON

Otley's winger Mark Kirkby nearly doubled the previous record of 12 on the way to a new record of 22. Kirkby's total included three hat tricks or more and came from 25 games for a strike record of a try every 1.14 games.

Evolution of record

10	Brendan Hanavan	Fylde	1987-88
12	Brendan Hanavan	Fylde	1993-94
12	Colin Phillips	Reading	1994-95
22	Mark Kirkby	Otley	1996-97

MOST CONVERSIONS IN A SEASON

This record dated back to the 1987-88 season and was the property of Fylde's Steve Burnage with 30. Last season 12 players broke the previous record with Harrogate's Ralph Zoing topping the list with 63 two ahead of Reading's Jason Dance. Burnage's Fylde record of 30 was beaten by Steve Gough with 57.

Evolution of record

30	Steve Burnage	Fylde	1987-88
63	Ralph Zoing	Harrogate	1996-97

MOST PENALTIES IN A SEASON

Four players broke the previous record of 56 set by Bedford's Andy Finnie in 1994-95. Top of the charts was Fylde's Steve Gough with a new record of 82. Hot on his heel's was Walsall's Richard Mills just one behind on 81. The two other players to break the record were Lydney's Paul Morris and London Welsh's Craig Raymond with 66 and 57 respectively.

Evolution of record

21	Ray Adamson	Wakefield	1987-88
22	Andy Higgin	Vale of Lune	1989-90
26	Mike Jackson	Fylde	1991-92
31	Andy Green	Exeter	1992-93
45	Andy Finnie	Bedford	1993-94
56	Andy Finnie	Bedford	1994-95
82	Steve Gough	Fylde	1996-97

ANALYSIS OF PLAYERS USED

Consistency breeds success as came be seen by the table below. The promoted pair of Exeter and Fylde used fewer players, had least number of players making their debuts and had most ever presents with three each. Exeter's players averaged 16.7 appearances each which put them top closely followed by Fylde with 15.5 while the Dalesman from Wharfedale finished third with 14.5 each.

Bottom club Clifton used a National League record 63 players of which an incredible 38 were making their debut ie 60%. Their players averaged just 7.14 appearances each which was two appearances less than the next worst club - Rosslyn Park.

	Players used	League debuts	Ever present	1	2
Clifton	63	38	-	60	7.1
Exeter	27(7)	7	3	26	16.7
Fylde	29(3)	7	3	24	15.5
Harrogate	35(3)	10	-	28	12.9
Havant	39(3)	18	-	46	11.5
Leeds	33(5)	15	-	45	13.6
Liverpool StH	42(1)	14	-	33	10.7
London Welsh	40(3)	20	-	50	11.3
Lydney	35(2)	9	1	26	12.9
Morley	35(2)	16	1	46	12.9
Otley	34(3)	14	2	41	13.2
Reading	38(1)	17	1	45	11.8
Redruth	43(2)	12	-	28	10.7
Rosslyn Park	48(5)	25	-	52	9.4
Walsall	42(3)		-		10.7
Wharfedale	31(4)	11	2	35	14.5

FAIR PLAY LEAGUE

This is another new feature which we will publish each season and hopefully get the RFU to make part of their awards evening.

Team	Yellow card	Red card	Total
Rosslyn Park	2	0	10
Wharfedale	4	0	20
Morley	3	1	25
Reading	4	1	30
London Welsh	4	1	30
Leeds	5	1	35
Fylde	6	1	40
Redruth	6	1	40
Clifton	8	1	50
Exeter	6	2	50
Lydney	11	0	55
Walsall	6	3	60
Liverpool St. H.	5	4	65
Otley	13	0	65
Havant	10	3	80
Harrogate	16	4	120

Rosslyn Park easily topped the 'Fair Play' table with just 10 points from two yellow cards. Both these cards were awarded against back row forward Simon Smith. Champions Exeter rattled up 50 points but only one yellow card was gained after they embarked on their 14 match unbeaten run. At the other end of the table Harrogate had the worst record in National League rugby. They had two players with three yellow cards against their name - Dean Holder and David Wheat and they were involved in one of two matches where four players were sent off. In their home game with Havant in April both sides had two players sent off in a touchline brawl late in the game. The other match with four players sent off was the Clifton v Liverpool St. Helens game early in the season. In that match Liverpool had three players sent off and Clifton one.

1 = % of players making league debut
2 = Average appearances per player

1996-97 DIVISION THREE

MOST TRIES

22	Mark Kirkby	Otley
21	Andrew Hodgson	Wharfedale
20	Mark Preston	Fylde
17	Ben Wade	Morley
16	Mark Appleson	Leeds
15	Sateki Tuipulotu	Leeds
15	Mark Woodman	Exeter
14	Gerry Ainscough	Leeds
14	Paul Brett	Liverpool StH
14	Jonathan Shepherd	Morley
13	Rob Bell	Harrogate
13	Mark Farrar	Harrogate
13	Kerry Morley	Harrogate
13	Tom Lewsey	London Welsh
13	Mark Buckingham	Clifton
13	Simon Dovell	Exeter
13	Simon Smith	Morley
13	Guy Spencer	Reading
12	Richard Matthias	Leeds
12	Christian Raducanu	Leeds
12	Nick Green	Leeds
11	Mark Sephton	Liverpool StH
11	Greg Anderton	Fylde
11	Sean Doyle	Exeter
11	Jerry Costeloe	Gloucester
10	Peter Congo	Redruth
10	Adam Mounsey	Wharfedale
10	Colin Stephens	Leeda
9	Hedley Verity	Wharfedale
9	Craig Walker	Wharfedale
9	Toby Rakison	Rosslyn Park
9	Danny Barrett	Reading
9	Steve Bartliffe	Leeds
9	Mike Cawthorne	Leeds
9	Chris O'Toole	Fylde
9	Andy Maunder	Exeter
9	Roger Hutchinson	Exeter

MOST PENALTIES

82	Steve Gough	Fylde
81	Richard Mills	Walsall
66	Paul Morris	Lydney
57	Craig Raymond	London Welsh
50	Andy Green	Exeter
49	Gerry Ainscough	Leeds
48	Ralph Zoing	Harrogate
45	Peter Rutledge	Otley
43	Jason Dance	Reading
31	Jamie Grayshon	Morley
25	Ian Morgan	Redruth
23	Nat Saumi	Redruth
23	Alan Peacock	Morley
23	Andy Holder	Rosslyn Park
20	Pete Russell	Havant
20	Paul Brett	Liverpool StH
19	Rob Ashworth	Havant
19	Andrew Hodgson	Wharfedale
18	Adam Mounsey	Wharfedale
16	Simon Humphreys	Liverpool StH
16	Sateki Tuipulotu	Leeds
13	Simon Hogg	Clifton
11	Phil Belshaw	Reading
9	Hamish Rushin	Havant
8	Alastair Sandilands	Rosslyn Park
7	Stacey Cady	Clifton
6	Colin Stephens	Leeds
6	John Fabian	Exeter
5	Rob Mills	Lydney
5	Phil O'Sullivan	Clifton
5	Dan Cottrell	Clifton
4	Andy Lewis	London Welsh
4	Mark Johnson	Lydney

MOST CONVERSIONS

63	Ralph Zoing	Harrogate
61	Jason Dance	Reading
58	Andy Green	Exeter
57	Steve Gough	Bristol
56	Peter Rutledge	Otley
45	Gerry Ainscough	Leeds
42	Richard Mills	Walsall
40	Paul Brett	Liverpool StH
40	Jamie Grayshon	Morley
39	Craig Raymond	Orrell
39	Adam Mounsey	Wharfedale
37	Sateki Tuipulotu	Leeds
31	Paul Morris	Lydney
27	Pete Russell	Havant
22	Alan Peacock	Morley
17	Andy Holder	Rosslyn Park
15	Ian Morgan	Redruth
14	Phil Belshaw	Reading
14	Nat Saumi	Redruth
12	Alex Howarth	Wharfedale
11	Simon Hogg	Clifton

MOST DROP GOALS

7	Craig Raymond	London Irish
5	Colin Stephens	Leeds
5	Ralph Zoing	Harrogate
4	John Firkin	Havant
4	Jamie Grayshon	Morley
3	Steve Gough	Fylde
3	Andy Green	Exeter
3	Brian Wellens	Liverpool StH
3	Anthony Cadman	Otley
3	Simon Hogg	Clifton
3	Pete Russell	Havant
2	Richard Mills	Walsall
2	Gordon Banks	Walsall
1	Chris O'Toole	Fylde
1	Andy Lewis	London Welsh
1	Matt Brain	Harrogate
1	Jason Thomas	Exeter

1996-97 DIVISION THREE

MOST POINTS IN THE SEASON

POINTS	PLAYER	CLUB	Tries	Cons.	Pens.	D.G.
404	Steve Gough	Fylde	7	57	82	3
338	Richard Mills	Walsall	1	42	81	2
307	Gerry Ainscough	Leeds	14	45	49	-
305	Ralph Zoing	Harrogate	4	63	48	5
300	Andy Green	Exeter	5	58	50	3
300	Craig Raymond	London Welsh	6	39	57	7
287	Peter Rutledge	Otley	8	56	45	-
281	Jason Dance	Reading	6	61	43	-
275	Paul Morris	Lydney	3	31	66	-
210	Paul Brett	Liverpool StH	14	40	20	-
197	Sateki Tuipulotu	Leeds	15	37	16	-
195	Jamie Grayshon	Morley	2	40	31	4
182	Adam Mounsey	Wharfdale	10	39	18	-
128	Alan Peacock	Morley	3	22	23	-
123	Pete Russell	Havant	-	27	20	3
121	Andy Holder	Rosslyn Park	3	17	23	1
120	Ian Morgan	Redruth	3	15	25	-
110	Mark Kirkby	Otley	22	-	-	-
105	Andrew Hodgson	Wharfedale	21	-	-	-
102	Nat Saumi	Redruth	1	14	23	-
101	Colin Stephens	Leeds	10	9	6	5
100	Mark Preston	Fylde	20	-	-	-
89	Mark Appleson	Leeds	16	3	-	1
86	Alex Howarth	Wharfedale	1	12	19	-
85	Ben Wade	Morley	17	-	-	-
80	Simon Hogg	Clifton	2	11	13	3
78	Mark Buckingham	Clifton	13	1	2	-
75	Mark Woodman	Exeter	15	-	-	-
73	Rob Ashworth	Havant	-	8	19	-
70	Jonathon Shepherd	Morley	14	-	-	-
69	Matt Dowse	Rosslyn Park	3	9	11	1
66	Phil Belshaw	Reading	1	14	11	-
65	Simon Dovell	Exeter	13	-	-	-
65	Rob Bell	Harrogate	13	-	-	-
65	Mark farrar	Harrogate	13	-	-	-
65	Kerry Morley	Harrogate	13	-	-	-
65	Tom Lewsey	London Welsh	13	-	-	-
65	Simon Smith	Morley	13	-	-	-
65	Guy Spencer	Reading	13	-	-	-

HARROGATE R.U.F.C.

NICKNAME: Gate

FOUNDED: 1871

President D Cunningham, c/o Harrogate RUFC, The County Ground, Claro Road, Harrogate HG1 4AG
01423 566966, 01423 562776 (Fax)

Chairman Allen Tattersfield, c/o Harrogate RUFC, as above

Club Secretary Rodney Spragg, Pear Tree Cottage, Nidd, Harrogate. HG3 3BJ.
01423 770126 (H) 01423 562634 (B) 01423 562776 (Fax)

Director of Rugby Jeff Young, c/o Harrogate RUFC, as above

Fixtures Secretary Malcolm Fleming, 29 Boroughbridge Road, Knaresborough. HG5 0LY.
01423 864618 (H) 0378 389280 (B)

The 125th anniversary season corresponded to the first full season of professionalism and this combined with the internecine strife within the game ensured that it was a memorable season in more ways than one.

Once again we had a poor start to the campaign when we were disrupted by injury and unavailability, but we gradually pulled round to end up in our highest ever league position of fifth. The more adventurous style of play was reflected in the number of tries scored by the backs, where wings Rob Bell and Kerry Morley together with scrum half Mark Farrar all scored thirteen tries to equal Jeremy Hopkinsons long standing record. Overall we averaged 3.5 tries per game the highest average we have achieved.

Among our more notable successes were home wins over promotion winners Exeter 15-12 and Fylde 27-19. We broke our biggest home win record against Clifton 79-7 and also recorded large winning margins against London Welsh 52-19 and Redruth 60-24. Unfortunately our poor track record in the Pilkington Cup continued when Widnes beat us by a well deserved 12-7.

Highlights included flanker David Wheat becoming the first Harrogate player to make 100 league appearances closely followed by Ian Hassall, Andy Simpson and Ralph Zoing. The latter achieving a notable double in reaching 100 league appearances and also becoming the first Harrogate player to score 1,000 league points in the same game at Havant. All these players played in the side which won promotion from North One in 1989-90. Andy Ludiman came on as a replacement for the North against New Zealand. Scrum half Mark Farrar in his first season won the players Player of the Year Award.

As part of the club's long term plan another notable first was achieved with the appointment of the former Welsh and British Lion hooker Jeff Young as director of rugby with the brief to oversee all playing activities. Jeff played for and captained the club in the 60s and his influence was reflected in the style of play and successful run in to the close of the season. Sadly following Jeff's appointment long standing team coach Peter Clegg decided to retire much to the regret of the club that he had coached through from North One to its present National Division One position.

Harrogate RUFC 96-97: Back Row (L-R); A Jones (Rugby Chr), B Forshaw (Hon Treas), R Spragg (Sec), S Young (Bar Chr), D Holder, A Pride, A Simpson, R Bell, P Taylor, S Brown, D Croft, A Caldwell, S Carbutt, D Cunningham (Pres), R Faulkner, A Tattersfield (Chr), R Guy (Vice Chr). Front Row; J Young (Dir of Rugby), G Siswick (Mgr), R Zoing, R Whyley, G Drane, M Farrar, R Marcroft (Cpt), L Feurer, M Brain, N Hill, C Reed.

Colours: Red, amber & black shirts & socks, black shorts.

Change colours: Red.

No	Ven.	Date	Opponents	Att.	Res.	Score	Scorers
1	(H)	31.08	v Reading		W	40-31	Dixon(t)Bell(t)Simpson(t)Wheat(t)Easterby(t)Zoing(3c3p)
2	(A)	07.09	v Rosslyn Park		L	16-19	Morley(t)Zoing(c3p)
3	(H)	14.09	v Wharfdale		W	23-18	Bell(2t)Zoing(2c3p)
4	(A)	21.09	v Exeter		L	7-22	Bell(t)Brain(c)
5	(A)	28.09	v Walsall		L	19-27	Whyley(t)Easterby(t)Dixon(3p)
6	(H)	05.10	v Leeds		L	26-35	Bell(t)Brain(t)P Taylor(t)PenTry(t)Dixon(3c)
7	(A)	12.10	v London Welsh		L	14-23	Bell(t)Simpson(t)Zoing(2c)
8	(H)	19.10	v Lydney		W	43-30	Bell(2t)Morley(t)Easterby(t)P Taylor(t)Zoing(3c3pdg)
9	(A)	26.10	v Redruth		W	32-20	Bell(t)Easterby(t)Morley(t)Brain(t)PenTry(t)Zoing(2cp)
10	(H)	09.11	v Morley		L	16-22	Farrar(t)Zoing(c3p)
11	(A)	16.11	v Clifton		W	41-13	Morley(2t)Farrar(2t)Brain(t)Zoing(5c2p)
12	(H)	21.12	v Fylde		W	27-19	Brain(t)Bell(t)P Taylor(t)Zoing(4p)
13	(A)	11.01	v Otley		L	8-17	Morley(t)Zoing(p)
14	(A)	18.01	v Reading		L	20-22	Wheat(t)Reed(t)Zoing(2c2p)
15	(H)	25.01	v Rosslyn Park		W	25-20	Holder(2t)Bell(t)Zoing(2cp)Brain(dg)
16	(A)	01.02	v Wharfdale		W	21-20	Wheat(t)Farrar(t)Zoing(c2pdg)
17	(H)	08.02	v Exeter		W	15-12	Brain(t)Easterby(t)Zoing(cp)
18	(H)	15.02	v Walsall		W	22-13	Hopkinson(t)Farrar(t)Morley(t)Zoing(2cdg)
19	(A)	22.02	v Leeds		L	3-28	Zoing(p)
20	(H)	01.03	v London Welsh		W	52-19	Farrar(3t)Brain(t)Dixon(t)Frerur(t)Hopkinson(t)Zoing(t6c)
21	(A)	08.03	v Lydney		W	38-18	Morley(2t)Caldwell(t)Dixon(t)Zoing(t5cp)
22	(H)	15.03	v Redruth		W	60-24	Dixon(2tc)Brain(2t)Reed(t)Bell(t)Farrar(t)Hopkinson(t)Easterby(t)Zoing(5cp)
23	(A)	22.03	v Morley		W	27-11	Dixon(2t)Holder(t)Zoing(3c2p)
24	(H)	05.04	v Clifton		W	79- 7	Hopkinson(3t)Farrar(2t)Hassell(t)Reed(t)Caldwell(t)Feurer(t)Hall(t) Marcroft(t)Zoing(2t7c)
25	(A)	12.04	v Fylde		L	17-22	Feurer(t)Zoing(4p)
26	(H)	19.04	v Havant		W	29-11	Morley(2t)Feurer(t)Farrar(t)Hassell(t)Zoing(2c)
27	(A)	26.04	v Liverpool StH		L	27-32	Morley(2t)Caldwell(t)Farrar(t)Zoing(2cp)
28	(H)	03.05	v Ptley		W	26-10	Caldwell(t)Reed(t)Zoing(2c2p2dg)
29	(A)	10.05	v Havant		L	15-30	Bell(t)Simpson(t)Zoing(cp)
30	(H)	17.05	v Liverpool StH		W	44-14	Marcroft(t)Feurer(t)P Taylor(t)Pride(t)Zoing(3c6p)

1996-97 HIGHLIGHTS

LEAGUE DEBUTS: Stuart Dixon, David Croft, Neil Hill, Simon Langstaff, Lee Feurer, Tim Barley, Mark Farrer, Gareth Drane, Dean Holder, Rob Faulkner.

TRY ON DEBUT: Stuart Dixon.

PLAYERS USED: 35 plus 3 as replacement.

EVER PRESENT: None - most appearances 27
- Ralph Zoing.

☐ Won 12 out of their last 16 games.

☐ Rob Bell, Mark Farrar and Kerry Morley all equal Jeremy Hopkinson's record of 13 ties in a season set in the 1991-92 season in Division Four North.

☐ Set a new record for consecutive defeats when losing four in a row early in the season.

☐ One of only 5 teams to score 100 tries in the season.

☐ That man Ralph Zoing was at it again breaking all the records. He topped the club's poits scoring list for the ninth year out of ten with a new record for points in a season. His 305 was 90 points more than the previous best set last season but his points average was down slightly.

	Pts	T	C	P	D	Apps	Ave.
96-97	305	4	63	48	5	27	11.29
95-96	215	3	19	51	3	18	11.94

Zoing set a new record for drop goals with five beating the previous record of three which he had achieved twice before. He also becomes one of a handful of players to have scored 1000 league points.

	Pts	T	C	P	D	Apps	Ave.
	1025		170	194	14		

Zoing also set a new record for scoring in consecutive matches with 24 the previous record was 13 which he himself held.

HARROGATE'S COURAGE LEAGUE MATCH DETAILS 1996-97

#	15	14	13	12	11	10	9	1	2	3	4	5	6	7	8	Replacements
1	Hassell	Morley	Dixon	Caldwell	Bell	Zoing	Brain	Simpson	Whyley	Field	Croft		Marcroft	Wheat	Easterby	Pride(5)Hopkinson(7)
2	Hassell	Morley	Dixon	Caldwell	Bell	Zoing	Brain	Simpson	Whyley	Field	Ruthin	Taylor	Marcroft	Wheat	Easterby	Ludiman(6)Hill(14)A Brown(3)Morris(6)
3	Hassell	Langstaff	Hill	Caldwell	Bell	Zoing	Brain	Simpson	Whyley	Field	Taylor	S Brown	Easterby	Wheat	Easterby	Seymour(4)
4	Hassell	Morley	A Taylor	Langstaff	Bell	Zoing	Brain	Simpson	Whyley	Pride	P Taylor	S Brown	Easterby	Wheat	Easterby	Field(3)Hill(12)Pride(7)
5	Hassell	Morley	Morley	Caldwell	Bell	Zoing	Brain	Simpson	Whyley	Taylor	S Brown	P Taylor	Easterby	Wheat	Easterby	Field(3)
6	Dixon	Feurer	Morley	Caldwell	Bell	Brain	Brain	Simpson	Whyley	A Brown	Taylor	P Taylor	Hopkinson	Wheat	Easterby	A Taylor(10)Marcroft(7)
7	Dixon	Feurer	Morley	Caldwell	Bell	Zoing	Barley	Simpson	Whyley	Ludiman	P Taylor	P Taylor	Hopkinson	Wheat	Easterby	S Brown(8)
8	Brain	Morley	Dixon	Caldwell	Bell	Zoing	Farrar	Simpson	Whyley	Ludiman	S Brown	P Taylor	Easterby	Wheat	Easterby	P Taylor
9	Brain	Morley	Caldwell	Caldwell	Bell	Zoing	Farrar	Simpson	Whyley	P Taylor	S Brown	Marcroft	Pride	Wheat	Easterby	Wheat(7)
10	Hassell	Morley	Brain	Caldwell	Bell	Zoing	Farrar	Simpson	Whyley	Ludiman	Pride	S Brown	Baker	Marcroft	Pride	Fuerer(12)Ruthen(5)
11	Brain	Morley	Dixon	Caldwe	Bell	Zoing	Farrar	Field	Whyley	P Taylor	S Brown	Marcroft	Pride	Wheat	Easterby	Drane(14)Feurer(13)A Brown(8)
12	Brain	Morley	Reed	Caldwell	Bell	Zoing	Farrar	Hall	Whyley	P Taylor	Ludiman	Marcroft	Marcroft	Wheat	Easterby	S Brown(6)
13	Brain	Morley	Reed	Caldwell	Bell	Zoing	Farrar	Field	Field	Ludiman	S Brown	Marcroft	Marcroft	Wheat	Easterby	Baker(8)Dixon(12)Ruthen(5)
14	Brain	Morley	Reed	Caldwell	Bell	Zoing	Farrar	Field	Hall	Ludiman	P Taylor	Marcroft	Holder	Wheat	Hopkinson	Reed(13)
15	Brain	Morley	Reed	Dixon	Bell	Zoing	Farrar	Field	Hall	Ludiman	P Taylor	Marcroft	Holder	Wheat	Hopkinson	Caldwell(11)
16	Bell	Morley	Reed	Caldwell	Bell	Zoing	Farrar	Field	Hall	Ludiman	P Taylor	Marcroft	Holder	Wheat	Hopkinson	Reed(13)
17	Hassell	Morley	Reed	Reed	Bell	Zoing	Farrar	P Taylor	Hall	Ludiman	P Taylor	Marcroft	Holder	Wheat	Hopkinson	Hopkinson(8)
18	Hassell	Morley	Reed	Reed	Bell	Zoing	Farrar	Field	Whyley	P Taylor	Ludiman	Marcroft	Holder	Wheat	Hopkinson	S Brown(4)
19	Hassall	Morley	Brain	Caldwell	Bell	Zoing	Farrar	Simpson	Field	Ruthen	Brown	Marcroft	Holder	Wheat	Hopkinson	Pride(4)
20	Brain	Morley	Dixon	Frurer	Bell	Zoing	Farrar	Field	Hall	Ludiman	Ludiman	Marcroft	Hopkinson	Wheat	Hopkinson	Hopkinson
21	Brain	Morley	Caldwell	Caldwell	Bell	Zoing	Field	Field	Hall	Taylor	Taylor	Marcroft	Hopkinson	WEheat	Hopkinson	Dixon(15)Simpson(1)Hopkinson(6)
22	Brain	Morley	Caldwell	Caldwell	Bell	Zoing	Simpson	Simpson	Whyley	S Brown	S Brown	Marcroft	Hopkinson	Wheat	Pride	Brain(11)Holder(6)
23	Dixon	Feurer	Caldwell	Caldwell	Bell	Zoing	Farrar	Field	Hall	S Brown	S Brown	Marcroft	Easterby	Easterby	Easterby	Holder(7)Drane(9)Simpson(8)Hassell(11)
24	Dixon	Feurer	Caldwell	Caldwell	Brain	Zoing	Farrar	Field	Hall	Ludiman	S Brown	Marcroft	Easterby	Easterby	Easterby	Hassell(15)Drane(9)Marcroft(4)Seymour(3)
25	Brain	Feurer	Reed	Caldwell	Brain	Zoing	Farrar	Field	Hall	S Brown	Brown	Marcroft	Easterby	Easterby	Hopkinson	Simpson(3)
26	Brain	Feurer	Reed	Morley	Feurer	Zoing	Field	Wade	Hall	Brown	Brown	Marcroft	Easterby	Easterby	Hopkinson	Hassell(15)Baker(8)
27	Dixon	Morley	Reed	Feurer	Zoing	Zoing	Farrar	Simpson	Whyley	Ruthen	P Taylor	Marcroft	Easterby	Marcroft	Hopkinson	Brain(12)
28	Cixon	Feurer	Reed	Caldwell	Bell	Zoing	Farrar	Carbutt	Faulkner	P Taylor	Brown	Marcroft	Easterby	Marcroft	Hopkinson	Hassell(15)Baker(8)Faulkner(1)
29	Hassell	Feurer	Reed	Caldwell	Bell	Zoing	Farrar	Simpson	Whyley	Brown	Brown	Marcroft	Easterby	Marcroft	Holder	Brain(15)Baker(8)Faulkner(1)
30	Brain	Feurer	Caldwell	Reed	Bell	Zoing	Farrar	Simpson	Whyley	Brown	Pride	Marcroft	Pride	Marcroft	Holder	Croft(8)Faulkner(1)

HARROGATE LEAGUE STATISTICS

(COMPILED BY STEPHEN McCORMACK)

Season	Div.	P	W	D	L	F	(Tries	Con	Pen	DG)	A	(Tries	Con	Pen	DG)	Most Points	Most Tries
87-88	N1	10	5	0	5	147	(17	8	21	0)	113	(11	6	19	0)	28 - Ralph Zoing	2 - Dave Bowe & Andy Caldwell
88-89	N1	01	7	1	2	204	(33	18	12	0)	120	(11	5	22	0)	64 - Ralph Zoing	8 - Clive Ware
89-90	N1	10	8	0	2	188	(20	12	26	2)	82	(10	6	9	1)	88 - Ralph Zoing	4 - Clive Ware
90-91	D4N	12	6	1	5	220	(35	16	16	0)	204	(22	14	27	3)	43 - Ralph Zoing	9 - Jeremy Hopkinson
91-92	D4N	12	6	0	6	170	(20	12	19	3)	175	(18	8	29	0)	45 - Ralph Zoing	3 - Steve Baker
92-93	D4N	12	10	1	1	363	(46	32	21	2)	115	(10	4	17	2)	131 - Ralph Zoing	9 - Steve Baker & Guy Easterby
93-94	4	18	14	2	2	479	(60	31	30	9)	219	(20	15	26	1)	105 - Ralph Zoing	13 - Jeremy Hopkinson
94-95	3	18	7	2	9	275	(27	16	34	2)	404	(45	25	39	4)	110 - Dan Clappison	7 - Rob Bell
95-96	3	18	6	3	9	333	(26	19	51	4)	387	(41	22	43	3)	215 - Ralph Zoing	5 - Richard Marcroft
96-97	3	30	18	0	12	832	(105	68	52	6)	595	(67	39	57	5)	305 - Ralph Zoing	13 - Rob Bell, Mark Farrar & Kerry Morley
Totals		150	87	10	53	3211	(389	232	281	28)	2418	(255	144	288	19)		

	HOME	AWAY
BIGGEST WIN	(72pts) 79-7 v Clifton 5.4.97	(28pts) 41-13 v Clifton 16.11.96
DEFEAT	(44pts) 15-59 v Bedford 15.4.95	(26pts) 13-39 v Bedford 12.11.94
MOST POINTS SCORED	79-7 v Clifton 5.4.97	41-13 v Clifton 16.11.96
AGAINST	15-59 v Bedford 15.4.95	13-39 v Bedford 12.11.94

MOST CONSECUTIVE VICTORIES - 5

MOST CONSECUTIVE DEFEATS - 4

MOST TRIES IN A MATCH
(FOR) 14 v Aspatria 30.4.94
(AGAINST) 9 v Otley 22.9.90 (H)

MOST APPEARANCES
FORWARD: 101(2) David Wheat
BACK: 98(4) Ian Hassell

CONSECUTIVE APPEARANCES
49 Rob Bell 9.92 - 9.9.95

CONSECUTIVE SCORING MATCHES
Scoring Tries - 6 - Clive Ware
Scoring Points - 24 - Ralph Zoing

MOST	in a SEASON	in a CAREER	in a MATCH
Points	305 Ralph Zoing 96-97	1025 Ralph Zoing 87-97	27 Ralph Zoing v Fylde 14.10.95 (H)
Tries	13 Jeremy Hopkinson 91-92 Rob Bell 96-97 Mark Farrar 96-97 Kerry Morley 96-97	38 Jeremy Hopkinson 90-97	5 Steve Baker v Lichfield 14.11.92 (H)
Conversions	63 Ralph Zoing 96-97	170 Ralph Zoing 87-97	9 Ralph Zoing v Towcestrians 13.3.93 (H)
Penalties	51 Ralph Zoing 95-96	194 Ralph Zoing 87-97	7 Ralph Zoing v Halifax 18.11.90 (H)
Drop Goals	5 Ralph Zoing 96-97	14 Ralph Zoing 87-97	2 Ralph Zoing v Askeans 20.11.93 (H)

HARROGATE PLAYING SQUAD

NAME	Ht	Wt	Birthdate	Birthplace	Club	Apps	Pts	T	C	P	DG
BACKS											
Ian Hassell											
					Harrogate	98+4	-	-	-	-	-
Kerry Morley					Wakefield	23	20	4	-	-	-
					Harrogate	29	70	14	-	-	-
Rob Bell											
					Harrogate	79	130	26	-	-	-
Craig Reed											
					Harrogate	70+1	83	16	-	-	-
Stuart Dixon											
					Harrogate	17+3	52	7	4	3	-
Lee Feurer											
					Harrogate	12+2	25	5	-	-	-
Andy Caldwell											
					Harrogate	59	36	8	-	-	-
Ralph Zoing											
					Harrogate	96	1025	13	170	194	14
Mark Farrar											
					Harrogate	22	65	13	-	-	-
Matt Brain											
					Harrogate	34+4	45	8	1	-	1
Gareth Drane											
					Harrogate	1+3	-	-	-	-	-
Neil Hill											
					Harrogate	1+2	-	-	-	-	-
Simon Langstaff											
					Harrogate	2	-	-	-	-	-
FORWARDS											
Andy Simpson											
					Harrogate	98+4	58	12	-	-	-
Richard Whyley											
					Harrogate	100	20	4	-	-	-
Jason Field											
					Harrogate	29+4	-	-	-	-	-
David Hall											
					Harrogate	50	10	2	-	-	-
James Wade											
					Harrogate	17	-	-	-	-	-
Simon Carbutt											
					Harrogate	14+1	-	-	-	-	-
Peter Taylor											
					Harrogate	89+1	55	11	-	-	-
Simon Brown											
					Harrogate	45+4	9	2	-	-	-
Dean Holder											
					Harrogate	11	15	3	-	-	-
Simon Easterby Ireland: u21.											
					Harrogate	28+1	40	8	-	-	-
Richard Marcroft											
					Harrogate	46+5	45	9	-	-	-
David Wheat											
					Harrogate	101	56	12	-	-	-
Jeremy Hopkinson											
					Harrogate	87+4	179	38	-	-	-
Alex Pride											
					Harrogate	19+12	4	1	-	-	-
Andy Ludiman											
					Harrogate	24+1	-	-	-	-	-
Mike Ruthen											
					Harrogate	20+8	-	-	-	-	-

County Ground, Claro Road, Harrogate. HG1 4AG.

Tel. Nos. 01423 566966   **Fax:** 01423 562776

Capacity: 5,000   **Seated:** 500   **Standing:** 4,500

Simple Directions:
    Claro Road is on the north side of the A59 (York Skipton road), just off the Stray (open grassed area adjacent to the town centre).

Nearest Railway Station: Harrogate (B.R.)
Car Parking: 400 at the ground, unlimited nearby
Admission: Season; Adult £55, OAPs £30 (includes parking) Children Free
              Matchday; Standing Adult £5, OAPs £2.50 Children Free, Seated Adult £6, OAPs £3.50, Children Free
Club Shop: Yes - matchdays only.
Clubhouse: Normal Licensing Hours, has two bars with snacks & bar meals available.
    Functions Facilities: Yes, capacity up to 120 seated

Training Nights: Monday and Thursday.

Harrogate Player of the Year 96-97; Mark Farrar.

MATCHDAY PROGRAMME

Size	A5
Number of pages	32
Price	£1
Programme Editor	Glyn Smith 01423 865763
Advertising Rates	Not available

LEEDS R.U.F.C.

FOUNDED: 1991

President Chips Browning, c/o Leeds RUFC, Headingley Stadium, St Michaels Lane, Leeds LS6 3BR.

Chairman Mike Palmer-Jones, c/o Leeds RUFC, as above

Club Secretary Mike Bidgood, 4 West Hill Avenue, Leeds. LS7 3QH.
0113 268 2784 (H), 0113 262 5382 (B), 0113 293 9494 (Fax), 0410 342054 (Mobile).

Fixtures Secretary Les Jackson, 4 Gledhow Wood Avenue, Leeds. LS8 1NY.
0113 266 5544 (H,B & Fax)

Director of Rugby Phil Davies, Chandos Park, Chandos Avenue, Leeds LS8 1QX
0410 342050 (Mobile), 0113 266 1406 (B & Fax)

Club Press Officer Mike Bidgood, c/o Leeds RUFC, as above
Rugby Press Officer Phil Davies, c/o Leeds RUFC, as above

This was the season that the Club finally started to move forward in concerted fashion. The second half of the 1995/96 promised much and the recruitment of a further dozen players completed a powerful squad. Most of the previous year's team also remained. Consequently the Roundheads (2nd XV) lost only to Gloucester and Doncaster in the Yorkshire Cup scoring a massive 1437 points in 30 games with Dan Eddie scoring 306 points.

In the Pilkington records tumbled as Redruth were eclipsed by 96-6 with Tonga international Sateki Tuipulotu scoring 4 tries. The form continued in the League and 7 days later the same opponents succumbed by 84-24. This set a new Club record total that was remarkably equalled in March and April. The season was completed with 11 straight wins including the demolition of League leaders Fylde by 34-0. 24 wins out of 30 were not enough as some enigmatic mid season away blues cost promotion by a single point. The massive points difference and the 186 tries scored in all 35 games counted for 'nowt' as the real objective was missed. The losses were at Wharfedale, Morley, Lydney, Fylde, Rosslyn Park and finally champions Exeter. All were comforably beaten in Leeds and the 100% home record was a fine tribute to the excellent Headingley Stadium. It allowed superb running rugby with over 100 tries at home. Seven players reached double figures with Mark Appleson sharing the lead on 19 with Tuipulotu.

All the leading players are again available and are joined by new recruits, Christian Saverimutto, Simon Easterby, Ralph Zoing, Tim Fourie and Steve Griffiths.

New training headquarters are planned and Academy and Apprenticeship schemes have been set up. The future must surely be rosy with Director of Rugby Phil Davies driving the Club forcefully forward!

Leeds RUFC 1997: Back Row (L-R); Les Woods (Manager), Jon Eagle (Coach), Richard Matthias, Mark Luffman, Jason Ashcroft, Sateki Tuipulotu, Simon Henry, Gavin Baldwin, Christian Radacanu, Paul Wood, Martin Whitcombe, Nick Green, Iain Salkeld, Dave Lowther (Coach), Chips Browning (President). Front Row (L-R); Steve Bartliff, Mike Cawthorn, Gerry Ainscough, Mark Appleson, Paul Johnson, Mike Shelley, Rhys Morgan, Kern Yates, Colin Stephens.
Photo - Photogenic, D J Williams

Colours: Royal blue, white, gold

Change colours: White, royal blue, gold

LEEDS

COURAGE LEAGUE MATCH DETAILS 1996-97

No	Ven.	Date	Opponents	Att.	Res.	Score	Scorers
1	(A)	31.08	v Otley		W	20-19	Coley(t)Ainscough(5p)
2	(A)	07.09	v Reading		W	35-16	Bartliffe(2t)Yates(t)Tuipulotu(t)Ainscough(3c3p)
3	(H)	14.09	v Rosslyn Park		W	49-5	Matthias(2t)Appleson(t)Tuipulotu(tc)Ainscough(2t4c3p)
4	(A)	21.09	v Wharfdale		L	18-23	Ainscough(3p)Stephens(2pdg)
5	(H)	28.09	v Exeter		W	33-24	Appleson(t)Bartliffe(t)Johnson(t)Ainscough(t2c3p)
6	(A)	05.10	v Harrogate		W	35-26	Johnson(t)Thornton(t)Appleson(dg)Ainscough(2c6p)
7	(A)	12.10	v Walsall		W	26-24	Morgan(t)Ainscough(t2c4p)
8	(H)	19.10	v London Welsh		W	22-17	Appleson(t)Ainscough(t2p)Stephens(2dg)
9	(A)	26.10	v Lydney		L	22-31	Raducanu(t)Matthias(t)Yates(t)Stephens(2cp)
10	(H)	09.11	v Redruth		W	84-24	Matthias(3t)Morgan(2t)Appleson(t)Cawthorne(t)Raducanu(t)Denham(t)Yates(t)Ashcroft(t)Shelley(t)Tuipulotu(t3c)Stephens(t4c)
11	(A)	16.11	v Morley		L	22-30	Matthias(t)Ashcroft(t)Ainscough(4p)
12	(H)	07.12	v Clifton		W	80-0	Matthias(4t)Appleson(t)Cawthorne(t)Raducanu(t)Green(t)Ashcroft(t)Tuipulotu(2tc)Ainscough(9c)
13	(A)	28.12	v Fylde		L	0-13	
14	(H)	04.01	v Havant		W	52-14	Cawthorne(2t)Raducanu(2t)Green(t)Morgan(t)Stephens(tc3p)Appleson(c)
15	(H)	18.01	v Otley		W	39-16	Raducanu(t)Appleson(t)Green(t)Shelley(t)Tuipulotu(2c5p)
16	(H)	25.01	v Reading		W	25-16	Appleson(2t)Shelley(t)Tuipulotu(t)Ainscough(cp)
17	(A)	01.02	v Rosslyn Park		L	14-20	Matthias(t)Ainscough(3p)
18	(H)	08.02	v Wharfdale		W	41-13	Yates(2t)Raducanu(t)Luffman(t)Walker(t)Ainscough(2c4p)
19	(A)	15.02	v Exeter		L	25-26	Griffin(t)Ainscough(c6p)
20	(H)	22.02	v Harrogate		W	28-3	Shelley(t)Ainscough(2c)Tuipolotu(2t3p)
21	(H)	01.03	v Walsall		W	84-3	Appleson(2t)Bartliffe(2t)Green(2t)Griffin(t)Baldwin(t)Stephens(t)Wood(t)Tuipolotu(tc)Ainscough(3t6c)
22	(A)	08.03	v London Welsh		W	28-17	Tuipulotu(t)Raducanu(t)Ashcroft(t)Stephens(t)Ainscough(c2p)
23	(H)	15.03	v Lydney		W	74-0	Stephens(4tc)Appleson(2t)Raducanu(t)Griffin(t)Perego(t)Eagle(t)Tuipulotu(t7cp)
24	(A)	22.03	v Redruth		W	27-10	Raducanu(2t)Green(t)Griffin(t)Stephens(2cdg)
25	(H)	05.04	v Morley		W	42-3	Green(t)Walker(t)Ainscough(t)PenTry(t)Tuipulotu(t4c3p)
26	(A)	12.04	v Clifton		W	84-9	Appleson(3t)Green(3t)Cawthorne(t)Griffin(t)Johnson(t)Perego(t)Baldwin(t)Whitcombe(t)Tuipulotu(t5p)Ainscough(3c)
27	(H)	20.04	v Fylde		W	34-0	Green(2t)Ainscough(T)Cawthorne(t)Stephens(t)Tuipulotu(3cp)
28	(A)	26.04	v Havant		W	74-10	Bartliffe(4t)Ainscough(2t6c)Appleson(t)Stephens(t)Cawthorne(t)Perego(t)Raducanu(t)Tuipulotu(tc)
29	(H)	03.05	v Liverpool St H		W	44-10	Shelley(2t)Johnson(t)Ainscough(t)Green(t)Luffman(t)Tuipulotu(4cp)Stephens(dg)
30	(A)	10.05	v Liverpool St H		W	48-0	Cawthorne(2t)Denham(2t)Morgan(t)PenTry(t)Ainscough(c)Tuipulotu(t4cp)

1996-97 HIGHLIGHTS

LEAGUE DEBUTS: Richard Matthias, Mike Cawthorne, Gavin Baldwin, Mark Luffman, Mike Shelley, Nick Green, Kern Yates, Sateki Tuipulotu, Phil Davies, Stuart Kneale, Simon Henry, Jason Ashcroft, Diccon Edwards, Paul Stirling, Mark Perego.

TRY ON DEBUT: Sateki Tuipulotu.

PLAYERS USED: 33 plus 5 as replacement.

EVER PRESENT: None - most appearances 29
- Mike Shelley (+ 1 as rep.) & Christian Raducanu.

❏ Broke or equalled all 15 scoring records in a remarkable season for a team not winning promotion.

❏ Gerry Ainscough, ex Orrell & Leicester utility back, demolished the season records for points, conversions and penalties with 307, 45 and 49. The previous records were 97, 12 and 20 by David Breakwell set in 93-94. He twice scored 27 points in a match beating the previous record of 20 set by David Breakwell v Aspatria in Oct. 93. He also set a new record of 9 conversions in a match beating the previous record of 4 held by Ben Lloyd and Ralph Bennett. He twice kicked 6 penalties to equal Colin Stephens's record set last season.

❏ Former Welsh international stand-off Colin Stephens set a new record for drop goals in a season with five and equalled the record of two drop goals in a match as he extended his career record to 11. Stephens also became one of three players to break the record of three tries in a match. Stephens along with Richard Matthias and Steve Bartliffe scored four tries in a match.

LEEDS'S COURAGE LEAGUE MATCH DETAILS 1996-97

#	15	14	13	12	11	10	9	1	2	3	4	5	6	7	8	Replacements
1	Coley	Matthias	Lloyd	Johnson	Thornton	Ainscough	Cawthorne	Baldwin	Luffman	Shelley	McCartney	Radacanu	Griffin	Lancaster	Green	
2	Appleson	Bartliffe	Tuipulotu	Johnson	Matthias	Ainscough	Cawthorne	Baldwin	Luffman	Shelley	McCartney	Radacanu	Griffin	Yates	Green	Morgan(10)
3	Appleson	Bartliffe	Tuipulotu	Johnson	Matthias	Ainscough	Cawthorne	Baldwin	Luffman	Shelley	Davies	Radacanu	Griffin	Yates	Green	Morgan(10)
4	Coley	Bartliffe	Tuipulotu	Johnson	Matthias	Stephens	Cawthorne	Baldwin	Kneale	Shelley	Henry	Henry	Griffin	Yates	Green	Ainscough(11)
5	Appleson	Bartliffe	Tuipulotu	Johnson	Thornton	Ainscough	Cawthorne	Baldwin	Luffman	Shelley	Davies	Radacanu	Green	Yates	Ashcroft	
6	Appleson	Edwards	Tuipulotu	Johnson	Thornton	Ainscough	Cawthorne	Baldwin	Luffman	Shelley	Davies	Radacanu	Green	Yates	Ashcroft	Swarbrigg(9)Salkeld(2)
7	Appleson	Edwards	Tuipulotu	Johnson	Thornton	Ainscough	Morgan	Baldwin	Luffman	Shelley	Davies	Radacanu	Green	Lancaster	Ashcroft	
8	Tuipulotu	Appleson	Ainscough	Johnson	Matthias	Stephens	Morgan	Whitcombe	Luffman	Shelley	Davies	Radacanu	Green	Yates	Ashcroft	Curtis(8)
9	Tuipulotu	Appleson	Edwards	Johnson	Matthias	Stephens	Morgan	Whitcombe	Kneale	Shelley	Davies	Radacanu	Green	Yates	Ashcroft	
10	Morgan	Matthias	Edwards	Tuipulotu	Appleson	Stephens	Cawthorne	Whitcombe	Kneale	Shelley	Davies	Radacanu	Denham	Yates	Ashcroft	Shelley(1)Green(6)
11	Morgan	Matthias	Tuipulotu	Ainscough	Appleson	Stephens	Cawthorne	Baldwin	Kneale	Shelley	Davies	Radacanu	Denham	Yates	Ashcroft	Johnson(14)Luffman(2)
12	Tuipulotu	Matthias	Edwards	Johnson	Appleson	Ainscough	Swarbrigg	Baldwin	Luffman	Shelley	Wood	Radacanu	Green	Griffin	Ashcroft	Morgan(14)Kelly(1)Henry(5)
13	Tuipulotu	Matthias	Edwards	Johnson	Ainscough	Stephens	Swarbrigg	Baldwin	Luffman	Shelley	Wood	Radacanu	Green	Griffin	Ashcrift	Morgan(14)
14	Morgan	Matthias	Edwards	Johnson	Sterling	Stephens	Cawthorne	Baldwin	Luffman	Shelley	Wood	Radacanu	Denham	Yates	Green	Thornton(13)Henry(5)
15	Tuipulotu	Bartliffe	Edwards	Johnson	Appleson	Stephens	Cawthorne	Baldwin	Luffman	Shelley	Wood	Radacanu	Yates	Green	Ashcroft	Morgan(11)
16	Appleson	Matthias	Tuipulotu	Johnson	Ainscough	Stephens	Cawthorne	Baldwin	Luffman	Shelley	Wood	Radacanu	Yates		Ashcroft	Whitcombe(1)
17	Appleson	Matthias	Tuipulotu	Johnson	Bartliffe	Ainscough	Cawthorne	Baldwin	Luffman	Shelley	Wood	Radacanu	Yates		Ashcroft	Davies(8)
18	Appleson	Matthias	Tuipulotu	Johnson	Appleson	Ainscough	Cawthorne	Baldwin	Luffman	Shelley	Wood	Radacanu	Yates	Griffin		Stephens(12)
19	Bartliffe	Matthias	Edwards	Walker	Matthias	Stephens	Cawthorne	Baldwin	Luffman	Shelley	Davies	Radacanu	Green	Yates	Griffin	Green(4)Salkeld(tr2)
20	Tuipulotu	Matthias	Ainscough	Walker	Morgan	Stephens	Cawthorne	Baldwin	Luffman	Shelley	Davies	Radacanu	Yates	Perego	Green	Ashcroft(6),Bartliffe(14)
21	Tuipulotu	Matthias	Ainscough	Walker	Appleson	Stephens	Cawthorne	Baldwin	Luffman	Shelley	Wood	Radacanu	Griffin	Perego	Green	Ashcroft(7),Kneale(4),Bartliffe(14)
22	Tuipulotu	Appleson	Ainscough	Johnson	Appleson	Stephens	Cawthorne	Baldwin	Luffman	Shelley	Wood	Radacanu	Green	Perego	Green	Griffin(8),Morgan(15),Whitcombe(1),Kneale(2)
23	Tuipulotu	Morgan	Ainscough	Johnson	Appleson	Stephens	Cawthorne	Baldwin	Luffman	Shelley	Wood	Radacanu	Griffin	Perego	Green	Eagle(14)Kelly(1)Salkeld(2)Ashcroft(6)
24	Tuipulotu	Morgan	Ainscough	Johnson	Appleson	Stephens	Cawthorne	Baldwin	Luffman	Shelley	Henry	Radacanu	Green	Perego	Ashcroft	Matthias(14)Whitcombe(1)Griffin(8)
25	Tuipulotu	Matthias	Walker	Johnson	Appleson	Stephens	Cawthorne	Baldwin	Luffman	Shelley	Henry	Radacanu	Green	Perego	Ashcroft	Ainscough(13)Griffin(6)Whitcombe(1)
26	Tuipulotu	Matthias	Ainscough	Johnson	Appleson	Stephens	Cawthorne	Whitcombe	Luffman	Shelley	Henry	Radacanu	Green	Perego	Green	Morgan(15)Kneale(2)Kelly(1)Williams(5)
27	Tuipulotu	Matthias	Ainscough	Johnson	Appleson	Stephens	Cawthorne	Whitcombe	Luffman	Shelley	Henry	Radacanu	Green	Perego	Green	Bartliffe(14)Ashcroft(7)
28	Tuipulotu	Bartliffe	Ainscough	Johnson	Appleson	Stephens	Cawthorne	Whitcombe	Luffman	Shelley	Henry	Radacanu	Griffin	Perego	Green	Morgan(15)Kneale(2)Williams(5)
29	Tuipulotu	Matthias	Ainscough	Johnson	Appleson	Stephens	Cawthorne	Baldwin	Luffman	Shelley	Henry	Radacanu	Green	Ashcroft	Perego	Griffin(6)Morgan(r/6)Kneale(5)
30	Tuipulotu	Bartliffe	Ainscough	Johnson	Appleson	Stephens	Cawthorne	Baldwin	Luffman	Shelley	Henry	Radacanu	Green	Ashcroft	Perego	Morgan(11)Kneale(2)Denham(4)

LEEDS LEAGUE STATISTICS
(COMPILED BY STEPHEN McCORMACK)

Season	Div.	P	W	D	L	F (Tries Con Pen DG)	A (Tries Con Pen DG)	Most Points	Most Tries
92-93	3	11	7	0	4	228 (28 17 16 2)	220 (24 11 24 2)	45 - Ben Lloyd	7 - Chris Thornton
93-94	4	18	7	0	11	243 (23 16 26 6)	318 (32 13 36 8)	97 - David Breakwell	3 - Penalty Tries
94-95	4	18	8	0	10	335 (36 19 35 4)	291 (30 15 34 3)	83 - Ralph Bennett	6 - Phil Griffin & Chris Thornton
95-96	4	18	9	1	8	312 (30 12 41 5)	347 (38 20 33 6)	67 - Colin Stephens	6 - Chris Thornton
96-97	3	30	24	0	6	1209 (158 94 71 6)	432 (48 27 42 4)	307 - Gerry Ainscough	16 - Mark Appleson
Totals		95	55	1	39	2327 (275 158 189 23)	1608 (172 86 169 23)		

	HOME	AWAY
BIGGEST WIN	(81pts) 84-3 v Walsall 1.3.97	(75pts) 84-9 v Clifton 12.4.97
DEFEAT	(6pts) 20-26 v Liverpool St. H. 25.3.94	(25pts) 10-35 v Liverpool St. H. 15.10.93
MOST POINTS SCORED	84-3 v Walsall 1.3.97	84-9 v Clifton 12.4.97
AGAINST	20-26 v Liverpool St. H. 25.3.94	10-35 v Liverpool St. H. 15.10.93

MOST CONSECUTIVE VICTORIES - 11 **MOST CONSECUTIVE DEFEATS - 5**

MOST TRIES IN A MATCH
(FOR) 14 v Redruth 9.1..96 (H)
v Walsall 1.3.97 (H)
(AGAINST) 6 v Aspatria 13.4.96 (A)

MOST APPEARANCES
FORWARD: 62(4) Phil Griffin
BACK: 62(1) Chris Thornton

CONSECUTIVE SCORING MATCHES
Scoring Tries - 4 - Chris Thornton, Richard matthias & Gerry Ainscough
Scoring Points - 11 - Sateki Tuipulotu

CONSECUTIVE APPEARANCES
24 David Breakwell 26.9.92 to 5.3.94

MOST	in a SEASON	in a CAREER	in a MATCH
Points	307 Gerry Ainscough 96-97	309 Gerry Ainscough 96-97	27 Gerry Ainscough v Rosslyn P. 14.9.96 (H) v Walsall 1.3.97 (H)
Tries	16 Mark Appleson 96-97	22 Chris Thornton 92-97	4 Richard Matthias v Clifton 7.12.96 (H) Colin Stephens v Lydney 15.3.97 (H) Steve Bartliffe v Havant 26.4.97 (A)
Conversions	45 Gerry Ainscough 96-97	46 Gerry Ainscough 96-97	9 Gerry Ainscough v Clifton 7.12.96 (H)
Penalties	49 Gerry Ainscough 96-97	49 Gerry Ainscough 96-97	6 Colin Stephens v Walsall 24.2.96 (H) Gerry Ainscough v Harrogate 5.10.96 (A) v Exeter 15.2.97 (A)
Drop Goals	5 Colin Stephens 96-97	9 Colin Stephens 95-97	2 Dan Eddie v Broughton Park 19.2.94 Colin Stephens v Exeter 9.9.95 (H) v London Welsh 19.10.96 (H)

LEEDS PLAYING SQUAD

NAME	Ht	Wt	Birthdate	Birthplace	Club	Apps	Pts	T	C	P	DG
BACKS											
Sateki Tuipulotu	6.0	13.13	03.07.71		Leeds (RL)						
Tonga.					Leeds	25	197	15	37	16	-
Richard Matthias	5.11	14.0	28.05.75	Llanelli	Orrell						
					Leeds	21+1	60	12	-	-	-
Mark Appleson	5.10	13.10	26.02.68	Islington	Prev. Clubs: Sale, London Scottish.						
Scotland: A.					Leeds	27	89	16	3	-	1
Paul Johnson	5.11	13.8	19.05.62	Huddersfield	Orrell	43	18	3	-	-	1
					Leeds	30+1	30	6	-	-	-
Gerry Ainscough	6.0	13.0	07.08.64	Wigan	Leicester	6	8	2	-	-	-
					Orrell	66+1	337	12	34	71	2
England: A. North.					Leeds	23+2	309	14	46	49	-
Colin Stephens	5.8	12.6	29.11.69	Swansea	Llanelli						
Wales.					Leeds	26+1	168	10	11	23	9
Mike Cawthorne	5.9	13.3	15.05.72	Bridlington	Wakefield	6	-	-	-	-	-
Yorkshire.					Leeds	25	45	9	-	-	-
Steve Bartliff	6.0	13.5	30.12.67								
Combined Services					Leeds	18+3	70	14	-	-	-
Rhys Morgan	6.1	13.3	30.07.67	High Wycombe	West Park Bramhope						
British Police.					Leeds	32+9	40	8	-	-	-
Damian Walker	6.1	12.11	03.10.74		Leeds	8	10	2	-	-	-
Jon Swarbrigg	5.9	12.11	16.09.69	Nuneaton	Nuneaton						
					Leeds	22+2	10	2	-	-	-
Matt Coley	6.3	14.0	29.11.73	Torquay	Leeds	10	14	1	-	3	-
Diccon Edwards	5.10	13.10	13.03.73	London	Wakefield	23	10	2	-	-	-
					Leicester	15	-	-	-	-	-
					Castleford (RL)		-	-	-	-	-
(Wales (RL). England u21. North)					Leeds	9	-	-	-	-	-
FORWARDS											
Gavin Baldwin	6.2	17.4	06.12.69	Wolverhampton	Wakefield	12+1					
England: A.					Leeds	26+1	5	1	-	-	-
Mark Luffman	5.10	14.12	17.08.71	Nottingham	Ilkley.						
					Otley	10	5	1	-	-	-
					Leeds	26+1	10	2	-	-	-
Mike Shelley	6.0	18.8	13.03.72	Leeds	West Hartlepool	18	20	4	-	-	-
North					Leeds	29+1	35	7	-	-	-
Christian Raducanu	6.5	16.11	02.10.67	Bucharest	Bradford & Bingley						
					Sale	7	4	1	-	-	-
Rumania					Leeds	47	80	16	-	-	-
Simon Henry	6.5	14.12	26.03.72	Leeds	Otley						
					Leeds	10+2	-	-	-	-	-
Phil Griffin	6.0	14.3	10.08.72		Vale of Lune						
Lancashire Schools					Leeds	63+4	65	13	-	-	-
Nick Green	6.4	16.7	26.01.68	Northampton	Wakefield	47	10	2	-	-	-
					Leeds	37+2	40	8	-	-	-
Kern Yates	6.0	14.4	12.02.74	Wegberg	Wakefield	12+1	5	1	-	-	-
England: Colts, Students.					Leeds	15+1	25	5	-	-	-
Stewart Kneale	5.10	14.9	30.04.74	Leeds	Morley						
Yorkshire.					Leeds	4+6	-	-	-	-	-
Martin Whitcombe	6.2	17.7	14.09.62	Keighley	Leicester						
					Sale	72	43	9	-	-	-
R.A.F.					Leeds	23+6	5	1	-	-	-
Mark Perego	6.1	16.0	08.02.64	Winchester	Llanelli						
Wales					Leeds	12	15	3	-	-	-
Lee Denham	6.1	16.2	05.03.74		Leeds	10+1	15	3	-	-	-
Jason Ashcroft	6.0	15.6	23.05.68		Waterloo						
					Leeds	17+4	25	5	-	-	-
Stuart Lancaster	6.0	13.3	09.10.69	Penrith	Leeds						
Paul Williams	6.6	15.8	06.03.76	Carmathen	Leeds Prev. Club: Fylde. Hons: Welsh Youth						
Phillip Davies	6.4	19.7	19.10.63	Seven Sisters	Leeds Prev. Club: Llanelli. Hons. Wales, British Lions						
Paul Wood	6.4	17.7	16.08.61	Halifax	Leeds Prev.: Bradford & Bingley, Wakefield. Hons. Yorkshire						
Ronnie Kelly	5.11	16.0	11.06.68		Leeds Prev. Club: Sale						
Iain Salkeld	5.9	13.10	08.06.71	Letchworth	Leeds Hons. Yorkshire						

Headingley Stadium, St Michaels Lane, Headingley, Leeds. LS6 3BR

Tel: 0113 278 6181

Fax: 0113 275 4284

Capacity: 27,000   **Seated:** 9,000   **Standing:** 18,000

Simple Directions: From East: M62 Junction 29 (M1). Follow signs Leeds M1, junction 43 (A61), Junc 47 leave motorway & follow signs City Centre. From City Centre: follow signs Otley, Skipton A660 to leave by Woodhouse Lane. In 2.3 miles turn left and then left again into St Michaels Lane. Ground on right.

Nearest Railway Station: Headingley & Leeds City

Car Parking: 450 at ground £1

Admission: Season - Adult £50, Children/OAPs £20: Matchday - Adult £5, Children/OAPs £3

Club Shop: Yes. Manager Alan Wright 0113 284 2525

Clubhouse: Open normal licensing hours, snacks available.

    Functions: Yes, capacity 150, contact Brian Hazelgrave c/o Leeds RUFC

Training Nights: Monday, Tuesday, Thursday.

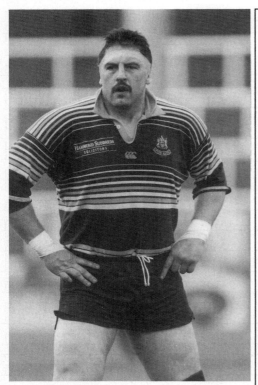

Leeds RUFC Director of Rugby; Phil Davies

MATCHDAY PROGRAMME

Size	A5
Number of pages	36 plus cover
Price	£1.50 Full colour
Programme Editor	
	Mike Bidgood, 0113 262 5382
Advertising Rates	Full page £500
	1/2 page £300
	1/4 page £150

LIVERPOOL St HELENS F.C.

NICKNAME: LSH

FOUNDED: 1857 (Merged 1986)

President Ian Clark
Chairman W S Magowan, MBE.
Club Secretary J D Robertson, 36 Beryl Road, Noctorum, Wirral. L43 9RT.
0151 677 5611 (H), 0151 427 7535 (B)
Fixtures Secretary R Hall, 21 Childwall Abbey Road, Liverpool. L16 0JL. 0151 722 3588 (H & Fax)
Press Officer C Brown, 47 Cowley Hill Lane, St. Helens. WA10 2AR. 01744 759075 (H), 01744 23281 (B)

In the three preceding campaigns Liverpool St. Helens had ended the scheduled fixtures just below the promotion zone, and yet the season began with more than a little trepidation. Unlike so many of our contemporaries we did not produce a major backer with money to burn and so it was with the majority of our squads from those three seasons that the campaign began.

For the duration of the 1995/96 season Moss Lane had become 'Fortress L.S.H.' with all invaders repelled, including First and Second Division opponents, but this proud record was not to be extended. The first visitors were London Welsh on a red hot August afternoon. The impression was that both sides were still on summer recess as the game struggled for life with the Exiles eventually winning 5-12. In the following weeks Lydney, Fylde, Walsall and Otley left Moss Lane with League points - Fortress L.S.H. had fallen.

Of the fifteen League games played at home six were lost by eleven points or less, while seven further games provided home victories, the only two major defeats being against Fylde (12-40) and Leeds (0-40). On the road there were also chances to improve our situation as seven of the fifteen away games were lost by twelve points or less - so near and yet so far.

After the first two games of the season we found ourselves fourth from bottom; with four to be relegated it was essential we improved. Despite numerous close calls it was only to be late in the season that we managed to move up into that almost illusive twelfth place and with it sanctuary.

It must be noted that the arrival of Paddy Mortimer played no little part in the improvement of the club's fortunes. A fresh approach, a fresh enthusiasm combined with the undoubted coaching qualities of Dave Buttery and his team stood us in good stead.

In what was a long, arduous season the highlights undoubtedly were the emergence of the 'young guns', Paul Brett, Phil Graham, Danny Jones, Simon Hazlett, Tommy Jackson, Mark Nolan and Martin Lloyd - to name but a few. The victories over Redruth (72-17), Harrogate (32-27) and Clifton (89-13) were others. Also the record points haul of Paul Brett came during the Clifton game, 39 (three tries and twelve goals).

The season's most negative aspect was surely the enforced retirement of Dr. Kevin Simms from the game on medical grounds. Kevin, of course, represented Cambridge (83/84/85), Lancashire, North Division (Captain in 1995) and England, for whom he gained fifteen caps.

Recruitment of quality footballers surely will be an ongoing concern during the season, but, in a new era when maintenance of last season's standards effectively means you are falling behind, one must be wary that consolidation is not the adopted buzz word for the season - realization both of potential and goals must be attained. Success is essential if we are to provide a team worthy of the ground improvements that at present are the focus for a bid to the Lottery Commission which, if realized, will provide one of the best sporting locations of any club outside the Premier Leagues.

Liverpool St Helens FC: Back Row (L-R); T Collins (Trainer), J A Walker (Ch of Rugby), D Lupton, N Hughes, M Nugent, K Davies, D Gaskell, S Hughes, D Pilkington, S Hazlett, M Sephton, J Turner (Ch of Selectors), P Mortimer & D Buttery (Coaches). Front Row; G Garvey (Team Sec), P Graham, S Humphreys, D Lever, M Nolan, B Wellens (Capt), T Jackson, C King, D Faulkner, J Hitchen. On ground; M Liddell, P Brett.

Colours: Red, white, black & blue hoops/navy.

Change colours: White with red trim/navy.

COURAGE LEAGUE MATCH DETAILS 1996-97

No	Ven.	Date	Opponents	Att.	Res.	Score	Scorers
1	(H)	31.08	v London Welsh		L	5-12	N Simms(t)
2	(H)	07.09	v Lydney		L	25-27	Jackson(t)Davies(t)Humphreys(5p)
3	(A)	14.09	v Redruth		L	6-12	Humphreys(2p)
4	(H)	21.09	v Morley		W	13-11	Brett(t)B Wellens(dg)Humphreys(cp)
5	(A)	28.09	v Clifton		L	16-23	Sephton(t)Graham(t)Humphreys(2p)
6	(H)	05.10	v Fylde		L	12-40	K Simms(t)Nugent(t)Humphreys(c)
7	(H)	12.10	v Havant		L	14-26	Graham(t)Humphreys(3p)
8	(H)	19.10	v Walsall		L	21-29	Brett(t)Eldoy(t)Humphreys(c3p)
9	(H)	26.10	v Otley		L	20-25	Salisbury(t)K Simms(t)Brett(tcp)
10	(A)	09.11	v Reading		L	26-65	Lupton(2t)Faulkner(2t)B Wellens(3c)
11	(H)	16.11	v Rosslyn Park		W	29-21	N Simms(t)Lupton(t)Graham(t)B Wellens(2t2c)
12	(A)	21.12	v Wharfdale		L	15-24	Brett(5p)
13	(A)	18.01	v London Welsh		W	17-15	Boyd(t)B Wellens(t)Brett(2cp)
14	(A)	25.01	v Lydney		L	19-23	B Wellens(t)Eldoy(t)Brett(t2c)
15	(H)	01.02	v Redruth		W	72-17	Gaskell(2t)Hendry(2t)Boyd(t)Graham(t)Sephton(t)Eldoy(t)Brett(3t6cp)
16	(A)	08.02	v Morley		L	36-41	Gaskell(t)Sephton(t)Jones(t)King(t)Brett(2c4p) B Wellens(c)
17	(H)	15.02	v Clifton		W	89-13	Sephton(4t)Gaskell(2t)B Wellens(t)Liddle(t)Graham(t)Jackson(t)Brett(3t12c)
18	(A)	22.02	v Fylde		L	13-30	Callaghan(t)Brett(c2p)
19	(H)	01.03	v Havant		W	22-10	Jackson(t)Sephton(t)Lupton(t)Brett(2c)Wellens(dg)
20	(A)	08.03	v Walsall		W	29-19	Sephton(2t)Davies(t)Graham(t)Brett(t2c)
21	(A)	15.03	v Otley		L	25-34	Walker(t)Gaskell(t)Callaghan(t)Brett(tcp)
22	(H)	22.03	v Reading		L	16-27	Walker(t)B Wellens(dg)Brett(tp)
23	(H)	29.03	v Exeter		L	18-25	Jones(3t)Brett(p)
24	(A)	05.04	v Rosslyn Park		L	7-25	Brett(tc)
25	(H)	12.04	v Wharfdale		W	30-25	Hazlett(t)Graham(t)Gaskell(t)Pilkington(t)Lupton(t)Brett(cp)
26	(A)	19.04	v Exeter		L	14-45	Eldoy(2t)Brett(2c)
27	(H)	26.04	v Harrogate		W	32-27	Hitchin(t)Boyd(t)Gaskell(t)Humphreys(t)Brett(3c2p)
28	(A)	03.05	v Leeds		L	10-44	Jackson(t)Liddle(t)
29	(H)	10.05	v Leeds		L	0-48	
30	(A)	17.05	v Harrogate		L	14-44	Sephton(t)Faulkner(t)Brett(2c)

1996-97 HIGHLIGHTS

LEAGUE DEBUTS: Mike Hitchin, Dave Faulkner, Ian Wellens, Tommy Jackson, Ian Brassington, Mark Nolan, James Salisbury, Alex Reay, Simon Hazlett, Dave Lever, John Hitchin, Ian Callaghan, John O'Boyle.

PLAYERS USED: 42 plus one as replacement.

EVER PRESENT: None - most appearances 27
- Mark Sephton & Dave Lupton (Paul Brett played 26+1)

❏ Scored more tries than promoted Fylde 96 to 90.

❏ Stuart Hughes extended his club record for consecutive appearances to 57.

❏ As well as their Division three record score of 89-13 v Clifton they also suffered their biggest ever home defeat losing 0-48 to promotion chasing Leeds.

❏ Young utility back Paul Brett made a record breaking start to league rugby.
He set a new record for points in a season with 210 beating the previous 155 set by Andy Higgin in 94-95, He also beat Higgin's record of scoring in 14 consecutive games - going one better with 15. In his 210 points were 14 tries which equalled Simon Humphrey's record for tries in a season set last season. His 40 conversions broke Andy Higgin's record of 24 from 94-95.

	Pts	T	C	P	D	Apps	Ave.
Paul Brett 96-97	210	14	40	20	-	25	8.40
Andy Higgin 94-95	155	4	24	27	2	17	9.12

❏ Brett twice broke the Division three record for points in a match. He first did it scoring 30 points against Redruth in February and then six weeks later he broke the record again. It was in the club's record 89-13 win over Clifton with Brett scoring 39 points which included another Division Three record of 12 conversions.

❏ Mark Sephton extended his all-time career record for tries to 52

LIVERPOOL ST HELEN'S COURAGE LEAGUE MATCH DETAILS 1996-97

15	14	13	12	11	10	9	1	2	3	4	5	6	7	8	Replacements	
BWellens	Yearsley	MHitchen	KSimms	Sephton	Eldoy	King	Grigg	Faulkner	S Hughes	Nugent	Sproston	N Hughes		Lupton		1
Humphreys	Yearsley	Davies	KSimms	Sephton	Eldoy	King	Grigg	Faulkner	S Hughes	Nugent	Sproston	N Hughes		Lupton	NSimms(13)	2
Humphreys	Graham	MHitchen	Davies	Sephton	I Wellens	King	Faulkner	S Hughes	Jackson	Nugent	Brassington	Williams		Lupton	Edgar(3)Brett(9)	3
Humphreys	Brett	KSimms	Davies	Sephton	I Wellens	King	Grigg	Faulkner	S Hughes	Nugent	Williams	Brassington		Lupton	Edgar(3)Brett(9)	4
Humphreys	Brett	Graham	Davies	Sephton	Eldoy	King	Grigg	Jackson	S Hughes	Nugent	Boyd	N Hughes		Lupton	Edgar(3)Graham(14)	5
Humphreys	Brett	KSimms	Davies	Sephton	Eldoy	King	Grigg	Jackson	S Hughes	Nugent	N Hughes	Hendry		Lupton	Edgar(11)	6
Humphreys	Brett	KSimms	Davies	Sephton	Eldoy	Grigg	Gill	Jackson	S Hughes	Nugent	N Hughes	Hendry		Lupton	Boyd(7)Jackson(4)	7
Humphreys	Brett	Brett	Davies	Sephton	Eldoy	Hudson	Edgar	Nolan	S Hughes	Boyd	N Hughes	Salisbury		Lupton	Jackson(3)Eldoy(9)	8
Graham	Brett	KSimms	Graham	NSimms	Ramsden	Gill	Reay	Jackson	S Hughes	Boyd	N Hughes	Salisbury		Lupton		9
Graham	Jones	NSimms	Brett	Sephton	Nolan	Nolan	Jackson	S Hughes	Nugent	Salisbury	Williams			Lupton	Faulkner(1)Liddell(9)Boyd(4)	10
Graham	Jones	NSimms	Brett	NSimms	Sephton	Faulkner	Nolan	S Hughes	Nugent	Williams	Williams			Lupton	Grigg(2)	11
Brett	Jones	Graham	Walker	Sephton	BWellens	King	Grigg	S Hughes	Nugent	Davies	Williams			Lupton	Hazlett(11)Nolan(2)	12
Graham	Jones	Graham	Walker	Sephton	BWellens	Liddell	Faulkner	S Hughes	Nugent	Williams	Hendry			Lupton	Eldoy(9)	13
Graham	Brett	Hazlett	Walker	Sephton	BWellens	Liddell	Faulkner	S Hughes	Nugent	Williams	Hendry			Lupton	Eldoy(9)	14
Graham	Brett	Hazlett	Davies	Sephton	BWellens	Liddell	Faulkner	Boyd	Nugent	Gaskell	Hendry			Lupton	Eldoy(9)Salisbury(8)Mills(2)Lever(1)	15
Graham	Jones	Brett	Davies	Sephton	NSimms	Liddell	Jackson	Boyd	Nugent	Gaskell	Hendry			Lupton	Eldoy(9)Jackson(3)J Hitchen(2)Callaghan(10)	16
Graham	Brett	Hazlett	Davies	Sephton	BWellens	King	S Hughes	Boyd	Nugent	Gaskell	Hendry			Lupton	N Hughes(6)Callaghan(10)	17
Graham	Brett	Davies	Hazlett	Sephton	BWellens	King	Faulkner	Faulkner	Boyd	Gaskell	Hendry			Lupton	Callaghan(12)Lever(1)	18
Graham	Brett	BWellens	Hazlett	Sephton	NSimms	King	S Hughes	Nugent	Boyd	Gaskell	Hendry			Lupton	Callaghan(13),Williams(7),Nolan(2),	19
Graham	Brett	Callaghan	Sephton	Sephton	BWellens	Liddle	Nolan	Jackson	Nugent	Boyd	Gaskell	Hendry		Lupton	Walker(13)	20
Graham	Brett	Callaghan	Jones	Sephton	BWellens	Liddell	Boyd	Jackson	Nugent	Gaskell	Hendry			Lupton	Liddell(9)	21
Brett	Walker	Callaghan	Jones	Sephton	BWellens	King	Boyd	Jackson	Nugent	Gaskell	N Hughes	Hendry		Lupton	Grigg(2)Wellens(15)	22
Brett	Callaghan	Callaghan	Jones	BWellens	King	J Hitchen	Nugent	Boyd	Gaskell	Lupton	Lupton				Walker(11)Eldoy(10)Nolan(2)	23
Graham	Brett	Callaghan	Jones	Pilkington	King	Jackson	Boyd	Nugent	Gaskell	Gaskell				Lupton	Eldoy(10)Nugent(8)Nolan(2)	24
Graham	Brett	Hazlett	Sephton	Pilkington	Lever	King	Boyd	Jackson	S Hughes	Gaskell	Gaskell			Lupton	NSimms(10)	25
Graham	Brett	Hazlett	Sephton	Pilkington	Liddle	King	Boyd	Jackson	S Hughes	N Hughes	Gaskell			Lupton	Eldoy(10)Nugent(8)	26
Graham	Humphreys	Brett	Hazlett	Pilkington	King	J Hitchen	Nolan	Jackson	Nugent	N Hughes	Gaskell			Lupton	Eldoy(10)Nolan(2)	27
Graham	Humphreys	Brett	Sephton	Pilkington	Nolan	Jackson	Boyd	Nugent	N Hughes	Gaskell				Lupton	S Hughes(8)Liddle(9)Lever(1)Hitchen(6)	28
Humphreys	O'Boyle	Davies	Hazlett	Callaghan	King	Jackson	Boyd	Nugent	N Hughes	Gaskell				Lupton	Eldoy(9)S Hughes(7)Lever(1)	29
Graham	Brett	Hazlett	Sephton	Pilkington	Lever	Jackson	S Hughes	Nugent	N Hughes	Gaskell				Lupton	Nolan(7)Callaghan(12)Faulkner(11)	30

LIVERPOOL St. HELENS LEAGUE STATISTICS
(COMPILED BY STEPHEN McCORMACK)

Season	Div.	P	W	D	L	F	(Tries	Con	Pen	DG)	A	(Tries	Con	Pen	DG)	Most Points	Most Tries
87-88	2	11	8	1	2	154	(18	8	19	3)	97	(10	6	13	2)	34 - Tosh Askew	3 - Ian Gibbons & John Shinwell
88-89	1	11	1	0	10	116	(9	4	22	2)	254	(37	20	22	0)	55 - Tosh askew	3 - Brendan Hanavan
89-90	2	11	8	2	1	154	(20	7	18	2)	106	(12	5	14	2)	66 - Tosh Askew	6 - Mark Sephton & Peter Buckton
90-91	1	12	0	0	12	88	(9	5	13	1)	349	(57	35	16	1)	31 - Andy Higgin	2 - Mark Sephton & Peter Buckton
91-92	2	12	0	0	12	87	(14	5	7	0)	418	(65	37	27	1)	26 - Paul Ramsden	4 - Mark Elliott
92-93	3	11	5	0	6	203	(22	12	19	4)	130	(13	4	18	1)	98 - Andy Higgin	8 - Mark Sephton
93-94	4	18	11	1	6	396	(44	22	43	1)	275	(25	12	37	5)	140 - Simon Mason	9 - Mark Sephton
94-95	4	18	10	3	5	374	(44	26	30	4)	243	(27	15	26	0)	155 - Andy Higgin	7 - Mark Sephton
95-96	4	18	11	1	6	471	(61	26	34	4)	343	(36	20	35	6)	120 - Mark Wellens	14 - Simon Humphreys
96-97	3	30	8	0	22	665	(90	49	36	3)	827	(99	61	66	4)	210 - Paul Brett	14 - Paul Brett
Totals		152	62	8	82	2508	(331	164	241	24)	3042	(381	215	274	22)		

HOME

BIGGEST WIN (76pts) 89-13 v Clifton 15.2.97
DEFEAT (48pts) 0-48 v Leeds 10.5.97
MOST POINTS SCORED 89-13 v Clifton 15.2.97

AGAINST 6-49 v Morley 14.3.92

MOST CONSECUTIVE VICTORIES - 6

MOST TRIES IN A MATCH
(FOR) 13 v Clifton 15.2.97 (H)
(AGAINST) 13 v Newcastle Gosforth 29.2.92

CONSECUTIVE APPEARANCES
57 Stuart Hughes 27.1.94 - 16.11.96

AWAY

(26pts) 31-5 v Broughton Park 23.10.93
(72pts) 4-76 v Newcastle Gosforth 29.2.92
36-28 v Aspatria 24.2.96
36-41 v Otley 8.2.97
4-76 v Newcastle Gosforth 29.2.92

MOST CONSECUTIVE DEFEATS - 24

MOST APPEARANCES
FORWARD:
BACK:

CONSECUTIVE SCORING MATCHES
Scoring Tries - 3 - Nick Walker, Simon Humphreys,
Mark Sephton & Dave Caskell
Scoring Points - 15 - Paul Brett

MOST	in a SEASON	in a CAREER	in a MATCH
Points	210 Paul Brett 96-97	353 Andy Higgin 90-96	39 Paul Brett v Clifton 15.2.97 (H)
Tries	14 Simon Humphreys 95-96 Paul Brett 96-97	52 Mark Sephton 89-96	4 Mark Sephton v Aspatria 13.3.93 (H) v Clifton 15.2.97 (H) Darren Crompton v Aspatria 13.3.93 (H)
Conversions	40 Paul Brett 96-97	46 Andy Higgin 90-96	12 Paul Brett v Clifton 15.2.97 (H)
Penalties	30 Simon Mason 93-94	70 Andy Higgin 90-96	6 Brian Wellens v Havant 14.10.95 (A)
Drop Goals	4 Andy Higgin 92-93	7 Andy Higgin 90-96	2 Nick Simms v Blackheath 9.1.88 (H) Tosh Askew v Headingley 14.10.89 (H)

LIVERPOOL ST HELENS PLAYING SQUAD

NAME	Ht	Wt	Birthdate	Birthplace	Club	Apps	Pts	T	C	P	DG

BACKS

NAME	Ht	Wt	Birthdate	Birthplace	Club	Apps	Pts	T	C	P	DG
Brian Wellens					Liverpool St Helens	80	230	10	24	35	9
Simon Humphreys					Liverpool St Helens	28+4	184	18	14	21	1
Ian Callaghan					Liverpool St Helens	5+5	10	2	-	-	-
Kevin Davies					Liverpool St Helens	66+2	65	13	-	-	-
Dave Pilkington					Liverpool St Helens	8	13	1	1	2	-
Mark Sephton					Liverpool St Helens	114	244	52	-	-	-
Matt Liddle					Liverpool St Helens	34+3	20	4	-	-	-
Graham Eldoy					Liverpool St Helens	66	95	19	-	-	-
Danny Jones					Liverpool St Helens	7	20	4	-	-	-
Chris Walker					Liverpool St Helens	8+2	10	2	-	-	-
Simon Hazlett					Liverpool St Helens	10+1	5	1	-	-	-
Paul Brett					Liverpool St Helens	30+1	220	16	40	20	-
Phil Graham					Liverpool St Helens	29+2	40	8	-	-	-

FORWARDS

NAME	Ht	Wt	Birthdate	Birthplace	Club	Apps	Pts	T	C	P	DG
Colin King					Liverpool St Helens	73	5	1	-	-	-
John Hitchen					Liverpool St Helens	11+3	5	1	-	-	-
Dave Lever					Liverpool St Helens	2+4	-	-	-	-	-
Mark Nolan					Liverpool St Helens	11+6	-	-	-	-	-
Tommy Jackson					Liverpool St Helens	20+2	20	4	-	-	-
Martin Boyd					Liverpool St Helens	27+2	10	2	-	-	-
Mike Nugent					Liverpool St Helens	49+1	5	1	-	-	-
Stuart Hughes					Liverpool St Helens	78	10	2	-	-	-
Neil Hughes					Liverpool St Helens	17+1	5	1	-	-	-
Dave Lupton					Liverpool St Helens	74	55	11	-	-	-
Dave Gaskell					Liverpool St Helens	53	80	16	-	-	-
James Salisbury					Liverpool St Helens	5+1	5	1	-	-	-
Dave Faulkner					Liverpool St Helens	8+3	15	3	-	-	-
John Crigg					Liverpool St Helens	58+2	20	4	-	-	-

Moss Lane (Off Rainford Rd.) Windle, St. Helens. WA11 7PL.

Tel. Nos. 01744 25708

Capacity: 2300   **Seated:** 300   **Standing:** 2000

Simple Directions:
M6 - Junction 23. A580 towards Liverpool for 5 miles. Then take A570 (Southport) for 100 yards - small lane on left to ground.
Car Parking: 200
Admission: Season tickets £40. Matchdays - adults £3.50 , children/OAPs £1.
Club Shop: Yes.
Clubhouse: with 3 bars & has food available. Functions up to 100 seated can be catered.
Training Nights: Tuesday & Thursday.

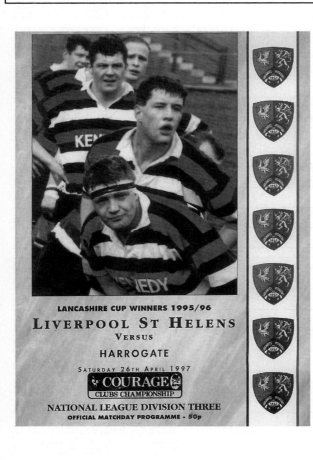

LANCASHIRE CUP WINNERS 1995/96
LIVERPOOL ST HELENS
VERSUS
HARROGATE
SATURDAY 26TH APRIL 1997
COURAGE
CLUBS CHAMPIONSHIP
NATIONAL LEAGUE DIVISION THREE
OFFICIAL MATCHDAY PROGRAMME - 50p

MATCHDAY
PROGRAMME

Size   A5

Number of pages 28 plus cover

Price   £1

Programme Editor
Ian Darlington.
01695 556662 (H)
01744 456387 (B)

Advertising Rates
Full page £300

LONDON WELSH R.F.C.

FOUNDED: 1885

President S J Dawes, c/o London Welsh RFC, Old Deer Park, Kew Road, Richmond, Surrey

Chief Executive Phil Lewis, c/o London Welsh RFC, as above

Club Secretary Tudor Roberts, Archers Hall, Westmill, Buntingford, Herts SG9 9LW.
01763 273827 (B), 01763 273994 (Fax)

Press Officer Allan Price, c/o London Welsh RFC, as above

Rugby Coach Clive Griffiths, c/o London Welsh RFC, as above

London Welsh were seldom seen at their best in 1996/97. Having won promotion in each of the previous two seasons, much was expected from Andy Tucker's squad. But in the end they had to settle for a disappointing eleventh place, which fairly reflected the side's form. Poor ball retention, lack of penetration, a break-up of one of the finest back rows in the division, and internal difficulties contributed to the decline. In fact, the Welsh scored only 69 tries in the league, a surprisingly low total from a club noted for its attacking flair.

Even so the Welsh had their moments against the leading sides. They did gain a double victory against relegated Clifton, but suffered double defeats at the hands of Exeter, Fylde, Leeds and Wharfedale. Against every other side in the division, however, honours were shared. Individually, Craig Raymond broke several club scoring records. His total of 325 points (300 in league games) was the best ever achieved by a London Welshman in a season, as was his haul of 28 points against Clifton, in December. Both Raymond and the club captain Andy Tucker played in all three London Division games against major international touring sides.

But the future for London Welsh seems immeasurably brighter. With the backing of the club's seven British Lions of 1971, a ten man consortium invested half a million pounds in the club to secure its position in the professional era. Their first appointment was the noted coach, Clive Griffiths, the former Llanelli and Wales full back, who also enjoyed a glittering playing and coaching career in rugby league. Under his direction a number of top players are expected to join the Welsh, who are determined to mount a more formidable challenge in 1997-98.

MATCHDAY PROGRAMME

Size	A5
Number of pages	36 + cover
Price	£1
Programme Editor	Paul Beker, c/o London Welsh RFC
Advertising Rates	Full Page £400, Half page £200
	Contact - Club

Colours: Scarlet

Change colours: Green.

LONDON WELSH

No	Ven.	Date	Opponents	Att.	Res.	Score	Scorers
1	(A)	31.08	v London Welsh		W	12- 5	Raymond(2p2dg)
2	(A)	07.09	v Otley		L	12-16	Raymond(4p)
3	(H)	14.09	v Reading		W	21-17	Lewsey(t)Vines(t)Raymond(c2pdg)
4	(A)	21.09	v Rosslyn Park		L	10-27	Raymond(tcp)
5	(H)	28.09	v Wharfdale		L	16-25	R Jones(t)Giraud(t)Raymond(2p)
6	(A)	05.10	v Exeter		L	17-18	Samuel(t)Lewsey(t)Raymond(2cp)
7	(H)	12.10	v Harrogate		W	23-14	Giraud2t)J Lewis(t)Raymond(c2p)
8	(A)	19.10	v Leeds		L	17-22	Shaw(t)S Thomas(t)Raymond(2cp)
9	(A)	26.10	v Walsall		L	20-32	Tucker(t)J Lewis(t)Raymond(2c2p)
10	(H)	09.11	v Lydney		W	37-23	Giraud(2t)Raymond(t2c6p)
11	(A)	16.11	v Redruth		L	23-27	Morgan(t)Tucker(t)Raymond(2c3p)
12	(H)	21.12	v Morley		W	27-22	Lubliner(t)Tucker(t)Raymond(t4p)
13	(H)	28.12	v Clifton		W	28-19	Raymond(tc6pdg)
14	(H)	11.01	v Havant		W	26-22	Lewsey(2t)Raymand(2c4p)
15	(H)	18.01	v Liverpool StH		L	15-17	Lewsey(t)P Harries(t)Raymond(cp)
16	(H)	25.01	v Otley		W	21-19	Lewsey(t)A Lewis(tc3p)
17	(A)	01.02	v Reading		L	17-32	Lewsey(t)Giraud(t)Morris(t)Raymond(c)
18	(H)	18.02	v Rosslyn Park		W	28-25	Lubliner(t)Raymond(c6pdg)
19	(A)	15.02	v Wharfdale		L	12-50	Lewsey(t)Raymond(tc)
20	(H)	22.02	v Exeter		L	15-36	Reynolds(t)Evans(t)Raymond(cp)
21	(A)	01.03	v Harrogate		L	19-52	Reynolds(t)Lewsey(2t)Raymond(2c)
22	(H)	08.03	v Leeds		L	17-28	Lubliner(t)Raymond(t2cp)
23	(H)	15.03	v Walsall		W	33-24	Riondet(t)Vines(t)Phillips(t)Tucker(t)Raymond(2c3p)
24	(A)	22.03	v Lydney		L	17-44	Muckalt(2t)Griffiths(t)Raymond(c)
25	(H)	29.03	v Fylde		L	9-13	Raymond(p2dg)
26	(H)	05.04	v Redruth		W	64-20	P Harries(2t)Riondet(2t)Muckalt(2t)Tucker(t)Samuel(t)Dawes(t)Lewsey(t) Raymond(7c)
27	(A)	12.04	v Morley		L	28-38	Lewsey(2t)Tucker(t)Lubliner(t)A Lewis(c2p)
28	(A)	19.04	v Clifton		W	15-13	Vines(t)Herbert(t)Raymond(cp)
29	(A)	26.04	v Fylde		L	9-39	Raymond(3p)
30	(A)	03.05	v Havant		L	26-38	Morgan(2t)M Lewis(t)Vines(t)Raymond(3c)

1996-97 HIGHLIGHTS

LEAGUE DEBUTS: Paul Morgan, Ian Davies, Goeff Crane, Dave Muckalt, Simon Pardoe, Tom Lewsey, Eldon Moors, Jamie Lewis, Peter Harries, Gareth Morris, Hew Roberts, Miles Hayman, James Reynolds, Peter Norvil, Andy Lewis, Jerome Riondet, Ross Evans, Alfie Harbinson, Matthew Lewis, Andrew Lewis.

TRY ON DEBUT: Tom Lewsey, Andy Lewis & Ross Evans.

PLAYERS USED: 40 plus 3 as replacement.

EVER PRESENT: None - most appearances 27+1
- Craig Raymond

❑ Scrum-half Tom Lewsey in his debut season breaks David Lubliner's record of nine tries in a season. Lewsey takes the record to 13 from 20 games.

❑ Had the joint third worst away record losing 13 of 15.

❑ Utility back five forward Graeme Peacock becomes the first Welsh player to reach 100 league appearances as he extends his club record to 102.

❑ Craig Raymond goes from strength to strength and now holds 12 of the Welsh's 15 scoring records - the only ones he does not hold are the try scoring ones. He set his third consecutive record for points in a season as he pushes the Welsh scoring record past 400, 500 and 600 to end on 613.

	Pts	T	C	P	D	Apps	Ave.
94-95	109	2	15	23	-	6	18.17
95-96	204	5	28	37	4	18	11.33
96-97	300	6	39	57	4	27	11.11
TOTAL	613	13	82	117	8	51	12.01

❑ Raymond set a new record by scoring in 20 consecutive matches.

LONDON WELSH'S COURAGE LEAGUE MATCH DETAILS 1996-97

#	15	14	13	12	11	10	1	2	3	4	5	6	7	8	Replacements
1	Shaw	Giraud	Morgan	Cedarwell	Vines	Raymond	GPhillips	Herbert	Tucker	Davies	Crane	DHarries	Muckalt	Peacock	Samuel(8)
2	Shaw	Giraud	Morgan	Cedarwell	AJones	Raymond	GPhillips	Herbert	Tucker	Davies	Crane	DHarries	Muckalt	Peacock	Samuel(7)RPhillips(11)
3	Vines	Giraud	Morgan	Pardoe	AJones	Raymond	GPhillips	Herbert	Tucker	Davies	Crane	DHarries	Peacock	Samuel	
4	Vines	A.Jones	Morgan	Pardoe	Giraud	Raymond	Lewsey	Herbert	Tucker	Crane	Moors	Muckalt	Peacock	Samuel	
5	Vines	Morgan	S Thomas	Cedarwell	Giraud	Raymond	GPhillips	Herbert	Davies	Crane	Moors	DHarries	Russell	Peacock	
6	Shaw	Morgan	S Thomas	Cedarwell	Giraud	Raymond	GPhillips	Herbert	RJones	Moors	Peacock	Muckalt	JLewis	Samuel	Morgan(12)Samuel(7)
7	Shaw	Morgan	S Thomas	Cedarwell	Giraud	Raymond	Lewsey	Herbert	RThomas	Moors	NThomas	DHarries	JLewis	Peacock	Morgan(12)
8	Shaw	Lubliner	S Thomas	Griffiths	Giraud	Raymond	Lewsey	Herbert	RThomas	Moors	NThomas	DHarries	Westlake	Peacock	Morgan(12)
9	Shaw	Lubliner	S Thomas	Griffiths	Giraud	Raymond	Lewsey	Tucker	RThomas	Moors	NThomas	DHarries	Westlake	Muckalt	Morgan(12)
10	Shaw	Morgan	S Thomas	Griffiths	Giraud	Raymond	Lewsey	Herbert	RThomas	Moors	Peacock	DHarries	Peacock	Peacock	Muckatt(6)
11	Shaw	Griffiths	S Thomas	Griffiths	Giraud	Raymond	GPhillips	Herbert	RThomas	Crane	NThomas	Moors	Peacock	Peacock	JLewis(4)SThomas(13)
12	PHarries	Lubliner	S Thomas	Griffiths	Giraud	Raymond	GPhillips	Herbert	Tucker	Crane	Peacock	Moors	Samuel	Crane	Morgan(13)Lewsey(9)DHarries(4)
13	PHarries	Lubliner	S Thomas	Riondet	Giraud	Raymond	Roberts	Davies	Tucker	Peacock	Peacock	DHarries	Westlake	Samuel	Crane(6)
14	PHarries	Lubliner	S Thomas	Riondet	Giraud	Raymond	Lewsey	Herbert	Davies	Moors	Hayman	Peacock	Westlake	Samuel	Crane()
15	PHarries	Lubliner	S Thomas	Riondet	Giraud	Raymond	Lewsey	Norvill	RThomas	Moors	Hayman	Peacock	Westlake	Peacock	Lubliner(13)Herbert(1)Crane(4)
16	PHarries	Reynolds	S Thomas	Riondet	Morris	Raymond	Lewsey	Davies	RThomas	NThomas	Hayman	Peacock	Westlake	Peacock	Morgan(14)
17	PHarries	Reynolds	S Thomas	Riondet	Morris	Raymond	Lewsey	Tucker	RThomas	NThomas	NThomas	Peacock	Westlake	Peacock	Raymond(10)Westlake(7)
18	PHarries	Lubliner	S Thomas	Riondet	Morris	Raymond	Lewsey	Tucker	RThomas	Moors	NThomas	Westlake	Muckalt	Peacock	Samuel(5)Herbert(3)
19	PHarries	Lubliner	Morris	S Thomas	Giraud	Raymond	Lewsey	Tucker	RThomas	Moors	Hayman	Westlake	Peacock	Peacock	ALewis(11)Pritchard(2)Samuel(6)
20	PHarries	Cedarwell	S Thomas	Riondet	Morris	Raymond	Lewsey	Harbison	RThomas	Moors	Hayman	Evans	Samuel	Crane	Crane()
21	PHarries	Cedarwell	Cedarwell	Riondet	Raymond	Reynolds	Lewsey	Davies	RThomas	Moors	Hayman	JLewis	Crane	Samuel	Griffiths(13)Muckalt(6)Herbert(8)
22	Vines	Griffiths	Griffiths	Riondet	Lubliner	Raymond	Lubliner	Davies	RJones	Moors	Hayman	JLewis	Samuel	JLewis	Phillips(9)Norvill(3)Cedarwell()
23	Vines	Griffiths	Griffiths	Riondet	PHarries	Raymond	Lubliner	Tucker	RThomas	Moors	Hayman	Peacock	Samuel	JLewis	Crane(8)SThomas(12)RThomas(3)
24	Vines	Lubliner	Griffiths	Riondet	GPhillips	Raymond	GPhillips	Tucker	Tucker	Moors	Hayman	JLewis	Samuel	JLewis	Lewsey(9)SThomas(13)Hayman(4)Agyemang(3)
25	Vines	Lubliner	Griffiths	Riondet	GPhillips	Raymond	Phillips	Tucker	Herbert	Moors	Harries	JLewis	Samuel	Peacock	Agyemang(5)
26	Vines	Lubliner	Griffiths	Riondet	PHarries	Raymond	Lewsey	Herbert	RThomas	Moors	Peacock	Muckatt	Samuel	Muckatt	Griffiths(13)JLewis(8)Herbert(3)
27	Vines	Lubliner	Griffiths	Riondet	PHarries	Raymond	ALewis	Tucker	RThomas	Moors	Peacock	Muckatt	Muckalt	Muckatt	Morgan(13)JLewis(7)
28	Vines	Dawes	Griffiths	Riondet	PHarries	Raymond	Lewsey	Herbert	RThomas	Moors	Peacock	DHarries	JLewis	Muckalt	Herbert(3)Samuel(7)SThomas(11)
29	Vines	Lubliner	Morgan	Riondet	PHarries	Raymond	Herbert	Tucker	Davies	Moors	Peacock	DHarries	Westlake	Peacock	Phillips(9)R.Jones(2)Muckatt(7)
30	Vines	Morgan	S Thomas	Riondet	PHarries	MLewis	Davies	R.Jones	RThomas	Moors	Hayman	Evans	Muckalt	Peacock	Reynolds(11)DHarries()

LONDON WELSH LEAGUE STATISTICS
(COMPILED BY STEPHEN McCORMACK)

Season	Div.	P	W	D	L	F	(Tries	Con	Pen	DG)	A	(Tries	Con	Pen	DG)	Most Points	Most Tries
87-88	2	11	3	2	6	153	(24	6	14	1)	185	(23	6	25	2)	25 - Nathan Humphreys	5 - Richard Wintle
88-89	2	11	1	1	8	125	(18	7	13	0)	235	(32	16	23	2)	23 - Nathan Humphreys	4 - Guy Leleu
89-90	3	11	3	0	8	141	(19	7	15	2)	179	(20	12	21	4)	25 - Lee Evans	3 - by 3 players - Gareth Hughes, Mark Thomas & Jim Williams.
90-91	D4S	12	7	0	5	235	(34	15	22	1)	165	(16	10	26	1)	30 - Gareth Hughes	6 - Mickey Bell
91-92	D4S	12	9	0	3	292	(49	21	16	2)	160	(15	8	25	3)	43 - Graeme Peacock	7 - Mark Douglas & Steve Thomas.
92-93	D4S	12	10	0	2	353	(50	29	15	0)	170	(19	9	18	1)	111 - Mike Hamlin	6 - Andy Tucker & Mickey Bell.
93-94	D4S	12	5	3	4	216	(25	11	22	1)	140	(9	4	28	1)	41 - David Shufflebotham	6 - Peter Walters
94-95	D4S	12	10	2	0	409	(52	28	31	0)	126	(8	4	25	1)	109 - Craig Raymond	7 - Colin Charvis & David Lubliner.
95-96	4	18	12	0	6	424	(49	28	37	4)	269	(28	15	31	2)	204 - Craig Raymond	9 - David Lubliner
96-97	3	30	12	0	18	634	(69	41	61	8)	777	(100	56	51	4)	300 - Craig Raymond	13 - Tom Lewsey
Totals		141	72	8	61	3002	(389	193	246	19)	2346	(220	140	273	21)		

	HOME	AWAY
BIGGEST WIN	(81pts) 88-7 v Sudbury 25.3.95	(43pts) 49-6 v Sidcup 16.11.91
DEFEAT	(25pts) 3-28 v Lydney 18.11.90	(38pts) 12-50 v Wharfedale 15.2.97
MOST POINTS SCORED	88-7 v Sudbury 25.3.95	49-6 v Sidcup 16.11.91
AGAINST	15-36 v Exeter 22.2.97	19-52 v Harrogate 1.3.97

MOST CONSECUTIVE VICTORIES - 10

MOST CONSECUTIVE DEFEATS - 6

MOST TRIES IN A MATCH
(FOR) 12 v Sudbury 25.3.95 (H)
(AGAINST) 8 v Wharfdale 15.2.97 (A)
v Harrogate 1.3.97 (A)

MOST APPEARANCES
FORWARD: 102 Graeme Peacock
BACK: 53 Tim Pike

CONSECUTIVE APPEARANCES
33 Graeme Peacock

CONSECUTIVE SCORING MATCHES
Scoring Tries - 5 - Mickey Bell (twice)
Scoring Points - 20 - Craig Raymond

MOST	in a SEASON	in a CAREER	in a MATCH
Points	300 Craig Raymond 96-97	613 Craig Raymond 94-97	28 Craig Raymond v Clifton 28.12.96 (H)
Tries	13 Tom Lewsey 96-97	21 Mark Douglas 87-96	4 Mickey Bell v N. Walsham 13.10.90 (H) David Lubliner v Sudbury 25.3.95 (H)
Conversions	39 Craig Raymond 96-97	82 Craig Raymond 94-97	7 Craig Raymond v Sudbury 25.3.95 (H) v Plymouth 30.9.95 (H) v Redruth 5.4.97 (H)
Penalties	57 Craig Raymond 96-97	117 Craig Raymond 94-97	6 Craig Raymond v Lydney 9.11.96 (H) v Clifton 28.12.96 (H) v Rosslyn Park 18.2.97 (H)
Drop Goals	7 Craig Raymond 96-97	11 Craig Raymond 94-97	2 Craig Raymond v Exeter 27.4.96 (A) v Liverpool St. H. 31.8.96 (A) v Fylde 29.3.97 (H)

LONDON WELSH PLAYING SQUAD

NAME	Ht	Wt	Birthdate	Birthplace	Club	Apps	Pts	T	C	P	DG
BACKS											
Jerone Riondet	5.11	14.4	19.04.71	Grenoble (Fra)	Prev. clubs: Racing Club de France, Harlequins.						
France: A, u21.					London Welsh	11	15	3	-	-	-
Matt Vines	6.0	13.8	11.05.76	S. Glamorgan	Prev. clubs: Llantiwt Major						
Welsh Exiles					London Welsh	16	20	4	-	-	-
Peter Harries	6.2	13.10	10.09.70	Romford	Prev. clubs: Pontypridd, Saracens.						
Wales: u21.					London Welsh	18	15	3	-	-	-
Tom Lewsey	5.11	13.9	03.05.75	Bromley	Prev. club: Bristol University						
English Universities					London Welsh	20+2	65	13	-	-	-
Craig Raymond	5.11	13.0	30.01.69	Llanlelli	Bath						
London Division					London Welsh	51+1	613	13	82	116	12
Steve Thomas	5.11	13.2	12.08.67	Singapore	Prev. club: Tenbury Wells						
E. Counties					London Welsh	43+5	58	13	-	-	-
David Lubliner	6.1	13.0	05.02.71	Roehampton	Prev. club: Mayfield (NZ)						
Mid Canterbury (NZ)					London Welsh	48+1	100	20	-	-	-
Martin Giraud	5.11	12.11	16.11.77	Essex							
Wales: u19.					London Welsh	21+1	40	8	-	-	-
Gerallt Phillips	5.9	12.8	04.08.69	Maesteg	Maesteg						
Welsh Exiles					London Welsh	43+7	24	5	-	-	-
Andy Lewis	5.9	11.7	30.06.74	Swansea	Prev. clubs: Dunvant, Exeter.						
Wales: Youth					London Welsh	3+1	24	1	2	4	1
David Griffiths	5.10	13.7	28.08.77	Aylesbury							
Welsh Exiles					London Welsh	14+2	5	1	-	-	-
Paul Morgan	5.9	12.2	03.10.74	Bridgend	Coventry						
Wales: u21.					London Welsh	9+5	15	3	-	-	-
Gareth Morris	6.3	11.7	23.03.76	Rhondda	Tylorstown						
Welsh Exiles					London Welsh	8	5	1	-	-	-
Nick Cederwell	5.11	13.4	26.10.67	London	Salisbury						
British Forces (Ger).					London Welsh	22+1	15	3	-	-	-
James Reynolds	5.8	11.7	06.12.72	Neath	Prev. clubs: Neath, Bridgend, Cambridge Univ.						
Wales: u21.					London Welsh	4+1	10	2	-	-	-
Peter Shaw	5.11	13.0	09.11.73	Hammersmith	Exeter University						
English Colleges					London Welsh	19	5	1	-	-	-
FORWARDS											
Mark Herbert	6.2	18.0	27.06.68	London	Saracens						
Essex					London Welsh	53+6	27	6	-	-	-
Andy Tucker	5.11	15.9	06.12.68	Pembroke	Prev. clubs: Whitland, Manly (Aus).						
London Division					London Welsh	82+1	116	24	-	-	-
Ian Davies	5.10	17.0	13.06.75	Abergavenny	Moseley						
North Midlands					London Welsh	23	-	-	-	-	-
Robbie Jones	5.8	13.3	12.05.66	Oxfordshire	Chinnor						
					London Welsh	12+4	5	1	-	-	-
Richard Thomas	5.11	15.6	23.11.67	Camberwell	London Welsh	76+1	9	2	-	-	-
Geoff Crane	6.5	18.0		Bristol	Prev. clubs: Bristol, Clifton.						
					London Welsh	18+6	-	-	-	-	-
Dai Harries	6.4	15.10	17.06.66	Dagenham	Cardiff						
Eastern Counties					London Welsh	63+6	27	6	-	-	-
Eldon Moors	6.5	17.4	26.12.71	Auckland(NZ)	Ebbw Vale						
North Harbour (NZ)					London Welsh	27	-	-	-	-	-
Miles Hayman	6.5	16.7	18.05.71	Hertfordshire	Lymm						
Army					London Welsh	11+1	-	-	-	-	-
Dave Muckalt	6.4	15.10	17.02.75	Lancaster	Saracens, Vale of Lune						
Middlesex					London Welsh	17+3	20	4	-	-	-
Alan Samuel	6.2	16.8	22.06.66	Surrey	London Welsh	11+7	10	2	-	-	-
Jamie Lewis	6.2	14.8	09.12.72	Cardiff	Swansea						
Wales: u19.					London Welsh	13+3	10	2	-	-	-
Graeme Peacock	6.5	15.7	15.04.66	Auckland (NZ)	Western Utd (N Harbour)						
North Harbour (NZ)					London Welsh	102+1	86	10	10	6	-
Ross Evans					London Welsh	2	5	1	-	-	-
Rowan Westlake	6.1	15.06	20.03.72	Isleworth	Rosslyn Park						
Surrey					London Welsh	29+2	5	1	-	-	-
Neil Thomas	6.6	17.5	07.11.62	Cardigan	Prev. clubs: Blackheath, Oxford Univ.						
Kent					London Welsh	36	-	-	-	-	-

Old Deer Park, Kew Road, Richmond, Surrey TW9 2AZ

Tel: 0181 940 1604   **Fax:** 0181 940 2368

Capacity: 7,200   **Seated:** 1.200   **Standing:** 6,000
Simple Directions: Half mile north of Richmond BR station, adjacent to south side of Kew Gardens
Nearest Railway Station: Richmond (BR & Underground)
Car Parking: 200
Admission: Season Adults £96, Juniors £16 existing members; Adults £120, Juniors £20 new members, Stand Supplement £3. Matchday £8-£10 includes programme (Non members). Stand Supplement £5. OAPs half price.
Club Shop: Yes, Manager TBA
Clubhouse: Three Bars, Food available
Training Nights: Tuesdays & Thursdays

Lydney's captain Nick Nelmes gets his man

Lydney going forward

LYDNEY R.F.C.

NICKNAME: Severnsiders   **FOUNDED:** 1887

President T C Bailey, Montrose, Highfield, Lydney, Gloucester
01594 842287 (H), 01594 842287 (B)

Chairman Dr. P Catlin, Gwynne Cottage, Saunders Green, Whitecroft, Lydney, Gloucester GL15 4PN.
01594 562404 (H)

Secretary A J Jones, 5 Kimberley Close, Lydney, Glos. GL15 5AE
01594 842709 (H), 01594 841470 (B), 01594 844604 (Fax)

Treasurer R A Jones, The Cottage, Staghill, Yorkley, Lydney, Gloucester, GL15 4TD
01594 563148 (H), 01594 845617 (B)

Fixtures Secretary R Powell, 'Skaint Mesto', Park Hill, Whitecroft, Lydney, Glos. GL15 4PL.
01594 562820 (H)

Referees J Powell, 01594 843180 (H): **Team Manager** G Sargent, 01594 562822 (H)

Lydney achieved their objective last season by retaining their place in National League Three and the club approaches next season with the same objective in mind.

Hooker Nick Nelmes will again captain the side and he will have the majority of last season's squad to support him.

Team manager Gordon Sargent has recruited a number of new players in order to add depth to his squad. He will be helped by a very successful 2nd XV who won the Forest of Dean Combination Cup and the 2nd XV South West Merit Table.

Last season's coaches Andy Wyman, John Saville and Paul Howell will be joined by Monmouth schoolmaster Peter Marriott who played for Bath.

Lydney have ambitious plans to develop their ground, the first stage of which will be to replace the grandstand at the river side of the ground.

The constitution has been changed and the club will now be run by a management committee to whom a number of sub committees will be responsible. An administrative officer has been appointed to deal with the club's finances and sponsorship.

Lydney is proud of its status in rugby bearing in mind the total population is less than ten thousand and it is also proud to be one of the best supported sides in the league. There is an air of optimism amongst players and the committee as the new season approaches with a mid table league position the target.

Lydney going forward

Colours: Black and white hoops.   **Change colours:** Red.

LYDNEY

No	Ven.	Date	Opponents	Att.	Res.	Score	Scorers
1	(H)	31.08	v Havant		W	28-15	Edwards(2t)Jewitt(t)Bendall(t)Mills(c2p)
2	(A)	07.09	v Liverpool StH		W	27-25	Nelmes(t)Stubbs(t)Knox(t)Morris(3c2p)
3	(H)	14.09	v Otley		W	34-22	Knox(t)Morris(c9p)
4	(A)	21.09	v Reading		L	11-25	Morris(t2p)
5	(H)	28.09	v Rosslyn Park		W	34-13	Stubbs(2t)Knox(t)R Williams(t)Edwards(t)Morris(3cp)
6	(A)	05.10	v Wharfdale		W	25-24	Stubbs(t)Nelmes(t)Knox(t)Morris(2c2p)
7	(H)	12.10	v Exeter		L	12-24	Nelmes(t)Morris(tc)
8	(A)	19.10	v Harrogate		L	30-43	Stubbs(t)Mills(t)Knox(t)Wakeham(t)Morris(2c2p)
9	(H)	26.10	v Leeds		W	31-22	Stubbs(2t)Davis(t)Morris(2c4p)
10	(A)	09.11	v London Welsh		L	23-37	Nelmes(t)Stubbs(t)Pentry(t)Morris(c2p)
11	(A)	16.11	v Walsall		L	15-20	Morris(5p)
12	(H)	21.12	v Redruth		W	35- 7	Saville(2t)Jewitt(t)Kilby(t)PenTry(t)Morris(2c2p)
13	(A)	11.01	v Fylde		L	16-24	Rees(t)Morris(c3p)
14	(A)	18.01	v Havant		W	25-10	Dunlop(t)Davis(t)Knox(t)Morris(2c2p)
15	(H)	25.01	v Liverpool StH		W	23-19	Dunlop(t)Morris(6p)
16	(A)	01.02	v Otley		L	17-27	Kilby(t)Morris(4p)
17	(H)	08.02	v Reading		L	18-25	Saville(t)Price(t)Morris(c2p)
18	(A)	15.02	v Rosslyn Park		L	3-22	Saville(p)
19	(H)	22.02	v Wharfdale		L	15-24	Nelmes(t)Meek(t)Imm(t)
20	(A)	01.03	v Exeter		L	9-60	Mills(3p)
21	(H)	08.03	v Harrogate		L	18-38	Morris(6p)
22	(A)	15.03	v Leeds		L	0-74	
23	(H)	22.03	v London Welsh		W	44-17	Hill(3t)G Williams(t)Knox(t)Price(t)PenTry(t)Morris(3cp)
24	(H)	29.03	v Clifton		W	56-13	Meek(2t)Saville(t)Davis(t)Price(t)Nelmes(t)G Williams(t)Wakeham(t)Morris(5c2p)
25	(H)	04.05	v Walsall		W	21-17	Hill(t)Morris(tc3p)
26	(A)	12.04	v Redruth		L	15-16	Wakeham(t)Davis(t)Morris(cp)
27	(H)	19.04	v Morley		L	15-25	Morris(5p)
28	(A)	26.04	v Clifton		W	49-25	Bendall(t)Hill(t)Jewitt(t)Meek(t)Wakeham(t)Davis(t)Knox(t)Johnson(t3cp)
29	(H)	03.05	v Fylde		L	6-20	Johnson(2p)
30	(A)	10.05	v Morley		L	13-33	G Williams(t)Bartlett(t)Johnson(p)

1996-97 HIGHLIGHTS

LEAGUE DEBUTS: Jimmy Roberts, Chris Dunlop, Phillip Imm, Leon Meek, Carl Watkins, Julian Hill, Mark Johnson, Andy Wintle, Paul Williams.

TRY ON DEBUT: Chris Dunlop, Phillip Imm & Leon Meek

PLAYERS USED: 35 plus 2 as replacement.

EVER PRESENT: Nick Nelmes

❑ Lost seven consecutive matches to equal their worst ever run.

❑ Nick Nelmes becomes the first player to reach 100 league appearances as he pushes his club record out to 116.

❑ Robert Mills becomes the first Back to reach 100 league appearances.

❑ Mike Stubbs and Adrian Knox set a new record of eight tries in a season. The previous record of seven was set by Stubbs himself in 94-95. This is the fourth time Stubbs has topped the try scoring list which is also a record.

❑ Paul Morris set new records for points, conversions and penalties in a season. His 275 points beat Richard Mill's record of 107 from last season. He also beat Mill's record of 19 conversions with 31. The penalty record of 25 was held by Andy Halford from 92-93 - Morris set a new mark of 66. He also set a new National League record of nine penalties in a match - also a club record, and by adding a conversion to the nine penalties, he set a new Division Three record of 29 points in a match - again a new club record.

LYDNEY'S COURAGE LEAGUE MATCH DETAILS 1996-97

	15	14	13	12	11	10	9	1	2	3	4	5	6	7	8	Replacements
1	Bendall	Stubbs	Chant	Jewitt	Edwards	Mills	J Davis	Nichols	Nelmes	G Williams	R Williams	Kilby	Knox	Wakeham	K Davis	Wakeham(-)
2	Bendall	Stubbs	Chant	Jewitt	Edwards	Morris	Powell	Nichols	Nelmes	G Williams	R Williams	Kilby	Knox	Wakeham	K Davis	
3	Bendall	Stubbs	Chant	Jewitt	Edwards	Morris	J Davis	Nichols	Nelmes	G Williams	R Williams	Kilby	Knox	Wakeham	K Davis	
4	Bendall	Stubbs	Chant	Jewitt	Edwards	Morris	J Davis	Nichols	Nelmes	G Williams	R Williams	Kilby	Knox	Wakeham	K Davis	
5	Morris	Stubbs	Chant	Jewitt	Edwards	Mills	J Davis	Nichols	Nelmes	G Williams	R Williams	Rees	Knox	Wakeham	K Davis	Wakeham(-)
6	Morris	Stubbs	Chant	Jewitt	Edwards	Mills	J Davis	Nichols	Nelmes	G Williams	R Williams	Kilby	Knox	Rees	K Davis	Roberts(-)
7	Morris	Stubbs	Chant	Jewitt	Edwards	Mills	J Davis	Nichols	Nelmes	G Williams	R Williams	Kilby	Knox	Wakeham	Rees	
8	Morris	Stubbs	Chant	Jewitt	Edwards	Mills	Davis	Smith	Nelmes	G Williams	R Williams	Kilby	Knox	Wakeham	Rees	Bendall(10)
9	Morris	Stubbs	Chant	Jewitt	Edwards	Mills	Davis	Smith	Nelmes	G Williams	R Williams	Kilby	Knox	Wakeham	Davis	
10	Morris	Stubbs	Chant	Jewitt	Saville	Mills	Davis	Smith	Nelmes	G Williams	R Williams	Kilby	Knox	Wakeham	Davis	
11	Morris	Stubbs	Chant	Jewitt	Edwards	Mills	Davis	Smith	Nelmes	G Williams	R Williams	Kilby	Knox	Wakeham	Davis	
12	Morris	Stubbs	Chant	Jewitt	Edwards	Mills	Davis	Smith	Nelmes	Bartlett	R Williams	Kilby	Knox	Wakeham	Davis	
13	Morris	Stubbs	James	Jewitt	Edwards	Mills	Davis	Price	Smith	Bartlett	R Williams	Kilby	Knox	Wakeham	Davis	Bendall(10)
14	Morris	Dunlop	Chant	Jewitt	Saville	Mills	Davis	Price	Nelmes	Bartlett	R Williams	Kilby	Knox	Wakeham	Davis	
15	Morris	Dunlop	Chant	Jewitt	Saville	Mills	Davis	Price	Nelmes	Bartlett	R Williams	Kilby	Knox	Wakeham	Davis	
16	Morris	Stubbs	Chant	Muyambizi	Saville	Mills	Davis	Price	Nelmes	Bartlett	R Williams	Kilby	Knox	Wakeham	Davis	
17	Morris	Stubbs	Chant	Muyambizi	Saville	Mills	Davis	Price	Nelmes	Bartlett	R Williams	Kilby	Knox	Wakeham	Kilby	Smith(-)
18	Saville	Stubbs	Chant	Muyambizi	Bendall	Mills	Davis	Price	Nelmes	Bartlett	R Williams	Roberts	Knox	Wakeham	Kilby	
19	Saville	Stubbs	Chant	Jewitt	Bendall	Mills	Davis	Price	Nelmes	G Williams	Hale	Kilby	Wakeham	Knox	Rees	Imm(8),R Williams(6),Meek(11)
20	Saville	Meek	Muyambizi	James	Saint	Mills	Edwards	Imm	Nelmes	G Williams	Hale	Roberts	Price	Knox	Rees	
21	Saville	Stubbs	Mills	James	Hill	Morris	Edwards	Price	Nelmes	G Williams	Hale	Roberts	Price	Knox	Rees	Lewis(5).
22	Chant	Johnson	Mills	Meek	Saville	Mills	Davis	Price	Nelmes	P Williams	Hale	Roberts	Rees	Knox	Kilby	
23	Mills	Saville	James	Meek	Hill	Mills	Davis	Price	Nelmes	G Williams	Hale	Roberts	Rees	Knox	Kilby	R Williams(-); J K Davis(-)
24	Mills	Saville	James	Meek	Hill	Morris	Davis	Price	Nelmes	G Williams	Hale	Roberts	Rees	Wakeham	Kilby	Jewitt(-); J K Davis(-)
25	Mills	Saville	Meek	Meek	Hill	Morris	Davis	Price	Nelmes	G Williams	Hale	Roberts	Rees	Wakeham	Kilby	Jewitt( )
26	Mills	Saville	James	Meek	Edwards	Morris	Davis	Price	Nelmes	G Williams	Roberts	Rees	Wakeham	Knox	Kilby	
27	Mills	Saville	James	Meek	Morris	Morris	Davis	Price	Nelmes	Hale	R Williams	Knox	Wakeham	Davis	Davis	R Williams(-); James(-)
28	Bendall	Hill	Meek	Meek	Wakeham	Johnson	Davis	Price	Nelmes	G Williams	Hale	Rees	Wakeham	Knox	Kilby	Bartlett(-); James(-)
29	Bendall	Saville	Meek	Jewitt	Wakeham	Johnson	Davis	Price	Nelmes	G Williams	R Williams	Hale	Rees	Knox	Kilby	Roberts(6)
30	Bendall	Wintle	Meek	Jewitt	Dunlop	Johnson	Davis	Price	Nelmes	G Williams	R Williams	Roberts	Watkins	Wakeham	Kilby	Beddis( )

LYDNEY LEAGUE STATISTICS

(COMPILED BY STEPHEN McCORMACK)

Season	Div.	P	W	D	L	F	(Tries	Con	Pen	DG)	A	(Tries	Con	Pen	DG)	Most Points	Most Tries
87-88	AL5	10	7	0	3	173	(25	11	16	1)	99	(			)	63 - Gerry Price	5 - David Ellis
88-89	AL5	10	8	1	1	240	(39	21	11	3)	98	(			)	65 - Gerry Price	6 - Mike Howells
89-90	3	11	3	0	8	153	(15	6	20	7)	166	(			)	79 - Mark Smith	3 - Simon Morris & Adrian Knox.
90-91	3	12	4	1	7	125	(12	7	21	0)	188	(			)	58 - Paul Morris	5 - Mike Stubbs
91-92	3	12	2	0	10	91	(12	5	11	0)	261	(			)	15 - Andy Berry	3 - Mark Fennell
92-93	D4S	12	8	0	4	187	(17	11	25	0)	170	(			)	102 - Andy Halford	6 - John Edwards
93-94	D5S	12	7	2	3	181	(16	7	27	2)	111	(			)	54 - Andy Halford	5 - Mike Stubbs & John Edwards.
94-95	D5S	12	10	1	1	263	(30	16	30	1)	131	(			)	70 - Andy Halford	7 - Mike Stubbs
95-96	D5S	12	11	1	0	320	(42	19	24	0)	132	(			)	107 - Robert Mills	6 - Nick Nelmes & Julian Davis
96-97	D3	30	13	0	17	668	(74	35	76	0)	766	(97	58	53	2)	275 Paul Morris	8 - Mike Stubbs Adrian Knox
Totals		133	73	6	54	2401	(208	103	185	13)	2022	(			)		

	HOME	AWAY
BIGGEST WIN	(47pts) 47-0 v Sidcup 8.4.89	(38Pts) 41-3 v High Wycombe 16.9.95
BIGGEST DEFEAT	(20pts) 18-38 v Harrogate 8.3.97	(74Pts) 0-74 v Leeds 15.3.97
MOST POINTS SCORED	56-13 v Clifton 29.3.97	41-3 v High Wycombe 16.9.95
AGAINST	18-38 v Harrogate 8.3.97	0-74 v Leeds 15.3.97

MOST CONSECUTIVE VICTORIES - 9
MOST CONSECUTIVE DEFEATS - 7 (twice)

MOST TRIES IN A MATCH
(FOR) 8 v Sidcup 8.4.89 (H)
v Clifton 29.3.97 (H)
(AGAINST) 11 v Leeds 15.3.97 (A)

MOST APPEARANCES
FORWARD: 116 Nick Nelmes
BACK: 109 Robert Mills

CONSECUTIVE APPEARANCES
53 Nick Nelmes 1989-94

CONSECUTIVE SCORING MATCHES
Scoring Tries - 5 - Mike Stubbs
Scoring Points - 16 - Paul Morris

MOST	in a SEASON	in a CAREER	in a MATCH
Points	275 Paul Morris 96-97	364 Paul Morris 88-97	29 Paul Morris v Otley (H) 14.9.96
Tries	8 Mike Stubbs 96-97 Adrian Knox 96-97	30 Mike Stubbs 90-97	4 David Ellis v Cheltenham (H) 31.10.87
Conversions	31 Paul Morris 96-97	41 Paul Morris 88-97	5 Gerry Price v Sidcup 8.4.89 (H) Paul Morris v Clifton 29.3.97 (H)
Penalties	66 Paul Morris 96-97	89 Paul Morris 88-97	9 Paul Morris v Otley 14.9.96 (H)
Drop Goals	6 Mark Smith 89-90	6 Mark Smith 88-90 Gerry Price 87-95	2 Mark Smith v Exeter 11.11.89 (H)

LYDNEY PLAYING SQUAD

NAME	Ht	Wt	Birthdate	Birthplace	Club	Apps	Pts	T	C	P	DG
BACKS											
Danny Bendall	5.11	11.12	23.04.75	Gloucester							
					Lydney	11+1	15	3	-	-	-
Mike Stubbs	5.11	14.2	29.08.64	Ireland	Gloucester						
Gloucestershire					Lydney	63	143	30	-	-	-
Stuart Chant	6.0	14.0	11.05.71	Gloucester	Prev. Clubs: Matson, Longlevens.						
					Lydney	40	15	3	-	-	-
Andy Jewitt	5.10	13.0	30.07.68	Wales	Prev. Clubs: Ebbw Vale, Newport.						
Gloucestershire					Lydney	32+2	20	4	-	-	-
Johnny Edwards	5.11	13.2			Lydney		-	-	-	-	-
Robert Mills	5.8	10.7	10.09.68	Gloucester							
Gloucestershire					Lydney	109	251	5	30	54	2
Paul Morris	5.11	12.0	08.04.71	Gloucester	Gloucester						
					Lydney	36	364	3	41	89	-
Mark Johnson	5.11	12.4	18.12.76	Gloucester							
					Lydney	3	23	1	3	4	-
Julian Hill	6.1	13.9	28.04.78	Gloucester							
					Lydney	5	25	5	-	-	-
Jason Meek	5.8	13.0	07.02.73	Gloucester	Drybrook						
					Lydney	10+1	20	4	-	-	-
Phillip Imm	6.2	17.7	15.03.63	Lydney	Bream						
					Lydney	1+1	5	1	-	-	-
Julian Davies	5.8	12.7	01.10.68	Gloucester	Prev. Clubs: Bristol, Gloucester						
S. Western Counties. Gloucestershire.					Bristol	27+1	40	10	-	-	-
					Lydney	58	80	16	-	-	-
Chad Mutyambizi	6.0	13.3	17.01.71	Zimbabwe							
					Lydney	7	-	-	-	-	-
Chris Dunlop	5.8	11.2	03.08.77	Birmingham							
					Lydney	3	10	2	-	-	-
Richard Saville	5.9	11.1	19.07.74	Gloucester							
					Lydney	22	33	6	-	1	-
Ashley James	5.10	13.0	25.05.68	Gloucester							
					Lydney	71+2	20	4	-	-	-
FORWARDS											
Nick Nelmes	5.11	14.12	11.09.66	Lydney							
Gloucestershire					Lydney	116	89	18	-	-	-
Nick Bartlett	6.0	17.0	10.04.69	Gloucester							
Royal Navy					Lydney	33+3	15	3	-	-	-
Paul Price	5.10	15.2	12.05.74	Gloucester	Prev. Clubs: Lydney, Gloucester.						
					Lydney	26	15	3	-	-	-
Richard Smith	5.10	15.8	21.08.62	Gloucester	Newent						
					Lydney	19	-	-	-	-	-
Gareth Williams	5.11	16.10	12.02.66	Gloucester	Gordon League						
Gloucestershire					Lydney	75	20	4	-	-	-
Robin Williams	6.4	17.3	19.08.63	Cinderford	Cinderford						
Gloucestershire					Lydney	80+4	38	8	-	-	-
Steve Hale	6.3	16.0	04.10.69	Gloucester							
					Lydney	64	-	-	-	-	-
Jimmy Roberts	6.3	16.6	24.08.77	Gloucester							
					Lydney	12+2	-	-	-	-	-
Adrian Knox	5.10	14.0	08.10.66	Lydney	Gloucester						
S. Western Counties. Gloucestershire.					Lydney	94	124	27	-	-	-
Noel Kilby	6.4	15.0	19.01.74	Gloucester							
					Lydney	31	15	3	-	-	-
Simon Wakenham	6.2	13.2	20.09.68	Bristol							
					Lydney	76	57	12	-	-	-
Rob Rees	6.4	15.2	01.08.72	Gloucester							
Gloucestershire					Lydney	60	15	3	-	-	-
Keith Davis	6.4	14.4	06.07.62	Lydney							
Gloucestershire					Lydney	60+2	14	3	-	-	-
Carl Watkins	6.0	14.10	25.05.62	Lydney							
					Lydney	2	-	-	-	-	-

Regentsholm, Regent Street, Lydney, Glos GL15 5RN

Tel. Nos. 01594 842479
Capacity: 3,320 +   **Seated:** 320   **Standing:** 3,000 +
Simple Directions: Turn into Swan Road off A48 in centre of Lydney. Take 1st turning left by garage,
    then 2nd turn right into ground
Nearest Railway Station: Lydney BR Appr 1 mile
Car Parking: Restricted on ground, spaces nearby
Admission: Season - Adults standing £35, seated £45, Children/OAPs standing £17.50, seated £22.50
    Matchday - Adults standing £4, seated £5, Children/OAPs standing £2, seated £2.50
Club Shop: Yes, Manageress Ann Sargent, 01594 562822
Clubhouse: Normal licensing hours, snacks available.
    Functions available contact Mrs Diane Emery 01594 841008 (H).
Training Nights: Tuesdays & Thursdays

Lydney captain, Nick Nelmes about to get his man

MATCHDAY PROGRAMME

Size	A5
Number of pages	36
Price	£1
Programme Editor	Dr D Dolan
Advertising Rates	Contact - Club

MORLEY R.F.C.

NICKNAME: The Maroons

FOUNDED: 1878

President Bruno Chorzeleski, c/o Morley RFC,
01937 586302 (H), 0113 250 2323 (B), 0113 250 9228 (Fax)

Chairman David Bradshaw, c/o Morley RFC, as above
0113 252 0412 (H), 0113 245 5438 (B).

Club Secretary Bob Lloyd, 5 Shepley Bridge, Mirfield, West Yorkshire, WF14 9HR
01924 494612 (H), 0585 741396 (Mobile), 0113 252 7050 (Fax).

Fixtures Secretary Peter Baxter, Apt 2, Fairfield House, 51 Scatherd Lane, Morley LS27 0PN.
0113 252 7050 (H), 0113 252 7050 (Fax)

Commercial Manager Alan Price, 5 Melbourne Mews, Kirkhamgate, Wakefield, WF2 0UG.
01924 384609 (H), 0113 252 7598 (B), 0113 253 4144 (Fax)

Chairman of Rugby Basil George, 0113 252 9856 (H), 0113 282 0088 (B)

Treasurer Ian Juniper, 0113 252 5371 (H), 0113 249 7511 (B)

Morley improved their League position of the previous two seasons by one place; they finished fourth. Maybe not a bad outcome for a club lacking much financial backing in this first season of professionalism, but nevertheless a disappointing one after the promise of mid-season.

In the second match, defeated at Fylde by a dropped goal in the last minute, and beaten at Liverpool St. Helens two weeks later when their goal kicking was unreliable, Morley overcame an indifferent start by winning their next eight games, the last being a victory over promotion rivals Leeds. Before Christmas they failed to win on their first visit to London Welsh, but early in 1997, after registering their highest League score (71 points at Clifton), they were in third place behind Fylde and Leeds with two games in hand. Prospects of returning to League Two after an absence of four seasons looked very possible.

However Fylde won at Scatcherd, despite the Maroons blitzing twelve points in six minutes. Hopes were revived when they were the only side to win at Rosslyn Park, but poor performances at home against Wharfedale and revitalised Harrogate interspersed with a demoralising defeat by an injury time penalty at Exeter put promotion out of Morley's own hands. A thrashing at Leeds preceded five successive victories at the end of the season that petered out and ended with a record 78 points against Walsall. After a poor start the season held the promise of promotion, but in the end it went on too long.

In the summer of 1996 the club lost Peter Massey to Wakefield, Craig Emmerson joined Gloucester and Stuart Kneale went to Leeds. Newcomers Alun Peacock, Mark Ireland, Brian Gabriel, Howard Graham, Simon Smith, Nick Sykes, Chris Bibb and Jamie Barker each at times made notable contributions and Eddie Rombo briefly set supporters agog with his pace, personality and seven tries in nine League appearances. When hooker Gordon Throup was injured after only eight matches, Andy Bemrose's decision to rejoin Morley could not have come at a better time.

Jonathon Shepherd and Craig Holdsworth played in every League match, Ben Wade missed one through injury, Howard Graham two and Jamie Grayshon's 195 points from twenty appearances put him top scorer for the tenth successive year.

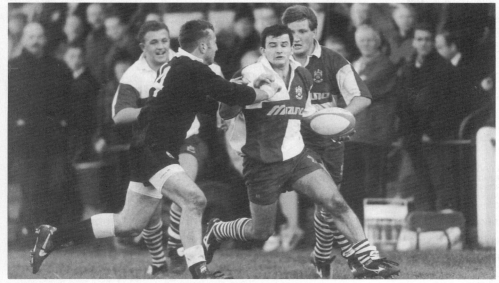

Morley's Simon Smith, Jonathon Shepherd & Andy Sales in action, last season

Photo - Gordon Bunney

Colours: Maroon & white quarters/maroon/maroon.

Change colours: All Blue.

MORLEY

No	Ven.	Date	Opponents	Att.	Res.	Score	Scorers
1	(H)	31.08	v Clifton		W	51-13	Wade(2t)Kinder(t)Smith(t)Barnes(t)Shepherd(t)PenTry(t)Peacock(5c2p)
2	(A)	07.09	v Fylde		L	17-19	Gabriel(t)Peacock(4p)
3	(H)	14.09	v Havant		W	42-13	Wade(2t)Holdsworth(t)Shepherd(t)PenTry(t)Peacock(4c3p)
4	(A)	21.09	v Liverpool StH		L	11-13	Rombo(t)Peacock(2p)
5	(H)	28.09	v Otley		W	37-13	Holdsworth(t)Shepherd(t)Naivalarua(t)Graham(t)Yule(t)Peacock(3c2p)
6	(A)	05.10	v Reading		W	34-24	Shepherd(2t)Rombo(t)Graham(t)Wade(t)Peacock(3cp)
7	(H)	12.10	v Rosslyn Park		W	15-14	Peacock(5p)
8	(A)	19.10	v Wharfdale		W	32-17	Gabriel(3t)Rombo(t)Clarke(t)Grayshon(2cp)
9	(H)	26.10	v Exeter		W	19- 9	Rombo(2t)Grayshon(3p)
10	(A)	09.11	v Harrogate		W	22-16	Graham(t)Barnes(t)Grayshon(3pdg)
11	(H)	16.11	v Leeds		W	30-22	Wade(t)Gabriel(t)Rombo(t)Grayshon(3c2pdg)
12	(A)	21.12	v London Welsh		L	22-27	Holdsworth(t)Crossley(t)Shepherd(t)Smith(t)Peacock(c)
13	(A)	18.01	v Clifton		W	71-25	Wade(4t)Naivalarua(2t)Clarke(2t)Holdsworth(t)Smith(t)Peacock(t5c2p)
14	(H)	25.01	v Fylde		L	18-30	Smith(t)PenTry(t)Peacock(c2p)
15	(A)	01.02	v Havant		W	51-15	Smith(2t)Graham(2t)Peacock(t)A Sales(t)Shepherd(t)Grayshon(5cpdg)
16	(H)	08.02	v Liverpool StH		W	41-36	Sykes(2t)Wade(2t)Smith(t)Holdsworth(t)Grayshon(4cp)
17	(A)	15.02	v Otley		W	31-24	A Sales(t)Smith(t)Enright(t)Grayshon(2c3p)Gabriel(dg)
18	(H)	22.02	v Reading		W	25-12	Peacock(t)Smith(t)Wade(t)Graham(t)Grayson(cp)
19	(A)	01.03	v Rosslyn Park		W	14- 8	Tiffin(t)Grayshon(3p)
20	(H)	08.03	v Wharfdale		L	10-13	Graham(t)Smith(t)
21	(A)	15.03	v Exeter		L	24-26	Smith(t)Shepherd(t)Grayshon(c4p)
22	(H)	22.03	v Harrogate		L	11-27	Sykes(t)Grayshon(2p)
23	(A)	29.03	v Redruth		W	29-16	Pierre(t)Barker(t)Shepherd(t)Yule(t)Grayshon(3cp)
24	(A)	05.04	v Leeds		L	3-42	Grayshon(p)
25	(H)	12.04	v London Welsh		W	38-28	Clarke(2t)Smith(t)Grayshon(t3c4p)
26	(A)	19.04	v Lydney		W	25-15	Tiffin(t)Clarke(t)Shepherd(t)Grayshontcp) Smith(t)Grayshon(2c)M Sales(2c)
27	(H)	26.04	v Redruth		W	58- 6	Shepherd(2t)Graham(t)Sykes(t)Enright(t)Wade(t)Barker(t)Clarke(t)Holdsworth(t)
28	(A)	03.05	v Walsall		W	36-17	Bibb(2t)Sykes(t)Pierre(t)Tiffin(t)Grayshon(4cdg)
29	(H)	10.05	v Lydney		W	33-13	Shepherd(2t)Naivalarua(2t)Wade(t)M Sales(c2p) Pierre(t)Grayshon(9c)
30	(H)	17.05	v Walsall		W	78-19	Naivalarua(2t)Holdsworth(2t)Tiffin(2t)Wade(2t)Graham(t)A Sales(t)Barker(t)

1996-97 HIGHLIGHTS

LEAGUE DEBUTS: Howard Graham, Alan Peacock, Brian Gabriel, Adam Goodwin, Simon Smith, Murray Withington, Eddie Rombo, Mark Ireland, David Hopton, Nick Sykes, Matthew Clough, Alan Pierre, Simon Chippendale, Chris Bibby, Jamie Barker, Mark Sales.

TRY ON DEBUT: Simon Smith.

PLAYERS USED: 35 plus 2 as replacement.

EVER PRESENT: Jonathan Shepherd.

❏ Achieved their best ever away win when they beat Clifton 71-25 to smash the previous record 49-6 v Liverpool St H in March 92.

❏ Jamie Grayshon set a unique record of topping the clubs points scoring charts for the tenth successive season with 195 points.
He also broke his own record of 21 points in a match which he had achieved twice. His new record is 23 and came in the 38-28 home win over London Welsh. In the 78-19 win over Walsall Grayshon set a new record of nine conversions in a match. That was also Morley's biggest ever win.
Grayshon became one of a handful of players to achieve the milestone of 1000 league points.
His 40 conversions doubled the previous best of 20 in a season from 95-96.

❏ Back row forward Ben Wade established a new record of 17 tries in a season. This easily beat the previous record of eight by Tony Clarke in 93-94. Wade also broke the record of three tries in a match with four against Clifton.

288

MORLEY'S COURAGE LEAGUE MATCH DETAILS 1996-97

	15	14	13	12	11	10	9	1	2	3	4	5	6	7	8	Replacements
1	Graham	Barnes	Shepherd	Naivalurua	Kinder	Peacock	Gabriel	Goodwin	Throup	McSwiney	Kenyon	Holdsworth	Wade	Yule	Smith	Tifin(15)
2	Graham	Barnes	Shepherd	Withington	Kinder	Peacock	Gabriel	Goodwin	Throup	McSwiney	Kenyon	Holdsworth	Wade	Yule	Smith	
3	Graham	Barnes	Shepherd	Withington	Rombo	Peacock	Gabriel	Goodwin	Throup	McSwiney	Kenyon	Holdsworth	Wade	Yule	Stowe	Anderson(8)
4	Graham	Barnes	Shepherd	Rombo	Rombo	Peacock	Gabriel	Ireland	Throup	McSwiney	Kenyon	Holdsworth	Wade	Yule	Wade	
5	Graham	Rombo	Shepherd	Naivalurua	Kinder	Peacock	Gabriel	Kenyon	Goodwin	McSwiney	Enright	Anderson Yule	Wade	Yule	Holdsworth	
6	Graham	Rombo	Shepherd	Naivalurua	Clarke	Tiffen	Tiffen	Ireland	Throup	McSwiney	Enright	Holdsworth	Hopton	Yule	Wade	
7	Graham	Rombo	Shepherd	Naivalurua	Clarke	Peacock	Tiffen	Ireland	Throup	McSwiney	Enright	Holdsworth	Wade	Yule	Smith	
8	Graham	Rombo	Shepherd	Naivalurua	Clarke	Peacock	Gabriel	Goodwin	McSwiney	Sykes	Enright	Holdsworth	Wade	Yule	Smith	Sykes(2)
9	Graham	Rombo	Shepherd	Naivalurua	A Sales	Grayshon	Gabriel	Ireland	Bemrose	McSwiney	Enright	Holdsworth	Wade	Yule	Smith	Goodwin(1)
10	Graham	Rombo	Shepherd	Naivalurua	Barnes	Grayshon	Gabriel	Ireland	Bemrose	Sykes	Enright	Holdsworth	Clough	Wade	Wade	
11	Graham	Rombo	Shepherd	Naivalurua	Barnes	Grayshon	Gabriel	Goodwin	Bemrose	Sykes	Enright	Holdsworth	Wade	Yule	Smith	
12	Graham	Crossley	Shepherd	Naivalurua	Clarke	Tiffin	Tiffin	Ireland	Bemrose	Sykes	Enright	Holdsworth	Wade	Yule	Smith	
13	Graham	Barnes	Shepherd	Naivalurua	Clarke	Peacock	Gabriel	Ireland	Bemrose	McSwiney	Enright	Holdsworth	Wade	Yule	Smith	Goodwin(2)Tiffin(15)Sykes(1)Pierre(5)
14	Graham	Barnes	Shepherd	Naivalurua	Clarke	Peacock	Gabriel	Ireland	Bemrose	McSwiney	Enright	Holdsworth	Wade	Yule	Smith	Tiffen(11)
15	Graham	Barnes	Shepherd	Naivalurua	Tiffin	Grayshon	Gabriel	Ireland	Bemrose	Sykes	Enright	Holdsworth	Wade	Hopton	Smith	A Sales(11)Acland(7)Chippendale(4)
16	Graham	Barnes	Shepherd	A Sales	Tiffin	Grayshon	Gabriel	Ireland	Bemrose	Sykes	Pierre	Holdsworth	Wade	Hopton	Smith	Enright(5)Acland(7)
17	Graham	Barnes	Shepherd	Naivalurua	Sales	Grayshon	Gabriel	Ireland	Bemrose	Sykes	Enright	Holdsworth	Stowe	Hopton	Smith	Yule(13),Campbell(12,Goodwin(1)
18	Graham	Tiffin	Shepherd	Peacock	Bibb	Grayshon	Gabriel	Ireland	Bemrose	McSwiney	Enright	Holdsworth	Wade	Yule	Smith	Campbell(12),Pierre(4)
19	Graham	Tiffin	Shepherd	Peacock	Bibby	Grayshon	Gabriel	Ireland	Bemrose	McSwiney	Enright	Holdsworth	Wade	Yule	Smith	Sykes(3)
20	Graham	Tiffin	Shepherd	Bibb	Bibb	Grayshon	Gabriel	Ireland	Bemrose	Sykes	Enright	Stowe	Wade	Yule	Smith	Holdsworth(5)
21	Graham	Tiffin	Shepherd	Peacock	Bibby	Grayshon	Gabriel	Ireland	Bemrose	Sykes	Enright	Holdsworth	Wade	Yule	Smith	Goodwin(3)Clough(7)
22	Graham	Barker	Shepherd	Naivalurua	Bibby	Grayshon	Gabriel	Ireland	Bemrose	Sykes	Enright	Holdsworth	Wade	Yule	Smith	Acland(7)Campbell(11)
23	Graham	Barker	Shepherd	Naivalurua	A Sales	Grayshon	Gabriel	Ireland	Bemrose	Sykes	Pierre	Acland	Wade	Yule	Wade	Smith(8)McSwiney(3)M.Sales(10)Chippendale(4)
24	Graham	Barker	Shepherd	A Sales	Bibby	Grayshon	Gabriel	Bemrose	Bemrose	Sykes	Enright	Holdsworth	Wade	Yule	Smith	Gabriel(11)McSwiney(3)Acland(8)
25	A Sales	Barker	Shepherd	Clarke	Bibby	Grayshon	Tiffin	Goodwin	Bemrose	Sykes	Enright	Holdsworth	Wade	Yule	Smith	Ireland(2)
26	A Sales	Barker	Shepherd	Clarke	Bibby	Grayshon	Tiffin	Bemrose	Bemrose	Sykes	Enright	Holdsworth	Wade	Yule	Smith	Graham(11)Ireland(1)Pierre(5)
27	Graham	Barker	Shepherd	Clarke	Grayshon	Grayshon	Tiffin	Ireland	Bemrose	Enright	Pierre	Holdsworth	Hopton	Yule	Smith	Holdsworth(4)M.Sales(10)
28	Graham	A Sales	Shepherd	Naivalurua	Clarke	Grayshon	Tiffin	Goodwin	Bemrose	Sykes	Pierre	Holdsworth	Hopton	Yule	Smith	Wade(7)Chippendale(6)M.Salesttr(11)
29	A Sales	Barker	Shepherd	Naivalurua	M Sales	Grayshon	Tiffin	Ireland	Bemrose	Sykes	Enright	Holdsworth	Wade	Yule	Smith	Throup(3)Grayshon(14)
30	Graham	A Sales	Shepherd	Naivalurua	Bibby	Grayshon	Tiffin	Goodwin	Bemrose	Ireland	Pierre	Holdsworth	Wade	Yule	Smith	Chippendale(5)Barker(15)M.Sales(10)

MORLEY LEAGUE STATISTICS
(COMPILED BY STEPHEN McCORMACK)

Season	Div.	P	W	D	L	F	(Tries	Con	Pen	DG)	A	(Tries	Con	Pen	DG)	Most Points	Most Tries
87-88	3	11	1	1	9	199	(14	8	8	1	235	(33	14	22	3)	37 - Jamie Grayshon	4 - Tony Clark
88-89	ALN	10	5	0	5	135	(12	6	23	2)	141	(13	7	22	3)	94 - Jamie Grayshon	6 - Tony Clark
89-90	ALN	10	8	0	2	169	(22	9	19	2)	115	(12	5	16	3)	78 - Jamie Grayshon	5 - Paul White
90-91	3	12	9	1	2	210	(30	15	19	1)	118	(12	5	18	2)	50 - Jamie Grayshon	5 - Mark Faulkner
91-92	2	12	4	0	8	171	(20	11	20	3)	202	(30	14	17	1)	57 - Jamie Grayshon	4 - Tony Clark
92-93	2	12	0	1	11	107	(7	3	19	3)	374	(45	28	28	3)	66 - Jamie Grayshon	2 - Tony Clark
93-94	3	18	6	0	12	245	(25	12	29	3)	334	(33	23	39	2)	117 - Jamie Grayshon	8 - Tony Clark
94-95	3	18	9	2	7	277	(23	12	41	5)	326	(33	19	39	2)	166 - Jamie Grayshon	7 - Tony Clark
95-96	3	18	9	2	7	336	(28	20	44	8)	328	(33	14	44	1)	206 - Jamie Grayshon	5 - Ben Wade
96-97	3	30	22	0	8	928	(123	65	56	5)	572	(56	32	69	7)	195 - Jamie Grayshon	17 - Ben Wade
Totals		151	73	7	71	2677	(304	161	288	33)	2745	(300	161	314	27)		

	HOME	AWAY
BIGGEST WIN	(59pts) 78-19 v Walsall 17.5.97	(46pts) 71-25 v Clifton 18.1.97
DEFEAT	(31pts) 7-38 v Wakefield 12.3.88	(78pts) 0-78 v Nottingham 24.10.92
MOST POINTS SCORED	78-19 v Walsall 17.5.97	71-25 v Clifton 18.1.97
AGAINST	7-38 v Wakefield 12.3.88	0-78 v Nottingham 24.10.92

MOST CONSECUTIVE VICTORIES - 8   **MOST CONSECUTIVE DEFEATS - 11**

MOST TRIES IN A MATCH
(FOR) 12 v Walsall 17.05.97 (H)
(AGAINST) 12 v Nottingham 24.10.92

MOST APPEARANCES
FORWARD: 61+2 Gordon Throup
BACK: 120(1) Jamie Grayshon

CONSECUTIVE SCORING MATCHES
Scoring Tries - 7 - Simon Smith
Scoring Points - 21 - Jamie Grayshon

CONSECUTIVE APPEARANCES
49 Gary Demaine

MOST	in a SEASON	in a CAREER	in a MATCH
Points	206 Jamie Grayshon 95-96	1063 Jamie Grayshon 87-97	23 Jamie Grayshon v Lon. Welsh 12.4.97 (H)
Tries	17 Ben Wade 96-97	45 Tony Clark 87-97	4 Ben Wade v Clifton 18.1.97 (A)
Conversions	40 Jamie Grayshon 96-97	123 Jamie Grayshon 87-97	9 Jamie Grayshon v Walsall 17.5.97 (H)
Penalties	44 Jamie Grayshon 95-96	226 Jamie Grayshon 87-97	7 Jamie Grayson v Rugby 21.10.95 (H)
Drop Goals	8 Jamie Grayshon 95-96	31 Jamie Grayshon 87-97	2 Jamie Grayshon v Wakefield 13.2.93 (A) v Richmond 13.11.93 (H) v Reading 14.6.95 (A) v Richmond 6.4.96 (H)

MORLEY PLAYING SQUAD

NAME	Ht	Wt	Birthdate	Birthplace	Club	Apps	Pts	T	C	P	DG

BACKS

NAME	Ht	Wt	Birthdate	Birthplace	Club	Apps	Pts	T	C	P	DG
Howard Graham					Morley	27+1	40	8	-	-	-
Jonathan Shepherd	5.9	13.7	31.07.74	Dewsbury	Morley	63	90	18	-	-	-
Tony Clarke	6.1	14.0	22.06.62	Dewsbury	Morley	117	207	45	-	-	-
Jamie Grayshon	5.11	13.0	21.11.68	Bradford	Morley	121+1	1063	10	123	226	31
Andy Sales	6.2	15.0	24.04.71	Morley	Morley	63+8	28	5	-	-	-
Alan Peacock					Orrell	8+2	10	-	2	2	-
					Morley	14	128	3	22	23	-
Jamie Barker					Morley	7+1	15	3	-	-	-
Chris Bibb					Morley	9	10	2	-	-	-
Mark Sales					Morley	2+3	12	-	3	2	-
Peter Naivalarua	6.4	16.0			Clifton						
					Morley	28	35	7	-	-	-
Brian Gabriel					Nottingham	36	30	6	-	-	-
					Morley	18+1	28	5	-	-	1
Jeremy Tiffen	6.0	13.0	16.02.71	Newcastle	Prev. Clubs: Northern, Roundhay, Richmond.						
					Morley	35+3	35	7	-	-	-
Andy Crossley	6.1	14.7	21.02.68	Huddersfield	Preston Grasshoppers						
					Morley	23+3	19	4	-	-	-

FORWARDS

NAME	Ht	Wt	Birthdate	Birthplace	Club	Apps	Pts	T	C	P	DG
Adam Goodwin	5.11	14.7	28.06.75	Leeds	Morley	11+4	-	-	-	-	-
Gordon Throup	5.10	15.0		Keighley	Wharfedale						
					Morley	69+5	10	2	-	-	-
Darryl McSwiney	5.11	16.7	08.02.70	Leeds	Morley	48+4	-	-	-	-	-
Nick Sykes					Morley	17+3	25	5	-	-	-
Andy Bemrose					Morley	29+2	-	-	-	-	-
Mark Ireland					Nottingham	14	-	-	-	-	-
					Morley	21+2	-	-	-	-	-
Craig Holdsworth	6.6	17.0	15.03.66	Leeds	Morley	53+2	59	12	-	-	-
Simon Enright	6.5	17.0	12.02.65	Birkenhead	Morley	45+1	10	2	-	-	-
Ben Wade	6.3	15.0	11.09.74	Leeds	Wakefield						
					Morley	52+5	115	23	-	-	-
Alastair Yule	6.0	14.0	11.07.63	Bakewell	Stirling County						
					Morley	82+3	25	5	-	-	-
Simon Smith					Morley	24+1	65	13	-	-	-
David Hopton	6.0	13.7	22.03.76	Dewsbury	Morley	6	-	-	-	-	-
Simon Chippendale	6.4	14.7	30.04.76	Pontefract	Morley	0+4	-	-	-	-	-
Nick Kenyon	6.3	15.0	01.02.60	Dewsbury	Wakefield	1	-	-	-	-	-
					Morley	57+2	5	1	-	-	-
Jonathan Stow	6.5	16.0	10.11.73	Bradford	Wakefield						
					Morley	51	15	3	-	-	-

Scatcherd Lane, Morley, West Yorkshire, LS27 0JJ

Tel. 0113 253 3487 Ground;   0113 252 7598 Office;   0113 253 4144 Fax

Capacity: 5,826   **Seated:** 826   **Standing:** 5,000

Simple Directions: From West; Leave M62 Jnc 27 Follow A650 towards Wakefield for 1.2 miles turn left St Andrews Ave. Ground 0.3 miles on left. From East; Leave M62 Jnc 28 follow A650 towards Bradford for 1.7 miles, turn right into St Andrews Ave.

Nearest Railway Station: Morley Low BR

Car Parking: 110 in & around ground

Admission: Season; Standing Adult £50, Family £100, Transfer to stand £1 Matchday; Standing Adults £5, Children/OAPs £2, Transfer to stand £1

Club Shop: Yes, Manager Mrs Amanda Binks 0113 253 3487

Clubhouse: Weekdays 18.30 - 23.00, Saturdays 13.00 - 23.00, Sundays 12.00 - 16.00, 20.30 - 23.00; Three bars with bar meals available
Functions: Yes, capacity 200 - contact Mandy Hudson 0113 253 3487/04325 165148

Training Nights: Mondays & Thursdays

Morley's Jamie Grayson, Andy Sales & Alistair Yule in action, last season.   Photo - Photogenic

MATCHDAY PROGRAMME

Size	A5
Number of pages	20
Price	£1
Programme Editor	
Advertising Rates	Full page £300
	Half page £175
	Qtr page £100

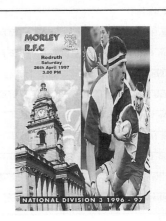

NEWBURY R.F.C.

NICKNAME: The Blues

FOUNDED: 1928

President To be elected

Chairman of Rugby David Barratt, White House Farm, Lambourn, Berkshire
01488 71793 (H), 0831 626470 (B Mobile)

Club Secretary To be elected

1st XV Coach Keith Richardson, c/o Newbury RFC, Monks Lane, Newbury, Berkshire RG14 7RW
01635 40103 (B), 01635 40533 (Fax)

After taking five years to win promotion into the National Leagues, the Blues took on the triple challenge of National League rugby, the open era and the move to a new ground. With the latter not available until mid October against Henley, the Blues played their first seven matches on the road and at that time there was only a slight inkling of what was to follow.

1996/97 was the best season in the club's history, probably any club's history, as Newbury won all 26 Leagues matches (Askeans by default), lost to winners Leicester in the Pilkington Cup by just five points (how many British Lions past and present played for Leicester that day?), and played the Western Samoans in that memorable November night formally to open the new ground at Monks Lane. The Leicester match followed a tough midweek win at Lydney (28-15), a match delayed by the mysterious outbreak of boils that struck down nine of the Newbury forwards. Newbury had not reached the second round before, let alone the fifth, so Leicester away was a tough as they get. At 23-3 the home side were coasting but the Blues finished the stronger and came back to 26-21 with tries from Julian Brammer, Brian Johnson and Tom Holloway. So near and yet so far from the greatest upset in the Cup competition.

Julian Brammer captained the side with great authority throughout the season and was ably supported by ever present players Colin Hall, Nick Grecian and Craig Davies. Five players played for England South West against Queensland, Argentina and South Africa 'A' and Brian Johnson played for England 'A' against South Africa 'A' at Gloucester. Brian and Nick Grecian were selected to play for the Barbarians, one of the greatest honours in the game, and Brian went on to become the top try scorer in English rugby and Nick would have been the top points scorer if Askeans had turned up. Over a 1000 league points were scored and a total of 200 tries recorded for the season. Brian Johnson and Craig Davies scored 31 tries for the club, a club record, and Nick Grecian established a new club points scoring record with 467, 386 in the league, to become the competition's leading scorer. Along the way Newbury played fast open rugby that brought the crowds flocking to the new Newbury Sports Arena. The Blues established new club league records firstly at home to Charlton Park (83-14), then Met. Police (87-0) and finally Tabard (91-17). The two matches with Henley were classic local derbies and it was the 11-9 win at Monks Lane in front of 2000 spectators that gave the Blues the impetus they were never going to lose as the season progressed.

With director of rugby, Terry Burwell, moving to a new post with the RFU at Twickenham, Newbury will look to Keith Richardson, the England 'A' coach recruited by Burwell last season, to maintain the momentum that has seen them rise from the bottom of South West Two to Natioinal Division One and the verge of the Premiership in seven memorable seasons.

Newbury's No 8, Craig Davis scores against North Walsham

Colours: Navy, sky & white irregular hoops

Change colours: White

NEWBURY

COURAGE LEAGUE MATCH DETAILS 1996-97

No	Ven.	Date	Opponents	Att.	Res.	Score	Scorers
1	(A)	31.08	v Charlton Park		W	46- 7	Davies(2t)Dangerfield(t)Stewart(t)Hall(t)NOsman(t)Johnson(t)POsman(4cp)
2	(A)	07.09	v High Wycombe		W	62-18	Davies(2t)Dangerfield(2t)Phillips(t)Johnson(t)Collins(t)McGeever(t)PenT(t)Grecian(7cp)
3	(A)	21.09	v Berry Hill		W	32- 8	Dangerfield(2t)Davies(t)Newman(t)Grecian(3c2p)
4	(A)	28.09	v Barking		W	35-11	Davies(2t)Brammer(t)Newman(t)Grecian(3c3p)
5	(A)	05.10	v Met Police		W	31-12	Duke(t)Johnson(t)McGeever(t)Grecian(tc3p)
6	(H)	19.10	v Henley		W	11- 9	Davies(t)Grecian(2p)
7	(A)	26.10	v Weston-S-M		W	28-22	Phillips(2t)Davies(t)Grecian(2c3p)
8	(H)	09.11	v Cheltenham		W	28-16	Phillips(t)Davies(t)Grecian(t2c3p)
9	(A)	16.11	v N Walsham		W	72-18	McGeever(3t)Holloway(2t)Smith(2t)N Osman(t)P Osman(t)Grecian(2t7cp)
10	(A)	11.01	v Plymouth		W	26-15	Johnson(2t)Smith(t)Grecian(c3p)
11	(A)	18.01	v Camberley		W	26-15	Hall(t)T Osman(t)Grecian(2c4p) Grecian(t11c2p)
12	(H)	25.01	v Charlton Park		W	83-14	Hall(3t)Holloway(2t)T Osman(t)N Osman(t)R Osman(t)Smith(t)Johnson(t)
13	(H)	02.02	v High Wycombe		W	49-10	Johnson(3t)Holloway(t)McCartney(t)Davies(t)Smith(t)Grecian(7c)
14	(H)	08.02	v Berry Hill		W	34- 0	Johnson(3t)McCartney(t)R Osman(t)Grecian(3cp)
15	(H)	15.02	v Barking		W	50-18	Johnson(3t)Holloway(2t)Kingdon(t)Grecian(4c4p)
16	(H)	22.02	v Met Police		W	87- 0	Davies(3t)Johnson(2t)Birch(t)Collins(t)Hall(t)T Osman(t)Phillips(t)Grecian(t2t2p8c)
17	(A)	02.03	v Henley		W	26- 8	Davies(2t)R Osman(t)Smith(dg)Grecian(c2p)
18	(A)	15.03	v Cheltenham		W	27-10	Holloway(2t)Johnson(t)Grecian(t2cp)
19	(H)	22.03	v North Walsham		W	63-13	Dangerfield(3t)Holloway(t)Prince(t)R Osman(t)Hall(t)Davies(t)Collins(t)McGeever(t)Grecian(t4c)
20	(H)	28.03	v Tabard		W	91-17	Holloway(3t)Davies(2t)Phillips(2t)Johnson(t)Prince(t)Collins(t)Hall(t)N Osman(t)R Osman(t)Grecian(2t8c)
21	(A)	05.04	v Tabard		W	31-13	Davies(2t)Phillips(t)McGeever(t)PenTry(t)Grecian(3c)
22	(H)	12.04	v Camberley		W	61-23	Holloway(3t)Duke(t)Phillips(t)Dangerfield(t)R Osman(t)T Osman(t)Grecian(t5c2p)
23	(A)	19.04	v Askeans		W	74- 5	Johnson(4t)Davies(3t)Hall(t)Smith(t)Holloway(t)PenTry(t)Grecian(t7c)
24	(H)	22.04	v Weston-S-M		W	54-13	Hall(2t)Brammer(t)Davies(t)McGeever(t)Holloway(t)T Osman(t)Grecian(5c3p)
25	(H)	26.04	v Plymouth		W	43- 0	Johnson(4t)McGeever(t)Holloway(t)Orr-Ewing(t)Grecian(4c)
26	(H)		v Askeans				Match not played

1996-97 HIGHLIGHTS

LEAGUE DEBUTS: Tom Holloway, Colin Phillips, Colin Hall, Ian McGeever, Brian Johnson, Richard McCartney,

PLAYERS USED: 32 plus three as replacement.

EVER PRESENT: Nick Grecian and Colin Hall.

❑ Full back Nick Grecian set a number of new records including 391 points in a season which was a new club record and Division Four South record .
In his total of 391 were 100 conversions which is also a club and Division Four South record.

❑ England A and The Army winger Brian Johnson set a new National Divisions record for tries in a season - 27. Not far behind was No 8 Craig Davies.

❑ Unable to complete final fixture of the season at home to Askeans who were unable to field a side.

Most points in a match

33 Nick Grecian v Charlton Park 25.01.97 (H)
32 Nick Grecian v Met Police 22.02.97 (H)
27 Nick Grecian v N Walsham 16.11.96 (A)
26 Nick Grecian v Tabard 28.03.97 (H)
21 Nick Grecian v Camberley 12.04.97 (H)
20 Nick Grecian v Barking 15.02.97 (H)
20 Brian Johnson v Askeans 19.04.97 (A)
20 Brian Johnson v Plymouth 26.04.97 (H)

Hat trick of tries in a match

4 Brian Johnson v Askeans 19.04.97 (A)
4 Brian Johnson v Plymouth 26.04.97 (H)
3 Ian McGeever v N Walsham 16.11.96 (A)
3 Brian Johnson v H Wycombe 02.02.97 (H)
3 Brian Johnson v Berry Hill 08.02.97 (H)
3 Brian Johnson v Barking 15.02.97 (H)
3 Craig Davies v Met Police 22.02.97 (H)
3 Matt Dangerfield v N Walsham 22.03.97 (H)
3 Tom Holloway v Tabard 28.03.97 (H)
3 Tom Holloway v Camberley 12.04.97 (H)
3 Craig Davies v Askeans 19.04.97 (A)

NEWBURY'S COURAGE LEAGUE MATCH DETAILS 1996-97

#	15	14	13	12	11	10	9	1	2	3	4	5	6	7	8	Replacement
1	Grecian	Johnson	NOsman	Clark	Dangerfield	P'Osman	Halley	Stewart	Winfield	Collins	Hall	Duke	Evans	McGeever	Davies	
2	Grecian	Johnson	NOsman	Clark	Dangerfield	P'Osman	Phillips	Stewart	Winfield	Collins	Hall	Duke	McGeever	Kingdom	Davies	Birch
3	Grecian	Newman	NOsman	Clark	Dangerfield	Smith	Halley	Stewart	Winfield	Collins	Hall	Duke	McGeever	Kingdom	Davies	Blower
4	Grecian	Newman	NOsman	TOsman	Dangerfield	Smith	Halley	Stewart	Brammer	Collins	Hall	Duke	McGeever	Kingdom	Davies	Birch
5	Grecian	Johnson	NOsman	TOsman	Dangerfield	Smith	Galley	Stewart	Brammer	Collins	Hall	Duke	McGeever	Kingdom	Davies	P'Osman
6	Grecian	Johnson	NOsman	TOsman	Dangerfield	Smith	Halley	Stewart	Brammer	Collins	Hall	Duke	McGeever	Kingdom	Davies	P'Osman
7	Johnson	Dangerfield	TOsman	TOsman	Holloway	Smith	Pinder	Stewart	Brammer	Collins	Hall	Newsham	Orr-Ewing	Knight	Davies	Blower
8	Clark	Johnson	Grecian	TOsman	Holloway	Smith	Phillips	Lowe	Brammer	Collins	Hall	Duke	McGeever	Kingdom	Davies	
9	Grecian	Johnson	Grecian	TOsman	Holloway	Smith	Phillips	Stewart	Brammer	Collins	Hall	Duke	McCartney	Kingdom	Davies	Little
10	Grecian	Johnson	NOsman	TOsman	Holloway	Smith	Halley	Stewart	Brammer	Collins	Hall	Duke	McCartney	McGeever	Davies	McGeever
11	Grecian	Johnson	NOsman	TOsman	Holloway	Smith	Phillips	Stewart	Brammer	Collins	Hall	Newsham	McCartney	Kingdom	McGeever	Davies,Halley
12	Grecian	Johnson	NOsman	TOsman	Holloway	Smith	Phillips	Stewart	Brammer	Collins	Hall	Newsham	McCartney	McGeever	Davies	Little,James,R'Osman
13	Grecian	Johnson	NOsman	R'Osman	Holloway	Smith	Halley	Stewart	Winfield	Little	Hall	Duke	McCartney	Kingdom	Davies	Phillips(11),McGeever(14),Lowe(1),Orr-Ewing(1)13
14	Grecian	Johnson	NOsman	R'Osman	Holloway	Smith	Phillips	Birch	Brammer	Collins	Hall	Duke	McCartney	McGeever	Davies	Orr-Ewing(6)
15	Grecian	Johnson	NOsman	TOsman	Holloway	Smith	Halley	Stewart	Brammer	Collins	Hall	Duke	McCartney	Kingdom	Davies	Orr-Ewing(7),Wagfer(9),R'Osman(13)
16	Grecian	Johnson	NOsman	TOsman	Holloway	Smith	Phillips	Stewart	Brammer	Collins	Hall	Duke	McCartney	Kingdom	Davies	McGeever( )Birch( )
17	Grecian	Johnson	R'Osman	TOsman	Holloway	Smith	Phillips	Stewart	Brammer	Collins	Hall	Duke	McCartney	Kingdom	Davies	P'Osman( )Birch( )
18	Grecian	Johnson	R'Osman	Prince	Holloway	Smith	Phillips	Stewart	Brammer	Collins	Hall	Duke	McCartney	Kingdom	Davies	Orr-Ewing(5)
19	Dangerfield	R'Osman	Prince	Prince	Holloway	Smith	Phillips	Stewart	Brammer	Collins	Hall	Newsham	McCartney	Kingdom	Davies	McCartney(7),N.Osman(10),N.James(1)
20	Grecian	Johnson	R'Osman	Prince	Holloway	Smith	Phillips	Stewart	Brammer	Collins	Hall	Newsham	McGeever	Kingdom	Davies	Evans(6)N.Osman(13)Dangerfield(14)
21	Grecian	Johnson	R'Osman	R'Osman	Holloway	Smith	Phillips	Stewart	Brammer	Collins	Hall	Duke	McGeever	Kingdom	Davies	Evans( )
22	Dangerfield	N'Osman	R'Osman	TOsman	Holloway	Smith	Phillips	Birch	Winfield	Collins	Hall	Duke	McGeever	Kingdom	Davies	R.Osman( )Evans( )
23	Johnson	N'Osman	R'Osman	TOsman	Holloway	Smith	Phillips	Birch	Winfield	Little	Hall	Duke	Orr-Ewing	Kingdom	Davies	T.Osman( )
24	Grecian	Johnson	N'Osman	TOsman	Holloway	Smith	Phillips	Stewart	Brammer	Collins	Hall	Duke	McGeever	Kingdom	Davies	Orr-Ewing( )Winfield( )P.Osman( )
25	Grecian	Johnson	R'Osman	TOsman	Holloway	P'Osman	Phillips	Stewart	Winfield	Collins	Hall	Duke	McGeever	Kingdom	Davies	N.Osman( )Orr-Ewing( )
26	MATCH VOID							MATCH VOID							MATCH VOID	

NEWBURY LEAGUE STATISTICS
(COMPILED BY STEPHEN McCORMACK)

Season	Div.	P	W	D	L	F	A	PD	Pts	Pos.	Coach	Captain
87-88	SW2	10	3	1	6	99	172	-73	7	10	E Butler	G Brown
88-89	SW2	10	4	0	6	102	134	-32	8	7	E Butler	R King
89-90	SW2	10	3	0	7	125	149	-24	6	9	E Cripps	R King
90-91	SW2	10	7	1	2	137	100	37	15	2p	T Burwell	A Widdop
91-92	SW1	10	5	0	5	142	145	-3	10	6	T Burwell	W Phillips
92-93	SW1	12	8	1	3	251	158	93	17	3	T Burwell	W Phillips
93-94	SW1	12	8	1	3	173	165	8	17	3	T Burwell	J Booth
94-95	SW1	12	9	1	2	376	113	263	19	2	S Czerpak	J Brammer
95-96	SW1	12	11	0	1	364	169	195	22	1p	S Czerpak	J Brammer
96-97	D4S	25	25	0	0	1170	295	875	50	1p	S Czerpak	J Brammer
Total		123	83	5	35	2939	1600	1339				

Colin Hall, former London Irish 2nd row, scores from close range.

NEWBURY PLAYING SQUAD

NAME	Ht	Wt	Birthdate	Birthplace	Club	Apps	Pts	T	C	P	DG

BACKS

NAME	Club	Apps	Pts	T	C	P	DG
Nick Grecian	London Scottish						
Scotland: 2.	**Newbury**	37	488	16	120	56	-
Brian Johnson							
England: A. The Army. South West.	**Newbury**	20	135	27	-	-	-
Tom Holloway	Wakefield	1+1	10	2	-	-	-
London u21.	**Newbury**	20	95	19	-	-	-
Colin Phillips	Reading	30	85	17	-	-	-
Berkshire. The Army.	**Newbury**	17+1	45	9	-	-	-
Kendal Smith							
Scotland: u19. Anglo-Scots u21.	**Newbury**	34	61	11	-	-	2
Matt Dangerfield							
	Newbury	15	93	12	6	7	-
Phil Osman							
	Newbury	3+2	11	-	4	1	-
Nick Osman							
England: u18, u16.	**Newbury**	17+3	20	4	-	-	-
Tim Osman							
	Newbury	16+1	30	6	-	-	-
Russell Osman							
	Newbury	10+3	30	6	-	-	-
Hugo Prince							
Queensland University.	**Newbury**	3	10	2	-	-	-
Simon Halley							
Berkshire u21.	**Newbury**	18+1	5	-	-	-	-
Jim Darragh	Rugby	9	-	-	-	-	-
	Newbury	-	-	-	-	-	-

FORWARDS

NAME	Club	Apps	Pts	T	C	P	DG
Julian Brammer							
Army. Combined Services. Oxfordshire. E. Counties.	**Newbury**	24	15	3	-	-	-
Colin Hall	Northampton	19	-	-	-	-	-
	London Irish	49+1	10	2	-	-	-
Army. Combined Services. British Police.	**Newbury**	26	55	11	-	-	-
Andy Duke							
London u21. Hampshire u21.	**Newbury**	19	10	2	-	-	-
Neil Collins	Reading	8	-	-	-	-	-
Berkshire.	**Newbury**	23	20	4	-	-	-
Pete Winfield							
Berkshire	**Newbury**	13+1	5	1	-	-	-
Craig Davies							
Wales u21, Students.	**Newbury**	36+1	165	31	-	-	-
Ian McGeever	Reading	?	43	9	-	-	-
Berkshire. Welsh Schools.	**Newbury**	16+2	45	9	-	-	-
John Kingdon							
Devon.	**Newbury**	27	5	1	-	-	-
Seb Stewart							
Army. Combined Services.	**Newbury**	20	-	-	-	-	-
Stuart Birch							
Berkshire.	**Newbury**	4+4	5	1	-	-	-
John McCartney							
Ulster u20.	**Newbury**	11+1	15	3	-	-	-
Dave Orr-Ewing	London Scottish						
Army. Combined Services.	**Newbury**	3+6	5	1	-	-	-
Ian Evans							
	Newbury	1+2	-	-	-	-	-
Simon Little							
	Newbury	14	10	2	-	-	-
Andy Newsham							
	Newbury	8	-	-	-	-	-

The Appearances and Points shown above are National Leagues' appearances & points only.

Monks Lane, Newbury, Berkshire RG14 7RW

Tel. Nos. 01635 40103

Capacity: 7,850   **Seated:** 350   **Standing:** 7,500

Simple Directions: From M4 take A34 to Newbury, at 4th r'about on Newbury ring road (A34) turn right. Keep left at mini-r'about, ground is half mile on left. From south turn left at 1st r'about on A34 ring road.

Nearest Railway Station: Newbury

Car Parking: 300 on ground, 1000 nearby @ £1.

Admission: Season - Adults Standing £90, Seated £150. Children/OAPs N/A
       Matchday - Standing; Adults £6, Children/OAPs £3. Seated; Adults £8, Children/OAPs £5.

Club Shop: Yes, Manageress Caroline Luker 01635 40103

Clubhouse: Normal Licensing hours, bar meals & restaurant available.
     Functions available capacity 250 contact Alan Judd 01635 40103

Training Nights: Tuesday & Thursday

Newbury's Brian Johnson, Unisys top try scorer, scoring one of his 27 league tries

MATCHDAY PROGRAMME

Size	A5
Number of pages	40 plus cover
Price	£1.50
Programme Editor	T B A
Advertising Rates	

Colour Full page £500, Half page £300, Qtr page £150
Mono Full page £250, Half page £150, Qtr page £75

NOTTINGHAM R.F.C.

NICKNAME: Green & Whites   **FOUNDED:** 1877

Chairman Bryan Ford, c/o Nottingham RFC, Ireland Avenue, Beeston, Nottingham NG9 1JD.
0115 925 4238
Director of Rugby Barrie Corless, c/o Nottingham RFC, as above
0370 674190 (Mobile). 0115 925 4238 (B), 0115 925 4255 (Fax)
Rugby Administrator David Shakespeare, c/o Nottingham RFC, as above
Club Secretary Audrey Gill, c/o Nottingham RFC, as above
Marketing Adrian Bentley & George Holloman, c/o Nottingham RFC, as above

It was to say the least a difficult season for the club both on and off the field. The team found itself ill equipped, particularly in the first half of the season, to compete in what had become a very strong league. Indeed a club record defeat was inflicted when the team lost to Coventry.

However, all was not doom and gloom and the team was strengthened after Christmas with the signing of three Canadian Internationals along with ex-international and experienced prop Gary Pearce.

There were encouraging signs with some spirited performances notably in difficult away fixtures at Newcastle and Richmond. Towards the end of the season Barrie Corless was appointed director of rugby and under the control of new chairman Bryan Ford the club is already regrouping with high hopes of bouncing straight back.

Nottingham RFC 1996-97 1st Team.   Photo - Nottingham Post

Colours: Green & white   **Change colours:** Yellow.

NOTTINGHAM

No	Ven.	Date	Opponents	Att.	Res.	Score	Scorers
1	(A)	07.09 v	Bedford	3100	L	23-41	Tomlinson(t)Brennan(t)Jackson(t)Carroll(c2p)
2	(H)	14.09 v	Newcastle	733	L	29-74	Tomlinson(2t)Royer(t)PTry(t)Carroll(3cp)
3	(A)	21.09 v	Moseley	883	L	22-34	Royer(t)Bygrave(t)Webster(t)Carroll(2cp)
4	(H)	28.09 v	London Scot	458	L	12-26	Carroll(3p)Hodgkinson(p)
5	(A)	05.10 v	Coventry	2500	L	22-102	Bygrave(t)Dawson(t)Jones(t)Beese(t)Craig(c)
6	(H)	12.10 v	Rotherham	646	L	21-44	Atkinson(t)Freer(t)Hodgkinson(c3p)
7	(H)	19.10 v	Blackheath	329	L	12-22	Hodgkinson(3p)Tomlinson(p)
8	(A)	26.10 v	Waterloo	450	W	20-19	Dawson(t)Bygrave(t)Tomlinson(2c2p)
9	(H)	02.11 v	Wakefield	495	L	18-40	Rees(t)PTry(t)Wills(c2p)
10	(A)	09.11 v	Rugby	514	L	12-20	Hartley(4p)
11	(H)	16.11 v	Richmond	611	L	5-70	Sussem(t)
12	(H)	28.12 v	Bedford	760	L	13-36	Rees(t)Carroll(c2p)
13	(A)	18.01 v	London Scot	1209	L	10-33	Dawson(t)Evans(cp)
14	(H)	02.02 v	Moseley	463	L	11-22	Bygrave(t)Evans(2p)
15	(H)	08.02 v	Coventry	422	L	0-29	
16	(A)	08.03 v	Rotherham	1100	L	24-30	Beatham(t)Jones(t)Wilcox(t)Evans(3cp)
17	(A)	16.03 v	Newcastle	1739	L	17-53	Claydon(t)Hall(t)Wilcox(t)Evans(c)
18	(A)	22.03 v	Blackheath	1287	L	0-24	
19	(H)	05.04 v	Waterloo	262	L	13-33	Evans(tc2p)
20	(A)	12.04 v	Wakefield	650	L	16-31	Byrom(t)Royer(t)Evans(2p)
21	(H)	19.04 v	Rugby	309	W	44-10	Hall(3t)Brennan(t)Bygrave(t)Dawson(t)Evans(4c2p)
22	(A)	26.04 v	Richmond	1658	L	0-34	

1996-97 HIGHLIGHTS

LEAGUE DEBUTS: Murray Craig, Stepen Spensley, Alex Dawson, Andy)'Kiwa, David Evans, Gavin Reynolds, Gary Pearce, Jason Hall, Simon Beatham, Elliott Spencer, Ian Gordon, Brian McCarthy, Guy Bibby, Alex Wilcox, Rob Merritt.

TRY ON DEBUT: Alex Dawson.

PLAYERS USED: 41 plus 3 as replacement.

EVER PRESENT: Alan Royer and Richard Bygrave. Richard Byrom started in 21 games and came on replacement in the other.

❏ Simon Hodgkinson extended his career record from 574 to 597.

	Pts	T	C	P	D	Apps	Ave.
Nottingham	597	5	54	142	14	67	8.91
Moseley	239	-	19	64	3	29	8.24
TOTAL	836	5	73	206	17	96	8.70

❏ Suffered a new club record of 12 consecutive defeats easily beating the previous record of six.

❏ Failed to score a try in six games - the worst record of any team in the top two divisions

❏ Suffered their worst ever defeat when going down 102-22 to Coventry in October. Their previous worst away defeat was just 41-7 at Sale in April 92.

❏ Also suffered their biggest ever home defeat going down 70-5 to the Champions Richmond in November. They also conceded 70+ points when losing 74-29 to Newcastle

❏ Prior to last season they had never conceded more than seven tries in a match - now they have done so on four occasions.

❏ Scrum-half Alan Royer moves into joint second place on the club's all-time try scoring list.

	Tries	Apps	Try Every
Richard Byrom	15	125	8.33 games
Andy Smallwood	12	47	3.92 games
Alan Royer	12	54	4.50 games

❏ Richard Byrom extended his Nottingham career record for appearances to 125 which puts him in the National League top ten.

❏ Richard Byrom topped the club's try scoring list in a season for a record third time. He previously shared the record of two with Andy Smallwood who has now moved on to Coventry.

NOTTINGHAM'S COURAGE LEAGUE MATCH DETAILS 1996-97

15	14	13	12	11	10	9	1	2	3	4	5	6	7	8	Replacements	
Byrom	Bygrave	Craig	Tomlinson	Webster	Carroll	Royer	Freer	Claydon	Jackson	Spensley	Sussum	Beese	Brennan	Atkinson		1
Byrom	Bygrave	Craig	Tomlinson	Webster	Carroll	Royer	Freer	Grantham	Downey	Spensley	Sussum	Beese	Brennan	Atkinson		2
Byrom	Bygrave	Craig	Tomlinson	Webster	Carroll	Royer	Freer	Grantham	Jackson	Sussum	Jones	Bradley	Brennan	Atkinson		3
Byrom	Smith	Tomlinson	Craig	Carroll		Royer	Freer	Grantham	Jackson	Sussum	Jones	Bradley	Claydon	Atkinson	Hodgkinson(10)Roberts(2)	4
Dawson	Bygrave	Smith	O'Kiwa	Wills		Royer	Downey	Roberts	Jackson	Sussum	Jones	Beese	Claydon	Atkinson	Grantham(10)Byrom(12)	5
Byrom	Bygrave	Craig	Tomlinson	Webster	Hodgkinson	Royer	Freer	Claydon	Jackson	Sussum	Jones	Beese	Rees	Bradley		6
Byrom	O'Kiwa	Tomlinson	Bygrave	Holland	Hodgkinson	Royer	Freer	Claydon	Jackson	Sussum	Jones	Bradley	Rees	Atkinson	Dawson(14)Ratcliffe(15)	7
Byrom	Dawson	Hartley	Holland	Hodgkinson	Tomlinson	Royer	Freer	Claydon	Jackson	Sussum	Jones	Bradley	Brennan	Atkinson		8
Byrom	Dawson	Hartley	Bygrave	Holland	Tomlinson	Royer	Freer	Claydon	Jackson	Sussum	Jones	Bradley	Brennan	Atkinson	Rees(7)Ratcliffe(14)	9
Byrom	Bygrave	Hartley	Smith	Holland	Musto	Royer	Freer	Claydon	Jackson	Sussum	Jones	Bradley	Rees	Atkinson		10
Byrom	Holland	Smith	Smith	O'Kiwa	Musto	Royer	Freer	Grantham	Jackson	Sussum	Jones	Beese	Claydon	Atkinson	Downey(3)	11
Byrom	Dawson	Carroll	Carroll	Hartley	Evans	Royer	Reynolds	Claydon	Pearce	Veldhuizen	Jones	Bradley	Atkinson		Rees(8)	12
Byrom	Bygrave	Beatham	Spencer	Spencer	Evans	Royer	Freer	Claydon	Pearce	Veldhuizen	Jones	Bradley	Brennan	Gordon	McCarthy(8)Dawson(14)	13
Byrom	Bygrave	Beatham	Spencer	Spencer	Evans	Royer	Freer	Claydon	Pearce	McCarthy	Jones	Bradley	Rees	Wilcox	Gordon(5)	14
Byrom	Bygrave	Beatham	Spencer	Spencer	Evans	Royer	Freer	Claydon	Pearce	McCarthy	Jones	Bradley	Rees	Gordon	Gordon(5)	15
Byrom	Bygrave	Beatham	Beatham	Holland	Evans	Royer	Freer	Claydon	Pearce	McCarthy	Jones	Bradley	Bibby	Wilcox		16
Byrom	Bygrave	Beatham	Beatham	Holland	Evans	Royer	Freer	Claydon	Pearce	McCarthy	Jones	Bradley	Bibby	Wilcox	Brennan(6)	17
Byrom	Bygrave	Beatham	Beatham	Holland	Evans	Royer	Freer	Claydon	Pearce	McCarthy	Jones	Gorcon	Bibby	Wilcox	Smith(13)Ratcliffe(10)Atkinson(7)	18
Byrom	Bygrave	Hall	Beatham	Holland	Evans	Royer	Reynolds	Merritt	Pearce	McCarthy	Gordon	Bradley	Brennan	Wilcox	Dawson(11)Gray(6)	19
Byrom	Bygrave	Beatham	Hall	Holland	Evans	Royer	Reynolds	Claydon	Pearce	McCarthy	Gordon	Bradley	Brennan	Wilcox	Dawson(15)Gray(6)	20
Byrom	Bygrave	Hall	Beatham	Dawson	Evans	Royer	Reynolds	Claydon	Pearce	McCarthy	Gordon	Bradley	Brennan	Wilcox	Freer(1)Grantham(6)Holland(11)Gray(5)Garnett(15)	21
Byrom	Hall	Smith	Holland	Evans		Royer	Freer	Claydon	Pearce	McCarthy	Sussum	Bibby	Brennan	Gordon	Atkinson(6)Reynolds(1)	22

NOTTINGHAM LEAGUE STATISTICS

(COMPILED BY STEPHEN McCORMACK)

Season	Div.	P	W	D	L	F	(Tries	Con	Pen	DG)	A	(Tries	Con	Pen	DG)	Most Points	Most Tries
87-88	1	11	4	1	6	146	(14	6	22	4)	170	(22	11	18	2)	86 - Simon Hodgkinson	5 - Clifton Jones
88-89	1	11	6	1	4	142	(10	6	24	6)	122	(7	5	26	2)	98 - Simon hodgkinson	2 - Lee Johnson
89-90	1	11	6	0	5	187	(22	15	19	4)	148	(21	8	15	1)	82 - Simon Hodgkinson	5 - Gary Hartley
90-91	1	12	6	0	6	138	(12	9	22	2)	194	(24	12	22	2)	80 - Simon Hodgkinson	3 - Richard Byrom
91-92	1	12	2	1	9	133	(11	7	22	3)	204	(24	12	27	1)	48 - Guy Gregory	4 - Martin Pepper
92-93	2	12	8	0	4	249	(22	14	28	9)	145	(13	4	21	3)	106 - Guy Gregory	3 - Richard Byrom
93-94	2	18	8	1	9	254	(17	11	44	5)	326	(31	18	38	7)	171 - Guy Gregory	5 - Andy Smallwood
94-95	2	18	8	1	9	299	(24	13	50	1)	322	(26	12	51	5)	97 - Ian Stent	4 - Andy Smallwood
95-96	2	18	5	1	12	333	(36	22	39	4)	433	(45	29	49	1)	158 - Simon Hodgkinson	7 - Alan Royer
96-97	2	22	2	0	20	344	(39	22	35	0)	827	(110	68	43	4)	55 - David Evans	5 - Richard Bygrave
Totals		145	55	6	84	2225	(207	125	305	38)	2891	(323	180	310	28)		

HOME
BIGGEST WIN (78pts) 78-0 v Morley 24.10.92
DEFEAT (65pts) 5-70 v Richmond 16.11.96
MOST POINTS SCORED 78-0 v Morley 24.10.92
AGAINST 29-74 v Newcastle 14.9.96

AWAY
(41pts) 46-5 v Blackheath 26.9.92
(80pts) 22-102 v Coventry 5.10.96
46-5 v Blackheath 26.9.92
22-102 v Coventry 5.10.96

MOST CONSECUTIVE VICTORIES - 5

MOST CONSECUTIVE DEFEATS - 12

MOST TRIES IN A MATCH
(FOR) 12 v Morley 24.10.92 (H)
v Newcastle 14.9.96 (H)
(AGAINST) 14 v Coventry 5.10.96 (A)

MOST APPEARANCES
FORWARD: 102(3) Chris Gray
BACK: 125(1) Richard Byrom

CONSECUTIVE SCORING MATCHES
Scoring Tries - 4 - Andy Smallwood
Scoring Points - 20 - Guy Gregory

CONSECUTIVE APPEARANCES
41 Guy Gregory 23.11.91 - 30.4.94

MOST	in a SEASON	in a CAREER	in a MATCH
Points	171 Guy Gregory 93-94	597 Simon Hodgkinson 87-93 & 95-97	25 Guy Gregory v Otley 11.9.93 (H)
Tries	7 Alan Royer 95-96	14 Richard Byrom 87-97	4 Gary Hartley v Morley 24.10.92 (H)
Conversions	18 Simon Hodgkinson 95-96	54 Simon Hodgkinson 87-93 & 95-97	9 Guy Gregory v Morley 24.10.92 (H)
Penalties	43 Guy Gregory 93-94	142 Simon Hodgkinson 87-93 & 95-97	6 Guy Gregory v Saracens 12.3.94
Drop Goals	9 Guy Gregory 92-93	19 Guy Gregory 91-94	2 Andy Sutton v Harlequins 31.3.90 (A) Guy Gregory v Rosslyn Park 4.4.92 (H) v Rosslyn Park 21.1.92 (A) v Fylde 9.1.93 (H) v Bedford 13.2.93 (A) Simon Hodgkinson v L Irish 17.2.96 (A)

NOTTINGHAM PLAYING SQUAD

NAME	Ht	Wt	Birthdate	Birthplace	Club	Apps	Pts	T	C	P	DG

BACKS

NAME	Ht	Wt	Birthdate	Birthplace	Club	Apps	Pts	T	C	P	DG
Richard Byrom	6.0	13.5	14.07.61	Kendal							
					Nottingham	125+1	62	14	-	-	-
Richard Bygrave	5.9	13.7	02.05.71	Rotherham							
					Nottingham	38+1	35	7	-	-	-
Alan Royer	6.0	12.7	01.12.70	Leicester	Leicester						
					Nottingham	54+1	60	12	-	-	-
Alex Dawson	5.10	12.0	22.02.76	Amersham	Northampton						
					Nottingham	5+4	20	4	-	-	-
Nick Carroll	5.11	12.7	09.01.70	Liverpool	Moderns						
					Nottingham	16	49	1	7	9	1
Jason Hall											
					Nottingham	10	20	4	-	-	-
David Evans											
					Nottingham	11	55	1	10	10	-
Mark Holland											
					Nottingham	11+1	-	-	-	-	-
Damian Smith	6.2	14.2	21.11.71	Nottingham	Moderns						
					Nottingham	5+1	-	-	-	-	-
Buster Musto			07.10.62								
					Nottingham	46	10	2	-	-	-
Simon Hodgkinson	5.10	12.0	15.12.62	Bristol	Moseley	29	239	-	19	64	3
					Nottingham	67+1	597	5	54	142	14
Paul Ratcliffe											
					Nottingham	0+3	-	-	-	-	-

FORWARDS

NAME	Ht	Wt	Birthdate	Birthplace	Club	Apps	Pts	T	C	P	DG
Martin Freer	5.11	15.7	15.10.63	Chatham	Blackheath						
					Nottingham	109+1	19	4	-	-	-
Charlie Claydon	5.10	13.10	24.07.68								
					Nottingham	28	10	2	-	-	-
Gary Pearce					Northampton	76	8	2	-	-	-
					Nottingham	11	-	-	-	-	-
Gavin Reynolds					Wakefield	1	-	-	-	-	-
					Nottingham	3+1	-	-	-	-	-
Robert Sussum			12.09.70								
					Nottingham	21	5	1	-	-	-
Brian McCarthy											
					Nottingham	9+1	-	-	-	-	-
Gareth Beese	5.11	14.10	14.11.72	Newport							
					Nottingham	19	25	5	-	-	-
John Brennan	5.11	14.0	20.12.71	Birmingham	Birmingham Solihull						
					Nottingham	17	10	2	-	-	-
Peter Atkinson	6.2	14.0	18.09.70	Wakefield	Prev. Clubs: Old Crossleyans, Headingley.						
					Nottingham	14+3	-	-	-	-	-
Ian Grantham	5.8	15.0	12.09.65	Nottingham							
					Nottingham	7+4	-	-	-	-	-
Lee Jones	6.4	17.0	16.06.71	Ilkeston	Ilkeston						
					Nottingham	25	10	2	-	-	-
Mark Bradley	6.3	15.7	21.12.69	Derby	Belper						
					Nottingham	77	35	7	-	-	-
Ian Gordon											
					Nottingham	6+2	-	-	-	-	-
Guy Bibby											
					Nottingham	5	-	-	-	-	-
Alex Wilcox											
					Nottingham	8	10	2	-	-	-

Tel: 0115 925 4255   **Fax:** 0115 925 4238

CAPACITY: 4,950   **SEATED:** 450   **STANDING:** 4,500

SIMPLE DIRECTIONS:
By Road: Off Queens Road, Beeston. Main Nottingham to Long Eaton Road
Nearest Railway Station: Beeston, left out of station to Main Queens Rd, left into Dovecote Lane, right into Ireland Ave, ground at end

CAR PARKING: 175 on ground

ADMISSION: Membership Standing; Adults £50, OAPs/Children £30: Seated; Adults £60, OAPs/Children £40. Matchday Standing; Adults £6, OAPs/Children £3: Seated; Adults £8, OAPs/Children £5

CLUB SHOP: Yes; Club Marketing 0115 925 4255

CLUBHOUSE: Matchday & training nights, snacks & bar meals available.
Function room: Yes, available for hire, capacity 100, contact Gary Tredwell-Stones

TRAINING NIGHTS: Mondays & Thursdays (Seniors); Sunday mornings (Mini's & Juniors).

Nottingham RFC's captain 1996-97 season scrum half Alan Royer.

MATCHDAY PROGRAMME

Size	A5
Number of pages	36 plus cover
Price	£1
Programme Editor	Adrian Bentley 0115 925 4255

Advertising Rates
Colour Full page £500, Half page £250
Mono Full page £300, Half page £150

OTLEY R.U.F.C.

President E Watson, c/o Otley RUFC.

FOUNDED: 1865

Chairman Paul Jacques, Springsyde, Birdcage Walk, Otley.
01943 462714 (H), 01132 591708 (B), 01132 589994 (Fax)

Club Secretary Marc Lawrence, 16 Bankfield Terrace, Baildon, BD17 7HZ
01274 593535 (H)

Director of Rugby Mike Wright, Cherry Tree Cottage, Dacre, Harrogate HG3 4ES
01423 780216 (H)

Director of Coaching Michael Barnett, 28 Beech Road, Harrogate HG2 8AG
01423 870467 (H)

Press Officer John C Finch, 9 Glen Mount, Menston, Ilkley. LS29 6DJ.
01943 872491 (H), 01943 461180 (Fax)

Training started early in 1997 and has never been better organised. Director of rugby Mike Wright has a fine team with Michael Barnett a diligent and active chief coach ably supported by ex Commonwealth Games athlete Mike Makin. Fitness overseer, and ex Leeds and Great Britain RL winger, John Atkinson's enthusiasm was matched by his success as demonstrated by the quality of play of the many young backs who were brought into the team over the season.

This fast tracking into League rugby was essential as seven members of the previous year's team had been lured away over the close season, including all but one experienced second row and these gaps had to be filled from the junior ranks.

It is to the credit of the club's magnificent youth structure that these replacements were in situ, albeit the young forwards were still short of bulk but their commitment and skills were never in question. Winger Mark Kirkby, who equalled the League record when scoring five tries at Redruth, is the latest to attract National attention. Last year it was Paul Sampson and incidently ten years ago John Bentley, so with the Colts XV making a regular habit of winning the County Cup there are more in the 'wings'.

It is a great relief that Peter Rutledge has decided on another season at Cross Green. The prolific scoring full back, having moved to Cheshire, reflects the superb spirit engendered by skipper Neil Hargreaves by rarely missing a training session. It will not be easy to replace such an artist even allowing for the fact that he is being given less goal chances as his captain prefers to run the ball at all times.

As the game progresses the matches get harder but they must also be enjoyed, both by players and by spectators alike and this is the intention of Neil as he continues at the helm.

Otley's scrum half Andy Brown in action against Wharfedale.

Photo - Wharfedale Observer

Colours: Black with irregular white hoops.

Change colours: Red with irregualr white hoops.

COURAGE LEAGUE MATCH DETAILS 1996-97

No	Ven.	Date	Opponents	Att.	Res.	Score	Scorers
1	(H)	31.08	v Leeds		L	19-20	Smith(t)Rutledge(c4p)
2	(H)	07.09	v London Welsh		W	16-12	Billington(t)Rutledge(c3p)
3	(A)	14.09	v Lydney		L	22-34	Clarke(t)Midgeley(t)PenTry(t)Rutledge(2cp)
4	(H)	21.09	v Redruth		W	41-34	Smith(2t)Billington(t)N Hargreaves(t)Rutledge(t5c2p)
5	(A)	28.09	v Morley		L	13-37	A Hargreaves(t)Rutledge(c2p)
6	(H)	05.10	v Clifton		L	29-42	Kirkby(3t)Walker(t)Rutledge(3cp)
7	(A)	12.10	v Fylde		L	14-28	Brown(t)Rutledge(3p)
8	(H)	19.10	v Havant		W	25-22	Wilson(t)Walker(t)Kirkby(t)Rutledge(2c2p)
9	(A)	26.10	v Liverpool StH		W	25-20	Brown(t)Midgeley(t)Rutledge(t2cp)Cadman(dg)
10	(H)	09.11	v Walsall		W	53-19	Clarke(2t)Kirkby(2t)Middleton(2t)Rutledge(t6c2p)
11	(H)	16.11	v Reading		W	31-20	Smith(t)Brown(t)Rutledge(t2c4p)
12	(H)	28.12	v Wharfdale		L	13-20	Walker(t)Burke(t)Rutledge(p)
13	(H)	11.01	v Harrogate		W	17- 8	Rutledge(t3p)Cadman(dg)
14	(A)	18.01	v Leeds		L	16-39	Kirkby(t)Rutledge(t2p)
15	(A)	25.01	v London Welsh		L	19-21	Burke(t)Rutledge(c4p)
16	(H)	01.02	v Lydney		W	27-17	Kelt(2t)Darby(t)Kirkby(t)Rutledge(2cp)
17	(A)	08.02	v Redruth		W	40-28	Kirkby(5t)Darby(t)Rutledge(5c)
18	(H)	15.02	v Morley		L	24-31	Midgeley(t)Darby(t)Rutledge(t3cp)
19	(A)	22.02	v Clifton		W	52-31	Billington(2t)Darby(2t)Cadman(t)Brown(t)N Hargreaves(t)Kirkby(t)Rutledge(6c)
20	(H)	01.03	v Fylde		L	7-22	PenTry(t)Rutledge(c)
21	(A)	08.03	v Havant		W	33-16	Billington(2t)Gardner(t)Cadman(dg)Hawkins(t2c2p)
22	(H)	15.03	v Liverpool StH		W	34-25	Kirkby(2t)Cadman(t)Smith(t)PenTry(t)Rutledge(3cp)
23	(A)	22.03	v Walsall		L	19-29	Kelley(t)Billington(t)Burke(t)Rutledge(2c)
24	(A)	29.03	v Rosslyn Park		L	15-39	Smith(t)Kirkby(t)Rutledge(cp)
25	(A)	05.04	v Reading		L	19-21	Billington(t)Brown(t)Rutledge(t2c)
26	(H)	12.04	v Rosslyn Park		W	39- 8	Kirkby(3t)Brown(t)A Hargreaves(t)Rutledge(4c2p)
27	(A)	19.04	v Wharfdale		L	15-23	A Hargreaves(t)PenTry(t)Rutledge(cp)
28	(H)	26.04	v Exeter		L	14-26	Kelt(t)Rutledge(3p)
29	(A)	03.05	v Harrogate		L	10-26	Kelt(t)Hawkins(t)
30	(A)	10.05	v Exeter		L	19-48	Kirkby(2t)Gardner(t)Hawkins(2c)

1996-97 HIGHLIGHTS

LEAGUE DEBUTS: Andy Clarke, Mark Nixon, Richard Kelt, Robert Gill, Chris Minchella, Greg Downes, Simon Middleton, Paul Coleman, Paul Kelley, Richard Smith, William Darby, Sam Gardner, Rob Whatmuff, Daniel Levi.

TRY ON DEBUT: William Darby.

PLAYERS USED: 34 plus 3 as replacement.

EVER PRESENT: Chris Baldwin and Neil Hargreaves.

❑ Captain Neil Hargreaves has now played 38 consecutive matches and is three short of Richard Petyt's record of 41.

❑ Mark Kirkby in his first full season breaks Jon Walker's 1990-91 record of 16 tries in a season. Kirkby took the record to 22 from 26 matches.
In the away fixture at Redruth he scored five tries to set a new Division Three record and club record for tries in a match. Both the previous records were four. Otley's was shared by Glyn Melville, Mark Farrar and John Walker. Kirkby's five tries gives him 25 points which is a record for points in a match - his third club record.

❑ Peter Rutledge tops the points scoring list for a fifth consecutive season and in the process sets a new club record of 287 points.
Rutledge breaks Jon Howarth's 1990-91 record of 17 conversions with 56. He also breaks his own record of 40 penalties with 45.

	Pts	T	C	P	D	Apps	Ave.
Total	841	21	104	176	-	90	9.34

❑ Rutledge breaks Glyn Melville's record of 72 appearances and takes the record to 90.

OTLEY'S COURAGE LEAGUE MATCH DETAILS 1996-97

#	15	14	13	12	11	10	9	1	2	3	4	5	6	7	8	Replacements
1	Rutledge	Walker	Smith	Billington	Kirkby	Cadman	Brown	Baldwin	Munro	Rice	Wilson	Clarke	Hall	N.Hargreaves	A.Hargreaves	Midgeley(6)
2	Rutledge	Walker	Smith	Billington	Kirkby	Cadman	Brown	Baldwin	Munro	Rice	Wilson	Clarke	Midgeley	N.Hargreaves	A.Hargreaves	
3	Rutledge	Walker	Smith	Billington	Kirkby	Hawkins	Farrar	Baldwin	Munro	Coleman	Wilson	Clarke	Hall	N.Hargreaves	A.Hargreaves	Brown(11)Nixon(6)Midgeley(8)
4	Rutledge	Walker	Kelt	Billington	Smith	Hawkins	Brown	Baldwin	Munro	Rice	Wilson	Nixon	Clarke	N.Hargreaves	Burke	
5	Rutledge	Walker	Smith	Billington	Kirkby	Hawkins	Brown	Baldwin	Munro	Rice	Wilson	Clarke	A.Hargreaves	N.Hargreaves	Burke	Gill(3)Clough(6)
6	Rutledge	Walker	Smith	Billington	Kirkby	Cadman	Brown	Minchella	Munro	Baldwin	Nixon	Clarke	Hall	N.Hargreaves	Burke	Midgeley(6)Henry(1)
7	Rutledge	Walker	Smith	Billington	Kirkby	Cadman	Brown	Baldwin	Munro	Henry	Wilson	Clarke	Downes	N.Hargreaves	Burke	Hall(6)
8	Rutledge	Walker	Middleton	Billington	Kirkby	Cadman	Brown	Baldwin	Munro	Coleman	Wilson	Clarke	Midgeley	N.Hargreaves	Burke	
9	Rutledge	Walker	Middleton	Billington	Kirkby	Cadman	Brown	Baldwin	Munro	Henry	Wilson	Nixon	Midgeley	N.Hargreaves	Burke	Kelt(12)
10	Rutledge	Walker	Middleton	Kelt	Kirkby	Cadman	Brown	Baldwin	Munro	Rice	Wilson	Clarke	Midgeley	N.Hargreaves	Burke	Smith(12)
11	Rutledge	Walker	Middleton	Smith	Kirkby	Hawkins	Brown	Baldwin	Munro	Rice	Wilson	Clarke	Midgeley	N.Hargreaves	Burke	
12	Rutledge	Walker	Middleton	Billington	Smith	Cadman	Brown	Baldwin	Kelley	Rice	Wilson	Clarke	Midgeley	N.Hargreaves	Burke	Elshaw(9)Munro(6)A.Hargreaves(5)
13	Rutledge	Smith	Middleton	Billington	Kirkby	Cadman	Brown	Baldwin	Kelley	Rice	Wilson	R.Smith	Midgeley	N.Hargreaves	Burke	A.Hargreaves(4)Darby(14)Gardner(11)
14	Rutledge	Smith	Middleton	Billington	Kirkby	Cadman	Brown	Baldwin	Kelley	Rice	R.Smith	Clarke	Midgeley	N.Hargreaves	Burke	Hall(5)Gardner(9)
15	Rutledge	Smith	Middleton	Billington	Kirkby	Cadman	Brown	Baldwin	Kelley	Rice	R.Smith	Clarke	Midgeley	N.Hargreaves	Burke	A.Hargreaves(5)
16	Rutledge	Darby	Billington	Kelt	Kirkby	Cadman	Brown	Baldwin	Kelley	Rice	R.Smith	Burke	Midgeley	N.Hargreaves	A.Hargreaves	
17	Rutledge	Darby	Billington	Kelt	Kirkby	Cadman	Brown	Baldwin	Kelley	Rice	R.Smith	Burke	Midgeley	N.Hargreaves	A.Hargreaves	
18	Rutledge	Darby	Billington	Kelt	Kirkby	Cadman	Brown	Baldwin	Kelley	Rice	R.Smith	Burke	Midgeley	N.Hargreaves	A.Hargreaves	
19	Rutledge	Darby	Kelt	Billington	Kirkby	Cadman	Brown	Baldwin	Munro	Rice	Smith	Burke	Midgeley	N.Hargreaves	A.Hargreaves	Henry(8),Whatmuff(13)
20	Rutledge	Darby	Billington	Kelt	Kirkby	Cadman	Brown	Baldwin	Munro	Rice	Smith	Wilson	Midgeley	N.Hargreaves	A.Hargreaves	Hawkins(15)
21	Hawkins	Kirkby	Smith	Billington	Gardner	Cadman	Browne	Baldwin	Kelly	Rice	Wilson	Nixon	Midgeley	N.Hargreaves	Burke	
22	Rutledge	Gardner	Smith	Billington	Kirkby	Cadman	Brown	Baldwin	Kelley	Rice	Wilson	Nixon	Midgeley	N.Hargreaves	Burke	Hawkins(10)A.Hargreaves(5)Greig(14)
23	Rutledgr	Greig	Smith	Billington	Kirkby	Hawkins	Brown	Baldwin	Kelley	Gill	Wilson	A.Hargreaves	Midgeley	N.Hargreaves	Burke	Levi(6)
24	Rutledge	Smith	Whatmuff	Billington	Kirkby	Hawkins	Brown	Baldwin	Kelley	Clarke	Smith	Wilson	Midgeley	N.Hargreaves	Burke	Cadman(10)Levi(5)
25	Rutledge	Smith	Whatmuff	Billington	Kirkby	Cadman	Brown	Baldwin	Kelley	Rice	Smith	Burke	Levi	N.Hargreaves	Midgeley	
26	Rutledge	Smith	Whatmuff	Billington	Kirkby	Cadman	Brown	Baldwin	Kelley	Rice	Smith	Wilson	Midgeley	N.Hargreaves	A.Hargreaves	Hawkins(10)Kelt(13)
27	Rutledge	Smith	Whatmuff	Billington	Kirkby	Hawkins	Cadman	Baldwin	Kelley	Rice	Smith	Wilson	Midgeley	N.Hargreaves	Burke	A.Hargreaves(6)
28	Rutledge	Darby	Kelt	Billington	Smith	Cadman	Brown	Baldwin	Kelley	Rice	Smith	Burke	Midgeley	N.Hargreaves	A.Hargreaves	
29	Rutledge	Smith	Kelt	Billington	Kirkby	Hawkins	Brown	Baldwin	Kelley	Rice	Smith	Wilson	Midgeley	N.Hargreaves	Burke	Levi(5)Munro(6)Cadman(3)
30	Hawkins	S.Smith	Billington	Kelt	Kirkby	Cadman	Browne	Baldwin	Munro	Knapton	R.Smith	Nixon	Midgeley	N.Hargreaves	Burke	Gardner(13)Darby(12)

OTLEY LEAGUE STATISTICS
(COMPILED BY STEPHEN McCORMACK)

Season	Div.	P	W	D	L	F (Tries Con Pen DG)					A (Tries Con Pen DG)					Most Points	Most Tries
87-88	N1	10	5	1	4	194	(30	13	16	0)	122	(			)	34 - Ian Colquhoun	8 - Glyn Melville
88-89	N1	10	5	0	5	197	(28	18	17	0)	112	(			)	59 - Robert Sharp	4 - Robert Sharp
89-90	N1	10	9	0	1	141	(20	8	14	1)	77	(			)	43 - David Lester	3 - John Walker & David Lester
90-91	D4N	12	11	0	1	426	(76	34	16	2)	89	(10	2	13	3)	77 - David Lester	6 - Adrian Scott
91-92	3	12	5	0	7	177	(24	9	19	2)	190	(24	8	24	2)	62 - Richard Petyt	4 - Mark Farrar
92-93	3	11	8	1	2	274	(32	15	28	0)	118	(14	6	11	1)	121 - Peter Rutledge	6 - Glyn Melville & Mark Farrar
93-94	2	18	4	1	13	235	(22	10	28	7)	449	(53	29	38	4)	119 - Peter Rutledge	7 - Sean Atkinson
94-95	3	18	9	0	9	278	(24	12	42	2)	258	(23	10	35	6)	167 - Peter Rutledge	6 - Peter Rutledge
95-96	3	18	6	1	11	278	(25	12	40	3)	441	(55	35	30	2)	147 - Peter Rutledge	3 - John Hall & Jon Flint.
96-97	3	30	13	0	17	720	(90	60	47	3)	766	(88	46	74	4)	287 - Peter Rutledge	22 - Mark Kirkby
Totals		149	75	4	70	2920	(371	191	267	20)	2622	(			)		

	HOME	AWAY
BIGGEST WIN	(55pts) 61-6 v Askeans 27.3.93	(30pts) 37-7 v Lichfield 13.10.90
DEFEAT	(26pts) 3-29 v Kendal 22.4.89	(79pts) 9-88 v Sale 12.2.94
MOST POINTS SCORED	61-6 v Askeans 27.3.93	52-31 v Clifton 22.2.97
AGAINST	29-42 v Clifton 15.10.96	9-88 v Sale 12.2.94

MOST CONSECUTIVE VICTORIES - 9

MOST CONSECUTIVE DEFEATS - 7

MOST TRIES IN A MATCH
(FOR) 10 v Hereford 1991
(AGAINST) 14 v Sale 12.2.94

MOST APPEARANCES
FORWARD: 117 Steve Rice
BACK: 90 Peter Rutledge

CONSECUTIVE APPEARANCES
41 Richard Petyt 11.11.91 to 30.4.94

CONSECUTIVE SCORING MATCHES
Scoring Tries - 5 - Glyn Melville
Scoring Points - 18 - Peter Rutledge

MOST	in a SEASON	in a CAREER	in a MATCH
Points	287 Peter Rutledge 96-97	841 Peter Rutledge 92-97	25 Mark Kirkby v Redruth 8.2.97
Tries	22 Mark Kirkby 96-97	41 Glyn Melville 87-96	5 Mark Kirkby v Redruth 08.02.97 (A)
Conversions	56 Peter Rutledge 96-97	104 Peter Rutledge 92-97	7 Ian Colquhoun v Birmingham 27.4.91 (H)
Penalties	45 Peter Rutledge 96-97	176 Peter Rutledge 92-97	6 Peter Rutledge v Harrogate 29.10.94 (A)
Drop Goals	7 Richard Petyt 93-94	10 Richard Petyt 91-94	2 Richard Petyt v Nottingham 11.9.93 (A)

OTLEY PLAYING SQUAD

NAME	Ht	Wt	Birthdate	Birthplace	Club	Apps	Pts	T	C	P	DG

BACKS

NAME	Ht	Wt	Birthdate	Birthplace	Club	Apps	Pts	T	C	P	DG
Peter Rutledge	6.1	13.7	05.04.65	Winnipeg	Prev. Clubs: Bradford & Bingley, Lewes.						
					Otley	90	841	21	104	176	-
Simon Smith											
					Otley	29+2	40	8	-	-	-
Mark Billington	6.1	14.0	14.06.71	Huddersfield	Huddersfield						
					Otley	45+3	50	10	-	-	-
Mark Kirkby	6.3	12.7	28.04.76	Otley							
					Otley	31+2	120	24	-	-	-
Richard Kelt											
					Otley	11+2	20	4	-	-	-
Simon Hawkin	5.7	13.0	31.03.75	Otley							
					Otley	36+4	52	4	4	5	3
Anthony Cadman	5.8	11.8	12.07.76	Portsmouth							
					Otley	33+4	24	2	1	-	4
Andy Brown											
					Otley	31+1	30	6	-	-	-
Tony Greig	6.0	14.0	01.09.71	Bebbington	Bradford & Bingley						
					Otley	6+1	-	-	-	-	-
William Darby											
					Otley	6+2	25	5	-	-	-
Rob Whatmuff											
					Otley	4+1	-	-	-	-	-
Sam Gardner											
					Otley	2+2	5	1	-	-	-
Simon Middleton											
					Otley	8	10	2	-	-	-

FORWARDS

NAME	Ht	Wt	Birthdate	Birthplace	Club	Apps	Pts	T	C	P	DG
Chris Baldwin	6.0	16.6	30.03.74	Sheffield	Prev. Clubs: Headingley, Rotherham						
					Otley	68+1	-	-	-	-	-
Alex Munro	5.10	14.7	11.02.67	Shipley	Prev. Clubs: Headingley, Leeds.						
					Otley	41+3	5	1	-	-	-
Steve Rice	6.1	16.8	10.06.63	Otley							
					Otley	117	9	2	-	-	-
Paul Kelley											
					Otley	16	5	1	-	-	-
Stephen Henry											
					Otley	6+2	-	-	-	-	-
Jonathan Burke	6.6	17.0	01.12.71	Bradford	Prev. Clubs: Leicester, Rugby.						
					Otley	43	25	5	-	-	-
Neil Hargreaves	6.1	14.0	22.04.65	Leeds	Headingley	33	12	3	-	-	-
					Leeds.	8	5	1	-	-	-
					Wakefield	9	-	-	-	-	-
					Otley	61	10	2	-	-	-
Andy Hargreaves	6.2	15.0	27.03.62	Bramley	Bramley						
					Otley	113+5	83	19	-	-	-
Steve Wilson	6.7	19.0	27.11.63	Leeds	Otlesians						
					Otley	57+1	10	2	-	-	-
Richard Smith											
					Otley	14	-	-	-	-	-
Mark Nixon											
					Otley	5+1	-	-	-	-	-
Andy Clarke											
					Otley	14	15	3	-	-	-
Richard Midgeley											
					Otley	29+4	15	3	-	-	-
Daniel Levi											
					Otley	1+2	-	-	-	-	-

Cross Green, Otley. LS21 1HE

Tel. Nos. 01943 850142.   **Fax.** 01943 461180

Capacity: 7,000   **Seated:** 850   **Standing:** 6,150
Simple Directions: Left hand side of Pool Road, leading to Harrogate, 1/2 mile from town centre.
Nearest Railway Station: Leeds BR
Car Parking: 100 on ground
Admission:
   Season - Adults VPs £65, £55, Children/OAPs £25
   Matchday - Standing Adults £5, Children/OAPs £1.50; Seated Adults £7, Children/OAPs £2.50
Club Shop: Yes, matchdays & Sunday lunchtime
Clubhouse: Normal Licensing hours, three bars with snacks available
Functions: Yes, capacity 130 seated, contact Steward Peter Longstaffe 01943 461180 or 01943 850142
Training Nights: Tuesdays & Thursdays

Otley's Simon Smith scoring a try.   Wharfedale Observer

MATCHDAY PROGRAMME

Size	A5
Number of pages	28 plus cover
Price	£1
Programme Editor	Peter Thompson, 01132 842134

Advertising Rates
   Mono Full page £200, Half page £120, Qtr page £60

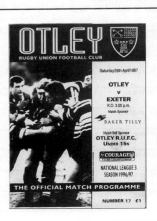

READING R.F.C.

NICKNAME: Green Machine

FOUNDED: 1898

President Sid Williams, c/o Reading RFC, Holm Park, Sonning Lane, Sonning, Reading, RG4 0ST
01734 696592, 01734 272622 (Fax)

Chairman Chris Horder, Suite 404, The Commercial Centre, Picket Piece, Andover, Hants, SP11 6RU
01980 626083 (H), 01204 366001 (B), 01204 366002 (Fax)

Club Secretary Phil Betts, 7 Sherwood Road, Winnersh, Wokingham RG41 5NH
0118 987 7064 (H)

Commercial Manager Craig Hunter, 4 Newcastle Road, Reading, RG2 7TR
0118 962 0693 (H), 0118 969 6592 (B), 0118 969 6592 (Fax)

Director of Rugby Mike Tewkesbury 01189 272622 (B)

Publicity Officer Craig Hunter as above

It was a record breaking season for Reading as they recovered from a poor start to finish sixth in National League Three.
They smashed their best score in league matches three times in as many months with 65 against Liverpool St. Helens, 71 at the expense of Redruth and 75 against Clifton. They also reached the Pilkington Cup fifth round for the first time before losing at home to star studded Saracens 41-3 and before that they achieved their biggest ever Pilkington win at home to Widnes 50-3. The Wanderers, Reading's second string, earned the club a record tenth Berkshire title by beating Bracknell's first team away 21-13 in an exciting final.

Jason Dance eclipsed Phil Belshaw's league points record with 281 and Guy Spencer's thirteen touchdowns edged past Colin Phillips best try mark established the previous season. Reading's first full time professional Andre Bachelet, his half back partner Jerry Costeloe, Danny Barrett, Tom Ellis and Greg Anstead, who won the Most Improved Player award, all proved valuable captures and Paul Neary's experience boosted the pack.

A new look side lost five of the first six National League Three encounters and after that promotion was always a forlorn hope, but the club rallied strongly in mid-season to gain their best ever placing in the national structure. Reading were the only club to win at promoted Fylde and they completed doubles over Clifton, Havant, Liverpool St. Helens, Lydney and Walsall the latter in a 44-42 triumph thanks to three late tries.

The only ever present Paul Guttridge was named Player of the Season, while the club had the honour of two players, Andre Bachelet and Mark Scharrenberg, representing the USA against Wales at Cardiff in January with Bachelet scoring the best try of the match.

Reading RFC; Back Row (L-R); Tewkesbury (Dir of Rugby), Ellis, H R Jones, Sparks, Nicholson, Spencer, Vatcher, Pratt, Till, Neary, Kemp, Turrell, Roberts (Asst Coach). Front Row; Stevenson, McCormack, Harris, Rolfe, Fanning, Wyeth, Dance, Dixon, Hopkins, Bachelet.

Colours: Myrtle & white irregular hoops/navy/myrtle.

Change colours: Navy with white 'V'.

COURAGE LEAGUE MATCH DETAILS 1996-97

No	Ven.	Date	Opponents	Att.	Res.	Score	Scorers
1	(A)	31.08	v Harrogate	Att.	L	31-40	Fanning(2t)Wyeth(t)Ellis(t)Dance(t3c)
2	(H)	07.09	v Leeds		L	16-35	Pratt(t)Guttridge(t)Boulard(2p)
3	(A)	14.09	v London Welsh		L	17-21	Sparkes(t)Belshaw(t2cp)
4	(H)	21.09	v Lydney		W	25-11	Ellis(t)Harris(t)Spencer(t)Belshaw(2c2p)
5	(A)	28.09	v Redruth		L	14-20	Harris(t)Belshaw(3p)
6	(H)	05.10	v Morley		L	24-34	Fanning(2t)Kemp(t)Spencer(t)Dance(2c)
7	(A)	12.10	v Clifton		W	40-22	HR Jones(2t)Ballard(t)C Hutson(t)Dance(t3c3p)
8	(H)	19.10	v Fylde		D	19-19	Dunn(t)Dance(c4p)
9	(A)	26.10	v Havant		W	30-21	Neary(2t)Spencer(t)Kemp(t)Dance(2c2p)
10	(H)	09.11	v Liverpool StH		W	65-26	Barrett(2t)Bachelet(2t)Vatcher(t)H Jones(t)Fanning(t)Costeloe(t)Pratt(t)Harris(t)Belshaw(6cp)
11	(A)	16.11	v Otley		L	20-31	Dunn(t)Martin(t)Belshaw(2c2p)
12	(H)	18.01	v Harrogate		W	22-20	Ellis(2t)Barrett(t)Dance(2cp)
13	(A)	25.01	v Leeds		L	16-25	Costeloe(t)Barrett(t)Dance(2p)
14	(H)	01.02	v London Welsh		W	32-17	Barrett(2t)Spencer(2t)Guttridge(t)Dance(2cp)
15	(A)	08.02	v Lydney		W	25-18	Spencer(3t)Dance(2c2p) Costeloe(t)Dance(9cp)
16	(H)	15.02	v Redruth		W	71- 3	Bachelet(2t)Spencer(2t)Ellis(t)Harris(t)Scharrenberg(t)Bachelet(t)Anstead(t)
17	(A)	22.02	v Morley		L	12-25	Costeloe(dg)Dance(3p) Sparkes(t)Hutson(t)PenTry(t)Dance(t10c)
18	(H)	01.03	v Clifton		W	75-12	Anstead(t)Costelloe(t)Spencer(t)Barrett(t)Fanning(t)Guttridge(t)Ellis(t)
19	(A)	08.03	v Fylde		W	21-16	Bachelet(t)Scharrenberg(t)Dance(c3p)
20	(H)	15.03	v Havant		W	54-13	Spencer(2t)Vatcher(t)Pratt(t)Costeloe(t)Hart(t)Scharrenberg(t)Dance(t7c)
21	(A)	22.03	v Liverpool StH		W	27-16	Scharrenberg(3t)Dance(3c2p)
22	(H)	29.03	v Walsall		W	49-16	Pratt(t)Guttridge(t)Harris(t)Costeloe(t)Harris(t)Dance(t5c3p)
23	(A)	02.04	v Rosslyn Park		L	25-29	Costeloe(t)Sparkes(t)Guttridge(t)Dance(2c2p)
24	(H)	05.04	v Otley		W	21-19	Ellis(t)Bachelet(t)Dance(c3p)
25	(A)	12.04	v Walsall		W	44-42	Costeloe(2t)C Hutson(t)Barrett(t)Vatcher(t)Fanning(t)Dance(4c2p)
26	(H)	19.04	v Rosslyn Park		W	17-12	Hart(t)Dance(4p)
27	(H)	26.04	v Wharfdale		W	25-10	Costeloe(2t)Sparkes(t)Belshaw(2c2p)
28	(A)	03.05	v Exeter		L	16-30	Pratt(t)Dance(c3p)
29	(A)	10.05	v Wharfdale		L	13-15	Dance(tc2p)
30	(H)	17.05	v Exeter		L	3-13	Ballard(dg)

1996-97 HIGHLIGHTS

LEAGUE DEBUTS: Malcolm Kemp, Andy Wyeth, Tom Ellis, Greg Anstead, Paul Neary, Huw R Jones, Paul Boulard, Paul Hopkins, Mike McCormack, Danny Barrett, Andre Bachelet, Jerry Costeloe, Chris Martin, Mark Scharrenberg, John Murley, Kevin Hughes, Adam Rolfe.

TRY ON DEBUT: Andy Wyeth, Tom Ellis and Chris Martin.

PLAYERS USED: 38 plus 1 as replacement.

EVER PRESENT: Paul Guttridge.

❑ Fourth highest try scorers in the division.

❑ Jason Dance breaks Phil Belshaw's 1994-95 record of 204 points in a season as he tops the points scoring list for the first time with 281.

	Pts	T	C	P	D	Apps	Ave.
Jason Dance 96-97	281	6	61	43	-	23	12.21
Phil Belshaw 94-95	204	1	26	49	-	17	12.00

Dance breaks Belshaw's record of 26 conversions with his 61. He also breaks Belshaw's record of six conversions in a match with 10 against Clifton in the 75-12 win.

❑ Ex Bournemouth winger Guy Spencer broke Colin Phillips record of 12 tries in a season set the previous year. Spencer goes one better to score 13 in 20 matches including a hat-trick against Lydney which equalled the club record for tries in a season.

❑ Mid season won 12 out of 14 but ended the season with three straight losses one short of their worst run.

READING'S COURAGE LEAGUE MATCH DETAILS 1996-97

	15	14	13	12	11	10	9	1	2	3	4	5	6	7	8	Replacements
1	Fanning	Kemp	Wyeth	Dixon	Spencer	Dance	Ellis	Guttridge	Stevenson	Anstead	Vatcher	Pratt	Neary	HR.Jones	Sparkes	
2	Fanning	Dunn	Kemp	Dixon	Spencer	Boulard	Ellis	Guttridge	Stevenson	Anstead	Vatcher	Pratt	Neary	HR.Jones	Sparkes	
3	Belshaw	Dunn	Kemp	Dixon	Spencer	Boulard	Ellis	Guttridge	Stevenson	Anstead	Vatcher	Pratt	Neary	HR.Jones	Sparkes	Harris(2)
4	Belshaw	Dunn	Kemp	Dixon	Spencer	Boulard	Ellis	Guttridge	Stevenson	Anstead	Vatcher	Pratt	Neary	HR.Jones	Sparkes	Dow(5)
5	Belshaw	Hopkins	Kemp	Dixon	Spencer	Ballard	Ellis	McCormack	Guttridge	Anstead	Vatcher	Pratt	Neary	HR.Jones	Sparkes	Dow(5)
6	Dance	Kemp	Fanning	Dixon	Spencer	Ballard	Ellis	McCormack	Guttridge	Anstead	Vatcher	Dow	Neary	HR.Jones	Sparkes	
7	Dance	Kemp	Fanning	Barrett	Spencer	Ballard	Bachelet	Guttridge	Harris	Anstead	Vatcher	Dow	Hart	HR.Jones	Sparkes	HR.Jones(7),C.Hutson(8)
8	Dance	Kemp	Fanning	Barrett	Spencer	Ballard	Bachelet	Guttridge	Harris	Anstead	C.Hutson	Dow	Hart	HR.Jones	Sparkes	Armstrong(6)
9	Dance	Kemp	Fanning	Spencer	Dunn	Costoloe	Bachelet	Guttridge	Harris	Anstead	C.Hutson	Pratt	Hart	HR.Jones	Vatcher	Martin(10)
10	Belshaw	Dunn	Fanning	Dunn	Spencer	Ballard	Bachelet	Guttridge	Harris	Anstead	C.Hutson	Pratt	Hart	HR.Jones	Vatcher	Martin(10)
11	Belshaw	Martin	Fanning	Ellis	Martin	Dunn	Bachelet	Guttridge	Hughes	Anstead	Vatcher	Pratt	Hart	HR.Jones	Neary	Sparkes(6)
12	Dance	Ellis	Fanning	Barrett	Spencer	Costoloe	Bachelet	Guttridge	Harris	Anstead	Vatcher	Pratt	Hart	HR.Jones	Neary	Sparkes(6)
13	Dance	Ellis	Scharrenberg	Barrett	Spencer	Costoloe	Bachelet	Guttridge	Perkin	Anstead	Vatcher	Pratt	Hart	HR.Jones	Hart	Sparkes(6)
14	Dance	Ellis	Fanning	Barrett	Spencer	Costoloe	Bachelet	Guttridge	Harris	Anstead	Vatcher	Pratt	Hart	HR.Jones	Sparkes	Perkin(12),Scharrenberg(14)
15	Dance	Ellis	Fanning	Barrett	Spencer	Costoloe	Bachelet	Guttridge	Harris	Anstead	Vatcher	Pratt	Murley	Hart	Hart	Perkin(12),Scharrenberg(14)
16	Dance	Scharrenberg	Fanning	Barrett	Spencer	Costoloe	Bachelet	Guttridge	Harris	Anstead	Vatcher	Pratt	Murley	HR.Jones	Hart	Neary(6)
17	Dance	Scharrenberg	Fanning	Barrett	Spencer	Costoloe	Bachelet	Guttridge	Harris	Anstead	Vatcher	Pratt	Hart	HR.Jones	Hart	Neary(6)
18	Dance	Ellis	Fanning	Barrett	Spencer	Costoloe	Bachelet	Guttridge	Harris	Anstead	Vatcher	Pratt	Murley	HR.Jones	Sparks	Scharrenberg(14),Hutson(7).
19	Dance	Ellis	Fanning	Barrett	Spencer	Costoloe	Bachelet	Guttridge	Harris	Anstead	Vatcher	Pratt	Murley	HR.Jones	Sparkes	Scharrenberg(14)
20	Dance	Martin	Fanning	Barrett	Spencer	Wells	Wells	Guttridge	Harris	Anstead	Vatcher	Pratt	Hart	HR.Jones	Scharrenberg	Scharrenberg(12)
21	Dance	Ellis	Fanning	Barrett	Spencer	Costoloe	Wells	Guttridge	Harris	Anstead	Vatcher	Pratt	Hart	Murley	Sparkes	Hutson(5)Dow(rr5)
22	Dance	Ellis	Fanning	Barrett	Spencer	Costoloe	Bachelet	Guttridge	Harris	Anstead	Vatcher	Pratt	Murley	Murley	Sparkes	Perkin(2)Barrett(12)Dow(8)
23	Dance	Ellis	Fanning	Scharrenberg	Scharrenberg	Costoloe	Bachelet	Guttridge	Harris	Anstead	Dow	Pratt	Murley	Murley	Vatcher	Perkin(2)Barrett(12)Dow(8)
24	Dance	Kemp	Fanning	Barrett	Spencer	Ballard	Bachelet	Guttridge	Perkin	Anstead	Vatcher	Pratt	Murley	HR.Jones	Sparkes	Harris(2)Costoloe(11)
25	Dance	Ellis	Fanning	Barrett	Spencer	Costoloe	Bachelet	Guttridge	Rolfe	Perkin	Vatcher	Pratt	Sparkes	HR.Jones	C.Hutson	Anstead(3)Stevenson(2)H.Jones(7)
26	Dance	Hopkins	Fanning	Barrett	Spencer	Costoloe	Bachelet	Guttridge	Harris	Anstead	Vatcher	Pratt	Hart	Murley	Belshaw	Belshaw(14)
27	Belshaw	R.Hutson	Fanning	Barrett	Spencer	Costoloe	Bachelet	Guttridge	Harris	Anstead	Vatcher	Pratt	Hart	Murley	Sparkes	HR.Jones(7)
28	Dance	Ellis	Fanning	Barrett	Spencer	Costoloe	Wells	Guttridge	Harris	Anstead	Vatcher	Pratt	Hart	Murley	Sparkes	Belshaw(14)H.Jones(10)
29	Dance	Kemp	Fanning	Warren	R.Hutson	Ballard	Ellis	Guttridge	Harris	Anstead	Vatcher	Pratt	Hart	Murley	Sparkes	C.Hutson(6)Rolfe(1)
30	Dance	R.Hutson	Fanning	Warren	Kemp	Ballard	Ellis	Guttridge	Harris	Anstead	Vatcher	Pratt	Hart	Murley	Sparkes	HR.Jones(4)

READING LEAGUE STATISTICS
(COMPILED BY STEPHEN McCORMACK)

Season	Div.	P	W	D	L	F	(Tries	Con	Pen	DG)	A	(Tries	Con	Pen	DG)	Most Points	Most Tries
87-88	SW2	10	7	1	2	146	(27	8	7	0)	75	(7	4	13	0)	27 - Neil Spencer	5 - Neil Spencer & Rodney Hutson
88-89	SW1	10	5	0	5	144	(22	10	11	1)	146	(24	7	11	1)	55 - Phil Belshaw	3 - Jon Deane & Curtis Hutson.
89-90	SW1	10	3	0	7	128	(22	8	7	1)	207	(30	15	18	1)	45 - Phil Belshaw	3 - Gary Williams & Alan Spence
90-91	SW1	10	7	1	2	208	(36	14	11	1)	100	(12	5	14	0)	43 - Phil Belshaw	6 - Paul Roberts & Curtis Hutson
91-92	SW1	10	4	0	6	120	(15	9	12	2)	163	(27	8	12	1)	36 - Martin Radford	4 - John Dixon & Rodney Hutson
92-93	SW1	12	11	0	1	267	(32	16	25	0)	99	(9	3	15	1)	104 - Phil Belshaw	6 Rodney Hutson & Mark Alexander
93-94	D5S	12	10	1	1	248	(26	8	34	0)	61	(5	3	10	0)	133 - Phil Belshaw	5 - Ian McGeevoer
94-95	4	18	14	1	3	435	(44	28	52	1)	319	(33	17	36	4)	204 - Phil Belshaw	6 - Curtis Hutson
95-96	3	18	5	1	12	397	(41	30	40	4)	484	(57	29	41	6)	103 - Phil Belshaw	12 - Colin Phillips
96-97	3	30	17	1	12	869	(109	75	56	2)	631	(74	45	54	3)	281 - Jason Dance	13 - Guy Spencer
Totals		140	83	6	51	2962	(374	206	255	12)	2285	(308	136	224	17)		

HOME
BIGGEST WIN	(68pts)	71-3 v Redruth 15.2.97
DEFEAT	(26pts)	27-53 v Coventry 27.4.96
MOST POINTS SCORED		75-12 v Clifton 1.3.97
AGAINST		27-53 v Coventry 27.4.96

AWAY
(36pts)	46-10 v Gordon League
(34pts)	10-44 v Harrogate 13.4.96
	46-10 v Gordon League
	10-44 v Harrogate 13.4.96

MOST CONSECUTIVE VICTORIES - 18

MOST CONSECUTIVE DEFEATS - 4

MOST TRIES IN A MATCH
(FOR) 11 v Salisbury (H), v Clifton 1.3.97 (H)
(AGAINST) 7 v Coventry 27.4.96 (H)

MOST APPEARANCES
FORWARD: Kevin Jones
BACK: Rodney Huston

CONSECUTIVE APPEARANCES
47 Ian Turnell

CONSECUTIVE SCORING MATCHES
Scoring Tries - 4 - Colin Phillips
Scoring Points - 34 - Phil Belshaw

MOST	in a SEASON	in a CAREER	in a MATCH
Points	281 jason Dance 96-97	771 Phil Belshaw 88-97	26 Greg Way v Harrogate 16.9.95 (H)
Tries	13 Guy Spencer 96-97	28 Curtis Hutson 87-97	3 Curtis Hutson v Torquay (H) Mark Alexander v Penry (A) Colin Phillps v Otley 6.4.96 (H) Guy Spencer v Lydney 8.2.97 (A) Mark Scharrenberg v L.St.H. 22.3.97 (A)
Conversions	61 Jason Dance 96-97	115 Phil Belshaw 88-97	10 Jason Dance v Clifton 1.3.97 (H)
Penalties	49 Phil Belshaw 94-95	165 Phil Belshaw 88-97	7 Phil Belshaw v Morley 14.10.95 (H)
Drop Goals	3 Dave Hill 95-96	3 Simon Rogers 87-95 Dave Hill 95-96	1 on 12 occasions by 8 players incl. Simon Rogers (x3) & Dave Hill (x3)

READING PLAYING SQUAD

BACKS

NAME	Ht	Wt	Birthdate	Birthplace	Club	Apps	Pts	T	C	P	DG
Lee Fanning	5.10	13.0	08.07.72	Romford							
					Reading	61	70	14	-	-	-
Malcolm Kemp											
					Reading	11	10	2	-	-	-
Guy Spencer	6.3	14.4	22.06.67	Wendover	Prev. Clubs: Biggleswade, Bournemouth						
					Reading	20	65	13	-	-	-
Jason Dance	5.8	12.10	08.11.70	Basingstoke	Exeter	3	12	-	3	2	-
					Reading	39	309	6	71	48	1
Tom Ellis	5.10	13.3	05.10.71	Kings Lynn	Saracens						
					Reading	24	40	8	-	-	-
Richard Ballard	5.10	11.6	28.09.74	Reading							
					Reading	10+2	8	1	-	-	1
Jerry Costeloe	5.10	12.4	25.11.74	Weston-s-Mare							
					Reading	18+1	58	11	-	-	1
Andre Baihelet U.S.A.	5.7	13.0	11.03.70	Sydney(Aus)	Old Blues (USA)						
					Reading	20	30	6	-	-	-
Mark Scharrenberg											
					Reading	5+4	30	6	-	-	-
James Warren	5.10	14.10	20.11.72	Reading	Redingensians						
					Reading	11+1	-	-	-	-	-
Danny Barrett English Universities	5.8	13.0	27.11.74	Brentwood	Saracens						
					Reading	19+1	45	9	-	-	-
Rodney Hutson	5.11	13.0	22.07.67	Reading							
					Reading	71	120	27	-	-	-
Paul Hopkins	5.10	12.4	05.08.70	Prev. Clubs: Dunvant, Newport.							
					Reading	3	-	-	-	-	-
Phil Belshaw	6.0	13.6	15.12.69	Reading	Bracknell						
					Reading	89+2	-	-	-	-	-

FORWARDS

NAME	Ht	Wt	Birthdate	Birthplace	Club	Apps	Pts	T	C	P	DG
Paul Guttridge	6.0	17.0	04.07.64	Reading	Prev. Clubs: Bristol, Richmond.						
					Reading	84	51	11	-	-	-
Greg Anstead	5.11	17.0	06.03.75	Bridgetown (Bar)	Bracknell						
					Reading	27+1	10	2	-	-	-
JJ Harris	5.9	15.0	22.10.72	Beaconsfield							
					Reading	37+2	25	5	-	-	-
Scott Perkin England: Colts, u18, u16.	5.7	14.0	19.03.74	Penzance	St. Ives						
					Reading	11+3	5	1	-	-	-
Mark Vatcher	6.4	17.7	08.03.71	Carshalton	Previous Clubs: Hull, Headingley, Rosslyn Park.						
					Reading	44+1	30	6	-	-	-
Danny Pratt England: Colts.	6.7	18.7	18.02.63	York	Wasps	1	-	-	-	-	-
					Reading	102	50	11	-	-	-
Graham Sparks	6.2	16.0	16.07.74	Taplow	Maidenhead						
					Reading	30+3	15	3	-	-	-
Curtis Hutson	6.4	19.5	28.02.65	Reading							
					Reading	109+5	137	28	-	-	-
Rub Dow	6.4	17.10	12.10.70		Prev. Clubs: Old Colfeians, Rosslyn Park						
					Reading	9+4	-	-	-	-	-
John Murley				Penzance	Prev. Clubs: Harlequins, Bracknell.						
					Reading	12	-	-	-	-	-
Martin Hart	6.4	17.5	23.02.63		Prev. Clubs: Maidenhead, Bracknell.						
					Reading	28	20	4	-	-	-
Huw Jones	5.11	14.4	25.10.70	Pontypridd							
					Reading	13+3	5	1	-	-	-
Huw R Jones	5.10	14.6	04.04.71	Carmarthen							
					Reading	9+3	10	2	-	-	-
Simon Stevenson	5.11	17.7	17.02.69	Oxford							
					Reading	9+1	-	-	-	-	-
Adam Rolfe	5.8	16.0	06.11.75	Bath	Bath						
					Reading	1+2	-	-	-	-	-

Holme Park Sonning Lane, Sonning, Reading RG4 0ST

Tel: 01734 696592   **Fax:** 01734 696592

Capacity: 2,500   **Seated:** 200   **Standing:** 2,300
Simple Directions: A4 Reading to Maidenhead Road, turn left 2 1/2 miles out of Reading, sign posted Sonning
Nearest Railway Station: Reading BR
Car Parking: 250 on ground, unlimited nearby
Admission: Season Price on aplication
Matchday; Adults non-members £5, members £4, Children members free, non-members £3.
Clubhouse: Normal Licensing Hours, snacks & bar meals available.
Function Facilities: Yes, capacity 80/200 - contact Tim Pratt 01189 696592
Clubshop: Yes, contact Tim Pratt 01189 696592
Training Nights: Tuesday & Thursday

Captain; Lee Fanning

Player of the Year; Paul Guttridge

MATCHDAY PROGRAMME

Size	A5
Number of pages	72
Price	Included with admission
Programme Editor	Nigel Sutcliffe 01189 696592
Advertising Rates	Mono Full page £200
	Half page £125
	Qtr page £75

ROSSLYN PARK F.C.

NICKNAME: The Park   FOUNDED: 1879

President Keith Young, 22 Holme Chase, St George's Avenue, Weybridge, Surrey KT13 0BZ
01932 847543 (H), 01932 568833 (B).

Chairman Geoff Bayles, Valley House, 6 Boyle Farm Road, Thames Ditton, Surrey KT7 0TS
0181 398 6656 (H), 0181 224 8607 (Fax)

Club Secretary David Whittam FRCS, 37 Queens Road, Kingston-on-Thames, Surrey. KT2 7SL.
0181 549 4209 (H), 0181 725 2052 (B), 0181 944 8059 (Fax)

Commercial Manager Alan Young, c/o Rosslyn Park RFC, Priory Lane, Roehampton, London SW15 5JH
0181 876 6044 (B), 0181 878 7527 (Fax)

Director of Rugby Robert Harding, 2 Barham Road, South Croydon, Surrey CR2 6LD
0181 688 5409 (H), 0181 640 9521 (B), 0181 681 0076 (Fax)

Chief Coach Frank Booth, 01439 788 277

Press Officer Bernard Wiggins, 01403 711299 (H), 01273 323434 (B), 01273 202627 (Fax)

Fixtures Secretary Charlie Addiman, 0181 874 6638 (H & Fax)

For Rosslyn Park the season 1996/97 could not have got off to a worse possible start. Of the first three matches, two being played away, Park suffered their heaviest defeat for some seasons, having 96 points scored against them in their first two away games. However, fortunately we were able to acquire the services of Frank Booth as coaching director to the club who soon acquainted himself with the task of reviving past fortunes and this he did in no small way. During the rest of the season Park won all their games at Home with the exception of Morley when they suffered a very narrow defeat, but it was not until the middle of February that Park were able to register their first away League match, but at least they managed to keep their winning ways at home for the remainder of the season. Amongst their notable wins at home were victories against Exeter and Leeds who in the first two matches of the season scored over 40 points against the Park.

Several games were lost over bad kicking, and failure to take opportunities to score when they arose, but gradually the team began to build in confidence and finish just above the middle of the table by the end of the season. Their success in the Pilkington Cup was short lived having dispatched Havant in the second round Park were quite well beaten by Rotherham in an away tie played in apparently appalling conditions.

During this season, Park have remained very much an amateur club. Players are not paid except for reasonable expenses although several clubs in lower leagues in the neighbourhood are paying their players albeit a fairly paltry match fee and also a fee for winning. There has clearly developed a large gulf between the fully professional clubs particularly in League One and the remainder of the Leagues. How long this will remain and whether it will be permanent only the future will tell. Clearly the lack of guidance this past season from the Rugby Union has to be addressed. There are many grievances which have not been settled, but as far as the Park are concerned with newly acquired players for next season every effort will be made to seek promotion to the higher leagues.

Rosslyn Park FC; 1st XV 1997

Colours: Red and white hoops.   **Change colours:** Dark blue and red hoop.

ROSSLYN PARK

No	Ven.	Date	Opponents	Att.	Res.	Score	Scorers
1	(A)	31.08	v Exeter		L	6-47	Maddock(2p)
2	(H)	07.09	v Harrogate		W	19-16	Henderson(2t)Springhall(t)Dowse(2c)
3	(A)	14.09	v Leeds		L	5-49	Marvel(t)
4	(H)	21.09	v London Welsh		W	27-10	Fennell(t)Boardman(t)Dowse(2t2cp)
5	(A)	28.09	v Lydney		L	13-34	Henderson(2t)Dowse(p)
6	(H)	05.10	v Redruth		W	37-23	Futter(t)C-Lamerton(t)Marvel(t)Maddock(t)Ruffell(t)Henderson(t)Dowse(2cp)
7	(A)	12.10	v Morley		L	14-15	Fennell(t)Dowse(3p)
8	(H)	19.10	v Clifton		W	22- 6	Sinclair(t)Rakison(t)Smith(t)Dowse(2cp)
9	(A)	26.10	v Fylde		L	8-40	Rakison(t)Dowse(p)
10	(H)	09.11	v Havant		W	22-17	Stratford(t)Sinclair(t)Sandilands(3p)Dowse(dg)
11	(A)	16.11	v Liverpool StH		L	21-29	Fennell(t)Dowse(tc3p)
12	(H)	18.01	v Exeter		W	36-10	C-Lamerton(t)Fennell(t)Currie(t)Middleton(t)Holder(t4cp)
13	(A)	25.01	v Harrogate		L	20-25	Currie(t)PenTry(t)Holder(2c2p)
14	(H)	01.02	v Leeds		W	20-14	Dalwood(t)Currie(t)Holder(tcp)
15	(A)	08.02	v London Welsh		L	25-28	Smither(2t)Springhall(t)Holder(2c2p)
16	(H)	15.02	v Lydney		W	22- 3	Ford(t)Smith(t)Ritchie(t)Holder(2cp)
17	(A)	22.02	v Redruth		W	25- 8	Sinclair(2t)Rakisson(t)Holder(2c2p)
18	(H)	01.03	v Morley		L	8-14	Strong(t)Holder(p)
19	(A)	08.03	v Clifton		W	13- 8	Holder(t)Smither(t)Booth(p)
20	(H)	15.03	v Fylde		W	18- 5	C-Lamerton(t)Fennell(t)Holder(cpdg)
21	(A)	22.03	v Havant		L	17-18	C-Lamerton(t)Futter(t)Holder(2cp)
22	(H)	29.03	v Otley		W	39-15	Rakison(4t)Currie(t)C-Lamerton(t)Maddock(3c)Booth(p)
23	(H)	02.04	v Reading		W	29-25	Fennell(t)Ritchie(t)McLeod(t)Futter(t)Maddock(2cp)Holder(c)
24	(H)	05.04	v Liverpool StH		W	25- 7	Booth(t)Smith(t)Smither(t)Currie(t)Maddock(c)Holder(p)
25	(A)	12.04	v Otley		L	8-39	Currie(t)Holder(p)
26	(A)	19.04	v Reading		L	12-17	Holder(4p)
27	(H)	26.04	v Walsall		W	25-19	Marvel(t)Fennell(t)Holder(5p)
28	(A)	03.05	v Wharfdale		L	31-45	Ford(t)Middleton(t)Currie(t)McLeod(t)Bailey(c3p)
29	(A)	10.05	v Walsall		W	35-13	Rakison(2t)Booth(t)Maslen(t)Sandilands(t2c2p)
30	(H)	17.05	v Wharfdale		W	28-21	Maslen(t)Henderson(t)Dalwood(t)Sandilands(t2c3p)

1996-97 HIGHLIGHTS

LEAGUE DEBUTS: Patrick Hartigan, Toby Rakison, Matt Dowse, Crawford Henderson, Richard Bailey, Dave Ruffell, Rupert Holt, Graham Boardman, Keith Middleton, Nick Marvel, John Moore, Ian Jardine-Brown, Paul Futter, Ray Brown, Olly Martin, Nick Coulter, Lysander Strong, Simon Thompson, Tony Dalwood, Ian McLeod, Alaster Sandilands, Richard Harding, Ben Maslen, Richard Booth, Charlie Abbon.

TRY ON DEBUT: Nick Marvel.

PLAYERS USED: 48 plus 5 as replacement only.

EVER PRESENT: None
— most appearances 27 Chris Ritchie.

❏ Achieved their best ever away win 35-13 at Walsall.

❏ Won 14 of 15 at home - the only defeat by Morley.

❏ Stand-off Andy Holder tops the club's points scoring list for the first time and in the process becomes the first man to score 100 points in a season for them.

	Pts	T	C	P	D	Apps	Ave.
Andy Holder 96-97	121	3	17	23	1	15	8.07
John Graves 90-91	92	2	12	20	-	12	7.66

Holder breaks Graves's record 13 conversions in a season set in 1988-89 with his 17 also broken was his record of 21 penalties with Holder getting 23.

❏ No 8 Toby Rakison equals Shane Roiser's record of 11 tries in a season dating back to 1993-94. Roiser's tries came in 16 matches compared to Rakison's 20. Rakison also broke Tony Brooks's record of three tries in a game with four at home to Otley.

ROSSLYN PARK'S COURAGE LEAGUE MATCH DETAILS 1996-97

#	15	14	13	12	11	10	9	1	2	3	4	5	6	7	8	Replacements	#
1	Dowse	Henderson	Hartigan	Maddock	Blake	Bailey	Springhall	Fennell	Ritchie	Vas	Ruffell	Gibson	Rakison	Nightingale	Smith	Geese(11),Holt(r11),Ford(3)	1
2	Dowse	Henderson	Currie	Maddock	Blake	Bailey	Springhall	Fennell	Ritchie	Vas	Ruffell	Gibson	Stratford	Boardman	Middleton	Hartigan(11)	2
3	Dowse	Currie	Marvel	Maddock		Bailey	Springhall	Fennell	Ritchie	Ford	Ruffell	Gibson	Stratford	Boardman	Middleton		3
4	Currie	Henderson	Marvel	Maddock	Bailey	Bailey	Springhall	Fennell	Ritchie	Ford	Ruffell	Gibson	Stratford	Boardman	Middleton		4
5	Maddock	Moore	Dickinson	Hartigan	Henderson	Dowse	Springhall	Fennell	Ritchie	Ford	Ruffell	Gibson	J-Brown	Boardman	Smith		5
6	Currie	Henderson	Maddock	Marvel	Futter	Dowse	Springhall	Fennell	Ritchie	Vas	Ruffell	C-Lamerton	Boardman	Rakison		Smyth(5)	6
7	Brown	Sinclair	Maddock	Marvel	Dowse	Dowse	Springhall	Fennell	Ritchie	Vas	Ruffell	C-Lamerton	Stratford	Martin	Rakison		7
8	Currie	Henderson	Maddock	Maddock	Dowse	Dowse	Springhall	Fennell	Ritchie	Ford	C-Lamerton	C-Lamerton	Smith	Boardman	Rakison	Gibson(6)	8
9	Currie	Giffin	Nickalls	Marvel	Sinclair	Dowse	Springhall	Fennell	Ritchie	Ford	C-Lamerton	Gibson	Smith	Boardman	Rakison	Gibson(6)	9
10	Brown	Sinclair	Nickalls	Dalwood	Sandilands	Dowse	Springhall	Fennell	Holt	Vas	Ruffell	Stratford	Strong	Boardman	Rakison	Futter(11),C-Lamerton(5),Henwood(tr1)	10
11	Brown	Simclair	Maddock	Nickalls	Futter	Dowse	Henwood	Fennell	Ritchie	Holt	C-Lamerton	Gibson	Strong	Boardman	Rakison	Thompson(3)	11
12	Currie	Henderson	Maddock	Marvel	Dowse	Coulter	Henwood	Fennell	Ritchie	Ford	C-Lamerton	Gibson	McLeod	Boardman	Rakison	Graves(15),Middleton(6)	12
13	Currie	Henderson	Maddock	Marvel	Sinclair	Springhall	Henwood	Fennell	Ritchie	Ford	C-Lamerton	Gibson	McLeod	Boardman	Middleton	Middleton(6)	13
14	Currie	Henderson	Maddock	Dalwood	Sinclair	Springhall	Henwood	Fennell	Ritchie	Ford	C-Lamerton	Gibson	Oliver	Boardman	Rakison	Strong(8)	14
15	Currie	Smither	Maddock	Dalwood	Futter	Springhall	Henwood	Fennell	Ritchie	Ford	C-Lamerton	Gibson	Strong	Boardman	Rakison	Hadley(15)	15
16	Graves	Smither	Maddock	Dalwood	Futter	Springhall	Henwood	Fennell	Ritchie	Ford	C-Lamerton	Gibson	Smith	Boardman	Rakison	Dickinson(15).	16
17	Dickinson	Smither	Maddock	Dalwood	Sinclair	Springhall	Henwood	Fennell	Ritchie	Ford	C-Lamerton	Gibson	Smith	Boardman	Rakison	Harding(2)Fennell(1)	17
18	Dickinson	Smither	Maddock	Dalwood	Sinclair	Springhall	Springhall	Fennell	Ritchie	Ford	Ruffell	Gibson	Oliver	McLeod	Rakison	Strong(6).	18
19	Currie	Henderson	Maddock	Dalwood	Smither	Holder	Booth	Fennell	Ritchie	Ford	Millward	Gibson	Smith	Rakison	Rakison	McLeod(5).	19
20	Currie	Smither	Maddock	Dalwood	Smither	Holder	Booth	Fennell	Ritchie	Ford	Millward	Gibson	Smith	Boardman	Middleton	Middleton	20
21	Currie	Maslen	Maddock	Dalwood	Futter	Holder	Booth	Fennell	Harding	Ford	Millward	Smith	Boardman	Boardman	Middleton	McLeod(7)	21
22	Currie	Smither	Maddock	Dalwood	Futter	Holder	Booth	Fennell	Ritchie	Ford	Millward	McLeod	McLeod	Boardman	Rakison	Dickinson(15)Smith(6)	22
23	Currie	Smither	Maddock	Dalwood		Holder	Booth	Fennell	Ritchie	Ford	Millward	McLeod	McLeod	Boardman	Smith	Smith	23
24	Currie	Smither	Maddock	Dalwood	Futter	Holder	Booth	Fennell	Ritchie	Ford	Millward	McLeod	McLeod	Boardman	Smith	Strong(tr8)	24
25	Currie	Abbon	Maslen	Dalwood	Smither	Holder	Booth	Fennell	Ritchie	Oliver	Millward	C-Lamerton	McLeod	Boardman	Smith	Middleton(8)Dickinson(14)	25
26	Currie	Smither	Maddock	Dalwood	Futter	Holder	Booth	Fennell	Ritchie	Ford	Millward	C-Lamerton	McLeod	Boardman	Rakison	Vas(3)Dickinson(13)	26
27	Dickinson	Currie	Maddock	Dalwood	Futter	Holder	Booth	Fennell	Vas	Ford	Millward	C-Lamerton	Rakison	Boardman	Smith	Fay(3)Maslen(13)	27
28	Currie	Henderson	Marvel	Dalwood	Abbon	Holder	Booth	Cooke	Ritchie	Ford	Millward	C-Lamerton	McLeod	Boardman	Middleton	Maslen(12)	28
29	Currie	Henderson	Marvel	Dalwood	Sandilands	Bailey	Cooke	Cooke	Ritchie	Ford	Millward	C-Lamerton	Middleton	Boardman	Rakison	McLeod(tr7)Hadley(tr13)	29
30	Slater	Henderson	Maslen	Dalwood	Sandilands	Bailey	Booth	Fennell	Ritchie	Ford	Millward	C-Lamerton	Middleton	Boardman	Rakison	Rakison	30

ROSSLYN PARK LEAGUE STATISTICS
(COMPILED BY STEPHEN McCORMACK)

Season	Div.	P	W	D	L	F	(Tries	Con	Pen	DG)	A	(Tries	Con	Pen	DG)	Most Points	Most Tries
87-88	2	11	8	2	1	155	(20	9	17	2)	83	(8	3	14	1)	73 - John Graves	6 - Tony Brooks
88-89	1	11	5	0	6	172	(20	13	21	1)	208	(22	12	30	2)	89 - John Graves	3 - by 3 players - Simon Hunter, Richard Crawford & Rob Nelson-Williams.
89-90	1	11	4	0	7	164	(19	8	21	3)	243	(40	19	15	0)	87 - John Graves	4 - Mark Jermyn
90-91	1	12	6	0	6	216	(30	12	20	4)	174	(15	9	27	5)	92 - John Graves	3 - by 3 players - Peter Taylor, Guy Leleu & Kelvin Wyles.
91-92	1	12	0	1	11	111	(12	3	17	2)	258	(24	18	36	6)	53 - John Graves	2 - Mark Thomas & Kelvin Wyles.
92-93	2	12	5	0	7	209	(17	5	36	2)	199	(13	7	34	6)	61 - John Graves & Gary Abraham	3 - Paul Essenhigh
93-94	3	18	10	1	7	372	(48	27	25	1)	240	(28	11	23	3)	59 - Paul Roblin	9 - Shane Roiser
94-95	3	18	10	0	8	313	(38	18	24	5)	280	(22	10	46	4)	54 - Mike Giffin	5 - Tim Smither & Adam Vander
95-96	3	18	3	2	13	290	(29	17	31	6)	426	(46	29	44	2)	45 - John Rowlands	5 - Mike Giffin
96-97	3	30	17	0	13	630	(80	37	50	2)	620	(70	45	58	2)	121 - Andy Holder	9 - Toby Rakison
Totals		153	68	6	79	2632	(313	149	262	28)	2731	(288	163	327	29)		

	HOME	AWAY
BIGGEST WIN	(48pts) 48-0 v Northampton 27.4.91	(22pts) 35-13 v Walsall 10.5.97
BIGGEST DEFEAT	(29pts) 17-46 v Coventry 2.3.96	(50pts) 14-64 v Orrell 28.4.90
MOST POINTS SCORED	48-0 v Northampton 27.4.91	50-35 v Harrogate 29.4.95
AGAINST	17-46 v Coventry 2.3.96	14-64 v Orrell 28.4.90

MOST CONSECUTIVE VICTORIES - 5

MOST CONSECUTIVE DEFEATS - 8

MOST TRIES IN A MATCH
(FOR) 9 v Northampton 27.4.91 (H)
(AGAINST) 11 v Orrell 28.4.90 (A)

MOST APPEARANCES
FORWARD: 87 David Barnett
BACK: 63 John Graves

CONSECUTIVE APPEARANCES
45 John Graves 19.9.87 to 27.4.91

CONSECUTIVE SCORING MATCHES
Scoring Tries - 3 - Shane Rosier, Dan Perret, Adam Vander, David Currie (x2) & Ian Campbell-Lamerton.
Scoring Points - 25 - John Graves

MOST	in a SEASON	in a CAREER	in a MATCH
Points	121 Andy Holder 96-97	454 John Graves 87-93&96	22 John Graves v Coventry 13.2.93 (H)
Tries	9 Shane Rosier 93-94 Toby Rakison 96-97	16 Tony Brooks 87-93	4 Toby Rakison v Otley 29.3.97 (H)
Conversions	17 Andy Holder 96-97	44 John Graves 87-93&96	5 Alex King v Harrogate 29.4.95 (A)
Penalties	23 Andy Holder 96-97	117 John Graves 87-93&96	6 Gary Abraham v Morley 27.3.93 (H)
Drop Goals	3 Andy Maddock 94-95 & 95-96 John Rowland 95-96	6 Andy Holder 89-95 Andy Maddock 94-96	2 Paul Roblin v Gloucester 4.1.92 (A) Andy Maddock v Rotherham 6.4.96 (A)

ROSSLYN PARK PLAYING SQUAD

NAME	Ht	Wt	Birthdate	Birthplace	Club	Apps	Pts	T	C	P	DG

BACKS

NAME	Ht	Wt	Birthdate	Birthplace	Club	Apps	Pts	T	C	P	DG
Crawford Henderson	6.1	14.0	11.02.69		ondon Scottish	7	-	-	-	-	-
					Harlequins	6	5	1	-	-	-
Scotland u21. Anglo Scots u21. Middlesex.					Rosslyn Park	14	30	6	-	-	-
David Currie			01.08.69		Harlequins	1	-	-	-	-	-
					Rosslyn Park	24	40	8	-	-	-
Alastair Sandilands			21.01.68		Prev. Clubs: Sheffield, London Welsh.						
Yorkshire u21.					Rosslyn Park	3	37	1	4	8	-
Andy Holder			27.03.66								
					Rosslyn Park	58	164	6	22	25	5
Richard Booth			18.01.70		Sale	21+1	127	-	17	31	-
England: u21, u18. Yorkshire.					Rosslyn Park	12	16	2	-	2	-
Ben Maslen			23.03.72		Gloucester	2	-	-	-	-	-
					Rosslyn Park	5+2	10	2	-	-	-
Tony Dalwood			12.10.70		Saracens						
England Schools. London.					Rosslyn Park	19	10	2	-	-	-
Tim Smither			26.02.72		Harlequins						
London u21. Surrey u21.					Rosslyn Park	29	35	7	-	-	-
Paul Futter			16.04.71		Clifton	20	14	2	1	-	-
London. Surrey.					Rosslyn Park	13+1	15	3	-	-	-
Andy Maddock			01.10.72		Wasps	8	16	1	1	3	-
England: u21, Students, u18. London.					Rosslyn Park	50	76	3	11	7	6
Richard Bailey			05.09.76		Harlequins						
England: Schools					Rosslyn Park	6	11	-	1	3	-
Nick Marvel					Bristol	3	-	-	-	-	-
					Rosslyn Park	8	15	3	-	-	-
Ed Dickinson			18.11.70		Worcester						
Oxford Univ. English Universities.					Rosslyn Park	26+5	5	1	-	-	-
Tim Springhall			13.05.68		Blackheath	25+1	10	2	-	-	-
					Rosslyn Park	25+1	10	2	-	-	-

FORWARDS

NAME	Ht	Wt	Birthdate	Birthplace	Club	Apps	Pts	T	C	P	DG
Ben Fennell			16.08.71								
					Rosslyn Park	33+1	40	8	-	-	-
Chris Ritchie			03.11.70								
London. Surrey. Welsh Univ.					Rosslyn Park	43+1	10	2	-	-	-
Jason Ford			11.08.71		Prev. Clubs: Basingstoke, Havant						
England u21 squad. Hampshire.					Rosslyn Park	24+1	10	2	-	-	-
Alex Millward			23.10.68								
					Rosslyn Park	64+2	5	1	-	-	-
Ian Campbell-Lamerton			14.07.62		London Scottish						
London. Army. Scottish Exiles.					Rosslyn Park	69	30	6	-	-	-
Ian McLeod			13.08.70		London Scottish						
Surrey. Scottish Exiles.					Rosslyn Park	9+3	5	1	-	-	-
Toby Rakison			29.09.74		Prev. Clubs: Blackheath, Harlequins.						
					Rosslyn Park	21	45	9	-	-	-
Simon Smith			06.08.72		Coventry	14	10	2	-	-	-
					Rosslyn Park	14+1	15	3	-	-	-
Keith Middleton			30.11.69		Prev. Clubs: Havant, Richmond.						
England: u18. British Universities.					Rosslyn Park	8+3	10	2	-	-	-
Graham Boardman			04.04.71		Prev. Clubs: Old Emmanuel, Watsonians						
Surrey. Scottish Universities.					Rosslyn Park	27	5	1	-	-	-
Darryl Vas											
					Rosslyn Park	21+1	-	-	-	-	-
Lysander Strong			13.08.74		Rugby						
E. Midlands Colts.					Rosslyn Park	2+3	5	1	-	-	-
Dave Ruffell											
					Rosslyn Park	10	5	1	-	-	-
Lee Gibson			12.08.72								
					Rosslyn Park	32+2	-	-	-	-	-

Priory Lane, Roehampton, London SW15 5JH

Tel: 0181 876 1879   **Fax:** 0181 878 7527

Capacity: 4,630   **Seated:** 630   **Standing:** 4,000

Simple Directions: Ground situated at the junction of Upper Richmond Rd (Sth Circular) and Roehampton Lane

Nearest Railway Station: Barnes BR Southern from Waterloo. Leave station on downside, cross strip of common to Upper Richmond Rd traffic lights. Turn right entrance on Upper Richmond Rd.

Car Parking: 150 in the ground @ £2

Admission: Season - Adult £58.75: Matchday - Adults £5,   Concessions for Children/OAPs

Club Shop: Yes, contact Alan Young 0181 876 6044

Clubhouse: 11.00-11.00 every day, except Wednesday. Snacks, barmeals & restaurant available.
     Functions: Yes, capacity 300, contact Doug Bradford 0181 876 1879

Training Nights: Tuesday & Thursday

ROSSLYN PARK FOOTBALL CLUB (RFU)

AUDENTES FORTUNA JUVAT

1996–97 SEASON

Sponsored by
William Jacks Motor Group JACKS

Official Programme £1.00

MATCHDAY PROGRAMME

Size
     A5

Number of pages
     32 plus cover

Price
     £1

Programme Editor
     Alan Young
     0181 876 6044

Advertising Rates

     Colour Full page £400,
     Half page £260

     Mono Full page £300,
     Half page £160

RUGBY LIONS F.C.

NICKNAME: The Lions

FOUNDED: 1994

President Peter Galliford, c/o Rugby FC, Webb Ellis Road, Rugby, Warwickshire CV22 7AU
01788 542433. 01788 561509 (Fax)

Chairman David Owen, c/o Rugby FC, as above.
01788 542433. 01788 561509 (Fax)

Commercial Director Mick Adnitt, c/o Rugby FC, as above.
01788 542433. 01788 561509 (Fax)

Secretary Roger Large, 3 Red Lodge Drive, Rugby. CV22 7TT.
01788 816363 (H), 01788 542433 (B), 01788 561509 (Fax)

Fixtures Secretary Richard Stocking, 5 Cunning Way, Rugby, Warks.
01788 816598 (H), 01664 813925 (B), 01788 561509 (Fax)

Press Officer Roger Large, as above.

For one glorious season we had a taste of professional rugby and what a feast. Although eventually relegated through our own minimal financial resources we enjoyed our taste of the big time and it is our declared ambition to bounce back immediately into League Two to enjoy it again.

Though outplayed by professionals on a number of occasions, the team worked hard, tackled hard and did not give up against the internationals pitted against them. Indeed, our best performances were saved for the promotion contenders. On the other hand there were games which we should have won particularly in the first half of the season but we failed to peak for those games and paid the eventual price.

Even in the Pilkington Cup Lady Luck deserted us with an away tie against League One leaders, Wasps, and another heavy defeat followed. In a somewhat gloomy season it was good to see that despite everything Stuart Glover, Steve Smith and Jim Quantrill were selected for the Midlands and Paul Thompson for the Scottish Exiles.

Jim Quantrill was leading points scorer with 133 whilst Eddie Saunders was leading try scorer with thirteen tries. Two more very important milestones occurred in this otherwise disappointing season when David Bishop and Phil Bowman passed 300 games for the club.

We look forward to next season in League Three, we know it will not be easy to regain our place in League Two but we have to be totally professional and dedicate our time and effort to achieve our goal.

Rugby FC squad.

Photo - Rugby Advertiser

Colours: White, black, red & white

Change colours: Orange, black & white.

RUGBY

No	Ven.	Date	Opponents	Att.	Res.	Score	Scorers
1	(A)	07.09	v London Scot	401	L	7-43	Broady(t)Quantrill(c)
2	(H)	14.09	v Coventry	1300	L	3-61	Cummins(p)
3	(A)	21.09	v Rotherham	750	L	18-49	Bale(2t)Bishop(t)Kennedy(dg)
4	(H)	29.09	v Bedford	1150	L	6-34	Quantrill(2p)
5	(A)	05.10	v Newcastle	2328	L	5-156	Pell(t)
6	(H)	12.10	v Moseley	530	W	29-22	Saunders(3t)Smith(t)Quantrill(3p)
7	(A)	19.10	v Richmond	1600	L	8-64	Bale(t)Quantrill(p)
8	(H)	26.10	v Wakefield	440	L	17-22	Saunders(t)Carter(t)PTry(t)Quantrill(c)
9	(A)	02.11	v Blackheath	1755	W	33-24	Bale(3t)Cummins(t)Baker(t)Quantrill(4c)
10	(H)	09.11	v Nottingham	514	W	20-12	Curll(t)Baker(t)Quantrill(2c2p)
11	(H)	16.11	v Waterloo	430	L	15-56	Oram(t)Gallagher(t)Quantrill(cp)
12	(A)	18.01	v Bedford	1696	L	6-57	Quantrill(2p)
13	(H)	08.02	v Newcastle	1190	L	8-70	Glover(t)Quantrill(p)
14	(A)	23.02	v Coventry	1900	L	10-24	Bale(t)Quantrill(cp)
15	(A)	08.03	v Moseley	477	L	11-34	Harrison(t)Quantrill(2p)
16	(H)	15.03	v Rotherham	360	L	16-41	Barr(tc3p)
17	(H)	22.03	v Richmond	575	L	31-72	Milner(2t)Jones(t)N Smith(t)Glover(t)Barr(2c)Quantrill(c)
18	(H)	29.03	v London Scot	520	L	16-45	Quantrill(t)Barr(c3p)
19	(A)	05.04	v Wakefield	550	L	12-53	Saunders(t)Milner(t)Barr(c)
20	(H)	12.04	v Blackheath	510	L	24-32	Saunders(t)Milner(t)Oram(t)Barr(3cp)
21	(A)	19.04	v Nottingham	309	L	10-44	Saunders(t)Barr(t)
22	(A)	26.04	v Waterloo	700	L	12-45	Saunders(t)Barr(tc)

1996-97 HIGHLIGHTS

LEAGUE DEBUTS: Damian Cummins, Paul Bale, Peter Jones, Jim Dicken, Mark Beauchamp, Alastair Kennedy, Greg Keyse, Mark Pincham, Rob Gallagher, Matt Curll, Paul Whitaker, Tom Harrison, Lawrence Little, Nick Smith, Wayne Barr, Andy Craig, John Cocks, Andrew Jarrett, Paul Smith.

TRY ON DEBUT: Tom Harrison and Wayne Barr.

PLAYERS USED: 45 plus 2 as replacement.

EVER PRESENT: Eddie Saunders.

☐ Set three unenviable Division Two record's of most points, tries and conversions against with 1060, 150 and 101.

☐ Jim Quantrill extended his career record for points, conversions and penalties to 388, 51 and 84 respectively.

☐ Suffered their worst ever run of consecutive defeats losing 12 in a row. The previous record was nine.

☐ Centre Nigel Hill extends his club record for appearances by a Back outright after having shared it with Ian Aitchison.

☐ Jim Quantrill equalled the club record for topping the leading points scoring list for a third consecutive year. The other two to achieve this were Chris Howard, in the first three laegue seasons and Mark Maoletoft immediately prior to Quantrill.

☐ Veteran winger Eddie Saunders topped the club's try scoring list for the seventh time in ten years which is a record for a player currently in the National divisions.
His career total now stands at 59 in 122 games which works out at a try every 2.07 games. During the Season Saunders scored his third league hat-trick of tries.

☐ Saunders catches scrum-half David Bishop's record of 122 appearances.

RUGBY'S COURAGE LEAGUE MATCH DETAILS 1996-97

#	15	14	13	12	11	10	9	1	2	3	4	5	6	7	8	Replacements	#
1	Quantrill	Saunders	Glover	Cummins	Bale	Pell	Bishop	Jones	Dicken	Broady	S Smith	Underhill	Gardner	Oram	Nicholls	Kirby(3)Hughes(6)	1
2	Beauchamp	Saunders	Glover	Cummins	Bale	Kennedy	Bishop	Jones	Dicken	Broady	S Smith	Ashmead	Oram	Nicholls		Baker(12)	2
3	Beauchamp	Saunders	Glover	Cummins	Bale	Kennedy	Bishop	Jones	Dicken	Broady	S Smith	Underhill	Keyse	Oram	Thompson	Baker(12)	3
4	Quantrill	Saunders	Glover	Cummins	Bale	Kennedy	Bishop	Jones	Dicken	Kirby	S Smith	Bowman	Keyse	Oram	Nicholls	Baker(15)	4
5	Beauchamp	Saunders	Glover	Cummins	Bale	Pell	Bishop	Jones	Kirby	Burdett	S Smith	Bowman	Keyse	Oram	Nicholls	Thompson(8)	5
6	Quantrill	Saunders	Glover	Gillooly	Bale	Cummins	Broady	Jones	Burdett	Mee	S Smith	Bowman	Hughes	Keyse		Beauchamp(13)	6
7	Quantrill	Saunders	Beauchamp	Gillooly	Bale	Cummins	Broady	Jones	Dicken	Mee	Pincham	Underhill	Carter	Hughes	Keyse	S Smith(6)	7
8	Quantrill	Saunders	Glover	Gillooly	Bale	Cummins	Baker	Jones	Burdett	Mee	S Smith	Underhill	Gallagher	Oram	Carter		8
9	Quantrill	Saunders	Glover	Cummins	Bale	Curll	Baker	Jones	Burdett	Mee	S Smith	Underhill	Gallagher	Oram	Gallagher	Gillooly(10)	9
10	Quantrill	Saunders	Glover	Cummins	Bale	Curll	Baker	Jones	Burdett	Mee	S Smith	Bowman	Carter	Gallagher	Gallagher	Keyse(6)	10
11	Quantrill	Saunders	Glover	Cummins	Bale	Curll	Baker	Broady	Burdett	Mee	S Smith	Underhill	Carter	Gallagher	Gallagher	Dicken(1)Evans(1)	11
12	Quantrill	Saunders	Glover	Whitaker	Bale	Cummins	Baker	Evans	Burdett	Kirby	S Smith	Underhill	Carter	Oram	Gallagher	Milner(2)Jones(1)Baker(13)Keyse(7)	12
13	Quantrill	Saunders	Glover	Gillooly	Bale	Cummins	Mee	Mee	Burdett	Kirby	S Smith	Bowman	Ashmead	Carter	Carter	Riely(1)Milner(2)Baker(9)Underhill(4)	13
14	Quantrill	Saunders	Glover	Gillooly	Bale	Cummins	Milner	Milner	Jones	Jones	Bowman	Smith	Ashmead	Carter	Ellis	S Baker(9)	14
15	Quantrill	Saunders	Glover	Gillooly	Bale	Cummins	Burdett	Burdett	Burdett	Bowman	Bowman	S Smith	Ashmead	Carter	Carter	Pell(15)Baker(12)Milner(6)	15
16	Quantrill	Saunders	Glover	Harrison	Harrison	Bishop	Jones	Riley	Mee	Mee	Bowman	S Smith	Oram	M R Ellis	Carter	Cummins(13)Jones(1)Thompson(6)	16
17	Quantrill	Saunders	Glover	T Harrison	W Barr	N Smith	Jones	Milner	Milner	Kirby	Underhill	Craig	Ashmead	Carter	Carter	Cummins(10)Jarrett(3)P Smith(4)Jenkins(6)	17
18	Quantrill	Saunders	Glover	N Smith	Bale	Bishop	Mee	Milner	Milner	Kirby	Underhill	Craig	Carter	M R Ellis	Cocks	Little(13)Baker(9)S Smith(6)Riely(1)Cummins(13)	18
19	Quantrill	Saunders	Glover	N Smith	Bale	Bishop	Jones	Milner	Milner	Kirby	Underhill	Craig	Hughes	M R Ellis	Cocks	Bishop(9)Thompson(6)Mee(1)Fry(2)	19
20	Quantrill	Saunders	Glover	Glover	Bale	Bishop	Jones	Jones	Bishop	Kirby	S Smith	Craig	Carter	Oram	Cocks	Cummins(13)	20
21	Quantrill	Saunders	Little	Glover	Bale	S Baker	S Baker	Milner	Milner	Kirby	S Smith	Craig	M R Ellis	Oram	Thompson	Cummins(12)Jones(3)Underhill(7)Cocks(6)Fry(tr1)	21
22	Quantrill	Saunders	Little	Harrison	Barr	Bishop	Riley	Milner	Milner	Jarrett	S Smith	Bowman	Cocks	Oram	P Smith	Watson(15)Underhill(12)S Baker(6)	22

RUGBY LIONS LEAGUE STATISTICS
(COMPILED BY STEPHEN McCORMACK)

Season	Div.	P	W	D	L	F	(Tries	Con	Pen	DG)	A	(Tries	Con	Pen	DG)	Most Points	Most Tries
87-88	4N	10	9	0	1	184	(15	15	17	1)	100	(9	2	18	2)	69 - Chris Howard	7 - Eddie Saunders
88-89	3	11	10	0	1	268	(41	19	19	3)	99	(8	5	19	0)	123 - Chris Howard	7 - Eddie Saunders & Chris Howard
89-90	2	11	5	0	6	238	(34	21	18	2)	172	(24	11	17	1)	100 - Chris Howard	7 - Eddie Saunders
90-91	2	12	10	0	2	252	(39	18	16	6)	146	(20	9	13	3)	68 - Stuart Vaudin	9 - David Bishop
91-92	1	12	2	3	7	124	(11	4	23	1)	252	(36	15	26	0)	60 - Mark Mapletoft	2 - Eddie Saunders & David Bishop
92-93	1	12	1	0	11	104	(10	6	11	3)	368	(50	26	19	3)	26 - Mark Mapletoft	3 - Eddie Saunders
93-94	2	18	5	1	12	186	(15	9	25	6)	302	(29	17	39	2)	115 - Mark Mapletoft	5 - Mark Mapletoft
94-95	3	18	11	0	7	355	(40	22	35	2)	271	(26	12	35	4)	131 - Jim Quantrill	8 - David Bishop
95-96	3	18	12	1	5	395	(41	26	44	2)	284	(23	14	26	1)	183 - Jim Quantrill	9 - Eddie Saunders
96-97	2	22	3	0	19	317	(40	20	23	1)	1060	(150	101	35	1)	72 - Jim Quantrill	8 - Eddie Saunders
Totals		144	68	5	71	2423	(286	160	229	27)	2954	(375	212	247	17)		

	HOME	AWAY
BIGGEST WIN	(40pts) 49-9 v Gosforth 11.11.89	(151pts) 5-156 v Newcastle 5.10.96
DEFEAT	(62pts) 8-70 v Newcastle 8.2.97	42-23 v Rosslyn Park 4.5.96
MOST POINTS SCORED	49-9 v Gosforth 11.11.89	5-156 v Newcastle 5.10.96
AGAINST	31-72 v Richmond 22.3.97	

MOST CONSECUTIVE VICTORIES - 8   **MOST CONSECUTIVE DEFEATS - 12**

MOST TRIES IN A MATCH
(FOR) 8 v Askeans 8.10.88
(AGAINST) 24 v Newcastle 5.10.96 (A)

MOST APPEARANCES
FORWARD: 107 Trevor Bevan
BACK: 122(1) David Bishop
122 Eddie Saunders

CONSECUTIVE APPEARANCES
42 Steve Smith 11.4.92 - 14.1.95

CONSECUTIVE SCORING MATCHES
Scoring Tries - 5 - Eddie Saunders
Scoring Points - 19 - Chris Howard

MOST	in a SEASON	in a CAREER	in a MATCH
Points	183 Jim Quantrill 95-96	388 Jim Quantrill 93-97	25 Chris Howard v Gosforth 1.11.89 (H)
Tries	9 David Bishop 90-91 Eddie Saunders 95-96	59 Eddie Saunders 87-97	3 Chris Howard v Vale of Lune 10.9.88 (H) Eddie Saunders v Bedford 12.4.95 (A) v Rotherham 23.9.95 (H) v Moseley 12.10.96 (H)
Conversions	21 Jim Quantrill 95-96	51 Jim Quantrill 93-97	6 Chris Howard v Gosforth 11.11.89 (H)
Penalties	42 Jim Quantrill 95-96	84 Jim Quantrill 93-97	7 Denzil Evans v Richmond 15.10.94 (H)
Drop Goals	4 Richard Pell 87-88	14 Richard Pell 87-95	1 by eight players Richard Pell (x14), Stuart Vaudin (x3), Mark Mapletoft (x3), Jim McLeod (x3), Chris Howard, David Bishop, Denzil Evans, Alastair Kennedy.

RUGBY PLAYING SQUAD

BACKS

NAME	Ht	Wt	Birthdate	Birthplace	Club	Apps	Pts	T	C	P	DG
Jim Quantrill	6.2	15.0	30.05.69	Poole	Birminghanm Solihull						
					Rugby	81	388	7	51	82	-
Stuart Glover	6.0	14.0	03.11.69	Bedford	Bedford						
					Rugby	54+1	25	5	-	-	-
Wayne Barr	5.10	13.7	07.02.70	Chiredzi (Zim)	Western Transvaal						
					Rugby	7	54	3	9	7	-
Paul Bale	5.11	13.0	20.12.76	Rugby	Newbold						
					Rugby	18	35	7	-	-	-
Damian Cummins	5.11	14.0	08.12.64	Tenby	Gloucester						
					Rugby	13+5	8	1	-	-	1
David Bishop	5.10	13.8	05.01.65	Westminster							
					Rugby	122+1	146	32	-	-	1
James Baker	6.2	15.7	10.09.74	Solihull	Rugby	2	-	-	-	-	-
Simon Baker	5.7	12.8	01.02.75	Coventry	Rugby	7+9	10	2	-	-	-
Lawrence Little	6.1	13.7	24.10.67	Tokorea (NZ)	North Harbour						
					Rugby	5+1	-	-	-	-	-
Nick Smith	6.0	13.5	14.07.72	Durban (SA)	Gloucester						
					Rugby	4	5	1	-	-	-
Eddie Saunders	6.0	12.7	02.11.60	Birmingham	Coventry						
					Rugby	118	265	59	-	-	-
Adrian Gillooly	6.0	14.11	06.04.70	Rugby	Rugby						
					Rugby	53+3	10	2	-	-	-
Dean Watson	5.9	13.0	08.11.65	Coventry	Coventry						
					Rugby	30+2	18	4	-	-	-
Tim Russell	5.8	11.7	03.10.75	Corby	Prev. Club: Walsall						
Paul Whittaker	5.8	11.7	07.01.77	Berkeley	Bristol						
					Rugby	1	-	-	-	-	-

FORWARDS

NAME	Ht	Wt	Birthdate	Birthplace	Club	Apps	Pts	T	C	P	DG
Neil Riley	5.10	16.7	29.12.64	Rugby							
Warwickshire.					Rugby	23+4	10	2	-	-	-
Peter Jones					Rugby	14+3	5	1	-	-	-
Richard Mee	6.0	18.7	25.05.67	Leicester	Leicester						
					Rugby	37+3	5	1	-	-	-
Rob Milner	5.11	14.9	05.06.68	Coventry	Nuneaton						
					Rugby	21+3	20	4	-	-	-
Russell Kirby	5.10	16.0	30.05.71	Stone	Stoke						
					Rugby	18+1	-	-	-	-	-
Rob Burdett	5.11	14.7	26.07.73	Rugby	Rugby	47+1	-	-	-	-	-
Steve Smith	6.6	17.3	20.06.68	Solihull	Prev. Clubs: Solihull, Coventry.						
					Rugby	90	-	-	-	-	-
Neil Underhill	6.10	17.0	23.06.72	Lutterworth							
					Rugby	24+3	-	-	-	-	-
Phil Bowman	6.5	17.10	16.02.65	Burton-on-Trent	Hinckley						
					Rugby	100	24	6	-	-	-
Dave Oram	6.2	14.4	25.02.68	Sutton Coldfield	Moseley						
					Rugby	44+1	25	5	-	-	-
Richard Hughes	6.2	14.7	28.05.70	Banbury							
					Rugby	11+1	-	-	-	-	-
Mark R Ellis	5.11	14.12	23.12.68	Kirby Muxloe	Prev. Clubs: Hinckley, Kenilworth.						
					Rugby	74+1	21	5	-	-	-
John Cocks	6.2	15.0	22.07.71	Epping	Cambridge Univ.						
					Rugby	4+1	-	-	-	-	-
Andy Craig	6.3	15.7	06.05.73	Thames (NZ)	Cambridge Univ.						
					Rugby	5	-	-	-	-	-
Paul Thompson	6.4	15.7	24.09.74	Warwick	Rugby	6+3	-	-	-	-	-
Paul Ashmead	6.1	15.2	03.01.66	Gloucester	Gloucester						
					Rugby	11	10	2	-	-	-
Andrew Jarrett	5.9	15.2	10.05.75	Chippenham	Rugby	1	Prev. Club: Gloucester				
James Bready	5.9	15.7	03.05.74	Gloucester	Rugby	11	Prev. Club: Gloucester				
Steve Carter	6.3	16.0	16.07.68	Nuneaton	Rugby	15+2	10	2	(ex Coventry)		

Tel: 01788 542433   **Fax:** 01788 561509

CAPACITY: 3,396   **SEATED:** 240   **STANDING:** 3,156

SIMPLE DIRECTIONS:
  By Road: Second turn right, half mile south west of town centre on A4071, Bilton Road.
  From NW; M6 Jnc 1 A426 Rugby A4071:
  From NE; M1 Jnc 20 A426 Rugby A4071:
  From SE; M1 Jnc 17/M45/A4071 towards Rugby.

  Nearest Railway Station: Rugby

CAR PARKING: 100 on ground

ADMISSION: Season: Adult £45, OAPs £10, Junior £5
                   Matchday: Adults standing £7, seated plus £1, OAPs/Juniors £2

CLUB SHOP: Yes; Manager Andrew Salter 01788 573350

CLUBHOUSE: Matchdays & training nights, snacks & bar meals available. Functions catered for, capacity 120, contact Bill Rees c/o Club

TRAINING NIGHTS: Tuesday & Thursday

Rugby Captain; Mark Ellis

THE
RUGBY LIONS
FOOTBALL CLUB

SATURDAY
12th OCTOBER 1996

RUGBY LIONS
v
MOSELEY

THE HOME OF RUGBY FOOTBALL
RUGBY CEMENT
THE LIONS SPONSORS

MATCHDAY PROGRAMME

Size   A5

Number of pages   20 plus cover

Price   £1

Programme Editor   D Keen 01788 331924

Advertising Rates

         Mono Full page £250,
         Half page £150,
         Qtr page £75

WHARFEDALE R.U.F.C.

NICKNAME: Green Machine / Dalesmen   **FOUNDED:** 1923

President John Spencer, High Pasture, Threshfield, Nr Skipton, N Yorks BD23 5NS
01756 752456 (H), 01756 753015 (B), 01756 753020 (Fax)

Club Secretary Gordon Brown, Wharfemead, Wood Lane, Grassington. Skipton, N. Yorks. BD23 5ND.
01756 752410 (H&B) 01756 752123 (Fax)

Director of Rugby/Fixture Secretary Michael Harrison, Old Hall Farm, Threshfield,
Skipton, N. Yorks. BD23 5PL 01756 752777 (H & B & Fax)

Press Officer Keith Lewis, Willow Bank, Bank Road, Cross Hills, Keighley, W. Yorks. BD20 8AA.
01535 634318 (H, B & Fax)

Chairman Frank House, Stocks House, Main Street, Threshfield, Nr Skipton,
N Yorks BD23 5HD. 01756 753546 (H)

Wharfedale may have raised a few eyebrows outside their close-knit Yorkshire Dales community by making what seemed a fairly comfortable transition from Regional to National level rugby, finishing the 1996/7 season a creditable 31st in the Courage Leagues with a squad of players mainly graduates from the club's mini and junior section but with a few highly committed newcomers. Many Wharfedale people will regard 96/97 as the clubs best league season so far but no one would overlook the hard work on and off the field which made it possible, underpinning the individual talents and the camaraderie which exists throughout the clubs six senior sides. In a marathon season with an intensity of competition never experienced before the Dalesmen chartered an aeroplane for the journeys to Redruth, Exeter and Havant, relied heavily on the talents of physios John Brewster and Stuart Cooper and often made up for their lack of bulk up front by trying to run their opponents off their feet!

After a heartening 34-19 win at Walsall on the opening day of the season the reality of what lay ahead dawned when Exeter visited Threshfield the following week and impressed everyone with the blend of power and style which eventually won them the title. Coached by Michael Harrison and Peter Hartley, the Dalesmen recovered to make the headlines with a 23-18 home win over promotion hopefuls Leeds and led by their inspirational captain John Lawn, with fullback Andy Hodgson (21 tries) and flanker Hedley Verity (9 tries) both playing in all 30 league games, the side then continud to learn and improve, confirming their growing reputation with a 13-10 victry at Morley and a league double over Otley which made up for a 27-34 reverse at Cross Green in the Third Round of the Pilkingon Cup.

Half backs Dan Harrison and Neil Heseltine and hooker John Lawn represented Yorkshire when the crowded League Three schedule permitted. Prop Ian Peel and full back Andy Hodgson played for North U-21 and flanker John Hartley represented Yorkshire in the U-21 final at Twickenham. Winger Adam Mounsey finished the season as leading scorer after joining the club from Morley and other newcomers to impress were lock David Lister from Keighley, centre/wing Steve McManus from West Hartlepool, Jonathan Davies from Anglesea and Sean Gilbert from Leeds, with former England 'A' scrum half Herbie Hancock making a telling contribution when needed.

Wharfedale look forward to making a strong challenge again in 1997/98 and extend a warm welcome to friends old and new at their picturesque Threshfield headquarters.
KEITH LEWIS

Wharfedale RUFC: 1st XV Squad 1996-97.   Photo - Keith Lewis

Colours: Emerald green/white/green.   **Change colours:** Scarlet & white hoops/white/

WHARFEDALE

COURAGE LEAGUE MATCH DETAILS 1996-97

No	Ven.	Date	Opponents	Att.	Res.	Score	Scorers
1	(A)	31.08	v Walsall		W	34-19	Hodgson(2t)Walker(t)D Harrison(t)PenTry(t)A Howarth(3cp)
2	(H)	07.09	v Exeter		L	17-29	Walker(t)A Howarth(4p)
3	(A)	14.09	v Harrogate		L	18-23	Verity(t)PenTry(t)A Howarth(c2p)
4	(H)	21.09	v Leeds		W	23-18	Verity(2t)Buckroyd(tdg)A Howarth(cp)
5	(A)	28.09	v London Welsh		W	25-16	I Peel(t)Rodgers(t)Walker(t)A Howarth(2c2p)
6	(H)	05.10	v Lydney		L	24-25	Hodgson(2t)A Howarth(c3p)Davies(dg)
7	(A)	12.10	v Redruth		L	22-25	McManus(t)Lister(t)Walker(t)A Howarth(2c)Davies(p)
8	(H)	19.10	v Morley		L	17-32	Hartley(t)A Howarth(4p)
9	(A)	26.10	v Clifton		W	32-19	Hodgson(t)Walker(t)McManus(t)Hezeltine(t)A Howarth(t2cp)
10	(H)	09.11	v Fylde		L	13-19	Lawn(t)McManus(t)A Howarth(p)
11	(A)	16.11	v Havant		W	27-13	McManus(2t)Hancock(t)Mounsey(t2cp)
12	(H)	21.12	v Liverpool StH		W	24-15	Walker(2t)Buckroyd(t)McManus(t)Davies(c)Mounsey(c)
13	(A)	28.12	v Otley		W	20-13	McManus(TOHodgson(t)Walker(t)Mounsey(cp)
14	(H)	18.01	v Walsall		W	37-27	Hodgson(3t)Hezeltine(t)Mounsey(t3c2p)
15	(A)	25.01	v Exeter		L	8-14	Mounsey(t)Buckroyd(p)
16	(H)	01.02	v Harrogate		L	10-21	Hodgson(t)Mounsey(cp)
17	(A)	08.02	v Leeds		L	13-41	I Peel(t)Mounsey(c2p)
18	(H)	15.02	v London Welsh		W	50-12	Hodgson(3t)Verity(t)D Harrison(t)Lister(t)Buckroyd(t)Mounsey(t5c)
19	(A)	22.02	v Lydney		W	24-15	D Harrison(t)Verity(t)Hodgson(t)Mounsey(3cp)
20	(H)	01.03	v Redruth		W	47-15	Lister(2t)Abbey(2t)Verity(t)Hezeltine(t)PenTry(t)Mounsey(6c)
21	(A)	08.03	v Morley		W	13-10	Buckroyd(t)McManus(t)Mounsey(p)
22	(H)	15.03	v Clifton		W	28-11	Walker(t)Hird(t)D Harrison(t)Mounsey(tc2p)
23	(A)	22.03	v Fylde		L	18-39	Davies(t)Mounsey(tc2p)
24	(H)	05.04	v Havant		W	27-22	Hezeltine(t)Gilbert(t)D Harrison(t)Mounsey(t2cp)
25	(A)	12.04	v Liverpool StH		L	25-30	Hodgson(2t)Davies(p)Mounsey(t2cp)
26	(H)	19.04	v Otley		W	23-15	Buckroyd(2t)Lawn(t)Mounsey(tp)
27	(A)	26.04	v Reading		L	10-25	Dickinson(t)Mounsey(cp)
28	(H)	03.05	v Rosslyn Park		W	45-31	Hodgson(3t)Verity(2t)Buckroyd(t)Mounsey(t5c)
29	(H)	10.05	v Reading		W	15-13	Hodgson(t)Verity(t)Mounsey(cp)
30	(A)	17.05	v Rosslyn Park		L	21-28	Hird(t)Davies(t)Hodgson(t)Mounsey(3c)

1996-97 HIGHLIGHTS

LEAGUE DEBUTS: Steve McManus, Mark Hancock, David Lister, Adam Mounsey, Jonathan Davies,

PLAYERS USED: 31 plus 4 as replacement.

EVER PRESENT: Hedley Verity and Andrew Hodgson.

❑ Winger Adam Mounsey in his debut season tops the points scoring list and breaks the record for points in a season with 182. The previous record set last season was 143 by Alex Howarth.

	Pts	T	C	P	D	Apps	Ave.
Adam Mounsey	182	10	39	18	-	20	9.10
Alex Howarth	143	2	23	29	-	12	11.92

Mounsey beats Howarth's record of 23 conversions by 16.

❑ Fifth best away record in the division.

❑ Second rower Denis Wood adds three to his record of consecutive appearances which now stands at 61.

❑ Andrew Hodgson breaks Les Ingham's 1991-92 record of 12 tries in a season with 21 in 30 games. That means Hodgson stands joint second on the all-time try scoring list with 27

❑ Alex Howarth passes Mark Toseland's career record of 77 penalties and extends it to 95 and his career record for points to 486.

	Pts	T	C	P	D	Apps	Ave.
Career	486	13	68	95	-	49	9.92

❑ One of only three teams to score tries in all 30 league matches - the other two were Havant and Otley.

❑ Just missed out on scoring 100 tries finishing on 96 - which was 10 more than promoted Fylde.

WHARFEDALE'S COURAGE LEAGUE MATCH DETAILS 1996-97

15	14	13	12	11	10	9	1	2	3	4	5	6	7	8	Replacements	
Hodgson	A.Howarth	Walker	M.Harrison	McManus	Hezeltine	D.Harrison	Metcalfe	Lawn	I.Peel	Lister	Cowley	Abbey	Verity	Buckroyd		1
Hodgson	A.Howarth	Walker	M.Harrison	Howarth	Hezeltine	Hancock	Metcalfe	Lawn	I.Peel	Lister	Cowley	Abbey	Verity	Buckroyd		2
Hodgson	A.Howarth	Walker	M.Harrison	S.Howarth	Hezeltine	Hancock	Metcalfe	Lawn	I.Peel	Wood	Cowley	Abbey	Verity	Buckroyd		3
Hodgson	A.Howarth	McManus	M.Harrison	Howarth	Hezeltine	Hancock	Metcalfe	Lawn	I.Peel	Wood	Cowley	Abbey	Verity	Buckroyd		4
Hodgson	A.Howarth	Walker	M.Harrison	Howarth	Hezeltine	Hancock	Metcalfe	Lawn	Rodgers	Lister	Cowley	Fitton	Verity	Buckroyd	Mounsey(11),Sugden(8),P.Peel(13)	5
Hodgson	A.Howarth	Walker	M.Harrison	Hancock	Hezeltine	Hancock	Metcalfe	Lawn	I.Peel	Lister	Cowley	Abbey	Verity	Buckroyd	Dickinson(1)	6
Hodgson	Mounsey	T.Harrison	M.Harrison	Davies	Hezeltine	Riddiough	Metcalfe	Lawn	I.Peel	Lister	Cowley	Hartley	Verity	Buckroyd	A.Howarth(10)	7
Hodgson	A.Howarth	Walker	M.Harrison	Mounsey	Hezeltine	D.Harrison	Metcalfe	Lawn	I.Peel	Lister	Cowley	Abbey	Verity	Buckroyd	Rodgers(3),Fitton(15)	8
Hodgson	A.Howarth	Walker	McManus	Mounsey	Hezeltine	D.Harrison	Metcalfe	Lawn	I.Peel	Lister	Cowley	Abbey	Verity	Buckroyd		9
Hodgson	A.Howarth	Walker	M.Harrison	McManus	Hezeltine	Hancock	Metcalfe	Lawn	I.Peel	Lister	Cowley	Abbey	Verity	Buckroyd	T.Harrison(12)	10
Hodgson	Mounsey	Walker	T.Harrison	McManus	Hezeltine	Hancock	Metcalfe	Lawn	I.Peel	Lister	Cowley	Abbey	Verity	Buckroyd	Wood(4),Rodgers(1)	11
Hodgson	Mounsey	Walker	M.Harrison	McManus	Hezeltine	Hancock	Metcalfe	Lawn	I.Peel	Lister	Cowley	Abbey	Verity	Buckroyd	Dickinson(1)	12
Hodgson	Mounsey	Walker	M.Harrison	Davies	Hezeltine	D.Harrison	Metcalfe	Lawn	I.Peel	Wood	Viner	Abbey	Verity	Buckroyd	Dickinson(1)	13
Hodgson	Mounsey	Walker	M.Harrison	McManus	Hezeltine	Hancock	Metcalfe	Lawn	I.Peel	Wood	Cowley	Abbey	Verity	Buckroyd	May(13)	14
Hodgson	Mounsey	Walker	M.Harrison	McManus	Hezeltine	Hancock	Metcalfe	Lawn	I.Peel	Lister	Cowley	Abbey	Verity	Buckroyd	Rodgers(1)	15
Hodgson	Walker	Walker	M.Harrison	McManus	Hezeltine	D.Harrison	Metcalfe	Lawn	Rodgers	Lister	Cowley	Abbey	Verity	Buckroyd	May(12),Metcalfe(3)	16
Hodgson	Davies	Walker	M.Harrison	McManus	Hezeltine	D.Harrison	Metcalfe	Lawn	I.Peel	Lister	Cowley	Abbey	Verity	Buckroyd		17
Hodgson	Davies	Davies	M.Harrison	Gilbert	Hezeltine	D.Harrison	Metcalfe	Lawn	I.Peel	Lister	Cowley	Abbey	Verity	Buckroyd	May(15),Hird(6),Lancaster(1)	18
Hodgson	Mounsey	Davies	M.Harrison	Gilbert	Hezeltine	D.Harrison	Metcalfe	Lawn	I.Peel	Lister	Cowley	Abbey	Hird	Buckroyd	S.Howarth(12)	19
Hodgson	Mounsey	Walker	M.Harrison	McManus	Hezeltine	D.Harrison	Metcalfe	Lawn	I.Peel	Lister	Cowley	Abbey	Verity	Buckroyd	Hird(6).	20
Hodgson	Mounsey	T.Harrison	Davies	McManus	Hezeltine	D.Harrison	Metcalfe	Lawn	I.Peel	Lister	Cowley	Hird	Verity	Buckroyd	Gilbert(11)	21
Hodgson	Mounsey	Walker	M.Harrison	McManus	Hezeltine	D.Harrison	Metcalfe	Lawn	I.Peel	Lister	Cowley	Abbey	Verity	Buckroyd	Hird(6)	22
Hodgson	Mounsey	Walker	M.Harrison	McManus	Hezeltine	D.Harrison	Metcalfe	Lawn	I.Peel	Lister	Cowley	Hird	Verity	Buckroyd	Metcalfe(2)P.Peel(15)Gilbert(1)	23
Hodgson	Mounsey	Walker	M.Harrison	Gilbert	Hezeltine	D.Harrison	Metcalfe	Lawn	I.Peel	Lister	Cowley	Abbey	Verity	Buckroyd	Hartley(6)	24
Hodgson	Mounsey	Walker	M.Harrison	McManus	Hezeltine	D.Harrison	Metcalfe	Lawn	Wood	Wood	Cowley	Lister	Fitton	Buckroyd	P.Peel(1)Gilbert(14)Stockton(8)	25
Hodgson	Mounsey	Walker	M.Harrison	McManus	Hezeltine	D.Harrison	Metcalfe	Lawn	Dickinson	Cowley	Viner	Fitton	Verity	Buckroyd	Viner(6)	26
Hodgson	Mounsey	Walker	M.Harrison	McManus	Hezeltine	D.Harrison	Lancaster	Lawn	P.Peel	Cowley	Viner	Fitton	Verity	Buckroyd	Sutcliffe(1)	27
Hodgson	Mounsey	Walker	M.Harrison	McManus	Hezeltine	D.Harrison	Lancaster	Lawn	Dickinson	Lister	Viner	Fitton	Verity	Buckroyd		28
Hodgson	Mounsey	Walker	M.Harrison	McManus	Hezeltine	D.Harrison	Lancaster	P.Peel	Dickinson	Lister	Cowley	Verity	Verity	Buckroyd	Dickinson(2)Gilbert(14)Hird(6)	29
Hodgson	Mounsey	Walker	Davies	Gilbert	Hezeltine	D.Harrison	Lancaster	I.Peel	Lister	Cowley	Hird	Verity	Buckroyd		McManus(13)Dickinson(1)Wood(tr1)	30

WHARFEDALE LEAGUE STATISTICS
(COMPILED BY STEPHEN McCORMACK)

Season	Div.	P	W	D	L	F	(Tries	Con	Pen	DG)	A	(Tries	Con	Pen	DG)	Most Points	Most Tries
87-88	NE1	10	8	0	2	145	(21	8	15	0)	70	(			)	37 - Mark Toseland	5 - Les Ingham & Steve Howarth.
88-89	N2	10	7	0	3	220	(26	19	24	2)	96	(			)	108 - Mark Toseland	7 - Les Ingham & Stuart Hird.
89-90	N2	10	5	1	4	161	(21	10	18	1)	134	(			)	72 - Mark Toseland	5 - Les Ingham & Glen Harrison.
90-91	N2	10	5	0	5	129	(16	7	15	2)	108	(			)	63 - Mark Toseland	3 - Steve Howarth & David Swinglehurst.
91-92	N2	10	10	0	0	254	(35	18	22	4)	55	(			)	111 - Russ Buckroyd	12 - Les Ingham
92-93	N1	12	7	0	5	216	(20	7	33	1)	207	(			)	45 - Mark Toseland	5 - Glen Harrison
93-94	N1	12	12	0	0	327	(48	18	17	0)	75	(			)	127 - Alex Howarth	8 - Alex Howarth & Simon Slater.
94-95	5N	12	6	1	5	209	(24	13	21	0)	206	(			)	94 - Alex Howarth	5 - Daniel Harrison
95-96	5N	12	12	0	0	331	(39	23	29	1)	146	(			)	143 - Alex Howarth	10 - Neil Heseltine
96-97	3	30	17	0	13	710	(96	52	40	2)	635	(			)	182 - Adam Mounsey	21 - Andrew Hodgson
Totals		128	89	2	37	2702	(346	175	235	13)	1732	(			)		

	HOME	AWAY
BIGGEST WIN	(54pts) 54-0 v Carlisle 4.1.92	(34pts) 68-34 v Lichfield 30.3.96
DEFEAT	(42pts) 8-50 v Walsall 25.3.95	(28pts) 13-41 Leeds 8.2.97
MOST POINTS SCORED	54-0 v Carlisle 4.1.92	68-34 v Lichfield 30.3.96
AGAINST	8-50 v Walsall 25.3.95	13-41 Leeds 8.2.97

MOST CONSECUTIVE VICTORIES - 14 (24.4.93 - 17.9.94)
MOST CONSECUTIVE DEFEATS - 3 - on three occasions

MOST TRIES IN A MATCH
(FOR) 12 v Sandbach 29.2.92
(AGAINST) 8 v Walsall 25.3.95

MOST APPEARANCES
FORWARD: 72 Stuart Hird 1987 - date
BACK: 76 Chris Davies 1987 - date

CONSECUTIVE APPEARANCES
61 Denis Wood 13.4.91 - 14.9.96

CONSECUTIVE SCORING MATCHES
Scoring Tries - 5 - Steve McManus
Scoring Points - 23 - Alex Howarth 1993-95

MOST	in a SEASON	in a CAREER	in a MATCH
Points	182 Adam Mounsey 96-97	486 Alex Howarth 93-97	24 Les Ingham v Sandbach 29.2.92
Tries	21 Andrew Hodgson 96-97	33 Les Ingham 87-93	6 Les Ingham v Sandbach 29.2.92
Conversions	39 Adam Mounsey 96-97	68 Alex Howarth 93-97	7 Mark Toseland v Huddersfield 12.11.88
Penalties	29 Alex Howarth 95-96	95 Alex Howarth 93-97	6 Mark Toseland v Lymm 14.1.89
Drop Goals	3 Russ Buckroyd 91-92	8 Russ Buckroyd 87-97	1 on 13 occasions including Russ Buckroyd - 8 times

WHARFEDALE PLAYING SQUAD

NAME	Ht	Wt	Birthdate	Birthplace	Club	Apps	Pts	T	C	P	DG

BACKS

NAME	Ht	Wt	Birthdate	Birthplace	Club	Apps	Pts	T	C	P	DG
Andrew Hodgson	5.11	13.0	09.02.76	Skipton							
Yorkshire, Colts, u21. North u21.					Wharfedale	43	130	26	-	-	-
Chris Walker	5.11	14.0	03.08.67	Keighley	Keighley						
Yorkshire Colts. North Colts.					Wharfedale	44	55	11	-	-	-
Jonathan Davies	6.0	14.0	28.03.72	Bangor	Bangor						
Wales: u19. Midland UAU					Wharfedale	17	26	3	1	2	1
Steve McManus	5.11	13.0	19.05.72	Keighley	West Hartlepool						
Yorkshire Colts. Midlands UAU					Wharfedale	26	40	8	-	-	-
Adam Mounsey	5.10	13.7	18.09.72	Bradford	Morley						
Yorkshire u18.					Wharfedale	22	182	10	39	18	-
Neil Hezeltine	5.9	13.0	16.07.68	Skipton	Kelso						
Yorkshire					Wharfedale	61	20	99	-	-	-
Daniel Harrison	5.11	13.0	26.10.71	Skipton							
Yorkshire					Wharfedale	51	70	14	-	-	-
Sean Gilbert	5.11	13.7	14.06.69	Norwich	Leeds	8	15	3	-	-	-
Yorkshire Colts. England Students (RL)					Wharfedale	4	5	1	-	-	-
Alex Howarth	6.0	14.0	30.11.68	Skipton							
Yorkshire					Wharfedale	48	486	13	68	95	-
Mike Harrison	5.11	14.5	31.01.65	Skipton							
Yorkshire u18.					Wharfedale	71	30	6	-	-	-
Tom Harrison	6.0	13.0	20.10.73	Keighley							
					Wharfedale	3	-	-	-	-	-
Mark Hancock	5.10	13.0	04.04.65	Southport	Richmond						
England: A. London. Barbarians					Wharfedale	8	5	1	-	-	-
Mark Viner	6.3	16.0	07.07.66	Bradford	Bradford Salem						
					Wharfedale	26	15	3	-	-	-
John Hartley	6.1	14.7	17.08.75	Skipton							
Yorkshire u21, Colts.					Wharfedale	1	5	1	-	-	-

FORWARDS

NAME	Ht	Wt	Birthdate	Birthplace	Club	Apps	Pts	T	C	P	DG
John Metcalfe	6.0	16.0	27.04.65	Bournemouth							
Yorkshire, Colts.					Wharfedale	78	20	4	-	-	-
John Lawn	5.7	14.0	07.08.70	Bradford							
Yorkshire					Wharfedale	74	35	7	-	-	-
Iain Peel	5.11	16.0	24.01.76	Harrogate							
Yorkshire Colts & u21. North u21.					Wharfedale	41	10	2	-	-	-
Phillip Peel	5.11	14.8	12.08.77	Harrogate							
Yorkshire Colts.					Wharfedale	2	-	-	-	-	-
Dennis Wood	6.3	16.8	22.11.60	Skipton	Ilkley						
Yorkshire Colts					Wharfedale	67	25	5	-	-	-
Rob Cowley	6.4	16.7	20.07.71	Skipton	Liverpool St. H.						
North UAU					Wharfedale	26	-	-	-	-	-
David Lister	6.5	16.0	19.01.73	Keighley	Keighley						
Yorkshire u21.					Wharfedale	26	20	4	-	-	-
Simon Abbey											
					Wharfedale	78	31	7	-	-	-
Hedley Verity	6.0	14.0	20.04.70	Harrogate							
					Wharfedale	88	102	21	-	-	-
Russ Buckroyd	6.0	14.7	31.01.67	Liverpool							
Yorkshire u21					Wharfedale	64	168	10	20	19	8
Neil Dickinson	6.0	15.7	30.07.69	Otley							
					Wharfedale	12	5	-	-	-	-
John Lancaster	6.0	16.0	11.06.68	Skipton							
					Wharfedale	42	-	-	-	-	-
Stuart Hird	6.3	14.7	01.09.58	Yockenthwaite							
					Wharfedale	76	99	23	-	-	-
Jonathan Fitton	6.0	16.0	24.05.70	Leeds							
					Wharfedale	3	-	-	-	-	-

Wharfeside Avenue, Threshfield, Skipton, N Yorks BD23 5ND

Tel. Nos. 01756 752547

Capacity: 3,000   **Seated:** 120   **Standing:** Covered 180, Uncovered 2,700
Simple Directions: Take B6256 from Skipton bypass, signed Grassington after 8 miles turn right after Old Hall Inn in Threshfield, left after 400 metres down 'The Avenue'
Nearest Railway Station: Skipton, no bus service. Group transport can be arranged through club secretary
Car Parking: 120 Adjacent
Admission: £4.00 by programme, U16 No Charge
Club Shop: Yes, Manager Barbara Brown   01756 752054
Clubhouse: Normal Licensing hours matchdays, snacks, bar meals & restaurant. Functions available, capacity 120, contact Club Secretary
Training Nights: Monday & Wednesday

Wharfedale's 96/7 leading scorer,
winger Adam Mounsey

Wharfedale's fly half Neil Heseltine
launches an attack

Photos - Keith Lewis

MATCHDAY PROGRAMME

Size	A5
Number of pages	48 plus cover
Price	£4 includes entry
Programme Editor	Bill Mann 01756 752687
Advertising Rates	Mono Full page £300
	Half page £150

WORCESTER R.F.C.

NICKNAME: Worcs

FOUNDED: 1871

President Roger Murray, 7 King Stephens Mount, Worcester.
01905 429016 (H)

Chairman Michael Robins, 8 Bromwich Lane, St Johns, Worcester WR2 4BH
01905 427973 (H), 01905 454183 (B), 01905 757222 (Fax)

Secretary Adrian Harling, 6 The Grove, Claines, Worcester. WR3 7NZ
01905 454900 (H), 01562 822295 (B), 01905 820083 (Fax)

Press Officer Nicola Goodwin, c/o Worcester RFC, Sixways. Pershore Lane, Hindlip, Worcester.
01432 273473 (H)

Director of Coaching Phil Maynard, 0121 458 5169 (H), 0831 659652 (Mobile)

Registrations Secretary Dick Cumming, c/o Worcester RFC, as above

At this time last season we were full of optimism and it's nice to report that it was not unfounded. We had a tremendous season, with only two losses and three draws including an undefeated league programme, which meant that promotion to League Three was achieved on 29th March. We had, therefore, the whole of April to build for and dream about next season.

Last summer was spent in recruiting high quality players to supplement our already talented squad. It was recognised that with 26 league matches strength in depth was going to be important, and so it proved. Bruce Fenley, our captain, Tim Smith and the rest of the ex-Gloucester lads provided a solid backbone to the team, but it's great to see last season's Worcester lads featuring highly throughout, with Nick Baxter once again leading try scorer.

Despite the league record we found the other sides in the league extremely competitive. Our local rivals Stourbridge and Birmingham/Solihull pushed us hard and there were tough encounters with Grasshoppers and Manchester as well as many of the other northern sides on their home patches. It's a league that we are pleased to be out of as the competition will only get stronger.

Mention should also be made of the contribution by our excellent Second XV. Four losses all season, including a close call in the North Midlands Cup Final, meant that a superb team spirit has developed as well as ensuring that quality players have been available when required.

Our new pitch, grandstand, clubhouse and indoor training centre are virtually complete and we now look forward to the 1997/98 season with confidence. With management, coaching and squad strengths being fine tuned to face the task ahead we begin operating at levels unheard of before in the club's history.

R. CUMMING

Worcester RFC: before their League clinching game with Hereford

Colours: Navy blue with gold band.

Change colours: White with navy blue & gold bands.

COURAGE LEAGUE MATCH DETAILS 1996-97

No	Ven.	Date	Opponents	Att.	Res.	Score	Scorers
1	(H)	31.08	v Stoke O T		W	58-14	Wootton(3t)Lyman(2t)Davies(t)Parsons(t)Baxter(t)Fenley(t)Smith(5c3p)
2	(A)	07.09	v Manchester		D	23-23	D Hughes(t)Lloyd(t)Smith(2c3p)
3	(A)	21.09	v Stourbridge		D	21-21	Wootton(t)Linnett(t)Smith(c3p)
4	(H)	28.09	v Kendal		W	30-10	Orgee(t)D Hughes(t)Harwood(dg)Smith(t3c2p)
5	(A)	05.10	v Birmingham S		W	19-11	Linnett(t)D Hughes(t)Smith(t2c)
6	(H)	19.10	v Lichfield		W	21-10	Wootton(t)Evans(t)Smith(c3p)
7	(A)	26.10	v Preston		W	11- 6	Fenley(t)Smith(2p)
8	(H)	09.11	v Sandal		W	64- 7	Baxter(3t)Tomlinson(2t)Cox(t)Miles(t)Parsons(t)Smith(t7c)
9	(A)	16.11	v Winnington P		W	32-27	Baxter(t)Fenley(t)Evans(t)Linnett(t)Bradley(t)Smith(2cp)
10	(H)	21.12	v Hereford		W	40- 3	Orgee(t)Fenley(t)PenT(t)Tomlinson(t)Bradley(t)G Hughes(t)Smith(5c)
11	(A)	28.12	v Aspatria		W	38-30	Fenley(t)Tisdale(t)Linnett(t)Humphries(t)Smith(3c4p)
12	(H)	18.01	v Sheffield		W	32-14	Humphries(2t)D Hughes(t)Fenley(t)Smith(3c2p)
13	(A)	25.01	v Stoke on Trent		W	45-14	Evans(3t)Raymond(t)Fenley(t)Smith(t3c3p)
14	(H)	01.02	v Manchester		W	17-10	Cox(t)Evans(t)Smith(tc)
15	(H)	08.02	v Stourbridge		W	32-30	Bradley(3t)G Hughes(t)Smith(3c2p)
16	(A)	15.02	v Kendal		W	19-12	Baxter(2t)Linnett(t)Smith(2c)
17	(H)	22.02	v Birmingham S		W	27-16	Fenley(2t)Mitchell(t)Baxter(t)Smith(2cp)
18	(A)	01.03	v Lichfield		W	32-16	Baxter(2t)Bradley(t)Evans(t)G Hughes(dg)Tomlinson(3cp)
19	(H)	08.03	v Preston G		D	13-13	D Hughes(t)G Hughes(dg)Smith(cp)
20	(A)	15.03	v Sandal		W	22-15	Fenley(t)Bradley(t)Houston(t)Smith(2cp)
21	(H)	22.03	v Winnington Park		W	28-23	Baxter(2t)Bradley(t)Tomlinson(tc2p)
22	(A)	26.03	v Nuneaton		W	37-19	Baxter(3t)Raymond(t)Wylde(t)Tomlinson(3c2p)
23	(A)	05.04	v Hereford		W	51- 0	Wilkinson(2t)Lyman(t)Baxter(t)Beard(t)Miles(t)Protherough(t)D Hughes(c) Harwood(c)Tomlinson(t2cp)
24	(A)	12.04	v Aspatria		W	61-22	Baxter(2t)PenTry(t)Linnett(t)Beard(t)Miles(t)Wilkinson(t)Houston(t)Smith(t8c)
25	(A)	19.04	v Sheffield		W	14- 6	Fenley(t)Tomlinson(2p)Yapp(dg)
26	(H)	26.04	v Nuneaton		W	43- 3	PenTry(t)D Hughes(t)Mitchell(t)Lyman(t)Evans(t)Tomlinson(t)Smith(5cp)

1996-97 HIGHLIGHTS

LEAGUE DEBUTS: Tim Smith

PLAYERS USED: 39 plus 3 as replacement.

EVER PRESENT: None - most appearances 25 +1
- Bruce Fenley

❑ Achieved promotion for the fourth time in six seasons.

❑ Have lost only three of their last 40 league games over three seasons.

❑ Ex Gloucester full back Tim Smith tops the points scoring list in his debut season and in the process sets a new club record of 242 points.

	Pts	T	C	P	D	Apps	Ave.
Tim Smith	242	6	61	30	-	21	11.52

Smith set new records for conversions and penalties in a season with 61 and 30 respectively.

❑ Winger Nick Baxter set a new record for tries in a season with his 18 from 19 matches.

WORCESTER'S COURAGE LEAGUE MATCH DETAILS 1996-97

#	15	14	13	12	11	10	9	1	2	3	4	5	6	7	8	Replacements
1	Smith	Baxter	D Hughes	Parsons	Wootton	Harwood	Fenley	Mitchell	Knight	Lyman	Tisdale	Lloyd	Orgee	Davies	Raymond	
2	Smith	Evans	D Hughes	Wilson	Baxter	Harwood	Fenley	Knight	Knight	Lyman	Tisdale	Lloyd	Orgee	Bradley	Raymond	Hart(8)
3	Smith	D Hughes	D Hughes	Spiller	Baxter	Harwood	Fenley	Linnett	Knight	Mitchell	Owen	Lloyd	Orgee	Bradley	Hart	Hart
4	Smith	Wootton	D Hughes	Spiller	Baxter	Harwood	Fenley	Linnett	Knight	Watts	Tisdale	Lloyd	Orgee	Beard	Hart	Miles(8)
5	Smith	Wootton	D Hughes	Parsons	Baxter	Harwood	Fenley	Linnett	Knight	Lyman	Tisdale	Lloyd	Orgee	Bradley	Miles	Hart(8)Spiller(12)
6	Smith	Wootton	D Hughes	Parsons	Evans	Harwood	Fenley	Linnett	Knight	Lyman	Tisdale	Lloyd	Orgee	Bradley	Miles	Miles(8)
7	Smith	Evans	D Hughes	Parsons	Woodon	Harwood	Fenley	Linnett	Knight	Lyman	Tisdale	Lloyd	Hart	Bradley	Cox	Hart
8	Smith	Baxter	D Hughes	Parsons	Evans	Harwood	Fenley	Linnett	Webster	Lyman	Tisdale	Cox	Hart	Bradley	Cox	Cox
9	Smith	Baxter	D Hughes	Parsons	Wylde	Harwood	Fenley	Linnett	Knight	Lyman	Miles	Hart	Hart	Bradley	Raymond	Blakeway(15)Humphreys(12)
10	D Hughes	Evans	D Hughes	Parsons	Evans	Harwood	Fenley	G Hughes	Knight	Raymond	Miles	Lloyd	Hart	Bradley	Hart	S Powell(8)Hart(8)
11	D Hughes	Tomlinson	Humphreys	Smith	Harwood	Fenley	Fenley	Linnett	Houston	Lyman	Raymond	Lloyd	Heaver	Bradley	Raymond	Beard(7)S Powell(9)G Hughes(15)
12	D Hughes	Parsons	Tomlinson	Humphreys	Baxter	Harwood	Fenley	Linnett	Houston	Lyman	Tisdale	Lloyd	Orgee	Bradley	Raymond	Raymond
13	Smith	Parsons	Tomlinson	Humphreys	G Hughes	Harwood	Fenley	Linnett	Houston	Mitchell	Tisdale	Owen	Orgee	Bradley	Raymond	Wilkinson(6)
14	Smith	Tomlinson	Humphreys Evans	Humphreys Evans	G Hughes	Harwood	Fenley	Linnett	Houston	Mitchell	Tisdale	Cox	Orgee	Bradley	Raymond	Miles(8)Baxter(15)
15	Smith	Tomlinson	Tomlinson	Tomlinson	G Hughes	Harwood	Fenley	Linnett	Houston	Mitchell	Tisdale	Cox	Cox	Bradley	Gibson	Miles(6)
16	Smith	Tomlinson	Tomlinson	Tomlinson	G Hughes	Harwood	Fenley	Linnett	Houston	Mitchell	Tisdale	Lloyd	Beard	Bradley	Raymond	Hart(8)
17	Smith	Tomlinson	Tomlinson	Tomlinson	G Hughes	Harwood	Fenley	Linnett	Houston	Mitchell	Tisdale	Lloyd	Beard	Bradley	Raymond	Raymond
18	Wylde	Tomlinson	Tomlinson	Tomlinson	G Hughes	Harwood	Fenley	Linnett	Houston	Mitchell	Tisdale	Miles	Beard	Bradley	Hart	
19	Smith	Tomlinson	Tomlinson	Tomlinson	G Hughes	Harwood	Fenley	Linnett	Houston	Mitchell	Tisdale	Beard	Beard	Bradley	Nicholls	
20	Smith	Tomlinson	Tomlinson	Tomlinson	G Hughes	Harwood	Fenley	Linnett	Houston	Mitchell	Lloyd	Beard	Beard	Nicholls	Nicholls	Raymond(8)
21	Wylde	Tomlinson	Tomlinson	Parsons	G Hughes	Harwood	Fenley	Linnett	Houston	Mitchell	Lloyd	Beard	Bradley	Nicholls	Hart	Tisdale(8)D Hughes(12)J Powell(tr6)
22	Wylde	Evans	Tomlinson	Tomlinson	Harwood	Fenley	Fenley	Linnett	Protherough	Mitchell	Tisdale	Lloyd	Beard	Bradley	Raymond	
23	Wylde	Evans	D Hughes	Tomlinson	Harwood	Fenley	Fenley	Linnett	Protherough	Mitchell	Tisdale	Lloyd	Beard	Wilkinson	Raymond	Blakeway(12)Miles(5)Linnett(1)Houston(6)
24	Wylde	Smith	D Hughes	Parsons	Baxter	Yapp	S Powell	Lyman	Houston	Mitchell	Tisdale	Lloyd	Beard	Wilkinson	Raymond	Fenley(9)Linnett(12)Tomlinson(12)Nicholls(7)
25	Wylde	Evans	D Hughes	Tomlinson	Baxter	Yapp	S Powell	Linnett	Houston	Mitchell	Tisdale	Miles	Beard	Wilkinson	Raymond	Smith(15)Lyman(3)Lloyd(5)
26	Smith	Evans	D Hughes	Tomlinson	Harwood	Fenley	Linnett	Houston	Houston	Lyman	Tisdale	Lloyd	Nicholls	Beard	Beard	Mitchell(1)Miles(4)Martin(9)

WORCESTER LEAGUE STATISTICS
(COMPILED BY STEPHEN McCORMACK)

Season	Div.	P	W	D	L	F	A	PD	Pts	Pos.	Coach	Captain
87-88	MID 2W	10	4	0	6	106	138	-32	8	8	P John	J Wooton
88-89	MID 2W	10	1	1	8	83	165	-82	3	11r	P John	J Wooton
89-90	NMID 1	10	8	0	2	237	72	165	16	1p	P John	R Everton
90-91	MID 2W	10	5	0	5	146	131	15	10	5	P John	R Everton
91-92	MID 2W	10	7	0	3	175	131	44	14	3		R Everton
92-93	MID 2	11	9	0	2	188	89	99	18	2p		
93-94	MID 1	12	8	0	4	234	104	130	16	2		
94-95	MID 1	12	11	1	0	278	82	196	23	1p	P Maynard	N Stoodley
95-96	D5N	12	9	0	3	317	187	130	18	2	P Maynard	
96-97	D4N	26	23	3	0	830	375	455	49	1p		
Total		123	85	5	33	2594	1474	1120				

A view of Worcester's magnificent new grandstand & floodlights. Unfortunately due to the print deadline we were unable await a photo with the posts in place. Photo: Courtesy Newsquest (Midlands South) Ltd.

WORCESTER PLAYING SQUAD

NAME	Ht	Wt	Birthdate	Birthplace	Club	Apps	Pts	T	C	P	DG

BACKS

NAME	Ht	Wt	Birthdate	Birthplace	Club	Apps	Pts	T	C	P	DG
Tim Smith	5.11	13.0	10.05.62	Gloucester	Gloucester	94	593	10	57	142	2
					Worcester	21+1	242	6	61	30	-
Rich Tomlinson	5.10	13.9	25.11.71	Worcester	Nottingham	16	28	3	2	3	-
					Worcester	18+1	72	6	9	8	-
Nick Baxter	6.0	14.7	13.04.73	Birmingham	Kings Norton						
					Worcester	29+1	115	23	-	-	-
Mark Humphries	5.10	13.0	10.11.75	Capetown	Villager(S.A.)						
					Worcester	4+1	15	3	-	-	-
Greg Harwood	5.7	11.7	28.01.67	Hereford	Prev. Clubs: Hereford, Coventry.						
Army.					Worcester	?	40	-	14	2	2
Bruce Fenley	5.8	12.0	07.09.68	Cheltenham	Moseley	35+3	18	4	-	-	-
					Gloucester	41	20	4	-	-	-
					Worcester	25+1	55	11	-	-	-
Gareth Hughes	5.10	13.7	25.07.66	Llaqnsysul	Askeans	17	83	1	11	17	2
					London Welsh		50	5	6	5	1
					Saracens	17+1	39	1	2	4	6
					Worcester	10+1	16	2	-	-	2
Duncan Hughes	5.11	14.0	14.07.72	Derby	Prev. Clubs: Newport, Llanelli.						
Wales: u21.					Worcester	24+1	32	6	1	-	-
Adrian Parsons	5.10	14.7	20.02.65	Wolverhampton	Moseley	23	8	2	-	-	-
England: Colts.					Worcester	14	20	4	-	-	-
Rich Wylde	5.10	12.7	09.11.73	Birkenhead	Saracens						
					Worcester	17	26	4	-	-	2
Barry Evans	6.0	14.0	10.10.62	Hinckley	Leicester	28	44	11	-	-	-
England Barbarians					Worcester	20	40	8	-	-	-
Dave Spiller	5.11	14.0	17.10.68	Melton Mowbray	Moseley	25	38	9	-	-	-
					Worcester	2+1	-	-	-	-	-

FORWARDS

NAME	Ht	Wt	Birthdate	Birthplace	Club	Apps	Pts	T	C	P	DG
Peter Mitchell	6.0	17.7	31.01.67	Cheltenham							
					Worcester	15+2	10	2	-	-	-
Mark Linnett	5.11	17.0	17.02.63	Rugby	Rugby						
England: B, u23, Colts.					Moseley	87	52	11	-	-	-
					Worcester	33+1	30	6	-	-	-
Neil Lyman	6.1	18.0	06.05.70	Bedford	Kidderminster						
					Moseley	13	-	-	-	-	-
					Worcester	27+2	25	5	-	-	-
Gordy Houston	6.1	14.9	22.03.67	Bangor (NI)	Instonians						
Scotland: Students.					Worcester	17+1	15	3	-	-	-
Nick Tisdale	6.5	16.6	26.08.69	Bridgenorth	Kidderminster						
					Worcester	32+1	5	1	-	-	-
Steve Lloyd	6.6	17.0	11.07.68	Montevideo (Uru.)	Harlequins	2	-	-	-	-	-
					Moseley	63	5	1	-	-	-
					Worcester	22+1	5	1	-	-	-
Spencer Bradley	5.11	14.7	24.05.69	Worcester							
					Worcester	27+1	90	18	-	-	-
Paul Beard	6.0	14.7	04.10.73	Pontypridd	Prev. Clubs: Cardiff, Newport.						
					Worcester	12+1	10	2	-	-	-
Peter Miles	6.6	16.7	04.06.65	Gloucester	Bath						
					Gloucester	9	12	3	-	-	-
					Worcester	7+6	15	3	-	-	-
Chris Raymond	6.5	17.0	01.03.68	Cheltenham	Moseley	42+2	5	1	-	-	-
					Gloucester	20+1	5	1	-	-	-
					Worcester	16+1	10	2	-	-	-
Leyton Wilkinson	6.3	15.2	19.10.74	Sutton-in-Ashfield	Kidderminster						
					Worcester	3+1	15	3	-	-	-
Mark Nicholls	6.4	16.7	07.07.71	Gloucester	Gloucester	5+1	-	-	-	-	-
					Rugby	6	5	1	-	-	-
					Worcester	4+1	-	-	-	-	-
Rich Protherough	5.8	13.0	09.11.76	Cheltenham							
England: Colt.					Worcester	2	5	-	-	-	-

The Appearances and Points shown above are National Leagues' appearances & points only.

Sixways, Pershore Lane, Hindlip, Worcester. WR3 8SU

Tel. Nos. 01905 454183.   **Fax:** 01905 757222.

Capacity: 3,500   **Seated:** 850   **Standing:** 2,650

Simple Directions:
   M5 junction 6 (Worcester North) take the B4168 to Droitwich and the ground is 300 yards on the left.
Nearest Railway Station: Worcester (Foregate Street).
Car Parking: 1,000 spaces at the ground.
Admission:
   Season - Adults £70, Members £65.
   Matchday - Adults Standing £5, Seated £6, U14's Free, 14-18 £1
Club Shop: Yes. Manager Brian Pugh - 01905 426498.
Clubhouse: Open matchdays & training nights, snacks, barmeals & restaurant available.
   Functions: Yes, capacity 250, contact Simon Lloyd 01905 454183

Worcester's Captain; Bruce Fenley

MATCHDAY PROGRAMME

Size   A5

Number of pages   56 plus cover

Price   £1 included with admission

Programme Editor
                     Nicola Goodwin 01432 273473 (H)
                     01432 271494 (Fax), 01905 454183

Advertising Rates
                     Mono Full page £250, Half page £150

DIVISION THREE

(THIS YEAR'S LEAGUE ONE)

RECORDS SECTION

DIVISION THREE - THE LAST TEN YEARS

	Champions	Runners-up	Relegated
1987-88	**WAKEFIELD**	WEST HARTLEPOOL	Morley, Birmingham
1988-89	**PLYMOUTH ALBION**	RUGBY	Maidstone, Met Police
1989-90	**LONDON SCOTTISH**	WAKEFIELD	None
1990-91	**WEST HARTLEPOOL**	MORLEY	Met Police, Vale of Lune
1991-92	**RICHMOND**	FYLDE	Lydney, Nuneaton
1992-93	**OTLEY**	HAVANT	Sheffield, Leeds, Clifton, Askeans, Liverpool, Aspatria, Plymouth, Broughton P.
1993-94	**COVENTRY**	FYLDE	Havant, Redruth
1994-95	**BEDFORD**	BLACKHEATH	Clifton, Exeter
1995-96	**COVENTRY**	RICHMOND	None
1996-97	**EXETER**	FYLDE	Walsall, Havant, Redruth, Clifton

	Most Points		Most Tries	
1987-88	121	Steve Burnage (Fylde)	10	Brendan Hanavan (Fylde)
1988-89	123	Chris Howard (Rugby)	8	Steve Walklin (Plymouth) Dave Scully (Wakefield)
1989-90	102	Andy Higgin (Vale of Lune)	7	Mike Harrison (Wakefield) Brendan Hanavan (Fylde)
1990-91	108	Mark Rodgers (Sheffield)	9	Jonathan Wrigley (W Hartlepool)
1991-92	106	Mike Jackson (Fylde)	8	Matt Brain (Clifton)
1992-93	122	Andy Green (Exeter)	8	Martin Kelly (Broughton Park) Mark Sephton (Liverpool StH)
1993-94	172	Andy Finnie (Bedford)	12	Brendan Hanavan (Fylde)
1994-95	228	Andy Finnie (Bedford)	8	David Bishop (Rugby)
1995-96	215	Ralph Zoing (Harrogate)	12	Colin Phillips (Reading)
1996-97	404	Steve Gough (Fylde)	22	Mark Kirkby (Otley)

	Most Penalties		Most Conversions		Most Drop Goals	
1987-88	30	Steve Burnage (Fylde)	22	John Stabler (W. Hartlepool)	4	Andy Green (Exeter)
1988-89	19	Chris Howard (Rugby)	24	Steve Burnage (Fylde)	2	4 players
1989-90	13	Gavin Hastings (L. Scottish)	25	Andy Green (Exeter)	4	Richard Cramb (L. Scot.)
1990-91	19	John Stabler (W Hartlepool)	22	Andy Green (Exeter) Mark Rodgers (Sheffield)	2	5 players
1991-92	16	Simon Hogg (Clifton)	26	Mike Jackson (Fylde)	2	5 players
1992-93	14	Peter Rutledge (Otley)	31	Andy Green (Exeter)	3	Andy Green (Exeter) Simon Hogg (Clifton)
1993-94	45	Andy Finnie (Bedford)	23	Richard Angell (Coventry)	3	Jamie Grayshon (Morley)
1994-95	56	Andy Finnie (Bedford)	24	Andy Finnie (Bedford)	5	Jamie Grayshon (Morley) Simon Hogg (Clifton)
1995-96	53	Ralph Zoing (Harrogate)	28	John Gregory (Richmond)	8	Jamie Grayshon (Morley)
1996-97	82	Steve Gough (Fylde)	63	Ralph Zoing (Harrogate)	7	Craig Raymond (L Welsh)

Team Records

Highest score:	Liverpool StH 89 Clifton 13. 15.2.97
Highest aggregate:	103: Clifton 19 Leeds 84. 12.4.97
Highest score by a losing side:	Walsall 42 Reading 44. 12.4.97
Highest scoring draw:	34-34 Reading v Rosslyn Park. 17.2.96
Most consecutive wins:	14 Exeter 1996-97
Most consecutive defeats:	13 Redruth 1996-97
Most points for in a season:	1209 Leeds 1996-97
Least points for in a season:	46 Birmingham 1987088
Most points against in a season:	1347 Clifton 1996-97
Least points against in a season:	89 Plymouth 1988-89
Most tries for in a season:	158 Leeds 1996-97
Most tries against in a season:	184 Clifton 1996-97
Least tries for in a season:	3 Birmingham 1987-88
Least tries against in a season:	5 Plymouth 1988-89
Most conversions for in a season:	94 Leeds 1996-97
Most conversions against in a season:	125 Clifton 1996-97
Most penalties for in a season:	85 Fylde 1996-97
Most penalties against in a season:	74 Otley 1996-97
Least penalties for in a season:	8 Morley 1987-88
Least penalties against in a season:	10 West Hartlepool 1990-91
Most drop goals for in a season:	8 Morley 1994-95 & London Welsh 1996-97
Most drop goals against in a season:	8 Rotherham 1995-96 & Havant 1996-97

Individual Records

Most points in a season:	404 Steve Gough (Fylde) 1996-97
Most tries in a season:	22 Mark Kirkby (Otley) 1996-97
Most conversions in a season:	63 Ralph Zoing (Harrogate) 1996-97
Most penalties in a season:	82 Steve Gough (Fylde) 1996-97
Most drop goals in a season:	8 Jamie Grayson (Morley) 1995-96
Most points in a match:	39 Paul Brett, **Liverpool StH** v Clifton 15.2.97
Most tries in a match:	5 Mark Kirkby, **Otley** v Redruth 8.2.97
Most conversions in a match:	12 Paul Brett, **Liverpool StH** v Clifton 15.2.97
Most penalties in a match:	9 Paul Morris, **Lydney** v Otley 14.9.96
	Rob Ashworth, **Havant** v Clifton 21.9.96
Most drop goals in a match:	4 Andy Rimmer, **Broughton Park** v Sheffield 17.11.90

The Wharfedale flanker, Hedley Verity, who was an ever-present during the 30-game 96-97 league season, is seen here in action against Lydney. Photo: Keith Lewis.

Gerry Ainscough getting set for another attempt, broke many goal kicking records for Leeds RUFC last season.

DIVISION THREE - ALL TIME RECORDS

100+ POINTS IN A SEASON

POINTS	PLAYER	CLUB	SEASON	Tries	Cons.	Pens.	D.G.
404	Steve Gough	Fylde	1996-97	7	57	82	3
338	Richard Mills	Walsall	1996-97	1	42	81	2
307	Gerry Ainscough	Leeds	1996-97	14	45	49	
305	Ralph Zoing	Harrogate	1996-97	4	63	48	5
300	Andy Green	Exeter	1996-97	5	58	50	3
300	Craig Raymond	London Welsh	1996-97	6	39	57	7
287	Peter Rutledge	Otley	1996-97	8	56	45	
281	Jason Dance	Reading	1996-97	6	61	43	
275	Paul Morris	Lydney	1996-97	3	31	66	
228	Andy Finnie	Bedford	1994-95		24	56	4
215	Ralph Zoing	Harrogate	1995-96	3	19	51	3
210	Paul Brett	Liverpool StH	1996-97	14	40	20	
206	Jamie Grayshon	Morley	1995-96	2	20	44	8
197	Sateki Tuipulotu	Leeds	1996-97	15	37	16	
196	John Gregory	Richmond	1995-96	4	28	40	
195	Jamie Grayshon	Morley	1996-97	2	40	31	4
183	Jim Quantrill	Rugby	1995-96	3	21	42	
182	Adam Mounsey	Wharfdale	1996-97	10	39	18	
172	Andy Finnie	Bedford	1993-94		14	45	3
167	Peter Rutledge	Otley	1994-95	6	13	37	
166	Jamie Grayshon	Morley	1994-95	2	12	39	5
155	Kevin Plant	Rotherham	1995-96		18	35	5
147	Sam Howard	Blackheath	1994-95	1	11	38	2
147	Peter Rutledge	Otley	1995-96	1	11	40	
138	Steve Gough	Fylde	1995-96	2	13	34	
133	John Gregory	Richmond	1994-95	1	19	30	
131	Jim Quantrill	Rugby	1994-95	2	20	27	
128	Alan Peacock	Morley	1996-97	3	22	23	
125	Andy Green	Exeter	1993-94	3	16	24	2
123	Chris Howard	Rugby	1988-89	7	19	19	
123	Pete Russell	Havant	1996-97		27	20	3
122	Andy Green	Exeter	1992-93		10	31	3
121	Steve Burnage	Fylde	1987-88	4	30	14	1
121	Peter Rutledge	Otley	1992-93	3	14	26	
121	Andy Holder	Rosslyn Park	1996-97	3	17	23	1
120	Ian Morgan	Redruth	1996-97	3	15	25	
117	Jamie Grayshon	Morley	1993-94		12	28	3
116	Simon Hogg	Clifton	1994-95	1	9	26	5
110	Dan Clappison	Harrogate	1994-95	1	12	26	2
110	Mark Kirkby	Otley	1996-97	22			
109	Andy Parker	Fylde	1993-94	3	17	20	
108	Martin Livsey	Plymouth	1987-88	2	23	17	1
108	Mark Rodgers	Sheffield	1990-91	7	7	22	
106	Mike Jackson	Fylde	1991-92	1	12	26	
105	Ray Adamson	Wakefield	1987-88	1	19	21	
105	Andrew Hodgson	Wharfdale	1996-97	21			
103	Phil Belshaw	Reading	1995-96	1	16	22	
102	Andy Higgin	Vale of Lune	1989-90		9	22	6
102	Nat Saumi	Redruth	1996-97	1	14	23	
101	Dominic Cundy	Plymouth	1988-89				
101	Colin Stephens	Leeds	1996-97	10	9	6	5
100	Simon Hogg	Clifton	1991-92	2	16	19	1
100	Mark Preston	Fylde	1996-97	20			

MOST POINTS IN A MATCH

39	Paul Brett	Liverpool StH v Clifton	15.02.97
30	Paul Brett	Liverpool StH v Redruth	01.02.97
29	Paul Morris	Lydney v Otley	14.09.96
29	Rob Ashworth	Havant v Clifton	21.09.96
28	Steve Burnage	Fylde v Birmingham	07.11.87
28	Craig Raymond	London Welsh v Clifton	28.12.96
27	Ralph Zoing	Harrogate v Fylde	14.10.95
27	Gerry Ainscough	Leeds v Rosslyn Park	14.09.96
27	Craig Raymond	London Welsh v Lydney	09.11.96
27	Gerry Ainscough	Leeds v Walsall	01.03.97
27	Nat Saumi	Redruth v Clifton	03.05.97
26	Greg Way	Reading v Harrogate	16.09.95
26	Andy Green	Exeter v Wharfdale	07.09.96
26	Richard Mills	Walsall v Clifton	07.09.96
25	Domonic Cundy	Plymouth v Met Police	26.11.89
25	Mark Rodgers	Sheffield v Askeans	13.03.93
25	Richard Angell	Coventry v Redruth	30.04.94
25	Steve Gough	Fylde v Rosslyn Park	26.10.96
25	Mark Kirkby	Otley v Redruth	08.02.97
25	Jason Dance	Reading v Clifton	01.03.97
25	Richard Mills	Walsall v Redruth	19.04.97
24	Chris Howard	Rugby v Maidstone	26.11.88
24	Richard Mills	Walsall v Leeds	12.10.96
24	Jason Dance	Reading v Walsall	29.03.97
24	Ralph Zoing	Harrogate v Clifton	05.04.97
24	Steve Gough	Fylde v London Welsh	26.04.97
24	Ralph Zoing	Harrogate v Liverpool StH	17.05.97
23	John Stabler	West Hartlepool v Broughton Park	09.03.91
23	Ralph Zoing	Harrogate v Reading	16.09.95
23	John Gregory	Richmond v Rotherham	30.09.95
23	Phil Belshaw	Reading v Morley	14.10.95
23	Peter Rutledge	Otley v Walsall	09.11.96
23	Craig Raymond	London Welsh v Rosslyn Park	18.02.97
23	Jamie Grayshon	Morley v London Welsh	12.04.97
22	Andy Atkinson	Wakefield v Met Police	24.09.88
22	Simon Hogg	Clifton v Lydney	28.03.92
22	Kevin O'Brien	Broughton Park v Askeans	11.04.92
22	Martin Livesey	Richmond v Blackheath	13.11.93
22	Peter Rutledge	Otley v Harrogate	29.10.94
22	Gerry Ainscough	Leeds v Harrogate	05.10.96
22	Sateki Tuipulotu	Leeds v Lydney	15.03.97
22	Richard Mills	Walsall v Reading	12.04.97
22	Gerry Ainscough	Leeds v Havant	26.04.97
21	John Stabler	West Hartlepool v Sheffield	03.10.87
21	Gareth Hughes	London Welsh v Fylde	13.01.90
21	Peter Rutledge	Otley v Askeans	27.03.93
21	Jason Hoad	Richmond v Fylde	05.02.94
21	Andy Finnie	Bedford v Coventry	23.04.94
21	Denzil Evans	Rugby v Richmond	15.10.94
21	Jamie Grayshon	Morley v Richmond	25.03.95
21	Jim Quantrill	Rugby v Fylde	09.09.95
21	Jamie Grayshon	Morley v Rugby	21.10.95
21	Marc Thomas	Coventry v Otley	02.03.96
21	Peter Rutledge	Otley v Redruth	21.09.96
21	Gerry Ainscough	Leeds v Walsall	12.10.96
21	Peter Rutledge	Otley v Reading	16.11.96
21	Alan Peacock	Morley v Clifton	18.01.97
21	Jason Dance	Reading v Redruth	15.02.97
21	Andy Green	Exeter v Fylde	05.04.97

MOST TRIES IN A MATCH

5	Mark Kirkby	Otley v Redruth	08.02.97
4	Brendan Hanavan	Fylde v Exeter	03.10.87
4	Steve Walklin	Plymouth v Birmingham	17.10.87
4	Ian Russell	Plymouth v Fylde	31.10.87
4	Brendan Hanavan	Fylde v Birmingham	07.11.87
4	Dan Cottrell	Clifton v Askeans	04.01.92
4	Mark Sephton	Liverpool StH v Aspatria	13.03.93
4	Dean Crompton	Liverpool StH v Aspatria	13.03.93
4	Mark Farrar	Otley v Askeans	27.03.93
4	Brendan Hanavan	Fylde v Redruth	09.04.94
4	Richard Matthias	Leeds v Clifton	07.12.96
4	Simon Dovell	Exeter v Havant	21.12.96
4	Ben Wade	Morley v Clifton	18.01.97
4	Mark Sephton	Liverpool StH v Clifton	15.02.97
4	Colin Stephens	Leeds v Lydney	15.03.97
4	Toby Rakison	Rosslyn Park v Otley	29.03.97
4	Steve Bartliffe	Leeds v Havant	26.04.97

3	Kevin Norris	Plymouth v Sheffield	12.09.87
3	Simon Cowling	Wakefield v Birmingham	31.10.87
3	Andy Holloway	Wakefield v Morley	12.03.88
3	Owen Evans	W Hartlepool v Nuneaton	23.04.88
3	Mike Harrison	Wakefield v Met Police	24.09.88
3	Simon Hughes	Plymouth v Fylde	19.11.88
3	Mike Murtagh	Wakefield v Askeans	11.11.89
3	Mike Harrison	Wakefield v Lon. Welsh	28.04.90
3	Andy Green	Exeter v Met Police	10.11.90
3	Peter Robinson	W Hartlepool v Vale of Lune	02.03.91
3	Mark Chatterton	Exeter v Headingley	23.11.91
3	Phil Della-Savina	Richmond v Nuneaton	28.03.92
3	Chris Thornton	Leeds v Exeter	13.03.93
3	Martin Kelly	Broughton Park v Exeter	24.04.93
3	Tony Brooks	Rosslyn Park v Havant	12.03.94
3	Eddie Saunders	Rugby v Bedford	12.04.92
3	Julian Horrobin	Coventry v Otley	30.03.96
3	Mark Preston	Fylde v Clifton	14.09.96
3	Mark Kirkby	Otley v Clifton	05.10.96
3	Bob Armstrong	Exeter v Redruth	19.10.96
3	Andrew Hodgson	Wharfedale v Walsall	18.01.97
3	Guy Spencer	Reading v Lydney	08.02.97
3	Paul Brett	Liverpool StH v Clifton	15.02.97
3	Brit Pearce	Havant v Walsall	22.02.97
3	Gerry Ainscough	Leeds v Walsall	01.03.97
3	Danny Jones	Liverpool StH v Exeter	29.03.97
3	Nick Green	Leeds v Clifton	12.04.97
3	Iain Dixon	Exeter v Otley	26.04.97

3	Mark Preston	Fylde v Morley	17.10.87
3	Simon Cowling	Wakefield v Nuneaton	05.12.87
3	Mike Cathery	Exeter v Birmingham	26.03.88
3	Chris Howard	Rugby v Vale of Lune	10.09.88
3	Andy Atkinson	Wakefield v Met Police	24.09.88
3	Paul Galvin	Met Police v Maidstone	14.01.89
3	Gareth Hughes	Lon. Welsh v Fylde	13.01.90
3	Dan Cottrell	Clifton v Broughton Park	13.10.90
3	Mark Spearman	Clifton v Exeter	17.11.90
3	Gary Walker	Roundhay v Askeans	06.04.91
3	Andy Ireland	Fylde v Askeans	14.12.91
3	Glyn Mellville	Otley v Aspatria	24.10.92
3	Harry Langley	Exeter v Broughton Park	24.04.93
3	Mike Friday	Blackheath v Morley	06.11.93
3	Tony Clark	Morley v Bedford	25.02.92
3	Eddie Saunders	Rugby v Rotherham	23.09.92
3	Andy Clarke	Richmond v Rosslyn Park	13.04.96
3	Simon Dovell	Exeter v Harrogate	21.09.96
3	Brian Gabrial	Morley v Wharfedale	19.10.96
3	Richard Matthias	Leeds v Redruth	09.11.96
3	Paul Brett	Liverpool StH v Redruth	01.02.97
3	Andrew Hodgson	Wharfedale v Lon. Welsh	15.02.97
3	Julian Hill	Lydney v Lon. Welsh	22.02.97
3	Mark Farrar	Harrogate v Lon. Welsh	01.03.97
3	Mark Scharrenberg	Reading v Liverpool StH	22.03.97
3	Mark Kirkby	Otley v Rosslyn Park	12.04.97
3	Mark Appleson	Leeds v Clifton	12.04.97
3	Andrew Hodgson	Wharfedale v Rosslyn Park	03.05.97

DIVISION THREE

MOST APPEARANCES

125	**Richard Byrom**	Nottingham	Full Back
122	**David Bishop**	Rugby	Scrum Half
121	**Jamie Grayshon**	Morley	Stand Off
118	**Eddie Saunders**	Rugby	Winger
117	**Tony Clarke**	Morley	Winger
	Steve Rice	Otley	Prop
116	**Nick Nelmes**	Lydney	Hooker
115	**Tim Smith**	Gloucester 94, Worcester 21.	Full Back
113	**Andy Hargreaves**	Otley	Flanker
111	**Neil Hargreaves**	Headingley 33, Leeds 8, Wakefield 9, Otley 61.	Flanker
109	**Curtis Hutson**	Reading	Lock
	Robert Mills	Lydney	Utility Back
	Martin Freer	Nottingham	Prop
103	**Jeremy Hopkinson**	Wharfedale 16, Harrogate 87.	Back Row
	Paul Gutteridge	Bristol 3, Richmond 16, Reading 84.	Prop
	Danny Pratt	Wasps 1, Reading 102.	Lock
102	**Graeme Peacock**	London Welsh	Back Five
	Chris Gray	Nottingham	Lock
101	**David Wheat**	Harrogate	Back Row
100	**Richard Whyley**	Harrogate	Prop
	Phil Bowman	Rugby	Lock
	Mark Appleson	Headingley 10, London Scottish 46, Sale 17, Leeds 27.	Winger
99	**Gordon Throup**	Wharfedale 30, Morley 69.	Hooker
98	**Ian Hassall**	Harrogate	Full Back
	Andy Simpson	Harrogate	Prop
96	**Simon Hodgkinson**	Moseley 29, Nottingham 67.	Full Back
	Ralph Zoing	Harrogate	Stand Off

DIVISION THREE - TEN YEAR RECORD

	87/88	88/89	89/90	90/91	91/92	92/93	93/94	94/95	95/96	96/97
ASKEANS	-	8	5	6	7	10	-	-	-	-
ASPATRIA	-	-	-	-	-	9	-	-	-	-
BIRMINGHAM	12	-	-	-	-	-	-	-	-	-
BROUGHTON PARK	-	-	-	8	6	11	-	-	-	-
BEDFORD	-	-	-	-	-	-	3	1	-	-
BLACKHEATH	-	-	-	-	-	-	4	2	-	-
CLIFTON	-	-	-	5	3	8	-	9	-	16
COVENTRY	-	-	-	-	-	-	1	-	1	-
EXETER	9	9	6	4	4	3	6	10	-	1
FYLDE	6	10	8	3	2	-	2	-	10	2
HARROGATE	-	-	-	-	-	-	-	7	6	5
HAVANT	-	-	-	-	-	2	9	-	-	14
HEADINGLEY	-	-	-	-	11	-	-	-	-	-
LEEDS	-	-	-	-	-	6	-	-	-	3
LIVERPOOL StH	-	-	-	-	-	7	-	-	-	12
LONDON SCOTTISH	-	-	1	-	-	-	-	-	-	-
LONDON WELSH	-	-	12	-	-	-	-	-	-	11
LYDNEY	-	-	11	11	13	-	-	-	-	10
MAIDSTONE	8	12	-	-	-	-	-	-	-	-
MET POLICE	7	11	-	12	-	-	-	-	-	-
MORLEY	11	-	-	2	-	-	8	5	5	4
NUNEATON	10	5	10	7	12	-	-	-	-	-
OTLEY	-	-	-	-	9	1	-	6	7	9
PLYMOUTH	3	1	-	-	-	12	-	-	-	-
READING	-	-	-	-	-	-	-	-	8	6
REDRUTH	-	-	-	-	5	4	10	-	-	15
RICHMOND	-	-	-	-	1	-	7	8	2	-
ROSSLYN PARK	-	-	-	-	-	-	5	4	9	8
ROTHERHAM	-	-	-	-	-	-	-	-	4	-
ROUNDHAY	-	-	7	9	10	-	-	-	-	-
RUGBY	-	2	-	-	-	-	-	3	3	-
SHEFFIELD	4	6	4	10	8	5	-	-	-	-
VALE OF LUNE	5	7	9	13	-	-	-	-	-	-
WAKEFIELD	1	3	2	-	-	-	-	-	-	-
WALSALL	-	-	-	-	-	-	-	-	-	13
WHARFDALE	-	-	-	-	-	-	-	-	-	7
WEST HARTLEPOOL	2	4	3	1	-	-	-	-	-	-

Kevin Hickey, flanked by Bob Browne (Secretary, left) and Roger Parkes (Chairman of Rugby, right) signs for Stourbridge RFC. He repaid the club with an excellent season ending up as top try scorer.

Kendal's 'Players' Player of the Year' Keith Robertson winning good lineout ball. Photo: Courtesy The Westmorland Gazette.

JEWSON

NATIONAL
League Two North

1996-97 DIVISION FOUR NORTH

PLAYING RECORD & breakdown

	Pd	W	D	L	Pts	HOME W	D	L	Pts	AWAY W	D	L	Pts
Worcester	26	23	3	0	49	12	1	0	25	11	2	0	24
Birmingham S.	26	19	0	7	38	11	0	2	22	8	0	5	16
Preston G.	26	17	2	7	36	10	0	3	20	7	2	4	16
Manchester	26	17	1	8	35	10	1	2	21	7	0	6	14
Sandal	26	15	1	10	31	11	0	2	22	4	1	8	9
Stourbridge	26	14	1	11	29	9	1	3	19	5	0	9	10
Winnington P.	26	14	1	11	29	7	1	5	15	7	0	6	14
Sheffield	26	11	2	13	24	8	1	4	17	3	1	9	7
Kendal	26	11	1	14	23	7	0	6	14	4	1	8	9
Aspatria	26	10	1	15	21	6	1	6	13	4	0	9	8
Lichfield	26	10	0	16	20	8	0	5	16	2	0	11	4
Nuneaton	26	8	1	17	17	6	1	6	13	2	0	11	4
Hereford	26	4	0	22	8	3	0	10	6	1	0	12	2
Stoke on Trent	26	2	0	24	4	2	0	11	4	0	0	13	0

POINTS FOR & breakdown

	Lge Pos	Pts	T	C	P	D	HOME Pts	T	C	P	D	AWAY Pts	T	C	P	D
1 **Worcester**	1	830	112	72	38	4	466	65	45	15	2	364	47	27	23	2
2 **Manchester**	4	795	101	64	53	1	449	60	40	23	0	346	41	24	30	1
3 **Birmingham S.**	2	746	101	50	46	1	431	58	33	24	1	315	43	17	22	0
4 **Stourbridge**	6	704	93	61	39	0	370	50	33	18	0	334	43	28	21	0
5 **Winnington P.**	7	651	87	45	38	4	305	39	25	20	0	346	48	20	18	4
6 **Sandal**	5	618	73	41	54	3	378	46	26	30	2	240	27	15	24	1
7 **Aspatria**	10	611	75	43	48	2	323	40	21	25	2	288	35	22	213	0
8 **Preston G.**	3	568	53	39	65	10	290	28	18	34	4	278	25	21	31	6
9 **Lichfield**	11	546	65	37	48	1	313	37	22	28	0	233	28	15	20	1
10 **Kendal**	9	541	50	36	60	3	331	35	24	35	1	210	21	12	25	2
11 **Sheffield**	8	484	43	25	73	0	297	27	18	42	0	187	16	7	31	0
12 **Nuneaton**	12	457	58	31	31	4	302	39	22	19	2	155	19	9	12	2
13 **Stoke on Trent**	14	391	41	21	48	0	224	23	11	29	0	167	18	10	19	0
14 **Hereford**	13	287	36	16	25	0	167	20	8	17	0	120	16	8	8	0

POINTS AGAINST & breakdown

	Lge Pos	Pts	T	C	P	D	HOME Pts	T	C	P	D	AWAY Pts	T	C	P	D
1 **Worcester**	1	375	35	25	48	2	175	15	11	25	1	200	20	14	23	1
2 **Birmingham S.**	2	391	48	26	33	0	181	25	13	10	0	210	23	13	23	0
3 **Preston G.**	3	394	41	18	49	2	184	19	7	24	1	210	22	11	25	1
4 **Kendal**	9	451	46	28	54	1	193	20	9	25	0	258	26	19	29	1
5 **Sheffield**	8	483	54	27	47	6	221	22	9	26	5	262	32	18	21	1
6 **Manchester**	4	504	62	37	40	0	206	25	15	17	0	298	37	22	23	0
7 **Winnington P.**	7	565	62	33	60	3	294	33	18	29	2	271	29	15	31	1
8 **Sandal**	5	573	70	41	46	1	212	26	14	18	0	361	44	27	28	1
9 **Stourbridge**	6	579	65	37	58	2	241	25	13	29	1	338	40	24	29	1
10 **Nuneaton**	12	667	84	50	48	1	318	44	25	16	0	349	40	25	32	1
=11 **Lichfield**	11	713	89	56	49	3	274	35	21	18	1	439	54	35	31	2
=11 **Aspatria**	10	713	92	50	43	8	278	34	18	19	5	435	58	32	24	3
13 **Stoke on Trent**	14	849	115	71	42	2	394	52	31	22	2	455	63	40	20	0
14 **Hereford**	13	972	131	82	49	2	412	52	31	29	1	560	79	51	20	1

1996-97 DIVISION FOUR NORTH

REVIEW

WORCESTER - Won the title comfortably by eleven points in their second season at National League rugby. They went undefeated with 23 wins and three draws. Topping the points and try scoring lists with 830 and 112 respectively. Winger Nick Baxter made a major contribution with a new club record of eighteen league tries in a season, which was also a Division record. Summer signing, Tim Smith from Gloucester, kicked well and ended the season with 242 points. Discipline was good with just four yellow cards which saw them finish fourth in the Fair Play League. They were defensively sound with the best record in the Division in terms of both points and tries conceded.

ASPATRIA - After relegation the previous season from National Four they finished a comfortable tenth. Were reasonably placed before losing six out of the last seven to drop a couple of places. Winger Craig Marriott set a new club record of seventeen League tries in a season, he also set a new club record of scoring tries in seven consecutive matches. Stand-off\full back Mike Scott set a new club record of 251 points in a season, scoring points in 25 of his 26 appearances. Used 45 players with only Nuneaton using more - 49.

BIRMINGHAM SOLIHULL - Achieved their best League finish since the 1978/88 season when they were in the Third Division. Showing good home form with just two defeats to Worcester and Manchester. Stand-off Jonathan Smart scored a club record 271 points which also included records for conversions and penalties with 47 and 43 respectively. They were one of three teams to score over 100 tries in the Division with the forwards outscoring the backs 51 to 50. Top of the try scoring list was Hooker David Cox with twelve, closely followed by flanker Bob Robinson and Jonathan Smart. They did not fair too well in the Fair Play League finishing twelth after having two players sent off and seven yellow carded.

HEREFORD - They finished bottom of the Fair Play League with 85 points from five sendings off and seven yellow cards. Suffering relegation after just one season having come up from Midlands One. They were always in the relegation area and their fate was sealed with seven straight defeats to end the season. They finished the season with just 36 tries and 287 points which were the lowest in the Division. Not surprisingly they collected most points and tries with 972 and 131 respectively.

KENDAL - Finished ninth, the same as the previous year, in a mixed season. They started and finished the season reasonably well but in the middle won just two out of fourteen. They managed the double over Sheffield and Aspatria. Coming second in the Fair Play League with ten points from two yellow cards which were against Jon Nicholson and Steve Whitehead. They used just 32 players the lowest in the Division by one from Sandal and Sheffield with Paul Dods and Billy Coxon being ever present. However, they did not score enough tries, managing just 50 with only Hereford, Stoke and Stourbridge scoring fewer.

LICHFIELD - Finished eleventh one place better than last season. Never managing to get a settled side, using 39 players. Andy Grey, centre and Matthew Brown being ever present. Their away record included just two wins at Kendal and Hereford. They won their last three league games having previously lost six in a row to add some respectability to their season. Coming tenth in the Fair Play League with 55 points from one sending off and nine yellow cards. Twenty of the points came from Hooker Will Parker with one red and two yellow cards.

MANCHESTER - Fourth place in their first season of National League rugby was an exceptional performance. They had a patchy start to the season with just two wins from eight before moving up a gear and then won fifteen out of their next eighteen games. Doing the double over second placed Birmingham Solihull. Manchester were the second highest points scorers in the Division behind Worcester and one of only three teams to top the 100 try mark. Finishing fifth in the Fair Play League with 30 points from one sending-off, Paul Burns, and four yellow cards. Only three teams, Aspatria, Hereford and Nuneaton used more players than Manchester's 41.

NUNEATON - Finished twelfth two places worse than last year. Having just five points out of 28 and looked to be relegation material. They then started their annual escape with five wins from seven to pull clear of Hereford and relegation. Using more players than any other side in the Division with 49, far more than next on the list Aspatria. They finished one from bottom in the Fair Play League with only Hereford having a worst record. Most of Nuneaton's 60 points came early in the season after which they cleaned up their game.

PRESTON GRASSHOPPERS - Finished third, five places higher than the previous season. They have now finished in the top four, seven seasons out of ten. They are one of three teams to have played all their league rugby in the Division along with Lichfield and Stourbridge. Having the fifth best home record and second best away record. Despite finishing second they scored just 53 tries which was only tenth best in the Division. At the other end of the scale only Worcester with 35 conceded less than Preston's 41 tries. They used just 35 players which was the fifth lowest total in the Division with Steve Kerry being the only ever present.

SANDAL - Their second season in National League rugby saw them finish fifth, a one place improvement on the previous season. Superb home record with eleven wins from thirteen matches and second only to Worcester who won twelve and drew one. their away record was far from impressive with just four fins. Had a good run near the end of the season to win six straight games including good wins over Birmingham, Solihull and Preston. Utility back Mark Wolff scored tries in five consecutive matches. Used just 33 players which was second only to Kendal's 32.

SHEFFIELD - Finished eighth three places worse than the previous season. Had a disappointing season being unable to get any sort of consistancy never winning more than two games in a row. Found scoring tries difficult with just 43, only Hereford 36 and Stoke 41, scored less. Came top of the Fair Play League with just one yellow card which was awarded against captain Nick Crapper for back chat.

STOKE ON TRENT - Came fourteenth and last to end their five season stay in the division. Had the distinction, along with West Hartlepool, as the only club not to win away in the National Leagues. Relied heavily on Simon Ashcroft who contributed 151 of their 391 points. Winger come Scrum Half, Simeon lloyd was easily the top try scorer with 11 - six more than Steve Maskery. Despite losing on a regular basis they kept their discipline to finish a highly creditable third in the Fair Play League.

STOURBRIDGE - Finished sixth one place better than the previous season. Had a stop start season never able to get any momentum going. Fourth highest try scorers in the Division with 93 which included 25 from their front row. Best of he front row as prop Simon Bayliewith twelve but top try scorer was No 8 Kevin Hickey with fifteen. Had the distinction of having two players sent off in the same match. Dale Smallman and John Taylor were dismissed in the 11-20 home defeat to Winnington Park. Taylor was sent-off after coming on as a replacement.

WINNINGTON PARK - finished seventh three places lower than the previous season. Had a terrible start to the season with just one point out of ten after five games. They got some consistancy and rattled up 18 points out of 24 to more up the table dramaticaly. Gary Bell had a superb season scoring a club record of 240 points. Used just 34 players, the third lowest after Kendal with 32 and both Sandal and Sheffield with 33. Front rowers Ian Taylor and Ian Davies were the only two ever presents. Had the fourth best away record in the Division with fourteen points from seven wins.

RECORD REVIEW

INDIVIDUAL RECORDS

MOST POINTS IN A SEASON

Preston's Steve kerry took back a record which he held from 1987-88 until 1990-91. Kerry's original record was 118 points set back in the inaugural season of league rugby 1987-88.
Since then the record has changed hands three times before Kerry's 1996-97 total of 317 regained it. His 317 points nearly doubled the previous record of 164, held by Walsall's Richard Mills

Evolution of record

118	Steve Kerry	Preston G'hoppers	1987-88
127	Paul Grayson	Preston G'hoppers	1991-92
131	Ralph Zoing	Harrogate	1992-93
164	Richard Mills	Walsall	1994-95
317	Steve Kerry	Preston G'hoppers	1996-97

MOST TRIES IN A SEASON

Worcester wing, Nick Baxter, broke the 6-year-old record for tries in a season with 18. The previous of record of 16 was set back in 1990-91 by Otley's winger Jon Walker. The two previous holders of this record are fairly well-known players - Eddie Saunders and Jim Mallinder.

Evolution of record

7	Eddie Saunders	Rugby	1987-88
10	Jim Mallinder	Roundhay	1988-89
16	on Walker	Otley	1990-91
18	Nick Baxter	Worcester	1996-97

MOST CONVERSIONS IN A SEASON

Worcester full back Tim Smith demolished the previous record of 29 conversions in a season with 61 in his side's Championship season. The previous record of 29 , set in the 1994-95 season, was achieved by Richard Mills in Walsall's Championship season.

12	Steve Kerry	Preston G'hoppers	1987-88
	Chris Howard	Rugby	1987-88
13	Gary Walker	oundhay	1988-89
17	Jon Howarth	Otley	1990-91
28	Ralph Zoing	Harrogate	1992-93
29	Richard Mills	Walsall	1994-95
61	Tim Smith	Worcester	1996-97

MOST PENALTIES IN A SEASON

Another record that was more than doubled last season with Preston's Steve Kerry setting a new total of 64. This beat the previous record of 31 which was shared by Simon Pennington of Stourbridge and Richard Mills of Walsall. Kerry had set the original record back in 1987-88 with 21.

21	Steve Kerry	Preston G'hoppers	1987-88
23	Jamie Grayshon	Morley	1988-89
28	Paul Grayson	Preston G'Hoppers	1990-91
31	Simon Pennington	Stourbridge	1992-93
31	Richard Mills	Walsall	1994-95
64	Steve Kerry	Preston G'hoppers	1996-97

MOST DROP GOALS IN A SEASON

Another record for Preston's Steve Kerry which again he originally set back in the 1987-88 season. Kerry kicked 9 drop goals to break the previous record of 6 set by another Preston player, Paul Grayson, during the 1991-92 season.

Evolution of record

5	Steve Kerry	Preston G'hoppers	1987-88
6	Paul Grayson	Preston G'hoppers	1991-92
9	Steve Kerry	Preston G'hoppers	1996-97

PLAYERS USED

	Players used	Ever present	
Aspatria	45(1)	1	Mike Scott
Birmingham	36(3)	2	Lee Baker, Andy Wood.
Hereford	42(3)	-	
Kendal	32(5)	2	Paul Dods, Billy Coxon.
Lichfield	39(7)	2	Andy Gray, Matthew Brown.
Manchester	41(6)	-	
Nuneaton	49(2)	-	
Preston	35(6)	1	Steve Kerry
Sandal	33(6)	-	
Sheffield	33(5)	-	
Stoke-on-Trent	41(2)	-	
Stourbridge	41(3)	-	
Winnington P.	34(4)	2	Ian Taylor, Ian Davies.
Worcester	39(3)	-	

FAIR PLAY LEAGUE

This is another new feature which we will publish each season and hopefully get the RFU to make part of their awards evening.

This season's Division Four award goes to Sheffield, who had the second best record in the National Leagues, after Second Division champions Richmond. Their one yellow card went to Nick Crapper for back chat.

Hereford were the team who had most players sent-off in League rugby with five - one more than Harrogate. They also had the second worst points total in National League rugby - behind Harrogate.

Team	Yellow card	Red card	Total
Sheffield	1	-	5
Kendal	2	-	10
Stoke-on-Trent	1	1	15
Worcester	4	-	20
Manchester	4	1	30
Sandal	2	2	30
Aspatria	7	-	35
Stourbridge	3	2	35
Preston	7	1	45
Lichfield	9	1	55
Winnington Park	9	1	55
Birmingham S.	7	2	55
Nuneaton	10	1	60
Hereford	7	5	85

PLAYERS SENT OFF - Division Four.

Steve Maskery	Stoke V Birmingham 21.9.96
Dwayne Edwards	Hereford v Stourbridge 28.9.96
Lee Baker	Birmingham v Stourbridge 26.10.96
Paul Burns	Manchester v Hereford 16.11.96
Simon Lewis	Hereford v Manchester 16.11.96
Nigel Hoyle	Sandal v Birmingham 21.12.96
Gareth Hughes	Hereford V Worcester 21.12.96
Will Parker	Lichfield v Aspatria 25.1.97
Chris Fairley	Hereford v Preston 25.1.97
Gareth Griffiths	Hereford v Preston 25.1.97
Dale Smallman	Stourbridge v Winnington P. 1.2.97
John Taylor	Stourbridge v Winnington P. 1.2.97
Richard McBride	Birmingham v Stourbridge 8.3.97
Mike Bebbington	Winnington v Kendal 5.4.97
Glen Barker	Sandal v Preston 3.5.97
Glyn Dewhurst	Preston v Sandal 3.5.97
Simon Lewis	Hereford v Lichfield 10.5.97

Matt Hoskin of Manchester FC (white shorts) breaks through the Stourbridge defence. The two players coming to support are from left Andy Murison and Tim Burgon. Photo: Courtesy The Stockport Express Advertiser.

Aspatria's captain Mark Richardson in action for Cumbria whom he captained to the County Championship. Mark was also chosen to play for the Barbarians. Photo: Courtesy Workington Times & Star.

1996-97 DIVISION FOUR NORTH

MOST TRIES

18	Nick Baxter	Worcester
17	Craig Marriott	Aspatria
15	Kevin Hickey	Stourbridge
15	Tim Burgon	Manchester
15	Glen Pearson	Manchester
12	Simon Baylie	Stourbridge
11	Bruce Fenley	Worcester
11	Jez Owens	Winnington Park
11	Gary Bell	Winnington Park
10	David Cox	Birmingham S
9	Ben Barton	Winnington Park
9	Adrian Bird	Winnington Park
9	Andrew Wolff	Sandal
9	Steve Swindells	Manchester
9	Bob Robinson	Birmingham S
9	Mark Chudleigh	Birmingham S
9	Clive Bent	Nuneaton
9	Mark Wolff	Sandal
9	Matthew Brown	Lichfield

MOST CONVERSIONS

61	Tim Smith	Worcester
50	Chris Mann	Stourbridge
49	Steve Swindells	Manchester
47	Jonathan Smart	Birmingham S
43	Mike Scott	Aspatria
40	Gary Bell	Winnington Park
40	Mark Hardcastle	Sandal
39	Steve Kerry	Preston G
33	David Richards	Lichfield
19	Jason Hudson	Kendal
16	Simon Ashcroft	Stoke on Trent
15	Jamie Morley	Sheffield
15	Gavin Henderson	Nuneaton
13	Jon Nicholson	Kendal
13	Marc Thomas	Nuneaton
12	Neil James	Manchester
9	Rich Tomlinson	Worcester
8	Rob Pound	Sheffield
8	Jim Reed-Daunter	Stourbridge
5	Dave Hill	Winnington Park
3	Gary Jeffreys	Stoke on Trent
3	Richard Gee	Nuneaton
3	Paul Dods	Kendal
3	Laurence Whitby-Smith	Lichfield
2	Nick Hillard	Stoke on Trent
2	Martin Kirk	Sheffield
2	Colin Taylor	Nuneaton
2	Jacob John	Stourbridge

MOST PENALTIES

64	Steve Kerry	Preston G
53	Mark Hardcastle	Sandal
48	Mike Scott	Aspatria
43	Jonathan Smart	Birmingham S
40	Jason Hudson	Kendal
39	Jamie Morley	Sheffield
38	Simon Ashcroft	Stoke on Trent
36	Steve Swindells	Manchester
35	Gary Bell	Winnington Park
32	Dave Richards	Lichfield
32	Chris Mann	Stourbridge
30	Tim Smith	Worcester
30	Rob Pound	Sheffield
19	Jon Nicholson	Kendal
16	Laurence Whitby-Smith	Lichfield
11	Gavin Henderson	Nuneaton
9	Phil Gee	Manchester
9	Nick Hillard	Stoke on Trent
9	Marc Thomas	Nuneaton
8	Rich Tomlinson	Worcester
6	Neil James	Manchester
5	Warwick Masser	Nuneaton
5	Colin Taylor	Nuneaton
4	Jim Reed-Daunter	Stourbridge
3	Dave Hill	Winnington Park
3	Matt Burgess	Sheffield
2	Dave Seales	Manchester
2	Simon Pennington	Stourbridge
1	David Bell	Kendal
1	Jacob John	Stourbridge
1	Simon Reid	Nuneaton
1	Andy Turton	Sandal
1	Rob Smith	Preston G
1	Steve Teasdale	Stoke on Trent
1	Nick Crapper	Sheffield

MOST DROP GOALS

9	Steve Kerry	Preston G
4	Dave Hill	Winnington Park
3	Mark Hardcastle	Sandal
3	David Bell	Kendal
3	Richard Gee	Nuneaton
2	Gareth Hughes	Worcester
2	Mike Scott	Aspatria
1	Jihn Bleasdale	Preston G
1	Tony Yapp	Worcester
1	Greg Harwood	Worcester
1	Warwick Masser	Nuneaton
1	David Richards	Lichfield
1	Jonathan Smart	Birmingham S
1	Phil Gee	Manchester

1996-97 DIVISION FOUR NORTH

MOST POINTS IN THE SEASON

POINTS	PLAYER	CLUB	Tries	Cons.	Pens.	D.G.
317	Steve Kerry	Preston G	4	39	64	9
271	Jonathan Smart	Birmingham S	9	47	43	1
251	Steve Swindells	Manchester	9	49	36	-
251	Mike Scott	Aspatria 1966-97	3	43	48	2
248	Mark Hardcastle	Sandal	2	40	53	3
242	Tim Smith	Worcester	6	61	30	-
240	Gary Bell	Winnington Park	11	40	35	-
206	Chris Mann	Stourbridge	2	49	32	-
175	David Richards	Lichfield	2	33	32	1
167	Jamie Morley	Sheffield	4	15	39	-
163	Jason Hudson	Kendal	1	19	40	-
151	Simon Ascroft	Stoke on Trent	1	16	38	-
111	Rob Pound	Sheffield	1	8	30	-
90	Nick Baxter	Worcester	18	-	-	-
85	Craig Marriott	Aspatria	17	-	-	-
83	Jon Nicholson	Kendal	-	13	19	-
75	Kevin Hickey	Stourbridge	15	-	-	-
75	Tim Burgon	Manchester	15	-	-	-
75	Glen Pearson	Manchester	15	-	-	-
72	Rich Tomlinson	Worcester	6	8	9	-
68	Gavin Henderson	Nuneaton	1	15	11	-
68	Marc Thomas	Nuneaton	3	13	9	-
60	Simon Baylie	Stourbridge	12	-	-	-
56	Richard Gee	Manchester	4	3	9	1
55	Bruce Fenley	Worcester	11	-	-	-
55	Jez Owens	Winnington Park	11	-	-	-
55	Simeon Lloyd	Stoke on Trent	11	-	-	-
54	Laurence Whitby-Smith	Lichfield	-	3	16	-
50	David Cox	Birmingham S	10	-	-	-
47	Neil James	Manchester	1	12	6	-
45	Ben Barton	Winnington Park	9	-	-	-
45	Adrian Bird	Winnington Park	9	-	-	-
45	Mark Wolff	Sandal	9	-	-	-
45	Andrew Wolff	Sandal	9	-	-	-
45	Clive Bent	Nuneaton	9	-	-	-
45	Matthew Brown	Lichfield	9	-	-	-
45	Mark Chudleigh	Birmingham S	9	-	-	-
45	Bob Robinson	Birmingham S	9	-	-	-

ASPATRIA R.U.F.C.

NICKNAME: Black/reds

FOUNDED: 1875

Chairman John Hunter, Summerhill, Fernbank, Cockermouth
0190082 5349 (H), 016973 20207 (B).
Director of Rugby/Press Officer M Hanley, 7 King Street, Aspatria, Cumbria, CA5 3AD.
016973 20328 (H), 01946 815111 (B), 01946 815082 (Fax)
President N Lazonby, Hawthorne House, Dubisath, Keswick. 017687 76363 (H)
Fixtures Secretary P Gray, Ingledene, Queen Street, Aspatria, Cumbria. CA5 3AP.
016973 21760 (H)   016973 31234 (B)
Treasurer W Bell, 01900 881200

The main objective for the season was to halt the slide and avoid relegation. This had occurred to so many clubs over the years. Whilst the objective was met, it was still classed as a disappointing season - losing Jason Spires, David Petch and George Doggart all early in the season meant that we played a large part of the league campaign without a recognised scrum-half. Clearly all the shortfalls in playing strength are being examined for the forthcoming season.

On a positive note, fly half Mike Scott scored nearly 400 points, which is a club record and captain Mark Richardson played for the Barbarians and led the Cumbrian team to victory in the County Championship. Over thirteen Aspatria players were involved in this victory which unfortunately took its toll on the club scene. The Second and Third XV teams won their County Shield Competitions as did the Colts, so all was not lost.

Off the field, the club is nearing completion of an all weather training area and gymnasium. These facilities give Aspatria some of the finest facilities in the north of England.

The new captain for the coming season is Prop Steven Irving.

Aspatria's Mike Scott - the club's top points scorer in the 1996-97 season, in action for Cumbria at Twickenham in the County Championship Final against Somerset.   Photo courtesy of The Cumberland News & Star.

Colours: Black & red hoops

Change colours: Black shirts

ASPATRIA

No	Ven.	Date	Opponents	Att.	Res.	Score	Scorers
1	(A)	31.08	v Lichfield		L	12-26	Marriott(t)Scott(tc)
2	(H)	07.09	v Preston		L	24-31	Marriott(t)Cook(t)Scott(c4p)
3	(A)	21.09	v Sandal		W	31-20	Marriott(2t)Cook(t)Scott(2c4p)
4	(H)	28.09	v Winnington p		W	30-22	Cook(t)Barton(t)Richardson(t)Branthwaite(t)Scott(2c2p)
5	(A)	05.10	v Hereford		L	12-34	Tinnion(t)Milnes(t)Scott(c)
6	(A)	19.10	v Stourbridge		W	45-34	Cook(2t)Bowe(t)Milnes(t)Branthwaite(t)Scott(4c4p)
7	(H)	26.10	v Sheffield		L	20-21	Davidson(t)Barton(t)Milnes(t)Scott(cp)
8	(A)	09.11	v Nuneaton		L	38-40	Marriott(2t)Tinnion(t)Milnes(t)Doggart(t)Southward(t)Scott(4c)
9	(H)	16.11	v Stoke O T		W	32-19	Doggart(t)Tinnion(t)Cook(t)Marriott(t)Richardson(t)Scott(2cp)
10	(A)	21.12	v Manchester		L	22-32	Richardson(2t)Southward(t)Scott(2cp)
11	(H)	28.12	v Worcester		L	30-38	Barton(t)Branthwaite(t)Scott(t3c3p)
12	(H)	25.01	v Lichfield		W	27-20	Marriott(t)Richardson(t)Scott(c4pdg)
13	(A)	01.02	v Preston G		L	11-23	Irving(t)Scott(2p)
14	(H)	08.02	v Sandal		D	27-27	Davidson(t)Cook(t)Richardson(t)Stephenson(t)Cockett(t)Scott(c)
15	(A)	15.02	v Winnington Park		L	19-40	Marriott(t)Southward(t)Scott(3p)
16	(H)	22.02	v Hereford		W	57- 0	Milnes(2t)Cusack(t)Marriott(t)Davidson(t)Southward(t)McCune(t) Cockett(t)Scott(7cp)
17	(H)	01.03	v Stourbridge		W	14-12	Marriott(t)Scott(2pdg)
18	(H)	15.03	v Nuneaton		W	18- 3	Marriott(t)Cockett(t)Scott(c2p)
19	(A)	22.03	v Stoke on Trent		W	38-22	Marriott(3t)Davidson(t)Southward(t)Cook(t)Scott(4c)
20	(H)	29.03	v Birmingham S		L	20-32	Marriott(t)Davidson(t)Scott(2c2p)
21	(H)	05.04	v Manchester		L	16-42	Marriott(t)Cusack(t)Scott(2p)
22	(A)	12.04	v Worcester		L	22-61	Scott(tc5p)
23	(H)	16.04	v Kendal		L	8-11	Richardson(t)Scott(p)
24	(A)	26.04	v Birmingham S		L	5-51	PenTry(t)
25	(A)	03.05	v Kendal		W	16-15	PenTry(t)Scott(c3p)
26	(A)	17.05	v Sheffield		L	17-37	J Miller(2t)Scott(2cp)

1996-97 HIGHLIGHTS

LEAGUE DEBUTS:

PLAYERS USED: 45 plus one as replacement only

EVER PRESENT: Mike Scott

☐ **Most points in a match**

22 Mike Scott v Worcester 12.04.97 (A)
20 Mike Scott v Stourbridge 19.10.96 (A)
20 Mike Scott v Worcester 28.12.96 (H)

☐ **Hat tricks of tries in a match**

3 Craig Marriott v Stoke on Trent 22.03.97 (A)

☐ Ended the season losing six out of last seven league games.

☐ Mike Scott set a new club record for points, conversions and penalties in a season. He now also holds the club career records for points, conversions, penalties and drop goals.

☐ **Most points in the season**

Pts	Player	T	C	P	D
251	Mike Scott	3	43	48	2
85	Craig Marriott	17	-	-	-
40	Graham Cook	8	-	-	-
35	Mark Richardson	7	-	-	-
30	Sephen Milnes	6	-	-	-

☐ **Most appearances**

26 Mike Scott
25 Stephen Irving
24 Craig Marriott, Mark Richardson and Stephen Milnes.

ASPATRIA'S COURAGE LEAGUE MATCH DETAILS 1996-97

No.	15	14	13	12	11	10	9	1	2	3	4	5	6	7	8	Replacements
1	Scott	Marriott	Davidson	Cook	Kyffen	Braithwaite	Pickering	Irving	Barton	Clemertson	Richardson	Simpson	Tinnion	Milnes	Hancock	Thwaites(4)/Dixon(2)/G.Miller(5)/Campbell(14)
2	Scott	Marriott	Davidson	Cook	McKellar	Braithwaite	Pickering	Irving	Dixon	Clemertson	Richardson	Tomlinson	Milnes	Maughan	Hancock	Gipp(5)
3	Braithwaite	Marriott	Davidson	Cook	Campbell	Scott	Pickering	Irving	Barton	Gipp	Clemertson	Tomlinson	Milnes	Maughan	Richardson	
4	Braithwaite	Marriott	Davidson	Cook	Mitchell	Scott	Pickering	Irving	Barton	Gipp	Clemertson	Tomlinson	Milnes	Maughan	Richardson	
5	Braithwaite	Marriott	Stephenson	Cook	Tinnion	Scott	Doggart	Irving	Dixon	Dowling	Clemertson	Tomlinson	Milnes	Maughan	Richardson	Simpson(6)
6	Braithwaite	McCartney	Cook	Davidson	Marriott	Scott	Doggart	Irving	Barton	Dowling	Richardson	Maughan	Simpson	Bowe	Hancock	Clemertson(3)
7	Braithwaite	McCartney	Southward	Davidson	Pickering	Scott	Doggart	Irving	Barton	Dowling	Richardson	Maughan	Simpson	Bowe	Milnes	Clemertson(4)/J.Miller(14)
8	Braithwaite	Marriott	Cook	Southward	Pickering	Scott	Doggart	Irving	Barton	Dowling	Richardson	Bowe	Benson	Tinnion	Milnes	Clemertson(6)/J.Miller(13)
9	Braithwaite	Marriott	Southward	Cook	Doggart	Scott	Pickering	Irving	Dixon	McClure	Clemertson	Bowe	Benson	Tinnion	Milnes	
10	Braithwaite	Cook	Davidson	Southward	Cockett	Scott	Doggart	Irving	Barton	McClure	Richardson	Clemertson	Simpson	Maughan	Milnes	Benson(5)/Dixon(8)
11	Braithwaite	Marriott	Stephenson	Southward	Cook	Scott	Doggart	Irving	Barton	McClure	Clemertson	Milnes	Ahlgren	Maughan	Milnes	Dixon(6)/Simpson(5)/Benson(3)
12	Braithwaite	Marriott	Stephenson	Southward	Davidson	Scott	Pickering	Irving	Barton	McClure	Richardson	Hancock	Benson	Maughan	Milnes	Barton(2)/Clemertson(5)
13	Braithwaite	Marriott	Davidson	Southward	Campbell	Scott	Petch	Irving	Barton	McClure	Richardson	Hancock	Benson	Cusack	Milnes	Cockett(11)
14	Cook	Cockett	Stephenson	Davidson	Marriott	Scott	Petch	Irving	Barton	McClure	Richardson	Lines	Maughan	Cusack	Milnes	
15	Cook	Cockett	Southward	Bowe	Kyffen	Scott	Petch	Irving	Barton	McClure	Hill	Lines	Simpson	Cusack	Milnes	Tomlinson(4)/N.Brown(2)
16	Cook	Marriott	Southward	Cockett	Cockett	Scott	Petch	Irving	Barton	McClure	Richardson	Lines	Simpson	Cusack	Milnes	Kyffen(9)/Maughan(8)/Brown(2)/Tomlinson(1)
17	Cook	Marriott	Davidson	Cockett	Cockett	Scott	Petch	Irving	Dixon	McClure	Richardson	Lines	Simpson	Cusack	Milnes	N.Brown(2)/Clemertson(6)/Maughan(7)
18	Cook	Marriott	Southward	Cockett	Cockett	Scott	Kyffen	Irving	Dixon	McClure	Richardson	Lines	Maughan	Cusack	Milnes	Clemertson(5)/N.Brown(2)
19	Cook	Marriott	Southward	Cockett	Kyffen	Scott	Pickering	Irving	Barton	McClure	Richardson	Lines	Maughan	Cusack	Milnes	Thwaites(8)/P.Miller(3)
20	Cook	Marriott	Davidson	Southward	Cockett	Scott	Pickering	Irving	Barton	McClure	Richardson	Lines	Maughan	Cusack	Milnes	N.Brown(2)/Sewell(3)
21	Pickering	Marriott	Davidson	Southward	Cockett	Scott	Bailiff	Irving	Barton	Sewell	Richardson	Thwaites	Lines	Cusack	Milnes	Hancock(8)/McClune(1)
22	Pickering	Marriott	Davidson	Kyffen	Cockett	Scott	Bailiff	Irving	Brown	Sewell	McClune	Clemertson	Bowe	Maughan	Hancock	Barton(4)
23	Cook	Marriott	Southward	Cockett	Cockett	Scott	Pickering	Irving	Barton	Sewell	Richardson	Hancock	Bowe	Maughan	Milnes	McClune(2)
24	Bailiff	Davidson	Davidson	Nicholls		Scott	Pickering	McClune	Dixon	Sewell	Richardson	Clemertson	Bowe	Maughan	Milnes	Thwaites(13)/P.Miller(1)
25	Davidson	Cockett	Southward	Marriott	Kyffen	Scott	Pickering	Irving	Barton	Sewell	Clemertson	Hancock	Bowe	Maughan	Milnes	Lines(4)
26	Cook	Cockett	Marriott	Barton	Cockett	Scott		Irving	Dixon	P.Miller	Richardson	Thwaites	Bowe	Bowyer	Benson	
28	J.Miller	Bond	Marriott	Barton	Cockett	Scott	Pickering	Irving	Dixon	P.Miller	Richardson	Thwaites	Bowe		Benson	

ASPATRIA LEAGUE STATISTICS
(COMPILED BY STEPHEN McCORMACK)

Season	Div.	P	W	D	L	F	(Tries	Con	Pen	DG)	A	(Tries	Con	Pen	DG)	Most Points	Most Tries
87-88	N2	10	8	0	2	263	(39	25	19	0)	60	(6	1	11	0)	108 - David Pears	13 - George Doggert
88-89	N1	10	7	1	2	206	(21	8	24	7)	100	(			)	99 - Andrew Harrison	4 David Murray & Malcolm Brown
89-90	N1	10	6	2	2	182	(19	10	19	2)	119	(			)	63 - Jimmy Miller	5 - Jimmy Miller
90-91	N1	10	8	0	2	178	(20	12	22	4)	93	(			)	59 - Andrew Harrison	5 - Jimmy Miller
91-92	D4N	12	11	0	1	253	(36	19	23	0)	100	(			)	55 - Andrew Harrison	7 - Jimmy Miller
92-93	3	11	3	1	7	170	(16	9	23	1)	308	(43	21	16	1)	84 - Andrew Harrison	2 - by 4 players
93-94	4	18	8	0	10	303	(27	14	43	1)	372	(42	21	36	4)	129 - Mike Scott	7 - Mark Richardson
94-95	4	18	7	1	10	265	(32	6	29	2)	378	(39	18	48	1)	98 - Mike Scott	7 - Mark Richardson
95-96	4	18	5	1	12	356	(46	27	23	1)	497	(63	37	34	2)	113 - Mike Scott	7 - Craig Marriott & Mark Richardson
96-97	4N	26	10	1	15	611	(75	43	48	2)	713	(92	50	43	8)	251 - Mike Scott	17 - Craig Marriott
Totals		143	73	7	63	2787	(331	173	273	20)	2740						

Welcome to
Bower Park
Season 1996/97

PROGRAMME DETAILS

SIZE: A5   **PRICE:** 50p

PAGES: 42

PROGRAMME EDITOR: Mrs A Quinn 016973 21610

ADVERTISING RATES
Mono Full Page £100
Half Page £50
Qtr Page £25

CLUB & GROUND DETAILS

Address: Bower Park, Station Road, Aspatria, Cumbria
Tel. Nos. 016973 20420

Capacity: 3,000   **Seated:** 300   **Standing:** 2,700

Simple Directions: Contact the Club Secretary,
Mr M Hanley (01697 320328 H).

Nearest Railway Station: Aspatria, 1/4 mile from ground
Car Parking: 200 on ground
Admission:
Matchdays - Adult £3, Children/OAPs £1
Clubhouse: Evenings 7.00-11.00, Matchday 12.00-11.00.
Snacks available. Functions available, capacity 200, contact
R Hewitson 016973 20420 or Mrs J Graham 016973 20379
Club Shop: Yes

Training Nights: Tuesday & Thursday

BIRMINGHAM & SOLIHULL RFC

NICKNAME: The Bees   **FOUNDED:** 1989 (Birmingham RFC & Solihull RUFC merged)

Club Secretary Kirk Simpson, 103 St Bernard's Road, Solihull, West Mids. B92 2NS.
0121 682 2708 (H), 0121 233 2298 (B).
Rugby Administrator Chris Gifford, 39 Beechwood Park Road, Solihull, West Mids B91 1ES
0121 705 2158 (H), 0121 359 0697 (B).
Commercial Manager David Radburn, 35 Yoxall Road, Shirley, Solihull, West Mids B90 3SD
0121 694 4864 (H), 0121 709 1088 (B)

Birmingham & Solihull RFC; Captain Keith Jervis

GROUND DETAILS

Address: Sharmans Cross Road, Solihull.
Tel. Nos. 0121 705 7995

Capacity: 3,000   **Seated:** None   **Standing:** 3,000
Simple Directions: From Solihull centre take Streetsbrook
Rd, through traffic lights, over hump back bridge. 2nd left
into Sharmana Cross Rd, grd 300 yards on left.
Nearest Railway Station: Solihull
Car Parking: 500 spaces are available at the ground.
Clubhouse: Saturdays 12.00-12.00, Sundays 10.00-3.00,
Tuesday & Thursday 7.00-11.30. Snacks & bar meals
available.
Functions; capacity 150, contact David Radburn
Club Shop: Yes. Manager - David Radburn.
Admission:
Season - Adults £45, OAPs £30, Children (U16) Free
Matchday - Adults £5, Children Free
Training Nights: Tuesday and Thursday

PROGRAMME DETAILS

SIZE:	A5
PRICE:	Included with entry
PAGES:	88 plus cover

PROGRAMME EDITOR:
David Radburn 0121 709 1088

ADVERTISING RATES
Mono - Full page £250
Half page NA.

Colours: Black with broad red & narrow amber hoops   **Change colours:** Red, black, amber & white quarters

BIRMINGHAM SOLIHULL | COURAGE LEAGUE MATCH DETAILS 1996-97

No	Ven.	Date	Opponents	Att.	Res.	Score	Scorers
1	(H)	31.08	v Sheffield		W	13- 8	Smart(2tp)
2	(A)	07.09	v Nuneaton		W	18- 8	Goodwin(2t)Robinson(t)Angell(p)
3	(H)	21.09	v Stoke O T		W	55-10	Angell(2t)Cox(2t)Robinson(2t)A Wood(t)Colburn(t)Smart(6cp)
4	(A)	28.09	v Manchester		L	15-18	Baker(t)S Adams(t)Smart(cp)
5	(H)	05.10	v Worcester		L	11-19	Taylor(t)Smart(2p)
6	(A)	19.10	v Kendal		W	11-10	Heaver(t)Smart(2p)
7	(H)	26.10	v Stourbridge		W	39-21	Hanson(t)Goodwin(t)Colburn(t)Heaver(t)Robinson(t)Smart(4c2p)
8	(H)	09.11	v Lichfield		W	52-18	Hanson(3t)Heaver(t)Cox(t)Baker(t)Robinson(t)Smart(t3c2p)
9	(A)	16.11	v Preston		W	18-11	A Wood(t)Smart(tc2p)
10	(H)	21.12	v Sandall		W	30-12	H Adams(t)Chudleigh(t)Taylor(t)Smart(3c3p)
11	(A)	28.12	v Winnington P		W	22-15	Dossett(t)Smart(c5p)
12	(H)	18.01	v Hereford		W	32- 5	Dossett(2t)Jones(t)Adams(t)Taylor(t)Smart(2cp)
13	(A)	25.01	v Sheffield		L	13-20	Cox(t)Smart(tp)
14	(H)	01.02	v Nuneaton		W	43-11	McCrainer(t)Dossett(t)G Wood(t)Cox(t)Smart(t3c4p)
15	(A)	08.02	v Stoke on Trent		W	48-14	Packer(3t)Cox(2t)adams(2t)G Wood(t)Jervis(t)Smart(4c)
16	(H)	15.02	v Manchester		L	32-39	Chapman(2t)Cox(t)Baker(t)Smart(2c2p)Angell(c)
17	(A)	22.02	v Worcester		L	16-27	G Wood(t)Hanson(t)Angell(2p)
18	(H)	01.03	v Kendal		W	13- 3	A Wood(t)Smart(c2p)
19	(A)	08.03	v Stourbricge		L	13-15	A Wood(t)Smart(c2p)
20	(A)	15.03	v Lichfield		W	42-13	Chudleigh(t)Packer(t)McLean(t)Chapman(t)Smart(t4c3p)
21	(H)	22.03	v Preston G		W	26- 6	Chapman(2t)Smart(2c4p)
22	(A)	29.03	v Aspatria		W	32-20	PenTry(t)A Wood(t)H Adams(t)Dossett(t)Smart(t2cp)
23	(A)	05.04	v Sandal		L	15-29	McLIdowney(2t)McCrainer(t)
24	(H)	12.04	v Winnington Park		W	34-24	Robinson(3t)Cox(t)Jones(t)Chudleigh(t)Smart(2c)
25	(A)	19.04	v Hereford		W	52-10	Jervis(2t)Chudleigh(t)A Wood(t)PenTry(t)Robinson(t)Cox(t)Goodwin(t)Smart(3c2p)
26	(H)	26.04	v Aspatria		W	51- 5	Baker(t)G Wood(t)Chapman(t)McCrainer(t)H Adams(tc)Chudleigh(2tc)Smart(t2cdg)

1996-97 HIGHLIGHTS

PLAYERS USED: 36 plus three as replacement only.

EVER PRESENT: Lee Baker

☐ Jonathan Smart set new club records for points, conversions and penalties in a season with 271, 47 and 43 respectively.

☐ One of only three teams to score 100 tries in the division.

112	Worcester
101	Manchester
101	Birmingham S

☐ Just 33 penalties scored against the lowest total in the division.

☐ **Most points in a match**
22 Jonathan Smart v Nuneaton 01.02.97 (H)
22 Jonathan Smart v Lichfield 15.03.97 (A)

☐ **Hat trick of tries in a match**
3 Dave Hanson v Lichfield 09.11.96 (H)
3 Richard Packer v Stoke onTrent 08.02.97 (A)
3 Bob Robinson v Winnington Park 12.04.97 (H)

☐ **Most points in the season**

Pts	Player	T	C	P	D
271	Jonathan Smart	9	47	43	1
50	David Cox	10	-	-	-
45	Bob Robinson	9	-	-	-
32	Mark Chudleigh	6	1	-	-
30	Richard Chapman	6	-	-	-
30	Andrew Wood	6	-	-	-

☐ **Most appearances**
26 Lee Baker.
25 David Cox and Jonathan Smart.
24 Gary Wood and Richard McCrainer.
23 Hamish Adams.

BIRMINGHAM SOLIHULL'S COURAGE LEAGUE MATCH DETAILS 1996-97

#	15	14	13	12	11	10	9	1	2	3	4	5	6	7	8	Replacements
1	Angell	Wilshaw	Shelton	S Adams	Goodwin	Smart	Colburn	Hetherington	Cox	Baker	GWood	Crees	Taylor	Robinson	A Wood	
2	Angell	Goodwin	Jervis	S Adams	Perry	Smart	Colburn	H Adams	Cox	Baker	GWood	Crees	Taylor	Robinson	A Wood	
3	Angell	Wilshaw	Jervis	S Adams	Perry	Smart	Colburn	H Adams	Cox	Baker	GWood	Crees	Taylor	Robinson	A Wood	Bastock(5)Tandy(8)S Jervis(12)
4	Angell	Hanson	Jervis	S Adams	Perry	Smart	Colburn	H Adams	Cox	Baker	GWood	McCrainer	Bastock	Robinson	A Wood	
5	Angell	Hanson	Jervis	S Adams	Perry	Smart	Colburn	H Adams	Cox	Baker	GWood	McCrainer	Taylor	Robinson	A Wood	Bastock(7)
6	Angell	Hanson	Jervis	Perry	Goodwin	Smart	Colburn	H Adams	Cox	Baker	GWood	McCrainer	Heaver	Robinson	A Wood	S Adams(15)
7	S Adams	Hanson	Jervis	McAldowney	Goodwin	Smart	Edwards	Eastgate	Cox	Baker	GWood	Heaver	Heaver	Robinson	A Wood	Colburn(9)S Adams(15)
8	Angell	Hanson	Jervis	McAldowney	Jones	Smart	Colburn	H Adams	Cox	Baker	GWood	McCrainer	Heaver	Robinson	A Wood	Eastgate(7)
9	S Adams	Hanson	Jervis	McAldowney	Jones	Smart	Cole	H Adams	Cox	Baker	GWood	McCrainer	Heaver	Robinson	A Wood	Colburn(9)S Adams(15)
10	Angell	Dossett	Jervis	McAldowney	Packer	Smart	Chudleigh	H Adams	Cox	Baker	GWood	McCrainer	Bastock	Taylor	A Wood	
11	Angell	Packer	Jervis	McAldowney	Dossett	Smart	Chudleigh	H Adams	Cox	Baker	GWood	McCrainer	Bastock	Robinson	A Wood	S Adams(11)Taylor(6)
12	Angell	Packer	Jervis	Dossett	Jones	Smart	Chudleigh	H Adams	Cox	Baker	GWood	McCrainer	Bastock	Robinson	A Wood	Taylor(6)Short(5)
13	Dossett	Packer	Jervis	McAldowney	Jones	Smart	Chudleigh	H Adams	Cox	Baker	GWood	McCrainer	Short	Robinson	A Wood	Bastock(7)
14	Dossett	Packer	Jervis	McAldowney	S Adams	Smart	Chudleigh	H Adams	Cox	Baker	GWood	McCrainer	Short	Robinson	A Wood	Taylor(4)Bastock(6)
15	Dossett	S Adams	McAldowney	McAldowney	Packer	Smart	Chudleigh	H Adams	Cox	Baker	Crees	McCrainer	McLean	Strong	A Wood	Angell(12)Taylor(4)Cole(9)
16	Angell	Dossett	Jervis	Chapman	Packer	Smart	Chudleigh	H Adams	Cox	Baker	Taylor	McCrainer	Short	McLean	A Wood	McCrainer(4)Bastock(7)McAldowney(10)
17	Dossett	Hanson	Shelton	Chapman	Packer	Smart	Chudleigh	H Adams	Cox	Baker	GWood	McCrainer	McBride	Robinson	Bastock	A Wood(4)Short(8)Hetherington(tr8)
18	Angell	Dossett	Jervis	Chapman	Packer	Smart	Chudleigh	H Adams	Blundell	Baker	GWood	McCrainer	McBride	Robinson	A Wood	Bastock(6)Hanson(9)
19	Angell	Hanson	Packer	Chapman	Dossett	Smart	Chudleigh	H Adams	Cox	Baker	GWood	McCrainer	McBride	Robinson	A Wood	Blundell(2),Bastock(8)Hetherington(11),Jones(12)
20	Shelton	Packer	Chapman	McAldowney	Jones	Smart	Chudleigh	H Adams	Cox	Baker	GWood	McCrainer	McLean	Robinson	Bastock	A Wood(7)
21	Angell	Jones	Chapman	McAldowney	Dossett	Smart	Chudleigh	H Adams	Cox	Baker	GWood	McCrainer	Bastock	Robinson	A Wood	Bentley(5)
22	Angell	Dossett	Chapman	McAldowney	Packer	Smart	Chudleigh	H Adams	Cox	Baker	GWood	McCrainer	Bastock	Robinson	A Wood	
23	Angell	Dossett	Chapman	McAldowney	Packer	Smart	Chudleigh	Hetherington	Cox	Baker	GWood	McCrainer	Bastock	McLean	A Wood	Goodwin(15)
24	Dossett	Jones	Chapman	Chapman	Packer	Smart	Chudleigh	H Adams	Cox	Baker	GWood	McCrainer	Bastock	Robinson	A Wood	McLean(6)
25	Dossett	Jones	Jervis	Chapman	Goodwin	Smart	Chudleigh	H Adams	Cox	Baker	GWood	McCrainer	Bastock	Robinson	A Wood	McLean(6)
26	Dossett	Packer	Jervis	Jervis	Chapman	Smart	Chudleigh	H Adams	Cox	Baker	GWood	McCrainer	Bastock	Robinson	A Wood	McLean(6)

BIRMINGHAM SOLIHULL LEAGUE STATISTICS
(COMPILED BY STEPHEN McCORMACK)

Season	Div.	P	W	D	L	F	A	PD	Pts	Pos.	Coach	Captain
87-88	3	11	0	1	10	46	381	-335	1	12r	B Wallace	W Hart
88-89	ALN	10	0	0	10	29	171	-142	0	11r		
89-90	MID	10	8	0	2	140	85	55	16	2p	R Smith	J Holliton
90-91	D4N	12	1	1	10	116	265	-149	3	13r	R Smith	R Richardson
91-92	MID1	10	3	1	6	126	151	-25	7	9	R Richardson	T Ryan
92-93	MID1	13	11	1	1	250	107	143	23	1p		
93-94	D5N	12	5	0	7	128	162	-34	10	9	M Swan	G Smith
94-95	D5N	12	5	0	7	167	226	-59	10	10	N Hurton	S Taylor
95-96	D5N	12	8	1	3	202	160	42	17	3		
96-97	D4N	26	19	0	7	746	391	355	38	2		
Total		128	60	5	63	1950	2099	-149				

Preston Grasshoppers' captain Steve Kerry, who broke his own Club points record with 444 and was the country's leading drop-goal exponent with 12 in the season.

Photo - Courtesy Lancashire Evening Post.

HINCKLEY R.F.C.

NICKNAME:

FOUNDED: 1893

President A Gildroy, 3 Shelley Gardens, Hinckley, Leics LE10 1TA
01455 632987 (H), 01455 238333 (B), 01455 251283 (Fax)

Chairman P B Walton, The Oaklands, Stanton Road, Elms Thorpe LE9 7SH
01455 273025 (H), 01455 634080 (B)

Secretary F J Swift, 8 The Rills, Hinckley, Leics LE10 1NA
01455 250270 (H), 01455 238866 (Fax as last resort only)

Treasurer M Roach, Flat 6, Desford Grange, Church Lane, Desford, Leics
01455 828959 (H).

Rugby Chairman P Green, 29 Windrush Drive, Hinckley, Leics LE10 0NY
01455 612498 (H)

Marketing Chairman Roger Edwards, Apple Orchard Farm, Dadlington, Nuneaton.
01455 213186

Hinckley started in mid League One and lost six games by three points or less to be relegated and were then relegated for the next three seasons ending up in Leicestershire League One. Since then they have been promoted five times out of seven years to reach their current position in National League Four or Two as it has been renamed. Their current secretary J. Swift took over as chairman in 1984 with the club £34,000 in the red and facing bankruptcy. Since then the club whilst being relegated became a stronger force thanks to the efforts of a few old stalwarts. With the debt written off and the purchase of the football club's buildings, Hinckley now find themselves second only to The Tigers in Leicestershire.

This year the club have made rugby history in winning promotion to National Four the first junior side in Leicestershire to gain such status. They also won the County Cup for a record seventh time. This followed by their Second XV winning their County Cup and the Colts winning theirs for the fourth consecutive year.

Not to be out done the ladies won Mid Four at their first attempt, surely a record that will never be surpassed.

Under the guidance of coach Bob Sulley, who has experienced relegation as a player, but the satisfaction of promotion as a coach, and who is ably aided by assistant Wayne Richardson, Hinckley look forward to the future.

They have achieved all this by their own efforts and a loyal band of support. A wonderful Colts side well respected throughout the whole of Leagues One and Two downwards. A committee who recognise the professional challenge but at the same time keep their feet on the ground to enjoy the rewards from our great game.

It is a credit to local lads that twelve out of nineteen that represented Hinckley through the latter stages of the season, winning eight of the last nine games, came through the junior/colts system.

Under the chairmanship of Peter Walton (Ex-Prop) they look forward to meeting old friends that were lost with relegation. With the support of sponsors BSS plc and BUPA Leicester plus Prestige Tools and eighty local businesses they hope to meet the future with confidence.

John Swift states "The challenge will not be easy but who would have thought we would be where we are now four years ago. We'll do our best, enjoy it in the process and in conclusion wish the very best of seasons to all the teams in Division Four."

Hinckley RFC: Back Row (L-R); Bob Sulley (Coach), John Bennett (President), Peter Walton (Chairman), Paul Garwood, Charlie Massarella, Chris Bennett, Mike Glew, Andy Poole, Karl Ashfield, Pete Goodall, Phil Wayne, Darren Barnes, Tom Walton, Dave Bennett, Phil Curtis, John Swift (Sec), Ken Chesterman (Physio), Wayne Richardson (Asst Coach). Front Row; Duncan Whitton, Craig Dutton, Eddie Brittain, Sam Bennett, Richard Massarella, Andy Goodall, Neil Castle, Dave Massarella, Paul Williams, John Newman, Simon Stratford.

Colours: Black & amber hoops, black shorts, black socks with amber tops **Change colours:** Red & green hoops

COURAGE LEAGUE MATCH DETAILS 1996-97

No	Ven.	Date	Opponents	Att.	Res.	Score	Scorers
1	(A)	07.09	v Stockwood Park Att.		W	29- 0	Dutton(2t)Green(t)Robinson(t)Brittian(t)Poole(2c)
2	(H)	21.09	v Syston		L	7- 8	R Masserella(t)Poole(c)
3	(A)	28.09	v Westleigh		W	27-22	Dutton(2t)Hilyer(t)Poole(t2cp)
4	(H)	06.10	v Whitchurch		W	48- 6	S Bennett(2t)Dutton(2t)D Bennett(t)R Masserella(t)Brittian(t)Castle(t)Poole(4c)
5	(A)	19.10	v Wolverhampton		W	63- 3	Dutton(2t)Brittian(2t)D Bennett(t)Castle(t)R Masserella(t)C Masserella(t)Kitching(t)Poole(5cp)
6	(H)	26.10	v Barker's Butts		W	68-28	Stratford(3t)Ashfield(t)Hilyer(t)Green(t)A Goodall(t)Castle(t)Kitching(t)Poole(5cp)
7	(A)	09.11	v Belgrave		W	18-16	Ashfield(t)Brittian(t)Poole(c2p)
8	(H)	16.11	v Broadstreet		W	25- 5	S Bennett(2t)Brittian(t)R Masserella(t)Poole(cp)
9	( )	25.01	v Burton		L	14-16	A Goodall(t)Brittian(t)Poole(2c)
10	( )	08.02	v Derby		W	51- 7	Dutton(2t)Poole(2t)R Masserella(2t)Wayne(t)C Masserella(t)Brittian(4cp)
11	( )	08.03	v Leamington		W	76-15	Brittian(5tc)S Bennett(2t)Poole(t)A Goodall(t)Walton(t)D Masserella(t)C Masserella(t)Dutton(tp3c)
12	( )	00.00	v Camp Hill		W	28- 7	Dutton(t)Garwood(t)Poole(t2c3p)
13	( )	00.00	v Leighton Buzzard		W	27-11	Green(t)D Bennett(t)Dutton(t)Poole(3c2p)
14	(H)	00.00	v Mansfield		W	31- 8	Dutton(2t)P Goodall(t)Brittian(t)Poole(t3c)
15	(A)	00.00	v Scunthorpe		W	15-11	Poole(5p)
16	( )	00.00	v Stafford		W	79-17	Dutton(3t)P Goodall(t)Walton(t)D Bennett(t)Brittian(t)R Masserella(t)C Masserella(t)Hilyer(t)Garwood(t)Poole(t8cp)

1996-97 HIGHLIGHTS

LEAGUE DEBUTS:

PLAYERS USED: 24

EVER PRESENT: Andy Goodall, Dave Bennett and Richard Massarella

❏ Most points in the season

Pts	Player	T	C	P	D
175	Andy Poole	9	38	18	-
99	Craig Dutton	18	3	1	-
83	Eddie Brittian	14	5	1	-
35	Richard Massarella	7	-	-	-
30	Sam Bennett	6	-	-	-
25	Dave Bennett	5	-	-	-

❏ Most points in a match

27 Eddie Brittian v Leamington 08.03.97 (H)
24 Andy Poole v Stafford
18 Andy Poole v Barkers Butts 26.10.96 (H)

❏ Hat trick of tries in a match

5 Eddie Brittian v Leamington 08.03.97 (H)
3 Simon Stratford v Barkers Butts 26.10.96 (H)
3 Craig Dutton v Stafford

❏ Most appearances

16 Andy Goodall, Dave Bennett and Richard Massarella
15 Craig Dutton and Charlie Massarella
14 Eddie Brittian, Paul Green, Simon Stratford, Paul Goodall, Tom Walton and Phil Wayne

HINCKLEY'S COURAGE LEAGUE MATCH DETAILS 1996-97

	15	14	13	12	11	10	9	1	2	3	4	5	6	7	8	Replacements	
1 Poole	Brittian	S Bennett	Durton	Robinson	C Massarella	R Massarella	Kitching		Hillier	Wayne	Green	P Goodall	A Goodall	Williams	D Bennett		1
2 Poole	Brittian	S Bennett	Durton	Garwood	Bunting	R Massarella	Kitching		Hillier	Wayne	Green	P Goodall	Williams	Williams	D Bennett	C Bennett(10)	2
3 Poole	Castle	Durton	S Bennett	Garwood	C Massarella	R Massarella	Kitching		Hillier	Wayne	Green	P Goodall	A Goodall	Walton	D Bennett		3
4 Poole	Brittian	S Bennett	Durton	Castle	C Massarella	R Massarella	Kitching		D Massarella	Wayne	Green	P Goodall	A Goodall	Walton	D Bennett		4
5 Poole	Brittian	S Bennett	Durton	Castle	C Massarella	R Massarella	Kitching		D Massarella	Wayne	Green	P Goodall	A Goodall	Walton	D Bennett		5
6 Poole	Castle	Durton	S Bennett	Brittian	C Massarella	R Massarella	Ashfield		Hillier	Wayne	Stratford	Green	A Goodall	Walton	D Bennett	Kitching(3)	6
7 Poole	Castle	S Bennett	Durton	Brittian	C Massarella	R Massarella	Kitching		Hillier	Ashfield	Green	P Goodall	A Goodall	Walton	D Bennett		7
8 Poole	Castle	S Bennett	Durton	Brittian	C Massarella	R Massarella	Kitching		Hillier	Ashfield	Green	P Goodall	A Goodall	Walton	D Bennett		8
9 Poole	Castle	S Bennett	Newman	Brittian	C Massarella	R Massarella	Ashfield		Hillier	Wayne	P Goodall	Stratford	A Goodall	Walton	D Bennett		9
10 Poole	Castle	Newman	Durton	Brittian	C Massarella	R Massarella	Ashfield		Hillier	Wayne	Stratford	P Goodall	A Goodall	Walton	D Bennett		10
11 Poole	Sharkey	S Bennett	Durton	Brittian	C Massarella	R Massarella	Ashfield			Wayne	Stratford	Green	A Goodall	Walton	D Bennett		11
12 Poole	Brittian	S Bennett	Durton	Sharkey	C Massarella	R Massarella	Ashfield			Wayne	P Goodall	Green	A Goodall	Walton	D Bennett	Garwood(14)	12
13 Poole	Garwood	Newman	Durton	Sharkey	C Massarella	R Massarella	Ashfield			Wayne	P Goodall	Green	A Goodall	Walton	D Bennett		13
14 Poole	Castle	Newman	Durton	Brittian	C Massarella	R Massarella	Ashfield			Wayne	P Goodall	Green	A Goodall	Walton	D Bennett		14
15 Poole	Garwood	S Bennett	Durton	Brittian	C Massarella	R Massarella	Ashfield			Wayne	P Goodall	Green	A Goodall	Walton	D Bennett		15
16 Poole	Garwood	S Bennett	Durton	Brittian	C Massarella	R Massarella	Ashfield			Wayne	P Goodall	Green	A Goodall	Walton	D Bennett	Hillier()	16

HINCKLEY LEAGUE STATISTICS
(COMPILED BY STEPHEN McCORMACK)

Season	Div.	P	W	D	L	F	A	PD	Pts	Pos.
87-88	M1	10	2	1	7	111	157	-46	5	10r
88-89	M2E	10	2	0	8	96	222	-126	4	11r
89-90	EM&L1	10	1	1	8	123	174	-51	3	11r
90-91	LEl1	10	10	0	0	236	49	187	20	1p
91-92	EM&L1	10	8	1	1	208	62	146	17	1p
92-93	ME1	12	10	1	1	296	119	177	21	2
93-94	ME1	12	10	0	2	223	97	126	20	1p
94-95	M2	12	8	1	3	286	134	152	17	4
95-96	M2	12	10	0	2	278	129	149	20	2p
96-97	M1	16	14	0	2	606	180	426	28	1p
Total		114	75	5	34	2463	1323	1140		

PROGRAMME DETAILS

SIZE: A5   **PRICE:**

PAGES: 22 plus cover

PROGRAMME EDITOR:

ADVERTISING RATES
Mono Full page £8

CLUB & GROUND DETAILS

Address: Leicester Road, Hinckley.
Tel. Nos. 01455 615010

Capacity: Unlimited **Seated:** None   **Standing:**

Simple Directions: Take the A47 out of Hinckley and the ground is situated about 1 mile past the golf club on the left hand side.

Nearest Railway Station: Hinckley, bus or taxi to town centre, follow A47 towards Leicester.

Car Parking: 200 on ground, 200+ nearby

Admission: Tickets - Concessions for Children & OAPs

Clubhouse: Tuesday, Thursday & Friday evenings. Saturday 12.00-Late. Sundays 12.00 onwards. Snacks & bar meals available

Functions: Yes, capacity 120 Club room, contact Carole Davies 01455 615010

Training Nights: Tuesday & Thursday

KENDAL R.U.F.C.

FOUNDED: 1905

President D Healey, c/o Kendal RUFC, Mint Bridge, Shap Road, Kendal LA9 6DL
01539 734039

Chairman Ian W Hutton, 168 Vicarage Drive, Kendal, Cumbria, LA9 5BX
01539 733152 (H), 01539 733333 (B).

Director of Rugby Chris Hayton, 106 Burneside Road, Kendal, Cumbria LA9 4RT
01539 724600 (H), 01539 725822 (B). 01539 730613 (Fax)

Fixture Secretary Andrew Quarry, 14 Collinfield, Kendal, Cumbria LA9 5SD
01539 731640 (H)   01539 720391 (B)   01539 720645 (Fax)

Match Secretary Roger Wilson, 31 Hills Wood Avenue, Kendal, Cumbria
01539 740449 (H), 01539 733333 (B)

Press Officer John Hutton, 168 Vicarage Drive, Kendal, Cumbria LA9 5BX.
01539 733152 (H), 01539 722112 (B)

Kendal started the season brilliantly winning six out of their first seven games, losing only to the eventual league champions at Worcester.

The victories included a first ever Pilkington Cup victory away at Stourbridge and an amazing second round victory at Sheffield after trailing by twenty points at half-time.

The league results became mixed by mid November and by early February defeat at Manchester was the start of a seven match losing streak, thankfully coming to an end with victory against Hereford on the 29th March, 1997. Kendal had dropped from top of the table into being possible relegation candidates but great character was shown and four league victories, including a club record 82-7 victory at Mintbridge against Hereford, at the back end of the season ensured league survival and the retention of National status.

The high points of the season were great successes in the Pilkington Cup competition. A third round victory at Sandal was 'rewarded' with a trip to Exeter and a thrilling 18-12 victory saw Kendal through to play Second Division Coventry in the fifth round, once again away from home. The Black & Ambers could not match the big spending Midlands side and an exciting Cup run came to an end.

After a record eight successive away ties please, please, can we have a home tie this season.
JOHN HUTTON

Kendal RUFC: Back Row (L-R); Peter Kremer (Director of Rugby), Mike Fell, Jason Hudson, Colin Wolstenholme, Billy Coxon, Mark Bowman, Harrie Nicholson, Rod Short (President), Dion Sieth, Mike Bowerbank, Richard Harryman, Nigel Pearson, Ian Stavert (1st Team Manager), Alison Bloxham (Physio). Front Row; Paul Dodds, Steve Healey, Mike Healey, Darren Sharpe, Jon Nicholson (Captain), Mark Airey, Steve Whitehead, Gavin Slater, David Bell.

Colours: Black and amber. **Change colours:** All green.

KENDAL

No	Ven.	Date	Opponents	Att.	Res.	Score	Scorers
1	(H)	31.08	v Nuneaton		W	30- 5	Bell(2t)S Healey(t)Hudson(3c3p)
2	(A)	07.09	v Stoke O T		W	21-12	S Healey(t)Slater(cp)Bell(tpdg)
3	(H)	21.09	v Manchester		W	30-21	Dodds(2t)Bowman(t)Hudson(2c2p)
4	(A)	28.09	v Worcester		L	10-30	S Healey(t)Hudson(cp)
5	(H)	05.10	v Stourbridge		W	25-21	Slater(t)Hudson(c6p)
6	(H)	19.10	v Birmingham S		L	10-11	Dodds(tc)Nicholson(p)
7	(A)	26.10	v Lichfield		L	23-25	Kremer(2t)Hudson(2c3p)
8	(H)	09.11	v Preston		L	13-19	S Healey(t)Hudson(c2p)
9	(A)	16.11	v Sandal		L	7-33	Downham(t)Dodds(c)
10	(H)	18.01	v Winnington Park		W	16-13	Dods(t)Hudson(c3p)
11	(A)	25.01	v Nuneaton		D	33-33	Moore(2t)J Slater(t)Bell(t)Hudson(2c3p)
12	(H)	01.02	v Stoke on Trent		W	40- 3	Dodds(t)Bracken(t)Wolstenholme(t)Hudson(t4c4p)
13	(A)	08.02	v Manchester		L	13-22	M Healey(t)Wolstenholme(t)Hudson(p)
14	(H)	15.02	v Worcester		L	12-19	Hudson(4p)
15	(A)	22.02	v Stourbridge		L	13-20	Bracken(t)Hudson(c2p)
16	(A)	01.03	v Birmingham S		L	3-13	Hudson(p)
17	(H)	08.03	v Lichfield		L	20-24	Harriman(t)Stephens(t)J Nicholson(2cp)Bell(dg)
18	(A)	15.03	v Preston G		L	14-15	J Slater(t)J Nicholson(3p)
19	(H)	22.03	v Sandal		L	23-24	Bell(t)Bowman(t)J Nicholson(2c3p)
20	(A)	29.03	v Hereford		W	35-11	Stephens(t)J Slater(t)Harriman(t)Bell(t)J Nicholson(3c3p)
21	(A)	05.04	v Winnington Park		L	13-24	Downham(t)J Nicholson(c2p)
22	(H)	12.04	v Hereford		W	82- 7	M Healey(3t)Airey(3t)Stephens(3tc)Dodds(tc)Moore(t)G Slater(t)H Nicholson(t) Wolstenholme(t)J Nicholson(4c)
23	(H)	16.04	v Aspatria		W	11- 8	Harriman(t)J Nicholson(2p)
24	(H)	26.04	v Sheffield		W	15-10	Bowerbank(t)G Slater(t)J Nicholson(cp)
25	(H)	03.05	v Aspatria		L	15-16	Hudson(5p)
26	(A)	10.05	v Sheffield		W	14-12	Dodds(t)J Nicholson(2p)Bell(dg)

1996-97 HIGHLIGHTS

LEAGUE DEBUTS:

PLAYERS USED: 34 plus three as replacement only.

EVER PRESENT: Billy Coxon and Paul Dodds.

❏ Only three teams scored less tries than Kendal's 50.
- 43 Sheffield
- 41 Stoke on Trent
- 36 Hereford

❏ Despite the above only two teams conceded less tries than Kendal.
- 35 Worcester
- 41 Preston G
- 46 Kendal

❏ Most points in a match
- 25 Jason Hudson v Stoke on Trent 01.02.97 (H)
- 20 Jason Hudson v Stiurbridge 05.10.96 (H)

❏ Hat trick of tries in a match
- 3 Mike Healey v Hereford 12.04.97 (H)
- 3 Dan Stephens v Hereford 12,04.97 (H)
- 3 Mark Airey v Hereford 12.04.97 (H)

❏ Most points in the season

Pts	Player	T	C	P	D
163	Jason Hudson	1	19	40	-
83	Jon Nicholson	-	13	19	-
42	David Bell	6	-	1	3
41	Paul Dodds	7	3	-	-

❏ Most appearances
- 26 Billy Coxon and Paul Dodds
- 24 Mike Healey
- 23 Jon Nicholson and Keith Robinson
- 20 Jason Hudson, IanDownham and David Bell

KENDAL'S COURAGE LEAGUE MATCH DETAILS 1996-97

	15	14	13	12	11	10	9	1	2	3	4	5	6	7	8	Replacements	
1	Hudson	Dodds	S Healey	M Healey	J Slater	Bell	Sharpe	Coxon	J Nicholson	Thompson	Bracken	Capstick	Downham	Wightman	Bowman		1
2	Hudson	Dodds	S Healey	M Healey	J Slater	Bell	Arey	Coxon	J Nicholson	Thompson	Bracken	Capstick	Downham	Wightman	Bowman		2
3	Hudson	Dodds	S Healey	M Healey	J Slater	Bell	Sharpe	Coxon	J Nicholson	Pearson	Bracken	Robinson	Downham	Wightman	Bowman		3
4	Hudson	Dodds	S Healey	M Healey	J Slater	Stephens	Sharpe	Coxon	J Nicholson	Thompson	Capstick	Capstick	Wolstenholme	Wightman	Bowman	Pearson(3)	4
5	Hudson	Dodds	S Healey	M Healey	J Slater	Stephens	Sharpe	Coxon	J Nicholson	Thompson	Bracken	Capstick	Wolstenholme	Wightman	Bowman	Pearson(3)	5
6	Dodds	Murray	S Healey	M Healey	Bell	Bell	Sharpe	Coxon	J Nicholson	Pearson	Capstick	Capstick	Downham	Wightman	Bowman		6
7	Dodds	Dodds	J Slater	M Healey	Murray	Bell	Sharpe	Coxon	N Robinson	Pearson	Bracken	K Robinson	Bowman	Wolstenholme	Kremer	H Nicholson(4)	7
8	Hudson	Dodds	S Healey	M Healey	J Slater	Stephens	Sharpe	Coxon	Whitehead	Pearson	Bracken	K Robinson	Downham	Wolstenholme	Bowman	H Nicholson(4)	8
9	Dodds	Dodds	J Slater	M Healey	Stephens	Bell	Sharpe	Coxon	J Nicholson	Pearson	Bracken	K Robinson	Downham	Wolstenholme	Bowman	H Nicholson(4)	9
10	Hudson	Dodds	J Slater	M Healey	Stephens	Bell	Sharpe	Coxon	J Nicholson	Pearson	Capstick	K Robinson	Downham	Bowman	Bowman	H Nicholson(4)	10
11	Hudson	Dodds	J Slater	M Healey	J Slater	Bell	Sharpe	Coxon	J Nicholson	Pearson	Bracken	K Robinson	Downham	Wolstenholme	Bowman	H Nicholson(4)	11
12	Hudson	Dodds	J Slater	M Healey	J Slater	Bell	Sharpe	Coxon	J Nicholson	Pearson	Bracken	K Robinson	Downham	Wolstenholme	Kremer	S Capstick(5)	12
13	Hudson	Dodds	J Slater	M Healey	J Slater	Bell	Sharpe	Coxon	J Nicholson	Pearson	Bracken	K Robinson	Downham	Wolstenholme	Kremer	Dolan(6)Harriman(3)H Nicholson(4)	13
14	Hudson	Dodds	J Slater	M Healey	J Slater	Bell	Sharpe	Coxon	J Nicholson	Pearson	Bracken	K Robinson	Wightman	Wightman	Kremer	Dolan(6)Harriman(3)H Nicholson(4)	14
15	Hudson	Dodds	J Slater	M Healey	J Slater	Bell	Sharpe	Coxon	J Nicholson	Pearson	Bracken	K Robinson	Whitehead	Wightman	Kremer	Kremer	15
16	Moore	Dodds	Dodds	M Healey	Fisher	Stephens	Sharpe	Coxon	J Nicholson	Harriman	Bracken	K Robinson	Downham	Kremer	Kremer	H Nicholson(4)S Slater(10)	16
17	Moore	Stephens	Stephens	M Healey	G Slater	Bell	Sharpe	Cox	J Nicholson	Harriman	Bracken	K Robinson	Whitehead	Whitehead	Robinson	H Nicholson(5),Kremer(7)	17
18	Moore	Stephens	Stephens	M Healey	J Slater	Bell	Sharpe	Coxon	J Nicholson	Pearson	Bowerbank	K Robinson	Downham	Wolstenholme	K Robinson	H Nicholson(5),Kremer(7)	18
19	Moore	Stephens	Stephens	M Healey	J Slater	Arey	Sharpe	Coxon	J Nicholson	Harriman	Bowerbank	K Robinson	Downham	Bowman	K Robinson	Robinson	19
20	Moore	Stephens	J Slater	G Slater	G Slater	Arey	Sharpe	Coxon	J Nicholson	Harriman	K Robinson	H Nicholson	Downham	Wolstenholme	K Robinson	K Robinson Wolstenholme(5)	20
21	Dodds	Stephens	J Slater	M Healey	J Slater	Bell	Sharpe	Coxon	J Nicholson	Harriman	H Nicholson	K Robinson	Downham	Wolstenholme	Bowman	Dolan(11)Bowerbank(5)Whitehead(7)	21
22	Dodds	Stephens	M Healey	G Slater	G Slater	Bell	Moore	Coxon	J Nicholson	Pearson	Bowerbank	K Robinson	Whitehead	Wolstenholme	Bowman	G Slater(11)	22
23	Dodds	Stephens	M Healey	G Slater	G Slater	Bell	Arey	Coxon	J Nicholson	Bowerbank	Bowerbank	K Robinson	Whitehead	Wolstenholme	Bowman	Harriman(3)D Slater(6)Wightman(11)Sharpe(11)	23
24	Dodds	Seith	Stephens	G Slater	G Slater	Sharpe	Arey	Coxon	J Nicholson	Bowerbank	K Robinson	Whitehead	Wolstenholme	Bowman	Bowman	Sharpe(9)Pearson(3)Nutter(6)J Slater(12)	24
25	Dodds	Seith	S Healey	M Healey	Hudson	Bell	Sharpe	Coxon	J Nicholson	Harriman	Bowerbank	Bowerbank	Whitehead	Wolstenholme	Bowman	Pearson(3)	25
26	G Slater	Dodds	Seith	M Healey	J Slater	Bell	Arey	Coxon	J Nicholson	Harriman	Bracken	Bowerbank	Downham	Wolstenholme	Bowman	Bracken(5)Pearson(3)	26

KENDAL LEAGUE STATISTICS
(COMPILED BY STEPHEN McCORMACK)

Season	Div.	P	W	D	L	F	A	PD	Pts	Pos.	Coach	Captain
87-88	NORTH1	10	7	0	3	135	104	31	14	2		
88-89	NORTH1	10	8	0	2	188	88	100	16	1p	R Lee	D Sharpe
89-90	ALN	10	6	0	4	130	136	-6	12	5	R Lee	D Sharpe
90-91	D4N	12	6	2	4	191	132	59	14	5	R Lee	S Hulme
91-92	D4N	12	8	1	3	157	123	34	17	3	R Lee	S Hulme
92-93	D4N	12	6	0	6	182	189	-7	12	6		
93-94	D5N	12	4	1	7	142	171	-29	9	10		
94-95	D5N	12	9	1	2	226	162	64	19	2	P Kremer	J Nicholson
95-96	D5N	12	5	0	7	215	227	-12	10	9		
96-97	D4N	26	11	1	14	541	451	90	23	9		
Total		128	70	6	52	2107	1783	324				

PROGRAMME DETAILS

SIZE: A5   **PRICE:** 50p extra to admission.

PAGES: 46 plus cover.

ADVERTISING RATES
Full page £160; half page £80; quarter page £50.

CLUB & GROUND DETAILS

Address: Mint Bridge, Shap Road, Kendal. LA9 6DL.
Tel. Nos. 01539 734039

Capacity: 1300   **Seated:** 300   **Standing:** 1000
Simple Directions: From the M6 junction 36 take A591.
Then A6 (Kendal to Penrith). Keep left at the 'Duke of
Cumberland' and the ground is 400metres on the left.
Nearest Railway Station: Kendal (via Oxenholme)
Car Parking: Space for 100 cars on ground.
Admission: Season - £30 for seated or standing
Matchdays - Members Adults £2.50, OAPs £1.
Non-members Adults £4.00, OAPs £1.
Club Shop: Yes. Shop manager - David Robinson, 01539
734039
Clubhouse: Matchdays & training nights. snacks available.
Functions available, capacity 200, contact Ron Hayes 01539
734039
Training Nights: Tuesday and Thursday

LICHFIELD R.U.F.C.

NICKNAME: Myrtle Greens   FOUNDED: 1874

President Paddy N Martin, 11 Church Road, Shenstone, Lichfield. 01543 480045 (H)

Chairman Jim Greenhorn, 47 Cherry Orchard, Lichfield. 01543 253825 (H).

Club Secretary Maurice Keenan, 61 Noddington Lane, Whittington, Lichfield.
01543 432804 (H)

Treasurer David Evans, 54 Curlew Close, Lichfield. 01543 255661 (H)

Fixtures Secretary Steve Barr, 2 Barley Croft, Whittington, Lichfield. WS14 9LY.
01543 432605 (H)

Director of Rugby Barry Broad, 01543 263355

Last season started in good style, with successful matches against Moseley and Rugby followed by an excellent First League match win over relegated Aspatria producing a sparkling brand of rugby prepared during pre-season. However in these games five key personnel received broken bones which upset continuity in team selection.

Fifty players played First XV rugby and the club experienced another seven players being forced into the captaincy role, far from ideal statistics. Too many enforced changes every week led to a season of underachievement. Eleventh place in the league but the club became Staffordshire Cup winners for a tenth time. Rob Smith represented the County whilst Brendon Langley and Lawrence Whitby-Smith were selected for British Police XV's tour to South Africa.

The 'myrtle greens' look forward to this season and continue to recruit quality players. A 'School of Excellence' to nurture the oldest talent available from local schools has been set up by Barry Broad who moves to director of rugby. Kris De Scossa takes charge of the coaching whilst Mark Roberts, at the tender age of twenty, has been appointed skipper.

Most appearances - Andy Gray - 33.

Leading points scorer, Dave Richards, 203 (from 20 games).

Leading try scorer, Matthew Brown - 12 tries.

Player of the Year - John Hicks.

The mini and junior section continues to flourish with many festivals, tournaments and County Cup wins. The Ladies XV gained promotion again and won the James Gilbert Cup (National Junior Cup Competition) beating Harlequins in the final at Stoope.

Lichfield RC.

Colours: Myrtle green, navy blue, red   Change colours: Myrtle green & yellow hoops/blue/red.

LICHFIELD

No	Ven.	Date	Opponents	Att.	Res.	Score	Scorers
1	(H)	31.08	v Aspatria		W	26-12	Brown(t)Grant(t)Lewis(t)Moysey(t)Richards(3c)
2	(A)	07.09	v Sheffield		L	15-76	Brown(t)Broomhall(t)Richards(cp)
3	(H)	21.09	v Nuneaton		W	27-10	Gray(t)Moysey(t)Richards(t3c3p)
4	(A)	28.09	v Stoke O T		L	20-29	Moysey(t)PenT(t)Richards(2c2p)
5	(H)	05.10	v Manchester		W	25-18	Ptolomey(t)Gray(t)Sebright(t)Richards(2c2p)
6	(A)	19.10	v Worcester		L	11-21	Ptolomey(t)Richards(cp)
7	(H)	26.10	v Kendal		W	25-23	Gray(t)Brown(t)Randolph(t)Richards(2c2p)
8	(A)	09.11	v Birmingham S		L	18-52	Lewis(t)Davies(t)Richards(c2p)
9	(H)	16.11	v Stourbridge		L	22-23	Prince(t)Richards(c5p)
10	(H)	18.01	v Preston G		L	10-23	Burden(t)W-Smith(cp)
11	(A)	25.01	v Aspatria		L	20-27	Miles(2t)Lewis(t)W-Smith(cp)
12	(H)	01.02	v Sheffield		W	12-11	W-Smith(4p)
13	(A)	08.02	v Hereford		L	19-22	Davies(t)Miles(t)Gray(t)Broomhall(c)Richards(c)
14	(H)	15.02	v Stoke on Trent		W	37-21	Burden(t)Davies(t)Robinson(t)Lewis(t)Richards(t3c2p)
15	(A)	22.02	v Manchester		L	8-31	Langley(t)Richards(p)
16	(H)	01.03	v Worcester		L	16-32	Brown(t)Broomhall(t)W-Smith(2p)
17	(A)	08.03	v Kendal		W	24-20	Mitchell(t)Grey(t)W-Smith(c4p)
18	(H)	15.02	v Birmingham S		L	13-42	Brown(2t)W-Smith(p)
19	(A)	22.03	v Stourbridge		L	19-48	Broomhall(t)Wills(t)W-Smith(3p)
20	(A)	29.03	v Sandal		L	5-42	R Smith(t)
21	(A)	05.04	v Preston G		L	9-18	Richards(3p)
22	(H)	12.04	v Sandal		L	14-27	Brown(t)Richards(3p)
23	(A)	19.04	v Winnington Park		L	25-36	Howes(2t)Miles(t)Richards(2cpdg)
24	(H)	26.04	v Hereford		W	46- 5	Howes(3t)Langley(t)Miles(t)Mitchell(t)Grey(t)B Davies(t)Richards(3c)
25	(H)	03.05	v Winnington Park		W	40-27	Grey(t)Sey(t)Brown(t)Langley(t)Richards(4c4p)
26	(A)	10.05	v Hereford		W	41-17	Brown(2t)Lewis(t)Howes(t)Broomhall(t)Roberts(t)Richards(4cp)

1996-97 HIGHLIGHTS

LEAGUE DEBUTS:

PLAYERS USED: 39 plus 7 as replacement.

EVER PRESENT: 2 - Andy Gray and Matthew Brown.

Most Appearances

26 Matthew Brown and Andy Gray.
24 Ben Davies.
21 Mark Moysey.

Most Points in Match

20pts Dave Richards v Winnington Park 03.05.97 (H)

Hat trick of tries in a match

3 Scott Howes v Hereford 26.04.97 (H)

Most Points in the season

Pts	Player	T	C	P	D
175	Dave Richards	2	33	32	1
54	Laurence W-Smith	-	3	16	-
45	Matthew Brown	9	-	-	-
35	Andy Gray	7	-	-	-
30	Scott Howes	6	-	-	-

Seventh highest try scorers away from home despite finishing 11th.

Only three teams conceded more tries than Lichfield's 89
131 Hereford
115 Stoke on Trent
92 Aspatria

LICHFIELD'S COURAGE LEAGUE MATCH DETAILS 1996-97

#	15	14	13	12	11	10	9	1	2	3	4	5	6	7	8	Replacements
1	Butler	Mitchell	Gray	Sebright	Brown	W-Smith	Richards	Cartwright	Parker	Robinson	Grant	Lewis	Davies	Moysey	Bourne	Sey(14)Childs(10)
2	Butler	Polomey	Gray	Sebright	Brown	Richards	Broomhall	Cartwright	Parker	Robinson	Grant	Hicks	Davies	Moysey	Bourne	Bartlwtt(13)Perry(8)Mitcherson(2)
3	Polomey	Sebright	Gray	Moysey	Brown	Bartlett	Richards	Bishop	Robinson	Randolph	Hicks	Hicks	Howes	Davies	Bourne	Davis(2)
4	Polomey	Brown	Gray	Moysey	Sebright	Richards	Childs	Bishop	Parker	Robinson	Grant	Hicks	Howes	Davies	Bourne	Smith(6)
5	Prince	Brown	Gray	Sebright	Brown	W-Smith	Richards	Bishop	Parker	Robinson	Lewis	Hicks	Davies	Moysey	Randolph	Bourne
6	Butler	Brown	Gray	Sebright	Polomey	W-Smith	Richards	Bishop	Parker	Robinson	Grant	Hicks	Davies	Moysey	Randolph	Randolph
7	Polomey	Brown	Gray	Sebright	Prince	W-Smith	Richards	Bishop	Parker	Robinson	Grant	Lewis	Davies	Moysey	Randolph	Bourne(4)
8	Polomey	Brown	Gray	Sebright	Prince	W-Smith	Richards	Bishop	Parker	Robinson	Lewis	Hicks	Davies	Moysey	Randolph	Randolph
9	Prince	Brown	Gray	Sebright	Burden	W-Smith	Richards	Bishop	Parker	Robinson	Grant	Lewis	Davies	Moysey	Lewis	Cartwright(6)
10	Wills	Brown	Gray	Sebright	Burden	W-Smith	Richards	Cartwright	Davis	Jackson	Grant	Bishop	Davies	Moysey	Lewis	Polomey(15)Hicks(4)
11	Wills	Brown	Gray	Smith	Burden	W-Smith	Miles	Cartwright	Parker	Jackson	Hicks	Hicks	Davies	Moysey	Lewis	Polomey(15)Davis(6)
12	Polomey	Brown	Gray	Smith	Broomhall	W-Smith	Miles	Cartwright	Parker	Jackson	Bishop	Hicks	Davies	Moysey	Lewis	van Block(6)
13	Polomey	Brown	Gray	Smith	Broomhall	W-Smith	Miles	Cartwright	Parker	Jackson	Hicks	Hicks	Davies	Moysey	Lewis	Bishop(3)Richards(10)
14	Wills	Brown	Gray	Smith	Burden	Richards	Miles	Cartwright	Parker	Robinson	Grant	Hicks	Davies	Moysey	Lewis	Grant(5)Broomhall(15)
15	Wills	Brown	Grey	Smith	Burden	Richards	Miles	Cartwright	Roberts	De Scossa	De Scossa	Lewis	Davies	Moysey	Langley	Hicks(12),Davis(tr 2)
16	Wills	Brown	Grey	Broomhall	Brown	W-Smith	Miles	Cartwright	Roberts	Jackson	Lewis	De Scossa	Hicks	Davies	Langley	Sey(5)
17	Wills	Brown	Grey	Broomhall	Brown	W-Smith	Miles	Cartwright	Roberts	Robinson	Hicks	Wedgewood	Davies	Moysey	Langley	Bishop(5)
18	Wills	Brown	Gray	Broomhall	Brown	W-Smith	Miles	Cartwright	Roberts	Robinson	Bishop	Hicks	Davies	Moysey	Langley	Langley
19	Wills	Brown	Gray	Broomhall	Brown	W-Smith	Robinson	Robinson	Roberts	Bishop	Hicks	De Scossa	Davies	Moysey	Langley	Wedgewood(5)
20	Wills	Mitchell	Gray	Moysey	W-Smith	W-Smith	R.Smith	Cartwright	Roberts	Jackson	Lewis	Lewis	Howes	Moysey	Langley	Langley
21	Wills	Mitchell	Gray	A.Smith	Brown	Richards	R.Smith	Cartwright	Roberts	Jackson	Grant	Grant	Davies	Moysey	Lewis	Broomhall(9)
22	Wills	Mitchell	Gray	A.Smith	Brown	Broomhall	Broomhall	Cartwright	Roberts	Jackson	Grant	Grant	Davies	Moysey	Langley	Howes(6)Davis(tr3)
23	Wills	Mitchell	Gray	A.Smith	Brown	Richards	Miles	Cartwright	Roberts	Jackson	Grant	Grant	Davies	Moysey	Harvey	Howes(7)Cobdan(12)Grimshaw(15)
24	Wills	Mitchell	Gray	Smith	Brown	Richards	Miles	Cartwright	Roberts	Jackson	Hicks	Lewis	Howes	Davies	Langley	DeScossa(7)Cobdan(13)Faulkner(15)
25	Wills	Mitchell	Gray	Broomhall	Brown	Richards	Miles	Cartwright	Roberts	Jackson	Hicks	Lewis	Howes	Sey	Langley	Davies(7)DeScossa(5)
26	Bartlett	Mitchell	Ryan	Brown	Brown	Richards	Broomhall	Mackin	Roberts	Jackson	Hicks	Randolph	Howes	Sey	Langley	Lewis(8)Davis(2)Moysey(7)

LICHFIELD LEAGUE STATISTICS
(COMPILED BY STEPHEN McCORMACK)

Season	Div.	P	W	D	L	F	A	PD	Pts	Pos.	Coach	Captain
87-88	ALN	10	4	0	6	150	165	-15	8	8	A Gouldstone	M Davis
88-89	ALN	10	4	1	5	112	113	-1	9	9	A Gouldstone	P Massey
89-90	ALN	10	5	0	5	110	121	-11	10	8	A Gouldstone	M Davis
90-91	D4N	12	8	1	3	177	152	25	17	2	A Gouldstone	T Butler
91-92	D4N	12	6	1	5	174	177	-3	13	5	B Broad	D Richards
92-93	D4N	12	6	1	5	221	224	-3	13	5	B Broad	D Richards
93-94	D5N	12	5	0	7	118	138	-20	10	7	B Broad	P Tinsley
94-95	D5N	12	6	0	6	217	208	9	12	5	B Broad	D Bourne
95-96	D5N	12	3	0	9	165	284	-119	6	12	B Broad	D Bourne
96-97	D4N	26	10	0	16	546	713	-167	20	11	B Broad	
Total		128	57	4	67	1990	2295	-305				

COURAGE LEAGUE
DIVISION 4 NORTH

SEASON 1996/97

Lichfield Rugby Club

1874
LICHFIELD RUFC

Club Sponsor

Beazer
HOMES

Lichfield RUFC Cooke Fields Tamworth Road Lichfield

OFFICIAL PROGRAMME

PROGRAMME DETAILS

SIZE: A5   **PRICE:** With admission

PAGES: 20 plus cover

PROGRAMME EDITOR: David Lewis 01543 254985

ADVERTISING RATES
Mono Full page £325, Half page £175, Qtr Page £100

CLUB & GROUND DETAILS

Address: Cooke Fields, Tamworth Road, Lichfield, Staffs.
Tel. Nos. 01543 263020

Capacity: 5,000   **Seated:** 200   **Standing:** 4,800

Simple Directions: Take the A51 towards Tamworth out of Lichfield for two miles. The club is situated, just after crossing the A38, on the left behind the 'Horse & Jockey' public house.
Nearest Railway Station:
Lichfield City or Lichfield Trent Valley
Car Parking: 1,000 spaces are available on the ground.
Admission: Season Adults £25, Children/OAPs £10
Matchday Adults £3, Children/OAPs £1
Club Shop: Yes, manager Keeley Grain 01543 432596
Clubhouse: Normal Licensing Hours, snacks & barmeals available. Functions available, capacity 330, contact Graham Ward 01283 790549
Training Nights: Tuesday and Thursday.

MANCHESTER F.C.

FOUNDED: 1860

President Alan Hanson, c/o Manchester FC, Grove Park, Grove Lane, Cheadle Hulme,
Cheshire SK8 7NB. 0161 485 1115
Chairman Russ Jenkins, c/o Manchester FC, as above
Club Secretary Norman R Thomas, 94, Kitts Moss Lane, Bramhall, Stockport, Cheshire. SK7 2BQ.
0161 439 3385 (H), 0161 367 9000 (B), 0161 439 0518 (Fax).
Fixtures Secretary Derek W Partington, 28 Crossfield Drive, Worsley, Manchester. M28 4GP.
0161 790 6742 (H)
Press Officer Alan S Hanson, 01625 261029 (H)   0161 236 4071 (B)
Director of Rugby Alex Keay, c/o Manchester FC, as above
0161 440 0147 (H), 0161 485 3733 (B & Fax)
Club Merchandise Stan Seales (Matchdays only), 0161 439 4893

Successful summer training and pre season games, including Munster, prepared Manchester for the fray of a new higher league.

Recruiting had gone well and the opening away win at Stourbridge augured well. Worcester were next and tipped for promotion. Manchester conceded fourteen points in the last ten minutes ending only with a draw. Birmingham, another fancied club, were beaten at Grove Park before things began to go wrong.

The side was hit with a succession of injuries and one Cup game and four League matches were lost in a row. The turning point came away at Hereford. The side ground out a win in the last quarter and smiles flickered round the faithful Alikadoo followers. From then on fourteen of the remaining seventeen league matches resulted in victories and Manchester ended their first season in the National Leagues in fourth position.

Captain Neil Hitchen led the team from the front until injury forced an early retirement and the captaincy passed to Steve Swindells. His goal kicking and vision from full-back had been missed through injury but he steadied the side and added an attacking edge to the backs.

Manchester's backs provided some breathtaking displays and exciting rugby. Wingers Glen Pearson, Matt Hoskin and Mike Blood showed pace, strength and finishing ability to collect a hat full of tries between them.

Centre combinations of Andy Murison, Gary Langhorn and Rod Ellis gave a solidity in defence and penetration when given a quick ball or half a gap. They too played their part in collecting the record number of points scored for the season for the club. Phil Jee's contribution at ten was considerable. His touch kicking accuracy sapped oppositions and his choice of options released the backs. Andy Jenn, who joined from Manchester University, gave good service at scrum-half.

Under the coaching influence of Alex Keay, now full time Director of Rugby, the pack improved and got fitter through the season. Nick Wheeler was a rock at prop, Guy Parker and Dave Craddock towered at lock and the back row combinations of Tim Burgon, Peter Craddock, Mark Dawson and the evergreen Jimmy Wilde often kept Manchester in the game. First team experience through the phase of injury helped the seconds to win the West 512 Merit Table.

Manchester FC: Back Row (L-R): Alex Kloss, Chris Marshall, Peter Craddock, Guy Parker, Gary Sawbridge, Will Robinson, Ben Gordon. Middle Row: Alex Keay (Director of Rugby), Anthony Hanson, Nick Wheeler, Glen Pearson, Gary Langham, Lewis Gross, Rod Ellis, Andy Jenn, Neil James, Norman Thomas (Secretary). Front Row: Jimmy Wilde, Mike Blood, John Wharton (Team Manager), Steve Swindells, Russ Jenkins (Chairman), Andy Murison, Stuart Dodds.

Colours: Red and white hoops/white/red.   Change colours: Maroon/white/red.

COURAGE LEAGUE MATCH DETAILS 1996-97

No	Ven.	Date	Opponents	Att.	Res.	Score	Scorers
1	(A)	31.08	v Stourbridge		W	26-13	Blood(t)Pearson(t)Murison(t)Swindells(c3p)
2	(H)	07.09	v Worcester		D	23-23	Wilde(t)Pearson(t)Swindells(2c3p)
3	(A)	21.09	v Kendal		L	21-30	A Nuttall(t)Gordon(t)Gee(c3p)
4	(H)	28.09	v Birmingham S		W	18-15	Burgon(t)PenT(t)Gee(c2p)
5	(A)	05.10	v Lichfield		L	18-25	Ellis(t)Pearson(t)Swindells(c2p)
6	(H)	19.10	v Preston G		L	18-19	A Hanson(t)Wilde(t)Seales(2p)Swindells(c)
7	(A)	26.10	v Sandal		L	19-31	Pearson(t)Robinson(t)James(3p)
8	(H)	09.11	v Winnington P		L	16-23	Pearson(t)James(c3p)
9	(A)	16.11	v Hereford		W	24- 8	Gordon(t)Dodds(t)Gee(c4p)
10	(H)	21.12	v Aspatria		W	32-22	Burgon(2t)Murison(t)Swindells(c5p)
11	(A)	28.12	v Sheffield		W	35-10	Burgon(2t)Murison(t)Ellis(t)Swindells(3c3p)
12	(H)	18.01	v Nuneaton		W	54- 3	Ellis(2t)Hoskins(2t)Murison(t)Dodds(t)Swindells(2t4c2p)
13	(H)	25.01	v Stourbridge		W	28-20	PenTry(t)P Craddock(t)Parker(t)Swindells(2c3p)
14	(A)	01.02	v Worcester		L	10-17	Hoskins(t)Swindells(cp)
15	(H)	08.02	v Kendal		W	22-13	Blood(t)Burgon(t)Swindells(t2cp)
16	(A)	15.02	v Birmingham S		W	39-32	Burgon(2t)Gee(2t)P Craddock(t)Swindells(t3cp)
17	(H)	22.02	v Lichfield		W	31- 8	Hoskins(2t)Gee(t)G Nuttall(t)Swindells(t3c)
18	(A)	01.03	v Preston G		L	10-18	Burgon(t)Swindells(cp)
19	(H)	08.03	v Sandall		W	43-17	Hoskins(t)Langhorn(t)Ellis(t)Blood(t)Burgon(t)D Craddock(t)Swindells(t4c)
20	(A)	15.03	v Winnington Park		L	31-46	Blood(t)Burgon(t)Crampton(t)Swindells(2c3p)Gee(dg)
21	(H)	22.03	v Hereford		W	73- 5	Pearson(3t)Burgon(2t)Parker(t)Gee(t)Dawson(t)P Craddock(t)Swindells(2t9c)
22	(A)	29.03	v Stoke on Trent		W	31-24	Pearson(2t)Burgon(2t)Swindells(c3p)
23	(A)	05.04	v Aspatria		W	42-16	Pearson(t)Ellis(t)PenTry(t)P Craddock(t)Swindells(t4c3p)
24	(H)	12.04	v Sheffield		W	46-17	Gross(t)Kloss(t)Murison(t)Dodds(t)PenTry(t)James(t2c)Swindells(3c2p)
25	(A)	19.04	v Nuneaton		W	40-28	Pearson(2t)PenTry(t)Ellis(t)Dawson(t)Gross(t)James(5c)
26	(H)	26.04	v Stoke on Trent		W	45-21	Pearson(3t)Langhorn(t)Gross(t)Dawson(t)Ellis(t)James(4c)Swindells(c)

1996-97 HIGHLIGHTS

LEAGUE DEBUTS:

PLAYERS USED: 41 plus 7 as replacement only.

EVER PRESENT: None - most appearances 24
- Pete Craddock & Nick Wheeler.

❏ Most points in a match
28 Steve Swindells v Hereford 22.03.97 (H)
24 Steve Swindells v Nuneaton 18.01.97 (H)
22 Steve Swindells v Aspatria 05.04.97 (A)

❏ One of only three teams to score 100 tries.
112 Worcester
101 Birmingham S
101 Manchester

❏ Hat trick of tries in a match
3 Glen Pearson v Hereford 22.03.97 (H)
3 Glen Pearson v Stoke on Trent 26.04.97 (H)

❏ Most points in the season

Pts	Player	T	C	P	D
251	Steve Swindells	9	49	36	-
75	Glen Pearson	15	-	-	-
75	Tim Burgon	15	-	-	-
56	Phil Gee	4	3	9	1
47	Neil James	1	12	6	-

❏ Second highest try scorers in home matches with 58 behind Worcester's 60.

❏ Most appearances
24 Nick Wheeler and Pete Craddock
22 Rod Ellis
20 Guy Parker

MANCHESTER'S COURAGE LEAGUE MATCH DETAILS 1996-97

#	15	14	13	12	11	10	9	1	2	3	4	5	6	7	8	Replacements
1	Swindells	Blood	Langhorn	Murison	Pearson	James	Hanson	Williamson	Hitchen	Wheeler	Parker	Robinson	PCraddock	Burgon	Wilde	Gordon(4)
2	Swindells	Medley	Langhorn	Murison	Pearson	James	Hanson	Williamson	Hitchen	Wheeler	Robinson	DCraddock	PCraddock	Burgon	Wilde	
3	Gee	Ellis	Langhorn	Murison	Pearson	James	Nuttall	Williamson	Hitchen	Wheeler	Gordon	Wilde	PCraddock	Burgon	Wilde	Marshall(5)Murray(10)
4	Buchanan	Ellis	Langhorn	Murison	Pearson	Gee	Nuttall	Williamson	Hitchen	Wheeler	Parker	Robinson	PCraddock	Burgon	Dawson	Sawbridge(2)Wilde(8)
5	Swindells	Pearson	Langhorn	Murison	Ellis	Hill	Hanson	Simpkins		Wheeler	Parker	Robinson	PCraddock	Burgon	Wilde	Dawson(7)Murray(13)
6	Buchanan	Hornby	Langhorn	Murison	Medley	Swindells	Hanson		Hitchen	Wheeler	Parker	Robinson	Burns	Herron	Wilde	Seales(10)Sawbridge(2)
7	Buchanan	Pearson	Langhorn	Murison	Lockett	James	Roberts		Hitchen	Wheeler	Parker	Robinson	Burns	Herron	Wilde	
8	Crampton	Langhorn	Murison	Lockett	James	Hanson	Roberts			Wheeler	Parker	Robinson	Burns	Herron	Wilde	Gee(9)
9	Buchanan	Lockett	Ellis	Langhorn	Pearson	Gee	Nuttall	Dodds	Hitchen	Wheeler	Gordon	DCraddock	Burns	PCraddock	Parker	Wilde(7)
10	Swindells	Hoskins	Ellis	Langhorn	Murison	Gee	Hanson	Dodds		Wheeler	DCraddock	Kloss	PCraddock	Burgon	Parker	Sawbridge(2)
11	Swindells	Hornby	Ellis	Murison	Pearson	Gee	Hanson	Dodds		Wheeler	DCraddock	Kloss	PCraddock	Burgon	Parker	Simpkins(4)
12	Swindells	Hoskins	Ellis	Murison	Langhorn	Gee	Nuttall	Dodds		Simpkins	DCraddock	Kloss	PCraddock	Burgon	Parker	Pearson(14)Roberts(1)Webster(13)Young(6)
13	Swindells	Hoskins	Ellis	Murison	Langhorn	Gee	Nuttall	Sawbridge		Wheeler	DCraddock	Kloss	PCraddock	Burgon	Parker	Dawson(5)
14	Swindells	Blood	Ellis	Murison	Ellis	Gee	Nuttall	Simpkins		Wheeler	DCraddock	Kloss	PCraddock	Burgon	Dawson	Wilde(8)Hornby(10)
15	Swindells	Blood	Murison	Ellis		Hoskins	James	Simpkins		Wheeler	DCraddock	Parker	PCraddock	Burgon	Dawson	Robinson(8)
16	Swindells	Blood	Murison	Ellis	Hoskins	Gee	Dodds	GNuttall		Wheeler	DCraddock	Parker	PCraddock	Burgon	Dawson	Langhorn(13)
17	Swindells	Blood	Langhorn	Ellis	Murison	Gee	Simpkins	GNuttall		Wheeler	DCraddock	Marshall	PCraddock	Burgon	Dawson	Murison(10)Sawbridge(2)
18	Swindells	Blood	Murison	Ellis	Hoskins	Gee		GNuttall		Wheeler	DCraddock	Parker	PCraddock	Burgon	Dawson	
19	Swindells	Hoskins	Langhorn	Ellis	Blood	Gee		GNuttall		Wheeler	DCraddock	Parker	PCraddock	Burgon	Dawson	Wilde(8)Webster(11)
20	Swindells	Blood	Crampton	Ellis	Blood	Gee	Dodds	GNuttall		Wheeler	Gordon	DCraddock	PCraddock	Burgon	Parker	Dawson(4)Seales(13)
21	Swindells	Blood	Ellis		Pearson	Gee	Dodds	GNuttall		Wheeler	Parker	DCraddock	PCraddock	Burgon	Dawson	James(14)Young(7)White(1)
22	Swindells	Pearson	Murison	Crampton		Gee	Jones	Dodds		Wheeler	Parker	DCraddock	PCraddock	Burgon	Dawson	
23	Swindells	Pearson	Ellis	Murison		Gee	Jenn	Dodds	Simpkins		Parker	DCraddock	PCraddock	Burgon	Dawson	Hyatt(7)Seales(10)Roberts(1)
24	Swindells	James	Ellis	Murison	Gross	Jenn	Dodds	Simpkins		Wheeler	DCraddock	Marshall	PCraddock		Dawson	Murray(12)Sawbridge(2)Kloss(5)Warhurst(15)
25	James	Pearson	Ellis	Langhorn	Gross	Gee	Jenn	Simpkins	Dodds	Wheeler		Kloss	PCraddock	Burgon	Dawson	Marshall(4)Sawbridge(1)Warhurst(9)
26	James	Pearson	Ellis	Langhorn	Gross	Gee	Jenn	Dodds	Sawbridge	Wheeler	Kloss	Marshall	PCraddock	Dawson	Wilde	Swindells(12)Blood(11)Roberts(2)Young(7)

MANCHESTER LEAGUE STATISTICS
(COMPILED BY STEPHEN McCORMACK)

Season	Div.	P	W	D	L	F	A	PD	Pts	Pos.	Coach	Captain
87-88	NORTH2	10	1	0	9	55	140	-85	2	10r	A Hanson	R Smith
88-89	NORTH W	10	3	0	7	115	128	-13	6	10r	A Hanson	D Kelly
89-90	NORTH W	20	8	1	1	212	62	150	17	1p	A Hanson	D Kelly
90-91	NORTH W	10	8	0	2	201	73	128	16	2	D Kelly	D Kelly
91-92	NORTH W	10	10	0	0	242	47	195	20	1p	D Kelly	D Kelly
92-93	NORTH2	12	10	0	2	302	103	199	20	1p		
93-94	NORTH1	12	8	0	4	208	159	49	16	4		
94-95	NORTH1	12	7	3	2	217	166	51	17	3		
95-96	NORTH1	12	10	1	1	362	124	238	21	1p		A Hanson
96-97	D4N	26	17	1	8	795	504	291	35	4		
Total		124	82	6	36	2709	1506	1203				

CHAMPIONS NORTH DIVISION ONE 1995/96
FOUNDED 1860 – MEMBER OF THE RUGBY FOOTBALL UNION – ELECTED 1872

MATCH PROGRAMME
SEASON 1996/97

PROGRAMME DETAILS

SIZE: A5   **PRICE:** With admission

PAGES: 36 plus cover

ADVERTISING RATES
Special location Full Page £250
Mono - Full Page £200
Half Page £125
Qtr Page £70

CLUB & GROUND DETAILS

Address: Grove Park, Grove Lane, Cheadle Hulme, Cheshire. SK8 7NB.
Tel. Nos. 0161 485 1115
Capacity: 3250   **Seated:** 250   **Standing:** 3000
Simple Directions: Exit junct.10 from M63 and head south on A34 (Wilmslow) for 2.5 miles to second roundabout. Exit left and club is 400 metres on the right.
From South: M56, Manchester Airport to A34, Wilmslow to B5095, Bramhall, club is about a mile.
Nearest Railway Station: Cheadle Hulme.
Car Parking: 200 spaces available within the ground.
Admission: Season - Adults £65, concession for OAPs.
Match day - Adults £4.00, OAPs £2.50, Children Free.
Club Shop: Yes. Manager - Stan Seales - 0161 439 4893.
Clubhouse: Normal Licensing hours, snacks & bar meals available. Functions available, capacity 150 seated, contact Bob or Sue Ashton 0161 485 1115
Training Nights: Tuesday and Thursday.

NUNEATON R.F.C.

NICKNAME: Nuns

FOUNDED: 1879

President Keith Howells,
RTS Arbury Road, Nuneaton, Warks, CV10 7NQ
01203 348286 (H), 01203 329821 (B), 01203 348286 (Fax)

Chairman Mo Burge,
45 Woodcote Avenue, Nuneaton, Warks, CV11 2DE
01203 386135 (H), 01827 718092 (B), 01926 415781 (Fax)

Secretary Maggie Mander,
7 Farriers Way, Crowhill, Nuneaton, Warks, CV11 6UZ
01203 381803 (H), 0171 462 4975 (B), 0171 636 6915 (Fax)

Treasurer Dick Sharrott,
183 Windermere Avenue, Nuneaton, Warks, CV11 6HW
01203 382119 (H), 01203 374437 (B), 01203 642092 (Fax)

Fixtures Secretary John Davies,
3 Saints Way, Nuneaton, Warks, CV10 0UU
01203 370011 (H), 01203 344800 (B)

Vice Chairman/Press Officer Paul Littlehales, 01203 341850 (H)
Club Coach Darren Grewcock, 01203 448282 (B)

The new season commenced with the official opening of the new club. Games were played by each section of the club including a demonstration 7-a-side by the ladies and cluminating in a representative game of the Nuneaton 1st XV versus a President's XV side which was made up of many ex-players who had agreed to don their boots again to mark this special occasion. Leicester and England player Graham Rowntree, who is an ex-Nun's player, unveiled the commemorative plaque. RFU Prsident John Richardson was also in attendance along with local dignitaries and members of the Sports Council.

Unfortunately, as with the previous season, the Nuns did not get off to a good start losing the first round of the Pilkington Cup and league defeats up to Christmas. The bad luck continued into the start of the New Year with the loss of several key senior players through injury, work commitments or transfers to other clubs. However, 1997 also brought with it a new club coach and the influx of some new players. The new coach Darren Grewcock, joined from nearby Coventry and instilled confidence and motivation into the side to ensure the Nuns retained their position in National League Two for the forthcoming season by winning the majority of the remaining fixtures.

The mini and junior section is an important part of the Nuns set up and was the starting ground for Internationals such as Graham Rowntree and Darren Garforth (Leicester and England). The section held a very successful Knock-Out Competition in March but sadly for the Nuns and the other English sides competing, the majority of the prizes were taken back to Wales. The ladies side folded at Christmas but some of the team have since joined other local sides.

For the new season a development squad has been formed with the intention of keeping players associated with the club as they progress from Colts to senior rugby and during their time away from the area whilst fulfilling their education.

MAGGIE MANDER

Colours: Red, black, white   **Change colours:** Green, black, white

COURAGE LEAGUE MATCH DETAILS 1996-97

No	Ven.	Date	Opponents	Att.	Res.	Score	Scorers
1	(A)	31.08	v Kendal		L	5-30	P Mitchell(t)
2	(H)	07.09	v Birmingham S		L	8-18	Bent(t)Henderson(p)
3	(A)	21.09	v Lichfield		L	10-27	Bent(t)Roberts(t)
4	(H)	28.09	v Preston		L	14-35	Warwood(t)Masser(3p)
5	(A)	05.10	v Sandal		L	13-24	Owen(t)Masser(c2p)
6	(H)	19.10	v Winnington P		L	16-25	Warwood(t)C Taylor(c3p)
7	(A)	26.10	v Hereford		L	16-21	PenT(t)C Taylor(c2p)Reid(p)
8	(H)	09.11	v Aspatria		W	40-38	Bent(2t)Roberts(t)A Taylor(t)M Mitchell(t)Henderson(3c3p)
9	(A)	16.11	v Sheffield		L	8-18	Owen(t)Henderson(p)
10	(A)	21.12	v Stourbridge		L	13-38	Carter(t)Masser(tdg)
11	(H)	28.12	v Stoke O T		W	22-18	A Taylor(2t)Masser(t)Warwood(t)Henderson(c)
12	(A)	18.01	v Manchester		L	3-54	Henderson(p)
13	(H)	25.01	v Kendal		D	33-33	Warwood(t)Bent(t)Alleyne(t)Henderson(3c4p)
14	(A)	01.02	v Birmingham S		L	11-43	Warwoood(t)Thomas(2p)
15	(H)	15.02	v Lichfield		W	22-19	Bent(t)Court(t)Taylor(t)Thomas(2p)
16	(A)	15.02	v Preston G		L	5-17	Gee(t)
17	(H)	22.02	v Sandal		W	29-15	Reid(t)Owen(t)Barry(t)Henderson(t)Thomas(2p)Gee(dg)
18	(A)	01.03	v Winnington Park		W	37- 0	Russell(2t)Bent(t)M Mitchell(t)Warwood(t)Thomas(3c2p)
19	(H)	08.03	v Hereford		W	34- 9	Sharp(t)Worwood(t)Snow(t)Gee(dg)Thomas(t4cp)
20	(A)	15.03	v Aspatria		L	3-18	Gee(dg)
21	(H)	22.03	v Sheffield		W	19- 5	Barden(2t)Court(t)Thomas(2c)
22	(H)	26.03	v Worcester		L	19-37	Bent(2t)Court(t)Thomas(2c)
23	(H)	05.04	v Stourbridge		L	18-26	Reid(t)Taylor(t)Thomas(tp)
24	(A)	12.04	v Stoke on Trent		W	28-16	Taylor(t)Court(t)M Mitchell(t)Russell(t)Henderson(4c)
25	(H)	19.04	v Manchester		L	28-40	Bates(t)M Mitchell(t)Court(t)Thomas(t)Henderson(4c)
26	(A)	26.04	v Worcester		L	3-43	Henderson(p)

1996-97 HIGHLIGHTS

PLAYERS USED: 48 plus three as replacement only.

EVER PRESENT: None - most appearances 21 by Mark Mitchell and Alan Taylor.

❏ Despite finishing 3rd bottom scored more tries than 5 teams including 3rd placed Preston Grasshoppers.

❏ Four teams conceded more tries than Nuneaton's 84

  89   Lichfield
  92   Aspatria
  115 Stoke on Trent
  131 Hereford

❏ Prop forward Craig Court scored four tries in the last six games of the season.

❏ **Most points in a match**

18 Gavin Henderson v Kendal 25.01.97 (H)
16 Marc Thomas v Hereford 08.03.97 (H)

❏ **Hat trick of tries in a match**

None - two was the best achieved five times by four players. Clive Bent (twice), Sam Russell, Alan Taylor and Stuart Barden.

❏ **Most points in the season**

Pts	Player	T	C	P	D
68	Marc Thomas	3	13	9	-
68	Gavin Henderson	1	15	11	-
45	Clive Bent	9	-	-	-
35	Alan Warwood	7	-	-	-
30	Warwick Masser	2	1	5	1
30	Alan Taylor	6	-	-	-

❏ **Most appearances**

21 Mark Mitchell and Alan Taylor.
20 Craig Court (2), and Clive Bent.
19 Alan Warwood and Gavin Henderson.

NUNEATON'S COURAGE LEAGUE MATCH DETAILS 1996-97

#	15	14	13	12	11	10	9	1	2	3	4	5	6	7	8	Replacements
1	May	P Jones	Baber	Warwood	Hiley	Henderson	P Mitchell	Ashfield	Owen	Moore	Brown	Roberts	Southwell	Lamb	Sharp	Nicol(8)
2	May	Baber	Baber	Warwood	P Jones	Henderson	P Mitchell	Ashfield	Owen	Cannon	Brown	Roberts	Southwell	Lamb	A Jones	
3	Bates	Bent	Webb	Warwood	P Jones	Henderson	Wesson	Owen	Owen	Brown	Brown	Roberts	A Jones	Nicol	Kalari	
4	Carter	Bent	Webb	Warwood	W Masser	Henderson	Wesson	Cannon	Owen	Brown	Brown	Roberts	Gill	Taylor	Kalari	
5	Carter	Bent	Baber	Warwood	W Masser	W Masser	P Mitchell	Moore	Owen	Court	Brown	Roberts	Taylor	Kalari	Kalari	C Taylor(10)
6	Carter	Webb	Warwood	Warwood	Bent	W Masser	P Mitchell	Owen	Owen	Court	Brown	Sharp	Taylor	Kalari	Kalari	Drew(1)
7	Reid	Bent	Warwood	Warwood	Barry	C Taylor	P Mitchell	Owen	Owen	Court	Brown	Sharp	M Mitchell	A Taylor	Kalari	Carter(11)Cannon(5)
8	Reid	Hiley	Warwood	Warwood	Bent	P Mitchell	P Mitchell	Owen	Flowers	Brown	Brown	Roberts	M Mitchell	A Taylor	Kalari	
9	Reid	Hiley	Warwood	W Masser	Bent	P Mitchell	P Mitchell	Owen	Flowers	Brown	Owen	Roberts	M Mitchell	A Taylor	Gill	Court(3)
10	Reid	Carter	Baber	Alleyne	Bent	Henderson	P Mitchell	Owen	Flowers	Brown	Brown	Bell	M Mitchell	A Taylor	Gill	Owen(2)Edwards(8)Court(3)
11	Reid	Baber	Warwood	Henderson	P Jones	Henderson	P Mitchell	Moore	Owen	Court	Brown	Roberts	M Mitchell	A Taylor	Edwards	Bent(14)Kalari(5)Savidge(9)
12	Reid	Bent	Warwood	W Masser	Barry	Henderson	Wesson	Wesson	Owen	Court	Bell	Sharp	M Mitchell	A Taylor	Kalari	
13	Reid	Bent	Warwood	Henderson	Alleyne	Henderson	Grewcock	Moore	Owen	Bell	Edwards	Sharp	M Mitchell	A Taylor	Kalari	
14	Thomas	Barry	Warwood	Reid	Bent	Savidge	Savidge	Moore	Owen	Court	Brown	Sharp	M Mitchell	A Taylor	Kalari	Owen(1)
15	Thomas	Barry	Warwood	W Masser	Bent	Grewcock	Grewcock	Moore	Gibson	Court	Brown	Edwards	M Mitchell	A Taylor	Russell	Bates(12)Drew(1)Savidge(9)O'Donoghue(5)
16	Henderson	Barry	Warwood	Alleyne	Bent	Savidge	Savidge	Moore	Gibson	Court	Brown	Sharp	M Mitchell	A Taylor	Russell	Owen(2)Gill(5)D Masser(12)
17	Thomas	Barry	Worwood	Henderson	Bent	S Brown	S Brown	Owen	Owen	Court	Sharp	Roberts	M Mitchell	A Taylor	Russell	Gibson(2)Reid(9)Savidge(R9)Donaghue(5)
18	Thomas	Barry	Worwood	Bent	Bent	Henderson	Henderson	Owen	Owen	Court	Sharp	Roberts	M Mitchell	A Taylor	Russell	O'Donoghue(5)Gibson(2)Carter(14)Evans(3)
19	Thomas	Barry	Worwood	Barden	Gee	Henderson	Henderson	Drew	Court	Court	Sharp	Roberts	M Mitchell	A Taylor	Russell	Snow(2)Kalari(6)W Masser(13).
20	Thomas	Barry	Worwood	Barden	Gee	Henderson	Henderson	Drew	Court	Court	Brown	Roberts	M Mitchell	A Taylor	Russell	Brown(4)Bent(14)Snow(tr1)
21	Thomas	May	Worwood	Barden	Gee	Grewcock	Grewcock	Drew	Court	Brown	Brown	Sharp	M Mitchell	A Taylor	Kalari	Henderson(4)Bent(14)Snow(tr1)
22	Thomas	Bent	W Masser	Barden	Gee	Grewcock	Grewcock	Owen	Gibson	Brown	Brown	Sharp	M Mitchell	A Taylor	Russell	Henderson(9)Kalari(2)Snow(14)Cannon(1)
23	Thomas	Barry	Worwood	Alleyne	Gee	Grewcock	Moore	Owen	Gibson	Court	Sharp	Roberts	M Mitchell	A Taylor	Russell	Snow(4)Cannon(1)Carter(15)
24	Thomas	Bates	Barden	Barden	Gee	Henderson	Cannon	Gibson	Gibson	Sharp	Sharp	King	M Mitchell	A Taylor	Russell	Snow(6)Brown(5)Evans(1)W Masser(10)
25	Thomas	W Masser	Barden	Bent	Gee	Henderson	Drew	Gibson	Gibson	Court	Sharp	Roberts	M Mitchell	Snow	Russell	Owen(3)Brown(4)Carter(1)Reid(9)
26	Reid	Gee	Barden	Carter	Carter	W Masser	Henderson	Gibson	Court	King	Gibson	Roberts	M Mitchell	Snow	Russell	Owen(2)Sharp(8)Newman(15)

NUNEATON LEAGUE STATISTICS
(COMPILED BY STEPHEN McCORMACK)

Season	Div.	P	W	D	L	F	A	PD	Pts	Pos.	Coach	Captain
87-88	3	11	2	1	8	94	157	-63	3	10	N Barker	R Massey
88-89	3	11	5	0	6	178	214	-36	10	5	T McCarthy	R Burton
89-90	3	11	4	0	7	127	196	-69	8	10	T McCarthy	R Burton
90-91	3	12	5	0	7	180	200	-20	10	7	T McCarthy	A Ambrose
91-92	3	12	1	2	9	153	237	-84	4	12r	M Lewis	A Ambrose
92-93	D4N	12	2	0	10	138	269	-131	4	12		
93-94	D5N	12	4	1	7	122	200	-78	9	11	S Redfern	P Flowers
94-95	D5N	12	4	0	8	129	161	-32	8	11	S Redfern	T Simms
95-96	D5N	12	4	1	7	178	329	-151	9	10		
96-97	D4N	26	8	1	17	457	667	-210	17	12		
Total		131	39	6	86	1756	2630	-874				

NUNEATON
RUGBY FOOTBALL CLUB
1996/1997 Season

FOUNDED · 1879

TNT Express

Sponsored by TNT Express
– Leading the Field in Express Delivery

PROGRAMME DETAILS

SIZE: A5 **PRICE:** £1
PAGES: 28 plus cover
EDITOR: Paul Littlehales
ADVERTISING RATES
Contact John Lumsden 01203 385559/325355

CLUB & GROUND DETAILS

Address: Liberty Way, Attleborough Fields, Nuneaton, Warks. CV11 6RR.
Tel. Nos. 01203 383206

Capacity Standing No limit
Simple Directions From M6 follow A444 to Nuneaton, follow ring road towards M69/A5. Ring road enters Eastborough Way, club just off mini round about
Nearest Railway Station: Nuneaton, Trent Valley, 30 mins walk.
Car Parking: Parking within the ground and nearby on Industrial Estate
Admission:
Season tickets: Adults £40 Children/OAPs £15.
Matchday: Adults £4 Children/OAPs £1
Club Shop: Yes. Manager Mo Burge.
Clubhouse: Normal licensing hours, some food available dependent on occasion. Functions for up to 100 seated can be catered for, contact Vanessa Jee 01203 383206
Training Nights: Tuesday and Thursday.

PRESTON GRASSHOPPERS RFC

NICKNAME: Hoppers
FOUNDED: 1869

President Les Anson, c/o Preston Grasshoppers RFC, Lightfoot Green, Fulwood, Preston, Lancs PR4 0AP
01772 863546, 01772 861605 (Fax)
Chairman David Taylorson, c/o Preston Grasshoppers RFC, as above.
Club Secretary Peter Ashcroft, c/o Preston Grasshoppers RFC, as above
01772 744066 (H), 01772 863546 (B), 01772 861605 (Fax)
Fixtures Secretary John Powell, 121 Bare Lane, Bare, Morecambe, Lancs. LA4 4RD.
01524 424514 (H), 01772 863546 (B), 01772 861605 (Fax)
Admin Officer Ken Moore, c/o Preston Grasshoppers RFC, as above
01772 720878 (H), 01772 863546 (B), 01772 861605 (Fax)
Press Officer John Herrington, 01772 712162 (H), 01772 863546 (B), 01772 861605 (Fax).

Hoppers' third place in the league was an improvement on the previous season, but again the Lightfoot Green side's promotion ambitions were frustrated after being in contention for three quarters of the season.

A best ever cup run took Hoppers to the fifth round with the defeats of Third League sides Fylde and Liverpool St. Helens providing evidence of the professional approach brought to the club by skipper Steve Kerry. The reward of a home tie with First Division Northampton meant that Paul Grayson returned to his roots and ensured a record crowd. A try from Ian Ashton and two penalties from Kerry produced a half time lead but the visitors asserted their authority to take control in the second half.

Narrow home defeats by Worcester and Birmingham/Solihull were the only other blemishes on an otherwise perfect record before Christmas, but a reverse at Winnington Park in January proved a major disappointment. The visit to Worcester in early March saw Hoppers become the only side in the season to take a point away from Sixways with a thrilling late rally. Injuries, particularly in the pack, led to a downturn in league fortunes in the final two months of the season but a successful Lancashire Cup run kept interest high. Although Hoppers' backs outplayed their Orrell counterparts in the final the strength of the First Division side's pack proved decisive.

On a personal front skipper Kerry equalled the league record for drop goals in a game with four at Aspatria on his way to collecting the Unisys award for his twelve in the season. Rob Smith looked a useful acquisition in the backs. The back row of Glyn Dewhurst and the brothers Ian and Neil Ashton gained respect throughout the league whilst the linking of former No 8, Mike Bailey, with Phil Crayston in the second row was an unqualified success.

Hoppers' Colts suggested that the stream of young talent will continue with a third successive Lancashire Cup win and Lightfoot Green's facilities continued to expand with the installation of a cricket wicket.

Preston Grasshoppers RFC: Back Row (L-R); W Johnston (Coach), C Dew (Head Coach), M Maddox, G Dewhurst, M Sword, N Ashton, M Bailey, I Ashton, P Crayston, L Bell, P Carter, D Chadwick, J Crayston (Manager), Mrs H Thompson (Physio), A Eccles (Manager). Front Row; N Bell, M Walker, J Bleasdale, J Chesworth, L Anson (President), S Kerry (Captain), J Lamb, B Greenwood, R Spicer, G Povall.

Photo courtesy Lancashire Evening Post.

Colours: Navy blue & white irregular hoops/navy blue/navy blue.   **Change colours:** Emerald green, red collar & cuffs.

COURAGE LEAGUE MATCH DETAILS 1996-97

No	Ven.	Date	Opponents	Att.	Res.	Score	Scorers
1	(H)	31.08	v Hereford		W	37-12	Greenwood(t)Lamb(t)Bleasdale(t)Kerry(2c6p)
2	(A)	07.09	v Aspatria		W	31-24	Greenwood(t)Bell(t)N Ashton(t)Kerry(2c4dg)
3	(H)	21.09	v Sheffield		W	18- 8	Bailey(t)Borowski(t)Kerry(c2p)
4	(A)	28.09	v Nuneaton		W	35-14	Greenwood(t)Walker(t)N Ashton(t)Kerry(t3c3p)
5	(H)	05.10	v Stoke O T		W	34- 9	Bailey(t)Dewhurst(t)Walker(t)N Ashton(2t)Kerry(3cp)
6	(A)	19.10	v Manchester		W	19-18	I Ashton(t)Kerry(c4p)
7	(H)	26.10	v Worcester		L	6-13	Kerry(pdg)
8	(A)	09.11	v Kendal		W	19-13	PenT9t)Kerry(c4p)
9	(H)	16.11	v Birmingham S		L	11-18	Smith(t)Kerry(2p)
10	(A)	11.01	v Winnington Park		L	3-10	Kerry(p)
11	(A)	18.01	v Lichfield		W	23-10	Smith(t)Kerry(t2c3p)
12	(A)	25.01	v Hereford		W	52- 3	Dewhurst(2t)N Ashton(t)Roberts(t)Chesworth(t)Walker(t)Kerry(t7cdg)
13	(H)	01.02	v Aspatria		W	23-11	Dewhurst(t)Vaughan(t)Kerry(2c2pdg)
14	(A)	08.02	v Sheffield		D	23-23	Dooley(t)Kerry(5pdg)
15	(H)	15.02	v Nuneaton		W	17- 5	Walker(t)Bleasdale(dg)Kerry(3p)
16	(A)	22.02	v Stoke on Trent		W	28-10	N Ashton(t)Whittingham(t)Smith(t)Kerry(2c3p)
17	(H)	01.03	v Manchester		W	18-10	Bleasdale(t)Chadwick(t)Kerry(c2p)
18	(A)	08.03	v Worcester		D	13-13	Dewhurst(t)Kerry(c2p)
19	(H)	15.03	v Kendal		W	15-14	Kerry(5p)
20	(A)	22.03	v Birmingham S		L	6-26	Kerry(2p)
21	(A)	29.03	v Stourbridge		L	13-18	Bailey(t)Kerry(2p)
22	(H)	05.04	v Lichfield		W	18- 9	Dooley(t)Smith(t)
23	(H)	12.04	v Stourbridge		W	41-21	Whittingham(2t)Chesworth(t)Dooley(t)Dewhurst(t)Smith(t)Kerry(4cp)
24	(A)	19.04	v Sandal		L	13-28	Kerry(tc2p)
25	(H)	26.04	v Winnington Park		L	20-27	Dewhurst(t)Bleasdale(t)Kerry(2c2p)
26	(H)	03.05	v Sandal		W	32-29	Bailey(2t)Kerry(2c6p)

1996-97 HIGHLIGHTS

PLAYERS USED: 35 plus six as replacement only.

EVER PRESENT: Steve Kerry.

Only Worcester with 35 conceded less than Preston's 41.

Steve Kerry with 317 points breaks the club record for points in a season as well as the National League Four record.

Most points in a match

22 Steve Kerry v Hereford 31.08.96 (H)
22 Steve Kerry v Hereford 25.01.97 (A)
22 Steve Kerry v Sandal 03.05.97 (H)
20 Steve Kerry v Nuneaton 28.09.96 (A)

Hat trick of tries in a match

None - four players scored two tries in a match.

Most poits in the season

Pts	Player	T	C	P	D
317	Steve Kerry	4	39	64	9
35	Glyn Dewhurst	7	-	-	-
28	Rob Smith	5	-	1	-
25	Mike Bailey	5	-	-	-
25	Neil Ashton	5	-	-	-

Most Appearances

26 Steve Kerry
25 Phil Crayston
24 John Chesworth, Mike Bailey & John Bleasdale (1)
23 Glyn Dewhurst
22 Mike Walker

Ex England international Wade Dooley had an eventful four matches scoring three tries and receiving two yellow cards.

PRESTON GRASSHOPPER'S COURAGE LEAGUE MATCH DETAILS 1996-97

	15	14	13	12	11	10	9	1	2	3	4	5	6	7	8	Replacements
1	Chesworth	Greenwood	N Bell	Lamb	Swarbrig	Kerry	Bleasdale	L Bell	Carter	Chadwick	Crayston	Bailey	Dewhurst	I Ashton	N Ashton	Povall(9)
2	Chesworth	Greenwood	N Bell	Lamb	Swarbrig	Kerry	Bleasdale	Spicer	Carter	Chadwick	Crayston	Bailey	Sword	I Ashton	N Ashton	Sword(6)
3	Chesworth	Greenwood	Borowski	Lamb	Walker	Kerry	Bleasdale	Spicer	Carter	Chadwick	Crayston	Bailey	Sword	I Ashton	N Ashton	Sword(6)
4	Chesworth	Greenwood	Borowski	Lamb	Walker	Kerry	Bleasdale	Chadwick	Carter		Crayston	Bailey	I Ashton	Dewhurst	N Ashton	Sword(8)Anderson(6)
5	Chesworth	Greenwood	N Bell	Lamb	Walker	Povall	Bleasdale	Spicer		Chadwick	Crayston	Bailey	Sword	Dewhurst	N Ashton	Bleasdale(9)
6	Chesworth	Greenwood	N Bell	Lamb	Walker	Kerry	Bleasdale		Carter	Chadwick	Crayston	Bailey	I Ashton	Dewhurst	N Ashton	
7	Chesworth	Greenwood	N Bell	Lamb	Walker	Kerry	Bleasdale	L Bell	Carter	Spicer	Crayston	Bailey	I Ashton	Dewhurst	N Ashton	
8	Chesworth	Smith	N Bell	Lamb	Walker	Kerry	Bleasdale	L Bell	Carter	Spicer	Crayston	Bailey	I Ashton	Dewhurst	N Ashton	
9	Chesworth	Smith	N Bell	Lamb	Walker	Kerry	Bleasdale	Spicer	Carter	Spicer	Crayston	Bailey	I Ashton	Dewhurst	N Ashton	Chadwick(5)
10	Chesworth	Smith	N Bell	Lamb	Walker	Kerry	Bleasdale	L Bell	Carter	Spicer	Crayston	Bailey	Sword	Dewhurst	N Ashton	Chadwick(3)
11	Chesworth	Smith	Hindle	Smith	Walker	Kerry	Bleasdale	L Bell	Carter	Spicer	Crayston	Bailey	Sword		N Ashton	Chadwick(1)Dewhurst(6)
12	Chesworth	N Bell	Hindle	Smith	Walker	Kerry	Bleasdale	McCarthy	Montgomery	Spicer	Crayston	Bailey	I Ashton		N Ashton	L Bell(8)Tyson(13)Roberts(5)
13	Chesworth	N Bell	Hindle	Smith	Walker	Kerry	Bleasdale	McCarthy	Montgomery	Spicer	Craston	Vaughan	I Ashton		N Ashton	Roberts(8)
14	Chesworth	N Bell	Hindle	Smith	Walker	Kerry	Bleasdale	L Bell	Carter	Spicer	Crayston	Dooley	I Ashton	Sword		N Ashton(6)
15	Chesworth	N Bell	Tyson	Smith	Walker	Kerry	Bleasdale	L Bell	Carter	Spicer	Crayston	Bailey	Sword	Dewhurst		Lamb(11)I Ashton(6)
16	Chesworth	Smith	Lamb	Tyson	Walker	Kerry	Bleasdale	Leeming	Carter	Chadwick	Crayston	Bailey	I Ashton		N Ashton	Whittingham(11),Montgomery(2)
17	Chesworth	Smith	N Bell	Whittingham	Walker	Kerry	Bleasdale	Chadwick	Montgomery	Spicer	Crayston	Bailey	I Ashton	Dewhurst	N Ashton	Sword(6),Tyson(11)
18	Chesworth	Smith	Bell	Tyson	Walker	Kerry	Bleasdale	Chadwick	Montgomery	Spicer	Crayston	Bailey	I Ashton	Dewhurst	N Ashton	Sword(6),Leeming(2).
19	Chesworth	Smith	N Bell	Whittingham	Walker	Kerry	Bleasdale	Chadwick		Spicer	Crayston	Bailey	Sword	Roberts	N Ashton	
20	Chesworth	Smith	N Bell	Whittingham	Walker	Kerry	Bleasdale	Ince		Spicer	Crayston	Bailey	I Ashton	Sword	Dewhurst	Kirkpatrick(1)Leeming(7)Chadwick(3)
21	Lamb	Smith	N Bell	Whittingham	Walker	Kerry	McCarthy	Ince		Chadwick	Crayston	Bailey	Roberts	Sword	Dewhurst	Tyson(11)Paresi(1)
22	Chesworth	Smith	N Bell	Whittingham	Walker	Kerry	Bleasdale	Leeming		Chadwick	Crayston	Dooley	Roberts	Dewhurst	Bailey	Paresi(3)
23	Chesworth	Greenwood	Kerry	Whittingham	Walker	Smith	Bleasdale	Maddox		Paresi	Crayston	Dooley	Sword	Dewhurst	Bailey	Povall(9)Roberts(8)
24	Chesworth	N Bell	Kerry	Whittingham	Walker	Smith	Bleasdale	Maddox		Paresi		Dooley	Roberts	Dewhurst	Bailey	Christopherson(12)Leeming(6)
25	Chesworth	N Bell	Kerry	Whittingham	Greenwood	Smith	Bleasdale	Montgomery		Paresi	Vaughan		Roberts	Dewhurst	Bailey	Lamb(13)Dransfield(6)Williams(3)
26	Lamb	Greenwood	Kerry	N Bell	Mulholland	Smith	Battersby	Vaughan				Roberts		Dewhurst	Bailey	Taylorson(I)

PRESTON GRASSHOPPERS LEAGUE STATISTICS
(COMPILED BY STEPHEN McCORMACK)

Season	Div.	P	W	D	L	F	A	PD	Pts	Pos.	Coach	Captain
87-88	ALN	10	5	1	4	178	149	29	11	4	M Alden	R Dransfield
88-89	ALN	10	5	0	5	161	141	20	10	6	K Aitchison	R Dransfield
89-90	ALN	10	5	0	5	122	109	13	10	6	J Greenwood	D Percy
90-91	D4N	12	8	0	4	192	109	83	16	3	J Greenwood	C Dew
91-92	D4N	12	8	0	4	195	123	72	16	4	J Greenwood	C Dew
92-93	D4N	12	8	0	4	144	140	4	16	3	J Greenwood	P Crayston
93-94	D5N	12	10	0	2	191	128	63	20	2	J Morgan	P Crayston
94-95	D5N	12	8	1	3	187	137	50	17	3	J Morgan	P Crayston
95-96	D5N	12	5	1	6	167	209	-42	11	8	J Morgan	M Bailey
96-97	D4N	26	17	2	7	568	394	174	36	3		
Total		128	79	5	74	2105	1639	466				

PROGRAMME DETAILS

SIZE: A5   **PRICE:** 50p

PAGES: 32 plus cover

PROGRAMME EDITOR
John Hetherington 01772 863546

ADVERTISING RATES
Mono Full page £200
Half page £120
Qtr page £70

CLUB & GROUND DETAILS

Address: Lightfoot Green, Fulwood, Preston, Lancs. PR4 0AP. **Tel. No.** 01772 863546 (Press Line: 01772 861605) Fax: 01772 861605

Capacity: 3,500   **Seated:** 250   **Standing:** 3,250
Simple Directions: Leave the M6 at Junct. 32 and head towards A6 Garstang. Turn left at the end of the slip road towards Preston. Take first left and follow signs for Ingol. The ground is 1/2 mile on the right.
Nearest Railway Station: Preston (BR) 3 miles, taxi £6
Car Parking: 400 spaces available adjacent to the ground.
Admission: Match days: Adults - Members £3, Others £4, Children/OAPs - 1/2 adult price, under 11 free.
Club Shop: Yes - contact K Moore 01772 863546
Clubhouse: Monday -Thursday 5.00-11.00, Friday 12.00-Midnight, Sat 12.00-11.00, Sun 12.00-10.30. Functions available, capacity 250, contact K Moore 01772 863546

SANDAL R.U.F.C.

NICKNAME: The Milnthorpers   FOUNDED: 1927

President Christopher Taylor, Woodside Farm, Woolley Edge, Wakefield. 01924 830448 (H).
Executive Chairman Howard Newton, 66 Manygates Lane, Sandal, Wakefield, W Yorks WF2 7DW.
01924 252411 (H)
Club Secretary Leonard Bedford, 14 Lindale Mount, Alverthorpe, Wakefield, W. Yorks. WF2 0BH
01924 782263 (H)
Chairman of Rugby Martin Shuttleworth, 66 Walton Drive, Crofton, Wakefield, WF2 6EU.
Press Officer P H Harrison, 46 Brandhill Drive, Crofton, Wakefield, W. Yorks. WF4 1PF.
01924 863457 (H)
Fixtures Secretary C Critchett, 01924 254329.   **Match Secretary & Referees** Malcolm Pashley, 01924 255020
Chairman Youth Rugby Clive Hoyland, 01924 830572. **Ladies Rugby Secretary** Ms J Dow, 01924 250661

This was arguably Sandal's most successful season ever. By finishing in fifth place in 4 North, Sandal achieved their highest ever position since Leagues began. Also, in their very last game of the season, victory over Doncaster in the final of the Yorkshire Cup ensured that the name of Sandal appears on the "T'Owd Tin Pot" trophy for the first time in the club's long history.

Perhaps the only disappointment of the season was the Third Round Pilkington Cup exit at the hands of Kendal, but a subsequent League double over the men from Cumbria made up for that earlier Cup defeat.

Sandal showed that they are a difficult side to beat on their own patch, having won all their home league games bar two, against Aspatria and Worcester. Away form however was inconsistent and only four games ended in Sandal victories - at Hereford, Stoke, Kendal and Lichfield. Improvement in away form needs to be addressed if Sandal are to maintain their position as a league front runner.

Top points scorer, for the eighth season in succcssion, was fly-half Mark Hardcastle who finished with 335 points, his best ever for the club. Top try scorer was versatile utility-back Andrew Wolff with 12, whilst elder brother full-back Mark Wolff was only one behind on 11 touch-downs. Danish RFU Internationals Jan Andersen and Michael Jeppesen were with the club for the first half of the season and others to make a significant impact in the side were former Rugby League backs Max Tomlinson and Henry Sharp. Evergreen former England centre Bryan Barley was once more coaxed out of retirement to feature prominently in key games, whilst the only ever-present in the side was Ken Fleming.

During the course of the season, a record six Sandal players gained deserved selection for Yorkshire, including second-row Glynn Thompson who skippered the County side, centre Jim Davis, scrum-half Andrew Turton, prop Nigel Hoyle, hooker Andrew Newton and back-row man Jason Mortimer.

Finally, worthy of mention are the Sandal Under 9s and Under 10s, both of whom won the Yorkshire Cup at their particular age groups, and the Sandal Under 14s, winners of the Yorkshire Plate competition.

Sandal RUFC: Celebrate their Yorkshire Cup Final truimph over Doncaster. Rear standing (L-R); Ken Fleming, Nick Jackson, Mark Prior, Andy Keay, Steve Barnes, Max Tomlinson, Don Angus, Glenn Barker, Mark Wolff, Martin Allchurch. Middle standing; Bryan Barley, Richard Wade, Jim Davis, Jason Mortimer, Jon Adams, Andrew Newton, Trevor Barker (Coach). Front kneeling; Eddie Dickinson, Andy Turton, Mark Rawnsley, Mark Hardcastle, Gary Lig, Henry Sharp

Colours: Maroon, gold & white hoops   **Change colours:** Gold with maroon & white hoops.

COURAGE LEAGUE MATCH DETAILS 1996-97

No	Ven.	Date	Opponents	Att.	Res.	Score	Scorers
1	(H)	31.08	v Winnington P		W	21-20	Kaye(t)Thompson(t)Hardcastle(c2pdg)
2	(A)	07.09	v Hereford		W	12- 3	Hardcastle(4p)
3	(H)	21.09	v Aspatria		L	20-31	Newton(t)Hodkinson(t)Dickinson(t)Hardcastle(cp)
4	(A)	28.09	v Sheffield		L	24-26	A Wolff(t)Hoyle(t)Hardcastle(c3pdg)
5	(H)	05.10	v Nuneaton		W	24-13	Dickinson(t)Hoyle(t)Hardcastle(c4p)
6	(A)	19.10	v Stoke O T		W	18-12	Hodkinson(t)A Wolff(t)Hardcastle(c2p)
7	(H)	26.10	v Manchester		W	31-19	Powell(2t)Burnham(t)Anderson(t)Hardcastle(c3p)
8	(A)	09.11	v Worcester		L	7-64	Anderson(t)Hardcastle(c)
9	(H)	16.11	v Kendal		W	33- 7	A Wolff(t)Lig(t)Turton(t)Barley(t)Anderson(t)Hardcastle(4c)
10	(A)	21.12	v Birmingham S		L	12-30	A Wolff(t)Jepperson(t)Hardcastle(c)
11	(A)	25.01	v Winnington Park		L	15-20	A Woolff(t)Sharp(t)Hardcastle(cp)
12	(H)	01.02	v Hereford		W	55.10	Hodkinson(2t)A Wolff(2t)Burnham(2t)Hoyle(t)Mortimer(t)Hardcastle(6cp)
13	(A)	08.02	v Aspatria		D	27-27	Sharp(t)Mortimer(t)M Wolff(t)Hardcastle(t2cp)
14	(H)	15.02	v Sheffield		W	23-13	Davis(2t)Burnham(t)Hardcastle(cpdg)
15	(A)	22.02	v Nuneaton		L	15-29	Turton(t)Davis(t)Hardcastle(cp)
16	(H)	01.03	v Stoke on Trent		W	25-13	A Wolff(t)PenTry(t)Hardcastle(t2c2p)
17	(A)	08.03	v Manchester		L	17-43	M Wolff(t)Barker(t)Hardcastle(2cp)
18	(H)	15.03	v Worcester		L	15-22	Barley(t)Davis(t)Hardcastle(cp)
19	(A)	22.03	v Kendal		W	24-23	Davis(2t)M Wolff(t)Hardcastle(3p)
20	(H)	29.03	v Lichfield		W	42- 5	M Wolff(t)A Wolff(t)Tomlinson(t)Hardcastle(3c7p)
21	(H)	05.04	v Birmingham S		W	29-15	Davis(t)M Wolff(t)Hardcastle(2c5p)
22	(A)	12.04	v Lichfield		W	27-14	M Wolff(t)Tomlinson(t)Hoyle(t)Hardcastle(3c2p)
23	(H)	19.04	v Preston G		W	28-13	M Wolff(2t)Sharp(2t)Hardcastle(c2p)
24	(H)	26.04	v Stourbridge		W	32-31	Tomlinson((2t)Pryor(2t)Rawnsley(t)Hardcastle(2cp)
25	(A)	03.05	v Preston G		L	29-32	Barley(2t)Pryor(t)Hardcastle(c4p)
26	(A)	10.05	v Stourbridge		L	13-38	M Wolff(t)Hardcastle(c2p)

1996-97 HIGHLIGHTS

PLAYERS USED: 33 plus five as replacement only.

EVER PRESENT: None - most appearances 25 Mark Hardcastle.

❏ Second best home record in the division after Champions Worcester. Suffered just two home defeats at home to Aspatria and Worcester.

❏ **Most points in a match**
26 Mark Hardcastle v Lichfield 29.03.97 (H)
19 Mark Hardcastle v Birmingham S 05.04.97 (H)

❏ **Hat tricks of tries in a match**
None - two tries was achieved 11 times by nine players. The only player to score two twice was centre Jim Davis.

❏ **Most points in the season**

Pts	Player	T	C	P	D
248	Mark Hardcastle	2	40	53	3
45	Andrew Wolff	9	-	-	-
45	Mark Wolff	9	-	-	-
35	Jim Davis	7	-	-	-

❏ **Most appearances**
25 Mark Hardcastle
24 Jason Mortimer
21 Andrew Wolff
20 Nigel Hoyle and Glen Barker

SANDAL'S COURAGE LEAGUE MATCH DETAILS 1996-97

15	14	13	12	11	10	9	1	2	3	4	5	6	7	8	Replacements	#
1 M Wolff	Kaye	Powell	A Wolff	Burnham	Hardcastle	Dickinson	Fleming	Lig	Hoyle	Thompson	Barker	Mortimer	Gibb	Rawnsley		1
2 M Wolff	Kaye	Powell	A wolff	Burnham	Hardcastle	Dickinson	Fleming	Lig	Hoyle	Thompson	Barker	Mortimer	Gibb	Rawnsley	Fleming(1)	2
3 Kaye	Hodkinson	Powell	A Wolff	Burnham	Hardcastle	Dickinson	Foreman	Newton	Hoyle	Mortimer	Thompson	Mortimer	Lig	Rawnsley		3
4 M Wolff	Hodkinson	Powell	A Wolff	Burnham	Hardcastle	Dickinson	Fleming	Newton	Hoyle	Thompson	Mortimer	Gibb	Lig	Rawnsley		4
5 M Wolff	Hodkinson	Burnham	Stead	A Wolff	Hardcastle	Dickinson	Fleming	Newton	Hoyle	Thompson	Mortimer	Gibb	Lig	Rawnsley		5
6 A Wolff	Hodkinson	Powell	Anderson	Burnham	Hardcastle	Dickinson	Fleming	Lig	Hoyle	Mortimer	Jepperson	Gibb	Barnes	Rawnsley	Bedford()	6
7 A Wolff	Hodkinson	Powell	Anderson	Burnham	Hardcastle	Turton	Fleming	Lig	Jepperson	Thompson	Barker	Gibb	Barnes	Rawnsley	Barker(Foreman t)	7
8 A Wolff	Hodkinson	Powell	Anderson	Stead	Hardcastle	Turton	Fleming	Lig	Hoyle	Thompson	Jepperson	Barnes	Barnes	Rawnsley	Barker(Fraser()	8
9 A Wolff	Hodkinson	Barley	Anderson	Burnham	Hardcastle	Turton	Fleming	Lig	Hoyle	Thompson	Barker	Mortimer	Barnes	Rawnsley	Barnes(O Fraser()	9
10 A Wolff	Hodkinson	Davis	Burnham	Burnham	Hardcastle	Turton	Fleming	Lig	Hoyle	Barker	Jepperson	Mortimer	Adams	Newton()	Newton()	10
11 A Wolff	Sharp	Davis	Hodkinson	Kaye	Hardcastle	Turton	Fleming	Lig	Hoyle	Thompson	Barker	Barnes	Adams	Mortimer		11
12 A Wolff	Sharp	Burnham	Burnham	Hodkinson	Hardcastle	Turton	Fleming	Newton	Hoyle	Thompson	Barker	Adams	Mortimer	Mortimer	Angus(3)Stollery(4)Kaye(15)	12
13 M Wolff	Sharp	Burnham	Burnham	Hodkinson	Hardcastle	Turton	Fleming	Newton	Hoyle	Thompson	Barker	Barnes	Mortimer	Mortimer		13
14 A Wolff	Tomlinson	Davis	Burnham	Hodkinson	Hardcastle	Dickinson	Fleming	Newton	Hoyle	Thompson	Barker	Stollery	Adams	Barnes	Foreman(3)Tomlinson(14)Barley(12)	14
15 A Wolff	Tomlinson	Adams	Hodkinson	Hodkinson	Hardcastle	Turton	Angus	Newton	Fleming	Barker	Barker	Stollery	Barnes	Barnes	M Wolff(11)Lig(4)	15
16 A Wolff	Tomlinson	Burnham	Burnham	M Wolff	Hardcastle	Turton	Fleming	Angus	Fleming	Mortimer	Barker	Stollery	Barnes	Barnes		16
17 A Wolff	Tomlinson	Burnham	Burnham	Tomlinson	Hardcastle	Dickinson	Lig	Newton	Hoyle	Thompson	Barker	Barnes	Adams	Mortimer	Barley(11).Key(2).	17
18 M Wolff	Davis	Barley	Burnham	Tomlinson	Hardcastle	Turton	Lig	Hoyle	Hoyle	Thompson	Barker	Barnes	Adams	Mortimer		18
19 M Wolff	Davis	Davis	Barley	Burnham	Hardcastle	Turton	Fleming	Newton	Hoyle	Thompson	Barker	Adams	Mortimer	Mortimer		19
20 M Wolff	Davis	Davis	Tomlinson	Burnham	Hardcastle	Turton	Fleming	Newton	Hoyle	Thompson	Barker	Barnes	Adams	Rawnsley	Dickinson(9)Wade(6)Angus(1)	20
21 M Wolff	Davis	Barley	Tomlinson	Burnham	Hardcastle	Turton	Fleming	Newton	Mortimer	Thompson	Barker	Barnes	Adams	Rawnsley	Key(7)	21
22 M Wolff	Burnham	Barley	Davis	Burnham	Hardcastle	Turton	Fleming	Newton	Thompson	Thompson	Barker	Mortimer	Adams	Rawnsley	Foreman(1)A Wolff(13)	22
23 M Wolff	Tomlinson	Davis	Sharp	Tomlinson	Hardcastle	Angus	Fleming	Fleming	Fleming	Barker	Mortimer	Adams	Wade	Rawnsley		23
24 Dickinson	Davis	Barley	Pryor	Dickinson	Hardcastle	Turton	Fleming	Newton	Foreman	Barker	Mortimer	Barnes	Adams	Rawnsley	Lig(2)Angus(3)Jackson(11)	24
25 M Wolff	Pryor	Barley	Dickinson	Tomlinson	Hardcastle	Turton	Fleming	Angus	Angus	Barker	Mortimer	Barnes	Adams	Rawnsley	Newton(2)	25
26 M Wolff	Tomlinson	Davis	Barley	Pryor	Hardcastle	Dickinson	Fleming	Newton	Angus	Barker	Mortimer	Wade	Adams	Rawnsley	Lig(6)Allchurch(11)Key(7)	26

SANDAL LEAGUE STATISTICS
(COMPILED BY STEPHEN McCORMACK)

Season	Div.	P	W	D	L	F	A	PD	Pts	Pos.	Coach	Captain
87-88	NORTH2	10	6	0	4	142	92	50	10	4	M Shuttleworth	N Powell
88-89	NORTH2	10	6	0	4	128	113	15	12	4	M Shuttleworth	N Powell
89-90	NORTH2	10	4	1	5	151	112	39	9	7	M Shuttleworth	N Powell
90-91	NORTH2	10	9	0	1	190	74	116	18	2p	M Shuttleworth	
91-92	NORTH1	10	5	0	5	140	115	25	10	4	M Shuttleworth	
92-93	NORTH1	12	6	1	5	205	129	76	13	4	M Shuttleworth	
93-94	NORTH1	12	9	0	3	219	131	88	18	2	M Shuttleworth	
94-95	NORTH1	12	8	3	1	227	126	101	19	1p	M Shuttleworth	A Turton
95-96	D5N	12	6	0	6	244	198	46	12	6	M Shuttleworth	B Barley
96-97	D4N	26	15	1	10	618	573	45	31	5		
Total		124	74	6	44	2264	1663	601				

CLARKS CLASH OF THE CODES

SANDAL R.U.F.C.
v
EASTMOOR A.R.L.F.C.

Wednesday, 7th August, 1996
Kick Off 7.30 p.m.
First Half Rugby League Rules - Second Half Rugby Union Rules

SANDAL
R.U.F.C.
SPONSORED BY
CLARKS BREWERY
WAKEFIELD

Tonights Big Match Sponsor:
H.B. CLARK & Co. (Successors) Ltd.

Official Souvenir Programme £1.00

PROGRAMME DETAILS

SIZE: A5   **PRICE:** With admission.

PAGES: 14 plus cover

PROGRAMME EDITOR
`Howard Newton 01924 252411

ADVERTISING RATES
Mono - Full page £200, 1/2 page £100,
1/4 page £50.

CLUB & GROUND DETAILS

Address: Milnthorpe Green, Standbridge Lane, Sandal, Wakefield, W. Yorks. WF2 7JD.
Tel. Nos. 01924 250661

Capacity: 1625   **Seated:** 75   **Standing:** 1500
Simple Directions: From the M1, junction 39, take the A636 to Wakefield. After 3/4 mile turn right at the roundabout into Ansdale Road, and after one mile the club will be found on the left.
Nearest Railway Station: Westgate, Wakefield.
Car Parking: 200 spaces available adjacent to ground.
Admission: Matchdays - Adults: £3 (League & Cup) Children/OAPs £1.
Club Shop: Yes. Manager - Howard Newton Tel. 01924 252411.
Clubhouse: Open matchdays & training nights, snacks & bar meals available. Functions available, capacity 120, contact Graham Holliday 01924 250661 (club)
Training Nights: Tuesday and Thursday.

SEDGELEY PARK RUFC

NICKNAME: Tigers **FOUNDED:** 1932

President John Widdup, 63 Greenleach Lane, Roe Green, Worsley, Manchester
0161 702 9264 (H), 0161 702 9264 (Fax)
Chairman David Smith, 95 Bury Old Road, Whitefield, Manchester.
0161 280 2921 (H), 0161 280 3509 (B), 0161 280 6226 (Fax).
Club Secretary Mark Mold, 32 Vicarage Avenue, Cheadle Hulme, Cheadle, Cheshire SK8 7JW
0161 486 0496 (H)
Fixture Secretary Rob Williamson, 17 Boundary Road, Bradley Fold, Bolton BL2 6SE
01204 705868 (H), 0161 202 1714 (B)
Commercial Manager Jeffry Coles, 334 Bradlesholme Road, Bury, Lancashire BL8 1EX
0161 764 4291 (H), 01282 778611 (B), 0161 763 5120 (Fax)
Press Officer John Lawrence, 56 Ringley Road West, Radcliffe, Manchester M26 9DJ
0161 723 5120 (H), 01254 392059 (B)
Director of Coaching Ken Fletcher, 01942 206215 (H)

Another memorable season was completed with not only the League Championship of North One but also the Lancashire Trophy. This meant three consecutive years of promotion and National League rugby to look forward to.

The arrival of open rugby clearly created the need to adjust and the administration of the club had also to be lifted to a new level and this was achieved, matching the success of the players, by recording a pofit at the end of the season, albeit a small one. This was a fine achievement when costs increased by 37 percent!

Success on the field was down to the inspirational leadership from director of coaching Ken Fletcher and club captain Bob Kimmens, the latter missing the last quarter of the season with a broken leg.

In total 34 games were played with 26 wins, 2 draws and just 4 defeats. The thousand points were exceeded (1060) with 152 tries (760 points) being scored. Leading scorer was Player of the Season Darren Weatherall, a product of the club's youth policy, with 186 points, of which 126 were scored in league matches.

Thirty players were used in league matches with the squad being strengthened as the season progressed and these players will form the nuclus of this years team.

The years success was based on a sound home record with only one point being dropped against New Brighton and that to the last kick of the match. Away from home defeat at Wigton at the end of September was followed by a run of eleven victories before an end of season wobble saw us go down at Stockton, Tynedale and West Park (Bramhope), although the league was secured at the latter thanks to other results.

Progress was made to the Fifth Round of the Intermediate Cup and in spite of leading by 22-5 just before half time we managed to snatch defeat from the jaws of victory losing 22-26.

During the season seven players were included in the Lancashire Senior squad whilst in the Under-13 and Under-16 teams 17 players represented the County with, on one occasion, six players being in the Under-13 team.

Our rapid rise through the leagues has meant that we have to look to developing our own players, so with in excess of 20 teams we are laying the foundations for the future. That combined with a current lottery application leaves the club in good heart and looking forward with great anticipation to life in the National Leagues.

Sedgley Park RUFC: Back Row (L-R); Kevin Williams, Rob Smith, Phil Donbavand, David Fell, Peter Renwick, Matt Alcock, John Gilfillan, Andy Kimmins, Kevin Talbot, Simon Joesbury, James Johnston, Simon Bond, Mike Blakely, Katie Tyle, Charles Austin. Front Row; Steve Haggleby, Matt Corns, Paul Morris, Scott Cunliffe, Ray Austin, Bob Kimmins, David Smith, Darren Weatherall, Keith Howie, Andy Morse, Mike Wilcock.

Colours: Claret with gold & black trimmings **Change colours:** Black shirts, maroon shorts.

SEDGELEY PARK

No	Ven.	Date	Opponents	Att.	Res.	Score	Scorers
1	(A)	07.09	v Hull Ionians		W	30-28	Renwick(2t)R Kimmins(t)Duncan(t)Ahearne(2cp)Smith(dg)
2	(H)	21.09	v Tynedale		W	36-20	Weatherall(2t)Webster(t)Talbot(t)Ahearne(2c4p)
3	(A)	28.09	v Wigton		L	10-34	Weatherall(t)R Kimmins(t)
4	(H)	05.10	v Stockton		W	41-19	Duncan(3t)Weatherall(t)Talbot(t)Smith(2t3c)
5	(A)	19.10	v New Brighton		W	26-18	Howie(t)Duncan(t)Wilcock(t)PenTry(t)Weatherall(3c)
6	(H)	26.10	v Macclesfield		W	46- 0	Talbot(3t)R Kimmins(2t)Gilfillan(t)Weatherall(t4cp)
7	(A)	09.11	v Bridlington		W	25-24	Duncan(2t)Talbot(t)Weatherall(2c2p)
8	(H)	16.11	v Widnes		W	26- 0	Joesbury(t)Morris(t)Wilcock(t)Weatherall(c3p)
9	(A)	18.01	v Bradford & Bingley		W	32- 8	Webster(2t)Wilcox(t)Smith(t)R Kimmins(t)Blakeley(2cp)
10	(A)	25.01	v Broughton Park		W	15- 8	Duncan(t)Weatherall(t)Blakeley(cp)
11	(H)	01.02	v Bradford & Bingley		W	64- 9	Alcock(2t)R Kimmins(2t)Wilcock(2t)Duncan(t)Talbot(T)Gilfillan(t)Blakeley(5c3p)
12	(A)	08.02	v Widnes		W	35-18	Weatherall(2t)R Kimmins(t)PenTry(t)Blakeley(3c3p)
13	(H)	15.02	v Bridlington		W	48-15	R Kimmins(2t)Joesbury(2t)Morris(t)Smith(t)Wilcock(t)Blakeley(5cp)
14	(A)	01.03	v Macclesfield		W	25-10	Duncan(t)Gilfillan(t)Webster(t)Blakeley(2c2p)
15	(H)	08.03	v New Brighton		D	17-17	A Kimmins(t)Wilcock(t)Blakeley(2cp)
16	(A)	15.03	v Stockton		L	17-38	A Kimmins(t)Wilcock(t)Talbot(t)Weatherall(c)
17	(H)	22.03	v Wigton		W	33-21	Talbot(2t)Fell(t)A Kimmins(t)Weatherall(tc2p)
18	(A)	05.04	v Tynedale		L	8-31	Joesbury(t)Blakeley(p)
19	(H)	12.04	v Hull Ionians		W	43-16	Wilcock(3t)Morris(t)Renwick(t)Smith(t)Donbavand(t)Weatherall(c2p)
20	(H)	19.04	v Broughton Park		W	27-10	Gilfillan(t)Cunliffe(t)Egan(t)Weatherall(t2cp)
21	(A)	26.04	v West Park Bramhope		L	28-31	Webster(2t)Wilcock(t)Morris(t)Weatherall(t)Smith(dg)
22	(H)	10.05	v West Park Bramhope		W	18-14	A Kimmins(t)Johnston(t)Weatherall(c2p)

1996-97 HIGHLIGHTS

LEAGUE DEBUTS:
Mark Ahearne, Simon Joesbury, John Gilfillan, Paul Morris, Mike Blakeley, Andy Morse, Mark Samfield, David Fell.

PLAYERS USED: 30 + 5 as replacement only.

EVER PRESENT: Darren Weatherall

❏ The forwards outscored the backs 50 - 41 in terms of tries, with 2 penalty tries.

❏ Their 650 points scored total is the most scored in a league season and was 98 points clear of the 2nd leading points scorers in the league.

❏ Tries were scored in every league game.

❏ Five players reached double figures for tries scored - Mike Wilcock (12), Darren Weatherall (11), Jon Duncan, Bob Kimmins and Kevin Talbot (10).

Three hat-tricks were scored - Jon Duncan v Stockton (H), Kevin Talbot v Macclesfield (H) & Mike Wilcock v Hull Ionians (H).

Nine tries were scored against Bradford & Bingley (H), and seven on 3 occasions v Stockton, Macclesfield & v Bridlington (H).

Only 43 of the 93 tries scored were converted.

❏ The club used four different goalkickers during the season - Darren Weatherall, Mike Blakeley, Rob Smith & Mark Ahearne.

❏ Each league match produced an average of 47.64 points - 29.55 FOR and 18.08 AGAINST.

❏ The biggest victory was a 64-9 win at home v Bradford & Bingley. On four further occasions more than 40 points were scored - v Stockton 41-19, v Macclesfield 46-0, v Bridlington 48-15 and v Hull Ionians 43-16.

SEDGELEY PARK'S COURAGE LEAGUE MATCH DETAILS 1996-97

#	15	14	13	12	11	10	9	1	2	3	4	5	6	7	8	Replacements
1	Wilcock	Weatherall	Kelly	Renwick	Ahearne	Corns	Smith	Alcock	Webster	Donbavand	R Kimmins	Egan	A Kimmins	Talbot	Duncan	
2	Wilcock	Weatherall	Smith	Renwick	Ahearne	Corns	Howie	Alcock	Webster	Donbavand	R Kimmins	Egan	Bond	Talbot	Duncan	
3	Wilcock	Weatherall	Barton	Renwick	Ahearne	Corns	Smith	Alcock	Webster	Fletcher	R Kimmins	Egan	Bond	Talbot	Duncan	
4	Wilcock	Weatherall	Barton	Renwick	Corns	Corns	Smith	Alcock	Webster	Donbavand	R Kimmins	Egan	Bond	Talbot	Duncan	
5	Wilcock	Weatherall	Gilfillan	Renwick	Corns	Corns	Howie	Alcock	Webster	Donbavand	R Kimmins	Egan	Joesbury	Hamilton	Duncan	
6	Smith	Weatherall	Gilfillan	Renwick	Barton	Corns	Howie	Alcock	Murray	Donbavand	R Kimmins	Egan	Hamilton	Talbot	Duncan	
7	Wilcock	Weatherall	Gilfillan	Renwick	Morris	Corns	Smith	Alcock	Webster	Donbavand	R Kimmins	Johnston	Hamilton	Talbot	Duncan	
8	Wilcock	Weatherall	Gilfillan	Renwick	Morris	Corns	Smith	Alcock	Webster	Donbavand	R Kimmins	Johnston	Joesbury	Talbot	Duncan	
9	Wilcox	Weatherall	Gilfillan	Blakeley	Morris	Corns	Smith	Alcock	Webster	Donbavand	A Kimmins	Johnston	Joesbury	Talbot	Duncan	
10	Wilcock	Weatherall	Gilfillan	Blakeley	Barton	Corns	Smith	Alcock	Webster	Murray	A Kimmins	Johnston	A Kimmins	Egan	Duncan	
11	Wilcock	Weatherall	Gilfillan	Blakeley	Morris	Corns	Smith	Alcock	Webster	Murray	R Kimmins	A Kimmins	Joesbury	Talbot	Duncan	
12	Wilcock	Weatherall	Gilfillan	Fell	Morris	Blakeley	Smith	Alcock	Webster	Donbavand	R Kimmins	A Kimmins	Joesbury	Talbot	Duncan	
13	Wilcock	Weatherall	Gilfillan	Fell	Morris	Blakeley	Smith	Alcock	Webster	Donbavand	R Kimmins	A Kimmins	Joesbury	Talbot	Duncan	
14	Wilcock	Weatherall	Gilfillan	Fell	Morris	Blakeley	Smith	Donbavand	Webster	Fletcher	R Kimmins	A Kimmins	Joesbury	Talbot	Duncan	
15	Wilcock	Weatherall	Gilfillan	Fell	Morris	Blakeley	Smith	Alcock	Webster	Murray	R Kimmins	A Kimmins	Joesbury	Talbot	Duncan	
16	Wilcock	Weatherall	Fell	Fell	Morris	Corns	Smith	Murray	Webster	Fletcher	R Kimmins	A Kimmins	Joesbury	Talbot	Duncan	
17	Wilcock	Weatherall	Gilfillan	Renwick	Fell	Corns	Smith	Alcock	Webster	Donbavand	Johnston	Johnston	Joesbury	Talbot	Talbot	
18	Wilcock	Weatherall	Gilfillan	Renwick	Blakeley	Blakeley	Smith	Alcock	Webster	Donbavand	Johnston	Egan	Joesbury	Duncan	Duncan	
19	Wilcock	Weatherall	Gilfillan	Renwick	Fell	Fell	Smith	Alcock	Webster	Donbavand	Johnston	Joesbury	A Kimmins	Cunliffe	Talbot	
20	Wilcock	Weatherall	Gilfillan	Renwick	Morris	Fell	Smith	Alcock	Webster	Donbavand	Johnston	Joesbury	Cunliffe	Cunliffe	Egan(/)	
21	Wilcock	Weatherall	Gilfillan	Blakeley	Morris	Fell	Smith	Alcock	Webster	Fletcher	Johnston	A Kimmins	Joesbury	Talbot	Duncan	
22	Wilcock	Weatherall	Gilfillan	Renwick	Morris	Fell	Howie	Alcock	Holse	Donbavand	Johnston	A Kimmins	Bond	Cunliffe	Talbot	

SEDGELEY PARK LEAGUE STATISTICS
(COMPILED BY STEPHEN McCORMACK)

Season	Div.	P	W	D	L	F	A	PD	Pts	Pos.	Coach	Captain
87-88	NW2	10	8	1	1	183	74	109	17	1p	R Sharp	R Hall
88-89	NW1	10	6	0	4	108	132	-24	12	3	A Bennett	R Hall
89-90	NW1	10	2	0	8	91	132	-41	4	9	R Sharp	P Egan
90-91	NW1	10	6	0	4	183	112	69	12	4	R Sharp	R Hall
91-92	NW1	10	5	1	4	119	145	-26	11	6	V Baker	R Hall
92-93	NW1	12	4	0	8	149	188	-36	*6	11	V Baker	P Renwick
93-94	NW1	12	5	2	5	201	134	67	12	5	C Hebbut	R Hall
94-95	NW1	12	12	0	0	421	60	361	24	1p	K Fletcher	P Egan
95-96	N2	12	10	0	2	257	141	116	20	2p	K Fletcher	R Kimmins
96-97	N1	22	17	1	4	650	398	252	35	1p	K Fletcher	R Kimmins
Total		120	75	6	40	2363	1516	847	142		* 2 points deducted.	

Sedgley Park
Rugby Union Football Club

Park Lane
Whitefield
0161 766 5050

Match Programme

PROGRAMME DETAILS

SIZE: A5   **PRICE:** £1

PAGES:

PROGRAMME EDITOR: Jeffry Coles 0161 764 4291, Fax 0161 763 5120

ADVERTISING RATES
Colour Full page £250.
Mono Full page 160, Half page £85, Qtr page £45

CLUB & GROUND DETAILS

Address: Park Lane, Whitefield, Manchester.
Tel. Nos. 0161 766 5050

Capacity: 1,000   **Seated:** None   **Standing:** 1,000
Simple Directions: From M62, junction 17 onto A56 for Bury. Take the left filter at the 2nd set of traffic lights, left at the next lights (Park Lane) and continue to the end.
Nearest Railway Station: N/A
Car Parking: 60 on ground, 50 nearby
Admission: Season tickets - Adult £40
Matchdays - Adult £3, Children/OAPs F.O.C.
Clubhouse: Evenings Monday - Thursday, **Matchdays** (Saturday & Sunday), snacks available. Functions available, capacity 135, contact John Grundy 0161 766 5050
Training Nights: Tuesday & Thursday

SHEFFIELD R.U.F.C.

FOUNDED: 1902

Chairman Steve Newsome, The Knoll, Over Road, Baslow, Bakewell DE45 1PL
01246 583135 (H), 01246 250044 (B), 01246 250055 (Fax)

President Keith Sugden, 45 Fairview Road, Dronfield, S18 6HF.
01246 412971 (H), 01142 432935 (B).

Club Secretary William Oliver, Cumberland House, Cumberland Street, Sheffield S1 4PT
01142 556817 (H), 01142 751501 (B), 01142 798804 (Fax)

Fixtures Secretary Bill Reid, c/o Sheffield RUFC, Abbeydale Park Sports Ground,
Abbeydale Road South, Sheffield S17 3LG. 0374 465995 (B)

Press Officer Ian Dawson, 15 Ladysmith Avenue, Sheffield S7 1SF
01142 250825 (H), 01246 250044 (B), 01246 250055 (Fax)

Internal Admin/Match Secretary Richard Fedyk, 01142 364785 (H), 01332 262951 (B), 01332 262846 (Fax)

Season 1996/97 for Sheffield RUFC can only be described as 'mixed'. A promising start was made (despite an early loss away to Birmingham) with a thumping victory over Lichfield followed by a run of closely fought games containing only four losses leaving the club well placed in the top half dozen at the close of 1996 and looking forward to the New Year. The disappointment of the year was definitely the exit from the Pilkington Cup to Kendal after relinquishing a fifteen point lead at half time to lose narrowly 29-31. Better luck next year!

1997 began on a low note with defeats against Lichfield and Worcester, although the team performance against the much fancied Midlands side gave causes for great optimism. The games to follow were a mixture of all that is good and bad about Sheffield rugby. Hard fought wins against Birmingham, Stourbridge and Aspatria were tempered by poor losses aganst Sandal, Nuneaton and Kendal to leave the club with a record of eleven wins and thirteen losses resulting in a final league position of below halfway, a situation we definitely need to improve upon in the coming season.

Season 1997/98 is eagerly awaited in Sheffield, as many changes have been made already during the close season to move Sheffield Rugby Club firmly forward both on and off the pitch. New club and kit sponsorship deals with major local firms, the appointment of an established coach (an ex Leicester 1st XV player) to work alongside the existing coaching set-up, the introduction of commercially minded individuals into the committee structure and active recruitment of new playing staff from both National League and local clubs are the 'building blocks' to assist our push towards Division Three and Two.

'Onwards and Upwards' is the new motto at Sheffield RUFC as we await with relish the oncoming season.

Sheffield RUFC: Back Row (L-R): Richard Armswood, Karl Holmes, Martin Fay (Coach), Rob Pound, Darren Cairns, Neil Pearson, Dave Watson, Martin Kirk, Adam Doran, Allen Broomhead (Coach), John Dale, Jim McKechnie, Richard Moss. Kneeling: Matt James, Ben Bryer, Nick Crapper (Capt 96/7), Jamie Morley (Capt 97/8), Chris Saul. Front Row: David Anderson, Mark Waugh.

Colours: Blue & white hoops/navy blue/red.   **Change colours:** Red/navy blue/red.

SHEFFIELD

No	Ven.	Date	Opponents	Att.	Res.	Score	Scorers
1	(A)	31.08	v Birmingham S		L	8-13	Allatt(t)Morley(p)
2	(H)	07.09	v Lichfield		W	76-15	Allatt(2t)Waugh(2t)Crapper(t)Pearson(t)Pound(c)Morley(3t7c5p)
3	(A)	21.09	v Preston		L	8-18	Graville(t)Morley(p)
4	(H)	28.09	v Sandal		W	26-24	Cairns(t)PenT(t)Morley(2c4p)
5	(A)	05.10	v Winnington P		D	21-21	Morley(7p)
6	(H)	19.10	v Hereford		W	21- 9	Kirk(t)Crapper(t)Morley(c3p)
7	(A)	26.10	v Aspatria		W	21-20	Allatt(2t)Morley(c3p)
8	(A)	09.11	v Stourbridge		L	25-28	PenT(t)Morley(c6p)
9	(H)	16.11	v Nuneaton		W	18- 8	Pound(p)Morley(5p)
10	(A)	21.12	v Stoke O T		W	23- 5	Pierre(t)Armswood(t)Morley(2c3p)
11	(H)	28.12	v Manchester		L	10-35	Beaumont(t)Morley(cp)
12	(A)	18.01	v Worcester		L	14-32	Anderson(t)Pound(3p)
13	(H)	25.01	v Birmingham S		W	20-13	Morley(t)Pound(5p)
14	(A)	01.02	v Lichfield		L	11-12	Pound(t2p)
15	(H)	08.02	v Preston G		D	23-23	Cairns(t)Kirk(t)PenTry(tPound(c2p)
16	(A)	15.02	v Sandal		L	13-23	Allatt(t)Pound(c2p)
17	(H)	22.02	v Winnington Park		L	18-31	Pound(6p)
18	(A)	01.03	v Hereford		W	11-10	N Pearson(t)Pound(2p)
19	(H)	15.03	v Stourbridge		W	21-12	Cairns(3t)Pound(3c)
20	(A)	22.03	v Nuneaton		L	5-19	Waugh(t)
21	(H)	29.03	v Stoke on Trent		W	9- 6	Burgess(3p)
22	(A)	05.04	v Manchester		L	17-46	Jones(t)Waugh(t)Watson(t)R Pearson(c)
23	(H)	19.04	v Worcester		L	6-14	Pound(2p)
24	(A)	26.04	v Kendal		L	10-15	Allatt(t)Pound(cp)
25	(H)	10.05	v Kendal		L	12-14	Pound(4p)
26	(H)	17.05	v Aspatria		W	37-17	Cairns(2t)R Pearson(t)Doran(t)D Holmes(t)Crapper(p)Kirk(t2c)

1996-97 HIGHLIGHTS

PLAYERS USED: 33 plus five as replacement only.

EVER PRESENT: None - most 24 Martin Kirk, Rob Pound and Dave Anderson(1)

❏ Kicked more penalties than any other side in the division.

73	Sheffield
65	Preston G
60	Kendal

❏ Third lowest try scorers in the division.

43	Sheffield
41	Stoke on Trent
36	Hereford

❏ Most points in a match

44 Jamie Morley v Lichfield 07.09.96 (H)
21 Jamie Morley v Winnington Park 05.10.96 (A)

❏ Hat trick of tries in a match

3 Darren Cairns v Stourbridge 19.03.97 (H)

❏ Most points in the season

Pts	Player	T	C	P	D
167	Jamie Morley	4	15	39	-
111	Rob Pound	1	8	30	-
35	Darren Cairns	7	-	-	-
35	Mark Allatt	7	-	-	-

❏ Most appearances

24 Dave Anderson(1), Martin Kirk and Rob Pound
23 Mark Waugh and Nick Crapper
22 Chris Saul and Jamie Morley
21 Mark Allatt

❏ Disciplinary

Best record in the division with just one yellow card. This was late in the season and went to Nick Crapper for being sarcastic to the referee. One yellow card left then joint second in the National Leagues behind Richmond and level with London Scottish,

SHEFFIELD'S COURAGE LEAGUE MATCH DETAILS 1996-97

No.	15	14	13	12	11	10	9	1	2	3	4	5	6	7	8	Replacements	No.
1	Allatt	Kirk	Saul	Morley	Amswood	Pound	D.Holmes	Anderson	Howard	Moss	Doran	Graville	Crapper	Waugh	Watson		1
2	Allatt	Kirk	Saul	Morley	Amswood	Pound	D.Holmes	Anderson	Howard	Moss	Doran	Graville	Crapper	Waugh	Watson	Broomhead(1)/Cotton(6)	2
3	Allatt	Kirk	Saul	Morley	R.Pearson	Pound	D.Holmes	McKechnie	Howard	Moss	Doran	Graville	Cotton	Waugh	Watson		3
4	Allatt	Kirk	Saul	Morley	R.Pearson	Pound	D.Holmes	Anderson	Howard	Moss	Doran	Graville	Cotton	Waugh	Crapper		4
5	Allatt	Kirk	Saul	Morley	Cairns	Pound	D.Holmes	Anderson	Howard	Moss	Dale	Graville	Watson	Waugh	Crapper	Broomhead(5)	5
6	Allatt	Saul	Kirk	Morley	Cairns	Pound	D.Holmes	Anderson	Howard	Moss	Taylor	Graville	Watson	Waugh	Crapper		6
7	Allatt	Kirk	Saul	Morley	Cairns	Pound	D.Holmes	Anderson	K.Holmes	Moss	Pierre	Graville	Watson	Waugh	Crapper		7
8	Allatt	Saul	Kirk	Morley	Cairns	Pound	D.Holmes	Anderson	K.Holmes	Moss	Pierre	Graville	Watson	Waugh	Crapper		8
9	Allatt	Kirk	Saul	Morley	Cairns	Pound	N.Pearson	Anderson	Howard	Moss	Pierre	Cotton	Watson	Waugh	Crapper	K.Holmes(2)	9
10	Allatt	Kirk	Saul	Morley	Amswood	Pound	N.Pearson	Anderson	Howard	Moss	Davies	Cotton	Watson	Waugh	Crapper		10
11	Allatt	Cairns	Kirk	Morley	Amswood	Pound	D.Holmes	Anderson	Howard	Moss	Graville	Davies	Beaumont	Waugh	Crapper	Doran(4)/Bradwell(10)/Briar(6)/Gilfillan(2)	11
12	Allatt	Cairns	Saul	Pound	Amswood	Kirk	D.Holmes	Anderson	Howard	Moss	Doran	Graville	Briar	Waugh	Watson	Jones(10)/White(5)	12
13	Pound	Cairns	Saul	Morley	Amswood	Kirk	Roberts	Anderson	Howard	Moss	Doran	Briar	Waugh	Watson		White(5)/D.Holmes(fr 10)	13
14	Pound	Cairns	Saul	Morley	Amswood	Kirk	Roberts	Anderson	Howard	Moss	Doran	Dale	Waugh	Watson	Briar	Davies(6)	14
15	Pound	Cairns	Saul	Morley	Kirk	Allatt	Roberts	Anderson	Howard	Moss	Doran	Dale	Crapper	Waugh	Briar	Watson(8)/N.Pearson(9)	15
16	Allatt	Cairns	Saul	Morley	Burgess	Pound	N.Pearson	Anderson	Howard	McKechnie	Doran	Cotton	Cotton	Waugh	Crapper	Jones(15)/Mayland(3)/Graville(5)	16
17	Burgess	Cairns	Saul	Morley	R.Pearson	Pound	N.Pearson	Anderson	K.Holmes	Moss	Doran	Crapper	Waugh	Briar		Briar	17
18	Pound	Saul	Morley	Morley	Cairns	Kirk	McKechnie	McKechnie	K.Holmes	Moss	Doran	Dale	Crapper	Waugh	White	Briar(6)/Anderson(1)	18
19	Pound	Amswood	Saul	Morley	Kirk	Kirk	N.Pearson	Anderson	K.Holmes	McKechnie	Doran	Dale	Crapper	Waugh	Watson	Jones(14)/Briar(9)	19
20	Pound	Allatt	Saul	Morley	Cairns	Kirk	N.Pearson	Anderson	K.Holmes	McKechnie	Dale	Crapper	Waugh	White		D.Holmes(10)/Graville(5)	20
21	Burgess	Burgess	Morley	Morley	Cairns	Kirk	N.Pearson	Anderson	K.Holmes	McKechnie	Graville	White	Crapper	Waugh	Watson	Mayland(1)	21
22	D.Holmes	D.Holmes	Saul	Morley	Cairns	Jones	N.Pearson	Anderson	Moss	McKechnie	Dale	Crapper	Waugh	Watson		Allison(4)/K.Holmes(2)	22
23	Pound	Allatt	Saul	Morley	Cairns	Kirk	N.Pearson	Anderson	Taylor	McKechnie	Graville	Allison	Crapper	Waugh	Watson	Parkin(7)K.Holmes(2)	23
24	R.Pearson	R.Pearson	Pound	Morley	Cairns	Kirk	N.Pearson	Anderson	Howard	McKechnie	Greville	Crapper	Waugh	Watson		Allison(5)/Parkin(2)	24
25	R.Pearson	R.Pearson	Saul	Saul	Cairns	Kirk	N.Pearson	Anderson	Howard	McKechnie	Dale	White	Crapper	Waugh	Watson	Graville(8)/K.Holmes(2)	25
26	Thirtle	Saul	R.Pearson	R.Pearson	Cairns	Kirk	N.Pearson	Anderson	K.Holmes	Moss	Doran	Dale	Allison	Waugh	Crapper	D.Holmes(14)/Parkin(2)/Broomhead(3)	26

SHEFFIELD LEAGUE STATISTICS
(COMPILED BY STEPHEN McCORMACK)

Season	Div.	P	W	D	L	F	A	PD	Pts	Pos.	Coach	Captain
87-88	3	11	7	1	3	134	161	-27	15	4		
88-89	3	11	4	1	6	170	182	-12	9	6		
89-90	3	11	6	0	5	176	174	2	12	4		
90-91	3	12	4	1	7	193	222	-29	9	10		
91-92	3	12	5	1	6	146	228	-82	11	8		
92-93	3	11	7	0	4	208	134	74	14	5		
93-94	4	18	5	1	12	287	310	-23	11	9		D Kaye
94-95	5N	12	5	0	7	156	197	-41	10	9	A Broomhead	N Crapper
95-96	5N	12	7	0	5	205	190	15	14	5	A Broomhead	N Crapper
96-97	4N	26	11	2	13	484	483	1	24	8	Most Points: 167 J Morley Most Tries: 7 M Allatt	
Total		136	67	7	68	2159	2281	-122				

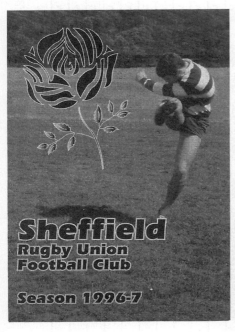

PROGRAMME DETAILS

SIZE: A5   **PRICE:** £3

PAGES: 48 plus cover

PROGRAMME EDITOR
C Roth, 01142 752575

ADVERTISING RATES
Full page £250, 1/2 page £125

CLUB & GROUND DETAILS

Address: Abbeydale Park Sports Club, Abbeydale Road South, Sheffield. S17 3LG.
Tel. Nos. 0114 236 7011

Capacity: 1200   **Seated:** 200   **Standing:** 1000
Simple Directions: The club is on the A621 (Bakewell to Baslow road) out of Sheffield.
Nearest Railway Station: Sheffield (BR) Dore & Totley (local)
Car Parking: 200 spaces are available at the club.
Admission: Matchday Adult £3.
Club Shop: Yes. manager Paul Bradwell 01142 553830
Clubhouse: Normal Licensing hours, bar meals available. Functions up to 150 can be catered for, contact Gary Roberts 01142 367011
Training Nights: Tuesday and Thursday.

STOURBRIDGE R.F.C.

FOUNDED: 1876

President Peter Thompson, 6 Ryecroft, Pedmore, Stourbridge.
01384 373800 (H), 0121 428 4000 (B), 0121 478 3000 (Fax)

Chairman Norman Robertson, 16A Middlefield Lane, West Hagley, Stourbridge
01562 886011 (H), 01384 455555 (B).

Fixture Secretary Alan McCreadie, 23 Norton Road, Stourbridge, DY8 2AG. 01384 373904 (H)

Press Officer Vernon Davies, 36 Beckman Road, Pedmore, Stourbridge. 01562 883640 (H)

Commercial Manager Ginny Truslove, 16 Cobden Street, Wollaston, Stourbridge DY8 3RY
01384 440283 (H), 01384 397555 (B)

A season full of promise as Stourbridge 1st XV slowly absorbed the philosophy and tactics of new coach Stewart Jardine. After many fluctuations it ended with a magnificent seven match unbeaten home run which captivated an enthusiastic home crowd. This was easily a club league record. The expansive fifteen man style favoured by Stewart and forwards coach Graham Smith benefited from close season law changes and was keenly adopted by a 1st team squad who maintained their confidence in the new style throughout the vagaries of this most arduous and demanding of all league seasons.

Ultimately, Stourbridge ended up in sixth position, highly satisfactory in view of the improved standards at the upper levels of this league, and this was amazingly similar to their last three outings when they were fifth, sixth and seventh respectively. However, the qualtity of play at its best has been the finest and certainly the most attractive seen at Stourton for many years. It was certainly the equal of the top sides as the home defeats of Birmingham-Solihull and Preston Grasshoppers and the draw against promoted Worcester illustrate. The Worcester game was chosen to inaugurate the magnificent 500 seat stand which topped off the excellent facilities at this most attractive of grounds. It was unfortunate that unseasonal Arctic weather marred the major representative game when the Midlands faced the Aussie team from tropical Queensland.

The club was led by Chris Mann for the second season. He continues to break all the club scoring records and has amassed 487 points in 53 games despite the fact that the drive for tries restricted him to two penalties in the last ten games. The try count at 95 was getting on for four per game and all try scoring records were smashed. Kevin Hickey led the try count with 15 and the changing nature of the modern game was highlighted by the fact that props scored 24 tries in total, led by the prolific Simon Baylie with 12 and Steve Phillips with 8.

A record 42 players represented the club, including many promising young Colts who can only benefit from the experience. Players like Matt Wynne-Hughes, Jacob John and Paul Meakin seem to have established themselves in a competitive and versatile squad. This versatility was illustrated by Simon Hill, hitherto wing or flanker, who stepped into the breach and performed competently in a second row depleted by injury.

Stourbridge RFC: Coach Stewart Jardine demonstrates the running game, which helped them develop into one of the leagues most exciting teams.

Colours: Navy blue with narrow white bands.   **Change colours:** Red & white hoops, trimmed navy blue.

COURAGE LEAGUE MATCH DETAILS 1996-97

No	Ven.	Date	Opponents	Att.	Res.	Score	Scorers
1	(H)	31.08	v Manchester		L	13-26	Phillips(t)Mann(c2p)
2	(A)	07.09	v Winnington Park		W	42-20	Baylie(2t)Badcock(t)John(t)Jardine(t)G Smith(t)Mann(3c2p)
3	(H)	21.09	v Worcester		D	21-21	John(t)Mann(tc3p)
4	(A)	28.09	v Hereford		W	35-27	Phillips(t)Hickey(t)Mann(2c7p)
5	(A)	05.10	v Kendal		L	21-25	Phillips(t)Badcock(t)Mann(c3p)
6	(H)	19.10	v Aspatria		L	34-45	Hickey(2t)Richardson(t)Phillips(t)John(t)Mann(3cp)
7	(A)	26.10	v Birmingham S		L	21-39	Phillips(2t)Jones(t)Mann(3c)
8	(H)	09.11	v Sheffield		W	28-25	Badcock(t)Hickey(t)Jardine(t)Mann(2c3p)
9	(A)	16.11	v Lichfield		W	23-22	Phillips(t)Baylie(t)Jardine(t)Pennington(c2p)
10	(H)	00.00	v Nuneaton		W	38-13	Baylie(2t)Hickey(t)Edwards(t)G Smith(t)Richardson(t)Reed-Daunter(4c)
11	(A)	18.01	v Stoke on Trent		W	40-19	Hickey(3t)Russell(t)Horton(t)Dickins(t)Reed-Daunter(2c2p)
12	(A)	25.01	v Manchester		L	20-28	Mann(t)Baylie(t)Reed-Daunter(2c2p)
13	(H)	01.02	v Winnington Park		L	11-20	J Smith(t)Mann(2p)
14	(A)	08.02	v Worcester		L	30-32	Hickey(t)Jardine(t)Protheroe(t)Mann(3c3p)
15	(H)	15.02	v Hereford		W	29- 5	Bratten(t)Dickins(t)Phillips(t)T J-Fellows(t)Mann(3cp)
16	(H)	22.02	v Kendal		W	20-13	Richardson(t)Edwards(t)Baylie(t)Mann(cp)
17	(A)	01.03	v Aspatria		L	12-14	Jardine(t)John(tc)
18	(H)	08.03	v Birmingham Sol		W	15-13	Jardine(t)Edwards(t)John(cp)
19	(A)	15/03	v Sheffield		L	12-21	Dickins(2t)Mann(c)
20	(H)	22.03	v Lichfield		W	48-19	Baylie(2t)Hill(t)Jardine(t)Maekin(t)Bratten(t)Richardson(t)Mann(5cp)
21	(H)	29.03	v Preston G		W	18-13	Baylie(t)Jardine(t)Mann(c2p)
22	(A)	05.04	v Nuneaton		W	26-18	Hill(t)Hickey(t)Bratten(t)Dickins(t)Mann(3c)
23	(A)	12.04	v Preston G		L	21-41	Hickey(2t)Protheroe(t)Mann(3c)
24	(H)	19.04	v Stoke on Trent		W	57-15	Badcock(2t)Bratten(2t)Dickins(t)Hickey(t)Pennington(t)Richardson(t)Mann(7cp)
25	(A)	26.04	v Sandal		L	31-32	Kiszka(2t)Hickey(t)Dickins(t)Badcock(t)Mann(3c)
26	(H)	10.05	v Sandal		W	38-13	Hickey(2t)Baylie(2t)John(t)Tibbitts(t)Mann(4c)

1996-97 HIGHLIGHTS

LEAGUE DEBUTS:

PLAYERS USED: 41 plus three as replacement only.

EVER PRESENT: None - most 25 John Russell

Most points in a match
25 Chris Mann v Hereford 28.09.96 (A)
17 Chris Mann v Stoke on Trent 19.04.97 (H)

Hat trick of tries in a match
3 Kevin Hickey v Stoke on Trent 18.01.97 (A)

Had an excellent record against Champions Worcester drawing 21 all at home and losing narrowly 30-32 away.

Had the unwanted distinction oif having two players sent off in the same match. Dale Smallman and

John Taylor were the culprits in the home game against Winnington Park.

Most points in the season
Pts	Player	T	C	P	D
206	Chris Mann	2	49	32	-
75	Kevin Hickey	15	-	-	-
60	Simon Baylie	12	-	-	-
40	Steve Phillips	8	-	-	-
40	Stewart Jardine	8	-	-	-

Most appearances
25 John Russell
23 Chris Mann and Kevin Hickey
22 James Richardson
21 Scott Badcock

No 8 Kevin Hickey tripled the previous record of five tries in a season held by Richard Trigg.

Stand off Chris Mann broke the club records for points, conversions and penalties in a season with 206, 49 and 32 respectively.

STOURBRIDGE'S COURAGE LEAGUE MATCH DETAILS 1996-97

15	14	13	12	11	10	9	1	2	3	4	5	6	7	8	Replacements	
R-Daunter	Jones	John	Badcock	Mann	Mann	L-Jones	Phillips	Hall	Baylie	DeScossa	Russell	Hill	Thomson	Hickey		1
John	Jones	Badcock	Edwards	James	Mann	Jardine	Smith	Baylie	Taylor	W+Hughes	Tippetts	Hill	Thomson	Hickey		2
John	S.Smith	Edwards	Badcock	S.Smith	Mann	Jardine	Merritt	Hall	Baylie	Taylor	Russell	W+Hughes	Tippetts	Hickey		3
John	S.Smith	Edwards	Badcock	Hill	Mann	Jardine	Merritt	Hall	Phillips	Taylor	Russell	Tippetts	Thomson	Hickey	Richardson(11)	4
John	S.Smith	Edwards	Badcock	Hill	Mann	Jardine	Merritt	Hall	Phillips	Taylor	Smallman	Tippetts	Thomson	Hickey	Perry(4)	5
John	Jones	Crowfoot	Badcock	Richardson	Mann	Jardine	Merritt	Phillips	Baylie	Taylor	Smallman	Horton	Thomson	Hickey	Hall(2)	6
John	S.Smith	Crowfoot	Badcock	Richardson	Mann	Jardine	Phillips	Baylie	Battie	Russell	Taylor	Smallman	Horton	Hickey	Hall(2)	7
Pennington	Edwards	Tapper	Badcock	Richardson	Mann	Jardine	Phillips	Merritt	Baylie	Russell	Baldwin	Smallman	Horton	Hickey	G.Smith(3)	8
Pennington	Edwards	Tapper	Badcock	Richardson	J.Smith	Jardine	Phillips	Merritt	Baylie	Russell	Baldwin	Smallman	Horton	Hickey	G.Smith(1)	9
R-Daunter	Edwards	Tapper	Badcock	Richardson	Hall	G.Smith	G.Smith	Merritt	Baylie	Taylor	Baldwin	Russell	Horton	Hickey	Thomson(5)J-Fellows(3)Meakin(.)	10
R-Daunter	Tapper	Bratten	Badcock	Richardson	Mann	Jardine	Smith	J-Fellows	Baylie	Russell	Baldwin	Horton	Horton	Hickey	Dickins(14)	11
R-Daunter	Richardson	Tapper	Bratten	Dickins	Mann	Jardine	G.Smith	J-Fellows	Baylie	Russell	Baldwin	Smallman	Horton	Hickey		12
J.Smith	Dickins	Meakin	Bratten	Richardson	Mann	Jardine	G.Smith	J-Fellows	Baylie	Russell	Whitehead	Smallman	Horton	Hickey	Taylor(5)	13
John	Richardson	Bratten	Badcock	Mann	Mann	Dickins	Phillips	G.Smith	Baylie	Taylor	Starynsky	Thomson	Horton	Hickey	Jardine(9)	14
J.Smith	Meakin	Bratten	Badcock	Richardson	Mann	Dickins	Phillips	Baylie	Baylie	Starynskyj	Taylor	Russell	Thomsom	Hickey	G.Smith(1),T.J-Fellows(2)	15
John	Meakin	Badcock	Badcock	Richardson	Mann	Dickins	G.Smith	Baylie	Starynskyj	Taylor	Russell	Russell	Tibbits	Hickey		16
John	Meakin	Badcock	Edwards	Richardson	Mann	Jardine	G.Smith	Baylie	Starynskyj	Hill	Russell	Tibbits	Tibbits	Hickey		17
John	Richardson	Badcock	Edwards	Meakin	Smith	Jardine	Phillips	Baylie	Hill	Russell	Russell	Tibbits	W+Hughes	Hickey	T.J-Fellows(8)	18
John	Badcock	Edwards	Edwards	Richardson	Smith	Dickins	Phillips	Baylie	Hill	Starynsky	W+Hughes	Tibbits	Russell	Hickey	N-Horton(.)N-Goodwin(.)	19
John	Meakin	Badcock	Badcock	Richardson	Mann	Jardine	Baylie	G.Smith	G.Smith	Russell	Hill	Tippetts	Thomson	W+Hughes	Starynsky(5)J-Fellows(2)	20
John	Meakin	Badcock	Edwards	Richardson	Mann	Jardine	Kiszka	Protheroe	Baylie	Hill	Russell	Thomson	Tibbits	Hickey	Dickins(15)Taylor(14)T.J-Fellows(6)	21
Dickins	Edwards	Bratten	Badcock	Richardson	Mann	Jardine	Phillips	Protheroe	Kiszka	Russell	Hill	Tippetts	W+Hughes	Hickey	Pennington(14)	22
Bratten	Edwards	Tapper	Badcock	Richardson	Mann	Jardine	Phillips	Protheroe	Kiszka	Smallman	Russell	Tippetts	W+Hughes	Hickey	Goodwin(1)	23
Pennington	Edwards	Bratten	Badcock	Richardson	Mann	Jardine	Phillips	Protheroe	Baylie	Starynsky	Hill	Russell	W+Hughes	Hickey	Tippetts(8)J-Fellows(7)	24
John	Edwards	Bratten	Badcock	Richardson	Mann	Dickins	Phillips	Protheroe	Kiszka	Russell	Hill	Horton	Tippetts	W+Hughes	Goodwin(3)Perry(12)Meakin(13)	25
John	Meakin	Bratten	Bratten	Richardson	Mann	Dickins	Baylie	Hall	Phillips	Russell	Hill	Horton	Tippetts	Hickey	W+Hughes(7)Kiszka(3)	26

STOURBRIDGE LEAGUE STATISTICS
(COMPILED BY STEPHEN McCORMACK)

Season	Div.	P	W	D	L	F	A	PD	Pts	Pos.	Coach	Captain
87-88	ALN	01	5	0	5	132	134	-2	10	7	D Fourness	J Shaw
88-89	ALN	10	6	0	4	118	79	49	12	3	D Fourness	K Astley
89-90	ALN	10	7	0	3	146	133	132	14	3	D Fourness	K Astley
90-91	D4N	12	5	1	6	134	161	-27	11	8	D Fourness	M Wilson
91-92	D4N	12	6	0	6	163	137	26	12	6	D Fourness	N Perry
92-93	D4N	12	5	1	6	161	144	17	11	9	D Fourness	N Perry
93-94	D5N	12	6	0	6	162	188	-26	12	5	D Fourness	T Jeavons-Fellows
94-95	D5N	12	6	0	6	166	174	-8	12	6	D Fourness	T Jeavons-Fellows
95-96	D5N	12	6	0	6	200	177	23	12	7	D Fourness	C Mann
96-97	D4N	26	14	1	11	704	579	125	29	6		C Mann
Total		128	66	3	59	2086	1906	180				

Stourbridge Rugby Football Club
Official Match Programme
1996-1997 Season

PROGRAMME DETAILS

SIZE: A5   **PRICE:** With admission.

PAGES: 40 plus cover

EDITOR: Vernon Davies 01562 886340

ADVERTISING RATES
Full page £100.

CLUB & GROUND DETAILS

Address: Bridgnorth Road, Stourton, Stourbridge, W. Midlands. DY7 6QZ.
Tel. Nos. 01384 393889.

Capacity: 3500   **Seated:** 499   **Standing:** 3001
Simple Directions: The ground is situated on the A458 (Bridgnorth road), two miles west of Stourbridge town centre. The ground is on the left hand side 1/2 mile past the 'Foresters Arms' public house.
Nearest Railway Station: Stourbridge Junction.
Car Parking: 200 spaces are available at the ground.
Admission: Matchday - £2.50 including programme.
Club Shop: Yes. matchdays & mini Sundays
Clubhouse: Matchdays 12.00-11.00, Sundays 12.00-2.00. Training nights 7.00-11.00, snacks & bar meals available. Functions available, capacity 150, contact P Purslow 01384 898142
Training Nights: Tuesday and Thursday.

WALSALL R.F.C.

FOUNDED: 1922

President, D E (Brains) Horton, c/o Walsall RFC, Broadway Ground, Delves Road, Walsall WS1 3JY.
Chairman R M Harding, 17 Belvedere Road, Walsall
01922 26576 (H), 01905 23204 (B), 01922 613310 (Fax)
Club Secretary Caleb Tillott, 6 Lichfield Road, Sandhills, Walsall Wood, Walsall. WS9 9PE.
01543 372667 (H), 01922 613310 (Fax)
Fixtures Secretary Tim Day, 20 Daffodil Place, Walsall. WS5 3DN. 01922 611729 (H), 01922 613310 (Fax)
Press Officer Howard Clews, 4 Binbrook Road, Short Heath, Walsall. WV12 4TW.
01902 631947 (H), 01922 613310 (Fax)
Director of Coaching Arnie Evans, 0121 353 1017 (H), 0121 378 1288 (B).
1st XV Coach Mick Trumper, 01952 403259 (H).

Walsall's 75th Anniversary Season, coincidentally the 35th season and 25th year respectively for the club's Colts and Mini/Juniors, had a double edged ending with celebrations after the commiserations.

First, after nine League seasons of steady rise from Midland Division One to National League Three, there was the club's first experience of relegation, a victim of the most extended League programme hitherto endured - 30 matches between 31st August and 17th May - and an RFU ruling that four teams, rather than two, would go down with Walsall the fourth and final one to suffer the dubious honour.

Despite a growing catalogue of long term injuries, all seemed well in the Autumn as Walsall won five of their first eleven League games, beating Clifton, Harrogate, London Welsh and Lydney at home and Liverpool away, and losing to eventual champions Exeter only to two breakaways (giveaway!) tries in the dying moments and to third placed, moneyed Leeds by just 24-26.

But after November they won only three more League matches out of nineteen, (all at home) over Clifton, Otley and Redruth, and were stretched physically in terms of weight and height and in personnel to the extent that they fielded a total of 46 different players, compared with just 26 the previous League campaign.

Damning defeats were those at home by Havant and Liverpool, who both climbed to safety over Walsall as a result, but most galling were the losses 22-24 away at Exeter, where Walsall sat in the home 22 for the final ten minutes without reward, and 42-44 at home to Reading; those 42 Walsall points were the highest score ever achieved by a losing side in the history of the National Leagues.

Major blows were the departure of charismatic coach Colin Jarvis to Australia for a year's teaching exchange in December and the posting to Germany by the RAF of Combined Services back Steve Lazenby in October. Lazenby returned in the Spring to captain the RAF in the Inter-Services Tournament and take his Twickenham appearance to 24, thereafter driving back each weekend in a vain effort to help Walsall avoid relegation.

After his fourteenth appearance for the Barbarians Richard Moon announced his retirement from a playing career embracing every England level bar a full cap and was honoured with a star-studded Charity Match to close his days on the field on 24th May.

In his fifth year as club chairman Rob Harding took his still-playing appearance record to 415 (126 in the Leagues), while Richard Mills increased his records to 368 points in the season (338 in the League) and 2010 in his Walsall career of 265 matches (1056 in 122 League games). HOWARD CLEWS

Walsall 1st XV: Back Row (L-R): Stacey McQueenie (Physio), Jim Deare (Team Asst), Mick Trumper, Mark Ellis, Gary Hill, Rob Harding (Chairman), Richard Coleman, Richie Morgan, Geraint Tillott, David Rose, Gary Green, Graham MacDonald (Asst Coach), Arnie Evans (Coach). Front Row: Andy Stewart, Richard Mills, Richard Moon, Daren Haley, Karl Jones, Malcolm Walker (Capt), Jon Lord, Matt McCluney, Steve Lazenby, Jon Rowe.
Photo - Wolverhampton Star & Express

Colours: Scarlet/black/scarlet.   **Change colours:** Black & white (scarlet hoops), black, black.

WALSALL

No	Ven.	Date	Opponents	Att.	Res.	Score	Scorers
1	(H)	31.08	v Wharfdale		L	19-34	Jones(t)Russell(t)Maughan(3p)
2	(A)	07.09	v Clifton		W	36-17	M Walker(2t)Mills(t3c5p)
3	(H)	14.09	v Exeter		L	11-35	Rowe(t)Mills(2p)
4	(A)	21.09	v Fylde		L	10-28	Tillott(t)Mills(cp)
5	(H)	28.09	v Harrogate		W	27-15	Rowe(t)Till(t)Mills(c5p)
6	(A)	05.10	v Havant		L	10-29	D Rose(t)Mills(cdg)
7	(H)	12.10	v Leeds		L	24-26	Mills(8p)
8	(A)	19.10	v Liverpool StH		W	29-21	M Walker(t)PenTry(t)Mills(2c5p)
9	(H)	26.10	v London Welsh		W	32-20	M Walker(t)Lazenby(t)Rowe(t)Moon(t)Mills(3c2p)
10	(A)	09.11	v Otley		L	19-53	Haley(t)Coleman(t)Jones(t)Mills(2c)
11	(H)	16.11	v Lydney		W	20-15	Taylor(t)M Walker(t)Mills(2c2p)
12	(A)	28.12	v Redruth		L	20-34	M Walker(t)Harding(t)Mills(2cp)Banks(dg)
13	(A)	18.01	v Wharfdale		L	27-37	Moon(t)Till(t)Harding(t)PenTry(t)Mills(2cp)
14	(H)	25.01	v Clifton		W	32-15	McCluney(t)Bamks(t)Coleman(t)Haley(t)Mills(3c2p)
15	(A)	01.02	v Exeter		L	22-24	Lea(t)Mills(c5p)
16	(H)	08.02	v Fylde		L	12-28	Mills(4p)
17	(A)	15.02	v Harrogate		L	13-22	D Rose(t)McCluney(t)Mills(p)
18	(H)	22.02	v Havant		L	24-45	A Walker(t)Dickson(t)Mills(c4p)
19	(A)	01.03	v Leeds		L	3-84	Mills(p)
20	(H)	08.03	v Liverpool StH		L	19-29	Coleman(t)Mills(c4p)
21	(A)	15.03	v London Welsh		L	24-33	Taylor(t)Wild(t)A Walker(t)Mills(3cp)
22	(H)	22.03	v Otley		W	29-19	A Walker(t)Burns(t)Mills(2c4p)M Walker(dg)
23	(A)	29.03	v Reading		L	16-49	A Walker(t)Mills(c3p)
24	(A)	05.04	v Lydney		L	17-21	Dicksen(t)Colemnan(t)Mills(2cp)
25	(H)	12.04	v Reading		L	42-44	A Walker(t)M Walker(t)Mallins(t)banks(t)Mills(2c5pdg)
26	(H)	19.04	v Rosslyn Park		W	35-25	N Rose(t)Coleman(t)Mills(2c7p)
27	(A)	26.04	v Rosslyn Park		L	19-25	Trumper(t)Mills(c4p)
28	(H)	03.05	v Morley		L	17-36	Lazenby(t)Dicksen(t)Mills(2cp)
29	(H)	10.05	v Rosslyn Park		L	13-35	Mallins(t)Mills(c2p)
30	(A)	17.05	v Morley		L	19-78	M Walker(t)Moon(t)N Rose(t)Banks(c)Mills(c)

1996-97 HIGHLIGHTS

LEAGUE DEBUTS: Ben Maughan, Mick Trumper, Richard Henwood, Mark Poole,

PLAYERS USED: 42 plus 3 as replacement only.

EVER PRESENT: Malcolm Walker

❏ Stand off Richard Mills re-wrote Walsall's points scoring records. In the 'in a match' section he set a new record of 26 points in the match against Clifton last September. In the home game against Leeds in October Mills kicked a record eight penalties to beat the previous record of six.
He set new records for points, conversions and penalties in a season with 338, 42 and 81 respectively. Later in the season he passed the 1000 point milestone for Walsall in league rugby and ended the season on 1056.
It was the sixth consecutive season that Mills had topped the points scoring list and the third consecutive season that he had broken the record for points in a season.

❏ Malcom Walker extended his career record for tries to 30 with eight more.
Walker topped the try scoring list for the third time with the first being back in 1988-89.

❏ Andy Walker equalled namesake Malcolm Walker's record of scoring tries in three consecutive matches.

❏ The 42 points they scored in losing to Reading was the highest total for a losing side in a National League match.

❏ SENT OFF: Dave Burns (v Havant) and
              Gary Till (v Fylde)

WALSALL'S COURAGE LEAGUE MATCH DETAILS 1996-97

15	14	13	12	11	10	9	1	2	3	4	5	6	7	8	Replacements	
Russell	Rowe	McCluney	Rose	M.Walker	Moon	Morgan	Haley	Jones	Harding	Trumper		Burns	Tillott	Coleman		1
Henwood	Rowe	McCluney	Rose	M.Walker	Mills	Morgan	Haley	Jones	Harding	Trumper	Godfrey	Burns	Tillott	Coleman	Harding(4)	2
Henwood	Rowe	McCluney	Rose	M.Walker	Mills	Morgan	Haley	Jones	Godfrey	Trumper	Harding	Burns	Tillott	Coleman		3
Lazenby	Rowe	McCluney	Rose	M.Walker	Mills	Morgan	Haley	Jones	Harding	Coleman	Trumper	Burns	Burns	Coleman		4
Lazenby	Rowe	McCluney	Rose	M.Walker	Mills	Morgan	Haley	Poole	Harding	Trumper	Coleman	Burns	Tillott	Coleman	Leaf(1)	5
Maughan	Rowe	McCluney	Rose	M.Walker	Mills	Morgan	Haley	Poole	Harding	Trumper	Burns	Trumper	Burns	Coleman	Stewart(15), Bambridge(14)	6
Lazenby	Russell	McCluney	Rose	M.Walker	Mills	Lea	Haley	Jones	Harding	Trumper	Coleman	Burns	Tillott	Coleman		7
Marshall	Russell	McCluney	Rose	M.Walker	Mills	Lea	Haley	Jones	Harding	Trumper	Coleman	Trumper	Till	Coleman		8
Lazenby	Rowe	McCluney	Rose	M.Walker	Moon	Morgan	Haley	Jones	Harding	Trumper	Wild	Trumper	Till	Coleman	Tillott(6), Lord(13)	9
Banks	Rowe	McCluney	Rose	M.Walker	Mills	Morgan	Haley	Jones	Harding	Ellis	Trumper	Tillott	Till	Coleman	King(6), Lane(8)	10
Banks	Rowe	McCluney	Rose	M.Walker	Mills	Lea	Haley	Jones	Harding	Ellis	Trumper	Trumper	Till	Coleman	Butler(9)	11
Banks	Rowe	McCluney	Rose	M.Walker	Mills	Poole	Green	Jones	Harding	Godfrey	Trumper	Trumper	Wild	Coleman	Lane(2), M.Jones(6)	12
Banks	Rowe	McCluney	Rose	M.Walker	Mills	Bloomfield	Haley	Jones	Harding	Ellis	Till	Till	Dicksen	Coleman	Tillott(7), Bateman(14)	13
Banks	Rowe	McCluney	Rose	M.Walker	Mills	Bloomfield	Haley	Jones	Harding	Ellis	Till	Till	Dicksen	Coleman	Godfrey(8)	14
Banks	Rowe	McCluney	Rose	M.Walker	Mills	Bloomfield	Haley	Jones	Harding	Ellis	Trumper	Till	Dicksen	Coleman	Godfrey(7), Leaf(1)	15
Banks	Rowe	McCluney	Rose	M.Walker	Mills	Bloomfield	Haley	Jones	Harding	Godfrey	Till	Till	Dicksen	Coleman		16
Banks	Rowe	Rose	M.Walker	M.Walker	Mills	Lea	Haley	Poole	Harding	Ellis	Godfrey	Till	Coleman	Coleman	A.Walker(15), Dicksen(7), Lord(12)	17
A.Walker	Rowe	Bambridge	M.Walker	M.Walker	Mills	Lea	Haley	Poole	Harding	Ellis	Godfrey	Godfrey	Till	Coleman	Taylor(3), Till(6)	18
A.Walker	Slattery	McCluney	Slattery	M.Walker	Stuart	Taylor	Haley	Poole	Harding	Ellis	Ellis	Godfrey	Dickson	Coleman	Tibbitts(9), Burns(12), Trumper(.)	19
A.Walker	McCluney	Bambridge	M.Walker	Mills	Mills	Taylor	Haley	Poole	Harding	Godfrey	Ellis	Burns	Dickson	Coleman	Tillott(6), Banks(13)	20
A.Walker	McCluney	M.Walker	M.Walker	Mills	Mills	Taylor	Haley	Lane	Harding	Godfrey	Godfrey	Burns	Dickson	Coleman	Jones(1), Dicksen(7)	21
A.Walker	McCluney	Rowe	Rowe	M.Walker	Mills	Taylor	Lane	Lane	Harding	Godfrey	Godfrey	Burns	Dickson	Coleman	Mallins(13), Leaf(1), Dicksen(11)	22
Mallins	McCluney	Bateman	Bateman	Bateman	Mills	Lea	Lane	Jones	Harding	Owen	Godfrey	Burns	Burns	Coleman	Stewart(9), Poole(1), Dicksen(14)	23
Mallins	Bateman	A.Walker	M.Walker	Dicksen	Mills	Lea	Jones	Jones	Harding	Godfrey	Godfrey	Burns	Burns	Coleman	Trumper(5), Lane(tr7)	24
Mallins	Rose	A.Walker	M.Walker	Dicksen	Mills	Lea	Jones	Jones	Harding	Godfrey	Godfrey	Burns	Burns	Coleman	Trumper(5), Banks(13)	25
Mallins	Rose	Lazenby	M.Walker	Dicksen	Mills	Lea	Haley	Jones	Harding	Godfrey	Godfrey	Burns	Burns	Coleman	Moon(9), Trumper(tr6)	26
Lazenby	A.Walker	A.Walker	M.Walker	Dicksen	Mills	Morgan	Haley	Jones	Harding	Godfrey	Godfrey	Burns	Burns	Coleman	Trumper(6)	27
Mallins	A.Walker	Lazenby	M.Walker	Dicksen	Mills	Morgan	Jones	Jones	Harding	Godfrey	Godfrey	Burns	Burns	Coleman	Leaf(1), Banks(11)	28
Mallins	Rose	Lazenby	M.Walker	Dicksen	Mills	Lane	Lane	Poole	Harding	Godfrey	Godfrey	Burns	Wild	Coleman	Leaf(3), Stewart(9), A.Walker(7), Trumper(tr1)	29
Mallins	Rose	Lazenby	M.Walker	Banks	Banks	Lane	Lane	Poole	Harding	Godfrey	Godfrey	Heaven	Wild	Coleman	Moon(9), Mills(6), Leaf(11), A.Walker(15)	30

WALSALL LEAGUE STATISTICS
(COMPILED BY STEPHEN McCORMACK)

Season	Div.	P	W	D	L	F	(Tries	Con	Pen	DG)	A	(Tries	Con	Pen	DG)	Most Points	Most Tries
87-88	MID1	10	5	2	4	183	(28	16	9	4)	100	(15	5	10	0)	53 - John Dowdswell	5 - Charlie Herriotts
88-89	MID1	10	10	0	0	210	(27	18	19	3)	71	(10	2	9	0)	95 - John Dowdswell	4 - Malcolm Walker
89-90	ALN	10	2	0	8	143	(17	9	15	4)	183	(22	10	23	2)	31 - John Dowdswell	4 Simon Leaver & Matt McCluney
90-91	ALN	12	5	0	7	149	(16	8	19	4)	176	(23	9	19	3)	75 - Richard Mills	3 - Dave Wild & Nick Millward
91-92	D4N	12	3	1	8	139	(11	4	24	5)	187	(24	14	20	1)	99 - Richard Mills	4 - Duncan Marshall
92-93	D4N	12	6	0	6	165	(15	9	24	0)	179	(19	15	16	2)	90 - Richard Mills	3 - by 3 players - Mike Friar, Gary Till & Jon Rowe.
93-94	D5N	12	7	0	5	166	(13	7	29	0)	148	(11	9	22	3)	81 - Richard Mills	3 - Gary Till
94-95	D5N	12	10	1	1	389	(47	29	31	1)	110	(10	3	17	1)	164 - Richard Mills	11 - Jon Rowe
95-96	4	18	10	0	8	406	(42	23	49	1)	324	(36	18	34	2)	193 - Richard Mills	10 - Malcolm Walker
96-97	3	30	8	0	22	640	(58	43	84	4)	980	(126	79	62	2)	338 - Richard Mills	8 - Malcolm Walker
Totals		138	66	3	69	2590	(274	166	303	26)	2458	(296	164	232	16)		

SEASON 1996-1997
OFFICIAL MATCH PROGRAMME £1

PROGRAMME DETAILS

SIZE: A5   **PRICE:** £1 (included in entry)

PAGES: 36 plus cover

PROGRAMME EDITOR Howard Clews 01902 631947

ADVERTISING RATES
Mono Full Page £75, Half £50

CLUB & GROUND DETAILS

Address: Broadway Ground, Delves Road, Walsall WS1 3 JY
Tel. Nos. 01922 26818, Fax 01922 613310

Capacity: 2,250   **Seated:** 250   **Standing:** 2,000
Simple Directions: From NE (A38.A461) almost into Town centre, take ring Rd left, grd 2 miles on right. From M6 Jnc 9, go left and fork 1st right at lights onto ring road. ground on left after 2miles.
Nearest Railway Station: Walsall BR 1.5 miles, hourly bus or taxi.
Car Parking: 100 adjacent to Clubhouse, 200 within 5 mins.
Admission: Match £5, inc programme, Members £3
Club Shop: Yes, Manager Martin McCluney 01922 33803
Clubhouse: Matchdays 12.00-23.00. Evenings (except Wed), 20.00-23.00. Sundays 12.00-16.30. Snacks & restaurant (by appointment for groups only). Contact Keith Oldnall 01922 29676 (H), 01922 26818 (Club)
Training Nights: Tuesday & Thursday

WINNINGTON PARK R.F.C.

NICKNAME: Park

FOUNDED: 1907

President R D Glenisten, 29 Brookside, Weaverham, Northwich, Cheshire, CW8 3HR
01606 851705 (H), 01565 632391 (B)

Chairman B Parkey, 1 Chilham Close, Winsford, Cheshire
01606 551188 (H), 0151 495 2222 (B)

Club Secretary J C W Downham, 216 London Road, Leftwich, Northwich, Cheshire. CW9 8AQ
01606 48962 (H), 01565 633294 (B)

Fixtures Secretary C F Gleare, Westerley, West Road, Weaverham, Northwich, Cheshire. CW8 3HH
01606 853999 (H)   01925 752016 (B)

Press Officer Bob Dean, 24 East Avenue, Rudheath, Northwich, Cheshire.
01606 43084 (H&B)

While secure in the knowledge that the side was largely intact, and had even gained valuable additions, the first season of professional rugby followed much discussion and heart searching at Winnington Park. In the event, players were not contracted, and things carried on as before. Hopefully, seeing the direction taken by other clubs would show the way ahead.

The season started badly with four defeats, injuries picked up in the first game disrupting the play for much of the season. A run of six consecutive wins brought the club to mid-way and safety, hopes began to rise but it was too late to challenge for promotion. Teams were overcome away that had succeeded at Burrows Hill, so that only Worcester and Birmingham managed the double.

Some defeats turned into landslide scores unexpectedly, but the morale stayed high and in the end it was a very respectable performance overall.

At the end of the season it turned out that the captain, having picked a date for his wedding after the league programme, ended up being married on the day of the last fixture. Being deprived of the services of Groom, Best Man and Usher, the remainder put up a good come back performance but failed to add the final points to gain a place above mid-way.

President Roy Palin had agreed to extend his period of office to cover the problems of the new game, and, having seen us through the storm, he steps down in favour of Bob Glenister, who has done wonders as chairman of the Colts.

Plans for ground improvements are showing signs of fruition, car parking and terracing have improved, and a stand may at last be a feature.

Winnington intend to maintain all sides, and continue to pursue Mini and Junior rugby as the life blood and future of the game.

Winnington Park v Wasps in 5th Round of Pilkington Cup

Colours: Royal & navy blue

Change colours: Red.

WINNINGTON PARK

COURAGE LEAGUE MATCH DETAILS 1996-97

No	Ven.	Date	Opponents	Att.	Res.	Score	Scorers
1	(A)	31.08	v Sandal		L	20-21	Farr(2t)Marshall(t)Hill(cp)
2	(H)	07.09	v Stourbridge		L	20-42	Gibson(t)Owens(t)Campbell(t)Bell(cp)
3	(H)	21.09	v Hereford		L	23-24	Barton(t)Ashall(t)Bell(tc2p)
4	(A)	28.09	v Aspatria		L	22-30	Barton(t)Farr(t)Taylor(t)Bell(2cp)
5	(H)	05.10	v Sheffield		D	21-21	Barton(t)PenT(t)Bell(c3p)
6	(A)	19.10	v Nuneaton		W	25-16	Staley(2t)PenT(t)Bell(2c2p)
7	(H)	26.10	v Stoke O T		W	23-10	Alcock(t)Davies(t)Bell(tc2p)
8	(H)	09.11	v Manchester		W	23-16	Bird(2t)Davies(t)Bell(c2p)
9	(H)	16.11	v Worcester		L	27-32	Campbell(2t)Owens(t)Bell(3c2p)
10	(H)	28.12	v Birmingham S		L	15-22	Bird(2t)Hill(cp)
11	(H)	11.01	v Preston G		W	10- 3	Basnett(t)Hill(cp)
12	(A)	18.01	v Kendal		L	13-16	Davies(t)Basnett(t)Bell(p)
13	(H)	25.01	v Sandal		W	20-15	Yardley(t)Owens(t)Bell(2c2p)
14	(A)	01.02	v Stourbridge		W	20-11	Bebbington(t)Yardley(t)Nicholls(t)(cp)
15	(A)	08.02	v Hereford		W	63- 5	Owens(3t)Edwards(t)Yardley(t)Davies(t)Farr(t)Bird(t)Bell(2t5cp)
16	(H)	15.02	v Aspatria		W	40-19	Yardley(3t)Hill(c)Bell(2t2c3p)
17	(A)	22.02	v Sheffield		W	31-18	Bird(2t)Owens(t)Taylor(t)Hill(dg)Bell(c2p)
18	(H)	01.03	v Nuneaton		L	0-37	
19	(A)	08.03	v Stoke on Trent		W	28-16	Barton(t)Bird(t)Campbell(t)Bell(2c2p)Hill(dg)
20	(H)	15.03	v Manchester		W	46-31	Barton(3t)Bebbington(t)Bird(t)Bell(t5c2p)
21	(A)	22.03	v Worcester		L	23-28	Owens(2t)Bell(2c2p)Hill(dg)
22	(H)	05.04	v Kendal		W	24-13	Davies(t)Barton(t)Bell(t3cp)
23	(A)	12.04	v Birmingham S		L	24-34	Basnett(t)Sproston(t)Green(t)Bell(t2c)
24	(H)	19.04	v Lichfield		W	36-25	Campbell(2t)Owens(t)Green(t)Bell(2t3c)
25	(A)	26.04	v Preston G		W	27-20	Yardley(2t)Davies(t)Bell(3p)Hill(dg)
26	(A)	03.05	v Lichfield		L	27-40	Shillabeer(t)Lloyd(t)Yardley(t)Owens(t)Barton(t)Bell(c)

1996-97 HIGHLIGHTS

LEAGUE DEBUTS:

PLAYERS USED: 34 plus four as replacement only.

EVER PRESENT: Ian Taylor and Ian Davies.

❏ Most points in a match
23 Gary Bell v Hereford 08.02.97 (A)
23 Gary Bell v Aspatria 15.02.97 (H)
21 Gary Bell v Manchester 15.03.97 (H)

❏ Hat trick of tries in a match
3 Jez Owens v Hereford 08.02.97 (A)
3 Nick Yardley v Aspatria 15.02.97 (H)
3 Ben Barton v Manchester 15.03.97 (H)

❏ Lost first four games of season before finding their form. Finished strongly losing just four of last 14.

❏ Were the only team to do the double over third placed Preston Grasshoppers.

❏ Most points in the season

Pts	Player	T	C	P	D
240	Gary Bell	11	40	35	-
55	Jez Owens	11	-	-	-
45	Ben Barton	9	-	-	-
45	Adrian Bird	9	-	-	-
45	Nick Yardley	9	-	-	-

❏ Most appearances
26 Ian Taylor and Ian Davies
25 Gary Bell
23 Jez Owens and Adrian Bird
22 Mike Bebbington
21 Matthew Farr and Dave Nicholls
20 Dave Alcock (1)

❏ Had more players with over 20 appearances, nine, than any other side in National League Four North and South.

WINNINGTON PARK'S COURAGE LEAGUE MATCH DETAILS 1996-97

	15	14	13	12	11	10	9	1	2	3	4	5	6	7	8	Replacements
1	Hall	Basnett	M Farr	Gibson	Bird	Hill	Pickering	Alcock	Taylor	Davies	Jones	Haddock	Bebbington	Yardley	David	David(10)
2	Owens	Bird	M Farr	Gibson	Ashall	Hill	Pickering	Alcock	Taylor	Davies	Haddock	Thomas	Bebbington	Yardley	Marshall	Conwood(1)
3	Gibson	Basnett	M Farr	Gibson	David	Hill	Bell	Alcock	Taylor	Davies	Nicholls	Haddock	Bebbington	Yardley	Potts	Marshall( )
4	Edwards	Higson	Barton	M Farr	Ashall	Hill	Samir	Alcock	Taylor	Davies	Haddock	Haddock	Potts	Marshall	Bebbington	Bryant(14)
5	Gibson	Owens	Barton	Edwards	Bell	Hill	Campbell	Alcock	Taylor	Davies	Nicholls	Haddock	Bebbington	Yardley	Sproston	
6	Owens	Basnett	M Farr	Barton	Bell	Hill	Pickering	Alcock	Taylor	Davies	Nicholls	Haddock	Jones	Staley	Bebbington	Ashall(9)
7	Owens	Basnett	M Farr	Barton	Bird	Bell	Samir	Alcock	Taylor	Davies	Nicholls	Haddock	Sproston	Bebbington	Bebbington	
8	Owens	Basnett	M Farr	Barton	Bird	Bell	Campbell	Alcock	Taylor	Davies	Nicholls	Sproston	Sproston	Staley	Bebbington	
9	Owens	Basnett	Barton	Barton	Bell	Bell	Campbell	Alcock	Taylor	Davies	Haddock	Sproston	Sproston	Staley	Bebbington	
10	Edwards	M Farr	Owens	Owens	Bird	Hill	Campbell	Alcock	Taylor	Davies	Nicholls	Green	Sproston	Staley	Bebbington	
11	Basnett	M Farr	Owens	Owens	Bird	Hill	Campbell	Alcock	Taylor	Davies	Nicholls	Green	Sproston	Yardley	Bebbington	Potts(8)
12	Basnett	M Farr	Owens	Owens	Bird	Hill	Bell	Alcock	Taylor	Davies	Nicholls	Green	Sproston	Staley	Staley	Potts(6)
13	Basnett	M Farr	Owens	Owens	Bird	Hill	Pickering	Alcock	Taylor	Davies	Haddock	Green	Hasler	Yardley	Bebbington	
14	Basnett	M Farr	Owens	Owens	Bird	Hill	Samir	Alcock	Taylor	Davies	Nicholls	Green	Staley	Yardley	Bebbington	Hall(11)Bocock(7)
15	Edwards	M Farr	Owens	Owens	Bird	Hill	Campbell	Alcock	Taylor	Davies	Nicholls	Green	Staley	Yardley	Bebbington	Hasler(8)
16	Edwards	M Farr	Owens	Owens	Bird	Hill	Campbell	Alcock	Taylor	Davies	Nicholls	Green	Staley	Yardley	Sproston	Hall(15)
17	Edwards	M Farr	Owens	Owens	Bird	Hill	Campbell	Alcock	Taylor	Davies	Nicholls	Green	Sposton	Yardley	Staley	
18	Bell	M Farr	Owens	Barton	Bird	Hill	Campbell	Alcock	Taylor	Davies	Nicholls	Green	Sproston	Bebbington	Bebbington	Haddock(4)
19	Bell	Hall	Owens	Barton	Bird	Hill	Campbell	Alcock	Taylor	Davies	Nicholls	Green	Sproston	Staley	Bebbington	
20	Bell	Hall	Owens	Barton	Bird	Hill	Campbell	Alcock	Taylor	Davies	Nicholls	Green	Sproston	Staley	Bebbington	Hasler(6)
21	Bell	Edwards	Owens	Barton	Bird	Hill	Campbell	Potts	Taylor	Davies	Nicholls	Hasler	Yardley	Staley	Bebbington	Alcock(1)
22	Bird	M Farr	Owens	Barton	Bird	Hill	Campbell	Alcock	Taylor	Davies	Nicholls	Green	Sproston	Bebbington	Bebbington	Haddock(4)
23	Basnett	Hall	Owens	Bird	Bird	Hill	Campbell	Potts	Taylor	Davies	Bebbington	Green	Sprostron	Yardley	Staley	Bocock(5)Ashall(13)
24	Bird	Owens	Hall	Barton	Bird	Hill	Campbell	Potts	Taylor	Davies	Nicholls	Green	Hasler	Yardley	Bebbington	
25	Bird	Owens	Hall	Barton	Hill	Hill	Campbell	Alcock	Taylor	Davies	Nicholls	Green	Hasley	Yardley	Sproston	Basnett(14)Potts(7)
26	Bird	Owens	Barton	Barton	Shilabeer	Lloyd	Campbell	Gleave	Taylor	Davies	Nicholls	Hasler	Bebbington	Yardley	Sproston	P Conwood(1)

WINNINGTON PARK LEAGUE STATISTICS
(COMPILED BY STEPHEN McCORMACK)

Season	Div.	P	W	D	L	F	A	PD	Pts	Pos.	Coach	Captain
87-88	NORTH1	10	8	0	2	211	74	137	16	1p	D Hill	K Curbishley
88-89	ALN	10	5	0	5	188	155	33	10	5	D Hill	R Allcock
89-90	ALN	10	4	0	6	142	152	-10	8	9	D Hill	R Allcock
90-91	D4N	12	7	1	4	167	148	19	15	4	D Hill	R Allcock
91-92	D4N	12	4	1	7	159	173	-14	9	8	D Hill	M Farr
92-93	D4N	12	5	1	6	167	165	2	11	10	D Hill	M Farr
93-94	D5N	12	6	1	5	227	132	95	13	4	V Murphy	D Nichols
94-95	D5N	12	5	1	6	173	214	-41	11	8	V Murphy	D Nichols
95-96	D5N	12	8	0	4	225	215	10	16	4	D Hill	
96-97	D4N	26	14	1	11	651	565	86	29	7	D Hill	
Total		128	66	6	46	2310	1993	317				

CLUB SPONSORED BY:
NALCO LIMITED

Founded 1907

W.P.R.U.F.C.

NATIONAL LEAGUE DIVISION 4 NORTH
WINNINGTON PARK R.F.C.

JANUARY 1996 - WINNINGTON PARK v WASPS IN 5th ROUND OF PILKINGTON CUP

FIRST XV SPONSORED BY
HEWLETT PACKARD

OFFICIAL PROGRAMME

PROGRAMME DETAILS

SIZE: A5   **PRICE:** With admission.

PAGES: 28 plus cover.

PPROGRAMME EDITOR: J J Palmer 01606 75817

ADVERTISING RATES
Full page £150, half page £75.

CLUB & GROUND DETAILS

Address: Burrows Hill, Hartford, Northwich, Cheshire. CW8 3AA.
Tel. Nos. 01606 74242

Capacity: 5000   **Seated:** None   **Standing:** 5000
Simple Directions: One mile from Hartford turn off A556, signed for Hartford, near Blue Weaver bridge. Turn right at church, left at the lights, right at T junction, then next left. Burrows Hill ground is second on the right.
Nearest Railway Station: Hartford.
Car Parking: 500 spaces are available on the ground.
Admission: Season - Adult £30. Matchdays - Adults £3. Children U13 Free. OAPs: £1
Clubhouse: Open matchdays & training nights, snacks available. Functions for up to 100 people can be catered for.
Training Nights: Tuesday and Thursday.

DIVISION FOUR NORTH

(PREVIOUSLY ALSO DIVISION FIVE NORTH & THIS YEAR'S LEAGUE TWO NORTH)

RECORDS SECTION

DIVISION FOUR NORTH - THE LAST TEN YEARS

	Champions	Runners-up	Relegated
1987-88	**RUGBY**	DURHAM	Derby, Solihull, Birkenhead P
1988-89	**ROUNDHAY**	BROUGHTON PARK	Birmingham
1989-90	**BROUGHTON PARK**	MORLEY	None
1990-91	**OTLEY**	LICHFIELD	Stoke on Trent, Birmingham S
1991-92	**ASPATRIA**	HEREFORD	Vale of Lune, Northern
1992-93	**HARROGATE**	ROTHERHAM	Towcestrians
1993-94	**ROTHERHAM**	PRESTON G.	Bradford & Bingley, Durham City
1994-95	**WALSALL**	KENDAL	Hereford, Barker's Butts
1995-96	**WHARFDALE**	WORCESTER	Broughton Park
1996-97	**WORCESTER**	BIRMINGHAM S	Hereford, Stoke on Trent

	Most Points		Most Tries
1987-88	118 Steve Kerry (Preston)	7	Eddie Saunders (Rugby)
1988-89	94 Jamie Grayshon (Morley)	10	Jim Mallinder (Roundhay)
1989-90	78 Jamie Grayshon (Morley)	5	Paul White (Morley)
1990-91	105 Paul Grayson (Preston)	16	Jon Walker (Otley)
1991-92	127 Paul Grayson (Preston)	7	Jimmy Miller (Aspatria)
1992-93	131 Ralph Zoing	9	Guy Easterby (Harrogate) Steve Baker (Harrogate)
1993-94	118 Kevin Plant (Rotherham)	8	John Dudley (Rotherham)
1994-95	164 Richard Mills (Walsall)	11	Jon Rowe (Walsall)
1995-96	143 Alex Howarth (Wharfedale)	10	Neil Hezeltine (Wharfedale) Spencer Bradley (Worcester)
1996-97	317 Steve Kerry (Preston G)	18	Nick Baxter (Worcester)

	Most Penalties	Most Conversions	Most Drop Goals
1987-88	21 Steve Kerry (Preston)	12 Steve Kerry (Preston) Chris Howard (Rugby)	5 Steve Kerry (Preston)
1988-89	23 Jamie Grayshon (Morley)	13 Gary Walker (Roundhay)	2 Jamie Grayshon (Morley)
1989-90	15 Jamie Grayshon (Morley)	8 Jamie Grayshon (Morley)	3 Jamie Grayshon (Morley)
1990-91	28 Paul Grayson (Preston)	17 Jon Howarth (Otley)	4 Richard Mills (Walsall)
1991-92	25 Paul Grayson (Preston)	13 Andrew Harrison (Aspatria)	6 Paul Grayson (Preston)
1992-93	31 Simon Pennington (Stourbridge)	28 Ralph Zoing (Harrogate)	N/A
1993-94	23 Richard Mills (Walsall)	22 Kevin Plant (Rotherham)	N/A
1994-95	31 Richard Mills (Walsall)	29 Richard Mills (Walsall)	N/A
1995-96	29 Alex Howarth (Wharfedale)	23 Alex Howarth (Wharfedale)	3 Warwick Masser (Nuneaton)
1996-97	64 Steve Kerry (Preston G)	61 Tim Smith (Worcester)	9 Steve Kerry (Preston G)

Team Records

Highest score:	Kendal 82 Hereford 7. 12.4.97
Highest aggregate:	91: Sheffield 76 Lichfield 15. 7.9.96
Highest score by a losing side:	Nuneaton 40 Aspatria 38. 9.11.96
Highest scoring draw:	23-23 Manchester v Worcester 7.9.96
	Sheffield v Preston 8.2.97
Most consecutive wins:	15 Worcester 1996-97
Most consecutive defeats:	18 Stoke on Trent 1996-97
Most points for in a season:	830 Worcester 1996-97
Least points for in a season:	29 Birmingham 1988-89
Most points against in a season:	972 Hereford 1996-97
Least points against in a season:	67 Roundhay 1987-88
Most tries for in a season:	112 Worcester 1996-97
Most tries against in a season:	131 Hereford 1996-97
Most conversions for in a season:	72 Worcester 1996-97
Most conversions against in a season:	82 Hereford 1996-97
Most penalties for in a season:	73 Sheffield 1996-97
Most penalties against in a season:	60 Winnington Park 1996-97
Most drop goals for in a season:	10 Preston Grasshoppers 1996-97
Most drop goals against in a season:	8 Aspatria 1996-97

Individual Records

Most points in a season:	317 Steve Kerry (Preston G) 1996-97
Most tries in a season:	18 Nick Baxter (Worcester) 1996-97
Most conversions in a season:	61 Tim Smith (Worcester) 1996-97
Most penalties in a season:	64 Steve Kerry (Preston G) 1996-97
Most drop goals in a season:	9 Steve Kerry (Preston G) 1996-97
Most points in a match:	44 Jamie Morley, **Sheffield** v Lichfield 7.9.97
Most tries in a match:	6 Simon Verbickas, **Sale** v Otley 12.2.94
Most conversions in a match:	9 Ralph Zoing, **Harrogate** v Towcestriamns 13.3.93
	Kevin Plant, **Rotherham** v Durham 19.2.94
Most penalties in a match:	8 Steve Baker, **Stourbridge** v Hereford 26.1.91
Most drop goals in a match:	4 Steve Kerry, **Preston G** v Aspatria 7.9.96

DIVISION FOUR NORTH - TEN YEAR RECORD

	87/88	88/89	89/90	90/91	91/92	92/93	93/94	94/95	95/96	96/97
Aspatria	-	-	-	-	1	-	-	-	-	10
Birkenhead P.	9	-	-	-	-	-	-	-	-	-
Birmingham	-	11	-	13	-	-	9	10	3	2
Broughton Park	6	2	1	-	-	-	-	-	13	-
Derby	10	-	-	-	-	-	-	-	-	-
Durham City	2	7	4	10	10	8	12	-	-	-
Harrogate	-	-	-	6	7	1	-	-	-	-
Hereford	-	-	-	11	2	11	8	13	-	13
Kendal	-	-	5	5	3	6	10	2	9	9
Lichfield	8	9	7	2	5	5	7	5	12	11
Manchester	-	-	-	-	-	-	-	-	-	4
Northern	5	4	8	7	13	-	-	-	-	-
Nuneaton	-	-	-	-	-	12	11	11	10	12
Preston G.	4	6	6	3	4	3	2	3	8	3
Otley	-	-	-	1	-	-	-	-	-	-
Morley	-	8	2	-	-	-	-	-	-	-
Barkers Butts	-	-	-	-	-	-	-	12	-	-
Bradford & Bingley	-	-	-	-	-	-	13	-	-	-
Rotherham	-	-	-	-	-	2	1	-	-	-
Roundhay	3	1	-	-	-	-	-	-	-	-
Rugby	1	-	-	-	-	-	-	-	-	-
Sandal	-	-	-	-	-	-	-	-	6	5
Sheffield	-	-	-	-	-	-	-	9	5	8
Stoke on Trent	-	10	11	12	-	4	6	7	11	14
Stourbridge	7	3	3	8	6	9	5	6	7	6
Solihull	11	-	-	-	-	-	-	-	-	-
Towcestrians	-	-	-	-	9	13	-	-	-	-
Walsall	-	-	10	9	11	7	3	1	-	-
Winnington Park	-	5	9	4	8	10	4	8	4	7
Worcester	-	-	-	-	-	-	-	-	2	1
Vale of Lune	-	-	-	-	13	-	-	-	-	-
Wharfedale	-	-	-	-	-	-	4	1	-	-

JEWSON

NATIONAL

League Two South

1996-97 DIVISION FOUR SOUTH

PLAYING RECORD & breakdown

	Pd	W	D	L	Pts	HOME W	D	L	Pts	AWAY W	D	L	Pts
Newbury	25	25	0	0	50	12	0	0	4	13	0	0	26
Henley	26	20	2	4	42	10	1	2	21	10	1	2	21
Barking	26	16	1	9	33	8	1	4	17	8	0	5	16
Camberley	26	15	2	9	32	8	1	4	17	7	1	5	15
Cheltenham	26	15	2	9	32	7	2	5	16	8	0	5	16
Plymouth	26	13	3	10	29	10	0	3	20	3	3	7	9
Met. Police	26	14	1	11	29	7	0	6	14	7	1	5	15
Tabard	26	10	3	13	23	6	2	5	14	4	1	8	9
Weston-s-Mare	26	11	0	15	22	7	0	6	14	4	0	9	8
N. Walsham	26	10	1	15	21	6	1	6	13	4	0	9	8
Berry Hill	26	10	0	16	20	8	0	5	16	2	0	11	4
High Wycombe	26	8	1	17	17	7	0	6	14	1	1	11	3
Charlton Park	26	3	1	22	7	1	1	11	3	2	0	11	4
Askeans	25	2	1	22	5	1	0	12	2	1	1	11	3

POINTS FOR & breakdown

	Lge Pos	Pts	T	C	P	D	HOME Pts	T	C	P	D	AWAY Pts	T	C	P	D
1 Newbury	1	1170	167	103	42	1	654	96	60	18	0	516	71	43	24	1
2 Henley	2	768	112	53	29	5	421	62	30	14	3	347	50	23	15	2
3 Barking	3	740	100	54	43	1	373	52	28	19	0	367	48	26	24	1
4 Plymouth	6	709	102	56	24	5	484	70	40	15	3	225	32	16	9	2
5 Camberley	4	688	92	51	38	4	437	62	38	14	3	251	30	13	24	1
6 Met. Police	7	661	82	46	52	1	377	45	25	34	0	284	37	21	18	1
7 High Wycombe	12	560	65	32	54	3	305	35	20	28	2	255	30	12	26	1
8 Cheltenham	5	559	71	39	35	7	284	35	20	19	4	275	36	19	16	3
9 Tabard	8	511	52	37	56	3	270	27	21	29	2	241	25	16	27	1
10 Weston-s-Mare	9	482	50	29	48	10	269	30	16	23	6	213	20	13	25	4
11 N. Walsham	10	426	54	21	38	0	263	32	14	25	0	163	22	7	13	0
12 Berry Hill	11	425	43	21	56	0	281	29	14	36	0	144	14	7	20	0
13 Charlton Park	13	352	45	23	26	1	220	27	14	18	1	132	18	9	8	0
14 Askeans	14	340	34	19	44	0	181	17	9	26	0	159	17	10	18	0

POINTS AGAINST & breakdown

	Lge Pos	Pts	T	C	P	D	HOME Pts	T	C	P	D	AWAY Pts	T	C	P	D
1 Newbury	1	295	36	14	26	3	133	17	6	10	2	162	19	8	16	1
2 Cheltenham	5	420	44	22	50	2	170	15	7	25	2	250	29	15	25	0
3 Henley	2	456	46	29	55	1	215	22	15	24	1	241	24	14	31	0
4 Barking	3	496	58	31	48	0	214	26	12	20	0	282	32	19	28	0
=5 Weston-s-Mare	9	515	60	34	45	4	225	27	15	19	1	290	33	19	26	3
=5 Camberley	4	515	64	30	41	4	222	26	13	20	2	293	38	17	21	2
7 Tabard	8	557	67	39	46	2	214	24	14	20	2	347	43	25	26	0
8 Met. Police	7	558	67	35	46	5	255	28	17	24	3	303	39	18	22	2
9 Plymouth	6	591	78	39	41	0	233	31	15	16	0	358	47	24	25	0
10 N. Walsham	10	605	79	42	37	5	296	41	23	14	1	309	38	19	23	4
11 Berry Hill	11	643	79	46	46	6	230	25	15	24	1	413	54	31	22	5
12 High Wycombe	12	707	97	51	36	4	317	45	22	16	0	390	52	29	20	4
13 Askeans	14	893	129	76	29	3	388	57	32	11	2	505	72	44	18	1
14 Charlton Park	13	1140	166	95	38	2	460	66	29	24	0	680	100	66	14	2

1996-97 DIVISION FOUR SOUTH

REVIEW

This was a one horse race if ever there was one.

Newbury were unbeaten throughout the season winning all 25 League games played, their final home fixture with Askean being void as the visiters were unable to field a side; they finished eight points clear of Henley.

Newbury, with director of rugby Terry Burwell at the helm, were easily the strongest side in the division and scored heavily throughout. They had the two top try scorers in National League rugby in England 'A' and the Army winger Brian Johnson and No 8 Craig Davies who scored 27 and 23 tries respectively. Full back Nick Grecian with 391 points was the second highest points scorer in League rugby after Fylde's Steve Gough.

Second place **Henley** went one better than the previous season. They lost their top points scorer Richard Perkins early in the season with injury after which he left the club. Injuries were a problem as they were unable to get a settled side. Late in the season winger Chris Spencer was a revelation, scoring 121 points in eight games.

Third placed **Barking** also went one better than the previous season. After an indifferent start, they came on strongly winning ten of their last eleven games including two wins over Cheltenham and one over Henley. Three of the nine defeats were by a point. Top try scorer was hooker Chris Tate with an excellent tally of fourteen.

Cheltenham too went one better than the previous season and achieved their highest ever league position. Their problem was that they failed to score enough tries, just 71, eighth best in the division. They started the campaign well winning thirteen out of sixteen before going into an end of season slump which saw them lose seven out of eight and slip down the table. They won more games away from home than at home and had the second best defensive record in the division after Newbury in terms of both points and tries conceded.

Camberley were another side to improve on last season's standing and achieved their highest ever league finish in fourth. They had a stop-start season with a mid season slump in which they managed just one win in seven. Twice scoring over 90 points in a League match, they were the only National League team to do so. The new half back partnership of Jason Hoad, ex-Richmond stand off, and Chris Hemming, an ex-Wasps scrum half, gave the side stability. Also impressive were winger Rory Jones and utility back Craig Greville.

Plymouth consolidated well after dropping a division the previous season; scoring tries was not a problem as they were third on the list with 102. Their problem was away from home, but that's nothing new, with just three wins from thirteen against a 10-3 home record.

Stand-off Martin Thompson finished top scorer and extended his career record to 439 whilst winger Steve Walklin set a new record for tries in a season, twelve, and extended his career record to 43.

Metropolitan Police's season was a tale of two halves. They started the season well with eleven wins in fifteen games - not bad by anyone's standards. The second half saw just three wins from eleven. They won more points away from home than at home. Back row forward Richard Galvin finished top try scorer with eleven, whilst winger Eddie Weatherley set a new club record of five tries in a game in the away fixture at Askean. Stand-off Mark Slevin had a highly productive season with 223 points at an average of just over ten per game.

Tabard had a real stop-start season which began badly with just one win from their first seven games. They relied heavily on stand-off Nick Churchman whose 264 points was over 50 of Tabard's League total of 511.

Churchman was the second highest scorer in the division after Newbury's Nick Grecian. Newbury had a settled side with 47 players used, but they only achieved one win against a team which finished above them when they beat Met. Police at home.

Weston-super-Mare suffered early on in the season with prolific points scorer Paul Thatcher being unavailable on a number of occasions. But they had good wins over Henley, Met. Police and Camberley to secure their league position, and they had the fifth best defensive record in terms of both points and tries conceded.

North Walsham escaped relegation by just one point thanks to a late surge of form which saw them win six of their last nine games, including a double over Met. Police. They lacked a consistent goal kicker with five players having a go but none of them having the consistency to do the job week in week out.

Berry Hill went into their last game of the season needing to beat Camberley to stave off relegation. They had won their previous six home games and won at Camberley a couple of weeks earlier but it was not to be and they lost narrowly and were relegated.

High Wycombe ended their six year stay in the division thanks to the worst away record in the competition along with bottom club Askean. They were another side who chopped and changed their goal kicker around and had two players score over 100 points, Chris Wyatt and Simon Shaw.

Charlton Park were relegated in their first season of National League rugby. They managed just three wins and although relegation was on the cards early on they carried on trying to play rugby and had an excellent reputation for good hospitality.

Askean finished bottom and so slipped out of National League rugby for the first time. They suffered very badly from injuries and on a number of occasions just managed to field a side and in one away trip had just fifteen players. They hope to have a settled side next season and bounce back.

RECORD REVIEW

INDIVIDUAL RECORDS

MOST POINTS IN A SEASON

Newbury full back Nick Grecian re-wrote the record book with 391 points in 25 matches at an average of 15.64 points per match. Gracian more than doubled the previous record of 176 set the previous season by Henley's Richard Pekins.

69	John Field	Askeans	1987-88
83	Simon Harvey	Clifton	1989-90
122	Melvin Badger	Weston-s-Mare	1990-91
129	Pete Russell	Havant	1991-92
133	Phil Belshaw	Reading	1993-94
176	Richard Perkins	Henley	1995-96
391	Nick Grecian	Newbury	1996-97

MOST TRIES IN A SEASON

Three Newbury players were among the six players who broke the previous record of 12 tries in a season set in the 1'992-93 season bu Sudbury's Steve Titcombe. Topping the list in 1996-97 was England A winger Brian Johnson with 27 tries, which included five hat-tricks.

7	john Willis	Redruth	1988-89
8	Melvin Badger	Weston-s-Mare	1990-91
9	Will Knight	Havant	1991-92
12	Steve Titcombe	Sudbury	1992-93
27	Brian Johnson	Newbury	1996-97

MOST CONVERSIONS IN A SEASON

Another record for Newbury kicking machine Nick Grecian who converted 100 of his sides 167 tries. This easily broke the previous record of 28 set by London Welsh's Mike Hamlin during the 1992-93 season.

9	John Field	Askeans	1987-88
10	Simon harvey	Clifton	1989-90
16	Simon Blake	Redruth	1990-91
23	Pete Russelll	Havant	1991-92
28	Mike hamlin	London Welsh	1992-93
100	Nick Grecian	Newbury	1996-97

MOST PENALTIES IN A SEASON

The record of 34 was beaten during the season by four players. Topping the list was Tabard stand-off Nick Churchman with 53. The previous record was set by Reading's Phil Belshaw during the 1993-94 season.

13	John Field	Askeans	1987-88
15	Simon Harvey	Clifton	1989-90
27	Rob Ashworth	Havant	1990-91
34	Phil Belshaw	Reading	1993-94
53	Nick Churchman	Tabard	1996-97

MOST DROP GOALS IN A SEASON

Weston-super-Mare's Simon Cattermole dropped 10 goals, including four in a match, to nearly double the previous record of six which was achieved by Clifton's Simon Harvey during their Championship season 1989-90.

Evolution of record

2	Andy Perry	Havant	1987-88
	Andy Perry	Havant	1988-89
6	Simon Harvey	Clifton	1989-90
10	Simon Cattermole	Weston-s-Mare	1996-97

PLAYERS USED

	Players used	1	Ever present	
Askeans	44(2)	8.5	-	
Barking	33(2)	11.8	-	
Berry Hill	33(4)	11.8	1	Pete Baldwin
Camberley	47(5)	8.3	-	
Charlton Park	50(1)	7.8	-	
Cheltenham	44(1)	8.7	-	
Henley	41(3)	9.5	-	
High Wycombe	42(1)	9.3	1	Simon Shaw
Met. Police	32(3)	12.3	-	
Newbury	32(3)	11.7	2	Colin Hall
				Nick Grecian
North Walsham	40(5)	9.7	-	
Plymouth	43(1)	9.1	1	Stuart Coleman
Tabard	47(4)	8.3	-	
Weston-s-Mare	42(2)	9.3	-	

1 - Average Appearances per player.

Newbury used just 32 players in winning the Division Four South title - the joint lowest figure in the division with seventh placed Metropolitan Police.

There were only five ever-presents in this division - the lowest of any of the national leagues.

	1	2	Ever Presents
DIVISION ONE	36.7	9.0	8
DIVISION TWO	37.3	8.8	11
DIVISION THREE	39.6	11.4	13
DIVISION FOUR SOUTH	37.9	10.3	5
DIVISION FOUR NORTH	38.6	10.1	10

1 - Average number of players used.
2 - Average number of matches per player.

FAIR PLAY LEAGUE

This is another new feature which we will publish each season and hopefully get the RFU to make part of their awards evening.

Cambereley topped the Division Four South Fair Play League with just one yellow card. The player who let the side down was lock Gary Hamer.

Of the players sent off in the division only two were backs - Barking's captain and scrum-half Dean Cutting, and Weston's stand-off Simon Cattermole.

Team	Yellow card	Red card	Total
Camberley	1	-	5
High Wycombe	4	-	20
North Walsham	4	-	20
Newbury	6	-	30
Plymouth	6	-	30
Met. Police	4	1	30
Berry Hill	7	-	35
Cheltenham	3	2	35
Barking	6	1	40
Henley	6	1	40
Charlton Park	7	1	45
Tabard	6	2	50
Weston-s-Mare	4	3	50
Askeans	7	2	55

DIVISION FOUR SOUTH PLAYERS SENT OFF

Simon Cattermole	Weston-s-M v Cheltenham 31.8.96
John Morris	Cheltenham v N. Walsham 21.9.96
Jed Sjollema	Tabard v Cheltenham 28.9.96
David Wilkie	Askeans v Weston-s-M 5.10.96
Steve Brain	Cheltenham v Plymouth 26.10.96
Andy Cunningham	Weston-s-M v Berry Hill 16.11.96
Dean Cutting	Barking v Weston-s-M 21.12.96
Jerry Stevens	Askeans v Tabard 16.3.97
Matthew Ford	Weston-s-M v Barking 5.4.97
Jason Lambert-Williams	Charlton P. v Askeans 5.4.97
Sean O'Leary	Henley v Cheltenham 29.4.97
Colin Bickle	Tabard v Berry Hill 3.5.97

A trio of Captains

MALCOLM PREEDY - Cheltenham Captain 1997-98.
Photo: Courtesy Gloucestershire Echo, Cheltenham.

RICHARD THOMPSON - Plymouth Albion Captain
& 1st XV Player of the Year. Andy Birkett looks on.
Photo: Courtesy Evening Herald, Plymouth.

MARK WELLS - Havant Captain 1997-98.　　　　　　　　　　Photo: Courtesy Portsmouth News.

1996-97 DIVISION FOUR SOUTH

MOST TRIES

27	Brian Johnson	Newbury
25	Craig Davies	Newbury
19	Tom Holloway	Newbury
14	Chris Tate	Barking
14	Nick Thomson	Barking
13	Craig Greville	Camberley
12	Matt Maudsley	Henley
12	Steve Walklin	Plymouth
12	Gavin Sharp	Henley
11	Chris Spencer	Henley
11	Ian Russell	Plymouth
11	Colin Hall	Newbury
11	Richard Galvin	Met Police
10	Ben Siaw	Barking
10	Rory Jones	Camberley
10	Willie Phillips	Henley
10	Andy Carter	Met Police
10	Tom Rains	Norht Walsham
10	Richard Thompson	Plymouth
9	Kerry Mapps	Berry Hill

MOST CONVERSIONS

100	Nick Grecian	Newbury
38	Nick Thomson	Barking
37	Mark Slevin	Met Police
36	Jason Hoad	Camberley
31	Nick Churchman	Tabard
30	Martin Thompson	Plymouth
28	Matt Maudsley	Henley
23	Paul Thatcher	Weston super Mare
19	Nick Birt	Plymouth
18	John Field	Charlton Park
17	Mike Crisp	Cheltenham
17	Matthew Watts	Cheltenham
13	Chris Wyatt	High Wycombe
12	Gary Cutting	Barking
12	Mike Mallalieu	Camberley
12	Chris Spencer	Henley
11	Simon Shaw	High Wycombe
10	Lee Osborne	Berry Hill
9	James Herring	Met Police
7	Steve Tunnicliffe	Askeans
7	Jon Perrins	North Walsham
6	Jeff Powell	Berry Hill
6	Richard Perkins	Henley
6	James Shanahan	North Walsham
6	Richard Thompson	Plymouth

MOST PENALTIES

53	Nick Churchman	Tabard
42	Mark Slevin	Met Police
42	Nick Grecian	Newbury
36	Paul Thatcher	Weston super Mare
34	Nick Thomson	Barking
22	Lee Osborne	Berry Hill
21	Simon Shaw	High Wycombe
21	Chris Wyatt	High Wycombe
21	Jeff Powell	Berry Hill
21	Mike Mallalieu	Camberley
21	John Field	Charlton Park
18	Matthew Watts	Cheltenham
14	Neil Fisher	Askeans
14	Jon Perrins	North Walsham
14	Chris Spencer	Hemley
13	Richard Larkin	Askeans
13	Jason Hoad	Camberley
13	Martin Thompson	Plymouth
12	Steve Tunnicliffe	Askeans
12	Mike Crisp	Cheltenham
11	James Shanahan	North Walsham
10	Gary Jones	Berry Hill
10	James Herring	Met Police
8	Gary Cutting	Barking
8	Matt Maudsley	Henley
7	Tony Kingsmill	North Walsham
7	Ken Cotter	High Wycombe
6	Simon Cattermole	Weston super Mare
6	Nick Birt	Plymouth
6	Stuart Dillon	North Walsham
5	Rob Hawkins	High Wycombe
4	Richard Thompson	Plymouth
4	Chris Sheryn	Weston super Mare
4	Torban Williams	Charlton Park

MOST DROP GOALS

10	Simon Cattermole	Weston super Mare
4	Martin Thompson	Plymouth
4	Jason Hoad	Camberley
3	Mike Crisp	Cheltenham
2	Phil Stanlake	Cheltenham
2	Benn Tubb	Henley
2	Chris Wyatt	High Wycombe
1	Steve Morritt	Barking
1	Matthew Watts	Cheltenham
1	Chris Holder	Henley
1	Phil New	Newbury
1	Rupert Potter	Henley
1	Richard Perkins	Henley
1	Ken Cotter	High Wycombe
1	Kendal Smith	Newbury
1	Andy Birkitt	Plymouth
1	Nick Churchman	Tabard
1	Giles Hewson	Tabard
1	Andy Elliott	Tabard
1	Mark Slevin	Met Police
1	Torban Williams	Charlton Park

1996-97 DIVISION FOUR SOUTH

MOST POINTS IN THE SEASON

POINTS	PLAYER	CLUB	Tries	Cons.	Pens.	D.G.
391	Nick Grecian	Newbury	13	100	42	-
264	Nick Churchman	Tabard	8	31	53	1
248	Nick Thomson	Barking	14	38	34	-
223	Mark Slevin	Met Police	4	37	42	1
164	Paul Thatcher	Weston super Mare	2	23	36	-
140	Matt Maudsley	Henley	12	28	8	-
138	Jason Hoad	Camberley	3	36	13	4
135	Brian Johnson	Newbury	27	-	-	-
131	Martin Thompson	Plymouth	4	30	13	4
126	Lee Osborne	Berry Hill	8	10	22	-
125	Craig Davies	Newbury	25	-	-	-
121	Chris Spencer	Henley	11	12	14	-
115	Simon Shaw	High Wycombe	6	11	21	-
114	Mike Crisp	Cheltenham	7	17	12	3
110	Chris Wyatt	High Wycombe	3	13	21	2
104	John Field	Charlton Park	1	18	21	-
95	Tom Holloway	Newbury	19	-	-	-
91	Matthew Watts	Cheltenham	-	17	18	1
87	Mike Mallallieu	Camberley	-	12	21	-
81	Nick Birt	Plymouth	5	19	6	-
75	Jeff Powell	Berry Hill	-	61	21	-
74	Richard Thompson	Plymouth	10	6	4	-
70	Chris Tate	Barking	14	-	-	-
70	James Shamahan	North Walsham	5	6	11	-
68	Gary Cutting	Barking	4	12	8	-
66	Simon Cattermole	Weston super Mare	2	4	6	10
65	Craig Greville	Camberley	13	-	-	-
61	Tony Kingsmill	North Walsham	6	5	7	-
61	Jon Perrins	North Walsham	1	7	14	-
60	Gavin Sharp	Henley	12	-	-	-
60	Steve Walklin	Plymouth	12	-	-	-
59	Andy Parton	Henley	8	5	3	-
55	Steve Tunnicliffe	Askeans	1	7	12	-
55	Richard Galvin	Met Police	12	-	-	-
55	Colin Hall	Newbury	11	-	-	-
55	Ian Russell	Plymouth	11	-	-	-
53	James Herring	Met Police	1	9	10	-

BARKING R.U.F.C.

NICKNAME: **FOUNDED:** 1930

President W Marshall, 3 Halsham Crescent, Barking, Essex IG11 9HQ. 0181 594 6086 (H)
Chairman Jim Marner, 239 Wingletye Lane, Hornchurch, Essex RM1 3BL.
01708 451723 (H), 01708 858136 (B)
Club Secretary George Darley, 12 Glenton Way, Romford, Essex. RM1 4AF
01708 764828 (H)
Treasurer Keith Parker, 1 St Andrews Place, Shenfield, Essex CM15 8HH 01277 227804 (H)
Director of Rugby John Davies, 8 Eddy Close, Romford, Essex RM7 9HS
01708 750868 (H), 01708 703535 (Fax)
Fixtures Secretary Graham Comley, 0181 591 5681 (H), 0171 696 3186 (B)

Barking finished the season 1996/97 in their highest ever league position, achieving a very creditable third. This position looked unobtainable in mid-February when the club was near the relegation area, after losing three games by one point, but ten wins from the last eleven games lifted the club's position and aspirations.

The season started with the appointment of John Davies in our newly created position of director of rugby joining the first team coach Mike Lovett. The club also attracted the services of five new young players moving to the area from university, with each of them making a big contribution to the success of the team, notably Nick Thompson, Nigel Blinkinsop and Paul Everitt.

Barking also won the Air-UK Essex Cup for the fifth consecutive year beating old rivals Harlow in the final 39-21.

Barking RUFC after winning the Essex Cup for the fifth time.

Colours: Cardinal and grey hoops.   **Change colours:** Yellow.

427

BARKING

No	Ven.	Date	Opponents	Att.	Res.	Score	Scorers
1	(H)	31.08	v Camberley		L	20-21	PenT(2t)G Cutting(2c2p)
2	(A)	07.09	v Askeans		W	39-12	Siaw(t)Rasmussen(t)Goody(t)Nicholson(t)Capaert(t)G Cutting(4c2p)
3	(H)	21.09	v Plymouth		D	15-15	Thompson(5p)
4	(H)	28.09	v Newbury		L	11-35	Everitt(t)Thompson(p)D Cutting(p)
5	(H)	05.10	v High Wycombe		W	42-23	Green(2t)Siaw(t)Tate(t)Rasmussen(t)Blenkinsop(t)Thompson(t2cp)
6	(A)	19.10	v Berry Hill		L	16-27	Blenkinsop(t)Tate(t)Thompson(2p)
7	(H)	26.10	v Charlton Park		W	56-20	Morritt(t)Blenkinsop(t)Tracey(t)Diable(t)Siaw(t)Rasmussen(t)Thomson(t5c2p)
8	(H)	09.11	v Met Police		L	18-19	Everitt(t)Rasmussen(t)Thompson(c2p)
9	(A)	16.11	v Henley		L	26-27	Rasmussen(2t)Thompson(2c4p)
10	(H)	21.12	v Weston-S-M		W	25-11	G Cutting(2t)Tate(t)Thompson(2c2p)
11	(H)	18.01	v N Walsham		W	11- 5	Blenkinsop(t)Thomson(2p)
12	(A)	25.01	v Camberley		L	18-41	Everitt(t)Morritt(dg)Thomson(tp)D Cutting(c)
13	(H)	01.02	v Askeans		W	50- 7	Whiteman(t)Stannard(t)Mahoney(t)Siaw(t)Thomson(4t5c)
14	(A)	08.02	v Plymouth		L	24-44	PenTry(2t)G Cutting(t3cp)
15	(A)	15.02	v Newbury		L	18-50	Tate(2t)Everitt(t)Thomson(p)
16	(A)	22.02	v High Wycombe		W	38- 0	Tate(t)Green(t)D Utting(t)Mahoney(t)Siaw(t)Thomson(t4c)
17	(H)	01.03	v Berry Hill		W	63- 7	Tate(4t)Goody(t)Green(t)Siaw(t)Mahoney(t)D Cutting(t)Thomson(2tc)G Cutting(3c)
18	(A)	08.03	v Charlton Park		W	68- 7	Tate(2t)Stannard(t)Mahoney(t)Hannon(t)Siaw(t)Thomson(2t2cp)D Cutting(3t3c)
19	(A)	15.03	v Met Police		W	40- 6	Tate(2t)Siaw(t)Turnell(t)Everitt(t)Thomson(3c3p)
20	(H)	22.03	v Henley		W	26-15	Green(2t)Tracey(t)Thomson(t3c)
21	(A)	29.03	v Cheltenham		W	15-12	Thomson(5p)
22	(A)	05.04	v Weston-S-M		W	27-17	Siaw(t)D Cutting(t)Blenkinsop(t)Stannard(t)Thomson(tc)
23	(H)	12.04	v Cheltenham		W	19- 3	D Cutting(t)Trowbridge(t)Capaert(t)Thomson(2c)
24	(A)	19.04	v N Walsham		W	14-12	G Cutting(t)Siaw(t)Thomson(2c)
25	(H)	26.04	v Tabard		L	17-33	Capaert(2t)Thomson(2cp)
26	(A)	10.05	v Tabard		W	24-20	Goody(t)Stannard(t)Thomson(cp)D Cutting(3p)

1996-97 HIGHLIGHTS

PLAYERS USED: 33 plus two as replacement only.

EVER PRESENT: None - most 25 Dean Cutting

❏ Finished the season strongly winning 10 out of the last 11.

❏ 3rd place highest ever finsh in their league history.

❏ One of only 4 sides to score 100 tries in the season.

167	Newbury
112	Henley
102	Plymouth
100	Barking

❏ Hat trick of tries in a match

4 Nick Thomson v Askeans 01.02.97 (H)
4 Chris Tate v Berry Hill 01.03.97 (H)
3 Dean Cutting v Charlton Park 08.03.97 (A)

❏ Most points in a match

30 Nick Thomson v Askeans 01.02.97 (H)
21 Nick Thomson v Charlton Park 26.10.96 (H)
21 Dean Cutting v Charlton Park 08.03.97 (A)
20 Chris Tate v Berry Hill 01.03.97 (H)

❏ Most points in the season

Pts	Player	T	C	P	D
248	Nick Thomson	14	38	34	-
70	Chris Tate	14	-	-	-
68	Gary Cutting	4	12	8	-
51	Dean Cutting	8	4	1	-

❏ Most appearances

25 Dean Cutting
24 Chris Tate
23 Nick Thomson, Paul Everitt, Ben Siaw & Lee Stannard.
22 Paul Tracey
21 Nigel Blenkinsop

BARKING'S COURAGE LEAGUE MATCH DETAILS 1996-97

Match	15	14	13	12	11	10	9	1	2	3	4	5	6	7	8	Replacements
1	G.Cutting	Slaw	Rasmussen	Brightwell	Dilley	Mahoney	D.Cutting	Wood	Tate	Reader	Tucker	Tracey	Trowbridge	Knowles	Stone	Capaert(12)Nicholson(')
2	G.Cutting	Slaw	Rasmussen	Diable	Brightwell	Mahoney	D.Cutting	Wood	Tate	Reader	Tucker	Tracey	Trowbridge	Knowles	Stannard	
3	Thomson	Green	Rasmussen	Diable	Slaw	Mahoney	D.Cutting	Usher	Tate	Reader	Armstrong	Tracey	Everitt	Knowles	Stannard	
4	Thomson	Green	Rasmussen	Diable	Capaert	Mahoney	D.Cutting	Usher	Tate	Reader	Armstrong	Tracey	Everitt	Goody	Stannard	Bushell(15)
5	Thomson	Green	Rasmussen	Diable	Slaw	Morritt	D.Cutting	Usher	Tate	Reader	Armstrong	Tracey	Everitt	Goody	Stannard	
6	G.Cutting	Slaw	Rasmussen	Diable	Green	Morritt	D.Cutting	Blenkinsop	Tate	Reader	Armstrong	Tracey	Everitt	Goody	Stannard	
7	Thomson	Brightwell	Rasmussen	Diable	Slaw	Morritt	D.Cutting	Blenkinsop	Tate	Reader	Armstrong	Tracey	Everitt	Goody	Stannard	Ansell(3)
8	Thomson	Brightwell	Diable	G.Cutting	Slaw	Morritt	D.Cutting	Blenkinsop	Tate	Reader	Armstrong	Tracey	Everitt	Goody	Stannard	Rasmussen(13)
9	Thomson	Brightwell	Rasmussen	G.Cutting	Slaw	Morritt	D.Cutting	Blenkinsop	Tate	Reader	M.Armstrong	P.Armstrong	Everitt	Goody	Stannard	
10	Thomson	Nicholson	Rasmussen	G.Cutting	Slaw	Morritt	D.Cutting	Usher	Tate	Reader	Tucker	Tracey	Everitt	Goody	Stannard	Diable(13)Hannon(11)
11	Thomson	Nicholson	Rasmussen	Diable	Slaw	Morritt	D.Cutting	Usher	Tate	Blenkinsop	Tucker	Tracey	Everitt	Goody	Stannard	
12	Thomson	Nicholson	Brightwell	Diable	Hannon	Morritt	D.Cutting	Usher	Tate	Blenkinsop	Martin	Tracey	Everitt	Goody	Stannard	Capaert(')Mahoney(')
13	Thomson	Slaw	Brightwell	Mahoney	Green	Morritt	D.Cutting	Usher	Tate	Blenkinsop	Martin	Tracey	Everitt	Goody	Stannard	G.Cutting(13)
14	Servini	Green	Mahoney	G.Cutting	Slaw	Whiteman	D.Cutting	Usher	Tate	Reader	Tucker	Tracey	Everitt	Goody	Stannard	
15	Thomson	Green	Mahoney	G.Cutting	Slaw	Whiteman	D.Cutting	Usher	Tate	Reader	Tucker	Tracey	Everitt	Goody	Stannard	Blenkinsop(1)Morritt(11)
16	Thomson	Green	Capaert	G.Cutting	Slaw	Mahoney	D.Cutting	Blenkinsop	Tate	Reader	Martin	Tracey	Everitt	Stannard	Trowbridge	Goody(8)Capaert(14)Tucker(5)
17	Thomson	Green	Capaert	G.Cutting	Slaw	Mahoney	D.Cutting	Usher	Tate	Blenkinsop	Tucker	Tracey	Everitt	Stannard	Trowbridge	Goody(8)Hannon(15)Martin(5)
18	Thomson	Green	Turnell	G.Cutting	Slaw	Mahoney	D.Cutting	Usher	Tate	Reader	Tucker	Tracey	Everitt	Stannard	Trowbridge	Goody(8),Martin(4),Hannon(13),
19	Thomson	Green	Turnell	G.Cutting	Slaw	Mahoney	D.Cutting	Blenkinsop	Tate	Reader	Tucker	Tracey	Everitt	Stannard	Trowbridge	Goody(')
20	Thomson	Green	Turnell	G.Cutting	Slaw	Mahoney	D.Cutting	Usher	Tate	Blenkinsop	Tucker	Tracey	Everitt	Stannard	Trowbridge	Reader(2)Goody(8)
21	Thomson	Green	Turnell	G.Cutting	Slaw	Mahoney	D.Cutting	Goody	Blenkinsop	Tucker	Martin	Tracey	Everitt	Stannard	Trowbridge	Reader(1)
22	Thomson	Green	Hannon	Turnell	Slaw	Mahoney	D.Cutting	Goody	Blenkinsop	Reader	Martin	Tracey	Everitt	Stannard	Trowbridge	
23	Thomson	Green	Turnell	Capaert	Slaw	Mahoney	D.Cutting	Usher	Tate	Blenkinsop	Tucker	Martin	Everitt	Stannard	Trowbridge	
24	Thomson	Green	Turnell	G.Cutting	Slaw	Mahoney	D.Cutting	Blenkinsop	Reader	Tucker	Martin	Tracey	Everitt	Goody	Stannard	Capaert(4)
25	Thomson	Green	Turnell	Capaert	Slaw	Mahoney	D.Cutting	Blenkinsop	Reader	Tucker	Martin	Tracey	Everitt	Goody	Stannard	Stannard
26	Thomson	Green	Capaert	G.Cutting	Slaw	Mahoney	D.Cutting	Usher	Tate	Blenkinsop	Tucker	Tracey	Everitt	Goody	Stannard	Trowbridge(2)Turnell(15)

BARKING LEAGUE STATISTICS
(COMPILED BY STEPHEN McCORMACK)

Season	Div.	P	W	D	L	F	A	PD	Pts	Pos.	Coach	Captain
87-88	LON3NE	10	8	1	1	204	61	143	17	1p		
88-89	LON2N	10	7	0	3	113	103	10	*12	5	T Wright	T Reader
89-90	LON2N	10	5	1	4	141	151	-10	11	4	T Wright	T Reader
90-91	LON2N	10	8	0	2	147	94	53	16	3	T Wright	T Reader
91-92	LON2N	10	7	1	2	187	140	47	15	2p	M Lovett	T Reader
92-93	LON1	12	6	1	5	183	171	12	13	7		
93-94	LON1	12	10	1	1	290	149	141	21	1p		
94-95	D5S	12	7	0	5	223	190	33	14	5	M Lovett	D Cutting
95-96	D5S	12	8	0	4	243	187	56	16	4	M Lovett	D Cutting
96-97	D4S	26	16	1	9	740	496	244	33	3		D Cutting
Total		124	82	6	36	2471	1742	729			* 2 pts deducted.	

BARKING RUGBY CLUB

OFFICIAL PROGRAMME

PROGRAMME DETAILS

SIZE: A5   **PRICE:** With admission

PAGES: 22 plus cover

PROGRAMME EDITOR
Contact Martin Dutt 0181 518 2472

ADVERTISING RATES
Colour Full Page £500
Half Page £300

CLUB & GROUND DETAILS

Address: Goresbrook, Gale St., Dagenham, Essex RM9 4TY
Tel. Nos. 0181 595 7324
Capacity: 1,000   **Seated:** None   **Standing:** 1,000
Simple Directions: A13 from London over Ripple Road flyover, 1st turning on left at 400 yards, Gale Street.
Nearest Railway Station: Becontree BR
Car Parking: 200
Admission: Matches £ 3.00
Club Shop: Yes; Manager J Logan 0181 924 8664
Clubhouse: Normal Licensing hours, snacks available. Functions available, capacity 120.
Training Nights: Tuesdays & Thursday

BRIDGWATER & ALBION RFC

NICKNAME: The Albion

FOUNDED: 1875

President Richard Bell. 01278 424883 (B) 01278 425944 (Fax).

Chairman Chris Heal, The Old Rectory, Otterhampton, Bridgwater, Somerset. TA5 2PT.
Tel: 01278 652190 (B)

Club Secretary Chris Llewelyn, 1A Roseberry Avenue, Bridgwater, Somerset TA6 4PB
0966 287092 (Mobile) 01278 431321 (T/Fax)

Asst. Sec./ Prog. Editor Karen Llewelyn. 01278 431321 (H - T/Fax) 0966 450724 (M)

Treasurer Christine Self, 52A Wembdon Rise, Bridgwater, Somerset. TA6 7QZ.
01278 450081 (H) 01278 455622 (B)

Fixtures Secretary Ralph Sealey, 12 Capes Close, Bridgwater, Somerset. TA6 5QS.
Tel: 01278 444757 (H) - but PLEASE confirm fixtures with John Lipscombe (below)

Asst. Fix. Sec. John Lipscomb. 01278 691345 (H) 01278 445859 (B).

On the field it was a season of many up and downs, the league season got off to a bad start with a loss to Barnstaple in the first match away in Devon. The following Saturday again a loss in the Pilkington Cup to Newbury 24 points to 46 (not a bad result considering their future form). Early season also left us with a few long term injuries, which meant a need to strengthen the 1st XV squad. At the half way mark at Christmas, spirits were high and promotion to the National Leagues considered more than a possibility. Following the restart of the league programme results went our way until February, when two losses left us third in the table and with little hope. Thanks go out to last year's coach Dave Egerton and the entire squad led by captain and outside half Nick Edmonds who rallied the troops and gave the spectators some excellent displays of fifteen man rugby. In three games we made up a 200 point points deficit to give us a fighting chance again. Finally it was all down to the last game against Stroud, we had to win and finish with a better points difference than Launceston. It was done with the team giving a tremendous all round performance.

The season on the field was also marked by Bridgwater & Albion winning the Somerset Cup beating Weston Hornets in the final. Also nine of the 1st XV squad respresented Somerset in the County Cup culminating with an appearance in the final at Twickenham, unfortunately they ended up losers on that day. With a good youth policy at the club the Colts also won a local cup and the under 15's won the Somerset Cup.

All in all a good season and a good stepping stone into the National Leagues.

Bridgwater & Albion RFC:

Colours: Scarlet, amber & black hoops

Change colours: White.

BRIDGWATER & ALBION | COURAGE LEAGUE MATCH DETAILS 1996-97

No	Ven.	Date	Opponents	Att.	Res.	Score	Scorers
1	(A)	07.09	v Barnstaple		L	9-14	Edmonds(2pdg)
2	(A)	21.09	v Camborne		W	40-10	Gwillam(t)Bennett(t)Saunders(t)Newnes-Smith(2t)Oliver(t)Edmonds(2p2c)
3	(H)	28.09	v Launceston		W	24-14	Thirwell(t)Webber(t)Edmonds(3pdgc)
4	(A)	01.10	v Matson		W	24-19	Gwillam(t)Veal(t)Edmonds(3pdgc)
5	(H)	19.10	v Salisbury		W	41-10	Gwillam(t)Rees(t)Newnes-Smith(t)Veal(2t)Waddon(t)Edmonds(p4c)
6	(A)	26.10	v Torquay Ath.		W	13-12	Veal(t)Edmonds(2pc)
7	(H)	09.11	v Brixham		W	47-16	Gwillam(t)Sluman(3t)Triggol(t)Wardle(t)Edmonds(3p4c)
8	(A)	16.11	v Gloucester O.B.		L	6-17	Edmonds(pdg)
9	(A)	11.01	v St. Ives		W	26- 9	Gwillam(t)Triggol(t)Edmonds(4p2c)
10	(H)	25.01	v Stroud		W	36-15	Gwillam(2t)Triggol(t)Ranson(t)Waddon(t)Edmonds(dg4c)
11	(A)	01.02	v Maidenhead		L	18-41	Newnes-Smith(t)Edmonds(tpdgc)
12	(H)	08.02	v Gloucester O.B.		W	28-15	Triggol(t)Barnes(t)Waddon(t)Edmonds(2pdg2c)
13	(A)	16.02	v Brixham		L	14-20	Waddon(t)Edmonds(3p)
14	(H)	01.03	v Torquay Ath.		W	35-10	Triggol(t)Newnes-Smith(2t)Pen.Try,Edmonds3p3c)
15	(H)	15.03	v Matson		W	24-17	Buller(2t)PenTry, Edmonds(p3c)
16	(A)	22.03	v Launceston		W	30-18	Gwillam(2t)Barnes(t)Edmonds(2p3c)Bennett(dg)
17	(H)	28.03	v Maidenhead		W	20-12	Bennett(t)Ranson(t)Edmonds(2p2c) — Edmonds(2p5c)
18	(A)	31.03	v Salisbury		W	61-12	Triggol(2t)Bennett(2t)Newnes-Smith(t)Buller(t)Pimm(2t)Crook(t)
19	(H)	05.04	v Camborne		W	96-10	Triggol(2t)Veal(t)Bennett(3t)Harris(t)Rackham(t)Newnes-Smith(t)Thirwell(t)Whitcombe(t)Buller(t)Crook(3t)Edmonds(t8c)
20	(H)	12.04	v Barnstaple		W	87- 7	Triggol(2t)Bennett(2t)Gwillam(3t)Barnes(t)Thirwell(t)Pimm(t)Baldwin(t)Edmonds(t2c)Buller(t9c).
21	(H)	26.04	v St. Ives		W	82-10	Veal(t)Gwillam(5t)Bennett(t)Ranson(t)Newnes-Smith(5t)Edmonds(p7c)
22	(A)	03.05	v Stroud		W	33-10	Triggol(t)Newnes-Smith(2t)Edmonds(4p3c)

Details provided by Michael R Berry.

1996-97 HIGHLIGHTS

PLAYERS USED: 30 + 5 as replacement only.

EVER PRESENT: Nick Edmonds, Ben Thirwell.
Jerry Barnes 21+1 as replacement

☐ Finished the season in rampant style. In their last 5 matches they scored 54 tries, 12 in their two away matches and 42 in their three home games.

☐ Only failed to score tries in two matches - both away from home.

☐ Hat trick of tries in a match
5 Nick Gwillam v St. Ives 26.04.97 (H)
5 Rob Newnes-Smith v St. Ives 26.04.97 (H)
3 Geoff Sluman v Brixham 09.11.96 (H)
3 Shaun Bennett v Camborne 05.04.97 (H)
3 Nick Gwillam v Barnstaple 12.04.97 (H)

☐ Most points in a match
25 Nick Gwillam v St. Ives 26.04.97 (H)
25 Rob Newnes-Smith v St. Ives 26.04.97 (H)
23 Derek Buller v Barnstaple 12.04.97 (H)

☐ Most points in the season
Fly-half Nick Edmonds scored 278 points during the season - this is more than the club have scored in any previous league season.

Pts	Player	T	C	P	D
278	Nick Edmonds	3	42	58	7
85	Nick Gwillam	17	-	-	-
75	Rob Newnes-Smith	15	-	-	-
60	Simon Triggol	12	-	-	-

☐ Most appearances
22	Nick Edmonds
22	Ben Thirwell
21+1	Jerry Barnes
21	Rob Newnes-Smith
20	Simon Triggol
20	Andy Webber

BRIDGWATER & ALBION'S COURAGE LEAGUE MATCH DETAILS 1996-97

	15	14	13	12	11	10	9	1	2	3	4	5	6	7	8	Replacements	
1	Whitington	Gwillam	Webber	Buller	Bennett	Edmonds	Ranson	Thirwell	Wills	Pinm	Waddon	Steward	Wilcox	Rees	Barnes		1
2	Oliver	Gwillam	Webber	Bennett	Veal	Edmonds	Newall	Newness-Smith	Wills	Sluman	Waddon	Thirwell	Harris	Rees	Barnes	Saunders,Pimm	2
3	Triggol	Gwillam	Webber	Oliver	Veal	Edmonds	Newall	Thirwell	Newness-Smith	Sluman	Waddon	Rackham	Harris	Rees	Barnes	Saunders,Pimm	3
4	Triggol	Gwillam	Webber	Oliver	Veal	Edmonds	Newall	Thirwell	Newness-Smith	Sluman	Waddon	Passmore	Harris	Rees	Barnes	Ranson	4
5	Triggol	Gwillam	Webber	Oliver	Veal	Edmonds	Newall	Thirwell	Newness-Smith	Sluman	Waddon	Rackham	Harris	Grove	Barnes	Wardle,Rees.	5
6	Triggol	Gwillam	Webber	Oliver	Veal	Edmonds	Ranson	Thirwell	Newness-Smith	Sluman	Waddon	Rackham	Wilcox	Rees	Barnes	Pimm,Wardle.	6
7	Triggol	Gwillam	Webber	Oliver	Duffy	Edmonds	Ranson	Thirwell	Newness-Smith	Sluman	Waddon	Rackham	Harris	Grove	Barnes	Wardle	7
8	Triggol	Gwillam	Webber	Oliver	Veal	Edmonds	Ranson	Thirwell	Newness-Smith	Wills	Waddon	Rackham	Harris	Grove	Buller	Buller	8
9	Triggol	Gwillam	Webber	Buller	Veal	Edmonds	Ranson	Thirwell	Newness-Smith	Sluman	Waddon	Rackham	Harris	Rees	Barnes	Whitcombe,Passmore.	9
10	Triggol	Gwillam	Webber	Bennett	Veal	Edmonds	Ranson	Thirwell	Newness-Smith	Sluman	Waddon	Rackham	Harris	Rees	Barnes	Whitcombe,Passmore.	10
11	Triggol	Gwillam	Webber	Bennett	Veal	Edmonds	Ranson	Thirwell	Newness-Smith	Sluman	Waddon	Rackham	Harris	Rees	Barnes	Buller,Passmore,Coleman,Whitcombe.	11
12	Triggol	Gwillam	Webber	Buller	Veal	Edmonds	Coleman	Thirwell	Newness-Smith	Sluman	Waddon	Rackham	Harris	Rees	Barnes	Grew,Bennett	12
13	Triggol	Buller	Webber	Bennett	Veal	Edmonds	Coleman	Thirwell	Newness-Smith	Sluman	Waddon	Passmore	Harris	Wilcox	Barnes	Barnes	13
14	Triggol	Gwillam	Webber	Bennett	Veal	Edmonds	Coleman	Newness-Smith	Sluman	Pinm	Thirwell	Rackham	Harris	Rees	Barnes	Baldwin	14
15	Triggol	Buller	Webber	Bennett	Veal	Edmonds	Ranson	Baldwin	Newness-Smith	Pinm	Thirwell	Rackham	Harris	Rees	Barnes	Coleman,Tompkins.	15
16	Triggol	Buller	Webber	Bennett	Veal	Edmonds	Ranson	Baldwin	Newness-Smith	Pinm	Thirwell	Rackham	Harris	Rees	Barnes	Veal,Coleman,Tompkins,Grove.	16
17	Triggol	Gwillam	Webber	Veal	Buller	Edmonds	Ranson	Baldwin	Newness-Smith	Pinm	Thirwell	Rackham	Harris	Rees	Barnes	Veal,Coleman,Tompkins.	17
18	Triggol	Crook	Webber	Veal	Buller	Edmonds	Coleman	Baldwin	Newness-Smith	Pinm	Thirwell	Rackham	Wilcox	Grove	Barnes	Innalls,Harris.	18
19	Triggol	Crook	Webber	Bennett	Veal	Edmonds	Coleman	Baldwin	Newness-Smith	Tompkins	Thirwell	Rackham	Harris	Rees	Barnes	Grove,Pimm,Whitcombe.	19
20	Triggol	Gwillam	Webber	Bennett	Buller	Edmonds	Ranson	Baldwin	Newness-Smith	Pinm	Thirwell	Rackham	Harris	Rees	Barnes	Veal,Coleman,Grove,Tompkins.	20
21	Triggol	Gwillam	Webber	Bennett	Buller	Edmonds	Ranson	Baldwin	Newness-Smith	Pinm	Thirwell	Rackham	Harris	Rees	Barnes	Veal,Whitcombe,Coleman.	21
22	Triggol	Gwillam	Webber	Bennett	Buller	Edmonds	Ranson	Baldwin	Newness-Smith	Pinm	Thirwell	Rackham	Harris	Rees	Barnes	Veal,Coleman.	22

Details provided by Michael R Berry.

BRIDGWATER & ALBION LEAGUE STATISTICS

Season	Div.	P	W	D	L	F	A	PD	Pts	Pos.	Coach	Captain
87-88	SW1	10	3	0	7	98	154	-56	6	9	G Cooper	P C L Burne
88-89	SW1	10	0	0	10	53	264	-211	0	11r	G Cooper	N G L Burne & A J Harris
89-90	SW2	10	2	1	7	122	158	-36	5	11r	J Davies	A J Harris
90-91	WC	10	7	0	3	145	105	30	14	3	J Davies	A J Harris
91-92	WC	10	8	0	2	266	74	192	16	2p	G Cooper	N P Edmonds
92-93	SW2	12	9	0	3	243	114	129	15	3	G Cooper	N P Edmonds
93-94	SW2	12	9	0	3	251	135	116	18	4	G Cooper	N P Edmonds
94-95	SW2	12	10	0	2	238	127	111	20	2p	G Cooper	N P Edmonds
95-96	SW1	12	8	0	4	241	195	46	16	4	D Egerton	G M Buller
96-97	SW1	22	18	0	4	794	318	476	36	1p	D Egerton	N P Edmonds
Total		120	74	1	45	2451	1644	807				

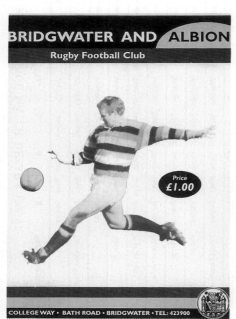

BRIDGWATER AND ALBION
Rugby Football Club
Price £1.00
COLLEGE WAY · BATH ROAD · BRIDGWATER · TEL: 423900

PROGRAMME DETAILS

SIZE: A5   **PRICE:** £1

PAGES: 40 plus cover.

PROGRAMME EDITOR: Karen Llewelyn.

ADVERTISING:
Full Page £130   Half Page £75 (+ VAT)

CLUB & GROUND DETAILS

Address: **Tel. No.:** 01278 423900
Bath Road, College Way, Bridgwater, Somerset. TA6 4TZ.

Capacity: 3000+ **Covered - Seating:** 500 **Standing:** 500

Simple Directions: Follow the A39 from Bridgwater towards Bath. The ground is situated adjacent to Bridgwater College, which is signposted.

Nearest Railway Station: Bridgwater (BR) (Bristol to Exeter line). 10 minute walk to the ground.

Car Parking: Plenty available at ground. Use of College car parking if necessary.

Admission: Season tickets - Adult £56. OAPs £28. Matchdays - Adult £4. OAPs £2. u16 Free.

Club Shop: Matchdays only. Contact Lionel Porter 01278 422973 (H) 01278 441498 (B)

Clubhouse: Open during normal licensing hours. Snacks available. Functions up to 300 can be catered for. Contact Roy Chidgey 01278 423900 (Clubhouse).

CAMBERLEY R.F.C.

NICKNAME: FOUNDED: 1931

President Peter Stevens, 17 Pine Avenue, Camberley, Surrey GU15 2LY. 01276 20839 (H)
Chairman Bob Hughes, 11 Beverley Close, Camberley, Surrey GU15 1HF.
01276 501729 (H), 0171 488 1616 (B)
Secretary Gwynne Evans, Woodcroft, 4 Paddock Close, Camberley, Surrey. GU15 2BN 01276 65170 (H)
Treasurer Mike Courtness, 12 Browning Close, Camberley, Surrey GU15 1DJ
01276 501974 (H), 01276 501974 (Fax)
Press Officer John Lightly, 204 Beaulieu Gardens, Blackwater, Camberley, Surrey. GU17 0LG.
0468 332870 (H), 01252 871657 (Fax)
Director of Rugby   Phil Moyle, 01923 824739
1st XV Coachs Dave Ball, 01344 778938, John Stonehouse 01483 473573
Fixtures Secretary Bill Fletcher, 01344 777701 (H)

Camberley successfully worked their way through the 1996/97 season and enjoyed the benefits of a much needed large first team squad. Fifty one players were used in the 26 league games as a continuous stream of injuries, notably in the front row, meant that it was rarely possible to field the same side in successive games. It says much for the determination of the players and coaching staff that, after a mid season lean spell, they were placed fourth in the league following a strong finish to the season.

The high points of the campaign were the games against Newbury, Henley and Barking in January when rugby of the highest quality was seen at Watchetts, but these games were quickly followed by the low points with the visits to Metropolitan Police and Weston. Perhaps the latter results were affected by the fact that both games were played on International weekends.

Camberley's Gary Hamer about to secure lineout ball, in their match with North Walsham

Players of the Year was a shared award between Craig Greville - centre and occasional scrum half - and Russel Kesley - a flanker who once he established himself in the team improved in every game. Outside half Jason Hoad was the leading points scorer with Craig Greville the top try scorer.

Jim Fowers, Rory Jones and Andy Dawling played for the army in the Inter Services Championship but the calls of service life together with a long term injury to Jim Fowers meant that their appearances for Camberley were somewhat infrequent.

The benefits of Camberley's youth policy was seen with the introduction to the squad of last season's colts scrum half, Andy Walshe, who won the Most Promising Newcomer award. The 1996/97 Colts again had a good season and reached the final of the Surrey County RFU Colts Cup.

The first ever season of 26 league games produced a steep learning curve with many lessons learned for the future. The coaching staff is being strengthened for 1997/98 with the introduction of former club captain and Surrey lock Dave Ball and John Stonehouse, whose playing career as a wing included representative rugby with Devon, Royal Navy and Combined Services.

Colours: Black with amber collar.   Change colours: Yellow with black collar.

CAMBERLEY

No	Ven.	Date	Opponents	Att.	Res.	Score	Scorers
1	(A)	31.08	v Barking		W	21-20	Smith(t)Dorling(t)Hoad(c3p)
2	(H)	07.09	v Met Police		W	15- 5	Endean(t)Scott(t)Hoad(cp)
3	(A)	21.09	v Henley		L	13-32	Jones(t)Dorling(t)Way(p)
4	(H)	28.09	v Weston-S-M		W	25-24	Endean(t)Another(t)Mallalieu(4p)Hoad(dg)
5	(A)	05.10	v Cheltenham		D	21-21	Mallalieu(6p)Hoad(dg)
6	(H)	19.10	v N Walsham		W	30-12	Hornung(t)Greville(t)Kearns(t)Mallalieu(3cp)Hoad(2dg)
7	(A)	26.10	v Tabard		W	22- 7	Haddingham(t)Endean(t)Greville(t)Mallalieu(2cp)
8	(A)	09.11	v Charlton Park		W	38-11	Jones(2t)Greville(2t)Dorling(t)Mallalieu(2c3p)
9	(H)	16.11	v Askeans		W	95-17	Jones(4t)Scott(2t)Greville(t)Hornung(t)Dorling(t)Ball(t)Walker(t)Hedge(t)Kearns(t)Hoad(2t10c)
10	(A)	21.12	v Plymouth		L	0-16	
11	(H)	18.01	v Newbury		L	15-26	PenTry(t)Ball(t)Mallalieu(cp)
12	(A)	25.01	v Barking		W	41-18	Stafford(2t)Marsh(t)Jones(t)Dorling(t)Davies(t)Hoad(4cp)
13	(A)	01.02	v Met Police		L	13-51	Haddingham(t)Hoad(c2p)
14	(H)	08.02	v Henley		L	18-23	Jones(t)Jennings(t)Mallalieu(c2p)
15	(A)	15.02	v Weston-S-M		L	10-25	Kesley(t)Mallalieu(cp)
16	(H)	22.02	v Cheltenham		L	10-25	Marsh(t)Jones(t)
17	(A)	01.03	v N Walsham		W	20-13	Smith(t)Kesley(t)Mallalieu(2c2p)
18	(H)	08.03	v Tabard		W	27- 9	Marsh(t)Greville(t)Jones(t)Ball(t)Hoad(2cp)
19	(H)	15.03	v Charlton Park		W	92- 8	Greville(2t)Scott(2t)Dorling(2t)McAllister(2t)Marsh(t)Brooks(t)Gill(t)Smith(t)Anderson(t)Hoad(t11c)
20	(A)	22.03	v Askeans		W	27-23	Anderson(t)Aldridge(t)Gill(t)Fleming(t)Hoad(2cp)
21	(H)	05.04	v Plymouth		D	17-17	Greville(t)Aldridge(t)Fleming(t)Hoad(c)
22	(A)	12.04	v Newbury		L	23-61	Greville(t)Smith(t)Haddingham(t)Hoad(c2p)
23	(H)	19.04	v High Wycombe		W	32-17	Greville(t)Haddingham(t)Marsh(t)Kesley(2t)Way(2cp)
24	(H)	26.04	v Berry Hill		L	20-21	Kesley(t)Hamer(t)Hoad(2c2p)
25	(A)	03.05	v High Wycombe		W	32- 7	Griffiths(2t)Greville(2t)Walsh(t)McAllister(t)Johnson(c)
26	(A)	10.03	v Berry Hill		W	11- 6	Hamer(t)Ticehurst(2p)

1996-97 HIGHLIGHTS

LEAGUE DEBUTS:

PLAYERS USED: 47 plus five as replacement only.

EVER PRESENT: None - most 25 Gary Hamer

❑ Twice scored 90+ points in a match. Newbury were the only other side to score 90 points in a match.

❑ Most points in a match
30 Jason Hoad v Askeans 16.11.96 (H)
27 Jason Hoad v Charlton Park 16.03.97 (H)
20 Rory Jones v Askeans 16.11.96 (H)

❑ Hat trick of tries in a match
4 Rory Jones v Askeans 16.11.96 (H)

❑ Most points in the season

Pts	Player	T	C	P	D
138	Jason Hoad	3	36	13	4
87	Mike Mallalieu	-	12	21	-
65	Craig Greville	13	-	-	-
50	Rory Jones	10	-	-	-
35	Andy Dorling	7	-	-	-

❑ Most appearances
25 Gary Hamer
23 Jason Hoad
22 Craig Greville
21 Chris Hornung
20 Rory Jones

❑ Started the season well but lost it mid season losing 6 out of 7 before going on to win 7 out of last 10.

CAMBERLEY'S COURAGE LEAGUE MATCH DETAILS 1996-97

	15	14	13	12	11	10	9	1	2	3	4	5	6	7	8	Replacements
1	Mallalieu	Jones	Greville	Keohane	Adamson	Hoad	Hornung	Mealin	Gill	Walker	Hamer	Ball	Dorling	Scott	Smith	Bentley(2)Milne(6)Johnson(12)
2	Smart	Adamson	Greville	Keohane	Endean	Hoad	Hornung	Mealin	Gill	Mealin	Hamer	Ball	Dorling	Scott	Smith	Walker(3)
3	Way	Griffiths	Greville	Keohane	Jones	Hoad	Hornung	Hedge	Jennings	Walker	Hamer	Ball	Dorling	Scott	Smith	Bentley(1)Jeffreys(14)Kesley(7)Davies(2)
4	Mallalieu	Endean	Greville	Keohane	Jones	Hoad	Hornung	Hedge	Jennings	Walker	Hamer	Ball	Dorling	Scott	Smith	Scott(6)
5	Mallalieu	Eccleston	Greville	Kearns	Jones	Hoad	Hornung	Hedge	Bentley	Walker	Hamer	Ball	Kesley	Dorling	Milne	Scott(6)
6	Mallalieu	Jones	Greville	Kearns	Jones	Hoad	Hornung	Hedge	Bentley	Mealin	Hamer	Ball	Kesley	Scott	Milne	
7	Mallalieu	Endean	Greville	Kearns	Jones	Hoad	Hornung	Mealin	Bentley	Hedge	Hamer	Ball	Kesley	Scott	Haddingham	Haddingham(6)
8	Mallalieu	Jones	Greville	Kearns	Endean	Hoad	Hornung	Mealin	Bradbury	Hedge	Hamer	Ball	Milne	Scott	Haddingham	Dorling(6)Davies(2)
9	Jeffreys	Jones	Greville	Kearns	Endean	Hoad	Hornung	Walker	Davies	Hedge	Hamer	Ball	Scott	Dorling	Haddingham	Payne(1)
10	Mallalieu	Jones	Greville	Stafford	Kearns	Hoad	Hornung	Mealin	Bentley	Hedge	Hamer	Ball	Milne	Dorling	Haddingham	Hackett(3)Stobbart(11)Batchelor(6)
11	Mallalieu	Jones	Greville	Stafford	Kearns	Hoad	Hornung	Fowers	Davies	Hedge	Hamer	Ball	Kesley	Scott	Haddingham	Mealin(1)Bentley(2)Milne(6)
12	Kearns	Jones	Stafford	McAllister	Marsh	Hoad	Hornung	Fowers	Davies	Mealin	Hamer	Ball	Scott	Smith	Haddingham	
13	Kearns	Jones	Stafford	McAllister	Marsh	Hoad	Hornung	Fowers	Davies	Hedge	Hamer	Ball	Milne	Scott	Haddingham	Brooks(6)Jennings(2)
14	Mallalieu	Jones	Stafford	McAllister	Kearns	Hoad	Hornung	Mealin	Jennings	Hedge	Hamer	Ball	Kesley	Scott	Haddingham	Batchelor(7)
15	Mallalieu	Marsh	Stafford	McAllister	Kearns	Hoad	Hornung	Mealin	Manthorpe	Batchelor	Ball	Ball	Milne	Glossop		Smith(8)Bradbury(2)Ruane(1)
16	Kearns	Marsh	Greville	McAllister	Marsh	Hoad	Anderson	Hedge	Anderson	Hedge	Ticehurst	Ball	Milne	Scott	Hamer	Glossop(5)Manthorpe(3)
17	Mallalieu	Marsh	Greville	McAllister	Fleming	Hoad	Anderson	Anderson	Gill	Mealin	Hamer	Brooks	Smith	Milne	Glossop	Glossop(6)
18	Marsh	Fleming	Greville	McAllister	Fleming	Hoad	Hornung	Anderson	Mealin	Hamer	Ball	Hamer	Kesley	Scott	Smith	Brooks(4)Dorling(6)
19	Marsh	Aldridge	Greville	McAllister	Fleming	Hoad	Hornung	Mealin	Gill	Mealin	Brooks	Brooks	Dorling	Scott	Smith	Ball(5)Jennings(2)Kesley(11)
20	Kearns	Aldridge	McAllister	Jones	Fleming	Head	Davies	Jennings	Anderson	Hamer	Brooks		Smith	Scott	Ticehurst	Ball(4)Gill(2)
21	Marsh	Aldridge	Aldridge	McAllister	Fleming	Head	Hornung	Mealin	Gill	Anderson	Ticehurst	Hamer	Kesley	Scott	Haddingham	Brooks(7)A Walsh(9)
22	Marsh	Davies	G Walsh	McAllister	Fleming	Head	Greville	Mealin	Gill	Anderson	Ticehurst	Hamer	Kesley	Smith	Haddingham	Ball(7)
23	Marsh	Aldridge	Greville	McAllister	Way	Way	Hornung	Gill	Anderson	Anderson	Ball	Hamer	Kesley	Gascoigne	Haddingham	
24	Marsh	Aldridge	McAllister	Jones	Head	Head	A Walsh	Mealin	Jennings	Anderson	Ticehurst	Hamer	Kesley	Gascoigne	Haddingham	Bradbury(2)Rise(1)
25	Marsh	Jones	G Walsh	McAllister	P Davies	Greville	Rise	Rise	Jennings	Anderson	Ticehurst	Hamer	Gascoigne	Haddingham	Smith	Smith(12)Bradbury(2)Milne(7)
26	Marsh	Endean	G Walsh	McAllister	Griffiths	P Davies	Greville	Payne	Jennings	Anderson	Ticehurst	Hamer	Kesley	Smith	Haddingham	

CAMBERLEY LEAGUE STATISTICS
(COMPILED BY STEPHEN McCORMACK)

Season	Div.	P	W	D	L	F	A	PD	Pts	Pos.	Coach	Captain
87-88	LON2S	10	7	0	3	139	122	17	14	4		
88-89	LON2S	10	6	1	3	123	112	11	13	4		C Gibson
89-90	LON2S	10	9	0	1	180	75	105	18	2	T Hart	C Gibson
90-91	LON2S	10	5	1	4	148	109	39	11	5	T Hart	C Gibson
91-92	LON2S	10	7	0	3	184	102	82	4	5	P Moyle	S Johnson
92-93	LON2S	12	10	2	0	241	94	147	72	1p	P Moyle	
93-94	LON1	12	9	0	3	242	137	105	18	3	P Moyle	
94-95	LON1	12	12	0	0	375	122	253	24	1p	P Moyle	
95-96	D5S	12	5	1	6	151	212	-61	11	7	P Moyle	
96-97	D4S	26	15	2	9	688	515	173	32	4		
Total		124	85	7	32	2471	1600	871				

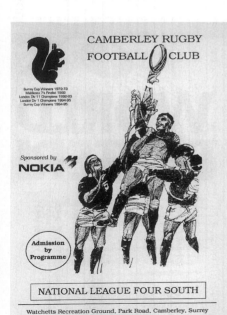

CAMBERLEY RUGBY
FOOTBALL CLUB

Surrey Cup Winners 1972-73
Middlesex 7's Finalist 1992
London Div 11 Champions 1992-93
London Div 1 Champions 1994-95
Surrey Cup Winners 1994-95

Sponsored by
NOKIA

Admission
by
Programme

NATIONAL LEAGUE FOUR SOUTH

Watchetts Recreation Ground, Park Road, Camberley, Surrey
Telephone: 01276 25395

PROGRAMME DETAILS

SIZE: A5   **PRICE:** £3 with entry
PAGES: 24 plus cover
PROGRAMME EDITOR
Contact Brian Divers 01276 20214
ADVERTISING RATES
Mono Full page £300, Half page £150, Qtr Page £100.

CLUB & GROUND DETAILS

Address: Watchetts Recreation Ground, Park Road, Camberley, Surrey GU15 2SR
Tel. Nos. 01276 25395
Capacity: 1,000   **Seated:** None
Simple Directions: M3 Jnc 4, follow signs for Frimley/Guildford. At 1st r'about turn left, sign Camberley, one & half miles to mini r'about turn right into Park Rd.
Nearest Railway Station: Camberley
Car Parking: 500 nearby
Admission: Matchday £3 with programme
Club Shop: Yes
Clubhouse: Monday 6.00-11.00, Saturday 11.00-11.00, Sunday 11.00-7.00, snacks available. Functions available - contact Alun Rise 01276 25395
Training Nights: Tuesday & Thursday

CHELTENHAM R.F.C.

NICKNAME: FOUNDED: 1889

Chairman John Costelloe, c/o Cheltenham RFC, Prince of Wales Stadium, Tommy Taylor's Lane,
Pittville, Cheltenham GL50 4NJ   01242 525393
President Peter Stephens, c/o Cheltenham RFC, as above.
Club Secretary   John Hannant, Shurdington Court Farm, Little Shurdington, Cheltenham GL51 5TX
01242 862319 (H)
Fixtures Secretary Tim Clink, 4 Leckhampton Road, Cheltenham, GL53 0AY
01242 236745 (H), 01242 255553 (B)
Coach Andy Cushing, Swanbrook Farmhouse, Pirton, Worcester WR8 9EL
01905 820759 (H), 01905 855270 (B)
Press Officer T Parker, 39 Long Mynd Avenue, Cheltenham GL51 5QT. 01242 694299 (H)

Cheltenham has had a mixed season in the National League scene, hitting the high spots on a few occasions but then unexpectedly failing when victory was in their grasp.

For most of the season they have had a small squad of players, which meant that a number were faced with the prospect of playing in almost all the league games, without having a rest period. This reflected on a number of matches in the latter half of the season when it was evident that some players were feeling the strain of constant league rugby every week.

At the same time the very same players had to face the Pilkington Cup rounds, in which through excellent commitment they won against Launceston, Worcester, Henley and Weston-super-Mare, before losing against Harlequins. The team went with high hopes of beating the 'Quins, but at least Cheltenham were not disgraced, and were supported on the Stoop ground by several hundred spectators.

A narrow win over Weston on the last day in August set the scene for several good league victories, but defeats from North Walsham and Newbury.

As with most other clubs, the weather caused problems in January, although four wins in February lifted spirits. But injuries to key players mounted up swiftly and several young players had an early opportunity to show their worth and hopefully will strengthen the squad this coming season. Thankfully after three defeats in a row, a draw against Henley and a fine win over Met. Police in early May restored morale.

With the stated aim of promotion there is need for a stronger squad to cover inevitable injuries and other problems which now arise in this new era of the game.

Congratulations to fly half, M Crisp, who topped the point scorers with 138 followed by centre\full back M Watts with 119.

Cheltenham's back row, Jamie Arthur on the attack with winger John Davis and Sam Masters (right) in support.

Photo - Gloucestershire Echo

Colours: Red & black shirts.   **Change colours:** Blue.

CHELTENHAM

No	Ven.	Date	Opponents	Att.	Res.	Score	Scorers
1	(A)	31.08	v Weston-S-M		W	8- 3	Williams(t)Watts(p)
2	(H)	07.09	v Charlton Park		W	37- 6	PenT(t)Loebenberg(t)Lodge(t)Fowke(t)Edwards(t)Ratcliffe(t)Crisp(2cp)
3	(H)	21.09	v N Walsham		L	15-18	Morris(t)Crisp(tcp)
4	(A)	28.09	v Tabard		W	26-19	Gilder(2t)Crisp(c4p)
5	(H)	05.10	v Camberley		D	21-21	Tarplee(t)Davis(t)Crisp(cp)Stanlake(pdg)
6	(A)	19.10	v Askeans		W	25-13	Crisp(2t)Williams(t)Watts(pdg)Stanlake(2c)
7	(H)	26.10	v Plymouth		W	34- 5	Fowke(2t)Davis(t)Harper(t)Masters(t)Watts(3cp)
8	(A)	09.11	v Newbury		L	16-28	Davis(t)Fowke(t)Watts(2p)
9	(H)	16.11	v High Wycombe		W	25-20	Cummins(t)Morris(t)Crisp(tdg)Watts(2cp)
10	(A)	18.01	v Berry Hill		W	23-20	Oakey(2t)Watts(2c2p)Crisp(dg)
11	(H)	25.01	v Weston-S-M		W	25-15	Clink(t)Turner(t)Ratcliffe(t)Stanlake(t)Crisp(c)Watts(p)
12	(A)	01.02	v Charlton Park		W	34- 9	Viall(2t)Freebury(t)Morgan(t)Crisp(tc)Stanlake(tc)
13	(A)	08.02	v N Walsham		W	43-18	Turner((3t)Mudway(t)Morgan(t)Oakey(t)Freebury(t)Crisp(4c)
14	(H)	15.02	v Tabard		W	23- 6	Turner(t)Viall(t)Watters(2c3p)
15	(A)	22.02	v Camberley		W	25-10	Edwards(2t)Crisp(t)Mudway(t)Watts(cp)
16	(H)	02.03	v Askeans		W	50-14	Lodge(3t)PenTry(t)Morris(2t)Edwards(t)Preedy(t)Watts(5c)
17	(A)	08.03	v Plymouth		L	8-39	Crisp(t)Watts(p)
18	(H)	15.03	v Newbury		L	10-27	Masters(t)Crisp(c)Stanlake(dg)
19	(A)	22.03	v N Walsham		L	18-22	Oakey(2t)Crisp(c2p)
20	(H)	29.03	v Barking		L	12-15	Crisp(3p)Watts(p)
21	(H)	05.04	v Berry Hill		W	16- 0	Brown(t)Watts(c3p)
22	(A)	12.04	v Barking		L	3-19	Watts(p)
23	(H)	19.04	v Met Police		L	10-17	Edwards(t)Watts(c)Crisp(p)
24	(A)	26.04	v Henley		L	10-19	Morgan(t)Watts(cp)
25	(H)	29.04	v Henley		D	6- 6	Watts(p)Stanlake(p)
26	(A)	03.05	v Met Police		W	36-31	Turner(3t)Pitman(2t)Crisp(4cp)

1996-97 HIGHLIGHTS

LEAGUE DEBUTS:

PLAYERS USED: 44 plus one as replacement only

EVER PRESENT: None - most 25 Mike Crisp

Second best defensive record in terms of both points and tries conceded.

POINTS		TRIES	
295	Newbury	36	Newbury
420	Cheltenham	44	Cheltenham
456	Henley	46	Henley

Hat trick of tries in a match

3 Ian Turner v N Walsham 08.02.97 (A)
3 Peter Lodge v Askeans 02.03.97 (H)
3 Ian Turner v Met Police 03.05.97 (A)

Most points in the season

Pts	Player	T	C	P	D
114	Mike Crisp	7	17	12	3
91	Matthew Watts	-	17	18	1
40	Ian Turner	8	-	-	-
28	Phil Stanlake	2	3	2	2

Most appearances

25 Mike Crisp
22 Ian Turner
20 Malcolm Preedy and Matt Mudway

Won more away games than home.

H/A	W	D	L	PTS
HOME	7	2	5	16
AWAY	8	0	5	16

CHELTENHAM'S COURAGE LEAGUE MATCH DETAILS 1996-97

No.	15	14	13	12	11	10	9	1	2	3	4	5	6	7	8	Replacements
1	Watters	Morgan	Williams	Watts	Davis	Crisp	Harper	Preedy	Newcombe	Phillips	Cuthbert	Lodge	Fowke	Morris	Masters	
2	Stanlake	Davis	Williams	Waters	Edwards	Crisp	Harper	Preedy	Ratcliffe	Phillips	Cuthbert	Lodge	Loebenberg	Morris	Masters	Masters(7)
3	Stanlake	Morgan	Davis	Turner	Edwards	Crisp	Mudway	Preedy	Ratcliffe	Phillips	Cuthbert	Lodge	Loebenberg	Morris	Arthur	Tunnicliffe( )
4	Watters	Morgan	Williams	Watts	Davis	Crisp	Glider	Preedy	Newcombe	Phillips	Cuthbert	Lodge	Clarke	Tarplee	Arthur	
5	Stanlake	Morgan	Williams	Turner	Davis	Crisp	Mudway	Preedy	Newcombe	Phillips	Cuthbert	Lodge	Arthur	Tarplee	Masters	Watts(15)Brown(2)
6	Watts	Morgan	Williams	Turner	Davis	Crisp	Preedy	Brown	Newcombe	Tunnicliffe	Clink	Oakey	Brain	Stanlake	Masters	Stanlake( )
7	Edwards	Morgan	Morgan	Turner	Davis	Crisp	Glider	Preedy	Ratcliffe	Phillips	Cuthbert	Oakey	Fowke	Morris	Masters	Watters(15)Brain(5)
8	Stanlake	Morgan	Morgan	Turner	Davis	Crisp	Harper	Preedy	Ratcliffe	Phillips	Cuthbert	Oakey	Fowke	Morris	Masters	Mudway(9)
9	Stanlake	Morgan	Morgan	Turner	Davis	Crisp	Harper	Preedy	Ratcliffe	Phillips	Cuthbert	Oakey	Loebenberg	Morris	Cummins	Pentigost(2)
10	Stanlake	Pitman	Watts	Turner	O'Sullivan	Crisp	Mudway	Preedy	Ratcliffe	Phillips	Clink	Oakey	Buxton	Tarplee	Masters	Oldham(14)
11	Stanlake	Oldham	Watts	Turner	Pitman	Crisp	Mudway	Preedy	Ratcliffe	Phillips	Clink	Oakey	Lodge	Tarplee	Masters	Viall(7)
12	Stanlake	Morgan	O'Sullivan	Turner	Viall	Crisp	Mudway	Tunnicliffe	Ratcliffe	Phillips	Clink	Oakey	Arthur	Freebury	Masters	Preedy(1)Tarplee(7)Betteridge(9)
13	Stanlake	Morgan	Pitman	Turner	Viall	Crisp	Mudway	Preedy	Ratcliffe	Tunnicliffe	Clink	Oakey	Arthur	Freebury	Masters	
14	Watters	Mudway	Pitman	Turner	Morgan	Crisp	Betteridge	Preedy	Ratcliffe	Phillips	Clink	Oakey	Arthur	Freebury	Masters	Morris(7)Viall(14)Lodge(9)
15	Stanlake	Edwards	Pitman	Watts	Morgan	Crisp	Mudway	Preedy	Ratcliffe	Phillips	Clink	Oakey	Arthur	Morris	Masters	Freebury(8)
16	Stanlake	Edwards	Watts	Turner	Pitman	Crisp	Mudway	Preedy	Ratcliffe	Phillips	Clink	Lodge	Arthur	Morris	Masters	
17	Stanlake	Edwards	Watts	Turner	Morgan	Crisp	Glider	Glider	Ratcliffe	Phillips	Clink	Freebury	Freebury	Morris	Masters	Denning(13)
18	Stanlake	Edwards	Turner	Denning	Morgan	Crisp	Mudway	Preedy	Ratcliffe	Phillips	Clink	Oakey	Buxton	Morris	Masters	Glider(1)
19	Stanlake	Edwards	Turner	Denning	Vaill	Crisp	Mudway	Preedy	Ratcliffe	Phillips	Clink	Lodge	Morris	Tarplee	Masters	
20	Surman	Edwards	Turner	Denning	Morgan	Crisp	Mudway	Preedy	Brown	Phillips	Clink	Lodge	Buxton	Tarplee	Masters	
21	Watts	Edwards	Turner	Denning	Stanlake	Crisp	Glider	Preedy	Brown	Phillips	Clink	Oakey	Arthur	Tarplee	Masters	Mico(6)Loebenberg(8)
22	Stanlake	Edwards	Watts	Turner	Morgan	Crisp	Mudway	Preedy	Hughes	Glider	Clink	Oakey	Arthur	Tarplee	Cummins	Denning(14)Holder(10)
23	Watts	Denning	Watts	Turner	Morgan	Crisp	Mudway	Brown	Hughes	Phillips	Clink	Oakey	Mico	Arthur	Arthur	Pitman(9)
24	Watts	Edwards	Pitman	Turner	Morgan	Crisp	Mudway	Preedy	Hughes	Phillips	Clink	Lodge	Mico	Tarplee	Arthur	Glider(6)Cummins(1)Oldham(9)
25	Stanlake	Edwards	Watts	Turner	Morgan	Crisp	Mudway	Preedy	Hughes	Phillips	Clink	Lodge	Mico	Tarplee	Masters	Preedy(1)Oakey(6)Oldham(14)Holder(10)
26	Crisp	Edwards	Pitman	Turner	Morgan	Holder	Mudway	Preedy	Hughes	Phillips	Clink	Lodge	Mico	Tarplee	Masters	Cummins(6)Oldham(11)

CHELTENHAM LEAGUE STATISTICS
(COMPILED BY STEPHEN McCORMACK)

Season	Div.	P	W	D	L	F	A	PD	Pts	Pos.	Coach	Captain
87-88	ALS	10	3	0	7	95	152	-57	6	10	R Akenhead	M Steele
88-89	ALS	10	4	2	4	122	151	-29	10	6	R Akenhead	C Kelly
89-90	ALS	10	2	0	8	107	201	-94	4	9	R Akenhead	D Kearsey
90-91	D4S	12	2	0	10	150	240	-90	4	13r	R Akenhead	P Sargison
91-92	SW1	10	6	0	4	164	142	22	12	4	J Moore	
92-93	SW1	12	6	0	6	221	197	24	12	6		
93-94	SW1	12	11	0	1	312	119	193	22	2		
94-95	SW1	12	11	1	0	275	112	163	21	1p		
95-96	D5S	12	6	0	6	194	173	21	12	6		S Masters
96-97	D4S	26	15	2	9	599	420	179	34	5		
Total		126	66	5	55	2239	1907	332				

1996-97 Season

National League Four(S)

PROGRAMME DETAILS

SIZE: A5   **PRICE:** 50p

PAGES: 24 plus cover

PROGRAMME EDITOR
T Parker 01242 694299

ADVERTISING RATES
Mono Full Page £150, Half page £100,
Qtr Page £50

CLUB & GROUND DETAILS

Address: Prince of Wales Stadium, Tommy Taylors Lane, Cheltenham, GLos GL50 4NJ
Tel. Nos. 01242 525393
Capacity: 4,500   **Seated:** 500
Standing: Covered 2,000, Uncovered 2,000
Simple Directions: M5 Jnc 10, 1.5 miles A4019 over t/lights to r'about, turn left Kingsditch Lane, 1st right, right into Windyridge Rd at end turn right, 200 yds turn right. Grd on right 500 yds.
Nearest Railway Station: Cheltenham (Taxi or bus)
Car Parking: 350 on ground
Admission: Season Adults £30, Children OAPs £15 Matchday Adults £3, Children/OAPs £1.50
Club Shop: Yes; Manager J G Pitman 01242 525393
Clubhouse: Normal Licensing hours, snacks available. Functions available, capacity 100, contact Reg Langley 01242 525393
Training Nights: Mondays & Wednesday

CLIFTON R.F.C.

NICKNAME: The Club

FOUNDED: 1877

Chairman John Raine, 1 Shumack House, High Street, Pensford BS18 4NN
01761 490717 (H), 01761 221190 (B)

Secretary Roger Bealin, 13 Frobisher Road, Ashton, Bristol. BS3 3AU.
01761 963 1832 (H), 01761 961 1532 (Fax)

Rugby Chairman Sheridan Smith, 11 Westfield Park, Clifton, Bristol
0117 908 0283 (H), 0117 929 4531 (B)

Press Officer/Fixtures Secretary/Administrator Brian Ben Jordan, 17 Royal Close, Henbury, Bristol BS10 7XP
0117 950 4723 (H), 0117 950 2855 (Fax)

President Grant Watson, Towerhurst, Leigh Woods, Bristol

Director of Coaching Peter Polledai, 8 Lampeter Road, Bristol BS9 3QQ
0117 962 8480 (H), 0117 929 8521 (B)

Commercial Peter Mitchell, 0117 968 3162

This was the season Clifton will wish to forget as it was full of disappointments and eventually ended in their relegation from National League Three.

Forced to rebuild through departures and retirements they again suffered a string of injuries pre-season which deprived them of the services of Justin Morris, Mark Wyatt, Henry Burlingham and Pat McCoy for the season.

Their rebuilt side lacked experience and found life difficult in what was to be a highly competitive league. They were also unable to field a settled side as the pre-season injury bug remained with them until the end of the season. The only time they were able to field a near full strength side they lost narrowly away to Fylde and this showed what might have been if the club had been injury free.

Such was the extent of the injury list that they used a total of 63 players in the league side with only seven playing in over half the game.

Despite these problems they were able to produce a competitive pack which gave little away in set piece play. South African Janik Hendriksz proved to be an outstanding lineout forward and youngster Tony Hussey was the epitomy of a modern mobile prop. Their problems were mainly outside the scrum where they were unable to find a consistent pair of halfbacks. Ryan Jamieson, Mark Harraway and Phil O'Sullivan all progressed from the newly formed development side and will be players to watch in the future.

The club believe they will bounce back after two poor seasons and are looking forward to celebrating their 125th season in style. Notwithstanding the disappontments of last season the players showed plenty of spirit and character and with the majority of a young squad remaining the future looks bright.

Clifton RFC squad: Back Row (L-R); John Raine (Chairman), Wayne Hone, Derek Farley (Vice President), Rob Amphlett, Alan Montgomery, Ryan Bent, Trevor Davis, Tony Hussey Janik Hendriksz, Mark Buckingham, Simon Dugan, Matt Snellus, Brian Jordan (Vice President and Fixture Secretary). Front Row; Norman Golding (Vice President), Phil O'Sullivan, Jon Phillips, Ray Wood, Paul Jeffery, Lee Ashford (Captain), Nick Lloyd, Kerry Lock, Dan Craven, Jo Seddon (Physio).

Colours: Lavender, black and white hoops.

Change colours: Yellow.

CLIFTON

No	Ven.	Date	Opponents	Att.	Res.	Score	Scorers
1	(A)	31.08	v Morley		L	13-51	Bull(t)Cottrell(c2p)
2	(H)	07.09	v Walsall		L	17-36	Hamid(t)Buckingham(t)Kerley(2cp)
3	(H)	14.09	v Fylde		L	17-45	Phillips(t)Buckingham(t)Kerley(2cp)
4	(A)	21.09	v Havant		L	19-34	Polledri(t)Cottrell(c3p)Pells(dg)
5	(H)	28.09	v Liverpool StH		W	23-16	Johnson(t)Pells(t)Simon Cady(2c3p)
6	(A)	05.10	v Otley		W	42-29	Lloyd(2t)Davis(t)Ashford(t)Heywood(t)Simon Cady(4c3p)
7	(H)	12.10	v Reading		L	22-40	Bull(t)Buckingham(t)PenTry(t)Simon Cady(2cp)
8	(A)	19.10	v Rosslyn Park		L	6-22	Hanks(p)Buckingham(p)
9	(H)	26.10	v Wharfdale		L	19-32	Bull(2t)Freeman(t)Hogg(2c)
10	(A)	09.11	v Exeter		L	10-71	Buckingham(t)Kerley(cp)
11	(H)	16.11	v Harrogate		L	13-41	Bull(t)Jamieson(c2p)
12	(A)	07.12	v Leeds		L	0-80	
13	(A)	28.12	v London Welsh		L	19-28	Harraway(t)Hogg(c4p)
14	(H)	11.01	v Redruth		W	28-17	Buckingham(2t)Hamid(t)Hussey(t)Hogg(tp)
15	(H)	18.01	v Morley		L	25-71	Jeffrey(t)Reece(t)Phillips(t)Hogg(2c2p)
16	(A)	25.01	v Walsall		L	15-32	Hendrick(t)Buckingham(tcp)
17	(A)	01.02	v Fylde		L	20-29	Buckingham(t)Hayward(t)Hogg(2cpdg)
18	(H)	08.02	v Havant		W	29-26	Ashford(t)Carr(t)Hogg(2c3p2dg)
19	(A)	15.02	v Liverpool StH		L	13-89	Buckingham(t)Phillips(t)Hogg(p)
20	(h)	22.02	v Otley		L	31-52	Phillips(t)Amphlett(t)Haywood(t)Jamieson(tc)Hogg(t2c)
21	(A)	01.03	v Reading		L	12-75	Carr(t)Davis(t)Phillips(c)
22	(H)	08.03	v Rosslyn Park		L	8-13	Hussey(t)Hogg(p)
23	(A)	15.03	v Wharfdale		L	11-28	Ashford(t)O'Sullivan(2p)
24	(H)	22.03	v Exeter		L	3-60	O'Sullivan(p)
25	(A)	29.03	v Lydney		L	13-56	Hendrick(t)Heywood(c2p)
26	(A)	05.04	v Harrogate		L	7-79	Phillips(t)O'Sullivan(c)
27	(H)	12.04	v Leeds		L	19-84	Buckingham(t)Craven(t)Locke(t)Hanks(2c)
28	(H)	19.04	v London Welsh		L	13-15	Craven(t)Hendrick(t)O'Sullivan(p)
29	(H)	26.04	v Lydney		L	25-49	Phillips(t)Smith(t)Hendrick(t)O'Sullivan(tcp)
30	(A)	03.05	v Redruth		L	26-47	Buckingham(2t)Phillips(t)Ashford(t)O'Sullivan(3c)

1996-97 HIGHLIGHTS

LEAGUE DEBUTS: Mike Pells, Ashley Johnson, Joe Newman, Simon Duggan, Simon Bull, Darren Watkins, Simon Cady, Phil Kerley, Martin Kent, Andy Morley, Simon Harvey, Andy Stephens, John Mead, Matt Snellus, Nick Lloyd, Paul Johnson, Brian Beattie, Janik Hendrikz, Mark Harraway, Eddie Smith, Mike Rees, Ryan Jamieson, Tony Hussey, Alan Montgomery, Rob Amphlett, James Alderson, Phil O'Sullivan, Yves Belanger, Wayne Davis, Tommaso Ravasini, Ryan Bent, Dan Cravan, John Carr, Paul Smith, Joel Pearson, Martin Hussan, Nick Cooper, Ray Woods.

PLAYERS USED: 63

EVER PRESENT: None - most appearances 26 Mark Buckingham

❑ Only away win at Otley.

❑ Clifton's 63 was the most players ever used in a National League season.

❑ Only Walsall, 58, scored less tries than Clifton's 62.

❑ Full back Mark Buckingham scores 13 tries in his first full season - second best in a season after Jon Phillips's 16 in 1993-94.

❑ Suffer worst ever run of defeats losing their last 12 games of the season. This easily beat the previous record of seven.

❑ Simon Hogg tops the clubs leading points scoring list for the sixth consecutive season.

❑ Gave league debuts to 39 players another National League record.

❑ Conceded more tries, 184, last season than in the previous nine added together - 173.

CLIFTON'S COURAGE LEAGUE MATCH DETAILS 1996-97

	15	14	13	12	11	10	9	1	2	3	4	5	6	7	8	Replacements	
1	Cottrell	Phillips	Hamid	Pells	Buckingham	Johnson	Wakler	Newman	Ashford	Duggan	Bull	Fletcher	Neary	Watkins	St Cady		1
2	Si Cady	Phillips	Hamid	Pells	Buckingham	Kerley	Wakler	Kent	Ashford	Duggan	Bull	Morley	Harvey	Watkins	Neary	Hodges(14),Stephens(1)St Cady(8)	2
3	Si Cady	Phillips	Hamid	Pells	Buckingham	Wakler	Kerley	Duggan	Ashford	Hough	Bull	Mead	Harvey	Watkins	St Cady	Hodges(14),Kerley(12),Snellus(14)	3
4	Cottrell	Hodges	Hamid	Pells	Buckingham	Wakler	Si Cady	Kent	Ashford	Hough	Bull	Mead	Polledri	Harvey	Haywood	Fletcher(8),Kerley(12),Snellus(14)	4
5	Cottrell	Phillips	Hamid	Pells	Buckingham	Si Cady	Lloyd	Johnson	Ashford	Hough	Bull	Morley	Polledri	Harvey	St Cady	Packer(6)	5
6	Cottrell	Phillips	Hamid	Pells	Buckingham	Si Cady	Lloyd	Johnson	Ashford	Hough	Bull	Morley	St Cady	Harvey	Haywood	Cottrell(14)	6
7	Buckingham	T Davis	Hamid	Locke	Phillips	Si Cady	Lloyd	Johnson	Ashford	Hough	Bull	Morley	St Cady	Harvey	Haywood	Stephens(2),Polledri(8),Snellus(14)	7
8	Freeman	Phillips	Hanks	Hamid	Buckingham	Rice	Lloyd	Johnson	Beattie	Hough	Bull	Mead	Powell	St Cady	Stephens	Stephens(2)	8
9	Freeman	Phillips	Hanks	Hamid	Buckingham	Hogg	Lloyd	Johnson	Stephens	Hough	Bull	Mead	Powell	St Cady	Haywood	Haywood	9
10	Si Cady	T Davis	Hamid	Hanks	Buckingham	Kerley	Jeffrey	Duggan	Ashford	Hough	Bull	Mead	Harvey	St Cady	Harvey	Polledri(5),Lloyd(9),Henrick(8)	10
11	Beresford	T Davis	Hanks	Pells	Buckingham	Jamieson	Jeffrey	Duggan	Packer	Hough	Bull	Blake	Harvey	Amphlett	Haywood	Amphlett,Wakler(9),Harvey(5),Rees(3)	11
12	Beresford	T Davis	Hanks	Pells	Buckingham	Jeffrey	Harraway	Packer	Ashford	Hough	Bull	Blake	Harvey	Blake	E Smith	Polledri(5),Ravasini(2)	12
13	Beresford	Carr	Pells	Buckingham	Hogg	Harraway	Hussey	Ravasini	Duggan		Bull	Hendrikz	Amphlett	Hone	Haywood	Alderson(12),Pearson(8),Jeffrey(9)	13
14	Buckingham	T Davis	Hamid	Carr		Hogg	Rice	Ravasini	Packer	Duggan	Bull	Hendrikz	Amphlett	Hone	Haywood	Haywood,Snellus(9)	14
15	Buckingham	T Davis	Hamid	Phillips		Hogg	Jeffrey	Hussey	Packer	Rees	Bull	Hendrikz	E Smith	Hone	Amphlett	Pearson(6),Rees(3),Stephens(2)	15
16	Buckingham	T Davis	Hamid	Carr	Locke	Jeffrey	Hussey	Ashford	Rees	Bull	Hendrikz	Pearson	Hone	Amphlett		Amphlett,Duggan(3),Lloyd(9),Packer(5),E Smith(8)	16
17	Buckingham	T Davis	Hamid	Carr	Phillips	Hogg	Hussey	Ashford	Bent	E Smith	Pearson	Amphlett	Haywood			Amphlett,Haywood,Jeffrey(5),Polledri(15)	17
18	Buckingham	Carr	Alderson	Phillips	Phillips	Hogg	Hussey	Ashford	Bent	Blake	Cooper	Pearson	Pearson	Haywood		Haywood	18
19	Buckingham	T Davis	Alderson	Phillips	Phillips	Hogg	Hussey	Ashford	Bent	Bull	Cooper	Amphlett	Haywood	Haywood		Haywood,Blake(5),Carl( ),Stephens( )	19
20	Snellus	T Davis	Jamieson Locke	Phillips	Phillips	Jeffrey	Lloyd	Bent	Ashford	Blake	Morley	Amphlett	Haywood	Haywood		Carl(15),Polledri(7),Packer(14)	20
21	Snellus	Jamieson Locke	Hamid	Phillips	Phillips	Jeffreys	Bent	Ashford	Duggan	Blake	Morley	Amphlett	Hendrikz	Hendrikz		Hendrikz	21
22	Buckingham	Carr	Hamid	Alderson	Phillips	Hogg	Rice	Hussey	Ashford	Duggan	Blake	Morley	Amphlett	Woods	Haywood	Jeffrey(11)Polledri(5)	22
23	Freeman	T Davis	Hamid	O'Sullivan	Phillips	Rice	Lloyd	Hussey	Ashford	Bent	Blake	Hendrikz	Powell	Pearson	Amphlett	Amphlett,Duggan(3)	23
24	Phillips	Alderson	O'Sullivan	Carr	Carr	Lloyd	Hussey	Ashford	Bent	Blake	Hendrikz	Powell	Pearson	Amphlett		Cravan(12)Haywood(6)	24
25	Buckingham	T Davis	Carr	Phillips	Phillips	Jeffrey	Lloyd	Stephens	Duggan	W Davis	Hendrikz	Amphlett	Hone	Haywood		Haywood,Snellus(13)Polledri(12)Ashford(r12)Bent(10)	25
26	Freeman	T Davis	Wood	O'Sullivan	Phillips	Lloyd	Hussey	Bent	W Davis	Belanger	Pearson	Hone	Amphlett			Amphlett,Stephens(7)Duggan(14)	26
27	Snellus	T Davis	Hanks	Lock	Phillips	Buckingham	Hussey	Bent	W Davis	Blake	Pearson	Hone	Amphlett			Amphlett,Duggan(3)Montgomery(4)	27
28	Snellus	T Davis	Lock	O'Sullivan	Phillips	Cravan	Hussey	Ashford	Bent	Smith	Montgomery	Pearson	Hone	Amphlett		Amphlett,Bent(1)	28
29	Snellus	T Davis	Lock	O'Sullivan	Phillips	Cravan	Bent	Ashford	Smith	Montgomery	Hendrikz	Pearson	Hone	Amphlett	Lloyd(9)	Lloyd(9)Stephens(8)Hussey(1)	29
30	Buckingham	T Davis	Lock	O'Sullivan	Phillips	Lloyd	Jeffrey	Hussey	Ashford	Bent	Montgomery	Hendrikz	Wood	Hone	Amphlett	Amphlett,Snellus(10)Cravan(9)Stephens(8)Duggan(r9)	30

Season	Div.	P	W	D	L	F (Tries Con Pen DG)	A (Tries Con Pen DG)	Most Points	Most Tries
87-88	SW1	10	6	0	4	210 (33 18 13 1)	112 (17 7 9 1)	60 - Roger Gilbert	7 - Mike Spearman
88-89	SW1	10	9	0	1	237 (28 16 25 6)	76 (6 2 15 1)	49 - Roger Gilbert	4 - Mark Trott
89-90	ALS	10	8	1	1	240 (31 16 21 7)	122 (18 7 10 2)	83 - Simon Harvey	6 - Mark Trott & Mark Wyatt
90-91	3	12	6	1	5	172 (25 12 13 3)	186 (23 4 18 3)	32 - Phil Cue	8 - Dan Cottrell
91-92	3	12	9	0	3	298 (44 22 25 1)	132 (14 5 19 3)	100 - Simon Hogg	8 - Matt Brain
92-93	3	11	4	2	5	206 (28 9 13 3)	175 (18 11 20 1)	71 - Simon Hogg	5 - Mark Wyatt & Doug Woodman
93-94	4	18	16	2	0	477 (54 24 39 14)	205 (17 6 35 1)	222 - Simon Hogg	16 - John Phillips
94-95	3	18	5	1	12	242 (25 12 26 5)	344 (33 19 40 7)	116 - Simon Hogg	4 - Matt Brain & Mark Wyatt
95-96	4	18	7	2	9	283 (27 14 38 2)	298 (27 17 41 2)	87 - Simon Hogg	5 - Malcolm Crane
96-97	3	30	4	0	26	518 (62 38 40 4)	1347 (184 125 58 1)	80 - Simon Hogg	13 - Mark Buckingham
Totals		149	74	9	66	2883 (218 181 253 46)	2997 (357 213 266 22)		

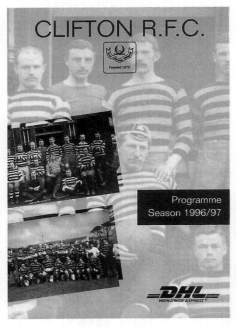

CLIFTON R.F.C.

Founded 1872

Programme Season 1996/97

DHL WORLDWIDE EXPRESS®

PROGRAMME DETAILS

SIZE: A5   **PRICE:** £1

PAGES: 40 plus cover.

PROGRAMME EDITOR: T B A

ADVERTISING RATES:
Mono Full page £250
Half page £125

CLUB & GROUND DETAILS

Address:
Station Road, Cribbs Causeway, Henbury, Bristol BS10 7TP.
Tel. Nos. 0117 950 0445   Fax: 0117 950 2855

Capacity: 2,500   **Seated:** 250   **Standing:** 2,250

Simple Directions: From M5 junction 17, take A4018 to Bristol West. At 3rd roundabout go right round and head back on opposite side of the road (towards the motorway). Turn left just after petrol station and then first right (signed Clifton RFC).

Nearest Railway Station: Bristol Parkway, taxi 15 minutes
Car Parking: 250 spaces on the ground.

Admission: Season - Adults £40;   Matchday - Adults £5, OAPs £2.50, Children Free

Club Shop: Yes, manager Mike Anderton 0117 568 8092
Clubhouse: Normal licensing hours, bar meals available. Function facilities, capacity 150

Training Nights: Monday & Wednesday

ESHER R.F.C.

FOUNDED: 1923-24

President R C Howard, c/o Esher RFC, The Rugby Ground, 369 Molesey Road, Hersham, Surrey KT12 3PF
Chairman T J Bale, c/o Esher RFC, as above
Club Secretary P Cook, c/o Esher RFC, as above
Fixtures Secretary S Gardner, 72 Chesil Street, Winchester, Hants SO23 0HX. 01962 869846 (H).
Director of Rugby H McHardy, c/o Esher RFC, as above
Rugby Managers J Inverdale & B Stratton, c/o Esher RFC, as above

For many years Esher have been the nearly-club of London rugby often aspiring to positions of pre-eminence that neither performances on the field nor organisationally off it they deserved. When 25 years ago the Surrey Cup was a regular visitor to the clubhouse and the fixture list included some of the most well-respected clubs in the country, maybe that vision of 'senior' status carried some weight.

When the League system was introduced more than a decade ago, the club, much to its consternation, was banished, so it thought, to the anonymity of London Division One. A measure of its ill-preparedness for the challenge ahead can be gleaned from the fact that half the team for the crucial match of the season that sealed relegation were unaware it was a league match at all. There was only one way to go, but it was a long way back.

So began Esher's renaissance five seasons ago. Inspired by recently retired Simon Halliday, the club re-grouped around half a dozen senior players with acres of rugby 'nous' if a little short on pace off the mark. Gone too was the snobby image the club had acquired in its halcyon period, when a huge City influence made the changing room appear more like a branch of the Stock Exchange.

In the past five years, two Surrey Cup victories, two promotions and three narrow misses, and two lucrative forays into the Pilkington Cup, coupled with a more measured and efficient approach from administrators and officials, have seen the club earn a place for the first time in the National Leagues. No-one is under-estimating the challenge ahead, not least because the number of league games is nearly double, and the travel costs to Redruth are slightly more than to Old Blues, three miles away. Nonetheless, this is the goal that was set at an AGM in 1992. Everyone involved is proud to have achieved it, and the style of rugby, notably in the 80-point demolition of Old Colfeians which won promotion last April, is worthy of a wider audience.

The club has made a definite decision to reward players on a nominal scale, because the sport at this level cannot sustain huge overheads. Perhaps, though, there is a level to be played at, where those involved remain in the game for fun because full-time rugby impinges on their more lucrative careers. Perhaps that is the future for the best clubs outside the Allied Dunbar Premiership and, consequently, for Esher.

Esher celebrate promotion.

Photo - courtesy of Simon Jones Associates

Colours: Black with amber band

COURAGE LEAGUE MATCH DETAILS 1996-97

No	Ven.	Date	Opponents	Res.	Score	Scorers
1	(A)	21.09	v Old Mid-Whitgiftians	W	37-16	
2	(H)	28.09	v Basingstoke	W	34- 7	
3	(A)	05.10	v Harlow	W	44-26	
4	(H)	19.10	v Wimbledon	W	13- 6	
5	(A)	26.10	v Sutton & Epsom	W	19-16	
6	(H)	09.11	v Staines	W	57- 3	
7	(A)	16.11	v Sudbury	W	28-10	
8	(H)	08.01	v Norwich	W	9- 5	
9	(A)	11.01	v Southend	W	37-20	
10	(H)	08.02	v Ruislip	L	8-17	
11	(H)	15.02	v Thurrock	W	61-13	
12	(A)	22.03	v Guildford & Godal	W	30-18	
13	(H)	05.04	v Old Colfeians	W	81-14	

SURREY KNOCK-OUT CUP CHAMPIONS

SEASON 1995/96

ESHER R.F.C. - A History
1923 - Date

In 1923, four rugby enthusiasts met, inevitably drinking beer in a pub, and decided to form a rugby club, presumably to improve their thirst. One - a Welshman, who like most of his race spoke faster and louder than the rest - insisted that the new club should adopt his Welsh club's colours. Hence, to this day, we wear the black and amber of Newport. The club's crest we 'borrowed' from the Coat of Arms of Henry VIII's ill-fated Cardinal Wolsey, who aroused his King's jealousy (by building nearby Hampton Court Palace) and his rage (by refusing him to divorce to re-marry) - two short-sighted failings which were leading him to the axe when, somewhat unsportingly, he died.

Thus equipped, the club now sought a pitch and found one on a friendly farmer's field. When not being used for rugby, the field was enjoyed by grazing cattle, whose activities added a new dimension to the hazards of the game. Two borrowed bedrooms and a bathroom at another local pub provided changing accommodation and Esher R.F.C. was in business.

By the outbreak of War in 1939 eight sides were being fielded each week and the club had moved to its present ground. The war scattered the members all over the world, the pitch was ploughed up for food production and for six years play was suspended.

The end of hostilities was the signal to restart and 1945/46 was the first post-war season. Alas, many members were never to return, but those who did lost nothing of their enthusiasm. By the 1950s Esher was back on its own re-sown pitch and the great post-war boom in rugby has begun.

A huge influx of players led eventually to as many as fifteen sides being fielded each Saturday, from the First XV, who were travelling all over the country to gain first class fixtures, and the Expendables, a team of over 30s (or 40s) who travelled as little as possible.

Whilst the creation of new junior clubs has removed the burden of organising so many sides, the growth of the club's playing stature has continued. During the past 25 years, Esher has bought its 27-acre ground, built a large stand, (seating 1200), become the first club in the London area to erect floodlights, and hosted more and more representative games, including an England trial and County Championship matches.

Our floodlights have given us the opportunity to play clubs from all over the world - Argentina, Belgium, France, Germany, Canada, Sweden, USA, Zambia, Spain, Italy, Romania, the Carribbean, and Holland. With the introduction of the League system, Esher were placed in London Division One but, after relegation in the first year, it took until 1993 to regain this status. The 1993/94 season was the most successful in the club's history with the Surrey Cup being added to promotion to London Division One, also election by Rugby World and Whitbread Brewery as Junior Club of the Year.

The following season 1994/95 we were second and in 1995/96 third, but we won the Surrey Cup. Apart from winning promotion to the National League this season, we managed to go through to the fifth round of the Pilkington Cup.

ESHER LEAGUE STATISTICS
(COMPILED BY STEPHEN McCORMACK)

Season	Div.	P	W	D	L	F	A	PD	Pts	Pos.
87-88	L1	10	1	1	8	53	141	-88	3	11r
88-89	L2S	10	4	0	6	77	180	-103	8	7
89-90	L2S	10	3	0	7	84	107	-23	6	8
90-91	L2S	10	5	1	4	149	139	10	11	6
91-92	L2S	10	5	0	5	153	146	7	9	6
92-93	L2S	12	7	0	5	201	189	12	14	3
93-94	L2S	12	10	2	0	382	95	287	22	1p
94-95	L1	12	10	0	2	344	132	212	20	2
95-96	L1	12	9	0	3	280	159	121	18	3
96-97	L1	13	12	0	1	458	171	287	24	1p
Total	-	111	66	4	41	2181	1459	722	-	-

PROGRAMME DETAILS

SIZE: A5   **PRICE:** With admission

PAGES: 28 plus cover

PROGRAMME EDITOR: contact Commercial Manager

ADVERTISING RATES
contact Commercial Manager

CLUB & GROUND DETAILS

Address: The Rugby Ground, 369 Molesey Road, Hersham, Surrey KT12 3PF
Tel. Nos. 01932 220295 (Office), 01832 254627 (Fax), 01932 224834 (Bar)

Capacity: Unlimited   **Seated:** 1,200   **Standing:** Unlimited
Simple Directions: M25 Junc 10, A3 to London. After 1 mile left to Walton-on-Thames (A245), after 1/4 mile right at lights into Seven Hills Road (B365). Turn right at r/about into Burwood Road & follow into Hersham Village, bear right into Molesey Road. After railway bridge (Hersham BR) ground 300yds left.
Nearest Railway Station: Hersham (Waterloo- Woking line)
Car Parking: Unlimited
Admission: Membership £25 per annum. Matchdays £3.
Clubhouse: Yes
Training Nights: Monday & Wednesday

HAVANT R.F.C.

NICKNAME: Hav   **FOUNDED:** 1951

President David Sparshatt, 16 Upperbere Wood, Waterlooville, Hants PO7 7HX
01705 268402 (H), 01264 366224 (B)

Chairman Harry Wilkinson, 83 East Lodge Park, Farlington, Portsmouth PO6 1AQ
01705 363246 (H)

Secretary Brian Hunter, 40 Fernhurst Close, Hayling Island, Hants PO11 0DT
01705 464870 (H).

Chairman of Rugby/Fixture Secretary Mick Chalk, 16 Highclere Avenue, Leigh Park,
Havant, Hants. PO9 4RB. 01705 472239 (H), 01705 723749 (B)

Press Officer Ray Quinn, c/o W W Fischer, Unit 6 Stratfield Park, Elletra Ave., Waterlooville. PO7 7XN.
01705 241122 (B)   01705 257596 (Fax)

Commercial Manager Terry Lovell, 01202 708968

Although there were many 'what might have beens' as we look back on the season, they didn't happen, so we are now just going to learn from the experience, get our act together and work our way back up again!

There were one or two score-lines that we'd rather forget, but in most matches we gave a good account of ourselves, and were definitely getting better as the season came to an end. Steve McC will do his usual magnificent job of providing the club statistics, so all that should be added is that Andy Pinnock was our Player of the Season and Matt Kell our most improved player.

We were pleased and proud to provide ten players to represent England London in the Counties of Origin Series before Christmas. Playing against Queensland, a South African 'A' XV and most particularly the Argentina national side, the last two at Twickenham, were experiences that our lads are unlikely ever to forget. We were also proud to provide the England London coach. New to the club at the beginning of the season, Simon Dear took over as 1st XV coach a few weeks in. The fact that he is continuing next season, supported by assistant coach Alan Rees, is one of our reasons for optimism.

Another reason is the recent link we have formed with Portsmouth University where, on behalf of the club, local businessmen have arranged rugby scholarships for the start of next season.

We are very much aware that dropping down a division (National 3 to National 4S?) can be followed quickly by further falls, particularly now that money can make a difference. We are not going to let that happen to us - we'll be back!

Havant RFC's Player of the Year 1996-97, Andy Pinnock

Colours: Navy and white/navy/navy.   **Change colours:** Red/navy/navy.

451

HAVANT

No	Ven.	Date	Opponents	Att.	Res.	Score	Scorers
1	(A)	31.08	v Lydney		L	15-28	Jewitt(t)Roach(Russell(cp)
2	(H)	07.09	v Redruth		L	23-25	Jones(t)Pinnock(t)Russell(2c3p)
3	(A)	14.09	v Morley		L	13-42	Jewitt(t)Russell(c)Firkin(2dg)
4	(H)	21.09	v Clifton		W	34-19	Firkin(t)Ashworth(c9p)
5	(A)	28.09	v Fylde		L	17-44	Jones(t)PenTry(t)Ashworth(2cp)
6	(H)	05.10	v Walsall		W	29-10	Moore(t)Reeve(t)Jones(t)Duffett(t)Ashworth(3cp)
7	(H)	12.10	v Liverpool StH		W	26-14	Oldham(t)Jewitt(t)Wells(t)Ashworth(c3p)
8	(A)	19.10	v Otley		L	22-25	Cowan(t)Moore(t)Ashworth(4p)
9	(H)	26.10	v Reading		L	21-30	Boydell(2t)Wells(t)Russell(3c)
10	(A)	09.11	v Rosslyn Park		L	17-22	Jewitt(t)Jones(t)Russell(c)Rushin(cp)
11	(H)	16.11	v Wharfdale		L	13-27	Boydell(t)Ashworth(c)Russell(pdg)
12	(A)	21.12	v Exeter		L	5-46	Pearce(t)
13	(A)	04.01	v eeds		L	14-52	Reeve(t)Rushin(2p)Firkin(dg)
14	(A)	11.01	v London Welsh		L	22-26	Pearce(t)Raubanheimer(t)Rushin(4p)
15	(H)	18.01	v Lydney		L	10-25	Wells(t)Russell(cp)
16	(A)	25.01	v Redruth		W	24-22	Oldham(t)Pearce(t)Pinnock(t)PenTry(t)Russell(2c)
17	(H)	01.02	v Morley		L	15-51	Mortley(t)Pearce(t)Russell(cp)
18	(A)	08.02	v Clifton		L	26-29	Reeve(t)Rees(t)Russell(2c4p)
19	(H)	15.02	v Fylde		L	13-60	PenTry(t)Russell(c2p)
20	(A)	22.02	v Walsall		W	45-24	Pearce(3t)Cowens(t)Wells(t)Raubanheimer(t)Firkin(t)Russell(5c)
21	(A)	01.03	v Liverpool StH		L	10-22	Kell(t)Russell(cp)
22	(H)	08.03	v Otley		L	16-33	Raubanheimer(t)Russell(c3p)
23	(A)	15.03	v Reading		L	13-54	Rees(t)Russell(c2p)
24	(H)	22.03	v Rosslyn Park		W	18-17	Wells(t)Jewitt(t)Firkin(c)French(p)Jones(p)
25	(A)	05.04	v Wharfdale		L	22-27	Burns(t)Kell(t)PenTry(t)French(c)Rushin(c)Firkin(p)
26	(H)	12.04	v Exeter		L	8-36	Jewitt(t)Rushin(p)
27	(A)	19.04	v Harrogate		L	11-29	Firkin(tdg)Rushin(p)
28	(H)	26.04	v Leeds		L	10-74	Jones(t)Pinnock(t)
29	(H)	03.05	v London Welsh		W	38-26	Oldham(t)Jones(t)Wells(t)Cowan(t)Jewitt(t)Sackeree(tp)Russell(cdg)
30	(H)	10.05	v Harrogate		W	30-15	Pinnock(2t)Raubenheimer(t)Russell(3c2pdg)

1996-97 HIGHLIGHTS

LEAGUE DEBUTS: Andy Pinnock, Derek Howard, Joe Duffett, Chris Cowan, Tony Leighton, Pony Moore, John Mills, Nick Oldham, Gareth Hughes, Matt Kell, Simon Lippiett, Dylan Raubanheimer, Rob Hutton, Nick French, Tim Nickals, Jamie McLoughlan, John Mangnall, John Sackeree.

TRY ON DEBUT: Andy Pinnock

PLAYERS USED: 39 plus 3 as replacement.

EVER PRESENT: None - most appearances 29 - Andy Pinnock.

❏ Full back Rob Ashworth set a new record for points in a match and penalties in a match with 29 and nine respectively v Clifton. The 29 beat the previous record

of 20 set in March 1992 by Pete Russell, whilst the nine penalties beat the previous record of five held jointly by Ashworth and Russell.

❏ Jon Firkin beat the club record of three drop goals in a season with four. That included two in the game v Morley in September which equalled Andy Perry's record set in November 87 v Lydney.

❏ Pete Russell topped the points scoring list for the fourth consecutive season - his fifth in all. It was the second time he'd topped the 100 point mark and was just six short of his record 129 set in 1991-92.
He kicked a record equalling five conversions in the away win at Walsall. This equalled his own record which he had achieved three times previously.

❏ Brit Pearce became the fourth Havant player to score a hat trick of tries in a League match when scoring three against Walsall in an away win.

HAVANT'S COURAGE LEAGUE MATCH DETAILS 1996-97

#	15	14	13	12	11	10	9	1	2	3	4	5	6	7	8	Replacements
1	Ashworth	Russell	Boydell	Pinnock	Jewitt	Firkin	Jones	Rees	Howard	Cameron	Duffett	Knight	Roach	Reeve	Davenport	Croket(1)Sibson(12)
2	Ashworth	Russell	Boydell	Pinnock	Jewitt	Firkin	Jones	Rees	Cowan	Cameron	Duffett	Knight	Leighton	Reeve	Wells	
3	Ashworth	Russell	Boydell	Pinnock	Jewitt	Firkin	Jones	Rees	Cowan	Cameron	Duffett	Knight	Leighton	Reeve	Wells	
4	Ashworth	Moore	Boydell	Pinnock	Jewitt	Firkin	Jones	Rees	Cowan	Mills	Duffett	Knight	Roach	Reeve	Wells	Leighton(6)
5	Ashworth	Moore	Boydell	Pinnock	Jewitt	Firkin	Jones	Rees	Cowan	Mills	Duffett	Knight	Leighton	Reeve	Wells	
6	Ashworth	Moore	Boydell	Pinnock	Jewitt	Firkin	Jones	Rees	Cowan	Mills	Duffett	Knight	Leighton	Pearce	Reeve	Matthews(8)
7	Ashworth	Moore	Boydell	Pinnock	Jewitt	Firkin	Jones	Rees	Cowan	Mills	Duffett	Knight	Wells	Reeve	Oldham	
8	Ashworth	Moore	Boydell	Pinnock	Jewitt	Firkin	Jones	Rees	Cowan	Mills	Duffett	Knight	Reeve	Wells	Oldham	Balls(7)Leighton(5)
9	Ashworth	Mortley	Boydell	Pinnock	Jewitt	Firkin	Jones	Hughes	Cowan	Rees	Duffett	Knight	Oldham	Reeve	Wells	Russell(15)
10	Rushin	Mortley	Boydell	Pinnock	Jewitt	Firkin	Jones	Hughes	Cowan	Mills	Duffett	Rouse	Oldham	Reeve	Davenport	Matthews(5)Firkin(15)
11	Ashworth	Mortley	Boydell	Pinnock	Rushin	Firkin	Jones	Hughes	Howard	Cameron	Duffett	Matthews	Oldham	Reeve	Pearce	Jewitt(14)Roach(8)
12	Rushin	Mortley	Boydell	Balls	Jewitt	Firkin	Jones	Rees	Howard	Cameron	Duffett	Knight	Oldham	Reeve	Pearce	Matthews(8)Lippiett(11)
13	Ashworth	Lippiett	Pinnock	Balls	Morley	Firkin	Jones	Rees	Howard	Cameron	Duffett	Knight	Oldham	Reeve	Pearce	Russell(14)Mills(7)Chapman(15)
14	Rushin	Pinnock	Balls	Lippiett	Firkin	Firkin	Jones	Rees	Howard	Cameron	Duffett	Knight	Wells	Reuebenhiemer	Wells	Morley(15)
15	Pinnock	Mortley	Boydell	Balls	Lippiett	Russell	Jones	Rees	Howard	Cameron	Duffett	Hutton	Wells	Reuebenhiemer	Wells	
16	Pinnock	Mortley	Boydell	French	French	Russell	Chapman	Rees	Howard	Cameron	Duffett	Knight	Wells	Pearce	Reuebenhiemer	Oldham(7)Jones(9)
17	Pinnock	Mortley	Boydell	Moore	Firkin	Russell	Chapman	Rees	Cameron	Cameron	Duffett	Knight	Oldham	Pearce	Jewitt	Jewitt(11)
18	Rushin	Mortley	Boydell	Jewitt	Moore	Russell	Chapman	Rees	Cameron	Cameron	Kell	Knight	Oldham	Reeve	Pearce	French(14)
19	Rushin	Mortley	Firkin	Pinnock	Pinnock	Russell	Chapman	Rees	Cameron	Mills	Kell	Knight	Wells	Reeve	Pearce	French(15)Nickolds(8)Cameron(3)
20	Pinnock	Jewitt	Boydell	Firkin	French	Russell	Chapman	Rees	Cowan	Burns	Kell	Knight	Oldham	Pearce	Wells(8)	Reuebenhiemer(7)
21	Pinnock	Jewitt	Balls	Balls	French	Russell	Jones	Rees	Cowans	Burns	Kell	Knight	Reuebenhiemer	Pearce	Pearce	
22	Pinnock	Mortley	Firkin	Mangnall	Russell	Russell	Jones	Rees	Burns	Burns	Kell	Roach	Roach	Roach	Pearce	Chapman(9)Roach(6)
23	Pinnock	Mortley	Firkin	French	Russell	Russell	Jones	Rees	Burns	Kell	Kell	Knight	Reuebenhiemer	Reuebenhiemer	Roach	Jones(14)
24	Pinnock	Jewitt	Boydell	French	Firkin	Russell	McLoughlan	Rees	Burns	Burns	Duffett	Wells	Oldham	Reeve	Pearce	Jones(14)
25	Pinnock	Jewitt	Boydell	Balls	Firkin	Russell	McLoughlan	Rees	Burns	Burns	Duffett	Wells	Oldham	Reeve	Pearce	Rushin(12)
26	Pinnock	Jewitt	Balls	Pinnock	Firkin	Russell	McLoughlan	Rees	Mills	Mills	Duffett	Wells	Oldham	Reeve	Pearce	Jones(9)Reuebenhiemer(6)
27	Rushin	French	Boydell	Jewitt	Firkin	Russell	Jones	Rees	Burns	Burns	Duffett	Kell	Reuebenhiemer	Knight	Wells	Cameron(3)Reeve(6)Mills(3)Sackeree(13)
28	Rushin	French	Davey	Jewitt	Firkin	Russell	Jones	Rees	Burns	Burns	Duffett	Kell	Wells	Reuebenhiemer	Knight	Russell(12)Cameron(3)McLoughlan(9)
29	Sackeree	French	Pinnock	Jewitt	Firkin	Russell	Jones	Rees	Cowan	Burns	Duffett	Kell	Oldham	Reeve	Wells	Leighton(6)
30	Sackeree	McLoughlan	Boydell	Pinnock	Jewitt	Russell	Jones	Rees	Cowan	Burns	Duffett	Matthews	Reuebenhiemer	Reeve	Leighton	

Reuebenhiemer(7)

HAVANT LEAGUE STATISTICS
(COMPILED BY STEPHEN McCORMACK)

Season	Div.	P	W	D	L	F	(Tries	Con	Pen	DG)	A	(Tries	Con	Pen	DG)	Most Points	Most Tries
87-88	ALS	10	5	0	5	116	(17	6	8	4)	102	(			)	39 - Chris Manktellow	3 - Chris Manktellow
88-89	ALS	10	8	1	1	177	(22	13	19	2)	92	(			)	61 - Peter Coomb	6 - Peter Coomb
89-90	ALS	10	5	1	4	132	(17	8	13	3)	126	(			)	43 - Rob Ashworth	5 - Andy Wilson
90-91	D4S	12	5	0	7	157	(15	8	27	0)	173	(			)	97 - Rob Ashworth	2 - by 4 players.
91-92	D4S	12	11	0	1	301	(45	23	24	1)	91	(			)	129 - Pete Russell	9 - Will Knight
92-93	3	11	8	1	2	185	(23	5	20	0)	93	(			)	54 - Rob Ashworth	3 - by 3 players - Mark Sheldon, Paul Jenkins & Andy Wilson.
93-94	3	18	3	0	5	203	(22	15	20	1)	432	(51	26	3	1)	32 - Pete Russell	4 - Nick Roach
94-95	4	18	10	2	6	390	(51	21	27	4)	330	(32	17	45	2)	85 - Pete Russell	10 - Nick Roach
95-96	4	18	7	1	10	287	(33	19	24	4)	368	(41	20	37	4)	80 - Pete Russell	4 - Nick Roach
96-97	3	30	8	0	22	589	(65	39	52	7)	954	(126	75	50	8)	123 - Pete Russell	7 - Brit Pearce & Andy Jewitt
Totals		139	70	6	63	2537	(310	157	234	26)	2761	(			)		

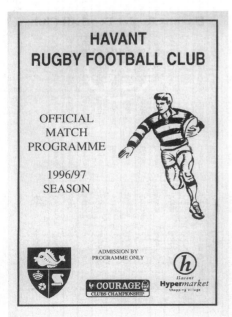

HAVANT RUGBY FOOTBALL CLUB

OFFICIAL MATCH PROGRAMME

1996/97 SEASON

ADMISSION BY PROGRAMME ONLY

COURAGE CLUBS CHAMPIONSHIP

Havant Hyper*market* Shopping Village

PROGRAMME DETAILS

SIZE: A5   **PRICE:** With admission.

PAGES: 36 plus cover

PROGRAMME EDITOR: Bill Sugden

ADVERTISING RATES
Full page £250, half page £150 & 1/4 page £85.

CLUB & GROUND DETAILS

Address: Hooks Lane, Fraser Road, Bedhampton, Havant, Hants. PO9 3EJ.
Tel. Nos. 01705 477843   Fax: 01705 492311
Capacity: 2,700   **Seated:** 200   **Standing:** 2,500
Simple Directions: From the A3(M) take the B2177 to roundabout. Follow the road signs to Bedhampton - straight on over mini-roundabout. Straight across traffic lights then bear left at level crossing. Take second left (James Road) then turn into Fraser Road at T-junction. Clubhouse is 200 yards on the right hand side.
Nearest Railway Station: Havant or Bedhampton (infrequent).
Car Parking: 200 spaces next to clubhouse.
Admission: Season tickets - Stand £60, Ground only £50. Matchdays - Adult £3, OAPs/Children £2. Extra for seat £2.
Club Shop: Yes Manager Jon Jones 01705 486516
Clubhouse: Normal licensing hours, snacks available. Functions for up to 100, contact Julian Davies 01705 473533
Training Nights: Tuesday and Thursday.

HENLEY R.F.C.

NICKNAME: Hawks

FOUNDED: 1930

President G Rae Jones, c/o Henley RFC, Dry Leas, Marlow Road, Henley-on-Thames, Oxfordshire
01491 574499/576561, 01491 412335 (Fax)

Chairman Graham Horner, c/o Henley RFC, as above

Director of Rugby/General Manager Tony MacArthur, Dry Leas, Marlow Road, Henley-on-Thames.
01491 574499/576561 (B), 01491 412335 (Fax)

Press Officer Noel Armstead, 01628 474398 (H & Fax).

Director of Coaching Jerry Bignall

1st Team Coach Nigel Dudding

Commercial Manager Alan Godwin

Fixture Secretary Paul Emerson, 0118 940 1526

Henley challenged strongly for promotion last season but had to bow out to Newbury, who alone amongst the Division Four (South) clubs had the means to adapt to the new professional era in an effective way. Both sides were undefeated when they met at Newbury in mid-October. The close result 11-9 in favour of the home side meant that they had their nose in front, bolstered by a superior points differential for the rest of the season. But Henley chased them hard until losing the return match at Dry Leas in March. This dented Henley's concentration and two further matches were lost to an improving Barking and a Weston-super-Mare side desperate to avoid relegation.

Forty-two players took part in First XV games as injuries played a significant part in testing the strength of the squad. None was more so than the No 10 position, where 1995/96 top scorer Richard Perkins (306 points) suffered a nasty AC joint injury in the second round Pilkington Cup game at Staines. His replacement, James Dunlop, then had to leave the field in the first game against Newbury the following week after just twenty minutes with a cruciate ligament injury which put him out for the rest of the season. To complete the trilogy, Ben Tubb who had stood in at fly-half for much of the season suffered a similar injury just seconds before the end of the penultimate game of 1996/97 against Cheltenham. Little wonder that Henley contemplate leaving the No 10 shirt out of their strip for next season!

Comfortable runners-up to Newbury in 1996/97 Henley are resolved again to challenge for promotion in the coming season. Some useful additions are expected to strengthen the squad and early signings include No 8 Alistair Mortimore (ex Bedford), Peter McAlister (ex Camberley and Blackheath), and also centre and halfback Ben Hobbs captain of Brunel University and Saracens Development XV. Last year's squad remains intact apart from lock Sean O'Leary, who has retired.

With one of the best playing surfaces in the country, Henley under new skipper Matt Maudsley will be looking to continue to play winning and entertaining rugby.

Henley RFC, 1st XV Squad 1996/97

Photo - Adrian Lewington

Colours: Gold, bottle green, navy hoops.

Change colours: Gold.

HENLEY

No	Ven.	Date	Opponents	Att.	Res.	Score	Scorers
1	(H)	31.08	v N Walsham		W	28- 6	Townsend(2t)Phillips(t)Hegginbotham(t)Tubb(dg)Perkins(cp)
2	(A)	07.09	v Tabard		W	45-22	Phillips(t)Parton(t)Tubb(t)Mahaffey(t)Townsend(t)Perkins(t3c2pdg)
3	(H)	21.09	v Camberley		W	32-13	Swadling(t)Wylder(t)Phillips(t)Mawdsley(t)Townsend(t)New(dg)Perkins(2c)
4	(A)	28.09	v Askeans		W	46-31	Swadling(2t)Hearn(t)Briton(t)New(t)Wylder(t)Mawdsley(2t3c)
5	(H)	05.10	v Plymouth		W	54-14	Townsend(3t)New(t)PenT(t)Phillips(t)Smye(t)Parton(c)Mawdsley(3tc)
6	(A)	19.10	v Newbury		L	9-11	Parton(2p)Dunlop(p)
7	(H)	26.10	v High Wycombe		W	28-21	Swadling(t)Walker(t)Phillip(t)Potter(dg)Mawdsley(2c2p)
8	(A)	09.11	v Berry Hill		W	38-30	Spencer(2t)Phillips(t)Parton(t)Hegginbotham(t)Mawdsley(5cp)
9	(H)	16.11	v Barking		W	27-26	Sharp(3t)Briton(t)Mawdsley(tc)
10	(A)	21.12	v Met Police		W	20-17	Sharp(2t)Rhymes(t)Mawdsley(cp)
11	(A)	18.01	v Charlton Park		W	29-11	Parton(t)Davidson(t)Briton(t)Spencer(t)Brown(t)Mawdsley(2c)
12	(A)	25.01	v N Walsham		W	22-16	Tubb(t)Townsend(t)Phillips(t)Mawdsley(tc)
13	(H)	02.02	v Tabard		W	31-25	Oswald(t)Sharp(t)Hegginbotham(t)Maudsley(t4cp)
14	(A)	08.02	v Camberley		W	23-18	Davidson(t)Tubb(tdg)Maudsley(tcp)
15	(H)	16.02	v Askeans		W	53- 3	Britton(t)Phillips(t)Sharp(t)Parton(2t3c)Maudsley(2t2cp)
16	(A)	22.02	v Plymouth		W	27-18	Sharp(t)Tubb(t)Parton(2tcp)Maudsley(c)
17	(H)	02.03	v Newbury		L	8-26	Swadling(t)Maudsley(p)
18	(A)	08.03	v High Wycombe		W	43-19	Turner(2t)Walker(2t)Hearn(t)Tubb(t)Higginbotham(t)Maudsley(4c)
19	(H)	15.03	v Berry Hill		W	34-19	Sharp(3t)Davidson(t)New(t)Daynes(t)Tubb(2c)
20	(A)	22.03	v Barking		L	15-26	Sharp(t)Swadling(t)Phillips(t)
21	(H)	29.03	v Weston-S-M		L	18-20	PenTry(t)Spencer(tc2p)
22	(H)	05.04	v Met Police		D	25-25	Horlar(t)Phillips(t)Spencer(t2c2p)
23	(A)	09.04	v Weston-S-M		W	24-16	Spencer(2tc4p)
24	(H)	12.04	v Charlton Park		W	64- 7	Davidson(2t)Bradbury(2t)Townsend(t)Walker(t)Spencer(4t7c)
25	(H)	26.04	v Cheltenham		W	19-10	Parton(t)Spencer(c4p)
26	(A)	29.04	v Cheltenham		D	6- 6	Spencer(2p)

1996-97 HIGHLIGHTS

SENT OFF: Sean O'Leary.

PLAYERS USED: 41 plus three as replacement only.

EVER PRESENT: Nick Bradbury and Willie Phillips.

□ Second top points scorers in the division.
  1170 Newbury
  768 Henley
  740 Barking

□ Most points in the season

Pts	Player	T	C	P	D
140	Matt Maudsley	12	28	8	-
121	Chris Spencer	11	12	14	-
60	Gavin Sharp	12	-	-	-
59	Andy Parton	8	5	3	-
50	Willie Phillips	10	-	-	-
45	Simon Townsend	9	-	-	-
35	Ben Tubb	5	2	-	2

□ Most points in a match
34 Chris Spencer v Charlton Park 12.04.97 (H)
24 Chris Spencer v Weston super Mare 05.04.97 (A)
20 Richard Perkins v Tabard 07.09.96 (A)

□ Hat trick of tries in a match
4 Chris Spencer v Charlton Park 12.04.97 (H)
3 Simon Townsend v Plymouth v Plymouth 05.10.96 (H)
3 Matt Maudsley v Plymouth 05.10.96 (H)
3 Gavin Sharp v Barking 16.11.96 (H)
3 Gavin Sharp v Berry Hill 15.03.97 (H)

□ Most appearances
26 Nick Bradbury and Willie Phillips
22 Matt Maudsley
21 Ben Tubb
20 Mike Turner

HENLEY'S COURAGE LEAGUE MATCH DETAILS 1996-97

	15	14	13	12	11	10	9	1	2	3	4	5	6	7	8	Replacements
1	Parton	Mahaffey	Swadling	Tubb	Townsend	Perkins	Davidson	Hegginbottam	Bradbury	New	O'Leary	Sampson	Horlar	Wylder	Phillips	Walker(5),Heuser(12)
2	Parton	Mahaffey	Swadling	Tubb	Townsend	Perkins	Davidson	Hegginbottam	Bradbury	New	Wylder	O'Leary	Horlar	Phillips	Walker	Scott(6),Wright(8),Dawes(12)
3	Parton	Townsend	Dawes	Swadling	Maudsley	Perkins	Smye	Hegginbottam	Bradbury	New	Fleming	O'Leary	Sowden	Sowden	Phillips	
4	Parton	Maudsley	Swadling	Hearn	Sharp	Perkins	Smye	Hegginbottam	Bradbury	New	Fleming	Wylder	Britton	Sowden	Phillips	
5	Parton	Maudsley	Swadling	Hearn	Townsend	Dunlop	Smye	Rhymes	Bradbury	New	O'Leary	Fleming	Sowden	Phillips	Wylder	Sharp(10)Wood(2)
6	Parton	Townsend	Maudsley	Hearn	Sharp	Dunlop	Davidson		Bradbury	New	O'Leary	Fleming	Sowden	Phillips	Taylor	Maudsley(10)Sowden(5)
7	Parton	Davidson	Swadling	Hearn	Maudsley	Potter	Smye	Rhymes	Bradbury	New	O'Leary	Turner	Sowden	Phillips	R.Walker	
8	Parton	McGregor	Maudsley	Tubb	Spencer	Smye			Bradbury	Maton	O'Leary	Turner	Britton	Britton		
9	Parton	McGregor	Maudsley	Tubb	Sharp	Spencer	Smye	Rhymes	Bradbury	New	O'Leary	Turner	Wylder	Britton	Britton	Swadling(12)Pollard(6)
10	Parton	Sharp	Maudsley	Tubb	Townsend	Spencer	Davidson	Maton	Rhymes	Bradbury	Turner	Wright	Phillips	Wylder	New	New(1)
11	Parton	Brown	Tubb	Maudsley	Townsend	Spencer	Davidson	Rhymes	Bradbury	New	O'Leary	Turner	Britton	Phillips	R.Walker	Hegginbottam(1)Sampson(5)Smye(9)
12	Parton	Brown	Tubb	Maudsley	Townsend	Spencer	Smye	Hegginbottam	Bradbury	New	O'Leary	Turner	Britton	Phillips	R.Walker	Davidson(9)Sharp(14)Sampson(4)
13	Parton	Maudsley	Hearn	Oswald	Sharp	Tubb	Smye	Hegginbottam	Bradbury	New	Sampson	Turner	Britton	Phillips	R.Walker	
14	Parton	Townsend	Maudsley	Oswald	Sharp	Tubb	Davidson	Hegginbottam	Bradbury	New	Sampson	Turner	Britton	Phillips	R.Walker	O'Leary(4)Rhymes(1)Spencer(tr12)
15	Parton	Townsend	Maudsley	Oswald	Sharp	Tubb	Davidson	Hegginbottam	Bradbury	New	Sampson	Turner	Britton	Phillips	R.Walker	Swadling(12)Smye(9)Maton(3)
16	Parton	Townsend	Swadling	Maudsley	Sharp	Tubb	Davidson	Hegginbottam	Bradbury	New	O'Leary	Sampson	Britton	Phillips	R.Walker	Hegginbottam(1)Turner(4)Daynes(14)
17	Parton	Maudsley	Swadling	Oswald	Sharp	Tubb	Davidson	Rhymes	Bradbury	New	O'Leary	Turner	Britton	Phillips	R.Walker	Hegginbottam(1)Smye(12)
18	Maudsley	Daynes	Swadling	Sharp	Sharp	Tubb	Smye	Rhymes	Bradbury	New	Sampson	Fleming	Britton	Phillips	Walker	Ventner(14),Hegginbottam(1),Pollard(4.
19	Daynes	Ventner	Maudsley	Swadling	Sharp	Tubb	Smye	Hegginbottam	Bradbury	New	Turner	Sampson	Fleming	Phillips	Walker	Wright(6),Spencer(9),Rhymes(1)
20	Davidson	Sharp	Maudsley	Ventner	Tubb	Smye	Rhymes	Bradbury	New	Turner	Sampson	Fleming	Phillips	Walker		Townsend(14),Wright(12),Hegginbottam(1)
21	Davidson	McGregor	Swadling	Oswald	Spencer	Tubb	Smye	Maton	Bradbury	Rhymes	Turner	Sampson	G.Walker	Phillips	R.Walker	O'Leary(4)Dawes(12)
22	Maudsley	Townsend	Swadling	Oswald	Spencer	Tubb	Davidson	Rhymes	Bradbury	Maton	Sampson	Turner	Horlar	Phillips	Wright	
23	Maudsley	Townsend	Swadling	Oswald	Spencer	Tubb	Davidson	Gavins	Bradbury	Hegginbottam	Sampson	Turner	Horlar	Phillips	R.Walker	
24	Maudsley	Townsend	Swadling	Oswald	Spencer	Tubb	Smye	Rhymes	Bradbury	Caudle	Sampson	Turner	Pollard	Phillips	R.Walker	Davidson(9)Horlar(6)Ventner(13)Gavins(1)
25	Parton	Maudsley	Swadling	Ventner	Spencer	Tubb	Davidson	Rhymes	Bradbury	Hegginbottam	Sampson	Turner	Horlar	Phillips	R.Walker	Fleming(6)McGregor(10)
26	Parton	Maudsley	Swadling	Ventner	McGregor	Spencer	Davidson	Gavins	Bradbury	Hegginbottam	O'Leary	Turner	Horlar	Phillips	R.Walker	Townsend(11)Caudle(1)Fleming(8)Smye(9)

HENLEY LEAGUE STATISTICS
(COMPILED BY STEPHEN McCORMACK)

Season	Div.	P	W	D	L	F	A	PD	Pts	Pos.	Coach	Captain
87-88	SW2	10	3	1	6	109	164	-55	7	10	G Horner	A Hooper
88-89	SW2	10	6	0	4	137	168	-31	12	5	G Horner	M Poulson
89-90	SW2	10	4	0	6	132	189	-57	8	8	C Woodward	M Duffelen
90-91	SW2	10	3	1	6	124	156	-32	7	8	C Woodward	M Duffelen
91-92	SW2	10	8	1	1	283	103	180	17	1p	C Woodward	M Duffelen
92-93	SW1	12	9	0	3	312	143	169	18	2	C Woodward	
93-94	SW1	12	12	0	0	328	125	203	24	1p	C Woodward	
94-95	D5S	12	5	0	7	190	299	-109	10	9	C Woodward	R Heginbotham
95-96	D5S	12	8	0	4	349	192	157	16	3	N Dudding	W Phillips
96-97	D4S	26	20	2	4	768	456	312	42	2		
Total		124	78	5	41	2732	1995	737				

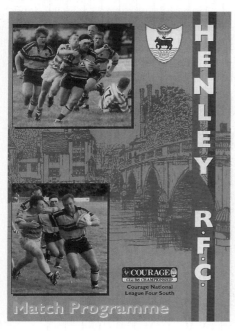

Match Programme

PROGRAMME DETAILS

SIZE: A5   **PRICE:** £1.50

PAGES: 48 plus cover

PROGRAMME EDITOR
Mick Dudding 01491 412288

ADVERTISING RATES
On Application

CLUB & GROUND DETAILS

Address:
Dry Leas, Marlow Rd, Henley-on-Thames, Oxon RG9 2JA
Tel. Nos. 0149 574499; Fax 01491 412335
Capacity: 2,000   **Seated:** None   **Standing:** 2,000
Simple Directions: Centre of Henley follow signs to Marlow, ground on left 100 yards past roundabout
Nearest Railway Station: Henley
Car Parking: 400 at ground
Admission: Season Adult £40, Matchday Adult £4, Children/OAPs £2
Club Shop: Yes manager Paul Emerson 0118 940 1526
Clubhouse: Tues, Wed, Thurs, Fri evenings. Saturday all day, Sunday lunchtime. Snacks & barmeals available. Functions available, capacity 150, contact Graham Cromack 01491 641282
Training Nights: Monday & Thursday; Women Wednesday

METROPOLITAN POLICE RFC

NICKNAME: Mets   FOUNDED: 1923

Club Secretary David Barham, MPAA Office, Room G11, Wellington House, Buckingham Gate, London. SW1E 6BE. 0181 422 4966 (H), 0171 230 7109 (B), 0171 230 7193 (Fax)

Fixtures Secretary Bob Williams, Enquiries Office, Colindale Police Station, Graham Parkway, Colindale, London NW9 5YW   0181 349 4966 (H), 0181 733 4570 (B), 0181 733 4490 (Fax)

Registration Officer John Packer, Marylebone Police Station, 1-9 Seymour Street, London. W1H 5AA. 0181 429 1935 (H), 0171 321 9482 (B), 0171 321 9346 (Fax)

President Sir Paul Condon QPM   **Chairman** Anthony Rowe QPM

In my report last year I said: "It will be interesting to see if we can come to terms with the demands of the first 'open' rugby season, but only the results of the next ten months will give an indication of our desire to continue playing at this level".

In my opinion we more than proved we had the desire, also a fair amount of ability and, at times, played our best rugby for many years. Unfortunately, we did not maintain this desire until the final whistle of the season, or perhaps at times played so well that our expectations could not be met. Whatever the reason both Jon Taylor (ably assisted by Nigel Botherwell) and John Packer worked miracles to produce many excellent results and confound our critics who had pencilled in the Met Police as prime condidates for the drop.

Overall we scored more points than in any previous season in the club's history, beating the 811 points scored in 71/72 by 51 points. Our league results were a vast improvement on previous seasons but could, and should, have been much better. In no fewer than eight of the matches lost there was only one score between the teams. We look forward with interest to the coming season.

Metropolitan Police RFC: Back Row (L-R); John Packer (Man.), Andy Smith, Frank Murray, Kevin Instance, Brian Keeley, Jeff Strickler, Jim Tunn, David Hay, Mark Slevin, Phil Thompson, Richard Galvin, Jamie Canham, Gordon Raybould, Jim Panter, Yogi Kerslake, Nick Thatcher, Julian Roe, Jon Taylor (Coach). Middle: Simon Stockton, Ray McGeary, Rob Kensey, Derek Barham, Paul Galvin, Richard Jenkins, Dean Jeffery (Capt), Kevin Walsh, Andy Carter, Graham Chesterton, Paul Kirby, Ziggy Banaghan. Front: Steve Wood, Eddie Weatherly, Rhos Cox, Steve Evans, Frank Armstrong, Ross Ferry, Mark Wood, James Herring, Gary Fryer, Jim Lunn, Damian McLoughlin

Colours: Blue and white hoops.   Change colours: Yellow with blue collar & cuffs.

COURAGE LEAGUE MATCH DETAILS 1996-97

No	Ven.	Date	Opponents	Att.	Res.	Score	Scorers
1	(H)	31.08	v Tabard		W	23-15	Carter(t)Woods(t)Slevin(2c3p)
2	(A)	07.09	v Camberley		L	5-15	Wakeford(t)
3	(H)	21.09	v Askeans		W	47- 9	Carter(2t)Lenthall(2t)Ferry(t)Canham(t)Slevin(4c3p)
4	(A)	28.09	v Plymouth		W	27-25	Carter(2t)R Galvin(t)Slevin(3c2p)
5	(H)	05.10	v Newbury		L	12-31	Slevin(4p)
6	(A)	19.10	v High Wycombe		W	23-13	Friar(t)Jeffrey(t)Wakeford(t)Slevin(c2p)
7	(H)	26.10	v Berry Hill		W	23-10	Weatherley(t)Jeffrey(t)Slevin(2c3p)
8	(A)	09.11	v Barking		W	19-18	Strickler(t)Slevin(c4p)
9	(H)	16.11	v Charlton Park		W	69- 0	Davies(2t)Carter(2t)R Galvin(2t)Thatcher(t)Thompson(t)Weatherley(t)Strickler(t)Slevin(t7c)
10	(H)	21.12	v Henley		L	17-20	Warlow(t)Slevin(4p)
11	(A)	28.12	v Weston-S-M		W	40-20	R Galvin(2t)Lunn(t)Thompson(t)Warlow(t)Davies(t)Slevin(5c)
12	(A)	25.01	v Tabard		L	12-20	Slevin(3pdg)
13	(H)	01.02	v Camberley		W	51-13	R Galvin(2t)Lunn(t)Canham(t)Friar(t)Weatherley(t)Slevin(t2c4p)
14	(A)	08.02	v Askeans		W	44-10	Weatherley(5t)Jenkins(t)Warlow(t)Slevin(3cp)
15	(H)	15.02	v Plymouth		W	31-20	Barham(t)Tovey(t)Jenkins(t)Slevin(tc3p)
16	(A)	22.02	v Newbury		L	0-87	
17	(H)	01.03	v N Walsham		W	42-25	Carter(2t)Davies(2t)Panter(t)Weatherley(t)Slevin(3c2p)
18	(A)	08.03	v Berry Hill		L	6- 8	Slevin(2p)
19	(H)	15.03	v Barking		L	6-40	Slevin(2p)
20	(A)	22.03	v Charlton Park		W	49-31	R Galvin(3t)Davies(t)Thatcher(t)Ferry(t)Herring(t4c2p)
21	(A)	05.04	v Henley		D	25-25	P Galvin(2t)Jeffrey(t)Herring(2c2p)
22	(H)	12.04	v Weston-S-M		L	8-14	R Galvin(t)Herring(p)
23	(A)	19.04	v Cheltenham		W	17-10	Jeffrey(t)P Galvin(t)Friar(t)Herring(c)
24	(H)	26.04	v N Walsham		L	17-22	Carter(t)Herring(4p)
25	(H)	03.05	v Cheltenham		L	31-36	Panter(t)PenTry(t)Tovey(t)Slevin(t3c)Herring(cp)
26	(A)	10.05	v N Walsham		L	17-21	Jeffrey(t)R Galvin(t)Canham(t)Herring(c)

1996-97 HIGHLIGHTS

LEAGUE DEBUTS:

PLAYERS USED: 32 plus three as replacement only

EVER PRESENT: None - most 25 Jamie Canham

❏ Had a better away record than home.

H/A	W	D	L	PTS
Home	7	0	6	14
Away	7	1	5	15

❏ **Most points in a match**
25 Eddie Weatherley v Askeans 08.02.97 (A)
21 Mark Slevin v Camberley 01.02.97 (H)
19 Mark Slevin v Charlton Park 16.11.96 (H)

❏ **Hat trick of tries in a match**
5 Eddie Weatherley v Askeans 08.02.97 (A)
3 Richard Galvin v Charlton Park 22.03.97 (A)

❏ **Most points in the season**

Pts	Player	T	C	P	D
223	Mark Slevin	4	37	42	1
55	Richard Galvin	11	-	-	-
53	James Herring	1	9	10	-
50	Andy Carter	10	-	-	-
45	Eddie Weatherley	9	-	-	-

❏ **Most appearances**
25 Jamie Canham
22 Ian Warlow
21 Nick Thatcher and Mark Slevin
20 Jim Lunn and Eddie Weatherley

METROPOLITAN POLICE COURAGE LEAGUE MATCH DETAILS 1996-97

No.	15	14	13	12	11	10	9	1	2	3	4	5	6	7	8	Replacements
1	Walsh	Carter	Ferry	Lunn	Wakeford	Slevin	Woods	Barham	Jeffrey	Thompson	Raybould	R Galvin	Panter	Canham		P Galvin(6)
2	Walsh	Carter	Ferry	Lenthall	Wakeford	Herring	Friar	Barham	Jeffrey	Thatcher	Tunn	P Galvin	Panter	Canham		Warlow(1)Roe(6)Woods(9)
3	Carter	Wakeford	Ferry	Lenthall	Weatherley	Slevin	Friar	Barham	Jeffrey	Thatcher	Canham	Thompson	Roe	Tovey	R Galvin	
4	Carter	Wakeford	Ferry	Lenthall	Weatherley	Slevin	Friar	Barham	Jeffrey	Thatcher	Canham	Thompson	Roe	Tovey	R Galvin	
5	Carter	Wakeford	Ferry	Lenthall	Weatherley	Slevin	Friar	Barham	Jeffrey	Thatcher	Canham	Thompson	Roe	Tovey	R Galvin	Herring(14)
6	Lunn	Carter	Ferry	Lenthall	Walsh	Wakeford	Friar	Thatcher	Jeffrey	Warlow	Canham	Thompson	Roe	Panter	R Galvin	Jenkins(9)
7	Lunn	Wakeford	Lenthall	Walsh	Weatherley	Slevin	Friar	Thatcher	Jeffrey	Warlow	Canham	Thompson	Roe	Tovey	R Galvin	
8	Lunn	Carter	Lenthall	Ferry	Weatherley	Slevin	Friar	Thatcher	Jeffrey	Warlow	Thompson	Canham	Williams	Tovey	R Galvin	R Galvin(5)Walsh(12)
9	Carter	Weatherley	Lenthall	Lunn	Davies	Slevin	Friar	Thatcher	Jeffrey	Warlow	Thompson	Canham	Roe	Strickler	R Galvin	Barham(1)
10	Lunn	Carter	Lenthall	Walsh	Davies	Slevin	Friar	Thatcher	Jeffrey	Warlow	Thompson	Canham	Roe	Strickler	R Galvin	Raybould(8)Chesterton(14)
11	Lunn	Weatherley	Lenthall	Walsh	Davies	Slevin	Friar	Thatcher	Instance	Warlow	Thompson	Canham	Roe	Strickler	R Galvin	R Galvin
12	Lunn	Panter	Weatherley	Walsh	Davies	Slevin	Friar	Thatcher	Instance	Warlow	Thompson	Canham	Strickler	Tovey	R Galvin	Jenkins(9)
13	Lunn	Weatherley	Lenthall	Walsh	Davies	Slevin	Friar	Thatcher	Jeffrey	Warlow	Thompson	Canham	Raybould	Tovey	R Galvin	Jenkins(9)
14	Lunn	Weatherley	Lenthall	Walsh	Davies	Slevin	Friar	Thatcher	Instance	Warlow	Thompson	Canham	Raybould	Tovey	R Galvin	Roe(8)Jenkins(9)
15	Carter	Weatherley	Lunn	Walsh	Davies	Slevin	Jenkins	Barham	Jeffrey	Warlow	Thompson	Canham	Roe	Tovey	R Galvin	Instance(2)McLoughlan(7)
16	Lunn	Weatherley	Walsh	Lenthall	Davies	Slevin	Jenkins	Barham	Instance	Warlow	Canham	Roe	McLoughlin	Panter	Panter	Hay(6),Chesterton(13)
17	Carter	Weatherley	Lunn	Ferry	Davies	Slevin	Jenkins	Barham	Instance	Warlow	Thompson	Canham	McLoughlin	Panter	Panter	Lenthall(14)
18	Carter	Weatherley	Ferry	Davies	Davies	Slevin	Jenkins	Barham	Jeffrey	Warlow	Thompson	Canham	Thompson	Panter	Panter	McLoughlin(6)
19	Lunn	Weatherley	Walsh	Davies	Davies	Slevin	Jenkins	Barham	Jeffrey	Warlow	Canham	Thompson	Raybould	Panter	R Galvin	Instance(5)Herring(10)Lenthall(2)
20	Carter	Weatherley	Lenthall	Davies	Davies	Slevin	Jenkins	Instance	Thatcher	Warlow	Canham	Thompson	Raybould	Panter	R Galvin	Walsh(13)Friar(9)Murray(5)
21	Walsh	Weatherley	Lenthall	Davies	Davies	Herring	Jenkins	Thatcher	Jeffrey	Warlow	Canham	Thompson	Panter	Keating	R Galvin	Friar(9)
22	Lunn	Weatherley	Lenthall	Ferry	Davies	Herring	Jenkins	Jeffrey	Thatcher	Warlow	Canham	Raybould	Roe	Roe	R Galvin	Keating (7)
23	Carter	Walsh	Ferry	Weatherley	Davies	Herring	Jenkins	Jeffrey	Thatcher	Warlow	Canham	Raybould	Roe	R Galvin	R Galvin	Instance(6)Keating(7)
24	Lunn	Carter	Slevin	Ferry	Weatherley	Herring	Friar	Thatcher	Jeffrey	Warlow	Canham	Raybould	Keating	Keating	R Galvin	Tovey(6)Panter(7)
25	Lunn	Carter	Slevin	Ferry	Weatherley	Herring	Friar	Instance	Jeffrey	Warlow	Canham	Raybould	Keating	Keating	R Galvin	Chesterton(10)Strickler(8)Barham(1)Jenkins(9)
26	Lunn	Weatherley	Slevin	Panter	Ferry	Herring	Friar	Instance	Thatcher	Warlow	Canham	Raybould	Raybould	Tovey	Keating	Jenkins(9)Jeffrey(2)Barham(8)

METROPOLITAN POLICE LEAGUE STATISTICS
(COMPILED BY STEPHEN McCORMACK)

Season	Div.	P	W	D	L	F	A	PD	Pts	Pos.	Coach	Captain
87-88	3	11	5	0	6	130	128	2	10	7	A Boddy	S O'Reilly
88-89	3	11	4	0	7	130	275	-145	8	11r	A Boddy	D Kyffin
89-90	ALS	10	9	0	1	255	74	181	18	1p	A Boddy	S Innes
90-91	3	12	4	0	8	130	188	-58	8	12r	A Boddy	S Innes
91-92	D4S	12	3	0	9	149	195	-46	6	10		N Sinclair
92-93	D4S	12	4	1	7	201	207	-6	9	9		
93-94	D5S	12	5	0	7	167	174	-7	10	10	R Williams	K Walsh
94-95	D5S	12	5	0	7	183	175	8	10	7	R Williams	K Walsh
95-96	D5S	12	2	1	9	130	204	-74	5	12	J Taylor	D Jeffrey
96-97	D4S	26	14	1	11	661	558	103	29	7		
Total		131	45	6	80	1960	2521	-561				

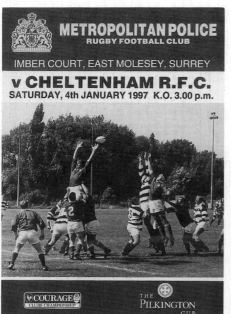

METROPOLITAN POLICE
RUGBY FOOTBALL CLUB

IMBER COURT, EAST MOLESEY, SURREY

v CHELTENHAM R.F.C.
SATURDAY, 4th JANUARY 1997 K.O. 3.00 p.m.

COURAGE
CLUBS CHAMPIONSHIP

THE PILKINGTON CUP

PROGRAMME DETAILS

SIZE: A5   **PRICE:** With entry

PAGES: 12 plus cover

PROGRAMME EDITOR
Contact David Barham 0171 230 7109

ADVERTISING RATES
Colour Full Page £250, Half page £175, Qtr page £100
Mono   Full page £100, Half page £75, Qtr page £50

CLUB & GROUND DETAILS

Address: Met Police (Imber Court) Sports Club, Ember Lane, East Molesey, Surrey KT8 0BT.
Tel. Nos. 0181 398 1267; Fax 0181 398 9755
Capacity: 3,250   **Seated:** 750   **Standing:** 2,500
Simple Directions: M25 Jnc 12, M3 towards London Jnc 1, take A308 to Hampton Court, turn right over bridge A309 to next r'about, turn right into Ember Court Rd, club at end.
Nearest Railway Station: Esher, turn right ground entrance 600 yds
Car Parking: 200 within ground
Admission: £3, Children/OAP £1
Club Shop: No
Clubhouse: Normal licensing hours, snacks & meals available. Functions available
Training Nights: Monday & Thursday

NORTH WALSHAM R.F.C.

NICKNAME: Walsh

FOUNDED: 1962

President Cyril Durrant MBE, Park Farm, Ashman Haugh, Norwich NR12 8YJ
01603 782546 (H)

Chairman Richard Flatters, Oak Apples, Lower Street, Salhouse, Norwich NR13 6RM
01603 721225 (H), 01603 684037 (B)

Club Secretary John Wheeley, Dubeck, Common Road, Thurne, Gt. Yarmouth. NR29 3BX.
01692 670294 (H)

Press Officer Tony Marcantonio, The White House, Southwood Road, Beighton, Norwich. NR13 3AB.
01493 751837 (H & Fax)

Fixtures Secretary K T Jarvis, The Chilterns, 2D Millfield Road, North Walsham. NR28 0EB.
01692 406429 (H), 01263 732341 (B)

Sighs of relief all round greeted the final whistle as North Walsham ended the last match of the season with a win against Metropolitan Police and the news came shortly afterwards that with Camberley winning at Berry Hill the Norfolk side would have another year in the National Leagues.

What a traumatic season it was, when a good start against Cheltenham away was followed by some frankly mediocre performances against sides that should and could have been beaten. Then came a horrendous run of injuries with as many as nine first team squad players injured, and at least three of them lasting for almost the whole season. One thing that was much in evidence even during a seven match losing run was the self belief engendered by skipper Jeff van Poortvliet that if Walsham stuck at it they would succeed. That belief was supported by last year's captain Nick Greenhall, who despite suffering a long term injury took on some of the coaching duties and players who were either asked to play out of position or had joined the club from sides lower down the Norfolk County structure had to raise their game and play at a level much higher than they were accustomed to.

So Walsham despite their limited resources and player catchment area will be staying in the National League, although the delight is somewhat tempered by the thought that they will no longer be able to visit and host clubs with whom they have built up such good relationships over past seasons.

North Walsham's No 8, Phil Anthony breaks out of defence against Plymouth with skipper Jeff Van Poortvliet in support.
Photo - Eastern Counties Newspapers

Colours: Green with 1 wide black & 2 narrow white bands/black/green.   Change colours: White/black/green.

NORTH WALSHAM

COURAGE LEAGUE MATCH DETAILS 1996-97

No	Ven.	Date	Opponents	Att.	Res.	Score	Scorers
1	(A)	31.08	v Henley		L	6-28	Perrins(2p)
2	(H)	07.09	v Weston-S-M		W	24-13	Smith(t)Sherman(t)PenT(t)Kingsmill(3cp)
3	(A)	21.09	v Cheltenham		W	18-15	Fox(t)Van Poortvliet(t)Perrins(c2p)
4	(H)	28.09	v Charlton Park		L	24-28	C Greenhall(t)Purling(t)Sherman(t)Van Poortvliet(t)Perrins(2c)
5	(H)	05.10	v Tabard		D	16-16	Shanahan(t)Perrins(c3p)
6	(A)	19.10	v Camberley		L	12-30	N Greenhall(t)Perrins(tc)
7	(H)	26.10	v Askeans		W	29-10	Purling(t)Rains(t)Smith(t)Kingsmill(c2p)Perrins(2p)
8	(A)	09.11	v Plymouth		L	22-41	Waight(t)Kingsmill(t)Smith(t)C Greenhall(t)Perrins(c)
9	(H)	16.11	v Newbury		L	18-72	Rains(2t)Pegden(t)Perrins(t)
10	(A)	21.12	v High Wycombe		L	8-33	Smith(t)Perrins(p)
11	(A)	18.01	v Barking		L	5-11	M Yaxley(t)
12	(H)	25.01	v Henley		L	16-22	Kingsmill(t)Perrins(c3p)
13	(A)	01.02	v Wesot-S-M		L	3-18	Kingsmill(p)
14	(H)	08.02	v Cheltenham		L	18-43	Rains(t)Balfour(t)Dillon(p)Kingsmill(cp)
15	(A)	15.02	v Charlton Park		W	16-11	Rains(2t)Dillon(2p)
16	(A)	22.02	v Tabard		L	8-23	Van Poorvtliet(t)KIngsmill(p)
17	(H)	01.03	v Camberley		L	13-20	Rains(t)Smith(t)Kingsmill(p)
18	(A)	08.03	v Askeans		W	22- 6	Kingsmill(t)Scott(t)Marlee(t)Shanahan(2cp)
19	(H)	15.03	v Plymouth		W	23-18	N Greenall(t)Hargrave(t)Shanahan(2c3p)
20	(A)	22.03	v Newbury		L	13-63	Rains(t)Shanahan(tp)
21	(H)	29.03	v Berry Hill		W	26- 8	Anthony(t)Shanahan(2tc3p)
22	(H)	05.04	v High Wycombe		W	23-15	Rains(2t)Dillon(c)Shanahan(t2p)
23	(A)	12.04	v Berry Hill		L	8-13	Smith(t)Shanahan(p)
24	(H)	19.04	v Barking		L	12-14	Kingsmill(t)Scott(t)Shanahan(c)
25	(A)	26.04	v Met Police		W	22-17	Loose(t)Girdler(t)Dillon(t2cp)
26	(H)	10.05	v Met Police		W	21-17	Kingsmill(2t)Smith(t)Dillon(2p)

1996-97 HIGHLIGHTS

LEAGUE DEBUTS:

PLAYERS USED: 40 plus five as replacement only

EVER PRESENT: None - most 25 Jeff van Poortvliet

❑ Won six of their last nine games to stave of relegation.

❑ Only three teams scored less points.

       340 Askeans
       352 Charlton Park
       425 Berry Hill
       426 North Walsham

❑ **Most points in a match**

21 James Shanahan v Berry Hill 29.03.97 (H)
13 James Shanahan v Plymouth 15.03.97 (H)

❑ **Hat trick of tries in a match**

None - two tries were scored five times with Tom Rains achieving the feat three times.

❑ **Most points in the season**

Pts	Player	T	C	P	D
70	James Shanahan	5	6	11	-
61	Tony Kingsmill	6	5	7	-
61	Jon Perrins	1	7	14	-
50	Tom Rains	10	-	-	-
35	David Smith	7	-	-	-
29	Stuart Dillon	1	3	6	-

❑ **Most appearances**

25 Jeff van Poortvliet
24 Rex Hargrave
22 Tony Kingsmill

NORTH WALSHAM'S COURAGE LEAGUE MATCH DETAILS 1996-97

No	15	14	13	12	11	10	9	1	2	3	4	5	6	7	8	Replacements
1	C Greenall	Kinsmill	Smith	NGreenall	Perrins	Shanahan	Hadridge	Loose	Hambling	Scott	Fletcher	Gibbs	Purling	Poortvliet	Anthony	Rains(15)O'Sullivan
2	Kingsmill	Smith	Fox	NGreenall	Sherman	Shanahan	Hadridge	Scott	Hambling	Waight	Hargrave	Carter	Purling	Poortvliet	Anthony	Davis(8)
3	Perrins	Sherman	Fox	NGreenall	Rains	Shanahan	Kelly	Scott	Hambling	Waight	Hargrave	Carter	Purling	Poortvliet	Browne	
4	Perrins	Sherman	Fox	NGreenall	C Greenall	Shanahan	Kelly	Scott	Evans	Waight	Hargrave	Carter	Purling	Poortvliet	Browne	Smith(13)
5	C Greenall	Kingsmill	Fox	NGreenall	Perrins	Shanahan	Hadridge	M Yaxley	Leonard		Hargrave	Carter	Purling	Poortvliet	Anthony	
6	Kingamill	Rains	Fox	Smith	Perrins	Shanahan	Hadridge	Colman	Nobbs	Scott	Hargrave	Carter	Purling	Poortvliet	Pegden	NGreenall(10)
7	Kingsmill	Rains	Smith	Fox	Bayliss	NGreenall	Kelly	Colman	Nobbs	Scott	Hargrave	B Yaxley	Purling	Poortvliet	Purling	Perrins(10)Waight(3)Fletcher(5)
8	Perrins	C Greenall	Fox	NGreenall	Smith	Kingsmill	Kelly	Scott	Nobbs	Waight	Hargrave	Carter	B Yaxley	Poortvliet	Pegden	Colman(1)
9	Perrins	Rains	Fox	Smith	C Greenall	Kingsmill	Hadridge	Scott	Nobbs	Waight	Hargrave	Carter	Purling	Poortvliet	Pegden	Fletcher(6)Balfour(15)Kelly(14)
10	Perrins	Rains	C Greenall	Fox	Smith	Kingsmill	Kelly	Colman	Hambling	Ridley	Gibbs	Hargrave	Purling	Poortvliet	Pegden	Hadridge(13)Pawson(10)Fletcher(8)
11	C Greenall	Rains	Perrins	Fox	Smith	Kingsmill	Hadridge	M Yaxley	Nobbs	M Yaxley	Hargrave	Purling	Poortvliet	Anthony		Chapman(8)Woodwark(10)
12	Perrins	Rains	Smith	Kingsmill	Woodwark	Shanahan	Loose	Nobbs	Leonard	Fletcher	Hargrave	Purling	Poortvliet	Anthony		Dillon(12)Gibbs(4)
13	Kingsmill	Rains	Smith	Kelly	Malone	Dillon	Loose	Nobbs	M Yaxley	Fletcher	Gibbs	Chapman	Poortvliet	Anthony		Girdler(2)Marlee(6)
14	Kingsmill	Rains	Smith	Kelly	Balfour	Dillon	Loose	Nobbs	M Yaxley	Hargrave	Carter	Marlee	Poortvliet	Anthony		Fletcher(5)Hood(13)
15	Shanahan	Rains	NGreenall	Kelly	Kingsmill	Dillon	Loose	Nobbs	M Yaxley	Hargrave	Gibbs	Marlee	Poortvliet	Anthony		Fletcher(8)Girdler(2)
16	Shanahan	Rains	Kelly	Green	Kingsmill	Dillon	Loose	Girdler	Nobbs	Girdler	Hargrave	Marlee	Poortvliet	Anthony		Moorfoot
17	Kingsmill	Rains	Kelly	NGreenall	Smith	Shanahan	Loose	Nobbs	Scott	Hargrave	Morefoot	Marlee	Poortvliet	Anthony		Fox(13).
18	Shanahan	Rains	Kelly	NGreenall	Kingsmill	Dillon	Hadridge	Loose	Girdler	Scott	Hargrave	Moorfoot	Marlee	Poortvliet	Anthony	Fletcher(4)
19	Rains	Fox	NGreenall	Smith	Shanahan	Kelly	Loose	Girdler	Scott	Hargrave	Morfoot	Marlee	Poortvliet	Anthony		
20	Dillon	Kingsmill	Fox	NGreenall	Rains	Shanahan	Kelly	Loose	Girdler	Scott	Gibbs	Gibbs	Davis	Anthony		Hadridge(12)Mason(5)Smith(14)
21	Dillon	Kingsmill	Fox	Kelly	Rains	Shanahan	Loose	Girdler	Scott	Hargrave	Morfoot	Marlee	Poortvliet	Anthony		Smith(11)
22	Dillon	Smith	Fox	Kelly	Rains	Shanahan	Hadridge	Loose	Hambling	Scott	Hargrave	Morfoot	Marlee	Poortvliet	Anthony	Girdler(2)
23	Dillon	Smith	Fox	Kelly	Rains	Shanahan	Hadridge	Loose	Hambling	Scott	Hargrave	Morfoot	Marlee	Poortvliet	Anthony	Kingsmill(14)Purling(8)
24	Dillon	Fox	Kelly	Smith		Shanahan	Hadridge	Loose	Scott	Hargrave	Morfoot	Marlee	Purling	Purling		
25	Dillon	Kingsmill	Fox	NGreenall	Smith	Shanahan	Kelly	Loose	Nobbs	Hambling	Hargrave	Morfoot	Marlee	Poortvliet	Anthony	Girdler(2)
26	Dillon	Kingsmill	Fox	NGreenall	Smith	Shanahan	Kelly	Loose	Girdler	Hambling	Hargrave	Morfoot	Purling	Poortvliet	Anthony	

NORTH WALSHAM LEAGUE STATISTICS
(COMPILED BY STEPHEN McCORMACK)

Season	Div.	P	W	D	L	F	A	PD	Pts	Pos.	Coach	Captain
87-88	LON2N	9	7	0	2	180	72	108	14	1p		
88-89	LON1	10	6	0	4	165	105	60	12	4		R Emblem
89-90	LON1	10	9	0	1	231	94	137	18	1p	D Brunton	S Rossi
90-91	D4S	12	5	2	5	170	180	-10	12	6	P Bryant	M Goodall
91-92	D4S	12	5	0	7	153	152	1	10	7	P Bryant	B Gardner
92-93	D4S	12	4	0	8	125	209	-84	8	11		
93-94	D5S	12	5	2	5	120	173	-53	12	8		
94-95	D5S	12	7	1	4	233	190	43	15	4	R Flatters	N Greenall
95-96	D5S	12	3	1	8	149	212	-63	7	11	N Youngs	N Greenall
96-97	D4S	26	10	1	15	426	605	-179	21	10		
Total		127	61	7	59	1952	1992	-40				

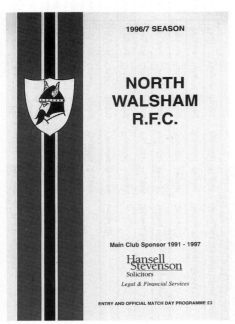

1996/7 SEASON

NORTH WALSHAM R.F.C.

Main Club Sponsor 1991 - 1997

Hansell Stevenson
Solicitors
Legal & Financial Services

ENTRY AND OFFICIAL MATCH DAY PROGRAMME £3

PROGRAMME DETAILS

SIZE: A5   **PRICE:** With Entry

PAGES: 20 plus cover

PROGRAMME EDITOR
Tony Marcantonio 01493 751837

ADVERTISING RATES
Contact Tony Marcantonio

CLUB & GROUND DETAILS

Address: Norwich Road, Scottow, Norwich, NR10 5BU

Tel. Nos. 01692 538461

Capacity: 1,000   **Seated:** None   **Standing:** 1,000

Simple Directions: From Norwich take B1150 to North Walsham, go through Coltishall towards N Walsham. Ground is on left just past "Three Horseshoes" Pub

Nearest Railway Station: North Walsham

Car Parking: Ample at ground

Admission: Adults £3 inc programme

Club Shop: Yes; Manager John Wheeley 01692 670294

Clubhouse: Open matchdays & training nights, snacks & barmeals available. Functions available, capacity 80, contact Secretary

Training Nights: Tuesday & Thursday 7.30pm

PLYMOUTH ALBION R.F.C.

FOUNDED: 1876

President Roger Harris   **Chairman** Paul Woods

Club Secretary Maureen Jackson, 27 Cardinal Avenue, St Budeaux, Plymouth, PL55 1UN
01752 363137 (H), 01752 777454 (B), 01752 777454 (Fax)

Director of Rugby Andy Johnson, c/o Plymouth Albion RFC, Beacon Park, Plymouth PL2 3JP
01752 8377425 (H), 01752 777454 (B), 01752 777454 (Fax)

Fixtures Secretary Terry Brown, c/o Plymouth Albion RFC, as above
01752 837742 (H), 01752 777454 (B), 01752 777454 (Fax)

Press Officer Paddy Marsh, 01752 343631 (H)

Club Coach Barry Trevaskis 01503 220462 (H)

After being relegated at the end of the previous season Plymouth Albion were pleased to occupy sixth position in the final league table.

Under the guidance of rugby director Andy Johnson and a team of experienced coaches, which included former Bath winger Barry Trevaskis, Albion played some entertaining rugby breaking a number of league scoring records along the way.

Centre Richard Thompson reluctantly took over the captaincy at the start of the season becoming one of Albion's youngest ever skippers. Throughout the campaign Thompson led his side from the front inspiring them with his no nonsense tackling. Unbeaten champions Newbury were given a shock at Beacon Park as Albion held the lead going into the final minutes only to run out of steam.

Drawing inspiration from this performance Albion recorded their first away league victory for three years, a sequence that involved 26 matches, when they beat Askeons 24-11 the following week. Although they didn't win many matches away from home they did draw three games on their travels, two of them at Camberley.

In the first round of the Pilkington Cup Albion equalised against Camberley in the final minute and progressed by virtue of scoring more tries. Later in the season they repeated the trick equalising late in the game to snatch a point. Their best performance of the season was a resounding 39-8 victory over high flying Cheltenham, while the worst performance came in Pilkington Cup exit at Devon rivals Barnstaple.

Influential players in Albion colours were Navy lock Gerard Harrison, young flanker Steve Dyer (voted Players' Player) and evergreen winger Steve Walklin who finished as Top Try Scorer, thus extending his own club record.

With a good blend of experience and youth, Albion eagerly await the new campaign, particularly as the travelling they have to do has been considerably reduced.
PADDY MARSH

Plymouth Albion RFC 1996-97:

Colours: White with broad cherry band edged with green.   Change colours: Cherry, green and white.

PLYMOUTH

COURAGE LEAGUE MATCH DETAILS 1996-97

No	Ven.	Date	Opponents	Att.	Res.	Score	Scorers
1	(A)	31.08	v High Wycombe		L	10-36	Coleman(t)I Goldsmith(t)
2	(H)	07.09	v Berry Hill		W	56-13	Russell(2t)Walklin(2t)Oman(t)Coleman(t)MacFarlane(t)Birkett(2tcp)R Thompson(3c)
3	(A)	21.09	v Barking		D	15-15	PenT(t)R Thompson(tcp)
4	(H)	28.09	v Met Police		L	25-27	Walklin(2t)Birkett(t)Birt(c)R Thompson(c2p)
5	(A)	05.10	v Henley		L	14-54	Manton(t)Oman(t)Birt(c)R Thompson(c)
6	(H)	19.10	v Weston-S-M		W	19- 8	Williams(t)Trinder(t)R Thompson(p)M Thompson(pdg)
7	(A)	26.10	v Cheltenham		L	5-34	Williams(t)
8	(H)	09.11	v N Walsham		W	41-22	Truman(2t)Pooley(t)R Thompson(t)Livingstone(t)Birt(t2c) M Thompson(2cp)
9	(A)	16.11	v Tabard		D	16-16	Walklin(t)I Goldsmith(t)M Thompson(2p)
10	(H)	21.12	v Camberley		W	16- 0	Armstrong(t)Manton(t)M Thompson(2p)
11	(H)	11.01	v Newbury		L	15-26	Walklin(t)James(t)M Thompson(cp)
12	(A)	18.01	v Askeans		W	24-11	Walklin(t)I Harrison(t)PenTry(t)Birt(c)
13	(H)	25.01	v High Wycombe		W	42-18	Russell(t)PenTry(t)Armstrong(t)R Thompson(t)Birt(tp)M Thompson(4cpdg)
14	(A)	01.02	v Berry Hill		L	24-33	Armstrong(t)G Harrison(t)Dyer(t)Coleman(t)Birt(c)M Thompson(c)
15	(H)	08.02	v Barking		W	44-24	R Thompson(2t)G Harrison(2t)Dyer(t)PenTry(t)Birt(2p)M Thompsom(4c)
16	(A)	15.02	v Met Police		L	20-31	Russell(t)G Harrison(t)M Thompson(2c2p)
17	(H)	22.02	v Henley		L	18-27	Russell(t)Pooley(t)Birt(p)M Thompson(cp)
18	(A)	01.03	v Weston-S-M		W	23-21	Dyer(t)PenTry(t)M Thompson(2c2pdg)
19	(H)	08.03	v Cheltenham		W	39- 8	G Harrison(2t)Russell(t)I Goldsmith(t)R Thompson(t)Livingstone(t) McFarlane(t)M Thompson(2c)
20	(A)	15.03	v North Walsham		L	18-23	Manton(t)Dyer(t)Birt(cp)Birkett(dg)
21	(H)	22.03	v Tabard		W	33-30	Trinder(2t)Livingstone(t)Enticknap(t)Russell(t)Birt(3c)M Thompson(c)
22	(H)	29.03	v Charlton Park		W	73-10	Dyer(2t)R Thompson(2t)Williams(t)Hewitt(t)Manton(t)Birt(3t5c)M Thompson(t4c)
23	(A)	05.04	v Camberley		D	17-17	R Thompson(t)Russell(t)M Thompson(tc)
24	(H)	12.04	v Askeans		W	63-20	Walklin(2t)Trinder(t)Dyer(t)Thomas(t)R Thompson(t)Durbin(t)Enticknap(t) M Thompson(2t2cdg)
25	(A)	19.04	v Charlton Park		W	39-24	Walklin(3t)Russell(3t)Trinder(t)Birt(2c)
26	(A)	26.04	v Newbury		L	0-43	

1996-97 HIGHLIGHTS

PLAYERS USED: 43 plus one as replacement only.

EVER PRESENT: Stuart Coleman

❏ 4th highest points scorers in the division and third highest try scorers.
Leading try scorers

167	Newbury
112	Henley
102	Plymouth

❏ Had the third best home record winning 10 out of 13 whilst having only the 11th best away record with just three wins.

❏ Kicked only 24 penalties the lowest total in the division.

❏ **Most points in a match**
25 Nick Birt v Charlton Park 29.03.97 (H)
19 Martin Thompson v Askeans 12.04.97 (H)

❏ **Hat trick of tries in a match**
3 Nick Birt v Charlton Park 29.03.97 (H)
3 Steve Walklin v Askeans 12.04.97 (H)

❏ **Most points in the season**

Pts	Player	T	C	P	D
131	Martin Thompson	4	30	13	4
81	Nick Birt	5	19	6	-
74	Richard Thompson	10	6	4	-
60	Steve Walklin	12	-	-	-
55	Ian Russell	11	-	-	-

❏ **Most appearances**
26 Stuart Coleman
25 Richard Thompson and Nick Birt
24 Mark Manton(2)
23 Steve Dyer
21 Martin Thompson and Ian Russell

PLYMOUTH'S COURAGE LEAGUE MATCH DETAILS 1996-97

No.	15	14	13	12	11	10	9	1	2	3	4	5	6	7	8	Replacements
1	Trinder	Walkin	Hawkins	Birt	Oman	Collins	Livingstone	Coleman	Pooley	Marton	Osborne	IGoldsmith	Cameron	Dyer	Lane	Hills(2)
2	RThompson	Walkin	Birt	Trinder	Oman	Birkitt	Maclarlane	Coleman	Pooley	Marton	Osborne	Russell	Cameron	Dyer	Truman	
3	RThompson	Walkin	Birt	Trinder	Oman	Birkitt	Livingstone	Coleman	Pooley	Marton	Russell		Cameron	Dyer	Polglase	
4	RThompson	Walkin	Birt	Trinder	Oman	Birkitt	Livingstone	Coleman	Pooley	Marton	Osborne	Russell	Short	Dyer	Polglase	
5	MThompson	Walkin	RThompson	Birt	Oman	Slade	Maclarlane	Coleman	Pooley	Marton	IHarrison	Short	Russell	Polglase	Russell	Birkitt(11)
6	RThompson	Walkin	Trinder	Birt	Williams	Birkitt		Coleman	Kirtley	Marton	IHarrison	Russell	Lane	Polglase	MGoldsmith	Osborne(4)
7	RThompson	Walkin	Trinder	Birt	Williams			Saunders	Marton	Kirtley	Russell		Lane	Dyer	Polglase	James(15)
8	RThompson	Walkin	Trinder	Birt	Williams	MThompson		Coleman	Pooley	Marton	IHarrison	Russell	Lane	Dyer	Truman	Birkitt(9)
9	RThompson	Walkin	Trinder	Birt	Erickknap	MThompson	Livingstone	Coleman	Pooley	Marton	Russell	IGoldsmith	Lane	Armstrong		Durbin(6)
10	RThompson	Walkin	James	Birt	Williams	MThompson	Livingstone	Coleman	Pooley	Marton	IGoldsmith	Russell	Dyer	Armstrong		Thomas(9)
11	RThompson	Walkin	James	Trinder	Williams	MThompson	Livingstone	Coleman	Pooley	Marton	IHarrison	IGoldsmith	Lane	Armstrong		Thomas(9)
12	RThompson	Walkin	James	Trinder	Williams	MThompson	Livingstone	Cockrill	Pooley	Marton	IHarrison	Lane	Cameron	Armstrong		IGoldsmith(15)Thomas(9)
13	Henwood	Walkin	Birt	RThompson	Williams	MThompson	Birkitt	Coleman	Pooley	Marton	IGoldsmith	Russell	Dyer	Armstrong		Livingstone(9)
14	Henwood	Birt	Birt	RThompson	Williams	MThompson	Birkitt	Coleman	Pooley	Marton	IGoldsmith	GHarrison	Dyer	Armstrong		Roberts(2)
15	Henwood	Birt	Birt	RThompson	Birt	MThompson	Birkitt	Coleman	Pooley	Marton	GHarrison	Russell	Dyer	Hewitt	Lane	
16	Henwood	Birt	Birt	RThompson	McFarlane	MThompson	Birkett	Coleman	Pooley	Marton	GHarrison	Lane	Dyer	Hewitt		Birkitt(8)James(12)Roberts(2)
17	Henwood	Williams	Birt	RThompson	McFarlane	MThompson		Coleman	Pooley	Marton	GHarrison	Russell	Dyer	Hewitt	Lane	Lane(8)
18	Henwood	McFarlane	Birkitt	RThompson	Erickknap	MThompson		Coleman	Pooley	Marton	GHarrison	Russell	Dyer	Russell		Marton(3)Kirtley(2)
19	Birkett	Walkin	RThompson	Birt	McFarlane	MThompson		Pooley	Marton	Cockrill	GHarrison	Lane	Dyer	Russell	Marton	IHarrison(6)
20	Birkett	Erickknap	Birt	Birt	McFarlane	MThompson		Pooley	Roberts	Marton	GHarrison	Cameron	Dyer	Russell		IHarrison(6)Roberts(2)Henwood(11)
21	Birkett	Birt	RThompson	Birt	Erickknap	MThompson		Coleman	Roberts	Marton	Goldsmith	Durbin	Dyer	Russell		Hewitt(4)Pooley(2)
22	Birkett	Trinder	RThompson	RThompson	Williams	MThompson		Coleman	Roberts	Marton	Goldsmith	Durbin	Dyer	Hewitt		Erickknap(15)Cockrill(1)Kirtley(2)Russell(6)
23	Trinder	Erickknap	Birt	RThompson	Williams	MThompson	Birkitt	Coleman	Roberts	Marton	IGoldsmith	Russell	Dyer	Hewitt		Oman(15)Durbin(8)
24	Trinder	Birt	Birt	RThompson	Erickknap	MThompson		Coleman	Coleman	Marton	IHarrison	Russell	Thomas	Woodruff		Cockrill(3)Durbin(8)Roberts(2)James(11)
25	Birkitt	Birt	Trinder	Birt	RThompson	Williams	RThompson	Livingstone	Coleman	Kirtley	Brooks	IGoldsmith	IGoldsmith	Dyer	Russell	Marton(3)McFarlane(10)
26	Birkitt	Walkin	Birt	Birt	RThompson	McFarlane	Livingstone	Coleman	Kirtley	Marton	GHarrison	Russell	Thomas	Russell		Lane(7)Rees(10)

PLYMOUTH ALBION LEAGUE STATISTICS
(COMPILED BY STEPHEN McCORMACK)

Season	Div.	P	W	D	L	F (Tries Con Pen DG)	A (Tries Con Pen DG)	Most Points	Most Tries
87-88	3	11	8	0	3	276 (41 23 21 1)	125 (11 3 22 3)	108 - Martin Livesey	8 - Kevin Nums
88-89	3	11	11	0	0	311 (47 27 19 4)	89 (5 3 18 3)	101 - Dominic Cundy	8 - Steve Walklin
89-90	2	11	5	0	6	206 (32 15 16 0)	164 (17 12 21 2)	36 - Charlie Gabbitas	4 Ian Russell & Steve Walklin
90-91	2	12	4	0	8	129 (9 6 23 4)	210 (30 15 18 2)	44 - Kevin Thomas	2 - Charlie Gabbitas
91-92	2	12	3	0	9	153 (16 7 25 0)	209 (23 12 27 4)	62 - Mark Slade	2 - by 5 players
92-93	3	11	0	0	11	130 (16 4 13 1)	305 (38 20 22 3)	26 - Martin Thompson	3 - Mark Haimes
93-94	4	18	9	0	9	286 (31 13 31 4)	416 (47 26 41 2)	90 - Martin Thompson	5 - Roger Bailey
94-95	4	18	4	2	12	324 (35 16 35 4)	381 (42 21 38 5)	129 - Martin Thomspon	6 - Steve Walklin
95-96	4	18	4	0	14	268 (31 16 21 6)	545 (69 40 24 4)	61 - Mark Slade	6 - Steve Walkin
96-97	4S	26	14	1	11	709 (102 56 24 5)	591 (78 39 41 0)	131 - Martin Thompson	12 - Steve Walkin
Totals		148	62	3	83	2792 (360 182 228 29)	3035 (360 191 272 29)		

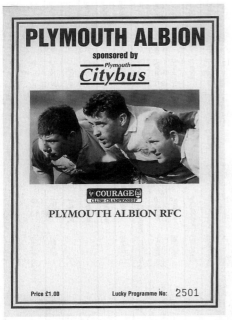

PLYMOUTH ALBION
sponsored by
Plymouth
Citybus

COURAGE
CLUBS CHAMPIONSHIP

PLYMOUTH ALBION RFC

Price £1.00   Lucky Programme No: 2501

PROGRAMME DETAILS

SIZE: A5   **PRICE:** £1

PAGES: 36 plus cover

PROGRAMME EDITOR
John Crow 01752 777454

ADVERTISING RATES
Contact John Crow

CLUB & GROUND DETAILS

Address: Beacon Park, Beacon Park Road, Plymouth, PL2 3JP
Tel. Nos. 01752 777454; Fax 01752 777454
Capacity: 3,000   **Seated:** 500   **Standing:** 2,500
Simple Directions: On approaching Plymouth follow signs for Plymouth Argyle FC. 200 yards past Safeway Superstore at 3rd traffic lights turn right, turn left at Cherry Tree Pub into Langstone Rd, ground 500yards on right.
Nearest Railway Station: Plymouth North Road
Car Parking: 50 within ground
Admission: Seated - Adults £4.
Standing - Adults £3, OAPs £1.50, Children Free
Club Shop: Yes; Manager Maureen Jackson 01752 777454
Clubhouse: Open during normal licensing hours - snacks & bar meals available. Functions catered for, capacity 150, contact Club Secretary
Training Nights: Monday & Thursday

REDRUTH R.F.C.

NICKNAME: The Reds   **FOUNDED:** 1875

President W J 'Bill' Bishop OBE, Lafrowda, Tregolls Road, Truro TR1 1LE
01872 276144 (H), 01209 313132 (B)

Chairman Gerald Curtis, Innsbruck, Trevingey Crescent, Redruth TR15 3DF
01209 216732 (H)

Secretary Ivor Horscroft, Silver Fields, Chapel Street, Redruth, Cornwall. TR15 2DT.
01209 215941 (H & B)   01201 214019 (Fax)

Fixtures Secretary Denzil Williams, 47 Madison Terrace, Hayle, TR27 4EE. 01736 752795 (H)

Press Officer Ivor Horscroft, (Secretary as above)

Treasurer Jerry Penna, Chy-Avalon, North Country, Redruth TR16 4BZ
01209 211520 (H), 01872 322000 Ext 3211 (B)

Club Coach Nick Brokenshire, Pennance Villa, Higher Pennance, Lanner, Redruth TR16 5TU.
01209 8213743 (H)

The 1996/97 season was approached with both hope and trepidation. Andy Hawken skippered the club for the second successive season, and from prior to Christmas gave a fair indication that the twenty point target, set at the beginning of the season, was achievable. Excellent home victories were achieved over Liverpool St. Helens, Wharfedale, Reading, London Welsh and Walsall with a solitary away victory at Havant. Away form, however, was pretty dismal with heavy defeats at Exeter, Rosslyn Park and Leeds.

Early in 1997 form plummeted, and defeats at home against Otley and Havant increased the pressure and relegation became a distinct possibility. Home victories late in the season against Lydney and Clifton were consolation but were not enough to retain the club's place in League Three.

The Pilkington Cup campaign was shrouded in controversy, with the club being placed in the North section and drawing Leeds away from home. Needless to say, the result went to Leeds with a 96 point victory.

Many players, ten in all, were placed in a "Club v County" dilemma in February, after the RFU scheduled quarter final matches in the County Championship on the same Saturday as League Three matches. Needless to say the players chose the club and were applauded for it.

Players to shine in a fairly dull season were youngsters Rocky Newton, who scored eight tries in his first eight appearances, Robert Thirlby, Andrew Joint, Dave Moyle, Ian Boase (when fit), Scott Wilkins and Simon O'Sullivan. The squad was strengthened with the arrival of Fijians Nat. Saumi and Ratu Aliféreti Doviverata and Cullam Osborne and Mark Goldsmith from Plymouth Albion.

Nick Brokenshire will be the new coach for 1997/98 with Dean Hussey as the new captain and hopes are high for a successful season.

Redruth RFC 1996-97:

Colours: Red with a green band/white/red.   **Change colours:** Green with a red band/white/red.

COURAGE LEAGUE MATCH DETAILS 1996-97

No	Ven.	Date	Opponents	Att.	Res.	Score	Scorers
1	(H)	31.08	v Fylde		L	16-28	Congo(t)Morgan(c3p)
2	(A)	07.09	v Havant		W	25-23	Hussey(t)Morgan(t5p)
3	(H)	14.09	v Liverpool StH		W	12- 6	Morgan(4p)
4	(A)	21.09	v Otley		L	34-41	Congo(2t)Mead(t)Douch(t)PenTry(t)Morgan(3cp)
5	(H)	28.09	v Reading		W	20-14	S Whitworth(t)Hawkin(t)Morgan(2c2p)
6	(A)	05.10	v Rosslyn Park		L	23-37	Gomez(2t)PenTry(t)Morgan(c2p)
7	(H)	12.10	v Wharfdale		W	25-22	Congo(t)Hawkin(t)Morgan(t2c2p)
8	(A)	19.10	v Exeter		L	0-44	
9	(H)	26.10	v Harrogate		L	20-32	Gomez(t)Douch(t)Morgan(2c2p)
10	(A)	09.11	v Leeds		L	24-84	Congo(2t)Douch(t)S Whitworth(3cp)
11	(H)	16.11	v London Welsh		W	27-23	Douch(t)Congo(t)Hawkin(t)Boase(t)Morgan(c)S Whitworth(cp)
12	(A)	21.12	v Lydney		L	7-35	Cook(t)S Whitworth(c)
13	(H)	28.12	v Walsall		W	34-20	Wilkins(2t)Douch(t)S O'Sullivan(t)Gomez(tcp)Hambley(2c)
14	(A)	11.01	v Clifton		L	17-28	Osborne(t)Gomez(2tc)
15	(A)	18.01	v Fylde		L	6-55	Sidwell(2p)
16	(H)	25.01	v Havant		L	22-24	Moyle(t)Knowles(t)PenTry(t)Gomez(2cp)
17	(A)	01.02	v Liverpool StH		L	17-72	Osborne(t)T O'Sullivan(t)Morgan(tc)
18	(H)	08.02	v Otley		L	28-40	Wilkins(t)Congo(t)Cook(t)Morgan(2c3p)
19	(A)	15.02	v Reading		L	3-71	S Whitworth(p)
20	(H)	22.02	v Rosslyn Park		L	8-25	Sibson(t)Morgan(p)
21	(A)	01.03	v Wharfdale		L	15-47	Stafford(t)P Congo(t)Saumi(cp)
22	(H)	08.03	v Exeter		L	18-31	Newton(t)Douch(t)Saumi(c2p)
23	(A)	15.03	v Harrogate		L	24-60	Congo(t)Wilkins(t)Hawkin(t)Saumi(3cp)
24	(H)	22.03	v Leeds		L	10-27	Newton(t)Saumi(cp)
25	(H)	29.03	v Morley		L	16-29	Newton(t)Saumi(c3p)
26	(A)	05.04	v London Welsh		L	20-64	Newton(t)Hussey(t)Saumi(2c2p)
27	(H)	12.04	v Lydney		W	16-15	Newton(2t)Saumi(2p)
28	(A)	19.04	v Walsall		L	25-35	Osborne(t)Wilkins(t)Saumi(t2c2p)
29	(A)	26.04	v Morley		L	6-58	Saumi(2p)
30	(H)	03.05	v Clifton		W	47-26	Newton(2t)Doviverata(t)Hawkin(t)Saumi(3c7p)

1996-97 HIGHLIGHTS

LEAGUE DEBUTS: Ian Morgan, Andrew Joint, Steve Farley, Jason Pengilly, James Grainey, Calum Osborne, Jason Chappell, Mark Goldsmith, Richard Newton, Ben Kingswood, Nat Saumi, Ratu Doviverata, Richard Thirlby, Tim Moore.

PLAYERS USED: 43 plus 2 as replacement.

EVER PRESENT: None - most appearances 29
- Andy Hawkin.

❏ Fijian full back Nat Saumi set a new record for points in a match with 27 in their final game of the season at home to Clifton. Included in his total was a record seven penalties. The previous records for the above were 20 and six and both were held by Simon Blake.

❏ Utility back Ian Morgan topped the points scoring list in his debut season and in the process became the third man to score 100 points in a season. Nat Saumi later in the season became the fourth man to achieve this feat.

❏ Young winger Richard Newton set a new record by scoring tries in four consecutive matches.

❏ Suffered a club record 13 successive defeats.

❏ Flanker Peter Congo set a new record of 10 tries in a season. Congo himself held the previous record of nine, set in 1995-96.

❏ Stand off Stuart Whitworth became the first Redruth player to reach 100 league appearances ending the season on 110.

REDRUTH'S COURAGE LEAGUE MATCH DETAILS 1996-97

#	15	14	13	12	11	10	9	1	2	3	4	5	6	7	8	Replacements
1	Gomez	Mead	Wilkins	Thomas	Penrose	Morgan	CWhitworth	Douch	Rutter	Tonkin	Joint	Cook	PCongo	Boase	Hawkin	Moylet(4)
2	Morgan	Mead	Wilkins	Hambly	Hussey	Morgan	CWhitworth	Douch	Rutter	Moyle	Cook	SO'Sullivan	PCongo		Hawkin	
3	Morgan	Mead	Wilkins	Hambly	Hussey	Hussey	CWhitworth	Douch	Rutter	Tonkin	SO'Sullivan	Cook	PCongo	Boase	Hawkin	
4	Morgan	Mead	Wilkins	Hambly	Hussey	SWhitworth	CWhitworth	Douch	Rutter	Tonkin	Joint	SO'Sullivan	PCongo	Boase	Hawkin	
5	Morgan	Mead	Hussey	Hambly	Gomez	SWhitworth	CWhitworth	Douch	Rutter	Tonkin	Joint	Cook	SO'Sullivan	Boase	Hawkin	Penrose(14)
6	Morgan	Farley	Hussey	Hambly	Gomez	SWhitworth	CWhitworth	Douch	Rutter	Tonkin	Joint	SO'Sullivan	PCongo	Boase	Hawkin	Moylet(5),Currow(13),Pengilly(12)
7	Morgan	Farley	Wilkins	Hambly	Gomez	SWhitworth	CWhitworth	Douch	Rutter	Tonkin	Joint		PCongo	Boase	Hawkin	Penrose(14)
8	Morgan	Farley	Wilkins	Hambly	Gomez	SWhitworth	CWhitworth	Moyle	Rutter	Tonkin	Joint		PCongo	Boase	Hawkin	Moylet(3),Penrose(14),SO'Sullivan(9)
9	Morgan	Penrose	Wilkins	Hambly	Gomez	SWhitworth	CWhitworth	Douch	Rutter	ACongo	Joint	Cook	SO'Sullivan	Boase	Hawkin	PCongo(6)
10	Penrose	Grainey	Wilkins	Hambly	Gomez	SWhitworth	CWhitworth	Douch	Rutter	Tonkin	Joint	Osbourne	PCongo	SO'Sullivan	Hawkin	
11	Morgan	Gomez	Wilkins	Hambly	Mead	SWhitworth	CWhitworth	Douch	Rutter	Moyle	Joint	Cook	PCongo	Boase	Hawkin	Penrose(15)
12	Morgan	Mead	Wilkins	Hambly	Gomez	SWhitworth	Chappell	Douch	Rutter	Moyle	Joint		TO'Sullivan	Boase	Hawkin	Sibson(15),SO'Sullivan(12)
13	Gomez	Sibson	Wilkins	Hambly	Mead	SWhitworth	CWhitworth	Douch	Rutter	Tonkin	Joint	Osbourne	SO'Sullivan	Boase	Hawkin	ACongo(4),Morgan(15)
14	Gomez	Mead	Wilkins	Hambly	Sibson	SWhitworth	Moyle	Douch	C-Griffiths	Tonkin	Joint	Osbourne		Boase	Hawkin	Morgan(14),Goldsmith(7)
15	Gomez	Knowles	Wilkins	Hambly	Sibson	Sidwell	CWhitworth	Douch	C-Griffiths	Tonkin	Joint	Osbourne		Goldsmith	Hawkin	Moylet(4),Morgan(15)
16	Gomez	Knowles	Wilkins	Hambly	Sibson	SWhitworth	CWhitworth	Douch	C-Griffiths	Tonkin	Moyle	Osbourne	SO'Sullivan		Hawkin	Moyle(4),Morgan(15)
17	Gomez	Knowles	Sibson	Hambly	Morgan	SWhitworth	CWhitworth	Douch	C-Griffiths	Tonkin	Joint	Osbourne	SO'Sullivan	TO'Sullivan	Hawkin	Grainey(14)
18	Gomez	Knowles	Wilkins	Sibson	Morgan	SWhitworth	CWhitworth	Douch	C-Griffiths	Moyle	Cook	Osbourne	SO'Sullivan	TO'Sullivan	Hawkin	
19	Gomez	Mead	Wilkins	Sibson	Newton	SWhitworth	CWhitworth	Douch	C-Griffiths	Cowie	Cook	Kingswood	TO'Sullivan		Hawkin	Knowles(15)
20	Morgan	Mead	Wilkins	Sibson	Newton	SWhitworth	CWhitworth	Douch	Eslick	Tonkin	Cook	Osbourne	PCongo		Hawkin	Goldsmith(7).
21	Saumi	Newton	Wilkins	Stafford	Sibson	SWhitworth	CWhitworth	Douch	Rutter	Tonkin	Cook	Osbourne	SO'Sullivan	Goldsmith	Hawkin	Goldsmith(7).
22	Saumi	Newton	Wilkins	Dovverata	Mead	SWhitworth	CWhitworth	Douch	Rutter	Tonkin	Joint	Osbourne	Goldsmith	Dovverata	PCongo	Phillips(2),PCongo(7),Cook(4).
23	Saumi	Newton	Wilkins	Dovverata	Newton	CWhitworth	CWhitworth	Douch	Rutter	Cook		Osbourne		Boase	Hawkin	Eslick(8).
24	Saumi	Thirlby	Wilkins	Dovverata	Newton	SWhitworth	CWhitworth	Douch	Rutter		Joint	Osbourne	SO'Sullivan	PCongo	Hawkin	Moyle(3),Eslick(7)
25	Saumi	Thirlby	Wilkins	Dov	Newton	SWhitworth	Hussey	Douch	Moyle		Joint	Osbourne	SO'Sullivan	Goldsmith	Hawkin	CWhitworth(9),Sibson(13),Eslick(3)
26	Saumi	Thirlby	Wilkins	Mead	Newton	SWhitworth	Hussey	Phillips	Moyle		Joint	Osbourne	SO'Sullivan	Goldsmith	Hawkin	Sibson(10)
27	Saumi	Mead	Wilkins	Newton	Sidwell	Hussey		Phillips			Joint	Osbourne	SO'Sullivan	Dovverata	Hawkin	Barnes(2)
28	Saumi	Mead	Wilkins	Gomez	Sidwell	Hussey				Tonkin	Cook	Osbourne	SO'Sullivan	Goldsmith	Hawkin	Cook(4)
29	Saumi	Newton	Wilkins	Pengilly	Sidwell	Hussey		Moore	Eslick		Joint	Osbourne	SO'Sullivan	Goldsmith	Hawkin	Dovverata(12)Kingswood(4)
30	Saumi	Sibson	Wilkins	Dovverata	Newton	Hussey		Douch	Moore	Eslick	Joint	Osbourne	SO'Sullivan	Goldsmith	Hawkin	Cook(5)Mead(12)

REDRUTH LEAGUE STATISTICS
(COMPILED BY STEPHEN McCORMACK)

Season	Div.	P	W	D	L	F	(Tries	Con	Pen	DG)	A	(Tries	Con	Pen	DG)	Most Points	Most Tries
87-88	SW1	10	9	0	1	214	(37	12	10	4)	107	(10	5	18	1)	48 - Simon Blake	6 - Jon Willis & Andy Knowles
88-89	ALS	10	6	1	3	136	(19	9	18	0)	81	(6	3	17	0)	29 - Gary Wills	7 - Jon Willis
89-90	ALS	10	7	0	3	151	(20	7	18	1)	84	(6	3	18	0)	34 - Gary Wills & Peter Harrison	4 - Jon Bowden & Marcel Gomez
90-91	D4S	12	12	0	0	225	(34	16	19	0)	79	(7	13	13	1)	95 - Simon Blake	6 - Andy Knowles
91-92	3	12	6	1	5	155	(14	3	28	3)	123	(10	1	23	4)	80 - Kevin Thomas	2 - by 4 players
92-93	3	11	7	2	2	175	(17	9	23	1)	125	(13	3	18	0)	89 - Kevin Thomas	6 - Andy Knowles
93-94	3	18	2	0	16	178	(9	2	41	2)	488	(63	34	33	2)	71 - Simon Blake	2 - Mark Rose & Chris Whitworth
94-95	4	18	6	2	10	309	(30	18	39	2)	387	(44	16	39	6)	179 - Simon Blake	4 - Simon Blake
95-96	4	18	7	2	9	358	(40	19	39	1)	392	(51	22	30	1)	126 - Stu Whitworth	8 - Peter Congo
96-97	3	30	7	0	23	565	(64	40	55	0)	1116	(159	96	40	3)	120 - Ian Morgan	10 - Peter Congo
Totals		149	69	8	72	2466	(284	135	284	14)	2982	(369	186	249	18)		

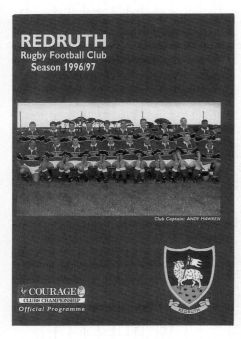

REDRUTH
Rugby Football Club
Season 1996/97

Club Captain: ANDY HAWKEN

COURAGE
CLUBS CHAMPIONSHIP
Official Programme

PROGRAMME DETAILS

SIZE: A5 **PRICE:** £1

PAGES: 30

PROGRAMME EDITOR Nick Serpell 01209 212611

ADVERTISING RATES
Colour Full page £500, Half page £350, Qtr page £200
Mono Full page £350, Half page £200, Qtr page £125

CLUB & GROUND DETAILS

Address:
The Recreation Ground, Redruth, Cornwall T15 1SY
Tel. Nos. 01209 215941, Fax 01209 314438
Capacity:15,675   **Seated:** 675   **Standing:** 15,000
Simple Directions: A30 West through Cornwall, leave at Redruth exit over twin roundabout, past Avers garage, ground signposted on left
Nearest Railway Station: Redruth
Car Parking: 100 on ground
Admission: Season Ticket £60, £35 OAP/children
Matchday Adults standing £5, seated £6, Children/OAPs £4
Club Shop: Yes, Manageress Christina Thomas 01209 215526
Clubhouse: Three bars, with snacks & bar meals available. Functions catered for contact Mrs Janet Johnson 01209 216097
Training Nights: Mondays & Wednesdays

TABARD R.F.C.

NICKNAME: Tabs

FOUNDED: 1951

President David Burrows, Bury Farm, Sandridgebury, St Albans, Herts
01727 854977

Fixtures Secretary Campbell Carmichael, 10 Chandos Road, Borehamwood, Herts.
0181 953 9006 (H)

Press Officer Peter Cook, 32 Pinewood Close, Borehamwood, Herts. WD6 5NW
0181 207 5564 (H), 0171 250 7499 (B), 0171 250 7447 (Fax)

1st XV Manager/Registration Geoff Bird, 1 Kendalls Close, Radlett, Herts
01923 852465 (H), 01923 852655 (B), 01923 852465 (Fax)

Head Coach Ivor Jones, 0181 953 1124

Tabard's season was a difficult one in which they showed that they had the capability but lacked the breaks necessary for a good league performance. Their first break was a bad one, captain Steve Armstrong breaking his leg training after only one game and, although he fought back to play again in the new year, his only reward was to break his arm playing against Plymouth Albion.

Tabard had three draws in the season, two of these coming in the dying minutes of close games, and on several occasions found themselves losing in injury time. Without their captain and with other injuries mounting up, they had to wait until the sixth game of the season for their first victory, against Charlton Park. However, as the season drew to a close and the relegation zone threatened, they played some of their best rugby to finish eighth in the table. Two good wins were against High Wycombe, where the backs turned in a fine performance in the opening quarter and old rivals Barking. This was perhaps the best game of the season cluminating in a 33-17 victory away from home.

In the Pilkington Cup Tabard made an early exit to up and coming Bracknell, but fought through to the final of the Herts Presidents Cup only to find the strain of two hard games in the weekend showing as they suffered a narrow defeat.

Of the players stand off Nick Churchman again topped the points scorers with a massive 432, which included twenty tries, making him top try scorer as well. Other fine performances came from the stalwart second row Richard Malone ably assisted by newcomer Colin Bickle, another newcomer hooker in Mark Sharp and fullback Mark Wilkins.

PETER COOK

Tabard RFC: Back Row (L-R); M Trippick, J Bambra, C Bickle, M Sharp, A Douglas, M Hanson, T Bennett, M Patrick, N Gough, T Smithers (Coach). Front Row; R Grice, S Dodge, N Churchman, D Robjohns, A Metcalf, S Dudley, M Wilkins, R McCabe, O Gardiner, P Luders.

Colours: Navy with broad yellow band edged with red.   **Change colours:** Blue, gold & red quadrants.

COURAGE LEAGUE MATCH DETAILS 1996-97

No	Ven.	Date	Opponents	Att.	Res.	Score	Scorers
1	(A)	31.08	v Met Police		L	15-23	Churchman(5p)
2	(H)	07.09	v Henley		L	22-45	Tooms(t)Sjollema(t)Hanson(t)Churchman(2cp)
3	(A)	21.09	v Weston-S-M		L	6-11	Churchman(2p)
4	(H)	28.09	v Cheltenham		L	19-26	Malone(t)Churchman(t3p)
5	(A)	05.10	v N Walsham		D	16-16	Tooms(t)Colstick(t)Churchman(2p)
6	(A)	19.10	v Charlton Park		W	37-18	Tooms(2t)Robjohns(t)Hunter(t)Churchman(4c3p)
7	(H)	26.10	v Camberley		L	7-22	Hewson(tc)
8	(A)	09.11	v Askeans		W	10- 3	PenT(t)Hewson(cp)
9	(H)	16.11	v Plymouth		D	16-16	Hanson(t)Churchman(c3p)
10	(H)	28.12	v High Wycombe		D	13-13	Armstrong(t)Churchman(c2p)
11	(H)	25.01	v Met Police		W	20-12	Jackson(t)Churchman(5p)
12	(A)	01.02	vHenley		L	25-31	West(2t)Armstrong(t)Churchman(2c2p)
13	(H)	08.02	v Weston-S-M		W	17- 7	Botterman(t)Churchman(4p)
14	(A)	15.02	v Cheltenham		L	6-23	Churchman(2p)
15	(H)	22.02	v N Walsham		W	23- 8	Churchman(2t2c2pdg)
16	(H)	01.03	v Charlton Park		W	32- 7	Armstrong(t)Robjohns(t)Sharp(t)Elliott(dg)Churchman(t3cp)
17	(A)	08.03	v Camberley		L	9-27	Churchman(3p)
18	(H)	15.03	v Askeans		W	38- 3	Gardner(2t)White(2t)Sharp(t)Churchman(5cp)
19	(A)	22.03	v Plymouth		L	30-33	PenTry(t)Armstrong(t)Gardner(t)Sharp(t)Churchman(2c2p)
20	(A)	28.03	v Newbury		L	17-91	Andrews(t)Lloyd(t)Hewson(2cdg)
21	(H)	05.04	v Newbury		L	13-31	P Bennett(t)Hewson(c2p)
22	(A)	12.04	v High Wycombe		W	30-19	Wilkins(2t)Robjohns(t)West(t)Churchman(2c2p)
23	(H)	19.04	v Berry Hill		W	30- 0	Metcalfe(t)West(t)Churchman(t3c3p)
24	(A)	26.04	v Barking		W	33-17	Luders(t)Metcalfe(t)Churchman(2t2c3p)
25	(A)	03.05	v Berry Hill		L	7-31	Botterman(t)Hill(c)
26	(H)	10.05	v Barking		L	20-24	Dogbe(t)Churchman(t2c2p)

1996-97 HIGHLIGHTS

LEAGUE DEBUTS:

PLAYERS USED: 47 plus four as replacement only

EVER PRESENT: None - most appearances 21
- Nick Churchman & Dick Malone

☐ Scored more penalties than everyone but Berry Hill.

56	Tabard
56	Berry Hill
54	High Wycombe
52	Met Police
48	Weston super Mare

☐ **Most points in a match**
23 Nick Churchman v N Walsham 22.02.97 (H)
23 Nick Churchman v Barking 26.04.97 (A)
20 Nick Churchman v Berry Hill 19.04.97 (H)

☐ **Hat trick of tries in a match**
None - two tries were scored on seven occasions by six
players with Nick Churchman achieving this feat twice.

☐ **Most points in the season**

Pts	Player	T	C	P	D
264	Nick Churchman	8	31	53	1
27	Giles Hewson	1	5	3	1
20	Roy Toms	4	-	-	-
20	Gareth West	4	-	-	-
20	Steve Armstrong	4	-	-	-

☐ **Most appearances**
21 Nick Churchman and Dick Malone
20 Dave Robjohns and Mike Hanson(1)

TABARD'S COURAGE LEAGUE MATCH DETAILS 1996-97

	15	14	13	12	11	10	9	1	2	3	4	5	6	7	8	Replacements	
1	Lloyd	Toms	Gilbert	Elliott	Churchman	Haxton	Gough	Dearsley	Lowde	P.Bennett	Spillema	Jeffreys	Hanson	Armstrong		Hewson(15)Sullivan(3)	1
2	Hewson	Toms	Elliott	Gilbert	Gardner	Haxton	Gough	Dearsley	Lowde	Bambra	Malone	Spillema	Jeffreys	Hanson	Lascelles	Welsh(1)Hunter(12)Douglas(6)	2
3	Wilkins	Toms	Colstick	Gilbert	Churchman	Haxton	Gough	Dearsley	Graham	Bambra	Bickle	Lascelles	Jeffreys	Hanson	P.Bennett	Hunter(12)	3
4	Wilkins	Toms	Colstick	Churchman	Gilbert	Haxton	Goff	Gough	Graham	Bambra	Malone	Spillema	Jeffreys	Hanson	Douglas		4
5	Wilkins	Toms	Elliott	Churchman	Colstick	Haxton	Goff	Gough	Graham	Bambra	Malone	Spillema	Henderson	Hanson	T.Bennett	Douglas	5
6	Wilkins	Toms	Robjohns	Elliott	Hunter	Haxton	Gough	Gough	Goff	Gough	Malone	Henderson	Douglas	Hanson	Patrick	Patrick	6
7	Wilkins	Toms	Robjohns	Elliott	Hunter	Haxton	Gough	Churchman	Goff	P.Bennett	Lascelles	Douglas	Jeffreys	Patrick	T.Bennett	T.Bennett	7
8	Wilkins	Toms	Luders	Elliott	Hunter	Haxton	Goff	Haxton	Goff	Bambra	Malone	Lascelles	Douglas	Jeffreys	T.Bennett	T.Bennett	8
9	Wilkins	Toms	Luders	Elliott	Hewson	Haxton	Goff	Haxton	Goff	Bambra	Bickle	Jeffreys	Douglas	Jeffreys	Jeffreys	Jeffreys	9
10	Wilkins	Toms	Robjohns	Elliott	Churchman	Haxton	Goff	Haxton	Goff	Bambra	Bickle	Malone	Douglas	Armstrong	T.Bennett	Hewson(12)Douglas(6)	10
11	Wilkins	Toms	Robjohns	Elliott	Churchman	Hewson	Goff	Haxton	Goff	Bambra	Bickle	Malone	T.Bennett	Armstrong	Armstrong	Spillema(4)	11
12	Toms	Toms	Robjohns	Elliott	West	Churchman	Goff	Haxton	Botterman	Bambra	Bickle	Malone	Douglas	T.Bennett	T.Bennett	Welsh(1)	12
13	Wilkins	Toms	Robjohns	Elliott	West	Churchman	Welsh	Welsh	Goff	Henderson	Bickle	Douglas	T.Bennett	T.Bennett	T.Bennett	Hanson(8)Trippick(tr3)	13
14	Wilkins	White	Luders	West	Churchman	Jackson	Goff	Goff	Trippick	Bickle	Malone	Armstrong	Metcalfe	Metcalfe	Metcalfe	Gilbert(11)	14
15	Gardiner	Luders	Elliott	Robjohns	Churchman	Jackson	Goff	Sharp	Bickle	Malone	Armstrong	Hanson	Metcalfe	Armstrong	Hewson(12)McCabe(13)		15
16	Wilkins	White	Elliott	Gardner	Churchman	Jackson	Goff	Goff	Sharp	Bickle	Malone	Hanson	Armstrong	Metcalfe	Grice(11)Spillema(8)Hewson(12)		16
17	Hewson	White	Gardner	Gilbert	Churchman	Jackson	Goff	Goff	Sharp	Malone	Bickle	Hanson	Armstrong	Metcalfe	McCabe(9),Colstick(1).		17
18	West	Hewson	Gardner	White	Churchman	McCabe	Goff	Goff	Trippick	Malone	Bickle	Hanson	Armstrong	Metcalfe	T.Bennett(6)		18
19	Hewson	White	Lloyd	Gardner	Churchman	Jackson	Goff	Goff	Trippick	Malone	Bickle	Hanson	Armstrong	Metcalfe	Jones(8)Williams(5)		19
20	West	Lloyd	Colstick	Gardner	Hewson	Andrews	Goff	Goff	Sharp	Bickle	Ricci	Malone	P.Bennett	Douglas	Henderson	White(12)	20
21	Wilkins	West	Gardner	Colstick	Hewson	Andrews	Gough	Botterman	Bambra	Bickle	Spillema	P.Bennett	Douglas	Jeffreys	Jeffreys		21
22	Wilkins	West	Dudley	Dogbe	Churchman	Andrews	Trippick	Sharp	Bambra	Bickle	Malone	P.Bennett	Hanson	Metcalfe	Douglas(6)Hewson(15)		22
23	West	White	Robjohns	Dudley	Churchman	Andrews	Andrews	Bambra	Sharp	Trippick	Bickle	Malone	T.Bennett	Hanson	Metcalfe		23
24	Wilkins	West	Luders	White	Churchman	McCabe	Andrews	Bambra	Sharp	Trippick	Bickle	Malone	T.Bennett	Hanson	Metcalfe		24
25	Elliott	Dogbe	Luders	West	Hill	McCabe	Bambra	Botterman	Trippick	Bickle	Malone	Douglas	Hanson	Patrick	Gough(1)		25
26	Wilkins	Grice	Robjohns	Dudley	Dogbe	Churchman	McCabe	Bambra	Sharp	Trippick	Malone	T.Bennett	Douglas	Hanson	Metcalfe	Gough(3)	26

TABARD LEAGUE STATISTICS
(COMPILED BY STEPHEN McCORMACK)

Season	Div.	P	W	D	L	F	A	PD	Pts	Pos.	Coach	Captain
87-88	LON3NW	10	7	1	2	104	87	17	15	4	I Jones	R Welsh
88-89	LON3NW	10	8	0	2	162	88	74	16	2	I Jones	T Smithers
89-90	LON3NW	10	10	0	0	264	75	189	20	1p	I Jones	T Smithers
90-91	LON2N	10	6	0	4	116	122	-6	12	4	T Smithers	N Churchman
91-92	LON2N	10	.9	1	0	167	59	108	19	1p	T Smithers	M Richards
92-93	LON1	12	10	1	1	230	127	103	21	1p		
93-94	D5S	12	6	2	4	183	136	47	14	3		
94-95	D5S	12	7	0	5	207	208	-1	14	6	I Jones	R Malone
95-96	D5S	12	4	1	7	195	244	-49	9	9	I Jones	M Trippick
96-97	D4S	26	10	3	13	511	557	-46	23	8		
Total		124	77	9	38	2139	1703	436				

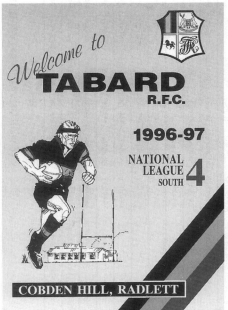

Welcome to
TABARD
R.F.C.

1996-97

NATIONAL LEAGUE SOUTH **4**

COBDEN HILL, RADLETT

PROGRAMME DETAILS

SIZE: A5   **PRICE:** £3 with entry

PAGES: 16 plus cover

PROGRAMME EDITOR
Dave Burrows 01727 854977

ADVERTISING RATES
Colour Full page £300, Half page £150, Qtr page £75

CLUB & GROUND DETAILS

Address: Cobden Hill, Radlett, Hertfordshire, WD7 7LN
Tel. Nos. 01923 855561
Capacity: 1,000   **Seated:** None   **Standing:** 1,000
Simple Directions: On A5183 Watling Street, from Elstree turn right after entry into Radlett, blind entrance by high brick wall nearly opposite "Cat & Fiddle" Pub.
Nearest Railway Station: Radlett
Car Parking: 250 adjacent to ground
Admission: Adult standing £3.00
Club Shop: Yes
Clubhouse: Matchday & training only. Bar meals available. Functions can be catered for contact Nick Gray 0831 668204
Training Nights: Tuesday & Thursday

WESTON SUPER MARE R.F.C.

NICKNAME: Seasiders

FOUNDED: 1875

President R H Main, 142 Quantock Road, Weston Super Mare, BS23 4DP. 01934 417860

Chairman J W Brentnall, c/o Messers J W Ward, 37 The Boulevard, Weston Super Mare. 0117 922 0208 (H), 01934 413535 (B)

Club Secretary H C Hope, 24 Feniton, Clovelly Rd., Worle, Weston Super Mare. BS22 0LN 01934 511834 (H), 01934 625643

Treasurer J Moon, 11 The Lindens, Worle, Weston Super Mare BS22 9LL 01934 514324 (H), 01934 625643 (B)

Club Manager/Coach Mick Reece, 11 Burnshill Drive, Taunton, Somerset TA2 6QF 01823 332101 (H), 01935 625643 (B), 0802 663888 (Mobile)

Season 95/96 was our most successful todate. So for season 96/97 there was a 'quiet air' of optimism. The pre-season training was going well, with the addition of two coaches, Derek Rowlands and Colin Reeves to help club coach Mick Reece. There was also the arrival of new players, Dave Underwood - Army/Som., Dave Bird - Som., and Calvin Venn - Army. All three players had completed their apprenticeship with local club, Hornets. In addition, Jim Morris a utility back and Jim Cooper a hooker joined us from Taunton and Somerset U21s.

The 'feel good' factor did not last long once the season was underway, when we were dealt a bitter blow with long term injuries sustained by five of our regular 1st XV members, including our captain, Paul Redman. More injuries were to follow as the season progressed.

The season was becoming one of 'make and do'. The early signing of Graham Buller from Bridgwater/Somerset proved to be more significant and successful throughout the season. The first half of the season did provide some success for the club, we reached Round Four of the Pilkington Cup once again and there was a superb match against league leaders Newbury losing by two late penalty goals.

We were pleased that Paul Thatcher, our prolific goal kicker was able, after his move from the area, to remain loyal to the club. He topped over 200 points yet again.

Our second half of the season saw a revival when six talented young players joined us from the Bristol area, and we went to mid May before our relegation struggle was over.

We won the games that mattered and once again we will compete to the best of our ability in League Two South next season.
H.C.HOPE

Weston Super Mare 1996-97 squad: Back Row (L-R); C Reeves (Asst Coach), C Venn, J Morris, J Robinson, L Walsh, S Cattermole, P Collins, J Hedges, R Main, A Fisher, A Croker, M Down, A Larkin, M Longdean, D Rowlands (Asst Coach). Middle Row; G Hill, R Hedges, D Steele, A Gaulton, P Redmance (Capt), B Sparks, P Popham, J Collard, Mick Reece (Club Coach). Front Row; D Underwood, D Bird, D Evans, N Coleman, C Sheryn, J Cooper.

Colours: Royal blue with red and white hoops   **Change colours:** Either Royal blue or Red

COURAGE LEAGUE MATCH DETAILS 1996-97

No	Ven.	Date	Opponents	Att.	Res.	Score	Scorers
1	(H)	31.08	v Cheltenham		L	3- 8	Cattermole(p)
2	(A)	07.09	v N Walsham		L	13-24	Underwood(t)Thatcher(c2p)
3	(H)	21.09	v Tabard		W	11- 6	Venner(t)Sheryn(2p)
4	(A)	28.09	v Camberley		L	24-25	Buller(t)Venner(t)PenT(t)Thatcher(3cp)
5	(H)	05.10	v Askeans		W	28-15	Venner(3t)Colard(2p)Sheryn(2cp)
6	(A)	19.10	v Plymouth		L	8-19	Gunningham(t)Sheryn(p)
7	(H)	26.10	v Newbury		L	22-28	Croker(t)Buller(t)Moore(t)Thatcher(2cp)
8	(A)	09.11	v High Wycombe		L	24-28	Venner(t)Buller(t)Thatcher(c4p)
9	(H)	16.11	v Berry Hill		W	29-18	Buller(t)Gaulton(t)Cattermole(2cp4dg)
10	(A)	21.12	v Barking		L	11-25	Gunningham(t)Thatcher(2p)
11	(H)	28.12	v Met Police		L	20-40	Buller(t)Pitt(t)Thatcher(c)Cattermole(tdg)
12	(A)	25.01	v Cheltenham		L	15-25	Thatcher(4p)Cattermole(dg)
13	(H)	01.02	v N Walsham		W	18- 3	Buller(t)Venner(t)Thatcher(c2p)
14	(A)	08.02	v Tabard		L	7-17	Cattermole(t)Thatcher(c)
15	(H)	15.02	v Camberley		W	25-10	Buller(t)Hanham(t)Underwood(t)Ford(t)Cattermole(cp)
16	(A)	22.02	v Askeans		W	18-10	Gaulton(t)Hiles(t)Cattermole(cpdg)
17	(H)	01.03	v Plymouth		L	21-23	Underwood(t)Buller(t)Thatcher(t3c)
18	(H)	15.03	v High Wycombe		W	19-13	Underwood(t)Bird(t)Cattermole(2pdg)
19	(A)	22.03	v Berry Hill		L	15-20	Down(t)Thatcher(tcp)
20	(A)	29.03	v Henley		W	20-18	Rutley(t)Barclay(t)Thatcher(2c2p)
21	(H)	05.04	v Barking		L	17-27	Havard(t)Thatcher(4p)
22	(H)	09.04	v Henley		L	16-24	Fisher(t)Thatcher(c3p)
23	(A)	12.04	v Met Police		W	14- 8	Underwood(t)Thatcher(2p)Cattermole(dg)
24	(A)	19.04	v Newbury		L	13-54	PenTry(t)Thatcher(cp)Cattermole(dg)
25	(H)	26.04	v Charlton Park		W	40-10	Croker(2t)Havard(2t)Bird(t)Thatcher(3c3p)
26	(A)	10.05	v Charlton Park		W	31-17	Gunningham(t)Underwood(t)Bird(t)Thatcher(2c4p)

1996-97 HIGHLIGHTS

LEAGUE DEBUTS:

PLAYERS USED: 42 plus two as replacement only.

EVER PRESENT: None - most appearances 23
- Graham Buller.

Only four sides scored less tries in the division.

34	Askeans
43	Berry Hill
45	Charlton Park
50	Weston super Mare

5th best defensive record in the division in terms of points against and tries conceded.

Won three of their last four away games to stave off any relegation threat.

Most points in a match
19 Simon Cattermole v Berry Hill 16.11.96 (H)
16 Paul Thatcher v Charlton Park 10.05.97 (A)

Hat trick of tries in a match
3 Mark Venner v Askeans 05.10.96 (H)

Most points in the season

Pts	Player	T	C	P	D
164	Paul Thatcher	2	23	36	-
66	Simon Cattermole	2	4	6	10
40	Graham Buller	8	-	-	-
37	Mark Venner	7	-	-	-

Most appearances
23 Graham Buller
22 Mark Venner, David Underwood, Andy Gunningham and David Bird.

WESTON SUPER MARE'S COURAGE LEAGUE MATCH DETAILS 1996-97

#	15	14	13	12	11	10	9	1	2	3	4	5	6	7	8	Replacements
1	Bamsey	Steele	Venn	Robinson	Underwood	Cattermole	Coleman	Popham	Bird	Croker	Main	Cottle	Venner	Walsh	Redman	Morris(11)Sparks(6)
2	Thatcher	Steele	Venn	Robinson	Underwood	Cattermole	Coleman	Popham	Bird	Fisher	Main	Cottle	Venner	Walsh	Redman	Redman
3	Sheryn	Steele	Venn	Robinson	Underwood	Bamsey	Coleman	Popham	Fisher	Main	Cottle	Brooks	Sparks	Venner	Walsh	Pitt(4)Croker(3)
4	Sheryn	Steele	Venn	Longdon	Underwood	Thatcher	Coleman	Popham	Gunningham	Main	Cottle	Pitt	Sparks	Walsh	Buller	Mitchell(2)Pitt(4)
5	Sheryn	Underwood	Venn	Colard	Underwood	Bamsey	Coleman	Popham	Bird	Croker	Cottle	Cottle	Walsh	Venner	Buller	Hanham(15)
6	Sheryn	Watley	Colard	Morris	Watley	Bamsey	Coleman	Gunningham	Gunningham	Croker	Brooks	Cottle	Walsh	Venner	Buller	Fisher(1)
7	Thatcher	Underwood	Colard	Robinson	Robinson	Bamsey	Moore	Gunningham	Mitchell	Croker	Pitt	Cottle	Walsh	Venner	Buller	Coleman(13)Sparks(5)
8	Thatcher	Morris	Hanham	Robinson	Steele	Cattermole	Gunningham	Mitchell	Fisher	Croker	Brooks	Cottle	Walsh	Venner	Buller	Sparks(8)
9	Morris	Underwood	Coleman	Evans	Steele	Moore	Thatcher	Collins	Collins	Popham	Brooks	Brooks	Sparks	Venner	Buller	Hedges(6)
10	Thatcher	Underwood	Robinson	Hiles	Steele	Moore	Moore	Bird	Bird	Croker	Pitt	Ford	Sparks	Venner	Buller	Sparks(4)
11	Thatcher	Underwood	Underwood	Hiles	Steele	Cattermole	Moore	Bird	Bird	Croker	Buller	Ford	Sparks	Venner	Buller	Sparks(6)Bamsey(13)
12	Thatcher	Rutley	Havard	Robinson	Steele	Cattermole	Gunningham	Hill	Fisher	Fisher	Buller	Cottle	Collins	Venner	Buller	Sparks(6)
13	Thatcher	Rutley	Havard	Venn	Steele	Cattermole	Gunningham	Bird	Croker	Buller	Brooks	Cottle	Ford	Venner	Ford	Sparks(4)
14	Hiles	Rutley	Havard	Rutley	Rutley	Cattermole	Gunningham	Bird	Croker	Croker	Brooks	Cottle	Ford	Venner	Buller	
15	Hiles	Underwood	Havard	Steele	Steele	Cattermole	Gaulton	Gunningham	Bird	Croker	Pitt	Cottle	Ford	Venner	Buller	Robinson(11)Fisher(3)
16	Hiles	Steele	Hanham	Underwood	Underwood	Cattermole	Gaulton	Gunningham	Croker	Fisher	Pitt	Pitt	Ford	Venner	Buller	Brooks(4),Thatcher(14)
17	Hiles	Underwood	Hanham	Thatcher	Underwood	Cattermole	Gaulton	Gunningham	Croker	Croker	Cottle	Brooks	Ford	Venner	Buller	Moore(12),Fear(6).
18	Bamsey	Rutley	Hanham	Havard	Underwood	Cattermole	Gaulton	Gunningham	Croker	Croker	Brooks	Brooks	Ford	Venner	Buller	Fear(7)
19	Thatcher	Steele	Hanham	Underwood	Underwood	Cattermole	Gaulton	Gunningham	Croker	Pitt	Brooks	Fear	Fear	Venner	Buller	Jones(1)Main(4)
20	Thatcher	Underwood	Hanham	Bamsey	Rutley	Cattermole	Gaulton	Gunningham	Croker	Croker	Main	Barclay	Ford	Venner	Buller	Pitt(4)Fisher(3)
21	Thatcher	Underwood	Hanham	Rutley	Bamsey	Bamsey	Jones	Gunningham	Croker	Main	Main	Barclay	Ford	Venner	Buller	Pitt(4)Fisher(1)
22	Thatcher	Underwood	Hanham	Rutley	Rutley	Down	Gunningham	Down	Croker	Main	Barclay	Ford	Venner	Buller	Fischer(3)Pitt(4)Mitchell(7)
23	Thatcher	Underwood	Hanham	Rutley	Rutley	Gaulton	Jones	Gunningham	Mitchell	Mitchell	Main	Barclay	Ford	Bird	Buller	Pitt(5)
24	Thatcher	Underwood	Hanham	Rutley	Rutley	Gaulton	Gaulton	Gunningham	Gaulton	Croker	Main	Barclay	Ford	Bird	Buller	Fisher(1)Pitt(4)Down(5)Jones(6)
25	Thatcher	Underwood	Hanham	Rutley	Cattermole	Down	Gaulton	Gunningham	Mitchell	Croker	Main	Pitt	Ford	Bird	Buller	Venn(12)Walsh(6)Brooks(6)
26	Thatcher	Underwood	Hanham	Rutley	Cattermole	Down	Gaulton	Gunningham	Mitchell	Croker	Main	Barclay	Ford	Bird	Buller	Bamsey(13)Down(6)
28	Thatcher	Underwood	Hanham	Rutley	Venn	Down	Jones	Mitchell	Fisher	Ford	Brooks	Barclay	Ford	Bird	Buller	Bamsey(13)Down(6)

WESTON SUPER MARE LEAGUE STATISTICS
(COMPILED BY STEPHEN McCORMACK)

Season	Div.	P	W	D	L	F	A	PD	Pts	Pos.	Most Points	Most Tries
87-88	SW1	10	4	0	6	146	107	39	8	8	40 - Paul Tincknell	7 - Charlie Larkin
88-89	SW1	10	4	0	6	188	183	5	8	7	33 - Andy Stewart	7 - Chris Brown
89-90	SW1	10	8	0	2	186	133	53	16	2p	66 - Melvin Badger	8 - Chris Brown
90-91	D4S	12	6	0	6	192	182	10	12	5	122 - Melvin Badger	8 - Melvin Badger
91-92	D4S	12	4	0	8	175	215	-40	8	9	39 - Jarad Collard	5 - Paul Whatley & Charlie Larkin
92-93	D4S	12	4	1	7	154	226	-72	9	10	81 - Paul Thatcher	3 - Barry Sparks
93-94	D5S	12	7	0	5	163	180	-17	14	5	91 - Paul Thatcher	2 Nell Coleman & Robert Chamberlain
94-95	D5S	12	8	0	4	194	160	34	16	3	119 - Paul Thatcher	2 - Mark Venner & Alan Baskerville
95-96	D5S	12	10	0	2	207	123	84	20	2	105 - Paul Thatcher	5 - Mark Venner
96-97	D4S	26	11	0	15	482	515	-33	22	9	164 - Paul Thatcher	8 - Graham Biller
Total		128	66	1	61	2087	2024	63				

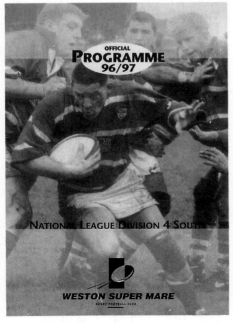

PROGRAMME DETAILS

SIZE: A5   **PRICE:** £1
PAGES: 16 plus cover
PROGRAMME EDITOR
Jon Cornish, 01275 340090
ADVERTISING RATES
T.B.A.

CLUB & GROUND DETAILS

Address: Recreation Ground, Drove Road, Weston Super Mare, North Somerset BS23 3PA
Tel. Nos. 01934 623118/625643
Capacity: 6,499   **Seated:** 499   **Standing:** 6,000
Simple Directions: M5 Jnc 21, follow new road into Weston, follow signs for town centre
Nearest Railway Station: Weston Super Mare, 100 yards from ground
Car Parking: 200 at ground, 50+ nearby
Admission: Season from £30, OAPs/Junior £15. Matchday £4, Children/OAPs £2
Club Shop: Yes; Manager John Fry 01934 415341
Clubhouse: Every evening (except Sunday) 7.00-11.00, matchdays 12.00-11.00, Sundays 12.00-3.00. Snacks available. Buffet, luncheons & functions (Capacity 150) available on request
Training Nights: Monday & Thursday

DIVISION FOUR SOUTH

(PREVIOUSLY ALSO DIVISION FIVE SOUTH & THIS YEAR'S LEAGUE TWO SOUTH)

RECORDS SECTION

DIVISION FOUR SOUTH - THE LAST TEN YEARS

	Champions	Runners-up	Relegated
1987-88	**ASKEANS**	SIDCUP	Streatham/Croydon
1988-89	**LYDNEY**	HAVANT	Sidcup, Stroud, Ealing
1989-90	**MET POLICE**	CLIFTON	Salisbury
1990-91	**RERUTH**	BASINGSTOKE	Maidenhead, Cheltenham
1991-92	**HAVANT**	BASINGSTOKE	Sidcup, Ealing
1992-93	**SUDBURY**	LONDON WELSH	Thurrock
1993-94	**READING**	LYDNEY	Southend, Maidstone
1994-95	**LONDON WELSH**	LYDNEY	Sudbury, Basingstoke
1995-96	**LYDNEY**	WESTON-S-MARE	Camborne
1996-97	**NEWBURY**	HENLEY	Berry Hill, Askeans, High Wycombe, Charlton Park

	Most Points		Most Tries
1987-88	69	John Field (Askeans)	N/A
1988-89			7 Jon Willis (Redruth)
1989-90	83	Simon Harvey (Clifton)	N/A
1990-91	122	Melvin Badger (W.S.M.)	8 Melvin Badger (W.S.M.)
1991-92	129	Pete Russell (Havant)	9 Will Knight (Havant)
1992-93	123	Steve Dybler (Sudbury)	12 Steve Titcombe (Sudbury)
1993-94	133	Phil Belshaw (Reading)	N/A
1994-95	119	Paul Thatcher (W.S.M.)	N/A
1995-96	176	Richard Perkins (Henley)	10 Richard Perkins (Henley) Tommy Adams (Camborne)
1996-97	391	Nick Grecian (Newbury)	27 Brian Johnson (Newbury)

	Most Penalties	Most Conversions	Most Drop Goals
1987-88	13 John Field (Askeans)	9 John Field (Askeans)	2 Andy Perry (Havant)
1988-89	N/A	N/A	2 Andy Perry (Havant)
1989-90	15 Simon Harvey (Clifton)	10 Simon Harvey (Clifton)	6 Simon Harvey (Clifton)
1990-91	27 Rob Ashworth (Havant)	16 Simon Blake (Redruth)	N/A
1991-92	24 Pete Russell (Havant)	23 Pete Russell (Havant)	4 Paul Tincknell (W.S.M.)
1992-93	25 Andy Halford (Lydney)	28 Mike Hamlin (Lon. Welsh)	4 M Gregory (Sudbury)
1993-94	34 Phil Belshaw (Reading)	N/A	5 Paul Tincknell (W.S.M.)
1994-95	31 Paul Thatcher (W.S.M.)	N/A	N/A
1995-96	28 Paul THatcher (W.S.M.) Richard Larkin (Askeans)	27 Richard Perkins (Henley)	4 Simon Cattermole (W.S.M.)
1996-97	53 Nick Churchman (Tabard)	100 Nick Grecian (Newbury)	10 Simon Cattermole (W.S.M.)

Team Records

Highest score:	Camberley 95 Askeans 17. 16.11.96
Highest aggregate:	112: Camberley 95 Askeans 17. 16.11.96
Highest score by a losing side:	N/A
Highest scoring draw:	25-25 Henley v Met Police 5.4.97
Most consecutive wins:	25 Newbury 1996-97
Most consecutive defeats:	14 Askeans 1996-97
Most points for in a season:	1170 Newbury 1996-97
Least points for in a season:	64 Maidstone 1989-90
Most points against in a season:	1140 Charlton Park 1996-97
Least points against in a season:	61 Reading 1993-94
Most tries for in a season:	167 Newbury 1996-97
Most tries against in a season:	166 Charlton Park 1996-97
Most conversions for in a season:	103 Newbury 1996-97
Most conversions against in a season:	95 Charlton Park 1996-97
Most penalties for in a season:	56 Berry Hill 1996-97
	Tabard 1996-97
Most penalties against in a season:	55 Henley 1996-97
Most drop goals for in a season:	10 Weston-Supre-Mare 1996-97
Most drop goals against in a season:	6 Berry Hill 1996-97

Individual Records

Most points in a season:	385 Nick Grecian (Newbury) 1996-97
Most tries in a season:	27 Brian Johnson (Newbury) 1996-97
Most conversions in a season:	96 Nick Grecian (Newbury) 1996-97
Most penalties in a season:	53 Nick Churchman (Tabard) 1996-97
Most drop goals in a season:	10 Simon Cattermole (Weston-S-M) 1996-97
Most points in a match:	34 Chris Spencer, **Henley** v Charlton Park 12.4.97
Most tries in a match:	5 Eddie Weatherley, **Met Police** v Askeans 8.2.97
Most conversions in a match:	11 Nick Grecian, **Newbury** v Charlton Park 25.1.97
Most penalties in a match:	7 Richard Larkin, **Askeans** v H Wycombe 30.9.95
Most drop goals in a match:	4 Simon Cattermole, **Weston-S-M** v Berry Hill
	16.11.96

DIVISION FOUR SOUTH - TEN YEAR RECORD

	87/88	88/89	89/90	90/91	91/92	92/93	93/94	94/95	95/96	96/97
Askeans	1	-	-	-	-	-	-	-	8	14
Barking	-	-	-	-	-	-	-	5	4	3
Basingstoke	-	-	8	2	2	5	11	13	-	-
Berry Hill	-	-	-	-	-	7	7	11	5	11
Camberley	-	-	-	-	-	-	-	-	7	4
Camborne	4	3	4	4	6	4	4	8	13	-
Charlton Park	-	-	-	-	-	-	-	-	-	13
Cheltenham	10	6	9	13	-	-	-	-	6	5
Clifton	-	-	2	-	-	-	-	-	-	-
Ealing	-	9	-	10	13	-	-	-	-	-
Havant	5	2	5	8	1	-	-	-	-	-
Henley	-	-	-	-	-	-	-	9	3	2
High Wycombe	-	-	-	-	5	8	9	10	10	12
London Welsh	-	-	-	3	3	2	6	1	-	-
Lydney	3	1	-	-	-	3	2	2	1	-
Maidenhead	-	-	-	12	-	-	-	-	-	-
Maidstone	-	-	10	11	8	12	13	-	-	-
Met. Police	-	-	1	-	10	9	10	7	12	7
Newbury	-	-	-	-	-	-	-	-	-	1
N. Walsham	-	-	-	6	7	11	8	4	11	10
Plymouth	-	-	-	-	-	-	-	-	-	6
Reading	-	-	-	-	-	-	1	-	-	-
Redruth	-	4	3	1	-	-	-	-	-	-
Salisbury	9	7	11	-	-	-	-	-	-	-
Sidcup	2	11	-	-	12	-	-	-	-	-
Southend	7	8	7	9	11	6	12	-	-	-
Stroud	6	10	-	-	-	-	-	-	-	-
Streatham/Croydon	11	-	-	-	-	-	-	-	-	-
Sudbury	8	5	6	7	4	1	-	12	-	-
Tabard	-	-	-	-	-	-	3	6	9	8
Thurrock	-	-	-	-	-	13	-	-	-	-
Weston-s-Mare	-	-	-	5	9	10	5	3	2	9

REGIONAL DIVISIONS

NORTHERN	488
MIDLAND	538
SOUTH WEST	585
LONDON & SOUTH EAST	637

Although the fixtures printed throughout this section of the book were correct at the time of going to press, it is most advisable that you check with club officials or your local press nearer to the time, as dates can be subject to change.

NORTHERN DIVISION

OFFICIALS 1997-98

CHAIRMAN, League Sub-Committee
Bob Archer, Brookfield House, Scotland Head, Winlaton, Tyne & Wear. NE21 6PL (H) 0191 414 3532

N.E. CO-ORDINATOR AND YORKSHIRE REPRESENTATIVE
Les Bentley, 32 Moorhead Terrace, Shipley, W. Yorkshire. BD18 4LB (H) 01274 585460

N.W. CO-ORDINATOR AND LANCASHIRE REPRESENTATIVE
Bill Chappell, Seawood House, Carter Road, Kents Bank, Grange-over-Sands, Cumbria. LA11 7AS (H) 01539 533456

LEAGUE SECRETARIES
North One A Johnson, 6 Rugby Drive, Tytherington, Macclesfield, Cheshire. SK10 2JD (H & Fax) 01625 614697 (Mbl) 0378 352857

North Two M S Smith, The Lowe, Wainstalls, Halifax, West Yorkshire. HX2 7TR (H & Fax) 01422 882879

North East One I Clarke, 109 Dryden Road, Low Fell, Gateshead, Tyne & Wear. NE9 5TS (H) 01914 218271

North East Two J Scott, 8 Main Street, Cherry Burton, Beverley, East Yorkshire. HU17 7RF (H) 01964 551340

North East Three G Gravil, 6 Grampian Way, Thorne, Doncaster, South Yorkshire. DN8 5YL (H) 01405 813642

Yorkshire One W F Cooper, "Moorcroft", Lucy Hall Drive, Baildon, Shipley, West Yorkshire. BD17 5BG (H) 01274 584355

Yorkshire Two R Lewis, 33 Swift Way, Sandal, Wakefield, West Yorkshire. WF2 6SQ (H) 01924 253049

Yorkshire Three J Cooper, 8 Otterwood Bank, Foxwood Hill, Acomb, York. YO2 3JS (H) 01904 797858 (B) 01904 452773

Yorkshire Four G Mapplebeck, 33 Oakley Street, Thorpe, Wakefield, West Yorkshire. WF3 3DX (H) 01924 828809

Yorkshire Five P Hazeldine, 90 Fairburn Drive, Garforth, Leeds, West Yorkshire. LS25 2JD (H) 0113 2866035

Durham & Northumberland One W G Scott, "Highbury", Main Road, Ryton, Tyne & Wear. NE40 3AG (H) 0191 4136293

Durham & Northumberland Two Mrs Joyce Baty, 5 Brooklands, Ponteland, Northumberland. NE20 9LZ (H) 01661 823527

Durham & Northumberland Three A R Brown, 22 Mill Crescent, Hebburn, Tyne & Wear. NE31 1UQ (H) 01914 693716

Durham & Northumberland Four J Ker, 4 Anlaby Close, Billingham, Cleveland. TS23 3RA (H & Fax) 01642 560536

North West One Ivon Hodgeson, Kimberley End, 22 Capesthorn Close, Holmes Chapel, Cheshire. CW4 7EW (H) 01477 533406

North West Two Ken Punshon, 24 Newcombe Road, Holcombe Brook, Nr Bury, Lancs (H) 01204 884886

North West Three Ian Scott Brown, Brumsholme, Pendleview, Grindleton, Nr Clitheroe, Lancs. BB7 4QU (H) 01200 440102 (B) 01254 582749/57346 (Mbl) 0973 819222

Cumbria & Lancashire North Roger Bott, 123 Albert Road West, Heaton, Bolton, Lancs. BL1 5ED (H) 01204 841376

Cumbria Bill Hopkinson, Far Hey Farm, Littleborough, Rochdale, Lancs. OL15 9NS (H) 01706 379879 (B) 01706 47474 x 4531

North Lancashire One Colin Barton, 4 Oulderhill Drive, Rochdale, Lancs. OL11 5LB (H) 01706 350312

North Lancashire Two Vic Thomas, 5 Portree Close, Winton, Eccles, Manchester. M30 8LX (H) 0161 788 7274

South Lancs & Cheshire One Mike Massey, Fieldside, Grange Road, Bowden, Cheshire. WA14 3EE (H) 0161 928 2997

South Lancs & Cheshire Two Brian Minor, 45 Gorton Street, Peel Green, Eccles, Manchester. M30 7LZ (H) 0161 789 4867

South Lancs & Cheshire Three Vic Thomas, 5 Portree Close, Winton, Eccles, Manchester. M30 8LX (H) 0161 788 7274

South Lancs & Cheshire Four Ken Potter, Lindesfarne, 97 The Farthing, Ashley Park, Chorley, Lancs. PR7 1SH (H) 01257 267411 (Fax) 01695 51205

NORTHERN DIVISION

NORTHERN DIVISION STRUCTURE 1996-97

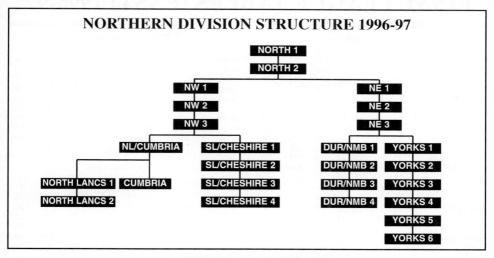

ADMINISTRATIVE RULES

On League Saturdays, both Clubs will telephone the match result to their League Secretary. Both clubs will also confirm within 48 hours the result and score in writing together with the list of players and replacements featuring in the match to the League Secretary on a card signed by the referee.

a.	In the case of Northern Division Leagues 1 and 2, North West Leagues 1, 2 and 3 and North East Leagues 1, 2 and 3, the League Secretary shall telephone the results not later than 5.15pm on the evening of the game to Snowdon Sports Editorial, PO Box 154, Sheffield, S10 4BW. Tel: 0114 230 3093. Fax: 0114 230 3094.

b.	For all other Leagues, the results shall be telephoned to Snowdon Sports Editorial by the League Secretary not later than 6.15pm on the evening of the match.

c.	In Northern Division Leagues 1 and 2 the League Secretaries will remit to the Chairman the scores and results in writing within 48 hours. The remaining League Secretaries will remit the results and the scores in writing to their North East or North West co-ordinator within 48 hours.

d.	In the case of an abandoned match the Secretary of the League must be supplied by the home Club with a certificate signed by the Referee indicating the point at which the match was abandoned, and the score.

e.	These arrangements do not prohibit local publicity and Clubs are advised to maintain and improve local publicity by informing their local press as usual.

f.	Any Club failing to notify the result in accordance with this Rule shall on the first occasion during a season be fined £15, on the second and third occasion £25. If the fines are not paid there will be a recommendation to the RFU that the Club be suspended or expelled from the League. Should

payment of fines not be honoured within 28 days of the date of the invoice, the offending club will lose 2 league points.

RESCHEDULED MATCHES

A match postponed or abandoned under Regulation 11(a) or (b) or a match not played on the appointed day for reasons acceptable to the Organising Committee SHALL be played on the NEXT AVAILABLE Saturday.

A Saturday is deemed to be "available" UNLESS one of the following conditions applies:

a)	Either Club has, on that day, a scheduled Courage League match.

b)	Either Club has, on that day, a Pilkington Cup or Shield match.

c)	Either Club has, on that weekend, a match in a Competition under the authority of their Constituent Body BUT NOT a Merit Table match.

d)	Either Club has a demand on one or more of their effectively registered players to play in a representative match under the authority of the RFU, their Division or their Constituent Body on that day.

e)	In addition, the Northern Division Organising Committee may - at its absolute discretion and usually at the start of a season - declare a specific Saturday "unavailable" where it falls on or close to a public holiday or where it is considered inappropriate to play for other particular reasons.

NORTHERN DIVISION
FINAL LEAGUE TABLES (EAST) 1996-97

NORTH ONE

	P	W	D	L	F	A	PT
Sedgley Park	21	16	1	4	632	384	33
Tynedale	21	14	1	6	546	311	29
New Brighton	21	14	1	6	484	381	29
Stockton	21	12	2	7	482	391	26
Wigton	21	12	1	8	467	331	25
Macclesfield	22	10	1	11	308	484	21
Bridlington	21	10	0	11	400	416	20
Widnes	21	10	0	11	240	431	20
Hull Ionians	22	7	2	13	359	456	16
West Park Bramhope	21	6	1	14	312	450	13
Broughton Park	22	6	0	16	358	425	12
Bradford & Bingley	22	6	0	16	312	540	12

NORTH TWO

	P	W	D	L	F	A	PTS
Doncaster	21	21	0	0	663	253	42
Middlebrough	21	18	0	3	685	280	36
Blaydon	22	14	0	8	479	382	28
Huddersfield	20	13	1	6	436	322	27
Alnwick	21	11	1	9	535	422	23
Northern	22	10	1	11	455	506	21
Driffield	21	10	1	10	410	470	21
Lymm	22	9	1	12	407	548	19
Vale of Lune	22	7	0	15	404	478	14
Halifax	22	6	0	16	366	509	12
York	22	4	1	17	357	504	9
Durham City	22	3	0	19	350	873	6

NORTH EAST ONE

	P	W	D	L	F	A	PTS
Morpeth	18	13	2	3	435	237	28
Old Crossleyans	18	13	2	3	388	213	28
Percy Park	18	12	1	5	397	307	25
Old Brodleians	18	8	2	8	458	401	18
Pontefract	18	9	0	9	345	358	18
Horden	18	7	1	10	371	412	15
Wheatley Hills	18	7	1	10	335	391	15
Gateshead Fell	18	6	2	10	287	328	14
Hartlepool Rovers	18	5	0	13	278	484	10
Keighley	18	4	1	13	218	381	9

NORTH EAST TWO

	P	W	D	L	F	A	PTS
Beverley	18	15	0	3	504	253	30
Goole	18	14	0	4	401	217	28
Ashington	18	11	1	6	489	360	23
Westoe	18	10	1	7	386	316	21
Cleckheaton	18	10	0	8	381	309	20
Darlington Mowden	18	9	1	8	417	330	19
Roundhegians	18	7	0	11	313	383	14
North Ribblesdale	18	6	1	11	339	489	13
Selby	18	4	0	14	281	396	8
Redcar	18	2	0	16	181	639	4

NORTH EAST THREE

	P	W	D	L	F	A	PTS
Darlington	18	16	0	2	702	274	32
Hull	18	14	0	4	452	229	28
Ripon	18	13	0	5	333	237	26
Sunderland	18	9	0	9	404	380	18
Pocklington	18	8	0	10	330	282	*14
Thornensians	18	7	0	11	297	356	14
Whitby	18	8	0	10	245	368	*14
Bramley	18	6	0	12	281	368	12
Whitley Bay Rockl.	18	5	0	13	241	468	10
Blyth	18	4	0	14	282	605	8

YORKSHIRE ONE

	P	W	D	L	F	A	PTS
Yarnbury	18	16	1	1	597	185	33
Ilkley	18	12	2	4	387	206	26
Bradford Salem	18	10	2	6	316	291	22
Malton &Norton	18	10	0	8	423	279	20
Northallerton	18	10	0	8	443	315	20
Wath	18	8	3	7	387	348	19
Leodiensians	18	8	2	8	359	340	18
Old Otlensians	18	5	0	13	273	335	*8
Moortown	18	4	1	13	301	466	*5
Wibsey	18	1	1	16	136	857	3

YORKSHIRE TWO

	P	W	D	L	F	A	PTS
Castleford	18	16	0	2	485	234	32
Dinnington	18	12	1	5	544	249	25
Barnsley	18	10	0	8	352	268	20
Hullensians	18	10	0	8	300	267	20
Scarborough	18	10	0	8	297	288	20
Halifax Vandals	18	8	2	8	247	297	18
Sheffield Oaks	18	6	3	9	236	211	15
Sheffield Tigers	18	7	0	11	295	387	14
Old Modernians	18	7	0	11	278	441	14
Phoenix Park	18	1	0	17	196	588	2

YORKSHIRE THREE

	P	W	D	L	F	A	PTS
Huddersfield YMCA	16	15	0	1	714	87	30
West Leeds	16	13	0	3	607	191	26
Stocksbridge	16	10	0	6	300	257	20
Hemsworth	16	10	0	6	330	353	20
Wetherby	16	8	2	6	339	324	18
Hessle	16	4	2	10	218	397	10
Aireborough	16	4	2	10	216	429	10
Skipton	16	4	0	12	187	483	8
Hornsea	16	1	0	15	142	532	2

YORKSHIRE FOUR

	P	W	D	L	F	A	PTS
York RI	16	14	0	2	396	187	28
Leeds Corinthians	16	10	1	5	279	175	21
Stanley Rodillians	16	9	0	7	310	193	18
Old Rishworthians	16	9	0	7	290	205	18
Knottingley	16	8	0	8	271	269	16
Heath	16	8	1	7	224	223	*15
Baildon	16	7	0	9	233	265	14
Mosborough	16	3	0	13	183	371	6
Knaresborough	16	3	0	13	159	457	6

YORKSHIRE FIVE

	P	W	D	L	F	A	PTS
Marist	14	13	0	1	415	127	26
Edlington & Wickersl	14	12	0	2	324	207	24
Burley	14	8	0	6	268	104	16
Garforth	14	7	0	7	202	187	14
Ossett	14	6	0	8	243	252	12
Rowntrees	14	6	0	8	245	231	*10
BP Chemicals	14	4	0	10	171	224	8
Danum Phoenix	14	0	0	14	83	649	*-4

YORKSHIRE SIX

	P	W	D	L	F	A	PTS
Adwick Le Street	12	8	1	3	234	116	17
De La Salle (Shef)	12	8	0	4	191	122	16
New Earswick	11	7	0	4	158	226	14
Rawmarsh	11	7	0	4	235	144	*12
Withernsea	12	5	1	6	200	167	*9
Leeds Medics &Denti	12	4	0	8	203	166	*6
Menwith Hill Quakers	12	1	0	11	86	366	2

DURHAM & NORTHMBERLAND ONE

	P	W	D	L	F	A	PTS
W Hartlepool TDSOB	18	18	0	0	643	175	468
Ryton	18	16	0	2	587	228	32
Acklam	18	11	0	7	428	255	22
North Shields	17	11	0	6	365	227	22
Medicals	18	8	0	10	308	345	16
Bishop Auckland	18	9	0	9	308	430	*16
Winlaton Vulcans	18	7	0	11	307	317	14
Novocastrians	18	4	0	14	254	365	8
Guisborough	17	3	0	14	165	560	6
Hartlepool	18	2	0	16	176	639	4

DURHAM & NORTHMBERLAND TWO

	P	W	D	L	F	A	PTS
Consett	18	15	2	1	545	178	32
North Durham	18	13	2	3	455	218	28
Barnard Castle	18	13	1	4	509	197	27
Ponteland	18	10	0	8	340	207	20
Chester-Le-Street	18	8	1	9	305	272	17
Seaton Carew	18	8	0	10	310	317	16
S Tyneside Coll	18	8	0	10	297	380	16
Wallsend	18	7	0	11	205	432	14
Darlington RA	18	3	0	15	115	424	6
Wensleydale	18	2	0	16	146	602	4

DURHAM & NORTHMB THREE

	P	W	D	L	F	A	PTS
Billingham	14	14	0	0	647	160	28
Seghill	14	11	0	3	362	128	22
Richmondshire	14	8	1	5	308	226	17
Seaham	14	8	1	5	282	216	17
Houghton	14	6	0	8	204	363	12
Sedgefield	14	4	0	10	192	339	8
Hartlepool	14	3	0	11	153	382	6
Wearside	14	1	0	13	139	473	2

DURHAM & NORTHMB FOUR

	P	W	D	L	F	A	PTS
Gosforth	12	12	0	0	721	36	24
Hartlepool Athletic	12	9	0	3	206	197	18
Jarrovians	12	7	0	5	221	234	14
Washington	12	6	0	6	120	272	12
Durham Constabulary	12	4	0	8	136	329	8
Newton Aycliffe	12	3	0	9	162	322	6
Prudhoe Hospital	12	1	0	11	86	262	2

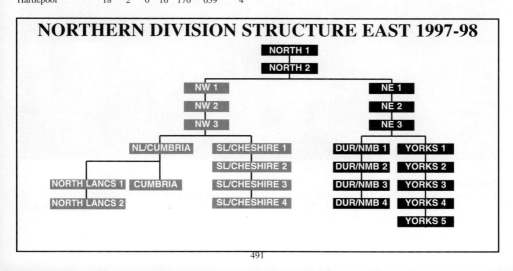

NORTHERN DIVISION STRUCTURE EAST 1997-98

491

NORTH ONE

North One 1997-98 Fixtures	Bridlington 1	Broughton Park 2	Doncaster 3	Hull Ionians 4	Macclesfield 5	Middlesborough 6	New Brighton 7	Stockton 8	Tynedale 9	West Park B. 10	Widnes 11	Wigton 12	
1 Bridlington	X	18/4	24/1	11/10	20/12	7/2	30/8	21/3	7/3	25/10	15/11	20/9	1
2 Broughton Park	10/1	X	15/11	7/2	4/4	25/10	21/3	20/9	11/10	24/1	25/4	7/3	2
3 Doncaster	8/11	17/1	X	20/9	18/10	7/3	7/3	18/4	21/3	11/10	31/1	30/8	3
4 Hull Ionians	14/2	18/10	14/3	X	18/4	4/4	31/1	8/11	20/12	6/9	27/9	17/1	4
5 Macclesfield	25/4	30/8	7/2	10/1	X	21/3	20/9	11/10	15/11	7/3	24/1	25/10	5
6 Middlesborough	18/10	31/1	27/9	30/8	6/9	X	8/11	17/1	18/4	14/3	14/2	20/12	6
7 New Brighton	4/4	6/9	25/4	25/10	14/3	24/1	X	7/3	7/2	15/11	10/1	11/10	7
8 Stockton	6/9	14/3	10/1	24/1	14/2	15/11	27/9	X	25/10	25/4	4/4	7/2	8
9 Tynedale	27/9	14/2	6/9	25/4	17/1	10/1	18/10	31/1	X	4/4	14/3	8/11	9
10 West Park Bramhope	31/1	8/11	14/2	21/3	27/9	20/9	17/1	20/12	30/8	X	18/10	18/4	10
11 Widnes	17/1	20/12	25/10	7/3	8/11	11/10	18/4	30/8	20/9	7/2	X	21/3	11
12 Wigton	14/3	27/9	4/4	15/11	31/1	25/4	14/2	18/10	24/1	10/1	6/9	X	12
	1	2	3	4	5	6	7	8	9	10	11	12	

Middlesbrough R.U.F.C. 1996/97.
Left to right, back, P.Tilson, D.Poole, P.Davidson, M.O'Halloran, M.Havelock and A.Flemming.
Centre, M.Read (President), A.Elwine, G.Pargeter (Chairman), K.Whitaker, L.Richardson, S.Jones, T.Lauriston, P.Evans, T.McGrath, N.Poole, J.Chapman, R.Lamprelle (Physio) and D.Brydon (Secretary).
Front, R.Horton, B.Addlington, P.Manders (Captain), P.Hodder (Coach) and J.Wrigley.

NORTH ONE CONTINUED

BRIDLINGTON RUFC
Ground Address: Dukes Park, Queensgate, Bridlington Tel: 01262 676405
Brief Directions: Follow signs to Bridlington, 1st traffic lights keep in n/s lane, right at roundabout, left at next lights, ground is 0.25 mile on right
Club Secretary: Allan Blackhall, 26 Viking Road,Bridlington YO16 5TW.   Tel: 01262 673567
Fixtures Secretary: J Chambers   Tel: (H) 01377 217532   (W) 01262 672088
Club Colours: Blue, yellow hoop around middle

BROUGHTON PARK FC
Ground Address: Chelsfield Grove, Off Mauldeth Rd West, Chorlton-cum-Hardy Manchester. M21 7SU Tel: 0161 8812481
Brief Directions: M56 J3, follow signs to Manchester A5103 (straight on) for 3 miles, left at Mauldeth Road West, ground is 0.75 mile on right
Club Secretary: Peter Oakes c/o Burymans Lace Mawer, Kingshouse, King St. West, Manchester. M3 2PW Tel: 0421 771325
Fixtures Secretary: Tom Barber   Tel: (H) 0161 998 8936   (W) 0161 226 2501
Club Colours: Black and white hoops

DONCASTER RFC
Ground Address: Armthorpe Road, Doncaster, South Yorkshire. DN9 3DG   Tel: 01302 770275
Brief Directions: From M18 J4, to Doncaster, 1st left , rt at roundabout, ground 1 mile on left. Or A1(M), A630 into Doncaster, anti clockwise round ring road,1st roundabout right after racecourse
Club Secretary: John Lowe, 57 Wroot Road, Finningley Village, Doncaster, South Yorkshire. DN9 3DR   Tel: (H) 01302 770275   (W) 0585 397 353
Fixtures Secretary: Harry Potts   Tel: (H) 01302 300319   (W) 01430 422 471 Ext 230
Club Colours: Blue with two red and white hoops

HULL IONIANS RUFC
Ground Address: Brantingham Park, Elloughton Road, Brantingham, East Yorkshire. HU15 1HY   Tel: 01482 667342
Brief Directions: From west, M62 onto A63 1st junction, follow signs for Brough, at 2nd Brantingham sign follow road to Brantingham, Club on right
Club Secretary: Peter Sharp, 38 Corby Park, North Ferriby, East Yorkshire. HU14 3AY   Tel: (H) 01482 631819   (W) 01482 803933
Fixtures Secretary: John Clayton   Tel: (H) 01482 651667
Club Colours: Red, white, blue, green quarters, blue shorts, red socks

MACCLESFIELD RUFC
Ground Address: Priory Park, Priory Lane, Macclesfield. SK10 4AE   Tel: 01625 827899
Brief Directions: From centre of Macclesfield follow signs for Leisure Centre, which is close to ground
Club Secretary: Terry McCreery, 20 Carnoustie Drive, Macclesfield. SK10 2TB   Tel: (H) 01625 615488   (W) 0161 832 5085
Fixtures Secretary: Alan Johnson   Tel: (H) 01625 614697
Club Colours: Blue and white hoops

MIDDLESBROUGH RUFC
Ground Address: Acklam Park, Green Lane, Middlesbrough   Tel: 01642 818567
Brief Directions: A19, A11330 exit to M'bro, immediate left at fork, right at bollards onto Croft Ave, straight over traffic lights onto Green Lane, club 400yds on right
Club Secretary: Don Brydon, 20 Westwood Ave, Linthorpe, Middlesborough. TS5 5PY   Tel: (H) 01647 819954   (W) 01642 264047
Fixtures Secretary: A.Murray   Tel: (H) 01287 637803
Club Colours: Maroon shirts, white shorts

NEW BRIGHTON FC(RU)
Ground Address: Reeds Lane, Moreton, Wirral. L46 3RS   Tel: 0151 677 1873
Brief Directions: M53 J1, direction of New Brighton, first turning left (sign posted to Club), approx 0.75 mile, turn left into Reeds Lane
Club Secretary: Brian Lawrence, 351 Leasowe Road, Moreton, Wirral. L46 2RE   Tel: (H) 0151 638 5379
Fixtures Secretary: Bernard Murphy   Tel:(H) 0151 625 8835   (W) 0151 637 0071
Club Colours: Navy blue, light blue, white

STOCKTON RFC
Ground Address: Norton (Teesside) Sports Complex, Station Road, Norton, Stockton, Cleveland. TS20 1PE Tel: 01642 554031
Brief Directions: From A19 take A1027 to Norton, at roundabout turn right into Station Rd, 60 yds on turn right, travel to end, clubhouse on left before Norton Tavern for dressing rooms
Club Secretary: John Robinson, 17 Rook Lane, Norton, Stockton, Cleveland. TS20 1SB   Tel: (H & W) 01642 892425
Fixtures Secretary: Brendon Thornton   Tel: (H) 01642 895825
Club Colours: Red shirts, white shorts, royal blue socks

TYNEDALE RFC
Ground Address: Tynedale Park, Corbridge, Northumberland. NE45 5AY   Tel: 01434 632996/7
Brief Directions: From north, across river bridge from Corbridge village to railway station, ground is adjacent. From south from Riding Mill to Corbridge, exit at railway station access
Club Secretary: N.S.Foster, 2 Tyne View Terrace, Corbridge, Northumberland NE45 5AJ   Tel: 01434 632262
Fixtures Secretary: R Halford   Tel: (H) 01661 842428
Club Colours: Jerseys royal blue with white horizontal stripes, white shorts, blue and white socks

WEST PARK BRAMHOPE RUFC
Ground Address: The Sycamores, Bramhope, Leeds. LS16 9JR   Tel: 0113 2671437
Brief Directions: From Leeds city centre take A660 sign posted Skipton & Otley, at Bramhope village turn left at roundabout direct to Club
Club Secretary: Martin Pearce, 12 Helmsley Drive, West Park, Leeds LS16 5AY   Tel: (H) 0113 2269913
Fixtures Secretary: Mike Openshaw   Tel: (H) 0113 2587338
Club Colours: Black and gold

WIDNES RUFC
Ground Address: Heath Road, Widnes, Cheshire. WA8 7NU   Tel: 0151 424 2575
Brief Directions: From M62 exit at J7, A57 to Warrington, right at 1st lights, right at junction up to roundabout, 1st left-Birchfield Rd, down to 1st major lights, right, right at 2nd lights, 1st right, club on left
Club Secretary: Alan Evans, 238 Mill Lane, Bold, Widnes,Lancs.   Tel: (H) 0151 424 3443
Fixtures Secretary: Raymond Heapey   Tel: (H) 0151 424 6565
Club Colours: Red and black hooped jerseys, black shorts

WIGTON RUFC
Ground Address: Lowmoor Road, Wigton, Cumbria. CA7 9QT   Tel: 016973 42206
Brief Directions: M6 J41 or A595 Carlisle to Cockermouth, both ways bring you to Wigton junction, follow road 0.5 mile to Wigton, club is the first stop
Club Secretary: Malcolm Sunter, Alpha, Lowmoor Road, Wigton, Cumbria. CA7 9QR   Tel: (H) 016973 42917
Fixtures Secretary: Allan Robson   Tel: (H) 016973 42310   (W) 01228 45810
Club Colours: Green shirts, white shorts, green socks

NORTH TWO

North Two 1997-98 Fixtures	Alnwick 1	Blackburn 2	Blaydon 3	Bradford & B 4	Driffield 5	Halifax 6	Huddersfield 7	Lymm 8	Morpeth 9	Northern 10	Vale of Lune 11	York 12	
1 Alnwick	X	8/11	17/1	7/2	18/4	30/8	20/12	11/10	25/10	20/9	21/3	7/3	1
2 Blackburn	24/1	X	25/4	7/3	20/9	11/10	30/8	21/3	7/2	15/11	25/10	10/1	2
3 Blaydon	15/11	20/12	X	25/10	30/8	21/3	18/4	7/2	24/1	7/3	20/9	11/10	3
4 Bradford & B	18/10	27/9	31/1	X		20/12	8/11	20/9	14/2	30/8	18/4	21/3	4
5 Driffield	10/1	14/3	4/4	15/11	X	7/3	6/9	24/1	25/4	7/2	11/10	25/10	5
6 Halifax	4/4	14/2	6/9	25/4	27/9	X	14/3	15/11	10/1	25/10	7/2	24/1	6
7 Huddersfield	25/4	4/4	10/1	24/1	21/3	20/9	X	25/10	15/11	11/10	7/3	7/2	7
8 Lymm	14/2	6/9	18/10	14/3	8/11	17/1	31/1	X	27/9	18/4	20/12	30/8	8
9 Morpeth	31/1	18/10	8/11	11/10	20/12	18/4	17/1	7/3	X	21/3	30/8	20/9	9
10 Northern	14/3	17/1	27/9	4/4	18/10	31/1	14/2	10/1	6/9	X	8/11	25/4	10
11 Vale of Lune	6/9	31/1	14/3	10/1	14/2	18/10	27/9	25/4	4/4	24/1	X	15/11	11
12 York	27/9	18/4	14/2	6/9	31/1	8/11	18/10	4/4	14/3	20/12	17/1	X	12
	1	2	3	4	5	6	7	8	9	10	11	12	

Morpeth R.F.C. Winners of North East One 1996/97.
Pictured with President, Chairman of Rugby, and Selectors, Club Coaches and 1st XV Team Manager.

NORTH TWO

ALNWICK RUFC
Ground Address: Greensfield, St James, Alnwick, Northumberland Tel: 01665 602342
Brief Directions: A1 slip (south) of Alnwick signed Alnwick from N/castle, after slip 1st left, club 300 yds on left. From Edinburgh, after slip straight over crossroads, Greensfield Ave as above
Club Secretary: Tim Flood, Witton Shield House, Netherwitton, Morpeth, Northumberland. NE61 4NL Tel: (H) 01670 772327   (W) 0191 252 6857
Fixtures Secretary: John Answorth Tel: (H) 01665 605196   (W) 01665 510505
Club Colours: Royal blue jersey with gold lion rampant badge

BLACKBURN RUFC
Ground Address: Ramsgreave Drive, Blackburn, Lancs. BB1 8NB Tel: 01254 247669
Brief Directions: M6 J31, follow signs to Blackburn, left at Moat House Hotel, club on left after 1 mile
Club Secretary: Mr L C Blow, 41 East Park Avenue, Blackburn, Lancs. BB1 8DT   Tel: (H & W) 01254 52705
Fixtures Secretary: Mr G Bancroft Tel: (H) 01254 201366   (W) 01850 920373
Club Colours: Blue top, white shorts

BLAYDON RFC
Ground Address: Crow Trees Ground, Hexham Road, Swalwell, Newcastle upon Tyne. NE16 3BM Tel: 0191 420 0505/6
Brief Directions: A1 north past Gateshead Metro Centre, take next exit for Swalwell
Club Secretary: G H March, c/o Ground as above. Tel: (H) 01207 545397
Fixtures Secretary: Jim Huxley Tel: (H) 0191 488 7280
Club Colours: Scarlet and white

BRADFORD & BINGLEY RFC
Ground Address: Wagon Lane, Cottingley Bridge, Bingley, Yorkshire Tel: 01274 775441
Brief Directions: M62 onto M606 to Bradford ring road, right to second roundabout, left onto A650 for 5 miles to Bingley, right by Beckfoot School onto Wagon Lane, ground 200yds along
Club Secretary: Mr J S Oddy, The Coach House, Warren Farm, Slate Quarry Lane, Eldwick, Bingley, Yorkshire. BD16 3NP Tel: (H) 01274 563254   (W) 01274 729792
Fixtures Secretary: W K Wilkinson Tel: (H & W) 01274 681231
Club Colours: Red, amber and black hoops, black shorts

DRIFFIELD RUFC
Ground Address: Kelleythorpe, Driffield, East Yorkshire. YO25 9DW Tel: 01377 256598
Brief Directions: South of Driffield town between Market Weighton Road roundabout and Beverley Road roundabout
Club Secretary: Stephen Edwards, Cedar Cottage, St Johns Road, Driffield, East Yorkshire. YO25 7RS   Tel: (H) 01377 253757   (W) 01653 697820
Fixtures Secretary: John Harrison Tel: (H & W) 01377 253032
Club Colours: Royal blue, black and white hoops

HALIFAX RUFC
Ground Address: Standeven Memorial Ground, Ovenden Park, Keighley Road, Ovenden, Halifax, West Yorkshire. HX2 8AR Tel: 01422 365926
Brief Directions: From Halifax town centre take main road to Keighley (A629), HRUFC is approx 2.5 miles from town centre on right behind Moorside Junior School
Club Secretary: M S Smith, The Lowe, Wainstalls, Halifax, West Yorkshire. HX2 7TR Tel: (H) 01422 882879   (W) 0850 233019
Fixtures Secretary: Glyn Kenyon, 18 Watkinson Rd, Illingworth, Halifax Tel: (H) 01422 245193
Club Colours: Dark blue, light blue and white bands

HUDDERSFIELD RUFC
Ground Address: Lockwood Park, Brewery Drive, Lockwood, Huddersfield. HD1 3UR Tel: 01484 423864
Brief Directions: Leave Huddersfield town centre on A616 signed Holmfirth, 0.75 mile straight across lights on B6108 signed Meltham, left after 300yds into ground
Club Secretary: Mark H Birch, c/o Club Tel: (H) 01484 852184
Fixtures Secretary: Barrie Starbuck Tel: (H) 01484 686059   (W) 01132 591999/0161 4458141
Club Colours: White shirts with claret and gold hoops, white shorts

LYMM   RFC
Ground Address: Crouchley Lane, Lymm, Cheshire. WA13 0AT Tel: 01925 753212
Brief Directions: M6 J20 to Lymm, 1.5 miles right at T junction, 0.5 mile turn right into Crouchley Lane, club 200 yds on right
Club Secretary: Johpn Cartwright, 12 Parke Gate Road, Stockton Heath, Warrington, WA4 2AP.
Fixtures Secretary: Chris Monks Tel: (H) 01925 262904
Club Colours: Black, green, white

MORPETH RFC (50TH ANNIVERSARY)
Ground Address: Grange House Field, Mitford Road, Morpeth. NE61 1RJ Tel: 01670 512508
Brief Directions: North from Newcastle on A1 from Morpeth centre travelling north, left after telephone exchange onto Mitford Road, entrance on right past the school
Club Secretary: Ken Fraser, Solway House, De Merley Road, Morpeth. NE61 1HZ Tel: (H) 01670 511208 (W) 01642 244144 Fax: 01642 245207
Fixtures Secretary: Bill Hewitt Tel: (H) 01670 787757
Club Colours: Red shirt with navy and white hoops, navy shorts.

NORTHERN FOOTBALL CLUB
Ground Address: McCracken Park, Great North Road, Gosforth, Newcastle upon Tyne. NE3 2DG Tel: 0191 236 3369
Brief Directions: From south & west, A1 western bypass north, take 'city north/Gosforth B1318' for 0.75 mile, ground on left. From north take B1318 from A1, ground 0.75 mile on left
Club Secretary: R M Gibson, 86 Pilgrim St., Newcastle-upon-Tyne. NE1 6SR.
Fixtures Secretary: Richard Kain Tel: (H) 0191 217 0362   (W) 0191 273 7965 Ext 148
Club Colours: White shirts, navy shorts, red socks

NORTH TWO CONTINUED

VALE OF LUNE RUFC
Ground Address: Powderhouse Lane, Lancaster. LA1 2TT   Tel: 01524 64029
Brief Directions: M6 J34 for Lancaster, follow signs for A589 Morecambe, approx 0.5 mile after crossing River Lune, turn right down Scale Hall, left at junction, ground 50yds on right
Club Secretary: c/o Vale of Lune RUFC, Powderhouse Lane, Lancaster. LA1 2TT   Tel: (H) 01524 416519
Fixtures Secretary: Mr F W Swarbrick   Tel: (H) 01524 37601   (W) 01524 64055
Club Colours: Cherry and white hoops, blue shorts, cherry and white socks

YORK RUFC
Ground Address: Clifton Park, Shipton Road, York YO3 6RE   Tel:01904 623602
Brief Directions: Turn south off York outer ring road (A10) towards York city centre on A19 from Thirsk, club situated on right after about 1.75 miles
Club Secretary: Brian McClure, 15 Stubden Grove, York. YO3 4UY   Tel: (H) 01904 691026
Fixtures Secretary: Peter Ayers   Tel: (H) 01904 470351
Club Colours: Green, black and white hoops with black shorts

NORTH EAST ONE

North East One 1997-98 Fixtures	Beverley	Durham City	Gateshead Fell	Goole	Horden	Old Brodleians	Old Crossleyans	Percy Park	Pontefract	Wheatley Hills	
	1	2	3	4	5	6	7	8	9	10	
1 Beverley	X	31/1	20/12	25/4	8/11	18/10	14/3	17/1	27/9	7/3	1
2 Durham City	11/10	X	14/2	20/9	14/3	25/4	10/1	20/12	25/10	24/1	2
3 Gateshead Fell	11/4	27/9	X	8/11	17/1	31/1	15/11	18/10	7/3	6/9	3
4 Goole	15/11	7/3	10/1	X	18/10	27/9	25/10	31/1	6/9	11/4	4
5 Horden	10/1	6/9	25/10	24/1	X	7/3	11/10	27/9	11/4	15/11	5
6 Old Brodleians	24/1	15/11	11/10	14/2	20/9	X	11/4	14/3	10/1	25/10	6
7 Old Crossleyans	6/9	8/11	25/4	17/1	31/1	20/12	X	7/3	18/10	27/9	7
8 Percy Park	25/10	11/4	24/1	11/10	14/2	6/9	20/9	X	15/11	10/1	8
9 Pontefract	14/2	17/1	20/9	14/3	20/12	8/11	24/1	25/4	X	11/10	9
10 Wheatley Hills	20/9	18/10	14/3	20/12	25/4	17/1	14/2	8/11	31/1	X	10
	1	2	3	4	5	6	7	8	9	10	

Wheatley Hills RUFC

NORTH EAST ONE CONTINUED

BEVERLEY RUFC
Ground Address: Beaver Park, Norwood, Beverley.
HU17 9HT Tel: 01482 870306
Brief Directions: Through Beverley centre, follow signs
for Hornsea, ground is just before level crossing behind
Lady le Gros pub
Club Secretary: Andrew Winter, 4 The Vineyards,
Leven, Beverley, East Yorkshire Tel: (H) 01964 543981
(W) 01482 884331
Fixtures Secretary: Rob Jenner Tel: (H) 01482
868944
Club Colours: Green, brown and white

DURHAM CITY RFC
Ground Address: Hollow Drift, Green Lane, Durham
City. DH1 3JU Tel: 0191 386 1172
Brief Directions: Take A1M, then A690, straight across
1st roundabout, left at next roundabout, left at traffic
lights, after 300 yards turn left into Green Lane, opposite
Durham Prison
Club Secretary: Mr R Elston, 18 Mayorswell Field,
Claypath, Durham City. DH1 1JW Tel: (H) 0191 386
3245 (W) 01207 507001
Fixtures Secretary: Mr J Thompson Tel: (H) 01388
528071 (W) 01388 762522
Club Colours: Blue and gold hoops, white shorts

GATESHEAD FELL RFC
Ground Address: Hedley Lawson Park, Eastwood
Gardens, Low Fell, Gateshead. NE9 5UB Tel: 0191
4200207
Brief Directions: Travelling north A167 into Gateshead,
pass 2 sets main lights, turn right Heavey Rd, 2nd left
Eastwood Gdns. Travelling south A167, left Springfield
Hotel, phone box turn left
Club Secretary: M A Nunn, 30 Limetrees Gardens,
Low Fell, Gateshead. NE9 5BE Tel: (H) 0191 4203089
Fixtures Secretary: Dr.W.D.Hetherington, 97 Kells
Lane, Lowfell, Gateshead NE9 5XX. Tel (H) 0191
4219487
Club Colours: Navy and sky narrow hoops

GOOLE RUFC
Ground Address: Westfield Sports Complex Ltd,
Westfield Lane, Hook, Goole, East Yorkshire. DN14
5PW Tel: 01405 762018
Brief Directions: M62 J36, straight through 2 sets of
traffic lights, continue on road out of Goole, right
towards Hook just before bridge into Westfield Lane
Club Secretary: I R Higgins, 14 The Meadows,
Howden, Goole, East Yorkshire. DN14 7DX Tel: (H)
01430 430037 (W) 01405 768621
Fixtures Secretary: P Shand Tel: (H) 01977 677660
(W) 01977 703357
Club Colours: Navy blue and gold quarters

HORDEN WELFARE RUFC
Ground Address: Northumberland Street, Horden,
Peterlee, County Durham Tel: 0191 5863501
Brief Directions: A19 into Peterlee, follow signs for
Horden, left onto Sunderland Rd, turn right at Bell
Hotel, 100 yards to club house
Club Secretary: William Featonby, 20 Morpeth Street,
Horden, Peterlee, County Durham. SR8 4BB Tel: (H)
0191 5866973
Fixtures Secretary: John Fenwick Tel: (H) 0191
5866540
Club Colours: Claret and sky blue

OLD BRODLEIANS RUFC
Ground Address: Woodhead, Denholme Gate Road,
Hipperholme, Halifax Tel: 01422 202708
Brief Directions: M62 J26, follow A58 signs to Halifax,
after 3.75 miles turn right at Hippodrome lights,
continue up hill for 0.5 mile, club on left about 250 yds
after Shell petrol station
Club Secretary: Mr Simon Heaton, Sutcliffe Wood
Farm, Woodbottom Lane, Hove Edge, Brighouse. HD6
2QW Tel: (H) 01484 721628 (W) 01274 700100
Fixtures Secretary: Mr M Hey, 2 Sunnybank Cres.,
Sowerby Bridge, Halifax. Tel: (H) 01422 839614 (W)
01924 490803
Club Colours: Black, red and white shirts, black shorts

OLD CROSSLEYANS RUFC
Ground Address: Standeven House, Broomfield
Avenue, Halifax, West Yorkshire. HX3 0JF Tel: 01422
363000
Club Secretary: Richard A Davies, 4 Warley Dene,
Holme Road, Warley, Halifax. HA2 7RS Tel: (H)
01422 832218
Fixtures Secretary: Derek Ainley Tel: (H) 01422
368233 (W) 01422 822217
Club Colours: Blue and amber

PERCY PARK RFC
Ground Address: Percy Park RFC, The Clubhouse,
Presenton Avenue, North Shields, Tyne & Wear. NE29
Tel: 0191 2575710
Brief Directions: Take east exit signed Tynem'th/N.
Shields/ W'tley Bay onto A1058 1 mile north of Tyne
Tunnel at the r'bout with A19/A1, rt at baths 2 r'bouts
later, 0.5mile lft, club 400yds lft
Club Secretary: A C Baker, 30 The Garth, Winlaton,
Tyne & Wear. NE21 6DD Tel: (W) 0191 4144869
(Fax) 0191 4148672
Fixtures Secretary: A I Carr Tel: (H) 0191 2587783
(W) 0191 2263000
Club Colours: Black and white hoops, black shorts,
black stockings with white tops

PONTEFRACT RFC
Ground Address: Moor Lane, Carleton, Pontefract,
West Yorkshire. WF8 3RX Tel: 01977 702650
Brief Directions: Exit A1 at Darrington, follow signs for
Pontefract, 2 miles to Moor Lane which is 1st left after
30mph sign on outskirts of Pontefract
Club Secretary: R Peacock, 12 Fair View, Carleton,
Pontefract, West Yorkshire. WF8 3NT Tel: (H) 01977
702284 (W) 01977 677421
Fixtures Secretary: M Higgitt Tel: (H) 01977 643605
Club Colours: Royal blue shirts and shorts

WHEATLEY HILLS DONCASTER RUFC
Ground Address: Wheatley Hills Sports Ground,
Brunel Road, York Road Industrial Estate, Doncaster.
DN5 8PT Tel: 01302 781472
Brief Directions: A638 into Doncaster, turn right at B &
Q depot, 1st right, follow road to bottom, club on right
Club Secretary: A R Dunkerley, 1 Mayfields,
Scawthorpe, Doncaster. DN5 7UA Tel: (H) 01302
782214 (W) 01132 446655
Fixtures Secretary: A R Dunkerley Tel: (H) 01302
782214 (W) 01132 446655
Club Colours: Maroon and gold quartered shirts,
maroon shorts

NORTH EAST TWO

North East Two 1997-98 Fixtures	Ashington	Cleckheaton	Darlington	Darl. Mols Plc	Hartlepool R.	Hull	Keighley	N. Ribblesdale	Roundhegians	Westoe	
	1	2	3	4	5	6	7	8	9	10	
1 Ashington	X	14/3	25/4	27/9	7/3	18/10	8/11	20/12	24/1	17/1	1
2 Cleckheaton	6/9	X	17/1	18/10	27/9	20/12	31/1	25/4	8/11	7/3	2
3 Darlington	15/11	25/10	X	6/9	11/4	27/9	18/10	10/1	7/3	24/1	3
4 Darlington Mols Plc	14/2	24/1	14/3	X	11/10	8/11	20/12	20/9	17/1	25/4	4
5 Hartlepool Rovers	20/9	14/2	20/12	31/1	X	17/1	25/4	14/3	18/10	8/11	5
6 Hull	24/1	11/4	14/2	10/1	25/10	X	20/9	11/10	15/11	14/3	6
7 Keighley	10/1	11/10	24/1	11/4	15/11	7/3	X	25/10	6/9	27/9	7
8 North Ribblesdale	11/4	15/11	8/11	7/3	6/9	24/1	17/1	X	27/9	18/10	8
9 Roundhegians	11/10	10/1	20/9	25/10	24/1	25/4	14/3	14/2	X	20/12	9
10 Westoe	25/10	20/9	11/10	15/11	10/1	6/9	14/2	24/1	11/4	X	10
	1	2	3	4	5	6	7	8	9	10	

ASHINGTON J.W.C. RFC
Ground Address: Recreation Ground, Ellington Road, Ashington, Northumberland Tel: 01670814123
Brief Directions: 1 mile north west of Ashington town centre on A1068. Map available on request
Club Secretary: Albert Armstrong, 25 Dundale Drive, Cramlington, Northumberland. NE23 9GA. Tel: (H) 01670 736891 (W) 01670 533303
Fixtures Secretary: A Armstrong Tel: (H) 01670 736891 (W) 01670 533303
Club Colours: Royal blue and amber hoops, white shorts.

CLECKHEATON RUFC
Ground Address: Moorend, Cleckheaton, West Yorkshire. BD19 3UD Tel: 01274 873410
Brief Directions: Situated 200 yards from J26 M62 on the Dewsbury Road
Club Secretary: Mr Ian Worley, 342 Whitehall Road, Westfield, Wyke, Bradford Tel: (H) 01274 677526
Fixtures Secretary: Mr Jack Wood Tel: (H) 01274 873532 (W) 01274 872423
Club Colours: Red and white shirts, black shorts, red socks with 2 white hoops

DARLINGTON MOWDEN PARK RFC
Ground Address: Yiewsley Drive, Mowden Park, Darlington
Brief Directions: From A1(M) follow A68 into Darlington, follow signs to Staindrop, left to Barnes Road, merges into Fulthorpe Ave, 2nd right is Yiewsley Drive
Club Secretary: Mike Charlton, Roadam House, 14 Kettle End, Barton, Richmond, North Yorkshire Tel: (H) 01325 377292 (W) 01325 368568
Fixtures Secretary: George Neville Tel: (H) 01325 469001 (W) 01325 387697
Club Colours: Blue and white hoops

DARLINGTON RFC
Ground Address: Blackwell Meadows, Grange Road, Darlington. DL1 5NR Tel: 01325 363777
Brief Directions: From south take A66, DRFC directly off Blands Corner roundabout. From north take A68 to Darlington and continue to A66 junction at Blands Corner roundabout at Blackwell
Club Secretary: Mr Andrew P F Foster, Cadogan, 45 Hartford Road, Darlington. DL3 8HF Tel: (H) 01325 466501 (Mbl) 0468 661266
Fixtures Secretary: Mr David Gardner Tel: (H) 01833 650543 (W) 01833 690305
Club Colours: Black, white and scarlet

HARTLEPOOL ROVERS
Ground Address: The Friaridge, Westview Road, Hartlepool Tel: 01429 267741
Brief Directions: Take A19 to the A179 turn off. Follow A1049 (Bypass Hartlepool) for 4 miles to the headland.
Club Secretary: Bill Dale, 21 Knapton Avenue, Billingham, Stockton-on-Tees. TS22 5DJ Tel: (H) 01642 863791
Fixtures Secretary: Tony Lowe, 8 Junction Rd., Norton, Stockton-on-Tees. TS20 1PJ. Tel: (H) 01624 530697
Club Colours: White shirts, black shorts, red socks

HULL RUFC
Ground Address: Haworth Park, Emmott Road, Hull. HU6 7AB Tel: 01482 802119
Brief Directions: Follow ring road signs onto Beverley Road Hull, the ground is signposted from there
Club Secretary: D J Ward, 78 St Margarets Avenue, Cottingham, Hull. HU16 5NB Tel: (H) 01482 842292 (W) 01482 325242
Fixtures Secretary: Robin Mason, 223 Beverley Rd, Kirkella, E. Yorks Tel: (H) 657495 (W) 652528
Club Colours: Black with gold and red hoop

KEIGHLEY RUFC
Ground Address: Skipton Road, Utley, Keighley, West Yorkshire. BD20 6DX Tel: 01535 602174
Brief Directions: Access to ground is from former A629 from Keighley to Skipton, ground is on right travelling north just on outskirts of town. NB no access from present A629 Aire V'ly rd
Club Secretary: M T Greaves, Holmlea, Summerhill Lane, Steeton, Keighley, West Yorkshire. BD20 6RX Tel: (H) 01535 653192   (W) 01535 605646
Fixtures Secretary: J Midgley Tel: 01535 214545 (W) 01535 605311
Club Colours: Scarlet, white and green hoops

NORTH RIBBLESDALE RUFC
Ground Address: Grove Park, Green Foot, Settle, North Yorkshire
Brief Directions: Leave A65 at roundabout on southern outskirts of town, into town turning right at Falcon Manor Hotel, ground 0.25 mile on left
Club Secretary: R T Graveson, Attermire House, Castle Hill, Settle, North Yorkshire. BD24 9EU Tel: (H) 01729 823559
Fixtures Secretary: A M Davidson, Gasker, Lawkland, Austwick Tel: (H) 01729 825595
Club Colours: Royal blue and white

ROUNDHEGIANS RUFC
Ground Address: Memorial Ground, Chelwood Drive, Roundhay, Leeds. LS8 2AT Tel: 0113 266 7377
Brief Directions: A61 to junction with Street Lane, follow Street Lane towards Roundhay Park, Chelwood Drive is a road off Street Lane
Club Secretary: Philip A Hobson, 3 Ashgrove Mount, Kippax, Leeds. LS25 7RD Tel: (H) 0113 286 7106 (W) 01422 362461
Fixtures Secretary: Glen English Tel: (H) 01924 265858
Club Colours: Green, black and white hooped shirts, black shorts

WESTOE RFC
Ground Address: Dean Road, South Shields, Tyne & Wear. Tel: 0191 456 1506
Brief Directions: Map available
Club Secretary: J R Wells, 240 Mowbray Road, South Shields. NE33 3NW Tel: (H) 0191 4552260
Fixtures Secretary: D Allen Tel: (H) 0191 4569531
Club Colours: Red, sky and dark blue hoops

NORTH EAST THREE

North East Three 1997-98 Fixtures	Bramley	Hartlepool TDSOB	Pocklington	Redcar	Ripon	Selby	Sunderland	Thornensians	Whitby	Yarnbury	
	1	2	3	4	5	6	7	8	9	10	
1 Bramley	X	24/1	11/10	20/12	14/3	8/11	25/4	17/1	14/2	20/9	1
2 Hartlepool TDSOB	18/10	X	27/9	31/1	17/1	20/12	7/3	8/11	6/9	25/4	2
3 Pocklington	31/1	14/2	X	25/4	20/12	17/1	8/11	18/10	20/9	14/3	3
4 Redcar	11/4	11/10	15/11	X	24/1	7/3	27/9	6/9	10/1	25/10	4
5 Ripon	6/9	25/10	11/4	18/10	X	27/9	31/1	7/3	15/11	10/1	5
6 Selby	10/1	11/4	25/10	20/9	14/2	X	14/3	15/11	24/1	11/10	6
7 Sunderland	15/11	20/9	10/1	14/2	11/10	6/9	X	11/4	25/10	24/1	7
8 Thornensians	25/10	10/1	24/1	14/3	20/9	25/4	20/12	X	11/10	14/2	8
9 Whitby	27/9	14/3	7/3	8/11	25/4	18/10	17/1	31/1	X	20/12	9
10 Yarnbury	7/3	15/11	6/9	17/1	8/11	31/1	18/10	27/9	18/4	X	10
	1	2	3	4	5	6	7	8	9	10	

THIS DIRECTORY IS NOT FOR CLUB OFFICIALS ONLY!

Do your club supporters know they can buy their own directory and help club funds?

BRAMLEY RUFC
Ground Address: The Warrels, Grosmount Terrace, Warrels Road, Bramley, Leeds. LS13 3NY   Tel: 0113 257 7787
Club Secretary: Andrew Hurdley, Hall Farm, Hall Road, Little Preston, Leeds. LS26 8UT   Tel: (H) 0113 286 0131   (W) 01274 741433
Fixtures Secretary: Brian Parkin   Tel: (H) 0113 256 3127
Club Colours: Green with black and gold band

HARTLEPOOL (WEST) TECHNICAL DAY SCHOOL OLD BOYS RUFC
Ground Address: Grayfields, Wiltshire Way, Hartlepool Tel: 01429 238548
Brief Directions: From A19 take A179 to Hartlepool, right at roundabout, continue for approx 2 miles, left into estate, right at T junction, club on left after 0.5 mile
Club Secretary: D Bramley, 63 Hutton Avenue, Hartlepool   Tel: (H) 01429 263157   (W) 01642 433363
Fixtures Secretary: A Cheshire   Tel: (H) 01429 234659 (W) 01642 604661
Club Colours: Blue and white

POCKLINGTON RUFC
Ground Address: Percy Road, Pocklington, East Yorkshire. YO4 2QB   Tel: 01759 303358
Brief Directions: Pocklington is situated 13 miles east of York off the A1079 towards Hull, ground located near town centre
Club Secretary: I Johnston, Fern Lea, 39 Percy Road, Pocklington, East Yorkshire. YO4 2LZ   Tel: (H) 01759 302967
Fixtures Secretary: Adrian Wilson   Tel: (H) 01759 305014
Club Colours: Navy and white quarters

REDCAR RUFC
Ground Address: McKinlay Park, Green Lane, Redcar. TS10 3RW   Tel: 01642 482733   (FAX) 01642 480830
Brief Directions: From A19 take A174 east towards Saltburn, take 2nd left (B1269), over level crossing, 1st right to coast road, continue to Green Lane on right at end of houses
Club Secretary: Alan Roebuck, c/o Club address as above   Tel: (H) 01642 486289
Fixtures Secretary: Terry Baxter, 12 The Crescent, Redcar.   Tel: (H) 01642 483900
Club Colours: Red, white, black

RIPON RUFC
Ground Address: Mallorie Park, Ripon, North Yorkshire. HG4 2QD   Tel: 01765 604675
Brief Directions: Mallorie Park is off main Ripon - Pateley Bridge Road, follow signs for Pateley Bridge via Skellbank
Club Secretary: M P P Viner, 20 Church Close, Tollerton, York. YO6 2ES   Tel: (H) 01347 838180   (W) 01904 626721
Fixtures Secretary: A W Proud   Tel: (H) 01765 605474 (W) 0113 292 6846
Club Colours: White, light blue and dark blue hoops

SELBY RUFC
Ground Address: Sandhill Lane, Leeds Road, Selby. YO8   Tel: 01757 703608
Brief Directions: Situated off Sandhill Lane, 1 mile west of town centre off A63 Leeds road
Club Secretary: Richard Besley, 20 Rowan Close, Thorpe Willoughby, Selby. YO8 9FJ   Tel: (H) 01757 708816   (W) 01924 411555
Fixtures Secretary: Michael Sullivan, 4 Millfield Drive Camblesforth, Selby, YO8 8JY.   Tel: (H) 01757 617183
Club Colours: Green, red and gold narrow hoops

SUNDERLAND RFC
Ground Address: Ashbrooke West Lawn, Sunderland, Tyne & Wear. SR2 7HH   Tel: 0191 528 4536
Brief Directions: A19 tow'ds Sunderland, exit Durham/S'land jcn, east 2.5 mls on Durham Rd to Barnes Htl, right then left into Qn Alex'a Rd, over 1st r'bout, 1st left W'bank Rd, left Ashbrk Rd, club 200yds left
Club Secretary: Mr J C Martin, 11 Roker Park Terrace, Sunderland, Tyne & Wear. SR6 9LY   Tel: (H) 0191 567 7045   (W) 0191 427 3562
Fixtures Secretary: Mr A Scott-Gray   Tel: (H) 0191 522 6188   (W) 0191 430 1446
Club Colours: Red, black and gold hoops

Selby RUFC

Photograph: Graham Cracknell Photography

NORTH EAST THREE CONTINUED

THORNENSIANS RUFC
Ground Address: Clubhouse, Coulman Road, Thorne, Doncaster, South Yorkshire   Tel: 01405 812746
Brief Directions: M18 J6 signed Thorne, 1 mile to town, left at traffic lights, right at crossroads, left at Church, club on left past school
Club Secretary: Ian Robson, Windyridge Cottage, Fieldside, Thorne, Doncaster, South Yorkshire. DN8 4BD   Tel: (H) 01405 812360   (W) 01405 812200
Fixtures Secretary: Bob Hutchinson   Tel: (H) 01405 813757
Club Colours: Blue, black and white hoops

WHITBY RUFC
Ground Address: Showfield, White Leys Road, Whitby, North Yorkshire. YO21 1L8   Tel: 01947 602008
Brief Directions: North West side of river, towards Sandend off Stakesby Road
Club Secretary: Mr F Howarth, 18 Lime Grove, Whitby, North Yorkshire   Tel: (H) 01947 600692
Fixtures Secretary: Mr T Cook   Tel: (H) 01947 600614
Club Colours: Maroon and black

YARNBURY (HORSFORTH) RFC
Ground Address: Brownberrie Lane, Horsforth, Leeds   Tel: 0113 2581346
Club Secretary: Paul Trigg, 3 Moorland Gardens, Moortown, Leeds. LS17 6JT   Tel: (H) 0113 2251389
Fixtures Secretary: John Riley   Tel: (H) 0113 2589131   (W) 01924 441818
Club Colours: Blue, black and white uneven hoops

West Hartlepool Technical Day School Old Boys R.U.F.C.
Winners Durham and Northumberland Division 1. 18 games undefeated in League Rugby 1996/97.

Do you know a rugby enthusiast with a birthday coming up?

This directory would make a perfect present.

So why not buy a copy from your club or from W H Smith.

DURHAM AND NORTHUMBERLAND ONE

Durham Northumberland One 1997-98 Fixtures	Acklam	Bishop Auckland	Blyth	Consett	Medicals	North Durham	North Shields	Ryton	WB Rockcliff	Winlaton Vulcans	
	1	2	3	4	5	6	7	8	9	10	
1 Acklam	X	8/11	18/10	7/3	25/4	17/1	27/9	14/3	31/1	20/12	1
2 Bishop Auckland	10/1	X	7/3	15/11	24/1	27/9	11/4	11/10	6/9	25/10	2
3 Blyth	24/1	20/9	X	25/10	14/2	14/3	10/1	11/4	15/11	11/10	3
4 Consett	20/9	25/4	17/1	X	20/12	8/11	31/1	14/2	18/10	14/3	4
5 Medicals	15/11	18/10	27/9	11/4	X	31/1	6/9	25/10	7/3	10/1	5
6 North Durham	25/10	14/2	6/9	10/1	11/10	X	15/11	20/9	11/4	24/1	6
7 North Shields	14/2	20/12	8/11	11/10	14/3	25/4	X	24/1	17/1	20/9	7
8 Ryton	6/9	31/1	20/12	27/9	17/1	7/3	18/10	X	8/11	25/4	8
9 WB Rockcliff	11/10	14/3	25/4	24/1	20/9	20/12	25/10	10/1	X	14/2	9
10 Winlaton Vulcans	11/4	17/1	31/1	6/9	8/11	18/10	7/3	15/11	27/9	X	10
	1	2	3	4	5	6	7	8	9	10	

ACKLAM RUFC
Ground Address: Talbot Park, Saltersgill Avenue, Middlesborough, Cleveland   Tel: 01842 321397
Club Secretary: Paul Pearson, 32 Foxgloves, Coulby Newham, Middlesborough, Cleveland. TS8 0XA   Tel: (H) 01642 597195   (W) 01325 461231
Fixtures Secretary: Dave Lynch   Tel: (H) 01642 486233
Club Colours: Black, green and white

BISHOP AUCKLAND RUFC
Ground Address: West Mills Playing Fields, Bridge Road, Bishop Auckland, Co Durham. DL14 7JH   Tel: 01388 602922
Brief Directions: From Bishop Auckland town centre leave to travel to Crook on A689 (not over viaduct), left along Bridge Rd just before crossing River Wear, club 0.5 mile along Bridge Rd
Club Secretary: K A Wilkinson Esq, 7 Victoria Avenue, Bishop Auckland, Co Durham. DL14 7JH   Tel: (H) 01388 605768   (W) 01388 603388
Fixtures Secretary: Mrs A Williamson, 19 Waddington Street, Bishop Auckland, DL14 6HG Tel: (H) 01388 600059
Club Colours: Navy and sky blue

BLYTH RFC
Ground Address: Plessey Road, Blyth, Northumberland Tel: 01670 352063
Brief Directions: From the south take A19 through Tyne Tunnel, continue on this until you pass Cramlington, take A1061 turn off into Blyth
Club Secretary: Mr D Reynolds, 20 Druridge Crescent, Newsham Farm Estate, Blyth, Northumberland. NE24 4SB   Tel: (H) 01670 360841   (W) 01670 352556
Fixtures Secretary: Mr Neil Richardson   Tel: (H) 01670 353605
Club Colours: Black and green hoops, black shorts

CONSETT & DISTRICT RFC
Ground Address: Belle Vue Park, Medomsley Road, Consett, Co Durham   Tel: 01207 590662
Brief Directions: Behind and to the side of Consett Civic Centre only 400m from centre of Consett
Club Secretary: John O'Connor, 26 Woodlands Road, Shotley Bridge, Consett, Co Durham. DH8 0DG   Tel: (H) 01207 501794
Fixtures Secretary: John McPherson, Hillhouse, Lobley Hill Road, Meadowfield, County Durham. DH7 8RQ. Tel: 0191 378041.
Club Colours: Black and amber hoops.

Consett & District RFC 1st XV

MEDICAL RFC
Ground Address: Cartington Terrace, Heaton, Newcastle   Tel: 0191 2761473
Club Secretary: Mr A, Crompton c/o Mr.D. Reeve, 3 Startion Rd., Forest Hall, Newcastle upon Tyne NE12 0AR   Tel: (H) 0191 2661610
Fixtures Secretary: Mr Phil Fisher   Tel: (H) 0191 2713559
Club Colours: Maroon with white shorts, maroon socks

NORTH DURHAM RFC
Ground Address: Prince Consort Road, Gateshead, Tyne & Wear. NE8 1RB   Tel: 0191 4783071
Brief Directions: Opposite the Civic Centre
Club Secretary: Bryan Dodds, 15 Ladyhaugh Drive, Whickham, Newcastle-upon-Tyne. NE16 5TE   Tel: (H) 0191 4886714   (W) 0191 4913030
Fixtures Secretary: John Davison   Tel: (H) 0191 4823778
Club Colours: Red and white hoops, navy shorts, bottle green stockings

NORTH SHIELDS RFC
Ground Address: Preston Playing Fields, Preston Village, North Shields, Tyne & Wear   Tel: 0191 257 7352
Brief Directions: From Tyne Tunnel (south) or A1/A19 (north) take A1058, follow signs for Tynemouth, club is situated next to Tynemouth Swimming Baths
Club Secretary: David Daniels, 1 Highcross Road, North Shields, Tyne & Wear   Tel: (H) 0191 252 6395 (W) 0191 253 1329
Fixtures Secretary: Mr.J. Blewitt, 4 Links Avenue, Whitley Bay   Tel: (H) 0191 259 0402
Club Colours: Royal blue and white hoops

RYTON RUFC
Ground Address: Main Road, Ryton, Tyne & Wear. NE40 3AG   Tel: 0191 413 3820
Brief Directions: On B6317 road to the west of Ryton, B6317 Ryton Road signposted from A695
Club Secretary: Gordon Wright, 30 South Grove, Ryton, Tyne & Wear, NE40 3JW   Tel 0191 4131986
Fixtures Secretary: Pauline Wright Tel: (H) 0191 413 1986
Club Colours: Royal blue and white

WHITLEY BAY ROCKCLIFF RFC
Ground Address: Lovaine Avenue, Whitley Bay, Tyne & Wear. NE25 8RW   Tel: 0191 2513704
Club Secretary: Mr Ian Richardson, 3 Westfield Avenue, West Munkseaton, Whitley Bay   Tel: (H & Fax) 0191 2512372   (W) 0191 2501864
Fixtures Secretary: Mr D Bennett   Tel: (H) 0191 2572174
Club Colours: Cardinal red shirts with gold trim, white shorts

WINLATON VULCANS RFC
Ground Address: Axwell View Playing Fields, Winlaton, Blaydon-on-Tyne. NE21 6EU   Tel: 0191 4142502
Brief Directions: From A1 take exit past Metro Centre signed Swalwell, take signs for Blaydon, just past Blaydon Pool turn left, continue up Shibdon Bank for 0.5 mile, club on left
Club Secretary: Timothy Williams, 29 Huntley Crescent, Winlaton, Blaydon-on-Tyne. NE21 6EU   Tel: (H) 0191 4144636
Fixtures Secretary: Ian Bilclough   Tel: (H) 0191 4147723
Club Colours: Black shirts, white collars, black shorts, black socks

Ryton R.U.F.C. 1996/97
Runners up Durham and Northumberland Division One.
Standing Left to Right, W.G. Scott (President), P.Higgins (Chairman), M.Phillips, J. Murray (Player Coach), P.Yielder, D.Reed, R.Pepper, J.Holmes, R.Malyon, S.Bennett, A.Child, G.Holmes, P.Ritson, N.Cameron, G.Jude (Physio), G.Wright (Fixture Secretary) and T.Mitchell (House Chairman).
Sitting Left to Right, R.Wearmouth, P.Elliott, O.Ingram, P.Kennedy (Captain), R.Scott and C.Oxley.

DURHAM AND NORTHUMBERLAND TWO

Durham Northumberland Two 1997-98 Fixtures	Barnard Castle	Billingham	Chester-le-Street	Guisborough	Hartlepool	Novocastrians	Ponteland	Seaton Carew	S. Tyneside Coll.	Seghill	
	1	2	3	4	5	6	7	8	9	10	
1 Barnard Castle	X	18/10	10/1	25/10	6/9	7/3	15/11	31/1	11/4	27/9	1
2 Billingham	24/1	X	25/10	11/10	11/4	6/9	10/1	27/9	15/11	7/3	2
3 Chester-le-Street	8/11	17/1	X	15/11	7/3	27/9	11/4	18/10	6/9	31/1	3
4 Guisborough	17/1	31/1	25/4	X	18/10	8/11	6/9	7/3	27/9	20/12	4
5 Hartlepool	14/3	20/12	20/9	24/1	X	17/1	14/2	25/4	11/10	8/11	5
6 Novocastrians	20/9	14/3	14/2	10/1	25/10	X	11/10	20/12	24/1	25/4	6
7 Ponteland	25/4	8/11	20/12	7/3	27/9	31/1	X	17/1	7/3	18/10	7
8 Seaton Carew	11/10	14/2	24/1	20/9	15/11	11/4	25/10	X	10/1	6/9	8
9 S. Tyneside Coll.	20/12	25/4	14/3	14/2	31/1	18/10	20/9	8/11	X	17/1	9
10 Seghill	14/2	20/9	11/10	11/4	10/1	15/11	24/1	14/3	25/10	X	10
	1	2	3	4	5	6	7	8	9	10	

BARNARD CASTLE RUFC
Ground Address: The Clubhouse, 7 Birch Road, Barnard Castle, Co Durham Tel: 01833 631766
Brief Directions: Follow main rd into town centre, turn left at market cross towards Bowes Museum, left into Birch Rd at Catholic Church, clubhouse on left approx 100 yards
Club Secretary: Mr T Worley, 17 Newgate, Barnard Castle, Co Durham. DL12 8NQ Tel: (H) 01833 637608 (W) 01833 690305
Fixtures Secretary: Mr D Jackson, c/o Headlam Hall Hotel, Headlam, Gainford, Darlington, DL2 3HA - Tel: 01325 730238
Club Colours: All black

BILLINGHAM RUFC
Ground Address: Greenwood Road, Billingham
Brief Directions: Adjacent to Belasis Hall Technology Park, Greenwood Road
Club Secretary: J M Ker, 4 Anlaby Close, Billingham. TS23 3RA Tel: (H & Fax) 01642 560536
Fixtures Secretary: Colin Wakenshaw Tel: (H) 01642 647813
Club Colours: Green and white hoops, white shorts

CHESTER-LE-STREET RFC
Ground Address: Donald Owen Clarke Centre, Riverside Park, Chester-Le-Street, Co Durham Tel: 0191 3871995
Brief Directions: Take A1(M) to Chester-Le-Street, follow directions to County Cricket Ground, Rugby Club is situated adjacent to ground in the Donald Owen Clarke Centre
Club Secretary: Paul Langley, 58 Rydal Road, Chester-Le-Street, Co Durham. DH2 3DT Tel: (H) 0191 3885989 (W) 0191 203 4207
Fixtures Secretary: Graham Rodger Tel: (H) 0191 389 1713
Club Colours: Navy blue shirts and shorts, red socks

GUISBOROUGH RUFC
Ground Address: Belmangate, Guisborough, Cleveland. TS14 7BB Tel: 01287 632966
Brief Directions: A19 to A174 (Redcar & Teesport), 3rd slip road to A172 at Marton, turn right, via Nunthorpe to pick up A171 to Guisborough, Belmangate from lights at Anchor Inn
Club Secretary: Dennis F Childs, 32 Boston Drive, Marton, Middlesborough. TS7 8LZ Tel: (H) 01642 314081
Fixtures Secretary: R I Atkinson, 60 Berkley Drive, Guisborough, Redcar & Cleveland, TS14 7LU Tel: (H) 01287 635939
Club Colours: Black and amber

HARTLEPOOL RFC
Ground Address: Mayfield Park, Easington Road, Hartlepool. TS24 9BA Tel: 01429 266445
Brief Directions: Leave A19 north of town on A179 over 2 roundabouts, right at 3rd, ground 500m on left
Club Secretary: Mr D.Jones, 14 Turnberry Crescent, Hartlepool TS 27 3PX Tel: (H) 01429 231125
Fixtures Secretary: Ken Thompson Tel: (W) 01642 279880
Club Colours: Black, Maroon and White

NOVOCASTRIANS RFC LTD
Ground Address: Sutherland Park, The Drive, High Heaton, Newcastle upon Tyne. NE7 7SY Tel: 0191 2661247
Brief Directions: From A19 or N'castle Central Motorway take A6127M and A1058 signed N'castle - Tynemouth. Exit on slip road A188 to Killingworth. N.O.V.O.S. RFC signs at The Drive. Club on left.
Club Secretary: Brian Chater, 100 Malvern Road, Preston Grange, North Shields, Tyne & Wear. NE29 9ES Tel: (H) 0191 2576885 (W) 01670 351532
Fixtures Secretary: Bob Fay Tel: (H) 0191 4873393 (W) 0191 3862714
Club Colours: Red, black and white hoops

PONTELAND RUGBY FOOTBALL CLUB
Ground Address: Ponteland Leisure Centre, Callerton Lane, Ponteland, Northumberland. NE20 9EG Tel: 01661 825441
Brief Directions: From north or south, enter village via A696, at lights by Diamond Inn turn to follow river, entrance to Sports Centre 150 yards on left just after zebra crossing
Club Secretary: Simon Philp, 61 Jackson Avenue, Ponteland, Northumberland. NE20 9UY Tel: (H) 01661 872773
Fixtures Secretary: Mrs Joyce Baty Tel: (H & Fax) 01661 823527
Club Colours: Maroon shirts with a black and white hoop, white shorts, maroon socks with a white top

SEATON CAREW RUGBY UNION FOOTBALL CLUB
Ground Address: Hornby Park, Elizabeth Way, Seaton Carew, Hartlepool. TS25 2AZ Tel: 01429 260945
Brief Directions: From A19 take A689 to Hartlepool, right at Owton Lodge pub onto B1276 to Seaton Carew seafront area, turn right and go along seafront past golf club, club on right in Elizabeth Way.
Club Secretary: Paul McManus, 9 Ruswarp Grove, Seaton Carew, Hartlepool. TS25 2BA Tel: (H) 01429 296327 (W) 01429 268821
Fixtures Secretary: Colin Chappell Tel: (H) 01429 868058 (W & Fax) 01429 269739
Club Colours: Maroon and amber quarters

SEGHILL RFC
Ground Address: Welfare Park, Seghill, Cramlington, Northumberland Tel: 0191 2370414
Brief Directions: A19 through Tyne Tunnel, take sliproad for Seghill, right at junction, left at next junction, right at mini r'bout then 2nd left, right at T junction, car park 150yds on right
Club Secretary: Stewart Grainger, 16 Carrick Drive, Parklands, Blyth, Northumberland Tel: (H) 01670 355909 (W) 01670 514141
Fixtures Secretary: Geoffrey Fenwick Tel: (H) 0191 2665146
Club Colours: Scarlet and black hoops

SOUTH TYNESIDE COLLEGE RUFC
Ground Address: Grosvenor Road, South Shields, Tyne & Wear. Tel: 0191 427 3500
Brief Directions: Travel to south side of Tyne Tunnel, take road to South Shields, travel to Westhoe area of South Shields, ground adjacent to S.T. College
Club Secretary: R Smith, 87 Colman Avenue, South Shields, Tyne & Wear. NE34 9AG Tel: (H) 0191 4242101 (W) 0191 4273571
Fixtures Secretary: C Moule Tel: (H) 0191 3887548 (W) 0191 4273577
Club Colours: Black with two red hoops and one gold hoop

DURHAM AND NORTHUMBERLAND THREE

Durham Northumberland Three 1997-98 Fixtures	Darlington RA	Gosforth	Hartlepool Ath.	Hartlepool BBOB	Houghton	Richmondshire	Seaham	Sedgefield	Wallsend	Wensleydale	
	1	2	3	4	5	6	7	8	9	10	
1 Darlington RA	X	20/12	11/10	20/9	8/11	24/1	17/1	14/3	25/4	14/2	1
2 Gosforth	11/4	X	15/11	25/10	7/3	11/10	6/9	24/1	27/9	10/1	2
3 Hartlepool Athletic	31/1	25/4	X	14/3	17/1	14/2	18/10	20/12	8/11	20/9	3
4 Hartlepool BBOB	7/3	17/1	6/9	X	31/1	15/11	27/9	8/11	18/10	11/4	4
5 Houghton	10/1	20/9	25/10	11/10	X	11/4	15/11	14/2	14/3	24/1	5
6 Richmondshire	18/10	31/1	27/9	25/4	20/12	X	8/11	17/1	7/3	6/9	6
7 Seaham	25/10	14/3	24/1	14/2	25/4	10/1	X	20/9	20/12	11/10	7
8 Sedgefield	6/9	18/10	11/4	10/1	27/9	25/10	7/3	X	31/1	15/11	8
9 Wallsend	15/11	14/2	10/1	24/1	6/9	20/9	11/4	11/10	X	25/10	9
10 Wensleydale	27/9	8/11	7/3	20/12	18/10	14/3	31/1	25/4	17/1	X	10
	1	2	3	4	5	6	7	8	9	10	

DARLINGTON RAILWAY ATHLETIC RFC
Ground Address: Brinkburn Road, Darlington Tel: 01325 468125
Brief Directions: From A1(M) Junction 58, take A68 into Darlington. After 1.75 miles turn left into Brinkburn Road (at The Brown Trout P.H.)
Club Secretary: Peter Sanderson, School House, Chapel Street, Middleton-St-George, Darlington Tel: (H) 01325 332986 (W) 01325 315444
Fixtures Secretary: Michael Thompson, 97 Bates Avenue, Darlington. Tel: (H) 01325 480547
Club Colours: Amber and black.

GOSFORTH RFC
Ground Address: Bullocksteads Sports Ground, Ponteland Road, Kenton Bank Foot, Newcastle-upon-Tyne NE13 8AH Tel: 0191 286 0088
Brief Directions: Turn off A1 at Airport, go westwards approx one mile and the ground is on right hand side of Ponteland Road.
Club Secretary: Trevor Hogg, 11 Launceston Close, Kingston Park, Newcastle-upon-Tyne. NE3 2XX Tel: (H) 0191 271 1120
Fixtures Secretary: Chris Atkinson Tel: (H) 0191 425 1159 Tel: (W) 0191 220 4114
Club Colours: Green and white hoops, white shorts, hooped socks.

HARTLEPOOL ATHLETIC RFC
Ground Address: Oakesway Estate, Hartlepool, Co Durham. TS24 0RE Tel: 01429 274715
Brief Directions: Leave A19 at A179 Hartlepool turn off, follow signs for Headland, ground 3 miles from A19
Club Secretary: Jim Ainslie, 10 Regent Street, Hartlepool, Co Durham. TS24 0QN Tel: (H) 01429 260003 (W) 0836 258317
Fixtures Secretary: John Bentham Tel: (H) 01429 222239
Club Colours: Sky blue

HARTLEPOOL BOYS BRIGADE OLD BOYS RFC
Ground Address: Old Friarage, Headland, Hartlepool (Ground only)
Brief Directions: From north or south, A19, take A179 Hartlepool exit, straight over 4 roundabouts, left at T junction, take left fork, Il Ponte pub, left at fire station, right onto seafront, ground on left
Club Secretary: G K Faint, 11 Nesbyt Road, Hartlepool. TS24 9NB Tel: (H) 01429 265674
Fixtures Secretary: I Mulrooney, 6 Carr Street, Hartlepool Tel: (H) 01429 278082 (W) 01429 276742
Club Colours: White with broad black band

HOUGHTON RUFC
Ground Address: Dairy Lane, Houghton le Spring, Tyne & Wear Tel: 0191 5841460
Brief Directions: Situated on A1052, Houghton to Chester-le-Street road, opposite Houghton Police Station, 0.25 mile west of A690
Club Secretary: David Winthrop, Hillcroft, 14 North Road, Hetton Le Hole. DH5 9JU Tel: (H) 0191 5170716 (W) 0191 5670094
Fixtures Secretary: John Felton Tel: (H) 0191 4161467 (W) 0191 4877171
Club Colours: Black shirts with white hoop, black shorts, black socks

RICHMONDSHIRE RUFC
Ground Address: The Playing Fields, Theakston Lane, Richmond, North Yorkshire. DL10 4LL Tel: 01748 850515
Brief Directions: A6136 out of Richmond, pass bus station approx 500 yards turn right, club situated on left approx 100 yards from junction
Club Secretary: Mr Russell Lord, 12 Whitefields Walk, Richmond, North Yorkshire. DL10 7DE Tel: (H) 01748 824273 (W) 01904 525844
Fixtures Secretary: Bob Dixon Tel: (H) 01748 825360
Club Colours: Red, yellow and white hoops

SEAHAM
Ground Address: New Olrive Playing Fields Club, 27 Cornelia Terrace, Seaham, Co Durham Tel: 0191 581 2331
Brief Directions: Come down A19 or A1, follow signs for Seaham, once in Seaham follow signs for harbour and ask for directions to club (everyone knows where it is)
Club Secretary: Mrs Carol Pinter, New Olrive Playing Fields Club, 27 Cornelia Terrace, Seaham Tel: (W) 0191 581 2331
Fixtures Secretary: Alan Mason Tel: (H) 0191 520 0282 (W) 0191 279 4342
Club Colours: Red jersey, white shorts, red socks

SEDGEFIELD RUFC
Ground Address: Sedgefield Community College, Sedgefield, Stockton-on-Tees, Cleveland Tel: 01740 621097
Club Secretary: Mr N Hetherington, 1 The Meadows, Sedgefield, Stockton-on-Tees, Cleveland Tel: (H) 01740 621179 (W) 0836 292665
Fixtures Secretary: Mr M Price Tel: (H) 01740 622792
Club Colours: Red and black quarters

WALLSEND RFC
Ground Address: Benfield Community Association Sam Smiths Pavilion, Benfield School Campus, Benfield Road, Walkergate, Newcastle. NE6 4NU Tel: 0191 265 9357.
Brief Directions: Just off A1058 Newcastle-Tynemouth (Coast rd), turn on to C127 to Benfield School, club at rear of school
Club Secretary: Brian J Thirlaway, 25 Blanchland Close, Battle Hill Estate, Wallsend, Tyne & Wear. NE28 9DU Tel: (H) 0191 234 4877
Fixtures Secretary: Robert Lowery Tel: (H) 0191 234 2400
Club Colours: Myrtle green jerseys with gold trim, white shorts.

WENSLEYDALE RUFC
Ground Address: Cawkhill Park, Wensley Road, Leyburn, North Yorkshire. DL8 5AR Tel: 01969 623067
Brief Directions: 1 mile west of Leyburn on the A684
Club Secretary: David Ward, 3 Kelberdale Terrace, Leyburn, North Yorkshire Tel: (H) 01969 624462 (W) 01969 622046
Fixtures Secretary: E Lowther Tel: (H) 01748 88473 (W) 01748 884473
Club Colours: Black and amber hoops

DURHAM AND NORTHUMBERLAND FOUR

Durham Northumberland Four 1997-98 Fixtures	Benton	Durham Const	Jarrovians	Newton Aycliffe	Prudhoe Hosp	Shildon Town	Washington	Wearside	
	1	2	3	4	5	6	7	8	
1 Benton	X	6/9	27/9	18/10	14/3	25/4	3/1	25/10	1
2 Durham Const	15/11	X	11/4	4/10	8/11	14/2	18/10	20/9	2
3 Jarrovians	14/2	25/10	X	15/11	20/9	28/3	25/4	4/10	3
4 Newton Aycliffe	28/3	14/3	6/9	X	27/9	3/1	25/10	25/4	4
5 Prudhoe Hosp	4/10	25/4	3/1	14/2	X	25/10	6/9	28/3	5
6 Shildon Town	8/11	27/9	18/10	20/9	11/4	X	14/3	15/11	6
7 Washington	20/9	28/3	8/11	11/4	15/11	4/10	X	14/2	7
8 Wearside	11/4	3/1	14/3	8/11	18/10	6/9	27/9	X	8
	1	2	3	4	5	6	7	8	

BENTON RFC
Ground Address: Civil Service Sports Club, Darsley Park, Old Whitley Road, Newcastle upon Tyne   Tel: 0191 2662727
Brief Directions: Ring Fixture Secretary
Club Secretary: Colin Reid, 114 Northumberland Street, Wallsend, Newcastle upon Tyne. NE28 7PX   Tel: (H) 0191 2624913   (W) 0191 2182931
Fixtures Secretary: G Parker   Tel: (H) 0191 2685821 (W) 0191 2254171
Club Colours: White top with blue horizontal stripe, black shorts, red socks

DURHAM CONSTABULARY RUFC
Ground Address: Durham Constabulary Police HQ, Aykley Heads, Durham. DH1 5TT   Tel: 0191 3864929 Ext 2295
Brief Directions: Ground is to the north west of the city, approaching on A167 or A1(M) join A691 and then B6532, Police HQ is well signposted, ground adjacent to HQ
Club Secretary: Mr Ray John, Support Services, Training Dept, Police HQ, Aykley, Heads, Durham   Tel: (W) 0191 3864929 Ext 2108
Fixtures Secretary: Mr Peter Davis   Tel: (H) 0191 3890848   (W) 0191 3752295
Club Colours: Royal blue and gold quarters

JARROVIANS RUFC
Ground Address: Lukes Lane Estate, Hebburn, Tyne & Wear   Tel: 0370 964 113
Brief Directions: North end of A1(M)/A194(M), continue north along A194, at 1st roundabout turn left, then immediate right, follow road along full length, ground on right
Club Secretary: Mr Stephen Softley, 20 Gladstone Street, Hebburn, Tyne & Wear. NE31 2XJ   Tel: 0191 4890789   (W) 0191 4772271 Ext 3250
Fixtures Secretary: Dave King.   Tel: (H) 0191 4891611   (W) 0191 4271717   Ex 5071
Club Colours: Black and amber hoops

NEWTON AYCLIFFE RUFC
Ground Address: Newton Aycliffe Sports Club, Moore Lane, Newton Aycliffe, Co Durham. DL5 5AG   Tel: 01325 312768
Brief Directions: Enter Newton Aycliffe on Central Ave, at the roundabout turn L. on Shafto Way take 3rd L. (Creighton Rd) then lst R. Moore Lane, carry on to the end of the road.
Club Secretary: Mr Sean Carroll, 91 Washington Crescent, Newton Aycliffe, Co Durham. DL5 4BE   Tel: (H) 01325 320874   (M) 0973 371971
Fixtures Secretary: Mr Charles Heslop, 35 Holly Hill, Shildon, Co. Durham, DL4 2DB.   Tel: 0976 305287
Club Colours: Green, amber and maroon

THIS DIRECTORY IS NOT FOR CLUB OFFICIALS ONLY!
Do your club supporters know they can buy their own directory and help club funds?

PRUDHOE HOSPITAL RFC
Ground Address: Prudhoe Hospital Sports & Social Club, Prudhoe, Northumberland
Brief Directions: A695 from Blaydon to Hexham, turn off for Prudhoe, look for Hospital sign on left just before Falcon pub on the right
Club Secretary: G Bridgewater, 15 Paddock Wood, Prudhoe, Northumberland. NE42 5BJ Tel: (H) 01661 832772
Fixtures Secretary: E.Walton,54 Moorlands, Prudhoe, Northumberland. NE42 5LS
Club Colours: Blue and red quarters, white collar, white shorts, red socks

SHILDON TOWN
Ground Address: Sunnydale Leisure Centre, Shildon, Co. Durham. Tel: 01388 777340
Club Secretary: P. Plews, 14 Alexandra Street, Shildon, Co. Durham. DL4 2EY. Tel: 01388 777334
Fixtures Secretary: Gary Mason, 24 Foundry Street, Shildon DL4 2HF. Tel: 01388 775584
Club Colours: Red and green quaters

WASHINGTON RUFC
Ground Address: Northern Arga Playing Fields, c/o Stephenson Industrial Estate, Washington, Tyne & Wear Tel: 0191 419 0258
Brief Directions: A194 from north or south, take the Washington North turn off (A195), left at 1st roundabout, left again
Club Secretary: Leslie Peter Cash, 206 Sulgrave Road, Washington, Tyne & Wear. NE37 3DD Tel: (H) 0191 417 6298
Fixtures Secretary: James Watlin Tel: (H) 0191 416 9599
Club Colours: Amber and blue hoops

WEARSIDE RUFC
Ground Address: Fulwell Quarry Reclamation Site, Newcastle Road, Sunderland, Tyne & Wear
Brief Directions: Leave A19, follow A184 (Newcastle rd) into Sunderland passing Regal Greyhound Stadium on left, turn right at roundabout to changing rooms
Club Secretary: Jonathon Ridley, 143 Atkinson Road, Fulwell, Sunderland, Tyne & Wear. SR6 9AY Tel: (H) 0191 5496523 (W) 0191 5656256 Ext 45441
Fixtures Secretary: Jeff Fowler Tel: (H) 0191 5345191 (W) 0191 2761161
Club Colours: Royal blue and scarlet hoops, white shorts, red socks

Washington RUFC
Back Row (L-R): J. Mould, A. Telford, C. Hepburn, G. Foster, B. Spencer, S. Harrison, P. guy, M. Donrin.
Front Row (L-R): D. Mills, J. Dale, J. McParlane, I. Dunn (Capt), W. Cash, S. Walsh, C. Gordon, P. Snell.

Do you know a rugby enthusiast with a birthday coming up?

This directory would make a perfect present.

So why not buy a copy from your club or from W H Smith.

YORKSHIRE ONE

Yorkshire One 1997-98 Fixtures	Bradford Salem	Castleford	Dinnington	Ilkley	Leodiensians	Malton & Norton	Moortown	Northallerton	Old Otliensians	W-on-Deas	
	1	2	3	4	5	6	7	8	9	10	
1 Bradford Salem	X	11/4	25/10	11/10	6/9	24/1	27/9	15/1	10/1	7/3	1
2 Castleford	20/12	X	20/9	24/1	17/1	14/3	25/4	11/10	14/2	8/11	2
3 Dinnington	17/1	7/3	X	15/11	1/4	8/11	18/10	6/9	11/4	31/1	3
4 Ilkley	31/1	18/10	25/4	X	8/11	17/1	7/3	27/9	6/9	20/12	4
5 Leodiensians	14/3	25/10	14/2	10/1	X	20/9	20/12	24/1	11/10	25/4	5
6 Malton & Norton	18/10	6/9	10/1	25/10	7/3	X	31/1	11/4	15/11	27/9	6
7 Moortown	14/2	15/11	24/1	20/9	11/4	11/10	X	10/1	25/10	6/9	7
8 Northallerton	25/4	31/1	14/3	14/2	18/10	20/12	8/11	X	20/9	17/1	8
9 Old Otliensians	8/11	27/9	20/12	14/3	31/1	25/4	17/1	7/3	X	18/10	9
10 Wath-on-Dearne	20/9	10/1	11/10	11/4	15/11	14/2	14/3	25/10	24/1	X	10
	1	2	3	4	5	6	7	8	9	10	

BRADFORD SALEM RFC
Ground Address: Shay Lane, Heaton, Bradford. BD9 6SL   Tel: 01274 496430
Brief Directions: From Bradford centre take A650 (Towards Keighley) along Manningham Lane. Left at 'The Park' (pub) and up hill turn right at top , past shops into Shay Lane. Ground is 100 yds on left.
Club Secretary: Mrs A Wheeler, 25 Ashwell Road, Heaton, Bradford BD9 4BA   Tel: 01274 487517
Fixtures Secretary: John Dobson   Tel: (H) 01274 487517
Club Colours: Royal blue, gold, black hoops, black shorts, blue socks

CASTLEFORD RUFC
Ground Address: Willow Bridge Lane, Whitwood, Castleford   Tel: 01977 554762
Brief Directions: M62E towards Hull, exit J31, 2nd turn left off roundabout, approx 1 mile through traffic lights, ground on right hand side
Club Secretary: M.Connell, 30 Church Avenue, Swillington , Leeds, LS26 8QH   Tel: (H) 0113 286 5231 (W) 01977 556565
Fixtures Secretary: Mr E Mills   Tel: (W) 0113 241 4056 (H) 01977 515784
Club Colours: Red and blue hoops

DINNINGTON RUFC
Ground Address: Lodge Lane, Dinnington, Sheffield, South Yorkshire. S31 7PB   Tel: 01909 562044
Club Secretary: Bill Gilbody, 16 Devonshire Drive, North Anston, Sheffield. S31 7AQ   Tel: (H) 01909 562997
Fixtures Secretary: Bill Gilbody   Tel: (H) 01909 562997
Club Colours: Gold, black and yellow hoops

ILKLEY RUFC
Ground Address: Stacks Field, Denton Road, Ilkley, West Yorkshire. LS29 0AD   Tel: 01943 607037
Brief Directions: From lights in town, turn towards the river down Brook Street, the ground is visible 300 metres on right
Club Secretary: Mr Gerald Whiteley, Springs End House, 44 Springs Lane, Ilkley, West Yorkshire. LS29 8TH   Tel: (H) 01943 609792   (W) 0113 2449254
Fixtures Secretary: Mr K Bernard   Tel: (H) 01943 602945   (W) 0113 2451000
Club Colours: Red, white and black hooped shirts

LEODIENSIAN RUFC
Ground Address: Crag Lane (off King Lane), Alwoodley, Leeds. LS17 5PR   Tel: 0113 2673409
Brief Directions: Leeds ringroad (outer) to Moortown Sainsburys, from Sainsburys travel away from Leeds on King Lane for 0.75 mile, ground on left hand side
Club Secretary: John Hastie, 132 Buckstone Avenue, Alwoodley, Leeds. LS17 5ET   Tel: (H) 01132 689881
Fixtures Secretary: Michael Crook   Tel: (H) 01132 260455   (W) 01535 636116
Club Colours: Navy blue and gold

MALTON & NORTON RUFC LTD
Ground Address: The Gannock, Old Malton, Malton, North Yorkshire   Tel: 01653 694657
Brief Directions: From A64 York to Scarborough - take bypass and enter Malton on the Pickering road, club is on left. From Malton head towards Old Malton and club is on right
Club Secretary: C J Whincup, Arboretum, Keld Head Hall, Middleton Road, Pickering. YO18 8NR   Tel: (H) 01751 477170
Fixtures Secretary: J Q Knock   Tel: (H & W) 01904 421105
Club Colours: Black shorts, red, white and black hooped shirts, black socks

MOORTOWN RUFC
Ground Address: Far Moss, off The Avenue, Alwoodley, Leeds, West Yorkshire Tel: 0113 2678243
Brief Directions: From the ring road turn up past the entrance to Sainsburys, 1.5 miles turn right onto The Avenue, 0.5 mile turn right into Far Moss
Club Secretary: Mr Graham Spark, 7 Hall Cliffe Grove, Horbury, Wakefield. WF4 6DE Tel: (H) 01924 271808
Fixtures Secretary: Mr Clive Forbes Tel: (H) 0113 2675974
Club Colours: Maroon, green and white hoops, blue shorts, maroon socks

NORTHALLERTON RUFC
Ground Address: Brompton Lodge, Northallerton Road, Brompton, Northallerton, North Yorkshire. DL6 2PZ Tel: 01609 773496
Club Secretary: G W Cartwright, 76 Thirsk Road, Northallerton, N. Yorkshire. DL6 1PL. Tel: (H) 01609 772881
Fixtures Secretary: A Bradley, 15 Borrowby Ave., Northallerton, N. Yorkshire. Tel: (H) 01609 772743
Club Colours: Green, amber and white

OLD OTLIENSIANS RUFC
Ground Address: Chaffer's Field, Pool Road, Otley, West Yorkshire Tel: 01943 461476
Brief Directions: From Otley town centre, take A659 to Harrogate, turn right at Stephen Smiths Garden Centre, follow sign to clubhouse
Club Secretary: D Taylor Esq, 39 The Whartons, Otley, West Yorkshire. LS21 2AG Tel: (H) 01943 850913 (W) 01274 334051
Fixtures Secretary: Dr A S Normanton Tel: (H) 01642 723199 (W) 01642 467144
Club Colours: Navy blue, royal blue and white hoops

WATH-UPON-DEARNE RUFC
Ground Address: Moor Road, Wath-Upon-Dearne, Rotherham Tel: 01709 872399
Brief Directions: Moor Road is adjacent to Wath Swimming Baths on the main Rotherham to Barnsley (A630) road
Club Secretary: Mr S Poxton, 19 Packham Way, Wath-Upon-Dearne, Rotherham, South Yorkshire. S63 6BR Tel: (H) 01709 874154 (W) 01226 282549
Fixtures Secretary: Mr S Corns Tel: (H) 01709 874911
Club Colours: Blue with maroon and gold bands

Bradford Salem
Back Row (L-R): J. Robinson (President),M. Benn, J. Hodgson, S. Schofield, D. Benn, P. Hodgson, S. Casey, A. Smith, J. Goodall, T. Brack, C. B. Tinker (Chairman).
Front Row (L-R): A. Cassar, P. Heap, P. Taylor, G. Durn, D. Smith, P. Durn, A. Garter, V. Potapi, A. Lazenby.

YORKSHIRE TWO

Yorkshire Two 1997-98 Fixtures	Barnsley	Halifax Vandals	Huddersfield YMCA	Hullensians	Old Modernians	Scarborough	Sheffield Oaks	Sheffield Tigers	West Leeds	Wibsey	
	1	2	3	4	5	6	7	8	9	10	
1 Barnsley	X	20/12	7/3	27/9	17/1	31/1	25/4	8/11	18/10	6/9	1
2 Halifax Vandals	11/4	X	14/3	25/10	14/2	20/9	11/10	15/11	10/1	24/1	2
3 Huddersfield YMCA	20/9	6/9	X	10/1	11/10	14/2	24/1	11/4	15/11	25/10	3
4 Hullensians	14/2	17/1	8/11	X	20/12	25/4	14/3	18/10	31/1	20/9	4
5 Old Modernians	25/10	22/9	31/1	11/4	X	18/10	10/1	7/3	6/9	15/11	5
6 Scarborough	11/10	7/3	27/9	15/11	24/1	X	25/10	6/9	11/4	10/1	6
7 Sheffield Oaks	15/11	31/11	18/10	6/9	8/11	17/1	X	27/9	7/3	11/4	7
8 Sheffield Tigers	10/1	25/4	20/12	24/1	20/9	14/3	14/2	X	25/10	11/10	8
9 West Leeds	24/1	8/11	25/4	11/10	14/3	20/12	20/9	17/1	X	14/2	9
10 Wibsey	14/3	18/10	17/1	7/3	25/4	8/11	20/12	31/1	27/9	X	10
	1	2	3	4	5	6	7	8	9	10	

BARNSLEY RUFC
Ground Address: Shaw Lane, Barnsley, South Yorkshire. S70 6HZ Tel: 01226 203509
Brief Directions: M1 J37, towards Barnsley, through 1st major lights, 2nd turning right into Shaw Lane, ground on right after school
Club Secretary: Michael Marshall, 4 Westbourne Grove, Barnsley. S75 1AE Tel: (H) 01226 771473
Fixtures Secretary: Steve Lumb, 49 Wood Lane, Carlton, Barnsley, S71 3JQ. Tel: 01226 726542
Club Colours: Red, white and navy hoops

HALIFAX VANDALS RUFC
Ground Address: Warley Town Lane, Warley, Halifax, West Yorkshire Tel: 01422 831704
Club Secretary: Andrew Ward, 124 Ravenstone Drive, Greetland, Halifax Tel: (H) 01422 377156 (W) 01422 347347
Fixtures Secretary: Mr Stephen C Beard Tel: (H) 01422 353099 (W) 01484 719642
Club Colours: Blue and white hoops, white shorts

HUDDERSFIELD YMCA RUFC
Ground Address: Lawrence Batley Sports Centre, Laund Hill, Huddersfield. HD3 4YS Tel: 01484 654052
Brief Directions: From west: M62 J23, follow Huddersfield signs, ground 0.5 mile on left. From east: M62 J24, Rochdale sign at r'bout, along A643 for 1 mile, left at r'bout, ground 0.5 mile left
Club Secretary: Ian Leask, 3 Cheviot Way, Mirfield, West Yorkshire. WF14 8HW Tel: (H) 01924 496448 (W) 01924 496007
Fixtures Secretary: Brian Castle Tel: (H) 01484 656120 (W) 01484 433836
Club Colours: Red and black hoops, black shorts

HULLENSIANS RUFC
Ground Address: Springhead Lane, Anlaby Common, Hull Tel: 01482 651086
Club Secretary: Mark Bayston, 31 Glenfield Drive, Kirkell, Hull. HU10 7UL Tel: (H) 01482 659793 (W) 01482 830367
Fixtures Secretary: Tim Robinson Tel: (H) 01482 348181 (W) 01482 323631
Club Colours: Red and black

Above: West Leeds RUFC

OLD MODERNIANS RUFC
Ground Address: The Clubhouse, Cookridge Lane, Cookridge, Leeds, West Yorkshire. LS16 7ND   Tel: 0113 267 1075
Club Secretary: Phillip Reasbeck
Fixtures Secretary: D Carter   Tel: (H) 0113 267 9718
Club Colours: Red and black hoops, black shorts

SCARBOROUGH RUFC
Ground Address: The Clubhouse, Scalby Road, Scarborough, North Yorkshire. YO12 6EE   Tel: 01723 363039
Brief Directions: Main Whitby Road out of Scarborough, approx 2 miles
Club Secretary: Mrs S E Hanson, The Clubhouse, Scalby Road, Scarborough   Tel: (W) 01723 363039
Fixtures Secretary: Mr D Prince   Tel: (H & Fax) 01723 377419
Club Colours: Maroon, navy and white

SHEFFIELD OAK RUFC
Ground Address: Malin Bridge Sports and Social Club, 22A Stannington Rd, Sheffield. S6 5TA   Tel: 01142 345349
Brief Directions: M1 J36 into Sheffield (north), A61 to Hillsborough Ground, 1st available right after Hillsborough Ground, Bradfield Rd, to Holme Lane, left at end of Holme Ln, 1st right after petrol station
Club Secretary: Andrew Thomas, 144 Lyminster Road, Wadsley Bridge, Sheffield. S6 1HZ   Tel: (H) 01142 326774
Fixtures Secretary: Glyn Davies   Tel: (H) 01142 2335829
Club Colours: Yellow with blue chevrons

SHEFFIELD TIGERS RUFC
Ground Address: Door Moor, Hathersage Road, Sheffield. S17 3AB   Tel: 0114 236 0075
Brief Directions: About 5 miles south west of Sheffield city centre on the A625 signed Hathersage. Ground just after Dore Moor Inn.
Club Secretary: Alick Bush, 210 Bradway Road, Sheffield. S17 4PE   Tel: (H) 0114 2361129   (W) 0114 2716950
Fixtures Secretary: Ron Lewis17 Harewood Drive, Wakefield. WF2 0DS.   Tel: (H) 01924 299874   (W) 0113 2435301
Club Colours: Maroon and white hoops, black shorts

WEST LEEDS RUFC
Ground Address: Blue Hill Lane, Wortley, Leeds. LS12 4NZ   Tel: 0113 2639869
Brief Directions: From Leeds ring road junction with Tong Road towards centre, 400 yards after Brick pub turn right then left Bluehill Lane, club 500 yards on right
Club Secretary: Ms Jill Dowson, 21 Butterbowl Road, Leeds. LS12 5JE   Tel: (H) 0113 279 6220   (W) 0113 2457111
Fixtures Secretary: Colin Edwards   Tel: (H) 0113 2522487   (W) 0850 226350
Club Colours: Navy, old gold and white

WIBSEY RUFC
Ground Address: Northfiel Road, Wibsey, Bradford. BD6   Tel: 01274 671643
Brief Directions: From top of M606 take 2nd exit towards Odsal roundabout, take 4th exit at side of Police station, 0.75 mile on left joined onto White Swan pub
Club Secretary: Martin Spencer, 188 St Enochs Road, Wibsey, Bradford. BD6 3BT   Tel: (H) 01274 605566 (W) 01274 739628
Fixtures Secretary: Mr Paul Knowles, 125 Poplar Grove, Bradford. BD7 4JX.   Tel: 01274 576373
Club Colours: Red and green hoops

Huddersfield YMCA RFC – 'The Yorkshire Trophy is Yorkshire's oldest and most valuable trophy. Huddersfield YMCA defeated Dinnington in the final. The picture shows the victorious squad'.
Back (L-R): McCrath, Throssell, Walker, A. Hunt, Newman, S. Harrison, Campbell, Kersay-Brown, Toomes, Moore, Metcalfe, Scott.
Front (L-R): P. Harrison, McAreavey, McCallion, M. Hunt (Capt), Hopkins, Bell, Ounsley.

YORKSHIRE THREE

Yorkshire Three 1997-98 Fixtures	Aireborough 1	Hemsworth 2	Hessle 3	Hornsea 4	Leeds Corinthians 5	Skipton 6	Stanley Rodillians 7	Stocksbridge 8	Wetherby 9	York RI 10	
1 Aireborough	X	14/2	25/4	14/3	20/9	25/10	11/10	24/1	10/1	20/12	1
2 Hemsworth	27/9	X	31/1	17/1	8/11	7/3	11/4	6/9	15/11	18/10	2
3 Hessle	15/11	11/10	X	20/9	14/2	10/1	24/1	25/10	11/4	14/3	3
4 Hornsea	6/9	25/10	7/3	X	24/1	11/4	10/1	15/11	11/10	27/9	4
5 Leeds Corinthians	7/3	10/1	27/9	18/10	X	6/9	15/11	11/4	25/10	31/1	5
6 Skipton	20/1	20/9	8/11	20/12	14/3	X	14/2	11/10	24/1	25/4	6
7 Stanley Rodillians	31/1	20/12	18/10	8/11	25/4	27/9	X	7/3	14/3	17/1	7
8 Stocksbridge	18/10	14/3	17/1	25/4	20/12	31/1	20/9	X	14/2	8/11	8
9 Wetherby	8/11	25/4	20/12	31/1	17/1	18/10	6/9	27/9	X	7/3	9
10 York RI	11/4	24/1	6/9	14/2	11/10	15/11	25/10	10/1	20/9	X	10
	1	2	3	4	5	6	7	8	9	10	

AIREBOROUGH RUFC
Ground Address: Green Lane Cricket Club, Nunroyd Park, Yeadon Tel: 01943 878299
Brief Directions: From M1 follow signs for airport. A65 to Yeadon follow signs for Guiseley. After J600 r'about Club 1 mile on right hand side of road.
Club Secretary: M Harper, 32 Aire View, Yeadon, West Yorkshire Tel: (H) 01132 504219   (W) 01132 505151
Fixtures Secretary: C Clarke, 51 Coppice View, Idle Bradford Tel: (H) 01274 610896
Club Colours: Maroon and white

HEMSWORTH RUFC
Ground Address: Moxon Fields, Lowfield Road, Hemsworth, Pontefract, West Yorkshire. WF9 4JT Tel: 01977 610078
Brief Directions: Pontefract Road from Town centre turn right after passing Hemsworth School.
Club Secretary: M ark Roberts, The Elms, Stockingate, South Kirkby, Pontefract. WF9 3QX Tel: (H) 01977 644379
Fixtures Secretary: Mark Roberts
Club Colours: Navy blue with red, gold and white band

HESSLE RUFC
Ground Address: Livingstone Road, Hessle, East Yorkshire Tel: 01482 643430
Brief Directions: Follow M62/A63 to Hull, 2 miles after traffic lights take Humber Bridge turn off, 2nd left at r'about to Hessle Foreshore, 1st right into Woodfield Ln, follow into L'stone Rd
Club Secretary: T J Sleight, 69 Tranby Avenue, Hessle. HU13 0PX Tel: (H) 01482 643262
Fixtures Secretary: P K Denton Tel: (H) 01482 561338
Club Colours: Green, black and white irregular hoops

HORNSEA RUFC
Ground Address: Clubhouse, Westwood Avenue, Hornsea. HU18 1BB Tel: 01964 534181
Club Secretary: Nic Marshall, 4 Paddock View, Beverley Road, Withernwick. HU11 4UA Tel: (H) 01964 527966   (W) 01964 536939
Fixtures Secretary: Ralph Robinson Tel: (H) 01964 533283
Club Colours: Black with green and white hoops across chest

LEEDS CORINTHIANS RUFC
Ground Address: Nutty Slack, Middleton District Centre, Leeds. 10-4RA Tel: 0113 2711574
Brief Directions: M62 J28 to Leeds or M1 city centre to Dewsbury follow signs for A653, turn onto Middleton ringroad at Tommy Wass pub, right at 1st r'bout and go to rear of supermarket onto shale track to club
Club Secretary: Glenn Maynard, 60 Middleton Park Grove, Leeds 10 4BQ Tel: 0113 2711728
Fixtures Secretary: Mr G Mapplebeck Tel: (H) 01924 828809   (W) 0113 2457205
Club Colours: Black with gold trim

SKIPTON RFC
Ground Address: Coulthurst Memorial Grounds, Carleton New Road, Skipton, North Yorkshire. BD23 2AZ Tel: 01756 793148
Brief Directions: Locate Skipton Railway Station - opposite car park, turn onto Carleton New Road, club 1st right after railway bridge
Club Secretary: H H Crabtree, 63 Raikes Road, Skipton, North Yorkshire. BD23 1LN Tel: (H & W) 01756 793083
Fixtures Secretary: A D Abell Tel: (H) 01756 798798 (W) 01423 539735
Club Colours: Cardinal red, white shorts

STANLEY RODILLIANS RUFC

Ground Address: Manley Park, Lee Moor Road, Stanley, Wakefield, West Yorkshire. WF3 4EF Tel: 01924 823619

Brief Directions: M62 J30, head towards Wakefield, turn right opposite Gordons Tyres, top of hill turn right, past double junction on left, turn left just after Lee Moor pub

Club Secretary: R J Matthews, 27 Newlands Walk, Stanley, Wakefield. WF3 4DT Tel: (H) 01924 828727

Fixtures Secretary: I Young   Tel: (H) 0113 282 6743 (W) 01742 671131

Club Colours: Green, black and white hoops

STOCKSBRIDGE RUFC

Ground Address: Stone Moor Road, Bolsterstone   Tel: 0114 288 5078

Brief Directions: A616 to Deepcar, go up hill at side of Royal Oak and opposite King & Miller, right to the top of hill, park in village square opposite Castle Inn

Club Secretary: Julian McGowan, 12 Keats Grove, Penistone, Sheffield. S30 6GU   Tel: (H) 01226 765814

Fixtures Secretary: C Lambert   Tel: (H) 0114 288 5223   (W) 0831 141732

Club Colours: Royal blue with two white hoops

WETHERBY RUFC

Ground Address: Grange Park, Wetherby, West Yorkshire   Tel: 01937 582461

Brief Directions: From Wetherby town centre head for A1 south, pass Police station on left, Jarvis Hotel on right, head for A1 south, having crossed A1 take left turn into Grange Park

Club Secretary: David Lewis, Linden Meadow, Grange Close, Bardsey, West Yorkshire. LS17 9AX   Tel: (H) 01937 572610   (W) 01132 361333

Fixtures Secretary: Keith Astbury   Tel: (H) 01132 862347

Club Colours: Red and white shirts, white shorts

YORK RAILWAY INSTITUTE RUFC

Ground Address: Railway Institute Sports Ground, New Lane, Acomb, York. YO2 4NU   Tel: 01904 798930

Brief Directions: From A1237 York ringroad, take B1224 signposted Acomb for 1.5 miles, after the Church of the Latter Day Saints on the right, take the 1st on the right (New Lane), sports ground at end

Club Secretary: Bryn D Bates, 16 Beech Place, Strensall, York. YO3 5AS   Tel: 01904 491296 (H) 01904 642961 (W)

Fixtures Secretary: W F Cooper   Tel: (H) 01274 584355

Club Colours: Royal blue and white hooped shirts, black shorts, royal blue socks

Above: Skipton RFC   *Photograph: David Hyde Photography*
Back Row (L-R): C. Bagnall, K. Coe, R. Robinson, T. Brown, W. Nicholson, D. Waltem, B. Burns (Coach), A. Winthrop, S. Williamson, P. Mason, R. Birks, A. Phillips, A. Abell (Rugby Chairman).
Back Row (L-R): R. Binns, I. Barraclough, I. Scriven, N. King (Capt), J. Sharpe, A. Dolan, D. Swinglehurst, P. Shearer.

Do you know a rugby enthusiast with a birthday coming up?

This directory would make a perfect present.

So why not buy a copy from your club or from W H Smith.

YORKSHIRE FOUR

Yorkshire Four 1997-98 Fixtures	Baildon 1	Burley 2	Edlington & W. 3	Garforth 4	Heath 5	Knaresborough 6	Knottingley 7	Marist 8	Mosborough 9	Old Rishworthians 10	
1 Baildon	X	10/11	14/3	17/1	18/10	7/3	25/4	27/9	20/12	31/1	1
2 Burley	10/1	X	11/10	27/9	7/3	17/11	24/1	11/4	25/10	6/9	2
3 Edlington & Wickers	6/9	31/1	X	7/3	20/12	27/9	17/1	18/10	25/4	10/11	3
4 Garforth	25/10	14/2	20/9	X	6/9	10/1	11/10	17/11	24/1	11/4	4
5 Heath	24/1	20/9	11/4	14/3	X	25/10	14/2	10/1	11/10	17/11	5
6 Knaresborough	20/9	25/4	14/2	10/11	17/1	X	20/12	31/1	14/3	18/10	6
7 Knottingley	17/11	18/10	25/10	31/1	27/9	11/4	X	6/9	10/1	7/3	7
8 Marist	14/2	20/12	24/1	25/4	10/11	11/10	14/3	X	20/9	17/1	8
9 Mosborough	11/4	17/1	17/11	18/10	31/1	6/9	10/11	7/3	X	27/9	9
10 Old Rishworthians	11/10	14/3	10/1	20/12	25/4	24/1	20/9	25/10	14/2	X	10
	1	2	3	4	5	6	7	8	9	10	

BAILDON RUFC
Ground Address: Jenny Lane, Baildon, Shipley, West Yorks. BD17 6RS Tel: 01274 582644
Brief Directions: A650 to centre of Shipley, follow Baildon signs in village centre, roundabout 3rd exit then left on Jenny Lane
Club Secretary: Mr G Porter, 100 Cliffe Avenue, Baildon, BRadford. BD17 6PD. Tel: 01274 419596
Fixtures Secretary: Roger Shuttleworth, 11 The Crescent, Otley, West Yorks. Tel: (H) 01943 467058
Club Colours: Red, white and black hoops

BURLEY RUFC
Ground Address: Club House, Abbey Road, Leeds. LS5 3NG Tel: 0113 275 7400
Brief Directions: A65 from Leeds city centre, Clubhouse 100 yds on left past Kirkstall Abbey opposite Vesper Gate pub
Club Secretary: Terry McCreedy, 42 Fearnville Place, Leeds. LS8 3DY Tel: (H) 0113 2655065 (W) 01274 770180
Fixtures Secretary: John Sanderson Tel: 0113 278 7772
Club Colours: Maroon and white

EDLINGTON AND WICKERSLEY RUFC
Ground Address: Granby Road WMC, Broomhouse Lane, Edlington, Doncaster, South Yorkshire
Brief Directions: A1(M) J36, A630 in direction of Rotherham for 0.25 mile, left at traffic lights, then 2nd left, right at T junction, Granby club and ground are 0.25 mile on left
Club Secretary: Michael Gulliver, 24 Elsham Close, Bramley, Rotherham. S66 0XZ Tel: (H) 01709 546823
Fixtures Secretary: Steven Houghton Tel: (H) 01709 531758
Club Colours: Yellow shirts, black shorts and socks

GARFORTH RUFC
Ground Address: Garforth Community College, Lidgett Lane, Garforth, Leeds. LS25 1LJ
Brief Directions: A63 Leeds to Selby road, left into Lidgett Lane, school on right, into main gate, proceed to changing facilities at back of school buildings
Club Secretary: George Shaw, 34 Rose Court, Garforth, Leeds. LS25 1NS Tel: (H) 0113 286 7193 (W) 01274 732707
Fixtures Secretary: John Daw Tel: (H) 0113 286 7338
Club Colours: Red, yellow, blue and black quarters, shorts and socks black

HEATH RUFC
Ground Address: North Dean, Stainland Road, West Vale, Halifax. HX4 8LS Tel: 01442 372920
Brief Directions: M62 J24, follow Halifax signs at bottom of hill (end of dual c'way), turn left towards Stainland, clubhouse approx 500m on left through used car lot
Club Secretary: Craig Bedford, 58 Hollins Lane, Sowerby Bridge. HX6 2RP Tel: (H) 0966 178947 (W & Fax) 01422 373462
Fixtures Secretary: Gary Mason Tel: (H) 01422 349271 (W) 01422 371909
Club Colours: Emerald, gold and claret

KNARESBOROUGH RUFC
Ground Address: Hay-A-Park, Park Lane, off Chain Lane, North Yorkshire Tel: 01423 862525
Brief Directions: Follow A59 to centre of Knaresborough, at traffic lights by Board Inn turn north, away from Calcutt (signpost), take 2nd right, at school, follow on to end of road
Club Secretary: Stephen Fuller, Walkingham Hill Cottage, Occaney Beck, Copgrove, Harrogate, North Yorkshire. HG3 3TD Tel: (H) 01423 340778 (W) 0113 2593454
Fixtures Secretary: Alf Burns Tel: (H) 01423 866703
Club Colours: Blue and gold hooped shirts, navy shorts and socks

KNOTTINGLEY RUFC
Ground Address: Knottingley RUFC, Howards Field, Marsh Lane, Knottingley. WF11 9DE Tel: 01977 672438
Brief Directions: Onto A645 main road toward Knottingley, turn off at town hall/St Botolophs Church, follow road 500m past Cherry Tree pub, turn left just before lights at bridge to Howards Field
Club Secretary: Adrian Carley, 50 Womersley Road, Knottingley, West Yorkshire Tel: (H) 01977 677690
Fixtures Secretary: John Alexander Tel: (H) 01977 673084
Club Colours: Blue and white

MARIST RUFC
Ground Address: Cranbrook Avenue, Cottingham Road, Hull Tel: 01482 859216
Brief Directions: From M62 follow signs for Universities, then continue to Cranbrook Avenue along Cottingham Road
Club Secretary: Kevin Johnson, 11 Roborough Close, Barnstaple Road, Hull Tel: (H) 01482 828973 (W) 01482 781202
Fixtures Secretary: Ralph Ayre, 92 Aukland Ave, Cottingham Road, Hull HU6 Tel: (H) 01482 804166
Club Colours: Blue

MOSBOROUGH RUFC
Ground Address: Mosborough WMC, Station Road, Mosborough, Sheffield, 19 Tel: 0114 248 5546
Brief Directions: M1 J30, take A616 towards Sheffield, at 2nd set of lights turn right, clubhouse on left
Club Secretary: Lawrence S Hannon, 12 Stonegravels Croft, Halfway, Sheffield. S19 5HP Tel: (H) 0114 248 8425 (W) 01246 854650
Fixtures Secretary: S C Collins Tel: (H) 0170 953 1732
Club Colours: Black and white hooped shirts, black shorts

OLD RISHWORTHIAN RUFC
Ground Address: The Clubhouse, Copley, Halifax, West Yorkshire. HX3 0UG Tel: 01422 353919
Brief Directions: M62 J24 follow signs to Halifax, at roundabout take 2nd exit, 2 miles turn left to Sowerby Bridge, enter Copley, turn left at Volunteer pub, follow road into Copley village, club on left
Club Secretary: D W Butler, Keepens, Shaw Lane, Holywell Green, Halifax. HX4 9DH Tel: (H) 01422 371672 (W) 01484 721223
Fixtures Secretary: R Wadsworth Tel: (H) 01422 323172 (W) 01484 845740
Club Colours: Maroon, white and black hoops

YORKSHIRE FIVE

Yorkshire Five 1997-98 Fixtures	Adwick-le-Street	BP Chemicals	Danum Phoenix	De La Salle	Leeds Med. & Den.	Menwith Hill Qua	Ossett	Rawmarsh	Rowntrees	Withersea	
	1	2	3	4	5	6	7	8	9	10	
1 Adwick-le-Street	X	10/11	25/4	20/12	17/1	31/1	14/3	18/10	27/9	7/3	1
2 BP Chemicals	10/1	X	24/1	25/10	27/9	6/9	11/10	7/3	11/4	17/11	2
3 Danum Phoenix	17/11	18/10	X	10/1	31/1	7/3	25/10	27/9	6/9	11/4	3
4 De La Salle	11/4	17/1	10/11	X	18/10	27/9	17/11	31/1	7/3	6/9	4
5 Leeds Medics & Den	25/10	14/2	11/10	24/1	X	11/4	20/9	6/9	17/11	10/1	5
6 Menwith Hill Qua	11/10	14/3	20/9	14/2	20/12	X	10/1	25/4	25/10	24/1	6
7 Ossett	6/9	31/1	17/1	25/4	7/3	10/11	X	20/12	18/10	27/9	7
8 Rawmarsh	24/1	20/9	14/2	11/10	14/3	17/11	11/4	X	10/1	25/10	8
9 Rowntrees	14/2	20/12	14/3	20/9	25/4	17/1	24/1	10/11	X	11/10	9
10 Withersea	20/9	25/4	20/12	14/3	10/11	18/10	14/2	17/1	31/1	X	10
	1	2	3	4	5	6	7	8	9	10	

THIS DIRECTORY IS NOT FOR CLUB OFFICIALS ONLY!

Do your club supporters know they can buy their own directory and help club funds?

YORKSHIRE FIVE CONTINUED

ADWICK-LE-STREET RUFC
Ground Address: Church Lane Playing Fields, Adwick-le-Street, Doncaster, South Yorkshire
Brief Directions: From A1 south take A638 Doncaster turn off, 1st left to Adwick-le-Street. Frm Doncaster take A638 Wakefield Rd (3 miles), right at Broad H'way pub, ground opp. Aldwick Station
Club Secretary: R J Terry, 7 Cranfield Drive, Skellow, Doncaster, South Yorkshire. DN6 8RS Tel: (H) 01302 727580 (W) 01977 605100
Fixtures Secretary: M A Leach-Flanagan Tel: (H) 01302 872429
Club Colours: Light blue and dark blue hoops, navy shorts, red hose

B P CHEMICALS RUFC
Ground Address: B P Chemicals Sports and Social Club, Salt End, Hedon, Hull. HU12 8DS Tel: 01482 896251
Brief Directions: M62 East, A63 East, Sports & Social Club off Rondabout opposite Chemical Works.
Club Secretary: Ben Glover, 61 Galfrid Road, Bilton, Hull. HU11 4HL Tel: (H) 01482 813260 (W) 01482 892450
Fixtures Secretary: Steve West Tel: (H) 01482 891371 (W) 01482 896251x2844
Club Colours: Maroon and dark green, gold hoops around middle

DANUM PHOENIX RUFC
Ground Address: Du Pont Sports and Social Club, Wheatley Hall Road, Doncaster Tel: 01302 364307
Club Secretary: Mr W G Hircock, Lloret, Littleworth Lane, Rossington, Doncaster. Dn11 0HD Tel: (H) 01302 867448 (W) 0385 522238
Fixtures Secretary: Paul Burgin Tel: (H) 01032 320374 (W) 01709 740750
Club Colours: Black with red and yellow band on shirt

DE LA SALLE (SHEFFIELD) RUFC
Ground Address: Lancaster Rd., Salford Tel: 0161 789 2261
Club Secretary: John Malone, 57 Hayfield Road, Salford, Manchester 6 8QA Tel; 0161 281 6011
Fixtures Secretary: Jim Collins Tel: 0161 281 3761
Club Colours: Scarlet and old gold hooped jerseys, black shorts

LEEDS MEDICS AND DENTISTS RFC
Ground Address: University of Leeds Playing Fields, Weetwood, Leeds
Club Secretary: Andy Cohen, 16 Norwood Grove, Leeds LS6 1DT
Fixtures Secretary: Mark Dodd same address as Secretary
Club Colours: White, black and burgandy hoops

MENWITH HILL QUAKERS
Ground Address: RAF Menwith Hill, Skipton Road, Harrogate, North Yorkshire Tel: 01423 777781/88
Brief Directions: 7 miles out of Harrogate on A59 road
Club Secretary: M Kirkbride, c/o RAF Menwith Hill, Harrogate Tel: (W) 01423 777781/88
Fixtures Secretary: M. Kirkbridge c/o ground.
Club Colours: Gold shirts with green trim

OSSETT RUFC
Ground Address: Ossett Cricket and Athletic Club, Queens Terrace, Ossett, West Yorkshire Tel: 01924 273618
Brief Directions: M1 J40, A638 to Wakefield, right at 1st lights, turn right up to Spring Mill after 0.5 mile
Club Secretary: Mr D J Dearnley, 4 Crown Point Close, Kingsway, Ossett. WF5 8RH Tel: (H) 01924 278991
Fixtures Secretary: Mr I Whitehead Tel: (H) 01924 264629
Club Colours: Red and black quarters

RAWMARSH RUFC
Ground Address: Rawmarsh Leisure Centre, Barbers Avenue, Rawmarsh, Rotherham, South Yorkshire Tel: 01709 719952
Brief Directions: From Sheffield or Doncaster approach the Rotherham ring road.Take A630 and enquire at Mushroom Garage.
Club Secretary: Alan Parker, 3 McManus Avenue, Rawmarsh, Rotherham Tel: (H) 01709 522795
Fixtures Secretary: Eric Perkins Tel: (H) 01709 526786
Club Colours: Black with amber trim

ROWNTREE RUFC
Ground Address: Mille Crux, Haxby Road, York Tel: 01904 623933
Brief Directions: From York outer ring road, take New Earswick turn off into York, and entrance on left of road, through village approx 1 mile
Club Secretary: C W Maher, 25 Towton Avenue, Tadcaster Road, York. YO2 2DW Tel: (H) 01904 638870
Fixtures Secretary: G Lavender Tel: (H) 01904 626897
Club Colours: Red, black and white

WITHERNSEA RUFC
Ground Address: Plough Inn, Hollym, nr. Withernsea, East Yorkshire. HU19 2RS Tel: 01964 612049
Brief Directions: Main road from Hull to Patrington, turn left into Hollym village at the crossroad, ground at rear of Plough
Club Secretary: Mr A C Ellis, 11-17 Seaside Road, Withernsea. HU19 2DL Tel: (H & W) 01964 613278
Fixtures Secretary: Mr D Thompson, 13 Manor Garth, Keyinham, HU12 9SQ. Tel: (H) 01964 624094
Club Colours: White and blue hoop

NORTHERN DIVISION
FINAL LEAGUE TABLES (WEST) 1996-97

NORTH WEST ONE

	P	W	D	L	F	A	PTS
Blackburn	18	14	0	4	410	205	28
West Park St Helens	18	11	1	6	340	311	23
Aspull	18	11	0	7	323	300	22
Chester	18	10	1	7	425	332	21
Penrith	18	10	0	8	342	343	20
Vagabonds (Isle of M)	18	9	1	8	386	381	19
Birkenhead Park	18	8	2	8	332	324	18
Oldershaw	18	6	0	12	345	403	12
Wilmslow	18	5	0	13	285	433	10
Netherhall	18	3	1	14	291	447	7

NORTH WEST TWO

	P	W	D	L	F	A	PTS
Old Aldwinians	18	15	0	3	401	167	30
Ashton on Mersey	18	13	0	5	423	236	26
Egremont	18	12	1	5	332	223	25
Leigh	18	10	0	8	337	383	20
Northwich	18	9	0	9	275	380	18
Kirby Lonsdale	18	8	1	9	376	330	17
Carlisle	18	8	0	10	311	290	16
Old Salians	18	6	0	12	227	346	12
Fleetwood	18	5	0	13	259	388	*8
Sandbach	18	3	0	15	240	438	6

NORTH WEST THREE

	P	W	D	L	F	A	PTS
Merseyside Police	18	14	0	4	400	172	28
Caldy	18	13	0	5	460	215	26
Workington	18	11	0	7	330	274	22
Rossendale	18	9	2	7	267	208	20
Stockport	18	9	2	7	304	325	20
Windermere	18	8	1	9	329	377	17
Cockermouth	18	8	1	9	188	251	17
Wigan	18	6	1	11	299	335	13
Calder Vale	18	6	0	12	258	343	12
Ruskin Park	18	2	1	15	201	536	5

S LANCS/CHESHIRE ONE

	P	W	D	L	F	A	PTS
Altrincham Kersal	18	18	0	0	567	162	36
Wirral	18	15	0	3	537	243	30
Warrington	18	13	0	5	418	221	26
St Edwards OB	18	10	1	7	348	352	21
South Liverpool	17	7	1	9	354	296	15
Eagle	18	7	1	10	317	334	15
Old Anselmians	18	6	0	12	282	436	12
Newton-Le-Willows	17	5	0	12	280	431	10
Birchfield	18	4	1	13	244	461	9
Old Parkonians	18	2	0	16	182	593	4

S LANCS/CHESHIRE TWO

	P	W	D	L	F	A	PTS
Southport	18	16	1	1	671	156	33
Crewe & Nantwich	18	16	0	2	638	191	32
Wallasey	18	10	1	7	305	249	21
Dukinfield	18	9	1	8	415	309	*17
Bowdon	18	8	1	9	302	391	*15
Congleton	18	9	0	9	342	350	*14
Didsbury TOC H	18	7	0	11	289	458	14
Sefton	18	6	0	12	241	450	12
Hoylake	18	4	0	14	233	637	8
Port Sunlight	18	3	0	15	190	435	*2

S LANCS/CHESHIRE THREE

	P	W	D	L	F	A	PTS
Marple	14	11	2	1	382	153	*22
St Marys OB	14	9	0	5	343	198	18
Prenton	14	10	2	2	307	188	*18
Douglas IOM	14	7	2	5	295	199	16
Helsby	14	5	1	8	261	217	11
Liverpool Collegiate	14	5	1	8	158	302	*9
Mossley Hill	14	2	1	11	116	415	5
Vulcan	14	2	1	11	140	452	*

S LANCS/CHESHIRE FOUR

	P	W	D	L	F	A	PTS
Shell Stanlow	8	6	0	2	267	95	12
Halton	8	6	0	2	199	120	12
Moore	8	5	0	3	178	163	10
Hightown	8	2	0	6	88	222	4
Holmes Chapel	8	1	0	7	68	200	2

N LANCS/CUMBRIA

	P	W	D	L	F	A	PTS
St Benedicts	18	17	0	1	493	173	34
Rochdale	18	14	0	4	546	196	28
Vickers	18	13	0	5	538	218	26
Trafford MV	18	10	0	8	390	305	20
Tydesley	17	8	1	8	385	327	17
Ashton-Under-Lyne	18	8	0	10	338	276	16
Ormskirk	18	7	0	11	248	452	14
Keswick	18	6	1	11	266	460	13
Upper Eden	18	4	0	14	268	489	8
Ambleside	17	1	0	16	190	766	2

NORTH LANCS ONE

	P	W	D	L	F	A	PTS
Blackpool	18	17	0	1	613	172	34
Broughton	18	14	0	4	407	222	28
De La Salle	17	14	0	3	362	232	*26
Bolton	17	11	0	6	445	276	22
Thornton Cleveleys	18	8	0	10	279	330	16
Bury	18	8	0	10	340	412	16
Littleborough	18	4	2	12	237	371	10
Old Bedians	18	6	0	12	206	327	*8
Haeton Moor	18	3	1	14	227	445	7
Colne & Nelson	18	2	1	15	194	523	5

NORTH LANCS TWO	P	W	D	L	F	A	PTS
Oldham	14	14	0	0	605	96	28
Eccles	14	12	0	2	412	125	24
Chorley	14	7	0	7	288	257	*12
Culcheth	14	5	1	8	194	298	11
Clitheroe	14	6	0	8	250	273	*10
North Manchester	14	6	0	8	181	313	*10
Burnage	14	5	1	8	231	257	*9
Lostock	14	0	0	14	85	627	0

CUMBRIA	P	W	D	L	F	A	PTS
Furness	14	13	0	1	625	100	26
Whitehaven	14	11	0	3	457	250	22
Moresby	14	9	1	4	303	137	19
Millom	14	6	1	7	213	315	13
Carnforth	14	5	0	9	176	337	10
Creighton	13	4	2	7	153	273	*8
Silloth	14	3	0	11	205	410	*2
Green Garth	13	2	0	11	130	483	*0

NORTHERN DIVISION STRUCTURE WEST 1996-97

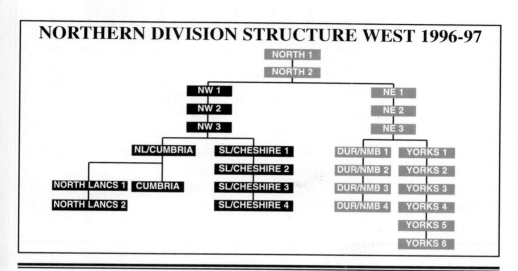

NORTHERN DIVISION LEAGUE STRUCTURE 1997-98

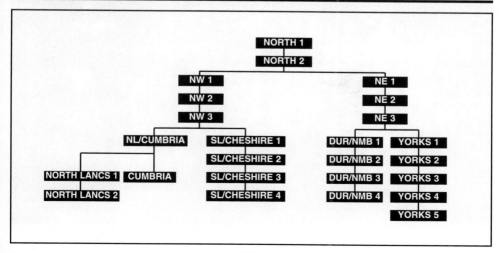

NORTH WEST ONE

North West One 1997-98 Fixtures	Ashton-on-M.	Aspull	Birkenhead Park	Chester	Old Aldwinians	Oldershaw	Penrith	Vagabonds	West Park St H.	Wilmslow	
	1	2	3	4	5	6	7	8	9	10	
1 Ashton-on-Mersey	X	20/12	10/1	25/10	14/3	20/9	25/4	24/1	11/10	14/2	1
2 Aspull	11/4	X	20/9	15/11	14/2	11/10	6/9	10/1	25/10	24/1	2
3 Birkenhead Park	8/11	7/3	X	18/10	31/1	17/1	20/12	27/9	6/9	25/4	3
4 Chester	17/1	25/4	24/1	X	20/12	14/3	8/11	11/10	14/2	20/9	4
5 Old Aldwinians	6/9	27/9	11/10	11/4	X	24/1	7/3	15/11	10/1	25/10	5
6 Oldershaw	7/3	31/1	25/10	6/9	18/10	X	27/9	11/4	15/11	10/1	6
7 Penrith	15/11	14/3	11/4	10/1	20/9	14/2	X	25/10	24/1	11/10	7
8 Vagabonds (IoM)	18/10	8/11	14/2	31/1	25/4	20/12	17/1	X	20/9	14/3	8
9 West Park St Helens	31/1	17/1	14/3	27/9	8/11	25/4	18/10	7/3	X	20/12	9
10 Wilmslow	27/9	18/10	15/11	7/3	17/1	8/11	31/1	6/9	11/4	X	10
	1	2	3	4	5	6	7	8	9	10	

Wilmslow R.U.F.C. 1st XV, after winning the Vandrey Middleton and Ashley Koenen Memorial against Stockport. April 1997.

ASHTON ON MERSEY RUFC
Ground Address: Banky Lane, off Carrington Lane, Ashton on Mersey, Cheshire   Tel: 0161 973 6637
Brief Directions: M63 J63 Carrington Spur, towards Carrington, right at lights, left at T junction, club 300 yards on right
Club Secretary: Steve Ruffley, 164 Bolton Road, Atherton, Manchester   Tel: (H) 01942 882856   (W) 01942 827640
Fixtures Secretary: P.Stokes.   Tel: (H) 0161 941 5641
Club Colours: Maroon and white hoops

ASPULL RFC
Ground Address: Woodshaw Park, Woods Road, Aspull, Wigan, Lancs   Tel: 01942 831611
Club Secretary: David Simpson, 5 Whitecroft, Wigan. WN3 5PS   Tel: (H) 01942 322968   (W & Fax) 01942 824773
Fixtures Secretary: G W Gregson   Tel: (H) 01257 421421   (W) 01772 267898   (F) 01772 885262
Club Colours: Sky and navy hoops

BIRKENHEAD PARK FC
Ground Address: Upper Park, Park Road North, Birkenhead. L41 8AA   Tel: 0151 652 4646
Brief Directions: M53 J4, take 4th exit off roundabout onto B5151 to Birkenhead, after 8 miles turn right at 4th lights into Upton Rd/Park Rd Nth, ground 0.5 miles on right
Club Secretary: G Reynolds, 13 Victoria Mount, Oxton, Birkenhead. L43 5TH   Tel: (H) 0151 653 0294
Fixtures Secretary: R C Hardman   Tel: (H) 0151 652 5204
Club Colours: Red, white and blue hoops

CHESTER RUFC
Ground Address: Hare Lane, Vicars Cross, Chester   Tel: 01244 336017
Brief Directions: From A55 (Chester Outer Ring Rd), take A51 then 1st left into Hare Lane.
Club Secretary: P W Rhodes, The Hollies, Off Carriage Drive, Frodsham, Cheshire. WA6 6EF   Tel: (H) 01928 731485   (W) 0151 225 2404
Fixtures Secretary: C Cawthorn, 21 Oaklands Ave, Tattenhall, Cheshire CH3 9QU   Tel: (H) 01829 770498 (W) 0122 603420
Club Colours: Red and white

OLD ALDWINIANS RUFC
Ground Address: Audenshaw Park, Droylsden Road, Audenshaw, Manchester. M34 5SN Tel: 0161 3011001
Brief Directions: East of Manchester, at junction of the A662 /635 Nr. Snipe Retail Park.
Club Secretary: Mr Chris Daly, 60 Green Lane, Hollingworth, Hyde, Cheshire. SK14 8JQ   Tel: (P&F 01457 762402 e.mail.Aldwinians@aol.com.
Fixtures Secretary: Alan Whalley, 190 Greenside Lane, Droylsden, Manchester. M35 6RR. Tel: (H)0161 3700921 (W)0161 2231353 Ext 246
Club Colours: Red and white hoops. Blue shorts/socks

OLDERSHAW RUFC
Ground Address: Belvidere Recreation Ground, Belvidere Road, Wallasey, Merseyside   Tel: 0151 638 4379
Brief Directions: M53 take Jcn for Wallasey Docks, follow road right, E. Falshaw grge on left, left at r'bout, over lights, left at lights after Funeral D'tors, over next lights, club down road on lft
Club Secretary: Mrs Stella Johnson, 26 Parkside, Wallasey, Merseyside. L44 9AJ   Tel: (H) 0151 638 1160 (W) 0151 227 5040
Fixtures Secretary: Mr Peter Purland   Tel: (H) 0151 733 4854   (W) 0151 724 4000
Club Colours: Navy blue with gold hoops

PENRITH RUFC
Ground Address: Winters Park, Penrith, Cumbria CA11 4RG.   Tel: 01768 863151
Brief Directions: M6 J40, A66 east for 0.5 mile, A686 east for 0,5 mile, PRUFC on left just past Police HQ
Club Secretary: Keith Davis, Ivy Bank, 59 Lowther Street, Penrith, Cumbria. CA11 7UQ   Tel: (H) 01768 866089
Fixtures Secretary: W F Mounsey   Tel: (H) 01768 881202
Club Colours: Myrtle green and white hooped shirts, white shorts.

VAGABONDS (I.O.M.) RUFC
Ground Address: Glencrutchery Road, Douglas, Isle of Man. IM2 6DA   Tel: 01624 661996
Brief Directions: Ask for T.T. Grandstand
Club Secretary: Stewart Halliday, 10 Kirkby Hall, Saddlestone, Braddan, Isle of Man. IM2 1PA   Tel: (H) 01624 624421
Fixtures Secretary: Stephen Wilson   Tel: (H) 01624 673029   (W) 01624 671118
Club Colours: White with black and yellow chest band, black shorts

WEST PARK (ST HELENS) RFC
Ground Address: Redrocks, Prescot Road, St Helens   Tel: 01744 26138
Brief Directions: On main Liverpool St Helens road, top of Eccleston Hill
Club Secretary: John B Fletcher, Ceklduminn, 7 Kings Road, Taylor Park, St Helens. WA10 3HT   Tel: (H) 01744 755895   (W) 01744 26138
Fixtures Secretary: J Eric Briers   Tel: (H) 01744 734665
Club Colours: Green and gold

WILMSLOW RUFC
Ground Address: Memorial Ground, Kings Road, Wilmslow. SK9 5PZ
Brief Directions: Kings Road is off the A538 from Wilmslow to Altrincham
Club Secretary: David Pike, 12 Fairbourne Drive, Wilmslow, Cheshire. SK9 6JF   Tel: (H) 01625 525616
Fixtures Secretary: Jim Blackburn   Tel: (H) 01625 532493
Club Colours: Sky blue, maroon and white jerseys, white shorts, maroon stockings

NORTH WEST TWO

North West Two 1997-98 Fixtures	Caldy	Carlisle	Egremont	Fleetwood	Kirby Lonsdale	Leigh	Merseyside Pol.	Netherhall	Northwich	Old Salians	
	1	2	3	4	5	6	7	8	9	10	
1 Caldy	X	20/12	7/3	27/9	31/1	6/9	8/11	18/10	25/4	17/1	1
2 Carlisle	11/4	X	14/3	25/10	20/9	24/1	15/11	10/1	11/10	14/2	2
3 Egremont	20/9	6/9	X	10/1	14/2	25/10	11/4	15/11	24/1	11/10	3
4 Fleetwood	14/2	17/1	14/2	X	25/4	20/9	18/10	31/1	14/3	20/12	4
5 Kirby Lonsdale	11/10	7/3	27/9	15/11	X	10/1	6/9	11/4	25/10	24/1	5
6 Leigh	14/3	18/10	17/1	7/3	8/11	X	31/1	27/9	20/12	25/4	6
7 Merseyside Police	10/1	25/4	20/12	24/1	14/3	11/10	X	25/10	14/2	20/9	7
8 Netherhall	24/1	8/11	25/4	11/10	20/12	14/2	17/1	X	20/9	14/3	8
9 Northwich	15/11	31/1	18/10	6/9	17/1	11/4	27/9	7/3	X	8/11	9
10 Old Salians	25/10	27/9	31/1	11/4	18/10	15/11	7/3	6/9	10/1	X	10
	1	2	3	4	5	6	7	8	9	10	

CALDY RFC
Ground Address: Paton Field, Thurstaston Road, Caldy, Wirral Tel: 0151 6258043
Club Secretary: Mrs B Barwood, 11 Covertside, New Ton, West Kirkby, Wirral
Fixtures Secretary: K Doolan Tel: (H) 0151 3480119
Club Colours: Sable, claret, silver and gold

CARLISLE RFC
Ground Address: Warwick Road, Carlisle Tel: 01228 21300
Brief Directions: M6 J43 on A69, head towards Carlisle, through 3 sets of lights, 150 yards after 3rd set turn right into ground
Club Secretary: N J Laycock, 90 Greystone Road, Carlisle. Cumbria, CA1 2DD Tel: (H & F) 01228 20277 (not after 10pm)
Fixtures Secretary: D D Morton, 14 Naworth Drive, Lowry Hill, Carlisle, Cumbria Tel: (H & Fax) 01228 515486
Club Colours: Red, navy blue and white

EGREMONT RUFC
Ground Address: Bleach Green, Egremont, Cumbria Tel: 01946 820645
Brief Directions: M6 J36, follow A595 north towards Workington, Egremont is approx 4 miles south of Whitehaven
Club Secretary: W H F Mornan, 58 Dent View, Egremont, Cumbria. CA22 2ET Tel: (H) 01946 822119 (W) 019467 71569 (Fx) 019467 75712
Fixtures Secretary: Mr D & Mrs C Ireland Tel: (H) 01946 822302 (W) 01946 599030 (Fx) 01946 599033
Club Colours: Black and gold

FLEETWOOD RUFC
Ground Address: Broadwaters, Melbourne Avenue, Fleetwood, Lancs Tel: 01253 874774
Brief Directions: Turn off M55 to Blackpool at Fleetwood/Kirkham exit, A585 to Fleetwood, 1st exit off roundabout at Nantieal College, sharp left at tram tracks into Crescent, follow round to Melbourne Ave
Club Secretary: Bryan Olsen, 32 Huntingdon Road, Thornton Cleveleys, Lancs FY5 1SR Tel: (H) 01253 854758 (W) 01253 866336
Fixtures Secretary: Andy Thompson, 67 Levens Drive, Poulton le Fylde, Lancs FY6 8EZ Tel: (H) 01253 882121 (H) 01253 300477
Club Colours: Green and gold hoops

KIRKBY LONSDALE RUFC
Ground Address: The Club House, Underley Park, Kirkby Lonsdale, via Carnforth, Lancs Tel: 015242 71780
Brief Directions: M6 J36, 1st left turn signpost town centre, keep left sign KL RUFC Old Huton, 0.5 mile turn right
Club Secretary: Richard Harkness, Meadowgarth, Fairbank, Kirkby Lonsdale, Via Carnforth, Lancs Tel: (H) 015242 71137 (W) 015242 72111
Fixtures Secretary: Paul Newell, Primrose Cottage, Thorns Lane, Sedbeigh
Club Colours: Red, black and amber hoops and socks, black shorts

LEIGH RUFC
Ground Address: Round Ash Park, Hand Lane, Leigh, Lancs. WN7 3RA Tel: 01942 673526
Brief Directions: Pennington Area of Leigh off St. Helens Road down Beech Walk to Hand Lane.
Club Secretary: Alban J. Westwell, 140 Chestnut Drive, South Leigh, Lancs. WN7 3JY. Tel: 01942 671017
Fixtures Secretary: Tom Hughes, 2 Launceston Road, Hindley Green, wigan, Lancs Tel: (H) 01942 257427
Club Colours: Black with amber hoops

NORTH WEST TWO CONTINUED

MERSEYSIDE POLICE RUFC
Ground Address: Police Sports Ground, Riversdale Road, Aigburth, L'pool 19, Merseyside Tel: 0151 427 2200
Brief Directions: Turn into Riversdale Road from Aigburth Road (A561) at Liverpool Cricket Club - half mile on Left before the river.
Club Secretary: D/Sgt Eric Sheppard, 38 Lynmouth Road, Aigburth, L'pool Merseyside. L17 6AW Tel: (H) 0151 427 4169 (W) 0151 777 6021
Fixtures Secretary: C. Evans, 42 Greenheys Rd, Wallasey, L44 5UP
Club Colours: Blue, black and white quarters

NETHERHALL
Ground Address: Netherhall Park, Netherhall Road, Maryport
Brief Directions: A66 to Cockermouth Head to Workington, right at roundabout for Maryport, turn left off bypass head into Maryport, right at lights A596 to Carlisle, club 400yds on right
Club Secretary: Paul Bartlett, 66 Garborough Close, Crosby, Maryport. CA15 6RZ Tel: (H) 01900 818420
Fixtures Secretary: L Rumney Tel: (H) 01900 811440
Club Colours: Claret and gold

NORTHWICH RUFC
Ground Address: Moss Farm Leisure Centre, Moss Road, Winnington, Northwich Tel: 01606 79987
Brief Directions: Follow directions from Northwich town centre to swimming pool
Club Secretary: Alan Langston, 25 Carlton Road, Witton Park. CW9 5PW Tel: (H) 01606 41039
Fixtures Secretary: Paul Taylor, 34 Ashwood Crescent, Barnton, Northwich, Cheshire Tel: (H) 01606 79662
Club Colours: Black shirts, black shorts

SALIANS (FORMERLY OLD SALIANS) RUFC
Ground Address: Rookwood, Clarendon Crescent, Sale, Cheshire
Brief Directions: M63 junction signposted to Sale B5166, at traffic lights turn right (Dane Road), Clarendon Crescent is 0.5 mile down Dane Road on the left
Club Secretary: Chris Armitage, 35 Willow Way, Didsbury, Manchester. M20 6JT Tel: (H) 0161 446 1134 (W) 01625 586677
Fixtures Secretary: Andy Parkinson Tel: (H) 0161 976 3904
Club Colours: Blue shirts with white hoop, blue shorts

NORTH WEST THREE

North West Three 1997-98 Fixtures	Altrincham K.	Calver Vale	Cockermouth	Rossendale	St Benedicts	Sandback	Stockport	Wigan	Windermere	Workington	
	1	2	3	4	5	6	7	8	9	10	
1 Altrincham Kersal	X	20/12	11/10	14/2	24/1	25/4	25/10	20/9	10/1	14/3	1
2 Calver Vale	11/4	X	25/10	24/1	10/1	6/9	15/11	11/10	20/9	14/2	2
3 Cockermouth	31/1	17/1	X	20/12	7/3	18/10	27/9	25/4	14/3	8/11	3
4 Rossendale	27/9	18/10	11/4	X	6/9	31/1	7/3	8/11	15/11	17/1	4
5 St Benedicts	18/10	8/11	20/9	14/3	X	17/1	31/1	20/12	14/2	25/4	5
6 Sandback	15/11	14/3	24/1	11/10	25/10	X	10/1	14/2	11/4	20/9	6
7 Stockport	17/1	25/4	14/2	20/9	11/10	8/11	X	14/3	24/1	20/12	7
8 Wigan	7/3	31/1	15/11	10/1	11/4	27/9	6/9	X	25/10	18/10	8
9 Windermere	8/11	7/3	6/9	25/4	27/9	20/12	18/10	17/1	X	31/1	9
10 Workington	6/9	27/9	10/1	25/10	15/11	7/3	11/4	24/1	11/10	X	10
	1	2	3	4	5	6	7	8	9	10	

THIS DIRECTORY IS NOT FOR CLUB OFFICIALS ONLY!

Do your club supporters know they can buy their own directory and help club funds?

Altringham Kersal 1st XV Squad which won all 18 games to be promoted to Northwest 3, in their Centenary Year.
Standing Left to Right, R.Salt (Coach), S.Domville, J.McCaffrey, S.Haliwell, M.Stoneman, J.Till, J.Orwin,
M.Faulkener, A.Gardiner, D.Jefferies, M.Chester, Mrs C.Purcell (Physio) and A.Forbes (President).
Kneeling , R.Wilks, J.Anderson, M.Wildegoose, W.Le Boutiller, P.Taylor (Captain), P.Moores, S.Gallimore, R.Neyton,
N.Hodgkinson, I.Wilson and H.Slack.

ALTRINCHAM (KERSAL) RFC
Ground Address: Stelfox Avenue, Timperley, Altrincham, Cheshire   Tel: 0161 972 9157
Brief Directions: M56 J3, take road towards Altrincham, after 3 miles 3rd exit off roundabout, Stelfox Ave 100 yds on right
Club Secretary: Dominic Leach, 5 Lisson Grove, Hale, Altrincham, Cheshire. WA15 9AE   Tel: (H) 0161 941 3085   (W) 0161 929 1851
Fixtures Secretary: George Brugnoli, 231 Brooklands Road, Sale, Greater Manchester.   Tel: (H) 0161 973 0194   (W) 0385 261743
Club Colours: Red, white and black hoops

CALDER VALE RUFC
Ground Address: Holden Road, Reedley, Burnley, Lancashire. BB10 2LE   Tel: 01282 424337
Brief Directions: M65 J12, right onto A682 towards Brierfield & Burnley North, through one set of traffic lights, Holden Road on left approx 0.5 mile, just past Oaks Hotel
Club Secretary: Mr W K Seed, 30 Moorland Drive, Brierfield, Nelson. BB9 5ER   Tel: (H) 01282 614172 (W) 01282 474291
Fixtures Secretary: Mr M Wilton, 93 Talbot Drive, Brier Cliffe, Burnley Lancs.   Tel: (H) 01282 457963
Club Colours: Royal blue and gold hoops

COCKERMOUTH RUFC
Ground Address: Laithwaite, Warrington Road, Cockermouth, Cumbria   Tel: 01900 824884
Brief Directions: A66 Penrith to Workington, 30 miles west of M6 J40, roundabout signed town centre, 0.75 mile to Main St, left & straight on 0.25 mile to Lloyds Garage, ground behind garage
Club Secretary: James McMullen, 128 High Brigham, Cockermouth, Cumbria. CA13 0Tj   Tel: (H) 01904 826432
Fixtures Secretary: A Quarry   Tel: (H) 01539 731640 (W) 01900 602623
Club Colours: Black and amber hoops

ROSSENDALE RUFC
Ground Address: Marl Pits Sports Ground, Newchurch Road, Rawtenstall, Lancashire   Tel: 01706 229152
Brief Directions: M66, A56, follow A682 St Mary's Way through 2 sets of traffic lights, right at 2nd set onto Newchurch Road, Marl Pits 0.5 mile on right
Club Secretary: Mr R J Sykes, 6 Holmes Wood Park, Holme Lane, Rawtenstall. BB4 6HZ   Tel: (H) 01706 213947
Fixtures Secretary: Mr T Kelly   Tel: 01706 217361
Club Colours: Maroon and white

SANDBACH RUFC
Ground Address: Bradwall Road, Sandbach, Cheshire. CW11 9AP   Tel: 01270 762475
Brief Directions: M6 J17, follow signs for Sandbach, turn right after 100 yds opposite Texaco garage, follow Offley Rd for 0.25 mile, turn right signed Bradwall, club 400 yards on right
Club Secretary: Mr Andrew Maddock, 40 Mortimer Drive, Sandbach, Cheshire. CW11 4HS   Tel: (H) 01270 759538   (W) 0113 204 4000
Fixtures Secretary: Mr Graham Armstrong   Tel: (H) 01270 760446
Club Colours: Green and red

ST BENEDICTS RUFC
Ground Address: Newlands Avenue, Mirehouse, Whitehaven, Cumbria,
Club House attached to St.Benedicts Social Club, Meadow Rd.
Mirehouse, Whitehaven, Cumbria.
Brief Directions: M6 to jct 40 (Penrith) A66 to A595 to Whitehaven-Barrow by pass and Pelican garage.Straight on to hospital over rouindabout then 1st rt down hill to green. Club by church.
Club Secretary: M J Morgan, 264 Meadow Road, Mirehouse, Whitehaven, Cumbria   Tel: (H) 01946 64076
Fixtures Secretary: C Dempsey   Tel: (H) 01946 590143 (W) 01946 74502
Club Colours: Amber and black hoops

STOCKPORT RUFC
Ground Address: Bridge Lane Memorial Ground, Headlands Road, Bridge Lane, Bramhall, Stockport, Cheshire. SK7 3AN Tel: 0161 439 2150
Club Secretary: Michael William Drew, 191 Moor Lane, Woodford, Stockport, Cheshire. SK7 1PF Tel: (H) 0161 439 5439 (W) 01625 525256
Fixtures Secretary: M J Wroe Tel: (H) 0161 440 8536
Club Colours: Red, green and white hoops

WIGAN RUFC
Ground Address: Douglas Valley, Wingates Road, Leyland Mill Lane, Wigan. WN1 2SA Tel: 01942 242556
Brief Directions: M6 J27, follow signs to Standish, take A49 towards Wigan, 2 miles, 1st left after Cherry Gardens Hotel into Leyland Mill Lane, then signposted
Club Secretary: Graham Heeley, 30 Darley Road, Hawkley Hall, Wigan. WN3 5PS Tel: (H) 01942 201360 (W) 01625 503050
Fixtures Secretary: David Clarke Tel: (H) 01942 207771
Club Colours: Black and white irregular hoops

WINDERMERE RUFC
Ground Address: Dawes Meadow, Longlands, Bowness on Windermere, Cumbria. LA23 3AS Tel: 015394 43066
Brief Directions: Drive towards Bowness & the lake from Windermere, coming in to Bowness, right just before cinema, right again past the bowling club, clubhouse is on the right.
Club Secretary: J C Stephenson, 46 Craig Walk, Windermere. LA23 2JT Tel: (W) 015394 88622
Fixtures Secretary: K E Williams, 2 Annesdale, Ambleside Road, Windermere. LA23 1BA. Tel: (W) 015394 47608
Club Colours: Amber and black

WORKINGTON RFC
Ground Address: Ellis Sports Ground, Mossbay Road, Workington. CA14 3XZ Tel: 01900 602625
Brief Directions: Adjacent to B5296, 0.5 mile south of town centre, 1st right after traffic lights at T A Centre
Club Secretary: M J Heaslip, 32 Elizabeth St, Workington. CA14 4DB Tel: (H) 01900 66339 (W) 01900 65656
Fixtures Secretary: J A Heaslip Tel: (H) 01900 602449
Club Colours: Black and white hoops

SOUTH LANCS & CHESHIRE ONE

South Lancashire/ Cheshire One 1997-98 Fixtures	Crewe & Nant.	Eagle	Newton-le-W.	Old Anselmians	Ruskin Park	St Edwards OB	South Liverpool	Southport	Warrington	Wirral	
	1	2	3	4	5	6	7	8	9	10	
1 Crewe & Nantwich	X	17/1	15/11	31/1	8/11	11/4	27/9	7/3	18/10	6/9	1
2 Eagle	25/10	X	11/10	7/3	24/1	10/1	6/9	11/4	27/9	15/11	2
3 Newton-le-Willows	25/4	31/1	X	20/12	17/1	6/9	8/11	18/10	7/3	27/9	3
4 Old Anselmians	11/10	20/9	11/4	X	14/2	24/1	15/11	10/1	14/3	25/10	4
5 Ruskin Park	10/1	18/10	25/10	27/9	X	15/11	7/3	6/9	31/1	11/4	5
6 St Edward's OB	20/12	8/11	14/3	18/10	25/4	X	31/1	27/9	17/1	7/3	6
7 South Liverpool	14/2	14/3	10/1	25/4	20/9	11/10	X	25/10	20/12	24/1	7
8 Southport	20/9	20/12	24/1	8/11	14/3	14/2	17/1	X	25/4	11/10	8
9 Warrington	24/1	14/2	20/9	6/9	11/10	25/10	11/4	15/11	X	10/1	9
10 Wirral	14/3	25/4	14/2	17/1	20/12	20/9	18/10	31/1	8/11	X	10
	1	2	3	4	5	6	7	8	9	10	

THIS DIRECTORY IS NOT FOR CLUB OFFICIALS ONLY!
Do your club supporters know they can buy their own directory and help club funds?

SOUTH LANCS & CHESHIRE ONE CONTINUED

CREWE AND NANTWICH RUFC
Ground Address: The Vagrants, Newcastle Road (A500), Willaston, Nantwich, Cheshire. CW5 7EP Tel: 01270 69506
Brief Directions: Situated on A500, opposite The Horseshoe pub, 2 miles east of Nantwich and 6 miles from J16 M6
Club Secretary: Alan Jones, 9 Gingerbread Lane, Nantwich, Cheshire. CW5 6NH Tel: (H & W) 01270 625737
Fixtures Secretary: Bob Christie Tel: (H) 01270 629637 (W) 01270 624160
Club Colours: Black Jersey with broad white band

EAGLE RUFC
Ground Address: Thornton Road, Great Sankey, Warrington Tel: 01925 632926
Brief Directions: A57 west from Warrington towards Liverpool onto the dual carriageway, where road splits at roundabout take left hand road (A562) and at lights turn left into Thornton Rd
Club Secretary: Vince Sandwell, 23 Waterworks Lane, Winwick, Warrington Tel: (H) 01925 650367 (W) 01925 830007
Fixtures Secretary: Dave Unsworth Tel: (H) 01925 727505
Club Colours: Black and white hoops

NEWTON-LE -WILLOWS RUFC
Ground Address: Crow Lane East, Newton-le-Willows, Merseyside Tel: 01925 224591
Brief Directions: M6 J23, take signs for Newton A49, continue down Ashton Rd (A49) until mini roundabout with Oak Tree pub on right, right into Crow Lane, club 300 yds on right
Club Secretary: Mr Philippe Boulton, 93 Winwick Road, Newton-le-Willows, Merseyside. WA12 8DB Tel: (H) 01925 229725
Fixtures Secretary: Mr Frank Rimmer Tel: (H) 01925 229152
Club Colours: Royal blue and gold hoops

OLD ANSELMIANS RUFC
Ground Address: Malone Field, Eastham Village Road, Eastham, Wirral Tel: 0151 327 1613
Brief Directions: M53 J5, take A41 towards Birkenhead, approx 400yds turn right into Eastham Village Rd, follow road for 0.5 mile, clubhouse on left opposite shops
Club Secretary: Tony Neville, 33 Stapleton Avenue, Greasby, Wirral. L49 2QT Tel: (H) 0151 678 4154 (W) 0151 350 1696
Fixtures Secretary: Tony McArdle Tel: 0151 342 1470
Club Colours: Blue, gold and white hoops

RUSKIN PARK RUFC
Ground Address: Ruskin Drive, St Helens Tel: 22893
Brief Directions: A580 - A570 St Helens bound
Club Secretary: Stephen Mitchell, 7 Larch Close, Billinge, Nr Wigan. WN5 7PX Tel: (H) 01744 893709 (W) 01744 20021
Fixtures Secretary: Geoff White Tel: (H) 01744 56478
Club Colours: Royal blue, black and white hoop

SOUTH LIVERPOOL RUFC
Ground Address: Dunlop Sports & Social Club, Speke Hall Avenue, Speke, Liverpool, L24 Tel: 0151 4861588
Brief Directions: Follow signs for Speke - Liverpool Airport.
Club Secretary: Lawrence Sherrington, 14 Brook Way, Great Sankey, Warrington, Cheshire. WA5 1RZ Tel: (H) 01925 726768
Fixtures Secretary: Dave Edge Tel: (H) 0151 425 4018
Club Colours: Amber and black quarters

Crewe and Nantwich R.U.F.C.
South Lancs / Cheshire 1 League. Promoted from runners up South Lancs / Cheshire 2 League 1996/97.
R.F. . . Junior Cup Finalists May 3rd Twickenham 1997.

SOUTHPORT RUFC
Ground Address: Waterloo Road, Hillside, Southport, Merseyside Tel: 01704 569906
Brief Directions: From north - through S/port via Lord St, past station on right, ground on right 50 yds after crossing. From south, A565 to S/port, straight through 3 lights, ground on left
Club Secretary: Ann Shorrock, 28a Alexander Rd.,Southport, Merseyside.PR9 9EZ Tel: 01704 537420
Fixtures Secretary: Mrs Margaret Jackson Tel: (H) 01704 578362
Club Colours: Red, black, amber hoops

ST EDWARDS OLD BOYS RUFC
Ground Address: Bishops Court, North Drive, Sandfield Park, West Derby, Liverpool. L12 2AR Tel: 0151 228 1414
Brief Directions: To end of M62, traffic lights, right onto Queens Drive (A5080), downhill through lights, right at next lights onto Alder Rd, left onto Eaton Rd, playing fields on left
Club Secretary: Simon J Smith, 107 Church Road, Woolton, Liverpool. L25 6OB Tel: (H) 0151 428 2799 (W) 0151 522 1234
Fixtures Secretary: B Reilly Tel: (H) 0151 428 3296
Club Colours: Royal blue shirt with gold band, white shorts, royal blue socks

WARRINGTON RUFC
Ground Address: Bridge Lane, Appleton, Warrington Tel: 01925 264591
Club Secretary: G P Robinson, 8 Bellhouse Lane, Warrington. WA4 2SD Tel: (H) 01925 261644
Fixtures Secretary: Paul Andrews Tel: (H) 01925 269154
Club Colours: Red, green, white

WIRRAL RFC
Ground Address: Old Wirralians Memorial Ground, Thornton Common Road, Clatterbridge, Wirral, Merseyside Tel: 0151 334 1309
Brief Directions: M53 J4, B5151 to Clatterbridge, past hospital on right, o.5 mile take left at crossroads, into Thornton Common Road
Club Secretary: Chris Whorton, 47 Meadow Lane, Willaston, Cheshire. L64 2TY Tel: 0151 327 5312
Fixtures Secretary: Mr A Hignett Tel: (H) 0151 327 1309
Club Colours: Maroon and white hoops

SOUTH LANCS & CHESHIRE TWO

South Lancashire/ Cheshire Three 1997-98 Fixtures	Douglas (IoM)	Halton	Helsby	Hoylake	Liverpool Coll.	Port Sunlight	St Mary's OB	Shell Stanlow	
	1	2	3	4	5	6	7	8	
1 Douglas (IoM)	X	11/4	4/10	20/9	18/10	14/2	8/11	15/11	1
2 Halton	25/10	X	15/11	4/10	25/4	28/3	20/9	14/2	2
3 Helsby	14/3	6/9	X	25/4	25/10	3/1	27/9	28/3	3
4 Hoylake	3/1	14/3	8/11	X	27/9	6/9	18/10	11/4	4
5 Liverpool Collegiate	28/3	8/11	11/4	14/2	X	4/10	15/11	20/9	5
6 Port Sunlight	27/9	18/10	20/9	15/11	14/3	X	11/4	8/11	6
7 St Mary's Old Boys	25/4	3/1	14/2	28/3	6/9	25/10	X	4/10	7
8 Shell Stanlow	6/9	27/9	18/10	25/10	3/1	25/4	14/3	X	8
	1	2	3	4	5	6	7	8	

BIRCHFIELD (LANCS) RUFC
Ground Address: Albright & Wilson Recreational Club, Birchfield Road, Widnes, Cheshire. WA8 0TB Tel: 0151 424 3222
Brief Directions: From M62 Junct. 7, follow A57 (Warrington) . Turn right at first set of lights, then right at T junction, 1st left at roundabout onto Birchfield Rd. Ground is 250 yds on the right.
Club Secretary: Stuart Ashton, 11 Eltham Close, Widnes, Cheshire. WA8 3RG Tel: (H) 0151 424 6344
Fixtures Secretary: Kevin McDonnell, 20 Newlyn Gardens, Penketh, Warrington. WA5 2UX. Tel: (H) 01925 722440 (W) 0151 424 4109 (M) 0802 400333
Club Colours: Maroon and black

BOWDEN RUFC
Ground Address: The Club House, Clay Lane, Timperley
Brief Directions: M56 J7, follow signs to Hale, after 1.5 turn right Delahays Rd, through next set of lights, after 0.5 mile up Thorley Lane turn right onto Clay Lane
Club Secretary: Tom St John Sloan, 7 Leigh Road, Hale, Cheshire Tel: (H) 0161 941 5865 (W) 0161 929 0105
Fixtures Secretary: Frank Norton, 36 Greenwall, Timperley. WA15 6JN Tel: (H) 0161 980 8195 (W) 01925 834639
Club Colours: Claret, white and black

CONGLETON RUFC
Ground Address: 78 Park Street, Congleton, Cheshire. CW12 Tel: 01260 273338
Brief Directions: Follow signs to Leisure centre
Club Secretary: Dennis Thorley, 46 Bladon Crescent, Alsager, via Stoke-on-Trent. ST7 2BG Tel: (H) 01270 878293 (W) 0161 223 1301 Ext 3132
Fixtures Secretary: Ken Williams Tel: (H) 01260 279202
Club Colours: Red, white, red, black hoops

DIDSBURY TOC H RFC
Ground Address: Ford Lane, Didsbury, Manchester Tel: 0161 446 2146
Brief Directions: M62 to M63 Stockport, take M56 turnoff, follow signs to Northenden, left at lights, right at next lights, right at next lights, through village and turn right into Ford Lane
Club Secretary: Peter J M Bradley, 8 Barnard Avenue, Heaton Moor, Stockport. SK4 4ED Tel: (H) 0161 432 0496 (W) 0161 788 9611
Fixtures Secretary: Richard Mortimer Tel: (H) 0161 976 5461
Club Colours: Black jersey with broad amber band

DUKINFIELD RUFC
Ground Address: Blocksages Playing Fields, Birch Lane, Dukinfield, Cheshire Tel: 0161 343 2592
Brief Directions: On B6170 between Hyde and Ashton-under-Lyne, next to the baths
Club Secretary: Ernie Taylor, 52 Gower Road, Hyde, Cheshire. SK14 5AD Tel: (H) 0161 3669541 (W) 01706 47422
Fixtures Secretary: Alan Hilton Tel: (H) 0161 338 3410
Club Colours: Royal blue and gold hoops

MARPLE RUFC
Ground Address: Wood Lane, Marple, Stockport
Brief Directions: Changing Rooms at Ridge College Marple, A626 into Marple, turn right into Cross Lane at Bowling Green pub, turn left into Buxton Lane, Ridge College on the right
Club Secretary: Mr M Cleverly, 16 Lyme Grove, Marple, Stockport, Cheshire Tel: (H) 0161 449 8393 (W) 0161 236 7733
Fixtures Secretary: Mr N Hawkley Tel: (H) 0161 449 9985 (W) 0161 273 3322
Club Colours: Red and black

PARKONIANS RUFC
Ground Address: H Martin Curphey Memorial Ground, Holm Lane, Oxton, Birkenhead, Wirral, Merseyside. L43 2HU Tel: 0151 652 3105
Brief Directions: M53 J3, A552 for Birkenhead, turn off into Holm Lane at the Swan Hotel, club is 200mtrs on left
Club Secretary: Mr P L Mullen, 8 Deerwood Crescent, Little Sutton, South Wirral. L66 1SE Tel: (H) 0151 339 1270 (W) 0151 448 6280
Fixtures Secretary: Mr E Potter Tel: (H) 0151 608 1582 (W) 0151 609 0202
Club Colours: Maroon, blue and white jerseys,stockings and white shorts

PRENTON RUFC
Ground Address: The Clubhouse, Prenton Dell, Prenton Dell Road, Prenton, Wirral, Merseyside. L43 3BS Tel: 0151 608 1501
Brief Directions: M53 Jct 3 Follow signs to Birkenhead. Pass under railway bridge(A551) 200 yds sign for golf range, Preston Dell Rd with club entrance half a mile on right.
Club Secretary: Paul Foster, 8 Rake Close, Upton, Wirral, Merseyside. L49 0XD Tel: (H) 0151 678 6643
Fixtures Secretary: George Pollock Tel: (H) 0151 653 5738
Club Colours: Maroon, gold and black

SEFTON RUFC
Ground Address: Thornhead Lane, Leyfield Road, West Derby, Liverpool. L12 9EY Tel: 0151 228 9092
Brief Directions: End of M62 take A5058 towards Bootle, at A57 turn right, left at lights, right in front of hospital, left at Bulldog pub (Leyfield Road), right into lane by electricity substation
Club Secretary: Roy Spencer, 8 Stoneycroft Close, Liverpool L13 0AT. Tel: (H) 0151 228 9833
Fixtures Secretary: B Houghton Tel: (H) 0151 428 3740
Club Colours: Red and white hooped shirts/socks, blue shorts

WALLASEY RUFC
Ground Address: Cross Lane, Leasowe Road, Wallasey, Wirral, Merseyside. L45 8NS Tel: 0151 638 1486
Brief Directions: Exit 1 on M53 towards Wallasey, take 2nd slip road to A551, turn right at lights
Club Secretary: J A Burton, 14 Seaview Lane, Irby, Wirral, Merseyside. L61 3UL Tel: (H) 0151 648 4341 (W) 0161 236 3707
Fixtures Secretary: A Rae Tel: (H) 0151 638 6903
Club Colours: Red, black, white hoops

SOUTH LANCS & CHESHIRE THREE

South Lancashire/ Cheshire Three 1997-98 Fixtures	Douglas (IoM) 1	Halton 2	Helsby 3	Hoylake 4	Liverpool Coll. 5	Port Sunlight 6	St Mary's OB 7	Shell Stanlow 8	
1 Douglas (IoM)	X	11/4	4/10	20/9	18/10	14/2	8/11	15/11	1
2 Halton	25/10	X	15/11	4/10	25/4	28/3	20/9	14/2	2
3 Helsby	14/3	6/9	X	25/4	25/10	3/1	27/9	28/3	3
4 Hoylake	3/1	14/3	8/11	X	27/9	6/9	18/10	11/4	4
5 Liverpool Collegiate	28/3	8/11	11/4	14/2	X	4/10	15/11	20/9	5
6 Port Sunlight	27/9	18/10	20/9	15/11	14/3	X	11/4	8/11	6
7 St Mary's Old Boys	25/4	3/1	14/2	28/3	6/9	25/10	X	4/10	7
8 Shell Stanlow	6/9	27/9	18/10	25/10	3/1	25/4	14/3	X	8
	1	2	3	4	5	6	7	8	

DOUGLAS (I.O.M.) RUFC
Ground Address: The Clubhouse, Port-E-Chee, Douglas, Isle of Man Tel: 01624 676493
Club Secretary: P E Garrett, 3 Ridgeway Street, Douglas, Isle of Man Tel: (H) 01624 629037 (W) 01624 624535
Fixtures Secretary: Sethin Taylor Tel: (H) 01624 672396 (W) 01624 626586
Club Colours: Maroon back, gold band

HALTON RUFC
Ground Address: ICI Recreation Ground, Liverpool Road, Widnes, Cheshire Tel: 0151 424 2355
Brief Directions: Frm M62 J7, A57 W'ington, rt at 1st lights, rt at T jcn, rt after 4th pelican, rt at lights, club on lft. Frm R'corn Brge, towncentre slip, under flyover, lft at r'bout, over next r'bout, rt at lights, club on lft
Club Secretary: A Pybus, 16 Durlston Close, Widnes, Cheshire. WA8 4GJ Tel: (H) 0151 423 3130
Fixtures Secretary: D Dyer Tel: (H) 0151 495 2402
Club Colours: Blue, green and white hoops

HELSBY RUFC
Ground Address: Helsby Sports and Social Club, Chester Road, Helsby, Cheshire Tel: 01928 722267
Brief Directions: Head west along M56 J14, left at roundabout, continue for 1 mile to lights, go straight ahead and pass the Helsby Arms pub, club is next turning on left
Club Secretary: Neil Birchall, 5 Wroxham Close, Helsby, Cheshire. WA6 0PZ Tel: (H) 01928 722563 (E mail) nbirchall@aol.com
Fixtures Secretary: A Ryder Tel: (H) 01928 723733
Club Colours: Black and gold hoops

HOYLAKE RUGBY FC
Ground Address: Melrose Avenue, Hoylake, Wirral, Merseyside Tel: 0151 632 2538
Brief Directions: M53 exit for West Kirkby and Moreton, travel through to Hoylake, left at roundabout, cross over level crossing at Hoylake Station and follow direction signs
Club Secretary: Mr D Western, The White Cottage, 118 Irby Road, Heswall, Wirral, Merseyside. L61 6XG Tel: (W) 0151 648 3208
Fixtures Secretary: J. McNeil, 6 Grove Terrace, Hoylake, Wirral. Tel: 0151 6321964
Club Colours: Red, green and white hoops

LIVERPOOL COLLEGIATE OLD BOYS RUFC
Ground Address: Liverpool Cricket Club, Aigburth Rd., Grassendale, Liverpool.19
Brief Directions: M62 Follow Queens Drive to Aigburth Road (Ohone secretary if further details are needed)
Club Secretary: M Hesketh, 37 Hattons Lane, Childwall, Liverpool 16. Tel: 0151 475 8495
Fixtures Secretary: P.Barnes Tel: (H) 0151 270 2146
Club Colours: Light blue, dark blue quarters

PORT SUNLIGHT RFC
Ground Address: Bromborough Playing Fields, Green Lane, Bromborough, Wirral Tel: 0151 334 3677
Brief Directions: A41 to Eastham, playing fields at Bromborough, Wirral
Club Secretary: Alan Haigh, 13 Charlotte's Meadow, Bebington, Wirral. L63 3JH Tel: (H) 0151 334 1304 (W) 0151 231 3132
Fixtures Secretary: Chris Dodd Tel: (H) 0151 608 7022
Club Colours: Black and white narrow hoops

SHELL (STANLOW) RUFC
Ground Address: The Shell Club, Chester Road, Whitby, Ellesmere Port, Cheshire   Tel: 0151 200 7050/7080   Fax: 0151 357 4175
Brief Directions: M53 J10, A5117 west to Strawberry public house, turn right at roundabout, club within 0.5 mile
Club Secretary: Mr A R J Dale, 12 Archers Way, Great Sutton, South Wirral, Cheshire. L66 2RY   Tel: (H) 0151 200 1860   (W) 0151 703 1398   (F) 703 1400
Fixtures Secretary: Mr G Fennion   Tel: (H) 0151 356 1952   (W) 01244 281281 Ext 523/510
Club Colours: Amber shirts, white shorts, red socks

ST MARYS OLD BOYS RUFC
Ground Address: Sandy Lane, off Gorsey Lane, Hightown, Merseyside   Tel: 0151 929 2020   HQ: 17 Moor Lane, Crosby. L23   Tel: 0151 924 1774
Brief Directions: Gorsey Lane is off a small road linking Little Crosby and Hightown, and can be reached from the A565 heading from Liverpool or Southport
Club Secretary: Mr Paul McCann 3 Dumfries Way, Melling Mount, Kirkby   Tel: (H) 0151 5480659
Fixtures Secretary: Mr Peter Moore   Tel: (H) 017048 78537
Club Colours: Maroon, yellow and blue hoops

SOUTH LANCS & CHESHIRE FOUR

South Lancashire/ Cheshire Four 1997-98 Fixtures	Hightown 1	Holmes Chapel 2	Moor 3	Mosley Hill 4	Vulcan 5	Whitehouse Park 6	
1 Hightown	X	25/10	6/9	20/9	4/10	3/1	1
2 Holmes Chapel	27/9	X	8/11	4/10	3/1	6/9	2
3 Moore	8/11	20/9	X	31/1	25/10	4/10	3
4 Mosley Hill	8/11	14/2	18/10	X	6/9	27/9	4
5 Vulcan	14/2	18/10	27/9		X	8/11	5
6 Whitehouse Park	18/10	8/11	14/2	25/10	20/9	X	6
	1	2	3	4	5	6	

GENTLEMEN OF MOORE RUFC
Ground Address: The Clubhouse, Moss Lane, Moore, Warrington. WA4 6UU   Tel: 01925 740473
Brief Directions: A56 from M56 towards Warrington, left at 1st set of traffic lights, right into Moss Lane in Moore Village
Club Secretary: John Stockton, 3 Hayes Lane, Appleton, Warrington. WA4 3DA   Tel: (H) 01925 266025   (W) 0161 973 1505
Fixtures Secretary: P J Woollacott   Tel: (H) 01925 266576   (W) 0161 228 6282
Club Colours: Black with gold band

HIGHTOWN RUFC
Ground Address: Sandy Lane, Hightown, Merseyside. L38   Tel: 0151 929 2330
Brief Directions: Main Liverpool/Southport Rd (was By-Pass) sign posts for Hightown left hand side before railwlay bridge
Club Secretary: Jem Barker, 28 Parkfield Road, Waterloo, Merseyside. L22 4RH   Tel: (H) 0151 474 0514
Fixtures Secretary: K. Lee, 10 Myrtle Grove, Crosby, Liverpool L23 Tel: 0151 9206315
Club Colours: Blue, white and brown Hoops

HOLMES CHAPEL RUFC
Ground Address: RPR Sports & Social Club, Brookl;ands, Holmes Chapel, CW4 8BE   Tel: 01477 532018
Brief Directions: Ground is on A54 (Holmes Chapel - Congleton Rd) on outskirts of village just beyond Railway Station
Club Secretary: Steve Ranger, 16 Balmoral Drive, Holmes Chapel, Cheshire. CW4 7HY   Tel: (H) 01477 533765   (W) 0850 003869
Fixtures Secretary: John Leary   Tel: (H) 01606 554614 (W) 01606 593411
Club Colours: Blue and gold hoops

MOSSLEY HILL RUFC
Ground Address: Mossley Hill Road, Liverpool 18 Tel: 0151 7244377
Brief Directions: From M62 take ring road towards Liverpool Airport. Turn left onto Allerton Rd, right onto Rose La. (at Tescos) Behind Church at top of Rose La.
Club Secretary: Mr A Pealing, 5 Fieldfare Close, Liverpool. L25 4HB   Tel: (H) 0151 280 1174
Fixtures Secretary: Mr J Parr, 30 Ridgtor Road, Liverpool 25   Tel: (H) 0151 4287625
Club Colours: Maroon and gold quarters or hoops

VULCAN RUFC
Ground Address: The Sportsfield, Wargrave Road, Newton-le-Willows, Merseyside Tel: 01925 224180
Club Secretary: Paul Tither, 19 Grosvenor Gardens, Newton-le-Willows, Merseyside. WA12 8LY   Tel: (H) 01925 222006   (W) 01925 417080
Fixtures Secretary: J Bajer Tel: (H) 01925 226653
Club Colours: Black and amber

WHITEHOUSE PARK RFC
Ground Address: Halton Sports, Murdishaw Avenue, Runcorn. WA7 6HP
Brief Directions: M56,A56,A533, Runcorn,Murdishaw,Halton Arms Pub off Murdishaw Avenue.
Club Secretary: Jeff Gore, 26 Tarnbeck, Norton, Runcorn, Cheshire WA7 6SF Tel: (H) 01928 712284
Fixtures Secretary: Peter Lyons Tel; (H) 01928 711869 (W) 0151 485 6717
Club Colours: Blue and White Hoops

NORTH LANCASHIRE & CUMBRIA

North Lancashire & Cumbria 1997-98 Fixtures	Ashton-under-L.	Blackpool	Furess	Keswick	Metrovick	Ormskirk	Rochdale	Tyldesley	Upper Eden	Vickers	
	1	2	3	4	5	6	7	8	9	10	
1 Ashton-under-Lyne	X	31/1	11/4	8/11	15/11	6/9	7/3	17/1	27/9	18/10	1
2 Blackpool	11/10	X	24/1	14/2	11/4	25/10	10/1	20/9	15/11	14/3	2
3 Furness	20/12	18/10	X	25/4	14/3	7/3	27/9	8/11	31/1	17/1	3
4 Keswick	10/1	27/9	15/11	X	25/10	11/4	6/9	18/10	7/3	31/1	4
5 Metrovick	25/4	20/12	6/9	17/1	X	27/9	18/10	31/1	8/11	7/3	5
6 Ormskirk	14/3	17/1	20/9	20/12	14/2	X	31/1	25/4	18/10	8/11	6
7 Rochdale	20/9	8/11	14/2	14/3	24/1	11/10	X	20/12	17/1	25/4	7
8 Tyldesley	25/10	7/3	10/1	24/1	11/10	15/11	11/4	X	6/9	27/9	8
9 Upper Eden	14/2	25/4	11/10	20/9	10/1	24/1	25/10	14/3	X	20/12	9
10 Vickers	24/1	6/9	25/10	11/10	20/9	10/1	15/11	14/2	11/4	X	10
	1	2	3	4	5	6	7	8	9	10	

THIS DIRECTORY IS NOT FOR CLUB OFFICIALS ONLY!
Do your club supporters know they can buy their own directory and help club funds?

NORTH LANCASHIRE & CUMBRIA CONTINUED

ASHTON-UNDER-LYNE RFC
Ground Address: Pavilion, Gambrel Bank, St Albans Avenue, Ashton-Under-Lyne. OL6 8TU   Tel: 0161 330 1361
Brief Directions: From Market Square Ashton, Henrietta Street to Broadoak Hotel, straight on to St Albans Avenue
Club Secretary: Mr Dennis Gee, 26 Burnedge Lane, Grasscroft, Oldham. OL4 4EA   Tel: (H) 01457 872823 (W) 0161 303 9482
Fixtures Secretary: Mr Neil Mather   Tel: (H) 0161 339 6697
Club Colours: Red, amber and black

BLACKPOOL RUFC
Ground Address: Fleetwood Road, Norbreck, Blackpool, Lancashire   Tel: 01253 853308
Brief Directions: M55 J4, right onto A583, right onto Whitegate Drive (still A583), bear right onto Devonshire Rd B5214, club on right 0.5 mile past Red Lion pub
Club Secretary: Cliff Wainscott, 15 Stafford Avenue, Poulton-Le-Fylde, Lancashire. FY6 8BJ   Tel: (H) 01253 885151
Fixtures Secretary: Ian Taylor   Tel: (H) 01253 358183 (W) 01253 751014
Club Colours: Red and blue hooped shirts and socks, blue shorts

FURNESS RUFC
Ground Address: Strawberry Grounds, Abbey Road, Barrow-in-Furness, Cumbria   Tel: 01229 825226
Brief Directions: A590 to Barrow-in-Furness and follow the old main road, Abbey Road, turn left into Crosslands Park Road
Club Secretary: John Maccinson, 64 Hawcoat Lane, Barrow-in-Furness, Cumbria   Tel: (H) 01229 823151 (W) 01229 837727
Fixtures Secretary: Martin Harbidge   Tel: (H) 01229 430276   (W) 01229 824532
Club Colours: Blue and white

KESWICK RUFC
Ground Address: Davidson Park, Keswick, Cumbria   Tel: 017687 72823
Club Secretary: Mr Tucker, Rocking House, Portinscale, Keswick   Tel: (H) 017687 75839
Fixtures Secretary: A J Branthwaite   Tel: (H) 017687 74234
Club Colours: Navy, green, gold hoops, white shorts

ORMSKIRK RUFC
Ground Address: Green Lane, Ormskirk, Lancs. L39   Tel: 01695 572523
Brief Directions: Adjacent A59 at junction with A570
Club Secretary: Mr L A Bumford, 28 Gores Lane, Formby, Nr Liverpool. L37 3NY   Tel: (H) 01704 878702   (W) 0151 934 4412
Fixtures Secretary: Mr A Worthington   Tel: (H) 01695 423762
Club Colours: Dark blue, light blue and green hoops

ROCHDALE RUFC
Ground Address: Moorgate Avenue, Bamford, Rochdale, Lancs. OL11 5LU   Tel: 01706 46863
Brief Directions: From Rochdale: B6222 to Bury past Cemetary Hotel, Moorgate Ave 3rd on right. From M62: J20 A627(M) to Rochdale, over 2nd r'bout B6452 left into B6222 at Cemetary Hotel
Club Secretary: John McManus, 27 Hunstanton Drive, Brandlesholme, Bury, Lancs. BL8 1EG   Tel: (H) 0161 761 4371   (W) 0161 740 4993   (F) 795 8094
Fixtures Secretary: Michael Deasey   Tel: (H) 01706 356094   (W) 01706 353208
Club Colours: Maroon and white hoops

TRAFFORD (METROVICK) RFCC
Ground Address: Macpherson Park, Finney Bank Road, Sale, Cheshire. M33 1LR   Tel: 0161 973 7061
Brief Directions: M63 J7, head for Altrincham, at 1st traffic lights turn right (Glebelands Rd), Finney Bank Rd is 0.5 mile along on right
Club Secretary: Mr Des French, 8 Shandon Avenue, Northenden, Manchester. M22 4DP   Tel: (H) 0161 902 9963
Fixtures Secretary: Mr M Pringle, Flat 4, 109 Edge Lane, Stretford, Manchester M32 8PU   Tel: (H) 0161 286 1775   (W) 0161 877 7760
Club Colours: Black and white hooped shirts, white shorts, black and white socks

TYLDESLEY RUFC
Ground Address: Well Street, Tyldesley M29 8HW   Tel: 01942 882967
Brief Directions: From A580 (East Lancs Road) take A577 (Mosley Common Road) until the start of the one way system, take a left down Well Street
Club Secretary: Mr H Hughes, 7 Finstock Close, Winton, Eccles, Manchester. M30 7NP   Tel: (H) 0161 707 8096   (W) 0161 600 4563
Fixtures Secretary: Mr A W Jones   Tel: (H) 01942 876938   (W) 01942 883348
Club Colours: Royal blue shirts, white shorts

UPPER EDEN RUFC
Ground Address: Pennine Park, Westgarth Road, Kirkby Stephen, Cumbria CA17 4DW   Tel: 017683 71585
Brief Directions: M6 J38, 12 miles to Kirkby Stephen, turn left by Spar shop (Westgarth), straight on to top of estate. A66 turn off at Brough, 4 miles to K. Stephen, right just after shop
Club Secretary: Stuart Reed, 4 Eastview Cottages, Redmayne Road, Kirkby Stephen   Tel: (H) 017683 72528
Fixtures Secretary: G Park   Tel: (H) 017683 71412
Club Colours: Black and white hoops

VICKERS RUFC
Ground Address: Hawcoat Park, Hawcoat Lane, Barrow in Furness, Cumbria   Tel:01229 825296
Brief Directions: M6 Jct 36. A590 to Barrow and follow signs for Furness General Hospital. Turn right at lights after hospital, ground is 200 yards on left.
Club Secretary: Mr A T Mason, 48 Crosslands Park, Barrow in Furness, Cumbria LA13 9NH Tel: (H) 01229 821624
Fixtures Secretary: MR C J High   Tel: (H) 01229 826886
Club Colours: Maroon and white shirts, white shorts and maroon socks.

NORTH LANCASHIRE ONE

North Lancashire One 1997-98 Fixtures		Bolton	Broughton	Bury	De La Salle	Eccles	Heaton Moor	Littleborough	Oldham	Old Bedians	Thornton Clev.	
		1	2	3	4	5	6	7	8	9	10	
1	Bolton	X	14/3	14/2	20/9	24/1	11/4	18/11	10/1	25/10	11/10	1
2	Broughton	6/9	X	11/10	14/2	25/10	20/9	11/4	18/11	10/1	24/1	2
3	Bury	27/9	31/1	X	18/10	18/11	25/10	7/3	6/9	11/4	10/1	3
4	De La Salle	7/3	27/9	24/1	X	10/1	11/10	6/9	11/4	18/11	25/10	4
5	Eccles	18/10	17/1	25/4	10/11	X	14/3	31/1	27/9	7/3	20/12	5
6	Heaton Moor	20/12	7/3	17/1	31/1	6/9	X	10/11	18/10	27/9	25/4	6
7	Littleborough	25/4	20/12	20/9	14/3	11/10	10/1	X	25/10	24/1	14/2	7
8	Oldham	10/11	25/4	14/3	20/12	20/9	24/1	17/1	X	11/10	20/9	8
9	Old Bedians	17/1	10/11	20/12	25/4	14/2	14/2	18/10	31/1	X	14/3	9
10	Thornton Cleveleys	31/1	18/10	10/11	17/1	11/4	18/11	27/9	7/3	6/9	X	10
		1	2	3	4	5	6	7	8	9	10	

NORTH LANCASHIRE TWO

North Lancashire Two 1997-98 Fixtures		Burnage	Chorley	Clitheroe	Colne & Nelson	Culcheth	Lostock	Montell Carr.	N. Manchester	
		1	2	3	4	5	6	7	8	
1	Burnage	X	3/1	6/9	27/9	18/10	14/3	25/10	25/4	1
2	Chorley	20/9	X	28/3	8/11	11/4	15/11	14/2	4/10	2
3	Clitheroe	15/11	18/10	X	11/4	4/10	8/11	20/9	14/2	3
4	Colne & Nelson	14/2	25/4	25/10	X	15/11	20/9	4/10	28/3	4
5	Culcheth	28/3	25/10	14/3	6/9	X	27/9	25/4	3/1	5
6	Lostock	4/10	6/9	25/4	3/1	14/2	X	28/3	25/10	6
7	Montell Carrington	11/4	27/9	3/1	14/3	8/11	18/10	X	6/9	7
8	North Manchester	8/11	14/3	27/9	18/10	20/9	11/4	15/11	X	8
		1	2	3	4	5	6	7	8	

NORTH LANCASHIRE ONE CONTINUED

BOLTON RUFC
Ground Address: Mortfield Pavilion, Avenue Street, Bolton. BL1 3AW   Tel: 01204 363710
Brief Directions: Head out of Bolton on Chorley Old Road, signposted near Morrisons supermarket
Club Secretary: David Powell, 39 Beaumont Chase, Knutshaw Bridge, Bolton   Tel: (H) 01204 658570   (W) 01524580309
Fixtures Secretary: David Patchett   Tel: (H) 017064 826298
Club Colours: Red and white hoops, black shorts

BROUGHTON RUFC
Ground Address: Yew Street, Broughton, Salford. M7 9HL   Tel: 0161 743 0902
Club Secretary: Paul Walsh, 6 Grassfield Avenue, Lower Broughton, Salford. M7 9HW   Tel: (H) 0161 792 1571
Fixtures Secretary: John Barrow   Tel: (H) 0161 743 0902
Club Colours: Blue with yellow, red, yellow stripe midway

BURY RUFC
Ground Address: Radcliffe Road, Bury, Lancashire   Tel: 0161 764 1528
Brief Directions: Exit off M62, A56 towards Bury, traffic lights at junction with Radcliffe Rd (4 miles) turn left, ground 200 yards on right
Club Secretary: G J Hilton, 66 Twiss Green Lane, Culcheth, Warrington, Cheshire   Tel: (H) 01925 762119   (W) 01925 762975
Fixtures Secretary: M Freschini   Tel: (H) 0161 764 9051
Club Colours: Red, gold and blue hoops, navy blue shorts, red stockings

DE LA SALLE (SALFORD) RUFC
Ground Address: Lancaster Road, Salford 6   Tel: 0161 789 2261
Brief Directions: Sth: off M602 Eccles Jcn 2 follow Salford past Hope Hsptl on rt, next lights left onto Lancaster Rd. From Nth: A580 East Lancs Rd towards Salford, right at Lancaster Rd, club halfway on right
Club Secretary: John Malone, 57 Hayfield Road, Salford. M6 8QA   Tel: (H) 0161 281 6011
Fixtures Secretary: Jim Collins   Tel: (H) 0161 281 3761   (W) 0161 775 7928
Club Colours: Red and gold hoops

ECCLES RFC
Ground Address: Gorton Street, Peel Green, Eccles   Tel: 0161 789 2617
Brief Directions: M63 J2 towards Eccles, Gorton Street 2nd on left
Club Secretary: A C Brunt, 12 Woodstock Drive, Worsley, Manchester. M28 2WW   Tel: (H) 0161 794 4114   (W) 01606 833333
Fixtures Secretary: A E Chettoe   Tel: (H) 0161 794 5642   (W) 0161 790 7711
Club Colours: Navy blue and white hoops

HEATON MOOR RUFC
Ground Address: Green Lane, Heaton Moor, Stockport   Tel: 0161 432 3407
Brief Directions: M63 J12, taking A5145 for Didsbury, at 1st set of traffic lights turn right (signed B5169 Heaton Moor/Reddish), Green Lane is 5th road on right
Club Secretary: Peter Jackson, 35 Stanley Road, Heaton Moor, Stockport   Tel: (H) 0161 442 9061   (W) 01928 717070
Fixtures Secretary: Alan Vose   Tel: (H) 0161 456 9362
Club Colours: Black, red and gold

LITTLEBOROUGH RUFC
Ground Address: Deep Lane, Rakewood, Hollingworth Lake, Littleborough, Lancashire. OL15 0AP   Tel: 01706 370220
Brief Directions: Take J21 off M62 .Left at r'about, rt at traffic lights and left into Kiln Lane. Then take left into Wild Horse Lane, rt at mini r'bout follow signs to Hollingworth Lake. Rt to Rakewood at Fish pub.
Club Secretary: Darren Mave, 11 Buersil Avenue, Balderstone, Rochdale.   Tel: 01706 32466
Fixtures Secretary: Mr Harry Hanson   Tel: (H) 0161 872 2141
Club Colours: Green, black and amber

OLD BEDIANS RFC
Ground Address: Underbank Farm, Millgate Lane, East Didsbury, Manchester. M20 5QX   Tel: 0161 445 8862
Club Secretary: Mr Ian Wilson, 7 Brooklands Close, Denton, Manchester. M34 3PL   Tel: (H) 0161 320 3392   (W) 0161 287 7760   (Fx) 287 7761
Fixtures Secretary: G Tucker   Tel: (H) 0161 445 2358
Club Colours: Royal blue shirts, white shorts

OLDHAM RUFC
Ground Address: Manor Park, Bryth Road, Bardsley, Oldham. OL8 2TJ   Tel: 0161 624 6383
Brief Directions: Off the main A627 Oldham to Ashton road, behind Bardsley Church
Club Secretary: T J Brown, 12 Tilton Street, Oldham. OL1 4JA   Tel: (H) 0161 620 1878   (W) 01254 57149
Fixtures Secretary: T Park   Tel: (H) 0161 832 8551
Club Colours: Red and white hoops

THORNTON CLEVELEYS RUFC
Ground Address: Fleetwood Road, Thornton Cleveleys, Lancashire   Tel: 01253 854104
Club Secretary: Michael Johnson, 15 Beryl Avenue, Thornton Cleveleys, Lancs. FY5 3PA   Tel: (H & W) 01253 822857
Fixtures Secretary: Bill Beckett   Tel: (H) 01253 884630
Club Colours: Red, black and amber hoops

BURNAGE RFC
Ground Address: Varley Park, Battersea Road, Heaton Mersey, Stockport. SK4 3EA Tel: 0161 432 2150
Brief Directions: M63 J12, A5145 to Station Road Heaton Mersey village, Industrial Estate Burnage RUFC is signposted to club
Club Secretary: Mr T Gregory, 22 Berwick Avenue, Heaton Mersey, Stockport. SK4 3AA Tel: (H) 0161 443 2761 (W) 01706 861341
Fixtures Secretary: Ivan Hodgson Tel: (H) 01477 33406
Club Colours: Black

CHORLEY
Ground Address: Brookfields, Chancery Road, Astley Village, Chorley, Lancashire PR71XP. Tel: 01257 268806
Club Secretary: Ken Potter, Lindisfarne, 97 The Farthings, Astley Park, Chorley. PR7 1SH Tel: (H) 01257 267411 (W) 01695 53485 (Fx) 01695 51205
Fixtures Secretary: Dave Nickease Tel: (H) 01772 451171 (W) 01704 303014
Club Colours: Black and white quarters

CLITHEROE RUFC
Ground Address: Littlemoor Park, Littlemoor Road, Clitheroe Tel: 01200 22261
Brief Directions: A59 from junction 32 M6. First Clitheroe turning. 1 mile turn R. into Littlemoor Road.
Club Secretary: John Hyde, Moor Hey Cottage, Knowle Green, Longridge, Preston Tel: (H) 01254 878402
Fixtures Secretary: Phil Isherwood Tel: (H) 01200 23781 (W) 01282 777368
Club Colours: Maroon and gold hoops

COLNE & NELSON RUFC
Ground Address: Holt House, Harrison Drive, Colne, Lancashire Tel: 01282 863339
Club Secretary: Keith Thornton, The Hawks, Massey Lane, Brierfield. BB9 5JT Tel: (W) 01282 415500
Fixtures Secretary: Duncan Bolton Tel: (H) 01282 869321 (W) 01282 818883
Club Colours: All black

CULCHETH RFC
Ground Address: Shaw Street, Culceth, Warrington, Cheshire. WA3 5SH Tel: 01925 763096
Club Secretary: Mr I Halliday, 23 Gosling Road, Croft, Warrington, Cheshire. WA3 7LN Tel: (H) 01925 765140
Fixtures Secretary: Mr S F Smith Tel: (H) 01925 766268 (W) 01942 272222
Club Colours: Red and black shirts, black shorts

LOSTOCK RFC
Ground Address: Lostock Lane, Lostock, Bolton, Lancashire
Brief Directions: M61 J6, turn right at roundabout on A6027 to Horwich, 1 mile on turn right before traffic lights, ground on left at BAC Lostock
Club Secretary: R Fletcher, 19 Shaftesbury Avenue, Lostock, Bolton. BL6 4AP Tel: (H) 01204 698362
Fixtures Secretary: S Curren Tel: (H) 01204 695928
Club Colours: Black shorts and shirts

MONTELL CARRINGTON
Ground Address: Carrington Works, Urmston, Manchester M31 4AJ
Club Secretary: Anthony Kelly, 332 Liverpool Road, Irlam, Manchester M30 6AN Tel: (H) 0161 775 7743
Fixtures Secretary: As Above
Club Colours: Red and yellow quarters

NORTH MANCHESTER & OLDHAM COLLEGES RUFC
Ground Address: Greengate/Victoria Avenue East, Moston, Manchester Tel: 0161 682 9234
Club Secretary: Brian H Stott, 8 Barlea Avenue, New Moston, Manchester. M40 3WL Tel: (H) 0161 682 0541 (W) 0161 681 1582
Fixtures Secretary: Jason Malone Tel: (H) 0161 653 5020
Club Colours: Green, black and white hoops

Cumbria 1997-98 Fixtures	Ambleside 1	Carnforth 2	Creighton 3	Green Garth 4	Millom 5	Moresby 6	Silloth 7	Whitehaven 8	
1 Ambleside	X	15/11	14/2	25/10	28/3	4/10	20/9	25/4	1
2 Carnforth	6/9	X	28/3	14/3	3/1	25/4	27/9	25/10	2
3 Creighton	27/9	18/10	X	6/9	25/4	25/10	14/3	3/1	3
4 Green Garth	11/4	4/10	15/11	X	14/2	20/9	18/11	18/10	4
5 Millom	18/10	20/9	8/11	27/9	X	15/11	11/4	14/3	5
6 Moresby	14/3	8/11	11/4	3/1	6/9	X	18/10	27/9	6
7 Silloth	3/1	14/2	4/10	25/4	25/10	28/3	X	6/9	7
8 Whitehaven	8/11	11/4	20/9	28/3	4/10	14/2	15/11	X	8
	1	2	3	4	5	6	7	8	

AMBLESIDE
Ground Address: Galava Park, Borrans Road, Ambleside, Cumbria LA22 0UL. Tel: 015394 32536
Club Secretary: Mrs. J. Irwin, 1 Hodge Howe Cottages, Windermere, Cumbria LA23 2EZ. Tel: (H) 015394 42025
Fixtures Secretary: Mr. N. Fecitt, Hart Head Farm, Rydal, Ambleside, cumbria. Tel: (H) 015394 33772 (W) 015394 32296
Club Colours: Black.

CARNFORTH RFC
Ground Address: Carnforth High School, Kellet Road, Carnforth, Lancashire
Club Secretary: P.D.Wetherill, 13 Hill St., Carnforth, Lancs. LA5 9DY Tel: 01524 73587
Fixtures Secretary: Steve Vose Tel: (H) 01524 832041
Club Colours: Green and black hoops

CREIGHTON RUFC
Ground Address: Carrs Field, Caxton Road, off Newton Road, Carlisle Tel: 01228 21169
Brief Directions: Follow signs to Cumberland Infirmary, 400 yards past on right hand side
Club Secretary: David J Thomlinson, 146 Moorhouse Road, Carlisle Tel: (H) 01228 35111 (W) 01228 24379
Fixtures Secretary: Ian Langley, Kiln Green House, Aikton, Wigton, CA7 0HY.
Club Colours: Navy blue, red collars and cuffs, white shorts, red sock

GREEN GARTH RUFC
Ground Address: Greengarth Hostel, Holmbrook, Cumbria Tel: 01946 725800
Club Secretary: Robert Eales, 20 Wholehouse Road, Scale, Cumbria. CA20 Tel: (H) 019467 28734
Fixtures Secretary: Steven Edgare Tel: (H) 019467 841534
Club Colours: Maroon and gold

MILLOM RUFC
Ground Address: Wilson Park, Haverigg, Millom, Cumbria. LA18 4LU Tel: 01229 770401
Brief Directions: Upon entering Haverigg, past Harbour pub towards the beach and play area, pass the Inshore Rescue Station, club house 200m down the tarmac lane
Club Secretary: G Edward Whitfield, 13 Willowside Park, Haverigg, Millom, Cumbria. LA18 4PT Tel: (H) 01229 774876
Fixtures Secretary: Ian Shovelton Tel: (H) 01229 773743
Club Colours: Blue and white

MORESBY RUFC
Ground Address: Walkmill Park, Old Pit Road, Moresby Parks, Whitehaven, Cumbria Tel: 01946 695984
Club Secretary: c/o The Clubhouse - at above address Tel: (H) 01946 695984
Fixtures Secretary: Syd Bray Tel: (H) 694199
Club Colours: Red shirts, white shorts

SILLOTH RUFC
Ground Address: Old Marshalling Yard,Eden Street, Silloth, Cumbria.CA5 4HE Tel: 016973 32299
Brief Directions: Lies in the centre of town
Club Secretary: David Henderson, 8 Beaconsfield Terrace, Silloth, Cumbria. CA5 4HE Tel: (H) 016973 31076
Fixtures Secretary: Richard Smith Tel: (H) 016973 31936
Club Colours: Green and black hoops

WHITEHAVEN RUFC
Ground Address: The Playground, Richmond Terrace, Whitehaven, Cumbria. CA28 7QR Tel: 01946 695253
Club Secretary: Mr E McConnell, 38 Loop Road South, Whitehaven, Cumbria. CA28 7SE Tel: (H) 01946 692225
Fixtures Secretary: Mr D Telford Tel: 01946 61355
Club Colours: Maroon and white hoops

MIDLAND DIVISION

MIDLAND DIVISION STRUCTURE 1997-98

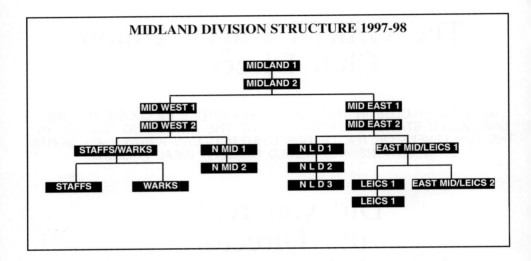

OFFICIALS 1997-98

CHAIRMAN
David I Robins, The Clubhouse, Upper Chase Road, Malvern. WR14 2BU (H) 01684 564826 (B) 01684 560247 (Fax) 01684 893125

LEAGUE SECRETARIES
Midland One David Coe, 4 Applegarth Close, Corby, Northants. NN18 8EU (H) 01536 460052 (B) 01536 402551 Ext 3107
Midland Two Geoff Goodall, 38 Presthills Road, Hinckley, Leics. LE10 1AJ (H) 01455 238742 (B) 01203 562650
Midland East One Mike Bracey, 154 Manor Road, Barton-le-Clay, Bedford. MK45 4NU (H) 01582 881237
Midland West One Brian Johnston, 9 Nursery Close, Atworth, Melksham, Wilts. SN12 8HX (H) 01225 790658 (B) 01249 442771 (Fax) 01249 442865
Midland East Two Philip Osborne, Ashthorne, Teeton Road, Ravensthorpe, Northampton. NN6 8EJ (H) 01684 770772 (B) 01327 705785
Midland West Two Nigel Banwell, 16 Riverside Close, Upton upon Severn, Worcester. WR8 0JN (H) 01684 592046
Staffs/Warks One Keith Dale, 14 St. Anthonys Drive, Newcastle, Staffs. ST5 2JE (H) 01782 615770
Staffordshire Bruce Braithwaite, 4 Badgers Croft, Eccleshall,

Staffs. ST21 6DS (H) 01785 851114 (B) 01785 277330 (F) 01785 277224
Warwickshire Ray Roberts, 261 Alwyn Road, Bilton, Rugby, Warks. CV22 7RP (H) 01788 810276 (F) 01788 816520
North Midlands One John McNally, 490 Brook Lane, Moseley, Birmingham. B13 0BZ (H) 0121 604 6180 (B) 0121 783 7232 (Fax) 0121 789 8306
North Midlands Two Alan Humphries, 26 Low Fold Close, St johns, Worcester WR8 5UE (H) 01905 422522
Notts/Lincs & Derby One Kevin Price, 10 Seagrave Road, Thrussington, Leicestershire. LE7 4UG (H) 01644 424388
Notts/Lincs & Derby Two Paul Raymont, 18 Longhill Rise, Kirkby-in-Ashfield, Nottinghamshire. NG19 9FL (H) 01623 750990
Notts/Lincs & Derby Three David H Murphy, The Old Carpenters Arms, 32 High Street, Little Bytham, Grantham, Lincolnshire. NG33 4QX (H) 01780 410692
East Midland/Leicestershire One Michael King, 53 Kettering Road, Market Harborough, Leics. LE16 8AN (H) 01858 467267
Leicestershire One & Two Clive Elliot, 9 Wavertree Close, Cosby, Leics LE9 1TN (H) 0116 284 1746 (B) 01709 550066
East Midlands Bob Ingledew, 15 Martin Close, Bedford. MK41 7JY (H) 01234 407521

MIDLAND DIVISION

ADMINISTRATIVE RULES

NOTIFICATION OF RESULTS

Club Secretaries are responsible for their club's compliance with the rules of notification of results.

Home clubs will telephone the match result to Russells News and Sports Agency. Tel: 0116 2332200 as soon as possible after the end of the game and certainly before 5.00 pm on the day of the match.

The match result card is the responsibility of the Home Club and must be completed by both Home and Away Clubs on the day of the game.

The Home Clubs will send to the League Secretary the Match Result Card. This must be by First Class Mail by the first post on the Monday following the game. It must be completed in all respects.

Failure to telephone or to post the card within the time limits will incur an immediate fine of £15. Any subsequent offense will incur a fine of £25. Offending club's will be notified, by the League Secretary, of fines imposed. Failure to pay within 28 days will result in the offending club having two points deducted.

A club with any fines outstanding at the end of the season will incur a recommendation to the RFU that the club be suspended or expelled from the League for the following season.

ADMINISTRATIVE INSTRUCTIONS

a.   League results to be telephoned to Russells by 5.00pm on the Saturday of the game.
Telephone: 0116 2332200 Fax: 0116 2332204.

b.   Match result card to be posted by first class mail on the Monday following the Saturday game.

c.   Notification and collection of fines will be administered by the appropriate League Secretary.

COMPUTER PRINTOUTS FOR PLAYERS' REGISTRATIONS

Clubs requiring updated printouts will send a request **together with a stamped addressed envelope** with the with the name of the club in the left hand corner to The Registrar, PO Box 183, Leicester LE3 8BZ.

CLUB REGISTRATION OFFICERS

It is essential that every club appoint an officer to be responsible for all registration matters. The Registration Officer must be fully aware of the RFU Registration of Players Regulations and the RFU Registration of Players Operating Procedures. These are published each year and sent to Club Secretaries.

POSTPONED GAMES

Clubs will notify the League Secretary immediately it is known that a match cannot be played. The League Secretary will also be informed within three days of that notification, the proposed re-arranged date. The Home Club must also notify the Referees Society to which the Club is affiliated the proposed re-arranged date.

RESCHEDULED MATCHES

A match postponed or abandoned under Regulation 11(a) or (b) or a match not played on the appointed day for reasons acceptable to the Organising Committee SHALL be played on the NEXT AVAILABLE Saturday.
A Saturday is deemed to be 'available' UNLESS one of the following conditions applies:

a.   Either Club has, on that day, a scheduled Courage League match.
b.   Either Club has, on that day, a Pilkington Cup or Shield match.

c.   Either Club has, on that weekend, a match in a Competition under the authority of their Constituent Body, but **NOT** a Merit Table match.

d.   Either Club has a demand on one or more of their effectively registered players to play in a representative match under the authority of the RFU, their Division or their Constituent Body on that day.

e.   In addition, the Midland Division Committee may - at its absolute discretion and usually at the start of a season declare a specific Saturday "unavailable" where it falls on or close to a public holiday or where it is considered by the committee inappropriate to play for other particular reasons.

MIDLAND DIVISION
FINAL LEAGUE TABLES (EAST) 1996-97

MIDLANDS ONE

	P	W	D	L	F	A	PTS
Hinckley	16	14	0	2	601	178	28
Burton	16	13	1	2	457	173	27
Belgrave	16	12	1	3	371	244	25
Scunthorpe	16	12	0	4	435	253	24
Broad Street	16	11	0	5	434	230	22
Whitchurch	16	9	1	6	435	304	19
Syston	16	9	0	7	253	253	18
Camp Hill	16	7	1	8	323	339	15
Wolverhampton	16	7	1	8	287	394	15
Lewighton Buzzard	16	7	1	8	285	407	15
Westleigh	16	5	3	8	307	283	13
Derby	16	5	3	8	319	412	13
Barkers Butts	16	6	0	10	329	441	12
Mansfield	16	5	1	10	238	323	11
Stafford	16	4	0	12	282	520	8
Leamington	16	2	0	14	268	556	4
Stockwood Park	16	1	1	14	198	512	3

MIDLANDS TWO

	P	W	D	L	F	A	PTS
Banbury	17	13	2	2	511	231	28
Kenilworth	17	14	0	3	442	283	28
Old Laurenthians	17	13	1	3	406	177	27
Kettering	17	13	1	3	457	234	27
Luctonians	17	12	2	3	426	168	26
Dudley	17	13	0	4	434	212	*24
Bedford Athletic	17	11	1	5	362	206	23
Bromsgrove	17	10	0	7	271	293	20
Ampthill	17	9	0	8	348	310	18
Sutton Coldfield	17	7	1	9	344	413	15
Newport	17	6	1	10	261	353	13
Towcestrians	17	7	0	10	286	283	*12
Paviors	17	4	2	11	286	442	10
Huntingdon	17	5	0	12	255	506	10
Keresley	17	4	0	13	218	352	*6
Long Buckby	17	3	0	14	269	550	6
Matlock	17	3	0	14	257	555	6
Bedworth	17	0	1	16	185	450	1

MIDLANDS EAST ONE

	P	W	D	L	F	A	PTS
Moderns	16	14	0	2	425	152	28
Old Northamptians	16	13	0	3	370	208	26
Wellingborough	16	10	1	5	379	269	21
Lutterworth	16	9	2	5	388	245	20
Lincoln	16	10	0	6	367	226	20
Stewarts & Lloyds	16	9	0	7	293	255	18
Ilkeston	16	9	0	7	222	241	18
Newark	16	8	0	8	255	264	16
Peterborough	16	7	1	8	266	310	15
Stoneygate	16	8	0	8	296	247	*14
Coalville	16	5	3	8	206	253	13
Ashbourne	16	6	1	9	227	275	13
Spalding	16	5	2	9	230	301	12
Vipers	16	5	3	8	170	219	*11
Amber Valley	16	5	1	10	222	419	11
Biggleswade	16	3	1	12	163	362	7
Northampton Boys B	16	2	1	13	213	446	5

MIDLANDS EAST TWO

	P	W	D	L	F	A	PTS
Nhampton Mens Own	16	15	0	1	594	220	30
Nhampton Old Scou	16	14	0	2	614	162	28
South Leicester	16	14	0	2	400	236	28
Dunstablians	16	12	0	4	433	268	24
West Bridgford	16	11	1	4	340	183	23
Loughborough	16	9	0	7	373	343	18
Nottingham Casuals	16	8	1	7	285	246	17
Long Eaton	16	7	2	7	307	312	16
Kibworth	16	8	0	8	232	382	16
Stamford	16	7	1	8	320	356	15
Oadby Wyggestonians	16	6	1	9	347	256	13
Grimsby	16	6	1	9	296	344	13
Kesteven	16	5	0	11	167	260	10
Bedford Queens	16	4	1	11	173	300	9
Mellish	16	4	0	12	180	369	8
East Retford	16	2	0	14	212	437	4
Chesterfield	16	0	0	16	141	740	0

EAST MIDLANDS/LEICS ONE

	P	W	D	L	F	A	PTS
Luton	15	15	0	0	609	183	30
Oakham	15	14	0	1	651	126	28
Market Bosworth	15	11	1	3	685	189	23
Bedford Swifts	15	11	1	3	426	183	23
Rushden & Higham	15	9	0	6	326	295	18
Daventry	15	9	0	6	258	248	18
Old Bosworthians	15	8	1	6	325	233	17
Bugbrooke	15	7	1	7	331	394	15
Colworth House	15	7	1	7	271	377	15
Aylestone St James	15	5	1	9	211	290	11
Brackley	15	5	1	9	252	418	11
St Neots	15	5	0	10	204	452	10
Melton Mowbray	15	5	1	9	244	257	*9
St Ives	15	3	0	12	160	574	6
Wellingborough	15	1	0	14	172	467	2
Old Ashbeians	15	1	0	14	144	583	2

EAST MIDLANDS

	P	W	D	L	F	A	PTS
Deepings	9	8	0	1	263	31	16
Northampton Casuals	9	8	0	1	291	80	16
Oundle	9	7	0	2	311	76	14
Thorney	9	5	0	4	201	174	10
Vauxhall Motors	9	5	0	4	162	173	10
Corby	9	4	1	4	175	135	9
Kempston	9	4	0	5	175	177	8
Northampton Heathens	9	2	1	6	260	225	5
Westwood	9	1	2	8	114	318	2
Biddenham	9	0	0	9	58	621	0

LEICS ONE

	P	W	D	L	F	A	PTS
Loughborough Student	10	9	0	1	377	75	18
Wigston	10	7	0	3	445	119	14
Old Newtonians	10	6	1	3	270	130	13
New Parks	10	5	1	4	206	159	*9
West Leicester	10	2	0	8	96	459	4
Aylestoniana	10	0	0	10	57	509	0

LEICS TWO

	P	W	D	L	F	A	PTS
Burbage	8	7	0	1	282	72	*12
Braunstone Town	8	6	0	2	195	118	*6
Aylestone Athletic	8	4	1	3	150	135	*5
Cosby	8	2	1	5	116	210	5
Shepshed	8	0	0	8	33	241	0

NOTTS, LINCS & DERBY ONE

	P	W	D	L	F	A	PTS
Buxton	16	14	1	1	433	153	29
Dronfield	16	12	2	2	305	131	26
Ashfield Swans	16	11	1	4	316	199	*21
Glossop	16	9	2	5	291	159	20
Southwell	16	9	2	5	343	216	20
Bakewell Mannerians	16	9	1	6	421	249	19
Keyworth	16	9	1	6	293	305	19
All Spartans	16	10	0	6	286	212	*18
Castle Donnington	16	7	1	8	197	252	15
Melbourne	16	8	0	8	274	212	*14
Leesbrook	16	6	1	9	233	274	13
Market Rasen * Louth	16	7	0	9	303	280	*12
Worksop	16	8	1	7	206	267	*11
Sleafford	16	3	1	12	134	289	7
Boston	16	4	0	12	188	298	*6
North Kesteven	16	2	0	14	131	482	4
East Leake	16	1	0	15	142	518	2

NOTTS, LINCS & DERBY TWO

	P	W	D	L	F	A	PTS
Boots Athletic	13	13	0	0	276	107	26
Stamford College	13	12	0	1	374	156	24
Cotgrave	13	9	0	4	245	125	18
Belper	13	9	0	4	219	140	*16
Nottinghamians	13	8	0	5	227	177	16
Rolle Royce	13	5	1	7	213	232	11
Barton & District	13	6	0	7	198	139	*10
Nottinghamshire Con	13	6	0	7	183	255	*10
Meden Vale	13	5	0	8	192	234	*8
Bourne	13	5	0	8	191	316	*8
Ollerton	13	3	1	9	127	287	7
Yarborough Bees	13	3	0	10	174	313	6
Cleethorpes	13	4	1	8	290	274	*3
University of Derby	13	1	1	11	134	288	*3

NOTTS, LINCS & DERBY THREE

	P	W	D	L	F	A	PTS
Hope Valley	12	11	1	0	499	53	23
Gainsborough	12	8	3	1	199	159	19
Skegness	12	7	1	4	364	160	15
Tupton	12	4	2	6	164	211	10
Bingham	12	5	0	7	148	233	10
Whitwell	12	2	0	10	94	430	4
Bilsthorpe	12	1	1	10	102	324	3

MIDLAND DIVISION STRUCTURE EAST 1997-98

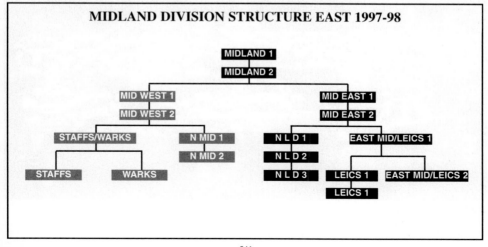

MIDLANDS ONE

Midlands One 1997-98 Fixtures	Banbury	Barkers' Butts	Belgrave	Broad Street	Burton	Camp Hill	Derby	Hereford	Kenilworth	Leighton Buzzard	Mansfield	Scunthorpe	Stoke-on-Trent	Syston	Westleigh	Whitchurch	Wolverhampton	
	1	2	3	4	5	6	7	8	9	10	11	12	13	14	15	16	17	
1 Banbury	X		15/11		10/1		24/1			7/3		11/4	6/9		27/9		25/10	1
2 Barkers' Butts	8/11	X		20/9		11/10				20/12		17/1	31/1		7/3		1/4	2
3 Belgrave		6/9	X		11/10		8/11	20/12	31/1		17/1			7/3		11/4		3
4 Broad Street	20/12		27/9	X	8/11						17/1	31/1	7/3		11/4		6/9	4
5 Burton		27/9		25/10	X		20/12	17/1	7/3		31/1			11/4		6/9		5
6 Camp Hill	17/1		25/10		15/11	X			31/1			7/3	11/4		6/9		27/9	6
7 Derby		25/10		15/11		10/1	X	31/1	11/4		7/3			6/9		27/9		7
8 Hereford	14/2	15/11		10/1		24/1		X	6/9		11/4		27/9			25/10		8
9 Kenilworth	25/4	24/1		14/2		14/3			X	20/9	11/10			15/11		10/1		9
10 Leighton Buzzard		10/1		24/1		14/2	14/3			X		6/9	27/9		25/10		15/11	10
11 Mansfield	14/3	10/1		24/1		14/2			27/9	25/4	X		25/10			15/11		11
12 Scunthorpe			24/1			14/2	14/3	25/4			20/9	X	25/10		15/11		10/1	12
13 Stoke-on-Trent			14/2			14/3	25/4	20/9	8/11		11/10		X		10/1		24/1	13
14 Syston	20/9	14/2		14/3	25/4					11/10		8/11	20/12	X		24/1		14
15 Westleigh			14/3		25/4		20/9	11/10	20/12		8/11			17/1	X		14/2	15
16 Whitchurch	11/10	14/3		25/4		20/9		8/11			20/12	17/1		31/1		X		16
17 Wolverhampton			25/4		20/9	11/10	8/11	17/1			20/12		31/1		7/3		X	17
	1	2	3	4	5	6	7	8	9	10	11	12	13	14	15	16	17	

Banbury R.U.F.C Season 1996/97
Courage League Champions, Midlands Division 2.
Photograph Banbury Guardian, Central Counties Newspapers LTD.

BANBURY RUFC
Ground Address: Bodicote Park, Oxford Road, Banbury, Oxon Tel: 01295 263862 (Ground)   01295 256298 (Clubhouse)
Brief Directions: M40 J11, follow signs town centre, hospital, Adderbury, continue to follow signs hospital, Adderbury, Ground on right 1.5 mile south of hospital on A4260
Club Secretary: Bryan A Davies, 34 Horton View, Banbury, Oxon. OX16 9HP Tel: (H) 01295 262027
Fixtures Secretary: Roger Croft Tel: (H) 01295 258289
Club Colours: Dark blue and white hoops

BARKERS' BUTTS RFC
Ground Address: Pickford Grange Lane, Allesley, Coventry. CV5 9AR Tel: 01676 522192
Brief Directions: A45 from Coventry to Birmingham, take left to Merden, 40yds turn left into Pickford Grange Lane, Club entrance 100yds on right
Club Secretary: R.G.Coward, c/o club at address above.
Fixtures Secretary: R.Hill   Tel: (H) 01676522887
Club Colours: Blue and gold hoops, navy shorts, blue and gold hooped socks

BELGRAVE RFC
Ground Address: Belgrave Pastures, Thurcaston Road, Abbey Lane, Leicester. Tel: 0116 2663033
Brief Directions: Ground situated where A6 Loughborough Road meets the Abbey Lane, opposite Mcdonalds
Club Secretary: Michael John Goddard, Grange Court, 271A Birstall Road, Birstall, Leics. LE4 4DJ Tel: (H) 0116 2677383   (W) 0802 263676
Fixtures Secretary: Kevin Hick Tel: (H) 0116 2608617   (W) 0116 2739501
Club Colours: Red and black hoops, black shorts

BROADSTREET RFC
Ground Address: The Ivor Preece Field, Brandon Road, Coventry.   Tel: 01203 453982 (Clubhouse), 01203 451706 (Caretaker)
Brief Directions: M6 Junction 2, take signs for Banbury, Stratford, Warwick. Along Coventry Eastern bypass. Ground entrance between TGI Fridays and Morrisons supermarket
Club Secretary: Mr C J McGinty, 14 Glendower Ave, Whoberley, Coventry. CV5 8BE Tel: (H) 01203 679261 or 0035373 23155
Fixtures Secretary: Mr Dave Wilkinson Tel: (H) 01203 543548
Club Colours: White shirts with red and green bands, white shorts

BURTON FC
Ground Address: Peelcroft, Lichfield Street, Burton upon Trent, Staffordshire. DE14 3RH Tel: 01283 564510
Brief Directions: Centre of Burton, adjacent to Safeways supermarket
Club Secretary: J D Lowe, 20 The Chevin, Stretton, Burton upon Trent, DE13 0XU Tel/Fax: (H) 01283 534422
Fixtures Secretary: P E Richard Tel: (H) 01332 516901
Club Colours: White jerseys with black diagonal band over right shoulder, white shorts, black socks

CAMP HILL RFC
Ground Address: Haslucks Green Road, Shirley, Solihull, West Midlands Tel: 0121 7444175
Brief Directions: Haslucks Green Road is off Stratford Road (A34) - at city centre end of Shirley - Junction 4 of M42
Club Secretary: Ken Birrell, 33 Ruskleigh Road, Shirley, Solihull. B90 1DQ Tel: (H) 0121 4304221
Fixtures Secretary: Graham Scutt Tel: (H) 0121 7444495
Club Colours: Maroon and light blue

Camp Hill R.F.C. 1st XV 1996/97 Season
Standing left to right: D.McConnell (Chairman), J.Ryan, D.Wildey (Manager-1), S.Smith, D.Shortt, A.Reynolds, P.Hinsley, B.Bowles (Chairman of Selectors), D.Roddy, S.Johnston, M.McWhirter, P.Strickland, J.Leyshon, B.Burton (Manager-2).
Seated M.Greaves (Physiotherapist), D.Lloyd, D.Pritchard, S.Morrissy, S.Tansley (Captain), M.Chetland (Vice Captain), M.Spencer, A.Wildey, J.Brown, K.Phillpots.

MIDLANDS ONEcontinued

DERBY RFC
Ground Address: The Pavilion, Kedleston Road, Derby. DE22 2TF Tel: 01332 344341
Brief Directions: Off A38 at Markeaton Park towards University of Derby campus - ground half a mile further on the left
Club Secretary: Mrs P.Dickens, 57 Wheeldon Avenue, Derby DE22 1HP Tel: 01332 341546
Fixtures Secretary: John Dickens Tel: (H) 01332 341546
Club Colours: Black and amber hoops, black shorts

HEREFORD RFC
Ground Address: Wyeside, Belvadere Lane, off Broomy Hill, Hereford HR4 9UT Tel: 01432 273410
Brief Directions: Follow ring road to Ross-On-Wye, turn right before bridge, over River Wye. 1st left after 'The Antelope' into Broomy Hill. 1st left, narrow lane clun is on riverside.
Club Secretary: M H V Littlrfirld, The Rides, 13 Burwood Close, Hereford HR1 1DQ Tel: (H) 01432 275468 (B) 01432 356310 (F) 01432 351310
Fixtures Secretary: Pete Greenow, Hackford Hose, Dinedor Cross, Hereford HR2 6PD Tel: (H&B) 01432 870874 (M) 0402 536620
Club Colours: Red and Black

KENILWORTH RFC
Ground Address: The Jack Davies Memorial Ground, Glasshouse Lane, Kenilworth. CV8 2AJ Tel: 01926 853945
Brief Directions: A452 off A46 into Kenilworth, turn right off roundabout into Birches Lane, Ground about 0.5 mile on right
Club Secretary: W J Whitesmith, 4 Glasshouse Lane, Kenilworth. CV8 2AJ Tel: (H) 01926 859465 (W) 01926 851113
Fixtures Secretary: Dai Davies Tel: (H) 01926 854824
Club Colours: Yellow and blue, dark blue shorts

LEIGHTON BUZZARD
Ground Address: Wright's Meadow, Leighton Buzzard, Stanbridge, Leighton Buzzard, Beds. LU7 9HR Tel: 01525 371322
Brief Directions: North: M1 J13, A507 through Woburn, South: M1 J9, then A5 to Dunstable, A505 to Aylesbury, 2nd turn right, Club 1 mile on right
Club Secretary: J W McCormack, 15 Neptune Gardens, Leighton Buzzard, Beds. LU7 8NW Tel: (H) 01525 378194 (W) 0181 427 4311
Fixtures Secretary: A Hodey, 36 Woodman Close, Leighton Buzzard, Beds. Tel: (H) 01525 379976 (W) 01462 851515
Club Colours: Navy blue & white regular hoops

MANSFIELD RUFC
Ground Address: Eakring Road, Mansfield, Notts. Tel: 01623 649834
Brief Directions: From south: M1 J27 onto A608, left to town centre, right onto A617, left onto Oak Tree Lane, right onto Eakring Road. Club 1 mile on right
Club Secretary: Keith Bingley, Keepers Cottage, Lamins Lane, Bestwood Park, Nottingham. NG6 8UJ Tel: (H) 0115 920 8943 (W) 01623 25821
Fixtures Secretary: Kevin Swithenbank Tel: (H) 01623 793726
Club Colours: Blue and white hoops, navy shorts, blue socks

SCUNTHORPE RUFC
Ground Address: Heslam Park, The Queensway, Scunthorpe, North Lincolnshire Tel: 01724 843013
Brief Directions: From end M181, roundabout 3rd exit, next roundabout 3rd exit, next roundabout 3rd exit Ashby Road, 400 mtrs signposted Heslam Park
Club Secretary: Mr Andrew S Bagshaw, 51 Old Brumby Street, Scunthorpe, North Lincolnshire. DN16 2AJ Tel: (H) 01724 849838 (W & Fax) 01652 652031
Fixtures Secretary: Mr Nigel Cleal Tel: (H) 01724 856801 (W) 01724 402763
Club Colours: Lincoln Greeb shirts with white & black bands,black shorts

Burton Midlands.

MIDLANDS ONE CONTINUED

STOKE - ON - TRENT RUFC
Ground Address: Hartwell Lane, Barlaston, Stoke on Trent, ST15 8TL
Brief Directions: From M1: A38 to A50. Left at lights (A520) at town outskirts. Take Rd. to Barlaston after 3m.Club 1m on left.From M6 leaveJ15(A34 South).to Barlaston club on right
Club Secretary: Stephen Beck, 10 Hillside Close, Fulford, Stoke on Trent St11 9RU Tel: 0121 212 5406
Fixtures Secretary: Eric Hardistry oit85813641
Club Colours: Dark Blue with Light Blue Hoops

SYSTON RUGBY FOOTBALL CLUB
Ground Address: Barkby Road, Queniborough, Leicester Tel: 0116 2601223
Brief Directions: Off A607 Melton Mowbray road (Ring secretary for map)
Club Secretary: Mr J D Newton, 62 Fosse Way, Syston, Leicester. LE7 1NE Tel: 0116 2694647
Fixtures Secretary: Mrs T Sturgess Tel: (H) 0116 2694250
Club Colours: Navy and saxe (light blue) hooped shirts, navy shorts

WESTLEIGH RFC
Ground Address: Lutterwirth Road, Blaby, Leicester Tel: 0116 2771010
Brief Directions: M1/M69 J21, take B4114 to Narborough, left at Foxhunter pub roundabout, right next roundabout, straight over next roundabout, left next roundabout, ground 150 yds on left
Club Secretary: D J Herd, 2 Ridgeway, Littlethorpe, Leicester. LE9 5JJ Tel: (H) 0116 2849318 (W) 0116 2415105
Fixtures Secretary: Mr C Barker, 66 Carisbrooke Rd., Leicester LE2 3PB Tel: (H) 0116 2708676
Club Colours: Black and white hooped jerseys, black shorts

WHITCHURCH RFC
Ground Address: Edgeley Park, Whitchurch. SY13 1EH Tel: 01948 663316
Brief Directions: South of the town, opposite Sir John Talbot's Comprehensive School - access via Edgeley Road
Club Secretary: Graham Kendall, Woodville, Armoury Lane, Preeswood, Whitchurch. SY13 2EN Tel: (H) 01948 666632 (W) 01244 321441
Fixtures Secretary: Neil Speakes Tel: 01948 665573
Club Colours: Red shirts, white shorts

WOLVERHAMPTON RUFC
Ground Address: Rear of Castlecroft Hotel, Castlecroft Road, Wolverhampton. WV3 8NA Tel: 01902 763900
Brief Directions: Wolverhampton ring road, take A454 Compton Rd/Bridgnorth Rd to traffic lights at Mermaid, turn left, 2nd right into Castlecroft Ave, ground straight ahead, behind hotel
Club Secretary: Dr D J Rutherford, Rose Cottage, 3 Woodland Cottages, Penn, Wolverhampton Tel: (H) 01902 335926 (W) 01902 24847
Fixtures Secretary: Mr.R.N.Astbury 1 Hamble Grove, Perton , South Staffs.WV6 7QW Tel: (H) 017902 741495
Club Colours: Black shirts, black shorts, black socks

Kenilworth R.F.C. 1996/97 Midlands 2 runners up.
Standing left to right: T.McCann, N.Glasheen, J.Fitzpatrick, T.Snelson, L.Blasdale, B.Doe, P.Whitehurst, D.F.Symons, P.Curbett, L.Sibley.
Front D.Perkins, G.Owen, B.Beach, J.Marvellt, M.Bennet (Captain), B.Pimlott, C.Sibley, C.Westrope, S.Brain, W.Murgan, T.Duckett.

MIDLANDS TWO

Midlands Two 1997-98 Fixtures*	Ampthill	Bedford Athletic	Bromsgrove	Dudley Kingswinford	Huntingdon	Kettering	Leamington	Longton	Luctonians	Moderns	Newport	Old Laurentians	Paviors	Stafford	Stockwood Park	Sutton Coldfield	Towcestrians	
	1	2	3	4	5	6	7	8	9	10	11	12	13	14	15	16	17	
1 Ampthill	X			10/1		24/1		25/10			14/2	14/3	15/11		27/9		25/4	1
2 Bedford Athletic	6/9	X	15/11		27/9		24/1		14/2	25/10				10/1		14/3		2
3 Bromsgrove	20/12		X	14/3	17/1	25/4				31/1	20/9	11/10					8/11	3
4 Dudley Kingswinford		20/12		X			20/9	31/1	11/10				7/3	25/4	17/1	8/11		4
5 Huntingdon	11/10			24/1	X	14/2		15/11			14/3	25/4	10/1			20/9		5
6 Kettering		17/1		6/9		X	11/10	7/3	8/11				11/4		31/1	20/12		6
7 Leamington	31/1		6/9		7/3		X		11/4	8/11	20/12		27/9				17/1	7
8 Longton		11/10	24/1				14/3	X	25/4	10/1			14/2	8/11	20/9			8
9 Luctonians	7/3		27/9		11/4		15/11		X	6/9			17/1	25/10			31/1	9
10 Moderns	8/11			14/2	20/12	14/3				X	25/4	20/9	24/1				11/10	10
11 Newport		31/1		27/9		25/10		11/4	20/12		X		6/9		7/3	17/1		11
12 Old Laurentians		7/3		25/10			15/11		6/9		10/1	X	27/9		11/4	31/1		12
13 Paviors		8/11	14/2				25/4	17/1	20/9				X	14/3	20/12	11/10		13
14 Stafford	17/1		11/4		31/1	20/9			7/3	11/10	8/11			X			20/12	14
15 Stockwood Park		20/9	10/1		25/10		14/2		14/3	15/11			24/1		X	25/4		15
16 Sutton Coldfield	11/4		25/10		6/9		10/1		24/1	27/9			15/11			X	7/3	16
17 Towcestrians		11/4		15/11		10/1		27/9			24/1	14/2	25/10		6/9		X	17
	1	2	3	4	5	6	7	8	9	10	11	12	13	14	15	16	17	

* Matches listed for 11th April 1998 may be rescheduled for 18th April 1998

AMPTHILL & DISTRICT
Ground Address: Dillingham Park, Woburn Road, Ampthill, Bedford. MK45 2HX Tel: 01525 403303
Brief Directions: Ground on right approaching Ampthill from Woburn
Club Secretary: Harry Cornforth, 43 Alameda Road, Ampthill, Bedford, MK45 2LA. Tel: (H) 01525 753277 (W) 01582 393700.
Fixtures Secretary: Graham Whitehall   Tel: (H) 752150
Club Colours: Maroon and amber

BEDFORD ATHLETIC RUFC
Ground Address: Putnoe Wood, Wentworth Drive, Bedford   Tel: 01234 214929
Club Secretary: B M Eynon, c/o Clubhouse at Ground
Fixtures Secretary: M Bowden, 5 Canbridge Road, Bedford, MK42 0LH Tel: (H) 01234 401718 (M) 0860 899078
Club Colours: Black and white hooped shirts, navy blue shorts, black socks

BROMSGROVE RFC
Ground Address: Finstall Park, Finstall Road, Bromsgrove, Worcs. B60 3DH Tel: 01527 874690
Brief Directions: Situated between Aston Fields and Finstall on Finstall Road (B4184), Bromsgrove
Club Secretary: Jon A Watson, 7 Bowmore Road, Bromsgrove, Worcs. B60 2HH Tel: (H) 01527 875467 (W) 01926 484000
Fixtures Secretary: Ralph M Gordon. Tel: (H & W) 01527 832003
Club Colours: White jerseys with red/black/red hoops, white shorts

DUDLEY KINGSWINFORD RFC
Ground Address: Heathbrook, Swindon Road, Wallheath, Kingswinford, West Midlands Tel: 01384 287006
Brief Directions: Just off A449 at Wallheath, halfway between Kidderminster and Wolverhampton
Club Secretary: David Evans, 156 Common Road, Woybourne, West Midlands. WV5 0LT Tel: (H) 01902 894463
Fixtures Secretary: Bill Jones Tel: (H) 01902 682056 (W) 0121 6067777
Club Colours: Cambridge blue and navy hoops, black shorts

546

MIDLANDS TWO CONTINUED

HUNTINGDON & DISTRICT RUFC
Ground Address: Huntingbroke School, Brampton Road, Huntingdon, Cambs. PE18 6BN
Brief Directions: Heading into Huntingdon from A14 or A1, Hinchingbroke School is adjacent to Hinchingbroke Hospital on the left.
Club Secretary: Jonathon C S Buckingham, The Gables, Chestnut Grove, Great Stukeley, Cambs. PE17 5AT   Tel: (H) 01480 455888
Fixtures Secretary: Tim Tack   Tel: (H) 01954 211140
Club Colours: Green shirts, blue shorts, green and white socks

KETTERING RUFC
Ground Address: Waverley Road (off Pipers Hill Road), Kettering, Northants   Tel: 01536 85588
Brief Directions: A14 J10, turn onto A6 to Kettering, at second traffic lights turn right, first left and first left again into Waverley Road, Ground is at end of road
Club Secretary: Peter May, 107 Pytchley Road, Kettering, Northants. NN15 6HA   Tel: (H) 01536 415804 (W)01536 85588
Fixtures Secretary: Rob Bowley   Tel: (H) 01832 205382   (W) 01536 722181
Club Colours: Blue and white hoops, blue shorts

LEAMINGTON RUFC
Ground Address: Moorefields, Kenilworth Road, Blackdown, Leamington Spa, Warwickshire. CV32 6RG Tel/Fax: 01926 425584
Brief Directions: Join A46 Warwick bypass (from North M6, J2, from South M40, J15). Leave bypass at Leamington/Kenilworth junction. Take A452 towards Leamington 1 mile, ground on left
Club Secretary: John Lyons, 3 Denewood Way, Kenilworth, CV8 2NY.   Tel: 01926 855787
Fixtures Secretary: Tony Grimes   Tel: (H) 01926 813501
Club Colours: Royal blue with single scarlet & gold hoop

LONGTON RFC
Ground Address: Roughcote Lane, Caverswall, Nr Stoke on Trent, Staffs. ST11 9EG   Tel: 01782 394449
Club Secretary: Mr Alan Miller, 5 The Dreys, Trentham, Stoke on Trent. ST4 8DU   Tel: (H) 01782 641845   (W) 01782 315188
Fixtures Secretary: Mr Dave Watt   Tel: (H) 01782 397292   (W) 01782 599052
Club Colours: Black and amber

LUCTONIANS RFC
Ground Address: Mortimer Park, Hereford Road, Kingsland, Leominster, Herefordshire   Tel: 01568 709080 (T/Fax)
Brief Directions: Opposite the Monument Inn, on the A4110 in the village of Kingsland, 4 miles north west of Leominster
Club Secretary: Huw Davies, The Bell House, Kingsland, Leominster, Herefordshire. HR6 9RU   Tel: (H) 01568 708450   (W) 01432 362130
Fixtures Secretary: Simon Green-Price, Luctonians RFC,Mortimer Park, Kingsland, Leominster, Herefordshire.   Tel: 01568 709080 (T/Fax)
Club Colours: Black and white shirts, black shorts.

MODERNS RUGBY FOOTBALL CLUB
Ground Address: Main Road, Wilford Village, Nottingham   Tel: 0115 981 1374
Brief Directions: Nottingham ring road until Clifton Bridge, leave at slip road taking B687 to traffic lights then left into main road Wilford, ground is at end of road
Club Secretary: Steve Strickland, 124 Highfield Road, Nuthall, Nottingham. NG16 1BP   Tel: (H) 0115 913 5944   (W) 01623 421210
Fixtures Secretary: Alistair Clark   Tel: (H) 0115 981 9207
Club Colours: Red and white quartered shorts, red shorts

Kettering R.F.C Season 1996/97
Back: Nick Dalziel, Peter Moss, Mark Wilson, Dave Fraser, Dave Newman, Shaun Parker, Mark Franklin, Barry Beal, Peter May (Club Administrator).
Middle: Doug Bridgeman (Club Coach), Kevin Buckby, Charlie Frost, Tony Oram, Chris Venn, Jason Fluester, Simon Handy.
Front: Russell Spencer, Creighton Wilson, Paul Gibson, Jim Groome, Martin Rogers, Steve Dawkins.
Photograph Courtesy of Northamptonshire Evening Telegraph.

NEWPORT (SALOP) RUFC

Ground Address: The Old Showground, Forton Road, Newport, Shropshire Tel: 01952 810021

Brief Directions: From the bypass, take turning to Newport on the roundabout that also signs to Shrewsbury, the ground is on the right

Club Secretary: Christopher Cann, 3 Chetwynd End, Newport, Shropshire. TF10 7JJ Tel: (H) 01952 810194 (W) 01952 820028

Fixtures Secretary: David Vasilionka Tel: (H) 01952 810755

Club Colours: Maroon and white hoops

OLD LAURENTIAN RFC

Ground Address: Fenley Field, Limetree Avenue, Rugby. CV22 7QT Tel: 01788 810855

Brief Directions: From A45 take A4071 from M6 through Rugby to Bilton Village

Club Secretary: Alan Willis, 45 Frobisher Road, Rugby. CV22 7HS Tel: (H) 01788 813481 (W) 01203 203564

Fixtures Secretary: Ray Roberts Tel: (H) 01788 810276

Club Colours: Maroon, green and gold hoops, green shorts

PAVIORS RFC

Ground Address: The Ron Rossin Ground, Burntstump Hill, Arnold, Nottingham. NG5 9PQ Tel: 0115 9630384

Brief Directions: A614 from Nottingham to Doncaster, 2 miles north of city turn left onto Burntstump Hill, first left pass the school on left to Rugby Club

Club Secretary: David Hudson, The School House, Eakring Road, Kneesall, Newark, Notts. NG22 0AG Tel & Fax: (H)01623 861072

Fixtures Secretary: Len Hines Tel: (H) 0115 9563654 (W) 0115 9492077

Club Colours: Green with red bands

STAFFORD RUFC

Ground Address: County Ground, Castlefields, Newport Road, Stafford. ST16 1BG Tel: 01785 211241

Brief Directions: M6 J13, A449 to Stafford for 1.5 miles, turn on left marked Rowley Park Westway, continue to junction with Newport Rd, turn right, Club 500 yds on left

Club Secretary: Mr P Hill, 39 Rising Brook, Stafford. ST17 0PV Tel: (H) 01785 259583

Fixtures Secretary: Mr B Bowen Tel: (H) 01785 603691

Club Colours: Black and amber hooped jerseys, black shorts

STOCKWOOD PARK RFC

Ground Address: Stockwood Park, London Road, Luton, Beds. LU1 4BH Tel: 01582 728044

Brief Directions: M1 J10, left at end of slip road, left at 1st set of traffic lights into Stockwood Park, Club on right

Club Secretary: N M Powley, 21 Folly Lane, Caddington, Luton, Beds. LU1 4AQ Tel: (H) 01582 420215 (W) 01582 548015

Fixtures Secretary: R A Poulter Tel: (H) 01462 456634 (W) 01582 742366

Club Colours: Red with yellow hoop, navy shorts, red socks

SUTTON COLDFIELD RFC

Ground Address: Walmley Road, Sutton Coldfield Tel: 0121 351 5323

Brief Directions: M6 north J5 take A452 (Brownhills) to Bagot Arms pub, then right onto B4148, ground is 0.5 mile on right from Walmley village shops

Club Secretary: Tim Gallagher, 61 Gorge Road, Sedgley, Dudley. DY3 1LE Tel: (H) 01902 887605 (W) 01902 305961

Fixtures Secretary: Dick Harris Tel: (H) 0121 353 1806

Club Colours: Emerald green shirts, white shorts

TOWCESTRIANS RFC

Ground Address: Towcestrians RFC, Greens Norton Road, Towcester, Northamptonshire. NN12 8AW Tel: 01327 350141

Brief Directions: From A43/A5 junction roundabout take exit for Greens Norton and Blakesley, ground situated approx 1 mile on right

Club Secretary: Richard Bodily, 35 Edgecote, Great Holm, Milton Keynes MK8 9ER Tel: (H) 01908 561279

Fixtures Secretary: Geoff Hanson Tel: (H) 01604 505491

Club Colours: Maroon with white edged amber band, black shorts, maroon socks

MIDLANDS WEST ONE

Midlands West One* 1997-98 Fixtures	Aston Old Edwardians (1)	Bedworth (2)	Keresley (3)	Kings Norton (4)	Leek (5)	Ludlow (6)	Malvern (7)	Newbold-on-Avon (8)	Nuneaton Old Eds (9)	Old Coventrians (10)	Old Halesonians (11)	Old Leamingtonians (12)	Selly Oak (13)	Stratford (14)	Telford (15)	Willenhall (16)	Woodrush (17)
1 Aston Old Edwardians	X		11/10	20/9			8/11		20/12		17/1		31/1	7/3		11/4	
2 Bedworth	6/9	X			11/10	8/11		20/12		17/1		31/1			7/3		11/4
3 Keresley		25/10	X		15/11		17/1		31/1		7/3		11/4	6/9		27/9	
4 Kings Norton		27/9	8/11	X			20/12		17/1		31/1		9/3	11/4		6/9	
5 Leek	27/9			25/10	X	20/12	17/1		31/1		7/3				11/4		6/9
6 Ludlow	25/10		10/1	15/11		X	31/1		7/3		11/4				6/9		27/9
7 Malvern		15/11			10/1	24/1	X		7/3		11/4		6/9	27/9		25/10	
8 Newbold-on-Avon	15/11		24/1	10/1			14/2	X		11/4		6/9			27/9	25/10	
9 Nuneaton Old Eds		10/1			24/1	14/2	14/3		X	6/9			27/9	25/10		15/11	
10 Old Coventrians	10/1		14/2	24/1			14/3		25/4	X			27/9		25/10		15/11
11 Old Halesonians		24/1			14/2	14/3	25/4		20/9		X		25/10	15/11		10/1	
12 Old Leamingtonians	24/1		14/3	14/2			25/4		20/9	11/10		X			15/11		10/1
13 Selly Oak		14/2			14/3	25/4	20/9		11/10		8/11		X	10/1		24/1	
14 Stratford		14/3			25/4	20/9	11/10		8/11		20/12			X	17/1	14/2	
15 Telford	14/2		25/4	14/3			20/9		11/10		8/11		20/12		X	24/1	
16 Willenhall		25/4			20/9	11/10	8/11		20/12		17/1			31/1		X	7/3
17 Woodrush		14/3	20/9	25/4			11/10		8/11		20/12		17/1	31/1			X

* Matches listed for 11th April 1998 may be rescheduled for 18th April 1998

ASTON OLD EDWARDIANS FC
Ground Address: Sunnybank Avenue, Perry Common, Birmingham. B44 0HP   Tel: 0121 373 5746
Brief Directions: Off College Road (A453) approx 1 mile south of Chester Road (A452)
Club Secretary: Mr Glyn Brazell, 167 Gravelly Lane, Erdington, Birmingham. B23 6LT   Tel: (H) 0121 382 1340   (W) 0121 607 0104
Fixtures Secretary: Mr Tony Stafford   Tel: (H) 0121 684 2653   (W) 0121 356 1395
Club Colours: Red, white and green hooped jerseys, white shorts

BEDWORTH RUFC
Ground Address: Rectory Fields, Smarts Road, Bedworth. CV12 0BP   Tel: 01203 312025
Brief Directions: Bedworth turn off A444 bypass, left at the bottom of slip road then left at Cross Keys pub into Smarts Road
Club Secretary: David Hatfield, 17 New Road, Ash Green, Coventry. CV7 9AS   Tel: (H) 01203 365160 (W) 01203 362399
Fixtures Secretary: Alan Sheppard   Tel: (H) 01203 353434
Club Colours: Green jerseys, white shorts

KERESLEY RFC
Ground Address: The John Radford Fields, Burrow Hill Lane, Chorley, Nr Coventry. CV7 8BE   Tel: 01676 540082
Brief Directions: Situated off Bennetts Road North, just past Keresley village
Club Secretary: John Frawley, 37 The Crescent, Keresley, Coventry.   Tel: (H) 01203 337537
Fixtures Secretary: L Casnell   Tel: (H) 01203 337219
Club Colours: Royal blue, scarlet and white jerseys and stockings, navy blue shorts

KINGS NORTON RFC
Ground Address: Ash Lane, Hopwood, Birmingham. B48 7BB   Tel: 0121 445 3340
Brief Directions: Near exit 2 from the M42, take Birmingham road and turn down Ash Lane, ground on right
Club Secretary: G S C Maciver, 11 Chapel Walk, Kings Norton, Birmingham. B30 3LW   Tel: (H) 0121 459 2279
Fixtures Secretary: K Evans   Tel: (H) 0121 501 1750 (W) 0121 444 2864
Club Colours: Red and gold hoops, white shorts, red socks

LEEK RUFC
Ground Address: Birchall Playing Fields, Cheddleton Road, Leek (A520) Tel: 01538 383697
Brief Directions: From M6 south, exit J14, A34 to Stone, A520 to Leek. From M6 north, exit J16, A500 exit Etruria roundabout, A53 to Leek, A520 right turn at lights
Club Secretary: Mike Clewes, 55 Westwood Park Drive, Leek. ST13 8NW Tel: (H) 01538 382922
Fixtures Secretary: Eric Birch Tel: (H) 01538 385963
Club Colours: Blue and white

LUDLOW RFC
Ground Address: The Linney, Ludlow. SY8 1EE Tel: 01584 875762
Brief Directions: Approaching Ludlow town centre from north, turn right just after Honda Equipe, follow narrow road for 0.5 mile, club on right behind football pitch
Club Secretary: Colin Spanner, 58 Henley Orchards, Ludlow. SY8 1TN Tel: (H) 01584 873107 (W) 01584 872333
Fixtures Secretary: Rob Flemons Tel: (H) 01568 780334 (W) 01562 820505 Ext 2545
Club Colours: Red shirts, black shorts

MALVERN
Ground Address: Spring Lane, Malvern Link, Worcester. WR14 1AJ Tel: 01684 573728
Brief Directions: Turn left at Texaco garage on approaching Malvern from Worcester on A449
Club Secretary: Ray Gillard, Lygon Cottage, Beauchamp Lane, Callow End, Worcester. WR2 4UQ Tel: (H & W) 01905 831777
Fixtures Secretary: W Pomeroy Tel: (H) 01684 562279
Club Colours: Maroon, gold and light blue jerseys, navy shorts

NEWBOLD-ON-AVON RFC
Ground Address: The Clubhouse, Parkfield Road, Newbold-on-Avon, Rugby. CV21 1EZ Tel: 01788 565811
Brief Directions: Take A426 Leicester road leaving Rugby, 1st r'bout B4112 signed Newbold/Nuneaton, approx 1 mile Xroads centre of Newbold left into Parkfield Rd, club 200yds on right
Club Secretary: Angenio Marsella, The Clubhouse, Parkfield Road, Newbold-on-Avon, Rugby. CV21 1EZ Tel: (H) 01788 565811
Fixtures Secretary: Ken Perks Tel: (H) 01788 577741 (W) 01788 572572
Club Colours: Red and black quarters

NUNEATON OLD EDWARDIANS RFC
Ground Address: Weddington Road, Nuneaton, Warwickshire Tel: 01203 386778
Brief Directions: Off M6 J3: follow A444 into and through Nuneaton, on left leaving town. Off A5 at A444 junction: A444 into Nuneaton for 2 miles, ground on right
Club Secretary: K McBride, 40 Somerset Drive, Nuneaton. CV10 8DD Tel: (H) 01203 347370
Fixtures Secretary: J F Sparkes Tel: (H) 01203 326029 (W) 01203 216331
Club Colours: Red and white hoops, black shorts

OLD COVENTRIANS RFC
Ground Address: Tile Hill Lane, Coventry. CV4 9DE Tel: 01203 715273
Brief Directions: Junction of A45 and B4101
Club Secretary: R C Richards, 28 Woodland Avenue, Coventry. CV5 6DB Tel: (H) 01203 670080
Fixtures Secretary: I Knowles Tel: (H) 01203 545692
Club Colours: Black, red and gold

Telford Hornets.
The champions of Midlands West 2 who gained promotion for their second year in succession and celebrated their 40th season in style.

MIDLANDS WEST ONE CONTINUED

OLD HALESONIANS RFC
Ground Address: Wassell Grove, Hagley, Stourbridge. DY9 9JD Tel: 01562 883036
Brief Directions: Wassell Grove is signposted on the A456, 4 miles from junction 3 of the M5 motorway
Club Secretary: Mr Simon J Hussey, 67 Carol Crescent, Halesowen, West Midlands. B63 3RR Tel: (H) 0121 550 5725   (W) 0121 322 6091
Fixtures Secretary: Mr Ian Glendinning, 39 Bloomfield Street North, West Midlands
Club Colours: Blue and amber hoops

OLD LEAMINGTONIANS RFC
Ground Address: The Crofts, Bericote Road, Blackdown, Leamington Spa. CV32 6QP Tel: 01926 424991
Brief Directions: From A46 take A452 towards Leamington Spa, after 600 yards take left fork towards Cubbington, ground 0.75 mile on right
Club Secretary: Dennis Fisher, 14 New Street, Cubbington, Leamington Spa. CV32 7LA Tel: (H) 01926 422131
Fixtures Secretary: Martyn Rawbone Tel: (H) 01926 497464 (not after 9pm) (W) 0121 698 4021
Club Colours: Blue and gold hoops, navy shorts

SELLY OAK RFC
Ground Address: Holders Lane, Moseley, Birmingham
Brief Directions: From Edgbaston Cricket Ground turn right into Russell Road, proceed until right turn into Moor Green Lane, Holders Lane is 1st right
Club Secretary: Simon Walster, 52 Wheats Avenue, Harborne, Birmingham B17 0RJ
Fixtures Secretary: Barry Pearce Tel: (H) 0121 358 4442   (W) 0121 360 8500
Club Colours: Blue and white hoops with red spangles

STRATFORD UPON AVON RFC
Ground Address: Pearcecroft Loxley Road, Stratford upon Avon Tel: 01789 297796
Brief Directions: Central Stratford, off Tiddington Road, alongside river on southern bank
Club Secretary: Mr R J Grant, 4 St Gregory's Road, Stratford upon Avon. CV37 6UH Tel: (H) 01789 266722   (W) 0121 502 7116
Fixtures Secretary: Mrs A Prentice Tel: (H) 01789 269892
Club Colours: Black and white hooped jerseys, white shorts

TELFORD HORNETS RFC
Ground Address: Town Park, Hinnshay Road, Dawley, Telford. TF4 3NZ Tel: 01952 505440
Brief Directions: M54, J4 for town centre, 2nd exit at roundabout, 1st exit next roundabout onto A442, continue to Cattlefield, 4th exit at roundabout to Dawley, 4th right, club 0.75 mile on left
Club Secretary: Martin Dolphin, 10 Canonbig Lea, Madeley, Telford. TF7 5RL Tel: (H) 01952 684904 (W) 01952 294424
Fixtures Secretary: Mary Cartwright Tel: (H) 01743 350056 (W) 0802 724134
Club Colours: Black and gold chest band

WILLENHALL RFC
Ground Address: Bognop Road, Essington, Nr Wolverhampton, S Staffordshire Tel: 01922 405694
Brief Directions: M6 M54 off at Junction 1, take road towards Wolverhampton, 1st left past traffic lights into Bognor Road, 1 mile towards Essington, club on right
Club Secretary: Elfyn Pugh, 9 Five-Fields Road, Willenhall, West Midlands. WV12 4NZ Tel: (H) 01902 607747   (W) 0197 885 2141
Fixtures Secretary: B Wood Tel: (H) 01922 516259
Club Colours: Maroon

WOODRUSH RFC
Ground Address: Icknield St, Forhill, Birmingham. B38 0EL Tel: 01564 822878
Brief Directions: M42 J3, take A435 to Birmingham, left to Weatheroak, over crossroads, past Kings Norton Golf Club, left at T junction, 1st right, ground on right
Club Secretary: Robin Caley, 75 Midhurst Road, Kings Norton, Birmingham. B30 3RA Tel: (H) 0121 458 4557 (W) 0121 455 0601
Fixtures Secretary: Steve Bent Tel: (H) 0121 459 3851
Club Colours: Emerald green and white hoops, black shorts

MIDLANDS WEST TWO

Midlands West Two 1997-98 Fixtures	1 Berks & Balsall	2 Birmingham Exiles	3 Coventry Saracens	4 Dixonians	5 Edwardians	6 Erdington	7 Evesham	8 GPT Coventry	9 Manor Park	10 Old Griffinians	11 Old Yardleians	12 Pershore	13 Shrewsbury	14 Southam	15 Stoke Old Boys	16 Tamworth	17 Warley
1 Berks & Balsall	X	11/4			15/11		10/1		24/1		7/3			6/9	27/9	25/10	
2 Birmingham Exiles		X		24/1		14/2		14/3	25/4		20/9			25/10	15/11	10/1	
3 Coventry Saracens	8/11	17/1	X		20/9		11/10			20/12			31/1	7/3	11/4		
4 Dixonians	20/9	8/11	14/2	X		14/3		25/4			11/10			20/12			24/1
5 Edwardians			6/9	7/3	X		11/10		8/11	20/12		17/1	31/1				11/4
6 Erdington	20/12	31/1			27/9	X		8/11			17/1			7/3	14/4	6/9	
7 Evesham			27/9	11/4		25/10	X		20/12	17/1		31/1	7/3				6/9
8 GPT Coventry	17/1	7/3			25/10		15/11	X				31/1		11/4	6/9	27/9	
9 Manor Park			25/10	6/9		15/11		10/1	X	31/1		7/3	11/4				27/9
10 Old Griffinians	14/2		15/11	27/9		10/1		24/1		X		11/4	6/9				25/10
11 Old Yardleians		6/9			10/1		24/1		14/2	14/3	X			27/9	25/10	15/11	
12 Pershore	14/3		10/1	25/10		24/1		14/2			25/4	X	27/9				15/11
13 Shrewsbury	25/4	11/10	24/1	15/11		14/2		14/3			20/9		X				10/1
14 Southam				14/2		14/3		25/4	20/9		11/10	8/11		X	10/1	24/1	
15 Stoke Old Boys				17/1	14/3		25/4		20/9	11/10		8/11	20/12		X	14/2	
16 Tamworth				31/1	25/4		20/9		11/10	8/11		20/12	17/1			X	7/3
17 Warley	11/10	20/12	14/3			25/4		20/9			8/11			17/1	31/1		X

BERKSWELL & BALSALL RFC
Ground Address: Meeting House Lane, Balsall Common, Nr Coventry Tel: 01676 533825
Brief Directions: From Birmingham turn left at roundabout in village, first right is Meeting House Lane, from Warwick turn right
Club Secretary: P C Wigley,23 Coplow Close, Balsall Common, Nr Coventry. CV7 7PQ Tel: (H) 01676 533036 (W) 01926 464306
Fixtures Secretary: S Weeks, 41 Sadler Rd.,Coventry CV6 2JY Tel: 01213 711510 (W) 0121 500 6168
Club Colours: Red and black shirts, black shorts

BIRMINGHAM EXILES
Ground Address: Catherine de Barnes Lane, Bickenhaill, Solihull, West Midlands B92 0DX Tel: 01675 442995
Brief Directions: Take A45 Coventry Road at NEC roundabout and exit at Catherine de Barnes Lane
Club Secretary: D.G. Armstrong, 6 Yenton Court, Chester Road, Erdington,Birmingham B24 OEB Tel: 0121 382 8513
Fixtures Secretary: Julian Griffiths Tel : 0121 449 2471
Club Colours: Blue and Red hoops, navy blue shorts

COVENTRY SARACENS
Ground Address: Bredon Avenue, Binley, Coventry Tel: 01203 453557
Brief Directions: From A46 (eastern bypass) take A428 to Coventry city centre for approx 1 mile, left into Bredon Ave, ground approx 200mtrs on left
Club Secretary: Brian Craner, 71 Westhill Road, Coundon, Coventry. CV 2AD Tel: (H) 01203 590280 (W) 01203 832996
Fixtures Secretary: Roger Hancox Tel: (H) 01203 542252 (W) 01203 687167
Club Colours: Black shirts with red and green 'V'

DIXONIANS RFC
Ground Address: 31A Fountain Road, Edgbaston, Birmingham. B17 8NJ Tel: 0121 434 3313
Brief Directions: From Five Ways Biringham A456 direction Kidderminster in 1.5 miles turn right Fountain Road/Stanmore Road
Club Secretary: Vivian Shingler, Timberhonger House, Timberhonger, Bromsgrove, Worcestershire. B61 9ET Tel: (H) 01527 861686
Fixtures Secretary: David Hall Tel: (H) 0121 378 2839
Club Colours: Maroon, green and black jerseys, black shorts and green stockings

EDWARDIAN FC
Ground Address: The Memorial Ground, Streetsbrook Road, Shirley, Solihull, West Midlands. B90 3PE   Tel: 0121 744 6831
Brief Directions: m42 J4, north up A34 Stratford Rd towards Birmingham for approx 2 miles, right at traffic lights, along road towards Crematorium, club directly opposite at next lights
Club Secretary: Chris Nevin, 21 Wroxall Road, Solihull, West Midlands. B91 1DR   Tel: (H) 0121 704 1870   (W) 0121 625 6621
Fixtures Secretary: Steve Abercrombie   Tel: (H) 0121 430 7508
Club Colours: Old gold, claret and navy

ERDINGTON RFC
Ground Address: Spring Lane Playing Fields, Kingsbury Road, Erdington, Birmingham 23   Tel: 0121 373 7597
Club Secretary: Derek Owen, 129 Bradbury Road, Solihull, West Midlands. B92 8AL   Tel: (H) 0121 706 4699   (W) 01527 64252
Fixtures Secretary: Keith Robinson   Tel: (H) 0121 351 2740
Club Colours: White shirts with single blue hoop

EVESHAM RFC
Ground Address: Albert Road, Evesham, Worcs   Tel: 01386 446469
Brief Directions: A435 south - over railway bridge, Albert Road is 2nd right, go to end, Evesham Sports Club
Club Secretary: J P Hartley, Nightingale Hill, Bishampton, Pershore, Worcs. WR10 2NH   Tel: (H) 01386 462325   (W) 01527 876776
Fixtures Secretary: I Moreton   Tel: (H) 01386 870566 (W) 01386 443311
Club Colours: Navy and maroon hoops

GPT (COVENTRY) RFC
Ground Address: GPT Sports Pavillion, Allard Way, coventry.   Tel: 01203 451157
Brief Directions: From M62 J2 join A46. After approx 2 miles rt at r'about. Left at next r'about. Rt at lights, rt at next lights, then left at 2nd set of lights. Ground 300 yds on the left.
Club Secretary: Richard Beddow, 26 Lilac Avenue, Coundon, Coventry CV6 1DE   Tel: (H) 01203 590 665
Fixtures Secretary: A Machin, 64 Stevenson Road, Kersley, Coventry. CV6 2JW.   Tel: 01203 338236
Club Colours: Red, green & blue hoops, black shorts.

MANOR PARK RFC
Ground Address: Griff & Coton Sports Club, Heath End Road, Stockingford, Nuneaton, Warks   Tel: 01203 386798
Brief Directions: M1-M6 J3, A444 Nuneaton, keep left at George Elliot hospital, into Heath End Road, turn into Griff & Coton Sports Ground on right
Club Secretary: W J Newcombe, 489 Heath End Road, Stockingford, Nuneaton, Warks. CV10 7HD   Tel: (H) 01203 374476
Fixtures Secretary: S Atkinson   Tel: (H) 01203 730606
Club Colours: Red and black hooped jerseys, black shorts and hose

OLD GRIFFINIANS RFC
Ground Address: Billesley Common, Kings Heath, Birmingham
Brief Directions: M42 J3, take A435 into B'ham, at Kings Heath turn right into Wheelers Lane and follow signs for Indoor Tennis Centre (B'ham A-Z page 106, grid ref C2)
Club Secretary: Mr R P Adie, 33 Middlemore Road, Northfield, Birmingham. B31 3UD   Tel: (H) 0121 624 7504   (W) 0121 453 1778
Fixtures Secretary: Mr B Malin   Tel: (H) 0121 475 3788
Club Colours: Black

OLD YARDLEIANS RFC
Ground Address: Tilehouse Lane, Shirley, Solihull, West Midlands   Tel: 0121 744 3380
Brief Directions: From nth, M42 J4 - Stratford Rd-Dog Kennel Ln - Dickens Heath Rd - Tythebarn Ln - Tilehouse Ln, From sth, M42 J3 - Alcetter Ln - Station Rd - Lowbrook Ln - Tilehouse Ln
Club Secretary: Ed Lewins, 50 Cottesbrook Road, Acocks Green, Birmingham. B21 6LE   Tel: (H) 0121 628 2175
Fixtures Secretary: Tom Power, 16 Charfield Road, Birmingham, B30 1QS.   Tel: (H) 0121 459 1622
Club Colours: Old gold, maroon and green

PERSHORE RFC
Ground Address: Piddle Park, Mill Lane, Wyre Piddle, Pershore, Worcestershire   Tel: 01386 554105
Brief Directions: Between Worcester and Evesham on B4538, turn off main road in middle of village on the corner by the War Memorial, club 0.5 mile down the lane
Club Secretary: Sam Cook, 7 Allsebrook Gardens, Badsey, Evesham, Worcs. WR11 5HJ.   Tel: (H) 01386 831494
Fixtures Secretary: Phil Green, 25 Drovers Way, Astwood Farm, Worcester. WR3 8QD.   Tel: (H) 01905 756442   (W) 01684 293482
Club Colours: Black shirts with two scarlet hoops, black shorts

SHREWSBURY RUFC
Ground Address: Sundorne Castle, Uffington, Shrewsbury. SY4 4RR   Tel: 01743 353380
Brief Directions: Follow M54/A5 extension from north or south to Shrewsbury, exit bypass at roundabout, marked B5062 Haughmond Abbey, ground 800 mtrs on left
Club Secretary: Graham S Jackson, 99 Highfields, Shrewsbury. SY2 5PJ   Tel: (H) 01743 361802
Fixtures Secretary: Nigel Hughes   Tel: (H) 01743 360383
Club Colours: Sky blue and navy blue narrow hooped shirts, navy shorts

SOUTHAM
Ground Address: Kineton Road, Southam, nr Rugby, Warwickshire   Tel: 01926 813674
Brief Directions: Take Leamington road (A425) off Southam by-pass(A423). Left at next roundabout, past ind.estate. Ground on right.
Club Secretary: Ivan Harvey, Rookery Nook, Priors Hardwick, nr Rugby, Warwickshire. CV23 8SL   Tel: (H) 01327 260709
Fixtures Secretary: Gary Gilks   Tel: (H) 01926 812370 (W) 0831 885150
Club Colours: Navy blue jerseys, white hoops

MIDLANDS WEST TWO CONTINUED

STOKE OLD BOYS RFC
Ground Address: A G Gale Field, Brookvale Avenue, Binley, Coventry. CV3 2RF   Tel: 01203 453631
Brief Directions: Off Binley Road, closest landmark is Binley Fire Station, 40 yards out of town
Club Secretary: Mr Brian Jose, 33 Hothorpe Close, Binley, Coventry. CV3 2HX   Tel: (H) 01203 457127 (W) 01203 335121 Ext 245
Fixtures Secretary: Mr J Monaghan   Tel: (H) 01203 451198
Club Colours: Maroon and white

TAMWORTH RUFC
Ground Address: Wigginton Lodge, Wigginton Park, Tamworth, Staffs   Tel: 01827 68794
Brief Directions: Head north out of town towards Burton, left turn into Thackeray Drive, right at T junction, 1st left, 1st left to park
Club Secretary: Michael Hobbs, 227 Hockley Road, Tamworth, Staffs   Tel: (H) 01827 288602
Fixtures Secretary: Gordon Penley Tel: (H) 01827 285211
Club Colours: Maroon, black and white

WARLEY RFC
Ground Address: St John's Recreation Grounds, St John's Road, Smethwick, Warley, West Midlands.
Club Secretary: Keiron Ward, 72 Oak Road, Oldbury, Warley. B68 0BD   Tel: (H) 0121 422 4639
Fixtures Secretary: Peter Davies Tel: (H) 0121 420 3141
Club Colours: Red and white hoops, black shorts

STAFFS & WARWICKS

Staffordshire/ Warwickshire One*
1997-98 Fixtures

	1 Alcester	2 Burntwood	3 Claverdon	4 Coventry Welsh	5 Dunlop	6 Earlsdon	7 GEC	8 Handsworth	9 Newcastle	10 Old Wheatleyans	11 Rugby St Andrews	12 Pinley	13 Shipston	14 Sillhillians	15 Spartans	16 Trentham	17 Trinity Guild	
	1	2	3	4	5	6	7	8	9	10	11	12	13	14	15	16	17	
1 Alcester	X		20/9	11/10		8/11		20/12				17/1		31/1		7/3	11/4	1
2 Burntwood	6/9	X			8/11		20/12		11/10	17/1	11/4		31/1		7/3			2
3 Claverdon		27/9	X	8/11		20/12		17/1				31/1		7/3		11/4	6/9	3
4 Coventry Welsh		25/10		X		17/1		31/1	15/11			7/3		11/4		6/9	27/9	4
5 Dunlop	25/10		15/11	10/1	X		31/1		7/3	27/9		11/4			6/9			5
6 Earlsdon		15/11			24/1	X		7/3	10/1			11/4		6/9		27/9	25/10	6
7 GEC	15/11		10/1	24/1		14/2	X		11/4	25/10		6/9		27/9				7
8 Handsworth		10/1			14/2		14/3	X	24/1			6/9		27/9		25/10	15/11	8
9 Newcastle	27/9		25/10	20/12		17/1			X	31/1	6/9	7/3		11/4				9
10 Old Wheatleyans	10/1	24/1	14/2			14/3		25/4		X	15/11	27/9		25/10				10
11 Rugby St Andrews	14/3		25/4	20/9		11/10		8/11			X	20/12		17/1		31/1		11
12 Pinley		24/1			14/3		25/4		14/2	20/9		X		25/10	15/11	10/1		12
13 Shipston	24/1		14/2	14/3		25/4		20/9		10/1	11/10		X		15/11			13
14 Sillhillians		14/2			25/4		20/9		14/3	11/10		8/11		X		10/1	24/1	14
15 Spartans	14/2		14/3	25/4		20/9		11/10			24/1	8/11		20/12	X			15
16 Trentham		14/3			20/9		11/10		25/4	8/11		20/12		17/1		X	14/2	16
17 Trinity Guild		25/4		11/10		8/11			20/9	20/12	7/3		17/1		31/1		X	17
	1	2	3	4	5	6	7	8	9	10	11	12	13	14	15	16	17	

* Matches listed for 11th April 1998 may be rescheduled for 18th April 1998

ALCESTER RFC
Ground Address: Birmingham Road, King's Coughton, Alcester, Warwickshire. B49 5QF Tel: 01789 764061
Brief Directions: The Ground is situated on the West side of the A435 between Studley and Alcester at Kings Coughton.
Club Secretary: Andu Hulburd, 35 Foregate Street, Astwood Bank, Redditch, Worcs. B96 6BW Tel: (H) 01527 892999 (W) 01789 761212
Fixtures Secretary: Alan Brookes Tel: (H) 01789 764076 (W) 01789 761210
Club Colours: Red and black

BURNTWOOD RUFC
Ground Address: Church Street, Chasetown, Nr Walsall. WS7 8QL Tel: 01543 676651
Brief Directions: From A5 follow directions to Chasetown Clubhouse at end of Church St. Club is next to CHasetown Football Club.
Club Secretary: Kevin Broadhead, 12 School Walk, Chaseterrace, Walsall. WS7 8NQ Tel: (H) 01543 279038
Fixtures Secretary: Alan Wood, 25 Boulton Close, Burntwood, Nr Walsall. WS7 Tel: (H) 01543 677513 (W) 01782 744111
Club Colours: Red, green and white hoops , black shorts.

CLAVERDON RFC
Ground Address: Ossetts Hole Lane, Yarningale Common, Claverdon, Warwicks. CV35 8HN Tel: 01926 843133
Brief Directions: From Henley in Arden to Warwick road, turn left before Claverdon village
Club Secretary: Basil Sayer, The White House, 45 Station Road, Balsall Common, Coventry. CV7 7FN Tel: (H) 01676 532164 (W) 01933 224444
Fixtures Secretary: Lindsey Shaw Tel: (H) 01564 795474 (W) 01789 41411 Ext 4595
Club Colours: Red and white

COVENTRY WELSH RFC
Ground Address: Burbages Lane, Longford, Coventry. CV6 6AY Tel: 01203 360303
Brief Directions: M6 J3, take bypass road A444 to next roundabout and the right hand turn at roundabout is Burbages Lane
Club Secretary: Jean Williams, 173 Goodyers End Lane, Bedworth, Nuneaton. CV12 0HH Tel: (H) 01203 364596
Fixtures Secretary: Gary Greenway Tel: (H) 01203 315403
Club Colours: Red

DUNLOP RFC
Ground Address: Dunlop Sports and Social Club, Burnaby Road, Radford, Coventry Tel: 01203 662394
Brief Directions: M6 J3, take 4th exit to Coventry, along bypass, over roundabout, right at 2nd roundabout, left at 3rd roundabout, turn right into Burnaby Rd, ground 0.5 mile on right
Club Secretary: Mrs Kim Challis, 24 Birchfield Road, Counden, Coventry. CV6 2BD Tel: (H) 01203 337152 (W) 01203 366416
Fixtures Secretary: Mr John Ormsby Tel: (H) 01203 410313
Club Colours: Black and amber hoops, black shorts

EARLSDON RFC
Ground Address: Mitchell Avenue, Canley, Coventry. CV4 8DY Tel: 01203 464467
Brief Directions: Along A45 to Police and Fire Stations, follow signs to Canley & Warwick University
Club Secretary: J Ward, 18 Wainbody Avenue, Green Lane, Coventry. CV3 6DB Tel: (H) 01203 419729
Fixtures Secretary: R Price, 25 Montrose Drive, Nuneaton. CV10 7LX Tel: (H) 01203 346190
Club Colours: Red and white

GEC ST LEONARDS RUFC
Ground Address: GEC Protection and Control, GEC St Leonards Social Club, St Leonards Avenue, Stafford, Staffs Tel: 01785 258070
Club Secretary: J A Waibley, 26 Hall Close, Stafford, Staffs. ST17 4JJ Tel: (H & W) 01785 253201
Fixtures Secretary: Mr I McLeod Tel: (H) 01889 579365 (W) 0860 694548
Club Colours: Black with a gold hoop

HANDSWORTH RUFC
Ground Address: 450 Birmingham Road, Walsall Tel: 0121 357 6427
Brief Directions: M6 J7, take A34 towards Walsall, ground at bottom of hill at end of dual carriageway on left
Club Secretary: Alec Hardy, 6 Freemount Square, Great Barr, Birmingham. B43 5QT Tel: (H) 0121 358 6612 (W) 01902 422399
Fixtures Secretary: D Mew Tel: (H) 0121 354 4518
Club Colours: Red and white hooped shirts, black shorts, red socks

NEWCASTLE (STAFFS) RUFC
Ground Address: Lilleshall Road, Claxton, Newcastle-under-Lyme, Staffordshire. ST5 3BX Tel: 01782 617042
Brief Directions: M6 J13 to Newcastle, turn left at 1st roundabout, over next roundabout, right at next roundabout, 3rd road on left
Club Secretary: Robin Websdale, 22 Cardington Close, Seabridge, Newcastle-under-Lyme. ST5 3LJ Tel: (H) 01782 633784 (W) 01782 839380
Fixtures Secretary: David Westrup Tel: (H) 01270 766538 (W & Fax) 01352 712536
Club Colours: Maroon and white

OLD WHEATLEYANS RFC
Ground Address: Norman Place Road, Coundon, Coventry Tel: 01203 334888
Brief Directions: At J9 on Coventry ring road, take A4170 (Radford Rd), after 1.5 miles turn left into Norman Place Rd, entrance is at the far end of road, on left
Club Secretary: Andrew Hibberd, 59 Frilsham Way, Allesley Park, Coventry. CV5 9LJ Tel: (H) 01203 711955 (W) 01203 563166
Fixtures Secretary: D Margetts Tel: (H) 01203 672952
Club Colours: Blue, maroon and gold

PINLEY RFC
Ground Address: The Croft, Wyken Croft, Coventry Tel: 01203 602059
Club Secretary: M D Brown,11 Minton Road,Minton Gardens,Coventry,CV2 2XH Tel: (H) 01203 363353 (W) 01203 003991
Fixtures Secretary: B Lester Tel: (H) 01203 443605
Club Colours: Red and black quarters

RUGBY ST ANDREWS RFC
Ground Address: Hillmorton Grounds, Ashlawn Road, Rugby. Tel: 01788 542786
Brief Directions: Ring Fixture Secretary
Club Secretary: Patricia Lee, 29 Faraday Road, Rugby CV22 5ND Tel: (H) 01788 570 707 (W) 01788 533708
Fixtures Secretary: John Hunt, 14 Northcott Road, Rugby. Tel: (H) 01788 574496
Club Colours: Sky Blue & navy hoops. Navy shorts.

SHIPSTON ON STOUR RFC
Ground Address: Mayo Road, Shipston on Stour, Warks Tel: 01608 662107
Brief Directions: From north, enter Shipston on A3400, turn right opposite hospital, 1st left then 1st right. From south enter on A3400, left opposite hospital, 1st left then 1st right
Club Secretary: Richard H Slatter, Woodhills Farm, Todenham, Moreton in Marsh, Gloucestershire. GL56 9PH Tel: (H) 01608 650453 (W) 01608 650453
Fixtures Secretary: Rob Hawkins Tel: (H) 01608 682216
Club Colours: Black shirts, shorts and socks

SILHILLIANS RUFC
Ground Address: Warwick Road, Copt Heath, Knowle, Solihull, West Midlands Tel: 01564 777680
Brief Directions: J5 M42, then towards Knowle, ground 50yds on left hand side
Club Secretary: G R Loader, 12 Stubbs Road, Penn, Wolverhampton, West Midlands. WV3 7DF Tel: (H) 01902 338474 (W) 01902 353522
Fixtures Secretary: M Walley Tel: (H) 0121 705 9182 (W) 01926 832754
Club Colours: Maroon and blue shirts, blue shorts

SPARTANS RUFC
Ground Address: Coppice Lane, Middleton, Nr Tamworth, Staffordshire. B78 2BS Tel: 0121 308 5857
Brief Directions: Club is situated by the junction of A446 and Coppice Lane, 0.25 mile on the Colehill side of the A453 at Bassetts Pole
Club Secretary: Miss Sarah McGrory, 33 Alexandra Mews, Victoria Road, Tamworth, Staffordshire. B79 7HT Tel: (H) 01827 63132 (W) 0121 322 6060
Fixtures Secretary: Paul Southam Tel: (H) 0121 353 4110
Club Colours: Black shirts and black shorts

TRENTHAM RUFC
Ground Address: Oaktree Road, Trentham, Stoke-on-Trent, Staffordshire Tel: 01782 642320
Brief Directions: M6 J15, A500 towards Stoke-on-Trent, A34 south signs to Trentham, at Trentham Gardens roundabout left onto A5035, Oakhill Road 0.5 mile on right
Club Secretary: Mr M S M Riley, 92 Eccleshall Road, Stafford, Staffordshire. ST16 1HS Tel: (H) 01785 811766 (W) 01925 824511
Fixtures Secretary: Mr C Bisson Tel: (H) 01782 659320
Club Colours: Green and white hoops, black shorts

TRINITY GUILD RFC
Ground Address: Rowley Road, Baginton, Coventry Tel: 01203 305928
Brief Directions: From north, follow A45 west of Coventry, follow airport signs. From south, follow A45 from M45. From west, follow A46 to A45
Club Secretary: D H Williams, 122 Grange Road, Longford, Coventry. CV6 6DA Tel: (H) 01203 360833 (W) 01203 666655 Ext 2420
Fixtures Secretary: K Lightowler Tel: (H) 01203 598932
Club Colours: Maroon, old gold and dark navy stripes

Staffordshire One 1997-98 Fixtures	Bloxwich 1	Cannock 2	Linley 3	Rubery Owen 4	Rugeley 5	Uttoxeter 6	Wednesbury 7	Wheaton Aston 8	
1 Bloxwich	X	20/9	7/3	8/11	17/1	20/1	31/1	11/10	1
2 Cannock	10/1	X	20/12	7/3	11/10	27/1	8/11	31/1	2
3 Linley	15/11	14/3	X	31/1	20/9	8/11	11/10	17/1	3
4 Rubery Owen	14/2	15/11	25/10	X	14/3	24/1	17/1	20/9	4
5 Rugeley	27/9	24/1	10/1	20/12	X	25/1	7/3	8/11	5
6 Uttoxeter	14/3	17/1	14/2	11/10	31/1	X	20/9	15/11	6
7 Wednesbury	25/10	14/2	24/1	27/9	15/11	10/1	X	14/3	7
8 Wheaton Aston	24/1	25/10	27/9	10/1	14/2	7/3	20/12	X	8
	1	2	3	4	5	6	7	8	

BLOXWICH RFC
Ground Address: Bloxwich Sports Club, Stafford Road, Bloxwich. WS3 3NJ   Tel: 01922 405891
Brief Directions: 0.25 mile outside Bloxwich town on A34 to Cannock, entrance between houses on left marked by black and white posts, 100yds past traffic lights
Club Secretary: Mr Anthony Allen, 16 Sorrel Close, Featherstone, Staffs. WV10 7TX   Tel: (H) 01902 739835   (W) 01902 864726
Fixtures Secretary: Mr Anthony Allen   Tel: (H) 01902 739835   (W) 01902 864726
Club Colours: Green with black and white chest hoops and black shorts

CANNOCK RUFC
Ground Address: The Morgan Ground, Stafford Road, Huntingdon, Staffordshire. WS12 4NU   Tel: 01543 467906
Club Secretary: Pauline Athersmith, 355 Cemetry Road, Cannock. WS11 2AY   Tel: (H) 01543 574711
Fixtures Secretary: Phil Pearson   Tel: (H) 01889 575 167   (W) 0121 544 2387
Club Colours: Blue and gold hoops

LINLEY & KIDSGROVE RUFC
Ground Address: Bathpool Park, West Morland Avenue, Kidsgrove, Stoke-on-Trent
Brief Directions: M6 J16, A500 towards Stoke-on-Trent, 2nd junction A34 Kidsgrove, follow signs for the Ski Centre
Club Secretary: Jason Swingewood, 48 Appledore Grove, Packmoor, Stoke-on-Trent. ST6 6XH   Tel: (H) 01782 816213   (W) 0151 934 6004
Fixtures Secretary: Mr Alan Hodgekinson   Tel: (H) 01782 838201
Club Colours: Green and gold quarters

RUBERY OWEN
Ground Address: High H ntre, High Hill, Essington, West Midlands. 1 2DW   Tel: 01922 492795
Brief Directions: M6 J11, 2 to Willenhall, 3 miles traffic lights turn right into er Sneyd Rd running into High Hill, club 0.5 mile on
Club Secretary: Michael andler, 32 Coppice Rd, Walsall Wood, Walsall. WS L   Tel: (H) 01543 370678   (W) 01384 40099
Fixtures Secretary: Graha nith   Tel: (H) 01922 400222
Club Colours: Red

RUGELEY RUFC
Ground Address: Hagley Youth Centre
Brief Directions: Turn off into A460 then take first right and ground entrance i the right.
Club Secretary: Mr D En Crabtree Way, Rugeley, Staffs. WS15 2PA   Tel: (H 89 579728
Fixtures Secretary: Mr.P. aman, 79 Brereton Rd.,Rugeley, Staffs. WS15   Tel: 0958 461146
Club Colours: Amber and k

UTTOXETER RFC
Ground Address: Oldfield orts Centre, Springfield Road, Uttoxeter, Staffs. T 889 564347
Brief Directions: From th tre of Uttoxeter, take Stone Road, after 200 yard at into Springfield Road. After 50 yards turn right.
Club Secretary: Simon B Stoneleigh Cottage, Gt. Cubley, Ashbourne, Derby DE6 2EY   Tel: (H) 01335 330306
Fixtures Secretary: Les H ries, 14 Eaton Road, Rocester, Stafffs.   Tel: (H 89 590604   Tel: (W) 01889 593680
Club Colours: Blue with e band

WEDNESBURY RUFC
Ground Address: Hydes Road Playing Fields, Hydes Road, Wednesbury Tel: 0121 502 2477
Brief Directions: M6 J9, to Wednesbury, straight on at traffic lights, take 5th left after that, playing fields 0.75 mile on right
Club Secretary: Peter Hughes , 28 Alder Road, Wednesbury, West Midlands. WS10 9PX Tel: (H) 0121 556 5005   (W) 01922 721898
Fixtures Secretary: Robert F Smith Tel: (H) 0121 556 6748   (W) 01902 757968
Club Colours: Black and white hoops, black shorts

WHEATON ASTON RUFC
Ground Address: Monckton Recreation Centre, Pinfold Lane, Penkridge, Staffordshire Tel: 01785 712264
Brief Directions: M6 J12, A5 towards Telford, at 1st island take A449 to Stafford, when you enter Penkridge take 1st left past Ford dealership, club 800 yds on left
Club Secretary: Mr Barry Dalby, 3 Kiddemore Green Road, Brewood, Staffs. St19 9BQ Tel: (H & W) 01902 850926
Fixtures Secretary: Mr David Tipton Tel: (H & W) 01902 850386
Club Colours: Black shirts with gold collar and cuffs, black shorts

WARWICKSHIRE

Warwickshire 1997-98 Fixtures	Atherstone	Coventrians	Coventry Tech	Ford (Leam)	Harbury	Old Warwickians	Rugby Welsh	Shuttery	Standard	Warwick	
	1	2	3	4	5	6	7	8	9	10	
1 Atherstone	X	11/10	10/1	20/9	24/1	14/2	25/10	14/3	15/11	20/12	1
2 Coventrians	31/1	X	18/10	7/3	8/11	25/4	6/9	17/1	27/9	11/4	2
3 Coventry Tech	6/9	14/2	X	24/1	11/10	25/10	14/3	15/11	25/4	17/1	3
4 Ford (Leam)	17/1	25/10	27/9	X	14/2	14/3	15/11	25/4	6/9	31/1	4
5 Harbury	27/9	14/3	31/1	18/10	X	15/11	25/4	6/9	17/1	7/3	5
6 Old Warwickians	18/10	20/12	7/3	8/11	11/4	X	17/1	27/9	31/1	6/9	6
7 Rugby Welsh	7/3	10/1	8/11	11/4	20/12	20/9	X	31/1	18/10	27/9	7
8 Shuttery	8/11	20/9	11/4	20/12	10/1	24/1	11/10	X	7/3	18/10	8
9 Standard	11/4	24/1	20/12	10/1	20/9	11/10	14/2	25/10	X	8/11	9
10 Warwick	25/4	15/11	20/9	11/10	25/10	10/1	24/1	14/2	14/3	X	10
	1	2	3	4	5	6	7	8	9	10	

ATHERSTONE RFC
Ground Address: Ratcliffe Road, Atherstone, Warks Tel: 01827 714934
Brief Directions: Drive into town centre, turn at Midland Bank into Ratcliffe Road, clubhouse approx 0.75 mile down on left
Club Secretary: David Boal, Thurmaston House, 74 South Street, Atherstone, Warks. CV9 1DZ Tel: (H) 01827 713145
Fixtures Secretary: Keith Berry Tel: (H) 01827 893138
Club Colours: Black

COVENTRIANS RFC
Ground Address: Black Pad, off Yelverton Road, Radford, Coventry. CV6 4NW Tel: 01203 682885
Brief Directions: M6 J3 onto A444 to Coventry, right at 2nd roundabout to Holbrook, at next 2nd roundabout Yelverton Road is 50yds on right
Club Secretary: J S Daniell, 116 Mill Farm Park, Marston Jabbett, Nuneaton, Warks. CV12 9SF Tel: (H) 01203 373470
Fixtures Secretary: J S Daniell Tel: (H) 01203 373470
Club Colours: Royal blue and white quarters

COVENTRY TECHNICAL R.F.C.
Ground Address: Mitchell Avenue, Canley, Coventry Tel: 01203 471733
Brief Directions: The club is only 5 mins from A45 Flethhampstead Highway, northbound take right turn into Charter Ave, southbound left at island by Canley fire and police station
Club Secretary: Stuart Kennedy, 48 Nutbrook Avenue, Tile Hill, Coventry. Tel: 01203 461063
Fixtures Secretary: Neil Franklin Tel: (H) 01203 335560
Club Colours: Green, gold and brown

FORD LEAMINGTON RFC
Ground Address: Newbold Comyn, Newbold Terrace, Leamington Spa, Warwickshire
Club Secretary: Hazel Tice, 35 Quarry Street, Leamington Spa, Warwickshire. W32 6AS Tel: (H) 01926 429999
Fixtures Secretary: Erich Newton Tel: (H) 01926 770624
Club Colours: Blue, black and white hoops, black shorts

HARBURY RFC
Ground Address: Waterloo Fields, Middle Road, Harbury, Warwickshire Tel: 01926 613462
Brief Directions: 0.5 mile off Fosse Way. From Leamington take left off Fosse Way (signposted Harbury), club on right before entering village
Club Secretary: Graham Lewis, Rose Cottage, Bridge Lane, Ladbroke, Warwickshire Tel: (H) 01926 815196
Fixtures Secretary: Jerry Birbeck Tel: (H) 01926 424053
Club Colours: Cherry and white hoops

OLD WARWICKIAN RFC
Ground Address: Sports Ground, Hampton Road, Warwick Tel: 01926 436235
Brief Directions: Follow road out of Warwick towards Henley in Arden pass the Warwick Horse Race Stadium and ground is on the right after bypass
Club Secretary: Patrick Wing, 57 Broadeers Road, Knowle, Solihull, West Midlands. B93 9OG Tel: (H) 01564 779947 (W) 0121 6267173
Fixtures Secretary: Andrew Marshall Tel: (H) 01926 651750
Club Colours: Maroon and white hoops

RUGBY WELSH RFC
Ground Address: Clubhouse: Bakehouse Lane, Rugby. CV21 2DB. Ground: (Council pitch remote from Clubhouse) Alwyn Road Recreation Ground, Bilton, Rugby. Tel: 01788 565605
Brief Directions: From Rugby town centre take A4071 at Bilton village turn left into Alwyn Road, Recreation Ground is on left after 0.5 mile
Club Secretary: Adrian Johnston, 46 Warren Road, Rugby. CV22 5LG Tel: (H) 01788 560804
Fixtures Secretary: John Rowland Tel: (H) 01788 574421 (W) 01788 563467
Club Colours: Red shirts, white shorts

SHOTTERY RFC
Ground Address: The Recreation Ground, SWans Nest Lane, Stratford-on-Avon
Brief Directions: Turn left by the SWans Nest hotel, bear right into car park, follow road to far end of recreation ground.
Club Secretary: Neil Povey, 11 Beechcroft, High Street, Henley in Arden, Solihull, West Midlands. B95 5AQ Tel: (H) 01564 793587 (W) 01386 830354
Fixtures Secretary: Shaun Brook, 35 Chepstow Close, Stratford-on-Avon, Warwickshire. Tel: 01789 415849
Club Colours: St. Andrew's blue

STANDARD RFC
Ground Address: Tanners Lane, Tile Hill, Coventry
Club Secretary: Chris Hughes, 108 Earlsdon Avenue South, Coventry. CV5 8DN Tel: (H) 01203 679552
Fixtures Secretary: Henry Kantor Tel: (H) 01203 463855 (W) 01926 643067
Club Colours: Dark blue, sky blue and white hoops

WARWICK RFC
Ground Address: Hampton Road, Warwick. CV34 6RD Tel: 01926 410972
Brief Directions: Exit M40, follow signs for Warwick, take left into Shakespeare Ave, club opposite junction, on Hampton Road
Club Secretary: Peter O Rourke, 96 Clinton Lane, Kenilworth, Warks. CV8 1AX Tel: (H) 01926 858239 (W) 0831 510696
Fixtures Secretary: John Eley Tel: (H) 01926 403144
Club Colours: Black and purple hoops, black shorts, black and purple hooped socks

Do you know a rugby enthusiast with a birthday coming up?

This directory would make a perfect present.

So why not buy a copy from your club or from W H Smith.

NORTH MIDLANDS ONE

North Midlands One* 1997-98 Fixtures	Birmingham Civil S. (1)	Bishops Castle (2)	Bridgnorth (3)	Bromyard (4)	Droitwich (5)	Five Ways Old Ed (6)	Kidderminster (7)	Kynoch (8)	Ledbury (9)	Old Centrals (10)	Old Saltleians (11)	Oswestry (12)	Redditch (13)	Ross-on-Wye (14)	Tenbury (15)	Upton-on-Severn (16)	Veseyans (17)	
1 Birmingham Civil Ser	X	6/9	11/10		8/11		20/12			17/1			31/1		7/3		11/4	1
2 Bishops Castle		X		11/10	8/11		20/12	20/9		17/1	11/4		31/1		7/3			2
3 Bridgnorth		27/9	X	20/12		17/1		25/10	31/1					7/3		11/4	6/9	3
4 Bromyard	25/10		15/11	X		17/1		31/1			7/3	27/9		11/4		6/9		4
5 Droitwich		25/10		10/1	X		31/1		15/11	7/3				11/4		6/9	27/9	5
6 Five Ways Old Ed	15/11		10/1	24/1		X	7/3				11/4	25/10		6/9		27/9		6
7 Kidderminster		15/11		24/1		14/2	X		10/1		11/4			6/9	27/9		25/10	7
8 Kynoch	10/1		24/1			14/2	14/3	X			6/9	15/11		27/9		25/10		8
9 Ledbury	27/9			8/11		20/12	17/1		X		31/1	6/9		7/3			11/4	9
10 Old Centrals		10/1		14/2		14/3	25/4	24/1		X		27/9		25/10			15/11	10
11 Old Saltleians	24/1			14/2		14/3	25/4		20/9		X		10/1	25/10		15/11		11
12 Oswestry	25/4		20/9	11/10	8/11					20/12		X	17/1	31/1		7/3		12
13 Redditch		24/1		14/3			25/4	20/9	14/2		11/10		X		15/11		10/1	13
14 Ross-on-Wye	14/2			14/3			25/4		20/9		11/10	24/1	8/11	X		10/1		14
15 Tenbury		14/2		25/4			20/9	11/10	14/3		8/11		20/12		X		24/1	15
16 Upton-on-Severn	14/3			25/4			20/9		11/10		8/11		14/2	20/12	17/1	X		16
17 Veseyans		14/3		20/9			11/10		8/11	25/4		20/12	17/1		31/1		X	17
	1	2	3	4	5	6	7	8	9	10	11	12	13	14	15	16	17	

* Matches listed for 11th April 1998 may be rescheduled for 18th April 1998

BIRMINGHAM CITY OFFICIALS RFC
Ground Address: Land Rover Sports & Social Club, Bilsmore Green, off Rowood Drive, Solihull, West Midlands. B92 9LN
Brief Directions: A45 Coventry Road, B425 Hobs Moat Road, pass Rover factory, further 0.5 mile to Social club
Club Secretary: David George Armstrong, 6 Yenton Court, Chester Road, Erdington, Birmingham. B24 0EB Tel: (H) 0121 382 2513   (W) 0121 200 1992
Fixtures Secretary: C Brecknell   Tel: (H) 0121 608 0781   (W) 0121 359 4911 (after 10pm)
Club Colours: Navy blue jersey with maroon and old gold chest band

BISHOPS CASTLE & ONNY VALLEY RFC
Ground Address: Love Lane, Bishops Castle   Tel: 01588 638816
Brief Directions: Changing rooms at Commjunity College in Bishop's Castle
Club Secretary: J A Smith, c/o Dr. N. Howell, Lower Gardens, Lydbury, North Shropshire, SY7 8AS.
Fixtures Secretary: R Jeavons-Fellows   Tel: (H) 01743 884088
Club Colours: Green and red stripes

BRIDGNORTH RFC
Ground Address: The Bull, Bridge Street, Bridgnorth, Shropshire. WV15 5AA Tel: 01746 762796
Brief Directions: The clubhouse is adjacent to the bridge over the river in Lowtown
Club Secretary: Pete Shimmin, 7 Buck Cottage, Sheinton, Cressage, Shropshire. SY5 6DJ Tel: (H) 01952 510604   (W) 01746 766488
Fixtures Secretary: Alun Stoll Tel: (H & W) 01902 332025
Club Colours: Black shirts, black shorts

BROMYARD RFC
Ground Address: The Clive Richards Sports Ground, Instone, Tenbury Road, Bromyard Tel: 01885 483933
Brief Directions: From Bromyard, take the B4214 towards Tenbury Wells, the ground is on the right hand side, approx 0.5 mile from the town
Club Secretary: Mick Warren, The Chestnuts, Munderfield, Bromyard, Hfds. HR7 4JT Tel: (H) 01885 490684   (W) 01885 490480
Fixtures Secretary: Mrs S Mann   Tel: (H) 01885 482332
Club Colours: Green and gold

DROITWICH RUFC
Ground Address: Hanbury Road, Droitwich, Worcs
Tel: 01905 770384
Brief Directions: M5 J5, A38 to Worcester, approx 2
miles turn left at traffic lights, left at next lights, ground
0.25 mile on left (B4090)
Club Secretary: Steve Bradbury, 61 Tagwell Road,
Droitwich, Worcs. WR9 7AQ   Tel: (H) 01905 772001
Fixtures Secretary: Rik Latham, 60 Showell Grove,
Droitwich, Worcs. Tel: (H) 01905 794638
Club Colours: Black and gold

FIVE WAYS OLD EDWARDIANS FC
Ground Address: Masshouse, Ash Lane, Hopwood,
Birmingham   Tel: 0121 445 4909
Brief Directions: M42 J2, signpost to Birmingham
reach roundabout to Birmingham, 100yds before garage
on right turn right into Ash Lane, club on right at end of
lane
Club Secretary: Richard Lisseter, 138 Chatsworth
Road, Halesowen, West Midlands. B62 8TH   Tel: (H)
0121 559 6549   (W) 0121 550 1724
Fixtures Secretary: Paul Hipkiss   Tel: (H) 0121 550
4280
Club Colours: Navy blue and gold

KIDDERMINSTER CAROLIANS RFC
Ground Address: Marlpool Lane, Kidderminster,
Worcs. DY11 4HP   Tel: 01562 740043
Brief Directions: Follow signs from Kidderminster
ringroad to Bridgnorth, at end Proud Cross Ringway is
Jackson pub, Marlpool Lane is to one side, ground 400m
from pub
Club Secretary: Mr Keith Stooksbury, 122 Crestwood
Avenue, Kidderminster, Worcs. DY11 6JS   Tel: (H)
01562 753916
Fixtures Secretary: Mr Tim Carder   Tel: (H) 01562
747910   (W) 01902 774217
Club Colours: Black with gold hoops

KYNOCH RFC
Ground Address: Holford Drive, Perry Barr,
Birmingham. B42 2TU   Tel: 0121 356 4369
Brief Directions: From Birmingham on right (after
UCE, Perry Barr) off Aldridge Road A453
Club Secretary: Mr.Paul L. Sturch, 132 Brantley Rd.,
Witton, Birmingham B67 DP   Tel: 0121 6862648
Fixtures Secretary: Ray Jones   Tel: (H) 0121 382 0310
Club Colours: Black and white hoops

LEDBURY RFC
Ground Address: Ross Road Playing Field, Ross Road,
Ledbury, Herefordshire, HR8 2LP   Tel: 01531 633926
Brief Directions: M50 Junction 2 follow signs to
Ledbury Left at lst Island 2nd L. at next, ground 200yds
on right
Club Secretary: Dominic Shaw, 1 Sunshine Close,
Ledbury, Herefordshire, HR8 2DZ Tel: (H) 01531
633674 (W) 01531 633181
Fixtures Secretary: Mike Nolan, Norwich House,
Oatleys Road, Ledbury. HR8 2BP   Tel: (H) 01531
635243 (W) 0121 3130813
Club Colours: Black and white hoops

OLD CENTRALS RFC
Ground Address: Bournvale, Hardwicke Road,
Aldridge, Staffs   Tel: 0121 353 2851
Brief Directions: Take Chester Road towards Brownhill,
turn left at Harwicke Arms, then right after 0.5 mile into
Bournvale
Club Secretary: D E Smith, 14 St Andrews, Allington,
Tamworth. B77 4RA   Tel: (H) 01827 50018   (W) 0121
384 7000
Fixtures Secretary: R Stain   Tel: (H) 0121 778 6804
Club Colours: Maroon, green and gold jerseys, navy
blue shorts

OLD SALTLEIANS RFC
Ground Address: Watton Lane, Water Orton, Coleshill,
Birmingham. B46 1PJ   Tel: 0121 748 3380
Brief Directions: Junction of Gilson Road/Watton Lane,
off A446, near Coleshill
Club Secretary: Matthew Lukeman, 20 Church Way,
Longdon, Nr Rugeley, Staffs. WS15 4PG   Tel: (H)
01543 490376   (W) 0121 323 2889
Fixtures Secretary: Kelvin Roberts   Tel: (H) 0121 351
1473
Club Colours: Red and yellow hooped shirts, navy
shorts, red, yellow and blue socks

OSWESTRY RFC
Ground Address: Park Hall, Oswestry   Tel: 01691
652949
Club Secretary: T Mark Jones, Park Issa, Whittington,
Oswestry. SY11 4NF   Tel: (H) 01691 657547   (W &
Fx) 01691 652120
Fixtures Secretary: John Wynn-Higgins   Tel: (H)
01939 235235
Club Colours: Black and red hoops, black shorts

REDDITCH RFC
Ground Address: Bromsgrove Road, Redditch
Brief Directions: Bromsgrove Highway - Birchfield
Road - Bromsgrove Road
Club Secretary: Brian Carr, 60 Wychbury Rd., Quarry
Bank, Brierley Hill, West Midlands   DY5 2XX   Tel:
(H) 01384 79092 (W & Fax) 01384 265001
Fixtures Secretary: Andy Barlow   Tel: (H) 01527
550695
Club Colours: Light and dark blue hoops, dark shorts

ROSS ON WYE RFC
Ground Address: Sports Centre, Wilton Rd, Ross-on-
Wye. Tel: 01989 563256
Brief Directions: Take Ross exit at Wilton roundabout,
Sports Centre 1st right over bridge. Wilton roundabout is
1st from south, 2nd from north, A40
Club Secretary: Miss Julie Price, 8 Eastern Avenue,
Mitcheldean, G;pocestershire   Tel: 01594 543787
Fixtures Secretary: Mr David Cooke   Tel: (H) 01989
564626   (W) 01594 542421 Ext 1348
Club Colours: Royal blue and white hoops

TENBURY RFC
Ground Address: Penlu, Worcester Road, Tenbury
Wells, Worcs. WR15 8AY   Tel: 01584 810456
Brief Directions: Nex to Tenbury Hospital
Club Secretary: Mr M Spicer, 19 Castle Close, Tenbury
Wells, Worcestershire. WR15 8AY. Tel: (H) 01584
819541
Fixtures Secretary: Mark Morgan, Deepcroft
Farmhouse, Newnham Bridge, Tenbury Wells, Worcs.
Tel: (H) 01584 781412
Club Colours: Green and black Hoops

UPTON-UPON-SEVERN RFC
Ground Address: Collingshurst Meadow, Old Street, Upton-upon-Severn   Tel: 01684 594445
Brief Directions: Opposite Upton-upon-Severn Church in the main street of the town. 10 miles south of Worcester and 7 miles north of Tewkesbury on the A38 trunk road
Club Secretary: Geoff Marchant, 48 Lansdowne Street, Worcester. WR1 1QF   Tel: (H) 01905 617007
Fixtures Secretary: Nigel Banwell   Tel: (H) 01684 592046
Club Colours: Black and white quarters, black shorts

VESEYANS RFC
Ground Address: Memorial Ground, Little Hardwick Road, Streetly, Sutton Coldfield, West Midlands   Tel: 0121 353 5388
Brief Directions: A452 to Brownhills. Turn left at the Hardwick pub and the ground is 1 mile further on the left.
Club Secretary: Mr Karl Ward, 52 Rosemary Hill Road, Sutton Coldfield. B74 4HJ.   Tel: (B) 07000 527592
Fixtures Secretary: Steve Smith, 206 Highbridge Road, Sutton Coldfield. B73 5QY.   Tel: (H) 0121 354 9633
Club Colours: Black and white hoops

NORTH MIDLANDS TWO

North Midlands Two 1997-98 Fixtures	Birchfield 1	Bourneville 2	Bredon Star 3	Cleobury Mortimer 4	Harborne 5	Stourport 6	Witton 7	Wulfrun 8	Yardley 9	
1 Birchfield	X	6/9	7/3	27/9	31/1	17/1	8/11	25/4	20/12	1
2 Bourneville	14/3	X	17/1	7/3	8/11	25/4	31/1	20/12	18/10	2
3 Bredon Star	20/9	25/10	X	10/1	14/2	11/10	11/4	24/1	6/9	3
4 Cleobury Mortimer	14/2	20/9	8/11	X	25/4	20/12	18/10	14/3	17/1	4
5 Harborne	11/10	10/1	27/9	15/11	X	24/1	6/9	25/10	7/3	5
6 Stourport	25/10	15/11	31/1	11/4	18/10	X	7/3	10/1	27/9	6
7 Witton	10/1	11/10	20/12	24/1	14/3	20/9	X	14/2	25/4	7
8 Wulfrun	15/11	11/4	18/10	6/9	17/1	8/11	27/9	X	31/1	8
9 Yardley	11/4	24/1	14/3	25/10	20/9	14/2	15/11	11/10	X	9
	1	2	3	4	5	6	7	8	9	

BIRCHFIELD RUFC
Ground Address: Birthwood Road Sports Ground, Kingstanding Road, Kingstanding, Birmingham
Club Secretary: Mr Robert Margeson, 438 Qweslett Road, Great Barr, Birmingham. B43 7EL   Tel: (H) 0121 360 3415
Fixtures Secretary: Roger Booth   Tel: (H) 0121 353 9332   (W) 0121 777 3222 Ext 3825
Club Colours: Green and black hoops

BOURNVILLE RFC
Ground Address: Rowheath, Heath Road, Bournville, Birmingham. B30   Tel: 0121 475 0480
Brief Directions: A38 out of B'ham city centre, after approx 5 miles turn left into Oaktree Ln and follow signs for Cadbury World, turn right into Maryvale Rd, ground 0.5 mile on left
Club Secretary: Mr Steve Hinton, 24 Woodgate Drive, Bartley Green, Birmingham. B32 4AE   Tel: (H) 0121 680 0952
Fixtures Secretary: Mr Michael Palmer   Tel: (H) 0121 475 0480   (M) 0802 935243
Club Colours: Blue, maroon and gold shirts, blue shorts

BREDON STAR RFC
Ground Address: Bredon Playing Fields, Kemerton Road, Bredon, Nr Tewkesbury, Glos   Tel: 01684 772831
Club Secretary: Carol Julie Malpass, 33 Plantation Crescent, Bredon, Nr Tewkesbury, Glos   Tel: (H) 01684 72831
Fixtures Secretary: Neil Evans   Tel: (H) 01684 772645 (W) 0973 171451
Club Colours: Red and black hoops

CLEOBURY MORTIMER RFC
Ground Address: Lacon Childe School, Love Lane, Cleobury Mortimer, Kidderminster, Worcs DY14 8PE Tel: 01299 271448
Brief Directions: To Cleobury along main street, then turn right just before the Three Horseshoes pub, left at mini roundabout, car park and ground 100 yards on left
Club Secretary: Mr P J Howman, 7 Lacon Close, Cleobury Mortimer, Kidderminster, Worcs. DY14 8EF Tel: (H & W) 01299 270462
Fixtures Secretary: MrT Wright.   Tel: (H) 01299 823293 (W) 0973 977176
Club Colours: Red and green quarters

HARBORNE RFC
Ground Address: Playing Fields, Metchley, Park Road, Harborne, Birmingham   Tel: 0121 427 2690
Club Secretary: Keith Barbaer, 186 Wecley Avenue, Selley Oak, Birmingham   Tel: (H) 0121 471 4085
Fixtures Secretary: Simon Parker   Tel: (H) 0121 420 3523
Club Colours: Green, red and black band

STOURPORT RFC
Ground Address: Starport Cricket and Rugby Club, Walshes Meadow, Dunley Road, Stourport-on-Severn, Worcestershire   Tel: 01299 822210
Brief Directions: From town centre follow signs for Great Witley, cross River Severn Bridge, turn left to Leisure Centre, ground straight ahead
Club Secretary: Andy Foster, Lime-Kilns, Pensax, Abberley, Worcs. WR6 6XH   Tel: (H) 01299 896631
Fixtures Secretary: Mark Shuter   Tel: (H) 01299 823903   (W) 0121 561 5561
Club Colours: Navy blue, gold V on chest

WITTON RFC
Ground Address: Bourne Vale, off Little Hardwick Road, Aldridge, West Midlands.   Tel: 0121 353 2856
Brief Directions: On Little Harwick Road look for signs Woodlands/Erdington Star/Old Centrals
Club Secretary: Mark Field, 47 Canberra Road, Walsall, West Midlands. WS5 3NN   Tel: (H) 01922 37588 (W) 0121 327 2205
Fixtures Secretary: Paul Hubbard, 77 Kirkwood Avenue, Erdington, Birmingham. B23 5QQ   Tel: (H) 0121 605 6946
Club Colours: Gold and black hoops

WULFRUN RUFC
Ground Address: Wednesfield High School, Lakefield Road, Wednesfield, Wolverhampton   Tel: 01902 732470
Brief Directions: M54 J1 signs to Wolverhampton, signs to Wednesfield, left at 2nd island, right at island, school is on the left. Or M6 J10 to Wednesfield. Rt Neachers Lane, left at island , school on Rt.
Club Secretary: C Withers, 1 Deyncourt Road, Wednesfield, Wolverhampton. WV10 0SG   Tel: (H) 01902 732809
Fixtures Secretary: C Turner, 148 Warstones Drive, Warstones, Woverhampton.   Tel: (H) 01902 653018
Club Colours: Emerald green with black V

YARDLEY & DISTRICT RFC
Ground Address: No 1 Cole Hall Lane, Stechford, Birmingham   Tel: 0121 789 8450
Brief Directions: B'ham outer ringroad A4040 to Stechford, at t/light jcn of A4040/ A47 take A47 Coleshill Rd, over 1st island, immediate right into H'way, 1st island right, over next island, ground left after bridge
Club Secretary: David Adderley, c/o Ground address Tel: (H) 0121 789 6735   (W) 0121 789 8450
Fixtures Secretary: Mr John Shaw   Tel: (H) 0121 705 3292
Club Colours: Royal blue, old gold bands

THE
OFFICIAL RUGBY UNION
CLUB DIRECTORY 1997-98

The Perfect Christmas Present

MIDLAND DIVISION
FINAL LEAGUE TABLES (WEST) 1996-97

MIDLANDS WEST ONE

	P	W	D	L	F	A	PTS
Longton	16	13	1	2	579	176	27
Malvern	16	12	0	4	425	198	24
Old Coventrians	16	12	0	4	381	274	24
Ludlow	16	10	1	5	258	211	21
Aston Old Edwardians	16	10	0	6	494	326	20
Selly Oak	16	10	1	5	382	292	*19
Old Halesonians	16	9	0	7	444	387	18
Stratford-Upon-Avon	16	9	0	7	258	300	18
Willenhall	16	8	1	7	316	257	17
Kings Norton	16	8	0	8	231	239	16
Newbold	16	7	0	9	272	213	14
Nuneaton Old Edw	16	7	0	9	262	441	14
Old Leamingtonians	16	5	2	9	289	361	12
Leek	16	4	2	10	243	333	10
Tamworth	16	4	2	10	163	331	10
Stoke Old Boys	16	2	0	14	189	555	4
Dixonians	16	1	0	15	144	436	2

MIDLANDS TWO

	P	W	D	L	F	A	PTS
Telford	16	12	1	3	456	207	25
Woodrush	16	12	0	4	387	208	24
Edwardians	16	12	0	4	348	174	24
Shrewsbury	16	12	0	4	343	184	24
Southam	16	12	0	4	336	186	24
Old Yardleians	16	11	0	5	391	214	22
Pershore	16	10	1	5	381	281	21
Erdington	16	9	0	7	319	273	18
Evesham	16	9	0	7	344	310	*16
Coventry Saracens	16	6	1	9	276	375	13
Warley	16	7	0	9	323	319	*12
Old Griffinians	16	6	0	10	333	399	12
GPT Coventry	16	5	0	11	199	383	10
Manor Park	16	4	1	11	278	382	*7
Rugby St Andrews	16	4	0	12	189	362	*2
Newcastle (Staffs)	16	1	0	15	162	393	2
Trinity Guild	16	2	0	14	182	597	*2

NORTH MIDLANDS ONE

	P	W	D	L	F	A	PTS
Birmingham City Off	16	16	0	0	520	136	32
Kidderminster	16	14	0	2	493	181	28
Bridgnorth	16	12	0	4	467	176	24
Redditch	16	12	0	4	396	179	24
Tenbury	16	12	0	4	409	235	24
Bromyard	16	11	0	5	290	222	22
Droitwich	16	10	0	6	409	297	20
Veseyans	16	9	0	7	315	262	18
Old Saltleians	16	8	0	8	304	250	16
Old Centrals	16	6	1	9	268	390	13
Kynoch	16	5	0	11	194	274	10
Upton-on-Severn	16	5	0	11	215	317	10
Birmingham Welsh	16	5	0	11	216	417	10
Birmingham Civil Ser	16	5	0	11	218	458	10
Five Ways Old Edw	16	2	1	13	208	343	5
Ross-on-Wye	16	1	2	15	147	649	4
Wulfrun	16	1	0	15	147	649	2

NORTH MIDLANDS TWO

	P	W	D	L	F	A	PTS
Ledbury	11	10	1	0	335	73	21
Bishops Castle	11	7	2	2	268	75	16
Oswestry	11	7	1	3	279	169	15
Harborne	11	7	0	4	246	188	14
Stourport	11	4	2	5	200	163	10
Bournville	11	5	0	6	212	220	10
Witton	11	4	2	5	164	203	10
Yardley & Dist	11	5	1	5	236	147	*9
Cleobury Mortimer	11	4	1	6	145	206	9
Birchfield	11	6	0	5	226	154	*6
Market Drayton	11	2	0	9	82	237	4
Bredon Star	11	0	0	11	90	648	*-2

MIDLAND DIVISION STRUCTURE WEST 1997-98

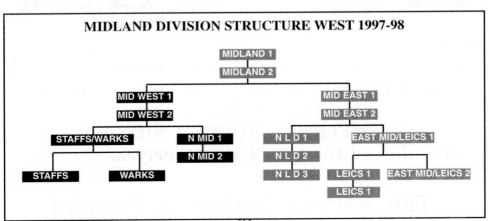

STAFFS/WARWICK ONE

	P	W	D	L	F	A	PTS
Berkswell * Balsall	14	13	1	0	308	100	27
Spartans	14	12	0	2	357	138	24
Alcester	14	9	2	3	266	191	20
Earlsdon	14	8	2	4	250	174	*16
Old Wheatleyans	14	8	0	6	329	283	16
Silhillians	14	7	2	5	280	250	16
Trentham	14	8	0	6	215	167	*14
Dunlop	14	6	1	7	216	137	13
Handsworth	14	6	1	7	222	208	*11
Pinley	14	5	1	8	191	178	11
Shipston-on-Stour	14	5	0	9	177	271	*8
GEC St Leonards	14	3	0	11	163	313	6
Coventry Welsh	14	4	0	10	230	286	*4
Coventrians	14	3	0	11	100	378	*4
Atherstone	14	3	0	11	180	410	*2

STAFFORDSHIRE

	P	W	D	L	F	A	PTS
Burntwood	16	14	1	1	482	165	29
Wednesbury	16	12	1	3	366	149	25
Wheaton Aston	16	11	0	5	372	266	22
Linley	16	8	1	7	293	271	17
Rubery Owen	16	8	0	8	328	295	16
Uttoxeter	16	8	0	8	279	370	16
Rugeley	16	5	0	11	190	284	10
Cannock	16	2	1	13	171	496	5
Bloxwich	16	2	0	14	208	393	4

WARWICKSHIRE

	P	W	D	L	F	A	PTS
Claverdon	16	14	1	1	403	112	29
Ford	16	12	2	2	469	110	26
Standard	16	12	0	4	502	181	24
Harbury	16	10	1	5	389	166	21
Old Warwickians	16	8	0	8	286	235	16
Shottery	16	6	1	9	201	458	*11
Rugby Welsh	16	4	1	11	149	336	9
Coventry Technical	16	2	0	14	150	410	*2
Warwick	16	1	0	15	79	620	*-2

MIDLAND DIVISION
LEAGUE STRUCTURE 1997-98

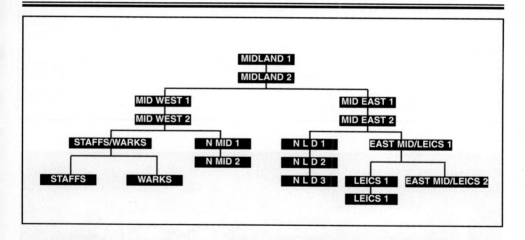

Do you know a rugby enthusiast with a birthday coming up?

This directory would make a perfect present.

So why not buy a copy from your club or from W H Smith.

MIDLANDS EAST ONE

Midlands East One 1997-98 Fixtures	Ashbourne 1	Coalville 2	Ilkeston 3	Lincoln 4	Long Buckby 5	Lutterworth 6	Matlock 7	Newark 8	Northampton Mens Own 9	Northampton Old Scouts 10	Old Northamptonians 11	Peterborough 12	Spalding 13	Stewart's & Lloyds 14	Stoneygate 15	Vipers 16	Wellingborough 17	
1 Ashbourne	X	11/10		8/11	6/9				20/12	17/1		31/1		7/3		11/4		1
2 Coalville		X		20/12	27/9		26/10		17/1	31/1		7/3		11/4		6/9		2
3 Ilkeston	26/10	15/11	X			11/1		31/1			7/3		11/4		6/9		27/9	3
4 Lincoln			10/1	X	26/10		15/11		31/1	7/3		11/4		6/9		27/9		4
5 Long Buckby			11/10		X	8/11	20/9	20/12			17/1		31/1		7/3		11/4	5
6 Lutterworth	15/11	10/1		24/1		X		7/3			11/4		6/9		27/9		26/10	6
7 Matlock	27/9		8/11			20/12	X	17/1			31/1		7/3		11/4		6/9	7
8 Newark	10/1	24/1		14/2				X	14/3		6/9		27/9		26/10		15/11	8
9 Northampton Mens Own		24/1		15/11	14/2	10/1			X	11/4		6/9		27/9		26/10		9
10 Northampton Old Scouts			14/2	10/1	14/3	24/1	25/4			X		27/9		26/10		15/11		10
11 Old Northamptonians	24/1	14/2		14/3					25/4	20/9	X		26/10		15/11		10/1	11
12 Peterborough			14/3		24/1	25/4	14/2	20/9			11/10	X		15/11		10/1		12
13 Spalding	14/2	14/3		25/4					20/9	11/10		8/11	X		10/1		24/1	13
14 Stewart's & Lloyds			25/4		14/2	20/9	14/3	11/10			8/11		20/12	X		24/1		14
15 Stoneygate	14/3	25/4		20/9					11/10	8/11		20/12		17/1	X		14/2	15
16 Vipers			20/9		14/3	11/10	25/4	8/11			20/12		17/1		31/1	X		16
17 Wellingborough	25/4	20/9		11/10					8/11	20/12		17/1		31/1		7/3	X	17
	1	2	3	4	5	6	7	8	9	10	11	12	13	14	15	16	17	

Northampton Mens Own - having beaten Hernani R.F.C. on their tour to the Basque region of Spain in May 1997. Also winners of Midlands East 2.

ASHBOURNE RUFC
Ground Address: The Recreation Ground, Ashbourne. DE6 1EJ
Brief Directions: From the centre of town, keep in right hand lane at junction, go straight on, playing field is 100 yds on right
Club Secretary: Peter J Fuller, Ednaston Lodge Farm, Ednaston, Derby. DE6 3BA Tel: (H) 01335 360381 (W) 01785 211414
Fixtures Secretary: Ian Jones Tel: (H) 01335 344894 (W) 01335 343243 Ext 2074
Club Colours: Navy and old gold hoops

COALVILLE RFC
Ground Address: Memorial Ground, Broomleys Road, Coalville, Leicester Tel: (H) 01530 812090
Club Secretary: Peter Smith, 50 Parkdale, Ibstock, Leics Tel: (H) 01530 262113 (W) 01530 832085
Fixtures Secretary: Charles Coulson Tel: (H) 01530 811280 (W) 01530 834079
Club Colours: Navy with amber band, white shorts

ILKESTON RUFC
Ground Address: Gallows Inn Fields, Nottingham Road, Ilkeston, Derbys Tel: 0115 9323088
Brief Directions: Nottingham to Ilkeston road, opposite Ford garage at the bottom of the hill
Club Secretary: John Braybrook, 16 Walker Street, Eastwood, Notts. NG16 3EH Tel: (H)01773 714856 Fax 01773 712767
Fixtures Secretary: Colin Fox Tel: (H) 0115 9308421 (W) 0115 9443569
Club Colours: Blue, green and white hoops, white shorts

LINCOLN RFC
Ground Address: Lindum Sports Ground, Wragby Road, Lincoln, Lincs Tel: 01522 526592
Club Secretary: John Graves, 7 Holdenby Road, Cherryfield, Lincoln. LN2 4TH Tel: (H) 01522 511500 (W) 01522 526352
Fixtures Secretary: C Buchanan-Smith Tel: (H) 01522 790959
Club Colours: Red, white, green hooped shirts, green shorts

LONG BUCKBY RFC
Ground Address: Station Road, Long Buckby, Northamptonshire Tel: 01327 842222
Brief Directions: 0.25 mile from market square, along Station Road towards Daventry
Club Secretary: P J Osborne, Ashthorne, Teeton Road, Ravensthorpe, Northampton Tel: (H) 01604 770772 (W) 01327 705785
Fixtures Secretary: S Ruddlesden Tel: (H) 01327 842933
Club Colours: Emerald green

LUTTERWORTH RFC
Ground Address: Ashby Lane, Bitteswell, Nr Lutterworth, Leics LE17 4SQ. Tel: 01455 557329
Brief Directions: Approx 1.5 miles north off Lutterworth on A426 at cross roads take turn for Ashby Parva & Ullesthorpe. Ground at end of lane approx 1 mile.
Club Secretary: Colin Hudson, Mason and Bowns Cottage, Ashby Parva, Nr Lutterworth, Leics LE17 5HY. Tel: (H) 01455 209053 Tel: (W) 01788 534606
Fixtures Secretary: Chris Payne, Cawder Ghyll, Shawell, Nr. Lutterworth, Leics. Tel: (H) 01788 860442
Club Colours: Red, green and white hoops blue shorts

MATLOCK RUFC
Ground Address: Cromford Meadows, Cromford, Matlock, Derbyshire Tel: 01629 822821
Brief Directions: Turn off A6 at Cromford towards Crich/Holloway, Ground 100yds on right
Club Secretary: C Baker, Badger House, Lumb Lane, Darley Dale, Matlock, Derbyshire. DE4 2HP Tel: (H & W) 01629 735294
Fixtures Secretary: D Pearson Tel: (H) 01629 55440
Club Colours: Royal blue, gold and grey quartered shirts, royal blue socks, navy blue shorts

NEWARK RFC
Ground Address: Kelham Road, Newark, Nottinghamshire Tel: 01636 702355
Brief Directions: From A1, A46 Newark bypass, ground is on Kelham Road on the road marked to Kelham on the right. From A46, take Newark bypass, left at roundabout, ground on right
Club Secretary: Mr Richard J H Ewens, 25/26 Market Place, Newark, Notts. NG24 1EA Tel: (H) 01949 850513 (W) 01636 72247 Fax: 01636 705672
Fixtures Secretary: Mr Hugh Daybell Tel: (H) 01636 702197
Club Colours: Blue shirts with single white hoop, blue shorts

NORTHAMPTON MENS OWN RFC
Ground Address: Stoke Road, Ashton, Northampton Tel: 01604 862463
Brief Directions: M1 J15, take A508 to Milton Keynes for 2.5 miles, through Roade village, take next left turning at crossroads, after 1 mile, signed Ashton, ground 0.5 mile on right
Club Secretary: John Goold, 38 Millway, Duston, Northampton. NN5 6ES Tel: (H) 01604 756297
Fixtures Secretary: Ernie Dalby Tel: (H) 01604 870609 (W) 01332 252132/0802 765527
Club Colours: White with blue hoop

NORTHAMPTON OLD SCOUTS RFC
Ground Address: Rushmere Road, Northampton. Tel: 01604 33639
Club Secretary: M. Heath, 16 Sandringham Road, Abington, Northampton. Tel: (H) 01604 38331 Tel: (W) 01604 643699
Fixtures Secretary: Keith Shurville, Tel: (H) 01604 494374 Tel: (W) 01908 690333 x 3406
Club Colours: Red, green, gold & navy hooped shirts, navy shorts.

OLD NORTHAMPTONIANS RFC
Ground Address: Billing Road, Northampton Tel: 01604 34045
Brief Directions: Follow signs for Northants County Cricket Ground and District of Abington
Club Secretary: T O Brien, 5 Ibstock Close, Billing Lane, Northampton. NN3 5DL Tel: (H) 01604 642758 (W) 01604 26004
Fixtures Secretary: D Summers Tel: (H) 01604 27910 (W) 01604 38430
Club Colours: Cardinal, navy, gold hoops

PETERBOROUGH RUFC
Ground Address: Second Drove, Fengate, Peterborough. PE1 5XA Tel: 01733 69413
Club Secretary: B A Hedges, 85 Apsley Way, Longthorpe, Peterborough. PE3 9NZ Tel: (H) 01733 332287
Fixtures Secretary: M Proud Tel: (H) 01487 822951
Club Colours: Red, silver, gold

SPALDING RFC
Ground Address: St Thomas' Road, Spalding, Lincs
Tel: 01775 725191
Brief Directions: From north, south & east, exit bypass at town centre sign, 1st left over river, immediate right, left into St Thomas Rd, From west, in town, 1st right after railway crossing
Club Secretary: J F Constable, 14 Amsterdam Gardens, Spalding, Lincs. PE11 3HY   Tel: (H) 01775 723790 (W) 01775 711911
Fixtures Secretary: T Hall   Tel: (H) 01775 762145 (W) 01406 422228
Club Colours: Maroon and blue hoops

STEWARTS & LLOYDS RFC
Ground Address: Occupation Road, Corby, Northants. NN17 1EH   Tel: 01536 400317
Brief Directions: From Kettering, A6003 towards Oakham, right at roundabout at top of Rockingham Hill, 0.75 mile, turn 1st right past Game Bird Pub into Occupation Rd, 1st right into ground
Club Secretary: J M Thompson, 5 Howe Crescent, Corby, Northants. NN17 2RY   Tel: (H) 01536 202433
Fixtures Secretary: Vernon Cook   Tel: (H) 01536 741971   (W) 0421 518320
Club Colours: Black shirts, black shorts

STONEYGATE FC
Ground Address: Covert Lane, Scraptoft, Leics. LE7 9SP   Tel: 0116 2419188
Brief Directions: A47 east out of Leicester (Signposted Peterborough), left at lights (Coles Nurseries) into Station La, turn right at bottom onto Covert Lane.
Club Secretary: S Morris, 203 Evington Lane, Leicester. LE5 6DJ   Tel: (H) 0116 2628596/2735927 (W) 0116 2628596
Fixtures Secretary: M C Herbert   Tel: (H) 0116 271 4229   (W) 0116 255 2694
Club Colours: Cardinal red and white hoops, navy shorts

VIPERS RFC
Ground Address: Blaby Bypass, Whetstone, Leicester
Tel: 0116 2864777
Brief Directions: M1 J21, follow A46 to roundabout at Fosse Park, right onto B4114, straight over next roundabout, next roundabout left, next roundabout right, club on left at end of d/c
Club Secretary: Paul Hutchinson, 20 Haddenham Rd.,Leicester LE3 2BF   Tel: (H) 0116 223 5683 (W) 0116 276 7000 (M) 0595 708 767
Fixtures Secretary: Ian Reid   Tel: (H) 0116 2810472
Club Colours: Green with gold and black hoops

WELLINGBOROUGH RFC
Ground Address: Cut Throat Lane, Great Doddington, Wellingborough, Northants. NN29 7TZ   Tel: 01933 222260
Brief Directions: Leave A45 at Earls Barton/Gt Doddington, turn left at end of exit road, left at small crossroads in approx 500mtr, clubhouse is at top of hill on right, approx 500 metres
Club Secretary: Bob Stevenson, 12 South Street, Wollaston, Northants. NN29 7RX   Tel: (H) 01933 664538   (W) 01933 226077
Fixtures Secretary: Ian Brown   Tel: (H & W) 01933 663622
Club Colours: White shirts with red hoop, navy shorts

THE
OFFICIAL RUGBY UNION
CLUB DIRECTORY 1997-98

The Perfect Christmas Present

MIDLANDS EAST TWO

Midlands East Two 1997-98 Fixtures	Amber Valley 1	Bedford Queens 2	Biggleswade 3	Buxton 4	Dunstablians 5	Grimsby 6	Kesteven 7	Kibworth 8	Long Eaton 9	Loughborough 10	Luton 11	Northampton BBOB 12	Nottingham Casuals 13	Oadby Wyggestonians 14	South Leicester 15	Stamford 16	West Bridgford 17	
1 Amber Valley	X	6/9	11/10	17/1			8/11		20/12			31/1		28/2		4/4		1
2 Bedford Queens		X		20/9	11/10		8/11		20/12	17/1		31/1		28/2		4/4		2
3 Biggleswade		27/9	X	31/1	11/10		20/12		17/1			28/2		4/4		6/9		3
4 Buxton		10/1		X	24/1	14/2		14/3		25/4		27/9		25/10		15/11		4
5 Dunstablians	27/9				X	8/11		20/12		17/1	31/1	28/2		4/4			6/9	5
6 Grimsby	25/10		15/11			X		17/1		31/1	28/2		4/4		6/9		27/9	6
7 Kesteven		25/10		28/2	15/11	10/1	X		31/1			4/4		6/9		27/9		7
8 Kibworth	15/11		10/1				24/1	X		28/2	4/4		6/9		27/9		25/10	8
9 Long Eaton		15/11		4/4	10/1	24/1		14/2	X			6/9		27/9		25/10		9
10 Loughborough	10/1		24/1				14/2		14/3	X	6/9		27/9		25/10		15/11	10
11 Luton	24/1		14/2	20/9			14/3		25/4		X		25/10		15/11		10/1	11
12 Northampton BBOB		24/1			14/2	14/3		25/4		20/9	11/10	X		15/11		10/1		12
13 Nottingham Casuals	14/2		14/3	11/10			25/4		20/9			8/11	X		10/1		24/1	13
14 Oadby Wyggestonians		14/2			14/3	25/4		20/9		11/10	8/11		20/12	X		24/1		14
15 South Leicester	14/3		25/4	8/11			20/9		11/10			20/12		17/1	X		14/2	15
16 Stamford		14/3			25/4	20/9		11/10		8/11	20/12		17/1		31/1	X		16
17 West Bridgford	25/4		20/9	20/12			11/10		8/11			17/1		31/1		28/2	X	17
	1	2	3	4	5	6	7	8	9	10	11	12	13	14	15	16	17	

AMBER VALLEY RUFC

Ground Address: Pye Bridge, Lower Somerscotes, Alfreton, Derbyshire DE55 INF.   Tel: 01773 541308
Club Secretary: Sue Ferguson, 60 Warwick Road, somercotes, Alfreton, derbyshire DE55 1SO.   Tel: (H) 01773 541308   Tel: (W) 01773 602106
Fixtures Secretary: Tom Uniache, Tel: (H) 01773 541953
Club Colours: Black, maroon and amber

BEDFORD QUEENS RUFC

Ground Address: Allen Park, Queens Park, Old Ford End Road, Bedford   Tel: 01234 211151
Brief Directions: From Northampton A428 to Bedford, 2nd R. as entering Bedford, R. at T junction, follow road appox. 1 mile, Nr. Bell Public House, ground on right, clubhouse just behind ground.
Club Secretary: J B G Cunningham, Flat 4, 16 Adelaide Square, Bedford. MT40 2RW   Tel: (H) 01234 269085 (W) 01234 347111
Fixtures Secretary: Andy Radnor   Tel: (H) 01462 816175   (W) 0385 372897
Club Colours: Maroon and white hoops, navy blue shorts

BIGGLESWADE RUFC

Ground Address: Langford Road, Biggleswade, Beds. SG18 9RA   Tel: 01767 312463
Brief Directions: On the A6001 Biggleswade to Henlow road, approx 1 mile from Biggleswade by the Broom turn off, on the right hand side coming from Biggleswade
Club Secretary: Mike Williams, 8 Laurel Way, Ickleford, Hitchin, Herts. SG5 3UP   Tel: (H) 01462 624925   (W) 01462 443091
Fixtures Secretary: Mike Pearson   Tel: (H) 01480 385077
Club Colours: Navy with red hoop

BUXTON RUFC

Ground Address: Fairfield Centre, Victoria Park Road, Buxton, Derbyshire   Tel: 01298 24081
Brief Directions: Follow A6 Stockport, up up Fairfield Rd. 1st R. Queens Rd becomes Bench Rd, left at T jcn with Victoria Park Rd, Centre on left after Royal Foresters
Club Secretary: David Robson, 20 Errwood Avenue, Buxton, Derbyshire. SK17 9BD   Tel: (H) 01298 22432 (W) 01298 26121 Ext 125
Fixtures Secretary: Marcus Savile Tel: 01298 25582(H) 0836 602477(W)
Club Colours: Blue, red and gold hoops, blue shorts

DUNSTABLIANS RUFC
Ground Address: Bidwell Park, Bedford Road, Houghton Regis, Dunstable, Beds. LU5 6JW Tel: 01582 866555/864107
Brief Directions: North out of Dunstable on A5, turn right after roundabout to Thorn, at end of road, ground is opposite, or M1 J12 through Toddington, ground is 3 miles on left
Club Secretary: Paul Freeman, 10B Tabor Close, Harlington, nr Dunstable, Beds. LU5 6PF Tel: (H) 01525 874550 (W) 01234 333492
Fixtures Secretary: Dai Gabriel Tel: 01582 606262
Club Colours: Red, black, silver

GRIMSBY RUFC
Ground Address: Springfield Road, Grimsby, North East Lincolnshire. DN33 3JF Tel: 01472 878594
Brief Directions: From M180/A180, take A1136, left at roundabout, right at Toothill roundabout, left at Bradley crossroads, right at Nuns corner, right fork, 1st right
Club Secretary: Mr T Horswood, 5 Ferriby Lane, Grimsby. DN34 3NU. Tel: 01472 872416
Fixtures Secretary: Roger Davies Tel: 01472 812763
Club Colours: Royal and black.

KESTEVEN RUFC
Ground Address: Wood Nook, High Dyke, Grantham, Lincs. Tel: 01476 564887
Brief Directions: A53 out of Grantham towards Spalding, past the R.A.F. camp then right at roundabout (B6403). Club on right about 400 yards.
Club Secretary: A J Snarey, The Mill, Manthorpe, Grantham, Lincs. NG31 8NH Tel: 01476 591941
Fixtures Secretary: P N White, 17 Wong Gardens, Barrowby, Grantham, Lincs. Tel: (H) 01476 571716
Club Colours: Black shirts, white shorts

KIBWORTH RUFC
Ground Address: Northampton Road, Market Harborough, Leicestershire Tel: 01858 464210
Brief Directions: From town centre, follow signs for Leisure Centre, club on right as you enter centre. From M1, M6, A14, follow A508 to Mkt Harborough, ground on left as entering town
Club Secretary: David R Coe, 4 Applegarth Close, Corby, Northamptonshire. NN18 8EU Tel: (H) 01536 460052 (W) 01536 402551 Ext 3107
Fixtures Secretary: David R Coe Tel: (H) 01536 460052 (W) 01536 402551 Ext 3107
Club Colours: Black

LONG EATON RUFC
Ground Address: West Park, Long Eaton, Nottingham. Tel: 0115 946 0907
Club Secretary: Tony Suiter, 102 Trowell Grove, Logn Eaton, Nottingham NG10 4BB. Tel: (H) 0115 972 1267 Tel: (W) 0115 934 4776
Fixtures Secretary: Martin Smith, Tel: (H & W) 0973 379510
Club Colours: Blue and white hoops, blue shorts.

LOUGHBOROUGH RFC
Ground Address: The Clubhouse, Derby Road Playing Fields, Derby Road, Loughborough (not a postal address) Tel: 01509 216093
Brief Directions: M1: J23, left at second roundabout, right at second roundabout-straight ahead at next roundabout then first left and follow signs for golf centre.
Club Secretary: Mr P.Talbot, 2 Poseiden Court, Cyclops Wharf, Homer Drive, London E14 3UG Tel: (H) 0171 5153073 (W) 0171 6174271 (FAX) 0171 617211
Fixtures Secretary: Nick Moore Tel: 01509 620703
Club Colours: Blue and old gold

LUTON RFC
Ground Address: Newlands Road, Luton, Beds Tel: 01582 20355
Brief Directions: M1 J10, take spur to roundabout, turn right, 200m turn right again, ground 1km on left
Club Secretary: P J Wilson, 17 Burghley Close, Flitwick, Bedford. MK45 1TF Tel: (H) 01525 713409 (W) 01480 52451 Ext 5232
Fixtures Secretary: Martin Alexander Tel: (H) 01582 598581 (W) 01582 22333
Club Colours: Green with red and white hoops, black shorts

NORTHAMPTON BOYS BRIGADE OLD BOYS RUFC
Ground Address: St Andrews Mill, St Andrews Road, Northampton. NN1 2PQ Tel: 01604 32460
Brief Directions: M1 J15A, follow signs for town centre, left at 1st lights just past 'Saints' Northampton RFC, cross 3 sets of lights, left into St Andrews Rd, ground entrance by Texaco garage
Club Secretary: Mrs Helen Bolden, 15 Berry Lane, Wootton, Northampton. NN4 6JU Tel: (H) 01604 766949
Fixtures Secretary: Peter Johnson Tel: 01604 586421
Club Colours: Light blue, dark blue, maroon hoops

NOTTINGHAM CASUALS RFC
Ground Address: Canal Side, Meadow Road, Beeston Rylands, Nottingham. NG9 1JG Tel: 0115 925 0135
Brief Directions: M1 J25, A52 to Nottingham, after 2nd roundabout, right at 2nd lights, straight across 2 crossroads, continue till road makes sharp right, over bridge, turn left
Club Secretary: John Littlestone, 87 Main Street, Loudham, Nottingham.NG14 7BN Tel: 0115 966 3869
Fixtures Secretary: Lech Kluk, 46 Springfiield Avenue,Sandiacre,Nottingham, NG10 5LZ Tel: 0115 946 2846
Club Colours: White with maroon hoops, black shorts

OADBY WYGGESTONIAN RFC
Ground Address: Oval Park, Wigston Road, Oadby, Leicester Tel: 0116 2714848
Brief Directions: M1 J21, follow Leicester South and East for 4 miles to A50, turn right, left at roundabout, ground 0.5 mile on left
Club Secretary: Jim Kilgallen, 75 Leicester Road, Oadby, Leicester. LE2 4DP Tel: (H) 0116 2713987 (W) 0116 285 8032
Fixtures Secretary: Tony Bayley, 27 Dover House, Dover St., Leicester. Tel: (H & W) 0116 255 3787
Club Colours: Black, white & gold hoops, black shorts

MIDLANDS EAST TWO CONTINUED

SOUTH LEICESTER RFC
Ground Address: Welford Road, Wigston, Leicester, LE18 1TE   Tel: 011 2882066
Brief Directions: M1/M69 J21, head east on ringroad towards Oadby & Wigston, take A50 towards Northampton, ground at the final roundabout of the built up area of Wigston
Club Secretary: Richard Dowdall, 4 Bodmin Avenue, Wigston Magna, Leicester. LE18 2HB   Tel: 0116 2885606
Fixtures Secretary: D Cottom   Tel: (H) 0116 2773615
Club Colours: Green and white hoops

STAMFORD RUFC
Ground Address: Hambleton Road, Stamford, Lincs Tel: 01780 52180
Brief Directions: Take Oakham/Melton Mowbray exit from A1, turn towards Stamford, approx 500 yds right turn into Lonsdale Rd, approx 200 yds fork left into Hambleton Rd
Club Secretary: N M Jolly, 21 Chatsworth Rd, Stamford, Lincs   Tel: (H) 01780 52134   (W) 01780 720501
Fixtures Secretary: A Baker   Tel: (H) 01780 56367
Club Colours: Purple, black and white shirts, black shorts

WEST BRIDGFORD RFC
Ground Address: The Memorial Ground, Stamford Road, West Bridgford, Nottingham   Tel: 0115 9232506
Brief Directions: Enter West Bridgford on A52, just over Gamston Bridge turn left, 1st left onto Brockley Rd, left at T junction, 2nd left onto Rufford Way, club on next bend
Club Secretary: K Howells, 117 Mount Pleasant, Keyworth, Nottingham. NG12 5ES   Tel: (H) 0115 9374468
Fixtures Secretary: N Davies, 17 Chantrey Road, West Bridford, Nottingham.   Tel: 0115 981 4344
Club Colours: Black shirts with red and gold hoops, black shorts and socks

NOTTS, LINCS AND DERBY ONE

Notts, Lincs & Derby One 1997-98 Fixtures

	Team	Ashfield	Bakewell Mannerians	Boots Athletic	Castle Donington	Chesterfield	Dronfield	East Retford	Glossop	Keyworth	Leesbrook Asterdale	Market Rasen & Louth	Melbourne	Mellish	Southwell	Stamford College OB	Worksop	
		1	2	3	4	5	6	7	8	9	10	11	12	13	14	15	16	
1	Ashfield	X		20/9	11/10			8/11		20/12		17/1		31/1	7/3			1
2	Bakewell Mannerians	6/9	X		11/10	8/11		20/12		17/1		31/1			7/3	20/9		2
3	Boots Athletic		27/9	X	8/11			20/12		17/1		31/1		7/3	6/9		11/10	3
4	Castle Donington		25/10		X	15/11		17/1		31/1		7/3		6/9	27/9		20/12	4
5	Chesterfield	27/9		25/10		X	20/12		17/1		31/1		7/3		6/9	8/11		5
6	Dronfield	25/10		15/11	10/1		X		31/1		7/3				27/9	17/1		6
7	East Retford		15/11			10/1	24/1	X		7/3		6/9		27/9	25/10		31/1	7
8	Glossop	15/11		10/1	24/1			14/2	X	6/9		27/9				25/10	7/3	8
9	Keyworth		10/1			24/1	14/2		14/3	X		27/9		25/10	15/11			9
10	Leesbrook Asterdale	10/1		24/1	14/2			14/3	20/9		X		25/10		15/11			10
11	market Rasen & Louth		24/1			14/2	14/3		20/9		11/10	X		15/11	10/1			11
12	Melbourne	24/1		14/2	14/3			20/9	11/10		8/11		X		10/1			12
13	Mellish		14/2			14/3	20/9		11/10	8/11			20/12	X	24/1			13
14	Southwell		14/3			20/9	11/10	8/11		20/12			17/1		X	31/1		14
15	Stamford College OB	14/2		14/3	20/9		11/10		8/11	20/12			17/1	17/1		X		15
16	Worksop	14/3								6/9	27/9	25/10	15/11	10/1	14/2	24/1	X	16
		1	2	3	4	5	6	7	8	9	10	11	12	13	14	15	16	17

ASHFIELD (Amalgamated SWANS & SPARTANS)
Ground Address: Oddicroft Lane off A38, Suttton in Ashfield, Nottingham
Brief Directions: M1 J28, follow signs to Mansfield A38, go through 3 sets of traffic lights, turn right (fire station opposite), follow road for 300 metres until school on right hand side of road
Club Secretary: Stephen Trainer, 12 Belfry Close, Broadlands Park, Kirkby in Ashfield, Notts. NG17 8NS Tel: (H) 01623 443744 (W) 0115 965 7276
Fixtures Secretary: John Chambers, 12Berry Hill Lane, Mansfield, Nottingham NG18 4BQ. Tel: 01623 641391
Club Colours: Navy , amber, red and black hoops

BAKEWELL MANNERIANS RUFC
Ground Address: The Showground, Coombs Road, Bakewell, Derbyshire
Brief Directions: Leave Bakewell on Sheffield/Chesterfield road, turn right immediately over river bridge, take 1st right (Coombs Road) to Showground, changing rooms nearby
Club Secretary: Terry Donnelly, 1 Commercial Road, Grindleford, Hope Valley, S32 2HA Tel: (H) 01433 631224
Fixtures Secretary: Joe Oldfield Tel: (H) 01629 814911 (W) 01629 813301
Club Colours: Dark blue, light blue and white hooped shirts, navy shorts

BOOTS ATHLETIC RFC
Ground Address: Boots Athletic Ground, Holme Road, Lady Bay, West Bridgford, Notts Tel: 01159 492388
Brief Directions: Follow signs to either Trent Bridge Cricket or Nottingham Forest, the Athletic Ground is on the south bank of the river Trent, next to Lady Bay bridge and Notts Forest
Club Secretary: Chris Harries, 218 Rutland Road, West Bridgford, Nottingham. NG2 5EB. Tel: 0115 982 2620
Fixtures Secretary: Greg Haywood, Slaughterhouse Cottage, Main St., Epperstone, Nottingham. NG14 6AD Tel: (H) 0115 9664629 (W) 0115 9712851
Club Colours: Dark blue and light blue quarters

CASTLE DONINGTON RUFC
Ground Address: The Spital Pavilion, The Spital, Castle Donington, Derbyshire Tel: 01332 812214 (pub)
Brief Directions: Travel into Donington from A6 turning right into the Spittal after the Tudor Inn, ground is situated 400yds on right
Club Secretary: A Hackett, The Old Bakery, Thringstone, Leicestershire. LE67 5AP Tel: (H) 01530 223599 (W) 0831 675987
Fixtures Secretary: Mr P Parry Tel: (H) 01509 670577
Club Colours: Red and black quartered shirts, black shorts, red and black socks

CHESTERFIELD RUFC
Ground Address: Sheffield Road, Stonegravels, Chesterfield Tel: 01246 232321
Brief Directions: M1 J29, town centre A61 to Sheffield (old road, not bypass), on left 1 mile town centre
Club Secretary: P I Jackson, 396 Old Road, Chesterfield. S40 3QF Tel: (H) 01246 568187 (W) 01246 270112
Fixtures Secretary: M Lord Tel: (H) 01246 274105
Club Colours: Red and white hoops, white shorts

DRONFIELD RUFC
Ground Address: Gosforth School, Carr Lane, Dronfield-Woodhouse, Dronfield.
Brief Directions: From north (Sheffield) into Dronfield, right at Coach & Horses, bear right under bridge, follow road at top of hill turn left (Stubley Drive), turn into school car park
Club Secretary: Bob Machin, 2 Hatton Close, Dronfield-Woodhouse, Dronfield. S18 5RW Tel: (H) 01246 411453
Fixtures Secretary: Mick Rodgers, 56 Ribblesdale Drive, Sheffield. S12 3XE. Tel: (H) 0114 247 2846 (W) 0114 271 6716
Club Colours: Red shirts, black shorts

Bakewell Mannerians R.U.F.C. 1997

EAST RETFORD RUFC
Ground Address: Ordsall Road, Retford, Nottinghamshire   Tel: 01777 703234
Brief Directions: From A1, join B620 from Worksop, past Ranby prison on left, through Babworth crossroads, right at mini roundabout, ground 0.5 mile on right
Club Secretary: E M Henderson, 51 Trent Street, Retford, Notts. DW22 6NG   Tel: (H) 01777 706987 (W) 01909 476724
Fixtures Secretary: Mr B Dudley   Tel: (H) 01777 818616
Club Colours: Emerald and amber hoops, navy blue shorts

GLOSSOP RUFC
Ground Address: Hargate Hill Lane, Charlesworth, Broadbottom, Hyde   Tel: 01457 864553
Brief Directions: Through Glossop on A57, take A626 signposted Marple, ground is 1.5 miles on left
Club Secretary: Alastair May, 6 Kinder Grove, Romiley, Stockport. SK6 4EU   Tel: (H) 0161 427 5774 (W) 01457 864553
Fixtures Secretary: Stephen Ford, Wood House, Swallow House Lane, Hayfield, Stockport SK12 5HB   Tel: 01663 744998 / 0850 871129
Club Colours: Royal blue shirts, black shorts

KEYWORTH RUFC
Ground Address: Willoughby Lane, Widmerpool, Nottingham. NG12 5BU
Brief Directions: Out of Nottingham on A606 Melton Rd, turn right taking signs for Widmerpool, on entering village turn left at T jctn, follow road to right, 1st left to Willoughby on the Wolds, ground on right
Club Secretary: Michael Waplington, 9 High Street, Carlton Le Moorland, Lincolnshire. LN5 9HT   Tel: (H) 01522 788387
Fixtures Secretary: Paul Stockbridge   Tel: (H) 01949 831270
Club Colours: Black with two amber hoops, black shorts and socks

LEESBROCK ASTERDALE RUFC
Ground Address: Asterdale Sports Centre, Borrowash Road, Spondon, Derby. DE21 7PH   Tel: 01332 668656
Brief Directions: M1 J25, 3rd turn marked Spondon. From city centre take A52, take turning marked Spondon (Ntm Old Road)
Club Secretary: John Borns, 160 Cole Lane, Borrowash, Derby, DE72 3GP   Tel: 01332 674216
Fixtures Secretary: Peter Albon   Tel: 01332 755225
Club Colours: Black, green, white and blue quarters

MARKET RASEN AND LOUTH RUFC
Ground Address: Willingham Road, Market Rasen   Tel: 01673 843162
Brief Directions: On entering Market Rasen, take A631 Louth road, on entering 40mph section ground is approx 100 yards on right
Club Secretary: B N Harper, Nongoby, Church Lane, Manby, Louth. LN11 8HL   Tel: (H & W) 01507 327318
Fixtures Secretary: J Holt   Tel: (H & W) 01472 852779   (FAX) 01472 851653
Club Colours: Red and green hoops, white shorts.

MELBOURNE RFC
Ground Address: Melbourne Recreation Ground, Cock Shut Lane, Melbourne, Derbyshire DE73 1DG   Tel: 01332 863674
Brief Directions: From M1, A453 to Melbourne. From Derby/Uttoxeter, A514 to Melbourne. Then B587 to Recreation Ground
Club Secretary: Miss Deborah Clarke, 48 Station Road, Melbourne, Derby. DE73 1EB   Tel: (H) 01332 864966
Fixtures Secretary: Hamish Walker   Tel: (H) 01332 864810
Club Colours: Bottle green and white

MELLISH RFC
Ground Address: War Memorial Ground, Plains Road, Mapperley, Nottingham. NG3 5RT   Tel: 0115 926 6653
Brief Directions: Ground situated on west side of B684 opposite The Travellers Rest, 2 miles east of the turn off the A614 and 2 miles north of the Plains squash club (national grid ref: 605463)
Club Secretary: J. R. B. Crisford, 3 Rushmere Walk, Arnold, Nottingham, NG5 6SH.   Tel: (H) 0115 9264259 (W) 0115 9787285
Fixtures Secretary: Syd Harris, 2 Tilstock Court, Watnam, Nottingham, NG16 1JR   Tel: (H) 01773 533405
Club Colours: Green, black, gold hooped jerseys, black shorts and socks

SOUTHWELL RUFC
Ground Address: Pentelowes, Park Lane, Southwell, Notts. NG25 0LA
Brief Directions: Park Lane is at the bottom of Brackenhurst Hill off Nottingham Road
Club Secretary: Nick Robinson, The Hall Farm, Main Street, Farnsfield, Notts. NG22 8EY   Tel: (H) 01623 882010   (W) 0116 289 2200
Fixtures Secretary: Phil Gordon   Tel: (H) 01636 830485
Club Colours: Maroon and blue

STAMFORD COLLEGE OLD BOYS RFC
Ground Address: Drift Road, Stamford, Lincs
Brief Directions: Follow signs to Stamford College, ground behind Leisure Centre
Club Secretary: Mr S Pulley, 5 Fir Road, Stamford. PE9 2FD   Tel: (H) 01780 66352   (W) 01476 566110
Fixtures Secretary: Mr F Simpson   Tel: (H) 01780 65341
Club Colours: Red and green hoops

WORKSOP RUFC
Ground Address: The Meadows, Stubbing Lane, Worksop, Notts. S80 1NF   Tel: 01909 484247
Brief Directions: Get onto Worksop bypass at roundabout with Mill House pub, take road to town centre then take 1st left into Stubbing Lane, club and grounds at end of road
Club Secretary: M E Murphy, 86 Bridge Street, Worksop, Notts. S80 1JF   Tel: (H) 01777 870952   (W) 01909 500544
Fixtures Secretary: N Gibson   Tel: (H) 01909 487506 (W) 01629 580000 Ext 7558
Club Colours: Black and white hooped shirts and socks, black shorts

Notts, Lincs & Derby Two Fixtures

	Barton & District (1)	Belper (2)	Boston (3)	Bourne (4)	Colgrave (5)	East Leake (6)	Gainsborough (7)	Hope Valley (8)	Meden Vale (9)	North Kesteven (10)	Nottingham Const. (11)	Nottinghamians (12)	Olletron (13)	Rolls Royce (14)	Sleaford (15)	
1 Barton & District	X		27/9	25/10	15/11			14/2		10/1		24/1		14/3		1
2 Belper	20/9	X				25/10	15/11		10/1	14/3		24/1		14/2		2
3 Boston		11/10	X	15/11	10/1			14/3			24/1		14/2		20/9	3
4 Bourne		8/11		X	24/1	20/12		20/9			14/2		14/3		11/10	4
5 Cotgrave		20/12			X	17/1	31/1	11/10			14/3		20/9		8/11	5
6 East Leake	11/10		8/11			X		10/1	24/1	20/9		14/2		14/3		6
7 Gainsborough	8/11		20/12	17/1			X	14/2	11/10		14/3		20/9			7
8 Hope Valley		7/3				11/4	27/9	X	25/10			15/11		10/1	31/1	8
9 Meden Vale	20/12		17/1	31/1	7/3				X	8/11		20/9		11/10		9
10 North Kesteven	7/3		11/4	27/9	25/10		24/1			X	15/11		10/1			10
11 Nottingham Const.		17/1				31/1	7/3	8/11	11/4		X	11/10		20/12		11
12 Nottinghamians	17/1		31/1	7/3	11/4					20/12	27/9	X		8/11		12
13 Olleston		31/1				17/3	11/4	20/12	27/9			25/10	X		17/1	13
14 Rolls Royce	31/1		7/3	11/4	27/9					17/1	25/10	15/11		X		14
15 Sleaford		11/4				27/9	25/10	15/11	14/2		10/1		24/1		X	15
	1	2	3	4	5	6	7	8	9	10	11	12	13	14	15	

BARTON & DISTRICT RUFC
Ground Address: Mill Lane, Barrow-on-Humber, North Lincolnshire
Club Secretary: T Phipps, 4 West Alridge, Barton-on Humber Tel: (H) 01652 63237 (W) 01724 847888
Fixtures Secretary: Andy Snowden Tel: (H) 01724 734629 (W) 01724 402372
Club Colours: Red and white

BELPER RUFC LTD
Ground Address: Herbert Strutt School Fields, Derby Road, Belper
Brief Directions: Ground is off A6 in Belper between Safeways supermarket and Babbington Hospital
Club Secretary: Chris Smith, Hillcrest, Hillcliff Lane, Turnditch, Belper, Derbyshire. DE56 2EA Tel: (H) 01773 550702 (W) 01332 332248
Fixtures Secretary: A Young Tel: (H) 01332 842768 (W) 01332 349457
Club Colours: Black and white hoops

BOSTON RFC
Ground Address: Great Fen Road, Wyberton, Boston, Lincs. PE21 7PB Tel: 01205 362683
Brief Directions: 0.25 mile west of Boston on A1121 next to airfield
Club Secretary: Mrs Lynn Creasey, 48 Glen Dr, Boston, Lincs. PE21 7QB Tel: (H) 01205 356753 (W) 01205 313000
Fixtures Secretary: Mr T Bembridge Tel: 01205 351973
Club Colours: Blue and white hoops, navy shorts, blue and white socks

BOURNE RUFC
Ground Address: Milking Nook Drive, Splading Road, Bourne, Lincs. Tel: 01778 393346
Club Secretary: Caroline Perkins, 91 Northorpe Lane, Thumby, Barne Tel: (H) 01778 422314
Fixtures Secretary: Martin Hunter Tel: (H) 01788 426536
Club Colours: Blue with gold band

NOTTS, LINCS AND DERBY TWO CONTINUED

COTGRAVE COLLIERY RUFC
Ground Address: Cotgrave Community Centre, Woodview, Cotgrave, Nottingham   Tel: 0115 9892916
Brief Directions: Cotgrave lies in triangle boarded by A52 Nottingham/ Grantham rd, A46 Leicester/Newark rd & A606 N'ham-Melton Mowbray rd, Community Centre is opposite the Miners Welfare
Club Secretary: Nicholas Webb, 30 Marwood, Cotgrave, Nottingham NG12 3NS   Tel: 0115 989 3038
Fixtures Secretary: Andrew Cooper   Tel: (H) 01332 873873   (W) 0116 234 0033 Ext 278
Club Colours: Claret and blue quarters

EAST LEAKE RFC
Ground Address: Costock Rd Playing Fields, Costock Road, East Leake, Loughborough, Leicestershire
Brief Directions: A60 N'gham tow'ds L'boro, right at Costock tow'ds E. Leake, ground on right. M1 J24, A6 tow'ds L'boro, left onto A6006 tow'ds Rempstowe, left where signed, thro' village, club on right
Club Secretary: Timothy Buffham, 10 Roberts Close, Kegworth, Derby. DE74 2HR   Tel: (H) 01509 670395 (W) 01509 223154
Fixtures Secretary: Andy D Noble   Tel: (H) 0116 237 6933   (W) 0116 262 8567/0973 172 928
Club Colours: Maroon & white hooped shirts, black shorts

GAINSBOROUGH RUFC
Ground Address: Castle Hills School, The Avenue, Gainsborough
Brief Directions: Follow signs for Leisure Centre, the school is next to it
Club Secretary: T Tanner, 11 Northolme, Gainsborough, Lincs. DN21 2QN   Tel: (H) 01427 610768   (W) 01246 451245
Fixtures Secretary: Howard Russel   Tel: (H) 01427 628265   (W) 01724 276221
Club Colours: 1st team: black shirt and shorts. 2nd team: black and yellow quarters

HOPE VALLEY RUFC
Ground Address: Castleton Playing Fields, Hollowford Road, Castleton, Derbyshire (No mail to this address)
Tel: (c/o The Peak Hotel) 01433 620247
Brief Directions: From Sheffield A625 through Hathersage and Hope to Castleton, 100 metres past Peak Hotel turn right into Back St, ground is 500 metres on right
Club Secretary: Ian Broad, 10 Farndale Road, Hillsborough, Sheffield. S6 1SH   Tel: (H) 0114 233 8264
Fixtures Secretary: Ian Broad   Tel: (H) 0114 233 8264
Club Colours: Purple, green and white quarters, black shorts

MEDEN VALE RFC
Ground Address: Welbeck Miners Welfare, Giksley Road, Meden Vale   Tel: 01623 842267
Brief Directions: From A60 turn towards Meden Vale, follow road until petrol station then turn left up the hill, take 2nd left into car park
Club Secretary: Mike Heaton, 5 Budby Crescent, Meden Vale, Mansfield, Notts   Tel: (H) 01623 846076 (W) 0115 9476091
Fixtures Secretary: Gary Heaton   Tel: (H) 01623 559434   (W) 01773 521881
Club Colours: Red with black collars

NORTH KESTEVEN RUFC
Ground Address: Pavilion Club (rear of Memorial Hall), Newark Road, North Hykeham, Lincoln
Brief Directions: From A46 south of Lincoln, take towards Lincoln, look for Memorial Hall sign on left opposite North Kesteven school and sports centre
Club Secretary: Graham Bennett, 36 Hood Street, Lincoln. LN5 7XB   Tel: 01522 887615
Fixtures Secretary: Nigel Thomas   Tel: (H) 01522 680193
Club Colours: Black jersey, white, red and green hoops

Hope Valley R.U.F.C.
Back: Rob Eyre, Bob Tann, Martin Hercock, Paul Oldridge (Captain), Jack Taylor, Nigel Winder, Sean Hickinson, Danny Driver.
Front: Paul Johnson, Jason Bradley, Richard Driver, Andy Stoddard, Graham Green, Nick Morgan, Richard Mosley.

NOTTINGHAMIANS
Ground Address: Adbolton Lane, West Bridgford, Nottingham Tel: 0115 981 1372
Club Secretary: David Hampson, 43 Lenton Manor, Lenton, Nottingham. NG7 2FW Tel: (H & W) 0115 946 2121
Fixtures Secretary: Phil Quinn Tel: (H) 01773 710668 (W) 0115 941 8418
Club Colours: Black, white and purple hoops

NOTTS CONSTABULARY RFC
Ground Address: Mellish RFC, Plains Road, Mapperley, Nottingham Tel: 0115 926 6655
Club Secretary: Mr Rushdale, c/o Radford Road Police Station, Radford, Notts Tel: (H) 0115 942 0999
Fixtures Secretary: Martin Hewitt Tel: (H) 0115 920 4996 (W) 0115 942 0999
Club Colours: Black and bottle green quarter

OLLERTON RFC
Ground Address: Boughton Sports Field, Church Road, Boughton, Newark, Notts
Brief Directions: From A614 take A6075 through New Ollerton and Boughton, turn left on apex of right hand bend at Harrow Inn, 200 yds right at Church, follow lane to the back of houses of Church Lane
Club Secretary: Dave Price, Lathmill, Harrow Farm, Tuxford Road, Boughton, Newark, Notts. NG22 9JZ Tel: (H) 01623 860871
Fixtures Secretary: Mark Woods Tel: (H) 01623 835123
Club Colours: Yellow and black hoops

ROLLS ROYCE RFC
Ground Address: Merrill Way, Allenton, Derby
Club Secretary: Nigel Calladine, 131 Marjorie Road, Chaddesden, Derby. DE21 4HP Tel: (H) 01335 344554
Fixtures Secretary: Cerith Davies Tel: (H) 01332 572256
Club Colours: Maroon and sky blue quarters

SLEAFORD RFC
Ground Address: Sleaford RFC, East Road Ground, East Road, Sleaford, Lincs. Tel: 01529 303335
Brief Directions: One mile north east of Sleaford on the A153 Skegness road, at the junction with the A17 Sleaford by-pass.
Club Secretary: Rick Mosley, 8 Millview Road, Heckington, Lincs. NG34 9JP. Tel: 01529 461710
Fixtures Secretary: George Marsh, 37 Meadow Field, Sleaford, Lincs. Tel: (H) 01529 303859
Club Colours: Red and black hoops, black shorts.

NOTTS, LINCS AND DERBY THREE

Notts, Lincs & Derby Three 1997-98 Fixtures	Bilsthorpe 1	Bingham 2	Cleethropes 3	Horncastle 4	Skegness 5	Tupton 6	University of Derby 7	Whitwell 8	Yarborough Bees 9	
1 Bilsthorpe	X	25/4	8/11	14/3	11/10	14/2	15/11	25/10	20/9	1
2 Bingham	24/1	X	14/3	11/10	14/2	25/10	10/1	20/9	15/11	2
3 Cleethorpes	11/4	27/9	X	14/2	25/10	20/9	24/1	15/11	10/1	3
4 Horncastle	27/9	7/3	18/10	X	20/9	15/11	11/4	10/1	24/1	4
5 Skegness	7/3	18/10	31/1	6/9	X	10/1	27/9	24/1	11/4	5
6 Tupton	18/10	31/1	6/9	17/1	20/12	X	7/3	11/4	27/9	6
7 University of Derby	17/1	20/12	25/4	8/11	14/3	11/10	X	14/2	25/10	7
8 Whitwell	31/1	6/9	17/1	20/12	25/4	8/11	18/10	X	7/3	8
9 Yarborough Bees	6/9	17/1	20/12	25/4	8/11	14/3	31/1	11/10	X	9
	1	2	3	4	5	6	7	8	9	

BILSTHORPE RUFC
Ground Address: Bilsthorpe Sports Ground, Eakring Road, Bilsthorpe, Newark, Notts
Club Secretary: Peter G Steffen, 55 Crompton Road, Bilsthorpe, Newark, Notts. NG22 8PS Tel: 01623 870906
Fixtures Secretary: Darren Wilford Tel: (H) 01623 824120
Club Colours: Green, gold and black hoops

BINGHAM RUFC
Ground Address: The Town Pavilion, Brendan Grove, Wynhill, Bingham, Notts. Tel: 01949 832874
Club Secretary: John Perry, 29 Cogley Lane, Bingham, Notts. Tel: (H) 01949 837777
Fixtures Secretary: R J Williams,
Tel: (H) 01636 8233076
Club Colours: Green & red hoops.

CLEETHORPES RUFC
Ground Address: Wilton Road, Cleethorpes, N E Lincs Tel: 01472 812936
Club Secretary: Alan Clark, 10 Cambridge Street, Cleethorpes. DN35 8HB Tel: (H) 01472 692716 (W) 01469 551017 (Fx) 01469 572988
Fixtures Secretary: Mr John Walsham Tel: (H) 01472 699322
Club Colours: Gold with blue hoops

HORNCASTLE
Ground Address: Horncastle Playing Fields, The Wong, Horncastle, Lincolnshire.
Club Secretary: Mrs. S Rinfret, Langley, Iddesleigh Road, Woodhall Spa, Lincolnshire LN10 6SR Tel: (H) 01562 352906 (W) 01526 353075
Fixtures Secretary: J I Bentley, 1 Albert Cottages, Chapel Lane, Legbourne, Louth, Lincolnshire LN11 8LW Tel: (H) 01507 600318

SKEGNESS RFC
Ground Address: Wainfleet Road, Skegness Tel: 01754 765699
Brief Directions: A153 turn right for town centre, 0.5 mile turn right at Highwayman pub, ground across A52
Club Secretary: Alan Hawkes, Grunters Grange, East Keal, Spilsby. PE23 4AY Tel: (H) 01790 752788
Fixtures Secretary: John Harris Tel: (H) 01754 765797
Club Colours: Royal blue and white hoops, navy shorts

TUPTON RUFC
Ground Address: The Recreation Ground, North Side, Tupton, Chesterfield Tel: (Tupton Social Club) 01246 862002
Brief Directions: From Chesterfield south A61 to Tupton, left at roundabout into Queen Victoria Road, then 2nd left into North Side
Club Secretary: Bob Curry, 170 Queen Victoria Road, Tupton, Chesterfield. S42 6DW Tel: (H) 01246 862059
Fixtures Secretary: Wayne Lilleyman Tel: (H) 01246 860545
Club Colours: Shirts-navy blue with 3 yellow bands, blue shorts and socks

UNIVERSITY OF DERBY MENS RUGBY
CLUBGround Address: Kedleston Campus, Kedleston Road. DE22 1GB Tel: 01332 633333
Brief Directions: A38 to Markeaton roundabout and follow directions to University at Kedleston Road Campus
Club Secretary: L Byrne, 24 Crown Street, Derby Tel: (H) 01332 349655
Fixtures Secretary: D R French Tel: (H) 01332 371275
Club Colours: Green and white quarters

WHITWELL RUFC
Ground Address: Markland Campus, N Derbyshire Tertiary College, Sheffield Road, Creswell, Notts. F80 4HW Tel: 01909 724908
Brief Directions: M1 J30, take A616 Newark road for approx 4 miles, take 1st right at Creswell, college on left
Club Secretary: Mrs Jill Marshall, 3 Duke Street, Whitwell, Worksop, Notts. S80 4TH Tel: (H) 01909 722 060
Fixtures Secretary: Mr Mark Passey Tel: (H) 01246 570645
Club Colours: Green and black

YARBOROUGH BEES RUFC
Ground Address: Yarborough Sports Centre, Riseholme Road, Lincoln Tel: 01522 524228
Brief Directions: Follow A46 to junction with A15 turn - signed Ermine, turn into Yarborough School 400 yards approx
Club Secretary: H Sampson, 7 Shannon Avenue, Lincoln. LN6 7JG Tel: (H) 01522 691631 (W) 01522 584510
Fixtures Secretary: Mr A Goulde Tel: (H) 01724 867048
Club Colours: Maroon and amber

EAST MIDLANDS

East Midlands 1997-98 Fixtures	Biddenham 1	Corby 2	Kempston 3	Northampton Casuals 4	Northampton Heathens 5	Oundle 6	Thorney 7	Vauxhall 8	Westwood 9	
1 Biddenham	X	25/4	6/9	17/1	8/11	27/9	18/10	31/1	7/3	1
2 Corby	15/11	X	18/4	8/11	27/9	6/9	7/3	17/1	18/10	2
3 Kempston	14/3	20/12	X	25/4	31/1	7/3	27/9	8/11	17/1	3
4 Northampton Casuals	25/10	10/1	15/11	X	7/3	18/4	6/9	18/10	31/1	4
5 Northampton Heathens	10/1	14/2	11/10	20/9	X	24/1	25/10	14/3	20/12	5
6 Oundle	14/2	14/3	20/9	20/12	18/10	X	31/1	25/4	8/11	6
7 Thorney	24/1	20/9	14/2	14/3	17/1	11/10	X	20/12	25/4	7
8 Vauxhall	11/10	25/10	10/1	24/1	6/9	15/11	18/4	X	27/9	8
9 Westwood	20/9	24/1	25/10	11/10	18/4	10/1	15/11	14/2	X	9
	1	2	3	4	5	6	7	8	9	

BIDDENHAM RFC
Ground Address: The Biddenham Pavilion, Biddenham, Beds
Club Secretary: Andrew Pryor, 43 Main Road, Biddenham, Bedfordshire. MK40 4BD   Tel: (H) 01234 325040   (W) 01234 350812
Fixtures Secretary: Trevor Sparks Tel: (H) 01234 327845
Club Colours: Bottle green and old english cream

CORBY RFC
Ground Address: Northen Park, Rockingham Triangle, Corby, Northants Tel: 01536 204466
Brief Directions: Junction of A6003 & A6116 to the north of Corby, next to Corby Football & Athletics Club and Post House Hotel
Club Secretary: George A Ewen, 24 Charnwood Road, Corby, Northants. NN17 1XS Tel: (H) 01536 201788 (W) 01536 265291
Fixtures Secretary: Charles Sanders, 21 Brunswick Gardens, Corby, Northants. Tel: (H) 01536 745440 (W) 01536 534760
Club Colours: Red and white yl's

KEMPSTON RFC
Ground Address: Cutler Hammer Sports & Social, Bell End, 134 High Street, Kempston, Bedfordshire. Tel: 01234 852499
Brief Directions: The ground is situated at the bottom of the hill from Sainsbury on the right hand side.
Club Secretary: Chris Pitts, 34 Park Road, Kempston, Beds. Tel: 01234 840921
Fixtures Secretary: Chris Pitts (as above).
Club Colours: Black with red 'V'

NORTHAMPTON CASUALS RFC
Ground Address: Rushmills House, Bedford Road, Rushmills, Northampton Tel: 01604 36716
Brief Directions: At J15 of M1 take A508 to Northampton and then 4th slip road and take A428 to Bedford. At first roundabout go right round and back towards Northampton, then take first left.
Club Secretary: Martyn Dimmock, 44A Park Drive, Kings Heath, Northampton NN5 7JU Tel: (H) 01604 457175
Fixtures Secretary: M D Askew Tel: (H) 01604 821148
Club Colours: Black with amber band

NORTHAMPTON HEATHENS RFC
Ground Address: The Racecourse, East Park Parade, Northampton. Tel: 01604 39250
Club Secretary: Martin Labrum, 101 Yoemans Meadow, Northampton NN4 9YX. tel: (H) 01604 765287
Fixtures Secretary: Derek Hodgkinson, Tel: (H) 01604 416442
OUNDLE RFC
Ground Address: Occupation Road, Oundle, Peterborough Tel: 01832 273101
Brief Directions: From Peterborough, cross bridge, turn right by garage, turn right then right again down single track road
Club Secretary: H Adams, Gilmour House, Lower Benefield, Peterborough. PE8 5AF Tel: (H) 01733 706962
Fixtures Secretary: Graham Snelling, 7 Wansford Road, Elton, Peterborough, PE8 6RZ. Tel: (H) 01832 280419 (W) 01832 272881
Club Colours: Red and white stripes on black

THORNEY RUFC
Ground Address: Thorney Ex Servicemens Club, Station Road, Thorney, Cambs. PE6 0QE   Tel: 01733 270283
Brief Directions: A47 from Peterborough towards Wisbech, at traffic lights on crossroads turn towards Crowland, club house 150 metres from crossroad
Club Secretary: Mr L Depwancke, 7 Headlands Way, Whittlesey. PE7 1RL   Tel: (H) 01733 204893
Fixtures Secretary: Mr R Turner   Tel: (H) 01733 571259
Club Colours: Navy and gold quarters

VAUXHALL MOTORS RUFC
Ground Address: 20 Gypsy Lane, Luton, Beds   Tel: 01582 748240
Brief Directions: Off M1 at J10, across 1st roundabout, down dual carriageway, left at roundabout then left immediately at next roundabout, entrance 200 yds on left
Club Secretary: Mr S. MacLaughlan, Adelaide House, 51 Adelaide Street, Luton, Beds. LU1 5BD. Tel: 01582 400138. Fax: 01582 411685
Fixtures Secretary: M Neate   Tel: (H) 01525 716393 (W) 01582 420565
Club Colours: Royal blue and gold shirts, black shorts

WESTWOOD RUFC
Ground Address: Phorpres Club, London Road, Peterborough   Tel: 01733 343501
Club Secretary: Ken Barnes, 17 St Peters Walk, Yaxley, Peterborough. PE7 3EY   Tel: (H) 01733 241382
Fixtures Secretary: Peter Tarttelin   Tel: (H) 01733 350632
Club Colours: Red and white hoops

EAST MIDLANDS AND LEICS ONE

East Midlands/Leicestershire One 1997-98 Fixtures	Aylestone St James	Bedford Swifts	Deepings	Brackley	Bugbrooke	Colworth House	Daventry	Loughborough Stud	Market Bosworth	Melton Mowbray	Oakham	Old Ashbeians	Old Bosworthians	Rushden & Higham	St Ives	St Neots	Wellingborough OG
	1	2	3	4	5	6	7	8	9	10	11	12	13	14	15	16	17
1 Aylestone St James	X	6/9		27/9		25/10		15/11		10/1		24/1		14/2		14/3	
2 Bedford Swifts		X	27/9		25/10		15/11		10/1		24/1		14/2		14/3		25/4
3 Deepings	20/9		X	25/10		15/11		10/1		24/1		14/2		14/3		25/4	
4 Brackley		11/10		X	15/11		10/1		24/1		14/2		14/3		25/4		20/9
5 Bugbrooke	11/10		8/11		X	10/1		24/1		14/2		14/3		25/4		20/9	
6 Colworth House		8/11		20/12		X	24/1		14/2		14/3		25/4		20/9		11/10
7 Daventry	8/11		20/12		17/1		X	14/2		14/3		25/4		20/9		11/10	
8 Loughborough Stud		20/12		17/1		31/1		X	14/3		25/4		20/9		11/10		8/11
9 Market Bosworth	20/12		17/1		31/1		7/3		X	25/4		20/9		11/10		8/11	
10 Melton Mowbray		17/1		31/1		7/3		11/4		X	20/9		11/10		8/11		20/12
11 Oakham	17/1		31/1		7/3		11/4		6/9		X	11/10		8/11		20/12	
12 Old Ashbeians		31/1		7/3		11/4		6/9		27/9		X	8/11		20/12		17/1
13 Old Bosworthians	31/1		7/3		11/4		6/9		27/9		25/10		X	20/12		17/1	
14 Rushden & Higham		7/3		11/4		6/9		27/9		25/10		15/11		X	17/1		31/1
15 St Ives	7/3		11/4		6/9		27/9		25/10		15/11		10/1		X	31/1	
16 St Neots		11/4		6/9		27/9		25/10		15/11		10/1		24/1		X	7/3
17 Wellingborough OG	11/4		6/9		27/9		25/10		15/11		10/1		24/1		14/2		X
	1	2	3	4	5	6	7	8	9	10	11	12	13	14	15	16	17

AYLESTONE ST JAMES RFC
Ground Address: Covert Lane, Scraptoft, Leicester
Tel: 01162 419202
Brief Directions: Out of Leicester on A47 Uppingham
Rd, left into Scraptoft Lane, top of lane go directly on to
Covert Lane, 2nd clubhouse on left
Club Secretary: K Wiridge, 5 Canons Close,
Narborough, Leicestershire. LE9 5FC Tel: (H) 01162
866481   (W) 01162 608187   (Fx) 640543
Fixtures Secretary: P Chapman Tel: (H) 01162
431826
Club Colours: Blue and white hoops, navy shorts

BEDFORD SWIFTS RUFC
Ground Address: Bedford Athletics Stadium, Newnham
Avenue/Barkers Lane, Bedford Tel: 01234 351115
Brief Directions: From A1, A428 west to Birmingham
and Northampton on outskirts of Bedford follow signs
left to Bedford Athletics Stadium or Priory Country Park
Club Secretary: Trevor N Stewart, 64 Ravensden Road,
Renhold, Bedford. MK41 0JY Tel: (H) 01234 771828
Fixtures Secretary: Mr Stan Davidson Tel: (H) 01234
857529
Club Colours: Gold and royal blue hooped shirts, navy
shorts

BRACKLEY RUFC
Ground Address: Springfield Way, off Pavillons Way,
Brackley, Northants. NN13 6LW Tel: 01280 700685
Club Secretary: Mrs Susan-Anne Cooper, 30 Octavian
Way, Brackley, Northants. NN13 7BL Tel: (H) 01280
704711 (Fax) 01280 703971
Fixtures Secretary: Chris Page Tel: (H) 01280 704711
Club Colours: Royal blue and white quarters

BUGBROOKE RUFC
Ground Address: Playing Fields, Pilgrims Lane,
Bugbrooke, Northants Tel: 01604 831137
Brief Directions: M1 J16, A45 towards Northampton, at
1st roundabout turn right onto B4525 towards
Bugbrooke, follow road through Kislingbury to
Bugbrooke
Club Secretary: Mr John Gowen, Alberts House,
Middle Street, Nether Heyford, Northants. NN7 3LL
Tel: (H) 01327 342422   (W) 01604 758857
Fixtures Secretary: Mr Terry Newcombe Tel: (H)
01604 831806
Club Colours: Bottle green shirts and shorts, gold
collar, green and gold striped socks

COLWORTH HOUSE RUFC
Ground Address: Unilever Research, Colworth House,
Sharnbrook, Bedford. MK44 1LQ Tel: 01234 222221
Brief Directions: Frm sth: A6 to Sharnbr'k, turning left,
thro' village to Colworth Hse sign, take sports field
signs. Frm north: A6 to Souldrop, turning right, thro'
S'drop to S'brook & C'wth Hse sign. as above
Club Secretary: Andrew Reynolds, 31Cheviot Close,
Bedford, MK 41 9EN. Tel: 01234 343248
Fixtures Secretary: Mark Forsyth, 41 Bedford
Road,Marston,Beds. MK43 0ND. Tel: 01234 705352.
Club Colours: Emerald green, scarlet band, black shorts
and socks

DAVENTRY RFC
Ground Address: Stepen Hill, Western Avenue,
Daventry, Northants. NN11 4ST Tel: 01327 703802
Brief Directions: M1 J16, A45 west to Daventry, upon
reaching Daventry, straight over roundabout heading for
Daventry town centre, 3rd road on left and the ground is
facing you
Club Secretary: Robin Bearne, 18 Kingsley Avenue,
Daventry, Northants. NN11 4AN Tel: (H) 01327
301678   (W) 0121 600 6646
Fixtures Secretary: Graham Woodliffe Tel: (H) 01327
261461   (W) 01327 305137
Club Colours: All black

DEEPINGS RUFC
Ground Address: Linchfield Road, Deeping St James,
Peterborough Tel: 01778 345228
Brief Directions: R'bout Market Deeping (Jcn of
A15/A16) take A16 towards Spalding, through town
until sight footbridge, left at Xroads before bridge,
immediate right thro' gates to ground
Club Secretary: Brian Kirby, 29 Tattershall Drive,
Market Deeping, Peterborough. PE6 8BS Tel: (H)
01778 343048   (W) 01733 556173
Fixtures Secretary: K Smith Tel: (H) 01778 346411
(W) 0116 276 5755
Club Colours: Green, black and gold hoops

LOUGHBOROUGH STUDENTS
Ground Address: Loughborough University, Leics.
LE11 3TU Tel: 01509 632009 (Athletic Union)
Brief Directions: M1 J21, head towards Loughborough
along Ashly Rd, follow directions into university, 1st XV
pitch immediately on left
Club Secretary: Steve Harrod
Fixtures Secretary: Glynn James Tel: (H) 01780
51793
Club Colours: White and maroon

MARKET BOSWORTH RFC
Ground Address: Cadeby Lane, Cadeby, Market
Bosworth, Nuneaton. CV13 0BE Tel: 01455 291340
Brief Directions: Off the A447, Hinckley to Ibstock
road, turn at signs for Cadeby and follow lane in
direction of Market Bosworth
Club Secretary: Zeb Shahin, Thistledown, 5Newton
Cottages, Main Road, Newton Regis, Warwicks. B79
0NE Tel: 01827 830160
Fixtures Secretary: P Spencer Tel: (H) 01455 633364
(W) 01455 230804
Club Colours: Blue, white and gold hoops, black shorts

MELTON MOWBRAY RFC
Ground Address: Burton Road, Melton Mowbray,Leics.
LE13 1DR Tel: 01664 63342
Brief Directions: Leave Melton Mowbray via the A606
to Oakham . Access is on the left past King Edward VII
upper school.
Club Secretary: P J Lee, 4 Torrance Drive, Melton
Mowbray, Leics. LE13 1HR Tel: (H) 01664 67452
(W) 01675 482060
Fixtures Secretary: T Middleton Tel: (H) 01664 67042
Club Colours: Maroon and white

OAKHAM RFC
Ground Address: The Showground, Barleythorpe Road,
Oakham Tel: 01572 724206
Club Secretary: Peter Bateman, 26 Well Street, Langham,
Oakham, Rutland. LE15 7JS Tel: 01572 756143
Fixtures Secretary: Peter Bateman Tel: 01572 756143
Club Colours: Black shirts with single amber band

OLD ASHBEIANS RFC
Ground Address: Nottingham Road, Ashby, Leicester LE65 1DQ. Tel: 01530 413992
Brief Directions: M42 junction 13, signposted Ashby (A50), right at next roundabout, signposted Lount Breedon (A453)
Club Secretary: John Mitchell, 50 Pennine Way, Ashby, Leicester LE65 1EW. Tel: (H) 01530 415284
Fixtures Secretary: Jim Grimsley, Tel: (H) 01530 414531 Tel: (W) 01530 416575
Club Colours: Maroon and light blue hoops.

OLD BOSWORTHIANS RFC
Ground Address: Hinckley Road, Leicester Forest East, Leicester Tel: 0116 238 7136
Brief Directions: Situated on A47 west of Leicester. From Leicester cross M1, pass Red Cow pub on right a mile further on, clubhouse on right, 5 miles short of Hinckley
Club Secretary: Richard Beason, The Laurels, Main Road, Claybrooke Magna, Lutterworth, Leics. LE17 5AJ Tel: (H) 01455 202605 (W) 0468 701741/01530 263323
Fixtures Secretary: Colin Hughes Tel: (H) 01530 834493 (W) 01509 631000
Club Colours: Navy shirts, navy shorts, navy and sky socks

RUSHDEN AND HIGHAM RUFC
Ground Address: Manor Park, Bedford Road, Rushden, Northants Tel: 01933 312071
Brief Directions: On main A6 Bedford side of Rushden, on the left leaving Rushden and the right when approaching Rushden from Bedford
Club Secretary: Steve Miles, Kialanga, The Green, Orlingbury, Kettering,Northants. NN14 1JA Tel: 01933 400123 (H) 01604 545410 (W)
Fixtures Secretary: Terry Dancer Tel: (H) 01933 624889
Club Colours: Black and white hoops

ST IVES (CAMBS) RUFC
Ground Address: Somersham Road, St Ives, Huntingdon, Cambs. PE17 4LY Tel: 01480 464455
Brief Directions: From the St Ives bypass, follow the B1040 towards Somersham, the ground is on the left
Club Secretary: Michael Prince,Vine Cottage, Church St, Woodhurst, Hunt'don Tel: 01487 822693
Fixtures Secretary: Nick Nicholson Tel: (H) 01480 381693
Club Colours: Royal blue and black shorts

ST NEOTS RUFC
Ground Address: The Common, St Neots. PE19 1HA Tel: 01480 474285
Brief Directions: Follow signs for Little Paxton from town centre, ground on left as you leave St Neots (1 mile from Town centre)
Club Secretary: Ray London, 14 James Court, Eynesbury, St Neots. PE19 2QQ Tel: (H) 01480 390135 (W) 01234 358 671 Ext 223
Fixtures Secretary: Keith Sanford, 366 Avenue Road, St. Neots, PE19 1LJ. Tel: (H) 01480 472812 (W) 01234 274049
Club Colours: Light blue with navy hoop

WELLINGBOROUGH OLD GRAMMARIANS RFC
Ground Address: Wellingborough O.G. New Memorial Sports Field, Sywell Road, Wellingborough, Northants NN8 8BS Tel: 01933 226188
Brief Directions: From Park Farm North go along Sywell Road, ground is on right.
Club Secretary: Ken Bernthal, 38 Torrington Road, Wellingborough ,Northants Tel: (H) 01933 679474 (W) 0171 887 5384
Club Colours: Claret and white hoops, black shorts

St. Ives 'Old Bulls'.

Back: Andy Frear, Rob Hogan, Andy Hogan, Dave Ruddy, Grame Morton, Ian Gammage, Big Stu Feering, Simon Chapman.

Front: Zinzan Pugh, Duncan Smith, Steve Burice, Andy Bottson, Ali Broom, Nick Nicholson (Captain), Martin Doughty, Phil Benton.

LEICESTERSHIRE ONE

Leicestershire One 1997-98 Fixtures	Aylestonians 1	Birstall 2	Burbage 3	New Parks 4	Old Newtonians 5	Wigston 6	
1 Aylestonians	X	8/11	20/9	24/1	11/10	7/3	1
2 Birstall	14/3	X	11/10	20/9	25/10	14/2	2
3 Burbage	31/1	7/3	X	25/10	14/3	8/11	3
4 New Parks	27/9	31/1	14/2	X	8/11	11/10	4
5 Old Newtonians	14/2	27/9	24/1	7/3	X	20/9	5
6 Wigston	25/10	24/1	27/9	14/3	31/1	X	6
	1	2	3	4	5	6	

AYLESTONIANS RFC
Ground Address: Knighton Lane East, Leicester   Tel: 0116 2834899
Club Secretary: Clive Cooper, 31 Rockingham Close, Leicester   Tel: (H) 0116 2740922
Fixtures Secretary: G Gaunt   Tel: (H) 01455 282052
Club Colours: Red, white and blue hoops

BIRSTALL RFC
Ground Address: Longslade Community College, Wanlip Lane, Birstall, Leicester   Tel: 0116 2674211
Brief Directions: From south - take A6 into Birstall, right at traffic lights (Sibson Rd). From north - A6 into Birstall, left at lights. When on Sibson Rd left at 1st island, college is 1.5-2 miles on left
Club Secretary: Mr C Blakesley, 39 Ashfield Drive, Anstey, Leicester. LE7 7TA   Tel: (H) 0116 2351254 (W) 0121 722 4000
Fixtures Secretary: Mr J Cross   Tel: (H) 0116 2673307
Club Colours: Black, green and white hoops, black shorts

BURBAGE RFC
Ground Address: John Cleveland College, Butt Lane, Hinckley, Leics
Brief Directions: From Jcn 2 M69/A5 towards Hinckley over island to traffic lights turn right, follow road to end turn left then 1st right after bridge, follow road to end turn right, JCC 500 yds on right
Club Secretary: C M Startin, 102 Strathmore Road, Hinckley, Leics. LE10 6LR   Tel: (H) 01455 634073 (W) 01455 637841
Fixtures Secretary: R Sansome   Tel: (H) 01455 610266
Club Colours: Green and white hoops

NEW PARKS RFC
Ground Address: New Parks Community College, St Oswalds Road Entrance, New Parks Estate, Leicester   Tel: 0116 2872115
Brief Directions: J21 off motorway, left towards A50, up to fire station, turn 1st right and 1st right towards the leisure centre, school on left
Club Secretary: T J Smith, 10 Birds Nest Avenue, New Parks Estate, Leicester. LE3 9NB   Tel: 0116 2911687
Fixtures Secretary: R Brooks   Tel: (H & W) 0116 2332536
Club Colours: Blue with black chevron

OLD NEWTONIANS RFC
Ground Address: Hinckley Road (A47), Leicester Forest East, Leicester   Tel: 0116 2392389
Brief Directions: Follow main A47 to Hinckley out of Leicester, pass Red Cow pub on right, ground 0.75 mile on right
Club Secretary: G A Clark, 250 Wigston Lane, Aylestone, Leicester. LE2 8DH   Tel: (H) 0116 2832309 (W) 0116 2785288
Fixtures Secretary: Peter Muggleton, 20 The Meadway, Birstall. LE4 4NS
Club Colours: Navy with white, red, green, white central band, navy shorts

WIGSTON RFC
Ground Address: Leicester Road, Countesthorpe, Leicester. LE18 3QU   Tel: 0116 277 1153
Brief Directions: From outer ring road take B5366 (Saffron Lane) to South Wigston, then Countesthorpe Rd-signed Countesthorpe, ground approx 1 mile on left
Club Secretary: Steve Benton, 5 Ramsdean Avenue, Wigston, Leicester. LE18 1DX   Tel: (H) 0116 288 9381 (W) 0116 255 6776
Fixtures Secretary: Richard Alexander   Tel: (H) 0116 288 0449
Club Colours: Purple with black, gold and silver chest and arm bands

LEICESTERSHIRE TWO

Leicestershire Two 1997-98 Fixtures	Anstey 1	Aylestone Ath. 2	Braunstone 3	Cosby 4	Shepshed 5	
1 Anstey	X	20/9	24/1	7/3	11/10	1
2 Aylestone Athletic	31/1	X	25/10	8/11	14/3	2
3 Braunstone	27/9	14/2	X	11/10	8/11	3
4 Cosby	25/10	27/9	14/3	X	31/1	4
5 Shepshed	14/2	24/1	7/3	20/9	X	5
	1	2	3	4	5	

ANSTEY RFC
Ground Address: Bennion Road, Beaumont Leys, Leicester
Brief Directions: From A46 (Leicester Western Bypass) take Anstey/Beaumont Leys exit. Follow signs to shopping centre, turn beside police station.
Club Secretary: Chris Apperley, 97 Link Road, Anstey, Leicester. LE7 7BZZ Tel: (H) 0116 234 0293 (W) 0860 487001
Fixtures Secretary: Ian Pollock, 14 Pinewood Close, Beaumont Leys, Leicester, LE4 1ER. Tel: 0116 2367364
Club Colours: Black shirt, black shorts, black socks with white hoops

AYLESTONE ATHLETIC RFC
Ground Address: Victoria Park Pavilion, Victoria Park, Leicester
Brief Directions: South from Railway Station, 1 mile along London Road, Park Pavilion on right hand side
Club Secretary: Robert Jackson, 9 Alder Close, Leicester Forest East, Leicester Tel: (H) 0116 299 3847
Fixtures Secretary: T Clay Tel: (H) 0116 2246808
Club Colours: Navy and scarlet hoops

BRAUNSTONE TOWN RFC
Ground Address: Mossdale Meadows, Kingsway, Braunstone, Leicester Tel: 0116 630018
Brief Directions: M69 - Narborough Road South - Kingsway
Club Secretary: Mrs Alison Tyers, 46 Salcombe Drive, Glenfield, Leicester. LE3 8F Tel: (H) 0116 2875276 (W) 01455 251200 Ext 8711
Fixtures Secretary: Mr Peter Tyers Tel: (H) 0116 2875276
Club Colours: Amber

COSBY RFC
Ground Address: Victory Park, Park Road, Cosby, Leics Tel: 0116 2849244
Brief Directions: M1 J21, follow signs for Narborough, at Narborough follow signs for railway station, cross level crossing, turn right and follow signs for Cosby, ground in centre of village
Club Secretary: C W Elliott, 9 Wavertree Close, Cosby, Leicester. LE9 5TN Tel: (H) 0116 2841746 (W) 01709 550066
Fixtures Secretary: C W Elliott Tel: (H) 0116 2841746 (W) 01709 550066
Club Colours: Black with Red & White chest bands

SHEPSHED RFC
Ground Address: Hindleys College, Forest Street, Shepshed, Loughborough, Leicestershire Tel: 01509 504511
Brief Directions: M1 J23 left A512 Ashby, 1st traffic lights right (Leicester Rd), 1st right past Jet Garages (Forest St), HLCC on right, 1st right
Club Secretary: Mr S Hughes, 76 Braddow Road, Loughborough. LE11 5YZ
Fixtures Secretary: M Timms Tel: (H) 01509 505331
Club Colours: Red and black quarters

Have you many Rugby enthusiasts at your Club ?
Does you Club need to raise extra funds ?

If the answer to these questions is Yes -
then place an order for

The Official Rugby Union Club Directory

WITH EVERY CLUB IN THE LEAGUE STRUCTURE INCLUDED AND ITS UNRIVALLED STATISTICAL COVERAGE OF THE CLUBS AND PLAYERS IN THE TOP LEVELS OF THE LEAGUE SYSTEM IT CAN ANSWER ALL SORTS OF QUESTIONS AND WOULD MAKE AN IDEAL PRESENT.

Did you realise the Directory is available to your club at very good discount rates.

If you order				Profit for Club
1	copy cost	£14.99		
2 or 3	copies cost	£13.50 each	£ 1.49 each	
between 4 & 9	copies cost	£10.00 each	£ 4.99 each	
between 10 & 19	copies cost	£ 9.00 each	£ 5.99 each	
20 or more	copies cost	£ 8.00 each	£ 6.99 each	

To find out more information or to place an order, contact the publishers:
Tony Williams Publications Ltd., Helland, North Curry, Taunton, Somerset. TA3 6DU.
or Telephone 01823 490080 or Fax 01823 490281

SOUTH WEST DIVISION

For the smooth operation of the English Clubs Championship it is essential each club appoints an official who will be responsible for receiving all correspondence in connection with the administration of the leagues. This will include results, tables, fines and registration matters. A Club will be deemed to have received notification if an item has been sent to this official - the Club's Nominated Contact. It is incumbent on this person to communicate the information to those within the club. Any changes to this officer during the season should be notified to the First Eleven Sports Agency in writing. Changes in officials should also be notified separately, to the RFU at Twickenham.

ADMINISTRATIVE RULES

1. MATCH RESULTS REPORTING INSTRUCTIONS FOR ALL LEAGUES

(i) Home clubs will telephone the First Eleven Sports Agency on 07071 611 611 as soon as possible after the end of each game and certainly before 6pm on Saturdays or within an hour of the end of the game on other days.

(ii) Both clubs in each game will complete a Match Result Card, listing the first names and surnames of the team and all replacements in block letters and the Match Result. The card must be signed by the Match Referee and officials from both clubs and posted, first class, to the First Eleven Sports Agency, by first post on Monday at the latest.

2. NOTIFICATION OF RESULTS

The Club's Nominated Contacts are responsible for their Club's compliance with the rules for notification of results. Failure to telephone and card-in the match result team and replacements lists, within the time limits laid down, will incur a fine for each offence of £15. Offending clubs will be notified of fines imposed, failure to pay within 28 days will result in the offending Club being deducted two Competition points. There is no right of appeal. Any outstanding fines at the end of the season can result in the South West Division requesting the RFU to expel the offending club from the leagues or deduct points at the start of the following season.

3. POSTPONED AND ABANDONED GAMES

The Nominated Contact of clubs with home matches must, in the event of a postponement or abandonment of any league match, immediately inform the First Eleven Sports Agency on 07071 611 611 and their appropriate League Secretary. This information should be relayed as soon as possible - clubs should not wait until the time the game would have finished before reporting the news. In the case of a game which is called off prior to kick off it is not necessary to complete a match card.

4. GENERAL ENQUIRIES

Apart from registration of players, see paragraph 6, and the telephoning of results, paragraph 1, a club's first point of contact over interpretation of the playing regulations or other matters involving the English Clubs Championship should be directed in the first instance to the club's League Secretary.

5. RESCHEDULED MATCHES

A match postponed or abandoned under Regulation 12 or a match not played on the appointed day for reasons acceptable to the Organising Committee SHALL be played on the NEXT AVAILABLE weekend.

A weekend is deemed to be "available" UNLESS one of the following conditions applies:

i) Either club has, on that weekend, a scheduled English Clubs Championship Match.

ii) Either Club has, on that weekend, a RFU Club Knockout Competition, Intermediate or Junior Knockout Cup tie.

iii) Either Club has, on that weekend, a match in an approved Competition under the authority of their constituent body BUT NOT a Merit Table match.

iv) Either Club has a demand on one or more of their effectively registered players to play in an approved representative match under the authority of the RFU, their Division or their Constituent Body on that weekend.

e) In addition, the South West Division Organising Committee, whose decision is final, may - at its absolute discretion and usually at the start of a season - declare a specific weekend "unavailable" where it falls on or close to a public holiday or where it is considered inappropriate to play for other particular reasons.

Each club involved in a postponed game will receive a letter from the First Eleven Sports Agency asking for details of the re-arranged fixture. Clubs must notify the Agency in writing and their League Secretary within SEVEN days of the original game of the date of the re-arranged fixture. Failure to do so, or to provide reasons why a date has not been agreed, will be subject to a £15 fine. It is also the responsibility of the home club to inform their referees' society of the date of the re-arranged game.

6. PLAYER REGISTRATION FORMS

All Player registration forms must, on completion, be forwarded to: The Registrar, The First Eleven Sports Agency, PO BOX 11, READING, RG6 3DT. Faxed registrations will not be accepted.

All enquiries regarding player registrations must be made, preferably in normal working hours, Monday to Saturday, to the Registrar by post, to the address above, by telephone to 07071 611 611, fax on 0118 9757764) or E-Mail to First11@aol.com.

The Agency shall keep computer images of the submitted forms and in the case of any dispute, these images will be accepted in place of the actual form at any hearing, appeal or other discussion about the registration.

7. CLUBS JOINING LEAGUES

All clubs wishing to join the English Clubs Championship must apply in writing to the South West Division Leagues Co-ordinating secretary no later than 14th April to qualify for entry the following season. By this same date, the club must have met all the entry criteria laid down in the English Clubs Championship Regulations and those applied, from time to time, by the Organising Committee.

8. CHANGE OF CLUB'S NAME

(i) Any proposals to change the name of a club must be notified to the Co-ordinating Secretary before 1st May for inclusion in the season commencing the August following.

(ii) Any clubs proposing a merger should note the regulation in respect of Club mergers contained in the Rugby Football Union's Handbook.

SOUTH WEST DIVISION

CHAIRMAN, League Sub-Committee
Dr C. V. Phillips, Barlowena, Alexandra Road, Illogan, REDRUTH, Cornwall. TR16 4EN (H) 01209 842660 (H/Fax) 01209 842892 (B)01209 714866 (B/Fax) 01209 716977

LEAGUE CO-ORDINATING SECRETARY
M. Gee, Lowenna, 70 Halsetown, ST IVES, Cornwall. TR26 3LZ (H/B/Fax) 01736 797777 EMAIL SWRFU@AOL.COM

DEPUTY LEAGUE CO-ORDINATING SECRETARY
B. Flanders, Old Cross House, Coscote, DIDCOT, Oxon. OX11 0NP (H/Fax) 01235 816523

LEAGUE SECRETARIES
South West One & Two J. D. Wooldridge, 16 Grange Drive, Durleigh, BRIDGWATER, Somerset. TA6 7LL (H/Fax) 01278 422009
Deputy: M. Gee, Lowenna, 70 Halsetown, ST IVES, Cornwall. TR26 3LZ (H/B/Fax) 01736 797777 EMAIL SWRFU@AOL.COM

Bucks/Oxon One & Two B. Flanders, Old Cross House, Coscote, DIDCOT, Oxon. OX11 0NP (H/Fax) 01235 816523
Deputy: H. Pocock, 10 Laceys Drive, Haslemere, HIGH WYCOMBE, Bucks. HP15 7JY (H) 01494 713879 (B) 0181 685 0444

Berks/Dorset & Wilts One & Two D. McAteer, 1 Rowlands Close, Mortimer West End, READING. RG7 3US (H/Fax) 0118 9701245
Deputy: K. Jones, 13 Stratfield Road, BASINGSTOKE, Hants. RG21 5RS (H) 01256 410461 (B) 0118 982 6750

Berks/Dorset & Wilts Three P. Richell, 26 Durweston, BLANDFORD FORUM, Dorset. DT11 0QE (H/Fax) 01258 452918 (B) 01258 472652
Deputy: A. Bott, Kew House, Anchor Road, CALNE, Wilts. SN11 8DL (H/Fax) 01249 821448 (M) 0410 017478

Cornwall/Devon League Mrs B. Davis, 8 Penrose Road, HELSTON, Cornwall. TR13 8TP (H/Fax 01326 563744 (B) 01209 215620
Deputy: G. Simpson, 108 Pattinson Drive, Mainstone, PLYMOUTH. PL6 8RU (H/Fax) 01752 707432

Cornwall One & Two N. J. Barber JP, 86 Dolcoath Road, CAMBORNE, Cornwall. TR14 8RP (H/Fax) 01209 710593 (B) 01752 665951
Deputy: D. Jenkins, 'Windward', St Ann's Chapel, GUNNISLAKE, Cornwall. PL18 9HQ (H/Fax) 01822 832785

Devon One R. Lovell, 4 Gillard Road, BRIXHAM, Devon. TQ5 8JX (H) 10803 855476 (B) 01803 859115
Deputy: G. Simpson, 108 Pattinson Drive, Mainstone, PLYMOUTH. PL6 8RU (H/Fax) 01752 707432

Devon Two & Three G. Hoggins, The Old Forge, North Street, NORTH TAWTON, Devon. EX20 2DE (H/Fax) 01837 82516
Deputy: G. Simpson, 108 Pattinson Drive, Mainstone, PLYMOUTH. PL6 8RU (H/Fax) 01752 707432

Gloucestershire & Somerset & Gloucestershire One & Two A. Townsend, 2 Kencourt Close, Kenilworth Avenue, GLOUCESTER. GL2 0QL (H/Fax) 01452 522721 (B) 01452 414403
Deputy: (G/S) A. Barnes, 18 Podsmead Place, Tuffley, GLOUCESTER. GL1 5PD (H) 01452 525530
(GL 1&2) Mrs E. Townsend (as above)

Gloucestershire Three C. Ravenhill, 18 Merevale Road, Longlevens, GLOUCESTER. GL2 0QY (H) 01452 304317
Deputy: A. Townsend, 2 Kencourt Close, Kenilworth Avenue, GLOUCESTER. GL2 0QL (H/Fax) 01452 522721 (B) 01452 414403

Southern Counties (North) M. Wild, 21 Westgate Crescent, Cippenham, SLOUGH. SL1 5BX (H/Fax) 01628 685528 (B) 01753 551066
Deputy: B. Flanders, Old Cross House, Coscote, DIDCOT, Oxon. OX11 0NP (H/Fax) 01235 816523

Southern Counties (South) A. Bott, Kew House, Anchor Road, CALNE, Wiltshire. SN11 8DL (H/Fax) 01249 821448 (M) 0410 017478
Deputy: N. Stafford, Veryan, 46 Bulkington, DEVIZES, Wilts. SN10 1SL (H) 01380 828264

Somerset One, Two & Three C. MacDonald, 8 Sycamore Drive, CREWKERNE, Somerset. TA18 7BT (H/Fax) 01460 76136
Deputy: R. Fisher, 20 Rookery Road, Knowle, BRISTOL. BS4 2DS (H) 0117 983 6325

Western Counties (North) W. Bishop, Hellvellyn, 1 Wiltshire Place, Kingswood, BRISTOL. BS15 4XA (H) 0117 957 5729 (B) 0117 935 2017 (Fax) 0117 9401290 EMAIL:BILLBISHOP1@COMPUSERVE.COM
Deputy: R. Fisher, 20 Rookery Road, Knowle, BRISTOL. BS4 2DS (H) 0117 983 6325

Western Counties (West) D. Jenkins, 'Windward', St Anns Chapel, Gunnislake, Cornwall. PL18 9HQ (H/Fax) 01822 832785
Deputy: A. Higgs, Roseleigh, Hollis Road, CHELTENHAM, Glos. GL51 6JG (H) 01242 230104

OTHER COMMITTEE MEMBERS
A. Boyer, 11 Christopher Court, Boundary Road, NEWBURY, Berks. RG14 7PQ (H/Fax) 01635 40574
J. Dance, Birch Cottage, Padworth Common, READING, Berks. RG7 4QG (H) 0118 970 0288/0118 970 1246 (Fax) 0118 970 1237
B. Morrison, First Eleven Sports Agency, PO BOX 11, READING. RG6 3DT (B) 07071 611 611 (Fax) 0118 975 7764 EMAIL FIRST11@AOL.COM
W. Wildash, 25 Marina Gardens, WEYMOUTH, Dorset. DT4 9QZ (H) 01305 773286 (B) 01305 212540 (Fax) 01305 212116

SOUTH WEST DIVISION
FINAL LEAGUE TABLES 1996-97

SOUTH WEST DIV ONE

	P	W	D	L	F	A	PTS
Bridgwater	22	18	0	4	794	318	36
Launceston	22	18	0	4	752	324	36
Maidenhead	22	16	1	5	648	285	33
Barnstable	22	14	0	8	487	403	28
Gloucester Old Boys	22	13	0	9	518	360	26
Torquay	22	10	1	11	364	354	21
Matson	22	10	1	12	355	362	20
Stroud	22	10	0	12	465	499	20
St Ives	22	8	0	14	313	725	16
Salisbury	22	7	0	15	394	686	14
Brixham	22	6	0	16	382	640	12
Camborne	22	1	0	21	253	769	*0

SOUTH WEST DIV 2E

	P	W	D	L	F	A	PTS
Bracknell	22	22	0	0	868	201	44
Swanage	21	16	0	5	628	321	32
Aylesbury	22	11	1	10	432	401	23
Dorchester	22	11	0	11	414	366	22
Amersham & Chiltern	20	11	0	9	340	312	22
Marlow	22	10	1	11	432	444	21
Oxford	22	10	0	12	476	538	20
Chinner	22	10	0	12	386	474	20
Sherborne	20	10	0	10	353	513	20
Bournemouth	22	7	0	15	369	497	14
Chippenham	22	6	0	16	381	587	12
Swindon	21	4	0	17	256	681	8

SOUTH WEST DIV 2W

	P	W	D	L	F	A	PTS
Penzance	21	18	0	3	636	244	36
Spartans	21	15	0	6	528	265	30
Cinderford	22	15	0	7	481	373	30
Old Pattesians	22	13	0	9	447	341	26
Dings Crusaders	22	12	2	8	470	415	26
Penryn	22	11	0	11	462	443	22
Clevedon	22	11	0	11	451	440	22
Tiverton	22	10	1	11	430	530	21
Taunton	22	8	3	11	444	511	19
Gordon League	22	8	2	12	420	520	18
Devenport Services	22	4	0	18	332	602	8
Combe Down	22	2	0	20	198	615	4

SOUTHERN COUNTIES NORTH

	P	W	D	L	F	A	PTS
Stow-on-the-Wold	18	17	0	1	722	120	34
Bicester	18	16	0	2	612	273	32
Olney	18	10	0	8	444	272	20
Buckingham	18	8	1	9	368	352	17
Oxford Harlequins	18	9	0	9	439	424	*16
Witney	18	8	0	10	334	453	16
Bletchley	18	8	0	10	277	448	16
Slough	18	7	1	10	335	422	15
Milton Keynes	18	5	0	13	304	452	10
Grove	18	1	0	17	144	763	*0

SOUTHERN COUNTIES SOUTH

	P	W	D	L	F	A	PTS
Abbey	18	18	0	0	703	154	36
Wimborne	18	16	0	2	608	165	32
Wootton Bassett	18	12	1	5	367	270	*23
Devizes	18	9	1	8	365	280	19
North Dorset	18	6	1	11	355	495	13
Blandford	18	5	3	10	232	375	13
Marlborough	18	6	0	12	254	520	12
Windsor	18	8	1	9	369	474	*11
Corsham	18	3	1	14	251	442	7
Redingensians	18	3	0	15	205	543	6

WESTERN COUNTIES NORTH

	P	W	D	L	F	A	PTS
Keynsham	15	14	1	0	584	180	29
St Mary's Old Boys	15	13	1	1	514	140	27
Hornets	15	13	1	1	432	145	27
Cleve	15	10	1	4	396	231	21
Cheltenham North	15	10	0	5	364	261	20
Cirencester	15	8	2	5	340	343	18
Old Redcliffians	15	8	0	7	261	248	16
Old Cilverhaysians	15	7	1	7	337	383	15
Drybrook	15	6	1	8	311	420	13
Oldfield Old Boys	15	5	0	10	257	386	10
Thornbury	15	5	0	10	254	395	10
North Bristol	15	4	1	10	224	317	9
Whitehall	15	4	1	10	234	336	*7
Bristol Harlequins	15	3	0	12	211	405	6
Avonmouth	15	3	0	12	195	429	6
Chard	15	2	0	13	187	482	*2

WESTERN COUNTIES WEST

	P	W	D	L	F	A	PTS
Okehampton	20	16	1	3	461	279	33
St Austell	20	15	0	5	531	288	30
Wellington	20	13	1	6	421	252	27
Paignton	20	11	1	8	365	329	23
Hayle	20	9	1	10	327	376	19
Bideford	20	9	0	11	350	348	18
Sidmouth	20	10	0	10	334	395	*18
Ivybridge	20	9	0	11	332	381	*16
Old Plymothian	20	7	0	13	260	361	14
Crediton	20	7	0	13	437	404	*12
Saltash	20	2	0	18	217	622	4

CORNWALL & DEVON

	P	W	D	L	F	A	PTS
Kingsbridge	14	13	0	1	340	108	26
South Molton	13	10	0	3	295	137	20
Teignmouth	13	8	0	5	260	169	16
Exmouth	14	8	1	5	255	242	*15
Bude	14	7	0	7	254	179	14
Honiton	14	4	1	9	220	339	9
Truro	14	2	0	12	151	347	*2
Plymouth C S	14	2	0	12	113	367	*2

CORNWALL ONE

	P	W	D	L	F	A	PTS
Falmouth	18	17	0	1	596	175	34
Newquay	18	17	0	1	527	121	34
Helston	18	9	2	7	477	290	20
Perranporth	18	9	0	9	324	285	18
Illogan Park	18	8	0	10	285	308	16
St Just	18	8	0	10	288	377	16
Liskeard	18	8	2	8	259	376	*16
St Agnes	18	7	0	11	360	440	*12
Stithians	18	5	0	13	207	408	10
Redruth Albany	18	0	0	18	97	640	0

CORNWALL TWO

	P	W	D	L	F	A	PTS
Bodmin	10	9	1	0	431	57	19
Wadebridge	10	8	1	1	326	42	17
St Day	10	5	0	5	153	173	10
Camborne S O M	10	4	0	6	146	191	*6
Roseland	10	3	0	7	98	236	6
Lankelly Fowey	10	0	0	10	56	511	0

DEVON ONE

	P	W	D	L	F	A	PTS
Withycombe	18	18	0	0	567	162	36
Newton Abbott	18	15	0	3	557	211	30
Tavistock	18	11	0	7	382	416	22
Topsham	18	9	1	8	412	404	19
Old Technicians	18	8	1	9	337	322	17
Old Public Oaks	18	8	0	10	371	288	16
Torrington	18	7	1	10	335	462	15
Exeter Saracens	18	5	0	13	260	517	10
Totnes	18	4	1	13	291	484	9
Tamar Saracens	18	3	0	15	186	432	6

DEVON TWO

	P	W	D	L	F	A	PTS
Ilfracombe	18	18	0	0	923	45	36
Dartmouth	18	12	0	6	570	296	24
Plymouth Argaum	18	11	0	7	323	293	22
Prince Rock	18	11	1	6	272	254	*21
North Tawton	18	9	0	9	296	317	18
Salcombe	18	8	0	10	266	410	16
Bovey Tracey	18	6	3	9	310	440	15
Cullompton	18	8	1	9	215	407	*13
Plymstock	18	4	1	13	208	438	9
St Columba	18	0	0	18	84	567	0

SOUTH WEST DIVISION STRUCTURE 1997-98

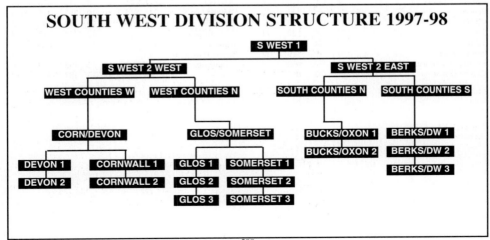

SOUTH WEST ONE

South West One 1997-98 Fixtures	Barnstaple	Berry Hill	Bracknell	Gloucester OB	High Wycombe	Launceston	Maidenhead	Matson	Penzance/Newlyn	St Ives	Stroud	
	1	2	3	4	5	6	7	8	9	10	11	12
1 *Barnstaple	X	4/4	?/9	27/9	14/3	14/2	18/10	31/1	17/1	8/11	20/12	10/1	1
2 Berry Hill	30/8	X	31/1	8/11	6/9	14/3	17/1	27/9	14/2	20/12	11/4	18/10	2
3 Bracknell	21/3	25/10	X	20/9	24/1	15/1	7/3	25/4	10/1	11/10	7/2	30/8	3
4 Gloucester Old Boys	7/3	24/1	14/3	X	15/11	25/4	11/10	10/1	4/4	7/2	25/10	6/9	4
5 *High Wycombe	20/9	21/3	8/11	17/1	X	27/9	20/12	14/2	18/10	18/4	30/8	31/1	5
6 Launceston	11/10	20/9	17/1	20/12	7/3	X	11/4	18/10	31/1	30/8	21/3	8/11	6
7 Maidenhead	7/2	15/11	27/9	14/2	25/4	10/1	X	4/4	6/9	25/10	24/1	14/3	7
8 Matson	25/10	7/3	20/12	11/4	11/10	7/2	30/8	X	8/11	21/3	20/9	17/1	8
9 Penzance/Newlyn	15/11	11/10	?/?	30/8	7/2	25/10	21/3	24/1	X	20/9	7/3	20/12	9
10 St Ives	24/1	25/4	14/2	18/10	10/1	4/4	31/1	6/9	14/3	X	15/11	27/9	10
11 Stroud	25/4	10/1	18/10	31/1	4/4	6/9	8/11	14/3	23/9	17/1	X	14/2	11
12 Torquay Athletic	11/4	7/2	4/4	21/3	25/10	24/1	20/9	25/11	25/4	7/3	11/10	X	12
	1	2	3	4	5	6	7	8	9	10	11	12	

BARNSTAPLE RFC
Ground Address: Pottington Road, Barnstable, North Devon Tel: 01271 45627
Brief Directions: Take A361 from Barnstable to Ilfracombe, turn left at 2nd traffic lights after Rolle Quay Bridge in Barnstable
Club Secretary: R Pettifer, Baileys Cottage, Lake, Barnstable. EX31 3HU   Tel: (H) 01271 73475
Fixtures Secretary: M Hughes Tel: (H) 01271 43547
Club Colours: Red shirts, white shorts, red socks

BERRY HILL
Ground Address: Lakers Road, Berry Hill, Coleford, Gloucestershire GL16 7LY Tel: 01594 833295
Brief Directions: From M4 Severn Bridge, M48 to Chepstow, B422B to Coleford, follow signs to Berry Hill. From M50 to Ross, A40 to Monmouth then A4136 to Berry Hill.
Club Secretary: T J Baldwin, Hill Brink, Coleford, Gloucestershire GL16 7AH Tel: (H) 01594 832539 (B) 01594 562631
Fixtures Secretary: G R Goddard, 71a Cheltenham Road, Glousestershire GL2 0JG Tel: (W) 01452 306749
Club Colours: Black and amber quarters

BRACKNELL RFC
Ground Address: Lily Hill Park, Lily Hill Road, Bracknell, Berkshire. RG12 2UG Tel: 01344 424013
Brief Directions: M4 J10, A329M Bracknell - A329 through town - Running Horse pub, ground at rear, or, M3 J3 - A322 Bracknell A329 - Ascot Road
Club Secretary: P J Denman, 57 Lingwood, Bracknell, Berks. RG12 7PZ Tel: (H) 01344 55400
Fixtures Secretary: S D Stevens, 18 Abbey Close, Harmanswater, Bracknell, Berks. Tel: 01344 422586
Club Colours: Green, gold and black

GLOUCESTER OLD BOYS RFC
Ground Address: Horton Road, Gloucester Tel: 01452 302390
Brief Directions: M5 J11A, follow signs to city centre, 3rd exit at roundabout adjacent to Wall's ice cream factory, 2nd left is Horton Road
Club Secretary: Ray Ellis, 15 Armscroft Way, Gloucester. GL2 0ST Tel: (H) 01452 525375 (W) 01452 416033
Fixtures Secretary: Bob Mansell Tel: (H) 01452 303055
Club Colours: Claret, gold and navy

HIGH WYCOMBE RUFC
Ground Address: Kingsmead Road, High Wycombe, Bucks. HP11 1JB. Tel: 01494 524407
Brief Directions: M40, J4 to A404 (Amersham) into town centre. A40 ((Beaconsfield). After 3rd mini r'about right into Abbey Barn Rd. After 800 yds sharp left into Kingsmead Rd.
Club Secretary: Don Dickerson, 3 Talbot Ave., High Wycombe, Bucks. HP13 5HZ. Tel: (H) 01494 532024 (B) 01494 479722
Fixtures Secretary: George Brown, Deerleap, Primrose Hill, Widmerend, High Wycombe, Bucks. HP15 6NU. Tel: (H) 01494 716700
Club Colours: Green with narrow black & white hoops

LAUNCESTON RFC
Ground Address: Polson, Launceston Tel: 01566 773406
Brief Directions: Leave A30 at Lifton Down junction, follow signs for Polson, LRFC situated at bottom of hill on left
Club Secretary: Bill Gladwell, 5 Hendra Tor View, Five Lanes, Altarnun,Cornwall PL15 7RG Tel: (H) 01566 86864 (W) 01208 77287 (FAX) 01208 73744
Fixtures Secretary: Mr W Gladwell Tel: 01566 86864
Club Colours: All black with white collar

SOUTH WEST ONE CONTINUED

MAIDENHEAD RUFC
Ground Address: Braywick Park, Braywick Road, Maidenhead, Berkshire   Tel: 01628 35452/29663
Brief Directions: M4 J8/9, A308(M) for Maidenhead town centre, 0.25 mile filter right across dual carriageway, Rugby club directly opposite
Club Secretary: Richard M Brown, 49 Bannard Road, Maidenhead, Berkshire. SL6 4NP   Tel: (H) 01628 70586   (W) 01628 25308
Fixtures Secretary: Chris Reeves   Tel: (H) 01628 20601
Club Colours: Magenta, violet and black

MATSON RFC
Ground Address: Redwell Road, Matson, Gloucester   Tel: 01452 528963
Brief Directions: 3 miles south of city centre on B4073, adjacent to dry ski slope
Club Secretary: Ron Etheridge, 63 Hawk Close, Abbeydale, Gloucester,GL4 8WE   Tel: 01452 539114
Fixtures Secretary: Andy James   Tel: (H) 01452 534525
Club Colours: Black shirts and white shorts

PENZANCE AND NEWLYN RFC
Ground Address: Westholme, Alexandra Road, Penzance, Cornwall. TR18 4LY   Tel: 01736 64227
Brief Directions: Follow sea front road until mini roundabout at Beachfield Hotel (Newlyn end of promenade) turn right 400yds up on the left
Club Secretary: T.Drew (Full time at club address above)
Fixtures Secretary: A Edwards   Tel: (H) 01736 731042 (W) 01736 331166
Club Colours: Black, white and red

ST IVES RFC
Ground Address: Alexandra Road, St Ives, Cornwall. TR26 1ER   Tel: 01736 795346
Brief Directions: A30 to St Erth, follow holiday route to St Ives (B3311), after passing Fire Station on right, Alexandra Road is 2nd left, ground is 200m on left
Club Secretary: Ms Carol Bell, Trerice, Clodgy View, St Ives, Cornwall. TR26 1JG   Tel: (H) 01736 797472
Fixtures Secretary: Mike Gee,Lowenna, 70 Halsetown, St Ives, Cornwall TR26 3LZ   Tel: (H) 01736 797168 (W) 01736 797777
Club Colours: Navy blue, and white

STROUD RFC
Ground Address: Fromehall Park, Stroud, Glos   Tel: 01453 763019
Brief Directions: 1 mile south of Stroud on A46
Club Secretary: Dennis Little, Lower Court, Selsley Road, Woodchester, Stroud, Glos. GL5 5PH   Tel: (H) 01453 872800   (Fax) 01453 872383
Fixtures Secretary: Russell Hillier   Tel: (H) 01453 764381   (W) 01275 464441
Club Colours: Blue and white hoops

TORQUAY ATHLETIC RFC
Ground Address: Torquay Recreation Ground, Seafront, Torquay, Devon   Tel: 01803 293842
Brief Directions: Head for seafront, ground on main seafront road adjacent to railway station
Club Secretary: J S Bradshaw, 6 All Hallows Road, Preston, Paignton TQ3 1EB   Tel: (H) 01803 521848 (W) 01392 204134 (FX) 0!392 204159
Fixtures Secretary: Dave Thompson   Tel: (H) 01803 845115 (W) 01803 858271
Club Colours: Black and white

High Wycome First XV Squad 1996/97.

SOUTH WEST TWO WEST

South West Two West 1997-98 Fixtures	Brixham	Camborne	Cinderford	Clevedon	Dings Crusaders	Keynsham	Okehampton	Old Patesians	Penryn	Spartans	Taunton	Tiverton	
	1	2	3	4	5	6	7	8	9	10	11	12	
1 Brixham	X	20/9	21/3	25/10	24/1	15/11	11/10	7/3	25/4	10/1	7/2	4/4	1
2 Camborne	14/3	X	7/3	24/1	15/11	25/4	7/2	11/10	10/1	4/4	25/10	6/9	2
3 Cinderford	6/9	27/9	X	4/4	14/3	14/2	8/11	18/10	31/1	17/1	20/12	28/3	3
4 Clevedon	31/1	8/11	30/8	X	6/9	14/3	20/12	17/1	27/9	14/2	18/4	18/10	4
5 Dings Crusaders	8/11	17/1	20/9	21/3	X	27/9	11/4	20/12	14/2	18/10	30/8	31/1	5
6 Keynsham	17/1	20/12	11/10	20/9	7/3	X	30/8	11/4	18/10	31/1	21/3	8/11	6
7 Okehampton	14/2	18/10	24/1	25/4	10/1	4/4	X	31/1	6/9	14/3	15/11	27/9	7
8 Old Patesians	27/9	14/2	7/2	15/11	25/4	10/1	25/10	X	4/4	6/9	24/1	14/3	8
9 Penryn	20/12	11/4	25/10	7/3	11/10	7/2	21/3	30/8	X	8/11	20/9	17/1	9
10 Spartans	18/4	30/8	15/11	11/10	7/2	25/10	20/9	21/3	24/1	X	7/3	20/12	10
11 Taunton	18/10	31/1	25/4	10/1	4/4	6/9	17/1	8/11	14/3	27/9	X	14/2	11
12 Tiverton	30/8	21/3	10/1	7/2	25/10	24/1	7/3	20/9	15/11	25/4	11/10	X	12
	1	2	3	4	5	6	7	8	9	10	11	12	

BRIXHAM RFC
Ground Address: Astley Park, Rea Barn Road, Brixham Tel: 01803 882162
Brief Directions: M5, then A380 to Torbay, follow signs for Brixham
Club Secretary: R B Houston, St Clwd, Cliff Park Road, Paignton   Tel: (H) 01803 550427
Fixtures Secretary: J D Irvine B.E.M.   Tel: (H) 01803 882219
Club Colours: Black with 6" white band

CAMBORNE RFC
Ground Address: The Recreation Ground, Camborne, Cornwall   Tel: 01209 713227
Brief Directions: Leave the A30 Camborne/Redruth bypass at junction for Camborne West following signs for the recreation ground
Club Secretary: W J C Dunstan, The Retreat, 11 Station Hill, Praze-an-Beeble, Camborne, Cornwall. TR24 0JT Tel: (H) 01209 831373   (W) 01736 795456
Fixtures Secretary: David Smith   Tel: (H)01209 716992
Club Colours: Cherry and white

CINDERFORD RFC
Ground Address: Dockham Road, Cinderford, Glos. GL14 2AQ   Tel: 01594 822673
Brief Directions: Centre of town close to bus station and Swan Hotel
Club Secretary: Mrs M Beavis, 5 Abbots Road, Cinderford, Glos. GL14 3BN   Tel: (H) 01594 823779
Fixtures Secretary: Mr A.J. Smith   Tel: 01594 822755
Club Colours: Red, black and amber

CLEVEDON RFC
Ground Address: Coleridge Vale Playing Fields, Southey Road, Clevedon, North Somerset. BS21 6PF Tel: 01275 877772
Brief Directions: M5 J20, 1st roundabout 12 o'clock exit, mini roundabout 12 o'clock exit, left at lights, 1st left by garage Binding & Payne which is signed for Clevedon RFC
Club Secretary: Robert G Legge, 2 Kingston Ave, Clevedon, North Somerset. BS21 6DS Tel: (H) 01275 874624 (Car) 0585 933142
Fixtures Secretary: John Evans Tel: (H) 01275 871443
Club Colours: Royal blue and old gold hoops

DINGS CRUSADERS RFC
Ground Address: Shaftesbury Crusade, Landseer Avenue, Lockleaze, Bristol. BS7   Tel: 0117 9691367
Brief Directions: Take J2 off M32 go towards Horfield and turn right at 2nd set of traffic lights (before bridge)After 1 mile turn left into Hogarth Walk and right at the end into Landseer Avenue.
Club Secretary: Rob Stevens , 4 Fonthill Way, B itton, Bristol BS15 6JT   Tel: (H) 0117 9329138
Fixtures Secretary: Terry Webb   Tel: 0117 9830273
Club Colours: Royal blue and black

KEYNSHAM RFC
Ground Address: The Crown Fields, Bristol Road, Keynsham, Bristol. BS18 2BE   Tel: 0117 987 2520
Brief Directions: Follow A4 from Bristol city centre, follow signs to Keynsham and Keynsham town centre. As you enter Keynsham the rugby cub is on the right hand side.
Club Secretary: Dermot Courtier, The Coach House, Eastover Farm, Manor Road, Saltford, Bristol. BS18 3AF. Tel: (H) 01225 874293 (B) 0171 250 2065
Fixtures Secretary: David Veal, 118 Harrington Road, Stockwood, Bristol. BS14 8JR.   Tel: (H) 01275 543416 (B) 01275 834628
Club Colours: Amber and black

OKEHAMPTON RUFC
Ground Address: Oaklands Park Showfield, Oaklands, Okehampton Tel: 01837 52508
Brief Directions: Off the Hatherleigh road, 250m from town centre
Club Secretary: Ted Cann, 11 Exeter Road, Okehampton. EX20 1NN Tel: (H) 01837 52759
Fixtures Secretary: David Dixon Tel: 01837 840818
Club Colours: Maroon and amber

OLD PATESIANS' RFC
Ground Address: Everest Road, Leckhampton, Cheltenham, Gloucestershire. Tel: 01242 524633
Brief Directions: Mini roundabout on London - M5 ring road, follow Old Bath Road, Everest Road on left opposite Wheatsheaf Inn
Club Secretary: P J McMurray, Avon, Victoria Terrace, Cheltenham, Gloucestershire. GL52 6BN
Tel: (H) 01242 570947 Tel: (W) 01242 515881
Fixtures Secretary: H Etheridge Tel: (H) 01242 238948 Tel:(W) 01242 221311 20674
Club Colours: Magenta, blue and white hoops

PENRYN RFC
Ground Address: The Memorial Ground, Kernick Road, Penryn Tel: 01326 372239
Brief Directions: From Exeter A38 to Plym'th Head twds L'keard, follow signs for Truro. From Truro A39 to Falm'th, continue to the Distribitor Rd, at r'bout turn to ind. est. (Asda), ground 2nd left
Club Secretary: Mr R Thomas, 44 Saracen Crescent, Penryn, Cornwall Tel: (H) 01326 377140
Fixtures Secretary: Mr P Webber Tel: (H) 01326 376613
Club Colours: Red and black hoops

SPARTANS RFC
Ground Address: Archdeacon Meadow, Cattle Market Complex, St Oswald Road, Gloucester Tel: 01452 410552
Brief Directions: M5 J12 for Gloucester, into Glos, take signs for docks, past docks, veer right just before Esso g'ge, take l/h lane, under railbridge, 1st left at Bell & Gavel, down as far as can go
Club Secretary: David Badham, 102 Deans Way, Gloucester. GL1 2QD Tel: (H) 01452 524252 (W) 01452 521521 Ext 2701
Fixtures Secretary: Paul Smith Tel: (H) 01452 533027
Club Colours: Red and black

TAUNTON RFC
Ground Address: Priory Park, Priory Bridge Road, Taunton, Somerset Tel: 01823 275670
Brief Directions: From M5 exit 25 follow signs to town centre, then county cricket ground and ground on right after roundabout by Great Mills store.
Club Secretary: George Wilson, 10 Obridge Road, Taunton. TA2 7PX Tel: (H) 01823 20495
Fixtures Secretary: Rodney Reed Tel: (H) 01823 276354 (W) 01823 337900 Ext 3375
Club Colours: Crimson, black and white hoops

TIVERTON RFC
Ground Address: Coronation Field, Bolham Road, Tiverton, Devon. EX16 7RD Tel: 01884 252271
Brief Directions: M5 J27 north towards Tiverton, 7 miles roundabout at end of d/carriageway left to Tiverton, ground 250mtrs on right just before footbridge over road
Club Secretary: David A J Baker, Millhouse, Burn, Silverton, Exeter, Devon. EX5 4BT Tel: (H) 01884 855548 (W) 01884 256412
Fixtures Secretary: Geoff D Bulley Tel: (H) 01884 259316 (W) 01392 382207
Club Colours: Light and dark blue

Okehampton R.F.C. XV 1996/97.
Champions Western Counties (West).

WESTERN COUNTIES WEST

Western Counties West 1997-98 Fixtures	Bideford	Devonport Serv.	Hayle	Ivybridge	Kingsbridge	Paignton	St Austell	Sidmouth	South Molton	Wellington	
	1	2	3	4	5	6	7	8	9	10	
1 Bideford	X	14/3	20/9	14/2	11/10	24/1	25/10	10/1	15/11	11/4	1
2 Devonport Services	6/9	X	25/10	20/9	10/1	14/2	15/11	11/10	11/4	24/1	2
3 Hayle	7/3	17/1	X	8/11	27/9	25/4	31/1	20/12	18/10	14/3	3
4 Ivybridge	27/9	7/3	10/1	X	15/11	11/10	11/4	24/1	6/9	25/10	4
5 Kingsbridge	31/1	8/11	14/2	25/4	X	20/12	18/10	14/3	17/1	20/9	5
6 Paignton	18/10	27/9	15/11	31/1	11/4	X	6/9	25/10	7/3	10/1	6
7 St Austell	17/1	25/11	11/10	20/12	24/1	14/3	X	20/9	8/11	14/2	7
8 Sidmouth	8/11	31/1	18/4	18/10	6/9	17/1	7/3	X	27/9	15/11	8
9 South Molton	25/4	20/12	24/1	14/3	25/10	20/9	10/1	14/2	X	11/10	9
10 Wellington	20/12	18/10	6/9	17/1	7/3	8/11	27/9	25/4	31/1	X	10
	1	2	3	4	5	6	7	8	9	10	

BIDEFORD RFC
Ground Address: King Georges Field, Riverside, Bank End, Bideford, Devon   Tel: 01237 474049
Brief Directions: N.D. link road, left end of Bideford New Bridge, into town until reach river, immediate left at Charles Kingsley statue, proceed River Bank Road to Bideford RFC car park
Club Secretary: Bernard A Ridd, The Firs, Glen Gardens, Bideford, Devon. EX39 3PH   Tel: (H) 01237 475180 (B) 01271 388617
Fixtures Secretary: Jilly Skinner, 95 Meddon Street, Bideford, Devon
Club Colours: Red and white hooped shirts, white shorts, red socks

DEVONPORT SERVICES RFC
Ground Address: The Rectory, 2nd Avenue, Devonport, Plymouth. PL1 5QE.   Tel: 01752 50559
Club Secretary: Mr M R Burningham, 1 Campbell Road, Plymstock, Plymouth, Devon. PL5 8UG. Tel: 01752 408874
Fixtures Secretary: Mr G Kelly, 24 Youldon Way, Morrabridge, Yelverton, Devon. PL20 7SN.
Club Colours: Navy shrits, scarlet shorts and socks

HAYLE RUGBY CLUB
Ground Address: Memorial Park, Marsh Lane, Hayle, Cornwall, TR27 4PS.
Brief Directions: Take A30 to first roundabout, ground immediately in front
Club Secretary: C Polkinghorne, 19 Meadowside Close, Hayle, Cornwall, TR27 4JL.   Tel: (H) 01736 753722
Fixtures Secretary: Mike Gee, Sunhail, 7 Hellesvean Close, St. Ives, Cornwall.   Tel: (H) 01736 797168
Club Colours: Green, black and white

IVYBRIDGE RFC
Ground Address: Cross-in Hand, Exeter Road, Ivybridge   Tel: 01752 894392
Brief Directions: From A38 Exeter/Plymouth main road, follow the `Park & Ride' signs. The ground is almost opposite the station entrance.
Club Secretary: John Naylor, Trem-Y-Wawr, Crescent Road, Ivybridge, Devon. PL21 0BP   Tel: (H) 01752 892412   (W) 01752 612138
Fixtures Secretary: Gary Aldridge, 99 Cleve Drive, Ivybridge.   Tel: (H) 01752 893773   (W) 01752 668351
Club Colours: Green, black and white

KINGSBRIDGE RFC
Ground Address: High House, Kingsbridge, Devon. TQ7 1JL   Tel: 01548 852051
Brief Directions: From centre of Kingsbridge take Dartmouth road alongside estuary, take 1st left and 1st right to the top of the hill
Club Secretary: Martin Newman, Fourwinds, 46 Saffron Park, Kingsbridge, Devon. TQ7 1RL   Tel: (H) 01548 853976   (W) 01548 853101
Fixtures Secretary: Derrick Marshall, 7 Welle House Gardens, Kingsbridge, Devon.   Tel: 01548 852618
Club Colours: Blue and white

PAIGNTON RFC
Ground Address: Queens Park, Queens Road, Paignton, Devon   Tel: 01803 557715
Brief Directions: Into Paignton town centre, over railway track towards beach, next right turn into Queens Road.
Club Secretary: David Siddal, 37 Dartmouth Road, Paignton   Tel: 01803 664691
Fixtures Secretary: Gary Moate, 12 Kapp Park Road, Goodrington, Paignton   Tel: 01803 555655
Club Colours: Red and white hoops

SIDMOUTH RFC
Ground Address: Blackmore Ground, Heydons Lane, Sidmouth Tel: 01395 516816
Brief Directions: Heydons Lane in the centre of town
Club Secretary: Brian Showell, 3 Connaught Close, Sidmouth, Devon. EX10 8TU Tel: (H) 01395 512055
Fixtures Secretary: T O'Brien Tel: (H) 01395 577403
Club Colours: Green, white shorts

SOUTH MOLTON RFC
Ground Address: Pathfields, Station Road, South Molton, Devon Tel: 01769 572024
Brief Directions: Taking Pathfields exit on the North Devon link road when reading signs for South Molton, take first right then first left
Club Secretary: Mrs Annie White, 8 Duke Street, South Molton, Devon. EX36 3AL Tel: (H) 01769 573741 (W) 01769 573204
Fixtures Secretary: Denis Cronk Tel: 01769 550402
Club Colours: Black

ST AUSTELL RFC
Ground Address: Tregorrick Park, Tregorrick Lane, St Austell, Cornwall. PL26 7AG Tel: 01726 76430
Brief Directions: Located on the road behind Asda superstore and next to Mount Edgecumbe Hospice. From St Austell By-Pass take turning to Penrice Hopital.First right before Hospital.
Club Secretary: Brian Perkins, 28 Duporth Bay, St.Austell.PL26 6AF
Fixtures Secretary: Mr Howard Roberts Tel: (H) 01726 812065
Club Colours: Red and white hoops

WELLINGTON RFC
Ground Address: The Athletic Ground, Corams Lane, Wellington, Somerset. TA21 8LL Tel: 01823 663758
Brief Directions: Leave M5 J25 or from A38 from Taunton, right at central traffic lights into North St, left at Sportsman Inn, enter via sports centre car park
Club Secretary: B K Colman, Meadowside, Mantle Street, Wellington, Somerset Tel: (H) 01823 663307
Fixtures Secretary: G R Vickery Tel: (H) 01823 664695 (W) 01823 335166
Club Colours: Red and black

CORNWALL AND DEVON

Cornwall/Devon 1997-98 Fixtures	Bude	Crediton	Exmouth	Falmouth	Honiton	Old Plymothians	Saltash	Teignmouth	Truro	Withycombe	
	1	2	3	4	5	6	7	8	9	10	
1 Bude	X	14/2	14/3	11/10	20/9	24/1	15/11	25/10	10/1	11/4	1
2 Crediton	27/9	X	7/3	15/11	10/1	11/10	6/9	28/3	24/1	25/10	2
3 Exmouth	6/9	20/9	X	10/1	25/10	14/2		15/11	11/10	24/1	3
4 Falmouth	31/1	25/4	8/11	X	14/2	20/12	17/1	18/10	14/3	20/9	4
5 Hontion	7/3	8/11	17/1	27/9	X	25/4	18/10	31/1	20/12		5
6 Old Plymothians	18/10	31/1	27/9	10/4	15/11	X	7/3	6/9	25/10	10/1	6
7 Saltash	25/4	14/3	20/12	25/10	24/1	20/9	X	10/1	14/2	11/10	7
8 Teignmouth	17/1	20/12	25/4	24/1	11/10	14/3	8/11	X	20/9	14/2	8
9 Truro	8/11	18/10	31/1	6/9	11/4	17/1	27/9	7/3	X	15/11	9
10 Withycombe	20/12	17/1	18/10	7/3	6/9	8/11	31/1	27/9	25/4	X	10
	1	2	3	4	5	6	7	8	9	10	

BUDE RFC
Ground Address: Bencoolen Meadow (off Kings Hill), Bude, Cornwall. EX23 8DG Tel: 01288 354795
Club Secretary: Mr F B Sykes, 65 Kings Hill, Bude, Cornwall. EX23 8QL Tel: (H) 01288 354210
Fixtures Secretary: Mr J A Boundy Tel: (H) 01288 381296 (W) 01288 353766
Club Colours: Maroon and sky blue hoops

CREDITON RFC
Ground Address: Blagdon, Exhibition Road, Crediton. EX17 1BY Tel: 01363 772784
Brief Directions: M5 to Exeter, A377 to Crediton then A3072 towards Tiverton, club on left hand side of road
Club Secretary: Jim Brown, 7 The Maltings, Penton Lane, Crediton, Devon. EX17 1HT
Fixtures Secretary: Captain Keith S Pitt (Retd) Tel: (H & W) 01363 82230
Club Colours: Black and amber

CORNWALL AND DEVON CONTINUED

EXMOUTH RFC
Ground Address: Imperial Recreation Ground, Royal Avenue, Exmouth. EX8 1DG Tel: 01395 263665
Brief Directions: M5 to Sandy Gate-Exeter, exit here, follow Exmouth signs 8 miles, enter Exmouth on town bypass from which ground can be seen adjacent to River Exe
Club Secretary: Mr B L Cornall, Hillside Court, 65 The Marles, Exmouth. EX8 4NE Tel: (H) 01395 275332
Fixtures Secretary: Mr C Wright Osborne House, The Strand, Lympstone, Exmouth. EX8 5JS Tel: (H) 01395 272411
Club Colours: Heliotrope, white hoops

FALMOUTH
Ground Address: Dracaena Avenue, Falmouth, Cornwall Tel: 01326 311304/316924
Brief Directions: Straight along Dracaena Avenue, visible from main road
Club Secretary: J K Dryden, 15 Pengarth Road, Falmouth, Cornwall Tel: (H & W) 01326 316644
Fixtures Secretary: Mr G V Wilkes Tel: (H) 01872 277249 (W) 01209 885605
Club Colours: Black and white

HONITON RFC
Ground Address: Allhallows Playing Fields, Northcote Lane, Honiton Tel: 01404 41239
Brief Directions: From traffic lights in High St, turn into Dowell St, continue for 0.5 mile, turn right at the Fire station into Northcote Lane, follow road around to the Sports Centre
Club Secretary: Dave Todd, Omega, Sidmouth Road, Honiton, Devon. EX14 8BE Tel: (H) 01404 41608
Fixtures Secretary: Roy Freemantle Tel: (H) 01404 41888
Club Colours: Red, amber and black hoops

OLD PLYMOTHIAN & MANNAMEADIAN RFC
Ground Address: King George V Playing Fields, Elburton, Plymouth, Devon
Brief Directions: A38 take 1st Plymouth junction to Marsh Mills roundabout, follow signs for Kingsb'dge for 3-4 miles, at r'bout (Plympton signed to left) 1st left, ground 0.25 mile on right
Club Secretary: Mr Ernie Bolster, 22 Carlton Close, Lower Compton, Plymouth, Devon Tel: (H) 01752 223908 (W) 01752 673626
Fixtures Secretary: Mr Simon Matthews Tel: (H) 01752 730114 (W) 01392 382222
Club Colours: Claret and blue quarters

SALTASH RFC
Ground Address: Moorlands Lane, Saltash, Cornwall Tel: 01752 847227
Brief Directions: From A38 westward over Tamar Bridge, through tunnel, left at 1st roundabout, right at lights, then 2nd right into Moorlands Lane, clubhouse at end of lane
Club Secretary: Mr D R Jenkins, Windward, St Anns Chapel, Gunnislake, Cornwall. PL18 9HQ Tel: (H) 01822 832785 (W) 01822 616977
Fixtures Secretary: Mr J Westaway Tel: (H) 01752 851727
Club Colours: Black, gold and red hoops

TEIGNMOUTH RFC
Ground Address: Bitton Sports Ground, Bitton Park Road, Teignmouth Tel: 01626 774714
Brief Directions: Adjacent to Shaldon Bridge, off main Teignmouth to Newton Abbot road
Club Secretary: Robert Lovendge, 59 Second Avenue, Teignmouth, Devon. TQ14 9DN Tel: (H) 01626 775891 (W) 01626 774556
Fixtures Secretary: Alan Norswathy Tel: (H) 01626 774946
Club Colours: Red, white and black hoops

TRURO RFC
Ground Address: St Clements Hill, Truro, Cornwall, TR1 1NY. Tel: 01872 274750
Brief Directions: A30, leave signpost for Trispen, to Truro at large roundabout, enter St Clements Hill next to Police station, ground on right at top of hill
Club Secretary: Mr Philip Rowe, 36 Chirgwin Road, Truro, Cornwall. TR1 1TT Tel: (H) 01872 71915 (W) 01872 224202
Fixtures Secretary: Mr Philip Lear Tel: (H) 01326 563370 (W) 01872 73479
Club Colours: Amber and blue

WITHYCOMBE RUGBY & RECREATION CLUB RFC
Ground Address: Raleigh Park, Hulham Road, Exmouth, Devon. EX8 3HS Tel: 01395 266762
Brief Directions: M5 south J30, take A376 to Exmouth, at 1st lights in Exmouth turn left at box junction into Hulham Rd, ground 200 yards on right
Club Secretary: David M Josey, 2 Larch Close, Marley Gardens, Exmouth, Devon. EX8 5NQ Tel: (H) 01395 275038 (W) 01395 264784
Fixtures Secretary: M J Norman Tel: (H) 01395 270644
Club Colours: Emerald green and black hoops

Do you know a rugby enthusiast with a birthday coming up?

This directory would make a perfect present.

So why not buy a copy from your club or from W H Smith.

CORNWALL ONE

Cornwall One 1997-98 Fixtures	Bodmin	Helston	Illogan Park	Liskeard/Looe	Newquay Hornets	Perranporth	St Agnes	St Just	Stithians	Wadebridge	
	1	2	3	4	5	6	7	8	9	10	
1 Bodmin	X	14/3	20/9	14/2	11/10	24/1	10/1	15/11	11/4	25/10	1
2 Helston	6/9	X	25/10	20/9	10/1	14/2	11/10	11/4	24/1	15/11	2
3 Illogan Park	7/3	17/1	X	8/11	27/9	25/4	20/12	18/10	14/3	31/1	3
4 Liskeard/Looe	27/9	7/3	10/1	X	15/11	11/10	24/1	6/9	25/10	11/4	4
5 Newquay Hornets	31/1	8/11	14/2	25/4	X	20/12	14/3	17/1	20/9	18/10	5
6 Perranporth	18/10	27/9	15/11	31/1	4/4	X	25/10	7/3	10/1	6/9	6
7 *St Agnes	8/11	31/1	11/4	18/10	6/9	17/1	X	27/9	15/11	7/3	7
8 St Just	25/4	20/12	24/1	14/3	25/10	20/9	14/2	X	11/10	10/1	8
9 Stithians	20/12	18/10	6/9	17/1	7/3	8/11	25/4	31/1	X	27/10	9
10 Wadebridge	17/1	25/4	11/10	20/12	24/1	14/3	20/9	8/11	14/2	X	10
	1	2	3	4	5	6	7	8	9	10	

BODMIN RFC
Ground Address: Clifton Park, Carminnow Cross, Bodmin, Cornwall   Tel: 01208 74629
Brief Directions: Off A38 before Flyover at A30 take B Road signed Lanhydrock 400yds turn right down private drive.
Club Secretary: Roy Whitehall, 16 Athelstan Park, Bodmin, Cornwall. PL31 1DS   Tel: (H) 01208 77528
Fixtures Secretary: Mike Roberts, 9 Church Park, Bodmin, PL31 2BU. Tel: 01208 74861
Club Colours: Light Blue/Dark Blue Hoops

HELSTON RFC
Ground Address: King George V Memorial Playing Fields, Clodgey Lane, Helston   Tel: 01326 573742
Brief Directions: A394 into north of town past Tesco superstore, 0.25 mile on right, before Flambards Theme Park
Club Secretary: Mrs Bev Davis, 8 Penrose Road, Helston, Cornwall. TR13 8NP   Tel: (H) 01326 563744 (W) 01209 215620
Fixtures Secretary: Mrs Bev Davis   Tel: (H) 01326 563744   (W) 01209 215620
Club Colours: Navy and white hoops

ILLOGAN PARK RFC
Ground Address: Illogan Park, New Inn, Park Bottom, Redruth, Cornwall
Brief Directions: Redruth to Illogan road, turn left before Pynter Lane End
Club Secretary: Mr G R Tonkins, 20 Lower Pengegon, Camborne, Cornwall. TR14 8RX   Tel: (H) 712395   (W) 218785
Fixtures Secretary: R J McLellan   Tel: (H) 01872 572696   (W) 712712
Club Colours: Yellow and black

LISKEARD - LOOE RFC
Ground Address: Lux Park, Coldstyle Road, Liskeard, Cornwall   Tel: 01579 342665
Brief Directions: Ask for the Leisure Centre, near town centre
Club Secretary: A C Patten, Beara Farm, Herodsfoot, Nr Liskeard, Cornwall. PL14 4RB   Tel: (H & W) 01579 321063
Fixtures Secretary: Peter Pascoe   Tel: (H) 01579 342956
Club Colours: Red and black hoops

NEWQUAY HORNETS RFC
Ground Address: Newquay Sports Centre, Tretherras Road, Newquay, Cornwall   Tel: 01637 875533
Brief Directions: Newquay via A3058, lft Chester Rd, 2nd lft Whitegate Rd, lft at T jcn, club 50 yds lft. Frm Redruth, N'quay via A392, across mini r'bouts into Edgcumbe Ave, rt Hilgrove Rd, 1st rt, club at end
Club Secretary: Ken Truscott, Homeleigh, 15 Quintrell Road, Newquay, Cornwall. TR7 3DX   Tel: (H) 01637 875698
Fixtures Secretary: Reg Roberts   Tel: (H) 01637 874568
Club Colours: Green and white

PERRANPORTH RC
Ground Address: Ponsmere Valley, Perranporth, Cornwall
Brief Directions: From Newquay turn right at Goonhavern roundabouts, continue approx 2 miles, past Golf Club on right, down steep hill, 1st turning left
Club Secretary: Mr Nik Lewis, Cornerways, Perranwell Road, Goonhavern, Nr Truro, Cornwall. TR4 9JL   Tel: (H) 01872 571217
Fixtures Secretary: Mr Bob Trevail   Tel: (H) 01872 573547
Club Colours: Green and gold

ST AGNES RFC
Ground Address: Enys Park, Trevaunance Road, St Agnes   Tel: 01872 553673
Brief Directions: Turn left opposite church, turn right after 800 yards, Enys Park is 200 yards on right
Club Secretary: Tim Barnes, c/o T & JB Produce Ltd, Gover Farm, Gover Hill, Mt Hawke, Truro. TR4 8BQ Tel: (H) 01209 890 218   (W) 01872 553311
Fixtures Secretary: Rob Penhaligon, 45 Penair View, Truro, Cornwall. TR1 1XR   Tel: 01872 275175
Club Colours: Black and red hoops

ST JUST RFC
Ground Address: St Just RFC, Tregeseal, St Just-in-Penwith, Cornwall. TR19 7PF   Tel: 01736 788593
Club Secretary: R W Bassett, 31 Boscathnoe Way, Heamdor, Penzance, Cornwall. TR18 3JS   Tel: (H) 01736 62311   (W) 01736 62341
Fixtures Secretary: P Whitman   Tel: (H) 01736 788150
Club Colours: All black

STITHIANS RFC
Ground Address: Playing Field, Stithians, Truro, Cornwall   Tel: 01209 860148
Brief Directions: Opposite the church in the centre of the village. The village lies in the centre of the triangle formed by Redruth, Falmouth and Helston.
Club Secretary: T J Knight, 6 Chainwalk Drive, Kenwyn, Truro, Cornwall. TR1 3ST   Tel: (H) 01872 270849   (W) 01872 276116
Fixtures Secretary: C Burley, 54 Collins Park, Stithians, Truro, Cornwall.   Tel: (H) 01209 860148 (W) 01209 860555
Club Colours: Maroon

WADEBRIDGE CAMELS RFC
Ground Address: Molesworth Field, Egloshayle, Wadebridge   Tel: 01208 815311
Brief Directions: Opposite Egloshayle Church
Club Secretary: M Richards, Perlees Farm, Wadebridge Tel: (H) 01208 812848   (W) 01726 860308
Fixtures Secretary: Chris Taylor   Tel: (H) 01208 813919
Club Colours: Chocolate and gold

CORNWALL TWO

Cornwall Two 1997-98 Fixtures	Callington 1	Camborne S of M 2	Llankelly Fowey 3	Redruth Albany 4	Roseland 5	St Day 6	Veor 7	
1 Callington	X	24/1	11/10	7/3	8/11	14/2	20/12	1
2 Camborne S of M	27/9	X	14/2	8/11	7/3	20/12	17/1	2
3 Llankelly Fowey	31/1	14/3	X	17/1	20/12	25/10	24/1	3
4 Redruth Albany	25/10	21/3	15/11	X	11/10	24/1	27/9	4
5 Roseland	17/1	15/11	27/9	10/1	X	11/4	14/2	5
6 St Day	15/11	11/10	10/1	14/3	31/1	X	8/11	6
7 Veor	14/3	10/1	11/4	31/1	25/10	7/3	X	7
	1	2	3	4	5	6	7	

CALLINGTON RFC
Ground Address: Duchy Agricultural College, Stoke Climsland, Callington, Cornwall
Brief Directions: Situated off main Callington to Launceston Road (A338) 3 miles outside Callington, the college is clearly signed..
Club Secretary: Michelle Campbell, 2 Chapel Street, Callington PL17 7BL   Tel: (H) 01579 382875   (W) 01579 386200
Fixtures Secretary: John Pritchard, 2 Delaware Court, Drakewalls, Gunnislake, Cornwall PL18 9BH.   Tel: (H) 01822 833371   (W) 01579 386241
Club Colours: Black and red quaters

CAMBORNE SCHOOL OF MINES RFC
Ground Address: The Memorial Ground, Boundervean Lane, Penponds, Camborne (not a postal delivery address)   Tel: 01209 612959 - Clubhouse Tel: 01209 711935
Brief Directions: Off Pendraves Road, Camborne, B3303 to Helson, turn right into Boundervean Lane. Before railway bridge, ground is 250m on right.
Club Secretary: Dr C V Phillips, Barlowena, Alexandra Road, Illogan, Redruth. Cornwall, TR16 4EN   Tel: (H) 01209 842660   (W) 01209 714866
Fixtures Secretary: N. R. Clarke, 2 Tremayne Close, Devoran, Truro, TR3 6QE.   Tel: (H) 01872 863139 (W) 01209 717724
Club Colours: Navy, gold and silver hoops

CORNWAL TWO CONTINUED

LANKELLY FOWEY RFC
Ground Address: Lankelly Farm, Lankelly Lane, Lankelly, Fowey, Cornwall
Brief Directions: On entering Fowey, turn right into Lankelly Lane, follow road until T junction, turn left, ground is 100yds on right
Club Secretary: David Taylor, Fourturnings, Fowey. PL23 1JU Tel: (H) 01726 832565
Fixtures Secretary: R Sainsbury Tel: (H) 01726 833050
Club Colours: Navy blue and white hoops

REDRUTH ALBANY RFC
Ground Address: Trewirgie Hill, Redruth, Cornwall. Tel: 01209 216945
Brief Directions: Adjacent to Redruth Cricket Club behind Trewirgie School, Falmouth Rd, Redruth, 0.5 mile from train station. Or ring club house for directions.
Club Secretary: Christophr Thomas, 67 Greenacre, Lanner Hill, Redruth, Cornwall TR16 6DD. Tel: (H) 01209 214871 (W) 01209 820983
Fixtures Secretary: W. J. Rogers, Pencoys, Roskear, Camborne, TR14 8DN. Tel: (H) 01209 714102
Club Colours: Royal blue shirts, black shorts, blue and white socks

ROSELAND RFC
Ground Address: Philleigh, Truro, Cornwall. TR2 5ET
Brief Directions: 15 miles from Truro on the Roseland Peninsula, signposted via Tregony and Towary, St Mawes.
Club Secretary: C R Thomas, Parton Vrane, Gerrans, Portscatho, Truro, Cornwall. TR2 5ET Tel: (H) 01872 580495
Fixtures Secretary: C J Trerise Tel: (H) 01872 560248
Club Colours: Navy and scarlet

ST DAY RFC
Ground Address: The Playing Field, St Day, Redruth, Cornwall
Brief Directions: Leave A30 at Scorrier exit, left past Cross Roads Hotel, at crossroads go straight across, ground just less than 1 mile on left
Club Secretary: P C Newcombe, 21 Martinvale Parc, Mount Ambrose, Redruth Tel: (H) 01209 212834
Fixtures Secretary: T Dunstan Tel: (H) 01209 821729
Club Colours: White with cherry band.

VEOR RFC
Ground Address: Wheal Gerry, Cliff View Road, Canborne, Cornwall
Brief Directions: Turn off A30 signed Canborne & Pool, right at traffic lights down hill, right again before pedestrian crossing, 0.5 mile right again after TA centre, ground 100 yds on right
Club Secretary: Bert Barber JP, 86 Dolcoath Road, Canborne, Cornwall. TR14 8RP Tel: (H & Fax) 01209 710593 (W) 01752 665951
Fixtures Secretary: Colin Pascoe Tel: 01209 716172
Club Colours: All black, amber trim

DEVON ONE

Devon One 1997-98 Fixtures	Dartmouth	Exeter Saracens	Ilfracombe	Newton Abbot	Old Public Oaks	Old Technicians	Plymouth Civ. S	Tavistock	Topsham	Torrington	
	1	2	3	4	5	6	7	8	9	10	
1 Dartmouth	X	18/10	7/3	27/9	15/11	31/1	10/1	11/4	6/9	25/10	1
2 Exeter Saracens	24/1	X	15/11	14/3	20/9	14/2	11/4	11/10	25/10	10/1	2
3 Ilfracombe	20/9	25/4	X	20/12	24/1	14/3	11/10	25/10	10/1	14/2	3
4 Newton Abbot	14/2	6/9	11/4	X	25/10	20/9	24/1	10/1	15/11	11/10	4
5 Old Public Oaks	25/4	7/3	11/10	17/1	X	8/11	14/3	27/9	31/1	20/12	5
6 Old Technicians	11/10	27/9	6/9	7/3	10/1	X	25/10	15/11	11/4	24/1	6
7 Plymouth Civil Serv	8/11	20/12	31/1	11/10	6/9	17/1	X	7/3	27/9	25/4	7
8 Tavistock	20/12	31/1	17/1	8/11	14/2	25/4	20/9	X	11/10	14/3	8
9 Topsham	14/3	17/1	8/11	25/4	11/10	20/12	14/2	24/1	X	20/9	9
10 Torrington	17/1	8/11	27/9	31/1	11/4	11/10	15/11	6/9	7/3	X	10
	1	2	3	4	5	6	7	8	9	10	

DARTMOUTH RFC
Ground Address: Dartmouth Community College, Norton Lane, Dartmouth, Devon TQ6
Brief Directions: Take A3122 Totnes to Dartmouth road, on arriving in Dartmouth take 1st right after Dartmouth United Football Club
Club Secretary: Miss J Evans, 8 Victoria Heights, Victoria Road, Dartmouth. TQ6   Tel: (H) 01803 833311
Fixtures Secretary: Mr S Atkins   Tel: (H) 01803 832381
Club Colours: Green and red hoops

EXETER SARACENS RFC
Ground Address: Exhibition Fields, Summer Lane, Whipton, Exeter, Devon   Tel: 01392 462651
Brief Directions: From M5 follow signs for Exeter Arena or from other direction follow Whipton signs then Exeter Arena signs
Club Secretary: David Mortimore, 39 lonsdale Road, Exeter. Tel: 01392 43305
Fixtures Secretary: Mr A Martin, 63 Parkers Cross Lane, Pinhoe, Exeter,   Tel: (H) 01392 464288
Club Colours: Red shirts, black shorts

ILFRACOMBE RFC
Ground Address: Brimlands, Hillsborough Road, Ilfracombe, North Devon   Tel: 01271 864249
Brief Directions: From town centre take road to east signed Combe Martin, look out for swimming pool, club on left close by
Club Secretary: Ian Roberts, Shortacombe, East Down, Barnstable, North Devon. EX31 4NT   Tel: (H) 01271 850542   (W) 01271 46677
Fixtures Secretary: Stuart Swanson   Tel: (H) 01271 850514
Club Colours: Blue and white hoops

NEWTON ABBOT RFC
Ground Address: Rackerhayes, Newton Road, Kingsteignton, Devon. TQ12 2LE   Tel: 01626 54150
Brief Directions: Follow signs for Racecourse, ground is opposite the course behind Fairway Furniture
Club Secretary: Mrs S Lock, 38 Mile End Road, Highweek, Newton Abbot. TQ12 1RW   Tel: (H) 01626 54835
Fixtures Secretary: Mr Gordon Hooper   Tel: (H) 01626 69791   (W) 01626 332160
Club Colours: All white

OLD PUBLIC OAKS RFC
Ground Address: King George V Playing Fields, Elburton
Brief Directions: On leaving A38 at Marsh Mills roundabout, take A374 towards city, turn left onto A379 Billacombe Rd, left at 3rd roundabout into Haye Rd, ground on right
Club Secretary: Mr G H Mathews, 25 Colwill Road, Mainstone, Plymouth   Tel: (H) 01752 707363
Fixtures Secretary: Mr R Boyle   Tel: (H) 01752 336502
Club Colours: Green and gold hoops

OLD TECHNICIANS RFC
Ground Address: Weston Mill Oak Villa, Ferndale Road, Weston Mill, Plymouth, Devon   Tel: 01752 363352
Brief Directions: A38 turn off onto B3396 to Devonport, left at 1st traffic lights, club approx 100 yards on left
Club Secretary: Tom Ozanne, 109 Townshend Avenue, Keyham, Plymouth, Devon   Tel: (H) 01752 606696 (W) 01752 553834
Fixtures Secretary: Keith Mills   Tel: (H & Fax) 01752 783776
Club Colours: Black with white circlet

PLYMOUTH CIVIL SERVICE RFC
Ground Address: Civil Service Sports Ground, Recreation Road, Beacon Down, Plymouth PL2 3HA.   Tel: 01752 702303
Brief Directions: Ground directly behind Plymouth Albion's ground at Beacon Park. Top of Ham Drive.
Club Secretary: Danny Avery, 25 Weston Mill Hill, Weston Mill, Plymouth PL5 2AR   Tel: (H) 01752 365890   Tel: (W) 01752 554586
Fixtures Secretary: Paul Routley, 1 Chaddlewood Close, Plympton. PL7 2HR.   Tel: 01752 338575
Club Colours: Red, white & black shirts, black shorts.

TAVISTOCK RFC
Ground Address: Sandy Park, Trelawney Road, Tavistock, Devon   Tel: 01822 618275
Brief Directions: From town centre take Brentor Road, under railway viaduct, 2nd right
Club Secretary: T Masters, St Peters, 10 Uplands, Tavistock, Devon. PL19 8ET   Tel: (H) 01822 614323
Fixtures Secretary: Martin Griffiths   Tel: (H) 01822 613030
Club Colours: Black and red hoops

TOPSHAM RFC
Ground Address: The Bonfire Field, Exeter Road, Topsham. EX3 0LY   Tel: 01392 873651
Brief Directions: From M5 follow signs to Topsham, club on left hand side
Club Secretary: Mark Bonning-Snook, 31 South Grange, Clyst Heath, Exeter, EX2 7EY.   Tel: (H) 01392 446363   (W) 01392 51056
Fixtures Secretary: Colin Bassent, Flat 7, 59 Fore Street, Topsham, EX3 0ML.   Tel: (H) 01392 874694
Club Colours: Light blue and dark blue hoops

TORRINGTON RUFC
Ground Address: Donnacroft, Torrington.   Tel: 01805 622202
Brief Directions: Situated on B3227 South Molton Road.
Club Secretary: Daren Nudds, 27 Holwill Drive, Tarka Hill, Torrington, North Devon.   Tel: (H) 01805 624899   Tel: (W) 01271 22561x2271
Fixtures Secretary: David Hickman,   Tel: (H) 01805 624196
Club Colours: Green black and white hoops

DEVON LEAGUE TWO

Devon Two 1997-98 Fixtures	Bovey Tracey	Cullompton	Marjons	North Tawton	Plymouth Argaum	Prince Rock	Salcombe	Tamar Saracens	Totnes	Wessex	
	1	2	3	4	5	6	7	8	9	10	
1 Bovey Tracey	X	14/3	20/9	11/10	24/1	10/1	21/3	14/2	25/10	15/11	1
2 Cullompton	6/9	X	25/10	10/1	14/2	11/10	24/1	20/9	15/11	11/4	2
3 Marjons	7/3	17/1	X	27/9	25/4	20/12	14/3	8/11	31/1	18/10	3
4 North Tawton	31/1	8/11	14/2	X	20/12	14/3	20/9	25/4	18/10	17/1	4
5 Plymouth Argaum	18/10	27/9	15/11	11/4	X	25/10	10/1	31/1	6/9	7/3	5
6 Prince Rock	8/11	31/1	18/4	6/9	17/1	X	15/11	18/10	7/3	27/9	6
7 Salcombe	20/12	18/10	29/11	7/3	8/11	25/4	X	17/1	27/9	31/1	7
8 Tamar Saracens	27/9	7/3	7/2	15/11	11/10	24/1	25/10	X	11/4	6/9	8
9 Totnes	17/1	25/4	11/10	24/1	14/3	20/9	14/2	20/12	X	8/11	9
10 Wessex	25/4	20/12	24/1	25/10	20/9	14/2	11/10	14/3	10/1	X	10
	1	2	3	4	5	6	7	8	9	10	

BOVEY TRACEY RFC
Ground Address: Bullands, Monks Way, Bovey Tracey, Devon
Brief Directions: Follow signs to Moreton Hampstead through Bovey Tracey, ground is on right hand side as you leave the town
Club Secretary: Carolyn Leigh, 34 East Street, Bovey Tracey, Devon. TQ13 9EJ Tel: (H) 01626 834432 (W) 01752 662051
Fixtures Secretary: M J Dyer Tel: (H) 01626 834337
Club Colours: Navy and white

CULLOMPTON RFC
Ground Address: Stafford Park, Knowle Lane, Cullompton, Devon. EX15 1PZ Tel: 01884 32480
Brief Directions: M5 J28 town centre, turn right by Manor Hotel, past fire station turn left to Langlands Rd, turn right at end of road, club at top of lane
Club Secretary: Dave Jewell, 34 Higher Street, Cullompton, Devon Tel: (H) 01884 35371
Fixtures Secretary: D J Keeling Tel: (H) 01823 660199
Club Colours: Scarlet and black hoops

MARJONS
Ground Address: The College of St Mark and St John, Driviford Road, Plymouth.
Club Secretary: Mr Simon Adams, 5 Dickenwall Lane, Honicknowle, Plymouth, Devon PL3 5NW. Tel: (H) 01752 7681411
Fixtures Secretary: As above.
Club Colours: Red and black quarters.

NORTH TAWTON RFC
Ground Address: The Butts, Barton Street, North Tawton, Devon
Brief Directions: On entering the town from De Bathe Cross, take the 1st turning right before reaching the square
Club Secretary: Mr C C Fear, 2 Boucher's Hill, North Tawton, Devon. EX20 2DG Tel: (H) 01837 82553
Fixtures Secretary: Mr Colin Sharp Tel: (H) 01837 82869
Club Colours: Black and amber

PLYMOUTH ARGAUM RFC
Ground Address: The Clubhouse, Bickleigh Down Road, Roborough, Plymouth. PL6 7AD Tel: 01752 772156
Brief Directions: At Roborough village turn down Bickleigh Down Rd, pass Medlands and carry on down lane, clubhouse on the right
Club Secretary: Mrs J L Davey, 3 Hazeldene Close, Lee Mill, Ivybridge, Devon. PL21 9EL Tel: (H) 01752 894453 (W) 01752 636000
Fixtures Secretary: Mrs T Truscott Tel: (H) 01752 707621
Club Colours: Black, bottle green, white

PRINCE ROCK RFC
Ground Address: King George V Playing Fields, Elburton, Plymouth Tel: (clubhouse) 01752 775727
Brief Directions: From Marshmills roundabout follow Plymouth Rd and signs for Plymstock, cross Laira Bridge along Billacombe Rd. and at third roundabout turn left then second right.
Club Secretary: Ian Radmore, 55 Lanhydrock Rd.,St Judes, Plymouth , DevonPL4 9HG Tel: (H) 01752 221235
Fixtures Secretary: Les Fowden 1 Hayes Rd., Oreston,Plymstock,Plymouth, Devon. PL9 7QA
Club Colours: Amber shirts, white shorts

SALCOMBE RFC
Ground Address: Twomeads, Camperdown Road, Salcombe Tel: 01548 842639
Brief Directions: On entering Salcombe take 1st left, 1st right, 2nd left
Club Secretary: Graham Jacobs, Cornerways, Bohaventure Road, Salcombe Tel: (H) 01548 842521
Fixtures Secretary: Robin Duhford Tel: (H) 01548 854022 (W) 01548 856222
Club Colours: Red shirts, white shorts, red and white socks

TAMAR SARACENS RFC
Ground Address: Parkway Sports Club, Ernesettle Lane, Ernesettle, Plymouth, Devon Tel: 01752 363080
Brief Directions: A38 to St Budeaux, turn off then towards Ernesettle
Club Secretary: Joe Jones, 18 Montacute Avenue, Honicknoule, Plymouth, Devon.
Fixtures Secretary: John Bentley Tel: (H) 01752 345020
Club Colours: Red , white and Green

TOTNES RFC
Ground Address: The Clubhouse, Borough Park, Totnes, Devon. TQ9 5XX Tel: 01803 867796
Brief Directions: Pitch on public park adjacent to British Rail station
Club Secretary: Mrs J V Guy, 50 Punchards Down, Follaton, Totnes, Devon. TQ9 5FD Tel: (H) 01803 864581 (Fax) 01803 867050
Fixtures Secretary: A Bourne Tel: (H) 01803 864462
Club Colours: Royal blue and white

WESSEX RFC
Ground Address: Flower Pots Fields, Exwick, Exeter
Brief Directions: Along Buddle Lane, turn right into Okehampton Road, turn left into Western Road
Club Secretary: Mr Phil Langford, 7 Kinnerton Way, Exwick Tel: (H) 01392 211959 (W) 01395 873781 Ext 4304
Fixtures Secretary: Mr R Roberts Tel: (H) 01395 271421
Club Colours: Bottle green and amber collars

DEVON LEAGUE THREE

Devon Three 1997-98 Fixtures	Axminster	Buckfastleigh	Devonport HSOB	Plymouth YMCA	Plympton Vic.	Plymstock	St Columba	Woodland Fort	
	1	2	3	4	5	6	7	8	
1 Axminster	X	8/11	25/10	17/1	14/3	24/1	7/3	10/1	1
2 Buckfastleigh	14/2	X	18/4	11/10	7/3	20/12	27/9	25/10	2
3 Devonport HSOB	31/1	10/1	X	7/3	11/10	17/1	20/12	8/11	3
4 Plymouth YMCA	27/9	24/1	15/11	X	10/1	25/10	14/2	14/3	4
5 Plympton Victoria	20/12	15/11	24/1	18/4	X	14/2	25/10	17/1	5
6 Plymstock	11/10	14/3	27/9	31/1	8/11	X	10/1	7/3	6
7 St Columba	15/11	17/1	14/3	11/4	31/1	8/11	X	11/10	7
8 Woodland Fort	11/4	31/1	14/2	20/12	27/9	15/11	24/1	X	8
	1	2	3	4	5	6	7	8	

AXMINSTER RUFC
Ground Address: Gammons Hill, Kilmington, Axminster (Change at Axminster Sports Hall, Chard St, Axminster)
Brief Directions: From Axminster take A35, turn left at Kilmington X and take 1st left, by Kilmington Quarry, ground at bottom of track. From Exeter, A35 at Kilmington X roads turn right and take 1st left.
Club Secretary: Mr Alan Beer, 8 Athelstan Close, Axminster, Devon. EX13 5RF   Tel: (H) 01297 34144 (W) 01297 33292
Fixtures Secretary: Nigel Powell   Tel: (H) 01297 34938
Club Colours: Red and royal blue

BUCKFASTLEIGH
Ground Address: The Cricket Club, Buckfastleigh, Devon   Tel: 01364 643895
Club Secretary: Mrs A Lawton, 10 Russell Road, Buckfastleigh, Devon TQ11 0DD   Tel: (H) 01364 642608   Tel: (W) 01364 643750
Fixtures Secretary: N Godwin, Tel: (H) 01364 642306
Club Colours: Black and yellow quarters

DEVONPORT HIGH SCHOOL OLD BOYS RFC
Ground Address: Devonport High School for Boys, Paradise Road, Millbridge, Plymouth, Devon. PL1 5QP   Tel: 01752 564682
Brief Directions: Next to Plymouth C.F.E.
Club Secretary: Mr G K Simpson, 108 Pattinson Drive, Mainstone, Plymouth, Devon. PL6 8RU   Tel: (H) 01752 707432   (W) 01752 563001
Fixtures Secretary: Mr C N Hill   Tel: (H) 01752 776792   (W) 01752 553965
Club Colours: Green, black and white

PLYMOUTH YMCA RFC
Ground Address: Suttons Field, John Kitto Community College, Burrington Way, Honicknowle, Plymouth   Tel: 011752 268169
Brief Directions: Turn off A38 at Manadon flyover, left onto Tavistock Road, right at lights, right at lights onto Honicknowle Road.
Club Secretary: Mr. M. J. Wilson, 8 Hilton Avenue, Manadon, Plymouth, Devon PL5 3HS
Fixtures Secretary: Mr. E. Hughes
Club Colours: Black and red striped shirts.

PLYMPTON VICTORIA RFC
Ground Address: King George V Playing Fields, Elburton, Plymstock, Plymouth, Devon.
Club Secretary: A.R.Dibble, 8 Wolrige Way, Plympton,Plymouth PL7 2RU   Tel: 01752 347 981
Fixtures Secretary: C.G.Mayne, 12 Canhaye Close, Plympton,Plymouth PL7

01752 335594
Club Colours: Black.

PLYMSTOCK RFC
Ground Address: Staddiscombe Playing Fields, Staddiscombe Road, Staddiscombe, Plymouth   Tel: 402751
Brief Directions: Leave Plymouth on A379 and follow signs to HMS Cambridge Playing Fields at top of Goosewell Road
Club Secretary: Lynda Stewart, Laburnam House, 4 Woodland Avenue, Elburton. PL9 8JE   Tel: (H) 402751
Fixtures Secretary: Paul Nicholson   Tel: (H) 402751
Club Colours: Blue

ST COLUMBA TORPOINT RFC
Ground Address: Defiance Field, Torpoint, Cornwall
Brief Directions: Torpoint Ferry, keep on main Liskeard road, in 2 miles ground on left
Club Secretary: P C Summers, 112 Rochford Crescent, Ernesettle, Plymouth. PL5 2QD   Tel: (H) 01752 362785
Fixtures Secretary: P C Summers   Tel: (H) 01752 362785
Club Colours: Scarlet with thin royal blue hoops

WOODLAND FORT RFC
Ground Address: Tanarfide Community College, Trevithick Road, Kingstamerton
Club Secretary: Steve Haif, 127 Devonfort Road, Stoke Village, Plymouth. PO1 5RQ   Tel: (H) 01752 563131 (W) 01752 765485
Fixtures Secretary: Paul Ashton   Tel: (H) 01752 367783
Club Colours: Green and white quarters

Western Counties North 1997-98 Fixtures

		Avonmouth OB	Bristol Harlequins	Cheltenham North	Cirencester	Cleve	Coney Hill	Drybrook	Gordon League	Hornets	North Bristol	Old Culverhaysians	Oldfield Old Boys	Old Redcliftians	Old Richians	St Marys Old Boys	Thornbury	Whitehall	
		1	2	3	4	5	6	7	8	9	10	11	12	13	14	15	16	17	
1	Avonmouth OB	X			11/10		20/9	8/11	20/12			17/1	31/1		4/4		28/2		1
2	Bristol Harlequins	6/9	X	11/10		8/11				20/12	17/1			31/1		7/3	28/3		2
3	Cheltenham North	27/9		X	20/12	25/10					17/1	31/1		7/3		11/4		6/9	3
4	Cirencester		25/10	15/11	X			17/1	31/1			7/3	11/4		27/9		*6/9		4
5	Cleve	25/10			10/1	X	15/11				31/1	7/3		11/4		6/9		27/9	5
6	Coney Hill		27/9		8/11		X	20/12	17/1			31/1	7/3		6/9		11/4		6
7	Drybrook		15/11	10/1			24/1	X	7/3			21/3	6/9		25/10		27/9		7
8	Gordon League		10/1	24/1			14/2		X	14/3		6/9	27/9		15/11		25/10		8
9	Hornets	15/11			24/1		10/1	14/2		X	11/4			6/9		27/9		25/10	9
10	North Bristol	10/1			14/2		24/1	14/3	25/4		X			27/9		25/10		15/11	10
11	Old Culverhaysians		24/1	14/2			14/3			25/4	20/9	X	25/10		10/1		15/11		11
12	Oldfield Old Boys		14/2	14/3			25/4			20/9	11/10		X	8/11	24/1		10/1		12
13	Old Redcliftians	24/1			14/3		14/2	25/4	20/9			11/10		X		15/11		10/1	13
14	Old Richians		25/4	20/9	11/10						8/11	20/12		17/1	X	31/1	7/3		14
15	St Mary's Old Boys	14/2			25/4		14/3	20/9	27/10			8/11	20/12			X		24/1	15
16	Thornbury		14/3	25/4	20/9					11/10	8/11			20/12	14/2	17/1	X		16
17	Whitehall	14/3			20/9		25/4	11/10	8/11			20/12	17/1			31/1		X	17
		1	2	3	4	5	6	7	8	9	10	11	12	13	14	15	16	17	

AVONMOUTH OLD BOYS RFC
Ground Address: Barracks Lane, Shirehampton, Bristol Tel: 0117 982 9093
Club Secretary: I K McNab, 48 Nibley Road, Shirehampton, Bristol, Avon. BS11 9XR Tel: (H) 0117 983 3380
Fixtures Secretary: A Woodruff Tel: (H) 0117 983 3066 (W) 0117 936 2173
Club Colours: Black with red chest band

BRISTOL HARLEQUINS RFC
Ground Address: Valhalla, Broomhill Road, Brislington, Bristol. BS4 Tel: 0117 972 1650
Club Secretary: Mr P Broome, 1 Ketch Road, Lower Knowle, Bristol Tel: (H) 0117 940 7929 (W) 0117 972 1261
Fixtures Secretary: Mr E Morrison Tel: (H) 01275 832580
Club Colours: Blue, black and white hoops

CHELTENHAM NORTH RFC
Ground Address: Stoke Orchard Road, Bishops Cleeve, Nr Cheltenham Tel: 01292 675968
Brief Directions: Junction 10 or 11 Cheltenham, head out of Cheltenham past racecourse on A435 towards Bishops Cleeve, turn toward Stoke Orchard village, 500 yards on left
Club Secretary: Andrew David Page, Baytrees, Chargrove Lane, Up Hatherley, Cheltenham Tel: (H) 01242 510932
Fixtures Secretary: Neil Carpenter Tel: 01242 252 554
Club Colours: Black with red band

CIRENCESTER RFC
Ground Address: The Whiteway, Cirencester, Glos Tel: 01285 654434
Brief Directions: Positioned at traffic lights on main Gloucester to Swindon A419 road, approx 1 mile from town centre
Club Secretary: R H Evans, 66 Rose Way, Cirencester, Glos. GL7 1PS Tel: (H) 01285 640954
Fixtures Secretary: J Lawrence Esq Tel: (H) 01285 821435
Club Colours: Red and black hoops, black shorts

CLEVE RFC
Ground Address: Cosham Street, Mangotsfield, Bristol
Brief Directions: M4 onto M32, M32 J1, carry straight through traffic lights to next roundabout, follow directions to Downend, then to Mangotsfield, turn into Cosasham St. Ground 300yds on Rt.
Club Secretary: Ron R G Pocock, 44 Spring Hill, Kingswood, Bristol Tel: (H) 0117 9611079
Fixtures Secretary: L A Millard Tel: (H) 0117 9654730 (W) 0976 154402
Club Colours: Maroon

CONEY HILL RFC
Ground Address: Metz Way, Coney Hill, Gloucester Tel: 01452 306238
Brief Directions: Gloucester ring road (Eastern Ave) to Texas DIY store, turn into Metz Way, club 0.25 mile on left
Club Secretary: D C Veale, 13 Stanway Road, Coney Hill, Gloucester. GL4 4RE Tel: (H) 01452 306510
Fixtures Secretary: Wes Hall Tel: (H) 01452 760798
Club Colours: Black, white and amber

DRYBROOK RFC
Ground Address: Mannings Ground, High Street, Drybrook, Glos Tel: 01594 542595
Brief Directions: Gloucester to Mitcheldean via Huntley, ground is on outskirts of village on Mitcheldean Road
Club Secretary: Glyn Tingle, Southview, Hazel Hill, Drybrook, Glos. GL17 9HH Tel: (H) 01594 543294 (W) 01594 542769
Fixtures Secretary: Derek Trigg Tel: (H) 01594 542258
Club Colours: Green with black on white band

GORDON LEAGUE RFC
Ground Address: Hempsted Lane, Gloucester. GL2 6JN Tel: 01452 303434
Brief Directions: Into Hempsted Lane past Colin Campbell pub, 500 yards on left
Club Secretary: Alan Barnes, 18 Podsmead Place, Tuffley, Gloucester. GL1 5PD Tel: (H) 01452 525530 (W) 01454 260681
Fixtures Secretary: W King, 361 Innsworth Lane, Churchdown, Glos. GL3 1EY Tel: (H) 01452 856787 (B) 01452 371171
Club Colours: White, red sash, black socks

HORNETS RFC
Ground Address: Hutton Moor Road, Weston-Super-Mare, North Somerset. BS22 8LY Tel: 01934 621433
Brief Directions: Follow new dual carriageway from M5 Weston turn off towards town centre, turn right at filter traffic lights following signs to Hutton Moor Sports Centre, ground directly opposite
Club Secretary: Anthony Wilson, 2a Grove Road, Weston-Super-Mare, North Somerset. BS23 8EY Tel: (H) 01934 415240 (W) 01684 297073
Fixtures Secretary: Mr Paul Davidson Tel: (H) 01934 414112
Club Colours: Black and amber

NORTH BRISTOL RFC
Ground Address: Oaklands, Gloucester Road, Almondsbury, Bristol. BS12 4AG Tel: 01454 612740
Brief Directions: M5 J16 onto A38, then to Gloucester, entrance 150 yards from Motorway
Club Secretary: C H Hill, 7 Keinton Walk, Henbury, Bristol. BS10 7EE Tel: (H) 0117 9508123
Fixtures Secretary: M Cottle Tel: (H) 0117 9506182
Club Colours: Royal blue and scarlet bands

OLD CULVERHAYSIANS RFC
Ground Address: The Clubhouse, Old Fosse Road, Odd Down, Bath Tel: 01225 832081
Brief Directions: Pitch at Bradford Road, Combe Down, Bath
Club Secretary: Mike Harding, 6 Gages Close, KIngswood, Bristol. BS15 2UH Tel: (H) 0117 947 5862 (W) 01453 835431
Fixtures Secretary: Bob Toghill Tel: (H) 01761 472219
Club Colours: Black

OLD REDCLIFFIANS RFC
Ground Address: Stockwood Lane, Brislington, Bristol Tel: 0117 9778501
Brief Directions: A34 from Bristol, turn right at McDonalds/Park & Ride, travel for 0.25 mile, ground on right hand side
Club Secretary: Richard Yandell, 11 Imperial Walk, Knowle, Bristol. BS14 9AD Tel: (H) 0117 9777657 (W) 0117 9873636
Fixtures Secretary: Russell Yandell Tel: (H) 01275 373444 (W) 01275 836077
Club Colours: Red and black hoops

OLD RICHIANS RFC
Ground Address: Sandyleaze, Longlevens, Gloucester. GL2 0PU Tel: 01452 524649
Brief Directions: Turn into Nine Elms Road from Cheltenham Road and follow to Sir Thomas Rich's School
Club Secretary: Paul Toleman, 4 Upper Rea, Hempsted, Gloucester. GL2 5LR Tel: (H) 01452 422274 (Fax) 01452 416138
Fixtures Secretary: Len Hayward Tel: (H) 01452 855769 (W) 01452 306181
Club Colours: Royal blue and gold hoops

OLDFIELD OLD BOYS
Ground Address: Shaft Road, Combe Down, Bath. Tel: 01225 834135
Brief Directions: Into Bath, follow signs for University, follow on towards Combe Down, turn down Shaft Road.
Club Secretary: Steve Godwin, 12 Lime Grove Gardens, Bath, Somerset BA2 4HE Tel: (H) 01225 318012 Tel (W) 01258 451441
Fixtures Secretary: Leon Book, 45 The Brow, Twerton, Bath. Tel: 01225 4802341
Club Colours: Maroon and gold.

ST MARY'S OLD BOYS RUFC
Ground Address: Northwood Trench Lane, Winterbourne Tel: 01454 250489
Brief Directions: M5 J16 towards Bristol, turn left at 1st roundabout then left again onto Woodlands Lane, Bradley Stoke ground 1 mile on left
Club Secretary: Mrs L Collins, 18 Belmont Road, St Andrews Bristol. BS6 5AS Tel: (H) 9249879
Fixtures Secretary: Mr W Hopkins Tel: (H) 0145 419571
Club Colours: Emerald green and black

THORNBURY RFC
Ground Address: Coopers Farm, Lower Morton, Thornbury, Bristol. BS12 1LG   Tel: 01454 412096
Brief Directions: From Thornbury: at Royal George pub take Gloucester rd out of town, after Anchor pub take 2nd left (ignore turn directly next to pub), club is down this lane approx 0.5 mile on the right
Club Secretary: Howard Roy Bowker, 2 Broncksea Road, Filton Park, Bristol. BS7 0SE   Tel: (H) 0117 969 8744
Fixtures Secretary: Maurice Carling   Tel: (H) 01454 885353
Club Colours: Black and amber hoops

WHITEHALL RFC
Ground Address: Foundry Lane, Speedwell, Bristol Tel: 0117 9659636
Brief Directions: Off B4465 Whitehall Road at Crofts End, turn right into Deep Pit Rd, take 2nd left. From M32 J2 follow sign post up Muller Rd, left at roundabout
Club Secretary: Kevin Smith, 150 Whitehall Road, Whitehall, Bristol. BS5 9BD   Tel: (H) 01179 351935 (F) 01179 847612   (W) 01179 847853
Fixtures Secretary: Alex Ferguson   Tel: (H) 0117 9772898
Club Colours: Myrtle green and gold

GLOUCESTERSHIRE AND SOMERSET

Gloucester/Somerset 1997-98 Fixtures

		1 Barton Hill	2 Bream	3 Bristol Saracens	4 Brockworth	5 Chard	6 Coombe Down	7 Frampton Cotterell	8 Gordano	9 Longlevans	10 Midsomer Norton	11 Old Sulians	12 St Bernadettes	13 Tor	14 Walcot Old Boys	15 Wells	16 Wiveliscombe	17 Yatton
1	Barton Hill	X			20/9	20/12		11/10		8/11		17/1		31/1		11/4	7/3	
2	Bream	6/9	X	11/10			17/1		8/11		20/12		31/1		7/3			7/2
3	Bristol Saracens	27/9		X	25/10		31/1		20/12		17/1		7/3		11/4			6/9
4	Brockworth		27/9		X	17/1		8/11		20/12		31/1		7/3		6/9	4/4	
5	Chard		10/1	24/1		X			14/2		14/3	6/9		27/9		15/11	25/10	
6	Combe Down	10/1			24/1	25/4	X	14/2		14/3			27/9		25/10		15/11	
7	Frampton Cotterell		25/10	15/11		31/1		X		17/1		7/3		11/4		27/9	6/9	
8	Gordano	25/10			15/11		7/3	10/1	X		31/1		11/4		6/9		27/9	
9	Longlevans		15/11	10/1		7/3			24/1	X		11/4		6/9		25/10	27/9	
10	Midsomer Norton	15/11			10/1		11/4	24/1		14/2	X		6/9		27/9			25/10
11	Old Sulians		24/1	14/2				20/9		14/3	25/4	X		25/10		10/1	15/11	
12	St Bernadettes	24/1			14/2	20/9		14/3		25/4	11/10		X		15/11			10/11
13	Tor		14/2	14/3			11/10		25/4		20/9	8/11		X		24/1	10/1	
14	Walcot Old Boys	14/2			14/3	11/10		25/4		20/9		8/11		20/12	X			24/1
15	Wells		25/4	20/9			20/12		11/10		8/11	17/1		31/1		X	7/3	
16	Wiveliscombe		14/3	18/4			8/11		20/9		11/10		20/12		17/1	14/2	X	
17	Yatton	14/3			25/4	8/11		20/9		11/10		20/12		17/1			31/1	X
		1	2	3	4	5	6	7	8	9	10	11	12	13	14	15	16	17

THIS DIRECTORY IS NOT FOR CLUB OFFICIALS ONLY!

Do your club supporters know they can buy their own directory and help club funds?

BARTON HILL OLD BOYS RFC
Ground Address: Duncombe Lane, Speedwell, Bristol.
Tel: 0117 987 2895
Brief Directions: M32 J2 (Kingswood). Follow thro'
Downend, Staple Hill to lights at Soundwell. Turn rt to
2nd set of lights. Turn rt then 2nd left into Argyle Rd.
Follow `Playing Field' to Duncombe Lane.
Club Secretary: Don Blackmore, 31 Battens Lane, St.
George, Bristol. BS5 8TG.   Tel: (H) 0117 961 1754 (B)
0117 936 5310
Fixtures Secretary: Paul Uppington, 18 Eaton Close,
Fishponds, Bristol.   Tel: (H) 0117 965 0340
Club Colours: White with a cherry band

BREAM RFC
Ground Address: High Street, Bream, Nr Lydney, Glos.
GL15 6JG   Tel: 01594 562320
Brief Directions: Approx 3 miles off main A48
Gloucester to Chepstow road, turn right after Westbury
Homes Site on right hand side
Club Secretary: John Grail, 31 Highbury Road, Bream,
Nr Lydney, Glos. GL15 6EF   Tel: (H) 01594 562737
Fixtures Secretary: Colin Henderson   Tel: (H) 01594
562430
Club Colours: Red and black

BRISTOL SARACENS RFC
Ground Address: Bakewell Memorial Ground, Station
Road, Cribbs Causeway, Henbury, Bristol   Tel: 0117
9500037
Brief Directions: M5 J17 towards Bristol city centre,
approx 1000 metres at 2nd roundabout on right
Club Secretary: A E Swash, 6 Downs Road, Westbury-
on-Trym, Bristol. BS9 3TX   Tel: (H) 01179 629047
(W) 01626 832283
Fixtures Secretary: C J Matthews   Tel: (H) 01179
243696   (W) 01454 419008
Club Colours: Myrtle green and white hooped shirts,
black shorts

BROCKWORTH RFC
Ground Address: Mill Lane, Brockworth.   Tel: 01452
862556
Brief Directions: From south: M5 turn off at junct. 11A,
follow signs to Gloucester, 1st left to Blockworth at
roundabout, straight over next, past Du-Pont, left at
lights into Vicarage Lane, straight over small
roundabout, 1st right into Mill Lane, 400 metres on
LHS.
Club Secretary: Andrew Yarworth, 288 Gloucester
Road, Cheltenham GL51 8NR   Tel: (H) 01242 242218
Tel: (W) 01452 333111/333114
Fixtures Secretary: Pete Hickey, Tel: (H & W) 01452
308819
Club Colours: Black shirts with white 'V'

CHARD RFC
Ground Address: The Park, Essex Close, Chard,
Somerset   Tel: 01460 62495
Brief Directions: Bottom of Chard High Street (by
Cerdic DIY shop), 100 yards up Essex Close
Club Secretary: Mr N J Urch, 2 South View, Listers
Hill, Ilminster, Somerset   Tel: (H) 01460 57864   (W)
01935 702913
Fixtures Secretary: Mr R Stuckey, 9 Cerdic Close,
Chard, Somerset   Tel: (H) 01460 63579   (W) 01460
63781
Club Colours: Black, red and gold

COMBE DOWN RFC
Ground Address: Holly's Corner, North Road, Combe
Down, Bath. BA2 5DE   Tel: 01225 832075
Brief Directions: Follow A3062 out of Bath to Combe
Down
Club Secretary: N Williams, 2 Abbey View Gardens,
Widcombe, Bath. BA2 6DQ   Tel: (H) 01225 312405
Fixtures Secretary: Nigel Clark   Tel: 01225 832634
Club Colours: Black and amber

FRAMPTON COTTERELL RFC
Ground Address: School Road, Frampton Cotterell,
Bristol   Tel: 01454 772947
Brief Directions: Off B3058 Winterbourne to Chipping
Sodbury road
Club Secretary: Mrs Sue Soper, 58 Lower Chapel Lane,
Frampton Cotterell, Bristol. BS17 2RH   Tel: (H) 01454
772095 (after 6pm)   (W) 01454 322422
Fixtures Secretary: Dave Moulsdale, 359 Church Rd.,
Frampton Cotterell, Bristol   Tel: 01454 250624
Club Colours: Green, black and gold

GORDANO RFC
Ground Address: The National Stadium, Caswell Lane,
Portbury, Nr Bristol BS20 9TH.   Tel: 01275 373486
Brief Directions: Take A369, head into village of
Portbury and bear left at the village green.
Club Secretary: Mrs R Pike, 10 Burtford Close, Portis
Head, Nr Bristol.   Tel: (H) 01275 847957
Fixtures Secretary: A Stanton, Tel: (H) 01275 877103
Club Colours: Red and black shirts, black shorts.

LONGLEVENS RFC
Ground Address: Longford Lane, Longlevens,
Gloucester   Tel: 01452 306880
Brief Directions: M5 J11 - Golden Valley bypass
towards Gloucester, right at 2nd lights into Old
Cheltenham Rd, Church Rd then Longford Ln. Or A38
T'kesbury rd turn right into Longford Ln past Queens
Head
Club Secretary: Colin Dunford, 66 Estcourt Road,
Gloucester. GL1 3LG   Tel: (H) 01452 522795   (W)
01452 529751
Fixtures Secretary: Greg Thomas   Tel: (H) 01452
526352
Club Colours: Red

MIDSOMER NORTON RFC
Ground Address: Norton Down Playing Fields,
Stratton-on-the-Fosse, Somerset. BA3 4RD   Tel: 01761
412827
Brief Directions: From centre of Midsomer Norton
follow Shepton Mallet road (B3355) for approx 800
yards
Club Secretary: John Presley, 73 Welton Grove,
Midsomer Norton, Somerset. BA3 2TT   Tel: (H) 01761
416089   (W) 01749 682267
Fixtures Secretary: Brian Wilcox   Tel: (H) 01761
241477
Club Colours: Red and white hoops, black shorts

OLD SULIANS RFC
Ground Address: Lansdown Road, Bath   Tel: 01225
310201
Brief Directions: Follow Lansdown Road from city
centre, ground is on left 400 m past MOD site
Club Secretary: Terry Haines, 24 Rockcliffe Avenue,
Bath. BA2 6QP   Tel: (H) 01225 465107   (W) 0117
9797540
Fixtures Secretary: Tony Slee   Tel: (H) 01225 317256
Club Colours: Blue with red band

ST BERNADETTE RFC

Ground Address: Hengrove Park, Bamfield, Whitchurch, Bristol   Tel: 01275 891500
Brief Directions: A37 out of town, turn right at Airport Rd traffic lights, turn left 0.5 mile by The Happy Cock pub, club is 0.25 mile on right
Club Secretary: Barry Taylor, 39 Woodleigh Gardens, Whitchurch, Bristol. BS14 9JA   Tel: (H) 01275 831880
Fixtures Secretary: Tony Aldridge   Tel: (H) 0117 9770075
Club Colours: Green and blue hoops

THE TOR RFC

Ground Address: Lowerside Park, Lowerside Lane, Glastonbury, Somerset   Tel: 01458 832236
Brief Directions: Adjacent to and signposted off A39 Glastonbury bypass
Club Secretary: Ms Carol Plenty, 26 Sheldon Drive, Wells, Somerset   Tel: (H) 01749 676754   (W) 01749 674949
Fixtures Secretary: Mr Keith Elver   Tel: (H) 01458 447284   (W) 01749 673199
Club Colours: Maroon

WALCOT OLD BOYS RFC

Ground Address: Albert Field, Lansdown, Bath   Tel: 01225 330199
Brief Directions: Follow signs from city centre to Lansdown, proceed along top to racecourse/golf club, halfway on right is ground opposite Bath car park & ride sign
Club Secretary: D J Bishop, 9 Sheridan Road, Twerton, Bath. BA2 1QY   Tel: (H) 01225 428942   (W) 01225 477540
Fixtures Secretary: S Sharp   Tel: (H) 01225 215821
Club Colours: Black and white hoops

WELLS RUFC

Ground Address: Charter Way, off Portway, Wells   Tel: 01749 672823
Brief Directions: Off the Portway A371 or follow signs to the Leisure Centre
Club Secretary: Mr Anthony C Cox, 10 Mount Pleasant Avenue, Wells, Somerset. BA5 2SQ   Tel: (H) 01749 673407
Fixtures Secretary: Mrs C Sullivan   Tel: 01749 679248
Club Colours: Black and white hoops

WIVELISCOMBE RFC

Ground Address: Recreation Ground, West Road, Wiveliscombe, Nr Taunton, Somerset. TA4 2TB   Tel: 01984 623897
Brief Directions: Take B3227 from Taunton to Barnstaple, ground is on left towards end of town
Club Secretary: G.Mabley, 3 Manor Park, Norton Fitzwarren, Taunton, Somerset   Tel: 01823 270002
Fixtures Secretary: C Mann   Tel: (H) 01823 400673 (Fax) 01823 400139
Club Colours: Blue with red sash

YATTON RFC

Ground Address: The Park, North End, Yatton, Avon   Tel: 01934 832085
Brief Directions: From centre of village, travel towards Clevedon, club is on right 300 yards after Railway bridge
Club Secretary: J G Crabtree, 11 Old Park Road, Clevedon, Avon   Tel: (H) 01275 876954   (W) 0117 943 2399
Fixtures Secretary: Nick Williams   Tel: (H) 01934 877250
Club Colours: Amber and black

Wells R.F.C. 1st XV Squad. Winners of Somerset Division and League 1996/97and unbeaten in League for two seasons.

Have you many Rugby enthusiasts at your Club ?
Does you Club need to raise extra funds ?

If the answer to these questions is Yes -
then place an order for

The Official Rugby Union Club Directory

WITH EVERY CLUB IN THE LEAGUE STRUCTURE INCLUDED AND ITS
UNRIVALLED STATISTICAL COVERAGE OF THE CLUBS AND PLAYERS IN
THE TOP LEVELS OF THE LEAGUE SYSTEM IT CAN ANSWER ALL SORTS
OF QUESTIONS AND WOULD MAKE AN IDEAL PRESENT.

Did you realise the Directory is available to your club at very good discount rates.

If you order				Profit for Club
1	copy cost	£14.99		
2 or 3	copies cost	£13.50 each	£ 1.49 each	
between 4 & 9	copies cost	£10.00 each	£ 4.99 each	
between 10 & 19	copies cost	£ 9.00 each	£ 5.99 each	
20 or more	copies cost	£ 8.00 each	£ 6.99 each	

To find out more information or to place an order, contact the publishers:
Tony Williams Publications Ltd., Helland, North Curry, Taunton, Somerset. TA3 6DU.
or Telephone 01823 490080 or Fax 01823 490281

GLOUCESTERSHIRE ONE

Gloucester One 1997-98 Fixtures	Ashley Down 1	Bristol Telephones 2	Cainscross 3	Cheltenham CS 4	Cheltenham Saracens 5	Chosen Hill 6	Hucclecote 7	Old Bristolians 8	Old Centrals 9	Old Cryptians 10	Painswick 11	Southmead 12	Tredworth 13	
1 Ashley Down	X		8/11		20/12			17/1		11/10	14/2	14/3		1
2 Bristol Telephones	25/10	X		17/1			14/2		14/3	15/11			27/9	2
3 Cainscross		10/1	X	14/2	15/11			14/3			27/9	25/10		3
4 Cheltenham CS	15/11		31/1	X			14/3		27/9	10/1			25/10	4
5 Cheltenham Saracens		31/1		7/3	X	10/1		27/9			25/10	15/11		5
6 Chosen Hill	27/9	8/11		20/12		X	17/1		14/2				14/3	6
7 Hucclecote	10/1		7/3	11/4			X		25/10	31/1			15/11	7
8 Old Bristolians		7/3		11/4	31/1	11/10		X	8/11		15/11	10/1		8
9 Old Centrals	31/1		11/4	11/10				8/11	X	7/3			10/1	9
10 Old Cryptians			20/12	17/1	25/10		14/2			X	14/3	27/9		10
11 Painswick		11/4		11/10		7/3	8/11	20/12			X	31/1		11
12 Southmead		11/10		8/11		11/4	20/12	17/1				X	14/2	12
13 Tredworth	7/3		11/10		8/11			20/12		11/4	17/1		X	13
	1	2	3	4	5	6	7	8	9	10	11	12	13	

ASHLEY DOWN OLD BOYS RFC
Ground Address: Lockleaze Combination Ground, Bonnington Walk, Lockleaze, Bristol   Tel: 0117 9312642
Brief Directions: From Filton Avenue, into Bonnington Walk, left at railway bridge, 0.25 mile along lane
Club Secretary: Peter Heath, 28 Carisbrook Close, Enfield, Middx EN1 3NB   Tel: 0181 245 5105
Fixtures Secretary: R Johnson   Tel: (H) 0117 9691581
Club Colours: Purple and white

BRISTOL TELEPHONE AREA RFC
Ground Address: B.T.R.A. Sports Ground, Stockwood Lane, Stockwood, Bristol. BS14   Tel: 01275 891776
Brief Directions: Take A37 (Wells Road) for approx 4 miles from city centre, left at Black Lion pub at Whitchurch, ground approx 1 mile on right
Club Secretary: Mike Cross, 21 Grangeville Close, Longwell Green, Bristol   Tel: (H) 0117 9325146   (W) 0117 9325146
Fixtures Secretary: Chris Watts   Tel: (H) 01275 543208   (W) 01454 611069
Club Colours: Red, white and blue hoops

CAINSCROSS RFC
Ground Address: Victory Park, Ebley, Stroud, Glos   Tel: 01453 766707
Brief Directions: M5 J13, between Stonehouse and Stroud on A417
Club Secretary: W R Tocknell, Pendaleon House, Selsley Road, North Woodchester, Stroud, Glos   Tel: (H) 01453 872333   (W) 01453 762773
Fixtures Secretary: D Roberts   Tel: (H) 01453 824964
Club Colours: Amber and blue

CHELTENHAM CIVIL SERVICE RFC
Ground Address: Civil Service Sports Ground, Tewkesbury Road, Uckington, Cheltenham   Tel: 01242 680424
Brief Directions: 2 miles from Cheltenham on the main road to Tewkesbury (A4019)
Club Secretary: Brian Didlick, 15 Stoneville Street, Cheltenham. GL51 8PH   Tel: (H) 01242 519285
Fixtures Secretary: Julie Mortlock   Tel: (H) 01242 582945
Club Colours: Navy blue

CHELTENHAM SARACENS RFC
Ground Address: King George V Playing Fields, Brooklyn Road, St Marks, Cheltenham, Glos
Brief Directions: From Gloucester & M5 follow dual carriageway to main GCHQ roundabout take 1st exit then right at square junction.
Club Secretary: Chris Whitelow, 110 Fairview Road, Cheltenham Glos.   Tel: (H) 01242 581257
Fixtures Secretary: Dave Henderson   Tel: (H) 01242 576030
Club Colours: Blue, black and gold hoops

CHOSEN HILL FP RFC
Ground Address: Brookfield Road, Churchdown, Gloucester   Tel: 01452 712384
Brief Directions: Equi-distant between Cheltenham/Gloucester on edge of village towards Cheltenham
Club Secretary: Colin Yeates, 14 Drews Court, Churchdown, Glos. GL3 2LD   Tel: (H) 01452 712827   (W) 01242 230881
Fixtures Secretary: Ian Yeates   Tel: (H) 01452 855839
Club Colours: Myrtle green and white

HUCCLECOTE OLD BOYS RFC
Ground Address: King George V Playing Fields, Upton Close, Hucclecote, Glos
Brief Directions: On Glos Eastern Ave bypass, turn towards Hucclecote at Walls ring road, right at lights at North Upton Lane, 2nd left into Upton Close, left at end of road for club
Club Secretary: John Ring, 9 Conway Road, Hucclecote, Glos. GL3 3PD Tel: (H) 01452 618920
Fixtures Secretary: Colin Bevan Tel: (H) 01452 863689
Club Colours: Black and amber

OLD BRISTOLIANS
Ground Address: Memorial Playing Field, Longwood Lane, Failand, Nr Bristol. Tel: 01275 392137
Brief Directions: M5 junction 19 head for Bristol, turn right at main lights onto B3129 for Failand, turn left after country club into Longwood Lane.
Club Secretary: Mr John Sisman, Flat 1, 39 Sydenham Hill, Cotham, Bristol. Tel: (H) 01179 232261 Tel: (W) 01179 885230
Fixtures Secretary: Mr Don Furze. Tel: (H) 01179 243182 Tel: (W) 01275 836077
Club Colours: Maroon, gold and green hoops.

OLD CENTRALIANS RFC
Ground Address: Saintbridge Sports Centre, Painswick Road, Gloucester. GL4 9QX Tel: 01452 303768
Club Secretary: Phil Niland, 12 Berry Lawn, Abbeydale, Gloucester. GL4 5YE. Tel: (H) 01452 387264 (M) 0802 760434
Fixtures Secretary: Andy Knight, 54 Bittern Ave., Abbeydale, Gloucester. GL4 8NB. Tel: (H) 01452 533744
Club Colours: Navy blue, royal blue and gold

OLD CRYPTIANS RFC
Ground Address: Memorial Ground, Tuffley Avenue, Gloucester. GL1 5NS Tel: 532002
Brief Directions: Off Bristol Road to Tuffley Avenue, ground 1 mile on right before Stroud Road
Club Secretary: Gordon Hill, 244 Stroud Road, Gloucester. GL4 0AU Tel: (H) 01452 521651 (W) 01454 260681 Ext 295/337
Fixtures Secretary: Derek Howell Tel: (H) 01452 414010 (W) 01452 425611
Club Colours: Yellow, maroon and navy blue

PAINSWICK RFC
Ground Address: Broadham Fields, Stroud Road, Painswick, Nr Stroud, Glos Tel: 01452 813861
Brief Directions: Situated adjoining the A46 on the southern edge of the village (on the Stroud side/Stroud Road)
Club Secretary: A T C Morgan, Pipers Edge, Cheltenham Road, Painswick, Nr Stroud, Glos. GL6 6SJ Tel: (H) 01452 814202 (W) 01452 521267
Fixtures Secretary: I J Hogg Tel: (H & W) 01452 728310
Club Colours: Cherry and white hoops, navy blue shorts

SOUTHMEAD RFC
Ground Address: Greenway Sports Centre, Greystoke Avenue, Southmead, Bristol Tel: 0117 9593060
Brief Directions: A38 to Filton, Southmead Road into Doncaster Road, Southmead
Club Secretary: Mr Mike Davies, 90 Twenty Acres, Brentry, Bristol. BS10 6PR Tel: (H) 0117 9497017
Fixtures Secretary: Mr Mike Haddow Tel: (H) 01454 614019
Club Colours: Blue shirt with emerald green hoop

TREDWORTH RUFC
Ground Address: The Lannet, King Edwards Avenue, Gloucester Tel: 01452 525465
Club Secretary: Mr Howard K Speck, Salem, 1 Ashcroft Close, St Leonards Park, Gloucester. GL4 6JX Tel: (H) 01452 302699
Fixtures Secretary: Mr K Broady Tel: (H) 01452 721450
Club Colours: Black and green

GLOUCESTERSHIRE TWO

Gloucester Two 1997-98 Fixtures	Aretians 1	Bishopston 2	Chipping Sodbury 3	Cotham Park 4	Dursley 5	Kingswood 6	Old Colstonians 7	Old Elizabethans 8	Smiths Industries 9	Tetbury 10	Tewkesbury 11	Westbury-on-Severn 12	Widden Old Boys 13	
1 Aretians	X	11/10			8/11		20/12		17/1	14/2		14/3		1
2 Bishopston		X	25/10		20/12		17/1		14/2	14/3		27/9		2
3 Chipping Sodbury	27/9		X	8/11		20/12		17/1			14/3		14/2	3
4 Cotham Park	25/10	15/11		X		17/1		14/2			27/9		14/3	4
5 Dursley			15/11	10/1	X		14/2		14/3	27/9		25/10		5
6 Kingswood	15/11	10/1			31/1	X		14/3			25/10		27/9	6
7 Old Colstonians			10/1	31/1		7/3	X			27/9	25/10	15/11		7
8 Old Elizabethans	10/1	31/1			7/3		11/4	X			15/11		25/10	8
9 Smiths Industries			31/1	7/3		11/4		11/10	X	15/11		10/1		9
10 Tetbury			7/3	4/4		11/10		8/11		X		31/1	20/12	10
11 Tewkesbury	7/3	28/2			11/10		8/11		20/12	17/1	X			11
12 Westbury-on-Severn			11/4	11/10		8/11		20/12			14/2	X	17/1	12
13 Widden Old Boys	31/1	7/3				11/4		11/10	8/11		10/1		X	13
	1	2	3	4	5	6	7	8	9	10	11	12	13	

ARETIANS RFC
Ground Address: Station Road, Little Stoke, Bristol. BS12 6HW   Tel: 01454 888069
Brief Directions: M5 J16, A38 into Bristol, at flyover turn left signed Yate (Gypsy Patch Ln), along road to railway bridge, directly left past bridge, ground approx 600yds on right on Station Rd
Club Secretary: Andy Vaughan, 42 Elm Close, Little Stoke, Bristol   Tel: (H) 0117 9756513   (W) 0117 9557767
Fixtures Secretary: Andy Williams   Tel: (H) 01454 886179   (W) 0117 9797187
Club Colours: Black

BISHOPSTON RFC
Ground Address: Bonnington Walk, Lockleaze, Bristol   Tel: 0117 969 1916
Brief Directions: From Almondsbury M'way interchange, A38 to Bristol, left at lights at end of Toronto Rd, cross lights at Filton Ave into B'nington Wk, ground on left straight after rail bridge
Club Secretary: Jim Hockley, 21 Pinewood Close, Westbury-on-Trym, Bristol. BS9 4AJ   Tel: (H) 0117 962 3509   (W) 0117 929 1031 Ext 2390
Fixtures Secretary: Stuart Brain   Tel: (H) 0117 958 5560
Club Colours: Red with black hoop edged in centenary gold

CHIPPING SODBURY RFC
Ground Address: The Ridings, Wickwar Road, Chipping Sodbury, South Gloucestershire   Tel: 01454 312852
Brief Directions: 2nd turning on the right on Wickwar Road out of Chipping Sodbury
Club Secretary: Mr N Jarrett, 62 Vayre Close, Chipping Sodbury, South Gloucestershire   Tel: (H) 01454 324807
Fixtures Secretary: Mr T Windsor   Tel: 01454 315959
Club Colours: Black

COTHAM PARK RFC
Ground Address: Beegar Bush Lane, Failand, Bristol   Tel: 01275 392501
Brief Directions: M5 J19, A369 towards Bristol, left on A3129 (Beegar Bush Lane)
Club Secretary: Frank Nesbitt, 94 Kenn Road, Clevedon, North Somerset. BS21 6EX   Tel: 01275 342334
Fixtures Secretary: Mike Gill   Tel: (H) 0117 9076387 (W) 0117 9306200
Club Colours: Black and white hoops

DURSLEY RFC
Ground Address: Stinchcombe Stragglers, Hounds Green, The Avenue, Stinchcombe, Dursley, Glos. GL11 6AJ   Tel: 01453 543693
Brief Directions: On the Dursley to Wotton-under-Edge Rd (B4060), on right just before entering Stinchcombe village
Club Secretary: Simon Bilous, 8 Ferney, Dursley, Glos. GL11 5AB   Tel: (H) 01453 545493   (B) 0117 908 8369
Fixtures Secretary: Steven Thompson, Graceland, Lower Kilcott, Millesley, Wotton-under-Edge, Glos. GL12 7RL.   Tel: (H) 01454 238753 (B) 01454 281149
Club Colours: Maroon and amber

KINGSWOOD RFC
Ground Address: The Pavilion, Deanery Road Playing Field, Grimsbury Road, Kingswood, Bristol. BS15   Tel: 0117 9675001
Brief Directions: Bristol on A420, turn right into Grimsbury Rd immediately before Tennis Court pub, ground is 1st left
Club Secretary: R Clease, 166 Mounthill Road, Kingswood, Bristol. BS15 2SX   Tel: (H) 0117 9750890
Fixtures Secretary: N Long   Tel: 0117 9608804
Club Colours: Sky blue and chocolate brown

OLD COLSTONIANS RFC
Ground Address: New Road, Stoke Gifford, Bristol
Tel: 0117 9690009
Brief Directions: Near Parkway Railway Station, next to Filton High School
Club Secretary: David Parker, 37 Ratcliffe Drive, Stoke Gifford, Bristol. BS12 6TX   Tel: (H) 0117 9697438 (W) 01275 555456
Fixtures Secretary: D. Parker, 37 Ratcliffe Drive, Stoke Gifford, Bristol.
Club Colours: Black, blue and gold hoops

OLD ELIZABETHANS RFC
Ground Address: Severn Road, Hallen, Bristol. BS10 7RZ   Tel: 0117 959 1072
Brief Directions: M5 J17, turn towards Pelning at roundabout then 1st left, continue for 2-3 miles until junction with King William IV pub on right, turn right, club 200 yards on left
Club Secretary: David Langdon, 13 Gloucester Street, Wotton-under-Edge, Glos. GL12 7DN   Tel: (H) 01453 845349   (W) 0117 966 8431
Fixtures Secretary: Amanda Heming   Tel: (H) 0117 9248053   (W) 0117 9876060
Club Colours: Blue, white and old gold hoops

SMITHS (INDUSTRIES) RFC
Ground Address: The Newlands, Evesham Road, Bishops Cleeve, Cheltenham, Glos   Tel: 01242 672752
Brief Directions: 2 miles due north of Cheltenham on A465
Club Secretary: Gerald Owen, 79 Station Road, Bishops Cleeve, Cheltenham, Glos   Tel: (H) 01242 676345   (W) 01242 673333 Ext 2912
Fixtures Secretary: Adrian Tedstone   Tel: 01242 570674
Club Colours: Royal blue and white

TETBURY RFC
Ground Address: Recreation Ground, Hampton Street, Tetbury, Glos   Tel: 01666 505052
Brief Directions: On the B4014 (Hampton St.) out of Tetbury towards Avening, the ground is situated on the right behind the betting shop.
Club Secretary: Sally Webber, 8 Clarrie Road, Tetbury, Glos. GL8 8EW.   Tel: 01666 504473
Fixtures Secretary: Ray McCarthy, 43 Conygar Rd., Tetbury. GL8 8JF.   Tel: (H) 01666 503870
Club Colours: Black and gold

TEWKESBURY RFC
Ground Address: The Moats, Lankett Lane, Tewkesbury, Glos.,   Tel: 01684 294364
Brief Directions: Behind Tewkesbury Abbey
Club Secretary: Claire Bowes, 31 Gould Drive, Northway, Tewkesbury, Glos.,   Tel: (H) 01684 850093 (W)0121 5576600
Fixtures Secretary: Paul Cole, 7 East Street, Tewkesbury, Glos.,   Tel: (H) 01684 295932
Club Colours: Black and amber hoops

WESTBURY-ON-SEVERN RFC
Ground Address: Westbury-on-Severn Parish Grounds, Westbury-on-Severn, Glos   Tel: 01452 760359
Brief Directions: A48 from Gloucester to Chepstow, Parish Ground on left hand side before Westbury-on-Severn village
Club Secretary: Phil Bleathman, The Hollies, Elton, Westbury-on-Severn, Glos. GL14 1JJ   Tel (H & W) 01452 760751/0831 184474
Fixtures Secretary: A Hyett, 1 Moyshill Villas, Strand Lane, Westbury-on-SEvern. GL14 1PG.
Club Colours: Royal blue and white hoops

WIDDEN OLD BOYS RFC
Ground Address: Memorial Ground, Tuffley Avenue, Gloucester   Tel: 01452 304080
Brief Directions: M5 north J12, right at 1st roundabout at end of bypass, left at next roundabout into Stroud Rd, approx 150 metres left into Tuffley Avenue
Club Secretary: Chris Hinde, 32 Millfields, Hucclecote, Gloucester   Tel: (H) 01452 617010   (W) 0378 205011
Fixtures Secretary: Andy Alder   Tel: 01452 721050
Club Colours: Myrtle green shirts, white shorts

Smiths Industries R.F.C. Displaying their new 'pink' colour clash strip on 'Ladies Day'.
Left to right standing, Simon North (Capt), John Smith, Carl Slatter, Dave Cole, Mark Plumb, Dennis Campbell, Adrian Randle, Rob James, Kevin Tyson, Mark Newman and Martin Cotter.
Left to Right Kneeling, Rich Torr, Jim Vallence, Tony Waterer, Nick Bishop, Matt Andrews, Alex Ayers and Martin Gilder.

Have you many Rugby enthusiasts at your Club ?
Does you Club need to raise extra funds ?

If the answer to these questions is Yes -
then place an order for

The Official Rugby Union Club Directory

WITH EVERY CLUB IN THE LEAGUE STRUCTURE INCLUDED AND ITS
UNRIVALLED STATISTICAL COVERAGE OF THE CLUBS AND PLAYERS IN
THE TOP LEVELS OF THE LEAGUE SYSTEM IT CAN ANSWER ALL SORTS
OF QUESTIONS AND WOULD MAKE AN IDEAL PRESENT.

Did you realise the Directory is available to your club at very good discount rates.

If you order				Profit for Club
1	copy cost	£14.99		
2 or 3	copies cost	£13.50 each		£ 1.49 each
between 4 & 9	copies cost	£10.00 each		£ 4.99 each
between 10 & 19	copies cost	£ 9.00 each		£ 5.99 each
20 or more	copies cost	£ 8.00 each		£ 6.99 each

To find out more information or to place an order, contact the publishers:
Tony Williams Publications Ltd., Helland, North Curry, Taunton, Somerset. TA3 6DU.
or Telephone 01823 490080 or Fax 01823 490281

GLOUCESTERSHIRE THREE

Gloucester Three 1997-98 Fixtures	Bristol Aeroplanes 1	Dowty 2	Gloucs. Civil Serv. 3	Gloucs. All Blues 4	Minchinhampton 5	Newent 6	Pilning 7	St Brendans 8	Wotton-under-Edge 9	
1 Bristol Aeroplanes	X		7/3	25/10	31/1			15/11		1
2 Dowty	11/4	X				7/3	15/11		31/1	2
3 Gloucester Civil Serv		14/3	X			31/1	25/10		15/11	3
4 Gloucester All Blues		8/11	11/4	X	7/3			31/1		4
5 Minchinhampton		14/2	10/1		X		14/3		25/10	5
6 Newent	14/2			14/3	15/11	X		25/10		6
7 Pilning	8/11			10/1		11/4	X		7/3	7
8 St Brendans		10/1	8/11		11/4		14/2	X		8
9 Wotton-under-Edge	10/1			14/2		8/11		14/3	X	9
	1	2	3	4	5	6	7	8	9	

BRISTOL AEROPLANE COMPANY RFC
Ground Address: Bristol Aerospace Welfare Association Sports Ground, 589 Southmead Road, Filton, Bristol. BS12 7DG   Tel: 0117 9768066
Brief Directions: Travel south along A38, right at the roundabout at top of Filton Hill into Southmead Road, ground on the right
Club Secretary: Neil Elliott, 4 The Bluebells, Bradley Stoke, Bristol. BS12 8BE   Tel: (H) 0117 9693714   (W) 0117 9795399
Fixtures Secretary: Trevor Curry   Tel: (H) 01275 876411
Club Colours: Red, white and blue hoops

DOWTY RFC
Ground Address: Sports & Social, Staverton, Gloucester   Tel: 01452 714567
Brief Directions: M5 J11 head for Gloucester, Elmbridge Court r'bout exit 4 - Churchdown, straight through 2 sets of lights, 1st left after golf course - down Hatherley, 1st right after factory
Club Secretary: Mrs G Blackwell, 6 Kaybourne Crescent, Churchdown, Gloucester. GL3 2HL   Tel: (H) 01452 859388
Fixtures Secretary: Mr A Nasrat   Tel: (H) 01452 713877
Club Colours: Blue and white hoops

GLOUCESTER ALL BLUES RFC
Ground Address: The Oxleaze, Westgate Bridge, Westgate Street, Gloucester   Tel: 01452 306984
Brief Directions: Bottom end of Westgate St over bridge, turn immediately left and club is about 100yards.
Club Secretary: Mr G R Selwyn, Millbank, Chessgrove Lane, Longhope, Gloucester. GL17 0LE.   Tel: (H) 01452 831215
Fixtures Secretary: Mr M Heath, 35 Dimore Close, Hardwicke, Glos.   Tel: (H) 01452 728159
Club Colours: Navy blue shirts, shorts and socks

GLOUCESTER CIVIL SERVICE TIGERS RFC
Ground Address: CSSA, Estcourt Road, Gloucester. GL1 3LG   Tel: 01452 528317
Brief Directions: M5 J11, A40 to Gloucester, continue on A40 to Longford roundabout, left at Longford Inn (Beefeater), left at next roundabout, ground is on immediate right
Club Secretary: Michael Hughes, 18 Coombe Glen Lane, Up Hatherley, Cheltenham, Glos. GL51 5LE   Tel: 01242 694243
Fixtures Secretary: Mr B Humphries   Tel: (H) 01452 728024
Club Colours: Red and blue hoops

MINCHINHAMPTON RFC
Ground Address: Minchinhampton Sports & Social Club, Tobacconist Road, Minchinhampton, Glos   Tel: 01453 88
Brief Directions: From centre of village take Tetbury road (Tetbury Street), 1st left, clubhouse straight ahead
Club Secretary: Rob Edmonds, Woodlands Cottage, 205 Slad Road, Stroud, Glos   Tel: (H) 01453 766662 (W) 01452 308989
Fixtures Secretary: Pete Weaving   Tel: (H) 01453 755561
Club Colours: Green, white and black hoops

NEWENT RFC
Ground Address: Recreation Ground, Watery Lane, Newent, Glos (Correspondence to: George Hotel, Newent)   Tel: 01531 820203
Brief Directions: Drive into centre of town, turn right into Watery Lane by the library/health centre, ground is on the right about 400 metres along Watery Lane
Club Secretary: Mark Smith, 2 Winfield, Newet, Glos., GL18 1QB.   Tel: 01531 822410
Fixtures Secretary: Alun Hunt, `Sunlight', Old Pike, Staunton, Glos., GL19 3QN   Tel: (H) 01452 840636
Club Colours: Green and gold

GLOUCESTERSHIRE THREE CONTINUED

PILNING RFC
Ground Address: The Pitch, Beach Road, Severn Beach, South Glos. BS12   Tel: 01454 653549
Brief Directions: Head for visitor's centre at second Severn crossing, turn into Beach Ave, Beach Road on right
Club Secretary: Lee Clarke, 122 Leinster Ave, Knowle West, Bristol. BS4 1NN   Tel: (W) 0117 9363472
Fixtures Secretary: Mike O'Brian   Tel: (H) 01454 633768
Club Colours: Blue and white hoops

ST BRENDANS OLD BOYS RFC
Ground Address: Combination Ground, Northway, Bristol. BS12 7QG   Tel: 0117 9692 793
Brief Directions: On the A38, opposite the main runway
Club Secretary: Richard A Kolanko, 91 Church Road, Horfield, Bristol. BS7 8SD   Tel: (H) 0117 9241390 (W) 0117 9666861
Fixtures Secretary: Frank Probert   Tel: (H) 0117 964779
Club Colours: Maroon and old gold hoops

WOTTON-UNDER-EDGE RFC
Ground Address: K L B School Ground, Kingswood Road, Wotton-under-Edge   Tel: 01453 842138 (Falcon Hotel)
Club Secretary: C R Baker, 13 Bradley Street, Wotton-under-Edge. GL12 7AP   Tel: (H) 01453 842455
Fixtures Secretary: R Flippance   Tel: (H) 01453 844958
Club Colours: Black and amber hoops

THE
OFFICIAL RUGBY UNION
CLUB DIRECTORY 1997-98

The Perfect Christmas Present

THE
OFFICIAL RUGBY UNION
CLUB DIRECTORY 1997-98

The Perfect Christmas Present

SOMERSET ONE

Somerset One 1997-98 Fixtures	Avonvale	Blagdon	Chew Valley	Frome	Imperial	Minehead	Nailsea & B.	North Petherton	Stothert & Pitt	Winscombe	
	1	2	3	4	5	6	7	8	9	10	
1 Avonvale	X	20/9	14/3	14/2	11/10	24/1	25/10	10/1	15/11	11/4	1
2 Blagdon	7/3	X	17/1	8/11	27/9	25/4	31/1	20/12	18/10	14/3	2
3 Chew Valley	6/9	25/10	X	20/9	10/1	14/2	15/11	11/10	11/4	24/1	3
4 Frome	27/9	10/1	7/3	X	15/11	11/10	11/4	24/1	6/9	25/10	4
5 Imperial	31/1	14/2	8/11	25/4	X	20/12	18/10	14/3	17/1	20/9	5
6 Minehead	18/10	15/11	27/9	31/1	11/4	X	6/9	25/10	7/3	10/1	6
7 Nailsea & Backwell	17/1	11/10	25/4	20/12	24/1	14/3	X	20/9	8/11	14/2	7
8 North Petherton	8/11	11/4	31/1	18/10	6/9	17/1	7/3	X	27/9	15/11	8
9 Stothert & Pitt	25/4	24/1	20/12	14/3	25/10	20/9	10/1	14/2	X	11/10	9
10 Winscombe	20/12	6/9	18/10	17/1	7/3	8/11	27/9	25/4	31/1	X	10
	1	2	3	4	5	6	7	8	9	10	

AVONVALE RFC
Ground Address: Bathford Playing Fields, Crown Field, Bathford, Bath, Avon   Tel: 01225 858295
Brief Directions: A4 out of Bath, through Batheaston, right at next roundabout, under railway bridge and next left, clubhouse is along a track next to phone box 200yds up Bathford Hill
Club Secretary: Mr C Burgess, 2 Cranmore Place, Odd Down, Bath. BA2 2UP   Tel: (W) 01225 477542
Fixtures Secretary: Steve Vowles, 77 Lockswood Road, Lower Weston, Bath BA1 3ES   Tel: (H) 01225 333852 (W) 01225 766451
Club Colours: Blue shirts with a white band

BLAGDON RFC
Ground Address: The Mead, Blagdon Village   Tel: 01761 463196
Brief Directions: Turn left off the A38 at Churchill traffic lights and follow road for approx 3 miles into Blagdon
Club Secretary: M Ryan, 3 The Old Rectory, Pilgrims Way, Chewstoke, Bristol. BS18 8TT   Tel: (H) 01275 333778   (W) 0117 9264662
Fixtures Secretary: M Ryan   Tel: (H) 01275 333778 (W) 0117 9264662
Club Colours: Green

CHEW VALLEY OLD BOYS RFC
Ground Address: Lobingtons, Chew Lane, Chew Stoke, Bristol
Brief Directions: Through Chew Magna, on to Chew Stoke, next to the school
Club Secretary: Timothy Weatherley, 10 Malago Walk, The Ridings, Bishopsworth, Bristol. BS13 8NZ   Tel: (H) 0117 9783216
Fixtures Secretary: Robert Martin   Tel: (H) 01275 832547
Club Colours: Green and white hoops

FROME RFC
Ground Address: Gypsy Lane, Frome, Somerset. BA11 2NA   Tel: 01373 462506
Brief Directions: Follow signs for Leisure Centre, Frome RFC is signposted from the Bath Road/Princess Anne Road traffic lights
Club Secretary: Paul Holdaway, 4 Market Place, Nunney, Nr Frome, Somerset. BA11 4LY   Tel: (H) 01373 836821
Fixtures Secretary: Symon Crouch Tel: 01373 465600
Club Colours: Red, black & white hoops

IMPERIAL RFC
Ground Address: Bristol Imperial Sports Ground, West Town Lane, Knowle, Bristol   Tel: 01275 546000
Brief Directions: From Wells road (A37) and Bath road (A4), turn into West Town Lane
Club Secretary: Stuart Eld, 43 Avonleigh Road, Bedminster, Bristol. B53 3HS   Tel: (H) 0117 9631 688
Fixtures Secretary: Jack Gommo   Tel: (H) 01275544811
Club Colours: Myrtle and amber shirts, blue shorts, myrtle and amber socks

MINEHEAD BARBARIANS RFC
Ground Address: Tom Stewart Field, Ellicombe, Minehead, Somerset. TA24 6TR   Tel: 01643 707155
Brief Directions: A39 to Minehead from Taunton/Bridgwater, left at roundabout signed Ellicombe, ground 100 metres
Club Secretary: Nick Demirtges, 34 St Georges Street, Dunster, Minehead, Somerset. TA24 6RS   Tel: (H) 01643 821349
Fixtures Secretary: The Club Seward, The Tom Stewart Field, Ellicombe, Minehead   Tel: (H) 01643 707155
Club Colours: Black and white hoops

NAILSEA & BACKWELL RFC
Ground Address: North Street, Nailsea   Tel: 01278 810818
Brief Directions: West down Silver Street, past Moor End Spout pub, 0.5 mile on left
Club Secretary: Anita Heappey, Wareham Lodge, Whitesfield Road, Naislsea BS19 2NF
Fixtures Secretary: Justin Siedle, 2 Huntley Grove, Nailsea, BS19 2UQ
Club Colours: Black

NORTH PETHERTON RFC
Ground Address: Beggars Brook, North Petherton, Nr Bridgwater, Somerset   Tel: 01278 663028
Brief Directions: M5 J24, A38 Taunton, through North Petherton, layby on left at exit of North Petherton
Club Secretary: Phil Ham, 45 Tudor Way, Bridgwater, Somerset TA6 6UE
Fixtures Secretary: Mr M House, 2 Hardings Close, North Petherton, Somerset   Tel: (H) 01278 663118
Club Colours: Black and white hoops / Black / Red, white and blue hoops

STOTHERT & PITT RFC
Ground Address: Adamsfield, Corston, Bath. BA1 9AY   Tel: 01225 874802
Brief Directions: On A4 road, Bristol side of Bath
Club Secretary: R V Garraway, 2 Westfield Park South, Lower Weston, Bath. BA1 3HT   Tel: (H) 01225 316863
Fixtures Secretary: P N Mitchell   Tel: (H) 01225 447112
Club Colours: Blue, black and amber

WINSCOMBE RFC
Ground Address: Longfield Recreation Ground, Winscombe, North Somerset   Tel: 01934 842720
Brief Directions: Turn off A38 into Winscombe, turn left at right hand bend to ground.
Club Secretary: Alun George, 3 Landseer Close, Worle, Weston-Super-Mare. BS22 9NL   Tel: (H) 01934 518270
Fixtures Secretary: Dave Sheppard, 14 Farm Road, Milton, Weston-Super-Mare.   Tel: 01934 629097
Club Colours: Black with white hoops

Chew Valley Somerset.

DO YOU KNOW A RUGBY ENTHUSIAST WITH A BIRTHDAY COMING UP?

This directory would make a perfect present.

So why not buy a copy from your club or from W H Smith.

SOMERSET TWO

Somerset Two 1997-98 Fixtures	Avon	British Gas	Broad Plain	Burnham-on-Sea	Castle Cary	Cheddar Valley	Crewkerne	Old Ashtonians	
	1	2	3	4	5	6	7	8	
1 Avon	X	14/2	31/1	11/10	20/12	27/9	15/11	11/4	1
2 British Gas	8/11	X	10/1	14/3		24/1	17/1	31/1	2
3 Broad Plain	25/10	11/4	X	27/9	24/1	15/11	14/3	14/2	3
4 Burnham-on-Sea	24/1	20/12	17/1	X	14/2	25/10	11/4	15/11	4
5 Castle Cary	14/3	7/3	11/10	8/11	X	10/1	31/1	27/9	5
6 Cheddar Valley	17/1	11/10	7/3	31/1	11/4	X	8/11	20/12	6
7 Crewkerne	7/3	27/9	20/12	10/1	25/10	14/2	X	24/1	7
8 Old Ashtonians	10/1	25/10	8/11	7/3	17/1	14/3	11/10	X	8
	1	2	3	4	5	6	7	8	

AVON RFC
Ground Address: Hicks Field, London Road East, Bath, Somerset Tel: 01225 852446
Brief Directions: On A4 towards Batheaston approx 0.5 mile from A46/A4 junction, entrance on right hand side
Club Secretary: Mr David Loader, 114 Southdown Road, Southdown, Bath, Somerset. BA2 1JJ Tel: (H)01225 316864 (W)01225 331116
Fixtures Secretary: Mr C Nicholson, 116 Free View Road, Twerton, Bath. BA2 1DZ Tel: (H) 01225 401623
Club Colours: Black and amber hoops

BRITISH GAS (BRISTOL) RFC
Ground Address: Norton Lane, Witchurch, Bristol
Brief Directions: Through Witchurch village, passed the Black Lion pub, over the bridge, and then next left. Ground is 1st on left.
Club Secretary: Colin Rowland, 57 Fitzgerald Road, Knowle, Bristol. BS3 5DH. Tel: 0117 977 5200
Fixtures Secretary: Les Brunyee, 43 Millmead House, Silcox Road, Hartcliffe, Bristol. BS3 Tel: 0117 964 4685
Club Colours: Blue and white hoops

BROAD PLAIN RFC
Ground Address: Hartcliffe School, Bishport Avenue, Hartcliffe, Bristol Tel: 0117 9552782
Brief Directions: South side of Bristol, between A37 and A38 roads
Club Secretary: Don Collins, 77 Lake Road, Henleaze, Bristol. BS10 5JE Tel: (H) 0117 9622094 (W) 0117 9248051
Fixtures Secretary: Ivan Gregory Tel: (H) 0117 9393713 (W) 0117 9552866
Club Colours: Blue, maroon and gold hoops

BURNHAM ON SEA RFC
Ground Address: B.A.S.C. Ground, Stoddens Road, Burnham on Sea, Somerset. TA8 2DE Tel: 01278 788355
Brief Directions: Signposted from M5 J22
Club Secretary: Lucy Harris, 50 Gloucester Road, Burnham on Sea, Somerset TA8 1JA
Fixtures Secretary: Andy Marsh, 217 Berrow Road, Burnham on Sea, Somerset TA8 2JG
Club Colours: Blue and white hoops

CASTLE CARY RUFC
Ground Address: Brookhouse Field, Sutton, Ditcheat, Shepton Mallet, Somerset Tel: 01963 351178
Brief Directions: A361 to Castle Cary from Shepton Mallet, turn right at Brookhouse Inn, 2nd on right
Club Secretary: Mr A J Bailey, 2 Enfield Terrace, Weymouth Road, Evercreech, Somerset Tel: (H) 01749 830268 (W) 0585 791109
Fixtures Secretary: Mr C Watts Tel: (H) 01963 350162
Club Colours: Red and black hoops

CHEDDAR VALLEY RFC
Ground Address: Sharpham Road Playing Fields, Cheddar, Somerset Tel: 01934 743623
Club Secretary: Ceri Davies, 16 Round Oak Grove, Cheddar, Somerset. BS27 3BW Tel: (H) 01934 744167
Fixtures Secretary: Callum Mackenzie Tel: (H) 01934 744277
Club Colours: Sky blue and scarlet hoops

CREWKERNE RFC
Ground Address: Henhayes, Main Car Park, South Street, Crewkerne, Somerset.
Club Secretary: Jeanette Collings, 59 Seycamore Close, Holway, Tournton, Somerstone. Tel: (H) 01823 279837
Fixtures Secretary: T Boyer, Tel: 01308 863169
Club Colours: Red and black hoops.

OLD ASHTONIANS RFC
Ground Address: Ashton Park School, Blackmoors Lane, Bower Ashton, Bristol Tel: c/o 0117 9877796
Brief Directions: From city follow signs for Portishead, school is indicated at 1st roundabout (turn left)
Club Secretary: Ian Reed, The Bear Inn, 261/3 Hotwells Road, Hotwells, Bristol. BS8 4SF Tel: (H & W) 0117 98777986
Fixtures Secretary: Tony Excell, 18 Perrycroft Rd., Bishopsworth, Bristol. BS13 7RY. Tel: (H) 0117 9642352
Club Colours: Blue shirt, yellow, green and white band, black shorts, yellow socks

Have you many Rugby enthusiasts at your Club ?
Does you Club need to raise extra funds ?

If the answer to these questions is Yes -
then place an order for

The Official Rugby Union Club Directory

WITH EVERY CLUB IN THE LEAGUE STRUCTURE INCLUDED AND ITS
UNRIVALLED STATISTICAL COVERAGE OF THE CLUBS AND PLAYERS IN
THE TOP LEVELS OF THE LEAGUE SYSTEM IT CAN ANSWER ALL SORTS
OF QUESTIONS AND WOULD MAKE AN IDEAL PRESENT.

Did you realise the Directory is available to your club at very good discount rates.

If you order				Profit for Club
1	copy cost	£14.99		
2 or 3	copies cost	£13.50 each	£ 1.49 each	
between 4 & 9	copies cost	£10.00 each	£ 4.99 each	
between 10 & 19	copies cost	£ 9.00 each	£ 5.99 each	
20 or more	copies cost	£ 8.00 each	£ 6.99 each	

To find out more information or to place an order, contact the publishers:
Tony Williams Publications Ltd., Helland, North Curry, Taunton, Somerset. TA3 6DU.
or Telephone 01823 490080 or Fax 01823 490281

SOMERSET THREE

Somerset Three 1997-98 Fixtures	Aller 1	Bath Old Edward. 2	Bath Saracens 3	Martock 4	Morgonians 5	Wincanton 6	
1 Aller	X	31/1	8/11	7/3	20/12	10/1	1
2 Bath Old Edwardians	25/10	X	14/3	10/1	15/11	14/2	2
3 Bath Saracens	14/2	20/12	X	31/1	11/4	15/11	3
4 Martock	15/11	11/4	25/10	X	14/2	14/3	4
5 Morganians	14/3	7/3	10/1	8/11	X	31/1	5
6 Wincanton	11/4	8/11	7/3	20/12	25/10	X	6
	1	2	3	4	5	6	

ALLER RFC
Ground Address: Westfield, Curry Rivel, Somerset. Tel: 01458 252687
Brief Directions: First right turn in Curry Rivel on the B3153 from Taunton.
Club Secretary: Mrs D Frome, 43 Chatham Place, Curry Rivel, Somerset TA10 0HR. Tel: (H) 01458 253050
Fixtures Secretary: Mark Roddie, Tel: (H) 01458 253599 Tel: (W) 01458 273740
Club Colours: Red and green hoops.

BATH OLD EDWARDIANS RFC
Ground Address: KES Sports Ground, Bathampton, Bath Tel: 01225 462354
Brief Directions: M4 J18, A46 to Bath, London Rd towards Batheaston, turn right over Tollbridge to Bathampton, ground next to canal
Club Secretary: Jonathon Miles, The Close, Gloucester Road, Upper Swainswick, Bath. BA1 8BR Tel: (H) 01225 859341 (W) 01225 443436 (F) 01225 443337
Fixtures Secretary: Rob Mitchell Tel: (H) 01225 310989 (W) 01373 463333 (F) 01373 451299
Club Colours: Gold, maroon and blue hoops

BATH SARACENS RFC
Ground Address: Civil Service Sports Ground, Claverton Down, Bath, Avon. Tel: 01225 832403
Brief Directions: From Bath take A367 to Frys Garage mini roundabout.Take first left, then straight on for 2 miles and turn right immediately after Ralph Allen School.
Club Secretary: Chris Curtis, 7 Seymor Court, Trowbridge, Wiltshire. Tel: (H) 01235 777169 Tel: (W) 01225 472362
Fixtures Secretary: Mr Rob Lawrence, Tel: (H) 01225 427356 Tel: (W) 01225 462039
Club Colours: Blue with red and gold hoops.

MARTOCK RFC
Ground Address: Martock Recreation Ground, Stoke Road, Martock
Brief Directions: Take Martock exit from A303 at Percombe Hill, left at T junction to join Stoke Road, ground on left after 1 mile
Club Secretary: Philip Jackson, Church Lodge Cottage, Church Street, Martock, Somerset. TA12 6JL Tel: (H) 01935 823514
Fixtures Secretary: Kevin Cox Tel: (H) 01935 825467
Club Colours: Green and black quarters

MORGANIANS RFC
Ground Address: Chedzoy Lane, Bridgwater, Somerset Tel: 01278 423434
Brief Directions: On A39 Bridgwater to Glastonbury road, over M5 motorway, 1st right into Chedzoy Lane opposite Mole Valley Farms
Club Secretary: Gordon Clark, 34 Plum Tree Close, Bridgwater, Somerset. TA6 4XG Tel: (H) 01278 452721
Fixtures Secretary: Gordon Clark Tel: (H) 01278 452721
Club Colours: Navy shirts with wide red and narrow yellow hoop

WINCANTON RUFC
Ground Address: Balsam Fields, Wincanton
Brief Directions: Into Wincanton from A303, after Fire station turn right down Moor Lane 0.5 mile
Club Secretary: Peter Gibson, Bayford East Lodge, Bayford Tel: (H) 01963 33121
Fixtures Secretary: Nick Duffin, 1 Ormsby House, Blandford Forum, Dorset Tel: 01963 370210
Club Colours: Black and amber

SOUTH WEST DIVISION
FINAL LEAGUE TABLES 1996-97

DEVON THREE

	P	W	D	L	F	A	PTS
Wessex	14	14	0	0	993	52	28
Marjons	14	12	0	2	963	157	24
Devonport HSOB	14	10	0	4	368	184	20
Buckfastleigh	14	8	0	6	289	372	16
Woodland Fort	14	4	1	9	174	556	9
Plympton Victoria	14	4	0	10	164	482	8
Axminster	14	2	1	11	186	613	5
Plymouth YMCA	14	1	0	13	121	842	*-4

GLOS & SOMERSET

	P	W	D	L	F	A	PTS
Coney Hill	15	15	0	0	704	122	30
Old Richians	15	11	0	4	461	227	22
Walcot Od Boys	15	10	0	5	380	257	20
Barton Hill	15	10	0	5	308	214	20
Gordano	15	10	0	5	363	288	20
St Bernadettes OB	15	10	0	5	299	256	20
Longlevens	15	10	0	5	280	268	20
Brockworth	15	8	0	7	318	330	16
Bream	15	6	0	9	203	235	12
Yatton	15	6	0	9	265	311	12
Midsomer Norton	15	6	0	9	335	401	12
Frampton Cotterell	15	6	0	9	246	413	12
Tor	15	5	0	10	213	354	10
Wiveliscombe	15	3	0	12	247	420	6
Old Sulians	15	3	0	12	177	376	6
Old Cryptians	15	1	0	14	218	545	2

GLOUCESTER ONE

	P	W	D	L	F	A	PTS
Bristol Saracens	12	11	0	1	326	87	22
Old Centralians	12	11	0	1	325	147	22
Painswick	12	7	1	4	224	185	15
Ashley Down O B	12	7	1	4	182	148	15
Old Bristolians	12	6	1	5	330	262	13
Tredworth	12	6	1	5	188	181	13
Hucclecote Od Boys	12	5	3	4	148	150	13
Cheltenham CS	12	5	2	5	197	198	12
Cainscross	12	4	2	6	164	234	10
Bristol Telephones	12	4	0	8	166	312	8
Cheltenham Saracens	12	3	1	8	108	219	7
Bishopston	12	2	1	9	182	250	5
Widden Old Boys	12	0	1	11	86	253	1

GLOUCESTER TWO

	P	W	D	L	F	A	PTS
Southmead	12	11	0	1	340	115	22
Chosen Hill FP	12	10	1	1	325	126	21
Westbury on Severn	12	10	0	2	316	127	20
Chipping Sodbury	12	9	0	3	350	123	18
Cotham Park	12	8	0	4	234	178	16
Smiths (Industries)	12	5	2	5	260	243	12
Tewkesbury	12	5	1	6	164	222	11
Aretians	12	5	1	6	211	295	11
Tetbury	12	4	1	7	197	190	9
Old Colstonians	12	4	0	8	232	294	8
Kingswood	12	3	0	9	176	307	6
Gloucester CS	12	1	0	11	120	493	2
St Brendans	12	0	0	12	143	355	0

GLOUCESTER THREE

	P	W	D	L	F	A	PTS
Dursley	8	8	0	0	230	54	16
Old Elizabethans	8	6	0	2	179	64	12
Bristol Aeroplanes	8	6	0	2	119	91	12
Minchinhampton	8	5	0	3	215	64	10
Pilning	8	4	0	4	67	69	8
Gloucester All Blues	8	3	0	5	89	114	6
Dowty	8	3	0	5	72	165	6
Newent	8	1	0	7	56	218	2
Wotton-under-Edge	8	0	0	8	58	246	0

SOMERSET ONE

	P	W	D	L	F	A	PTS
Wells	18	17	1	0	606	172	35
Frome	18	15	0	3	599	206	30
Minehead Barbarians	18	10	2	6	390	214	22
North Petherton	18	9	1	8	371	261	19
Chew Valley	18	8	2	8	298	279	18
Imperial	18	9	1	8	329	299	*17
Stothert & Pitt	18	8	1	9	285	446	17
Avonvale	18	6	1	11	242	415	13
Nailsea & Backwell	18	3	0	15	223	560	*4
Crewkerne	18	0	1	17	144	635	*-1

SOMERSET TWO

	P	W	D	L	F	A	PTS
Winscombe	16	15	0	1	536	144	30
Blagdon	16	13	0	3	456	185	26
Avon	16	12	0	4	522	210	24
Cheddar Valley	16	8	0	8	201	295	16
Broad Plain	16	6	1	9	260	359	13
Castle Cary	16	7	0	9	261	319	*12
Old Ashtonians	16	5	1	10	235	334	11
Bath Saracens	16	5	0	11	268	335	10
Bath Old Edwardians	16	0	0	16	110	668	*-2

SOMERSET THREE

	P	W	D	L	F	A	PTS
British Gas	10	10	0	0	362	45	20
Burnham on Sea	10	7	0	3	206	85	*12
Morganians	10	5	0	5	97	148	10
Wincanton	10	5	0	5	139	299	*8
Martock	10	3	0	7	283	257	*4
Aller	10	0	0	10	24	277	0

BERK/DORSET/WILT ONE

	P	W	D	L	F	A	PTS
Weymouth	18	16	1	1	513	174	33
Westbury	18	13	0	5	350	215	26
Melksham	18	12	1	5	399	241	25
Calne	18	11	1	6	324	243	*21
Aldermaston	18	11	0	7	292	264	*20
Trowbridge	18	6	1	11	341	269	13
Bridport	18	6	0	12	203	301	12
Thatcham	18	6	0	12	239	344	12
Lytchett Minister	18	6	0	12	195	416	12
Supermarine	18	1	0	17	102	491	2

BERK/DORSET/WILT TWO

	P	W	D	L	F	A	PTS
Tadley	14	13	1	0	448	95	27
Ivel Barbarians	14	10	2	2	552	139	22
Colerne	14	9	0	5	257	315	18
Swindon College	14	7	1	6	303	256	15
Oakmedians	14	7	1	6	242	397	15
Portcastrians	14	4	0	10	210	242	8
Berkshire Shire Hall	14	1	1	12	194	397	3
Pewsey Vale	14	2	0	12	144	509	*2

BERK/DORSET/WILT THREE

	P	W	D	L	F	A	PTS
Minety	12	11	0	1	246	77	22
Christchurch	12	9	1	2	314	101	19
Hungerford	12	7	0	5	171	110	14
Warminster	12	5	2	5	188	188	*10
Bournemouth Univ	12	3	1	8	273	254	7
Puddletown	12	3	0	9	139	311	6
Poole	12	2	0	10	108	398	4

BUCKS OXON LEAGUE

	P	W	D	L	F	A	PTS
Chipping Norton	12	11	0	1	362	64	22
Beaconsfield	12	10	0	2	547	127	20
Cholsey	12	10	0	2	416	97	20
Phoenix	12	10	0	2	265	101	*18
Drifters	12	7	0	5	289	204	14
Littlemore	12	7	0	5	218	153	14
Wheatley	12	7	0	5	249	208	14
Pennanians	12	6	0	6	212	251	12
Chesham	12	4	0	8	208	252	8
Abingdon	12	3	0	9	79	370	*4
Gosford All Blacks	12	2	0	10	85	374	*2
Harwell	12	1	0	11	126	416	2
Didcot	12	0	0	12	62	501	0

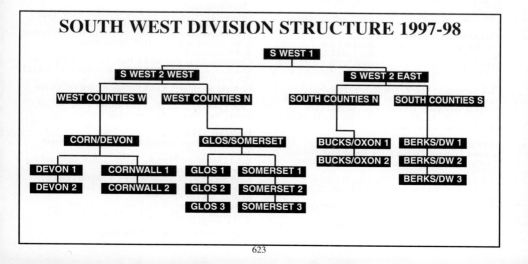

SOUTH WEST DIVISION STRUCTURE 1997-98

S WEST 1

S WEST 2 WEST

S WEST 2 EAST

WEST COUNTIES W

WEST COUNTIES N

SOUTH COUNTIES N

SOUTH COUNTIES S

CORN/DEVON

GLOS/SOMERSET

BUCKS/OXON 1

BERKS/DW 1

BUCKS/OXON 2

BERKS/DW 2

BERKS/DW 3

DEVON 1

CORNWALL 1

GLOS 1

SOMERSET 1

DEVON 2

CORNWALL 2

GLOS 2

SOMERSET 2

GLOS 3

SOMERSET 3

South West Two East 1997-98 Fixtures	Abbey 1	Amersham & C. 2	Aylesbury 3	Bournemouth 4	Chinnor 5	Dorchester 6	Maslow 7	Oxford 8	Salisbury 9	Sherborne 10	Stow-on-the-Wold 11	Swanage & RW 12	
1 Abbey	X	20/9	21/3	8/11	17/1	20/12	14/2	18/4	27/9	18/10	31/1	30/8	1
2 Amersham & Chil	14/3	X	4/4	6/9	27/9	18/10	31/1	8/11	14/2	17/1	4/4	20/12	2
3 Aylesbury	6/9	30/8	X	31/1	8/11	17/1	27/9	20/12	14/3	11/10	18/10	18/4	3
4 Bournemouth	24/1	21/3	25/10	X	20/9	7/3	25/4	11/10	15/11	10/1	4/4	7/2	4
5 Chinnor	15/11	7/3	24/1	14/3	X	11/10	10/1	7/2	25/4	4/4	6/9	25/10	5
6 Dorchester	25/4	7/2	15/11	27/9	14/2	X	4/4	25/10	10/1	6/9	14/3	24/1	6
7 Maslow	11/10	25/10	7/3	20/12	4/4	30/8	X	21/3	7/2	8/11	17/1	20/9	7
8 Oxford	10/1	24/1	25/4	14/2	18/10	31/1	6/9	X	30/8	14/3	27/9	15/11	8
9 Salisbury	7/3	11/10	20/9	17/1	20/12	4/4	18/10	4/4	X	31/1	8/11	21/3	9
10 Sherborne	7/2	15/1	7/2	4/4	30/8		24/1	20/9	25/10	X	20/12	7/3	10
11 Stow-on-the-Wold	25/10	10/1	7/2	30/8	21/3	20/9	15/11	7/3	24/1	25/4	X	11/10	11
12 Swanage & RW	4/4	25/4	10/1	18/10	31/1	8/11	14/3	17/1	6/9	27/9	14/2	X	12
	1	2	3	4	5	6	7	8	9	10	11	12	

ABBEY RFC
Ground Address: Rosehill, Peppard Road, Emmer Green, Reading, Berkshire. RG4   Tel: 01734 722881
Brief Directions: On B481 from Reading through Caversham & Emmer Green to Peppard & Nettlebed, after leaving Borough Boundary, 2 sharp bends later, Abbey on the left
Club Secretary: Mrs Lynne Lee, Cotswold, Behoes Lane, Woodcote, nr Reading. RG8 0PP Tel: (H) 01491 680102
Fixtures Secretary: Mrs Lynne Lee   Tel: (H) 01491 680102
Club Colours: Navy blue with green and white hoops

AMERSHAM & CHILTERN RFC
Ground Address: Ash Grove, Weedon Lane, Amersham, Bucks. HP6 5QU   Tel: 01494 725161
Brief Directions: From Amersham/Chesham road, take Copperkings Lane (signed Hyde Heath), Weedon Lane is 2nd left
Club Secretary: I McKenzie Esq, 17 Highover Park, Amersham, Bucks. HP7 0BN   Tel: (H) 01494 431966
Fixtures Secretary: R Cook, 120 Chestnut Lane, Amersham, Bucks. HP6 6DZ.   Tel: (H) 01494 433144
Club Colours: Claret and white

AYLESBURY RFC
Ground Address: Ostlers Field, Brook End, Weston Turville, Aylesbury, Bucks. HP22 5RN   Tel: 01296 612556
Club Secretary: Graham N Roberts, Burghley, 2 Wheelwrights, Weston Turville, Bucks. HP22 5QS Tel: (H) 01296 612925
Fixtures Secretary: James P Williams   Tel: (H) 01296 688249
Club Colours: Black and magenta hooped shirts, black shorts and socks

BOURNEMOUTH RFC
Ground Address: Bournemouth Sports Club, Chapel Gate, Bast Parley, Christchurch, Dorset. BH23 6BD Tel: 01202 581933
Brief Directions: Alongside Bournemouth Airport, approach from A338 dual carriageway.
Club Secretary: Mike Wilkes, 581 Christchurch Road, Bournemouth, Dorset. BH1 4BU   Tel: 01202 3923454
Fixtures Secretary: Ian Mure   Tel: (H) 01202 696331
Club Colours: Sable and black, small gold hoops on shirts

CHINNOR RFC
Ground Address: The Pavilion, Kingsey Road, Thame, Oxon. OX9 3PB   Tel: 01844 213735/213907
Brief Directions: Situated on the Thame Western bypass at the junction with the a4129 Thame-Princes Risborough road
Club Secretary: Richard J P Hall, 7 Limes Way, Shabbington, Bucks. HP18 9HB   Tel: (H) 01844 201332 (W) 01844 201045
Fixtures Secretary: Kevin Robinson   Tel: (H) 01844 217900   (W) 01844 213822
Club Colours: Wide black and narrow white hooped jersey, black shorts, black and white hooped socks

DORCHESTER RFC
Ground Address: Coburg Road, Dorchester, Dorset Tel: 01305 265692
Brief Directions: From the bypass, follow signs to West Dorset Leisure Centre
Club Secretary: Graham Aspley, 5 Nappers Court, Charles Street, Dorchester. DT1 1EE   Tel: (H) 01305 814802   (W) 01305 269944
Fixtures Secretary: Tony Foot, 25 Cromwell road, Dorchester DT1 2D   Tel: (H) 01305 250137   (W) 01305 251400
Club Colours: Green and white hoops

SOUTH WEST TWO EAST CONTINUED

MARLOW RUFC
Ground Address: Riverwoods Drive, Marlow, Bucks
Tel: 016284 77054/83911
Club Secretary: Graham Cutts, 6 Eastern Dene,
Hazlemere, Bucks. HP15 7BT   Tel: (H) 01494 711391
(W) 01494 431717
Fixtures Secretary: Graham Cutts   Tel: (H) 01494
711391   (W) 01494 431717
Club Colours: Black and white hoops, black shorts

OXFORD RFC
Ground Address: Southern by pass, North Hinksey
Village, Oxford   Tel: 01865 243984
Brief Directions: Ground can only be approached from
A34 going south, turn left off A34, sign posted
Club Secretary: Mrs Mary Bagnall, 3 Appleford Rd.,
Sutton Courtney, Oxon OX14 4NG   Tel: (H) 01865
390630
Fixtures Secretary: Roger Mountford   Tel: (H) 01993
812389
Club Colours: Green, black and silver

SALISBURY RFC
Ground Address: Castle Road, Salisbury   Tel: 01722
325317
Brief Directions: On A345 Salisbury to Amesbury
Road, just to the south of Old Sarum
Club Secretary: Dr G W Jack, 14 Windlesham Road,
Salisbury, Wiltshire. SP1 3PY   Tel: (H) 01722 335542
(W) 01980 612388
Fixtures Secretary: R H Rowland   Tel: 01725 512064
Club Colours: Green and white

SHERBORNE RFC
Ground Address: The Terrace, Sherborne, Dorset.   Tel:
01935 812478
Brief Directions: The ground is on the A352, half a mile
south of the town centre going towards Dorchester.
Club Secretary: Rod Liddiard, 6 Vincents Close,
Alweston, Sherborne, Dorset. DT9 5JH   Tel: (H) 01963
23402
Fixtures Secretary: Mrs V Rushton   Tel: (H) 01258
820195
Club Colours: All black

STOW-ON-THE-WOLD & DISTRICT RFC
Ground Address: Oddington Road, Stow-on-the-Wold,
Cheltenham, Glos (No post box)   Tel: 01451 830887
Brief Directions: From 'Unicorn' traffic lights in Stow
take Oddington/Chipping Norton road, ground is 1.5
miles on right
Club Secretary: N Drury, 2 Chestnut Corner, White
Hart Lane, Stow-on-the-Wold, Cheltenham, Glos   Tel:
(H) 01451 831686   (W) 01608 650428
Fixtures Secretary: A Jones   Tel: (H) 01993 842757
Club Colours: Black and white hoops

SWANAGE & WAREHAM RFC
Ground Address: Bestwall, Wareham, Dorset   Tel:
01929 552224
Brief Directions: Traffic lights at town centre, take
Bestwall to end, turn left into ground
Club Secretary: Mr Kevin Large, 20 Gannetts Park,
Swanage, Dorset   Tel: (H) 01929 426523   (W) 01929
425818
Fixtures Secretary: Mr John Hopkins   Tel: (H) 01202
886804
Club Colours: Maroon shirts and socks, white shorts

Abbey R.F.C.
Abbey won all of its 18 matches in Southern Counties South Division in 1996/97 and the photograph shows the
team immediately after the final league game of the season.
Photograph courtesy of Reading Chronicle.

SOUTHERN COUNTIES NORTH

Southern Counties North 1997-98 Fixtures	Beaconsfield	Bicester	Bletchley	Buckingham	Chipping Norton	Milton Keynes	Olney	Oxford Harleq.	Slough	Witney	
	1	2	3	4	5	6	7	8	9	10	
1 Beaconsfield	X	27/9	7/3	10/1	6/9	15/11	11/10	11/4	24/1	25/10	1
2 Bicester	14/2	X	14/3	20/9	15/11	11/10	24/1	25/10	10/1	18/4	2
3 Bletchley	20/9	6/9	X	25/10	11/4	10/1	14/2	15/11	11/10	24/1	3
4 Buckingham	8/11	7/3	17/1	X	18/10	27/9	25/4	31/1	20/12	14/3	4
5 Chipping Norton	14/3	25/4	20/12	24/1	X	25/10	20/9	10/1	14/2	11/10	5
6 Milton Keynes	25/4	31/1	8/11	14/2	17/1	X	20/12	18/10	14/3	20/9	6
7 Olney	31/1	18/10	27/9	15/11	7/3	4/4	X	6/9	25/10	10/1	7
8 Oxford Harlequins	20/12	17/1	25/4	11/10	8/11	24/1	14/3	X	20/9	14/2	8
9 Slough	18/10	8/11	31/1	28/3	27/9	6/9	17/1	7/3	X	15/11	9
10 Witney	17/1	20/12	18/10	6/9	31/1	7/3	8/11	27/9	25/4	X	10
	1	2	3	4	5	6	7	8	9	10	

BEACONSFIELD RFC
Ground Address: Oak Lodge Meadow, Windsor End, Beaconsfield, Buckinghamshire Tel: 01494 673783
Brief Directions: A40 to Beaconsfield, Saracens Head roundabout turn south down Windsor End, ground and club house 400 yards on left
Club Secretary: Philip Raw, Edgemoor, Britwell, Salome, Oxfordshire. OX9 5LF Tel: (H) 01491 612090
Fixtures Secretary: Malcolm Ridgley Tel: (H) 01494 718173
Club Colours: Green and gold hoops

BICESTER RUFC
Ground Address: Oxford Road, Bicester, Oxon. OX6 8AB Tel: 01869 241000
Brief Directions: As you approach Bicester from south on A34, the ground is on the right on the edge of town just past Tescos
Club Secretary: Mrs Jane Feist , 37 Moor Pond Close, Bicester, Oxon.
Fixtures Secretary: G Davies Tel: (H & W) 01869 241993
Club Colours: Red, amber and brown hooped shirts, navy blue shorts, red or hooped socks

BLETCHLEY RUFC
Ground Address: Manor Fields, Bletchley, Milton Keynes, Bucks Tel: 01908 372298
Brief Directions: On B488 from Leighton Buzzard, fork right at 'The Plough', from this fork take 3rd right - Manor Road, proceed down road over bridge to ground
Club Secretary: C W Spence, 17 Milesmere, Two Mile Ash, Milton Keynes. MK8 8QP Tel: (H) 01908 561876 (W) 0171 374 3051
Fixtures Secretary: I Punter Tel: (H) 01908 642994
Club Colours: Burgundy and white hoops

BUCKINGHAM RUFC
Ground Address: Floyd Field, Moreton Road, Maids Moreton, Buckingham Tel: 01280 815474
Brief Directions: From Buckingham town centre, take A413 to Towcester, after approx 0.5 mile ground is on the left
Club Secretary: Finlay Gemmell, 22 Elmfields Gate, Winslow, Bucks. MK18 3JG Tel: (H) 01296 714640 (W) 01628 893772
Fixtures Secretary: Anthony Smith Tel: (H) 01280 815634
Club Colours: Green and white hoops

CHIPPING NORTON RUFC
Ground Address: Greystones, Burford Road, Chipping Norton, Oxon. OX7 5UZ Tel: 01608 643968
Brief Directions: Follow A361 to Burford out of Chipping Norton
Club Secretary: Mrs T King, 24 Cross Keys, Chipping Norton, Oxon. OX7 5HG Tel: (H) 01608 643097
Fixtures Secretary: Mr T Cripps, 4 Portland Place, Chipping Norton, Oxon Tel: (H) 01608 641182 (W) 01608 643911
Club Colours: Black and red hoops

MILTON KEYNES RUFC
Ground Address: Sam Coster Pavilion, Field Lane, Greenleys, Wolverton, Milton Keynes, Bucks. MK12 6AZ Tel: 01908 313858
Brief Directions: Travel from Stony Stratford town centre towards Wolverton, rt at double r'bout into Gt Monics St (V5), proceed across r'bout, rt into Field Ln, rt at T j'tion, next left to clubhouse
Club Secretary: Mr Peter Hemingway, 6 Malvern Drive, Hilltop, Stony Stratford, Milton Keynes. MK11 2AE Tel: (H) 01908 564931 (W) 0181 863 5611 Ext 2474
Fixtures Secretary: Mr Veral Wilcox Tel: (H) 01908 313083
Club Colours: All black, wide white chest hoop, white collars

OLNEY RFC
Ground Address: Recreation Ground, East Street, Olney, Bucks Tel: 01234 71288
Brief Directions: From Newport Pagnell & Milton Keynes take A509, on entering Olney past church & right at market place, left into East St, ground 300 yards on right
Club Secretary: Stuart Parkin, West View Farm, Olney, Bucks. MK46 5EX Tel: (H) 01234 713165 (W) 01234 711792
Fixtures Secretary: Alec Tebby Tel: (H) 01933 663385 (W) 0850 560660
Club Colours: Cerise and french grey

OXFORD HARLEQUINS RFC
Ground Address: * Horspath Rd Rec., Cowley, Oxford. Tel: 01865 775765
Marston Ferry Road, Oxford. Tel: 01865 552813
Brief Directions: * Off the Eastern ring road sign-posted to Horspath
By the Rover Car works
Club Secretary: A W G Barson, 97 Oxford Road, Garsington, Oxford OX44 9AD. Tel: (H) 01865 361540
Fixtures Secretary: P Cox, 43 Oxford Road, Garsington, Oxford. Tel: 01865 361267
Club Colours: Amber, dark blue, white and maroon quarters

SLOUGH RFC
Ground Address: Tamblyn Fields, Upton Court Park, Upton Court Road, Langley, Slough, Berkshire. SL3 7LT Tel: 01753 522107/692115
Brief Directions: M4 J5 towards Slough on A4 (London Rd), left at 2nd traffic lights into Upton Court Rd, club entrance approx 500 metres on left, 200 metres down Dedicated Drive
Club Secretary: Mike Wild, 21 Westgate Crescent, Cippenham, Slough, Berkshire. SL1 5BX Tel: (H & FAX) 01628 685528
Fixtures Secretary: Clive Blackman Tel: (H) 01753 684403 (W) 01895 836579
Club Colours: Sage green jersey with single white hoop, blue shorts, green socks

WITNEY RFC
Ground Address: The Clubhouse, Hailey Road, Witney, Oxon. OX8 5UH Tel: 01993 771043 Fax: 01993 779985
Brief Directions: Leave Witney centre by Bridge St, towards Oxford & Bicester, left at mini roundabout, keep along main road passing garage on right, ground on left after about 1 mile
Club Secretary: Chris Birks, 112 Colwell Drive, Witney, Oxon. OX8 7NH Tel: (H) 01993 778341 (W) 0589 444655
Fixtures Secretary: Pete Holliday Tel: (H) 01993 705327 (W) 01527 498259
Club Colours: Black hoops on sky blue

THE
OFFICIAL RUGBY UNION
CLUB DIRECTORY 1997-98

The Perfect Christmas Present

BUCKINGHAMSHIRE AND OXFORDSHIRE ONE

Bucks/Oxon One 1997-98 Fixtures	Cholsey 1	Drifters 2	Grove 3	Littlemore 4	Pennanians 5	Phoenix 6	Wheatley 7	
1 Cholsey	X	24/1	11/10	7/3	8/11	14/2	20/12	1
2 Drifters	27/9	X	24/2	8/11	7/3	20/12	17/1	2
3 Grove	31/1	14/3	X	17/1	20/12	25/10	24/1	3
4 Littlemore	25/10	11/4	15/11	X	11/10	24/1	27/9	4
5 Pennanians	17/1	15/11	27/9	10/1	X	11/4	24/2	5
6 Phoenix	15/11	11/10	10/1	14/3	31/1	X	8/11	6
7 Wheatley	14/3	10/1	11/4	31/1	25/10	7/3	X	7
	1	2	3	4	5	6	7	

CHOLSEY RFC
Ground Address: Hithercroft Road, Wallingford, Oxon
Tel: 01491 835044
Brief Directions: Situated on Wallingford bypass on
west side of town, bypass signposted on all approaches
to Wallingford
Club Secretary: T N Harding, 24 Roding Way, Didcot,
Oxon. OX11 7RQ Tel: (H) 01235 510602 (W) 0860
154217
Fixtures Secretary: M Porter Tel: (H) 01734 410946
Club Colours: Amber and black

DRIFTERS RFC
Ground Address: Farnham Common Sports Club, One
Pin Lane, Farnham Common, Bucks Tel: 01753 644190
Brief Directions: From M40 J2, or M4 J6 take A355
`One Pin Lane' half mile north of Farnham Common.
Club Secretary: Dave Hancock, 19 Thurston Road,
Slough, Berks, SL1 3JW. Tel: 01753 576512
Fixtures Secretary: Alan Pearce, 9 Stevenson Road,
Hedgerley, Bucks.
Club Colours: Black with magenta and gold chest band

GROVE RFC
Ground Address: Recreation Ground, Cane Lane,
Grove, Wantage, Oxfordshire Tel: 01235 762750
Brief Directions: Frm Oxford (A338), turn right into
village, rt at r'bout, lft at r'bout (Brereton Dv), lft at end
to Cane Ln. Frm sth enter vlge at lights, lft at r'bout into
D'worth Rd, follow as above
Club Secretary: Bryan L Evans, Stradey, 5 Farmstead
Close, Grove,Oxon. OX12 0BD Tel: (H) 01235 760747
Fixtures Secretary: Kevin Sanders Tel: (H) 01235
771549
Club Colours: Red, white and blue hoops

LITTLEMORE RFC
Ground Address: Peers School, Sandy Lane West,
Littlemoor, Oxon. OX4 5JY Tel: 01865 715776
Brief Directions: Oxford ring road to Cowley (eastern
bypass A4142), past the Rover plant on left, left turn and
signpost to Peers School
Club Secretary: Mr M Boyle, 40 Tallis Lane, Browns
Wood, Milton Keynes. MK7 8OZ Tel: (H) 01908
645949 (W) 01908 853723
Fixtures Secretary: C Wright Tel: (H) 01865 374420
Club Colours: White shirts, white shorts, royal blue socks

PENNANIANS RUFC
Ground Address: Farnham Park, Beaconsfield Road,
Farnham Royal, Bucks. SL2 3BU Tel: 01753 646252
Club Secretary: Mr Martin James, 47 Pearl Gdns,
Slough, Berks. SL1 2YX Tel: (H) 01753 734910 (W)
01344 28821
Fixtures Secretary: Richard Kearney Tel: 01753 581963
Club Colours: Black shirt with 2 white hoops

PHOENIX RFC
Ground Address: The Sports Ground, Institute Road,
Taplow, Bucks. SL6 0NS Tel: 01628 664319
Brief Directions: M4 J7, take A4 towards Maidenhead,
after Sainsburys superstore take next right (0.5 mile)
then 1st left after the bridge is Institute Road
Club Secretary: S K Turner, 20 Balmoral Close,
Cippenham, Slough. Sl1 6JP Tel: (H) 01628 661660
(W) 01344 746052
Fixtures Secretary: N Bennett Tel: (H)01753 570341
(W) 01753 615693
Club Colours: Red and black quarters

WHEATLEY RUFC
Ground Address: Playing Fields, Holton, Wheatley,
Oxford Tel: 01865 873476
Brief Directions: Leave A40 at Wheatley signs in
Oxford towards London, turn left at T junction and
ground is on left about 500 yards from the turn
Club Secretary: Mrs Elaine Murray, The Mead, 56
Clifden Road, Worming Hall, Bucks. HP18 9JP Tel:
(H) 01844 358940 (W) 01865 785414
Fixtures Secretary: Bryn Davies Tel: (H)01844
292846
Club Colours: Purple, white and black bands, black
shorts

Bucks/Oxon Two 1997-98 Fixtures	Abingdon 1	Chesham 2	Didcot 3	Gosford All Blacks 4	Harwell 5	Winslow 6	
1 Abingdon	X	31/1	8/11	7/3	20/12	10/1	1
2 Chesham	25/10	X	14/3	10/1	15/11	14/2	2
3 Didcot	14/2	20/12	X	10/1	18/4	15/11	3
4 Gosford All Blacks	15/11	11/4	25/10	X	14/2	14/3	4
5 Harwell	14/3	7/3	10/1	8/11	X	10/1	5
6 Winslow	11/4	8/11	7/3	20/12	25/10	X	6
	1	2	3	4	5	6	

ABINGDON RUFC
Ground Address: Southern Sports Park, Lambrick Way, Abingdon. OX14 5TJ   Tel: 01235 553810
Club Secretary: Michael D Fox, 31 Peachcroft Road, Abingdon, Oxon. OX14 2NA   Tel: (H) 01235 523522
Fixtures Secretary: Peter Shufflebotham   Tel: (H) 01235 528730
Club Colours: Green and gold hooped shirts, black shorts, green socks

CHESHAM RUFC
Ground Address: Chesham Park Community College, Chartridge Lane, Chesham, Bucks. HP5 2RG Tel: 01494 793827
Brief Directions: Chartridge Lane of St. Marys Way in central Chesham. Club is 400 metres on L. Furthest College gate is entrance
Club Secretary: M M Hogg, 37 Lye Green Road, Chesham, Bucks. HP5 3LS   Tel: (H) 01494 771576
Fixtures Secretary: Dick King   Tel: (H) 01494 780056
Club Colours: Blue and claret hoops

DIDCOT RUFC
Ground Address: Edmonds Park, Park Road, Didcot
Brief Directions: From roundabout at Georgetown filling station/Wallingford Arms, take road to West Hagbourne, ground is about 0.5 mile on left
Club Secretary: Mrs Jane Llewellyn, 54 Loyd Road, Didcot, Oxon. OX11 8JT   Tel: (H) 01235 813634   (W) 01235 512902
Fixtures Secretary: Mark Maidment, Sprat Public House, Hagbourne Road, Didcot, Oxon   Tel: 01235 812224
Club Colours: Red and white hoops

GOSFORD ALL BLACKS RFC
Ground Address: Langford Lane, Kidlington, Oxon Tel: 01865 373994
Brief Directions: Take A44 Evesham road from Oxford, follow signs to Oxford Airport, club is opposite airport
Club Secretary: Steve Butcher, Gosford All Blacks RFC, Langford Lane, Kidlington, Oxon
Fixtures Secretary: c/o Brian Strong   Tel: (H) 01865 378525
Club Colours: Black

HARWELL RUFC (50TH ANNIVERSARY SEASON)
Ground Address: Central Sports Field, Aere Harwell Laboratory, Nr Didcot, Oxon
Brief Directions: To the left of main gate at Harwell Laboratory on old Newbury-Abingdon road
Club Secretary: Colin Bartlett, 66 Upthorpe Drive, Wantage, Oxon. OX12 7DG   Tel: (H) 01235 767596
Fixtures Secretary: Jenny Bosley   Tel: (H) 01235 833688
Club Colours: Royal blue, light blue and white hoops

WINSLOW RUFC
Ground Address: The Winslow Centre, Park Road, Winslow, Buckingham. MK18
Brief Directions: A413 through Winslow, 0.5 mile towards Buckingham from town centre, turn left into Avenue Road, 1st right into Park Road
Club Secretary: Simon Drakeford, 31 Green Way, Newton Longville, Bucks. MK17 0AP   Tel: (H) 01908 644239
Fixtures Secretary: Colin Brown, Gardeners Cottage, 27 Horn Street, Winslow. MK18 3AP   Tel: (H) 01296 714312
Club Colours: Blue and gold hoops

SOUTHERN COUNTIES SOUTH

Southern Counties South 1997-98 Fixtures	Blandford	Chippenham	Devizes	Marlborough	North Dorset	Swindon	Westbury	Weymouth	Wimborne	Wootten Bassett	
	1	2	3	4	5	6	7	8	9	10	
1 Blandford	X	6/9	20/9	10/1	14/2	25/10	25/4	11/4	11/10	24/1	1
2 Chippenham	14/3	X	14/2	11/10	24/1	20/9	25/10	15/11	10/1	21/3	2
3 Devizes	7/3	27/9	X	15/11	11/10	10/1	11/4	6/9	24/1	25/10	3
4 Marlborough	8/11	31/1	25/4	X	20/12	14/2	18/10	17/1	14/3	20/9	4
5 North Dorset	27/9	11/10	31/1	28/3	X	15/11	6/9	7/3	25/10	10/1	5
6 Swindon	17/1	7/3	8/11	27/9	25/4	X	31/1	11/10	20/12	14/3	6
7 Westbury	15/11	17/1	20/12	24/1	14/3	11/10	X	8/11	20/9	14/2	7
8 Weymouth	20/12	25/4	14/3	25/10	20/9	24/1	10/1	X	14/2	11/10	8
9 Wimborne	31/1	8/11	11/10	6/9	17/1	14/4	7/3	27/9	X	15/11	9
10 Wootten Bassett	11/10	20/12	17/1	7/3	8/11	6/9	27/9	31/1	25/4	X	10
	1	2	3	4	5	6	7	8	9	10	

BLANDFORD RFC
Ground Address: Larks Mead, Blandford
Brief Directions: From A354 across roundabout, 2nd left opposite cemetary, 1st left in housing estate
Club Secretary: Tony Moogan, Langdale Cottage, 34 Anvil Rd., Pimperne, Blandford Forum, Dorset DT11 8UQ
Fixtures Secretary: Dave Stringer   Tel: (H) 01258 456954
Club Colours: Gold, brown, white and red

CHIPPENHAM RFC
Ground Address: Allington Field, Frogwell, Chippenham. SN14 0YZ   Tel: 01249 446997
Brief Directions: A420 twoards Bristol. Turn left by Allington Farm shop for Corsham & Sheldon Manor. After 600 yards turn sharp left, entrance on left. NB Now no entrance from Frogwell.
Club Secretary: H Whiteman, 31 Wells Close, Chippenham. SN14 0QD.   Tel: 01249 651176
Fixtures Secretary: A Lloyd, 27 Lords Mead, Chippenham.   Tel: (H) 01249 656793
Club Colours: Black and white

DEVIZES RFC
Ground Address: Chivers Ground, Sports Club, London Road, Devizes, Wiltshire   Tel: 01380 723763
Brief Directions: Beside the Wiltshire Constabulary H.Q. on the A361 in DEvizes town centre.
Club Secretary: Paul Rumbold, Belmont, Potterne Road, Devizes, Wiltshire. SN10 5DB   Tel: (H) 01380 724497   (W) 01672 517237
Fixtures Secretary: Andy Quinn, 13 Stockwell Road, Devizes.   Tel: (H) 01380 728230   (W) 01380 722341
Club Colours: Black shirts with broad white band, white shorts

MARLBOROUGH
Ground Address: Elcot Lane, Marlborough, Wilts   Tel: 01672 514717
Club Secretary: Mrs Joyce Adams, 10 Ailesbury Way, Burbage, Marlborough, Wilts. SN8 3TD   Tel: (H) 01672 810718
Fixtures Secretary: Mr Alec Thomas   Tel: (H) 01672 512296
Club Colours: Black and amber

NORTH DORSET RFC
Ground Address: Slaughtergate, Longbury Hill Lane, Gillingham, Dorset   Tel: 01747 822748
Brief Directions: Take Wincanton road (B3081) from town centre, Longbury Hill Lane is on right about 1 mile from the town, 300 yds after the end of 30mph zone
Club Secretary: Paul Phillips, 3 Buttercup Close, Gillingham, Dorset. SP8 4XB   Tel: (H) 01747 825271
Fixtures Secretary: Clive Drake   Tel: (H) 01747 825856
Club Colours: Green and navy

SWINDON RFC
Ground Address: Greenbridge Road, Swindon, Wilts. SN3 3LA   Tel: 01793 521148
Club Secretary: Liz Banovic, 286 Cricklade Road, Swindon. SN2 6AY   Tel: (H) 01793 525689
Fixtures Secretary: David McAteer,   Tel: 01793 643985
Club Colours: Blue and amber hoops, white shorts

WESTBURY RFC
Ground Address: Leighton Sports Ground, Wellhead Lane, Westbury, Wiltshire   Tel: 01373 826438
Brief Directions: Warminster road (A350), opposite Cedar Hotel turn into Welland Lane, ground 300 metres on left
Club Secretary: Mrs Carole Jones, 36 Westbury Road, Yarnbrook, Nr. Trowbridge, Wiltshire. BA14 6AG   Tel: (H) 01225 766647   (W) 01373 828400
Fixtures Secretary: Mr Mark Knott   Tel: (H & W) 01985 215054
Club Colours: Green and black hoops

WEYMOUTH RFC
Ground Address: Monmouth Avenue, Weymouth, Dorset   Tel: 01305 778889
Brief Directions: 3rd turn left after passing Safeways supermarket
Club Secretary: Mrs G Llewellyn, 2 Goulds Hill Close, Upwey, Weymouth   Tel: (H) 01305 812415
Fixtures Secretary: Dick Foyle   Tel: (H) 01305 266144
Club Colours: Light blue, dark blue circle, black shorts

WIMBORNE RFC
Ground Address: Leigh Park, Wimborne, Dorset   Tel: 01202 882602
Brief Directions: A31, take B3073 to Wimborne, approx 1.5 miles turn left into Gordan Rd, Leigh Park immediately ahead, approx 400yds
Club Secretary: Michael Moysey, 42 Lacy Drive, Wimborne, Dorset. BH21 1DG   Tel: (H) 01202 841478
Fixtures Secretary: D. Noyce   Tel: (H) 01258 451608
Club Colours: All black

WOOTTON BASSETT RFC
Ground Address: Rylands Field, Stoneover Lane, Wootton Bassett, Wiltshire   Tel: 01793 851425
Brief Directions: M4 J16, past Sally Pussey's and Churchill House pubs, turn left along Stoneover Lane, Rugby ground is 200yds along on left
Club Secretary: Phil James, 7 Middleground, Wootton Bassett, Wilts SN4 8LJ   Tel: (H) 01793 855064   (W) 01793 497721
Fixtures Secretary: Jim Brierley   Tel: (H) 01793 731780
Club Colours: Black

Westbury Rugby Club, after beating Aldermaston, at Aldermaston by 18 points to 3, in the last game of the season to gain pormotion to Southern Counties (South). The second promotion in two seasons.

THIS DIRECTORY IS NOT FOR CLUB OFFICIALS ONLY!
Do your club supporters know they can buy their own directory and help club funds?

BERKSHIRE, DORSET AND WILTSHIRE ONE

Berks, Dorset & Wilts One 1997-98 Fixtures	Aldermaston	Calne	Corsham	Ivel Barbarians	Melksham	Redingensians	Tadley	Thatcham	Trowbridge	Windsor	
	1	2	3	4	5	6	7	8	9	10	
1 Aldermaston	X	20/9	14/3	14/2	11/10	24/1	15/11	25/10	10/1	4/4	1
2 Calne	7/3	X	17/1	8/11	27/9	25/4	18/10	31/1	20/12	14/3	2
3 Corsham	6/9	25/10	X	20/9	10/1	14/2	11/4	15/11	11/10	24/1	3
4 Ivel Barbarians	27/9		7/3	X	15/11	11/10	6/9	11/4	24/1	25/10	4
5 Melksham	31/1	14/2	8/11	25/4	X	20/12	17/1	18/10	14/3	20/9	5
6 Redingensians	18/10	15/11	27/9	31/1	11/4	X	7/3	6/9	25/10	10/1	6
7 Tadley	25/4	24/1	20/12	14/3	25/10	20/9	X	10/1	14/2	11/10	7
8 Thatcham	17/1	11/10	25/4	20/12	24/1	14/3	8/11	X	20/9	14/2	8
9 Trowbridge	8/11	28/3	31/1	18/10	6/9	17/1	27/9	7/3	X	15/11	9
10 Windsor	20/12	13/2	18/10	17/1	7/3	8/11	31/1	27/9	25/4	X	10
	1	2	3	4	5	6	7	8	9	10	

ALDERMASTON RFC
Ground Address: Aldermaston Recreational Society Sports Ground, Tadley, Hants   Tel: 01189 817233
Brief Directions: From Basingstoke follow directions for Tadley on A340, then for Awe Aldermaston, then for Recreational Society.
Club Secretary: Kevin Jones, 13 Stratford Road, Basingstoke, Hants. RG21 5RS   Tel: (H) 01256 410461 (W) 01189 826750
Fixtures Secretary: David Jenkins   Tel: (H) 01189 813078   (W) 01189 837487
Club Colours: Scarlet shirts, black shorts

CALNE RFC
Ground Address: The Recreation Ground, Anchor Road, Calne, Wiltshire. SN11 8DX   Tel: 01249 812206
Brief Directions: Turn into Bank Row opposite Lansdowne Strand Hotel, past Somerfields into Mill St, follow road uphill into Anchor Rd, car park on left after 500 yards
Club Secretary: Steve Gill, 1 Heddington Wick, Heddington, Calne, Wiltshire   Tel: (H) 01380 850909
Fixtures Secretary: Ian West   Tel: (H) 01249 813737
Club Colours: Blue with red and white hoop

CORSHAM RFC
Ground Address: Lacock Road, Corsham
Brief Directions: Off A4 at the Hare & Hounds, keep straight down Pickwick Rd 0.5 mile past War Memorial on Lacock Rd
Club Secretary: J G Wiltshire, 84 Springfield Close, Rudloe, Corsham, Wilts. SN13 0JR   Tel: (H) 01225 810800
Fixtures Secretary: R Slade   Tel: (H) 01249 712683
Club Colours: Red and white hoops

IVEL BARBARIANS RFC
Ground Address: Johnson Park, Yeovil, Somerset   Tel: 01935 411636 (club)   01935 74433 (ground)
Brief Directions: A37 from Ilchester, on seeing built up area right at roundabout then left at mini roundabout, ground on right opposite garden centre
Club Secretary: V J Jenkins, 7 Chestnut Drive, Yeovil, Somerset. BA20 2NL   Tel: (H & W) 01935 29770
Fixtures Secretary: R. Reeves, 220 Preston Road, Yeovil, Somerset   Tel: (H) 01935 473927   Tel: (B) 01935 410911
Club Colours: Black and white quarters

MELKSHAM (AVON) RFC
Ground Address: Melksham (Avon) Sports & Social Club, Melksham, Wiltshire   Tel: 01225 704982
Club Secretary: Mr A C Butcher, 14 Lowbourne, Melksham, Wilts. 7SN12 7DZ   Tel: 01225 707426 (H), 01225 702400 (W) 01225 702011 (Fax)
Fixtures Secretary: Vanessa Petty   Tel: (H) 01225 705936
Club Colours: Blue and sky blue hoops

REDINGENSIANS RFC
Ground Address: Old Bath Road, Sonning. Tel: 0118 9695259
Brief Directions: On the A4 east of Reading, next to Sonning Golf Club
Club Secretary: J H Cook, 95 Century Court, Grove End Rd, London. NW8 9LD   Tel: (H) 0171 289 1887 (W) 0171 444 8178
Fixtures Secretary: G F Nattriss, 64 Broadwater Rd, Twyford, Berks. RG10 0EU   Tel: (H) 0118 9340685 (W) 0181 3917070
Club Colours: Dark blue, light blue and white hoops

TADLEY RUGBY CLUB RFC
Ground Address: Red Lane, Aldermaston, Reading, Berks
Brief Directions: Frm M3: A340 Basingstoke into Tadley, take road to Burghfield/ Reading, left into Red Ln. Frm M4: Theale A4 to Newbury, turn left A340 to Aldermaston/Tadley, left into A'maston into Red Ln
Club Secretary: R W Mears, 22 Winchfield Gardens, Tadley, Hants. RG26 3TX   Tel: (H) 01189 811648
Fixtures Secretary: R W Mearsas above
Club Colours: Black with amber hoop

THATCHAM RFC
Ground Address: Henwick Worth Playing Fields,Henwick Lane, Thatcham, berkshire.
Brief Directions: Henwick Playing Fields are on the north side of the A4 which runs from Newbury through Thatcham to Reading. The entrance in Henwick Lane is on the eastern side of Thatcham.
Club Secretary: Mr R B Morris, 182 Bath Road, Thatcham, Berkshire. RG18 3HJ Tel: (H) 01635 826985   (W) 0118 9817474
Fixtures Secretary: Mrs Kathi Surtees Tel: (H) 01635 868285   (W) 017Ï 2101387
Club Colours: Red and blue quarters

TROWBRIDGE RFC
Ground Address: Green Lane, Trowbridge, Wiltshire. BA14 7DH   Tel: 01225 761389
Brief Directions: Head for West Ashton from County Way
Club Secretary: Bryn Parfitt, 60 Paxcroft Way, Trowbridge, Wiltshire. BA14 7DJ Tel: (H) 01225 351044
Fixtures Secretary: Mickey Milton, 13 Blair Road, Trowbridge, Wilts. Tel: 01225 767204
Club Colours: Dark blue, light blue and gold hoops

WINDSOR RFC
Ground Address: Home Park, Datchet Road, Windsor, Berkshire Tel: 01753 860807
Brief Directions: Off M4, signed Windsor, follow d/carriageway to 1st slip road off left, left at roundabout, left at next roundabout, keep left past railway station, next left into Home Park
Club Secretary: Sean Leone, 35 Bell View, Windsor, Berks. SL4 4ET Tel: (H) 01753 863713   (W) 0181 848 8881
Fixtures Secretary: Peter Davison Tel: (H) 01753 840559
Club Colours: Black, green, gold and maroon quarters

BERKSHIRE, DORSET & WILTSHIRE TWO

Berks, Dorset & Wilts Two 1997-98 Fixtures	Berkshire Shire H	Bridport	Christchurch	Colerne	Lytchett Minster	Minety	Oakmedians	Portcastrians	Supermarine	Swindon College	
	1	2	3	4	5	6	7	8	9	10	
1 Berkshire Shire Hall	X	14/3	14/2	20/9	11/10	25/10	24/1	10/1	18/4	15/11	1
2 Bridport	6/9	X	20/9	25/10	10/1	15/11	14/2	11/10	24/1	11/4	2
3 Christchurch	27/9	7/3	X	10/1	15/11	18/4	11/10	24/1	25/10	6/9	3
4 Colerne	7/3	17/1	8/11	X	27/9	31/1	25/4	20/12	14/3	18/10	4
5 Lytchett Minster	31/1	8/11	25/4	14/2	X	18/10	20/12	14/3	20/9	17/1	5
6 Minety	17/1	25/4	13/12	11/10	24/1	X	14/3	20/9	14/2	8/11	6
7 Oakmedians	18/10	27/9	31/1	15/11	4/4	6/9	X	25/10	10/1	7/3	7
8 Portcastrians	8/11	31/1	18/10	11/4	6/9	7/3	17/1	X	15/11	27/9	8
9 Supermarine	20/12	18/10	17/1	6/9	7/3	27/9	8/11	25/4	X	31/1	9
10 Swindon College	25/4	20/12	14/3	24/1	25/10	10/1	20/9	14/2	11/10	X	10
	1	2	3	4	5	6	7	8	9	10	

THIS DIRECTORY IS NOT FOR CLUB OFFICIALS ONLY!

Do your club supporters know they can buy their own directory and help club funds?

BERKSHIRE SHIRE HALL RUFC
Ground Address: Royal County of Berkshire Sports &
Social Club, Sonning Lane, Sonning, Reading Tel:
01734 691340
Brief Directions: From Reading head towards A4 up
Sheppards House Hill, pass Mobil garage on right, take
left Sonning Lane, 2nd turning on the right
Club Secretary: Dave Norris, 74 Caldbell Drive,
Woodey, Reading, Berks. RG5 4JX Tel: (H) 01734
696439 (W) 01344 713582
Fixtures Secretary: Steve Bentey Tel: (H) 01491
872509
Club Colours: Blue, yellow hoop

BRIDPORT RFC
Ground Address: Bridport Leisure Centre, Skilling Hill
Road, Bridport, Dorset. DT6 3LN Tel: 01308 420555
Brief Directions: Take A35 Bridport By-Pass, at R'bout
south of Town turn R. (North). After 300yds turn L. at
Traffic Lights opp. Safeway store.
Club Secretary: Richard Salt, 21 South Street, Bridport,
Dorset. DT6 3NR Tel: (H) 01308 458347 (W) 01308
422236
Fixtures Secretary: John Greig Tel: (H) 01308 456692
(W) 01308 424600
Club Colours: Dark blue

CHRISTCHURCH
Ground Address: Grange Road, Somerford,
Christchurch, Dorset BH23 4JE. Tel: 01202 404279
Club Secretary: Kieran Newell, 3 Brabazon Drive,
Christchurch, Dorset. Tel: 01425 278276
Fixtures Secretary: Tim Morgan, Tel: 01202 823752
Club Colours: Sky blue, white and black hoops

COLERNE RFC
Ground Address: Bath Road, Colerne, Wiltshire
Brief Directions: Under water tower on main road past
village
Club Secretary: Mrs Karen Sayers, 8 Cleaves Avenue,
Colerne, Wiltshire. SN14 8BX Tel: (H) 01225 744355
Fixtures Secretary: Mr Chris Moore, 12 Fossway
Close, Colerne, Wilts. Tel: (H) 01225 742380
Club Colours: Black

LYTCHETT MINSTER RFC
Ground Address: South Manor Drive, Lytchett Minster,
Poole
Brief Directions: Follow A35 Poole to Dorchester, at
end of dual carriageway follow signs to village,
changing accommodation next to church
Club Secretary: D H Smurthwaite, Staddlestones,
Cheselbourne, Dorchester. DT2 7NJ Tel: (H) 01258
837796 (W) 01202 622413
Fixtures Secretary: M Hobson Tel: (H) 01202 623287
Club Colours: Red and blue hoops, white shorts

MINETY RUGBY FOOTBALL CLUB
Ground Address: The Playing Fields, Minety, Nr
Malmesbury, Wiltshire Tel: 01666 860 680
Brief Directions: From Swindon take A419 to
Cirencester, turn off at Cricklade, through Cricklade to
Minety, right at Q8 garage (Minety Motors) to the
playing fields
Club Secretary: Kevin Vancil, 12 Essex Walk, Walcot,
Swindon. SN3 3EY Tel: (H) 01793 525898 (W)
01793 504945
Fixtures Secretary: Mark Turner Tel: (H) 01666
860680
Club Colours: Green and purple hoops

OAKMEDIANS RUFC
Ground Address: Meyrick Park Pavilion, Bournemouth.
BH2 6LJ Tel: 01202 789497
Brief Directions: Bournemouth town centre then head
for Meyrick Park Golf Club, approx 0.5 mile from town
centre
Club Secretary: Sarah Palmer, 48 Nursery Road,
Moordown, Bournemouth. BH9 3AT Tel: (H) 01202
528466
Fixtures Secretary: Jenny Phillips Tel: (H) 01202
525311
Club Colours: Blue and white hoops with black shorts

PORTCASTRIAN RFC
Ground Address: Iford Lane Playing Fields, Iford Lane,
Southbourne, Bournemouth, Dorset. BH6 5NF Tel:
01202 434565
Brief Directions: Turn towards Southbourne off A228
(Wessex Way) into Iford Lane, past Bournemouth
Hospital to Iford Lane, playing fields on left
Club Secretary: Graeme Willard, 54 Ensbury Park
Road, Moordown, Bournemouth, Dorset. BH9 2SJ Tel:
(H & W) 01202 524472
Fixtures Secretary: Paul Smith,53 Watermill
Rd.,Fairmile, Christchurch,Dorset. Tel: (H) 01202
490353 (W) 01202 490019
Club Colours: Royal blue, yellow and red hoops

SUPERMARINE RFC
Ground Address: Supermarine Sports and Social Club,
Highworth Road, South Marston, Nr Swindon, Wiltshire
Tel: 01793 824828
Brief Directions: Take A419 M4 to Cirencester Rd, turn
off at north or south 'Honda' junction, follow A361
signed Highworth, club entrance off roundabout for
industrial estate
Club Secretary: Geoff Bath, 2 Folly Drive, Highworth,
Wiltshire Tel: (H) 01793 861619
Fixtures Secretary: Ian Frizzle Tel: (H) 01793 763135
Club Colours: Royal and dark blue quarters

SWINDON COLLEGE OL BOYS RFC
Ground Address: Croft Sports Centre, Marlborough
Lane, Swindon. Tel: 01793 526622
Club Secretary: T Davis, 15 Sandown Road, Swindon,
wiltshire SN13 1QD. Tel: (H) 01793 694006 Tel: (W)
01488 73444
Fixtures Secretary: Mr P Tyler, Tel: (H) 01367 242386
Club Colours: Red and black quarters

THIS DIRECTORY IS NOT FOR CLUB OFFICIALS ONLY!

Do your club supporters know they can buy their own directory and help club funds?

BERKSHIRE, DORSET & WILTSHIRE THREE

Berks, Dorset & Wilts Three 1997-98 Fixtures	Cholsey 1	Drifters 2	Grove 3	Littlemore 4	Pennanians 5	Phoenix 6	Wheatley 7	
1 Honda	X	11/10	24/1	8/11	14/2	7/3	20/12	1
2 Hungerford	31/1	X	14/3	20/12	25/10	17/1	24/1	2
3 Pewsey Vale	27/9	14/2	X	7/3	20/12	8/11	17/1	3
4 Poole	17/1	27/9	15/11	X	14/?	10/1	14/2	4
5 Puddletown	15/11	10/1	11/10	31/1	X	11/4	8/11	5
6 Verwood	25/10	15/11	11/4	11/10	24/1	X	27/9	6
7 Warminster	14/3	11/4	18/10	25/10	7/3	31/1	X	7
	1	2	3	4	5	6	7	

HONDA
Ground Address: Supermarine Sport & Social Club, Highworth Road, South Marston, Swindon, Wilts SN3 4TZ Tel: 01793 824828
Club Secretary: Mr Tom Lee, c/o Honda Engineering Europe, Highworth Road, South Marston, Swindon, Wilts SN3 4TZ Tel: (H) 01793 695448 (W) 01793 416500/416533 (F) 01793 458363
Fixtures Secretary: Nigel Harper, 22 Stapleford Way, Penhill, Swindon, Wilts Tel: (H) 01793 721540 (W)01793 831183 Ext 3003 (F) 01793 454416
Club Colours: Green and white quarters, green shorts and socks

HUNGERFORD RFC
Ground Address: The Cricket Pavilion, Hungerford Common, Hungerford, Berks Tel: 01488 682663
Club Secretary: Angus Russel, 39 Chilton Way, Hungerford, Berks. RG17 0JR Tel: (H) 01488 683993 (W) 01635 506297
Fixtures Secretary: Peter Goodwin Tel: (H) 01635 45887 (W) 01635 48222
Club Colours: Claret and porter

PEWSEY VALE RFC
Ground Address: Pensey Vale Comprehensive School, Wilcot Road, Pewsey, Wiltshire
Brief Directions: A345 to Pewsey, into Wilcot Road, 2nd left into Pewsey Vale School car park, change at the adjacent Sports Centre, pitches are to the back of the school
Club Secretary: Mr David Steven Aroskin, 20a Rawlins Road, Pewsey, Wiltshire. SN9 5EB Tel: (H & W) 01672 562218 (W) 0976 882103
Fixtures Secretary: Mr Kevin Robinson Tel: (H) 01672 562989
Club Colours: Red, white, royal blue and black quarters

POOLE RFC
Ground Address: hamworthy Rec., Turlin Moor , Blandford Road, Hamworthy, Poole, Dorset
Brief Directions: From Poole quay, follow directions for Hamworthy, over the lifting bridge and continue for 2 miles.
Club Secretary: Mrs Tessa Ingle-Finch, 6 Mansfield Avenue, Parkstone, Poole, Dorset. BH14 0DQ Tel: (H) 01202 241993
Fixtures Secretary: Miles Cosslett, 54 Marshwood Ave., Canford Heath, Poole, Dorset. Tel: (H) 01020 690641(B) 01712 768067
Club Colours: Blue and amber

PUDDLETOWN
Ground Address: Greenfields, Puddletown, Dorchester, Dorset. Tel: 01305 848808
Brief Directions: Leave Dorchester on A35 east, after 1/4 mile turn left on B3143, 3 miles on RHS, old army camp club.
Club Secretary: Mr David Smith, Providence House, 39 Dorchester Road, Maiden Newton, Dorset DT2 0BZ. Tel: (H) 01300 320209 Tel: (W) 01305 251111
Fixtures Secretary: Mr P Smeeth, Tel: (H) 01300 348310
Club Colours: Red shirts, black shorts, red socks

VERWOOD
Ground Address: Potterne Park, Potterne Way, Verwood, Dorset
Club Secretary: M Cockram, 145 Ringwood Road, Verwood, Dorset BH31 7AE Tel: (M) 0402 034238 (W) 01202 821111   (F) 01202 813455
Fixtures Secretary: Robin Oliver Peirce, c/o 145 Ringwood Road, Verwood, Dorset BH31 7AE Tel: (H) 01202 826372   (W) 01483 750814   (F) 01483 295140
Club Colours: Red and white quarters

WARMINSTER RFC
Ground Address: Warminster Cricket Club, Sambourne Road, Warminster, Wiltshire Tel: 01985 219039
Club Secretary: Simon Pick, 95 Portway, Warminster, Wiltshire. BA12 0AA Tel: (H) 01985 847756
Fixtures Secretary: Steve Evans Tel: (H) 01985 212750
Club Colours: Royal blue and gold hoop

Have you many Rugby enthusiasts at your Club ?
Does you Club need to raise extra funds ?

If the answer to these questions is Yes -
then place an order for

The Official Rugby Union Club Directory

WITH EVERY CLUB IN THE LEAGUE STRUCTURE INCLUDED AND ITS UNRIVALLED STATISTICAL COVERAGE OF THE CLUBS AND PLAYERS IN THE TOP LEVELS OF THE LEAGUE SYSTEM IT CAN ANSWER ALL SORTS OF QUESTIONS AND WOULD MAKE AN IDEAL PRESENT.

Did you realise the Directory is available to your club at very good discount rates.

If you order				Profit for Club
	1	copy cost	£14.99	
2 or 3		copies cost	£13.50 each	£ 1.49 each
between 4 & 9		copies cost	£10.00 each	£ 4.99 each
between 10 & 19		copies cost	£ 9.00 each	£ 5.99 each
20 or more		copies cost	£ 8.00 each	£ 6.99 each

To find out more information or to place an order, contact the publishers:
Tony Williams Publications Ltd., Helland, North Curry, Taunton, Somerset. TA3 6DU.
or Telephone 01823 490080 or Fax 01823 490281

LONDON & SOUTH EAST DIVISION

COMPETITON SUB-COMMITTEE

CHAIRMAN
R Tennant, Esq., 57 Boveney Road, Forest Hill, London. SE23 3NL (H) 0181 699 9025

SECRETARY
M A Ward Esq., Courage Clubs Championship, P.O. 12, Beccles, Suffolk. NR34 9HZ (W) 01502 711343 (Fx) 01502 712660

EASTERN COUNTIES
F A G Ford, Esq., 'Fairhaven', 36 Haynes Road, Hornchurch, Essex. RM11 2HT (H) 01708 457807

HAMPSHIRE
D McF Hathorn, 3 Broomacres, Fleet, Aldershot, Hampshire. GU13 9UU (H) 01252 621565 (W) 01276 65155 Ext 201

HERTFORDSHIRE
D J Williams, Esq., 7 Sadlers Way, Hertford, Herts. SG14 2DZ (H) 01992 586744

KENT
D Attwood, Esq., 6 Somerset Gardens, Lewisham, London. SE13 7SY (H) 0181 691 2820

MIDDLESEX
P Astbury, Esq., 32 Kneller Gardens, Isleworth, Middlesex. TW7 7NW (H) 0181 898 5372

SURREY
H Brady, Esq., 29 St Bodolphs Road, Worthing, Sussex BN11 4J5 (H) 0171 370 1078

SUSSEX
B. Vincent, Esq., 29 St. Botolphs Road, Worthing, Sussex. BN11 4JS (H) 01903 206516

CO-OPTED L.E.A.F. MANAGER
I Reeve, Esq., The Croft, Romsey Road, Kings Somborne, Hampshire. SO20 6PP (H) 01794 388064
The phone number of the East India Club is 0171 930 1000

LEAGUE OFFICERS & ADDRESSES

London One F A G Ford, Esq., 'Fairhaven', 36 Haynes Road, Hornchurch, Essex. RM11 2HT (H) 01708 457807

London Two North D J Williams, Esq., 7 Sadlers Way, Hertford, Herts. SG14 2DZ (H) 01992 586744

London Two South D McF Hathorn, 3 Broomacres, Aldershot, Hampshire. GU13 9UU (H) 01252 621565 (W) 01276 65155 Ext 201

London Three North East M J Stott, Esq., Brick Kiln Farm, North Walsham, Norfolk (H) 01692 403096

London Three North West D Gerschlick, Esq., 20A The Avenue, Potters Bar, Hertfordshire. EN6 1EB (H) 01707 644433

London Three South East D Attwood, Esq., 6 Somerset Gardens, Lewisham, London. SE13 7SY (H) 0181 691 2820

London Three South WestD McF Hathorn, 3 Broomacres, Fleet, Aldershot, Hampshire. GU13 9UU (H) 01252 621565 (W) 01276 65155 Ext 201

Eastern Counties One & Two M Tuck, Esq., 51 Highfield Road, Billericay, Essex. CM11 2PE (H) 01277 655483

Eastern Counties Three North & South R Hatch, Esq., 99 Ernest Road, Wivenhoe, Essex. CO7 9LJ (H) 01206 823548

Eastern Counties Four North & South R Wyartt, Esq., Stone Cottage, The Green, Beyton, Bury St Edmunds, Suffolk. IP30 9AF (H) 01359 270410

Hampshire all leagues J Sneezum, Bursledon Lodge, Salterns Lane, Old Bursledon, Southampton, Hampshire. SO3 8DH (H) 01421 212286

Hertfordshire/Middlesex One R Willingale, Esq., Fairmile Farm Cottage, Cobham, Surrey. KT11 1JY (H) 01932 866927

Hertfordshire/Middlesex Two N Alway, Esq., 20 Herndon Road, London. SW18 2DG (H) 0181 870 6818

Hertfordshire/Middlesex Three A Rabjohn, Esq., 62 Central Avenue, Hounslow, Middlesex. TW3 2QL (H) 0181 894 1850

Hertfordshire/Middlesex Four North J Gregory, Esq., 58 Luton Road, Redbourne, Hertfordshire. AL3 6PY (H) 01582 792798

Hertfordshire/Middlesex Four South B East, Esq., 64 Station Road, Harpenden, Herts. AL5 4TL (H & Fx) 01582 762209

Kent all leagues J Carley, Esq., 11 Vlissingen Drive, Deal, Kent. CT14 6TZ (H) 01304 381273

Surrey General R Greer Kirkwood, Esq., 63 Shaftsbury Way, Strawberry Hill, Twickenham. TW2 5RW (H) 0181 898 1767

Surrey One J S Laidman, Esq., 2 West Dene, Park Lane, Cheam, Surrey. SM3 8BW (H) 0181 643 2919

Surrey Two M P Tanner, Esq., 1 Woodland Way, Morden, Surrey. SM4 4DS (H) 0181 540 5784 (W) 01923 214123

Surrey Three J Mason, Esq., 30 Ryefield Road, London. SE19 3QU (H) 0181 771 5815

Surrey Four P. Lovering Esq., Mynthurst Garden, Leigh, Reigate, Surrey. RH2 8RJ (H) 01293 862331

Sussex all leagues J M Carrington, Esq., 115 Cootes Avenue, Horsham, West Sussex. RH12 2AF (H) 01403 260556

LONDON & SOUTH EAST DIVISION R.F.U. OFFICIALS & RFU COMPETITION SUB-COMMITTEE

LONDON & SOUTH EAST DIVISION
CHAIRMAN R Tennant, Esq., 57 Boveney Road, Forest Hill, London. SE23 3NL (H) 0181 699 9025
SECRETARY D S Straw, Esq., 161 High Street, Hampton Hill, Hampton, Middlesex. TW12 1NL (W) 0181 941 7610
TREASURER G C Cattermole, Esq., 62 George V Avenue, Pinner, Middlesex. HA5 5SW (H) 0181 863 1304 (W) 0171 491 3311

RFU REPRESENTATIVES (COMPETITION SUB-COMMITTEE)

B Williams, Esq., Chez Nous, Main Road, Westerfield, Ipswich, Suffolk. IP6 9AJ (H) 01473 213339
G G Smith, Esq., The Old Rectory, Provender Lane, Norton, Near Faversham, Kent. ME13 0SU (H) 01795 521166

LONDON & SOUTH EAST DIVISION

LONDON & SOUTH EAST DIVISION STRUCTURE 1996-97

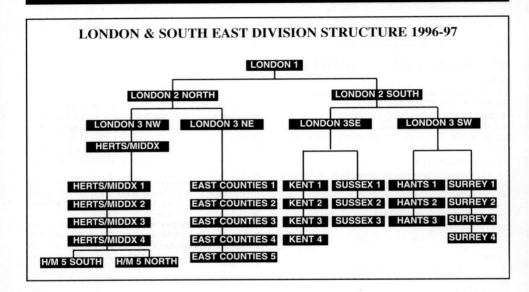

ADMINISTRATIVE RULES

1. REPORTING OF MATCH RESULTS
Match results shall be reported by the time specified on the particular instructions to each club. This report of results is a FACT and is not open to excuse or reason for failure. Accordingly NO APPEAL will be accepted for failure to comply.

2. REPORTING OF POSTPONED MATCHES
Fixtures are scheduled for a particular day and the Results Service MUST receive a report of postponement in just the same way as if the game had been played. Please note that the Results Service OPENS 15 minutes BEFORE the notional time of no-side ie. the service recognises the NORMAL kick-off time according to the time of the season. The Results Service and the League Administration are NOT one and the same thing and it is, therefore, insufficient simply to tell your League Secretary of a postponement. Failure to comply will incur the same penalty as failure to lodge a result.

3. PLAYING OF POSTPONED MATCHES
A match postponed or abandoned under Regulation 11(a) or (b) or a match not played on the appointed day for reasons acceptable to the Organising Committee SHALL, henceforth, be played on the NEXT AVAILABLE SATURDAY.
A Saturday is deemed to be 'available' UNLESS one of the following conditions applies:
a. 		either Club has, on that day, a scheduled Courage League match.

b. 		either Club has, on that day, a Pilkington Cup or Shield match.
c. 		either Club has, on that weekend, a match in a Competition within the authority of the Constituent Body, BUT NOT a Merit Table game.
d. 		either Club has, on that day, a demand on one or more of their 'effectively registered' players to play in a Representative game within the authority of the RFU, the Division or Constituent Body.
e. 		In addition, the Organising Committee (that is the London & SE Division Sub-committee) may - at its absolute discretion and usually at the start of any season - declare that a specific Saturday be deemed 'unavailable' where it falls on or close to a public holiday or where it is considered by the Committee inappropriate to play for another particular reason.

4. NEW APPLICATIONS TO JOIN LEAGUE
Application to join a league MUST be made IN WRITING and shall be in the hands of the Divisional Competition Secretary NOT LATER THAN 30th April. By this same date, the Club MUST have met ALL the entry criteria laid down in Courage League Regulation and those applied, from time to time, by the Organising Committee.

LONDON & SOUTH EAST DIVISION FINAL LEAGUE TABLES 1996-97

LONDON LEAGUE ONE

	P	W	D	L	F	A	PTS
Esher	13	12	0	1	458	171	*22
Norwich	13	9	1	3	267	181	19
Ruislip	13	8	0	5	235	207	16
Harlow	13	7	1	5	405	311	15
Basingstoke	13	7	1	5	237	246	15
Staines	13	7	0	6	345	289	14
Guildford & God	13	7	0	6	321	279	14
Sutton & Ewell	13	6	0	7	288	225	12
Wimbledon	13	6	0	7	286	235	12
Old Colfeians	12	7	0	5	258	347	*12
Sudbury	12	5	1	6	204	232	*9
Old Mid Whitgiftian	13	3	0	10	170	321	6
Southend	13	3	0	10	197	413	6
Thurrock	13	1	0	12	179	393	2

LONDON TWO NORTH

	P	W	D	L	F	A	PTS
Cheshunt	11	9	1	1	319	152	19
Bishops Stortford	11	8	0	3	336	159	16
Romford & Gidea P	11	8	0	3	275	216	16
Cambridge	11	7	0	4	267	203	14
Ipswich	11	6	0	5	290	252	12
Old Albanians	11	6	0	5	257	254	12
Old Verulamians	11	5	0	6	185	261	10
Finchley	11	4	0	7	200	253	8
Colchester	11	4	1	6	185	252	*7
Brentwood	11	3	0	8	151	227	6
Woodford	11	3	0	8	220	310	6
Ealing	11	2	0	9	180	326	4

LONDON TWO SOUTH

	P	W	D	L	F	A	PTS
Thanet Wanderers	12	11	0	1	392	172	22
Gravesend	12	10	0	2	380	158	20
Beckenham	12	9	0	3	312	201	18
Westcombe Park	12	7	0	5	414	228	14
Horsham	12	7	0	5	283	238	14
Old Blues	12	7	0	5	298	265	14
Old Wimbledonians	12	6	0	6	253	233	12
Old Juddian	12	7	0	5	238	236	*12
Old Guildfordians	12	4	0	8	235	289	8
Dorking	12	4	0	8	224	281	8
Streatham-Croydon	12	3	0	9	142	498	6
Old Reigatian	12	2	0	10	198	308	*2
Brockleians	12	1	0	11	152	414	2

LONDON THREE N E

	P	W	D	L	F	A	PTS
Diss	12	10	1	1	378	131	21
Chingford	12	10	1	1	334	157	21
Braintree	11	9	1	1	263	198	19
Canvey Island	12	6	1	5	238	306	13
Lowestoft & Yarm	12	5	1	6	205	216	11
Woodbridge	12	5	0	7	252	245	10
Bury St Edmunds	12	6	0	6	247	258	*10
Maldon	12	5	0	7	217	289	10
Eton Manor	11	4	1	6	222	249	9
West Norfolk	12	4	2	6	218	232	*8
Chelmsford	12	4	0	8	177	233	*6
Rochford	12	4	0	8	212	291	*4
Old Edwardians	12	1	0	11	132	290	2

LONDON THREE NW

	P	W	D	L	F	A	PTS
Old Merchant Taylors	12	10	1	1	415	202	21
Welwyn	12	10	1	1	323	146	21
Barnet	12	9	0	3	415	134	18
Hertford	12	9	0	3	305	153	18
Grasshoppers	12	7	1	4	275	193	15
Old Gaytonians	12	5	3	4	267	267	13
Letchworth	12	6	0	6	287	312	12
Hampstead	12	5	1	6	346	280	11
Old Millhillians	12	5	1	6	226	223	11
Lensbury	12	3	0	9	289	337	6
Fullerians	12	3	0	9	210	315	6
Kingsburians	12	1	0	11	103	555	2
Haringey	12	1	0	11	147	491	*-2

LONDON THREE SE

	P	W	D	L	F	A	PTS
Lewes	12	11	0	1	301	182	22
Sevenoaks	12	10	0	2	506	146	20
Haywards Heath	12	10	0	2	475	126	20
Maidstone	12	9	0	3	273	141	18
Worthing	12	6	0	6	326	257	12
Canterbury	12	6	0	6	245	235	12
Park House	12	6	0	6	285	302	12
Tunbridge Wells	12	6	0	6	243	323	12
Sidcup	12	5	0	7	237	323	10
Chichester	12	4	0	8	154	246	*6
Bognor	12	3	0	9	174	362	*4
Old Beccehamian	12	1	0	11	167	325	2
Brighton	12	1	0	11	124	542	2

LONDON THREE SW

	P	W	D	L	F	A	PTS
Winchester	12	10	0	2	344	133	20
Warlingham	12	9	1	2	330	168	19
Portsmouth	12	9	1	2	351	205	19
Gosport	12	9	0	3	328	183	18
Alton	12	8	0	4	263	218	16
Old Alleynian	12	7	0	5	296	233	14
Jersey	12	6	0	6	322	235	12
Old Emanuel	12	6	0	6	252	296	12
Old Whitgiftians	12	4	2	6	188	286	10
Purley	12	3	0	9	246	345	6
Old Walcountians	12	2	1	9	158	369	5
Guy's Hospital	12	2	0	10	221	348	*2
Barnes	12	0	1	11	126	406	1

EASTERN COUNTIES TWO

	P	W	D	L	F	A	PTS
Hadleigh	12	12	0	0	724	74	24
Bancroft	12	10	0	2	345	176	20
Felixstowe	12	9	0	3	297	114	18
Westcliff	12	8	0	4	287	202	16
Old Cooperians	12	8	0	4	194	160	16
Thetford	12	7	0	5	361	225	*12
Loughton	12	6	0	6	255	260	12
Met Pol Chigwell	12	4	1	7	203	285	9
Old Palmerians	12	4	0	8	127	247	8
Fakenham	12	4	0	8	147	394	8
Thames	12	2	1	9	102	348	5
Southwold	12	2	0	10	180	433	4
Ravens	12	1	0	11	117	421	2

EASTERN COUNTIES ONE

	P	W	D	L	F	A	PTS
Basildon	12	12	0	0	395	125	24
Campion	12	10	0	2	359	127	20
Upminster	12	9	0	3	233	211	18
Holt	12	8	0	4	258	238	16
Wymondian	12	7	0	5	332	190	14
Newmarket	12	7	0	5	204	183	14
Shelford	12	6	0	6	310	218	12
Cantabrigan	12	5	0	7	263	244	10
Ilford Wanderers	12	5	0	7	197	235	10
Ely	12	4	0	8	208	301	8
Wanstead	12	3	0	9	181	351	6
Harwich & Dover	12	1	0	11	154	394	2
Saffron Walden	12	1	0	11	118	395	*0

EASTERN COUNTIES THREE

	P	W	D	L	F	A	PTS
S Woodham Ferrers	11	11	0	0	336	84	22
Mersea	11	9	0	2	272	125	18
Crusaders	11	8	0	3	279	112	16
Billericay	11	8	0	3	283	141	16
Beccles	11	8	0	3	266	174	16
Broadland	11	5	0	6	212	215	*8
Ipswich	11	4	0	7	186	192	8
East London	11	3	0	8	177	221	6
Stowmarket	11	2	0	9	102	290	4
Lakenham Hewett	11	2	0	9	106	304	4
Thurston	11	2	0	9	115	431	4
Wisbech	11	4	0	7	126	171	*2

LONDON & SOUTH EAST DIVISION STRUCTURE 1997-98

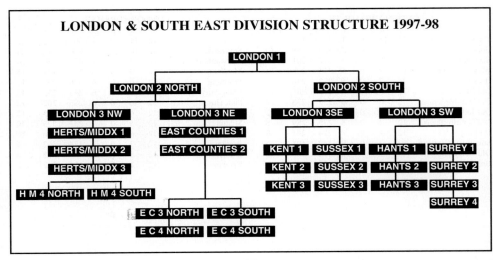

LONDON ONE

London One 1997-98 Fixtures

	Askeans	Basingstoke	Charlton Park	Cheshunt	Guildford & Godalming	Harlow	Norwich	Old Corfeians	Old Mid-Whitgiftians	Ruislip	Southend	Staines	Sudbury	Sutton & Epsom	Thanet Wanderers	Thurrock	Wimbledon	
	1	2	3	4	5	6	7	8	9	10	11	12	13	14	15	16	17	
1 Askeans	X			17/1	7/3	27/9			6/9		20/12		8/11	18/10	31/1			1
2 Basingstoke	20/9	X		28/2		8/11		11/10			31/1		17/1	20/12	14/3			2
3 Charlton Park	14/2	6/9	X				8/11	7/3		20/12		18/10				17/1	27/9	3
4 Cheshunt			10/1	X	24/1	7/3			14/2		18/10		27/9	6/9	15/11			4
5 Guildford & Godalming		27/9	28/2		X		20/12	6/9		17/1		8/11			31/1	18/10		5
6 Harlow			20/9		11/10	X	31/1		25/10	28/2		17/1			14/3	20/12		6
7 Norwich	15/11	24/1		11/10			X	10/1			20/9	7/3			25/10		14/2	7
8 Old Corfeians	14/3		31/1		18/10			X	27/9		17/1		20/12	8/11	28/2			8
9 Old Mid-Whitgiftians		18/10	14/3		20/9		17/1		X	31/1		20/12				28/2	8/11	9
10 Ruislip	10/1	14/2		25/10			27/9	24/1		X		6/9			15/11		7/3	10
11 Southend			15/11		10/1	14/2			24/1	11/10	X		6/9	7/3		25/10		11
12 Staines	25/10	10/1		20/9			15/11			14/3		X	28/2		11/10		24/1	12
13 Sudbury			25/10		15/11	24/1	14/3		10/1	20/9			X	14/2		11/10		13
14 Sutton & Epsom			11/10		25/10	10/1	28/2		15/11	14/3		31/1		X		20/9		14
15 Thanet Wanderers			24/1	20/12	14/2	6/9		7/3		8/11		18/10	27/9		X			15
16 Thurrock	24/1	7/3					18/10	14/2		8/11		27/9			10/1	X	6/9	16
17 Wimbledon	11/10	15/11		14/3				25/10			28/2		31/1	17/1	20/9		X	17
	1	2	3	4	5	6	7	8	9	10	11	12	13	14	15	16	17	

ASKEAN R.F.C.
Ground Address: 60A Broad Walk, Kidbrooke, London. SER3 8NB Tel: 0181
Brief Directions: A2 from London, Broad Walk is first left off Rochester way, which is reached by following signs for local traffic at Kidbrooke turn off
Club Secretary: Graham Terry, Endwaye, Brookhurst Gardens, Tunbridge Wells, Kent TN4 0UA Tel: (H & FAX) 01892 528996
Fixtures Secretary: Mike Sidgwick Tel: 01689 857436
Club Colours: White with blue and white bands

BASINGSTOKE RFC
Ground Address: Down Grange, Pack Lane, Basingstoke RG22 5HN Tel:01256 323308
Brief Directions: Frm east, M3 J6, A339, left at rndabout, straight over rndabout, left next rndabout, 4th exit next rndabout signed Down Grange Sports Complex, 1 mile left Coniston Rd, 1st left
Club Secretary: Brian Anderson, 9 Pelham Close, Old Basing, Basingstoke, Hants. RG24 7HU Tel:(H) 01256 59687
Fixtures Secretary: Kevin Barrett Tel: (H) 01734 700906
Club Colours: Amber shirts, blue

CHARLTON PARK RFC
Ground Address: Pippenhall Sports Ground, Avery Hill Park, Footscray Road, Eltham SE9
Brief Directions: From A2 to A20 follow signs for Eltham High Street, turn into Southend Crescent or Footscray Road, Entrance at junction Southend Crescent and Footscray road.
Club Secretary: Nick Hollier, 5 Brunswick Road, Bexleyheath, Kent DA6 8EL Tel: (H) 0181 301 1210 (W) 0181 303 7777
Fixtures Secretary: Roger Foxon Tel: 0181 311 3498
Club Colours: Blue/Blue/Red

CHESHUNT RFC
Ground Address: Rosedale, Andrews Lane, Cheshunt, Herts. EN7 6TB Tel: 01992 623983
Brief Directions: M25 J25, north on A10, left at 1st roundabout, straight over next 2 roundabouts, 1st left into Andrews Lane, club is 200 yds on left
Club Secretary: Huw Davies, 43 Roydon Rd., Stanstead Abbotts, Herts SG12

8HG Tel: (H) 01920 872490 (W) 01992 645100
Fixtures Secretary: Peter Thompson, 7Harrison Walk, Cheshunt Herts EN8 8PT Tel: 01992 633027
Club Colours: Green and white

LONDON ONE CONTINUED

GUILDFORD & GODALMING RFC
Ground Address: Broadwater, Guildford Road (A3100), Godalming, Surrey. GU7 3BU   Tel: 01483 416199
Brief Directions: From A3 take B3000 towards Godalming, turn right at A3100, ground 400yds on right
Club Secretary: David Gambold, 10 Treebys Avenue, Jacobs Well, Guildford, Surrey. GU4 7NT   Tel: (H) 01483 566304   (W) 01483 561365
Fixtures Secretary: Len Bodill   Tel: (H) 01483 570580
Club Colours: Green and white

HARLOW RUFC
Ground Address: Ram Gorse, Elizabeth Way, Harlow, Essex. CM20 2JQ   Tel: 01279 426 389
Club Secretary: David Eynon, 12 Highfield, Harlow, Essex. CM18 6HE   Tel: (H) 01279 426 389   (W) 0181 554 1607
Fixtures Secretary: John Pendleton   Tel: (H) 01729 439265
Club Colours: Red shirts, green trimmings and shorts

NORWICH RFC
Ground Address: Beeston Hyrne, North Walsham Road, Norwich. NR12 7BW.   Tel: 01603 426259/454561
Brief Directions: From ring road go North on B1150 (North Walsham Road), ground on LHS 1 mile from ring road.
Club Secretary: K. E. C. Searle, Alan Boswell Insurance Services, Cedar House, 115 Carrow Road. NR1 1HP.   Tel: (H) 01508 480564   Tel: (W) 01603 218000
Fixtures Secretary: Steven Henson   Tel: (H) 01603 748351   (W) 01603 687552
Club Colours: Maroon, gold and green

OLD COLFEIANS RFC
Ground Address: Horn Park, Eltham Road, Lee, London. SE12   Tel: 0181 852 1181
Brief Directions: Ground is in Eltham Rd, opposite Weigal Rd, on the A20, 600m in the direction of Lee, Lewisham and London from the intersection of the A20 & A205 roundabout
Club Secretary: Dai Andrew, 80 Dallinger Road, Lee, London. SE12 0TH   Tel: (H) 0181 857 4036   (W) 0171 924 8252
Fixtures Secretary: John Nunn   Tel: (H) 0181 265 7447   (W) 0181 850 1853
Club Colours: Blue, black, maroon and old gold bands, navy shorts and socks

OLD MID-WHITGIFTIAN RFC
Ground Address: Lime Meadow Avenue, Sanderstead, Surrey. CR2 9AS   Tel: 0181 657 2014
Brief Directions: From Stanstead Hill rndabout, 0.75 mile along Limpsfield Rd towards Warlingham, past old fire station & garage, left into Sanderstead Crt Ave, 100yds right, club at end
Club Secretary: John Crate, 16 Mallard Way, Wallington, Surrey. SM6 9LZ   Tel: 0181 647 9081
Fixtures Secretary: Andy Hillburn   Tel: (H) 0181 657 1825   (W) 0181 917 8888 Ext 4571
Club Colours: Dark blue shirts, dark blue shorts

Thanet Wanderers R.U.F.C.
After beating Sudbury in the semi-final of the Intercup at Henley, March 1997.

LONDON ONE CONTINUED

RUISLIP RFC
Ground Address: West End Road, Ruislip, Middlesex. HA4 6DR Tel: 01895 633102
Brief Directions: In West End Rd near junction with Wood Lane. By train to Ruislip Underground Station, turn left out of station, over bridge and clubhouse on right after Wood Lane
Club Secretary: Michael Searls, 16 Park Way, Rickmansworth, Herts. WD3 2AT Tel: 01923 773903
Fixtures Secretary: Steve Hazell Tel: (H) 01932 354060 (W) 0181 641 8510
Club Colours: Maroon and white hooped shirts, white shorts, maroon socks

SOUTHEND RFC
Ground Address: Warners Bridge Park, Sumpters Way, Southend on Sea SS2 5RR Tel: 01702 546682
Brief Directions: From London A127 to Southend, go past park & large garage, left at roundabout into Sutton Rd, 0.5 mile left at mini roundabout, ground at end through ind. est.
Club Secretary: David Dilley, 106 Woodside, Leigh on Sea, Essex. SS9 4RB Tel: (H) 01702 75075
Fixtures Secretary: Charlie Painter Tel: 01702 546682
Club Colours: Brown and white

STAINES RFC
Ground Address: The Reeves, Feltham Hill Road, Hanworth, Middlesex. TW13 7NB Tel: 0181 890 3051
Brief Directions: Take the Lower Feltham exit from A316, Great Chertsey Rd, turn left past United Dairy into Feltham Hill Rd, ground 400 yards on left
Club Secretary: Kevin McMahon,23 Cherry Orchard, Staines, Middlesex. TW13 7NB 0181 890 3051
Fixtures Secretary: E J de Voil Tel: 0181 890 6643
Club Colours: Blue and red jerseys, white shorts

SUDBURY RUFC
Ground Address: Moorsfield, Rugby Road, Great Cornard, Sudbury, Suffolk Tel: 01787 377547
Brief Directions: Ground on B 1508 Colchester, Bures, Sudbury road, 1.5 miles from Sudbury town centre in Great Cornard. From town centre left after Kings Head, 1st right into Rugby Rd
Club Secretary: P M E Maddocks, 8 Nether Court, Halstead, Essex. CO9 2HE Tel: (H) 01787 473027
Fixtures Secretary: G Underwood Tel: 01787 373045
Club Colours: Blue jersey and wide white hoop

SUTTON & EPSOM RFC
Ground Address: Cuddington Court, Rugby Lane, West Drive, Cheam, Surrey. SM2 7NF Tel: 0181 642 0280
Club Secretary: R R Poole, Well Cottage, Loxwood Road, Wisborough Green, West Sussex. RH14 0DJ Tel: (H) 01403 700594 (W) 0181 643 3443
Fixtures Secretary: Ian Frazer Tel: (H) 0181 643 4835 (W) 0171 542 5649
Club Colours: Black and white hoops

THANET WANDERERS RUFC
Ground Address: St Peters Rec. Ground, Callis Court Road, Broadstairs, Kent. CT10 3AE Tel: 01843 866763
Brief Directions: From Broadstairs Broadway traffic lights proceed along St Peters Park Rd, take 1st right under railway bridge and ground is on left
Club Secretary: Peter Hawkins, 51 Park Rd, Ramsgate, Kent. CT11 9TL Tel & Fax: (H & W) 01843 593142
Fixtures Secretary: Peter Hawkins Tel & Fax: (H & W) 01843 593142
Club Colours: Blue, black and yellow hoops

THURROCK RFC
Ground Address: Oakfield, Long Lane, Grays, Essex Tel: 01375 374877
Brief Directions: M25 from north J31/A13 direction Southend, 2nd exit (Grays), 4th exit from 2nd roundabout, off 1st left (Long Lane), 3 miles east to above address, left at flats.
Club Secretary: D H Evans, 29 Mayfield, Connaught Ave, Grays, Essex. RM16 2XL Tel: 01375 382458
Fixtures Secretary: K. Hymas "Clearwater", Argent Street, Grays, Essex, RM17 6PG
Club Colours: Black and white hoops

WIMBLEDON RFC
Ground Address: Beverley Meads, Barham Road, Wimbledon, London. SW20 0ET
Brief Directions: Barham Rd off Copse Hill, off Coombe Lane which is off A3. Nearest train station Raynes Park (BR, Network SE), take No 57 bus to Copse Hill, club at end of Barham Rd
Club Secretary: David Dixon-Smith, 42 Princes Road, Wimbledon, London. SW19 8RB Tel: (W) 0181 543 6244 Fax: 0181 543 5377
Fixtures Secretary: Richard Baker Tel: (H) 01372 729331 (W) 0171 254 2491
Club Colours: Maroon and cambridge blue

Sudbury R.U.F.C. London One.
Back left to right: M.Harris (Manager), C.Pinnegar (Coach), T.Hogsbjerg. I.Howlett, R.Ward, S.Bull,
M.Burman, S.Jenkins, S.Pinnegar, A.Wisbey, D.Gowler.
Front left to right: I.Brown, S.Harries, D.Beanland, A.Tibbles, C.Donnelly (President), J.Cowling (Captain),

LONDON TWO NORTH

London Two North 1997-98 Fixtures

	1 Barnet Elizabethans	2 Bishop's Stortford	3 Braintree	4 Brentwood	5 Cambridge	6 Chingford	7 Colchester	8 Diss	9 Ealing	10 Finchley	11 Ipswich	12 Old Albanians	13 Old Merchant Taylors	14 Old Verulamians	15 Romford & Gidea Pk	16 Welwyn	17 Woodford	
1 Barnet Elizabethans	X	17/1		6/9			27/9	31/1	7/3			18/10			8/11	20/12		1
2 Bishop's Stortford		X	15/11	14/2			7/3		24/1			6/9			27/9	18/10	6/9	2
3 Braintree	24/1		X		18/10		10/1		24/1			6/9	7/3	14/2			6/9	3
4 Brentwood			28/2	X	17/1	28/2			20/9	20/12	31/1	18/10				8/11		4
5 Cambridge	15/11	11/10			X			25/10		7/3		24/1	10/1		20/9	14/2		5
6 Chingford	14/2		17/1		8/11	X			18/10	20/12		6/9	7/3			27/9		6
7 Colchester			28/2	25/10	31/1	20/9	X		11/10	17/1	28/2					20/12		7
8 Diss		20/12		7/3		24/1	6/9	X	14/2			27/9			18/10	8/11		8
9 Ealing			31/1		20/12	28/2		X		8/11	17/1	27/9	6/9				18/10	9
10 Finchley	25/10	20/9					11/10		X			10/1	15/11	28/2	14/3	24/1		10
11 Ipswich	10/1	25/10		27/9			15/11		6/9	X		14/2	24/1			7/3		11
12 Old Albanians			20/9	15/11	28/2	11/10	10/1	25/10	31/1	28/2	X							12
13 Old Merchant Taylors	20/9	28/2					8/11	28/2				20/12	X	11/10	17/1	31/1		13
14 Old Verulamians	28/2	31/1		27/9			18/10	28/2			8/11			X	20/12	17/1		14
15 Romford & Gidea Pk			11/10	10/1	14/3	25/10	24/1		15/1		20/9	14/2			X			15
16 Welwyn			25/10	24/1		15/11	14/2		10/1		11/10	7/3			6/9	X		16
17 Woodford	11/10	28/2					20/9					17/1	15/11	25/10	31/1	28/2	X	17

BARNET ELIZABETHANS
Ground Address: Byng Road, Barnet, Hertfordshire
Tel: 0181 449 0040
Brief Directions: From Wood St, coming from A1 Sterling Corner, left at Black Horse p.h. bear left into The Avenue, 2nd left into Wentworth Rd, 1st left into Byng Rd
Club Secretary: Mike Parker, 1Cedar Avenue, East Barnet, Herts EN4 8DY Tel: (H)0181 368 4767 (W) 0171 290 4042
Fixtures Secretary: Peter Glenister Tel: (H) 01438 820692
Club Colours: Navy blue and claret

BISHOPS STORTFORD RFC
Ground Address: Silver Leys, Hadham Road, Bishops Stortford, Herts. CM23 2QE Tel: 01279 652092
Brief Directions: From north/south, M11 J8, A120 signed Puckeridge. From east/west, A120 to Tesco roundabout, Tesco on right, ground 400m left
Club Secretary: R M Liddle, 95 Parsonage Lane, Bishops Stortford, Herts. CM23 5BA Tel: (H) 01279 651330
Fixtures Secretary: T.Swanson
Tel: (H)01279 651658 (W) 0171 579 6390
Club Colours: Royal blue and white hoops

BRAINTREE RUFC
Ground Address: the Clubhouse, Beckers Green Road, Braintree, essex CM7 6PR. Tel: 01376 311181
Brief Directions: From Braintree bypass A120 exit at Galleys Corner roundabout to Braintree East (B1018 Cressing Road), 300 metres turn right into Beckers Green Road, Ground at end of road.
Club Secretary: Mrs C Wadford, 8 Chelmer Road, Braintree, Essex CM7 3PY. Tel: (H) 01376 341642
Fixtures Secretary: Mrs D Nightingale, Tel: (H) 01371 850013
Club Colours: Black with amber collar.

BRENTWOOD RFC
Ground Address: King Georges Playing Fields, Ingrave Road, Brentwood, Essex. CM13 2AQ Tel: 01277 210267
Club Secretary: Mr Paul Kehoe, 11 Clifton Way, Hutton, Brentwood, Essex. CM13 2QR Tel: (H)01277 215821
Fixtures Secretary: Nick Priddle, Foxhurst, Coxes Farm Rd, Billericay. CM11 2UA Tel: (H) 01277 656685
Club Colours: Claret, grey and white hoops, black shorts

CAMBRIDGE RUFC
Ground Address: Grantchester Road, Cambridge Tel: 01223 312437
Brief Directions: M11 J12, follow signs to Cambridge, Grantchester Rd is 1st right when you pass Cambridge City Welcome sign, ground is 200 mtrs on right
Club Secretary: David Martin, 45 York Street, Cambridge. CB1 2PZ Tel: (H) 01223 314705
Fixtures Secretary: Mrs P. Sumpter Tel: (H) 01954 260410
Club Colours: Blood and sand hoops with white shorts

CHINGFORD RFC
Ground Address: Lea Valley Playing Fields, Waltham Way, Chingford, London. E4 8AQ Tel: 0181 529 4879
Brief Directions: M11 to A406 westbound,approx 3miles to Cook's ferry junction. Signs to Chingford, around roundabout,under viaduct and led into 1009.over mini roundabout then 1 mile on left.
Club Secretary: Howard Hartley, 85 Whitehall Gardens, Chingford, London. E4 6EJ Tel: (H) 0181 559 4821
Fixtures Secretary: David Butler Tel: (H) 0181 529 3412 (W) 0181 529 4879
Club Colours: Black jerseys with royal blue and white hoops

COLCHESTER RFC
Ground Address: Mill Road, Colchester. CO4 5JF Tel: 01206 851610
Brief Directions: Turn off A12 onto A1232, right at roundabout into business park, right at next roundabout, straight over next roundabout into Mill Road, ground is 400yds on right
Club Secretary: Ron Hatch, 99 Ernest Road, Wivenhoe. CO7 9LJ Tel: (H) 01206 823548
Fixtures Secretary: Jon Roberts Tel: (H) 01621 854043
Club Colours: Black

DISS RFC
Ground Address: Mackenders, Bellrope Lane, Roydon, Diss, Norfolk Tel: 01379 642891
Brief Directions: 1 mile west of Diss on A1066 through Roydon village, at end of 40mph limit turn into Bellrope Lane opposite White Hart pub, club 150 yards on left
Club Secretary: N P Kingsley, Diss RFC, c/o S Smith, Unit 1, Diss Business Centre, Frenze, Diss, Norfolk. IP21 4EY Tel: (H) 01379 641717 (Fax) 01379 651177
Fixtures Secretary: J Green Tel: (H) 01379 741705
Club Colours: Royal blue and white

EALING
Ground Address: Berkeley Avenue, Greenford, Middlesex. UB6 0NZ Tel: 0181 422 0868
Brief Directions: Take A40 - Western Ave to Greenford Rd fly over, turn north onto A4127 (Greenford Rd), Berkeley Ave 1 mile up on right just past canal bridge, opposite Glaxo offices
Club Secretary: Hugh Hutchinson, 19 Kent Avenue, Ealing, London. W13 8BE Tel: (H) 0181 991 1389
Fixtures Secretary: Paul Monteith Tel: (H) 01572 757021 (W) 0171 204 2932
Club Colours: White shorts, green and white stripes

FINCHLEY RFC
Ground Address: Summers Lane, Finchley, London. N12 0PD Tel: 0181 445 3746
Brief Directions: From North Circular Rd (A406) take A1000 north towards Barnet/N Finchley, past Leisure centre on right, turn right at lights into Summers Ln, ground 100yds on right
Club Secretary: D G Wedderburn Esq, 41 Oxford Gardens, Whetstone, London. N20 9AG Tel: (H) 0181 446 2430 (W) 0171 378 9988
Fixtures Secretary: Kevin Egan Esq Tel: (H) 0181 346 1882 (W) 0181 244 1956
Club Colours: Scarlet and white 2.25" hoops

Welwyn R.F.C. 1st XV.
Promoted to London North 2 after 8 seasons in London NW3.

IPSWICH RUFC
Ground Address: Humber Doucy Lane, Ipswich. IP4 3PZ Tel: 01473 724072 Fax: 710439
Brief Directions: A12 ToysRus r'bout straight over towards Ipswich at 3rd traffic light garage on L&R Turn L. go over 2 sets lights. 2 r'bouts. Over bridge turn L. at end T.Junction
Club Secretary: Mrs Lisa Greetham, 159 Woodbridge Road, Ipswich IP4 2PE Tel: (H) 01473 233731 (W) 01473 724072
Fixtures Secretary: Mrs Lisa Greetham Tel: (H) 01473 233731 (W) 01473 724072
Club Colours: Black and amber

OLD ALBANIAN RFC
Ground Address: Beech Bottom, Old Harpenden Road, St Albans, Herts Tel: 01727 864476
Brief Directions: Approx 1 mile from centre of St Albans on A1081 towards Luton, 150 yards from Ancient Briton public house
Club Secretary: Peter Lipscomb, 35 Gurney Court Road, St Albans, Herts. AL1 4QU Tel: (H) 01727 760466 (W) 0181 784 5924
Fixtures Secretary: Mr David Verdon Tel: (H) 0171 538 0184 (W) 0171 712 8947
Club Colours: Red, blue and gold hooped shirts, blue shorts

OLD MERCHANT TAYLORS' FC
Ground Address: Durrants, Lincoln Way, Croxley Green, Herts. WD3 3ND Tel: 01923 773014
Brief Directions: From Watford take signs for Saratt at Two Bridges p.h. onto Baldwins Ln, right at 1st mini r'bout into Durrants Dv, 1st left Kenilworth Dv, 1st right into Rochester Way
Club Secretary: M G Foster, Durrants, Lincoln Way, Croxley Green, Herts. WD3 3ND Tel: (H) 0973 657412 (W) 0973 657412
Fixtures Secretary: G W Shilling Tel: (H) 01923 774506 (W) 01923 774506
Club Colours: White jerseys, black shorts

OLD VERULAMIAN RFC
Ground Address: Cotlandswick, London Colney, nr St Albans, Hertfordshire. AL2 1DW Tel: 01727 822929
Brief Directions: Take A405 towards M10, ground 400 yds on left
Club Secretary: A B Charlwood, 12 Waverley Road, St Albans, Hertfordshire. AL3 5PA Tel: (H) 01727 846923 (W) 0171 634 3054
Fixtures Secretary: Mrs V Halford Tel: (H) 01727 830732 (W) 01920 830230
Club Colours: Royal blue with gold 'V', white shorts

ROMFORD & GIDEA PARK RFC
Ground Address: Crowlands, Crow Lane, Romford, Essex. RM7 0EP Tel: 01708 760068
Brief Directions: A12 to Moby Dick pub, from London right, from east left,into Whalebone Ln Nth,at lights left Londn Rd, 0.5 mile right Jutsums Ln,under bridge,left Crow Ln,ground 100m right
Club Secretary: D G E Davies, 25 Stanley Avenue, Gidea Park, Romford, Essex. RM2 5DL Tel: (H) 01708 724870 (W) 0181 592 4193
Fixtures Secretary: G Finch Tel: (H) 01277 229817 (W) 0181 804 1980
Club Colours: Black, purple and white

WELWYN RUGBY CLUB
Ground Address: Hobbs Way, Colgrove, Welwyn Garden City, Herts Tel: 01707 329116
Brief Directions: A1(M) J4, follow signs to Gosline sports park, bear left into Parkway, left at next r'bout into Turmore Dale, 1st left into Colgrove, 30 yds right into Hobbs Way
Club Secretary: J M Sargeant, 67 Woodhall Lane, Welwyn Garden City, Herts. AL7 3TG Tel: (H) 01707 331186
Fixtures Secretary: K Smith Tel: (H & W) 01438 351807 (Fax) 01438 249129
Club Colours: Maroon and white hoops, blue shorts, maroon socks

WOODFORD RFC
Ground Address: Highams, High Road, Woodford Green, Essex. IG8 9LB Tel: 0181 504 6769
Brief Directions: Woodford tube station, north via Snakes Ln to Woodford High Rd, turn left for 500yds, club entrance on right 25 yds off main road next to Woodford High School
Club Secretary: N.A.R. Pearce, 33 Forest Drive West, Leytonstone, London E11 1JZ Tel: (H) 0181 539 8184
Fixtures Secretary: Mr M Whiteley Tel: 0181 524 2737(H) 0171 865 5972 (W)
Club Colours: White, Lavender, Black and Purple

THIS DIRECTORY IS NOT FOR CLUB OFFICIALS ONLY!
Do your club supporters know they can buy their own directory and help club funds?

LONDON THREE NORTH EAST

London Three North East 1997-98 Fixtures	Basildon	Bury St Edmonds	Campion	Canvey Island	Chelmsford	Eton Manor	Holt	Lowestoft & Yarmouth	Maldon	Newmarket	Old Edwardians	Rochford	Shelford	Upminster	West Norfolk	Woodbridge	Wymondham	
	1	2	3	4	5	6	7	8	9	10	11	12	13	14	15	16	17	
1 Basildon	X			8/11	17/1			7/3	27/9	31/1	18/10	6/9					20/12	1
2 Bury St Edmonds	15/11	X	14/2		11/10	10/1				25/10				24/1	7/3	20/9		2
3 Campion	11/10		X	31/1	14/3	25/10				20/9	17/1				15/11		28/2	3
4 Canvey Island		14/3		X			11/10	15/11	24/1		14/2	10/1	25/10	20/9				4
5 Chelmsford			27/9		X		15/11	24/1	7/3		6/9	14/2	10/1			18/10		5
6 Eton Manor	14/3			20/12	31/1	X			18/10	28/2	8/11	27/9					17/1	6
7 Holt	24/1	18/10	6/9			14/2	X			10/1				8/11	7/3	27/9		7
8 Lowestoft & Yarmouth		20/12	18/10			6/9	31/1	X				28/2	17/1	27/9	8/11			8
9 Maldon		31/1	20/12				14/3	11/10	X			25/10	20/9	28/2		17/1		9
10 Newmarket				18/10	20/12			14/2	6/9	X	27/9	7/3	24/1			8/11		10
11 Old Edwardians		28/2					20/9	25/10	10/1		X	15/11	11/10	14/3		31/1		11
12 Rochford		17/1	8/11				28/2	20/9				X	14/3	31/1	18/10	20/12		12
13 Shelford	14/2	8/11	27/9			7/3	17/1						X	20/12	6/9	18/10		13
14 Upminster	10/1	27/9	7/3		25/10	24/1				15/11				X	14/2	6/9		14
15 West Norfolk	20/9			17/1	28/2	11/10		8/11	14/3	20/12					X		31/1	15
16 Woodbridge	25/10		24/1	28/2	20/9	15/11				11/10					10/1	X	14/3	16
17 Wymondham				6/9			25/10	10/1	14/2			7/3	24/1	15/11	11/10		X	17
	1	2	3	4	5	6	7	8	9	10	11	12	13	14	15	16	17	

BASILDON RFC
Ground Address: Gardiners Close, Basildon, Essex. SS14 2AW Tel: 01268 533136
Brief Directions: Frm wst: A127 London/S'thend arterial rd, past 1st signs for B'don, rt A132, rt at 2nd r'bout A1235, rt at 1st lights (not Zebra) Gardiners Lans south is first left-ground at end.
Club Secretary: T.Ramsbottom, 12 Stafford Green, Basildon SS16 6DY Tel: 01268 492558
Fixtures Secretary: Len Hymans Tel: (H) 01268 693899 (W) 0850 500159
Club Colours: Bottle green with two white hoops

BURY ST EDMONDS RFC
Ground Address: The Haberden, Southgate Green, Bury St Edmonds Tel: 01284 753920
Brief Directions: Leave A14 on A134 (B.S.E. east & Sudbury), ground is 400 yards on right, next to Mobil Petrol Station
Club Secretary: Mr R M Peacock, 31 Plovers Way, Bury St Edmonds. IP33 2NJ Tel: (H) 01284 761536 (W) 01284 754450
Fixtures Secretary: Mr S Lord Tel: (H) 01284 769722 (W) 0171 720 2188
Club Colours: Green and yellow quarters

CAMPION RFC
Ground Address: Cottons Park, Cottons Approach, Romford, Essex. RM7 7AA Tel: 01708 753209
Brief Directions: Frm W. exit A12 at lights after Moby Dick pub, rt -Mawney Rd, before T junction rt -Marks Rd, ground 1st left. Frm E., A12 thro' 3 lights after Gallows Crnr, lt-Hawney Rd-as above
Club Secretary: P O'Brien, 68 Lancaster Drive, Elm Park, Hornchurch, Essex. RM12 5ST Tel: (H) 01708 446980 (W) 01708 342453
Fixtures Secretary: K O'Neill Tel: (H) 01277 811742 (W) 0181 522 2349
Club Colours: Red and black hoops

CANVEY ISLAND RUFC
Ground Address: Trewkes Creek, Dovervelt Road, Canvey Island, Essex Tel: 01268 681881
Brief Directions: A130 to Canvey Island, straight across 2 roundabouts, turn left at 3rd Climmen Road, follow road, club on left
Club Secretary: Mr Stephen Clarke, 26 Thelma Avenue, Canvey Island, Essex. SS8 9DT Tel: (H) 01268 699858 (W) 0171 473 1144
Fixtures Secretary: G M Henderson, 3 Brindles, Canvey Island. Tel: (H) 01268 681121 (M) 0802 700886
Club Colours: Red and blue

CHELMSFORD RFC
Ground Address: Coronation Park, Timsons Lane, Springfield, Chelmsford, Essex. CM2 6AF Tel: 01245 261159
Brief Directions: A12 - take Boreham/North Springfield turning, head for Chelmsford, over 1st roundabout, 2nd roundabout 3rd exit, over roundabout, 1st turning after Plough pub Timsons Lane
Club Secretary: Peter Willis, 9 Burton Place, Chelmsford, Essex. CM2 6TY Tel: (H) 01245 469411 (W) 01245 702703
Fixtures Secretary: I. Stuart, 49 Hillside Grove, Chelmsford, Essex CM2 9DA Tel: 01245 604670.
Club Colours: Blue

ETON MANOR RFC
Ground Address: Eastway Sports Centre, Quartermile Lane, London. E10 Tel: 0181 555 2670
Club Secretary: Mr John Ayling, 44 Lytton Road, Leytonstone, London. E11 1JH Tel: (H) 0181 558 1800 (W) 0171 831 3666
Fixtures Secretary: Martin Scott Tel: (H) 0181 530 4451
Club Colours: Dark blue with light blue hoops dark blue shorts

HOLT RFC
Ground Address: Bridge Road, High Kelling, Holt, Norfolk. NR25 6QT Tel: 01263 712191
Brief Directions: Take Crome Road (A148) from Holt, after approx 1 mile turn left into Bridge Road (signposted Holt RFC)
Club Secretary: P J Lockhart, April Cottage, The Rosary, Millbarton, Norwich. NR14 8AL Tel: (H) 01508 570835 (W) 01603 628251
Fixtures Secretary: P J Lockhart Tel: (H) 01508 570835 (W) 01603 628251
Club Colours: All black

LOWESTOFT & YARMOUTH RUFC
Ground Address: Gunton Park, off Corton Long Lane, Old Lane, Corton, Nr Lowestoft, Suffolk
Brief Directions: Frm L'toft A12 to Gt Yarm'th, at start of d. c'way (past Pleasure wood Hills) turn right into Corton Long Ln, 200yds right to Old Ln, ground at end. Frm Gt Yarm'th left at end of d. c'way off A12
Club Secretary: June Nelson, 70 Upper Cliff Road, Gorleston, Gt Yarmouth. NR31 6AJ Tel: (H) 01494 653095 (W) 01493 656071
Fixtures Secretary: Tex Colby Tel: (H) 01502 585924
Club Colours: Blue and white hoops

MALDON RUFC
Ground Address: Drapers Farm Sports Club, Drapers Chase, Heybridge, Maldon, Essex. Tel: 01621 852152
Brief Directions: A414 to Maldon. Then northern by-pass to Heybridge.Follow signs to Goldhanger. Half a mile up Goldhanger road on left.
Club Secretary: S.R.Knight, 2 Suffolk Rd., Maldon, Essex CM9 6AY Tel : 01621 853089
Fixtures Secretary: Norman Manning Tel: 01621 856073
Club Colours: Royal blue and white hoops

NEWMARKET RUFC
Ground Address: Sports Pavilion, Scaltback Middle School, Elizabeth Avenue, Newmarket, Suffolk. CB8 0JJ Tel: 01638 663082
Brief Directions: A14 (Newmkt bypass), A142 towards Newmkt, right at Tesco r'bout, left at T junction, past 3 factories on right, turn right into Elizabeth Ave, clubhouse at rear of school
Club Secretary: Robert Voss, 58 King Edward VII Road, Newmarket, Suffolk. CB8 0EU Tel: (H) 01638 669596 (W) 01763 260421
Fixtures Secretary: John Taylor Tel: (H) 01638 507483 (W) 01638 507483
Club Colours: Emerald green and black hoops

Holt London 3.
Back left to right: A.Formosa, C.Palmer, B.Rosser, M.Evans, D.Wolff, A.Bowen, J.Cole, G.Brown, A.Brown,
A.Jenkins (Coach), J.Birca (Touch Judge).
Front left to right: M.Collins, R.Bruce, E.Lassman, M.Jacobs, G.Hewitt-Coleman, G.Ebdon-Hussey,
M.Redding, C.Humphrey, I.Hoare.

OLD EDWARDIANS RFC
Ground Address: Westlands Playing Fields, London Road, Romford, Essex
Brief Directions: On A118 towards London from Romford (known locally as London Road)
Club Secretary: Mrs C Hunt, Orchard End, St James Court, Billericay, Essex   Tel: (H) 01708 764429
Fixtures Secretary: Mr P Griffith   Tel: (H) 01708 450022
Club Colours: Navy blue shirts, white shorts

ROCHFORD HUNDRED RFC
Ground Address: The Clubhouse, Magnolia Road, Hankwell, Essex. SS4 3AD   Tel: 01702 544021
Club Secretary: Mr R Simon Wakefield, 54 Parklands Drive, Springfield, Chelmsford, Essex. CM1 7SP   Tel: (H) 01245 266158   (W) 01702 541581
Fixtures Secretary: Mr Colin Chandler   Tel: (H) 01277 766748
Club Colours: Black shirt and shorts, black socks with white tops

SHELFORD RUFC
Ground Address: Davey Field, Cambridge Road, Gt Shelford, Cambridge   Tel: 01223 843357
Brief Directions: M11 J11 heading into Cambridge, right at traffic lights into Shelford Rd, continue for 1 mile, club is on the right opposite Scotsdale Garden Centre
Club Secretary: Lydia D Cangenheim, 37 Rock Road, Cambridge. CB1 4UG   Tel: (H) 01223 245446   (W) 01223 314988
Fixtures Secretary: Mr Mike Whibley   Tel: (H) 01223 214070   (H) 01223 248061
Club Colours: Maroon and white hoops

UPMINSTER RFC
Ground Address: Hall Lane Playing Fields, Hall Lane, Upminster, Essex   Tel: 01708 220320
Brief Directions: From M25 take A127 towards Romford, take Upminster turn off, ground 0.5 mile on left over mini roundabout
Club Secretary: M Eve, 142 Cranson Park Avenue, Upminster, Essex. RM14 3XJ   Tel: (H) 01708 225383 (W) 01708 858935
Fixtures Secretary: Shaun Neale   Tel: (H) 01708 445423
Club Colours: Yellow and blue hoops

WEST NORFOLK RUFC
Ground Address: Gatehouse Lane, North Wootton, Kings Lynn   Tel: 01553 631307
Brief Directions: A149 to K. Lynn to Hunstanton bypass A148 to K. Lynn r'bout at top of hill, right at lights in Castle Rising Rd, left at T junction to North Wootton, through village to green, left at Gatehouse Lane
Club Secretary: J A Williams, 1 Courtwell Place, Springwood, Kings Lynn   Tel: (H) 01553 760968   (W) 01842 765577
Fixtures Secretary: D Kingdon   Tel: (H) 01553 776331
Club Colours: French grey with cerise band, navy shorts

WOODBRIDGE RUFC
Ground Address: Hatchley Barn, Bromeswell, Woodbridge, Suffolk. IP12 2PP   Tel: 01394 466630
Brief Directions: From A12 take B1084 to Orford, after passing junction to Eyke, entrance is approx 600 yards on right
Club Secretary: K J Blow, 14 Cobbold Road, Woodbridge, Suffolk. IP12 1HA   Tel: (H) 01394 384642 (W) 01473 643417
Fixtures Secretary: Ian Rafferty   Tel: (H) 01394 382369   (W) 01473 383100
Club Colours: Blue

WYMONDHAM RUFC
Ground Address: Foster Harrison Memorial Ground, Tuttles Lane, Wymondham, Norfolk   Tel: 01953 607332
Brief Directions: To Wymonham on A11, onto the Wy'ham bypass until slip road marked Wy'ham & E. Dereham B1135, past Somerfield on left, thro' next r'bout, ground 0.25 mile right
Club Secretary: Martin Warren, 14 Newark Close, Thorpe St Andrew, Norwich. NR7 0YJ   Tel: (H) 01603 437805   (W) 01603 616112
Fixtures Secretary: M.Berry   Tel: (H) 01359 233078 (M) 0410 411047
Club Colours: Red and black hooped shirts, black shorts and socks

EASTERN COUNTIES ONE

Eastern Counties One 1997-98 Fixtures	Bancroft	Cantabrigians	Ely	Felixstowe	Hadleigh	Harwich & D	Ilford Wanderers	Saffron Walden	Wanstead	Westcliff	
	1	2	3	4	5	6	7	8	9	10	
1 Bancroft	X	6/9	11/10	14/2	20/9	10/1	25/10	14/3	24/1	15/11	1
2 Cantabrigians	7/3	X	14/2	20/9	14/3	25/10	24/1	15/11	11/10	10/1	2
3 Ely	31/1	27/9	X	18/10	25/10	14/3	15/11	28/2	10/1	6/9	3
4 Felixstowe	27/9	28/2	24/1	X	11/10	15/11	10/1	6/9	25/10	14/3	4
5 Hadleigh	28/2	20/12	17/1	31/1	X	27/9	6/9	8/11	28/3	18/10	5
6 Harwich & Dovercourt	8/11	17/1	20/12	28/3	14/2	X	20/9	18/10	7/3	31/1	6
7 Ilford Wanderers	17/1	18/10	28/3	8/11	7/3	28/2	X	31/1	20/12	27/9	7
8 Saffron Walden	20/12	28/3	20/9	7/3	10/1	24/1	11/10	X	14/2	25/10	8
9 Wanstead	18/10	31/1	8/11	17/1	15/11	6/9	14/3	27/9	X	28/2	9
10 Westcliff	28/3	8/11	7/3	20/12	24/1	11/10	14/2	17/1	20/9	X	10
	1	2	3	4	5	6	7	8	9	10	

BANCROFT RFC
Ground Address: Buckhurst Way, Buckhurst Hill, Essex. IG9 6JD   Tel: 0181 504 0429
Brief Directions: M11/A406 to 'Waterworks' junction, exit & take A104 to Woodford, at Castle pub turn right (Broadmead Rd), left at 2nd traffic lights, ground 1mile on right before railway bridge
Club Secretary: S B Thirsk, 4 Bentley Way, Woodford Green, Essex. IG8 0SE   Tel: (H) 0181 504 1468   (W) 01279 441111
Fixtures Secretary: G Wiseman   Tel: (H) 0181 504 7647   (W) 0171 930 9711
Club Colours: Blue, black, light blue, claret hoops

CANTABRIGIAN RFC
Ground Address: Sedley Taylor Road, Cambridge. CB2 2PW   Tel: 01223 516061
Club Secretary: R L Ladds, 4 Flamstead Road, Cambridge. CB1 3QU   Tel: (H) 01223 249008   (W) 01223 553888
Fixtures Secretary: J Edmonds   Tel: (H) 01223 563256 (W) 01223 844123
Club Colours: Navy blue and white hoops

ELY RUFC
Ground Address: Downham Road Playing Fields, Ely, Cambs   Tel: 01353 662363
Brief Directions: Just North of Ely. L.H.S. of A10 bypass which is signed Downham Market, King's Lynn.
Club Secretary: Christopher Ormerod, 20 Brays Lane, Ely, Cambs., CB7 4QJ.   Tel: 01353 661629
Fixtures Secretary: Martin Hammond, Hillcrest House, 110 Bexwell Road, Downham Market, Norfolk, PE388 9LH.
Tel: (H) 01366 384990 Fax: 01366 85739
Club Colours: Yellow and black hoops

FELIXSTOWE RUFC
Ground Address: Coronation Sports Ground, Mill Lane, Felixstowe, Suffolk. IP11 8LN   Tel: 01394 270150
Brief Directions: Follow A14 to Felixstowe, at roundabout take right to dock, 1st slip road come off, left at bottom, right at mini roundabout, next mini roundabout turn right
Club Secretary: Mr D J Cain,16 Berners Rd., Felixstowe, 1P11 7LF   Tel: (H) 01394 278112   (W) 01473 217261
Fixtures Secretary: Dave Rose, 19 Victoria Street, Felixstowe   Tel: 01394 673846
Club Colours: Black and white hooped shirts, black shorts

HADLEIGH RUFC
Ground Address: Layham Road Sports Ground, Hadleigh, Ipswich, Suffolk. IP7 5NE   Tel: 01473 824217
Brief Directions: From Hadleigh High St turn into Layham Rd (flanked by library and chemist), over bridge and go on round bends, ground is on the left
Club Secretary: Andrew Hunkin, 7 Yeoman Way, Hadleigh, Ipswich. IP7 5HW   Tel: (H) 01473 824448 (W) 01473 825745
Fixtures Secretary: Chris Lander   Tel: (H) 01473 824757   (W) 0802 968415
Club Colours: Maroon and white

EASTERN COUNTIES ONE CONTINUED

HARWICH AND DOVERCOURT RUFC
Ground Address: Swimming Pool Road, Wick Lane, Dovercourt, Harwich, Essex. CO12 3TS   Tel: 01255 240225
Brief Directions: A120 to Ramsey roundabout, 3rd exit, right at War Memorial into Fronks Rd, 2nd right into Hall Lane, left into Wick Lane, right towards swimming pool, clubhouse past pool
Club Secretary: Keiran Coyles, 4 Acorn Close, Dovercourt, Harwich, Essex. CO12 4XF   Tel: (H) 01255 504432   (W) 01255 508117
Fixtures Secretary: Barry Male   Tel: (H) 01255 886165   (W) 01255 244838
Club Colours: Black shirts with one white hoop, black shorts, black socks with white top

ILFORD WANDERERS RFC
Ground Address: The Club House, Forest Road, Barkingside, Ilford, Essex. IG6 3HJ   Tel: 0181 500 4622
Brief Directions: By road: A12 to Gants Hill r'bout take Cranbrook Rd to Barkingside High St, into Forest Rd at Fulwell Cross R/A Fairlop Oak pub, ground 1 mile left, signposted
Club Secretary: Steve Ward, 37 Sedley Rise, Loughton, Essex. IG10   Tel: (H) c/o 0181 5971158   (W) 0181 5944894 (league contact)
Fixtures Secretary: Beiron Harding   Tel: (H) 0181 597 1158   (W) 0181 592 7861
Club Colours: Red, green and white hoops

SAFFRON WALDEN RFC
Ground Address: Springate, Henham, Nr Bishops Stortford   Tel: 01279 850791
Club Secretary: B Peachey, 2 Gloucester Place, Clare, Suffolk. CO10 8QR   Tel: (H) 01787 278464   (W) 01277 260600
Fixtures Secretary: M Flood   Tel: (H) 01279 657772   (W) 01628 771800
Club Colours: Myrtle green

WANSTEAD RFC
Ground Address: Roding Lane North, Woodford Bridge, Essex
Club Secretary: Neil Joyce, 21 Grosvenor Road, Leyton, London E10 6LG.   Tel: (H) 0181 556 9125
Fixtures Secretary: Terry Elliot, Tel: (H) 0181 599 2743
Club Colours: Blue and white hoops.

WESTCLIFF RFC
Ground Address: The Gables, Aviation Way, Southend-on-Sea, Essex. SS2 6UN   Tel: 01702 541499
Brief Directions: A127 turn left at Perrys Ford Garage at Kent Elms corner about .5 mile from Southend. After 200yds turn R. in to Snakes Lane go to end turn R and L at 4th r'about to Aviation Way . Ground 600yds.
Club Secretary: T J Eastwell, 21 Dawlish Drive, Leigh-on-Sea, Essex. SS9 1QX   Tel: (H) 01702 542311
Fixtures Secretary: Tony Pendry, 71A Burdett Avenue, Westcliff-on-Sea, Essex, SS0 7JN.   Tel: 01702 334872
Club Colours: Maroon and old gold hoops

EASTERN COUNTIES TWO

Eastern Counties Two 1997-98 Fixtures	Fakenham	Loughton	Mersea Island	Met Police, Chigwell	Old Cooperians	Old Palmerians	Southwold	Sth Woodham F.	Thames	Thetford	
	1	2	3	4	5	6	7	8	9	10	
1 Fakenham	X	8/11	17/1	7/3	31/1	18/10	28/2	28/3	27/9	20/12	1
2 Loughton	10/1	X	27/9	11/10	6/9	28/2	15/11	24/1	14/3	25/10	2
3 Mersea Island	25/10	14/2	X	20/9	14/3	6/9	10/1	11/10	15/11	24/1	3
4 Met Police, Chigwell	6/9	31/1	28/2	X	8/11	20/12	27/9	17/1	18/10	28/3	4
5 Old Cooperians	11/10	7/3	20/12	10/1	X	28/3	24/1	20/9	25/10	14/2	5
6 Old Palmerians	24/1	20/9	7/3	14/3	15/11	X	25/10	14/2	10/1	11/10	6
7 Southwold	20/9	28/3	8/11	14/2	18/10	17/1	X	20/12	31/1	7/3	7
8 Sth Woodham Ferrers	15/11	18/10	31/1	25/10	28/2	27/9	14/3	X	6/9	10/1	8
9 Thames	14/2	20/12	28/3	24/1	17/1	8/11	11/10	7/3	X	20/9	9
10 Thetford	14/3	17/1	18/10	15/11	27/9	31/1	6/9	8/11	28/2	X	10
	1	2	3	4	5	6	7	8	9	10	

FAKENHAM RUFC
Ground Address: Old Wells Road, Fakenham, Norfolk Tel: 01328 851007
Brief Directions: From A148 take roundabout at edge of town and go towards town centre, 1st left into Old Wells Road, turn right at far end to clubhouse
Club Secretary: Nicola Walton, The Old School House, Kilmodeston, Fakenham, Norfolk. NR21 0AT Tel: (H) 01328 878732
Fixtures Secretary: Chris Evans Tel: (H) 01362 694537
Club Colours: Light blue and black

LOUGHTON RFC
Ground Address: Squirrels Lane, Hornbeam Road, Buckhurst Hill, Essex. Tel: 0171 504 0065
Brief Directions: A11 out of NE London to Woodford Green, turn right following police station into Monkhams Lane, follow to end and straight over crossroads into Chesnut Avenue, continue onto Squirrels Lane.
Club Secretary: Craig Clark, 15 Herenard Green, Coughton, Essex. Tel: (H) 0181 502 4854
Fixtures Secretary: Brian Westley, Tel: (H) 01689 819365 Tel: (W) 0171 777 2883
Club Colours: White with green hoop between black hoops.

MERSEA ISLAND RFC
Ground Address: E.C.C. Youth Camp, East Road, East Mersea, Colchester
Brief Directions: From Colchester - over Causeway, turn left East Road, 3rd turning right, lane to Youth Camp
Club Secretary: Tony Eves, Dormy House, Lower Road, Peldon, Colchester, Essex. CO5 7QR Tel: (H & W & Fax) 01206 735537
Fixtures Secretary: Graham Woods Tel: (H) 01206 383525
Club Colours: Blue and white

MET POLICE CHIGWELL RFC
Ground Address: Metropolitan Police Sports Ground, Chigwell Hall, High Road, Chigwell, Essex Tel: 500 2735
Brief Directions: From A406 north circular road, take A113 Chigwell road, pass under M11 up hill, take left fork (A113) straight on 1st & 2nd mini roundabouts, ground 100 yds on left
Club Secretary: Malcolm Bartlett, 11 Fairfield Rd, Ongar, Essex. CM5 9HJ Tel: (H) 01277 364206 (W) 01426 241278
Fixtures Secretary: James Handing Tel: (H) 0181 501 3981 (W) 01975 709578
Club Colours: Blue shirts, black shorts

OLD COOPERIANS RUFC
Ground Address: Blake Hall Sports Ground, Blake Hall Road, Wansted, London Tel: 0181 989 1673
Brief Directions: From Leytonstowe Green main roundabout down Bush Rd, right at traffic lights, ground 50 yards on left
Club Secretary: John C Green, Greenlow House, Melbourn, Herts. SG8 6OG Tel: (H) 01763 260624 (W) 01279 652214
Fixtures Secretary: Chris Nicholls Tel: (H & Fax) 0181 592 9450
Club Colours: Dark blue with gold and light blue hoops

OLD PALMERIANS RFC
Ground Address: Palmers Cottage, Chadwell Road, Grays, Essex Tel: 01375 370121
Brief Directions: A13 take A1012 towards Grays, at next roundabout take B149 to Palmers College (follow signposts Palmers College)
Club Secretary: Mr Carwyn Owen, 1b Rose Cottage, Mill Lane, Grays, Essex. RM20 4YD Tel: (H) 01375 378668
Fixtures Secretary: Mr Andrew Cresswell Tel: (H) 01394 670885 (W) 01394 675811
Club Colours: Light blue and dark blue hoops

SOUTH WOODHAM FERRERS RFC
Ground Address: Saltcoats Playing Fields, Saltcoats Pavilion, South Woodham Ferrers, Essex Tel: 01245 320041
Club Secretary: Mrs S Williams, 11 Drywoods, South Woodham Ferrers, Essex Tel: (H) 01245 325987
Fixtures Secretary: Mr Barry Gittos Tel: (H) 01245 324603
Club Colours: Black shirts, black shorts and black socks

SOUTHWOLD RFC
Ground Address: The Pavilion, The Common, Southwold, Suffolk
Brief Directions: First right at Kings Head Hotel and proceed towards water tower
Club Secretary: Andy Toone, 17 Portsch Close, Carlton Colville, Lowestoft, Suffolk. NR33 8TY Tel: (H) 01502 515649 (W) 01502 566321
Fixtures Secretary: John Winter Tel: (H) 01986 875994 (W) 01986 784234
Club Colours: Black and single old gold chest band

THAMES RUFC
Ground Address: St Cedds Playing Field, Garron Lane, Aveley, South Ockendon, Essex
Brief Directions: Turn off Tunnel Junction, down Ship Lane, right at T junction, second off roundabout. First left, second left.
Club Secretary: David Northfield, 179 Blackshots Lane, Grays, Essex. RM16 2LL Tel: (H) 01375 407043 (W) 01268 402239
Fixtures Secretary: Tony Lincoln, 65 Victoria Avenue, Grays, RM16 2RN. Tel: 01375 391404.
Club Colours: Emerald Green and black hoops

THETFORD RFC
Ground Address: Two Mile Bottom, Mundford Road, Thetford Tel: 01842 755176
Brief Directions: From A11 take the A134 Kings Lynn/Mundford road, travel for 1 mile and take the first turning on the right
Club Secretary: P Candlin, 67 Nunnery Drive, Thetford. IP24 3EP Tel: (H) 01842 750416 (W) 01842 750415
Fixtures Secretary: W Smith Tel: (H) 01842 766113 (W) 01359 269681
Club Colours: Red and white hoops

EASTERN COUNTIES THREE NORTH

Eastern Counties Three North 1997-98 Fixtures	Beccles	Brightlingsea	Broadland	Crusanders	Lakenham-Hewitt	March	Stowmarket	Thurston	
	1	2	3	4	5	6	7	8	
1 Beccles	X	20/9	7/3	14/2	15/11	31/1	18/10	10/1	1
2 Brightlingsea	17/1	X	10/1	20/12	31/1	18/10	28/2	8/11	2
3 Broadland	20/12	6/9	X	28/2	18/10	17/1	8/11	31/1	3
4 Crusanders	8/11	7/3	15/11	X	17/1	6/9	31/1	18/10	4
5 Lakenham-Hewitt	28/2	25/10	24/1	20/9	X	14/2	10/1	20/12	5
6 March	25/10	24/1	20/9	10/1	8/11	X	20/12	28/2	6
7 Stowmarket	24/1	15/11	14/2	25/10	6/9	7/3	X	17/1	7
8 Thurston	6/9	14/2	25/10	24/1	7/3	15/11	20/9	X	8
	1	2	3	4	5	6	7	8	

BECCLES RUFC
Ground Address: Beef Meadow, Common Lane, Beccles Tel: 01502 712016
Brief Directions: Into Beccles from Safeway roundabout, over mini roundabout, follow road left over railway, 1st left is Common Lane
Club Secretary: W J Wells, Cliff Cottage, Puddingmoor, Beccles. NR34 9PP Tel: (H & Fax) 01502 715509
Fixtures Secretary: Miles James Tel: (H) 01502 716334 (W) 01603 612513 (Pager)
Club Colours: Green and black quarters

BRIGHTLINGSEA RFC
Ground Address: Colne Community School, Church Rd., Brightlingsea Tel: 01206 304946
Brief Directions: Follow signs for Thorrington on A1027 Colchester/Clacton Rd, at Thorrington Cross take A1029 to B'sea, follow road towards Church at top of hill, approx 2 miles, Sports Centre on left
Club Secretary: Roger Kemble, 8 Tabor Close, Brightlingsea, Essex. CO7 0QS Tel: (H) 01206 302432
Fixtures Secretary: Trevor Andrews Tel: (H) 01206 302235
Club Colours: Scarlet, black socks and shorts

BROADLANDS RFC
Ground Address: Cobham Playing Field, Cobham, Great Yarmouth, Norfolk Tel: 01493 657052
Brief Directions: Just off main New Bridge to Gonigston or Norwich - A47
Club Secretary: S Watson, 44A Southam Road, Great Yarmouth, Norfolk. NR31 0DT Tel: (H) 01493 748775 (W) 01493 657052
Fixtures Secretary: Mr D Todd Tel: (H) 01493 512671
Club Colours: Red, white and blue hoops

CRUSADERS RUFC
Ground Address: Beck Hythe, Little Melton, Nr Norwich, Norfolk Tel: 01603 811157
Brief Directions: Situated in Little Melton, S.E. of Norwich. From southern bypass take Watton Rd (B1108), turn left past the garden centre, thro' village, pass village inn, next left, 1st right, club 400yds right
Club Secretary: John Alton Jones, Norwich Food Co, 19 Alston Rd, Hellesden Pk, Norwich Tel: 01603 486666
Fixtures Secretary: Michael Bridgman Tel: 01603 250926
Club Colours: Gold and emerald green hoops, black shorts, green socks

LAKENHAM - HEWETT RFC
Ground Address: Hilltops, Norwich Road, Swardeston, Norwich, Norfolk Tel: 01508 578826
Brief Directions: Approach Norwich on the Southern bypass, leave on Norwich/Ipswich exit (A140), head to Norwich, turn 1st left (B1113), ground 1.25 miles on right
Club Secretary: Phil Boyce, 2 Branksome Road, Norwich. NR4 6SN Tel: (H) 01603 454208
Fixtures Secretary: Bruce Ridgeway Tel: (H) 01603 897771 (W) 01603 628333 Ext 271
Club Colours: Red

MARCH BRAZA RUFC
Ground Address: Braza Sports Pavilion, Elm Road, March, Cambridgeshire. Tel: 01354 59741
Brief Directions: Follow signs for HMP Whitemoor Sportsfield, on junction off side road to prison.
Club Secretary: Andrew Wollard, 14 Highfield Road, March. Tel: (H) 01354 653154 Tel: (W) 01354 651214
Fixtures Secretary: John Hopkins , 20 Highfield Rd., March, Cambs. Tel: 01354 660509
Club Colours: Maroon and white hoops.

STOWMARKET RUFC
Ground Address: Chilton Fields Sports Club, Chilton Way, Stowmarket, Suffolk Tel: 01449 613181
Brief Directions: From Bury St Edmonds direction along A14, take exit marked Stowmarket, 2nd exit at roundabout, left onto housing estate, follow road, last road on the right
Club Secretary: Mrs Sharon Crowe, 1 Lime Tree Place, Stowmarket. IP14 1BU
Fixtures Secretary: Mr Darryl Chapman Tel: (H) 01449 672787
Club Colours: Navy blue, white and red

THURSTON RUFC
Ground Address: Robinson Field, Ixworth Road, Thurston, Suffolk Tel: 01359 232450
Brief Directions: Exit A14 Thurston, follow Thurston signs, along Thurston Rd past Cracknells garage, under r/way bridge, head out of village (school on left), 200 yds on right
Club Secretary: Mick Thomas Tel: (H) 01284 700429
Fixtures Secretary: Bruce Workmaster Tel: (H) 01284 702693 (W) 01284 756565
Club Colours: Royal blue shirts with red collar & cuffs, blue shorts and stockings

EASTERN COUNTIES THREE SOUTH

Eastern Counties Three South 1997-98 Fixtures	Billericay	Burnham-on-C.	East London	Haverhill	Ipswich YMCA	Ongar	Ravens	Sawston	
	1	2	3	4	5	6	7	8	
1 Billericay	X	8/11	31/1	17/1	6/9	28/2	18/10	20/12	1
2 Burnham-on-Crouch	14/2	X	17/1	7/3	15/11	25/10	6/9	24/1	2
3 East London	25/10	20/9	X	15/11	14/2	24/1	7/3	6/9	3
4 Haverhill	20/9	20/12	28/2	X	24/1	10/1	8/11	25/10	4
5 Ipswich YMCA	10/1	28/2	8/11	18/10	X	20/12	31/1	17/1	5
6 Ongar	15/11	31/1	18/10	6/9	7/3	X	17/1	8/11	6
7 Ravens	24/1	10/1	20/12	14/2	25/10	20/9	X	28/2	7
8 Sawston	7/3	18/10	10/1	31/1	20/9	14/2	15/11	X	8
	1	2	3	4	5	6	7	8	

BILLERICAY RFC
Ground Address: Willowbrook Sports & Social Club, Stock Road, Billericay, Essex
Club Secretary: Neil Jarvis, Brenenden, North Road, Crays Hill, Billericay, Essex. CM11 2XD   Tel: (H) 01268 289481   (W) 0171 797 8000
Fixtures Secretary: Sean Norris   Tel: 01277 654952
Club Colours: Black with gold band, black shorts, black and gold socks

BURNHAM-ON-CROUCH RUFC
Ground Address: Dengie Hundred Sports Centre, Millfields, Station Rd, Burnham-on-Crouch, Essex. CM0 8HS   Tel: 01621 784633 (Off.)   01621 784656 (Bar)
Brief Directions: From all main routes continue east (north of River Crouch), pick up B1010 into B.-0-Crouch, right at T jcn, over rail bridge into town centre, library on right, entrance to ground immediate right
Club Secretary: Mr Warwick H Bridge, 12 Glendale Road, Burnham-on-Crouch, Essex. CM0 8LY   Tel: (H) 01621 783807
Fixtures Secretary: Mr Warwick H Bridge   Tel: (H) 01621 783807
Club Colours: Navy blue and amber hoops, navy shorts

EAST LONDON RUFC
Ground Address: Holland Road, West Ham, London. E15 3BP   Tel: 0171 476 5526
Brief Directions: From Canning Town roundabout proceed down Manor Road, turn right before West Ham tube station follow road round, right at Holland Road
Club Secretary: Ian Bessant,, 111Croydon Road, Plaistow, London E13 8EP   Tel: (H) 0171 474 3770 (W) 0171 9767213
Fixtures Secretary: Rob Williams   Tel: (H) 0181 558 8651   (W) 0181 5563322
Club Colours: Maroon and navy hoops

HAVERHILL & DISTRICT RFC
Ground Address: Castle Playing Fields, School Lane, Haverhill, Suffolk. CB9 9DE   Tel: 01440 702871
Brief Directions: Take Haverhill bypass. Junction signed Clements Estate. Take 2nd left up School Lane.
Club Secretary: Mr Ian Stewart, 7 Minster Road, Haverhill, Suffolk, CB9 0DR.   Tel: (H) 01440 706076 (W) 01279 442611
Fixtures Secretary: Gordon Anderson, 2 Arundel Walk, Haverhill, Suffolk, CB9 9BE.   Tel: 01440 763555
Club Colours: Maroon and blue checks, black shorts and socks

IPSWICH YM RUFC
Ground Address: The Street, Rushmere, Ipswich, Suffolk   Tel: 01473 713807
Brief Directions: From A14 west, exit on A1156 (Ipswich W & N), 1st exit at r'bout tow'ds town centre, under r/w bridge, left at dbl mini r'bout, over lights, left at 4th r'bout Rushmere Rd, past church, ground on rt
Club Secretary: Mr R Daniels, 85 Western Avenue, Felixstowe, Suffolk. IP11 9NT   Tel: (H) 01394 283907 (W) 01473 553149
Fixtures Secretary: Mr R Hullis   Tel: (H) 01473 625027   (W) 01473 622701
Club Colours: Maroon and amber hoops

ONGAR RFC
Ground Address: Love Lane, Ongar, Essex   Tel: 01277 363838
Brief Directions: To Ongar from Brentwood A128, turn right into town, along High St, before tube station on left turn right into Love Lane, ground 300 metres
Club Secretary: Nigel Doubleday, 105 Roundhill, Waltham Abbey, Essex. BN9 1TF   Tel: (H) 01992 768950   (W) 0802 284346
Fixtures Secretary: Peter Hodgson   Tel: (H) 01277 354404   (W) 0468 277258
Club Colours: Blue with amber band

RAVENS RFC
Ground Address: Ford Sports and Social Club, Aldborough Road South, Newbury Park, Ilford, Essex. Tel: 0181 590 3797.
Brief Directions: From North M11 then A406 (North Circular Road) to junction with A12 and Eastbound along A12 past Newbury Park Underground then right at lights. Ground on left.
Club Secretary: Gary Bishop, c/o BACB Ltd, 30 Gresham Street, London, EC2V 7LP.   Tel: 0181 788 7962
Fixtures Secretary: A C Guest, 57 Shaftsbury Road, Forest Gate, London, E7 8PD   Tel:(H) 0181 471 7571
Club Colours: Navy blue and gold hoops

SAWSTON RFC
Ground Address: Sawston Village College, New Road, Sawston, Cambs. CB2 4BP   Tel: 01223 836615
Brief Directions: M11 J10, take A505 to Sawston, next roundabout take A1301 marked Sawston/Cambridge, after 1 mile turn right to Sawston then 1st left New Road, College on left
Club Secretary: Paul Clerke, 1 Crossways, Linton, Cambridge. CB1 6NQ   Tel: (H) 01223 843985   (W) 01223 834555 Ext 3575
Fixtures Secretary: Philip Mason   Tel: (H) 01279 812545   (W) 0171 377 6161 Ext 289
Club Colours: Black, navy and white quarters

THIS DIRECTORY IS NOT FOR CLUB OFFICIALS ONLY!
Do your club supporters know they can buy their own directory and help club funds?

EASTERN COUNTIES FOUR NORTH

Eastern Counties Four North 1997-98 Fixtures	Clacton 1	Mistley 2	Norwich Union 3	RAF Lakenheath 4	Swaffham 5	Watton 6	Wisbech 7	
1 Clacton	X	10/1	8/11	20/12	24/1	28/2	11/10	1
2 Mistley	27/9	X	17/1	31/1	7/3	18/10	15/11	2
3 Norwich Union	14/2	11/10	X	10/1	25/10	20/12	24/1	3
4 RAF Lakenheath	7/3	25/10	27/9	X	15/11	17/1	14/2	4
5 Swaffham	18/10	20/12	31/1	28/2	X	8/11	10/1	5
6 Watton	15/11	24/1	7/3	11/10	14/2	X	25/10	6
7 Wisbech	17/1	28/2	18/10	8/11	27/9	31/1	X	7
	1	2	3	4	5	6	7	

CLACTON RUFC
Ground Address: Clacton Rugby Clubhouse, Recreation Ground, Valley Road, Clacton-on-Sea, Essex. CO15 4NA Tel: 01255 421602
Club Secretary: David Jaffray, 30 Craigfield Avenue, Clacton-on-Sea, Essex. CO15 4HS Tel: (H) 01255 429762 (W) 01255 678793
Fixtures Secretary: Damian Williams Tel: 01255 222823
Club Colours: Maroon jersey, navy shorts, maroon socks with white tops

RAF LAKENHEATH
Club Secretary: D Rees, c/o Rugby Club RAF Lakenheath, Mildenhall, Suffolk. Tel: (H) 01638 751552 Fax: 01638 542118
Fixtures Secretary: D Rees, as above.
Club Colours: Navy and amber quarters.

MISTLEY RFC
Ground Address: Mistley Parish Playing Fields, Furzehill, Mistley, Manningtree, Essex. CO11 2QL
Club Secretary: Mrs S Tate, Amir, Mill Lane, Bradfield, Manningtree, Essex. CO11 2UT Tel: (H) 01255 870596
Fixtures Secretary: James Tate Tel: (H) 01255 870596
Club Colours: Red and purple quarters

NORWICH UNION RFC
Ground Address: Pinebanks Sports and Leisure Club, White Farm Lane, off Harvey Lane, Norwich, Norfolk Tel: 01603 433752
Brief Directions: Approach city from S.E. A47 bypass, at end enter city towards Thorpe St Andrew, right into Pound Ln, immediate left before lights onto B1150, 1st left at r'bout Harvey, 4th left, club at end
Club Secretary: Adam Fox, 56 Cremorne Lane, Norwich, Norfolk. NR1 1YW Tel: (H) 01603 767150 (W) 01603 681303
Fixtures Secretary: Mark Howell Tel: (H) 01603 501503 (W) 01603 622200
Club Colours: Green and white quarters, white shorts, green socks

SWAFFHAM RUFC
Ground Address: North Pickenham Road, Swaffham, Norfolk Tel: 01760 724829
Brief Directions: Into town centre, at traffic lights take A47 towards E. Dereham, turn right at Gradys Hotel along North Pickenham Road, ground 400 metres on right
Club Secretary: Hugh Green, Gemini Cottage, Weasenham St Peter, Kings Lynn, Norfolk. PE32 2TD Tel: (H) 01328 838269
Fixtures Secretary: Dew Humphreys Tel: (H) 01362 692863 (W) 01760 337261 Ext 7249
Club Colours: Amber shirts, black shorts

WATTON
Ground Address: Dereham Road sports centre, Watton, Norfolk. Tel: 01953 881281
Club Secretary: Mr Mark Robert Thorpe, 11 Suffolk Road, Gaywood, Kings Lynn, Norfolk. PE30 4AH Tel: 01553 771319
Fixtures Secretary: S Blackwood, 36 Queensway, Watton, Norfolk. IP25 6BL Tel: 01953 884103 Ex 249
Club Colours: Red and black quaters

**EASTERN COUNTIES FOUR NORTH
WISBECH RUFC**
Ground Address: Chapel Road, Wisbech, Cambridgeshire. PE1 1RG Tel: 01945 463666
Brief Directions: Along South Brink, proceed to Old Market Place, turn left, ground approx 200 yards on right after garage
Club Secretary: J R C Pallant, 139 Lynn Road, Wisbech, Cambs. PE13 3DH Tel: 01945 588147/01354 622 421.
Fixtures Secretary: David Dobson Tel: (H) 01945 461223
Club Colours: Red shirts, blue shorts

EASTERN COUNTIES FOUR SOUTH

Eastern Counties Four South 1997-98 Fixtures	Dagenham	Fairbairn-C.	May & Baker	Millwall Albion	Old Brentwoods	Rayleigh	Stanford	Witham	
	1	2	3	4	5	6	7	8	
1 Dagenham	X	14/2	25/10	24/1	28/2	20/12	11/10	10/1	1
2 Fairbairn-Chigwell	8/11	X	24/1	11/10	25/10	28/2	10/1	20/12	2
3 May & Baker	31/1	18/10	X	10/1	17/1	8/11	20/12	28/2	3
4 Millwall Albion	18/10	17/1	27/9	X	20/12	31/1	28/2	8/11	4
5 Old Brentwoods	15/11	31/1	11/10	7/3	X	10/1	14/2	18/10	5
6 Rayleigh	7/3	15/11	14/2	25/10	27/9	X	24/1	11/10	6
7 Stanford	17/1	27/9	7/3	15/11	8/11	18/10	X	31/1	7
8 Witham	27/9	7/3	15/11	14/2	24/1	17/1	25/10	X	8
	1	2	3	4	5	6	7	8	

DAGENHAM RFC
Ground Address: Central Park Pavilion, Central Park, Rainham Rodd North, Dagenham, Essex. RM10 Tel: 0181 593 8302
Club Secretary: R J Moreton, 21 Central Park Avenue, Dagenham, Essex. RM10 7DA Tel: (H) 0181 984 8444
Fixtures Secretary: R J Moreton Tel: 0181 984 8444
Club Colours: Red and white quarters

FAIRBAIRN AND CHIGWELLL
Ground Address: Wanstead Flats Playing Fields, Capel Road, Forest Gate, London E11.
Club Secretary: Peter Evans, 350 Ripple Road, Barking, Essex. Tel: (H) 0181 591 8085
Fixtures Secretary: Peter Evans, as above.
Club Colours: Marron shirts and blue shorts.

MAY AND BAKER
Ground Address: Dagenham Road, Dagenham, Essex. Tel: 0181 919 3156
Club Secretary: Terry Simmons, 105 Albion Road, Dagenham Essex RM10 8DE. Tel: (H) 0181 593 2630 Tel: (W) 0181 919 2579
Fixtures Secretary: Mike Parnell, Tel: 01245 231302
Club Colours: Black with single red band.

MILLWALL ALBION
Ground Address: Mellend Stadium, Rhodeswell Road, London E14
Club Secretary: B Lancaster, 14 Reef house, Manchester Road, London E14. Tel: 0171 538 0453
Fixtures Secretary: G Batley, c/o B Lancaster as above.
Club Colours: Black and white quarters with red collars.

OLD BRENTWOODS
Ground Address: Ashwells Road, Kelvedon Hatch, Brentwood , Essex. CM15 9SE Tel: 01277 374070
Brief Directions: not found
Club Secretary: T.J. Faiers, Archdale, 1 Woodway, Shenfield, Essex. CM15 8LP. Tel: 01277 214503 (B) 0181 270 4567/4561 (F) 0181 270 4545.
Fixtures Secretary: R.Seaman, 5 The Knoll, Rayleigh, Essex. SS6 7HD. TEL: (H) 01268 774113 (B) 01268 560040.
Club Colours: Dark/Light Blue Hoops.

RAYLEIGH WYVERNS RFC
Ground Address: John Fisher Playing Fields, Little Wheatleys Chase, Rayleigh, Essex
Brief Directions: From A127 take A130 towards Chelmsford, next roundabout turn right, towards Rayleigh (A129), take 1st right Little Wheatleys Chase, ground 500 yds on right after school
Club Secretary: S J Earl, 22 The Fairway, Leigh-on-Sea, Essex. SS9 4QL Tel: (H) 01702 524111
Fixtures Secretary: M Sheppard Tel: (H) 01268 781152 (W) 0171 587 4139
Club Colours: Scarlet and emerald quarters

STANFORD LE HOPE RFC
Ground Address: Stanford Recreation Ground, Corringham Rd.,Stanford-le Hope. Tel: 01375 640957
Brief Directions: A13 to Stanford-le-Hope then turn off at A1014. Right at roundabout into Corringham Rd. First left Rainbow Lane, First Right Billet Lane. Clubhouse at far end on right.
Club Secretary: Darren Watkins, 169 London Road, Grays, Essex RM17 5YP. Tel: (H) 01375 374776
Fixtures Secretary: Kyran McDonald, Tel: (H) 01375 360801/403520
Club Colours: Red and White.

WITHAM RUFC
Ground Address: Spa Road, Witham, Essex. CM8 1UN Tel: 01376 511066
Brief Directions: Frm A12 Col'ter: Witham turn, right at 4th lights, right at end, left under rail bridge. Frm A12 Chelmsf'd: Witham turn, left at 1st lights, right at end, left under bridge. Frm B1018 B'tree: over r'bouts to centre, right at lights, right at next lights, right at end
Club Secretary: Miss Heather Turner, 48 Mulberry Gardens, Witham, Essex. CM8 2PX Tel: (H) 01376 520866 (W) 01284 768911
Fixtures Secretary: Mr Gus Downes Tel: (H) 01621 857593 (W) 01376 501818
Club Colours: Brown and white engineers stripes

LONDON THREE NORTH WEST

London Three North West 1997-98 Fixtures	Chiswick	Fullerians	Grasshoppers	Hackney	Hampstead	Haringey	Harpenden	Hertford	Kingsburians	Lensbury	Letchworth	Mill Hill	Old Gaytonians	Old Millhillians	St Albans	Tring	Uxbridge	
	1	2	3	4	5	6	7	8	9	10	11	12	13	14	15	16	17	
1 Chiswick	X	20/12	27/9	14/2			6/9		8/11	7/3		17/1				18/10		1
2 Fullerians		X	7/3	10/1	25/10		14/2		27/9	24/1					15/11	6/9		2
3 Grasshoppers			X	11/10	14/3		15/11	31/1		25/10			17/1	10/9			28/2	3
4 Hackney				X	17/1	7/3		8/11			6/9	31/1	27/9	18/10	31/1		20/12	4
5 Hampstead	10/1				X	24/1		27/9			14/2	15/11	7/3	6/9			18/10	5
6 Haringey	28/2	17/1	18/10			X		20/12	6/9			27/9	31/1			8/11		6
7 Harpenden				20/9	28/2		X	17/1				8/11	20/12	14/3			31/1	7
8 Hertford	25/10	20/9			15/11			X	14/3		10/1	11/10	24/1	14/2				8
9 Kingsburians			14/2	15/11	11/10		24/1		X	10/1					25/10	7/3	20/9	9
10 Lensbury					31/1			20/12		X	27/9		18/10	8/11	28/2		17/1	10
11 Letchworth	14/3	31/1	8/11	14/3		20/9	18/10		17/1		X	28/2				20/12		11
12 Mill Hill		8/11	6/9	24/1			7/3		18/10	11/10		X			10/1	27/9		12
13 Old Gaytonians	20/9	28/2	20/12			11/10			31/1		25/10	14/3	X			17/1		13
14 Old Millhillians	11/10	14/3			25/10				28/2		15/11	20/9	10/1	X		31/1		14
15 St Albans	24/1				20/12	14/2		18/10			7/3		6/9	27/9	X		8/11	15
16 Tring			24/1	25/10	20/9		10/1	28/2		15/11					11/10	X	14/3	16
17 Uxbridge	15/11	11/10				10/1		6/9			24/1	25/10	14/2	7/3			X	17
	1	2	3	4	5	6	7	8	9	10	11	12	13	14	15	16	17	

CHISWICK RFC (FORMERLY KNOWN AS OLD MEADONIANS)
Ground Address: Riverside Lands, Chiswick. W4   Tel: 0181 995 6956
Brief Directions: A316 to Chiswick bridge, turn left along Riverside Lands
Club Secretary: D K Samual, 39 Weavers Close, Isleworth, Middlesex TW7 6ET   Tel: (H) 0181 569 8691   (W) 0181 6004818
Fixtures Secretary: Roger Willmgale   Tel: (H) 01932 866927
Club Colours: Sky blue and maroon

FULLERIANS RFC
Ground Address: Watford Grammar School, New Field, Coningesby Drive (end of Parkside Dr), Watford, Herts   Tel: 01923 237974
Brief Directions: From A41 Hunton Bridge Roundabout (J13 M25) follow Hempstead Rd towards Watford town centre, right at lights into Langley Way, turn right at end into Coningesby Drive
Club Secretary: Chris Windsor, 5 Nascot Road, Watford, Herts WD1 3RD   Tel: (H) 01923 442355 (W) 0171 738 0455
Fixtures Secretary: J. Ayres, 20 Church Street, Quawton, Aylesbury, Bucks HP22 4AP
Club Colours: Red, green and black hooped shirts & stockings, black shorts

GRASSHOPPERS RFC
Ground Address: Macfarlane Sports Field, Macfarlane Lane, off Syon Lane, Osterley   Tel: 0181 568 0010
Brief Directions: Train: to Syon stn, lft out of stn to major Xroads, straight on across Gt Wst Rd (A4), ground 0.5 mile on right after Tescos. Road: Frm L'don on A4, rt into Syon Ln at Gillette Cnr
Club Secretary: Tom Walsh, 26 Ravenswood Gardens, Isleworth, Middlesex. TW7 4JG   Tel: (H) 0181 560 4804   (W) 0181 585 4007
Fixtures Secretary: Andy Brown   Tel: (H) 0181 560 4844   (W) 0181 560 2583
Club Colours: Green, gold and black

HACKNEY RFC
Ground Address: Spring Hill, Clapton, London. E5   Tel: 0181 806 5289
Club Secretary: David Clarke, 31 Cowley Road, Wanstead, London. E11 2HA   Tel: (H) 0181 926 2310 (W) 0181 262 5000
Fixtures Secretary: G.Noga   Tel: (H) 0181 304 2577 (W) 0181 985 2349
Club Colours: Gold, blue and green quarters

LONDON THREE NORTH WEST CONTINUED

HAMPSTEAD RFC
Ground Address: Hampstead Heath Extension, Hampstead Way, London. NW11 Tel: 0181 458 4548/0181 731 7183
Brief Directions: North End Rd (between Jack Straws & Golden Green) opposite Solders Hill Park turn into Hampstead Way, changing rooms are in middle of Heath Extension
Club Secretary: Mr S J Loffler, 14 Grey Close, London. NW11 6QG Tel: (H) 0171 458 6512 (W) 0181 759 4822
Fixtures Secretary: Mr C Scully (will change late summer 96) Tel: (H) 0181 987 9000 (W) 01426 912234
Club Colours: Maroon and gold halves separated by a white band

HARINGEY RFC
Ground Address: New River Sports Centre, White Hart Lane, Wood Green. N22 5QW
Brief Directions: By tube to Wood Green, then W3 bus to White Hart Lane. By road: New River Sports Centre is positioned towards the Wood Green end of White Hart Lane
Club Secretary: Glynne Jones, 44 Park Hall Road, East Finchley. N2 9PX Tel: (H) 0181 883 8091
Fixtures Secretary: Colin Field Tel: (H) 01707 645557
Club Colours: Green, scarlet and white

HARPENDEN RFC
Ground Address: Redbourn Lane, Harpenden, Herts. AL5 2BA Tel: 01582 460711
Brief Directions: Take B487 off A1081 (was A6) on south side of Harpenden Ground is 400 metres past entrance to Golf Club
Club Secretary: Trevor Hawkins, 27 Monks Close, Redbourne, Herts.AL3 7LY Tel: (H) 01582 793621 (W) 01256 811466 (FAX) 01256 811400
Fixtures Secretary: Michael Parker Tel: (H) 01582 713010 (W) 0181 201 5840
Club Colours: Brown and white quarters

HERTFORD RFC
Ground Address: Tel: 01920 462 975
Club Secretary: Adrian Sparks, 29 Wilton Crescent, Hertford, Herts. SG13 8JS Tel: (H) 01992 589364 (W) 01279 866101
Fixtures Secretary: David J Williams Tel: (H) 01992 586744 (W) 01279 655261 Ext 426
Club Colours: Black, royal blue and gold shirts, black shorts

KINGSBURIANS RFC
Ground Address: Northwick Park Pavilion, Northwick Park Open Space, The Fairway, North Wembley, Middlesex Tel: 0181 904 4414
Brief Directions: Frm nth: To Harrow, Watford Rd at N'wick r'bout (A404), left - Norval Rd, 1st left - Fairway. Frm S. & W.: M40/A40 - Gr'nford Rd, north - J. Lyon r'bout, left - Watford Rd
Club Secretary: Neil Keeler, 25 Lansdown Road, Stanmore, Middlesex. HA7 2RX Tel: (H) 0181 954 7211 (W) 01442 844342
Fixtures Secretary: Bruce Bland Tel: (H) 0181 868 5244 (W) 0181 204 4442
Club Colours: Black and amber hooped shirts, black shorts

LENSBURY RFC
Ground Address: Broom Road, Teddington, Middlesex. TW11 9NU Tel: 0181 977 8821
Brief Directions: By rail: Teddington Station, through High St towards river, over traffic lights into Broom Road
Club Secretary: Simon G Duffay, 229 richmond Road, Kingston U Thames, Surrey KT2 5DQ Tel: (H) 0181 549 0831 (W) 0171 521 3888
Fixtures Secretary: Ross Cardew, 11 Westfield Road, Surbiton, Surrey KT6 4EZ Tel: (H) 0181 339 9563 (W) 0181 332 3751
Club Colours: Purple, gold and black hoops

LETCHWORTH GARDEN CITY RUFC
Ground Address: Baldock Road, Letchworth, Herts Tel: 01462 682554
Brief Directions: Turn off A1 to Letchworth, turn right at A505 towards Baldock, turn right at mini roundabout. Ground situated behind North Herts Laisure Centre.
Club Secretary: I.Johal,17 Howards Wood, Letchworth, Herts. SG6 2DM Tel: (H) 01462 482658
Fixtures Secretary: R G Steele Tel: (H) 01462 676985
Club Colours: Black and amber hoops

MILL HILL RUFC
Ground Address: Mill Hill RFC, Page Street, London. NW7 2EJ Tel: 0181 203 0685
Brief Directions: Next to J2 of M1, follow signs for Barnet Copthall and club is next to school just off Page St on entrance to stadium
Club Secretary: Tom Maison, 60 Pursley Road, London. NW7 2BS Tel: (H) 0181 959 7005
Fixtures Secretary: P J Braddock Tel: (H & W) 0181 953 6500
Club Colours: Chocolate and gold hoops

OLD GAYTONIANS RFC
Ground Address: South Vale, Harrow, Middlesex HA1 3PN. Tel: 0181 423 4133
Brief Directions: A40 leaving London for Greenford fly over exit. turn right into A4127. Southvale is first turning on left after Sudbury Hill B.R.station.
Club Secretary: D A Garvey, 17 Lowlands Road, Eastcote, Pinner, Middlesex HA5 1TP. Tel: (H) 0181 866 5850
Fixtures Secretary: B A C Kennet, Tel: 0181 998 2879
Club Colours: White with thin chocolate, green and blue bands.

OLD MILLHILLIANS RFC
Ground Address: Pinner Park, Headstone Lane, Middlesex. HA2 6BR Tel: 0181 428 2281
Brief Directions: Entrance to ground 20 yds to left of Headstone Lane station, exit on opposite side, 5 minutes walk from station
Club Secretary: M Leon, Wildacre, Bushfield Road, Bovingdon, Herts. HP3 0DR Tel: (H) 01442 833665
Fixtures Secretary: P Foottit Tel: (H) 0181 906 3060 (W) 0181 367 7711
Club Colours: Chocolate and white hoops

ST ALBANS RFC
Ground Address: Boggey Mead Spring, Oaklands Lane, Smallford, St Albans, Herts. AL4 0HR Tel: 01727 869945
Club Secretary: N J Millar, 39 Watford Road, St Albans, Herts. AL1 2AE Tel: (H) 01727 830169 (W) 01582 794007
Fixtures Secretary: Gerry Thomas Tel: (H) 01727 873004
Club Colours: Royal blue and gold hoops, navy shorts

TRING RUFC
Ground Address: Pendley Sports Centre, Cow Lane, Tring, Herts Tel: 01442 825710
Brief Directions: A41, junction to Tring/Berkhamsted. Head towards Berkhamstead after 200 meters turn left into Cow Lane club at bottom of hill on right
Club Secretary: Paul Tarpey, Barnsite, Lycrome Road, Lye Green, Bucks. HP5 3LQ Tel: (H & W) 01494 771115
Fixtures Secretary: Ian Wright, 8 New Road, Northchurch, Berkhamsted, Herts Tel: (H) 01442 875983
Club Colours: Black and gold hoops

UXBRIDGE RFC
Ground Address: Uxbridge Cricket Club, Gatting Way, Park Road, Uxbridge, Middlesex. UB10 0SL Tel: 01895 237571
Club Secretary: Mr Kieran Dineen, 6 Asa Court, Old Station Road, Hayes, Middlesex. UB3 4NA Tel: (H) 0181 561 7763 (W) 0171 594 6069
Fixtures Secretary: B McPherson Tel: (H) 01895 852065
Club Colours: Black, red, white hooped shirts and socks, black shorts

The Official Rugby Union Club Directory

Did you realise the Directory is available to your club at very good discount rates.

HERTS AND MIDDLESEX ONE

Hertfordshire/Middlesex One 1997-98 Fixtures	Centaurs	Civil Service	Enfield Ignatians	HAC	Harrow	Hemel Hempstead	Hendon	Imperial Medicals	London New Zealand	London Nigerians	Old Haberdashers	Old Hamptonians	Stevenage Town	Twickenham	Upper Clapton	Wembley	
	1	2	3	4	5	6	7	8	9	10	11	12	13	14	15	16	
1 Centaurs	X	11/10	10/1		25/10		15/11		7/3			31/1		20/9			1
2 Civil Service		X		27/9				14/3	8/11	17/1	24/1	18/10		20/12		14/2	2
3 Enfield Ignatians		20/9	X	20/12	11/10		25/10		31/1			17/1		7/3			3
4 HAC	17/1			X		31/1		15/11			11/10		20/9		7/3	25/10	4
5 Harrow		31/1		18/10	X			27/9	20/12		8/11		17/1		14/3		5
6 Hemel Hempstead	14/2	25/10	24/1	15/11		X	10/1		20/9	14/3			11/10				6
7 Hendon		7/3		20/9	8/11		X	18/10		17/1			20/12	31/1			7
8 Imperial Medicals	20/12		8/11			17/1		X			20/9			7/3	31/1	11/10	8
9 London New Zealand				14/2				24/1	X	27/9	15/11	14/3	25/10		11/10	10/1	9
10 London Nigerians	24/1		15/11	10/1	7/3		11/10	25/10		X						20/9	10
11 Old Haberdashers	18/10		27/9		14/2	8/11		14/3		31/1	X		17/1	20/12			11
12 Old Hamptonians			24/1		7/3		10/1			14/2	25/10	X	11/10	20/9	15/11		12
13 Stevenage Town	27/9	10/1	14/3		24/1	18/10	14/2			20/12			X	8/11			13
14 Twickenham				14/3				14/2	18/10	8/11	10/1	27/9	15/11	X		24/1	14
15 Upper Clapton	14/3	15/11	14/2		10/1	27/9	24/1			18/10			25/10		X		15
16 Wembley	8/11		18/10			20/12	27/9				7/3		31/1	17/1		X	16
	1	2	3	4	5	6	7	8	9	10	11	12	13	14	15	16	17

CENTAURS RFC
Ground Address: Gower Road, Syon Lane, Osterley, Middlesex. TW7 5PY Tel: 0181 560 4500
Brief Directions: A4 to Gilette Corner, take Syon Lane, north past Tescos, Gower Road is next right
Club Secretary: M W Root, 116 Uxbridge Rd, Hatch End, Middlesex. HA5 4DS Tel: (H & W) 0181 421 5988
Fixtures Secretary: Jerry Goldie Tel: (H) 0181 568 7240 (W) 0181 891 4886
Club Colours: Light blue and dark blue quarters

CIVIL SERVICE FC (RU)
Ground Address: Dukes Meadows, Riverside Drive, Chiswick. W4 Tel: 0181 994 1202
Club Secretary: N G Alway, 20 Herndon Road, London. SW18 2DG Tel: (H) 0181 8706818 (W) 0171 583 5333
Fixtures Secretary: R Hulme Tel: (H) 01438 832 054 (W) 0171 270 5821
Club Colours: White shirts

ENFIELD IGNATIANS RFC
Ground Address: Queen Elisabeth Stadium, Donkey Lane, Enfield, Middlesex Tel: 0187 363 2877
Brief Directions: M25 J25 south on A10 to Carterhatch Lane, follow signs
Club Secretary: Glyn Jones, 45 Halifax Rd, Enfield, Middx Tel: (H) 0181 366 3207 (W) 0181 967 9474
Fixtures Secretary: Pete Tiernan Tel: 0181 529 8130
Club Colours: Blue and gold

HONOURABLE ARTILLERY COMPANY RFC
Ground Address: Armoury House, City Road, London. EC1Y 2BQ Tel: 0171 606 4644
Brief Directions: Metropolitan/Northern & Circle lines to Moorgate station, go north, past Finsbury Square on City Road, entrance to Artillery ground 200m on left
Fixtures Secretary: Colin Pritchard, 31 Bedford Avenue, Little Chalfont, Buckinghamshire. HP6 6PS Tel: (H) 01494 76 2982 (W) 0171 439 1791
Club Colours: Broad dark blue and red hoops

HARROW RFC
Ground Address: Grove Field, Wood Lane, Stanmore, Middlesex. HA7 4LF. Tel: 0181 954 2615
Brief Directions: Nearest tube station is Stanmore (Jubilee line). 142 bus up Stanmore Hill, alight at `Vine' PH. Ground is 5 mins walk along Wood Lane.
Club Secretary: Andrew Olie, 14 Stanmore Road, Watford. WD2 5ET. Tel: (H) 01923 242738
Fixtures Secretary: Peter Pope, 16 Kenilworth Drive, Croxley Green, Watford. WD3 3NW. Tel: 01925 241504
Club Colours: Navy blue with white hoops

HEMEL HEMPSTEAD (CAMELOT) RFC
Ground Address: Club House, Chaulden Lane, Hemel Hempstead, Herts Tel: 01442 230353
Brief Directions: A41 to Berkhamstead, right at Hemel Station roundabout, left at next roundabout into Northridge Way, Chaulden Lane 300 yards on left
Club Secretary: John Clapham, 49 Brook Court, Watling Street, Radlett. WD7 7JA Tel: 01923 542104
Fixtures Secretary: Mrs D Gooding Te 01442 255891
Club Colours: Royal Blue and white hoops

HENDON RFC
Ground Address: Copthall Playing Fields, Great North Way, Hendon. NW4   Tel: 0181 203 1737
Brief Directions: From north - M1 J2, ground 200 yards on left behind garage. Elsewhere - follow signs to Barnet Copthall stadium. Half mile south on A1 of junction(five ways corner) with A41.
Club Secretary: T Brownsell, 9 Winscombe Way, Stanmore, Middlesex. HA7 3AX   Tel: (H) 0181 954 7060
Fixtures Secretary: C Silver   Tel: (H) 0181 954 9641
Club Colours: Bottle green, white, black unequal horizontal stripes

IMPERIAL MEDICAL
Ground Address: St Mary's Hospital Athletic Ground, Udney Park Road, Teddington, Middlesex
Brief Directions: Teddington Station (SW Network). Exit to (East, Garden Centre) Station Road. Turn right and then take the third left.
Club Secretary: Ral Young FRCS, West Middlesex Hospital, Twickenham Road, Isleworth. TW7 6AF   Tel: (H) 0181 891 0638   (W) 0181 565 5768
Fixtures Secretary: Professor P S Sever, Dept. Clinical Pharmacology, St Mary's Hospital, Praed St. , Paddington, London. W2 1NY.   Tel: (W) 0171 725 1117
Club Colours: Blue, white, green & red.

LONDON NEW ZEALAND RFC
Ground Address: c/o Osterley Sports & Social Club, Tentelow Lane, Osterley, Middlesex   Tel: 0181 574 3774
Club Secretary: Tudor Davies, 46 Lamorna Grove, Stanmore, Middlesex. HA7 1PQ   Tel: (H) 0181 952 6822   (W) 0171 723 0022
Fixtures Secretary: Richard Peacock   Tel: (H) 0181 952 6822   (W) 0171 723 0022
Club Colours: All black

LONDON NIGERIAN RFC
Ground Address: Copthall Playing Fields, Great North Way, Hendon, London. NW4   Tel: 0181 203 1737
Brief Directions: Frm Hendon Cntral: Watford Way north at Page St turn, cross to sthbnd lane, take lft fork (to Gt Nth Way), ground 500yds by NorthWays Tyres. Frm north: M1 J2, ground 200 yds
Club Secretary: John Orchard, 43 Portland Place, London. W1N AG   Tel: (H) 0831 304 126   (W) 0171 636 9386
Fixtures Secretary: Babs Kehinde   Tel: (H) 0171 366 7036
Club Colours: Green and white quarters

OLD HABERDASHERS
Ground Address: Old Haberdashers' Sports Ground, Croxdale Road, Theobald Street, Boreham Wood, Hertfordshire WD6 4PY.   Tel: 0181 9531987
Club Secretary: M S Baker, Rookwood, Hedsor Road, Bourne End, Bucks, SL8 5EE.   Tel: 0181 5876399
Fixtures Secretary: A Gray.   Tel: 01494 778127
Club Colours: Blue, white and magenta.

OLD HAMPTONIANS RFC
Ground Address: The Pavilion, Dean Road, Hampton, Middlesex. TW12 1AQ   Tel: 0181 979 2784
Brief Directions: Leave A316 (London to M3) at signs for A316 Hampton proceed on Uxbridge Road for half mile. R. into Hanworth Road pass 3 schools on R. before turning R into Dean Road
Club Secretary: Bob Hudson, 50 Rydens Rd, Walton-on-Thames, Surrey, KT12 3DL.   Tel: 01932 880173
Fixtures Secretary: Peter Dendy, 62 Myrtle Road, Hampton Hill, Middlesex, TW12 1QO.   Tel: 0181 941 4416
Club Colours: Gold, silver and black hoops

STEVENAGE TOWN RFC
Ground Address: North Road, Stevenage, Herts. SG1 4BB   Tel: 01438 359788
Brief Directions: Take A1M Stevenage North Jcn 7, take road towards Graveley, 1st right (past garden centre) towards St'age, ground 400yds on right, parking on access road by pitches
Club Secretary: Richard Stephens, 18 Russell Close, Stevenage, Herts. SG2 8PB   Tel: (H) 01438 351971 (answerphone)   (W) 01438 355751
Fixtures Secretary: Fred McCarthy   Tel: (H) 01438 811590
Club Colours: Black shirts with green hoop, black shorts, green socks

TWICKENHAM RFC
Ground Address: Park Fields, South Road, Hampton, Middlesex   Tel: 0181 979 2427
Brief Directions: A316 to Unigate Dairy, take road to Hampton, turn right into Oak Ave, South Rd on right by Royal Oak public house
Club Secretary: J. N. Francis, 50 Hatherop Road, Hampton, Middlesex, TW12 2RF.   Tel: (H) 0181 9410877 (W) 0181 5808094
Fixtures Secretary: Tony Kaye   Tel: (H & W) 0181 898 7210
Club Colours: Red and black hoops

UPPER CLAPTON FOOTBALL CLUB
Ground Address: Upland Road, Thornwood Common, Epping, Essex. CM16 6NL   Tel: 01992 572588
Brief Directions: M11 north, jct 7.Follow signs to B1393 to Epping. Upland Rd. on right after 500yds after Rooky Garage.
Club Secretary: Kevin Hewitt-Devine, 10 Cedar Court, Epping, Essex. CM16 4HL   Tel: 0171 278 7706
Fixtures Secretary: David Miller   Tel: (H) 01279 724849   (W) 0860 427651
Club Colours: Red and white hoops.

WEMBLEY RFC
Ground Address: Roger Bannisters Playing Fields, Uxbridge Road, Harrow Weald, Middlesex   Tel: 0181 420 1789
Brief Directions: From Harrow on Hill take Harrow View to roundabout, ground on right. From Watford take Oxley Lane, ground on left
Club Secretary: J. Williams, 111 Eastcote Road, Pinner, Middlesex HA5 1ET   Tel: (H & Fax) 0181 868 2892
Fixtures Secretary: Chris Green   Tel: (H) 0181 537 9544
Club Colours: Maroon and amber quarters

HERTS AND MIDDLESEX TWO

Hertfordshire/ Middlesex Two 1997-98 Fixtures	1 Bank of England	2 Barclays Bank	3 Datchworth	4 Feltham	5 Hitchin	6 London Exiles	7 London French	8 Old Abbotstonians	9 Old Actonians	10 Roxeth Manor OB	11 Sudbury Court	12 UCS Old Boys	13 Watford	
1 Bank of England	X	20/12	14/2			25/10		11/10	17/1	20/9				1
2 Barclays Bank		X			8/11	7/3	18/10	31/1		10/1			27/9	2
3 Datchworth		25/10	X		31/1	11/10		20/9	20/12	7/3				3
4 Feltham	27/9	17/1	14/3	X		20/12		25/10	14/2					4
5 Hitchin	7/3			20/9	X		17/1				11/10	25/10	20/12	5
6 London Exiles					18/10	X	27/9	10/1		8/11		14/2	14/3	6
7 London French	31/1		10/1	7/3			X				20/9	11/10	25/10	7
8 Old Abbotstonians					27/9		14/3	X		18/10	20/12	17/1	14/2	8
9 Old Actonians		11/10			10/1	20/9	8/11	7/3	X	31/1				9
10 Roxeth Manor OB				11/10	14/3		14/2			X	25/10	20/12	17/1	10
11 Sudbury Court	18/10	14/2	27/9	8/11		17/1			14/3		X			11
12 UCS Old Boys	8/11	14/3	18/10	10/1					27/9		31/1	X		12
13 Watford	10/1		8/11	31/1					18/10		7/3	20/9	X	13
	1	2	3	4	5	6	7	8	9	10	11	12	13	

BANK OF ENGLAND RFC
Ground Address: Priory Lane, Roehampton, London. SW15 5JQ Tel: 0181 876 8417
Brief Directions: A205 (Upper Richmond Rd) towards Richmond, past junction with Roehampton Lane and Rocks Lane then left into Priory Lane
Club Secretary: Mike Anderson, 4 Charles Street, Barnes, London, SW13 0NZ Tel: (H) 0181 781341 (W) 0171 4919600
Fixtures Secretary: Mike Anderson
Club Colours: Old gold, blue and white hoops

BARCLAYS BANK RFC
Ground Address: Park View Road, Ealing, London. W5 2JF Tel: 0181 998 4904
Brief Directions: Piccadilly Line to North Ealing Station, Central Line to Ealing Broadway. By car to Hanger Lane, turn into Woodville Gardens and then into Park View Road
Club Secretary: S C Payne, 36 Glenfield Road, Banstead, Surrey SM7 2DG Tel: (H) 0181 898 4107 (W) 0171 699 3732
Fixtures Secretary: D M Bevan-Jones Tel: (H) 0181 898 4107 (W) 0171 699 3732
Club Colours: Maroon jersey with silver edged gold band

DATCHWORTH RFC
Ground Address: Datchworth Green, Datchworth, Herts. SG3 6TL Tel: 01438 812490
Brief Directions: Leave A1(M) at J6 (Welwyn) on B197 north towards Stevenage, at Woolmer Green turn right towards Datchworth, pitches and clubhouse behind tennis courts
Club Secretary: Mrs L D Wyatt, 7 Hazeldell, Watton-at-Stone, Hertford. SG14 3SL Tel: (H) 01920 830407
Fixtures Secretary: (Pre-season) Mr P Nightingale Tel: (H) 01438 820500 (During season) Mr T Johnson Tel: (H) 01438 814460
Club Colours: Green shirts and socks, black shorts

FELTHAM RFC
Ground Address: Park Road, Hanworth, Middlesex Tel: 0181 894 3609
Brief Directions: Hanworth Rd (located by the air park)
Club Secretary: S C Griffiths, 27 Fosse Way, Ealing, London. W13 0BZ Tel: (H) 0181 997 6153 (W) 0181 861 1313
Fixtures Secretary: W.Orrell, 52 Ormond Drive, Hampton, TW12 2TN Tel: 0181-941 2877
Club Colours: Dark blue, light blue and gold

HITCHIN RFC
Ground Address: King George V Recreation Ground, Old Hale Way, Hitchin, Herts Tel: 01462 432679
Brief Directions: At Angel Reply pub turn into Bearton Road, take 2nd left into Old Hale Way, turn into ground by phone box
Club Secretary: G Morgan, 209 Cambridge Road, Hitchin, Herts. SG4 0JP Tel: (H) 01462 431781 (W) 01582 27315
Fixtures Secretary: G Morgan Tel: (H) 01462 431781 (W) 01582 27315
Club Colours: Maroon shirts, white shorts

LONDON EXILES RUFC
Ground Address: Barn Elms Sports Centre, Queen Elizabeth Walk, Barnes, London. SW13 0DG
Brief Directions: South over Hammersmith Bridge, down Castelnau Rd to join with Rocks Ln at lights, take sharp left next to Red Lion pub into Queen E'beth Walk, ground at end of road
Club Secretary: Tim Edghill, 586 Gosberton Road, London. SW12 8LF Tel: (H) 0181 673 2628 (W) 0171 413 1313
Fixtures Secretary: Tim Edghill Tel: (H) 0181 673 2628 (W) 0171 413 1313
Club Colours: Claret, white and navy hoops, white shorts, claret, white and navy socks

LONDON FRENCH RFC
Ground Address: Barn Elms, Rocks Lane, Barnes, London. SW20
Club Secretary: Jeremy O'Dwyer, 117 Sugden Road, London. SW11 5ED Tel: (H) 0171 223 2274 (W) 0171 814 2166
Fixtures Secretary: Chris Hutton Tel: (H) 0181 287 9892 (W) 0181 490 1538
Club Colours: French blue shirt, white shorts, red socks

OLD ABBOTSTONIANS RFC
Ground Address: Pole Hill Open Spaces, Raeburn Road, Hayes, Middlesex Tel: 0181 845 1452
Brief Directions: A40 exit for Hillingdon Long Lane towards Uxbridge Rd, left at BP station, left into Pole Hill Rd (Midland Bank at corner),round bend, 1st left after bus stop, club at end
Club Secretary: Mr Denis Halloran, 8 Swallow Drive, Northolt, Middlesex. UB5 6UH Tel: (H) 0181 842 2154 (W) 0171 707 2203
Fixtures Secretary: Mr Mark Nettleton Tel: (H) 01895 440714
Club Colours: Blue and red

OLD ACTONIANS RFC
Ground Address: Gunnersbury Drive (off Paper Lane), London. W5 Tel: 0181 567 4556
Brief Directions: Coming west from Acton Town tube station, cross North Circular Rd, take 1st right (opposite Gunnersbury Park main entrance), ground 50yds on left of G'sbury Drive
Club Secretary: Peter Mullen, 77 Warwick Road, Ealing, London. W55 Q6 Tel: (H) 0181 840 9235 (W) 0171 962 3426
Fixtures Secretary: Tom Lepsky Tel: (H) 0181 993 2616 (W) 0171 229 2404
Club Colours: Royal blue, white hoops, red collar

ROXETH MANOR OLD BOYS RFC
Ground Address: Queensmead School, Queens Walk off Victoria Road, Ruislip, Middlesex Tel: 0181 845 6010
Club Secretary: Mr D Peacham, 26 Yeading Avenue, Harrow, Middlesex. HA2 9RN Tel: (H) 0181 868 1799
Fixtures Secretary: Mr P Noot Tel: (H) 01753 888775
Club Colours: Black

SUDBURY COURT RFC
Ground Address: East Lane Pavilion, East Lane, North Wembley, Middlesex Tel: 0181 904 8485
Brief Directions: By road: at junction of Watford Road and East Lane turn into East Lane, ground 400 yards on right. By train: To North Wembley station turn left ground 600yds on left.
Club Secretary: Derek Gray, 33 Northwick Park Road, Harrow, Middlesex. HA1 2NY Tel: (H) 0181 427 4155
Fixtures Secretary: David Keeling, 17 Nunnery Lane, Luton, Bed. Tel: 01582 652417
Club Colours: Red and white on dark blue shirts, navy shorts, red socks with white tops

UCS OLD BOYS RFC
Ground Address: Farm Avenue, London. NW2 Tel: 0181 452 4337
Club Secretary: Paul Gee, 63 Blackhorse Lane, South Mimms, Herts. EN6 3PS Tel: (H) 01707 662 748 (W) 0402 803961
Fixtures Secretary: Frank Butterworth Tel: (H) 0181 2033369 (W)01189 734003
Club Colours: Maroon, black and white

WATFORD RFC
Ground Address: Knutsford Playing Fields, Radlett Road, Watford, Herts Tel: 01923 243292
Brief Directions: From A41 (M1 J5) take Watford/ town centre link road, right at 1st roundabout, over bridge, car park on left, ground on right.
Club Secretary: Steve Kiely, 30 Sheepcot Lane, Watford. WD2 6DH. Tel: (H) 01923 680914
Fixtures Secretary: Liam Dalmon, 10 Derwent Road, Leverstock Green. Tel: (H) 01442 219350
Club Colours: Red, white and blue hoops

THIS DIRECTORY IS NOT FOR CLUB OFFICIALS ONLY!
Do your club supporters know they can buy their own directory and help club funds?

HERTS AND MIDDLESEX THREE

Hertfordshire/ Middlesex Three 1997-98 Fixtures	Hammersmith & F	Millfield Old Boys	Northolt	Old Ashmoleans	Old Grammarians	Old Isleworthians	Old Standfordians	Pinner & Gramarians	Royston	St Nicholas Old Boys	Southgate	
	1	2	3	4	5	6	7	8	9	10	11	
1 Hammersmith & Fulham	X	31/1	27/9	18/10	8/11			14/3				1
2 Millfield Old Boys		X				27/9	14/3	18/10		8/11	17/1	2
3 Northolt	11/10		X					17/1	25/10	14/2	20/9	3
4 Old Ashmoleans		25/10	31/1	X					20/12	20/9	11/10	4
5 Old Grammarians		20/12	14/3	27/9	X				31/1		25/10	5
6 Old Isleworthians	20/9		8/11	17/1	14/2	X	11/10					6
7 Old Standfordians	14/2		18/10	8/11	17/1		X		27/9			7
8 Pinner & Gramarians	11/10			14/2	20/9	20/12	25/10	X				8
9 Royston		20/9				18/10		8/11	X	17/1	14/2	9
10 St Nicholas Old Boys	25/10				11/10	31/1	20/12	14/3		X		10
11 Southgate	20/12					14/3	31/1	27/9		18/10	X	11
	1	2	3	4	5	6	7	8	9	10	11	

HAMMERSMITH & FULHAM RFC
Ground Address: Hurlingham Park, Hurlingham Road, London. SW6   Tel: 0171 736 5186
Brief Directions: From Putney Bridge (southside) turn right into New Kings Rd (A308) and right again under rail bridge into Hurlingham Rd, Hurlingham Park is 300m on right
Club Secretary: Chris Cuthbertson, 17 Wheatsheaf Lane, London. SW6 6LS Tel: (H) 0171 381 5064
Fixtures Secretary: Lyndon Walters   Tel: (H) 0171 790 1233   (W) 0171 962 8047
Club Colours: Red with navy and white bands

MILLFIELD OLD BOYS RFC
Ground Address: Harrow RFC, Wood Lane, Stanmore, Middlesex Tel: 0181 954 2615
Club Secretary: Angela Lesly, Westmill Fisheries, PO Box 24, Ware, Herts. SG12 0YN Tel: (H) 01920 486534
Fixtures Secretary: Alan Burns Tel: (H) 01920 486534
Club Colours: Red, green and blue hoops

NORTHOLT RFC
Ground Address: Cayton Green Park, Cayton Road, Greenford, Middlesex. UB6 8BJ Tel: 0181 813 1701
Brief Directions: A40 Western Av to Greenford (Bridge Htl jcn/A4127 G'ford Rd), go as if to join A40 to London but stay lft & join slip parallel with A40 (R'mede Gdns), to end, left into Cayton Rd, ground at end
Club Secretary: Chris Haynes, 12 Montcalm Close, Hays, Middlesex Tel: (H) 0181 841 3546
Fixtures Secretary: Geoff Payne Tel: (H) 0181 845 0874
Club Colours: Sky and navy blue hoops

OLD ASHMOLEAN RFC
Ground Address: Ashmole School, Burleigh Gardens, Southgate, London. N14
Brief Directions: At Southgate underground station roundabout, turn into Ashfield Parade, bear right into Burleigh Gardens, school entrance 250 metres on left
Club Secretary: Mr G Bull, 60 Ladysmith Road, Enfield, Middlesex. EN1 3AA Tel: (H) 0181 363 5991 (W) 0973 347235
Fixtures Secretary: Mr S Stamp Tel: (H) 0181 364 3212   (W) 0171 494 2785
Club Colours: Scarlet and emerald hoops, black shorts

OLD GRAMMARIANS RFC
Ground Address: The Sports Field, Corner of Worlds End Lane/Green Dragon Lane, Enfield.
Brief Directions: M25 J24 (Potters Bar), A1005 towards Enfield, after about 3 miles right down Slades Hill, 4th left into Bincote Rd to Worlds End Ln, L turn to Green Dragon Ln entrance 80yds on left.
Club Secretary: Brian Calderwood, 17 Birch Crescent, Aylesford, Kent. ME20 7QE Tel: (H) 01622 718350 (W) 01622 710811
Fixtures Secretary: Mike Holt, 60 Chandos Road, East Finchley, London. Tel: (H) 0181 883 4016
Club Colours: Navy, red and light blue band

OLD ISLEWORTHIANS RFC
Ground Address: Memorial Ground, Wood Lane, Isleworth, Middlesex Tel: 0181 560 7949
Brief Directions: A4 (Great West Road) or London Road to Isleworth
Club Secretary: Huw Davies, 230 Whitton Dene, Isleworth, Middlesex. TW7 7LU   Tel: (H) 0181 898 5924   (W) 0171 528 1995
Fixtures Secretary: Steve Rac   Tel: (H) 0181 898 8982 (W) 01734 442333
Club Colours: Blue jersey with a horizontal red band and grey stripe

OLD STANDFORDIANS RFC
Ground Address: Old Kents Lane, Standon, Herts
Brief Directions: At the junction between A10/A120 at Puckeridge, take A120 towards Bishops Stortford, pitch on right after 0.5 mile opposite Heron public house
Club Secretary: Ted Modoy, 522 Hatfield Road, St Albans, Herts   Tel: (H) 01727 834413
Fixtures Secretary: Adrian Watson   Tel: (H) 01763 271139
Club Colours: Black with pink hoop

PINNER & GRAMMARIANS RFC
Ground Address: Shaftesbury Playing Fields, Grimsdyke Road, Hatchend Pinner, Middlesex   Tel: 0181 428 3136
Brief Directions: By rail: Hatchford (NSG & B'loo), west A410 Uxbrge Rd to Hatch End B'way Shps, rt G'sdyke Rd, 2nd rt H'view, 1st lt C'burn Ave, club lt. Road: frm E. same, frm W. A410 Uxbrg Rd, lt G'dyke Rd
Club Secretary: David Hiles, 31 Lulworth Close, South Harrow, Middlesex. HA2 9NR   Tel: (H & Fax) 0181 864 0787
Fixtures Secretary: Mick Hawgood   Tel: (H) 0181 845 5901 (W) 0181 424 2001
Club Colours: Navy and 1" scarlet hoops

ROYSTON RUFC
Ground Address: Heath Sports Club, Baldock Road, Royston. SG8   Tel: 01763 243613
Brief Directions: A10 north or south to roundabout by cinema, turn west through town centre, past golf club on left, A505 from Baldock turn right at Little Chef, club on right
Club Secretary: Miss Jo Buck, Caylers Farm, Nuthampstead. SG8 8NA   Tel: (H) 01763 848249
Fixtures Secretary: Godfrey Everett   Tel: 01763 243846
Club Colours: Black and white hoops, black shorts, black socks

SOUTHGATE RFC
Ground Address: Nortel Ltd, Oakleigh Road South, New Southgate, London. N11 1HB   Tel: 0181 945 2655/2181
Brief Directions: A406 frm E., exit for Arnos Grove, pass Arnos Grve stn to r'bout, 2nd exit for Oakl'gh Rd Sth. A406 frm W., left for New Southgate stn, right at Turrets pub, 1st exit r'bout for Oakl'gh Rd Sth
Club Secretary: David Hockey, 5 The Vineries, Enfield, Middlesex. EN1 3DQ   Tel: (H) 0181 342 0202   (W) 0171 270 3874
Fixtures Secretary: Simon Shuttler   Tel: (H) 0181 368 5025   (W) 0181 446 8324
Club Colours: Dark blue, light blue and gold irregular hoops

ST NICHOLAS OLD BOYS RFC
Ground Address: c/o Ickenham Cricket Club, Oak Avenue, Ickenham, Middlesex   Tel: 01895 639366
Brief Directions: From Hillingdon turn off A40, follow signs to Ickenham and Ruislip, turn left after 2nd petrol station into Oak Avenue
Club Secretary: Mr M J Lafford, 44 Haydon Drive, Eastcote, Pinner, Middlesex   Tel: (H) 0181 868 1321 (W) 0181 756 2647
Fixtures Secretary: S Telfer   Tel: (H) 01895 624199 (W) 0181 246 9771
Club Colours: Red shirts, white shorts

HERTS AND MIDDLESEX FOUR NORTH

Hertfordshire/ Middlesex Four North 1997-98 Fixtures	Belsize Park	Cuffley	Hatfield	Kilburn Cosmos	Kodak	Old Streetonians	Old Tottonians	QE II Hospital	
	1	2	3	4	5	6	7	8	
1 Belsize Park	X	8/11	31/1	14/3					1
2 Cuffley		X			14/3	25/10	31/1	17/1	2
3 Hatfield		14/2	X		25/10	17/1		11/10	3
4 Kilburn Cosmos		11/10	8/11	X		14/2		31/1	4
5 Kodak	14/2			17/1	X		11/10		5
6 Old Streetonians	11/10			31/1	X	8/11	14/3		6
7 Old Tottonians	17/1		14/3	25/10			X		7
8 QE II Hospital	25/10				8/11		14/2	X	8
	1	2	3	4	5	6	7	8	

BELSIZE PARK RFC
Ground Address: c/o Hendon RFC, Copthall Stadium, Hendon, Middlesex
Brief Directions: As for Hendon RFC
Club Secretary: Sebastian Colquhoun, 9 Regency Lawn, Croftdown Road. NW5 1HF   Tel: (H) 0171 485 5767   (W) 0171 355 0219
Fixtures Secretary: Hugh Reeve-Tucker   Tel: (H) 0181 874 5907   (W) 0171 234 4822
Club Colours: Lavender and black

CUFFLEY RFC
Ground Address: Cheshunt School, College Road, Cheshunt, Herts. EN7 9LY
Brief Directions: Approx 2 miles north of J25 on M25 on the A10, turn left by 1st set of traffic lights, school 50 yards on left opposite Crocodile public house
Club Secretary: C A Palmer, 10 Connaught Road, Harpenden, Herts. AL5 4HF   Tel: (H) 01582 768152 (W) 0171 895 1515
Fixtures Secretary: P Cushing   Tel: (H) 01455 5557568   (W) 01582 470605
Club Colours: Red with black hoop

HATFIELD RFC
Ground Address: Roe Hill Hall, Briars Lane, Hatfield, Hertfordshire   Tel: 01707 269814
Brief Directions: A1(M) J3, A1001 towards Galleria shopping centre, 1st r'bout 3rd exit crossing motorway, next roundabout left into Cavendish Way, right at next roundabout into Briars Lane, club at top of hill
Club Secretary: Ian Cranforth, 15 Little Thistle, Welwyn Garden City, Herts. Tel: 01707 334258
Fixtures Secretary: Mr G Waddingham   Tel: (H) 01707 663659   (W) 01707 666013
Club Colours: Green, white, brown and gold

KODAK RFC
Ground Address: Kodak Sports Ground, Harrow View, Harrow, Middlesex. HA1 4TY   Tel: 0181 427 2642
Brief Directions: Ground is 1.5 miles north of Harrow-on-Hill (A4008)
Club Secretary: Mr B J Haynes, 139 Queenswalk, Ruislip, Middlesex. HA4 0NW   Tel: (H) 0181 841 4545 (W) 0181 559 9555
Fixtures Secretary: Mr B J Haynes   Tel: (H) 0181 841 4545   (W) 0181 559 9555
Club Colours: Gold and green

OLD STREETONIANS
Ground Address: Hackney Marshes, Homerton Road, London E9.   Tel: 0181 985 8206
Club Secretary: D Stringer, Unit 1, Victoria Wharf, Palmers Road, London E2.   Tel: (H) 0181 858 8837 Tel: (W) 0181 983 0460
Fixtures Secretary: Chris Rummage, Tel: (H) 0171 359 1739   Tel: (W) 0171 778 3289
Club Colours: Red and royal blue quarters.

OLD TOTTONIANS RFC
Ground Address: Churchfields Playing Fields, Great Cambridge Road/Harrow Drive, Edmonton, London. N9 Tel: 0181 364 3099
Club Secretary: Trevor De La Salle, 55 Welsummer Way, Le Motte Chase, Cheshunt, Herts. EN8 0UG   Tel: (H) 01992 638492   (W) 01494 444811
Fixtures Secretary: John Cockrill   Tel: (H) 01707 872507   (W) 0171 421 2039
Club Colours: Blue and amber hooped shirts, blue shorts

QUEEN ELIZABETH II RFC
Ground Address: Hatfield Hyde Sports Club, King George V Playing Fields, Beehive Lane, Welwyn Garden City, Hertfordshire. Al7 4BP   Tel: 01707 326700
Brief Directions: From A1 take WGC exit, follow signs to QE II Hospital, when in the road "Howlands" turn into Beehive Lane, turn left past Beehive public house
Club Secretary: Steve Murray, 73 Howicks Green, Welwyn Garden City, Hertfordshire. AL7 4RJ   Tel: (H) 01707 887324
Fixtures Secretary: Peter Kelly   Tel: (H) 01707 338897
Club Colours: Myrtle green and amber

Do you know a rugby enthusiast with a birthday coming up?

This directory would make a perfect present.

So why not buy a copy from your club or from W H Smith.

HERTS AND MIDDLESEX FOUR SOUTH

Hertfordshire/ Middlesex Four South 1997-98 Fixtures	British Airways	GWR	Hayes	Meadhurst	Orleans FP	Osterley	Quintin	Thamesians	
	1	2	3	4	5	6	7	8	
1 British Airways	X	11/10				8/11	14/2	31/1	1
2 GWR		X	31/1		14/3		25/10	17/1	2
3 Hayes	25/10		X	17/1		14/3			3
4 Meadhurst	14/3	8/11		X		31/1			4
5 Orleans FP	17/1		11/10	14/2	X				5
6 Osterley		14/2			25/10	X	17/1	11/10	6
7 Quintin			8/11	11/10	31/1		X	14/3	7
8 Thamesians				14/2	25/10	8/11		X	8
	1	2	3	4	5	6	7	8	

BRITISH AIRWAYS RFC
Ground Address: Concorde Centre, Crane Lodge Road, Craneford, Middlesex   Tel: 0181 562 0291
Brief Directions: M4 Junction 3, Follow signs to A312 to Feltham.Follow dual carriageway and left at lights,then right at mini roundabout.
Club Secretary: Andrew Lord, 37 Thames Close, Thame Street, Hampton, Middlesex   Tel: (H) 0181 941 1525   (W) 0141 848 4773   (M) 0370 574754
Fixtures Secretary: Pete Attard   Tel: (W) 0956 511460 (M) 0956 511460
Club Colours: Red, white & blue quarters, white shorts

GREAT WESTERN RAILWAY RFC
Ground Address: G. W. Railway (London) RFC, Castle Bar Park, Vallis Way, West Ealing W13.   Tel: 0181 998 7928
Brief Directions: By train to Ealing Broadway, then to Castle Bar Park Halt via E1, E2 or E9 buses.
Club Secretary: Peter Allsop, 41 Lyncroft Avenue, Pinner, Middlesex HA5 1JU.   Tel: (H) 0181 866 0532
Fixtures Secretary: Roy Sullivan, Tel: (H) 0181 575 6074
Club Colours: Cardinal and black jerseys.

HAYES RFC
Ground Address: Grosvenor Playing Fields, Kingshill Avenue, Hayes, Middlesex   Tel: 0181 845 4963
Brief Directions: From A40, off at "Target" roundabout head south, at next roundabout (White Hart) take Yeading Lane, at 1st major set of lights turn right into Kingshill Ave, ground is 1 mile on right
Club Secretary: Gary Peacock, 13 Ivy Cottages, Uxbridge Road, Hillingdon. UB10 09J   Tel: (H) 01895 232079   (W) 0956 937883
Fixtures Secretary: Alun Davies   Tel: (H) 0181 248 7640   (W) 0956 304909
Club Colours: Navy blue and yellow quarters

MEADHURST
Ground Address: Meadhurst Sports and Social Club, Chertsey Road, Sunbury on Thames, Middlesex TW16 7LN.   Tel: 01932 763500
Club Secretary: Brian Messenger, BP Chemicals Limited, Poplar House, Chertsey Road, Sunbury on Thames, Middlesex TW16 7LL.   Tel: (H) 01784 464548 Tel: (W) 01932 774054
Fixtures Secretary: Keith Wills, Tel: (H) 0181 840 0297   Tel: (W) 0181 965 6031
Club Colours: Green and Gold.

ORLEANS F.P. RFC
Ground Address: Orleans Park, off Richmond Road, Twickenham   Tel: 0181 892 5743
Brief Directions: Off Richmond Road, between Crown pub and Orleans Park School
Club Secretary: Steve Frost, 13 Langham Place, Chiswick, London. W4 2QL   Tel: (H) 0181 747 5026 (W) 0181 943 5331
Fixtures Secretary: Graham Todd   Tel: 0181 898 4982
Club Colours: Gold, maroon and white

OSTERLEY RFC
Ground Address: Tentelow Lane, Norwood Green, Southall, Middlesex   Tel: 0181 574 3774
Brief Directions: From A4 Great West Road: north from Gilette Corner up Windmill Lane
Club Secretary: Richard Evans, 111 Rowlands Avenue, Pinner, Middlesex. HA5 4AW   Tel: (H) 0181 428 5797
Fixtures Secretary: John Green   Tel: 0181 568 5557
Club Colours: Black and white hoops

QUINTIN RFC
Ground Address: Hartington Road, Chiswick, London. W4   Tel: 0181 994 0467
Brief Directions: Go north from Chiswick Bridge 1st L. Hartington Rd (Pitches on L.) continue turn 1st R. Cavendish Rd for entry to Pavilion on right side of road.
Club Secretary: Nigel Smith, 4 Australia Avenue, Maidenhead, Berks. SL6 7DJ   Tel: (H) 01628 75899 (W) 01494 488493
Fixtures Secretary: Colin Smith   Tel: 0181 337 9631
Club Colours: Red and green hoops, blue shorts

THAMESIANS RFC
Ground Address: Ricmond upon Thames College, Egerton Road, Twickenham, Middlesex. TW2 7SJ   Tel: 0181 894 3110
Brief Directions: Entrance to ground is in Egerton Road off Chertsey Road (A316) and adjacent to Harlequin FC Ground
Club Secretary: E J Burrows, 133 Cranleigh Road, Lower Feltham, Middlesex. TW13 4QA   Tel: (H & W) 0181 890 7162
Fixtures Secretary: David Munday   Tel: (H) 0181 979 9265   (W) 0181 547 3300
Club Colours: Maroon and green

LONDON & SOUTH EAST DIVISION FINAL LEAGUE TABLES 1996-97

EASTERN COUNTIES FOUR

	P	W	D	L	F	A	PTS
March	9	9	0	0	343	67	18
Burnham on Crouch	9	8	0	1	345	101	16
Haverhill	9	6	0	3	143	107	12
Ongar	9	5	0	4	209	185	10
Sawston	9	5	0	4	132	128	10
Stanford	9	4	0	5	162	185	8
Brightlingsea	9	3	0	6	168	184	6
Norwich Union	9	3	0	6	96	267	6
Witham	9	2	0	7	184	261	*2
Clacton	9	0	0	9	53	350	0

EASTERN COUNTIES FIVE

	P	W	D	L	F	A	PTS
Millwall Albion	8	7	0	1	282	84	14
Swaffham	8	6	0	2	196	145	12
May & Baker	8	5	1	2	264	110	11
Rayleigh	8	5	1	2	141	142	11
Fairbairn-Chigwell	8	5	0	3	120	100	10
Dagenham	8	3	1	4	173	138	*5
Mistley	8	1	1	6	172	305	3
RAF Lakenheath	7	1	0	6	161	169	2
Orwell	7	0	0	7	62	378	0

HAMPSHIRE ONE

	P	W	D	L	F	A	PTS
Esso	12	11	0	1	285	152	22
Southampton	12	10	0	2	503	179	20
Farnborough	12	11	0	1	399	99	*20
US Portsmouth	12	9	0	3	367	163	18
Millbrook	12	9	0	3	362	176	18
Andover	12	6	0	6	358	186	12
Isle of Wight	12	5	0	7	221	311	10
Eastleigh	12	4	0	8	126	292	8
Guernsey	12	4	0	8	246	445	8
Petersfield	12	3	0	9	306	313	6
Tottonians	12	3	0	9	262	272	6
Ventnor	12	3	0	9	187	467	6
Fordingbridge	12	0	0	12	57	624	*-4

HAMPSHIRE TWO

	P	W	D	L	F	A	PTS
Overton	14	11	1	2	473	132	23
New Milton	14	11	1	2	442	203	*21
Trojans	14	10	0	4	381	176	20
Romsey	14	8	3	3	294	236	19
Sandown & Shanklin	14	6	1	7	268	287	*11
Fareham Heathens	14	5	0	9	262	397	10
Nomads	14	2	0	12	105	400	4
Alresford	14	0	0	14	103	497	*-2

HAMPSHIRE THREE

	P	W	D	L	F	A	PTS
Southampton Inst	12	11	1	0	555	146	23
AC Delco	12	9	0	3	380	174	18
Hamble	12	8	0	4	335	134	16
Waterlooville	12	7	0	5	320	224	14
Fleet	11	3	1	7	191	279	7
Ellingham	11	1	0	10	86	563	2
Kingsclere	12	1	0	11	92	439	*0

HERTS/MIDDS ONE

	P	W	D	L	F	A	PTS
Harpenden	12	11	0	1	388	128	22
St Albans	12	9	0	3	374	181	18
Old Meadonians	12	9	0	3	271	156	18
Tring	12	8	0	4	267	199	16
Old Elizabethans	12	9	0	3	233	193	*16
Hackney	12	6	0	6	282	233	12
Uxbridge	12	6	0	6	204	159	12
Mill Hill	12	6	0	6	202	235	12
Hemel Hempstead	12	6	0	6	254	173	*8
St Mary's Hospital	12	4	0	8	264	272	8
Old Hamptonians	12	2	0	10	199	312	4
Hendon	12	2	0	10	136	335	4
Centaurs	12	0	0	12	122	620	*-2

HERTS/MIDDS TWO

	P	W	D	L	F	A	PTS
Harrow	12	12	0	0	394	130	24
Upper Clapton	12	9	1	2	265	159	19
Twickenham	12	9	0	3	287	172	18
Wembley	12	8	0	4	258	181	16
Old Paulines	12	7	1	4	212	233	15
H.A.C.	12	6	0	6	270	282	12
London New Zeal	12	4	2	6	168	216	10
Enfield Ignatians	12	4	1	7	230	227	9
Civil Service	12	4	1	7	170	183	9
Old Haberdashers	12	3	3	6	170	218	9
Stevenage Town	12	1	3	8	159	259	5
Datchworth	12	2	1	9	133	274	5
Old Actonians	12	2	1	9	118	300	5

HERTS/MIDDS THREE

	P	W	D	L	F	A	PTS
London Nigerians	11	11	0	0	595	163	22
U.C.S. Old Boys	11	9	1	1	330	132	19
Old Abbotstonians	11	9	1	1	313	119	19
Hitchin	11	6	0	5	212	224	12
London French	11	5	0	6	244	307	10
London Exiles	11	5	0	6	171	265	10
Roxeth Manor OB	11	4	0	7	117	236	8
Barclays Bank	11	5	0	6	264	218	*6
Antlers	11	4	0	7	218	277	*6
Bank of England	11	3	0	8	209	334	6
Watford	11	3	0	8	113	318	6
Sudbury Court	11	1	0	10	99	292	2

HERTS/MIDDS FOUR

	P	W	D	L	F	A	PTS
Feltham	11	11	0	0	397	109	22
London Cornish	11	10	0	1	372	119	*18
Old Ashmoleans	11	7	0	4	299	308	14
Royston	11	6	1	4	175	125	13
Hammersmith & Ful	11	7	0	4	277	113	*10
Southgate	10	5	0	5	162	188	10
Old Islworthians	11	4	1	6	182	194	9
Old Grammarians	11	4	0	7	201	230	8
Old Stanfordians	11	4	1	6	155	214	*7
Pinner & Gramm	11	1	0	10	82	276	2
Hayes	11	0	0	11	50	568	*-2
Royal Hospital	10	4	1	5	296	204	*-11

KENT TWO

	P	W	D	L	F	A	PTS
Folkstone	12	11	0	1	527	123	22
Whitstable	12	9	1	2	254	86	19
Snowdown CW	12	8	0	4	202	142	16
Deal	12	7	1	4	269	191	15
Nat West Bank	12	7	1	4	250	186	15
Sittingbourne	12	6	2	4	220	120	14
Lordswood	12	7	1	4	241	185	*13
Tonbridge	12	6	0	6	319	196	12
Aylesford	12	3	2	7	97	239	8
Old Gravesendians	12	4	0	8	185	350	8
Old Williamsonians	12	3	0	9	158	302	6
Old Elthamians	12	3	0	9	147	304	6
Greenwich	12	0	0	12	70	515	*-4

HERTS/MIDDS 5N

	P	W	D	L	F	A	PTS
Millfield Old Boys	6	6	0	0	222	93	12
St Nicholas Old Boys	6	5	0	1	225	46	10
Cuffley	6	4	0	2	117	140	8
Old Tottonians	6	2	0	4	129	134	4
Old Streetonians	6	2	0	4	122	153	*2
QE II Hospital	6	1	0	5	54	168	2
Hatfield	6	1	0	5	36	171	2

KENT THREE

	P	W	D	L	F	A	PTS
Midland Bank	9	9	0	0	332	105	*16
New Ash Green	9	7	0	2	200	79	14
Bexley	9	6	0	3	171	128	12
Vigo	9	5	0	4	181	118	10
Edenbridge	9	4	1	4	122	130	9
STC Footscray	9	2	1	6	94	225	5
Citizens	9	3	0	6	81	137	*4
Orpington	9	2	0	7	114	227	4
Old Olavians	9	2	0	7	78	205	4
Canterbury Exiles	9	4	0	5	161	180	*-22

HERTS/MIDDS 5S

	P	W	D	L	F	A	PTS
Northolt	5	5	0	0	311	6	10
G.W.R.	7	5	0	2	136	105	10
Quintin	7	3	2	2	92	106	8
Orleans FP	7	3	1	3	106	148	7
British Airways	7	4	0	3	58	111	*6
Osterley	6	1	1	4	46	202	3
Meadhurst	6	1	1	4	73	115	*1
Middlesex Hospital	5	0	1	4	64	93	*-7

KENT FOUR

	P	W	D	L	F	A	PTS
Darenth Valley	8	6	0	2	225	91	12
Greenwich	8	6	0	2	173	94	12
Faversham	8	6	0	2	146	53	*10
Meopham	8	2	0	6	59	183	4
Westerham	8	0	0	8	75	257	0

KENT ONE

	P	W	D	L	F	A	PTS
Cranbrook	11	10	1	0	277	153	21
Medway	11	9	0	2	198	111	18
Sheppey	11	7	1	3	306	229	15
Old Dunstonians	11	7	0	4	302	216	14
Gillingham Anchorian	11	7	1	3	263	154	*13
Dartfordians	11	6	0	5	214	229	12
Betteshanger	11	5	1	5	258	164	11
Old Shootershillians	11	4	1	6	178	253	9
Ashford	11	4	0	7	139	175	8
Bromley	11	2	0	9	130	294	4
Met Pol Hayes	11	1	1	9	131	288	3
Dover	11	1	0	10	190	320	2

SURREY ONE

	P	W	D	L	F	A	PTS
Old Reedonians	12	10	0	2	418	138	20
Effingham	12	9	0	3	265	113	18
University Vandals	12	9	0	3	294	195	18
Cranleigh	12	9	1	2	234	132	*17
Chobham	12	7	0	5	282	219	14
Chipstead	12	7	0	5	236	207	*12
Woking	12	6	0	6	231	203	12
Old Caterhamians	12	4	0	8	209	248	8
Old Cranleighans	12	4	0	8	166	262	8
KCS Old Boys	12	4	0	8	185	319	8
Battersea Ironsides	12	3	0	9	152	300	6
John Fisher Old Boys	12	2	1	9	127	275	5
Kingston	12	3	0	9	139	327	*4

SURREY TWO

	P	W	D	L	F	A	PTS
Raynes Park	12	12	0	0	440	109	24
Wandsworthians	12	9	1	2	323	160	19
Farnham	12	9	0	3	335	159	18
Merton	12	8	1	3	227	154	17
Old Rutlishians	12	6	2	4	290	221	14
Old Haileyburians	12	6	1	5	336	216	13
London Media	12	6	0	6	319	291	12
Cobham	12	5	0	7	257	227	10
Old Tiffinians	12	4	0	8	219	301	8
Law Society	12	4	0	8	225	439	8
Shirley Wanderers	12	3	1	8	197	225	7
Old Freemans	12	3	0	9	162	399	6
Old Suttonians	12	0	0	12	107	536	0

SUSSEX ONE

	P	W	D	L	F	A	PTS
Heathfield & Waldron	12	12	0	0	428	102	24
Uckfield	12	10	0	2	401	117	20
East Grinstead	12	9	0	3	409	113	18
Crawley	12	8	1	3	357	151	17
Eastbourne	12	8	1	3	289	132	17
Hove	12	7	0	5	242	173	14
Ditchling	12	7	0	5	194	245	14
Hastings & Bexhill	12	3	2	7	256	254	8
Crowborough	12	3	1	8	168	254	7
Old Brightonians	12	3	1	8	158	438	7
Seaford	12	3	0	9	215	298	*4
Pulborough	12	2	0	10	110	392	4
Burgess Hill	12	0	0	12	121	679	0

SURREY THREE

	P	W	D	L	F	A	PTS
Old Wellingtonian	10	9	0	1	316	75	18
Reigate & Redhill	10	8	1	1	282	133	17
Mitcham	10	7	0	3	167	94	*12
Kings Coll Hosp	10	6	0	4	230	183	12
Lightwater	10	5	1	4	199	155	11
Croydon	10	5	0	5	125	230	10
Worth Old Boys	10	4	0	6	222	202	8
London Fire Brigade	10	3	0	7	166	236	6
Old Bevonians	10	2	0	8	151	275	4
Egham	10	2	0	8	110	334	4
BEC Old Boys	10	3	0	7	136	187	*2

SUSSEX TWO

	P	W	D	L	F	A	PTS
BA Wingspan	12	10	1	1	297	78	21
Sun Alliance Horsham	12	9	0	3	223	103	18
Newick	12	8	1	3	174	99	17
St Francis	11	5	0	6	215	112	10
Hellingly	12	5	0	7	187	222	10
Sussex Police	11	3	0	8	101	232	6
Plumpton	12	0	0	12	57	408	0

SURREY FOUR

	P	W	D	L	F	A	PTS
Haslemere	7	6	0	1	212	101	12
Old Johnians	7	6	0	1	139	87	*10
St Georges Hospital	7	4	0	3	124	15	8
Racal Decca	7	4	0	3	92	144	8
Surrey University	7	3	0	4	136	138	6
Economicals	7	3	0	4	85	104	6
Surrey Police	7	1	0	6	103	156	2
Oxted	7	1	0	6	41	187	2

SUSSEX THREE

	P	W	D	L	F	A	PTS
Shoreham	10	10	0	0	292	51	20
Rye	10	5	2	3	143	113	12
Midhurst	10	5	1	4	130	179	11
Robertsbridge	10	4	0	6	189	145	8
Barns Green	10	2	1	7	132	203	5
Arun	10	2	0	8	89	284	4

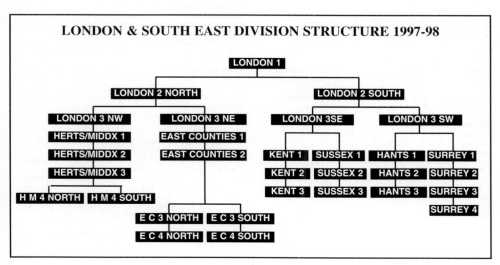

LONDON & SOUTH EAST DIVISION STRUCTURE 1997-98

LONDON TWO SOUTH

London Two South 1997-98 Fixtures	Beckenham	Brockleians	Dorking	Gravesend	Haywards Heath	Horsham	Lewes	Old Blues	Old Guildfordians	Old Juddian	Old Reigatian	Old Wimbledonians	Sevenoaks	Streatham & Croydon	Warlingham	Westcombe Park	Winchester	
	1	2	3	4	5	6	7	8	9	10	11	12	13	14	15	16	17	
1 Beckenham	X			20/12		17/1	27/7	18/10			6/9		31/1		28/2	8/11		1
2 Brockleians	10/1	X				11/10			6/9	14/2		24/1	25/10	7/3	15/11			2
3 Dorking	24/1	18/10	X					27/9		7/3		14/2	15/11	6/9	10/1			3
4 Gravesend		20/9	11/10	X	25/10		24/1	14/2			10/1				7/3	15/11		4
5 Haywards Heath	14/2	8/11	20/12		X			18/10	6/9			7/3		27/9	24/1			5
6 Horsham			25/10	27/9	15/11	X	14/2	7/3			24/1				6/9	11/10		6
7 Lewes		31/1	28/2		14/3		X		17/1	8/11	11/10			20/12		20/9		7
8 Old Blues		28/2	14/3		20/9	15/11		X	31/1		25/10		17/1			11/10		8
9 Old Guildfordians	15/11			14/3		20/9			X	24/1		10/1	11/10	14/2	25/10			9
10 Old Juddian	11/10			31/1		28/2		20/12		X		25/10	14/3		20/9	17/1		10
11 Old Reigatian		17/1	31/1		28/2				20/12	18/10	X	27/9		8/11			14/3	11
12 Old Wimbledonians	20/9			17/1		31/1		18/10	8/11			X	28/2		14/3	20/12		12
13 Sevenoaks				18/10	10/1	8/11	7/3	6/9			14/2		X			27/9	24/1	13
14 Streatham & Croydon	25/10			28/2		14/3				10/1		15/11	20/9	X	11/10	31/1		14
15 Warlingham				8/11		20/12	6/9	27/9			7/3		17/1		X	18/10	14/2	15
16 Westcombe Park		14/3	20/9		11/10		10/1	24/1	28/2		18/11					X	25/10	16
17 Winchester	7/3	20/12	17/1		31/1				8/11	27/9		6/9		18/10			X	17
	1	2	3	4	5	6	7	8	9	10	11	12	13	14	15	16	17	

BECKENHAM RFC
Ground Address: Balmoral Avenue, Elmers End, Beckenham, Kent. BR3 3RD   Tel: 0181 650 7176
Brief Directions: Entrance in Balmoral Ave which runs between Eden Park Ave & Upper Elmers End Rd (A214). From bottom of Beckenham High St take Croydon Rd (A222), left into Eden Pk
Club Secretary: Mr M L Parker, c/o H & V Controls Ltd, Orchard Business Centre 2, Kangley Bridge Road, Sydenham. SE26 5AQ   Tel: (W) 0181 776 7272
Fixtures Secretary: Mr J M Arger   Tel: 01580 891550
Club Colours: Royal blue and old gold hoops

BROCKLEIANS RFC
Ground Address: Eltham Palace Road, Eltham, London. SE9 5LX   Tel: 0181 8508650
Brief Directions: A20 to junction with South Circular, turn into Eltham Palace Road at World of Leather.
Club Secretary: Gordon Robertson, New Lodge, 37 Holbrook Lane, Chislehurst, Kent. BR7 6PE   Tel: (H) 0181 467 1997
Fixtures Secretary: George Wright   Tel: (H) 01622 738396
Club Colours: Chocolate, emerald and old gold

DORKING RFC
Ground Address: The Pavilion, The Big Field, Brockham, Betchworth, Surrey. RH3 7LZ   Tel: 01737 843928
Brief Directions: From Dorking take A25 to Reigate after 2miles turn right towards Brockham, then first left into Kiln Lane
Club Secretary: Mr Mark Gardner, 30 The Borough, Brockham, Betchworth, Surrey. RH3 7NB   Tel: (H) 0173 784 4258   (W) 01372 378 788
Fixtures Secretary: Mr Philip Parrot, 15 Rothes Rd., Dorking, Surrey. RH4 1LG   Tel: 01306 877103
Club Colours: Red and white

GRAVESEND RFC
Ground Address: The Rectory Field, Milton Road, Gravesend, Kent. DA12 2PP
Brief Directions: M25 A2 intersection, head towards Dover, leave A2 at Gravesend East (Valley Drive), follow 1.75 mile to end, right at roundabout, 1st left, ground 0.75 miles on left
Club Secretary: John Moore, 375A Singlewell Road, Gravesend, Kent. DA11 7RL   Tel: (H) 01474 362998
Fixtures Secretary: Bobby Wright   Tel: (H) 01474 327303
Club Colours: Four inch black and white hoops

LONDON TWO SOUTH CONTINUED

HAYWARDS HEATH RFC
Ground Address: Whitemans Green, Cuckfield, Haywards Heath, West Sussex   Tel: 01444 413950
Brief Directions: On B2114 about 0.5 mile west of Cuckfield
Club Secretary: M K Cook, Tinkers, Summerhill Lane, Haywards Heath, West Sussex. RH16 1RL   Tel: (H) 01444 452327   (W) 0171 753 1972
Fixtures Secretary: I Beckett   Tel: (H) 01444 412576   (W) 01737 224828
Club Colours: Red and black quarters, black shorts

HORSHAM RUFC
Ground Address: Coolhurst Ground, Hammer Pond Road, Horsham, West Sussex. RH13 6PJ   Tel: 01403 265027
Brief Directions: Leave Horsham town centre on A281 (Brighton), past garden centre on right, left into Magpie Lane, right into Hammer Pond Road
Club Secretary: Peter Robbins, 4 Holming End, Horsham RH12 4UW   Tel: (H) 01403 270715   (W) 01483 862019
Fixtures Secretary: Nick Brown, 21 Crawley Rd., Horsham, RH12 4DS   Tel: (H) 01403 250892   (W) 01403 234449
Club Colours: Emerald green shirts and white shorts

LEWES RFC
Ground Address: Stanley Turner Ground, Kingston Road, Lewes, East Sussex   Tel: 01273 473732
Brief Directions: From railway station take road to Newhaven, passing Swan Inn on right, cross bypass bridge and entrance is on the left
Club Secretary: A J Page, 13 Greater Paddock, Ringmer, Lewes, East Sussex. BN8 5LH   Tel: (H) 01273 813419
Fixtures Secretary: S Rhodes   Tel: (H) 01323 492245
Club Colours: Blue and white hoops

OLD BLUES RFC
Ground Address: Dornan Fields, Arthur Road, Motspur Park, Nr New Malden, Surrey   Tel: 0181 336 2566
Brief Directions: From London A3, along Kingston bypass, take sliproad signed Worcester Pk & Cheam, 1st left after pillarbox into Motspur Pk, over levelcrossing into W. Barnes Ln, 2nd right
Club Secretary: Giles Simons, 66B Gowrie Rd, London, SW11 5NR. Tel: (H) 0171 2070010 (W) 0171 6282441
Fixtures Secretary: Alistair Burns, 47 Becmead Avenue, London, SW16 0UJ. Tel: (H) 0181 7697045 (B) 0171 5011344
Club Colours: French Navy, cardinal & old gold

OLD GUILDFORDIANS RFC
Ground Address: Stoke Park, London Road, Guildford, Surrey   Tel: 01483 300752
Brief Directions: A3 turn off to Burpham, follow signs for Guildford town centre, Stoke Park on right after large roundabout, club house at northern end of Stoke Park
Club Secretary: David Bedford, 23 Brodie Road, Guildford, Surrey. GU1 3KZ   Tel: 01483 502023   (W) 0171 240 0074
Fixtures Secretary: Terry Maguire   Tel: (H) 01483 36514   (W) 0181 788 4351
Club Colours: Green with red & white hoops, green shorts

OLD JUDDIANS RFC
Ground Address: Tonbridge Sports Ground, The Slade, Tonbridge, Kent. TN9 1HR   Tel: 01732 358548
Brief Directions: From Tonbridge High St turn into Castle St signed Swimming Pool, bear right, left, then right again through bend, next right into The Slade, fork right at end into car park
Club Secretary: Steve Davey, 35 Dowgate Close, Tonbridge, Kent. TN9 2EH   Tel: (H) 01732 357429 (W) 01732 866066
Fixtures Secretary: Tony Russell   Tel: 01732 355582
Club Colours: Claret & light blue hoops, navy blue shorts

Haywards Heath London 2 South.
Promoted as Champions from London 3 South East.

OLD REIGATIAN RFC
Ground Address: Park Lane, Reigate, Surrey RH2 9DL. Tel: 01737 245634
Brief Directions: Park La on A25 Reigate ³/₄ mile on RHS
Club Secretary: D Forsyth, 2 high Street, Redhill, Surrey RH1 1RA.   Tel: (H) 01883 743654   Tel: (W) 01737 646089
Fixtures Secretary: D Payton, Tel: (H) 01737 221129   Tel: (W) 0171 488 8049
Club Colours: Green and blue hoops.

OLD WIMBLEDONIANS RFC
Ground Address: 104, Cottenham Park Road, London. SW20 0TZ   Tel: 0181 879 0700
Club Secretary: Mrs Margaret Parsons, Hawth, Glaziers Lane, Normandy, Guildford, Surrey. GU3 2EA   Tel: (H) 01483 811103   (W) 0171 257 1827
Fixtures Secretary: Mr Des Hawken   Tel & Fax: (H) 0181 643 2833
Club Colours: Green, maroon and gold

SEVENOAKS RUFC
Ground Address: Knole Paddock, Plymouth Drive, Sevenoaks, Kent. TN13 3RP   Tel: 01732 452027
Brief Directions: A225 to Sevenoaks railway station, 1st left St Botolpus Rd, turn right at top, 50 yds take a double left, 1st right Plymouth Drive
Club Secretary: John Maslin, 198 Chesterfield Drive, Sevenoaks, Kent. TN13 2EH Tel: (H) 01732 460910 (W) 0171 5281888
Fixtures Secretary: Howard Pearl   Tel: (H) 01732 763431   (W) 0171 240 7171
Club Colours: Blue and yellow hoops

STREATHAM-CROYDON RUFC
Ground Address: Rosevale, 159 Brigstock Road, Thornton Heath, Surrey. CR7 7JP   Tel: 0181 684 1502
Brief Directions: A23 turn off at Thornton Heath Pond, 1st left is Brigstock Road, club 400 yards on right
Club Secretary: Ian Stevenson, 18 Crown Woods Way, Eltham, London. SE9 2NN   Tel: (H) 0181 850 9061
Fixtures Secretary: R V Towers   Tel: (H) 0181 658 2333   (W) 0181 698 8911
Club Colours: Maroon shirts, white shorts

WARLINGHAM RFC
Ground Address: Limpsfield Road, Hamsey Green, Warlingham, Surrey. CR6 9RB   Tel: 01883 62 2825
Brief Directions: Frm A235 Sth Croydon, B269 - Hamsey Green, on leaving H. Green ground on rt after H.G. Gardens. Frm M25 J6, A22 4 miles, rt on B270, 1st lft, right at T jcn, ground on right
Club Secretary: Peter Wrightson, 2 Markville Gardens, Caterham, Surrey CR3 6RJ
Fixtures Secretary: Paul Fettes   Tel: (H) 0181 657 7628
Club Colours: Royal blue and white hoops, navy shorts

WESTCOMBE PARK RFC
Ground Address: Goddington Dene, Goddington Lane, Orpington, Kent. BR6 9SH   Tel: 01689 834902
Brief Directions: From M25 or A20, take A224 to Orpington, Goddington Ln is off A224 opposite parade of shops and garage, on left towards Sevenoaks or on right from M25
Club Secretary: Robin Taylor, 24 Pinchbeck Road, Green Street Green, Orpington, Kent. BR6 6DR   Tel: (H) 01689 855052   (W) 0181 319 7768
Fixtures Secretary: John Bellinger   Tel: (H) 0181 850 7280   (W) 0171 481 5507
Club Colours: Navy with white hoops

WINCHESTER RFC
Ground Address: St Bartholomew Playing Field, North Walls Park, Nuns Road, Winchester. SO23 7EF   Tel: 01962 867021
Brief Directions: Take J7 off M3 and on to A33. After approx. 12 mright to Kingsworthy. Approx. 1m left into Russell Rd. WRFC directly in front of you.
Club Secretary: Phil Davies, Kings School House, Sarum Road, Winchester, Hampshire. SO22 5HA   Tel: (H) 01962 852059
Fixtures Secretary: James Jermain   Tel: (H) 01962 620230
Club Colours: Amber and Black

Sevenoaks R.F.C.
Promoted from London 3 South East.

LONDON THREE SOUTH EAST

London Three South East 1997-98 Fixtures	Beccehamians	Bognor	Brighton	Canterbury	Chichester	Cranbrook	Crawley	East Grinstead	Heathfield & Waldron	Maidstone	Medway	Park House	Sheppey	Sidcup	Tunbridge Wells	Uchfield	Worthing	
	1	2	3	4	5	6	7	8	9	10	11	12	13	14	15	16	17	
1 Beccehamians	X		15/11	14/3		20/9	10/1	11/10					25/10	14/2		24/1		1
2 Bognor	20/12	X		17/1		27/9			28/2		14/3			8/11		18/10	31/1	2
3 Brighton		6/9	X	20/12		17/1		31/1		18/10		27/9	28/2		8/11			3
4 Canterbury		10/1		X	20/9				25/10	14/2	15/11	24/1		7/3		11/10		4
5 Chichester	6/9		10/1		X	11/10	24/1	25/10					15/11	7/3		14/2		5
6 Cranbrook		24/1		27/9		X			15/11	7/3	10/1	14/2		6/9		25/10		6
7 Crawley			20/9	17/1		31/1	X	28/2			8/11		18/10	14/3	20/12			7
8 East Grinstead		14/2		18/10		8/11		X	10/1	6/9	24/1	7/3			27/9			8
9 Heathfield & Waldron	18/10		14/2		8/11		7/3		X				24/1	27/9		6/9	20/12	9
10 Maidstone	31/1	25/10		28/2				20/9		X	11/10	15/11		17/1			14/3	10
11 Medway	8/11		7/3	20/12		6/9			31/1		X		18/10			27/9	17/1	11
12 Park House	17/1	11/10			31/1				14/3		20/9	X		20/12		8/11	28/2	12
13 Sheppey		7/3		8/11		20/12		17/1		27/9	14/2	6/9	X		18/10			13
14 Sidcup			25/10	28/2		14/3	15/11	20/9					11/10	X	31/1	10/1		14
15 Tunbridge Wells	28/2	15/11		14/3					11/10	24/1	25/10	10/1			X		20/9	15
16 Uchfield			11/10	31/1		28/2	25/10	14/3		20/12			20/9		17/1	X		16
17 Worthing	27/9		24/1	18/10		14/2	15/11						10/1	6/9		7/3	X	17
	1	2	3	4	5	6	7	8	9	10	11	12	13	14	15	16	17	

BECCEHAMIAN RFC
Ground Address: Sparrows Den, Corkscrew Hill, West Wickham, Kent   Tel: 0181 777 8105
Brief Directions: Corner of Corkscrew Hill and Addington Road (A2022)
Club Secretary: Alan Pitt, 3 Kent Road, West Wickham, Kent   Tel: (H) 0181 289 6629   (W) 01923 817537
Fixtures Secretary: C Putmer   Tel: (H) 0181 777 6307
Club Colours: Maroon, black and silver hoops

BOGNOR RFC
Ground Address: The Clubhouse, Hampshire Avenue, Bognor Regis, West Sussex. PO21 5JY   Tel: 01243 824000
Brief Directions: Proceed along main A259 Bognor to Chichester road, turn south into Hampshire Avenue, ground is 100mtrs on left
Club Secretary: Steve Emmett, Chimneys, Bilsham Road, Yapton-Arundel, West Sussex. BN18 0JU   Tel: (H) 01243 554022   (W) 01903 884667
Fixtures Secretary: Dean Dewey   Tel: (H) 01243 266185
Club Colours: Purple, green and white hoops, black shorts, green socks

BRIGHTON FOOTBALL CLUB (RFU)
Ground Address: Waterhall Playing Fields, Waterhall Road, Brighton, East Sussex. BN1 8YR   Tel: 01273 562729
Brief Directions: From London A23 to Patcham roundabout, round roundabout, turn into Hill Rd, underneath Railway arch, 1st right, under road arch, 1st left, straight up to clubhouse
Club Secretary: Miss Colette Duggan, 42 Woodland Drive, Hove, Sussex. BN3 6DL   Tel: (H) 01273 500440 (W) 01903 524157
Fixtures Secretary: R Greenwood   Tel: (H) 01273 502898
Club Colours: Royal Blue shirts, dark blue shorts and red socks

CANTERBURY RFC
Ground Address: Merton Lane (North), Nackington Road, Canterbury, Kent   Tel: 01227 768958
Brief Directions: Exit A2 for Canterbury, at 4th roundabout take 3rd exit, proceed over traffic lights, turn right after cricket ground on B2068, 9-10 miles turn right to ground
Club Secretary: T D O Hall Esq, Whiteacre Farmhouse, Whiteacre Lane, Waltham, Canterbury. CT4 5SR   Tel: (H) 01227 700344   (W) 01227 768155
Fixtures Secretary: Dennis Creed   Tel: (H) 01227 750747   (W) 01227 766161
Club Colours: Black and amber

CHICHESTER RFC
Ground Address: Oaklands Park, Wellington Road, Chichester, West Sussex Tel: 01243 779820
Club Secretary: Simon Hill, St Ronans, 8 Clayton Ave, Selbey, West Sussex. PO20 4OB   Tel: (H) 01243 602598   (W) 01243 781000
Fixtures Secretary: Mike French   Tel: (H) 01705 482383   (W) 01243 787641
Club Colours: Dark blue and light blue hoops

CRANBROOK RFC
Ground Address: Tomlin Ground, Angley Road, Cranbrook, Kent. TN17 3LB   Tel: 01580 712777
Brief Directions: Off A229 Hastings road, 14 miles south of Maidstone, 4 miles north of Hawkhurst at junction of Cranbrook bypass with Whitewell Lane
Club Secretary: David Davies, Beeches, Station Road, Staplehurst, Kent. TN12 0QG Tel: (H) 01580 891448 (W) 01580 891448
Fixtures Secretary: Alan Shorter, 2 Thornden Cottages, Rolvenden Layne, Cranbrook. TN17 4PS Tel: (H) 01580 241409 (W) 01580 890095
Club Colours: Magenta and white

CRAWLEY RFC
Ground Address: Willoughby Fields, 1 Field Avenue, Cranley   Tel: 01293 533995
Brief Directions: Off A23 Crawley bypass from north take M23 J10 onto A23 bypass, 1.5 miles pass Sainsburys, right at next roundabout into Field Ave towards Charlwood, ground approx 0,75 mile on right
Club Secretary: Ray Lloyd, 105 Gales Drive, Three Bridges, Crawley. RH10 1QD   Tel: (H) 01293 536664 (W) 0171 865 5723
Fixtures Secretary: Dave Haime   Tel: (W) 01293 410648
Club Colours: Maroon and blue

EAST GRINSTEAD RFC
Ground Address: Saint Hill Green, East Grinstead, West Sussex. RH19 4JU   Tel: 01342 322338
Brief Directions: On Minor Road to Horsted Keynes off B2110 Turners Hill Road
Club Secretary: Mrs Carol Chandler, Rushbrook, Little Frenches Farm, Snowhill, Copthorne, Surrey. RH10 3EG Tel: (H) 01342 834648
Fixtures Secretary: R P Russell   Tel: (H) 01342 834648
Club Colours: Blue shirts with broad white hoop

HEATHFIELD & WALDRON RFC
Ground Address: Hardy Roberts Recreation Ground, Cross in Hand, Heathfield, East Sussex   Tel: 01435 868747
Brief Directions: Adjacent to Cross in Hand public house in centre of village opposite Esso garage
Club Secretary: Peter R Mercer, Mapsedge, Cross in Hand, Heathfield, East Sussex. TN21 0TA   Tel: (H) 01435 863396   (W) 01424 775999
Fixtures Secretary: Phil Bell   Tel: (H) 01435 882871 (W) 01424 774433
Club Colours: Green and white quarters

MAIDSTONE FC
Ground Address: The William Harvey Memorial Ground, The Mote, Willow Way, Maidstone, Kent. ME16 0RY   Tel: 01622 754159
Brief Directions: Leave M20 at A249, follow signs to Maidstone
Club Secretary: Jim Griffiths, 11 Tichborne Close, Allington Park, Maidstone, Kent. ME15 9UF   Tel: (H) 01622 681802   (W) 01622 710108
Fixtures Secretary: A F Kellener   Tel: (H & W) 01622 754872
Club Colours: Red, white and black hoops

MEDWAY RFC
Ground Address: Priestfield, Rochester, Kent
Brief Directions: M2 J3, follow A249 to Chatham, at Bridgewood roundabout left (Maidstone/Rochester road), past Comet on right, take left turn signed B, ground 200m on left
Club Secretary: Mr A D D Green, 18a City Way, Rochester, Kent. ME1 2AB   Tel: (H) 01634 818428
Fixtures Secretary: Mr G Farrow   Tel: (H) 01634 666255   (W) 01622 883608
Club Colours: Yellow and red

PARK HOUSE FC
Ground Address: Barnet Wood Road, Hayes, Kent. BR2 7AA   Tel: 0181 462 7318
Brief Directions: A21 to Bromley (or from M25 J4), turn off on A233 (Oakleigh Rd) towards Biggin Hill, Barnet Wood Road is a turning on the right
Club Secretary: Robert D Elves, 47 Ramillies Road, Sidcup, Kent. DA15 9JA   Tel: (H) 0181 304 9170   (W) 01474 853731
Fixtures Secretary: G Bunnage   Tel: (H) 0181 467 1447   (W) 0181 401 0111
Club Colours: Black shirts with red circlet, black shorts

SHEPPEY FOOTBALL CLUB LTD
Ground Address: The Clubhouse, Lower Road, Minster, Sheerness, Kent   Tel: 01795 872082
Brief Directions: A249 to Sheppey, from M2 or M20 on Sheppey, at 1st roundabout take
Club Secretary: Mrs Carole Payne, 40 Dumergue Avenue,Queenborough, Sheerness, Kent ME11 5BH Tel: (H) 01795 875120   (W) 01795 660756
Fixtures Secretary: Mr Gerry Lawson   Tel: (H) 01795 875120   (W) 01795 660756
Club Colours: White with single red hoop, black shorts

SIDCUP FC (RFU)
Ground Address: Crescent Farm, Sydney Road, Sidcup, Kent. DA14 6RA   Tel: 0181 3002336
Brief Directions: A20-A222 towards Sidcup (Chislehurst Rd), proceed to 1st traffic lights (Police Station), left into Main Road, left just past fire station into Sydney Rd, ground 200mtrs on left
Club Secretary: Allan Jones, 53 Goodwin Drive, Sidcup, Kent. DA14 4NX   Tel: (H & W) 0181 302 2382
Fixtures Secretary: Malcolm Leamon   Tel: (H) 0181 8595598
Club Colours: Maroon, white and navy blue squares

676

TUNBRIDGE WELLS RFC
Ground Address: St Marks Recreation Ground, Frant Road, Tunbridge Wells   Tel: 01892 527448
Club Secretary: M.M.Stickler, 79 Upper Grosvenor Rd., Tunbridge Wells, KentTN1 2DZ   Tel : 01892 533687 (Day and evening)
Fixtures Secretary: Stuart Montgomery   Tel: (H) 01892 530130
Club Colours: Navy blue and white quarters

UCKFIELD RFC
Ground Address: Hempsted Playing Fields, Nevill Road, Manor Park, Uckfield Tel: 01825 768956
Brief Directions: The Manor Park Estate is on northern outskirts of the town, turn into Browns Ln entrance & take 2nd road on left, the ground is at the end of the 3rd road on the right
Club Secretary: Mrs D. Wickham, 26 Rocks Park Road, Uckfield.   Tel: (H) 01825 762855
Fixtures Secretary: Mrs Maureen Poole   Tel: (H) 01825 761151
Club Colours: Amber with purple and white hoops

WORTHING RFC
Ground Address: The Rugby Park, Roundstone Lane, Angmering, West Sussex Tel/Fax: 01903 784706
Brief Directions: Turn right at `Roundstone' pub on A259 (Worthing to Littlehampton road) signposted Angmering. The ground is on the RHS approx 1/4 mile up the road.
Club Secretary: Brian Vincent, 29 St. Botolph's Rd., Worthing, W. Sussex. BN11 4JS. Tel: (H) 01903 206516 (B) 01903 821981
Fixtures Secretary: Paul Hughes, 74 Lanfranc Road, Worthing, W. Sussex. BN14 4JS. Tel: (H) 01903 784706 (M) 0370 850462
Club Colours: Royal blue, chocolate and gold hoops

The Official Rugby Union Club Directory

Did you realise the Directory is available to your club at very good discount rates.

KENT ONE

Kent One 1997-98 Fixtures	Ashford 1	Belteshanger 2	Bromley 3	Dartfordians 4	Deal Wanderers 5	Dover 6	Folkestone 7	Gillingham Anchorians 8	Lordswood 9	Met Police, Hayes 10	Nat West Bank 11	Old Dunstonians 12	Old Shootershillians 13	Sittingbourne 14	Snowdown CW 15	Whitstable 16	
1 Ashford	X	15/11		11/10	27/9		14/3			10/1		24/1	14/2	25/10			1
2 Belteshanger		X		20/12	31/1			14/2	14/3		18/11			17/1	8/11	27/9	2
3 Bromley	8/11	24/1	X		17/1	20/12	18/10			14/2		14/3	27/9				3
4 Dartfordians		15/11		X	18/10	25/10		10/1	24/1		14/3				27/9	14/2	4
5 Deal Wanderers					X			7/3	11/10	20/9	24/1	25/10	10/1			15/11	5
6 Dover	18/10	10/1		8/11		X	27/9			24/1		14/2	14/3	15/11			6
7 Folkestone		25/10		20/9	14/2		X		15/11			10/1	24/1	11/10	7/3		7
8 Gillingham Anchorians	20/12		31/1			17/1	8/11	X		14/3		27/9	18/10				8
9 Lordswood	17/1		7/3		31/1	20/12	20/9		X			18/10	8/11				9
10 Met Police, Hayes		7/3		17/1				27/9		X	8/11			31/1	20/12	18/10	10
11 Nat West Bank	7/3		11/10		20/9	31/1	25/10	15/11			X					10/1	11
12 Old Dunstonians		20/9		31/1				11/10	20/12			X		7/3	17/1	8/11	12
13 Old Shootershillians		11/10		7/3				25/10	17/1	15/11			X	20/9	31/1		13
14 Sittingbourne				10/1	8/11	20/12		14/2	24/1			27/9		X	18/10	14/3	14
15 Snowdown CW	20/9	25/10			14/3	11/10		15/11	10/1			14/2			X	24/1	15
16 Whitstable	31/1		20/9				7/3	17/1	11/10	25/10			20/12			X	16
	1	2	3	4	5	6	7	8	9	10	11	12	13	14	15	16	

ASHFORD (KENT) RFC LTD
Ground Address: Kinneys Field
Brief Directions: A28 from Ashford to Canterbury, 400 yards after crossing M20 motorway, the ground narrow entrance is on right directly opposite the Fire Station
Club Secretary: D G Humphreys, Withersdane Green Farmhouse, Wye, Ashford, Kent. TN25 5DL Tel: (H) 01233 813263 (W) 0181 7002201
Fixtures Secretary: Colin Yalden Tel: (H) 01233 640905 (W) 01233 622444
Club Colours: Red, gold and black

BETTESHANGER CW RFC
Ground Address: Welfare Ground, Cavill Square, Deal, Kent. Clubhouse: Welfare Club 1st floor, Condray Square, Deal, Kent Tel: 01304 365090
Brief Directions: A258 to Walmer, 3rd left Church St, right at T junction Court Rd, left at T junction St Richards Rd, past water tower turn right Mill Hill, 2nd left, 2nd left Cavell Sq, 1st left to ground & changing
Club Secretary: Simon Rickatson, 40 Mongeham Rd, Gt. Mongeham, Deal, Kent. CT14 9PQ Tel: 01304 361178
Fixtures Secretary: Bob Pinnick Tel: (H) 01227 750530 (W) 01843 822686
Club Colours: Red and white hoops

BROMLEY RFC
Ground Address: Barnet Wood Road, Hayes, Kent Tel: 0181 462 3430
Club Secretary: John Marriot, 6 Ravenleigh Cart, 89 Bromley Common, Bromley, Kent. BR2 9RN Tel: (W) 01622 672541
Fixtures Secretary: Alex Mackintosh Tel: (H) 0181 460 8049 (W) 0181 460 8049
Club Colours: Black jerseys, amber hoops, black shorts

DARTFORDIANS RUFC
Ground Address: Bourne Road, Bexley, Kent Tel: 01322 669817
Club Secretary: Jack Morris, 7 Irving Way, Swanley, Kent. BR8 7EP Tel: (H) 01322 669817
Fixtures Secretary: D Rapley Tel: (H) 0181 857 6198
Club Colours: Maroon and old gold shirts, navy shorts

DEAL WANDERERS RFC
Ground Address: Clubhouse, Western Road, Deal, Kent. Tel: 01304 365892
Fixtures Secretary: Mr R Dorling, 13 Halsatt Road, Deal, Kent. CT14 9ED Tel: (H) 01304 373112
Club Colours: Blue and amber.

DOVER RFC
Ground Address: Crabble Athletic Ground, Crabble Road, River, Dover, Kent Tel: 01304 210296
Brief Directions: From M2/A2, at Esso garage take River exit, left at mini r'bout, sharp right at lights, 300m on left. From M20/A20 leave Dover to Canterbury, fork left at lights on Crabble Hill, 300m on left
Club Secretary: J D Thomas, Karma, Minnis Lane, River, Dover. CT17 0PT Tel: (H) 01304 822169
Fixtures Secretary: R Dixon Tel: (H) 01304 852776
Club Colours: Light and dark blue hoops

FOLKESTONE RFC
Ground Address: New Burlington Field, Bargrove, Newington, Folkestone, Kent. CT18 8BH   Tel: (H) 01303 266887
Brief Directions: Take the Hythe Road (B2065) from the A20 (Ashford to Folkestone road), 1 m on left. From London M20 Exit J12 (Cheriton).Follow A20 for 1m then B2065 to Hythe.1/4m on Rt.
Club Secretary: Barry Keating, Carbery, Church Hill, Hythe, Kent. CT21 5DW   Tel: (H) 01303 264604
Fixtures Secretary: A D Ruddock   Tel: (H) 01303 276530
Club Colours: Green and white hooped shirts, white shorts, green and white socks

GILLINGHAM ANCHORIANS RFC
Ground Address: Watling Street Playing Fields, off Darland Avenue, Gillingham, Kent   Tel: 01634 851495
Brief Directions: Leave M2 by A278, turn left at terminal roundabout (signed A2 Gillingham), across new roundabout, left at 2nd traffic lights at Darland Ave, ground 200 yards on left
Club Secretary: R.E.Ferguson,, 81 Marshall Road, Gillingham, Kent ME8 0AN   Tel: (H) 01634 231774
Fixtures Secretary: Neil Cripps   Tel: (H) 01634 378140   (W) 01322 336060
Club Colours: Purple, black and white hoops

LORDSWOOD RUFC
Ground Address: Martin Grove, North Dane Way, Lordswood, Chatham, Kent   Tel: 01634 669138
Brief Directions: M2 J3, A229 t'wd Chatham, 3rd exit at 3rd r'bout (Walderslade), over 1st r'bout, 3rd exit at 2nd r'bout (Lordswood Lane), 3rd exit at r'bout (Albermarle Rd), left at end, clubhouse 500yds on right
Club Secretary: Mr Huw Thomas, 97 Ballens Road, Lordswood, Kent. ME5 8PD   Tel: (H) 01634 867045 (W) 01634 271511
Fixtures Secretary: Mr Peter O Neil   Tel: (H) 01634 201006   (W) 01634 687166
Club Colours: Amber and black irregular hoops

METROPOLITAN POLICE (HAYES) RFC
Ground Address: The Warren Sports & Social Club, Hayes Common Road, Hayes, Kent   Tel: 0181 462 1266
Brief Directions: A232 Hayes Common, from M25 J4 north on A21 then east on A232
Club Secretary: Gary D Morant, 57 Orchard Way, Shirley, Croydon. Tel: 0181 777 3700
Fixtures Secretary: George Strachan, 244 Pickhurst Lane, West Wickham, Kent. Tel: (H) 0181 462 7996
Club Colours: Burgundy and royal blue quarters

NATIONAL WESTMINSTER BANK RFC
Ground Address: Copers Cope Road, Beckenham, Kent. BR3 1NZ   Tel: 0181 650 4559/650 9217
Brief Directions: Freq trains to Charing X and London Bridge to Lower Sydenham. Out of Station on down side. Turn right at bottom into Worsley Bridge Rd. 1st Right (100yds) into Coopers Cope Rd, on right.
Club Secretary: C J Longhurst, 12 Churchfields Rd, Beckenham, Kent BR3 4QW
Fixtures Secretary: G W C Teale   Tel: (H) 0181 462 9288   (W) 0171 398 8540
Club Colours: Light and dark blue hoops

OLD DUNSTONIAN RFC
Ground Address: St Dunstan's Lane, Langley Park, Beckenham, Kent. BR3 3SS   Tel: 0181 650 1779
Brief Directions: Frm Bromley Sth station, rt at lights Westmoreland Rd, rt at next lights Hayes Ln, 2nd lft Brabourne Rs, at the bottom entrance to St D'stans Ln is almost opp. between no's 114/6 Wickham Way
Club Secretary: Mike Rogers, Aboyne, Pickhurst Lane, West Wickham, Kent. BR4 0HN   Tel: (H) 0181 462 3064   (W) 0171 447 2238
Fixtures Secretary: Philip France   Tel: (H) 0181 776 2335
Club Colours: Navy and white circlet

OLD SHOOTERSHILLIAN S RFC
Ground Address: 123/125 Mayday Gardens, Kidbrooke, London. SE3   Tel: 0181 856 1511
Brief Directions: Frm Well Hall r'bout take signs for Woolwich & Ferry, over lights at top of hill, next left Broadwalk, over 4 humps, left Mayday Gdns, follow road to green on left, entrance to ground in corner
Club Secretary: Kevin Bailey, 15 Grace Avenue, Allington, Nr Maidstone, Kent. ME16 0BS   Tel: (H) 01622 675930   (W) 01206 767763   (M) 0589 216801
Fixtures Secretary: Ian Trevett   Tel: (H) 0181 859 0746
Club Colours: Red, blue, green and yellow

SITTINGBOURNE RUFC
Ground Address: Gore Court Sports Club, The Grove, Key Street, Sittingbourne, Kent. ME10 1YT   Tel: 01795 423813
Brief Directions: From M2 eastbound, A249 to Sittingbourne & Sheerness, after 2 mile take A2 towards Sittingbourne, after 0.5 mile turn left just after Sports ground, left again into club car park
Club Secretary: Steve Smith, 34 Crouch Hill Court, Lower Halstow, Sittingbourne, Kent. ME9 7EJ   Tel: (H) 01795 843356
Fixtures Secretary: Denise Smith   Tel: (H) 01795 843356
Club Colours: Blue and gold hoops

SNOWDON COLLIERY WELFARE RFC
Ground Address: Welfare Ground, Aylesham, Canterbury, Kent   Tel: 01304 840278
Brief Directions: Take A2, 8 miles south of Canterbury, take Aylesham turn off, ground 2 miles further along this road
Club Secretary: Eddie Sullivan, 4 Burgess Road, Aylesham, Canterbury, Kent. CT3 3AU   Tel: (H) 01304 840052
Fixtures Secretary: Alan Booth   Tel: (H) 01304 840619
Club Colours: Red and blue hoops

WHITSTABLE RFC
Ground Address: Reeves Way, Chestfield, Whitstable, Kent. CT5 3QS   Tel: 01227 794343
Brief Directions: A299 Thanet Way to Whitstable, by Chestfield roundabout. The ground is opposite Chestfield & Swalecliffe Railway Station
Club Secretary: Colin James, 71 Swalecliffe Court Drive, Whitstable, Kent. CT5 2NF   Tel: (H) 01227 793031
Fixtures Secretary: Roger Dengate, 70 Regent St. Whitstable, Kent. CT5 1JQ.   Tel: (H) 01227 264604
Club Colours: Blue and white.

KENT TWO

Kent Two 1997-98 Fixtures

	Aylesford	Bexley	Citizens	Edenbridge	Footscray	Greenwich Acads	Midland Bank	New Ash Green	Old Elthamians	Old Gravesendians	Old Olavians	Old Williamsonian	Orpington	Tonbridge	Vigo	
	1	2	3	4	5	6	7	8	9	10	11	12	13	14	15	
1 Aylesford	X		31/1		11/10	15/11			17/1	20/9			25/10	73		1
2 Bexley	14/3	X			10/1	14/2			27/9		15/11	18/10	24/1			2
3 Citizens		11/10	X	25/10			15/11	10/1		14/2		24/1	20/9			3
4 Edenbridge	27/9	20/12		X	24/1	14/3			18/10				8/11	14/2		4
5 Footscray				8/11	X		14/2	14/3		18/10	17/1	27/9			20/12	5
6 Greenwich Acads			17/1		20/9	X				20/12	7/3	8/11		11/10	31/1	6
7 Midland Bank	18/10	17/1		31/1		27/9	X		8/11				20/12	14/3		7
8 New Ash Green	8/11	31/1		7/3		18/10	20/9	X	20/12				17/1			8
9 Old Elthamians	24/1		7/3		25/10	10/1			X		11/10			15/11	20/9	9
10 Old Gravesendians		20/9		11/10			25/10	15/1	31/1	X		10/1	7/3			10
11 Old Olavians			18/10	10/1			24/1	14/2		27/9	X	14/3		8/11		11
12 Old Williamsonian	20/12	7/3		20/9			11/10	25/10	17/1			X	31/1			12
13 Orpington	14/2				15/11	24/1			14/3		25/10		X	10/1	11/10	13
14 Tonbridge			20/12		7/3				27/9	8/11	31/1	18/10		X	17/1	14
15 Vigo		25/10	27/9	15/11			10/1	24/1		14/3		14/2			X	15
	1	2	3	4	5	6	7	8	9	10	11	12	13	14	15	

AYLESFORD RFC
Ground Address: ADJ Ferry Field, Hall Road, Aylesford
Brief Directions: From M20 J5, 3rd exit at roundabout (if coastbound) 1st exit (if London bound), next roundabout 2nd exit (A20 London bound), to 2nd set of lights turn right, right at T junction, car park on right
Club Secretary: Rick Bryant, 9 Tollgate Way, Sandling, Maidstone, Kent. ME14 3DF Tel: (H) 01622 683951 (W) 01634 874994
Fixtures Secretary: Dave Enston Tel: (H) 01732 842666
Club Colours: Red shirts, black shorts, red socks

BEXLEY RFC
Ground Address: Hall Place Park, Bourne Road, Bexley, Kent
Club Secretary: Peter Butler, 194 Claremont Road, Hextable, Kent. BR8 7QU Tel: (H) 01322 664389
Fixtures Secretary: Paul Herbert Tel: (H) 01322 555556
Club Colours: Royal blue and white hooped shirts, blue shorts, blue socks with white tops

CITIZENS RFC
Ground Address: Old Dunstonian Sports Ground, St Dunstans Lane, Langley Park, Beckenham, Kent. BR3 3SS Tel: 0181 650 1779
Brief Directions: St Dunstans Lane is off Wickham Way, in Eden Park, Beckenham, nearest station is West Wickham
Club Secretary: R Lewis Esq, 22 Eastnor Road, London. SE9 2BG Tel: (H) 0181 859 1094 (W) 0181 850 8170
Fixtures Secretary: R J Mannell Esq Tel: (H) 0181 857 3057
Club Colours: Black with maroon and white hoops

EDENBRIDGE RFC
Ground Address: The Pavilion, Lingfield Road Recreation Ground, Lingfield Road, Edenbridge, Kent. TN8 Tel: 01732 862435
Brief Directions: From Edenbridge High Street travelling south, turn right into Stangrove Road, left into Crouch House Road, right into Lingfield Road.
Club Secretary: N. A. Dearmer, 13 Court Drive, Sutton, Surrey, SM1 3RG. Tel: (H) 0181 6437791 (W) 01707 662662
Fixtures Secretary: John Martin, Little Acre, Swan Lane, Edenbridge, Kent, TN8 6AJ. Tel: (H) 01732 862761
Club Colours: Black and yellow hoops

FOOTS CRAY RUFC
Ground Address: 239A Foots Cray Road, New Eltham, London. SE9 2EL
Club Secretary: Stephen Roberts, 279 Burnt Oak Lane, Sidcup, Kent. DA15 8LR Tel: (H) 0181 302 7141 (W) 01753 679253
Fixtures Secretary: Tony Codd Tel: (H) 0181 857 6040
Club Colours: Blue and gold hoops

GREENWICH ACADEMICALS RFC
Ground Address: Poly Sports and Social Club, Kidbrooke Lane, Eltham, London. SE9 6TA Tel: 0181 850 0210
Brief Directions: Kidbrooke Lane is a turning off the South Circular - called Westhorne Ave at this point - and is 300 yards from the intersection of the A2 and the South Circular
Fixtures Secretary: G O Miller Tel: (H & W) 0181 850 2794
Club Colours: Green with gold and red bands

MIDLAND BANK RFC
Ground Address: Lennard Road, Beckenham, Kent Tel: 0181 778 7784
Club Secretary: C Rouse, 59 Crantock Road, London. SE6 Tel: (H) 0181 698 4527
Fixtures Secretary: J R D Hayhow Tel: (H) 0181 467 3314 (W) 0171 623 9333
Club Colours: Green shirts, blue shorts

NEW ASH GREEN RFC
Ground Address: Punch Croft, New Ash Green, Kent. Tel: 01474 874660
Club Secretary: David McLlaren, Lynwood, Wrotham Road, Fairseat, Sevenoaks, Kent. TN15 7JR. Tel: (H) 01732 822552
Fixtures Secretary: Paul Martin, Tel: (H) 01474 874513
Club Colours: Dark green and black quarters, black shorts.

OLD ELTHAMIANS RFC
Ground Address: War Memorial Sports Ground, Foxbury, Perry Street, Kent Tel: 0181 467 1035
Brief Directions: At Sidcup turn off of A20, follow directions for Chislehurst (War Memorial) via Perry Street, Foxbury Ave is on the right after approx 0.75 mile, club house at very end of private road
Club Secretary: Ian McKinnon, 25 The Gardens, Beckenham, Kent. BR3 2PH Tel: (H) 0181 650 1936 (W) 01634 200844
Fixtures Secretary: David Organ Tel: (H) 0181 464 2542
Club Colours: Royal blue and amber horizontal bands

OLD GRAVESENDIANS RFC
Ground Address: Fleetway Sports Ground, Bronte View, Parrock Road, Gravesend, Kent DA12 1PX. Tel: 01474 365503
Club Secretary: Tony Collins, 41 Barleycorn, Leybourne Kent ME19 5PS Tel: 01732 847722
Fixtures Secretary: A. Ennis Tel: (H) 01474 327674
Club Colours: Light blue and dark blue hoops

OLD OLAVIANS RUFC
Ground Address: St Olaves School, Goddington Lane, Orpington, Kent Tel: 01689 830744
Club Secretary: Adam Watson, 310A High Street, Orpington, Kent. BR6 0NG Tel: (H) 01689 875044 (W) 0171 406 8421
Fixtures Secretary: Neil Hayward Tel: (H) 01689 820556 (W) 0171 459 2000
Club Colours: Purple, black and white hoops

OLD WILLIAMSONIAN RFC
Ground Address: Maidstone Road, Rochester, Kent. Tel: 01634 842883
Club Secretary: Andy Campbell, 85 Seal Hollow Road, Sevenoaks, Kent. TN13 3SA Tel: (H) 01732 453623 Tel: (W) 0171 283 3434
Fixtures Secretary: Dean Painter Tel: (H)01634 260892
Club Colours: Navy blue, single gold hoop

ORPINGTON RFC
Ground Address: Hoblingwell Wood, Leesons Way, St Pauls Cray, Orpington, Kent. BR5 2QB Tel: 01689 823913
Club Secretary: Ken Hall, The Lodge, ORFC, Leesons Way, St Pauls Cray, Orpington, Kent. BR5 2QB Tel: (H) 01689 896262 (W) 01689 823913
Fixtures Secretary: Chris Evans Tel: (H) 01689 896709
Club Colours: Black and amber hoops

TONBRIDGE RFC
Ground Address: The Clubhouse, Avebury Avenue, Tonbridge, Kent Tel: 01732 350067
Brief Directions: A26 (High Street) exit, at roundabout by Station Bridge, down Avebury Avenue
Club Secretary: Malcolm Yates, 8 Cardinal Close, Tonbridge, Kent, TN9 2EN Tel: 01732 357964
Fixtures Secretary: David Carver, 50 Pennington Place, Southborough, Tunbridge Wells, Kent. Tel: (H) 01892 543736
Club Colours: Chocolate and old gold hoops, black shorts, chocolate and old gold socks

VIGO RFC
Ground Address: Swanswood Field, Vigo Village, Havvel Road, Vigo, Kent Tel: 01732 823830
Club Secretary: N W Simpson, Pitfield House, Meopham Green, Meopham, Kent. DA13 0PZ Tel: (H) 01474 812407 (W) 0181 8541331
Fixtures Secretary: John Taylor Tel: (H) 01322 227363 (W) 0171 488 0733
Club Colours: Red shirts, black shorts

KENT THREE

Kent Three 1997-98 Fixtures	Canterbury Exiles 1	Darenth Valley 2	Erith 3	Faversham 4	Greenwich 5	Meophan 6	
1 Canterbury Exiles	X	10/1	27/9	18/10	8/11	14/2	1
2 Darenth Valley	11/10	X	25/10	15/11	24/1	8/11	2
3 Erith	15/11	14/2	X	20/9	11/10	18/10	3
4 Faversham	24/1	27/9	8/11	X	25/10	10/1	4
5 Greenwich	20/9	18/10	10/1	14/2	X	27/9	5
6 Meophan	25/10	20/9	24/1	11/10	15/11	X	6
	1	2	3	4	5	6	

CANTERBURY EXILES
Ground Address: 'The Pound', Stodmarsh Road, Stodmarsh, Nr Canterbury, Kent.
Club Secretary: Stephen Gile, Edelweiss, 97 The Street, Adisham, Canterbury, Kent CT3 3JW. Tel: (H) 01304 842644 Tel: (W) 01304 616191
Fixtures Secretary: Littlehammill, Hammill Nr Woodnesborough, Sandwich, Kent CT13 0EH. Tel: (H) 01304 617030 Tel: (W) 01622 750131
Club Colours: Red, black and amber hoops.

DARENTH VALLEY RFC
Ground Address: The Leigh Clubhouse, Leigh City Technical College, Green Street, Dartford, Kent Tel: 01322 290801
Brief Directions: M25 J1, take road towards Dartford (across M25), 1st left at roundabout (past petrol garage) and 1st right onto College campus
Club Secretary: Mrs Shelley Carey, 23 Hamilton Walk, Erith Kent, DA8 2JP Tel: 01322 330544
Fixtures Secretary: Will Willets Tel: 01622 891866
Club Colours: Black with white V

ERITH RFC
Ground Address: Sussex Road, Northumberland Heath Playing Fields, Northumberland Heath, Erith, Kent Tel: 01322 432295
Brief Directions: A2 towards London, Blackprince turn off towards Erith, turn left into Brook St and left into Sussex Road
Club Secretary: R W Shepherd, 24 Lesney Park, Erith, Kent. DA8 3DN Tel: (H) 01322 341073 (W) 0181 285 7082
Fixtures Secretary: S Button Tel: (H) 01322 387689
Club Colours: Light and dark blue hoops, blue shorts

FAVERSHAM RUFC
Ground Address: Faversham Recreation Ground Lodge, Faversham, Kent. ME13 8HA Tel: 01795 530651
Club Secretary: Pat Rowan, 14 Abbey Street, Faversham, Kent. ME13 7BE Tel: (H) 01795 530651
Fixtures Secretary: Pat Rowan Tel: (H) 01795 530651
Club Colours: Sky blue and white squares

GREENWICH RFC
Ground Address: The Pavilion, Old Mill Road, Plumstead, London SE18. Tel: 0181 854 8637
Club Secretary: Bob Keyes, 24 Burwood Road, Plumstead SE18 7QZ. Tel: (H) 0181 854 2847
Fixtures Secretary: Steve Raker, Tel: 0181 311 8227
Club Colours: Red and black quarters, black shorts.

MEOPHAM
Ground Address: New ground being built, using school ground near King's Arms.
Club Secretary: P. Cornell, The Kings Arms, Meopham Green, Meopham, Kent. DA13 0QB. Tel: (H) 01474 813323
Fixtures Secretary: Shaun Ellis Tel: (H)01474 812650
Club Colours: Navy Blue with 2 white hoops

SUSSEX ONE

Sussex One 1997-98 Fixtures	BA Wingspan 1	Crowborough 2	Ditchling 3	Eastbourne 4	Hastings & Bexhill 5	Hove 6	Pulborough 7	Seaford 8	Sun Alliance, Hor. 9	
1 BA Wingspan	X	18/10	6/9	28/2	14/3	31/1	15/11	25/10	10/1	1
2 Crowborough	24/1	X	14/3	6/9	15/11	27/9	10/1	11/10	25/10	2
3 Ditchling	7/3	20/12	X	17/1	11/10	28/3	14/2	24/1	20/9	3
4 Eastbourne	20/9	7/3	25/10	X	24/1	20/12	11/10	10/1	14/2	4
5 Hastings & Bexhill	20/12	18/3	31/1	18/10	X	8/11	20/9	14/2	7/3	5
6 Hove	11/10	14/2	15/11	14/3	10/1	X	25/10	6/9	24/1	6
7 Pulborough	28/3	8/11	27/9	31/1	28/2	17/1	X	7/3	20/12	7
8 Seaford	17/1	31/1	18/10	8/11	27/9	28/2	6/9	X	28/3	8
9 Sun Alliance, Horsham	8/11	17/1	28/2	27/9	6/9	18/10	14/3	15/11	X	9
	1	2	3	4	5	6	7	8	9	

BRITISH AIRWAYS WINGSPAN RUFC
Ground Address: Bewbush Leisure Centre, Coachmans Drive, Bewbush, Crawley   Tel: 01293 546477
Brief Directions: Turn west off A23 at Cheals roundabout, signed Horsham, on A264, 3rd exit at 2nd roundabout (Breezehurst Drive), sports centre is 0.5 mile on left
Club Secretary: Mike Duff, 10 Brooklands Road, Tollgate Hill, Crawley, Sussex. RH11 9QQ   Tel: (H) 01293 409908   (W) 01293 662258
Fixtures Secretary: Harry Townsend   Tel: (H & W) 01342 322508
Club Colours: Red, white and blue

CROWBOROUGH RFC
Ground Address: Steel Cross, Crowborough, East Sussex   Tel: 01892 654832
Brief Directions: South on A26 from Tunbridge Wells, Club signposted at roundabout after village of Boarshead
Club Secretary: Gavin Tyler, 3 Wallis Close, Crowborough, East Sussex. TN6 2YA   Tel: (H) 01892 665153   (W) 01892 506155
Fixtures Secretary: Alex Stephenson   Tel: (H) 01892 669843
Club Colours: Red with white hoops, blue shorts

DITCHLING RFC
Ground Address: The Playing Fields, Lewes Road, Ditchling, East Sussex   Tel: 01273 843423
Brief Directions: From the village crossroads, head east on the Lewes Road and the ground is approx 0.25 mile down on the left
Club Secretary: John Magrath, 10 Copythorne House, Gordon Road, Haywards Heath, West Sussex. RH16 1EL   Tel: (H) 01444 415182   (W) 01403 233606
Fixtures Secretary: Chris Atkinson   Tel: (H) 01444 416174   (W) 0181 681 5500
Club Colours: Myrtle green shirts, white shorts

EASTBOURNE RFC
Ground Address: Park Avenue, Hampden Park, Eastbourne, East Sussex. BN22 9QN   Tel: 01323 503076
Brief Directions: 500yds north of Eastbourne District General Hospital, clearly signposted.
Club Secretary: Hugh Graham, 17A Pashley Road, Eastbourne, East Sussex. BN20 8DU   Tel: (H) 01323 646600
Fixtures Secretary: Bob Waite, 'Safari', Lion Hill, Stone Cross. Tel: (H) 01323 766708
Club Colours: Navy blue and gold

HASTINGS AND BEXHILL RFC
Ground Address: William Parker School Site, Park Avenue, hastings, East Sussex. Tel 01424 444255
Club Secretary: L Morgan, 10 Delaware Road, St Leonards-on-Sea, East Sussex. Tel: (H) 01424 855040
Fixtures Secretary: P Knight Tel: (H) 01424 731379
Club Colours: Blue and white hoops.

HOVE RFC
Ground Address: Hove Park, Goldstone Crescent, Hove, East Sussex. Tel: 01273 505103
Brief Directions: Adjacent to Brighton and Hove FC on A27 Coast Road.
Club Secretary: Graham J. L. Gordon, 9 Albany Towers, 6 St. Catherine's Terrace, Hove, East Sussex. BN3 2RQ   Tel: (H) 01273 726081   Tel: (W) 0171 412 4377
Fixtures Secretary: Mike Richardson Tel: (H) 01273 500512   Tel: (W) 0171 0181 644 4388
Club Colours: Maroon and sky blue hoops.

PULBOROUGH RFC
Ground Address: Sports & Social Club, Rectory Lane, Pulborough, West Sussex   Tel: 01798 873020
Brief Directions: Approach by Rectory Lane branching north off east end of Lower Street opposite Arundale School
Club Secretary: Chris Brazier, 2 Heather Farm Cottages, Chobham Rd., Horsell Common, Woking, Surrey GU21 4XY   Tel: (W) 01798 812345
Fixtures Secretary: Michael Ford   Tel: (H) 01903 745697
Club Colours: Black and white hoops

SEAFORD RFC
Ground Address: The Salts Recreation Ground, The Esplanade, Seaford   Tel: 01323 892355
Brief Directions: Situated on the sea front just off the A259
Club Secretary: E A Pugh, Shottery, 19 Chyngton Road, Seaford, Sussex   Tel: (H) 01323 892020
Fixtures Secretary: P Ungoed   Tel: (H) 01323 893688
Club Colours: Scarlet

SUN ALLIANCE, HORSHAM
Ground Address: Royal & Sun Alliance Club, North Heath Lane, Horsham, West Sussex RH12 4PJ
Brief Directions: A264 leave at roundabout for Ruffey, 3rd exit at next roundabout, go half mile and turn left into North Heath Lane at mini roundabout, ground is half mile on LHS.
Club Secretary: K.J.Reed, 38 Red Admiral Street, North Heath Lane, Horsham, West Sussex RH12 5YJ
Fixtures Secretary: S West   Tel:(H) 01403 269838 (W) 01403 234285
Club Colours: Navy Blue with yellow, Green,and White chevron

SUSSEX TWO

Sussex Two 1997-98 Fixtures	Burgess Hill	Hellingly	Old Brightonians	Newich	Rye	St Francis	Shoreham	Sussex Police	
	1	2	3	4	5	6	7	8	
1 Burgess Hill	X	20/12	11/10	24/1	10/1	25/10	14/2	15/11	1
2 Hellingly	20/9	X	10/1	11/10	15/11	24/1	25/10	14/2	2
3 Old Brightonians	17/1	27/9	X	25/10	18/10	14/2	15/11	20/12	3
4 Newich	18/10	17/1	31/1	X	14/2	15/11	20/12	27/9	4
5 Rye	27/9	7/3	24/1	8/11	X	20/12	11/10	31/1	5
6 St Francis	31/1	18/10	8/11	7/3	20/9	X	27/9	17/1	6
7 Shoreham	8/11	31/1	7/3	20/9	17/1	10/1	X	18/10	7
8 Sussex Police	7/3	8/11	20/9	10/1	25/10	11/10	24/1	X	8
	1	2	3	4	5	6	7	8	

BURGESS HILL RFC
Ground Address: Poveys Close, Burgess Hill, West Sussex   Tel: 01444 232221
Brief Directions: Royal George Road turn into Southway at Weald public house right intoPoveys Close - ground at end.
Club Secretary: Mike Bushell, 4 Kirdford Close, Burgess Hill, West Sussex. RH15 0BW   Tel: (H) 01444 246795 (W) 01444 252205
Fixtures Secretary: Tony Balsdon, 102 Marlborough Drive, Burgess Hill, West Sussex. RH15 0EU.   Tel: (H) 01444 246170   (W) 01273 273234
Club Colours: All black

HELLINGLY RFC
Ground Address: Hellingly Sports Clubs, Upper Horsebridge, Hailsham, East Sussex
Brief Directions: Turn east off A22 onto A271, ground half mile on right opposite White Hart pub
Club Secretary: Peter Stotesbury, 10 Hawkswood Drive, Hailsham, East Sussex. BN27 1UR   Tel: (H) 01323 844648   (W) 01323 841666
Fixtures Secretary: Jim Bedford   Tel: 01323 845660
Club Colours: Amber and black

NEWICK RFC
Ground Address: King GeorgeV Playing Ground, Newick, Nr Lewes, East Sussex
Brief Directions: A272 from Haywards Heath, right at village green, 2nd right, playing field Allington Road, on first bend, left into field
Club Secretary: Diane Thomas, Pinecroft, Allington Rd., Newick, East Sussex BN8 4NA Tel: (H) 01825 723624
Fixtures Secretary: Martin Barling Tel: (H) 01825 722666
Club Colours: Dark blue and maroon hooped jerseys and socks

OLD BRIGHTONIAN RFC
Ground Address: Share with Brighton FC (RFU). Waterhall Playing Fields, Mill Road, Patcham, Brighton Tel: 01273 562729
Brief Directions: From London & north- A23 turn right at 1st roundabout entering Brighton, past garage under railway bridge, 100 metres sign post, turn right
Club Secretary: C D Loadsman, 20 Meadow Close, Hove, Sussex Tel: (H) 01273 552988 (W) 01273 736000
Fixtures Secretary: P Rumney Tel: (H) 01273 504981
Club Colours: Light blue and magenta hoops on navy

RYE RFC
Ground Address: Rye RFC, New Road, Rye, East Sussex Tel: 01797 224867
Brief Directions: Situated east of main town on the A259 coast road
Club Secretary: Jason Bowen, 15 Southundercliff, Rye, East Sussex. TN31 7HN Tel: (H) 01797 226597 (W) 0468 453671
Fixtures Secretary: Graham Nunn Tel: (H) 01797 280517
Club Colours: Red and white quarters, black shorts, black socks

SHOREHAM RFC
Ground Address: Kings Manor School, Kingston Lane, Shoreham-by-Sea, West Sussex Tel: 01273 597625
Brief Directions: Take A27 to Shoreham (Old Shoreham road) westward Kingston Lane is on left at traffic lights before Holmbush shopping centre r'bout, Kings Manor School 0.5 mile on right
Club Secretary: Simon Edgar, 17 Newtimber Gardens, Shoreham-by-Sea, West Sussex BN43 5GQ. Tel: (H) 01273 701618 (W) 0831 236918
Fixtures Secretary: Mrs Sandy Beal Tel: (H) 01273 884827
Club Colours: Amber and bottle green quarters

ST FRANCIS RFC
Ground Address: Southgate Playing Fields
Brief Directions: M23 J11, take A23 to Crawley, right at roundabout into Southgate Ave, ground approx 1 mile on right hand side
Club Secretary: Iain Mitchell, 9 Tangmead Road, Ifield, Crawley, Sussex Tel: (H) 01293 516108 (W) 0171 599 3223
Fixtures Secretary: Vince McGahan Tel: (H) 01293 547194 (W) 01293 503278
Club Colours: Black with white and royal blue band

SUSSEX POLICE RFC
Ground Address: Brighton Rugby Club, Patcham, Waterhall, Brighton, Sussex Tel: 01273 562729
Brief Directions: A23 London to Brighton road, turn right at Patcham along Mill Road, then left into Waterhall ground
Club Secretary: P Johnson, Police Station, Kingsham Road, Chichester, Sussex Tel: (H) 01243 825408 (W) 01243 520230
Fixtures Secretary: C Gale Tel: (H) 01444 458482 (W) 01444 451555
Club Colours: Blue and gold quarters, blue shorts, blue socks

SUSSEX THREE

Sussex Three 1997-98 Fixtures	Arun 1	Barns Green 2	Chichester Institute 3	Midhurst 4	Plumpton 5	Robertsbridge 6	
1 Arun	X	8/11	14/3	11/10	31/1	25/10	1
2 Barns Green	28/2	X	11/10	25/10	17/1	31/1	2
3 Chichester Institute	17/1	24/1	X	31/1	25/10	28/2	3
4 Midhurst	24/1	14/2	18/10	X	28/2	17/1	4
5 Plumpton	18/10	14/3	14/2	8/11	X	24/1	5
6 Robertsbridge	14/2	18/10	8/11	14/3	11/10	X	6
	1	2	3	4	5	6	

ARUN RUFC
Ground Address: The Littlehampton School, Hill Road, Littlehampton, West Sussex Tel: 01903 713944
Brief Directions: Off Horsham Road, Littlehampton
Club Secretary: S White, 66 Holmes Lane, Rustington, West Sussex. BN16 3PU Tel: (H) 01903 774434
Fixtures Secretary: P Best Tel: (H) 01903 723969
Club Colours: Red, white and navy quarters

BARNS GREEN RFC
Ground Address: Christ's Hospital School, Horsham, West sussex.
Club Secretary: Miss Sue Blanchard, 42 Finians Field,Barns Green, West Sussex RH13 7PW.
Tel: (H) 01403 731652
Fixtures Secretary: Mr P A Bailey,
Tel: (H) 01403 730058 Tel: (W) 0181 667 5504
Club Colours: Gold & green quarters.

CHICHESTER INSTITUTE FOR HIGHER EDUCATION
Ground Address: Bishop Otter College, College Lane, Chichester, West Sussex. PO19 4PE. Tel:01243 787137.
Club Secretary: G.A. Jones, Bishop Otter College, College Lane, Chichester, West Sussex. PO19 4PE. (H) 01243 539857 (B) 01243 787137.
Fixtures Secretary: As Above.
Club Colours: No Details?

MIDHURST RFC
Ground Address: Cowdray Ruins, Cowdray Park, Midhurst, West Sussex Tel: 01730 816658
Brief Directions: At mini roundabout junction of A286 and A272 take entrance to Cowdray Park, turn left 200 yards along drive
Club Secretary: Simon Flint, Broadoak, Chichester Road, Midhurst, West Sussex. GU29 9PF Tel: (H) 01730 816465 (W) 0181 390 1144
Fixtures Secretary: Simon Fay Tel: (H) 01730 813357
Club Colours: Amber with royal blue band/hoop.

PLUMPTON RFC
Ground Address: The Racecourse, Plumpton, East Sussex
Brief Directions: Plumpton Racecourse opposite railway station
Club Secretary: Mr C Woodward, 2 Monks Way, Lewes, East Sussex. BN7 2EX Tel: (H) 01273 476219 (W) 01273 526110
Fixtures Secretary: Mr G Glendenning Tel: (H) 01273 620585
Club Colours: Maroon and gold

ROBERTSBRIDGE RUFC
Ground Address: Robertsbridge Community College, Knelle Road, Robertsbridge, East Sussex. TN32 5EA
Brief Directions: From the village follow signs to the railway station, go over the level crossing, take the 2nd right then go straight up to the college
Club Secretary: Grant Vincent, Upper Maisonette, 120 Braybrooke Road, Hastings, East Sussex. TN34 1TG Tel: (H) 01424 438984 (W) 01424 853481
Fixtures Secretary: Gareth Stoten Tel: (H) 01580 880174 (M) 0370 959648 (W) 0181 905 1661
Club Colours: Purple with single white hoop

LONDON THREE SOUTH WEST

London Three South West 1997-98 Fixtures	Alton	Barnes	Effingham	Esso	Farnborough	Gosport	Guy's Hospital	Jersey	Old Alleynian	Old Emanuel	Old Reedonians	Old Walcourtians	Old Whitgiftians	Portsmouth	Purley	Southampton	University Vandals	
	1	2	3	4	5	6	7	8	9	10	11	12	13	14	15	16	17	
1 Alton	X	20/9		11/10					28/2	10/1			14/3	17/1		15/11	25/10	1
2 Barnes		X	10/1		7/3	24/1	14/2		27/9		15/11	6/9	18/10					2
3 Effingham	18/10		X					8/11		6/9	17/1			27/9	20/12	7/3	14/2	3
4 Esso		20/12	24/1	X	6/9	14/2	7/3		18/10			27/9	8/11					4
5 Farnborough	17/1		20/9		X	11/10	25/10	31/1			14/3			20/12	28/2			5
6 Gosport	8/11	28/2				X		20/12		27/9	31/1			18/10	17/1	6/9		6
7 Guy's Hospital	20/12		14/3		20/9		X	17/1		18/10	28/2			8/11	31/1			7
8 Jersey	7/3	11/10		25/10				X		17/1				20/9	14/2	10/1	15/11	8
9 Old Alleynian		25/10		17/1	15/11	10/1	14/3		X		11/10	14/2		20/9				9
10 Old Emanuel		28/2		14/3	8/11			17/1		X		20/12	31/1			11/10	20/9	10
11 Old Reedonians	27/9			10/1				18/10		7/3	X			6/9	8/11	14/2	24/1	11
12 Old Walcourtians	31/1		11/10		10/1	25/10	15/11	28/2			20/9	X			14/3			12
13 Old Whitgiftians		15/11		14/2	10/1	24/1		6/9		25/10	7/3		X	11/10				13
14 Portsmouth		14/3		20/9					31/1	15/11	17/1	28/2		X		25/10	11/10	14
15 Purley	6/9	25/10		15/11					27/9		14/2			7/3	X	24/1	10/1	15
16 Southampton		31/1		28/2	18/10		27/9		20/12			8/11	17/1			X	14/3	16
17 University Vandals		17/1		31/1	27/9	7/3	6/9		8/11			18/10	20/12				X	17
	1	2	3	4	5	6	7	8	9	10	11	12	13	14	15	16	17	

ALTON RFC
Ground Address: Anstey Park, Anstey Road, Alton, Hampshire. GU34 2RL   Tel: 01420 82076
Brief Directions: From A31 take A339 towards Alton Town. After approx half a mile ground on right.
Club Secretary: Keith Page, 31 Nursery Rd, Alresford, Hampshire. SO24 9JW   Tel: (H) 01962 734302   (W) 01483 573727
Fixtures Secretary: Martin Simpson, 10 Gauvain Cl, Alton, Hampshire. GU34 2SB   Tel: (H) 01420 86880
Club Colours: Red

BARNES RFC
Ground Address: Barnes Harrodians Sports Club, Barn Elms, Queen Elizabeth Walk, Barnes, London SW13 8DG.   Tel: 0181 876 7685
Brief Directions: From Hammersmith and Kensington cross Hammersmith Bridge, down Castlenau for 3/4 mile, left into Quenn Elizabeth Walk at Red Lion PH, Ground at end of road 1/2 mile long. (Plenty parking).
Club Secretary: Paul Kirby, 53 Stanhope Gardens, London SW7 5RF.   Tel: (H) 0171 373 9120   Tel: (W) 0171 602 5678
Fixtures Secretary: Andy Long: Tel: (H) 0181 948 3809   (W) 01784 474746
Club Colours: Green and gold shirts, green shorts.

EFFINGHAM RFC
Ground Address: King George V Playing Fields, Browns Lane, Effingham, Surrey   Tel: 01372 458845
Brief Directions: A3 to M25 junction, Effingham signpost left on slip road south bound, follow road until right at Lord Howard pub, then right then left, forward until lights then left and 1st left
Club Secretary: Mike Wheeler, 34 Oakfields, Broadacres, Guildford, Surrey. GU3 3AU   Tel: (H) 01483 835262
Fixtures Secretary: E Newton   Tel: (H) 01708 754434 (W) 0171 738 1122
Club Colours: Emerald green and amber hoops, black shorts

ESSO (FAWLEY) RFC
Ground Address: Esso Recreation Ground, 179-181 Long Lane, Holbury, Southampton.   Tel: 01703 893750
Brief Directions: From M27 J2 follow A326 to Fawley for approx 8 miles. Ground on right after Haraley Roundabout.
Club Secretary: Gary Locke, 40 Hillview Road, Hythe, Southampton, SO45 5GL.   Tel: 01703 849035
Fixtures Secretary: Gary Locke
Club Colours: Red shirts, Navy blue shorts, red socks

FARNBOROUGH RUFC
Ground Address: Tilebarn Close, Cove, Farnborough, Hampshire. GU14 8LS   Tel: 01252 542750
Brief Directions: M3 J4, follow road signs to A325 Farnborough, at 1st set of lights, follow direction signs to Rugby Club
Club Secretary: Paul L Davies, 7 Woodcut Road, Wrecclesham, Farnham, Surrey. GU10 4QF   Tel: (H) 01252 716088   (W) 01252 342266
Fixtures Secretary: Barry Mackay   Tel: 01252 512363
Club Colours: Dark and light blue hoops

GOSPORT AND FAREHAM RFC
Ground Address: Gosport Park, Dolphin Crescent, Gosport, Hants. PO12 2HE   Tel: 01705 353235
Brief Directions: M27 J11, A32 Gosport at dble r'bout, lft at 2nd r'bout, past HMS Sultan lft at r'bout, r.h. lane after Kellys Hotel & immediate left, 5th rt (Molesw'th Rd), turn right & left over bridge
Club Secretary: Ian Rackham, 265 Hawthorn Crescent, Cosham ,Portsmouth PO6 2TL   Tel: (H) 01705 796625
Fixtures Secretary: Mr P Tomlinson   Tel: 01705 617673
Club Colours: Royal blue and old gold

GUYS HOSPITAL RFC
Ground Address: Honor Oak Park, London. SE23 1NW   Tel: 0181 690 1612
Brief Directions: South Circular A205 onto B218 (Brockley Rise), crossroads B238 turn right 200 yards club on right
Club Secretary: Richard Clinton, 385 Southwark Park Road, Bermondsey. SE16   Tel: (H) 0171 237 0522   (W) 0171 955 5000 Ext 5430
Fixtures Secretary: Graham Cawtom   Tel: (H) 0171 735 3857   (W) 0171 955 4255
Club Colours: Blue and gold hoops

JERSEY RFC
Ground Address: Ruedes Landes, St Peter, Jersey C I. JE3 7BG   Tel: 01534 499929
Brief Directions: Opposite airport
Club Secretary: Mr.R.Shambrook, Maufont Lodge, Jardin de la Fontaine, St. Saviour, Jersey. Channel Islands   Tel: 01534 855645
Fixtures Secretary: Mr C Chipperfield   Tel: 01534 811961
Club Colours: Red shirts, white shorts

OLD ALLEYNIAN FC
Ground Address: Dulwich Common, Dulwich, London. SE21 7HA   Tel: 0181 693 2402
Brief Directions: On the south side of the South Circular (A205), 0.5 mile east of Dulwich College
Club Secretary: R A (Joe) Crow, 99 Burbage Road, Dulwich, London. SE24 9HD   Tel: (H) 0171 274 2659
Fixtures Secretary: Alastair N Capon, 182 Hayes Lane, Bromley, Kent. BR2 9EL.   Tel: 0181 462 0886
Club Colours: Dark blue, light blue and black hoops

OLD EMANUEL RFC
Ground Address: Blagdons, Blagdon Lane, New Malden, Surrey   Tel: 0181 942 3857
Brief Directions: From Burlington Rd Roundabout on A3 at New Malden. Using north bound slip road to London ground situated 200 yards on left
Club Secretary: I A Blair, 28 Hunters Road, Chessington, Surrey. KT9 1RV   Tel: (H) 0181 397 1272   (W) 0171 872 3349
Fixtures Secretary: J Monkhouse   Tel: (H) 01483 827323   (W) 01483 764114
Club Colours: White

OLD REEDONIANS
Ground Address: North Avenue, Whiteley Village, Walton-on-Thames, Surrey. KT12 4DX   Tel: 01932 849616
Brief Directions: From A3/A245 junction towards Woking. After 1/4 mile turn right on B365 (Seven Hills Road). At 1st r'about turn right into Burwood Rd. Enter village & ground is 1/4 mile on right.
Club Secretary: John B Rogers, 8 Model Cottages, East Sheen, London. SW14 7PH.   Tel: (H) 0181 876 1512   Tel: (W) 01932 864335
Fixtures Secretary: David Nash, 41 Kennel Road, Fetcham, Surrey. KT12 2JR.   Tel: (H) 01372 452601   (W) 0181 560 4111.
Club Colours: Dark blue, light blue, red and white hoops.

OLD WALCOUNTIANS RFC
Ground Address: Clockhouse, Carshalton Road, Woodmansterne, Banstead, Surrey. SM7 3HU   Tel: 01737 354348
Brief Directions: Carshalton Rd is approx 2 miles from A217, off Croydon Lane, the clubhouse is approx 0.5 mile along Carshalton Rd on the left
Club Secretary: Michael Swettenham, 4 Blakehall Rd., Carshalton, Surrey SM5 3EZ
Fixtures Secretary: Mr R McDowell   Tel: (H) 0181 669 6801
Club Colours: Black, blue and gold

OLD WHITGIFTIAN RFC
Ground Address: Croham Manor Road, South Croydon, Surrey. CR2 7BG   Tel: 0181 686 2127 (office) 0181 688 3248 (bar)
Brief Directions: 1 mile south of Central Croydon on A235, fork left at The Swan & Sugarloaf pub into Selsdon Rd, 300 yds mini r'bout 2nd exit into Croham Rd, ground 0.5 mile on right
Club Secretary: Geoff Austin, 97 Clifton Road, Kingston-upon-Thames, Surrey. KT2 6PL   Tel: (H) 0181 549 3757   (W) 0171 926 5400
Fixtures Secretary: Geoff Austin   Tel: (H) 0181 549 3757   (W) 0171 926 5400
Club Colours: Red, black and blue hooped shirts, white shorts

PORTSMOUTH RFC
Ground Address: Norway Road, Hilsea, Portsmouth   Tel: 01705 660610
Club Secretary: Roger T Hollis, 69 Blackbrook Road, Fareham, Hampshire. PO15 5DE.   Tel: 01329 236506
Fixtures Secretary: Mr W. Arnold, 61 Chetwynd Road, Southsea, Hampshire.   Tel: (H) 01705 821109   (W) 01705 819125
Club Colours: Black with 3 white & gold hoops

PURLEY RFC
Ground Address: Parsons Pightle, Coulsdon Road, Old Coulsdon, Surrey. CR5 1EE   Tel: 01737 553042
Brief Directions: M25 J7 - M23-A23, turn right in Coulsdon to Marl Pit Lane, to end turn right, Coulsdon Road, ground 0.5 mile on right
Club Secretary: Simon Witham, 2 Kingswood Avenue, Sanderstead, Surrey. CR2 9DQ   Tel: (H) 0181 657 2089   (W) 0171 247 4466
Fixtures Secretary: Martin Bazley   Tel: (H) 0181 660 2157   (W) 0171 377 5423
Club Colours: Black and white

SOUTHAMPTON RFC
Ground Address: Lower Brownhill Road, Millbrook, Southampton, Hants   Tel: 01703 737777
Brief Directions: M27 onto M271, take 1st slip road, 1st exit off roundabout towards Lordshill, after 150 yds turn right into Lower Brownhill Road
Club Secretary: Paul Raine, 7 Beattie Rise, Hedge End, Southampton. SO30 4RF   Tel: (H) 01489 788460   (W) 01489 575420
Fixtures Secretary: George Materna   Tel: (H) 01489 786704   (W) 01489 886611
Club Colours: Red and white hoops

UNIVERSITY VANDALS RFC
Ground Address: Brownacres, The Towing Path, Walton-on-Thames, Surrey   Tel: 01932 227659
Club Secretary: A Williams, 7 Clarence Close, Walton-on-Thames, Surrey. KT12 5JX   Tel: (H) 01932 229727 (W) 0171 259 6633
Fixtures Secretary: C J Cockrean   Tel: (H) 01932 226837
Club Colours: Black, purple and emerald green

SURREY ONE

Surrey One 1997-98 Fixtures	Battersea Ironsides	Chobham	Chipstead	Cranleigh	Farnham	John Fisher Old Boys	KCS Old Boys	Kingston	Old Caterhamians	Old Cranleighans	Old Paulines	Raynes Park	Wandsworthians	Woking	
	1	2	3	4	5	6	7	8	9	10	11	12	13	14	
1 Battersea Ironsides	X	10/1		14/2	15/11	24/1			11/10			27/9		25/10	1
2 Chobham		X			20/9			20/12	17/1		18/10		8/11	31/1	2
3 Chipstead	18/10	24/1	X	27/9	10/1	14/2						8/11		15/11	3
4 Cranleigh		15/11		X	25/10	10/1		31/1	20/9					11/10	4
5 Farnham					X			8/11	20/12	14/2	27/9	31/1	18/10	17/1	5
6 John Fisher Old Boys		25/10			11/10	X		17/1	31/1				20/12	20/9	6
7 KCS Old Boys	8/11	14/2	20/12	18/10	24/1	27/9	X					17/1			7
8 Kingston	20/9		11/10				25/10	X	15/11		10/1		24/1		8
9 Old Caterhamians			25/10				15/11	27/9	X	10/1	24/1	18/10	14/2		9
10 Old Cranleighans	20/12	27/9	17/1	8/11		18/10	31/1			X					10
11 Old Paulines	17/1		31/1	20/12		8/11	20/9		11/10		X				11
12 Raynes Park		11/10		24/1		15/11		14/2		20/9	25/10	X	10/1		12
13 Wandsworthians	31/1		14/9	17/1			11/10			25/10	15/11		X		13
14 Woking							10/1	18/10	8/11	24/1	14/2	20/12	27/9	X	14
	1	2	3	4	5	6	7	8	9	10	11	12	13	14	

THIS DIRECTORY IS NOT FOR CLUB OFFICIALS ONLY!
Do your club supporters know they can buy their own directory and help club funds?

BATTERSEA IRONSIDES RFC
Ground Address: Garret Green, Burntwood Lane, Earlsfield, London. SW17   Tel: 0181 879 9913
Brief Directions: From south: turn left at Tooting Broadway towards Wandsworth, after 2nd r'bout Burntwood Ln is 1st main road on right, Garret Green is 500m on right, club a further 300m on left
Club Secretary: Martin Paul Tanner, 1 Woodland Way, Morden, Surrey. SM4 4DS   Tel: (H) 0181 540 5784 (W) 0585 778712
Fixtures Secretary: Tony Szulc   Tel: (H) 0171 622 7694
Club Colours: Green jerseys with white band, white shorts, red socks

CHIPSTEAD RFC
Ground Address: The Meads, High Road, Chipstead, Surrey   Tel: 01737 553035
Club Secretary: Tony Greig, 8 Yew Tree Close, Chipstead, Surrey CR5 3LH   Tel: (W) 0171 327 3415 Tel: (H) 01737 552396
Fixtures Secretary: R. W. Adair, 56 Woodcrest Road, Purley, Surrey CR8 4JB   Tel: (H) 0181 668 3428   (W) 0181 686 8911
Club Colours: Gold and royal blue

CHOBHAM RFC
Ground Address: Fowlers Wells, Windsor Road, Chobham, Woking, Surrey. GU24 8NA   Tel: 01276 858616
Brief Directions: Take road to Sunningdale out of village centre (B383), ground is 500 yards on right behind Cobham Working Mens Club
Club Secretary: Mrs Pam Squire, Cobbitts, Guildford Road, Chobham, Woking, Surrey. GU24 8EA   Tel: (H) 01276 858438
Fixtures Secretary: John Shalley, Tudor Cottage, 61 Chertsey Rd, Chobham, Woking, Surrey, GU24 8PT Tel (H) 01276 855410
Club Colours: Scarlet and gold hoops on navy blue

CRANLEIGH RFC
Ground Address: Wildwood Lane, Alfold, Cranleigh, Surrey   Tel: 01483 275843
Brief Directions: From Guildford A281 towards Horsham, left turn after Bookers Lea Farm, signed Cranleigh Brickworks. From Cranleigh High St, via Knowle Lane turn right at Wildwood Lane
Club Secretary: Mrs Christine Williams, 36 Sylvaways Close, Cranleigh, Surrey. GU6 7HG   Tel: (H) 01483 276928
Fixtures Secretary: Mr Derek Coward, 2 Dover Court, Cranleigh, Surrey, GU6 7EZ.   Tel: (H) 01483 271247 (W) 01483 275248
Club Colours: Red and navy blue quarters, red socks, blue shorts

Old Pauline F.C. transfer to 'Surrey One' from 'Herts/Middx Two'.
The Club celebrated its 125th Anniversary Season by holding a full C.L.O.B. XV to 24-27 on 7th May 1997, when the President of the R.F.U, John Richardson, also planted a tree.
Back: (Referee), Dave Bridgeman, Andy Tyson, Duncan Gordon-Smith, Mike French, Chris Matthews, Dave Clein, Alex York, John Kirkpatrick, Mike Bell, John Errington (Club Captain), Dick Bayne, Des Beirne (Coach).
Front: Guy Gibbs, Alan Sullivan, Neil Robinson, Pat Venning, Dave Taylor (1st XV Captain), Ali Greer, Jason Mawer, John Patterson, (Absent: Mike J.A. Freeman).

FARNHAM RUFC
Ground Address: Westfield Lane, Wreulesham, Farnham, Surrey. GU10 4QP   Tel: 01252 721138
Brief Directions: Take A325 to Petersfield from A31 Farnham bypass, after 0.75 mile pass Bear & Ragged Staff pub on right turn next right into Riverdale, 1st left onto recreation ground
Club Secretary: Derek R Wall, 22 Hope Lane, Farnham, Surrey. GU9 0HZ   Tel: (H) 01252 710476
Fixtures Secretary: J F Robertson   Tel: (H) 01252 712387   (W) 01344 850414
Club Colours: Black and white 2" hoops, black shorts

JOHN FISHER OLD BOYS RFC
Ground Address: 198 Limpsfield Road, Hamsey Green, Warlingham, Surrey   Tel: 01883 625149
Brief Directions: M25 J6 (Godstone), follow A22 towards Whyteleafe & Purley, right at 2nd roundabout, straight over mini roundabout, 1st left to end, right onto Limpsfield Rd, club 0.25 mile on right
Club Secretary: Chris Mallows, 14 Braemar Avenue, South Croydon, Surrey. CR2 0QA   Tel: (H) 0181 660 4756   (W) 01737 782805
Fixtures Secretary: Chris Doyle   Tel: (H) 01279 722588   (W) 0171 816 1015
Club Colours: Blue, gold and white hoops

K.C.S. OLD BOYS RFC
Ground Address: Arthur Road, Motspur Park, New Malden, Surrey. KT3 6LX   Tel: 0181 336 2512
Brief Directions: 10 mins walk from Motspur Park station. From A3 at New Malden underpass, south along A2043, approx 400m left into Motspur Park (Rd), cto Arthur Rd, 2nd right after level crossing
Club Secretary: Noel M Crockford, 78 Claygate Lane, Hinchley Wood, Surrey. KT10 0BJ   Tel: (H) 0181 398 7474   (W) 0181 398 6499
Fixtures Secretary: Andy Todd   Tel: (H) 0181 942 0048   (W) 0181 395 3808
Club Colours: Red, blue and old gold hoops

KINGSTON RFC
Ground Address: King Edward Recreation Ground, Hook Road, Chessington, Surrey. KT9 1PL   Tel: 0181 397 8385
Brief Directions: Leave A3 at Hook roundabout, follow sign for A243 Chessington, entrance approx 200 yards on the right
Club Secretary: Nick Deere, 14 Bolton Road, Chessington, Surrey KT9 2JB Tel: (Day) 01737 784258
Fixtures Secretary: Robin Wilcox, 17 Warren Drive North, Surbiton, Surrey   Tel: 0181 399 6029
Club Colours: Maroon and white hoops, blue shorts

OLD CATERHAMIAN RFC
Ground Address: Park Avenue, Caterham, Surrey. CR3 6AH   Tel: 01883 343488
Brief Directions: From Caterham Station up Church Hill, 1st left into Stansted Road, Park Avenue 1st on right
Club Secretary: Mrs L Myland, Ash Trees, 15 Portley Lane, Caterham, Surrey. CR3 5JR Tel: (H&B 01883 343319
Fixtures Secretary: M Rowland   Tel: (H) 01342 842115   (W) 01737 775160
Club Colours: Black, amber, silver, mauve, black shorts

OLD CRANLEIGHAN RFC
Ground Address: Old Portsmouth Road, Thames Ditton, Surrey. KT7 0HB   Tel: 0181 398 3092
Club Secretary: Mark Lubbock, 52 Sarsfield Road, London. SW12 8HN   Tel: (H) 0181 398 3092
Fixtures Secretary: Tony Price   Tel: (H) 0181 949 1194   (W) 0181 533 7588
Club Colours: Blue, white and gold hoops

OLD PAULINE FC
Ground Address: St Nicholas Road, off Speer Road, Thames Ditton, Surrey. KT7 0PW   Tel: 0181 398 1858
Brief Directions: From r'bout in Hampton Court Way (A309) turn east, 400m to Thames Ditton Station, after railway arch 1st left into Speer Rd, 2nd right into St Nicholas Rd
Club Secretary: John Howard, 93A Richmond Park Road, Kingston, Syrrey. KT2 6AF   Tel: (H) 0181 541 3817   (W) 01372 464470 (FX) 0171 982 2258
Fixtures Secretary: John Howard   Tel: (H) 0181 541 3817   (W) 01372 464470
Club Colours: Red, white and black hoops

RAYNES PARK RFC
Ground Address: Raynes Park Sports Ground, Taunton Avenue, Raynes Park, London. SW20
Brief Directions: Shannon Corner exit A3 to Raynes Park, last turning left (Camberley Ave) before Coombe Lane/West Barnes Lane traffic lights
Club Secretary: Russell Price, 101 Belmont Avenue, New Malden, Surrey. KT3 6QE   Tel: (H) 0181 949 2448   (W) 0171 299 5082
Fixtures Secretary: As for Secretary
Club Colours: Blue and gold jerseys, blue shorts and stockings

WANDSWORTHIANS RFC
Ground Address: Kings College Sports Ground, Windsor Avenue, New Malden, Surrey. KT3 5HA   Tel: 0181942 0495
Club Secretary: Ian Maclean, 45 More Lane, Esher, Surrey   Tel: (H) 01372 463121
Fixtures Secretary: Gary Kirkwood   Tel: (H) 0181 640 0263   (W) 0181 665 3756
Club Colours: Maroon, white and gold hoops

WOKING RFC
Ground Address: Byfleet Recreation Ground, Stream Close, off Rectory Lane, Byfleet, Surrey   Tel: 01932 343693
Brief Directions: Leave A3 at Painshill (Cobham & Byfleet) junction A245 to Byfleet, over 3 main roundabouts, turn left at 4th into High Rd and then right into Rectory Lane
Club Secretary: Andrew Jones, 66 Kings Rd, New Haw, Surrey KT15 3BQ   Tel: (H) 01932 880936   (W) 0181 214 2525
Fixtures Secretary: Mr Ian Vousden   Tel: (H) 01483 836817
Club Colours: Blue and gold hoops, black shorts

SURREY TWO

Surrey Two 1997-98 Fixtures	Antlers 1	Cobham 2	Law Society 3	London Medic 4	Merton 5	Old Freemans 6	Old Haileyburians 7	Old Rutlishians 8	Old Suttonians 9	Old Tiffinians 10	Old Wellingtonians 11	Reigate & Redhill 12	Shirley Wanderers 13	
1 Antlers	X				11/10	17/1	20/9	8/11			14/2		20/12	1
2 Cobham	27/9	X			20/12	7/3		17/1	25/10				31/1	2
3 Law Society	25/10	10/1	X			27/9		31/1	15/11				7/3	3
4 London Medic	10/1	14/2	20/9	X		15/11			24/1	11/10				4
5 Merton			17/1	7/3	X		15/11			31/1	25/10	27/9		5
6 Old Freemans					20/9	X	14/2	11/10			24/1	10/1	8/11	6
7 Old Haileyburians		8/11	20/12	31/1			X			17/1	27/9	7/3		7
8 Old Rutlishians				27/9	24/1		10/1	X		7/3	15/11	25/10		8
9 Old Suttonians	7/3				8/11	31/1	11/10	20/12	X				17/1	9
10 Old Tiffinians	15/11	24/1	14/2		25/10			10/1		X		27/9		10
11 Old Wellingtonians		11/10	8/11	17/1					20/9	20/12	X	31/1		11
12 Reigate & Redhill	24/1	20/9	11/10	20/12					14/2	8/11		X		12
13 Shirley Wanderers				25/10	14/2		24/1	20/9			10/1	15/11	X	13
	1	2	3	4	5	6	7	8	9	10	11	12	13	

ANTLERS RFC
Ground Address: Bushy Park, Teddington, Middlesex Tel: 0181 977 4989
Brief Directions: Ground adjacent to Teddington Cricket Club in Bushy Park, at the rear of N.P.L.
Club Secretary: Peter Woolgar, 114 Elgin Avenue, Ashford, Middlesex. TW15 1QG Tel: (H) 01784 259734 (W) 01268 564113
Fixtures Secretary: Rod Bromfield Tel: (H) 0181 979 5635
Club Colours: Dark blue

COBHAM RFC
Ground Address: The Memorial Ground, Fairmile Lane, Cobham, Surrey Tel: 01932 863245
Brief Directions: Ground situated on junction of Fairmile Lane and the Portsmouth road (A307) approx 3 miles from Esher, 1 mile from Cobham opposite Fairmile Hotel
Club Secretary: Andrew Harburn, 21 The Avenue, Surbiton, Surrey, KT5 8JW/ Tel: 0181 8482738
Fixtures Secretary: Ian Johnson, 209 Portsmouth Road, Cobham, Surrey, KT11 1JR. Tel: (H) 01932 862694 (W) 0181 942 1033
Club Colours: Blue, maroon and gold quarters

LAW SOCIETY RFC
Ground Address: Beverly Meads, Barham Road, Copse Hill, Wimbledon. Sw20
Club Secretary: Adam Walker, Wedlake Bell, 16 Bedford Street, London W2E 9HF. Tel: (W) 0171 876 5542 Tel: (H) 0171 379 7266
Fixtures Secretary: Harold Young Tel: (W) 0171 737 7610 Tel: (H) 0171 542 6273
Club Colours: Black , Maroon and White Hoops.

LONDON MEDIA RUFC
Ground Address: Battersea Park, London
Brief Directions: Albert Bridge Road entrance to Battersea Park (near Albert Bridge)
Club Secretary: Nick Field, 315a Cavendish Road, Balham, London. SW12 0PQ Tel: (H) 0181 673 3809 (W) 0171 734 5358
Club Colours: Black and white quarters

MERTON RFC
Ground Address: Morden Recreation Ground, Faversham Road, Morden, Surrey
Brief Directions: From Rose Hill roundabout take St Helier Ave (A297), 1st left into Middleton Rd, then 4th exit from roundabout into Faversham Rd, entrance to ground is 100 yards on left
Club Secretary: Robert Smith, SCCS, Charrington Street, London. NW1 1RG Tel: (W) 0171 387 0126
Fixtures Secretary: Paul Webster Tel: (H) 0171 736 0149 (W) 0181 874 8182
Club Colours: Gold, black and white quarters

OLD FREEMANS RFC
Ground Address: City of London Freemen's School, Ashtead Park, Ashtead, Surrey. KT21 1ET   Tel: 01372 274158
Brief Directions: From Epsom Leatherhead A24 road turn into Park Lane Epsom end of Ashstead take 1st left through gates into park. Entrance to school ground 400 yards on right.
Club Secretary: Peter Ling, 74 Woodlands Road, Bookham, Surrey. KT24 4HH.   Tel: 01372 459172.
Fixtures Secretary: M J Bailey, 123 Overdale, Ashstead, Surrey. KT21 1PZ.   Tel: (H) 01372 278505 (W) 0181 642 3419
Club Colours: Dark blue, maroon & gold shirts, dark blue shorts

OLD HAILEYBURIANS
Ground Address: 27 Ruxley Lane, Kingston Road, Ewell, Surrey. KT19 0JB   Tel: 0181 393 3901
Brief Directions: Reached from London by Portsmouth Rd (A3), take left filter to Epsom about 200 yds from Tolworth underpass along Kingston Rd, after 1 mile right into Ruxley Lane, 100 yards on left
Club Secretary: Roderick Sheen, 29 Kenilworth Avenue, London. SW19 7LN   Tel: (H) 0181 879 7851 (W) 0171 782 0990
Fixtures Secretary: Peter Blackmore 19 St, Andrews Street, Hertford, Herts. SG14 1HZ
Club Colours: Magenta and white hoops

OLD RUTLISHIANS RFC
Ground Address: Old Rutlishians Association, Poplar Road, Merton Park. SW19   Tel: 0181 542 3678
Brief Directions: Kingston Rd Merton to Dorset Rd by Merton Park level crossing, proceed along Dorset Rd to Melrose Ave, take left fork for Poplar Road
Club Secretary: W H Griffin, 68 Love Lane, Morden, Surrey. SM4 6LP   Tel: (H) 0181 395 1875
Fixtures Secretary: John Petrides   Tel: (H) 0181 657 7750   (W) 0181 679 6233
Club Colours: Gold, silver, azure and black

OLD SUTTONIANS RFC
Ground Address: Walch Pavilion, Priest Hill, Banstead Road, Ewell, Surrey   Tel: 0181 393 7427
Brief Directions: By road: travel east on A232, pass TJ Ribs, under rail bridge, 1st right into Banstead Rd. By train: Network SE to Ewell East station, club behind station
Club Secretary: Mr S J Udall, 16 Kingsdown Road, Cheam, Surrey. SM3 8NY   Tel: (H) 0181 644 7259 (W) 01992 560330
Fixtures Secretary: Mr I M Connell   Tel: (H) 0181 642 8915
Club Colours: Red, white and black

OLD TIFFINIAN RFC
Ground Address: Grist Memorial Ground, Summer Road, off Hampton Court Way, East Molesey, Surrey   Tel: 0181 398 1391
Brief Directions: Hampton Court roundabout along Hampton Court way (A309).To turn into Summer Road you have to go to roundabout and come back , it is then first left.
Club Secretary: Mr A Green, 2 Caroline Court, 25 Lovelace Road, Surbiton, Surrey   Tel: (H) 0181 399 9223   (W) 0181 330 8201
Fixtures Secretary: Mr R G Kirkwood   Tel: (H) 0181 898 1767
Club Colours: Violet, white and navy blue

OLD WELLINGTONIAN RFC
Ground Address: 27 Ruxley Lane, Kingston Road, Ewell, Surrey (Shared with Old Haileyburians RFC)   Tel: 0181 393 3901
Brief Directions: East off the A3 from Tolworth Roundabout.
Club Secretary: Nick Dennis, 24 Coleford Road, London SW18 1AD.   Tel: (H) 0181 874 8486 (B) 0171 600 2801
Fixtures Secretary: Nick Prichard, 86a Iffley Road, London. W6 0PF.   Tel: (H) 0181 748 4002 (B) 01784 452600
Club Colours: Black with orange, light blue & yellow stripes

REIGATE & REDHILL RFC
Ground Address: Eric Hodgkins Memorial Ground, Colley Lane, Reigate, Surrey   Tel: 01737 221110
Brief Directions: M25 J8 south on Reigate Hill, turn right before level crossing, to end of road turn right then keep left into Colley Lane, club 200m on right
Club Secretary: Norman Phillips, 28 Hurstleigh Drive, Redhill, Surrey. RH1 2AA   Tel: (H) 01737 212912
Fixtures Secretary: Mick Blackie   Tel: (H) 01737 247418
Club Colours: Royal blue with 2 white, 1 light blue hoop

SHIRLEY WANDERERS RUFC
Ground Address: Kent Gate, Addington Road, West Wickham, Kent   Tel: 0181 777 5298
Club Secretary: Martin Stone, 251 Quentin Court, Regency Walk, Shirley, Croydon, Surrey   Tel: (H) 0181 777 6712
Fixtures Secretary: Geoff Jeffcoat   Tel: (H) 0181 777 5174   (W) 0181 761 3000
Club Colours: All white

SURREY THREE

Surrey Three 1997-98 Fixtures	Bec Old Boys 1	Croydon 2	Egham 3	Haslemere 4	King's Coll. Hos. 5	Lightwater 6	London Cornish 7	London Fire Brig 8	Mitcham 9	Old Bevonian 10	Old Johnians 11	Worth Old Boys 12	
1 Bec Old Boys	X		25/10		15/11	10/1			24/1	27/9			1
2 Croydon	20/9	X		10/1			24/1	25/10	27/9			15/11	2
3 Egham	17/1	8/11	X	20/9	20/12		11/10					24/1	3
4 Haslemere				X		8/11		31/1	17/1	20/12		27/9	4
5 King's College Hospital	8/11	11/10		24/1	X		20/9	15/11				10/1	5
6 Lightwater		17/1	27/9		31/1	X	20/12			25/10			6
7 London Cornish				15/11			X	27/9	31/1	17/1		25/10	7
8 London Fire Brigade	20/12		10/1			20/9		X	8/11	11/10	24/1		8
9 Mitcham	11/10		15/11		25/10	24/1			X	20/9	10/1		9
10 Old Bevonian		31/1	25/10		27/9	10/1				X	15/11		10
11 Old Johnians		20/12	31/1	11/10	17/1		8/11				X		11
12 Worth Old Boys	31/1					11/10		17/1	20/12	8/11	20/9	X	12
	1	2	3	4	5	6	7	8	9	10	11	12	

BEC OLD BOYS
Ground Address: Sutton Manor Sports & Social Club, Northey Avenue, Cheam, Surrey. SM2 7HJ Tel: 0181 642 3423
Brief Directions: Right off of A217 into Northey Avenue
Club Secretary: Mr Nick Ryan, 201 Lennard Road, Beckenham, Bromley. BR3 1QN Tel: (H) 0181 778 9984 (W) 0171 247 7441
Fixtures Secretary: Mr Rick Mayhew Tel: (H) 0181 286 2463
Club Colours: Blue, old gold and white hoop

CROYDON RFC
Ground Address: Layhams Road (junction with King Henry's Drive), Keston, Bromley, Kent Tel: 01959 573409
Brief Directions: A2022 to Addington Village, at r'bout 200yds beyond Gravel Hill, fork south to New Addington as signed up Lodge Ln, left at next r'bout into King Henry's Drive, left at end into Layhams Rd
Club Secretary: Trevor Davies, 62 Coulsdon Road, Coulsdon, Surrey. CR5 2LB Tel: (H) 0181 668 4864 (W) 0171 976 0066
Fixtures Secretary: Bob Goodwin Tel: (H) 0181 653 9819
Club Colours: Black, magenta, white hoops

EGHAM RFC
Ground Address: Coopers Hill Sports Club, Coopers Hill Lane, Engleffield Green, surrey, TW20 0LB.
Brief Directions: M25 J13 onto A30 towards Egham, along Egham bypass (Runneymede on right), turn into High St at r'bout at bottom of hill, ground on left just past Crown public house
Club Secretary: Robert John Deacon, 2 Hythe Park Road, Egham, Surrey. TW20 8BW Tel: (H) 01784 740640 (W) 01784 436502
Fixtures Secretary: Paul Garrett Tel: (H) 01784 477151
Club Colours: Mid blue with gold hoop

HASLEMERE
Ground Address: The Pavilion, Woolmer Hill Sports Ground, Haslemere, Surrey Tel: 01428 643072
Brief Directions: Off A3 turn down Sandy Lane at Bramshott Chase towards Hammer Vale, turn left to Woolmer Hill and then left to Woolmer Hill Sports Ground and school
Club Secretary: David Cooper, The Wood Pigeon, Combe Lane, Initley, Wormley, Surrey. GU8 5TB Tel: (H & W) 01428 682362
Fixtures Secretary: Tony Griffin Tel: (H) 01428 661985 (W) 0171 405 4446
Club Colours: Light blue and white hoops

KINGS COLLEGE HOSPITAL
Ground Address: The Griffin Sportsground, 12 Dulwich Village, Dulwich, London SE21 7AL Tel: 0181 693 6900/2330.
Club Secretary: N. Bunker, 24 Maxted Road, Peckham, London SE15 4LL. Tel: (H) 0171 277 6919 (B) 0171 737 4000 ext 4050/4051 (F) 0171 733 0210
Fixtures Secretary: As Above.
Club Colours: Navy, Sky Blue, Maroon Hoops.

LIGHTWATER RFC
Ground Address: The Sports Centre, The Avenue, Lightwater, Surrey. GU18 5RQ Tel: 01276 472664
Club Secretary: Anthony Sharp, 65 Cedar Close, Bagshot, Surrey. GU19 5AB Tel: (H) 01276 472994 (W) 01483 729661
Fixtures Secretary: Dave Forsaith Tel: (H) 01252 871400
Club Colours: Green and white quarters, black shorts

LONDON CORNISH RFC
Ground Address: Richardson Evans Memorial Ground, Roehampton Lane, Kingston, Surrey Tel: 0181 788 3628
Brief Directions: On main A3, 200 yards north of Robin Hood roundabout
Club Secretary: Dave Fletcher, 27 Riverbank, Laceham Road, Staines, Middlesex. TW18 2QE Tel: (H) 01784 461927 (W) 0181 813 9494
Fixtures Secretary: Angus Milne Tel: (H) 0171 735 5100 (W) 0171 716 6645
Club Colours: Black with narrow gold hoops

LONDON FIRE BRIGADE RFC
Ground Address: Priest Hill Sports Ground, Banstead Road, Ewell, Surrey. KT17 3HG Tel: 0181 394 1946
Brief Directions: Junction of Cheam Road and Banstead Road, Ewell, next to Ewell East railway station
Club Secretary: Charlie Gilbert, 15 Park Road, Banstead, Surrey. SM7 3BY Tel: (H) 01737 362191
Fixtures Secretary: David Yates Tel: (H) 0181 974 1092
Club Colours: Flame, ember, charcoal

MITCHAM RUFC
Ground Address: Rosehill Recreation Ground, Rosehill, Sutton, Surrey
Club Secretary: Dave Starling, 28 Poole Road, West Ewell, Surrey Tel: (H) 0181 394 2672 (W) 0171 926 3995
Fixtures Secretary: Tony Antoniou Tel: (H) 0181 679 5644 (W) 0171 525 3316
Club Colours: Lavender and green

OLD BEVONIANS RFC
Ground Address: Ballard Coombe, Robin Hood Way, London. SW15 3QF Tel: 0181 942 2907
Brief Directions: Along A3, London bound side between New Malden & Robin Hood R'about.
Club Secretary: Mrs A. Lefeure, 100 Longfellow Road, Worcester Park, Surrey. KT4 8BR Tel: 0181 3302278
Fixtures Secretary: Peter Hunt, 29 Cleves Court, Mill Road, Epsom, Surrey. KT17 4AQ Tel: (H) 01372 748493
Club Colours: Black, amber and green hoops

OLD JOHNIAN RFC
Ground Address: Oaken Lane, Hinchley Wood, Surrey Tel: 0181 398 0535
Club Secretary: Mike Stuttard, 8 Woodside Avenue, Esher, Surrey. KT10 8JQ Tel: (H) 0181 398 9417 (W) 01372 379011
Fixtures Secretary: David Robinson Tel: (H) 01243 775901 (W) 01243 770374
Club Colours: Bottle green and white hoops

WORTH OLD BOYS SOCIETY RFC
Ground Address: c/o 27 Ruxley Lane, Ewell Tel: 0181 393 3901
Brief Directions: Take A240 towards Epsom from A3 at Tolworth Tower exit, after 1 mile at 3rd lights, Ruxley Lane is on the right
Club Secretary: Mr M Madsen, Little Friars, Great Chart, Nr Ashford, Kent Tel: (H) 01233 625441 (W) 0171 629 8863
Fixtures Secretary: Mr S Taylor Tel: (H) 0181 878 9065 (W) 0171 488 4000
Club Colours: Blue and gold quarters

SURREY FOUR

Surrey Four 1997-98 Fixtures	Economicals 1	Oxted 2	Racal Decca 3	St George's Hosp. 4	Surrey Police 5	Surrey University 6	
1 Economicals	X	15/11	8/11	17/1	11/10	20/12	1
2 Oxted	20/9	X	17/1	20/12	8/11	11/10	2
3 Racal Decca	24/1	25/10	X	11/10	20/12	20/9	3
4 St George's Hospital	25/10	27/9	20/12	X	20/9	24/1	4
5 Surrey Police	20/12	24/1	27/9	15/11	X	25/10	5
6 Surrey University	27/9	20/12	15/11	8/11	17/1	X	6
	1	2	3	4	5	6	

ECONOMICALS RUFC
Ground Address: LSE Sports Ground, Windsor Avenue, New Malden, Surrey   Tel: 0181 942 1229
Brief Directions: A3 southbound, right at New Malden roundabout, 3rd left into Presbury Rd leads into Windsor Ave. A3 north, left into South Lane, 2nd left Thetford Rd leads into Windsor Ave
Club Secretary: Steve Bowen, 60 South Eden Park Road, Beckenham, Kent, BR3 3BG.   Tel: 0181 7762953
Fixtures Secretary: Steve Bowen   Tel: (H) 0181 7762953
Club Colours: Green and white hoops

OXTED RFC
Ground Address: Holland Fields, Holland Road, Hurst Green, Oxted, Surrey   Tel: 01883 717468
Brief Directions: M25 J6, follow sign to Oxted, turn left onto A25, right into Woodhurst Lane (under railway viaduct), follow for 2 miles, club on right
Club Secretary: Mick Berry, 12 Coldshot Lane, Hurst Green, Oxted, Surrey   Tel: (H) 01883 717261
Fixtures Secretary: Steve Taylor   Tel: (H) 01883 716899
Club Colours: Red hoop on blue shirt, blue shorts, red socks

RACAL DECCA RFC
Ground Address: Decca Sports and Social Club, Kingston Road, Tolworth, Surrey   Tel: 0181 337 9190
Brief Directions: A3 from Guildford/London, turn off at Tolworth junction then A240 towards Ewell, approx 200 yards turn left at traffic lights, ground on left
Club Secretary: Andrew Howard, Flat 7, 18-24 Warwick Way, Pimlico, London. SW1V 1RX Tel: (H) 0171 8345956 (W) 0171 4124607
Fixtures Secretary: Andrew Howard - As above
Club Colours: Blue and white hoops

ST GEORGES HOSPITAL MEDICAL SCHOOL RFC
Ground Address: St George's Hospital Sports Ground, Stoke Road, Cobham, Surrey. Tel: 01932 864341
Club Secretary: Paul Guyver, Camner Terrace, Tooting, London. SW17 0RE   Tel: (H) 0181 767 0440   Tel: (W) 0181 725 2709
Fixtures Secretary: M Manchief   Tel: 0181 725 5077

SURREY POLICE RFC
Ground Address: Police HQ, Mount Browne, Sandy Lane, Guildford. GU1 3HG   Tel: 01483 571212
Brief Directions: From Guildford Town centre take A3100 towards Godalny, 1 mile at Ships PH turn R. into Sandy Lane and HQ is 600 yds on Left
Club Secretary: S P Burrows, 4 Junewood Close, Woodham, New Haw, Addlestone, Surrey. KT15 3PX Tel: (H) 01932 344607   (W) 01483 482757
Fixtures Secretary: Jim Bennett, 49 Coltsfoot Drive, Burpham, Guildford, GU1 1YG. Tel: (H) 01483 826149   (W) 01483 31111 Ext 3167
Club Colours: Black top with red V, black shorts

UNIVERSITY OF SURREY RFC
Ground Address: Varsity Centre Sports Pavilion, Egerton, Guildford, Surrey   Tel: 01483 259242
Club Secretary: Matt Phillips, c/o Sports Office, Union House, University of Surrey, Guildford. GU2 5XH   Tel: (H) 01483 259981
Fixtures Secretary: Dan Wilton
Club Colours: Black

HAMPSHIRE ONE

Hampshire One 1997-98 Fixtures	Andover 1	Eastleigh 2	Guernsey 3	Isle of Wight 4	Millbrook 5	Overton 6	Petersfield 7	Tottonians 8	US Portsmouth 9	
1 Andover	X	20/12	14/2	20/4	28/3	24/1	17/1	7/3	11/10	1
2 Eastleigh	14/3	X	10/1	25/10	27/9	11/10	6/9	24/1	15/11	2
3 Guernsey	27/9	8/11	X	20/12	17/1	7/3	31/1	28/3	28/2	3
4 Isle of Wight	28/2	17/1	14/3	X	18/10	15/11	27/9	8/11	6/9	4
5 Millbrook	15/11	14/2	25/10	24/1	X	20/9	14/3	11/10	10/1	5
6 Overton	18/10	31/1	6/9	28/3	28/2	X	8/11	17/1	27/9	6
7 Petersfield	25/10	7/3	11/10	14/2	20/12	10/1	X	20/9	24/1	7
8 Tottonians	6/9	18/10	15/11	10/1	31/1	25/10	28/2	X	14/3	8
9 US Portsmouth	31/1	28/3	20/9	7/3	8/11	14/2	18/10	20/12	X	9
	1	2	3	4	5	6	7	8	9	

ANDOVER RFC
Ground Address: The Goodship Ground, Foxcotte Park, Hatherden Road, Andover, Hants   Tel: 01264 339518
Brief Directions: From town centre take ring road to Portway Ind Estate, turn into Goch Way, right onto Hatherden Rd, follow road for 0.75 mile to roundabout, turn into Sports Centre
Club Secretary: R J Smith, 17 Longstock Close, Andover, Hants. SP10 3UN   Tel: (H) 01264 359491 (W) 01264 332299
Fixtures Secretary: R J Smith   Tel: (H) 01264 359491 (W) 01264 332299
Club Colours: Black

EASTLEIGH RFC
Ground Address: Bishopstoke Playing Fields, Bishopstoke Road, Eastleigh   Tel: 01703 641312
Brief Directions: From Eastleigh Railway station take turning over railway bridge to Fair Oak and ground is approx 600 yards up on the left
Club Secretary: Mr B M Booth, Redlynch, 72 Station Road, Netley Abbey, Southampton. SO31 5AF   Tel: (H) 01703 452718
Fixtures Secretary: Dr J S Sneezum   Tel: (H) 01703 402286   (W) 01703 616941
Club Colours: Red, amber and black hoops

GUERNSEY RUFC
Ground Address: Footes Lane, St Peter Port, Guernsey   Tel: 01481 54590
Club Secretary: B J Mildon, P O Box 181, St Peter Port, Guernsey   Tel: (H) 01481 65493   (W) 01481 715055
Fixtures Secretary: S W Sidwell   Tel: (H) 01481 711751
Club Colours: Green and white

ISLE OF WIGHT RFC
Ground Address: The Clubhouse, Wootton Recreation Ground, Wootton, Isle of Wight. PO33 4NQ   Tel: 01983 883240
Brief Directions: Right at the Cedars, Wootton, into Church Road, left into Footways, left onto Recreation Ground
Club Secretary: Tracy Allen, 19 Victoria Grove, East Cowes, Isle of Wight. PO32 6DJ   Tel: (H) 01983 280549
Fixtures Secretary: Mr Dave Metcalfe   Tel: (H) 01983 755339
Club Colours: Navy, gold hoops

MILLBROOK RUFC
Ground Address: Lordshill Outdoor Recreation Centre, Redbridge Lane, Lordshill, Southampton   Tel: 01703 739759
Brief Directions: M27 J3 to M271 to J1, A3051, 1st left into Redbridge Lane, 1 mile on right
Club Secretary: Mrs J Ings, 27 Gemini Close, Lordshill, Southampton   Tel: (H)01703 345559
Fixtures Secretary: Wayne Renwick   Tel: (H) 01489 892231
Club Colours: Emerald and scarlet hoops

OVERTON RFC
Ground Address: Town Meadow, High Street, Overton, Basingstoke, Hants
Brief Directions: Basingstoke B3400 through village on right hand side
Club Secretary: Colin Gordon, 6 Waltham Court, Overton, Hants. RG25 3NY   Tel: (H) 01256 771671 (W) 01264 334477
Fixtures Secretary: Alec Coles   Tel: (H) 01256 410836
Club Colours: Royal blue

HAMPSHIRE ONE CONTINUED

PETERSFIELD RFC
Ground Address: Penns Place, Petersfield, Hants.
GU31 4EP Tel: 01730 264588
Brief Directions: East edge of town, co-located with
East Hants District Council offices and Taro Sports
Centre as signed
Club Secretary: Geoff Litchfield, 13 Copse Close,
Petersfield. GU31 4DL Tel: (H) 01730 265072
Fixtures Secretary: Tim Dilks Tel: (H) 01730 267966
Club Colours: Red with white band

TOTTONIANS RFC
Ground Address: Water Lane, Totton, Southampton
Tel: 01703 663810
Brief Directions: Take West Totton Bypass from M27,
turn left at Safeway , right into Calmore Road, left into
Water Lane. Ground on the left.
Club Secretary: Mr G Searle, Meadow End, Romsey
Road, Kings Somborne, Stockbridge Tel: (H) 01794
388779   (W) 01256 482572
Fixtures Secretary: Chris Edwards, 22 Ash Road,
Ashurst, Southampton. Tel: 01703 293294
Club Colours: Green, black and white hoops

UNITED SERVICES PORTSMOUTH RFC
Ground Address: Burnaby Road, Portsmouth,
Hampshire. Tel: 01705 830125
Brief Directions: Enter Portsmouth via M275, follow
signs to Isle of Wight Car Ferries, ground on right under
railway bridge
Club Secretary: John Collins, 4 Neelands Grove,
Paulsgrove, Portsmouth, Hants. PO6 4QL Tel: (H)
01705 380859   (B) 01705 312856
Fixtures Secretary: Bob Gray, 11 Chatham Drive, Old
Portsmouth. Tel: (H) 01705 341375 (B) 01705 726610
Club Colours: Navy blue & red hoops, navy blue shorts

HAMPSHIRE TWO

Hampshire Two 1997-98 Fixtures	Fareham Heathens	Fordingbridge	New Milton	Nomads	Romsey	Sandown & S.	Southampton I.	Trojans	Ventnor	
	1	2	3	4	5	6	7	8	9	
1 Fareham Heathens	X	31/1	20/12	28/2	28/3	7/3	27/9	17/1	8/11	1
2 Fordingbridge	11/10	X	14/2	24/1	20/9	10/1	25/10	20/12	7/3	2
3 New Milton	14/3	27/9	X	6/9	8/11	15/11	28/2	18/10	17/1	3
4 Nomads	20/9	18/2	7/3	X	20/12	14/2	31/1	8/11	28/3	4
5 Romsey	15/11	28/2	10/1	14/3	X	25/10	6/9	31/1	18/10	5
6 Sandown & Shanklin	6/9	8/11	28/3	27/9	17/1	X	18/10	28/2	31/1	6
7 Southampton Institute	14/2	17/1	20/9	11/10	7/3	24/1	X	28/3	20/12	7
8 Trojans	25/10	14/3	24/1	10/1	11/10	20/9	15/11	X	14/2	8
9 Ventnor	10/1	6/9	25/10	15/11	24/1	11/10	14/3	27/9	X	9
	1	2	3	4	5	6	7	8	9	

FAREHAM HEATHENS RFC
Ground Address: Cams Alders Sports Centre, Highfield Avenue, Fareham Tel: 01329 221793
Brief Directions: From Fareham centre A27 west signed S'hampton, at Firestation r'bout stay on A27 for 100m, rt at lights Redlands Ln, rt at next j'tion by pub/church, Sports C'tre next left
Club Secretary: R Townsend, 9 Daisy Lane, Locksheath, Southampton. SO31 6RA Tel: (H) 01489 574945
Fixtures Secretary: Pete Mitchell, 2 Chilworth Gardens, Clanfield, Portsmouth, PO8 0LD. Tel: 01705 348744
Club Colours: Red and black quarters

FORDINGBRIDGE RFC
Ground Address: Recreation Ground, Fordingbridge, Hants Tel: 01425 652047
Brief Directions: Off A338 (12 miles south of Salisbury and 15 miles north of Bournemouth) alongside by- pass, western side adjacent to river .
Club Secretary: Mrs Nicola Stockley, 59 Shaftesbury Street, Fordingbridge, Hants. SP6 1JG Tel: (H) 01425 657204   (W) 01202 664781
Fixtures Secretary: John Trim Tel: (H) 01425 655156 (W) 01202 664781
Club Colours: Sky blue

NEW MILTON RFC
Ground Address: The Sports Ground, Ashley Road, Ashley, New Milton, Hants Tel: 01425 610401
Brief Directions: From centre of town, to Ashley Ground next to Junior School and behind Ashley Hotel
Club Secretary: N E Hanmer, Walsingham, Andrew Lane, Ashley, New Milton, Hants Tel: (H) 01425 612613   (W) 01590 682495
Fixtures Secretary: A Williams, 57 Oakwood Avenue, New Milton, Hants.
Club Colours: Green and white quarters

NOMADS RFC
Ground Address: Farlington's Recreation Ground, Eastern Road, Portsmouth, Hampshire. Tel: 01705 691574
Brief Directions: North side of A27, behind Hilton International Hotel.
Club Secretary: Ken Walker, 38 Warblington Road, Emsworth, Hampshire. PO10 7HQ. Tel: (H) 01243 375263   Tel: (W) 01705 671969
Fixtures Secretary: Ken Walker, as above.
Club Colours: Red and black irregular hoops.

ROMSEY RUFC
Ground Address: Romsey Sports Centre, Lower Southampton Road, Romsey, Hampshire. SO51 8AF Tel: 01794 519400
Brief Directions: M27 J3, follow signs to Romsey, straight over 1st roundabout, left at 2nd roundabout, at end of long wall turn left into Sports Centre
Club Secretary: Andrew Mott, 3 South Close, Romsey, Hampshire. SO51 7UP Tel: (H) 01794 515295
Fixtures Secretary: Malcolm Pain, 2 Nursery Road, Bitterne Park, Southampton. SO2 4NS Tel: 01703 557972
Club Colours: Royal blue with gold hoops

SANDOWN & SHANKLIN RUFC
Ground Address: The Clubhouse, The Fairway Lake, Sandown, Isle of Wight. PO36 9ES Tel: 01983 404707
Club Secretary: Janice Routledge, 27 Atherley Road, Shanklin, Isle of Wight. PO37 7AU Tel: (H) 01983 863994 (W) 01983 273029
Fixtures Secretary: Colin Bond Tel: (H) 01983 402374
Club Colours: Blue and white close hoops

SOUTHAMPTON INSTITUTE
Ground Address: Hardmoor Playing Fields, Stoneham Lane, Eastleigh. So5 3HT Tel: 01703 617574
Brief Directions: Exit junction 5 on M27 (Airport turn off)
Club Secretary: D H Prout, 38 Chessel Avenue, Bitterne, Southampton. SO2 4DX Tel: (H) 01703 394795   (W) 01703 319343
Fixtures Secretary: Martin Hughes , Southampton Institute, East Park Terrace

Southampton
Club Colours: Maroon and white

TROJANS RFC
Ground Address: Stoneham Park, Stoneham Lane, Eastleigh, Hants. SO50 9HT Tel: 01703 612400/613068
Brief Directions: M27 J5, proceed south signed Southampton on A335 to 1st lights, right into Bassett Green Rd, right at next lights into Stoneham Ln, under motorway and immediate left
Club Secretary: J W J Mist, Westbury House, 14 Bellevue Road, Southampton. SO15 2AY Tel: (H) 01703 583450   (W) 01703 332844
Fixtures Secretary: C G Holt Tel: (W) 01703 771195
Club Colours: Blue with narrow red hoops

VENTNOR RUGBY FOOTBALL CLUB
Ground Address: The New Pavilion, Watcombe Bottom, Whitwell Road, Upper Ventnor, Isle of Wight Tel: 01983 834155
Brief Directions: Just outside Ventnor on the Whitwell road
Club Secretary: John Owen, Appuldurcombe Farm, Wrexall,Ventnor I.O.W. Tel: 01983 840188
Fixtures Secretary: Gary Stirling Tel: (H) 01983 761494 (W) 01983 822811
Club Colours: Blue with white band

HAMPSHIRE THREE

Hampshire Three 1997-98 Fixtures	AC Delco 1	Alresford 2	Ellingham 3	Fleet 4	Hamble 5	Hampshire C. 6	Kingsclere 7	Waterlooville 8	
1 AC Delco	X	17/1	10/1	7/3	14/2	24/1	8/11	18/10	1
2 Alresford	27/9	X	7/3	8/11	18/10	10/1	14/2	24/1	2
3 Ellingham	14/3	15/11	X	14/2	24/1	8/11	18/10	27/9	3
4 Fleet	15/11	28/2	25/10	X	27/9	31/1	24/1	14/3	4
5 Hamble	25/10	31/1	11/10	17/1	X	7/3	10/1	28/2	5
6 Hampshire Const.	11/10	14/3	28/2	18/10	15/11	X	17/1	14/2	6
7 Kingsclere	28/2	25/10	31/1	11/10	14/3	27/9	X	15/11	7
8 Waterlooville	31/1	11/10	17/1	10/1	8/11	25/10	7/3	X	8
	1	2	3	4	5	6	7	8	

AC DELCO RFC
Ground Address: AC Delco (Southampton) Sports and Social Club, Sports Ground, Stoneham Lane, Eastleigh, Southampton, Hants   Tel: 01703 613334
Club Secretary: Chris Jackson, 56 Gramby Grove, High Field, Southampton. SO17 3RZ   Tel: (H) 01783 558576
Fixtures Secretary: Richard Legge   Tel: 01703 261830
Club Colours: Navy blue and red squares

ALRESFORD RFC
Ground Address: Bighton Cricket Club, Brighton, Nr Alresford
Brief Directions: Contact Club House (Horse & Groom 01962 734809)
Club Secretary: Mark Elliott, c/o Horse & Groom, Broad Street, Alresford, Hampshire   Tel: 01962 734809
Fixtures Secretary: Robin Howard   Tel: 01962 734809
Club Colours: Gold, green and black

ELLINGHAM & RINGWOOD RFC
Ground Address: Picket Post, Ringwood, Hants   Tel: 01425 476668
Club Secretary: Douglas Middleton, 56 Eastfield Lane, Ringwood, Hants. BH24 1UP   Tel: (H) 01425 475521 (W) 01202 893000
Fixtures Secretary: Philip Lambert   Tel: 01425 476643
Club Colours: Blue and amber

FLEET RUFC
Ground Address: Wavell-Cody School, Lynchford Road, Farnborough, Hants. GU14 6BH
Brief Directions: M3 J4 follow signs for A331, turn right at first roundabout (Lynchford Road), ground is on left just past Fire station and opposite Forte Post House Hotel on A325
Club Secretary: Merrik Knight, 31 Osborne Road, Farnborough, Hants. GU14 6AE   Tel: (H) 01252 654818   (M) 0802 976691
Fixtures Secretary: David Cave   Tel: 01252 651314
Club Colours: Red and Royal Blue hoops blue shorts and red socks.

HAMBLE
Ground Address: The College Playing fields, Baron Road, Hamble, Southampton.   Tel: 01703 452117
Brief Directions: Into Hamble Village along Hamble Lane, left into Aquilla Way (off fire station), right, left into Baron Road.
Club Secretary: Helen Adams, 48 Woolwich Close, Bursledon, Southampton. SO31 8GE   Tel: ((H) 01703 406465
Fixtures Secretary: D Thompson, Tel: (H) 01703 457466
Club Colours: Blue, light blue and white quarters

HAMPSHIRE CONSTABULARY
Ground Address: Southern Support Headquarters, Hamble Lane, Hamble, Southhampton, Hants. SO3 5TS   Tel: 01703 456464
Club Secretary: A. Pragnell, Cranford, Station Road, Soberton, Hampshire SO32 3QU   Tel: (H) 01489 877316 (B) 01705 32111 ext 6124   (F) 01705 371221
Fixtures Secretary: C.Small, 1 Peregrine Close, Totton, Southampton SO40 8UG Tel: (H) 01703 868435   (B) 0976 301539
Club Colours: Red/Black Hoops.

KINGSCLERE
Ground Address: Fieldgate Centre, Fieldgate Drive, Kingsclere, Newbury, Berkshire.
Club Secretary: Chris Smith, 30 Oakfield Close, Ecchinswell, Newbury, Berkshire. Tel: (H) 01635 298006
Fixtures Secretary: Jeremy Dickins, Tel: 01488 686218
Club Colours: Red and white hoops.

WATERLOOVILLE RFC
Ground Address: Jubilee Park, Rowlands Avenue, Waterlooville, Hants.
Club Secretary: Ray Mowatt, 9 Holst Way, Waterlooville, Hants. PO7 5SJ   Tel: (H) 01705 269275
Fixtures Secretary: Ian Day   Tel: (H) 01705 264080
Club Colours: Sky blue and red halves

OTHER COMPETITIONS

FIVE NATIONS CHAMPIONSHIP

SATURDAY 18th JANUARY 1997

At Lansdowne Road, Dublin.

At Murrayfield.

IRELAND 15 v 32 FRANCE
H.T. 12-12

IRELAND:
C O'Shea (London Irish); J Topping (Ballymena), M Field (Malone), J Bell (Northampton), D Crotty (Garryowen); E Elwood (Lansdowne), N Hogan (Terenure College/Oxford University); N Popplewell (Newcastle), K Wood (Harlequins) (captain), P Wallace (Saracens), D Corkery (Bristol), P Johns (Saracens), J Davidson (London Irish), D McBride (Malone), E Miller (Leicester).
Replacements: A Clarke (Northampton) for Wood 38 minutes, K McQuilken (Lansdowne) for Field 47 minutes, P Flavin (Blackrock College) for Popplewell 80 minutes.
New cap: Flavin.

SCORER:
Pens: Elwood (5).

FRANCE:
J-L Sadourny (Colomiers); D Venditti (Brive), T Castaignede (Toulouse), S Glas (Bourgoin), E Ntamack (Toulouse); A Penaud (Brive), F Galthie (Colomiers); C Califano (Toulouse), M Dal Maso (Agen), F Tournaire (Narbonne), A Benazzi (Agen)(captain), O Merle (Montferrand), H Miorin (Toulouse), P Benetton (Agen), F Pelous (Dax).
Replacements: P Carbonneau (Brive) for Galthie 43 minutes, R Castel (Toulouse) for Miorin 62 minutes.
New caps: none
Yellow cards: Merle, Pelous.

SCORERS:
Tries: Venditti (3), Galthie (1).
Pens: Castaignede (2).
Cons: Castaignede (3).

Referee: A Watson, South Africa.

SCOTLAND 19 v 34 WALES
H.T. 13-10

SCOTLAND:
R Shepherd (Melrose); A Stanger (Hawick), S Hastings (Watsonians), G Townsend (Northampton), K Logan (Stirling County); C Chalmers (Melrose), G Armstrong (Newcastle); D Hilton (Bath), G Ellis (Currie), M Stewart (Northampton), P Walton (Newcastle), G Weir (Newcastle), A Reed (Wasps), M Wallace (Glasgow High-Kelvinside), R Wainwright (Watsonians) (captain).
Replacements: S Munro (Glagsow High-Kelvinside) for Reed 55 minutes, D Stark (Melrose) for Chalmers 78 minutes.
New cap: Ellis, who became the first player from Currie to be capped by Scotland.
SCORERS:
Try: Hastings.
DG: Chalmers.
Pens: Shepherd (3).
Con: Shepherd.

WALES:
N Jenkins (Pontypridd); I Evans (Llanelli), A Bateman (Richmond), S Gibbs (Swansea), G Thomas (Bridgend); A Thomas (Swansea), R Howley (Cardiff); C Loader (Swansea), J Humphreys (Cardiff)(captain), D Young (Cardiff), S Williams (Neath), Gareth Llewellyn (Harlequins), M Rowley (Pontypridd), C Charvis (Swansea), S Quinnell (Richmond).
Replacements: C Quinnell (Richmond) for Rowley 67 minutes, G Jones (Cardiff) for Charvis 76 minutes, J Davies (Cardiff) for Gibbs 78 minutes.
New caps: None
SCORERS:
Tries: S Quinnell, Jenkins, A Thomas, Evans.
Pens: Jenkins (2).
Cons: Jenkins (4).

Referee: H A Smith, Ireland.

SATURDAY, 1st FEBRUARY 1997

At Twickenham (for Calcutta Cup).

ENGLAND 41 v 13 SCOTLAND
H.T. 16-10

ENGLAND:
T Stimpson (Newcastle); J Sleightholme (Bath), W Carling (Harlequins), P de Glanville (Bath) (captain), T Underwood (Newcastle); P Grayson (Northampton), A Gomarsall (Wasps); G Rowntree (Northampton), M Regan (Bristol), J Leonard (Harlequins), L Dallaglio (Wasps), M Johnson (Leicester), S Shaw (Bristol), R Hill (Saracens), T Rodber (Northampton/Army).
Replacements: None
New cap: Hill.

SCORERS:
Tries: Gomarsall, Carling, de Glanville, penalty-try.
Pens: Grayson (5).
Cons: Grayson (3).

SCOTLAND:
R Shepherd (Melrose); D Stark (Melrose), A Stanger (Hawick), R Eriksson (London Scottish), K Logan (Stirling County); G Townsend (Northampton), B Redpath (Melrose); T Smith (Watsonians), G Ellis (Currie), M Stewart (Northampton), P Walton (Newcastle), G Weir (Newcastle), A Reed (Wasps), T Smith (Gloucester), R Wainwright (Watsonians) (captain).
Replacement: S Hastings (Watsonians) for Ericksson 71 minutes.
New cap: T Smith.

SCORERS:
Try: Ericksson.
Pens: Shepherd (2).
Con: Shepherd.

Referee: P O'Brien, New Zealand.

At Cardiff Arms Park.

WALES 25 v 26 IRELAND
H.T. 10-20

WALES:
N Jenkins (Pontypridd); I Evans (Llanelli), G Thomas (Bridgend), S Gibbs (Swansea), D James (Bridgend); A Thomas (Swansea), R Howley (Cardiff); C Loader (Swansea), J Humphreys (Cardiff)(captain), D Young (Cardiff), S Williams (Neath), Gareth Llewellyn (Richmond), M Rowley (Pontypridd), C Charvis (Swansea), S Quinnell (Richmond).
Replacements: C Quinnell (Richmond) for Rowley 63 minutes, K Jones (Ebbw Vale) for Charvis 70 minutes.
New Caps: None

SCORERS:
Tries: Evans (2), S Quinnell.
Pens: Jenkins (2).
Cons: Jenkins (2).

IRELAND:
J Staples (Harlequins)(captain); D Hickie (St Mary's College), J Bell (Northampton), M Field (Malone), D Crotty (Garryowen); E Elwood (Lansdowne), N Hogan (Terenure College/Oxford University); N Popplewell (Newcastle), R Nesdale (Newcastle), P Wallace (Saracens), D Corkery (Bristol), P Johns (Saracens), J Davidson (London Irish), D McBride (Malone), E Miller (Leicester).
Replacement: G Fulcher (London Irish) for Johns 74 minutes.
New Caps: Hickie, Nesdale.

SCORERS:
Tries: Bell, Miller, Hickie.
Pens: Elwood (3).
Con: Elwood.

Referee: W Erickson, Australia.

SATURDAY, 15th FEBRUARY 1997.

At Parc des Princes, Paris.

At Lansdowne Road, Dublin.

FRANCE 27 v 22 WALES
H.T. 20-10

IRELAND 6 v 46 ENGLAND
H.T. 6-11

FRANCE:

J-L Sadourny (Colomiers); L Leflammand (Bourgoin), R Dourthe (Dax), S Glas (Bourgoin), D Venditti (Brive); C Lamaison (Brive), P Carbonneau (Brive); C Califano (Toulouse), M Dal Maso (Agen), J-L Jordana (Toulouse), A Benazzi (Agen), O Merle (Montferrand), H Miorin (Toulouse), R Castel (Beziers), F Pelous (Dax).
Replacements: D Aucagne (Pau) for Dourthe 21 minutes, O Magne (Dax) for Miorin 55 minutes.
New caps: Leflammand, Aucagne.

SCORERS:
Tries: Leflammand (2), Venditti, Merle.
Pen: Aucagne.
Cons: Dourthe, Aucagne.

WALES:

N Jenkins (Pontypridd); I Evans (Llanelli), A Bateman (Richmond), S Gibbs (Swansea), G Thomas (Bridgend); A Thomas (Swansea), R Howley (Cardiff); C Loader (Swansea), J Humphreys (Cardiff)(captain), D Young (Cardiff), S Williams (Neath), Gareth Llewellyn (Richmond), M Rowley (Pontypridd), C Charvis (Swansea), S Quinnell (Richmond).
Replacement: J Davies (Cardiff) for Evans 55 minutes.
New Cap: None

SCORERS:
Tries: Thomas, Howley, Bateman.
Pen: Jenkins.
Cons: Jenkins (2).

Referee: P Marshall, Australia.

IRELAND:

J Staples (Harlequins)(captain); D Hickie (St Mary's College), J Bell (Northampton), M Field (Malone), J Topping (Ballymena); E Elwood (Lansdowne), N Hogan (Terenure College/Oxford University); N Popplewell (Newcastle), R Nesdale (Newcastle), P Wallace (Saracens), D Corkery (Bristol), P Johns (Saracens), J Davidson (London Irish), D McBride (Malone), E Miller (Leicester).
Replacements: A Foley (Shannon) for Miller 12 minutes, D Humphreys (London Irish) for Elwood 25 minutes, B O'Meara (Cork Constitution) for Hogan 65 minutes.
New cap: O'Meara.

SCORER: Pens: Elwood (2).

ENGLAND:

T Stimpson (Newcastle); J Sleightholme (Bath), W Carling (Harlequins), P de Glanville (Bath)(captain), T Underwood (Newcastle); A Gomarsall (Wasps); G Rowntree (Leicester), M Regan (Bristol), J Leonard (Harlequins), L Dallaglio (Wasps), M Johnson (Leicester), S Shaw (Bristol), R Hill (Saracens), T Rodber (Northampton/Army).
Replacements: A Healey (Leicester) for Gomarsall 73 minutes, J Guscott (Bath) for Carling 77 minutes.
New Cap: None

SCORERS:
Tries: Sleightholme (2), Underwood (2), Gomarsall, Hill.
Pens: Grayson (4).
Cons: Grayson (2).

Referee: C Hawke, New Zealand.

SATURDAY, 1st MARCH 1997.

At Twickenham.

ENGLAND 20 v 23 FRANCE
H.T. 14-6

At Murrayfield.

SCOTLAND 38 v 10 IRELAND
H.T. 14-6

ENGLAND:

T Stimpson (Newcastle); J Sleightholme (Bath), W Carling (Harlequins), P de Glanville (Bath)(captain), T Underwood (Newcastle); P Grayson (Northampton), A Gomarsall (Wasps); G Rowntree (Leicester), M Regan (Bristol), J Leonard (Harlequins), L Dallaglio (Wasps), M Johnson (Leicester), S Shaw (Bristol), R Hill (Saracens), T Rodber (Northampton/Army).

Replacements: None

New Caps: None

SCORERS:

Try: Dallaglio.

DG: Grayson.

Pens: Grayson (4).

FRANCE:

J-L Sadourny (Colomiers); L Leflammand (Bourgoin), C Lamaison (Brive), S Glas (Bourgoin), D Venditti (Brive); A Penaud (Brive), P Carbonneau (Brive); M Dal Maso (Agen), F Tournaire (Narbonne), C Califano (Toulouse), A Benazzi (Agen) (captain), H Miorin (Toulouse), O Merle (Montferrand), O Magne (Dax), F Pelous (Dax).

Replacements: R Castel (Beziers) for Miorin 49 minutes, M de Rougemont (Toulon) for Benazzi 66 minutes.

New Caps: None.

SCORERS:

Tries: Leflammand, Lamaison.

DG: Lamaison.

Pens: Lamaison (2).

Cons: Lamaison (2).

Referee: J Fleming, Scotland.

SCOTLAND:

R Shepherd (Melrose); A Stanger (Hawick), A Tait (Newcastle), G Townsend (Northampton), K Logan (Stirling County); C Chalmers (Melrose), B Redpath (Melrose); T Smith (Watsonians), G Ellis (Currie), M Stewart (Northampton), R Wainwright (Watsonians) (captain), A Reed (Wasps), G Weir (Newcastle), I Smith (Moseley), P Walton (Newcastle).

Replacements: None.

New Caps: None.

SCORERS:

Tries: Tait, Walton, Weir, Townsend, Stanger.

Pen: Shepherd.

Cons: Shepherd (5).

IRELAND:

J Staples (Harlequins)(captain); D Hickie (St Mary's College), M Field (Malone), K McQuilkein (Lansdowne), J Bell (Northampton); D Humphreys (London Irish), B O'Meara (Cork Constitution); P Flavin (Blackrock College), R Nesdale (Newcastle), P Wallace (Saracens), D Corkery (Bristol), P Johns (Saracens), W Davidson (London Irish), D McBride (Malone), B Cronin (Garryowen).

Replacements: C O'Shea (London Irish) for Staples 25 minutes, P Burke (Bristol) for McQuilken 65 minutes, S McIvor (Garryowen) for O'Meara 67 minutes.

New Caps: None.

SCORERS:

Try: Hickie.

Pen: Humphreys.

Con: Humphreys.

Referee: G Simmonds, Wales.

FIVE NATIONS CHAMPIONSHIP
SATURDAY, 15th MARCH 1997.

At Parc des Princes, Paris.

FRANCE 47 v 20 SCOTLAND
H.T. 26-13

FRANCE:
J-L Sadourny (Colomiers); L Leflammand (Bourgoin), C Lamaison (Brive), S Glas (Bourgoin), D Venditti (Brive); D Aucagne (Pau), G Accoceberry (Begles-Bordeaux); F Tournaire (Narbonne), M Dal Maso (Agen), D Casadie (Brive), A Benazzi (Agen)(captain), O Merle (Montferrand), H Miorin (Toulouse), O Magne (Dax), F Pelous (Dax).
Replacements: R Castel (Beziers) for Miorin 55 minutes, M de Rougemont (Toulouse) for Dal Maso 73 minutes, P Carbonneau (Brive) for Accoceberry 75 minutes, U Mola (Dax) for Leflammand 75 minutes, P Bondouy (Narbonne) for Venditti 75 minutes.
New caps: Casadei, Mola, Bondouy.

SCORERS:
Tries: Benazzi, Leflammand, Dal Maso, Magne.
DG: Sadounry.
Pens: Lamaison (6).
Cons: Lamaison (3).

SCOTLAND:
R Shepherd (Melrose); T Stanger (Hawick), A Tait (Newcastle), G Townsend (Northampton), K Logan (Wasps); C Chalmers (Melrose), B Redpath (Melrose); T Smith (Watsonians), G Ellis (Currie), M Stewart (Northampton), R Wainwright (Watsonians)(captain), G Weir (Newcastle), A Reed (Wasps), I Smith (Moseley), P Walton (Newcastle).
Replacements: D Cronin (Wasps) for Walton 15 minutes, D Hodge (Watsonians) for Chalmers 55 minutes, C Glasgow (Heriot's FP) for Tait 75 minutes.
New Caps: Hodge, Glasgow.

SCORERS:
Tries: Tait (2).
Pens: Shepherd (2).
Cons Shepherd (2).

Referee: E Morrison, England.

This was the last international match played on the Parc des Princes.

At Cardiff Arms Park.

WALES 13 v 34 ENGLAND
H.T. 3-6

WALES:
N Jenkins (Pontypridd); S Hill (Cardiff), A Bateman (Richmond), N Davies (Bridgend), G Thomas (Bridgend); J Davies (Cardiff), R Howley (Cardiff); C Loader (Swansea), J Humphreys (Cardiff)(captain), D Young (Cardiff), S Williams (Neath), G Llewellyn (Richmond), M Voyle (Llanelli), K Jones (Ebbw Vale), S Quinnell (Richmond).
Replacements: W Proctor (Llanelli) for Jenkins 14 minutes, S John (Llanelli) for Loader 22 minutes, D McIntosh (Pontypridd) for K Jones 64 minutes, C Quinnell (Richmond) for Voyle 67 minutes.
New Caps: None.

SCORERS:
Try: Howley.
Pens: J Davies (2).
Con: J Davies.

ENGLAND:
T Stimpson (Newcastle); J Sleightholme (Bath), W Carling (Harlequins), P de Glanville (Bath)(captain), T Underwood (Newcastle), M Catt (Bath), A Healey (Leicester); G Rowntree (Leicester), M Regan (Bristol), J Leonard (Harlequins), B Clarke (Richmond), M Johnson (Leicster), S Shaw (Bristol), R Hill (Saracens), T Rodber (Northampton/Army).
Replacements: J Guscott (Bath) for Sleightholme 40 minutes, P Greening (Gloucester) for Regan 40 minutes, C Sheasby (Wasps) for Clarke 69 minutes, R Andrew (Newcastle) for Catt 72 minutes, D Garforth (Leicester) for Rowntree 77 minutes.
New cap: Garforth.

SCORERS:
Tries: Stimpson, Underwood, Hill, de Glanville.
Pens: Catt (2).
Cons: Catt (4).

Referee: J Dume, France.

This was England's fourth consecutive victory over Wales, who still lead their series with 48 wins against 43; 12 matches have been drawn. After the match work commenced on building a new stadium on the Arms Park site in time for the 1999 Rugby World Cup.

This was France's first Grand Slam since 1987.

FINAL TABLE

	P	W	L	F	A	Pts
France	4	4	0	129	77	8
England	4	3	1	141	55	6
Wales	4	1	3	94	106	2
Scotland	4	1	3	90	132	2
Ireland	4	1	3	57	141	2

THE BRITISH LIONS
in South Africa 1997

PLAYERS (England unless stated)
with appearances & Test match appearances (bracketed)
Replacement appearances are marked "+"

Full-backs

Neil Jenkins (Pontypridd/Wales)	6+2	(3)
Tim Stimpson (Newcastle)	6+1	(0+1)

Wings

Nick Beal (Northampton)	5	-
John Bentley (Newcastle)	8	(2)
Ieuan Evans (Llanelli/Wales)	5	(1)
Tony Underwood (Newcastle)	7+1	(1)
*Tony Stanger (Hawick/Scotland)	1	-

Centres

Alan Bateman (Richmond/Wales)	6+1	(0+1)
Scott Gibbs (Swansea/Wales)	5+1	(0+1)
Will Greenwood (Leicester/England 'A')	5+1	-
Jeremy Guscott (Bath)	7	(3)
Alan Tait (Newcastle/Scotland)	5+1	(2)

Outside-halves

Paul Grayson (Northampton)	1	-
Gregor Townsend (Northampton/Scotland)	6	(2)
*Mike Catt (Bath)	5+1	(1)

Scrum-halves

Matt Dawson (Northampton)	4+2	(3)
Austin Healey (Leicester)	4+3	(0+2)
Rob Howley (Cardiff/Wales)	4	-
*Kyran Bracken (Saracens)	1	-

Props

Jason Leonard (Harlequins)	5+3	(0+1)
Graham Rowntree (Leicester)	5+1	-
Tom Smith (Watsonians/Scotland)	7	(3)
Paul Wallace (Saracens/Ireland)	5+1	(3)
David Young (Cardiff/Wales)	4+2	-

Hookers

Mark Regan (Bristol)	5+1	(1)
Barrie Williams (Neath/Wales)	3+1	-
Keith Wood (Harlequins/Ireland)	5	(2)

Locks

Jimmy Davidson (London Irish/Ireland)	7+1	(3)
Martin Johnson (see captain)	6	(3)
Simon Shaw (Bristol)	6+1	-
G (Doddie) Weir (Newcastle/Scotland)	3	-
*Nigel Redman (Bath)	4	-

Back-row

Neil Back (Leicester)	7+1	(1+1)
Lawrence Dallaglio (Wasps)	7	(3)
Richard Hill (Saracens)	5	(2)
Eric Miller (Leicester/Ireland)	4+1	(0+1)
Scott Quinnell (Richmond/Wales)	2+1	-
Tim Rodber (Northampton & Army)	5	(2)
Rob Wainwright (Watsonians & Army/Scotland)	7	(1)
*Tony Diprose (Saracens)	2	-

* Replacement during tour.

MANAGEMENT

Manager: Fran Cotton (England).
Coach: Ian McGeechan (Scotland).
Assistant Coach: Jim Telfer (Scotland).
Captain: Martin Johnson (Leicester & England).

ITINERARY

Date	Opponent	Venue / Result
Sat, 24th May 1997	Eastern Province Invitation XI	Port Elizabeth W 39-11
Wed, 28th May 1997	Border	East London W 18-14
Sat, 31st May 1997	Western Province	Cape Town W 38-21
Wed, 4th Jun 1997	Mpumalanga	Witbank W 64-14
Sat, 7th Jun 1997	Northern Transvaal	Pretoria L 30-35
Wed, 11th Jun 1997	Gauteng Lions	Johannesburg W 20-14
Sat, 14th Jun 1997	Natal Sharks	Durban W 42-12
Tue, 17th Jun 1997	Emerging Springboks	Wellington W 51-22
Sat, 21st Jun 1997	SOUTH AFRICA	Cape Town W 25-16
Tue, 24th Jun 1997	Free State Cheetahs	Bloemfontein W 52-30
Sat, 28th Jun 1997	SOUTH AFRICA	Durban W 18-15
Tue, 1st July 1997	Northern Free State	Welkom W 67-39
Sat, 5th July 1997	SOUTH AFRICA	Johannesburg L 16-35

TOP POINTS SCORERS

Tim Stimpson	111
Neil Jenkins	110
Tony Underwood	35
John Bentley	35
Jeremy Guscott	23

Eastern Province Invit. XI   11
British Lions   39

Referee: A Turner, Transvaal.   H.T.: 6-10.

EASTERN PROVINCE: T van Rensburg; D Keyser, R van Jaarsveld, H le Roux, K Pedro; K Ford, C Alcock; D Saayman, J Kirsten, W Enslin, M Webber, K Wiese, A du Preez, S Scott-Young, J Greeff. Replacements: W Lessing for Enslin 40 mins., M van der Merwe for Webber 44 mins., R Fourie for Ford 45 mins..
Scorers: Try: Keyser. Pens: Van Rensburg (2).

BRITISH LIONS: N Jenkins; I Evans, J Guscott, W Greenwood, N Beal; G Townsend, R Howley; T Smith, K Wood, J Leonard (captain), L Dallaglio, G Weir, S Shaw, R Hill, S Quinnell. Replacements: B Williams for Wood 66 mins., T Underwood for Evans 66 mins., J Davidson for Shaw 72 mins..
Scorers: Tries: Guscott (2), Weir, Underwood, Greenwood. Pens: Jenkins (2). Cons: Jenkins (4).

Border   14
British Lions   18

Referee: A Burger, Gauteng.   H.T.: 8-10.

BORDER: R Bennett; K Hilton-Green, G Hechter, K Malotana, A Claasen; G Miller, J Bradbrook; H Kok, R van Zyl, D du Preez, M Swart, S Botha, J Gehring, A Botha, A Fox. Replacements: D Maidza for Malotana 45 mins., L Blakeway for Gehring 74 mins., D Coetzer for A Botha 79 mins..
Scorers: Try: Claasen. Pens: Miller (3).

BRITISH LIONS: T Stimpson; J Bentley, A Bateman, S Gibbs, T Underwood; P Grayson, A Healey; G Rowntree, M Regan, D Young, R Wainwright (captain), G Weir, J Davidson, N Back, E Miller. Replacements: A Tait for Gibbs 45 mins., M Dawson for Healey 55 mins., P Wallace for Young 68 mins..
Scorers: Tries: Bentley, Regan, Wainwright. Pen: Stimpson.

Western Province   21
British Lions   38

Referee: A Schoonwinkel, Free State. H.T.: 14-18.

WESTERN PROVINCE: J Swart; J Small, R Fleck, D Muir (captain), P Rossouw; P Montgomery, S Hatley; G Pagel, A Paterson, K Andrews, R Brink, F van Heerden, L Louw, M Krige, A Aitken. Replacements: A van der Linde for Pagel 57 mins., R Skinstad for Krige 65 mins.. Temp. replacement: L Koen for Muir 57-68 mins..
Scorers: Tries: Muir (2), Brink. Cons: Montgomery (3).

BRITISH LIONS; T Stimpson; I Evans, J Guscott, A Tait, J Bentley; G Townsend, R Howley; G Rowntree, B Williams, J Leonard, L Dallaglio, M Johnson (captain), S Shaw, R Hill, T Rodber. Replacements: S Quinnell for Rodber 63 mins., W Greenwood for Tait 73 mins..
Scorers: Tries: Bentley (2), Tait, Evans. Pens: Stimpson (4). Cons: Stimpson (3).

Mpumalanga   14
British Lions   64

Referee: C Spannenberg, W. Province. H.T.: 7-35.

MPUMALANGA: E van Gericke; J Visagie, R Potgieter, G Gendall, P Nel; R van As, D van Zyl; A Botha, H Kemp, H Swart, P Joubert, M Bosman, E van der Berg, F Roussouw, T Oosthuizen. Replacements: J Beukes for Oosthuizen 72 mins., A van Rooyen for Nel 78 mins..
Scorers: Tries: Joubert (2). Cons: van As (2).

BRITISH LIONS: N Beal; I Evans, A Bateman, W Greenwood, T Underwood; N Jenkins, M Dawson; T Smith, K Wood, P Wallace, R Wainwright, G Weir, J Davidson, N Back, T Rodber (captain). Replacements: M Regan for Wood 53 mins., S Shaw for Weir 57 mins., D Young for Regan 75 mins..
Scorers: Tries: Wainwright (3), Underwood (2), Evans (2), Dawson, Jenkins, Beal.

Northern Transvaal   36
British Lions   30

Referee: A Watson, E. Province.   H.T.: 18-17.

NORTHERN TRANSVAAL: G Bouwer; C Steyn, J Schutte, D van Schalwyk, W Lourems; R de Marigny, C Breytenbach; L Campher, H Tromp, P Boer, N van der Walt, D Grobbelaar, D Badenhorst, S Bekker, A Richter (captain). Replacements: G Esterhuizen for Lourens 35 mins., G Laufs for Grobbelaar 41 mins., J Brooks for Tromp 41 mins., R Shroeder for van der Walt 66 mins., A Proudfoot for Boer 71 mins.. Temp. replacement: J Taliaard for Bouwer 38-40 mins..
Scorers: Tries: Van Scalwyk (2), Steyn, Richter. Pens: Steyn (3). Cons: Steyn (3).

BRITISH LIONS: T Stimpson; J Bentley, A Tait, J Guscott, T Underwood; G Townsend, R Howley; G Rowntree, M Regan, J Leonard, L Dallaglio, M Johnson (captain), S Shaw, E Miller, S Quinnell. Replacements: S Gibbs for Bentley 60 mins., D Young for Leonard 75 mins..
Scorers: Tries: Guscott (2), Townsend. Pens: Stimpson (3). Cons: Stimpson (3).

Gauteng Lions   14
British Lions   20

Referee: T Henning, N. Transvaal.   H.T.: 9-3.

GAUTENG LIONS: D Du Toit; J Gillingham, J van der Walt, H Le Roux, P Hendriks; L van Rensburg, J Roux; R Grau, C Rossouw, K van Greuning, A Vos, K Wiese (captain), B Thorne, P Krause, W Brosnihan. Replacements: J Dalton for Rossouw 53 mins., B Swart for Grau 65 mins..
Scorers: Try: Vos. Pens: Du Toit (3).

BRITISH LIONS: N Beal; J Bentley, J Guscott, W Greenwood, T Underwood; M Catt, A Healey; T Smith, B Williams, P Wallace, R Wainwright, N Redman, J Davidson, N Back, T Rodber (captain). Replacement: N Jenkins for Underwood 56 mins..
Scorers: Tries: Healey, Bentley. Pens: Catt, Jenkins. Cons: Jenkins (2).

Saturday 14th June 1997
Durban

Natal Sharks   12
British Lions   42

Referee: J Meuwesen, Eastern Province.H.T.: 9-16.

NATAL SHARKS: G Lawless; J Joubert, J Thompson, P Muller, S Payne; H Scriba, R du Preez; R Kempson, J Allan, A-H le Roux, W van Heerden, N Wegner, J Slade, W Fyvie (captain), D Kriese.
Replacement: R Strudwick for van Heerden 6-10 mins. (temporary) and 30 mins. (permanent), J Smit for Le Roux 77 mins..
Scorer: Pens: Lawless (4)

BRITISH LIONS: N Jenkins; I Evans, A Bateman, S Gibbs, A Tait; G Townsend, R Howley; T Smith, K Wood, D Young, L Dallaglio, M Johnson (captain), S Shaw, R Hill, E Miller. Replacements: M Dawson for Howley 13 mins., M Catt for Bateman 60 mins., J Leonard for Smith 65 mins.. Temp. replacement: R Wainwright for Johnson 26-32 mins..
Scorers: Tries: Townsend, Catt, Dallaglio. DG: Townsend. Pens: Jenkins (4). Cons: Jenkins (3).

Tuesday 17th June 1997
Wellington

Emerging Springboks   22
British Lions   61

Referee: I Rogers, Natal.

EMERGING SPRINGBOKS: M Smith (Free State); D Kayser (Eatern Province), P Montgomery (Western Province), M Hendricks (Boland), P Treu (South-West Districts); L van Rensburg (Gauteng), J Adlam (North-West); R Kempson (Natal), D Santon (Boland)(captain), N du Toit (Boland), W Brosnihan (Gauteng), R Opperman (Free State), B Els (Free State), P Smit (Griqualand West), J Coetzee (Free State). Replacements: K Myburgh (Griqualand West) for Adlam 11 mins., M Goosen (Boland) for van Rensburg 21 mins., K Malotana (Border) for Smith 62 mins., L Campher (Northern Trsnsvaal) for Kempson 65 mins., J Brooks (Northern Transvaal) for Santon 67 mins., T Arendse (Western Province) for Brosnihan 71 mins..
Scorers: Tries: Brosnihan, Goosen, Treu. Pen: Smith. Cons: Smith, Montgomery.

BRITISH LIONS: T Stimpson; J Bentley, A Bateman, W Greenwood, N Beal; M Catt, A Healey; G Rowntree, M Regan, J Leonard (captain), R Wainwright, N Redman, J Davidson, N Back, A Diprose.
Scorers: Tries: Beal (3), Rowntree, Stimpson, Catt. Pens: Stimpson (3). Cons: Stimpson (6)

TOP TRY SCORERS

7	Underwood & Bentley.
4	Guscott, Beal, Wainwright & Stimpson.
3	Evans & Dawson.
2	Tait, Regan, Jenkins, Townsend, Catt & Shaw.
1	Greenwwod, Weir, Healey, Dallaglio, Rowntree, Bateman, Bracken & Back.

Hat-tricks
Wainwright (v Mpumalanga), Beal (v Emerging Springboks), Bentley (v Free State) and Underwood (v Northern Free State).

1st TEST MATCH

Saturday 21st June 1997
Newlands, Cape Town

SOUTH AFRICA   16
BRITISH LIONS   26

Referee: C Hawke, New Zealand   H.T.: 8-9.

SOUTH AFRICA; A Joubert (Natal); J Small (Western Province), J Mulder (Gauteng), E Lubbe (Griqualand West), A Snyman (Northen Transvaal); H Honiball (Natal), J van der Westhuizen (Northern Transvaal); J Du Randt (Free State), A Drotske (Free State), A Garvey (Natal), R Kruger (Northern Transvaal), M Andrews (Natal), J Strydom (Gauteng), A Venter (Free State), G Teichmann (Natal)(captain). Replacement: R Bennett (Border) for Lubbe 40 mins.. No new caps.
Scorers: Tries: Du Randt, Bennett. Pens: Lubbe, Honiball.

BRITISH LIONS:
N Jenkins (Pontypridd/Wales); I Evans (Llanelli/-Wales), J Guscott (Bath/England), S Gibbs (Swansea/Wales), A Tait (Newcastle/Scotland); G Townsend (Northampton/Scotland), M Dawson (Northampton/England); T Smith (Watsonians/-Scotland), K Wood (Harlequins/Ireland), P Wallace (Saracens/Ireland), L Dallaglio (Wasps/England), M Johnson (Leicester/England), J Davidson (London Irish/Ireland), R Hill (Saracens/England), T Rodber (Northampton & Army/England). Replacement: J Leonard (Harlequins/England) for Smith 79 mins.. All bar Evans, Guscott, Gibbs, Johnson and Leonard were making their first test appearances for the British Lions.
Scorers: Tries: Dawson, Tait. Pens: Jenkins (5).

Tuesday 24th June 1997
Bloemfontein

Free State Cheetahs   30
British Lions   52

Referee: J Kaplan, Natal.   H.T.: 13-31.

FREE STATE CHEETAHS: M Smith; J-H van Wyk, H Muller (captain), B Venter, S Brink; J de Beer, S Fourie; D Groenewald, C Marais, W Meyer, C van Rensburg, R Opperman, B Els, J Erasmus, J Coetzee. Replacements: H Jacobs for Fourie 40 mins., D Heymans for Meyer 60 mins..
Scorers: Tries: Brink (2), de Beer. Pens: De Beer (3). Con: De Beer.

BRITISH LIONS: T Stimpson; J Bentley, A Bateman, W Greenwood, T Underwood; M Catt, A Healey; G Rowntree, B Williams, D Young, R Wainwright, N Redman (captain), S Shaw, N Back, E Miller. Replacements: N Jenkins for Greenwood 40 mins., J Leonard for Rowntree 71 mins.. Temp. replacement: Leonard for Rowntree 16-20 mins..
Scorers: Tries: Bentley (3), Stimpson, Bateman, Jenkins, Underwood. Pens: Stimpson (3). Cons: Stimpson (4).

2nd TEST MATCH

Saturday 28th June 1997
Kingsmead, Durban

SOUTH AFRICA 15
BRITISH LIONS 18
Referee: D Mene, France.   H.T.: 5-6.

SOUTH AFRICA: A Joubert (Natal); A Snyman (Northern Transvaal), P Montgomery (Western Province), D van Schalkwyk (northern Transvaal), P Rossouw (Western Province); H Honiball (Natal), J van der Westhuizen (Northern Transvaal); J Du Randt (Free State), A Drotske (Free State), A Garvey (Natal), R Kruger (Northern Transvaal), M Andrews (Natal), J Strydom (Gauteng), A Venter (Free State), G Teichmann (Natal)(captain). Replacements: A van Heerden (Western Province) for Kruger 50 mins., D Theron (Griqualand West) for Garvey 67 mins.. Temp. replacement: Van Heerden for Teichmann 2-5 mins.. Scorers: Tries: Van der Westhuizen, Montgomery, Houbert.

BRITISH LIONS: N Jenkins (Pontypridd/Wales); J Bentley (Newcastle/England), J Guscott (Bath/-England), S Gibbs (Swansea/Wales), A Tait (Newcastle/Scotland); G Townsend (Northampton/-Scotland), M Dawson (Northampton/England); T Smith (Watsonians/Scotland), K Wood (Harlequins/-Ireland), P Wallace (Saracens/Ireland), L Dallaglio (Wasps/England), M Johnson (Leicester/England)-(captain), J Davidson (London Irish/Ireland), R Hill (Saracens/England), T Rodber (Northampton & Army/England). Replacements: N Back (Leicester/-England) for Hill 56 mins., A Healey (Leicester/England) for Tait 76 mins., E Miller (Leicester/Ireland) for Rodber 77 mins.. New British Lions caps: Bentley, Back, Healey, Miller. Scorers: DG: Guscott. Pens: Jenkins (5).

Tuesday 1st July 1997
Welkom
Northern Free State 39
British Lions 67
Referee: D de Villiers, Western Province.

NORTHERN FREE STATE: T Ehrentraut; R Harmse, A van Buuren, T de Beer, W Nagel; E Herbert, J Jering (captain); K Applegryn, O Wagener, B Nel, H Kershaw, K Heydenrich, S Nieuwenhuyzen, E Delport, M Venter. Replacements: J Burrows for Ehrentraut 67 mins., A Fouche for Delport 75 Minutes, C Dippenaar for Wagener 78 mins.. Scorers: Tries: Ehrentraut, Wagener, de Beer, Herbert, penalty-try. Pens: Herbert (2). Cons: Herbert (4).

BRITISH LIONS: T Stimpson; A Stanger, A Bateman, N Beal, T Underwood; M Catt, K Bracken; J Leonard (captain), M Regan, D Young, R Wainwright, N Redman, S Shaw, N Back, A Diprose. Replacements: G Rowntree for Leonard 40 mins., A Healey for Bracken 54 mins.. Scorers: Tries: Underwood (3), Stimpson (2), Shaw (2), Back, Bracken, Regan. Pen: Stimpson. Cons: Stimpson (7).

3rd TEST MATCH

Saturday, 5th July 1997
Ellis Park, Johannesburg.

SOUTH AFRICA 35
BRITISH LIONS 16
Referee: W Erickson, Australia.   H.T.: 13-9.

SOUTH AFRICA: R Bennett (Border); A Snyman (Northern Transvaal), P Montgomery (Western Province), D van Schalkwyk (Northern Transvaal), P Rossouw (Western Province); J de Beer (Free State), J van der Westhuizen (Northern Transvaal); J du Randt (Free State), J Dalton (Gauteng), D Theron (Griqualand West), J Erasmus (Free State), J Strydom (Gauteng), K Otto (Northern Transvaal), A Venter (Free State), G Teichmann (Natal)(captain). Replacements: H Honiball (Natal) for Montgomery 53 mins., N Drotske (Free State) for Dalton 66 mins., A Garvey (Natal) for du Randt 64 mins., J Swart (Western Province) for de Beer 68 mins., F van Heerden (Western Province) for Teichmann 70 mins., W Swanepoel (Free State) for van der Westhuizen 78 mins.. New caps: De Beer, Swart, Swanepoel. Scorers: Tries: Montgomery, van der Westhuizen, Snyman, Rossouw. Pens: De Beer (3). Cons: De Beer (2), Honiball.

BRITISH LIONS (England unless stated): N Jenkins (Pontypridd/Wales); J Bentley, S Gibbs (Swansea/Wales), J Guscott (Bath), T Underwood (Newcastle); M Catt (Bath), M Dawson (Northampton); T Smith (Watsonians/Scotland), M Regan (Bristol), P Wallace (Saracens/Ireland), R Wainwright (Watsonians/Scotland), M Johnson (Leicester)(captain), J Davidson (London Irish/-Ireland), N Back (Leicester), L Dallaglio (Wasps/England). Replacements: T Stimpson (Newcastle) for Underwood 30 mins., A Bateman (Richmond/Wales) for Guscott 41 mins., A Healey (Leicester) for Dawson 70 mins.. New British Lions caps: Underwood, Catt, Regan, Wainwright, Stimpson, Bateman. Scorers: Try: Dawson. Pens: Jenkins (3). Con: Jenkins.

SUMMARY

PLAYED	**13**
WON	**11**
LOST	**2**
POINTS SCORED	**480**
TRIES	56
DROPPED GOALS	2
PENALTY GOALS	38
CONVERSIONS	40
POINTS AGAINST	**278**

HEINEKEN EUROPEAN CUP

POOL A

Saturday, 12th October 1996

Bath 55 v 26 Edinburgh
H.T. 38-9

Bath: J Callard; A Robinson, H Paul, J Guscott, A Adebayo; M Catt, C Harrison; K Yates, G Adams, V Ubogu, A Robinson (captain), N Redman, B Cusack, R Webster, S Ojomoh. Replacements: M Perry for Paul 61 minutes, N Thomas for Webster 72 minutes. Scorers: Tries: Guscott (2), Adebayo, Callard, Ubogu, Ojomoh, A Robinson. Pens: Callard (2). Cons: Callard (7).

Edinburgh: D Lee (Watsonians); S Reed (Boroughmuir), S Hastings (Watsonians)(captain), C Simmers (Edinburgh Academicals), S Lang (Heriot's FP); D Hodge (Watsonians), G Burns (Watsonians); A Watt (Currie), G Ellis (Currie), B Stewart (Edinburgh Academicals), B Ward (Currie), P Jennings (Boroughmuir), A Lucking (Currie), G Dall (Heriot's FP), D Clark (Currie). Replacement: C Mather (Watsonians) for Jennings.
Scorers: Tries: Hodge, Lee. Pens: Hodge (4). Cons: Hodge (2). Half-time: 38-9

Referee: G Simmonds, Wales.

Pontypridd 28 v 22 Treviso
H.T. 15-16

Pontypridd: K Morgan; D Manley, J Lewis, S Lewis, P Ford; N Jenkins (captain), Paul John; N Eynon, Phil John, A Griffiths, M Lloyd, G Prosser, M Rowley, D McIntosh, M Williams. Replacement: R Collins for Lloyd 67 minutes. Temporary replacement: C Cormack for Morgan 22-25 minutes.
Scorers: Try: M Williams. Pens: Jenkins (7). Con: Jenkins.

Treviso: P Dotto; L Perziano, I Francescato, P F Donati, L Manteri; F Mazzariol, A Troncon; M Dal Sie, A Moscardi, A Castellani, A Sgorlon, C Signori, D Scaglia, V Cristofoletto, L Bot. Replacement: S Rigo for Cristofoletto 66 minutes.
Scorers: Try: Mazzariol. Pens: Mazzariol (5). Con: Mazzariol.
Half-time: 15-16

Referee: S Lander, England.

Wednesday, 16th October 1996 (at Myreside)

Edinburgh 10 v 32 Pontypridd
H.T. 0-15

Edinburgh: D Lee (Watsonians); S Reed (Boroughmuir), S Hastings (Watsonians)(captain), C Simmers (Edinburgh Academicals), S Lang (Heriot's FP); D Hodge (Watsonians), G Burns (Watsonians); A Watt (Currie), G Ellis (Currie), B Stewart (Edinburgh

Academicals), B Ward (Currie), P Jennings (Boroughmuir), A Lucking (Currie), C Mather (Watsonians), S Reid (Boroughmuir). Replacement: M Blair (Currie) for Mather 75 minutes.
Scorers: Try: Reed. Pen: Hodge. Con: Hodge.

Pontypridd: C Cormack; D Manley, J Lewis, S Lewis, O Robins; N Jenkins (captain), Paul John; N Eynon, J Evans, A Griffiths, M Spiller, G Prosser, P Owen, R Collins, D McIntosh. Replacements: S Enoch for Manley 41 minutes, M Lloyd for Spiller 67 minutes.
Scorers: Tries: Enoch (3), S Lewis, Owen. Pen: Jenkins. Cons: Jenkins (2). Half-time: 0-15

Referee: R Duhau, France.

Treviso 14 v 34 Dax
H.T. 9-17

Treviso: P Dotto; L Perziano, I Francescato, P-F Donati, L Manteri; F Mazzariol, A Troncon (captain); M Dal Sie, A Moscardi, A Castellani, A Sgorlon, C Signori, D Scaglia, L Bot, V Cristofoletto.
Scorers: Try: Perziano. Pens: Mazzariol (3).

Dax: R Dourthe; P Giordani, F Duberger, F Tauzin, P Labeyrie; U Mola, N Morlaes; O Gouaillard, R Ibanez, D Laperen, O Magne, F Lalanne, F Pelous, F Dupleichs, R Berek.
Scorers: Tries: Tauzin, Magne, Duberger, Mola. Pens: Dourthe (2). Cons: Dourthe (3), Tauzin.

Referee: R Davies, Wales.

Saturday, 19th October 1996.

Pontypridd 19 v 6 Bath
H.T. 13-3

Pontypridd: K Morgan; P Ford, J Lewis, S Lewis, S Enoch; N Jenkins (captain), Paul John; N Eynon, Phil John, A Griffiths, M Lloyd, G Prosser, M Rowley, M Williams, D McIntosh. Temporary replacement: R Collins for Williams 40-41 minutes.
Scorers: Try: Paul John. Pens: Jenkins (4). Con: Jenkins.

Bath: J Callard; J Sleightholme, A Adebayo, M Perry, J Robinson; M Catt, C Harrison; K Yates, G Adams, J Mallett, A Robinson (captain), M Haag, N Redman, R Webster, E Peters.
Scorers: Pens: Callard (2). Half-time: 13-3

Referee: J Fleming, Scotland.

Sunday, 20th October 1996.

Dax 69 v 12 Edinburgh
H.T. 31-9

Dax: R Dourthe; U Mola, P Giordani, F Duberger, P Labeyrie; M Dourthe, J Daret; W Rebeyrotte, T Rechou, O Gouillard, O Magne, F Lalanne, O Roumat (captain), R Berek, F Pelous. Replacements: F Dupleichs for Pelous 43 minutes, R Ibanez for

711

Rechou 44 minutes, D Laperne for Roumat 50 minutes.
Scorers: Tries: R Dourthe (3), Magne (2), Labeyrie (2), M Dourthe (2), Mola. Pen: R Dourthe. Cons: R Dourthe (8).

Edinburgh: D Lee (Watsonians); S Lang (Heriot's FP), S Hastings (Watsonians)(captain), C Simmers (Edinburgh Academicals), S Reed (Boroughmuir); D Hodge (Watsonians), G Burns (Watsonians); A Watt (Currie), G Ellis (Currie), B Stewart (Edinburgh Academicals), B Ward (Currie), P Jennings (Boroughmuir), A Lucking (Currie), D Clark (Boroughmuir), G Dall (Heriot's FP). Replacements: G Beveridge (Boroughmuir) for Burns 70 minutes, M Blair (Currie) for Dall 75 minutes, R McNulty (Boroughmuir) for Watt 79 minutes.
Scorers: Pens: Hodge (4). Half-time: 31-9

Referee: L Mayne, Ireland.

Saturday, 26th October 1996.
Bath 25 v 15 Dax
H.T. 16-13

Bath: J Callard (captain); J Robinson, H Paul, J Guscott, A Adebayo; M Catt, C Harrison; D Hilton, G Adams, J Mallett, N Thomas, M Haag, N Redman, R Webster, S Ojomoh. Replacements: B Cusack for Redman 58 minutes, M Perry for Callard 72 minutes.
Scorers: Try: Paul. Pens: Callard (5), Catt. Con: Callard.

Dax: R Dourthe; U Mola, P Giordani, F Tauzin; P Labeyrie, J Daret; O Gouillard, R Ibanez, D Laperne, O Magne, F Lalanne, O Roumat (captain), R Berek, F Pelous. Replacements: V Dubois for Duberger 56 minutes, F Dupleichs for Magne 60 minutes, G Norris for Pelous 70 minutes.
Scorers: Try: Mola. Pens: Dourthe (3). Con: Dourthe.

Half-time: 16-13

Referee: B Smith, Ireland.

Sunday, 27th October 1996. At Myreside.
Edinburgh 23 v 43 Treviso
H.T. 11-26

Edinburgh: D Lee (Watsonians); S Lang (Heriot's FP), S Hastings (Watsonians)(captain), D Hodge (Watsonians), S Reed (Boroughmuir); A Donaldson (Currie), G Beveridge (Boroughmuir); A Watt (Currie), G McKelvey (Watsonians), B Stewart (Edinburgh Academicals), B Ward (Currie), P Jennings (Boroughmuir), A Lucking (Currie), G Dall (Heriot's FP), D Clark (Currie).
Scorers: Tries: Lee, Donaldson, Lucking. Pens: Hodge (2). Con: Hodge.

Treviso: P Dotto; L Perziano, I Francescato, P-F Donati, L Manteri; F Mazzariol, A Troncon (captain); M Dal Sie, A Moscardi, G Grespan, A Sgorlon, C Signori, D Scaglia, V Cristofoletto, J Gardner. Replacement: P Pellarini for Cristofoletto 70 minutes.
Scorers: Tries: Perziano (2), Troncon (2), Grespan, Mazzariol, Sgorlon. Cons: Mazzariol (4).

Referee: A Spreadbury, England.

Saturday, 2nd November 1996.
Dax 22 v 18 Pontypridd
H.T. 12-7

Dax: R Dourthe; U Mola, P Giordani, F Tauzin, P Labeyrie; J-F Dubois, N Morlaes; O Gouillard, R Ibanez, D Laperne, O Magne, F Lalanne, O Roumat (captain), R Berek, F Pelous. Replacement: W Rebeyrotte for Laperne 63 minutes.
Scorers: Try: Mola. Pens: Dourthe (5). Con: Dourthe.

Pontypridd: K Morgan; D Manley, J Lewis, S Lewis, P Ford; N Jenkins (captain), Paul John; N Eynon, Phil John, A Griffiths, M Lloyd, G Prosser, M Rowley, M Williams, D McIntosh.
Scorers: Pens: Jenkins (6). Half-time: 12-7.

Referee: C Muir, Scotland.

Treviso 27 v 50 Bath
H.T. 8-28

Treviso; F Donati; L Perziano, T Visentin, I Francescato, L Manteri; F Mazzariol, A Troncon (captain); G Grespan, A Moscardi, A Castellani, A Sgorlon, V Cristofoletto, D Scaglia, S Rigo, J Gardner. Replacements: P Dotto for Visentin 39 minutes, P Pellarini for Rigo 60 minutes, M Perziano for L Perziano 69 minutes, M Dal Sie for Castellani 72 minutes.
Scorers: Tries: Francescato, Troncon, Donati, Mazzariol. Pen: Mazzariol. Cons: Mazzariol (2).

Bath: J Callard; J Robinson, P de Glanville (captain), J Guscott, A Adebayo; M Catt, C Harrison; D Hilton, G Dawe, J Mallett, N Thomas, M Haag, S Ojomoh, E Peters. Replacement: V Ubogu for Mallett 72 minutes. Temporary replacement: H Paul for Catt 14-20 minutes.
Scorers: Tries: Catt (4) Adebayo (2), Hilton. Pen: Catt. Cons: Catt (5), Harrison. Half-time: 8-28.

Referee: D Gillet, France.

FINAL POOL 'A' TABLE

	P	W	L	F	A	Pts
Dax	4	3	1	141	69	6
Bath	4	3	1	136	88	6
Pontypridd	4	3	1	97	60	6
Benetton Treviso	4	1	3	106	135	2
Edinburgh	4	0	4	71	199	0

Dax and Bath qualify for quarter-finals

POOL B

Llanelli 34 v 17 Leinster
H.T. 16-17

Llanelli: G Evans; A Richards, M Wintle, N Boobyer, D Evans; F Botica, R Moon; R Jones, R McBryde (captain), S John, H Jenkins, S Ford, V Cooper, C Wyatt, I Jones. Replacement: P Morris for Jenkins 71 minutes.
Scorers: Tries: Wyatt , Moon , Boobyer . Pens: Botica (5). Cons: Botica (2).

Leinster: P McKenna (Old Belvedere); P Gavin (Old Belvedere), R McIlreavy (St Mary's College), K McQuilken (Lansdowne), D O'Mahoney (Lansdowne); R Governey (Lansdowne), A Rolland (Blackrock College); H Hurley (Moseley), M McDermott (Lansdowne), P Wallace (Saracens), C Pim (Old Wesley)(captain), N Francis (Old Belvedere), M O'Kelly (London Irish), S Rooney (Lansdowne), V Costello (London Irish). Replacement: N Hogan (Oxford University) for Rolland 48 minutes.
Scorers: Tries: Gavin , McKenna , O'Mahoney . Con: Governey.

Referee: J Bacigalupo, Scotland.

Pau 85 v 28 Scottish Borders
H.T. 31-0

Pau: N Brusque; B Lande, D Dantiaca, C Paille, S Claverie; D Aucagne, F Torssain; P Triep-Clapdevielle, J Rey, S Bria, S Keith, A Lagouarde, T Cleda, F Rolles, P Ebel (captain). Replacements: T Baleix for Bria 48 minutes, N Baque for Ebel 65 minutes, T Duces for Dantiaca 65 minutes.
Scorers: Tries: Lande (4), Keith (2), Aucagne (2), Brusque , Cleda , Paille , Lagouarde , penalty try. Pens: Aucagne (2). Cons: Aucagne (5), Brusque (2).

Scottish Borders (Melrose unless stated): C Murray (Hawick); M Moncrieff, S Nichol, D Bain, G Parker; C Chalmers, B Redpath (captain); M Browne, S Brotherstone, P Wright, S Bennett (Kelso), R Brown, I Elliot (Hawick), N Broughton, C Hogg. Replacements: S Mitchell, C Turnbull (Hawick) for Bain 61 minutes.
Scorers: Tries: Hogg , Mitchell , Turnbull , Moncrieff . Cons: Parker (4).

Referee: G Black, Ireland.

Wednesday, 16th October 1996. At Lansdowne Road, Dublin.

Leinster 10 v 27 Leicester
H.T. 10-13

Leinster: P McKenna (Old Belvedere); P Gavin (Old Belvedere), K McQuilkin (Lansdowne), M Ridge (Old Belvedere), D O'Mahony (Lansdowne); A McGowan (Blackrock College), A Rolland (Blackrock College); H Hurley (Moseley), M McDermott (Lansdowne), P Wallace (Saracens), C Pim (Old Wesley), N Francis (Old Belvedere), M O'Kelly (London Irish), S Rooney (Lansdowne). Replacements: C Clarke (Terenure College) for McKenna 9 minutes, R Governey (Lansdowne) for McQuilkin 67 minutes.
Scorers: Try: Penalty-try. Pen: McGowan. Con:

McGowan.

Leicester: G Austin; S Hackney, S Potter, W Greenwood, L Lloyd; R Liley, A Kardooni; G Rowntree, R Cockerill, D Garforth, J Wells, M Johnson (captain), M Poole, E Miller, W Johnson. Replacement: N Malone for Greenwood 27 minutes.
Scorers: Tries: Rowntree , Kardooni , Wells . Pens: R Liley (2). Cons: R Liley (3).

Referee: J Dume, France.

In Hawick.

Scottish Borders 24 v 16 Llanelli
H.T. 3-9

Scottish Borders (Melrose unless stated): C Turnbull (Hawick); M Moncrieff, C Murray (Hawick), S Nichol, G Parker; C Chalmers, B Redpath (captain); N McIlroy (Jed-Forest), S Brotherstone, S Ferguson (Peebles), S Bennett (Kelso), R Brown, S Aitken, N Broughton, C Hogg.
Scorers: Pens: Parker (8).

Llanelli: G Evans; A Richards, M Wintle, N Boobyer, C Warlow; F Botica, R Moon; R Evans, R McBryde (captain), S John, P Morris, S Ford, V Cooper, C Wyatt, I Jones. Replacement: J Williams for Morris 78 minutes.
Scorers: Try: Richards. Pens: Botica (3). Con: Botica.

Referee: G Crothers, Ireland.

Saturday, 19th October 1996.
Leicester 43 v 3 Scottish Borders
H.T. 14-3

Leicester: J Liley; S Hackney, S Potter, N Malone, R Underwood; R Liley, A Healey; D Jelley, D West, D Garforth, O Wingham, M Johnson (captain) M Poole, W Johnson, E Miller. Replacement: D Drake-Lee for Miller 40 minutes.
Scorers: Tries: Miller , Underwood , Hackney , Poole , J Liley , West . Pen: R Liley. Cons: R Liley (5).

Scottish Borders (Melrose unless stated): C Turnbull (Hawick); A Stanger (Hawick), S Nichol, C Murray (Hawick), G Parker; C Chalmers, B Redpath (captain); N McIlroy (Jed-Forest), S Brotherstone, S Ferguson (Peebles), S Bennett (Kelso), R Brown, S Aitken, N Broughton, C Hogg. Replacement: D Bain for Murray 26 minutes.
Scorers: Pen: Parker.

Referee: G Simmonds, Wales.

Llanelli 31 v 15 Pau
H.T. 21-12

Llanelli: S Jones; A Richards, M Wintle, N Boobyer, G Evans; F Botica, R Moon; R Jones, R McBryde (captain), S John, C Wyatt, S Ford, V Cooper, I Jones, J Williams. Replacements: P Morris for Cooper 64 minutes, R Evans for R Jones 78 minutes. Sent-off: I Jones 62 minutes.
Scorers: Tries: Boobyer , S Jones , Moon , Botica . Pen: Botica. Cons: Botica (4).

Pau: N Brusque; S Claverie, C Paille, D Dantiacq, Y Martin; D Aucagne, F Torossian; P Mayrin, J Rey (captain), P Triep-Capdeville, S Keith, T Mentieres, A Lagouarde, N Bacque, F Rolles. Replacements: S

Bria for Rey 55 minutes, T Ebel for Rolles 58 minutes, T Cleda for Lagouarde 67 minutes. Sent-off: Bacque 60 minutes, Torossian 77 minutes.
Scorers: Tries: Brusque , Claverie . Pen: Aucagne. Con: Aucagne.

Referee: C Lander, England.

Saturday, 26th October 1996.
Pau 14 v 19 Leicester
H.T. 14-6

Pau: N Brusque; B Lhande, D Dantiacq, C Paille, S Claverie; D Aucagne, C Passicos; P Triep-Capdeville, J Rey, S Bria, S Keith, T Cleda, A Lagouarde, F Rolles, P Ebel (captain).
Scorers: Try: Rey. DG: Aucagne. Pens: Aucagne (2).

Leicester: J Liley; S Hackney, S Potter, N Malone, R Lloyd; R Liley, A Healey; G Rowntree, R Cockerill, D Garforth, J Wells, M Johnson, M Poole, B Drake-Lee, D Richards (captain). Replacements: G Austin for Potter 14 minutes, R Underwood for Lloyd 64 minutes.
Scorers; Try: Lloyd. Pens: R Liley (4). Cons: R Liley.

Referee: I Ramage, Scotland.

In Melrose.
Scottish Borders 25 v 34 Leinster
H.T. 22-11

Scottish Borders (Melrose unless stated): C Turnbull (Hawick); M Changleng (Gala), A Stanger (Hawick), S Nichol, G Parker; C Chalmers, B Redpath (Captain); N McIlroy (Jed-Forest), S Brotherstone, S Ferguson (Peebles), S Bennett (Kelso), I Elliot (Hawick), S Aitken, K Armstrong (Jed-Forest), C Hogg. Replacement: D Bain for Chalmers 63 minutes.
Scorers: Tries: Changleng , Parker , Aitken . Pens: Parker (2). Cons: Parker (2).

Leinster: C Clarke (Terenure College); D Hickie (St Mary's College), K McQuilkin (Lansdowne), D O'Mahony (Lansdowne); A McGowan (Blacrock College), N Hogan (Oxford University); H Hurley (Moseley), M McDermott (Lansdowne), A McKeen (Lansdowne), C Pim (Old Wesley)(captain), N Francis (Old Belvedere), M O'Kelly (London Irish), D Oswald (Blackrock College), V Costello (London Irish). Replacements: C Dempsey (Terenure College) for Clarke 60 minutes, S Rooney (Lansdowne) for Oswald 78 minutes.
Scorers: Tries: Oswald , Clarke , McGowan , Hickie . Pens: McGowan (4). Con: McGowan.

Referee: S Piercy, England.

Saturday, 2nd November 1996.
Leicester 25 v 16 Llanelli
H.T. 10-9

Leicester: J Liley; S Hackney, W Greenwood, N Malone, L Lloyd; R Liley, A Healey; G Rowntree, R Cockerill, D Garforth, J Wells, M Johnson, M Poole, W Drake-Lee, D Richards. Replacement: A Kardooni for Healey 77 minutes.
Scorers: Tries: Drake-Lee , Lloyd , Healey , Rowntree . Pen: R Liley. Con: R Liley.

Llanelli: W Proctor; I Evans (captain), M Wintle, N Boobyer, A Richards; F Botica, R Moon; R Evans, R McBryde, S John, P Morris, S Ford, V Cooper, M Perego, C Wyatt. Replacement: H Williams-Jones for R Evans 74 minutes. Temporary replacements: H Williams-Jones for R Evans 10-16 minutes, L Williams for Perego 32-38 minutes.
Scorers: Try: Wintle. DG: Botica. Pens: Botica (2). Con: Botica.

Referee: P Thomas, France.

At Donnybrook, Dublin.
Leinster 25 v 23 Pau
H.T. 16-15

Leinster: C Clarke (Terenure College); D Hickie (St Mary's College), M Ridge (Old Belvedere), K McQuilkin (Lansdowne), D O'Mahony (Lansdowne); A McGowan (Blackrock College), N Hogan (Terenure College); H Hurley (Moseley), M McDermott (Lansdowne), P Wallace (Saracens), C Pim (Old Wesley)(captain), M O'Kelly (London Irish), N Francis (Old Belvedere), D Oswald (Blackrock College), V Costello (London Irish). Replacements: S Rooney (Lansdowne) for Oswald 51 minutes, J Blaney (Terenure College) for McDermott 60 minutes.
Scorers: Try: McQuilkin. Pens: McGowan (6). Con: McGowan.

Pau: N Brusque; S Claverie, D Dantiaq, C Paille, B Lhande; D Aucagne, C Passicos; P Triep-Capdeville, J Rey, S Bria, S Keith, T Mentieres, T Cleda, F Rolles, P Ebel (captain). Replacements: J-M Souverbie for Claverie 41 minutes, P Maurin for Triep-Capdeville 60 minutes, T Duces for Brusque 69 minutes, T Baleix for Rey 72 minutes.
Scorers: Tries: Paille (10, Claverie , Aucagne . Pens: Aucagne (2). Con: Aucagne.

Referee: P Bolland, Wales.

FINAL POOL 'B' TABLE

	P	W	L	F	A	Pts
Leicester	4	4	0	114	43	8
Llanelli	4	2	2	97	81	4
Leinster	4	2	2	86	109	4
Pau	4	1	3	137	103	2
Scottish Borders	4	1	3	80	178	2

Leicester and Llanelli qualify for quarter-finals

POOL C

Brive 34 v 19 Neath
H.T. 19-5

Brive: S Viars; M Heymans, C Lamaison, G Fabre, S Carrat; A Penaud (captain), P Carbonneau; D Casadei, L Travers, R Crespy, Y Domi, E Allegret, T rees, F Duboisset, G Kacala. Replacements: G Ross for Allegret 58 minutes, T Labrousse for Duboisset 58 minutes, E Bouti for Casadei 70 minutes, S Bonnet for Carrat 72 minutes.
Scorers: Tries: Carrat (4), Viars . Penalty-goals: Viars (3).

Neath: P Williams; C Higgs, D Hawkins, G Evans, Richard Jones; D Morris, C Bridges; L Gerrard, B Williams, J Davies (captain), S Martin, M Glover, A Kembery, Robin Jones, C Scott. Replacement: P Horgan for Bridges 28 minutes, I Boobyer for Robin Jones 60 minutes.
Scorers: Tries: Higgs, Horgan, penalty try. Cons: Morris (2).

Referee: B Campsall, England.

Sunday, 13th October 1996. At McDiarmid Park, Perth.

Caledonia 34 v 41 Ulster
H.T. 18-15

Caledonia: R Shepherd (Melrose); N Renton (Boroughmuir), P Rouse (Dundee High School FP), A Carruthers (Kirkcaldy), J Kerr (Watsonians); J Newton (Dundee High School FP), P Simpson (Edinburgh Academicals); T Smith (Watsonians), S Brown (Kirkcaldy), D Herrington (Kirkcaldy), D McIvor (Glenrothes)(captain), S Grimes (Watsonians), S Hamilton (Hamilton Academicals), M Waite (Edinburgh Academicals), C Allan (Edinburgh Academicals). Replacement: D Officer (Currie) for Kerr 80 minutes.
Scorers: Tries: Shepherd , Rouse , Grimes . DG: Newton. Pens: Shepherd (4). Cons: Shepherd (2).

Ulster: R Morrow (Queen's University); J Topping (Ballymena), M Field (Malone), S Coulter (Ballymena), J Cunningham (Dublin University); D Humphreys (London Irish), S Bell (Dungannon); R Mackey (Malone), S Ritchie (Ballymena), G Leslie (Dungannon), S Duncan (Malone), P Johns (Saracens), J Davidson (London Irish), S McKinty (Bangor), D McBride (Malone)(captain). Replacement: N McClusky (Queen's University) for Coulter 40 minutes, S Laing (Instonians) for Field 75 minutes.
Scorers: Tries: Humphreys (2), Cunningham (2), McKinty . DG: Humphreys. Pens: Humphreys (2), Laing . Cons: Humphreys (2).

Referee: J-C Gastou, France.

Wednesday, 16th October 1996.

Neath 27 v 18 Caledonia
H.T. 13-3

Neath: G Davies; C Higgs, David Hawkins, D Evans, Richard Jones; P Williams, P Horgan; L Gerrard, M Thomas, J Davies (captain), S Martin, M Glover, A Kembery, Robin Jones, I Boobyer.
Scorers: Tries: Hawkins , Evans . Pens: G Davies (5).

Con: G Davies.

Caledonia: R Shepherd (Melrose)(captain); N Renton (Boroughmuir), P Rouse (Dundee High School FP), A Carruthers (Kirkcaldy), D Officer (Currie); J Newton (Dundee High School FP), P Simpson (Edinburgh Academicals); T Smith (Watsonians) S Brown (Kirkcaldy), D Herrington (Kirkcaldy), S Hannah (Kirkcaldy), S Grimes (Watsonians), S Hamilton (Hamilton Academicals), M Waite (Edinburgh Academicals), C Allan (Edinburgh Academicals).
Scorers: Tries: Shepherd , Smith . Pens: Shepherd (2). Con: Shepherd.

Referee: J Pearson, England.

In Belfast.

Ulster 15 v 21 Harlequins
H.T. 12-10

Ulster: R Morrow (Queen's University); N McCluskey (Queen's University), J Topping (Ballymena), S Coulter (Ballymena), J Cunningham (Dublin University); D Humphreys (London Irish), A Matchett (Portadown); R Mackey (Malone), S Ritchie (Ballymena), G Leslie (Dungannon), S Duncan (Malone), P Johns (Saracens), J Davidson (London Irish), S McKinty (Bangor), D McBride (Malone)(captain). Replacement: J Patterson (Dungannon) for McBride 60 minutes.
Scorers: DG: Humphreys. Pens: Humphreys (4).

Harlequins: J Staples; D O'Leary, G Connolly, R Paul, P Mensah; W Carling, H Harries; J Leonard (captain), K Wood, L Benezech, R Jenkins, Gareth Llewellyn, Glyn Llewellyn, M Watson, B Davison.
Scorers: Tries: Watson , O'Leary . Pens: Carling (3). Con: Carling.

Referee: K McCartney, Scotland.

Saturday, 19th October 1996.

Harlequins 44 v 22 Neath
H.T. 24-8

Harlequins: J Staples; D O'Leary, G Connolly, R Paul, P Mensah; W Carling, H Harries; J Leonard (captain), K Wood, L Benezech, L Cabannes, Gareth Llewellyn, Glyn Llewellyn, B Davison, M Watson. Replacements: J Williams for Mensah 41 minutes, P Challinor for Connolly 68 minutes. Temporary replacement: R Jenkins for Gareth Llewellyn 16-22 minutes.
Scorers: Tries: Williams (3), O'Leary (2), Cabannes (2), Mensah . Cons: Carling (2).

Neath: G Davies; C Higgs, H Woodland, G Evans, Richard Jones; P Williams, P Horgan; L Gerrard, B Williams, J Davies (captain), S Martin, M Glover, A Kembery, Robin Jones, S Williams. Replacement: I Boobyer for Kembery 15 minutes.
Scorers: Tries: S Williams (2), Boobyer . Pen: G Davies. Cons: G Davies (2).

Sunday, 20th October 1996. At McDiarmid Park, Perth.

Caledonia 30 v 32 Brive
H.T. 8-14

Caledonia: R Shepherd (Melrose); D Officer (Currie), P Rouse (Dundee High School FP), A Carruthers (Kirkcaldy), N Renton (Boroughmuir); J Newton (Dundee High School FP), P Simpson (Edinburgh Academicals); T Smith (Watsonians), S Brown (Kirkcaldy), D Herrington (Kirkcaldy), G Flockhart

(Stirling County), S Hamilton (Hamilton Academicals), S Grimes (Watsonians), D McIvor (Glenrothes) (captain), M Waite (Edinburgh Academicals). Replacements: J Mitchell (Kirkcaldy) for Shepherd 40 minutes, W Anderson (Kirkcaldy) for Herrington 45 minutes, S Pearson (Dundee High School FP) for Carruthers 59 minutes.
Scorers: Tries: Rouse , Officer , Simpson , Grimes . Pens: Shepherd (2). Cons: Shepherd , Newton .

Brive: S Viars; G Fabre, C Lamaison, R Paillat, S Carrat; A Penaud (captain), P Carbonneau; D Casadei, L Travers, R Crespy, Y Domi, E Allegret, A Rees, G Kalala, F Duboisset. Replacements: D Venditti for Fabre 33 minutes, A Boudi for Duboisset 43 minutes, G Ross for Allegret 79 minutes.
Scorers: Tries: Carrat (2), Fabre , Casadei . DG: Venditti. Pen: Lamaison. Cons: Lamaison (3).

Referee: N Whitehouse, Wales.

Saturday, 26th October 1996.

Neath 15 v 13 Ulster
H.T. 7-6

Neath: G Davies; C Higgs, R Jones, G Evans, D Case; P Williams, P Horgan; L Gerrard, B Williams, J Davies (captain), S Martin, M Glover, P Matthews, I Boobyer, S Williams. Replacements: L Griffiths for Martin 70 minutes, G Newman for Boobyer 75 minutes.
Scorers: Tries: S Williams , Gerrard . Pen: G Davies. Con: G Davies.

Ulster: R Morrow (Queen's University); J Topping (Ballymena), M Field (Malone), M McCall (Dungannon), J Cunningham (Dublin University); D Humphreys (London Irish), A Matchett (Portadown); R Mackey (Malone), S Ritchie (Ballymena), G Leslie (Dungannon), S Duncan (Malone), G Longwell (Ballymena), J Davidson (London Irish), S McKinty (Bangor), D McBride (Malone)(captain).
Scorers: Try: McKinty. Pens: Humphreys (2). Con: Humphreys.

Referee: C Muir, Scotland.

Sunday, 27th October 1996.

Brive 23 v 10 Harlequins
H.T. 12-10

Brive: S Viars; G Fabre, C Lamaison, D Venditti, S Carrat; A Penaud (captain), P Carbonneau; D Casadei, L Travers, R Crespy, Y Domi, E Allegret, T Rees, T Labrousse, G Kacala. Replacements: F Duboisset for Domi 65 minutes, G Ross for Rees 67 minutes, E Bouti for Crespy 67-70 minutes (temporary) & 79 minutes, R Paillat for Fabre 79 minutes.
Scorers: Try: Carrat. DGs: Penaud , Carbonneau . Pens: Lamaison (4).

Harlequins: J Staples; J Williams, W Carling, R Paul, G Connolly; P Challinor, H Harries; J Leonard (captain), K Wood, L Benezech, B Davison, Gareth Llewellyn, Glyn Llewellyn, M Watson, L Cabannes. Replacements: S Pilgrim for Staples 16 minutes, D Luger for Pilgrim 60 minutes, R Jenkins for Watson 68 minutes.
Scorers: Try: Challinor. Pen: Carling. Con: Carling.

Referee: B Stirling, Ireland (replaced 57 minutes by G Crothers, Ireland).

Saturday, 2nd November 1996.

Harlequins 56 v 35 Caledonia
H.T. 20-16

Harlequins: J Staples; D O'Leary, R Paul, G Connolly, J Williams; W Carling, H Harries; J Leonard (captain), K Wood, A Mullins, R Jenkins, Gareth Llewellyn, A Snow, L Cabannes, B Davison. Replacements: P Challinor for Williams 41 minutes, D Luger for Connolly 78 minutes. Temporary replacement: M Watson for Davison 37-41 minutes.
Scorers: Tries: Staples (3), Williams (2), O'Leary (2), Challinor , Paul . Pen: Carling. Cons: Carling (4).

Caledonia: R Shepherd (Melrose); D Officer (Currie), P Rouse (Dundee High School FP), A Carruthers (Kirkcaldy), J Kerr (Watsonians); J Newton (Dundee High School FP), P Simpson (Edinburgh Academicals); T Smith (Watsonians), K McKenzie (Stirling County), D Herrington (Kirkcaldy), D McIvor (Glenrothes) (captain), S Hamilton (Hamilton Academicals), S Grimes (Watsonians), M Waite (Edinburgh Academicals), G Flockhart (Stirling County). Replacements: W Anderson (Kirkcaldy) for Smith 41 minutes, J Thompson (Kirkcaldy) for Rouse 65 minutes, C MacDonald (Kirkcaldy) for Hamilton 65 minutes, S Hannah (Kirkcaldy) for Flockhart 65 minutes.
Scorers: Tries: McIvor (2), Officer , Newton . Pens: Shepherd (3). Cons: Shepherd (3).

Referee: L Mayne, Ireland.

Ulster 6 v 17 Brive
H.T. 6-5

Ulster: R Morrow (Queen's University); J Topping (Ballymena0, M Field (Malone), M McCall (Dungannon), J Cunningham (Dublin University); D Humphreys (London Irish), A Matchett (Portadown); R Mackey (Malone), S Ritchie (Ballymena), G Leslie (Dungannon), S Duncan (Malone), P Johns (Saracens), J Davidson (London Irish), S McKinty (Bangor), D McBride (Malone)(captain). Replacement: J Patterson (Dungannon) for McKinty 28 minutes.
Scorers: DG: Humphreys. Pen: Humphreys.

Brive: D Venditti; S Viars, R Paillat, C Lamaison, S Carrat; A Penaud (captain), P Carbonneau; D Casadei, L Travers, E Bouti, Y Domi, E Allegret, G Ross, G Kacala, F Duboisset. Replacements: R Crespy for Travers 60 minutes, C Heymans for Venditti 62 minutes, S Bonnet for Penaud 79 minutes.
Scorers: Tries: Duboisset , Carrat , Viars . Con: Penaud.

Referee: H F Lewis, Wales.

FINAL POOL 'C' TABLE

	P	W	L	F	A	Pts
Brive	4	4	0	106	65	8
NEC Harlequins	4	3	1	131	95	6
Neath	4	2	2	83	109	4
Ulster	4	1	3	75	87	2
Caledonia	4	0	4	117	156	0

Brive and NEC Harlequins qualify for quarter-finals

POOL D

Saturday, 12th October 1996. In Cork.

Munster 23 v 5 Milan
H.T. 17-0

Munster: D Crotty (Garryowen); R Wallace (Saracens), B Walsh (Cork Constitution), S McCahill (Sunday's Well), B Begley (Old Crescent); K Keane (Garryowen), S McIvor (Garryowen); J Fitzgerald (Young Munster), T Kingston (Dolphin), P McCarthy (Cork Constitution), A Foley (Shannon), G Fulcher (London Irish), M Galwey (Shannon)(captain), B Cronin (Garryowen), L Toland (Old Crescent). Replacements: P Murray (Shannon) for Crotty 41 minutes, B O'Meara (Cork Constitution) for McIvor 70 minutes.
Scorers: Try: Begley. Pens: Begley (5), Keane (1).

Milan: F Williams; R Crotti, M Bonomi, M Tommasi, Marcello Cuttitta; D Dominguez, F Gomez; Massimo Cuttitta (captain), C Orlandi, F Properzi, D Beretta, F Berni, G Croci, O Arancio, T Ciccio. Replacements: O Rovelli for Ciccio 11 minutes, M Vaghi for Massimo Cittitta 30 minutes, S Tassi for Rovelli 30 minutes, A Stoica for Bonomi 70 minutes.
Scorers: Try: Williams.

Referee: D R Davies, Wales.

Sunday, 13th October 1996.

Wasps 24 v 26 Cardiff
H.T. 15-13

Wasps: J Ufton; P Sampson, N Greenstock, V Tuigamala, L Scrace; G Rees, A Gomarsall; M Griffiths, S Mitchell, W Green, M White, D Cronin, M Greenwood, L Dallaglio (captain), C Sheasby. Temporary replacements: M Fraser for Ufton 21-30 minutes, J Worsley for White 31-40 minutes.
Scorers: Pens: Rees (8).

Cardiff: J Thomas; S Hill, M Hall, G Jones, N Walker; J Davies, R Howley; L Mustoe, J Humphreys, D Young, H Taylor (captain), J Wakeford, D Jones, E Lewis, J Ringer. Replacement: M Bennett for Ringer 51 minutes.
Scorers: Tries: Howley (2), Lewis. DGs: Davies (2). Pen: Davies. Con: Davies. .gap 5
Referee: B Stirling, Ireland.

Wednesday, 16th October 1996.

Cardiff 48 v 18 Munster
H.T. 24-18

Cardiff: J Thomas; N Walker, M Hall, G Jones, S Hill; J Davies, R Howley; L Mustoe, J Humphreys, D Young, H Taylor (captain), J Wakeford, D Jones, M Bennett, E Lewis. Replacements: P Booth for Young 50 minutes, K Stewart for D Jones 52 minutes, I Jones for Thomas 53 minutes, L Jarvis for Davies 65 minutes.
Scorers: Tries: Howley (3), Lewis (3), Hill (1), Taylor (1). Cons: Davies (4).

Munster: D Crotty (Garryowen); R Wallace (Saracens), S McCahill (Sunday's Well), B Walsh (Cork Constitution), B Begley (Old Crescent); K Keane (Garryowen), S McIvor (Garryowen); I Murray (Shannon), T Kingston (Dolphin) P McCarthy (Cork Constitution), A Foley (Shannon), M Galwey (Shannon)(captain), G Fulcher (London Irish), B Cronin (Garryowen), L Toland (Old Crescent).
Replacements: L Dineen (Old Crescent) for Foley 48 minutes, P Murray (Shannon) for Begley 72 minutes. Temporary replacement: Dineen for Galwey 14-24 minutes.
Scorers: Tries: Begley (1), Foley (1). Pens: Begley (1), Keane (1). Con: Begley.

Milan 26 v 44 Toulouse
H.T. 12-29

Milan: F Williams; R Crotti, M Tommasi, M Bonomi, Marcello Cuttitta; D Dominguez, F Gomez; M Varghi, C Orlandi, F Properzi, O Orancio, G Croci, F Berni, P Pedroni (captain), D Beretta.
Scorers: Tries: Gomez (1), Properzi (1). Pens: Dominguez (4). Cons: Dominguez (2).

Toulouse: S Ougier; E Ntamack, T Castaignede, M Marfaing, D Berti; C Deylaud, J Tilloles; J-L Jordana, P Soula, C Califano, R Sonnes, H Miorin, F Bellot, S Dispagne, J-L Cester. Replacements: O Carbonneau for Deylaud 40 minutes, D Lacroix for Dispagne 48 minutes, P Lassere for Jordana 61 minutes.
Scorers: Tries: Berty (1), Ntamack (1), Deylaud (1), Califano (1), Ougier (1), penalty-try. Pens: Castaignede (2). Cons: Castaignede (3), Deylaud (1).

Referee: B Campsall, England.

Saturday, 19th October 1996. In Limerick.

Munster 49 v 22 Wasps
H.T. 16-5

Munster: P Murray (Shannon); R Wallace (Saracens), B Walsh (Cork Constitution), S McCahill (Sunday's Well), D Crotty (Garryowen); K Keane (Garryowen), S McIvor (Garryowen); J Fitzgerald (Young Munster), T Kingston (Dolphin), N Healy (Shannon), D Conroy (Shannon), G Fulcher (London Irish), M Galwey (Shannon)(captain), A Foley (Shannon), B Cronin (Garryowen).
Scorers: Tries: Keane (1), Foley (1), Galwey (1), Cronin (1), Wallace (1), Crotty (6), penalty-try. Pens: Keane (2). Cons: Keane (4).

Wasps: J Ufton; P Sampson, N Greenstock, V Tuigamala, S Roiser; G Rees, A Gomarsall; M Griffiths, S Mitchell, W Green, M White, D Cronin, M Greenwood, L Dallaglio (captain), C Sheasby.
Scorers: Tries: Sheasby (1), Ufton (1), Greenwood (1), Roiser (1). Con: Ufton.

Referee: D Mene, France.

Toulouse 36 v 20 Cardiff
H.T. 11-12

Toulouse: S Ougier; E Ntamack (captain), M Marfaing, T Castaignede, D Berty; C Deylaud, J Tilloles; C Califano, P Soula, J-L Jordana, D Lacroix, H Miorin, F Belot, H Manent, S Dispagne. Replacement: C Guiter for Lacroix 70 minutes. Sent-off: Soula 22 minutes.
Scorers: Tries: Berty (2), Castaignede (1), Ntamack (1). DGs: Castaignede (1), Deylaud (1). Pens: Castaignede (2). Cons: Castaignede (2).

Cardiff: J Thomas; S Hill, M Hall, G Jones, N Walker; L Jarvis, R Howley; L Mustoe, J Humphreys, D Young, H Taylor (captain), J Wakeford, D Jones, M Bennett, E Lewis. Replacements: P Booth for Mustoe 57 minutes, J Ringer for Bennett 70 minutes, P Young

for Humphreys 79 minutes.
Scorers: Try: G Jones. Pens: Jarvis (2).

Referee: R Megson, Scotland.

Saturday, 26th October 1996.

Wasps 77 v 17 Toulouse
H.T. 23-10

Wasps: J Ufton; P Sampson, N Greenstock, V Tuigamala, S Roiser; A King, A Gomarsall; D Molloy, S Mitchell, W Green, L Dallaglio (captain), D Cronin, A Reed, M White, C Sheasby. Replacements: M Greenwood for Cronin 65 minutes, L Scrace for Roiser 75 minutes, D Macer for Green 76 minutes, M Fraser for Gomarsall 77 minutes, I Dunstan for Molloy 78 minutes. Temporary replacement: A Volley for White 38-42 minutes.
Scorers: Tries: Greenstock (2), Reed (1), Roiser (1), Mitchell (1), Sampson (1), Sheasby (1), King (1), penalty-try. DG: King. Pens: Ufton (5). Cons: Ufton (6), King (1).

Toulouse: S Ougier; E Ntamack (captain), M Marfaing, T Catsaignede, D Berty; C Deylaud, J Tilloles; C Califano, C Guiter, J-L Jordana, J-L Cester, H Miorin, F Belot, H Manent, S Dispagne. Replacements: O Carbonneau for Castaignede 24 minutes, P Lassere for Guiter 40 minutes, X Garbojasa for Berty 44 minutes, F Cazaux for Ougier 67 minutes. Temporary replacement: D Lacroix for Cester 44-50 minutes.
Scorers: Tries: Ntamack (1), Lassere (1). Pen: Castaignede. Cons: Deylaud (2).

Referee: G Simmonds, Wales.

Sunday, 27th October 1996.

Cardiff 41 v 19 Milan
H.T. 23-12

Cardiff: J Thomas; N Walker, M Hall, L Davies, S Hill; L Jarvis, R Howley; A Lewis, J Humphreys, D Young, H Taylor (captain), J Wakeford, K Stewart, J Ringer, M Bennett. Replacements: L Jones for Stewart 25 minutes, L Mustoe for Lewis 73 minutes. Temporary replacement: I Jones for Thomas 17-34 minutes.
Scorers: Tries: Hall (1), Howley (1), Thomas (1), Bennett (1). Pens: Jarvis (5). Cons: Jarvis (3).

Milan: F Williams; R Crotti, M Bonomi, M Tommasi, Marcello Cuttitta; D Dominguez, F Gomez; S Cerioni, A Marengoni, F Properzi, O Orlandi, P Pedroni (captain), G Croci, D Beretta, O Arancio. Replacement: M Platania for Williams 45 minutes.
Scorers: Try: Marengoni. Pens: Dominguez (4). Con: Dominguez.

Referee: B Perez, France.

2nd November 1996.

Toulouse 60 v 19 Munster
H.T. 17-9

Toulouse: S Ougier; E Ntamack (captain), M Marfaing, T Castaignede, D Berty; C Deylaud, J Cazalbou; C Califano, P Lassere, J-L Jordana, D Lacroix, H Miorin F Belot, R Sonnes, S Dispagne. Replacements: O Carbonneau for Castaignede 48 minutes, H Manent for Belot 48 minutes, W Begarie for Jordana 69 minutes.
Scorers: Tries: Marfaing (3), Califano (2), Ntamack

(2), Berty (1), Ougier (1). Pen: Deylaud. Cons: Deylaud (6).

Munster: P Murray (Shannon); R Wallace (Saracens), B Walsh (Cork Constitution), S McCahill (Sunday's Well), D Crotty (Garryowen); K Keane (Garryowen), S McIvor (Garryowen); J Fitzgerald (Young Munster), T Kingston (Dolphin), N Healy (Shannon), A Foley (Shannon), M Galwey (Shannon), G Fulcher (London Irish), D Corkery (Bristol), B Cronin (Garryowen). Replacements: P McCarthy (Cork Constitution) for Healy 6 minutes, I Murray (Cork Constitution) 68 minutes, L Dineen (Old Crescent) for Cronin 68 minutes.
Scorers: Try: Corkery. Pens: Keane (4). Con: Keane (1).

Referee: T Spreadbury, England.

Milan 23 v 33 Wasps
H.T. 16-12

Milan: M Bonomi; P Scanziani, A Stoica, M Tommasi, Marcello Cuttitta; D Dominguez, F Gomez; Massimo Cuttitta (captain), A Marangoni, F Properzi, C Orlandi, P Pedroni, G Croci, D Beretta, O Arancio. Replacement; S Tassi for Orlandi 50 minutes.
Scorers: Tries: Gomez (1), Massimo Cuttitta (1). Pens: Dominguez (3). Cons: Dominguez (2).

Wasps: J Ufton; P Sampson, N Greenstock, V Tuigamala, S Roiser; A King, A Gomarsall; D Molloy, D Macer, I Dunston, L Dallaglio (captain), M Greenwood, A Reed, M White, C Sheasby. Replacement: M Wood for Gomarsall 79 minutes.
Scorers: Tries: Sampson (2), Dallaglio (1), King (1). DG: King. Pens: Ufton (2). Cons: Ufton (2).

Referee:

FINAL POOL 'D' TABLE

	P	W	L	F	A	Pts
Cardiff	4	3	1	135	97	6
Toulouse	4	3	1	157	142	6
Wasps	4	2	2	156	115	4
Munster	4	2	2	109	135	4
Milan	4	0	4	73	141	0

Leicester and Llanelli qualify for quarter-finals.

HEINEKEN EUROPEAN CUP 1997-98

Teams entered - () to be confirmed)

POOL 'A':
Leicester, Leinster, Milan, Toulouse.

POOL 'B':
Glasgow, Swansea, Ulster, Wasps.

POOL 'C':
Bath, Borders, Brive, Pontypridd.

POOL 'D':
Bourgoin, (Cardiff), Harlequins, Munster.

POOL 'E':
Caledonia, (Llanelli), Pau, Treviso.

QUARTER-FINALS

Saturday, 16th November 1996.

Cardiff 22 v 19 Bath

H.T. 16-9   Attendance: 12,000

Cardiff: J Thomas; N Walker, M Hall, L Davies, S Hill; J Davies, R Howley; A Lewis, J Humphreys, D Young, M Bennett, J Wakeford, D Jones, J Ringer, H Taylor (captain). Replacements: O Williams for Bennett 13 minutes, L Jarvis for Thomas 62 minutes.
Scorers: Try: Walker. Pens: J Davies (3), Jarvis (2). Con: J Davies.

Bath: J Robinson; H Paul, P de Glanville (captain), J Guscott, A Adebayo; M Catt, A Nicol; D Hilton, D French, V Ubogu, N Thomas, M Haag, N Redman, E Peters, S Ojomoh. Replacement: I Sanders for Nicol 3 minutes.
Scorers: Try: Thomas. Pens: Catt (4). Con: Catt.

Referee: G Black, Ireland.

Dax 18 v 26 Toulouse

H.T. 18-16   Attendance: 14,000

Dax: R Dourthe; U Mola, P Giordani, F Tauzin, P Labeyrie; J-F Dubois, N Morlaes; O Gouaillard, R Ibanez, D Laperne, R Berek, P Beraud, G Roumat (captain), O Magne, F Pelous. Replacements: F Duberger for Mola 44 minutes, F Dupleichs for Beraud 51 minutes, W Rebeyrotte for Gouaillard 63 minutes, T Rechou for Ibanez 72 minutes.
Scorers: Tries: Mola (2). Pens: Dourthe (2). Con: Dourthe.

Toulouse: S Ougier; E Ntamack (captain), M Marfaing, T Castaignede, D Berty; C Deylaud, J Cazalbou; C Califano, P Soula, J-L Jordana, D Lacroix, H Miorin, F Belot, S Dispagne, R Sonnes. Replacement: H Manent for Sonnes 48 minutes.
Scorers: Tries: Marfaing, penalty try. Pens: Deylaud (2), Castaignede (2). Cons: Deylaud, Castaignede .

Referee: P Thomas, France.

Leicester 23 v 13 Harlequins

H.T. 3-5   Attendance: 10,263

Leicester: R Liley; S Hackney, W Greenwood, S Potter, L Lloyd; R Liley, A Healey; G Rowntree, R Cockerill, D Garforth, J Wells, M Johnson, M Poole, N Back, D Richards (captain). Replacements: E Miller for Back 33 minutes, R Field for Poole 55 minutes, R Underwood for Lloyd 63 minutes.
Scorers: Tries: Cockerill, R Liley . Pens: R Liley (3). Cons: R Liley.

Harlequins: J Staples; D O'Leary, G Connolly, W Carling, D Luger; P Challinor, H Harries; J Leonard (captain), K Wood, L Benezech, R Jenkins, Gareth Llewellyn, Glyn Llewellyn, L Cabannes, B Davison.
Scorers: Tries: Luger, Carling . Pen: Challinor.

Referee: C Thomas, Wales.

Sunday, 3rd November 1996.

Brive 35 v 14 Llanelli

H.T. 26-7   Attendance: 14,000

Brive: S Viars; G Fabre, C Lamaison, D Venditti, S Carrat; A Penaud (captain), P Carbonneau; D Casadei, L Travers, R Crespy, Y Domi, E Allegret, T Rees, G Kacala, T Labrousse. Replacements: F Duboisset for Domi 32 minutes, E Bouti for Travers 56 minutes, A Boudi for Crespy 76 minutes, C Heymans for Penaud 78 minutes.
Scorers: Tries: Labrousse, Venditti . Penalty-goals: Lamaison (7). Cons: Lamaison (2).

Llanelli: W Proctor; I Evans (captain), M Wintle, N Boobyer, G Evans; F Botica, R Moon; R Jones, R McBryde, S John, M Perego, S Ford, V Cooper, I Jones, C Wyatt. Replacement: P Morris for Perego 41 minutes.
Scorers: Tries: I Evans (2). Cons: Botica (2).
Half-time: 26-7. Attendance: 14,000.

Referee: B Campsall, England.

SEMI-FINALS

Saturday, 4th January 1997.
At Welford Road, Leicester.

Leicester 37 v 11 Toulouse

H.T. 20-6   Attendance: 16,300

Leicester: J Liley; S Hackney, S Potter, W Greenwood, L Lloyd; R Liley, A Healey; G Rowntree, R Cockerill, D Garforth, J Wells, M Johnson, M Poole, N Back, D Richards (captain). Replacement: R Underwood for Hackney 73 minutes.
Scorers: Tries: Hackney, Back, Garforth, Healey, Penalty-try. Pens: J Liley (2). Cons: J Liley (3).

Toulouse: S Ougier; E Ntamack (captain), M Marfaing, T Castaignede, D Berty; C Deylaud, J Cazalbou; C Califano, P Soula, J-L Jordana, D Lacroix, H Miorin, F Belot, R Sonnes, S Dispagne. Replacements: H Manent for Sonnes 65 minutes, O Lassere for Soula 71 minutes.
Scorers: Try: Marfaing. Pens: Deylaud (2).

Referee: J Fleming, Scotland.

Sunday, 5th January 1997.
At Parc Municipal des Sports, Brive.

Brive 26 v 13 Cardiff

H.T. 9-3   Attendance: 14,000

Brive: S Viars; G Fabre, C Lamaison, D Venditti, S Carrat; A Penaud (captain), P Carbonneau; D Casadie, I Travers, R Crespy, L van der Linden, E Allegret, G Ross, G Cacala, F Duboisset. Replacements: A Rees for Allegrat 58 minutes, E Bouti for Casadei 61 minutes, C Heymans for Carrat 64 minutes, S Bonnet for Carbonneau 75 minutes, Y Dommi for Van der Linden 76 minutes.
Scorers: Tries: Venditti, Duboisset . Pens: Lamaison (4). Cons: Lamaison (2).

Cardiff: J Thomas; S Hill, M Hall, L Davies, N Walker; J Davies, R Howley; A Lewis, J Humphries, L Mustoe, H Taylor (captain), J Wakeford, D Jones, G Jones, E Lewis. Replacement: P Young for D Jones 52 minutes. Yellow card: Humphreys. Sent-off: Humphreys 52 minutes.
Scorers: Try: Penalty-try. Pens: J Davies (2). Con: J Davies.

Referee: B Stirling, Ireland.

HEINEKEN CUP FINAL

Saturday, 25th January 1997.
Cardiff Arms Park   Attendance: 40,664

BRIVE 28   9 LEICESTER

Half Time: 8-6

Tries	Carrat (2)	
	Viars	
	Fabre	
Penalties	Lamaison	J Liley (3)
Conversions	Lamaison	
Drop Goals	Lamaison	

15	S Viars	J Liley	15
14	G Fabre	S Hackney	14
13	C Lamaison	W Greenwood	13
12	D Venditti	S Potter	12
11	S Carrat	R Underwood	11
10	(Captain) A Penaud	R Liley	10
9	P Carbonneau	A Healey	9
1	D Casadei	G Rowntree	1
2	L Travers	R Cockerill	2
3	R Crespy	D Garforth	3
4	L van der Linden	J Wells	4
5	E Allegret	M Johnston	5
6	G Ross	M Poole	6
7	G Kacala	N Back	7
8	F Duboisset	D Richards (Captain)	8

Replacements:

T Labrousse for Duboisset 49 minutes.
A Rees for Allegret 67 minutes.
R Paillat for Penaud 69 minutes.
E Bouti for Casadei 70 minutes.
Y Domi for van den Linden 77 minutes.

Replacements

E Miller for Richards 68 minutes
T Lloyd for Underwood 72 minutes.
Temporary Replacement
P Freshwater for Garforth 17-22 minutes.

Competition Leading Scorers

Points

Richard Dourthe	Dax	82
Christophe Lamaison	Brive	70
Rob Liley	Leicester	62
Neil Jenkins	Pontypridd	62
Frano Botica	Llanelli	61
Rowen Shepherd	Caledonia	57
Francesco Mazzariol	Treviso	56
David Aucagne	Pau	53
David Humphreys	Ulster	52
Sebastian Carrat	Brive	50
Mike Catt	Bath	50
Gary Parker	Scottish Borders	50

Tries

Sebastian Carrat	Brive	10
Robert Howley	Cardiff	6
Ugo Mola	Dax	6
Darren O'Leary	Harlequins	5
Jamie Williams	Harlequins	5
Emile Ntamack	Toulouse	5
Michel Marfaing	Toulouse	5
Mike Catt	Bath	4
Emyr Lewis	Cardiff	4
Benjamin Lhande	Pau	4
David Berty	Toulouse	4

EUROPEAN CONFERENCE

POOL 'A'

Saturday, 12th October 1996
Agen 32 Newport 13
Newbridge 38 Glasgow 62
Sale 12 Montferrand 17

Wednesday, 16th October 1996
Agen 27 Montferrand 17
Glasgow 9 Sale 26 (at Hughenden)
Newport 24 Newbridge 9

Saturday, 19th October 1996
Montferrand 76 Glasgow 9
Newbridge 13 Agen 30
Sale 52 Newport 22

Saturday, 26th October 1996
Agen 33 Sale 16
Newbridge 12 Montferrand 46
Newport 25 Glasgow 10

Wednesday, 30th October 1996
Glasgow 23 Agen 34 (at Hughenden)

Saturday, 2nd November 1996
Sale 57 Newbridge 34
Montferrand 55 Newport 14

FINAL TABLE

	P	W	D	L	F	A	Pts
Agen	5	5	0	0	156	82	10
Montferrand	5	4	0	1	211	74	8
Sale	5	3	0	2	166	115	6
Newport	5	2	0	3	98	158	4
Glasgow	5	1	0	4	113	202	2
Newbridge	5	0	0	5	106	219	0

Agen and Montferrand qualify for quarter-finals

POOL 'B'

Saturday, 12th October 1996
Bridgend 23 Castres 36
Bristol 53 Treorchy 5
Narbonne 73 Dinamo Bucharest 22

Wednesday, 16th October 1996
Bridgend 30 Bristol 27
Castres 67 Dinamo Bucharest 6
Treorchy 19 Narbonne 26

Saturday, 19th October 1996
Bridgend 24 Dinamo Bucharest 24
Bristol 16 Narbonne 18
Castres 61 Treorchy 7

Saturday, 26th October 1996
Bristol 14 Castres 27
Dinamo Bucharest 38 Treorchy 31
Narbonne 33 Bridgend 17

Saturday, 2nd November 1996
Narbonne 11 Castres 16
Dinamo Bucharest 19 Bristol 18
Treorchy v Bridgend
Not played.

TABLE

	P	W	D	L	F	A	Pts
Castres	5	5	0	0	207	71	10
Narbonne	5	4	0	1	161	90	8
Din. Bucharest	5	2	1	2	109	213	5
Bridgend	4	1	1	2	94	120	3
Bristol	5	1	0	4	128	99	2
Treorchy	4	0	0	4	72	178	0

Castres and Narbonne qualify for quarter-finals

POOL 'C'

Saturday, 12th October 1996
Connacht 34 Padova 12 (in Galway)
Orrell 32 Dunvant 29

Sunday, 13th October 1996
Toulon 29 Northampton 38

Wednesday, 16th October 1996
Dunvant 26 Connacht 9
Northampton 61 Orrell 7
Toulon 32 Padova 23

Saturday, 19th October 1996
Connacht 11 Northampton 31 (in Galway)
Orrell 23 Toulon 28
Padova 49 Dunvant 11

Saturday, 26th October 1996
Northampton 48 Dunvant 32
Orrell 42 Padova 25

Sunday, 27th October 1996
Toulon 44 Connacht 10

Saturday, 2nd November 1996
Connacht 30 Orrell 18
Dunvant 8 Toulon 31
Padova 9 Northampton 29

FINAL TABLE

	P	W	D	L	F	A	Pts
Northampton	5	5	0	0	207	88	10
Toulon	5	4	0	1	164	102	8
Connacht	5	2	0	3	94	131	4
Orrell	5	2	0	3	122	173	4
Padova	5	1	0	4	118	148	2
Dunvant	5	1	0	4	106	169	2

Northampton and Toulon qualify for quarter-finals

POOL 'D'

Saturday, 12th October 1996
    Bourgoin 45 Begles 22
    Gloucester 59 Ebbw Vale 7
    Swansea 63 London Irish 38

Wednesday, 16th October 1996
    Ebbw Vale 3 Swansea 32
    Gloucester 10 Begles Bordeaux 17
    London Irish 13 Bourgoin 34

Saturday, 19th October 1996
    Begles-Bordeaux 32 London Irish 6
    Bourgoin 39 Ebbw Vale 3
    Swansea 62 Gloucester 12

Saturday, 26th October 1996
    Ebbw Vale 28 London Irish 20
    Swansea 31 Begles-Bordeaux 31

Sunday, 27th October 1996
    Gloucester 9 Bourgoin 24

Saturday, 2nd November 1996
    Begles-Bordeaux 93 Ebbw Vale 7
    Bourgoin 54 Swansea 19
    London Irish 13 Gloucester 29

FINAL TABLE

	P	W	D	L	F	A	Pts
Bourgoin	5	5	0	0	196	66	10
Begles-Bordeaux	5	3	1	1	195	99	7
Swansea	5	3	1	1	207	138	7
Gloucester	5	2	0	3	119	123	4
Ebbw Vale	5	1	0	4	48	243	2
London Irish	5	0	0	5	90	186	0

Bourgoin & Begles-Bordeaux qualify for quarter-finals

QUARTER-FINALS

Saturday, 16th November 1996

Agen 20 Begles-Bordeaux 15 (after extra-time)
Bourgoin 17 Montferrand 15
Castres 23 Toulon 15
Northampton 22 Narbonne 23

SEMI-FINALS

Saturday, 4th January 1997

BOURGOIN 29 v 6 NARBONNE

Scorers: Bourgoin - Tries: Laflammand (1), N
    Geany (1). Pens: Peclier (5). Cons:
    Peclier (2).
    Narbonne - Pens: Valls (2)

CASTRES 23 v 6 AGEN

Scorers: Castres - Tries: Aue (1), Garrigues (1).
    Pens: Paillat (3). Cons: Paillat (2).
    Agen - Pens: Prosper (2).

FINAL

Sunday, 26th January 1997.
Beziers

BOURGOIN 18 v 9 CASTRES

Scorers: Bourgoin - D.G. Peclier. Pens: Favre (3),
    Peclier (2)
    Castres - Pens: Savy (2), Paillat.

Northampton were the only English club to progress to the quarter finals where they lost narrowly to Narbonne.

The photo shows their half back pair of Matt Dawson and Paul Grayson in league action against Harlequins.

Photo:
Joe McCabe.

722

COUNTY CHAMPIONSHIP

SOUTH

POOL ONE

Saturday, 30th November 1996
Oxfordshire 10 Hertfordshire 66 (at Oxford)

Saturday, 7th December 1996
Hertfordshire 24 Surrey 8 (at Hertford)

Saturday, 14th December 1996
Surrey 24 Oxfordshire 30 (at Imber Court)

FINAL TABLE	P	W	L	F	A	Pts
Hertfordshire	2	2	0	90	18	4
Oxfordshire	2	1	1	40	90	2
Surrey	2	0	2	32	54	0

POOL TWO

Saturday, 30th November 1996
Middlesex 34 Buckinghamshire 22 (at Old Merchant Taylors RFC)
Somerset 29 Devon 19 (at Weston-super-Mare)

Saturday, 7th December 1996
Buckinghamshire 7 Devon 48 (at Aylesbury)
Middlesex 15 Somerset 29 (at Old Merchant Taylors')

Saturday, 14th December 1996
Devon 17 Middlesex 37 (at Bideford)
Somerset 90 Buckinghamshire 12 (at Bridgwater)

FINAL TABLE	P	W	L	F	A	Pts
Somerset	3	3	0	148	46	6
Middlesex	3	2	1	86	68	4
Devon	3	1	2	84	73	2
Buckinghamshire	3	0	3	41	172	0

POOL THREE

Saturday, 30th November 1996
Dorset & Wiltshire 33 Berkshire 13 (at Salisbury)
Hampshire 31 Eastern Counties 19 (at Havant)

Saturday, 7th December 1996
Berkshire 37 Eastern Counties 30 (at Bracknell)
Dorset & Wiltshire 19 Hampshire 10 (at Bournemouth)

Saturday, 14th December 1996
Eastern Counties 18 Dorset & Wiltshire 17 (at Braintree)
Hampshire 58 Berkshire 7 (at Basingstoke)

FINAL TABLE	P	W	L	F	A	Pts
Hampshire	3	2	1	99	45	4
Dorset & Wiltshire	3	2	1	79	41	4
Eastern Counties	3	1	2	67	85	2
Berkshire	3	1	2	57	131	2

POOL FOUR

Saturday, 30th November 1996
Cornwall 29 Sussex 10 (at Camborne)
Kent 20 Gloucestershire 21 (at Maidstone)

Saturday, 7th December 1996
Gloucestershire 54 Sussex 29 (at Cheltenham)
Kent 11 Cornwall 32 (at US, Chatham)

Saturday, 14th December 1996
Cornwall 15 Gloucestershire 10 (at Redruth)
Sussex 57 Kent 10 (at Worthing)

FINAL TABLE	P	W	L	F	A	Pts
Cornwall	3	3	0	76	31	6
Gloucester	3	2	1	82	64	4
Sussex	3	1	2	96	90	2
Kent	3	0	3	41	110	0

NORTH

POOL ONE

Saturday, 30th November 1996
Cumbria 48 Lancashire 12 (at Aspatria)
East Midlands 8 Leicestershire 53 (at Towcestrians)

Saturday, 7th December 1996
Cumbria 71 East Midlands 3 (at Workington)
Lancashire 24 Leicestershire 6 (at Waterloo)

Saturday, 14th December 1996
East Midlands 7 Lancashire 90 (at Bedford)
Leicestershire 27 Cumbria 15 (at Syston)

FINAL TABLE	P	W	L	F	A	Pts
Cumbria	3	2	1	136	42	4
Lancashire	3	2	1	126	61	4
Leicestershire	3	2	1	86	47	4
East Midlands	3	0	3	18	216	0

POOL TWO

Saturday, 30th November 1996
Northumberland 21 Cheshire 3 (at Northern RFC)
Notts., Lincs. & Derbys. 22 Warwickshire 27 (at Newark)

Saturday, 7th December 1996
Cheshire 24 Warwickshire 12 (at Birkenhead Park)
Northumberland 17 Notts., Lincs. & Derbys. 21 (at Tynedale)

Saturday, 14th December 1996
Notts., Lincs. & Derbys 41 Cheshire 17 (at Newark)
Warwickshire v Northumberland postponed

Saturday, 18th January 1997
Warwickshire 20 Northumberland 33 (at Rugby)

FINAL TABLE	P	W	L	F	A	Pts
Northumberland	3	2	1	71	44	4
Notts., Lincs & Derbys.	3	2	1	86	61	4
Warwickshire	3	1	2	59	79	2
Cheshire	3	1	2	44	74	2

POOL THREE

Saturday, 30th November 1996
Staffordshire 10 North Midlands 44 (at Burton-on-Trent)
Yorkshire 36 Durham 5 (at Hull Ionians)

Saturday, 7th December 1996
Durham 38 North Midlands 37 (at Blaydon)
Yorkshire 77 Staffordshire 15 (at Halifax)

Saturday, 14th December 1996
North Midlands 17 Yorkshire 69 (at Stourbridge)
Staffordshire 19 Durham 80 (at Burton)

FINAL LEAGUE	P	W	L	F	A	Pts
Yorkshire	3	3	0	182	37	6
Durham	3	2	1	123	87	4
North Midlands	3	1	2	98	117	2
Staffordshire	3	0	3	39	201	0

Quarter-finals
(Saturday, 18th January 1997)

Cornwall 20 Hertfordshire 15 (at Redruth)
Cumbria 34 Yorkshire 19 (at Aspatria)
Somerset 23 Hampshire 21 (at Bridgwater)

(Saturday, 22nd February 1997)
Northumberland 16 Lancashire 7 (at Tynedale)

Semi-finals
(Saturday, 8th March 1997)
Cornwall 24 Cumbria 38
(at Camborne)

CORNWALL (Launceston unless stated): D Sloman; I Veal (Bridgwater & Albion), B Stafford (Redruth), K Thomas (Redruth), M Bradshaw; J Tucker, R Nancekivell; P Risdon, P Lucas, P Brooks, J Atkinson (St Ives)(captain), G Hutchings, J Wilcocks, M Addinall (Penryn), D Shipton. Replacements: C Monk (Penryn) for Nancekivell 40 minutes, A Borradaile (Wasps) for Bradshaw 53 minutes, S Warring for Brooks 83 minutes.
SCORERS: Tries: Atkinson (1), Tucker (1). Pens: Sloman (4). Con: Sloman.

CUMBRIA (Aspatria unless stated): G Cook; S Davidson, P Burns (Furness), M Lynch (Wigton), D Warwick (Waterloo); M Scott, P Thompson (Wigton); S Irving, M Armstrong (Wigton), J McCune, S Milnes, A Bell (Wigton), G Atkinson (Egremont), S Cusack, M Richardson (captain). Replacement: J Slater (Kendal) for Atkinson 60 minutes.
SCORERS: Tries: Thompson (2), Davidson (1), Cook (1). Pens: Scott (4). Cons: Scott (3).

Somerset 14 Northumberland 10
(at Bridgwater)

SOMERSET (Bridgwater & Albion unless stated): M Westcott (Keynsham); D Underwood (Weston-super-Mare), D Fox (Keynsham), A Webber, P Blackett (Keynsham); N Edmunds, N Lloyd (Clifton); J Barnes, C Rees, T Harris, M Venner (Weston-super-Mare)(captain), M Rackham, M Curry (Exeter), J King (Hornets), S Withey (Keynsham). Replacement: B Thurwell for Withey 65 minutes.
SCORERS: Try: Lloyd. Pens: Edmunds (3).

NORTHUMBERLAND (Tynedale unless stated): P Singleton (Percy Park); N Gandy (Northern), A Moses (Alnwick), T Kirkup (Morpeth), M Carr (Percy Park); D Wilson (Medicals), S Manners (Alnwick); R Parker (captain), E Parker, E Winter, H Burn (Alnwick), S Dunn, M Curry (Alnwick), I Ponton, H Vyvyan (Newcastle University). Replacements: M Walker (Newcastle University) for Gandy 22 minutes, S Clayton-Hibbert for Manners 40 minutes, D Hutton (Morpeth) for Curry 65 minutes, A Nellis (Morpeth) for Ponton 78 minutes.
SCORERS: Try: Moses. Pen: Moses. Con: Moses.
Half-time: 6-10.

FINAL
(Saturday, 19th April 1997. At Twickenham)

CUMBRIA 21 SOMERSET 13
H.T. 11-8

CUMBRIA (Aspatria unless stated): G Cook; S Davidson, P Burns (Furness), M Lynch (Wigton), D Warwick (Waterloo); M Scott, P Thompson (Wigton); S Irving, M Armstrong (Wigton), J McCune, S Milnes, A Bell, B Atkinson, S Cusack, M Richardson (captain). Replacements: J Cartmell (Wigton) for Cusack 25 minutes, D Johnston (Wigton) for McCune 67 minutes, P Cusack (Cockermouth) for Cook 70 minutes, P Hancock (for Atkinson 72 minutes.
SCORERS: Tries: Bell (1), Milnes (1). Pens: Scott (3). Con: Scott.

SOMERSET (Bridgwater & Albion unless stated): M Westcott (Keynsham); D Underwood (Weston-super-Mare), D Fox (Keynsham), A Webber, P Blackett (Keynsham); N Edmunds, L Hirons (Keynsham); J Barnes, C Rees, A Harris, J King (Hornets), M Rackham, M Curry (Exeter), M

Venner (Weston-super-Mare)(captain), S Withey (Keynsham). Replacements: S Bennett (Keynsham) for Fox 40 minutes, B Thirlwall for Venner 40 minutes, N Lloyd (Clifton) for Hirons 77 minutes.
SCORERS: Tries: Rees (1), King (1). Pen: Edmunds.

Referee: B Campsall, Yorkshire.

Under-21 COUNTY CHAMPIONSHIP

Royal Navy 24 Oxfordshire 29
Oxfordshire 43 Brookes University 29

East Midlands 33 Warwickshire 17
Notts., Lincs & Derbys 27 Staffordshire 0
North Midlands 15 Warwickshire 17

Hertfordshire 29 Kent 31
Surrey 35 Middlesex 16
Eastern Counties 21 Army 20
Sussex 48 Hampshire 23

(Surrey and Sussex qualified for SE Counties play-off)

Play-off (Saturday, 18th January 1997)
Sussex 10 Surrey 18

NORTH
(Sunday, 26th January 1997)
Cheshire 28 Yorkshire 39 (at Wilmslow)

Semi-finals
(Sunday, 9th March 1997)

Dorset & Wiltshire 10 Surrey 10
(at Bournemouth)
(Dorset & Wilts progress - scoring more tries)

(Sunday, 23rd March 1997)
Notts., Lincs. & Derbys 9 Yorkshire 27
(at Beeston)

FINAL
(Saturday, 19th April 1997. At Twickenham).

DORSET & WILTS 3-27 YORKSHIRE

Dorset & Wiltshire Scorer: Pen: Maycock
Yorkshire Scorers: Tries: Kirkby (2), Hyde, Harrison. Pen: Dixon. Cons: Dixon (2).

IRELAND

INSURANCE CORPORATION LEAGUE
Final Tables

DIVISION ONE

	P	W	D	L	F	A	Pts
Shannon	13	12	0	1	345	174	24
Lansdowne	13	9	0	4	349	184	18
Terenure College	13	9	0	4	301	179	18
St Mary's College	13	8	1	4	305	279	17
Ballymena	13	8	0	5	241	230	16
Cork Constitution	13	7	1	5	283	262	15
Blackrock College	13	7	0	6	288	278	14
Garryowen	13	7	0	6	287	283	14
Young Munster	13	6	0	7	243	265	12
Dungannon	13	5	0	8	324	344	10
Old Crescent	13	4	0	9	239	281	8
Old Belvedere	13	4	0	9	193	287	8
Old Wesley	13	3	0	10	206	327	6
Instonians	13	1	0	12	173	404	2

Champions: Shannon
Relegated: Old Wesley and Instonians

DIVISION TWO

	P	W	D	L	F	A	Pts
Clontarf	13	11	0	2	329	167	22
Dolphin	13	9	1	3	294	236	19
Bective Rangers	13	9	0	4	261	146	18
Skerries	13	9	0	4	225	193	18
De la Salle-Pal'stn	13	6	2	5	285	243	14
Monkstown	13	6	2	5	242	244	14
Univ College Cork	13	7	0	6	245	273	14
Malone	13	6	0	7	261	255	12
Greystones	13	6	0	7	242	260	12
Sunday's Well	13	5	1	7	282	337	11
Wanderers	13	5	1	7	223	280	11
City of Derry	13	3	0	10	217	303	6
North of Ireland FC	13	2	1	10	183	324	5
Highfield	13	2	0	11	205	286	4

Champions: Clontarf. Promoted: Dolphin
Relegated: North of Ireland FC and Highfield

DIVISION THREE

	P	W	D	L	F	A	Pts
Buccaneers	10	9	1	0	201	112	19
Galwegians	10	8	1	1	206	106	17
Bohemians	10	8	0	2	249	110	16
Portadown	10	7	0	3	337	135	14
Univ Coll Dublin	10	6	1	3	162	179	13
Queen's Univ Bel'ft	10	5	0	5	166	157	10
Collegians	10	4	0	6	153	221	8
Galway Corinthians	10	3	1	6	150	164	7
Dublin University	10	2	0	8	172	298	4
Bangor	10	1	0	9	96	262	2
Waterpark	10	0	0	10	107	261	0

Champions: Buccaneers. Promoted: Galwegians
Relegated: Bangor and Waterpark

DIVISION FOUR

	P	W	D	L	F	A	Pts
Suttonians	9	9	0	0	359	102	18
Ballynahinch	9	8	0	1	295	96	16
Ards	9	7	0	2	202	117	14
Ballina	9	5	1	3	142	153	11
Richmond	9	5	0	4	156	127	10
Creggs	9	4	0	5	149	180	8
CIYMS	9	2	0	7	125	180	4
Sligo	9	2	0	7	62	176	4
Armagh	9	1	1	7	87	308	3
Univ Coll Galway	9	1	0	8	82	220	2

Champions: Suttonians. Promoted: Ballynahinch

SCOTLAND

SRU TENNANTS PREMIERSHIP
Final Tables

DIVISION ONE	P	W	D	L	F	A	Pts
Melrose	14	14	0	0	582	215	28
Watsonians	14	13	0	1	678	226	24
Currie	14	9	0	5	394	244	18
Boroughmuir	14	6	1	7	391	325	13
Hawick	14	5	0	8	268	397	10
Jed-Forest	14	4	0	10	217	506	8
Heriot's FP	14	3	0	11	224	416	6
Stirling County	14	2	1	11	220	524	5

DIVISION TWO	P	W	D	L	F	A	Pts
Edinburgh Acads	14	11	0	3	388	187	22
West of Scotland	14	10	1	3	395	264	21
Dundee High Sch FP	14	10	1	3	334	205	21
Glasgow High-Kelv	14	8	1	5	339	265	17
Glasgow Acads	14	6	0	8	292	339	12
Kelso	14	5	0	9	308	431	10
Gala	14	2	1	11	314	392	5
Biggar	14	2	0	12	187	474	4

DIVISION THREE	P	W	D	L	F	A	Pts
Kirkcaldy	14	12	0	2	489	203	24
Kilmarnock	14	10	0	4	344	298	20
Preston Lodge FP	14	9	0	5	358	287	18
Peebles	14	8	0	6	302	304	16
Musselburgh	14	7	0	7	283	258	14
Selkirk	14	6	0	8	288	348	12
Glasgow Southern	14	2	0	12	249	335	4
Stewart's-Melville	14	2	0	12	199	479	4

DIVISION FOUR	P	W	D	L	F	A	Pts
Gordonians	14	12	0	2	299	176	24
Ayr	14	9	0	5	283	205	18
Hillhead-Jordanhill	14	8	1	5	388	225	17
Grangemouth	14	8	1	5	255	228	17
Glenrothes	14	6	1	7	247	211	13
Corstorphine	14	5	1	8	245	260	11
Langholm	14	3	0	11	206	308	6
Haddington	14	2	2	10	180	464	6

TOP SCORERS

POINTS

Duncan Hodge (Watsonians)	252
John Mitchell (Kirkcaldy)	179
Ally Donaldson (Currie)	176
Bob Stewart (Hillhead-Jordanhill)	175
Gary Parker (Melrose)	171

TRIES

Scott Nichol (Melrose)	16
John Kerr (Watsonians)	14
James Craig (West of Scotland)	13
Derek Stark (Melrose)	11
John Mitchell (Kirkcaldy)	11

DROPPED-GOALS

Erin Cossey (Glasgow Southern)	5
Ricjie Thom (Musselburgh)	4
Duncan Hodge (Watsonians)	3
Jon Newton (Kirkcaldy)	3

HIGHEST SCORING CLUBS

Watsonians	587
Melrose	582
Kirkcaldy	493
West of Scotland	395
Boroughmuir	394

TOP TRY TALLY

Melrose	82
Watsonians	70
Kirkcaldy	68
Boroughmuir	54
West of Scotland	52

SRU TENNENTS NATIONAL LEAGUES

1996-97

(as at 20th April 1997)

DIVISION ONE

	P	W	D	L	F	A	Pts
Aberdeen GS FP	18	16	0	2	608	189	32
Stewartry	18	13	0	5	513	247	26
East Kilbride	18	10	2	6	466	430	22
Dunfermline	18	10	1	7	436	376	21
Duns	18	10	1	7	467	415	21
Trinity Academicals	18	8	3	7	516	332	19
Edinburgh Univ	18	7	0	11	397	397	14
Portobello FP	18	6	1	11	222	464	13
Edinburgh Wands	18	4	2	12	220	414	10
Wigtownshire	18	1	0	17	187	878	0*

DIVISION TWO

	P	W	D	L	F	A	Pts
Hutchesons'-Aloys	18	17	0	1	619	196	34
Berwick	18	15	0	3	743	199	30
Livingston	18	12	0	6	443	305	24
Dalziel HSFP	18	9	0	9	410	282	18
Royal High	18	9	0	9	316	332	18
Cambuslang	18	8	0	10	297	386	16
St Boswells	18	7	0	11	339	590	14
Allan Glen's	18	6	0	12	319	501	12
Dumfries	18	4	1	13	231	542	7*
Ardrossan Acads	18	2	1	15	176	560	5

DIVISION THREE

	P	W	D	L	F	A	Pts
Annan	18	17	0	1	580	184	34
Howe of Fife	18	13	0	5	359	277	26
Linlithgow	18	12	1	5	463	251	25
Lismore	18	10	1	7	336	279	21
Morgan Academy	18	10	0	8	392	362	20
Perthshire	18	9	0	9	482	399	18
Cartha Queen's Park	18	8	0	10	329	358	16
Alloa	18	4	0	14	194	585	8
Leith Academicals	17	3	0	14	243	466	6
Cumbernauld	17	2	0	15	181	399	4

DIVISION FOUR

	P	W	D	L	F	A	Pts
Ross High	18	17	0	1	580	184	34
Madras College FP	18	15	1	2	496	241	31
Highland	17	10	0	7	331	285	20
Clydebank	18	8	2	8	284	262	18
Penicuik	18	8	1	9	336	387	17
Aberdeenshire	18	8	0	10	359	325	16
Hillfoots	18	8	0	10	287	413	16
Paisley	18	6	1	11	210	335	13
North Berwick	18	5	1	12	354	558	9*
Waysiders/D'pellier	17	2	1	14	173	512	5

DIVISION FIVE

	P	W	D	L	F	A	Pts
Garnock	18	17	0	1	738	130	34
Murrayfield	18	12	1	5	552	238	25
Lochaber	18	10	1	7	417	270	21
Falkirk	18	10	1	7	317	349	21
Lenzie	18	10	0	8	313	337	20
Dunbar	18	8	0	10	463	449	16
Greenock Wanderers	18	8	0	10	246	450	16
Aberdeen University	18	6	0	12	342	496	10*
Irvine	18	5	1	12	247	614	9*
Forrester FP	18	2	0	16	233	535	4

DIVISION SIX

	P	W	D	L	F	A	Pts
Whitecraigs	16	13	0	3	379	162	26
Lasswade	16	13	0	3	354	166	26
Earlston	16	10	0	6	305	218	20
Moray	16	8	1	7	304	321	17
RAF Kinloss	16	6	1	9	232	244	13
Marr	16	6	0	10	205	283	12
Cumnock	16	6	0	10	206	289	12
St Andrews Univ	16	6	0	10	253	364	12
Inverleith	16	3	0	13	174	365	6
Walkerburn	0	0	0	0	0	0	0*

DIVISION SEVEN

	P	W	D	L	F	A	Pts
Carnoustie HSFP	18	16	0	2	481	203	32
Helensburgh	18	15	1	2	520	124	31
Hamilton Academical	18	13	2	3	627	149	28
Panmure	18	9	1	8	378	255	19
RAF Lossiemouth	18	10	0	8	481	257	18*
Broughton FP	18	8	0	10	239	265	16
Dalkeith	18	5	0	13	230	471	10
Rosyth & District	18	5	0	13	189	486	10
Harris Academy FP	18	5	0	13	193	652	8*
Waid Academy FP	18	2	0	16	206	682	2*

* Denotes points deducted

728

SRU TENNENTS 1556 CUP

First Round

(Saturday, 7th September 1996)

Mackie Academy FP 22 Howe of Fife 60
Garnock 67 Perthshire 7
Walkerburn 45 Earlston 18
Helensburgh 70 Broughton FP 0
Falkirk 89 Aberdeen University 3
Dunfermline 47 Penicuik 0
Newton Stewart 13 Aberdeen Grammar School FP 47
Stewartry 27 Clydebank 13
Moray House 0 Livingston 112
Birkmyre 0 Dalziel 36
Strathclyde Police 29 Irvine 14
Ellon 16 Hawick Trades 36
Berwick 63 Dalkeith 12
Ardrossan Academicals 37 Edinburgh Northern 14
Isle of Arran 17 Cambuslang 40
Greenock Wanderers 32 Hyndland FP 17
Lenzie 25 Dalgety Bay 17
Aberdeen Wanderers 12 Lochaber 41
Hawick Lindeen 114 Lanark 7
Cartha Queens Park 63 Portobello 17
Edinburgh University 32 Inverleith 8
Dundee University v Rosyth & District postponed
Waysiders/Drumpellier 9 Madras College FP 34
Hamilton Academicals 11 Forrester FP 3
Bute 41 North Berwick 10
Lasswade 15 Dunbar 22
Linlithgow 50 RAF Lossiemouth 33
Hutchesons'/Aloysians 32 Hawick Harlequins 0
Strathclyde University 22 Trinity Academicals 53
Murrayfield 29 Paisley 20
Wigtownshire 15 Allan Glen's 21
Morgan Academy FP 33 Carnoustie High School FP 22
Gala YM 25 Cumbernauld 17
St Andrews University 12 Aberdeenshire 81
Waid Academy FP 15 Leith Academicals 63
Liberton FP 0 Strathmore 37
Panmure 0 Annan 52
Strathendrick 35 Bishopton 5
St Boswells 81 RAF Kinloss 21
Alloa 21 Hillfoots 11
Oban Lorne 0 Duns 50
Edinburgh Wanderers 15 Ross High 33
Lismore 32 Marr 37
Cumnock 12 Dumfries 12
(after extra-time - Dumfries win on away tries rule)
Royal High 46 Highland 9
East Kilbride 59 Orkney 10
Whitecraigs 83 Harris Academy FP 21

Second Round

(Saturday, Sunday, 2nd & 3rd November 1996)

Bute 9 Earlston 5
Helensburgh 25 Moray 6
Aberdeenshire 34 Alloa 16
Allan Glen's 8 St Boswells 177
Annan 13 Aberdeen Grammar School FP 17
Berwick wo Greenock Wanderers
Cambuslang 8 Hamilton Academicals 8
(Hamilton Academicals win on away tries rule -
after extra time)
Dunbar 5 Morgan Academy FP 25
Dunfermline 36 Strathclyde Police 25
Duns 28 Madras College FP 5
Edinburgh University 30 Royal High 0
Falkirk 3 Linlithgow 43
Garnock 23 Hutcheson's-Alloysians 12
Howe of Fife 22 Dalziel 8
Leith Academicals 13 Trinity Academicals 60
Lenzie 18 Hawick Trades 52
Livingston 34 Gala YM 24
Murrayfield 7 East Kilbride 29
Ross High 108 Ardrossan Academicals 5
Stewartry 32 Dumfries 0
Strathendrick 45 Rosyth & District 0
Strathmore 18 Cartha Queen's Park 22
Whitecraigs 12 Hawick Linden 48

(Saturday, 14th December 1996)
Lochaber 35 Marr 0

Third Round

(Sunday, 19th January 1996)

Ayr 23 Ross High 3
Berwick 14 Gordonians 6
Biggar 6 Gala 27
Corstorphine 41 Howe of Fife 22
Dundee High School FP 48 Hillhead-Jordanhill 13
Duns 20 Glasgow Academicals 37
Edinburgh University 33 East Kilbride 27
Glasgow High-Kelvinside 65 Helensburgh 13
Glenrothes 19 Langholm 5
Grangemouth 12 Glasgow Southern 24
Haddington 26 Kilmarnock 49
Hamilton Academicals 21 Cartha Queen's Park 17
Hawick Trades 3 Garnock 0
Kelso 67 Livingston 3
Kirkcaldy 55 Dunfermline 3

Linlithgow 7 Hawick Linden 13
Lochaber 17 Musselburgh 43
Morgan Academy 15 West of Scotland 56
Peebles 27 Preston Lodge FP 6
St Boswells 20 Bute 9
Selkirk 14 Stewartry 15
Stewart's-Melville FP 37 Aberdeenshire 6
Strathendrick 3 Edinburgh Academicals 69
Trinity Academicals 13 Aberdeen Grammar School FP 16

Fourth Round

(Saturday, 8th March 1997)
Watsonians 60 Hawick Trades 3

(Saturday, 22nd March 1997)
Ayr 3 Kelso 9
Berwick 34 Corstorphine 0
Currie 20 Gala 32
Dundee High School FP 41 Glasgow Academicals 5
Edinburgh Academicals 17 Kilmarnock 32
Edinburgh University 14 Glenrothes 13
Glasgow Southern 58 Aberdeen Grammar School FP 17
Hawick 6 Boroughmuir 19
Hawick Linden 15 Stewart's-Melville FP 9
Heriot's FP 24 Jed-Forest 11
Kirkcaldy 16 Hamilton Academicals 3
Peebles 32 Musselburgh 8
St Boswells 10 Melrose 70
Stirling County 31 Stewartry 7
West of Scotland 33 Glasgow High-Kelvinside 10

Fifth Round

(Sunday, 5th April 1997)
Boroughmuir 71 Stirling County 9
Dundee High School FP 31 Hawick Linden 6
Edinburgh University 8 Kirkcaldy 48
Gala 20 Watsonians 59
Glasgow Southern 10 West of Scotland 15
Heriot's FP 37 Berwick 17
Melrose 71 Kelso 37
Peebles 22 Kilmarnock 10

Quarter-finals

(Sunday, 20th April 1997)

Boroughmuir 42 Watsonians 29
Kirkcaldy 33 Dundee High School FP 18
Peebles 16 Heriot's FP 18
West of Scotland 23 Melrose 45

Semi-finals

(Sunday, 27th April 1997)

Boroughmuir 45 Heriot's FP 0
Kirkcaldy 9 Melrose 36

FINAL

Saturday, 10th May 1997
Murrayfield.

BOROUGHMUIR 23 v 31 MELROSE

Half-time: 13-8.
Referee: E Murray, Greenock Wanderers.

BOROUGHMUIR: C Aitken; N Renton, D Laird, S
Lineen, A McLean; D Wyllie, G Beveridge; S Paris,
K Allan, S Penman, A Cadzow, D Burns, G
McCallum, R Kirkpatrick, S Reid (captain).
Replacements: S Wands for Kirkpatrick, D
Cunningham for Allan 57-59 minutes (temporary)
and 62 minutes.
Scorers: Tries: McLean (2), Wyllie (1). Pens: Aitken
(2). Con: Aitken.
MELROSE: R Shepherd; D Stark, S Nichol, Ross
Brown, M Moncrieff; C Chalmers, B Redpath
(captain); M Browne, S Brotherstone, P Wright, M
Donnan, Robbie Brown, S Aitken, C Hogg, N
Broughton.
Scorers: Tries: Shepherd (3), Moncrieff (1). Pens:
Shepherd (3). Con: Shepherd.

SRU TENNENTS 1556 BOWL

First Round

(Saturday, 22nd March 1997)
Biggar 24 Gordonians 13
Bute 13 Dunfermline 27
Grangemouth 27 Howe of Fife 11
Haddington 10 Selkirk 30
Helensburgh 12 Cartha Queen's Park 19
Livingston 46 Aberdeenshire 5
Preston Lodge FP 22 Garnock 7
Trinity Academicals 48 Langholm 25

Byes: Duns, East Kilbride, Hillhead-Jordanhill,
Linlithgow, Lochaber, Morgan Academy FP,
Ross High, Strathendrick.

Second Round
(Saturday, 5th April 1997)
Cartha-Queen's Park 27 Hillhead-Jordanhill 54
Lochaber 7 Biggar 26
(matches Sunday, 6th April 1997)
Duns 16 Linlithgow 27
East Kilbride 8 Selkirk 32
Grangemouth 19 Dunfermline 10
Livingston 13 Preston Lodge 31
Morgan Academy FP 15 Trinity Academicals 49
Ross High 33 Strathendrick 3

Quarter-finals
(Saturday, 19th April 1997)
Grangemouth 12 Ross High 29
(Sunday, 20th April 1997)
Linlithgow 23 Biggar 33
Preston Lodge 19 Selkirk 27
Trinity Academicals 24 Hillhead-Jordanhill 23

Semi-finals
(Sunday, 27th April 1997)
Biggar 27 Ross High 13
Trinity Academicals 14 Selkirk 22

FINAL
Saturday, 10th May 1997
Murrayfield.

BIGGAR 15 v 23 SELKIRK
Half-time: 10-11.
Referee: J Bacigalupo, Edinburgh Wanderers.

BIGGAR: M Bruce; S Harrison, L Graham (captain),
E Bulman, S Armstrong; D Lavery, N Abernethy; D
Fleming, A Yates, F Campbell, S Sheridan, D
Ireland, K Ollerenshaw, E McAlpine, M Scott.
Replacements: R Young for Abernethy 66 minutes,
F Smith for Fleming 66 minutes, I Barr for Ireland
71 minutes, J Humble for Sheridan 71 minutes.
Scorers: Tries: Ollerenshaw (1), Campbell (1). Pen:
Lavery. Con: Lavery.
SELKIKR: S Tomlinson (captain); D Hulme, M
Jaffray, A Dickson, B Armstrong; J Brett, A
Lindores; S McColm, D Graham, D Clarkson, B
Gentleman, S Hamilton, D Cameron, P Minto, S
Laurie. Replacement: D Lawson for Gentleman 70
minutes.
Scorers: Try: Hulme. DG: Brett. Pens: Brett (5).

SRU TENNENTS 1556 SHIELD

First Round
(Saturday, 5th April 1997)
Glenrothes 22 Glasgow Academicals 15
Hawick Trades 16 Currie 30
(matches Sunday, 6th April 1997)
Aberdeen Grammar School 58 Hamilton
Academicals 9
Corstorphine 16 Glasgow High-Kelvinside 54
Hawick 58 Stewart's-Melville FP 16
Jed-Forest 42 Ayr 17
Musselburgh 8 Edinburgh Academicals 62
St Boswells 22 Stewartry 8

Quarter-finals
(Sunday, 20th April 1907)
Aberdeen Grammar School FP 24 Glenrothes 18
Edinburgh Academicals 16 Currie 22
Glasgow High-Kelvinside 42 Jed-Forest 27
St Boswells 12 Hawick 35

Semi-finals
(Sunday, 27th April 1997)
**Glasgow High-Kelvinside 51 Aberdeen
Grammar School FP 16**
Hawick 43 Currie 20

FINAL
Saturday, 10th May 1997.
At Murrayfield.

GLASGOW HIGH-KELVINSIDE 46 v 18 HAWICK
Half-time: 15-3.
Referee: R Megson, Edinburgh Wanderers.

GLASGOW HIGH-KELVINSIDE: G Breckenridge
(captain); G Cladwell, A Common, H Bassi, G
Hawkes; C Little, A Kerr; G McIlwham, M Blackie,
E Logan, A Ness, N Adams, K Wilson, S Unkles, F
Wallace. Replacements: Barrett for Caldwell 61
minutes, W Hamilton for Unkles 62 minutes, J
MacLay for Blackie 68 minutes, P Manning for
Hawkes 71 minutes, B Irvine for Adams 79 minutes.
Scorers: Tries: Hawkes (3), Common (2), Wallace
(1). Pens: Breckenridge (2). Cons: Breckenridge (5).
HAWICK: G Oliver; D Grant, T Stanger, C Murray,
G Sharp; B Wear, K Reid; B McDonnell, J Hay
(captain), M Landels, C Cottrill, I Elliot, A
Stevenson, J Graham, J Parkes.
Scorers: Tries: Graham (1), Stanger (1), Hay (1).
Pen: Sharp.

WALES

Champions Challenge Trophy
Sunday, 1st September 1996. At Cardiff Arms Park.

NEATH 19 v 60 PONTYPRIDD

H.T. 12-17

Referee: P Adams, WRU.

NEATH: M Williams; C Higgs, R Jones, J Funnell, B Grabham; P Williams, D Hawkins; L Gerrard, B Williams, J Davies (captain), I Boobyer, A Kembery, N Watkins, G Newman, S Gardner. Replacements: K Phillips for B Williams 51 minutes, P Matthews for Watkins 68 minutes, G Taylor for Boobyer 69 minutes, M Harris for Davies 76 minutes.
SCORERS: Tries: Jones, Funnell, Higgs. Cons: M Williams (2).

PONTYPRIDD: K Morgan; D Manley, J Lewis, S Enoch, G Wyatt; N Jenkins (captain), Paul John; N Eynon, Phil John, A Metcalfe, P Collins, G Prosser, N Jones, P Thomas, D McIntosh. Replacements: M Williams for Thomas 28 minutes, I Jones for Metcalfe 32 minutes, J Evans for Phil John 46 minutes, M de Maid for Paul John 56 minutes.
SCORERS: Tries: Manley (3), Enoch (2), Morgan (2), Paul John (2), McIntosh. Cons: Jenkins (5).

NATIONAL LEAGUES
Final Tables

DIVISION ONE

	P	W	D	L	T	B	Pts
Pontypridd	22	20	0	2	124	22	62
Swansea	22	14	0	8	128	22	50
Llanelli	22	16	2	4	111	16	50
Cardiff	22	14	1	7	99	12	41
Bridgend	22	10	1	11	79	10	31
Newport	22	12	2	8	71	5	31
Ebbw Vale	22	12	2	8	50	4	30
Neath	22	10	0	12	74	9	29
Dunvant	22	10	2	10	69	5	27
Caerphilly	22	2	0	20	59	10	14
Treorchy	22	3	0	19	57	4	10
Newbridge	22	4	0	18	45	0	8

Champions: Pontypridd   Runners-up: Swansea
Qualified for Heineken Cup: Llanelli and Cardiff
Qualified for European Conference: Bridgend, Newport, Ebbw Vale and Neath
Relegated: Dunvant, Caerphilly, Treorchy and Newbridge

DIVISION TWO

	P	W	D	L	T	B	Pts
Aberavon	22	16	1	5	107	20	53
Llandovery	22	16	0	6	109	20	52
Cross Keys	22	18	0	4	96	14	50
S Wales Police	22	12	1	9	82	8	33
Pontypool	22	11	2	9	71	9	33
UWIC (Card Ins)	22	10	1	11	86	11	32
Abertillery	22	13	0	9	54	6	32
Bonymaen	22	11	1	10	65	8	31
Maesteg	22	9	0	13	53	7	25
Blackwood	22	7	0	15	44	3	17
Abercynon	22	4	0	18	40	4	10*
Ystradgynlais	22	2	0	20	36	2	6

* Two points deducted for failing to field a team against Aberavon on 19.10.96

Champions: Aberavon
Relegated: Abercynon and Ystradgynlais

DIVISION THREE

	P	W	D	L	T	B	Pts
Rumney	22	17	1	4	114	17	52
Merthyr	22	15	1	6	85	14	45
Tondu	22	15	1	6	78	13	44
Pyle	22	11	0	10	87	14	38
Kenfig Hill	22	12	0	10	75	9	33
Tenby United	22	12	0	10	53	5	29
Llanharan	22	8	1	13	55	6	23
Mountain Ash	22	10	0	12	44	3	23
Tredegar	22	8	0	14	48	6	22
Narberth	22	9	2	11	40	2	22
Builth Wells	22	9	0	13	48	3	21
Penarth	22	2	1	19	39	2	7

Promoted: Rumney (champions) & Merthyr
Relegated: Builth Wells and Penarth

DIVISION FOUR

	P	W	D	L	T	B	Pts
St Peter's	22	16	1	5	95	14	47
Whitland	22	16	1	5	90	14	47
Oakdale	22	16	1	5	79	12	45
Carmarthen Qns	22	14	1	7	89	15	44
Kidwelly	22	13	1	8	88	13	40
Llantrisant	22	11	1	10	57	6	29
Glynneath	22	12	0	10	50	5	29
Glamorgan Wand	22	8	1	13	69	10	27
Rhymney	22	9	0	13	51	5	23
Blaina	22	9	0	13	50	4	22
Vardre	22	4	1	17	46	2	11
Tumble	22	0	0	22	40	4	4

Promoted: St Peter's (champions) and Whitland
Relegated: Tumble and Vardre

DIVISION FIVE

	P	W	D	L	T	B	Pts
Ystrad Rhondda	22	17	0	5	91	18	52
Felinfoel	22	17	1	4	94	11	46
Bedwas	22	14	0	8	85	11	39
Tonmawr	22	14	1	7	85	11	39
Resolven	22	13	0	9	79	8	34
Aberavon Quins	22	11	1	10	60	11	34
Abergavenny	22	11	0	11	56	10	32
Garndiffaith	22	10	1	11	62	6	27
Seven Sisters	22	8	0	14	54	9	25
Waunarlwydd	22	8	0	14	62	4	20
Cardiff HSOB	22	4	0	18	45	4	12
Pontypool Utd	22	2	2	18	46	5	11

* Denotes points deducted

Promoted: Ystrad Rhondda (champions) and
Felinfoel
Relegated: Waunarlwydd, Cardiff HSOB and
Pontypool United

DIVISION SIX

Promoted: Bedwas (East), Waunarlwydd (West),
Resolven (Central)

LEADING SCORERS

POINTS

N Jenkins (Pontypridd)	285
G Rees (Newport)	282
K Thomas (Felinfoel)	222
J Williams (Pontypool)	220
S Hancox (Tumble)	219
B Hayward (Ebbw Vale)	205
A Williams (Swansea)	198
J Mason (Rumney)	187
J Davies (Hendy)	187
W Jervis (Llanharan)	183
A Dragone (Carmarthen Quins)	183

TRIES

S Ford (Cardiff)	21
M Evans (Kidwelly)	20
W Proctor (Llanelli)	17
C Higgs (Neath)	15
K Hocking (Tondu)	14
Paul John (Pontypridd)	14
J Beynon (Vardre)	13
J Sims (Blackwood)	13
G Jones (Cardiff & Bridgend)	*13
A Harris (Swansea)	12
D Manley (Pontypridd)	12

* 11 for Cardiff, 2 for Bridgend

TOP TEAM - TRIES

Neath	121
Cardiff	119
Pontypridd	98
Kidwelly	94
Llanelli	88
Merthyr	85
Swansea	83
Rumney	79
Dunvant	78
Blackwood	78

TOP TEAM - BONUS POINTS

Neath	37
Cardiff	35
Kidwelly	29
Llanelli	29
Pontypridd	28
Merthyr	28
Dunvant	24
Blackwood	23
Swansea	22
Bridgend	22

SWALEC CUP 1996-97

1st Round
(Saturday, 31st August 1996)

Amman United 20 Furnace United 12
Banwen 22 Skewen 18
Barboed 38 Welshpool 13
Barry 18 Pontycymmer 24
Bethesda 21 BP Llandarcy 0
Bridgend Athletic 27 Crumlin 20
Bridgend Sports 66 Aberystwyth University 7
British Steel 27 New Tredegar 15
Brynmawr 35 Bala 18
Bynea 18 Lampeter Town 7
Caldicot 18 Fishguard & Goodwick 6
Canton 19 Rhiwbina 13
Cefn Cribbwr 13 Trebanos 17
Cefneithin 11 Morriston 24
Croesyceiliog 29 Llantwit Major 8
Crymych 15 Penygraig 61
Crynant 37 Pontarddulais 0
Cwmavon 39 Llandaff North 19
Cwmgors 13 Tylorstown 13
(Cwmgors win on try count)
Cwmgwrach 52 Cefn Coed 8
Cwmllynfell 17 Hoel y Cyw 5
Denbigh 6 RTB Ebbw Vale 39
Deri 21 Penygroes 20
Gwernyfed 32 Ogmore Vale 13
Haverfordwest 28 New Dock Stars 22
Llandaff 7 Pill Harriers 18
Llandeilo 29 Usk 23
Llanhilleth 12 Carmarthen Athletic 32
Llantwit Fardre 28 Blaengarw 3
Machen 5 Taibach 11
Mold 5 Abercarn 21
Monmouth 21 Nantymoel 9
Neath Athletic 90 Cardiff University 22
Newtown 17 Cwmbran 66
Newport H.S. O.B. 11 Maesteg Quins 20
Old Penarthians 17 Chepstow 32
Pembroke Dock Quins 7 Nantyffylon 20
Penclawdd 25 Llandybie 12
Pentyrch 0 Taff's Well 40
Pontardawe 15 Llandudno 13
Pontyates 10 Treherbert 29
Pontyberem 13 Bangor 7
Porthcawl 19 Colwyn Bay 5
Rhyl & District 50 Tonna 10
Ruthin 28 Cwmtyrch 10
St Joseph's 12 Rhydyfelin 10
Swansea Uplands 10 Old Illtydians 31
Tonyrefail 43 Loughor 13
Trimsaran 11 Abercrave 39
Trinant 30 Newport Saracens 23
Tycroes 27 Llandybydder 0
UWIN 3 Hirwaun 90
Ynysddu 5 Beddau 15

2nd Round
(Saturday, 21st September 1996)

Aberavon Green Stars 15 St Josephs 38
Abercarn 27 Pembroke 10
Abercrave 6 Haverford West 22
Amman United 14 Cwmgors 13
Ammanford 62 Blaenavon 0
Beddau 13 Maesteg Quins 12
Bethesda 14 St David's 3
Birchgrove 29 Penclawdd 15
Blaenau Gwent 10 Aberaeron 15
Bridgend Athletic 44 Bargoed 15
Bridgend Sports 44 Monmouth 0
Briton Ferry 22 Milford Haven 5
Burry Port 31 Llandeilo 51
Bynea 61 Llangwm 0
Cardiff Medics 7 Dinas Powys 76
Cardigan 9 Nelson 7
Carmarthen Athletic 19 Llantwit Fardre 17
Chepstow 14 Hirwaun 21
Croesyceiliog 16 Canton 9
Crynant 11 Brecon 45
Cwmbran 16 St Albans 13
Cwmgrach 45 Caldicott 27
Dolgellau 31 Baglan 6
Hartridge HS OB 6 Gilfach Goch 29
Hollybush 16 Fairwater 21
Gorseinon w/o Lampeter College
Laugharne 8 Cwmavon 21
Llanelli Wanderers 23 Newcastle Emlyn 48
Llangenneth 29 Treherbert 11
Morriston 26 Trebanos 13
Mumbles 18 Taibach 13
Nantyffylon 25 Penlan 5
Neath Athletic 28 Aberystwyth 22
New Tredegar 10 RTB Ebbw Vale 35
Old Illtydians 10 Cwmllynfell 22
Pencoed 42 Pontyclun 7
Penygraig 8 Cilfynydd 0
Pill Harriers 23 Gowerton 10
Pontardawe 9 Pontycymmer 20
Pwllheli lost to Banwen
Risca 40 Gwernyfed 10
Ruthin 43 Rhyl & District 10
Senghenydd 25 Pontyberem 7
Taff's Well 34 Porthcawl 26
Talywain 25 Brynamman 22
Tonyrefail 40 Penygroes 12
Trynant 11 Brynmawr 7
Tycroes 10 Glais 28
Watterstown 5 Aberdare 17
Wrexham 95 Fleur-de-Lys 3
Ynysbwl 40 Cowbridge 25
Ystalefera 38 Bryncoch 35

3rd Round

(Saturday, 19th October 1996)

Abercarn 11 Cardigan 6
Aberdare 3 Pencoed 18
Abergavenny 32 Beddau 13
Banwen 9 Bridgend Athletic 12
Bedwas beat Ystalyfera
Bethesda 5 Tonyrefail 40
Birchgrove 29 Llangenneth 13
Bridgend Sports 16 Trinant 9
Briton Ferry 24 Cwmavon 10
Carmarthen Athletic 12 Senghenydd 6
Cwmbran 25 Cwmgwrach 22
Cwmllynfell 34 Bynea 11
Dinas Powys 23 Garndiffaith 12
Dolgellau 33 Risca 20
Felinfoel 51 Aberaeron 6
Glais 16 Croesyceiliog 14
Gorseinon 10 Pill Harriers 33
Morriston 17 Haverfordwest 8
Mumbles 15 Pontypool United 5
Nantyffyllon 9 Waunarlwydd 3
Neath Athletic 13 Ammanford 21
Penygraig 10 Fairwater 8
Pontycymmer 20 Aberavon Quins 16
Resolven 27 Cardiff HS OB 26
RTB Ebbw Vale 51 Llandeilo 10
Ruthin 18 Amman United 16
St Joseph's 17 Newcastle Emlyn 22
Seven Sisters 0 Taff's Well 26
Talywain 18 Brecon 7
Wrexham 9 Gilfach Goch 15
Ynysbwl 30 Hirwaun 38
Ystrad Rhondda 18 Tonmawr 5

4th Round

(Saturday, 23rd November 1996)

Abercarn 27 RTB Ebbw Vale 6
Abergavenny 14 Penarth 10
Bridgend Sports 6 Narberth 9
Briton Ferry 13 Whitland 21 (AET)
Builth Wells 15 Rumney 13
Carmarthen Athletic 47 Glamorgan Wanderers 5
Cwmllynfell 15 Bedwas 17
Dinas Powys 39 Merthyr 33
Felinfoel 34 Ystrad Rhondda 19
Gilfach Goch 30 St Peter's 8
Glais 15 Ammanford 28
Glynneath 36 Blaina 22
Llantrisant 21 Oakdale 19
Morriston 19 Carmarthen Quins 26
Mountain Ash 9 Kenfig Hill 8
Mumbles 21 Tredegar 24 (AET)
Nantyffyllon 9 Tonyrefail 13
Newcastle Emlyn 48 Cwmbran 7
Pencoed 15 Llanharan 9
Penygraig 34 Bridgend Athletic 8
Pill Harriers 10 Dolgellau 15
Pontycymmer 21 Tumble 12

Taff's Well 15 Resolven 35
Tenby United 10 Hirwaun 19
Tondu 9 Pyle 26
Vardre 18 Kidwelly 29

(Saturday, 30th November 1996)

Rhymney 23 Talywain 5
Ruthin 22 Birchgrove 27

Fifth Round

(Saturday, 14th December 1996)

Bedwas 10 Abercynon 23
Cross Keys 39 Tonyrefail 20
Felinfoel 34 Narberth 3
Kidwelly 16 Carmarthen Quins 22
Llandovery 22 Birchgrove 8
Llantrisant 10 Dinas Powys 27
Maesteg 22 Aberavon 39
Mountain Ash 5 Gilfach Goch 28
Pencoed 33 Glynneath 8
Penygraig 32 Tredegar 16
Pontycymmer 17 Abergavenny 10
Pontypool 12 Dolgellau 3
Pyle 11 Carmarthen Athletic 0
South Wales Police 13 Bonymaen 3

(Saturday, 21st December 1996)

Abercarn 22 Ystradgynlais 31
Newcastle Emlyn 29 Resolven 12
Rhymney 31 Ammanford 19
UWIC (Cardiff Institute) 6 Abertillery 11
Whitland 18 Builth Wells 0

(Wednesday, 22nd January 1997)

Blackwood 44 Hirwaun 10

Sixth Round

(Friday, 24th January 1997)

Bridgend 26 Newbridge 20

(Saturday, 25th January 1997)

Aberavon 8 Ebbw Vale 32
Caerphilly 17 Llanelli 20
Cross Keys 13 Abertillery 13
(Abertillery win on try count)
Dinas Powys 18 Pontycymmer 5
Felinfoel 10 Pontypridd 90
Llandovery 18 Pyle 16
Newcastle Emlyn 24 Gilfach Goch 16
Penygraig 12 Carmarthen Quins 18
Pontypool 21 Pencoed 9
Rhymney 11 Treorchy 59
South Wales Police 39 Blackwood 7
Swansea 71 Dunvant 10
Whitland 18 Ystradgynlais 8

(Sunday, 26th January 1997)

Neath 57 Abercynon 6
Newport 30 Cardiff 44

Seventh Round

(Saturday, 22nd February 1997)

Abertillery 10 Llanelli 27
Cardiff 99 Dinas Powys 7
Carmarthen Quins 19 Neath 44
Llandovery 19 South Wales Police 29
Newcastle Emlyn 0 Ebbw Vale 43
Pontypool 26 Whitland 24
Swansea 20 Pontypridd 19
Treorchy v Bridgend postponed

(Saturday, 1st March 1997)

Treorchy 13 Bridgend 22

QUARTER-FINALS

(Saturday, 22nd March 1997)

Cardiff 57 South Wales Police 30
Llanelli 59 Pontypool 17

(Saturday, 29th March 1997)

Ebbw Vale 17 Bridgend 16
Neath 24 Swansea 32

SEMI-FINALS

(Saturday, 12th April 1997. In Cardiff)

Ebbw Vale 15 v 26 Swansea
Half-time: 0-5.　　Referee: D Bevan, Clydach.

EBBW VALE: A Harries; I Jeffreys, J Hawker, M Boys, S Marshall; B Hayward, D Llewellyn; A Phillips, S Jones, D Bell, B Watkins, C Billen, J Lillas, K Jones (captain), M Jones. Replacement: A Lamberton for S Jones 73 minutes.
SCORERS: Tries: Harries, Jeffreys. Pen: Hayward. Con: Hayward.

SWANSEA: M Back; W Leach, M Taylor, S Gibbs, Simon Davies; A Williams, A Booth; I Buckett, G Jenkins (captain), S Evans, A Reynolds, S Moore, P Arnold, R Appleyard, Stuart Davies. Replacements: L Davies for Back 39 minutes, D Thomas for Appleyrad 53 minutes, R Jones for Simon Davies 72 minutes. SCORERS: Tries: Simon Davies, Taylor, Williams. DG: Booth. Oens: Williams (2). Con: Williams.

(Sunday, 13th April 1997. In Swansea)

Cardiff 36 v 26 Llanelli
Half-time: 28-9.　　Referee: C Thomas, Skewen.

CARDIFF: J Thomas; N Walker, M Hall, L Davies, S Hill; L Jarvis, R Howley; A Lewis, J Humphreys (captain), L Mustoe, M Bennett, K Stewart, D Jones, J Ringer, O Williams. Replacements: L Jones for Stewart 66 minutes, H Taylor for Bennett 66 minutes. SCORERS: Tries: Howley (3), Walker. Pens: Jarvis (4). Cons: Jarvis (2).

LLANELLI: W Proctor; A Richards, N Davies, N Boobyer; G Evans; F Botica, R Moon; R Jones, R McBryde (captain), S Gale, H Jenkins, S Ford, M Voyle, I Jones, C Wyatt. Replacements: S Jones for Richards 40 minutes, P Morris for Jenkins 40 minutes, H Williams-Jones for R Jones 50 minutes, V Cooper for Ford 53 minutes. SCORERS: Tries: N Davies, Moon. Pens: Botica (4). Cons: Botica (2).

FINAL

Saturday, 26th April 1997　　　Cardiff Arms Park

CARDIFF　33-26　SWANSEA

Attendance: 40,000　　　　Half-time: 9-14.　　　Referee: D Davies, Llanbradach.

CARDIFF: J Thomas; S Hill, M Hall, L Davies, N Walker; L Jarvis, R Howley; A Lewis, J Humphries, L Mustoe, H Taylor (captain), K Stewart, D Jones, G Jones, O Williams. Temporary replacements: P Young for Humphries 16-21 minutes, J Davies for L Davies 22-30 minutes.
SCORERS: Tries: Walker, Thomas, Hall. Pens: Jarvis (4). Cons: Jarvis (3).

SWANSEA: M Back; A Harris, M Taylor, S Gibbs, Simon Davies; A Williams, A Booth; I Buckett, G Jenkins (captain), S Evans, A Reynolds, S Moore, P Arnold, R Appleyard, Stuart Davies. Replacement: K Colclough for Evans 80 minutes. Temporary replacement: D Niblo for Reynolds 16-22 minutes.
SCORERS: Tries: M Taylor (2), Moore, penalty-try. Cons: A Williams (3).

OTHER TOURS 1996-97

BARBARIANS

Sat,	17th Aug 1996	Scotland	Murrayfield	W 48-45
Sat,	24th Aug 1996	Wales	Cardiff	L 10-31
Tue,	8th Oct 1996	Newport	Newport	W 86-33
Sat,	7th Dec 1996	Australia	Twickenham	L 12-39
Tue,	25th Feb 1997	Leicester	Leicester	W 38-22
Wed,	5th Mar 1997	East Midlands	Northampton	W 72-38

Summary: Played 6, Won 4, Lost 2, Points For 266, Against 208.

AUSTRALIA TO ITALY & BRITISH ISLES

Sat,	19th Oct 1996	Italy 'A'	Sicily	W 55-19
Wed,	23rd Oct 1996	ITALY	Padova	W 40-18
Wed,	30th Oct 1996	Scotland 'A'	Hawick	W 47-20
Sat,	2nd Nov 1996	Glasgow & Edinburgh	Old Anniesland	W 37-19
Tue,	5th Nov 1996	Scottish Select XV	McDiarmid Park, Perth	W 25- 9
Sat,	9th Nov 1996	SCOTLAND	Murrayfield	W 29-19
Wed,	13th Nov 1996	Connacht	Galway	W 37-20
Sat,	16th Nov 1996	Ulster	Belfast	W 39-26
Tue,	19th Nov 1996	Leinster	Dublin	Cancelled
Sat,	23rd Nov 1996	IRELAND	Lansdowne Road, Dublin	W 22-12
Tue,	26th Nov 1996	Munster	Limerick	W 55-19
Sun,	1st Dec 1996	WALES	Cardiff Arms Park	W 28-19
Sat,	7th Dec 1996	Barbarians	Twickenham	W 39-12

Summary: Played 12 (one cancelled and not included), Won 12, Points For 406, Against 192. This was the first time Australia had won all their matches on a British Isles tour.

6th Match. v SCOTLAND. Saturday, 9th November 1996. At Murrayfield.

SCOTLAND 19-29 AUSTRALIA   (Half-time: 6-19)

SCOTLAND: R Shepherd (Melrose); A Stanger (Hawick), G Townsend (Northampton)(captain), R Eriksson (London Scottish), K Logan (Stirling County); C Chalmers (Melrose), G Armstrong (Newcastle); D Hilton (Bath), K McKenzie (Stirling County0, B Stewart (Edinburgh Academicals), M Wallace (Glasgow High-Kelvinside), D Cronin (Wasps), G Weir (Newcastle), I Smith (Gloucester), E Peters (Bath). Replacement: B Redpath (Melrose) for Armstrong 75 minutes. New cap: Wallace.
SCORERS: Tries: Logan, Stanger, Pens: Shepherd (3).

AUSTRALIA (New South Wales unless stated): M Burke; T Horan (Queensland), D Herbert (Queensland), P Howard (Australian Capital Territory), J Roff (Australian Capital Territory); D Knox (Australian Capital Territory), S Payne; R Harry, M Foley (Queensland), A Blades, O Finegan (Australian Capital Territory), W Waugh, J Eales (Queensland)(captain), D Wilson (Queensland), D Manu. Replacement: B Robinson (Australian Capital Territory) for Finegan 64 minutes. No new caps.
SCORERS: Tries: Waugh, Herbert. Pens: Burke (5). Cons: Burke (2).

Referee: P Thomas, France.

10th Match. v IRELAND. Saturday, 23rd November 1996. At Lansdowne Road, Dublin.

IRELAND 12-22 AUSTRALIA   (Half-time: 9-6)

IRELAND: J Staples (Harlequins); J Topping (Ballymena0, J Bell (Northampton), M McCall (Dungannon), D Crotty (Garryowen); P Burke (Bristol), S McIvor (Garryowen); N Popplwwell (Newcastle), K Wood (Harlequins)(captain), P Wallace (Saracens), D Corkery (Bristol), G Fulcher (London Irish), J Davidson (London Irish), D McBride (Malone), A Foley (Shannon). Replacement: M Field (Malone) for Staples 14 minutes. New cap: Crotty.
SCORER: Pens: P Burke (4)

AUSTRALIA (Queensland unless stated): M Burke (New South Wales); J Little, D Herbert, T Horan, J Roff (Australian Capital Territory); D Knox (Australian Capital Territory), G Gregan (Australian Capital Territory); D Crowley, M Foley, A Blades (New South Wales), D Manu (New South Wales), W Waugh (New South Wales), J Eales (captain), D Wilson, M Brial (New South Wales). Replacement: B Robinson (Australia Capital Territory) for Eales 65 minutes. No new caps.
SCORERS: Try: Knox. Pens: M Burke (5). Con: M Burke.

Referee: B Campsall, England.

12th Match. v WALES. Sunday, 1st December 1996. At Cardiff Arms Park (National Stadium).

WALES 19-28 AUSTRALIA   (Half-time: 6-18)

WALES: W Proctor (Llanelli); I Evans (Llanelli), G Thomas (Bridgend), I Gibbs (Swansea), D James (Bridgend); J Davies (Cardiff), R Howley (Cardiff); C Loader (Swansea), J Humphreys (Cardiff)(captain), D Young (Cardiff), H Taylor (Cardiff), Gareth Llewellyn (Harlequins), D Jones (Cardiff), K Jones (Ebbw Vale), S Williams (Neath). Replacements: C Charvis (Swansea) for Williams 17 minutes, N Jenkins (Pontypridd) for Proctor 48 minutes, C Quinnell (Richmond) for D Jones 69 minutes. New cap: Charvis.
SCORERS: Try: Thomas. Pens: Davies (4). Con: Davies.

AUSTRALIA: M Burke (New South Wales); J Roff (Australian Capital Territory), J Little (Queensland), T Horan (Queensland)(captain), D Campese (New South Wales); P Howard (Australian Capital Territory), G Gregan (Australian Capital Territory); D Crowley (Queensland), M Foley (Queensland), A Blades (New South Wales), O Finegan (Australian Capital Territory), T Gavin (New South Wales), D Giffin (Australian Capital Territory), D Wilson (Queensland), M Brial (New South Wales). New cap: Giffin.
SCORERS: Tries: Burke, Brial. penalty-try. Pens: Burke (3). Cons: Burke (2).

Referee: I Ramage, Scotland.

NB: This was David Campese's 101st and last cap.

WESTERN SAMOA IN ENGLAND, IRELAND & WALES

Sat, 2nd Nov 1996	Saracens	Enfield	L	40-53
Tue, 5th Nov 1996	Oxford University	Iffley Road, Oxford	W	58-27
Sat, 9th Nov 1996	Munster	Cork	W	35-25
Tue, 12th Nov 1996	IRELAND	Lansdowne Road, Dublin	W	40-25
Tue, 19th Nov 1996	Cambridge University	Grange Road, Cambridge	W	14-13
Sat, 23rd Nov 1996	Llanelli	Stradey Park, Llanelli	L	15-23
Tue, 26th Nov 1996	Cardiff	Cardiff	W	53-29
Fri, 29th Nov 1996	Newbury	Newbury	W	35-21
Mon, 2nd Dec 1996	Bath	Bath	L	17-36
Wed, 4th Dec 1996	Leicester & Northampton	Leicester	W	33-20
Tue, 10th Dec 1996	Richmond	Richmond	W	32-12

Summary: Played 11, Won 8, Lost 3, Points For 372, Against 284.

4th Match. v IRELAND. Tuesday, 12th November 1996. At Lansdowne Road, Dublin.

IRELAND 25-40 WESTERN SAMOA   (Half-time: 12-22)

IRELAND: S Mason (Richmond); R Wallace (Saracens), R Henderson (London Irish), J Bell (Northampton), J Topping (Ballymena); D Humphreys (London Irish), N Hogan (Oxford University)(captain); H Hurley (Moseley), A Clarke (Northampton), P Wallace (Saracens), D Corkery (Bristol), M Galwey (Shannon), J Davidson (London Irish), D McBride (Malone), P Johns (Saracens). Replacement: V Costello for McBride 72 minutes. New caps: Henderson, Topping.
SCORERS: Try: P Wallace. Pens: Mason (6). Con: Mason.

WESTERN SAMOA; V Patu (Vaiala); A So'oalo (Marist-St Joseph's), T Vaega (Te Atatu), G Leaupepe (Te Atatu), V Tuigamala (Wasps); E Va'a (Wellington), J Filemu (Wellington); B Reidy (Marist-St Pat's), T Eiasamaivao (Avalon), A Le'uu (Otahuhu), S Ta'ala (Wellington), P Leavasa (Apia), M Birtwhistle (Suburbs), P Lam (Canterbury)(captain), I Feaunati (Marist-St Pat's). Replacement: J Paramore (Bedford) for Leavasa 58 minutes.
SCORERS: Tries: Vaega (2), So'oalo, Leaupepe, Patu. Pens: Va'a (30. Cons: Va'a (3).

Referee: S Borsani, Argentina.

SOUTH AFRICA 'A' TO BRITISH ISLES

Sat, 2nd Nov 1996	Cambridge University	Cambridge	W	57-11
Fri, 8th Nov 1996	Scotland 'A'	Hawick	L	19-32
Tue, 11th Nov 1996	Ireland 'A'	Dublin	L	25-28
Sat, 16th Nov 1996	Oxford University	Oxford	W	49-12
Wed, 19th Nov 1996	Western Counties	Exeter	W	62-20
Sat, 23rd Nov 1996	London Counties	Twickenham	W	43-17
Wed, 26th Nov 1996	Northern Counties	Huddersfield	W	29-13
Sun, 1st Dec 1996	South West Counties	Exeter	W	22-20
Mon, 9th Dec 1996	Cardiff	Cardiff	W	40- 7
Wed, 11th Dec 1996	England 'A'	Gloucester	W	35-20
Sat, 14th Dec 1996	Emerging Wales	Swansea	W	42-26

Summary: Played 11, Won 9, Lost 2, Points For 423, Against 206.

9th Match. v England 'A'. Wednesday, 11th December 1996. In Gloucester.

ENGLAND 'A' 20-35 SOUTH AFRICA 'A' (Half-time: 7-18)

ENGLAND 'A': C Catling (Gloucester); B Johnson (Newbury/Army), J Baxendell (Sale), N Greenstock (Wasps), S Bromley (Harlequins); M Mapletoft (Gloucester), A Healey (Leicester); M Volland (Northampton), S Mitchell (Wasps), N Webber (Moseley), G Allison (Harlequins), D Grewcock (Coventry), R Fidler (Gloucester), R Jenkins (Harlequins), S Ojomoh (Bath)(captain). Replacement: P Sampson (Wasps) for Catling 78 minutes.
Scorers: Tries: Bromley, Healey. Pens: Mapletoft (2). Cons: Mapletoft (2).

SOUTH AFRICA 'A': A du Toit (Northern Transvaal); M Hendricks (Boland), J Joubert (Natal), E Lubbe (Griqualand West), M Goosen (Boland); L Koen (Western Province), G Scholtz (Western Province); O le Roux (Natal), N Drotske (Orange Free State)(captain), W Mayer (Eastern Province), C Krige (Western Province), R Opperman (Orange Free State), H Louw (Western Province), P Smit (Griqualand West), R Erasmus (Orange Free State). Temporary replacement: J Coetzee (Boland) for Krige 20-22 minutes.
Scorers: Tries Krige (2), Goosen, Hendricks, Erasmus. Pens: Koen (2). Cons: Koen (2).

Referee: D McHugh, Ireland.

SOUTH AFRICA IN ARGENTINA, FRANCE & WALES

Tue, 5th Nov 1996	Rosario	Rosario	W 45-36
Sat, 9th Nov 1996	ARGENTINA	Buenos Aires	W 46-15
Tue, 12th Nov 1996	Cuyo	Mendoza	W 89-19
Sat, 16th Nov 1996	ARGENTINA	Buenos Aires	W 44-21
Sat, 23rd Nov 1996	French Barbarians	Brive	L 22-30
Tue, 26th Nov 1996	South East France	Lyon	W 36-20
Sat, 30th Nov 1996	FRANCE	Bordeaux	W 22-12
Tue, 3rd Dec 1996	French Universities	Lille	L 13-20
Sat, 7th Dec 1996	FRANCE	Paris	W 13-12
Sun, 15th Dec 1996	WALES	Cardiff	W 37-20

Summary: Played 10, won 8, lost 2, points for 367, against 205.

10th Match. Sunday, 15th December 1996. At Cardiff Arms Park.

WALES 20-37 SOUTH AFRICA (Half-time: 12-23)

WALES: N Jenkins (Pontypridd); I Evans (Llanelli), S Gibbs (Swansea), A Bateman (Richmond), G James (Bridgend); A Thomas (Swansea), R Howley (Cardiff); C Loader (Swansea), J Humphreys (Cardiff)(captain), D Young (Cardiff), D McIntosh (Pontypridd), Gareth Llewellyn (Harlequins), M Rowley (Pontypridd), C Charvis (Swansea), S Williams (Neath). Replacement: N Thomas (Bath) for McIntosh 69 minutes. New caps: Rowley, McIntosh, N Thomas.
Scorers: Try: A Thomas. Penalty-goals: Jenkins (5).

SOUTH AFRICA: A Joubert (Natal); J Small (Natal), J Mulder (Transvaal), H le Roux (Transvaal), J Olivier (Northern Transvaal); H Honiball (Natal), J van der Westhuizen (Northern Transvaal); D Theron (Griqualand West), J Dalton (Transvaal), A Garvey (Natal), R Kruger (Northern Transvaal), J Wiese (Transvaal), M Andrews (Natal), A Venter (Orange Free State), G Teichmann (Natal)(captain). Replacements: A van der Linde (Western Province) for Theron 21 minuyes, J Strydom (Transvaal) for Andrews 40 minutes, A Snyman (Northern Transvaal) for Olivier 76 minutes. No new caps.
Scorers: Tries: Van der Westhuizen (3), Joubert, Olivier. Pens: Honiball (2). Cons: Honiball (2), Joubert.

Referee: S Lander, England.

QUEENSLAND IN BRITISH ISLES

Wed, 13th Nov 1996	Cambridge University	Cambridge	L 20-27
Sun, 17th Nov 1996	Michael Lynagh XV	Saracens RFC	W 28- 5
Wed, 20th Nov 1996	North Counties	Huddersfield	W 27-18
Sun, 24th Nov 1996	Midland Counties	Stourbridge	W 29-25
Thu, 28th Nov 1996	South West Counties	Newbury	W 30- 9
Sun, 1st Dec 1996	London Counties	Sunbury	W 64-16
Wed, 4th Dec 1996	Pontypridd	Pontypridd	W 28-19
Tue, 10th Dec 1996	Scottish Development XV	McDiarmid Park, Perth	W 63-31
Fri, 13th Dec 1996	England 'A'	Gateshead	W 25-22

Summary: Played 8, won 7, lost 1, ponts for 314, against 172.

2nd Match. Saturday, 30th November 1996. At Twickenham.

ENGLAND 19-34 NEW ZEALAND BARBARIANS   (Half-time: 9-8)

ENGLAND: T Stimpson (Newcastle); J Sleightholme (Bath), W Carling (Harlequins0, P de Glanville (Bath)(captain), A Adebayo (Bath); M Catt (Bath), A Gomarsall (Wasps); G Rowntree (Leicester), M Regan (Bristol), J Leonard (Harlequins), T Rodber (Nortampton/Army), M Johnson (Leicester), S Shaw (Bristol), L Dallaglio (Wasps), C Sheasby (Wasps).
Scorers: Tries: Sleightholme, Stimpson. Pens: Catt (3).

NEW ZEALAND BARBARIANS: C Cullen (Manawatu); J Vidiri (Counties), A Ieremia (Wellington), L Stensness (Auckland), J Lomu (Counties); A Mehrtens (Canterbury), J Marshall (Counties); M Allen (Taranaki), S Fitzpatrick (Auckland)(captain), O Brown (Auckland), M Jones (Auckland), I Jones (North Auckland), R Brooke (Auckland), T Randell (Otago), A Blowers (Auckland). Replacements: D Mika (Auckland) for Randell 55 minutes. C Spencer (Auckland) for Mehrtens 58 minutes, G Osborne (North Harbour) for Vidiri 79 minutes.
Scorers: Tries: Brooke, Blowers, Spencer, Vidiri. Pens: Mehrtens (2), Spencer (2). Con: Spencer.

Referee: C Thomas, Wales.

ITALY IN WALES & IRELAND

Tue, 31st Dec 1996	Llanelli	Llanelli	Cancelled
Sat, 4th Jan 1997	IRELAND	Dublin	W 37-29

2nd Match Saturday, 4th January 1997. At Lansdowne Road, Dublin.

IRELAND 29-37 ITALY (Half-time: 18-17)

IRELAND: C O'Shea (London Irish); J Topping (Ballymena), J Bell (Northampton), M McCall (Dungannon), D Crotty (Garryowen); P Burke (Bristol), S McIvor (Garryowen); N Popplewell (Newcastle), K Wood (Harlequins)(captain), P Wallace (Saracens), D Corkery (Bristol), G Fulcher (London Irish), J Davidson (London Irish), E Miller (Leicester), A Foley (Shannon). Replacements: D McBride (Malone) for Miller 33 minutes, P Johns (Saracens) for Fulcher 66 minutes. New cap: Miller.
Scorers: Try: Bell. Pens: Burke (8).

ITALY: J Pertile (Roma); P Vaccari (Calvisano), A Stoica (Milan), S Bordon (Rovigo), Marcello Cuttitta (Milan); D Dominguez (Milan), A Troncon (Treviso); Massimo Cuttitta (Milan)(captain), C Orlandi (Milan), F Properzi Curti (Milan), J Gardner (Treviso), W Cristofoletto (Treviso), G Croci (Milan), A Sgorlon (Treviso), O Arancio (Milan). Replacements: N Mazzucato (Padova) for Marcello Cuttitta 43 minutes, C Checchinato (Treviso) for Cristofoletto 67 minutes. Yellow card: Gardner.
Scorers: Tries: Vaccari (2), Massimo Cuttitta, Dominguez. Pens: Dominguez (3). Cons: Dominguez (4).

Referee: R Davies, Wales.

UNITED STATES EAGLES IN WALES

Wed, 1st Jan 1997	Emerging Wales	Newport	Cancelled
Sat, 4th Jan 1997	Neath	Cardiff Arms Park	L 15-39
Tue, 7th Jan 1997	Pontypridd	Cardiff Arms Park	W 15-13
Sat, 11th Jan 1997	WALES	Cardiff	L 14-34

Summary: Played 3, won 1, lost 2, points for 44, against 86.

OTAGO IN ENGLAND & SCOTLAND

Sat, 18th Jan 1997	Cambridge University	Cambridge	W 47-23
Sun, 26th Jan 1997	London Irish	Sunbury	W 82-14
Tue, 28th Jan 1997	Scottish Development XV	Stirling	W 44-19
Fri, 31st Jan 1997	England 'A'	Bristol	W 42-15
Tue, 4th Feb 1997	Bath	Bath	W 31-18
Tue, 11th Feb 1997	Northampton-Leicester	Northampton	W 37- 8
Thu, 13th Feb 1997	Richmond	Richmond	W 70- 0

Summary: Played 7, won 7, points for 353, against 97.

AUCKLAND BLUES IN ENGLAND

Thu, 13th Feb 1997	Bristol	Bristol	W 62-21
Tue, 18th Feb 1997	Harlequins	Stoop Memorial Ground	W 33-29
Sat, 22nd Feb 1997	Brive	Brive	W 47-11

Summary: Played 3, won 3, points for 142, against 61.

REGIONAL DIVISIONS' CLUB INDEX

To locate a club, find its name in the Regional Divisions' Club Index, and check the league in which it plays. You can then find the league's page number on page 752.

REGIONAL DIVISIONS' CLUB INDEX

To locate a club, find its name in the Regional Divisions' Club Index, and check the league in which it plays. You can then find the league's page number on page 752.

BLACKBURN RUFC	N - N 2	BROUGHTON RUFC	N - NL 1
BLACKPOOL RUFC	N - NLC	BUCKFASTLEIGH	SW - D 3
BLAGDON RFC	SW - S 1	BUCKINGHAM RUFC	SW - SCN
BLANDFORD RFC	SW - SCS	BUDE RFC	SW - C D
BLAYDON RFC	N - N 2	BUGBROOKE RUFC	M - EML
BLETCHLEY RUFC	SW - SCN	BURBAGE RFC	M - L 1
BLOXWICH RFC	M - S	BURGESS HILL RFC	L - SX 2
BLYTH RFC	N - DN 1	BURLEY RFC	N - Y 4
BODMIN RFC	SW - C 1	BURNAGE RFC	N - NL 2
BOGNOR RFC	L - L 3 SE	BURNHAM ON SEA RFC	SW - S 2
BOLTON RUFC	N - NL 1	BURNHAM-ON-CROUCH RUFC	L - EC 3S
BOOTS ATHLETIC RFC	M - NLD 1	BURNTWOOD RUFC	M - SW
BOSTON RFC	M - NLD 2	BURTON FC	M - M 1
BOURNE RUFC	M - NLD 2	BURY RUFC	N - NL 1
BOURNEMOUTH RFC	SW - SW 2 E	BURY ST EDMONDS RFC	L - L 3 NE
BOURNVILLE RFC	M - NM 2	BUXTON RUFC	M - ME 2
BOVEY TRACEY RFC	SW - D 2	CAINSCROSS RFC	SW - G 1
BOWDEN RUFC	N - SLC 2	CALDER VALE RUFC	N - NW 3
BRACKLEY RUFC	M - EML	CALDY RFC	N - NW 2
BRACKNELL RFC	SW - SW 1	CALLINGTON	SW - C 2
BRADFORD & BINGLEY RFC	N - N 2	CALNE RFC	SW - BDW 1
BRADFORD SALEM RFC	N - Y 1	CAMBORNE RFC	SW - SW 2 W
BRAINTREE RUFC	L - L 2 N	CAMBORNE SCHOOL OF MINES RFC	SW - C 2
BRAMLEY RUFC	N - NE 3	CAMBRIDGE RUFC	L - L 2 N
BRAUNSTONE TOWN RFC	M - L 2	CAMP HILL RFC	M - M 1
BREAM RFC	SW - GS	CAMPION RFC	L - L 3 NE
BREDON STAR RFC	M - NM 2	CANNOCK RUFC	M - S
BRENTWOOD RFC	L - L 2 N	CANTABRIGIAN RFC	L - EC 1
BRIDGNORTH RFC	M - NM 1	CANTERBURY EXILES	L - K 3
BRIDLINGTON RUFC	N - N 1	CANTERBURY RFC	L - L 3 SE
BRIDPORT RFC	SW - BDW 2	CANVEY ISLAND RUFC	L - L 3 NE
BRIGHTLINGSEA RFC	L - EC 3N	CARLISLE RFC	N - NW 2
BRIGHTON FOOTBALL CLUB	L - L 3 SE	CARNFORTH RFC	N - C
BRISTOL AEROPLANE COMPANY	SW - G 3	CASTLE CARY RUFC	SW - S 2
BRISTOL HARLEQUINS RFC	SW - WCN	CASTLE DONINGTON RUFC	M - NLD 1
BRISTOL SARACENS RFC	SW - GS	CASTLEFORD RUFC	N - Y 1
BRISTOL TELEPHONE AREA RFC	SW - G 1	CENTAURS RFC	L - HM 1
BRITISH AIRWAYS RFC	L - HM 4S	CHARD RFC	SW - GS
BRITISH AIRWAYS WINGSPAN RUFC	L - SX 1	CHARLTON PARK RFC	L - L 1
BRITISH GAS (BRISTOL) RFC	SW - S 2	CHEDDAR VALLEY RFC	SW - S 2
BRIXHAM RFC	SW - SW 2 W	CHELMSFORD RFC	L - L 3 NE
BROAD PLAIN RFC	SW - S 2	CHELTENHAM CIVIL SERVICE RFC	SW - G 1
BROADLANDS RFC	L - EC 3N	CHELTENHAM NORTH RFC	SW - WCN
BROADSTREET RFC	M - M 1	CHELTENHAM SARACENS RFC	SW - G 1
BROCKLEIANS RFC	L - L 2 S	CHESHAM RUFC	SW - BO2
BROCKWORTH RFC	SW - GS	CHESHUNT RFC	L - L 1
BROMLEY RFC	L - K 1	CHESTER RUFC	N - NW 1
BROMSGROVE RFC	M - M 2	CHESTER-LE-STREET RFC	N - DN 2
BROMYARD RFC	M - NM 1	CHESTERFIELD RUFC	M - NLD 1
BROUGHTON PARK FC	N - N 1	CHEW VALLEY OLD BOYS RFC	SW - S 1

REGIONAL DIVISIONS' CLUB INDEX

To locate a club, find its name in the Regional Divisions' Club Index, and check the league in which it plays. You can then find the league's page number on page 752.

REGIONAL DIVISIONS' CLUB INDEX

To locate a club, find its name in the Regional Divisions' Club Index, and check the league in which it plays. You can then find the league's page number on page 752.

DURHAM CONSTABULARY RUFC .....N - DN 4
DURSLEY RFC ....SW - G 2
EAGLE RUFC ....N - SLC 1
EALING ....L - L 2 N
EARLSDON RFC ....M - SW
EAST GRINSTEAD RFC ....L - L 3 SE
EAST LEAKE RFC ....M - NLD 2
EAST LONDON RUFC ....L - EC 3S
EAST RETFORD RUFC ....M - NLD 1
EASTBOURNE RFC ....L - SX 1
EASTLEIGH RFC ....L - H 1
ECCLES RFC ....N - NL 1
ECONOMICALS RUFC ....L - SY 4
EDENBRIDGE RFC ....L - K 2
EDLINGTON AND WICKERSLEY RUFC ...N - Y 4
EDWARDIAN FC ....M - MW 2
EFFINGHAM RFC ....L - L 3 SW
EGHAM RFC ....L - SY 3
EGREMONT RUFC ....N - NW 2
ELLINGHAM & RINGWOOD RFC ....L - H 3
ELY RUFC ....L - EC 1
ENFIELD IGNATIANS RFC ....L - HM 1
ERDINGTON RFC ....M - MW 2
ERITH RFC ....L - K 3
ESSO (FAWLEY) RFC ....L - L 3 SW
ETON MANOR RFC ....L - L 3 NE
EVESHAM RFC ....M - MW 2
EXETER SARACENS RFC ....SW - D 1
EXMOUTH RFC ....SW - C D
FAIRBAIRN AND CHIGWELLL ....L - EC 4S
FAKENHAM RUFC ....L - EC 2
FALMOUTH ....SW - C D
FAREHAM HEATHENS RFC ....L - H 2
FARNBOROUGH RUFC ....L - L 3 SW
FARNHAM RUFC ....L - SY 1
FAVERSHAM RUFC ....L - K 3
FELIXSTOWE RUFC ....L - EC 1
FELTHAM RFC ....L - HM 2
FINCHLEY RFC ....L - L 2 N
FIVE WAYS OLD EDWARDIANS FC ....M - NM 1
FLEET RUFC ....L - H 3
FLEETWOOD RUFC ....N - NW 2
FOLKESTONE RFC ....L - K 1
FOOTS CRAY RUFC ....L - K 2
FORD LEAMINGTON RFC ....M - W
FORDINGBRIDGE RFC ....L - H 2
FRAMPTON COTTERELL RFC ....SW - GS
FROME RFC ....SW - S 1
FULLERIANS RFC ....L - L 3 NW
FURNESS RUFC ....N - NLC

GAINSBOROUGH RUFC ....M - NLD 2
GARFORTH RUFC ....N - Y 4
GATESHEAD FELL RFC ....N - NE 1
GEC ST LEONARDS RUFC ....M - SW
GENTLEMEN OF MOORE RUFC ....N - SLC 4
GILLINGHAM ANCHORIANS RFC ....L - K 1
GLOSSOP RUFC ....M - NLD 1
GLOUCESTER ALL BLUES RFC ....SW - G 3
GLOUCESTER CIVIL SERVICE TIGERS .SW - G 3
GLOUCESTER OLD BOYS RFC ....SW - SW 1
GOOLE RUFC ....N - NE 1
GORDANO RFC ....SW - GS
GORDON LEAGUE RFC ....SW - WCN
GOSFORD ALL BLACKS RFC ....SW - BO2
GOSFORTH RFC ....N - DN 3
GOSPORT AND FAREHAM RFC ....L - L 3 SW
GPT (COVENTRY) RFC ....M - MW 2
GRASSHOPPERS RFC ....L - L 3 NW
GRAVESEND RFC ....L - L 2 S
GREAT WESTERN RAILWAY RFC ....L - HM 4S
GREEN GARTH RUFC ....N - C
GREENWICH ACADEMICALS RFC ....L - K 2
GREENWICH RFC ....L - K 3
GRIMSBY RUFC ....M - ME 2
GROVE RFC ....SW - BO1
GUERNSEY RUFC ....L - H 1
GUILDFORD & GODALMING RFC ....L - L 1
GUISBOROUGH RUFC ....N - DN 2
GUYS HOSPITAL RFC ....L - L 3 SW
HONOURABLE ARTILLERY COMPANY .L - HM 1
HACKNEY RFC ....L - L 3 NW
HADLEIGH RUFC ....L - EC 1
HALIFAX RUFC ....N - N 2
HALIFAX VANDALS RUFC ....N - Y 2
HALTON RUFC ....N - SLC 3
HAMBLE ....L - H 3
HAMMERSMITH & FULHAM RFC ......L - HM 3
HAMPSHIRE CONSTABULARY ....L - H 3
HAMPSTEAD RFC ....L - L 3 NW
HANDSWORTH RUFC ....M - SW
HARBORNE RFC ....M - NM 2
HARBURY RFC ....M - W
HARINGEY RFC ....L - L 3 NW
HARLOW RUFC ....L - L 1
HARPENDEN RFC ....L - L 3 NW
HARROW RFC ....L - HM 1
HARTLEPOOL ATHLETIC RFC ....N - DN 3
HARTLEPOOL BOYS BRIGADE OB RFC .N - DN 3
HARTLEPOOL RFC ....N - DN 2
HARTLEPOOL ROVERS ....N - NE 2

REGIONAL DIVISIONS' CLUB INDEX

To locate a club, find its name in the Regional Divisions' Club Index, and check the league in which it plays. You can then find the league's page number on page 752.

HARTLEPOOL (WEST) T D S O B RUFC . .N - NE 3
HARWELL RUFC . . . . .SW - BO2
HARWICH AND DOVERCOURT RUFC . . .L - EC 1
HASLEMERE . . . . .L - SY 3
HASTINGS AND BEXHILL RFC . . . . .L - SX 1
HATFIELD RFC . . . . .L - HM 4N
HAVERHILL & DISTRICT RFC . . . . .L - EC 3S
HAYES RFC . . . . .L - HM 4S
HAYLE RUGBY CLUB . . . . .SW - WCW
HAYWARDS HEATH RFC . . . . .L - L 2 S
HEATH RUFC . . . . .N - Y 4
HEATHFIELD & WALDRON RFC . . . . . .L - L 3 SE
HEATON MOOR RUFC . . . . .N - NL 1
HELLINGLY RFC . . . . .L - SX 2
HELSBY RUFC . . . . .N - SLC 3
HELSTON RFC .SW - C 1
HEMEL HEMPSTEAD (CAMELOT) RFC .L - HM 1
HEMSWORTH RUFC . . . . .N - Y 3
HENDON RFC . . . . .L - HM 1
HEREFORD RFC . . . . .M - M 1
HERTFORD RFC . . . . .L - L 3 NW
HESSLE RUFC . . . . .N - Y 3
HIGH WYCOMBE RUFC . . . . .SW - SW 1
HIGHTOWN RUFC . . . . .N - SLC 4
HITCHIN RFC .L - HM 2
HOLMES CHAPEL RUFC . . . . .N - SLC 4
HOLT RFC . . . . .L - L 3 NE
HONDA . . . . .SW - BDW 3
HONITON RFC .SW - C D
HOPE VALLEY RUFC . . . . .M - NLD 2
HORDEN WELFARE RUFC . . . . .N - NE 1
HORNCASTLE . . . . .M - NLD3
HORNETS RFC . . . . .SW - WCN
HORNSEA RUFC . . . . .N - Y 3
HORSHAM RUFC . . . . .L - L 2 S
HOUGHTON RUFC . . . . .N - DN 3
HOVE RFC . . . . .L - SX 1
HOYLAKE RUGBY FC . . . . .N - SLC 3
HUCCLECOTE OLD BOYS RFC . . . . . . .SW - G 1
HUDDERSFIELD RUFC . . . . .N - N 2
HUDDERSFIELD YMCA RUFC . . . . .N - Y 2
HULL IONIANS RUFC . . . . .N - N 1
HULL RUFC . . . . .N - NE 2
HULLENSIANS RUFC . . . . .N - Y 2
HUNGERFORD RFC . . . . .SW - BDW 3
HUNTINGDON & DISTRICT RUFC . . . . . .M - M 2
ILFORD WANDERERS RFC . . . . .L - EC 1
ILFRACOMBE RFC . . . . .SW - D 1
ILKESTON RUFC . . . . .M - ME 1
ILKLEY RUFC . . . . .N - Y 1

ILLOGAN PARK RFC . . . . .SW - C 1
IMPERIAL MEDICAL . . . . .L - HM 1
IMPERIAL RFC . . . . .SW - S 1
IPSWICH RUFC . . . . .L - L 2 N
IPSWICH YM RUFC . . . . .L - EC 3S
ISLE OF WIGHT RFC . . . . .L - H 1
IVEL BARBARIANS RFC . . . . .SW - BDW 1
IVYBRIDGE RFC . . . . .SW - WCW
JARROVIANS RUFC . . . . .N - DN 4
JERSEY RFC .L - L 3 SW
JOHN FISHER OLD BOYS RFC . . . . .L - SY 1
K.C.S. OLD BOYS RFC . . . . .L - SY 1
KEIGHLEY RUFC . . . . .N - NE 2
KEMPSTON RFC . . . . .M - EM
KENILWORTH RFC . . . . .M - M 1
KERESLEY RFC . . . . .M - MW 1
KESTEVEN RUFC . . . . .M - ME 2
KESWICK RUFC . . . . .N - NLC
KETTERING RUFC . . . . .M - M 2
KEYNSHAM RFC . . . . .SW - SW 2 W
KEYWORTH RFC . . . . .M - NLD 1
KIBWORTH RUFC . . . . .M - ME 2
KIDDERMINSTER CAROLIANS RFC . . .M - NM 1
KILBURN COSMOS . . . . .L - HM 4N
KINGS COLLEGE HOSPITAL . . . . .L - SY 3
KINGS NORTON RFC . . . . .M - MW 1
KINGSBRIDGE RFC . . . . .SW - WCW
KINGSBURIANS RFC . . . . .L - L 3 NW
KINGSCLERE . . . . .L - H 3
KINGSTON RFC .L - SY 1
KINGSWOOD RFC . . . . .SW - G 2
KIRKBY LONSDALE RUFC . . . . .N - NW 2
KNARESBOROUGH RUFC . . . . .N - Y 4
KNOTTINGLEY RUFC . . . . .N - Y 4
KODAK RFC . . . . .L - HM 4N
KYNOCH RFC .M - NM 1
LAKENHAM - HEWETT RFC . . . . .L - EC 3N
LANKELLY FOWEY RFC . . . . .SW - C 2
LAUNCESTON RFC . . . . .SW - SW 1
LAW SOCIETY RFC . . . . .L - SY 2
LEAMINGTON RUFC . . . . .M - M 2
LEDBURY RFC .M - NM 1
LEEDS CORINTHIANS RUFC . . . . .N - Y 3
LEEDS MEDICS AND DENTISTS RFC . . . . .N - Y 5
LEEK RUFC . . . . .M - MW 1
LEESBROCK RUFC . . . . .M - NLD 1
LEIGH RUFC . . . . .N - NW 2
LEIGHTON BUZZARD . . . . .M - M 1
LENSBURY RFC . . . . .L - L 3 NW
LEODIENSIAN RUFC . . . . .N - Y 1

REGIONAL DIVISIONS' CLUB INDEX

To locate a club, find its name in the Regional Divisions' Club Index, and check the league in which it plays. You can then find the league's page number on page 752.

REGIONAL DIVISIONS' CLUB INDEX

To locate a club, find its name in the Regional Divisions' Club Index, and check the league in which it plays. You can then find the league's page number on page 752.

REGIONAL DIVISIONS' CLUB INDEX

To locate a club, find its name in the Regional Divisions' Club Index, and check the league in which it plays. You can then find the league's page number on page 752.

OLD PUBLIC OAKS RFC . . . . .SW - D 1	PENZANCE AND NEWLYN RFC . . . . . .SW - SW 1
OLD REDCLIFFIANS RFC . . . . .SW - WCN	PERCY PARK RFC . . . . .N - NE 1
OLD REEDONIANS . . . . .L - L 3 SW	PERRANPORTH RC . . . . .SW - C 1
OLD REIGATIAN RFC . . . . .L - L 2 S	PERSHORE RFC . . . . .M - MW 2
OLD RICHIANS RFC . . . . .SW - WCN	PETERBOROUGH RUFC . . . . .M - ME 1
OLD RISHWORTHIAN RUFC . . . . .N - Y 4	PETERSFIELD RFC . . . . .L - H 1
OLD RUTLISHIANS RFC . . . . .L - SY 2	PEWSEY VALE RFC . . . . .SW - BDW 3
OLD SALTLEIANS RFC . . . . .M - NM 1	PHOENIX RFC . . . . .SW - BO1
OLD SHOOTERSHILLIAN S RFC . . . . .L - K 1	PILNING RFC .SW - G 3
OLD STANDFORDIANS RFC . . . . .L - HM 3	PINLEY RFC . . . . .M - SW
OLD STREETONIANS . . . . .L - HM 4N	PINNER & GRAMMARIANS RFC . . . . . . .L - HM 3
OLD SULIANS RFC . . . . .SW - GS	PLUMPTON RFC . . . . .L - SX 3
OLD SUTTONIANS RFC . . . . .L - SY 2	PLYMOUTH ARGAUM RFC . . . . .SW - D 2
OLD TECHNICIANS RFC . . . . .SW - D 1	PLYMOUTH CIVIL SERVICE RFC . . . . . .SW - D 1
OLD TIFFINIAN RFC . . . . .L - SY 2	PLYMOUTH YMCA RFC . . . . .SW - D 3
OLD TOTTONIANS RFC . . . . .L - HM 4N	PLYMPTON VICTORIA RFC . . . . .SW - D 3
OLD VERULAMIAN RFC . . . . .L - L 2 N	PLYMSTOCK RFC . . . . .SW - D 3
OLD WALCOUNTIANS RFC . . . . .L - L 3 SW	POCKLINGTON RUFC . . . . .N - NE 3
OLD WARWICKIAN RFC . . . . .M - W	PONTEFRACT RFC . . . . .N - NE 1
OLD WELLINGTONIAN RFC . . . . .L - SY 2	PONTELAND RFC . . . . .N - DN 2
OLD WHEATLEYANS RFC . . . . .M - SW	POOLE RFC . . . . .SW - BDW 3
OLD WHITGIFTIAN RFC . . . . .L - L 3 SW	PORT SUNLIGHT RFC . . . . .N - SLC 3
OLD WILLIAMSONIAN RFC . . . . .L - K 2	PORTCASTRIAN RFC . . . . .SW - BDW 2
OLD WIMBLEDONIANS RFC . . . . .L - L 2 S	PORTSMOUTH RFC . . . . .L - L 3 SW
OLD YARDLEIANS RFC . . . . .M - MW 2	PRENTON RUFC . . . . .N - SLC 2
OLDERSHAW RUFC . . . . .N - NW 1	PRINCE ROCK RFC . . . . .SW - D 2
OLDFIELD OLD BOYS . . . . .SW - WCN	PRUDHOE HOSPITAL RFC . . . . .N - DN 4
OLDHAM RUFC . . . . .N - NL 1	PUDDLETOWN . . . . .SW - BDW 3
OLLERTON RFC . . . . .M - NLD 2	PULBOROUGH RFC . . . . .L - SX 1
OLNEY RFC .SW - SCN	PURLEY RFC . . . . .L - L 3 SW
ONGAR RFC . . . . .L - EC 3S	QUEEN ELIZABETH II RFC . . . . .L - HM 4N
ORLEANS F.P. RFC . . . . .L - HM 4S	QUINTIN RFC . . . . .L - HM 4S
ORMSKIRK RUFC . . . . .N - NLC	RACAL DECCA RFC . . . . .L - SY 4
ORPINGTON RFC . . . . .L - K 2	RAF LAKENHEATH . . . . .L - EC 4N
OSSETT RUFC .N - Y 5	RAVENS RFC . . . . .L - EC 3S
OSTERLEY RFC . . . . .L - HM 4S	RAWMARSH RUFC . . . . .N - Y 5
OSWESTRY RFC . . . . .M - NM 1	RAYLEIGH WYVERNS RFC . . . . .L - EC 4S
OUNDLE RFC .M - EM	RAYNES PARK RFC . . . . .L - SY 1
OVERTON RFC .L - H 1	REDCAR RUFC . . . . .N - NE 3
OXFORD HARLEQUINS RFC . . . . .SW - SCN	REDDITCH RFC . . . . .M - NM 1
OXFORD RFC . . . . .SW - SW 2 E	REDINGENSIANS RFC . . . . .SW - BDW 1
OXTED RFC . . . . .L - SY 4	REDRUTH ALBANY RFC . . . . .SW - C 2
PAIGNTON RFC . . . . .SW - WCW	REIGATE & REDHILL RFC . . . . .L - SY 2
PAINSWICK RFC . . . . .SW - G 1	RICHMONDSHIRE RUFC . . . . .N - DN 3
PARK HOUSE FC . . . . .L - L 3 SE	RIPON RUFC .N - NE 3
PARKONIANS RUFC . . . . .N - SLC 2	ROBERTSBRIDGE RUFC . . . . .L - SX 3
PAVIORS RFC .M - M 2	ROCHDALE RUFC . . . . .N - NLC
PENNANIANS RUFC . . . . .SW - BO1	ROCHFORD HUNDRED RFC . . . . .L - L 3 NE
PENRITH RUFC . . . . .N - NW 1	ROLLS ROYCE RFC . . . . .M - NLD 2
PENRYN RFC . . . . .SW - SW 2 W	ROMFORD & GIDEA PARK RFC . . . . . . .L - L 2 N

REGIONAL DIVISIONS' CLUB INDEX

To locate a club, find its name in the Regional Divisions' Club Index, and check the league in which it plays. You can then find the league's page number on page 752.

REGIONAL DIVISIONS' CLUB INDEX

To locate a club, find its name in the Regional Divisions' Club Index, and check the league in which it plays. You can then find the league's page number on page 752.

STANDARD RFC	.M - W
STANFORD LE HOPE RFC	.L - EC 4S
STANLEY RODILLIANS RUFC	.N - Y 3
STEVENAGE TOWN RFC	.L - HM 1
STEWARTS & LLOYDS RFC	.M - ME 1
STITHIANS RFC	.SW - C 1
STOCKPORT RUFC	.N - NW 3
STOCKSBRIDGE RUFC	.N - Y 3
STOCKTON RFC	.N - N 1
STOCKWOOD PARK RFC	.M - M 2
STOKE OLD BOYS RFC	.M - MW 2
STOKE - ON - TRENT RUFC	.M - M 1
STONEYGATE FC	.M - ME 1
STOTHERT & PITT RFC	.SW - S 1
STOURPORT RFC	.M - NM 2
STOW-ON-THE-WOLD & DISTRICT	.SW - SW 2 E
STOWMARKET RUFC	.L - EC 3N
STRATFORD UPON AVON RFC	.M - MW 1
STREATHAM-CROYDON RUFC	.L - L 2 S
STROUD RFC	.SW - SW 1
SUDBURY COURT RFC	.L - HM 2
SUDBURY RUFC	.L - L 1
SUN ALLIANCE, HORSHAM	.L - SX 1
SUNDERLAND RFC	.N - NE 3
SUPERMARINE RFC	.SW - BDW 2
SURREY POLICE RFC	.L - SY 4
SUSSEX POLICE RFC	.L - SX 2
SUTTON COLDFIELD RFC	.M - M 2
SUTTON & EPSOM RFC	.L - L 1
SWAFFHAM RUFC	.L - EC 4N
SWANAGE & WAREHAM RFC	.SW - SW 2 E
SWINDON COLLEGE OL BOYS RFC	.SW - BDW 2
SWINDON RFC	.SW - SCS
SYSTON RUGBY FOOTBALL CLUB	.M - M 1
TADLEY RUGBY CLUB RFC	.SW - BDW 1
TAMAR SARACENS RFC	.SW - D 2
TAMWORTH RUFC	.M - MW 2
TAUNTON RFC	.SW - SW 2 W
TAVISTOCK RFC	.SW - D 1
TEIGNMOUTH RFC	.SW - C D
TELFORD HORNETS RFC	.M - MW 1
TENBURY RFC	.M - NM 1
TETBURY RFC	.SW - G 2
TEWKESBURY RFC	.SW - G 2
THAMES RUFC	.L - EC 2
THAMESIANS RFC	.L - HM 4S
THANET WANDERERS RUFC	.L - L 1
THATCHAM RFC	.SW - BDW 1
THE TOR RFC	.SW - GS
THETFORD RFC	.L - EC 2
THORNBURY RFC	.SW - WCN
THORNENSIANS RUFC	.N - NE 3
THORNEY RUFC	.M - EM
THORNTON CLEVELEYS RUFC	.N - NL 1
THURROCK RFC	.L - L 1
THURSTON RUFC	.L - EC 3N
TIVERTON RFC	.SW - SW 2 W
TONBRIDGE RFC	.L - K 2
TOPSHAM RFC	.SW - D 1
TORQUAY ATHLETIC RFC	.SW - SW 1
TORRINGTON RUFC	.SW - D 1
TOTNES RFC	.SW - D 2
TOTTONIANS RFC	.L - H 1
TOWCESTRIANS RFC	.M - M 2
TRAFFORD (METROVICK) RFCC	.N - NLC
TREDWORTH RUFC	.SW - G 1
TRENTHAM RUFC	.M - SW
TRING RUFC	.L - L 3 NW
TRINITY GUILD RFC	.M - SW
TROJANS RFC	.L - H 2
TROWBRIDGE RFC	.SW - BDW 1
TRURO RFC	.SW - C D
TUNBRIDGE WELLS RFC	.L - L 3 SE
TUPTON RUFC	.M - NLD3
TWICKENHAM RFC	.L - HM 1
TYLDESLEY RUFC	.N - NLC
TYNEDALE RFC	.N - N 1
UCKFIELD RFC	.L - L 3 SE
UCS OLD BOYS RFC	.L - HM 2
UNITED SERVICES PORTSMOUTH RFC	.L - H 1
UNIVERSITY OF DERBY MENS RUGBY CLUB	.M - NLD3
UNIVERSITY OF SURREY RFC	.L - SY 4
UNIVERSITY VANDALS RFC	.L - L 3 SW
UPMINSTER RFC	.L - L 3 NE
UPPER CLAPTON FOOTBALL CLUB	.L - HM 1
UPPER EDEN RUFC	.N - NLC
UPTON-UPON-SEVERN RFC	.M - NM 1
UTTOXETER RFC	.M - S
UXBRIDGE RFC	.L - L 3 NW
VAGABONDS (I.O.M.) RUFC	.N - NW 1
VALE OF LUNE RUFC	.N - N 2
VAUXHALL MOTORS RUFC	.M - EM
VENTNOR RUGBY FOOTBALL CLUB	.L - H 2
VEOR RFC	.SW - C 2
VERWOOD	.SW - BDW 3
VESEYANS RFC	.M - NM 1
VICKERS RUFC	.N - NLC
VIGO RFC	.L - K 2
VIPERS RFC	.M - ME 1

REGIONAL DIVISIONS' CLUB INDEX

To locate a club, find its name in the Regional Divisions' Club Index, and check the league in which it plays. You can then find the league's page number on page 752.

VULCAN RUFC . . . . .N - SLC 4
WADEBRIDGE CAMELS RFC . . . . .SW - C 1
WALCOT OLD BOYS RFC . . . . .SW - GS
WALLASEY RUFC . . . . .N - SLC 2
WALLSEND RFC .N - DN 3
WANDSWORTHIANS RFC . . . . .L - SY 1
WANSTEAD RFC .L - EC 1
WARLEY RFC . . . . .M - MW 2
WARLINGHAM RFC . . . . .L - L 2 S
WARMINSTER RFC . . . . .SW - BDW 3
WARRINGTON RUFC . . . . .N - SLC 1
WARWICK RFC . . . . .M - W
WASHINGTON RUFC . . . . .N - DN 4
WATERLOOVILLE RFC . . . . .L - H 3
WATFORD RFC . . . . .L - HM 2
WATH-UPON-DEARNE RUFC . . . . .N - Y 1
WATTON . . . . .L - EC 4N
WEARSIDE RUFC . . . . .N - DN 4
WEDNESBURY RUFC . . . . .M - S
WELLINGBOROUGH
    OLD GRAMMARIANS . . . . .M - EML
WELLINGBOROUGH RFC . . . . .M - ME 1
WELLINGTON RFC . . . . .SW - WCW
WELLS RUFC . . . . .SW - GS
WELWYN RUGBY CLUB . . . . .L - L 2 N
WEMBLEY RFC .L - HM 1
WENSLEYDALE RUFC . . . . .N - DN 3
WESSEX RFC . . . . .SW - D 2
WEST BRIDGFORD RFC . . . . .M - ME 2
WEST LEEDS RUFC . . . . .N - Y 2
WEST NORFOLK RUFC . . . . .L - L 3 NE
WEST PARK BRAMHOPE RUFC . . . . .N - N 1
WEST PARK (ST HELENS) RFC . . . . .N - NW 1
WESTBURY RFC . . . . .SW - SCS
WESTBURY-ON-SEVERN RFC . . . . .SW - G 2
WESTCLIFF RFC . . . . .L - EC 1
WESTCOMBE PARK RFC . . . . .L - L 2 S
WESTLEIGH RFC . . . . .M - M 1
WESTOE RFC . . . . .N - NE 2
WESTWOOD RUFC . . . . .M - EM
WETHERBY RUFC . . . . .N - Y 3
WEYMOUTH RFC . . . . .SW - SCS
WHEATLEY HILLS DONCASTER RUFC . .N - NE 1
WHEATLEY RUFC . . . . .SW - BO1
WHEATON ASTON RUFC . . . . .M - S
WHITBY RUFC .N - NE 3
WHITCHURCH RFC . . . . .M - M 1
WHITEHALL RFC . . . . .SW - WCN
WHITEHAVEN RUFC . . . . .N - C
WHITEHOUSE PARK RFC . . . . .N - SLC 4

WHITLEY BAY ROCKCLIFF RFC . . . . . . .N - DN 1
WHITSTABLE RFC . . . . .L - K 1
WHITWELL RUFC . . . . .M - NLD3
WIBSEY RUFC . . . . .N - Y 2
WIDDEN OLD BOYS RFC . . . . .SW - G 2
WIDNES RUFC . . . . .N - N 1
WIGAN RUFC . . . . .N - NW 3
WIGSTON RFC . . . . .M - L 1
WIGTON RUFC . . . . .N - N 1
WILLENHALL RFC . . . . .M - MW 1
WILMSLOW RUFC . . . . .N - NW 1
WIMBLEDON RFC . . . . .L - L 1
WIMBORNE RFC . . . . .SW - SCS
WINCANTON RUFC . . . . .SW - S 3
WINCHESTER RFC . . . . .L - L 2 S
WINDERMERE RUFC . . . . .N - NW 3
WINDSOR RFC . . . . .SW - BDW 1
WINLATON VULCANS RFC . . . . .N - DN 1
WINSCOMBE RFC . . . . .SW - S 1
WINSLOW RUFC . . . . .SW - BO2
WIRRAL RFC . . . . .N - SLC 1
WISBECH RUFC . . . . .L - EC 4N
WITHAM RUFC . . . . .L - EC 4S
WITHERNSEA RUFC . . . . .N - Y 5
WITHYCOMBE RUGB
    & RECREATION CLUB RFC . . . . . . .SW - C D
WITNEY RFC . . . . .SW - SCN
WITTON RFC . . . . .M - NM 2
WIVELISCOMBE RFC . . . . .SW - GS
WOKING RFC . . . . .L - SY 1
WOLVERHAMPTON RUFC . . . . .M - M 1
WOODBRIDGE RUFC . . . . .L - L 3 NE
WOODFORD RFC . . . . .L - L 2 N
WOODLAND FORT RFC . . . . .SW - D 3
WOODRUSH RUFC . . . . .M - MW 1
WOOTTON BASSETT RFC . . . . .SW - SCS
WORKINGTON RUFC . . . . .N - NW 3
WORKSOP RUFC . . . . .M - NLD 1
WORTH OLD BOYS SOCIETY RFC . . . . .L - SY 3
WORTHING RFC . . . . .L - L 3 SE
WOTTON-UNDER-EDGE RFC . . . . .SW - G 3
WULFRUN RUFC . . . . .M - NM 2
WYMONDHAM RUFC . . . . .L - L 3 NE
YARBOROUGH BEES RUFC . . . . .M - NLD3
YARDLEY & DISTRICT RFC . . . . .M - NM 2
YARNBURY (HORSFORTH) RFC . . . . .N - NE 3
YATTON RFC . . . . .SW - GS
YORK RAILWAY INSTITUTE RUFC . . . . . . .N - Y 3
YORK RUFC . . . . .N - N 2

REGIONAL DIVISIONS' LEAGUE INDEX

To locate a club in the Regional Club Index, simply find the club by name in the Club Index and then look up the league code in the League Index below.